THE BUILDINGS OF ENGLAND

FOUNDING EDITOR: NIKOLAUS PEVSNER

ESSEX

JAMES BETTLEY AND NIKOLAUS PEVSNER

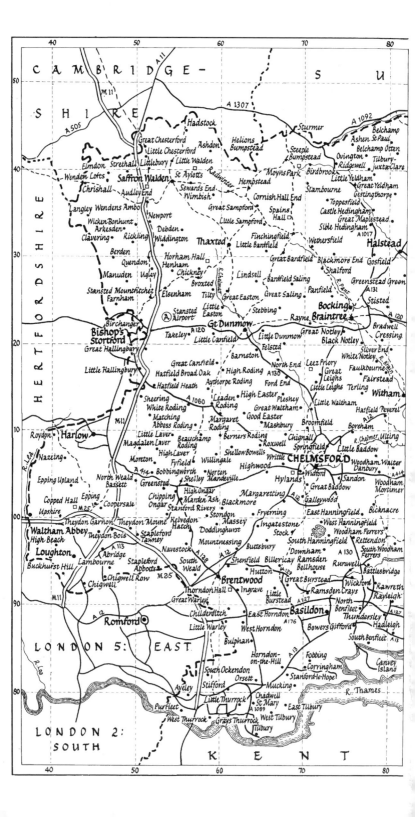

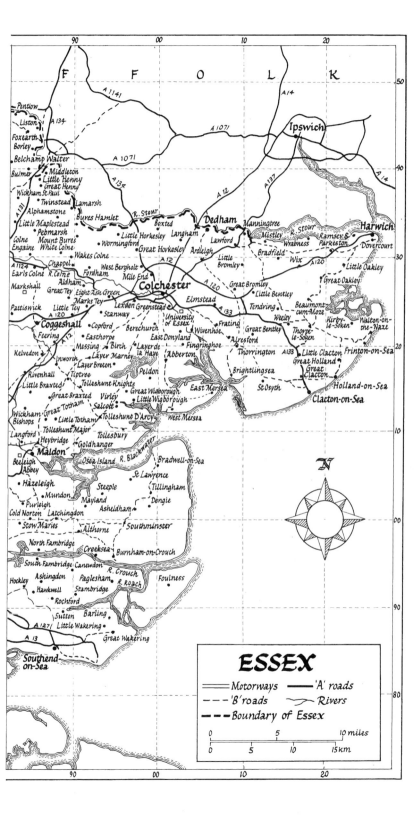

ESSEX

Motorways ——— 'A' roads ———
'B' roads - - - - Rivers ～～～
- - - Boundary of Essex

0   5   10 miles
0   5   10   15km

PEVSNER ARCHITECTURAL GUIDES

The Buildings of England series was created and
largely written by Sir Nikolaus Pevsner (1902–83).
First editions of the county volumes were published by
Penguin Books between 1951 and 1974. The continuing
programme of revisions and new volumes has been
supported by research financed through
the Buildings Books Trust since 1994

THE BUILDINGS BOOKS TRUST

was established in 1994, registered charity number 1042101.
It promotes the appreciation and understanding
of architecture by supporting and financing
the research needed to sustain new and revised volumes of
The Buildings of England, Ireland, Scotland and *Wales*

The Trust gratefully acknowledges
assistance from

ENGLISH HERITAGE

with photography for this book

and all those who have contributed toward the costs of
research, writing and illustrations, including major grants from:

ESSEX HERITAGE TRUST

FRIENDS OF HISTORIC ESSEX

THE C.J. ROBERTSON TRUST

Essex

BY

JAMES BETTLEY

AND

NIKOLAUS PEVSNER

WITH CONTRIBUTIONS FROM

DAVID ANDREWS

NIGEL BROWN

AND

JAMES KEMBLE

THE BUILDINGS OF ENGLAND

YALE UNIVERSITY PRESS
NEW HAVEN AND LONDON

YALE UNIVERSITY PRESS
NEW HAVEN AND LONDON
302 Temple Street, New Haven CT 06511
47 Bedford Square, London WC1B 3DP
www.pevsner.co.uk
www.lookingatbuildings.org
www.yalebooks.co.uk
www.yalebooks.com
for
THE BUILDINGS BOOKS TRUST

Published by Yale University Press 2007
2 4 6 8 10 9 7 5 3 1

ISBN 978 0 300 11614 4

Printed in China
through World Print
Set in Monotype Plantin

CONTENTS

LIST OF TEXT FIGURES AND MAPS   x

PHOTOGRAPHIC ACKNOWLEDGEMENTS   xiii

MAP REFERENCES   xiv

FOREWORD   xv

INTRODUCTION   1

    TOPOGRAPHY   1

    GEOLOGY   4

    THE PREHISTORY OF ESSEX, BY NIGEL BROWN   6

    ROMAN ESSEX, BY JAMES KEMBLE   12

    THE MIDDLE AGES   18

    TIMBER-FRAMED BUILDINGS, *c.* 1200–1700, BY DAVID ANDREWS   31

    MAJOR SECULAR BUILDINGS, 1400–1660   42

    POST-REFORMATION CHURCHES TO 1660   45

    SECULAR BUILDINGS, 1660–1830   47

    CHURCHES AND CHAPELS, 1700–1840   52

    VICTORIAN ESSEX   55

    ESSEX SINCE 1914   66

    WARFARE AND DEFENCE   75

    COUNTY SURVEYORS AND ARCHITECTS   77

    FURTHER READING   78

ESSEX   85

GLOSSARY   865

INDEX OF ARCHITECTS, ARTISTS, PATRONS AND RESIDENTS   891

INDEX OF PLACES   923

LIST OF TEXT FIGURES AND MAPS

Every effort has been made to contact or trace all copyright holders. The publishers will be glad to make good any errors or omissions brought to our attention in future editions.

Landscape regions of Essex (J. Hunter, *The Essex Landscape*, 1999) 4

Great Totham, Lofts Farm. Late Bronze Age enclosure as it might have appeared *c.* 800 B.C. (by Roger Massey-Ryan) 10

Roman Essex (J. Hunter, *The Essex Landscape*, 1999) 13

Stondon Massey, St Peter and St Paul. Isometric of belfry and spire (by Barbara Basini. Reproduced by kind permission of Essex County Council) 26

High Laver, Mashams. Plan (by D.H. Scott) 36

High Laver, Mashams. Isometric (by John Walker) 36

Sketch of mews court (Essex County Council, *A Design Guide for Residential Areas*, 1973) 72

Audley End. Henry Winstanley's 'General Prospect', *c.* 1676 96

Audley End. Plan of ground floor (based on English Heritage guidebook, 1997) 99

Audley End. Plan of park (based on H.M.S.O. guidebook, 1984) 103

Berechurch Hall (*Building News*, 42, 1882) 134

Boreham, New Hall. Plan of the house between *c.* 1573 and 1738 (based on *History of the King's Works*, Vol. IV, 1982) 156

Boreham, New Hall. South range of Henry VIII's mansion (engraving by George Vertue for the Society of Antiquaries, 1786) 157

Brentwood, Essex County Lunatic Asylum (*Builder*, 15, 1857) 175

Chigwell, St Mary. Brass to Archbishop Samuel Harsnett †1631 227

Chrishall, Holy Trinity. Brass to Sir John de la Pole and wife Joan, *c.* 1380 236

Colchester. Balkerne Gate, reconstruction (VCH, Vol. III, 1963) 259

Colchester Castle. Plans of ground and first floors (E.C. Fernie, *The Architecture of Norman England*, 2000) 275

Copped Hall. Elevation of John Sanderson's house
(P. Morant, *History and Antiquities of the County of
Essex*, Vol. I, 1768)   308
Cressing Temple. Plan (based on a plan kindly supplied
by Essex County Council)   313
Dovercourt, 'New Town'. Garden and principal fronts
of £650 houses (J. Weale, *Designs and Examples of
Cottages, Villas, and Country Houses*, 1857)   329
Ford End, St John the Evangelist (*Building News*, 26,
1884)   365
Great Bardfield, Brick House. By Edward Bawden,
1950 (Fry Art Gallery)   390
Greenstead, Wivenhoe New Park. Linocut by Quinlan
Terry of Raymond Erith's design (R.A. 1963)   435
Harlow, St Mary and St Hugh. Brass to W. Newman
†1602   467
Ingatestone, Lightoaks (*British Architect*, 23, 1885)   505
Lawford Hall. Model farm (*Building News*, 37, 1879)   524
Layer Marney. Plan, including conjectured extent of
planned house (based on RCHME, *Essex*, Vol. III,
1922, and material kindly supplied by Nicholas
Charrington)   526
Leez Priory. Plan, including outline of demolished
portions (based on RCHME, *Essex*, Vol. II, 1921)   532
Little Easton, Easton Lodge (P. Morant, *History and
Antiquities of the County of Essex*, Vol. I, 1768)   552
Mistley Towers. The church as remodelled by Robert
Adam (*The Works in Architecture of Robert and James
Adam*, 1778–9)   601
Pebmarsh, St John the Baptist. Brass to Sir William
Fitzralph, *c*. 1331–8   623
St Osyth Priory. Plan (based on RCHME, *Essex*,
vol. III, 1922)   672
Southend-on-Sea. Leigh-on-Sea, National Schools
(J. Clarke, *Schools and School Houses*, 1852)   703
Stansted Mountfitchet, Blythwood. Model dairy
(*Builder*, 87, 1904)   740
Thorndon Hall. Design for formal gardens and
landscaping by Sieur Bourginion (Essex Record
Office)   777
Thorndon Hall. Elevation (J. Paine, *Plans, Elevations and
Sections of Noblemen and Gentlemen's Houses*, Vol. II,
1783)   778
University of Essex (based on material kindly supplied by
the University of Essex Estate Management Section)   798
Waltham Abbey, Holy Cross and St Lawrence. Plan,
including demolished portions of the abbey (based on
material kindly supplied by P.J. Huggins)   805

MAPS

Essex	ii–iii
Basildon	112–3
Bocking	146
Braintree	167
Chelmsford	202–3
Clacton-on-Sea	238–9
Coggeshall	247
Colchester	256–7
Colchester. Roman Colchester	258
Frinton-on-Sea	369
Harlow	448–9
Harwich	473
Loughton	567
Maldon	578
Saffron Walden	655
Southend-on-Sea	692–3
Southend-on-Sea. Central Area	694
Stansted Mountfitchet	737
Witham	842

PHOTOGRAPHIC ACKNOWLEDGEMENTS

We are grateful to English Heritage and its photographers Jonathan Bailey and Patricia Payne, who took most of the photographs in this volume (© English Heritage Photo Library), and also to the sources of the remaining photographs as shown below. We are grateful for permission to reproduce them as appropriate.

Colchester Borough Council: 6

English Heritage Picture Library: 67

The Highways Agency: 122

Morley von Sternberg: 113

Norman Foster, Foster & Partners: 117

Steve Stephens: 120

University of Essex: 116

The photographs are included in the indexes, and references to them are given by numbers in the margin of the text.

MAP REFERENCES

The numbers printed in italic type in the margin against the place names in the gazetteer of the book indicate the position of the place in question on the index map (pp. ii–iii), which is divided into sections by the 10-kilometre reference lines of the National Grid. The reference given here omits the two initial letters (formerly numbers) which in a full grid reference refer to the 100-kilometre squares into which the country is divided. The first two numbers indicate the *western* boundary, and the last two the *southern* boundary, of the 10-kilometre square in which the place in question is situated. For example, Abberton (reference 0010) will be found in the 10-kilometre square bounded by grid lines 00 (on the *west*) and 10, and 10 (on the *south*) and 20; Writtle (reference 6000) in the square bounded by the grid lines 60 (on the *west*) and 70, and 00 (on the *south*) and 10.

The map shows all those places, whether towns, villages, or isolated buildings, which are the subject of separate entries in the text.

FOREWORD

'Essex is not as popular a touring and sight-seeing county as it deserves to be. People say that is due to the squalor of Liverpool Street Station. Looking round the suicidal waiting-room on platform 9 and the cavernous left luggage counters behind platforms 9 and 10, I am inclined to agree.'

Pevsner's wonderfully evocative opening of the Introduction to the first edition of *Essex* (1954) remains true as far as the first sentence is concerned, although one can no longer blame Liverpool Street Station, which was so successfully rebuilt in the 1980s.* One gets the impression that Pevsner did not altogether enjoy Essex. There was too much travelling, and the county might well have seemed rather shabby and unenticing in 1954, when so many buildings were suffering from neglect and lack of maintenance resulting from the Second World War: bomb damage still awaiting repair, no materials or cash forthcoming to refurbish country houses that had been requisitioned, and ordinary houses simply looking unloved. It is now extremely rare to find a cottage that has not been recently restored, or a church that is damp and neglected. All this has an effect upon the attitude of the visitor and chronicler, and is inclined to make one more receptive 'to the charms and the little problems of village churches and farmhouses' than Pevsner admitted he sometimes was.

But there have been more fundamental changes. The most obvious is that the boundaries of Essex changed in 1965, meaning that twenty-five places in the SW of the county included in the first edition and its revision (by Enid Radcliffe, 1965) are now in Greater London, and are included in *Buildings of England: London 5: East* (2005). On the borders, this has created some anomalies, but on the whole this volume has not suffered unduly, as far as architectural history is concerned, from the absence of those places. Without them, it has proved possible – but only just – to keep Essex in one volume. It has, however, been a struggle. The sheer quantity of worthwhile buildings in Essex will perhaps surprise some: with over 14,000 listed buildings it ranks seventh in England, with nearly forty per cent more listed buildings than Norfolk. Much of this, as David Andrews points out in the Introduction, is accounted for by timber-framed buildings, and here lies perhaps the greatest change that has taken place in the last fifty years: the vastly improved knowledge and understanding of vernacular buildings. I have still had to be very selective, but I

---

* See *Buildings of England: London 1: The City of London* (1997), 311–12.

hope with better judgement than was possible in 1954. Pevsner's main source was the Royal Commission's volumes, which are still useful, but assigned most timber-framed farmhouses and cottages to the C17. Improved dating techniques, above all tree-ring dating (or dendrochronology), have shown many of these to be C15 or earlier. Those wanting more comprehensive coverage of timber-framed buildings must resort to the statutory lists; I have aimed to include here every building listed Grade I and II*, and a selection of others.

Other building types and features now seem, because of changing tastes, to have been unduly neglected in previous editions: these would include industrial buildings (including railway buildings and workers' housing); agricultural buildings; and gardens, parks, and landscape. There is more on the C19 and C20, where Pevsner can seem at his most arbitrary in his selection: why ignore the Frinton Park estate, when his entries for Silver End and East Tilbury show that he valued the Modern Movement buildings there? Sometimes his zeal for recent buildings, especially post-war schools, now seems excessive, although one must remember that the general condition of buildings in 1954 would have made these new ones particularly welcome. Unfortunately, they have not all lasted as well as their C19 predecessors, which are now better appreciated and in many cases have been successfully refurbished and sympathetically extended. Pevsner's enthusiasm for the oil refinery at Coryton (*see* Corringham) is also now hard to agree with, although it underlines the point that beauty is often to be found in unexpected places in Essex (e.g. West Thurrock).

Otherwise, the criteria for selection remain much the same. All Anglican and Roman Catholic churches built before 1914, and Nonconformist churches and chapels before 1840, should be included, as well as a high proportion of those built since. Most church furnishings of any importance have been included, especially for Anglican churches, but not bells and plates nor, as a rule, chairs or other easily movable objects, or organs. Country houses and castles are all included, although in the case of the former access has not always been possible. This is indicated in the text; otherwise I have visited all the buildings described, although not necessarily inside. Domestic furniture is very rarely mentioned, the description of interiors usually being confined to such architectural features as plasterwork, staircases, fireplaces and panelling, although even so security is a concern and it cannot be stressed too often that most of the buildings described here are in private ownership and public access is seldom possible. Security is just as much an issue for churches, but the trend seems to be, surprisingly, for more to be open on a regular basis than has been the case.

Perhaps the most noticeable difference between this and previous editions is the space given to perambulations, which again have benefited from recent research, whether as part of statutory re-listing or for publications: the increased length of some entries is to be expected (Coggeshall, Colchester, Maldon, Saffron

Walden), of others perhaps more surprising (Loughton, Witham). On the other hand, pressure of space has meant less by way of scene-setting for smaller towns and villages than is now usual in revisions of other counties. The entries for Harlow and Basildon may seem excessive to some, but they have required almost complete rewriting. In 1965, the New Towns and the villages they absorbed were not fully integrated in the text, while the sections on recent buildings were written by their chief architects, Sir Frederick Gibberd and Anthony B. Davies. While these accounts now have historic interest in themselves, they were hardly objective. The revised entries treat the two New Towns as fully developed settlements, a mix of old and new, much like any other town.

In 1965, South Woodham Ferrers was not even on the drawing board, still less Great Notley, so these account for two new entries. A few places were omitted altogether by Pevsner, whether deliberately or accidentally one can only guess, or now merit separate entries: Battlesbridge, Blackmore End, Buckhurst Hill, Bures Hamlet, Childerditch, Eight Ash Green, Greenstead Green, Hatfield Heath, Hazeleigh, Highwood, Holland-on-Sea, Little Henny, Marden Ash, Osea Island, Wenden Lofts, West Horndon. Copped Hall, Hylands, Stansted Airport and the University of Essex also have separate entries, whereas some country houses are now to be found under their parishes: Belhus (Aveley), Stanstead Hall (Greenstead Green), Broadoaks and Tiptofts (Wimbish), Warlies Park (Upshire). Langenhoe and Shopland, their churches demolished, no longer have entries at all. The reorganization and renaming of civil parishes has led to the amalgamation of Great and Little Coggeshall and Great and Little Stambridge, now simply Coggeshall and Stambridge. The Bartlow Hills (Ashdon) now find themselves in Cambridgeshire.

Pevsner got round Essex in six or eight weeks, some of that time at least spent in a caravan lent to him by H. de Cronin Hastings, his editorial colleague at the *Architectural Review* (Pevsner said this made 'life and work comfortable'; one would like to know more). It took me five years, admittedly not full-time, which leaves me with an overwhelming admiration for what Pevsner managed to achieve, especially when one looks at the scrappy notes from which he wrote up his entries; no word processor, no digital camera. Pevsner's writing is incredibly concise and carefully constructed; altering an entry can have the effect of removing a stone from an arch – the whole thing is liable to collapse. Although this new edition is about twice as long as the old one, it has been more a question of adding to what Pevsner wrote rather than changing it.* He made very few actual errors, and in the process of correcting those I fear that many more will have crept in. Pevsner certainly did get some things wrong, but we only know that with the benefit of hindsight and new research; what he wrote was correct according to the current

---

* Original entries on prehistoric and Roman antiquities were by Jon Manchip White, and many of these remain unaltered.

state of knowledge. As ever, corrections and comments from readers are welcomed, and will be incorporated when the opportunity arises.

Five years' travelling and even more years' research have resulted in a staggeringly long list of those who have helped in one way or another, wittingly or not, with this revised edition. Such a venture is very much a collaborative effort, and among Essex friends and colleagues it is hard to know where to begin, but Julia Abel Smith and David Andrews have, in different ways, provided help and support throughout. In addition, David Andrews has written the sections on timber-framed buildings, church roofs, and timber-framed belfries and bell-towers for the Introduction; other sections were written by Nigel Brown (Pre-historic Essex) and James Kemble (Roman Essex), for whose expertise I am most grateful. Michael and Lucy Archer, Michael Beale, Nancy Briggs (who was also thanked by Pevsner for help with the second edition), Jane Cole, Sir Howard Colvin, Paul Drury, Canon John Fitch, Chris French, the late Adrian Gibson, Professor and Mrs Andor Gomme, Angela Green, Sarah Green, Michael Hall, Elain Harwood, Anne Holden, Jill Holman, Peter Howell, the late John Hunter, Paul Joyce, Michael Kerney, K. F. Langford, Michael Leach, David W. Lloyd, Alison Maguire, Adam Menuge, Paul Moynihan, Kenneth Neale, Stephen Oliver, Anne Padfield, Chris Palmer, Michael Pearson, Andrew Phillips, Professor John F. Potter, Alan Powers, Peter Richards, Pat Ryan, Maureen Scollan, Martin Scott, Richard Shackle, David Stenning, Sir Alastair and Lady Stewart, Alan Teulon, Robert Thorne, Glenys Thornton, Roy Tricker, Paul Tritton, Pam Walker, and Brenda and Elphin Watkin, have generously shared their knowledge on a wide variety of topics.

Adrian Corder-Birch and Chris Pond must be singled out for the very generous amount of time they gave to showing me (respectively) Halstead and surrounding villages, and Loughton. They read the entries for those places and corrected my mistakes; others who performed this valuable service were Harry Bacon and Clive Plumb (Basildon), Philip Crummy (Colchester), John Came (Maldon), Nicholas Antram and Trudi Hughes (Saffron Walden), James Boutwood (Thaxted), Bridget Cherry and Peter Huggins (Waltham Abbey). Such mistakes as remain are entirely my fault, not theirs.

Individual owners, incumbents and churchwardens are alas too many to mention, but those who were particularly helpful and hospitable include Mr and Mrs Charles Ashton, Ronald Blythe, Mr and Mrs Ian Burnett, Lady Butler, G.R. Capel Cure, Mr and Mrs Nicholas Charrington, Michael Clark, Mrs Sonia Coode-Adams, Rev. J.R. Corbyn, George Courtauld, William Courtauld, Fiona Cowell, Brian Creasey, Gillian Darley, Lord Dixon-Smith, Professor R.F. Dyson, Robert Erith, Christopher Foyle, Mrs Gnade Gray, Mr and Mrs Roger Hadlee, Dr D.G. Hessayon, Mr and Mrs M. Hindmarch, Howard Hughes, Mr and Mrs Hugh Johnson, David Keddie, the late Lord Kelvedon, the Hon. Thomas Lindsay, Mrs Fiona Mallinson, Mrs Sarah Micklem,

Col. Geoffrey Morgan, Rev. David Nash, Mr and Mrs Robin
Newman, Francis Nichols, C.W.O. Parker, Mrs V. Pedley, Lord
Petre, Mr and Mrs Tim Pratt, Lord and Lady Rayleigh, Charles
Raymond, Mr and Mrs T. Ruggles-Brise, Mrs Charlotte Ryder,
Philip Seers, D.J. Serrell-Watts, the late Humphrey Spender,
Christopher Stewart-Smith, the late James Sunnucks, P.T.
Thistlethwayte, Mr and Mrs Vincent Thompson, Mrs Nigel
Turner, Dr Louise Villar, Mr and Mrs Michael Ward-Thomas,
and Darrell Webb.

On specific topics, I am immensely grateful to the following:
Rt Rev. Thomas McMahon and Father Stuart Foster (R.C.
churches); Clyde Binfield and Rosalind Kaye (Nonconformist
churches and chapels); David Park (pre-Reformation wall paintings); Peter Cormack, Martin Harrison, and Michael Kerney
(stained glass); Geoffrey Fisher and Adam White (church monuments; their attributions are identified in the text as GF and
AW respectively); Angela Goedicke, Anne Haward, Rosanne Kirk-
patrick, and Marion Scantlebury (church furnishings generally);
Muriel Carrick (domestic wall paintings); Peter Kay (railways).
Architects and artists who generously provided information
about their own and others' work include James Boutwood,
Nancy Coulson, John Doubleday, Ben Downie, Melville Dunbar,
John Fairhead, David Ferguson, Benjamin Finn, Ronald Geary,
Trisha Gupta, Robin Matthews, Simon Plater, Quinlan Terry,
Geoffrey Vale, Tim Venn and Alan Willis.

At the University of Essex, I was greatly helped by Professors
Tim Gray and Jules Lubbock, and Maz Brook; at Anglia Ruskin
University by Ian Mehrtens; at Chigwell School by Marian
Delfgou; and at the Friends' School, Saffron Walden, by Roger
Buss. Robert Gammie and Ray Vango opened the doors of
(respectively) Chelmsford Prison and the Bank of England Print-
ing Works at Loughton, while Annette Cowper-Coles guided me
through Chelmsford Cathedral's archive. At English Heritage,
Wayne Cocroft drove me round the Waltham Abbey Gunpowder
Works and Gareth Hughes showed me unfamiliar parts of Audley
End, as well as providing much background information. Peter
Berridge and Tom Hodgson of Colchester Museums were particularly helpful. I owe a collective debt to members, past and
present, of the Essex Society for Archaeology and History, the
Essex Gardens Trust, and the Vernacular Architecture Group, not
only for their individual knowledge and experience, which is far
greater than I could ever hope to achieve, but also for fortuitously
arranging visits to buildings which had proved inaccessible to this
individual. Thanks are also due to colleagues on the Chelmsford
Diocesan Advisory Committee, who may not have realized the
extent to which their brains were being picked.

From the first edition, Pevsner's thanks to Mary Mouat 'for
creating and keeping all the files' should be repeated, as they
explain the dedication to 'The Mouats of Shenfield', and from
the second edition those to Enid Radcliffe for the 'intricate and
thankless job of all the necessary correspondence and re-editing'.
Among those who have sent in corrections and suggestions since

the publication of the second edition in 1965, the following must be mentioned, in addition to some already acknowledged above: Geoff Brandwood, Lt Col C.A. Brooks, Rev. F.T. Dufton, D.J. Emery, Ellis Gummer, J.A. Finch, J. Fisher, R.N. Hadock, B.M. Kettle, John McCann, George McHardy, H.E. Scarlett, Michael Shearer, Richard Slaughter, G. Spain, and Roger White.

As far as research is concerned, Essex is blessed with a particularly fine Record Office, whose new building in Chelmsford and computerized catalogue were both ready just as I was embarking upon this project. Both have contributed considerably, but not as much the staff at Chelmsford and Colchester, who have been unfailingly helpful. I must also thank former colleagues at the Royal Institute of British Architects and Victoria and Albert Museum, who may not have been aware that preliminary research for this volume was going on while I was still among them. Karen Evans has kindly carried out additional research in these and other libraries when I could not face another visit to London. National Monuments Record staff at Swindon have also been obliging in getting out large quantities of material (including Pevsner's notes for the first edition), as have librarians at Lambeth Palace.

This revision was initiated at Penguin Books and completed at Yale University Press, but I am grateful to the Buildings of England team for ensuring that the transition was seamless. John Newman endured increasingly less subtle hints about my ambitions vis-à-vis Essex while supervising my Ph.D. at the Courtauld before finally succumbing, while Bridget Cherry failed to dissuade me from the folly of giving up my job at the V&A in order to take the task on; I am grateful to both. Bridget Cherry scrutinized my early efforts, and since her retirement Simon Bradley and, especially, Charles O'Brien have kept the project on the right track, and have never failed to be encouraging in their support, and perceptive and positive in their criticism. Production of the volume has been calmly managed by Emily Winter, with Emily Wraith in the important supporting role of picture researcher. New photographs were taken with great enthusiasm by Jonathan Bailey and Pat Payne of English Heritage. The county map was drawn by Reg Piggott, the town maps and other plans by Alan Fagan. Bernard Dod has copy-edited the manuscript, and Judith Wardman was responsible for the epic indexes.

Research for the revised editions in this series is supported financially by the work of the Buildings Books Trust and I am indebted to its Secretary, Gavin Watson, for all his efforts. Valuable additional funding for the revision of Essex was provided by the Essex Heritage Trust and the Friends of Historic Essex, to whom we are extremely grateful.

As with every volume in the series, the author and publishers will be very grateful for information on errors and omissions.

James Bettley
January 2007

INTRODUCTION

TOPOGRAPHY

Essex is a large county, with great variety of character. The historic county ranked eighth in size after Yorkshire, Lincolnshire, Devon, Norfolk, Northumberland, Lancashire, and Somerset, with 978,000 acres, although in 1965 it was reduced to 907,798 acres following the creation of Greater London, into whose eastern boroughs were absorbed much of the county's built-up areas.* But the population remained relatively large – in 2001 it was over 1.6 million – and overall it is two-and-a-half times as densely populated as its neighbour Suffolk, three times as much as Norfolk. Yet there are parts of Essex – farmland in the N of the county, marshland in the SE – as empty of people as any parts of those two counties; 72 per cent of the land is still given to farming. The N shore of the River Thames, on the other hand, from Purfleet to Southend, is almost continuously built up with housing, light industry, retail parks, and the roads connecting them. It is for that part of the county, as well as the brash resorts of Clacton and Walton on the E coast and the New Towns of Basildon and Harlow, that Essex is best known to those who do not live there. Moreover, it is often treated as a thoroughfare rather than a destination. It is crossed by the M11 leading from London to Cambridge and Norfolk, and the A12 for those heading to Suffolk; there are major sea terminals and docks at Tilbury, Harwich, and Parkeston; and there is London's third airport at Stansted. Most travellers wish to put these places behind them as quickly as possible, although if they lingered to explore Harwich, for example, or turned off the main roads, they would be well rewarded.

The largest town is Southend, a conurbation of former villages whose urban development began only in the late C18 (it is also no longer part of the administrative county of Essex, but a unitary authority, as is Thurrock, centred on Grays Thurrock and extending from Aveley in the W to Fobbing in the E, and from Tilbury in the S to Bulphan in the N). The principal historic towns are Colchester and Chelmsford, which have vied for supremacy over the centuries. Colchester is older, a flourishing regional capital before the Romans, and was granted its first charter in 1189; Chelmsford's market came ten years later, but although

---

* Covered by *The Buildings of England: London 5: East* (2005).

it did not return members to parliament it became, under the influence of the bishops of London and because of its central location, the county town and the centre of secular and, more recently, ecclesiastical administration. With its castle, town hall, and university, Colchester feels more like a city, Chelmsford Cathedral failing to be a sufficient make-weight. Historically, the other important towns were Maldon (first charter 1171), Harwich (1318), Saffron Walden (1549), Thaxted (1554), and Great Dunmow (1555). Many other small towns are recognizable from their layout as having once had markets – e.g. Braintree, Chipping Ongar, Coggeshall, Rayleigh, Rochford – but one of the characteristics of Essex is the predominance of scattered villages. The traditional village, with church and houses clustered round a green, can certainly be found; one such is Finchingfield, justly celebrated for its picturesque composition, with its pond and bridge and little street rising to the church; although the less concentrated centres of Great Bardfield and Wethersfield compete with it for charm. More typical, however, are the many villages which have a church and manor house relatively isolated, the other houses scattered about the parish, perhaps centred on another feature such as a crossroads that has gained in importance over the years. Elmstead, Great Totham, High Roding are three examples among many, but the most extreme instance is Felsted, with no fewer than eleven 'greens' forming satellite settlements around the parish centre. 'End' is also used to denote these subdivisions of parishes. No satisfactory explanation for this pattern of settlement has been advanced.

The two great influences on the county's character, which have contributed to this great variety, are its physical make-up and its proximity to London. Until 1965, the border between Essex and London was the River Lea, w of Stratford. Over the centuries Essex provided much of the capital's firewood, hay, dairy produce, and other supplies, receiving in return much of the capital's waste with which to manure its fields, while in the C19 it found a new industrial role as London's oil and petroleum depot (at Corringham), and Tilbury provided an alternative to the docks further upstream. In the C20, Essex provided housing for over-populated London, with large 'out-county' council estates at Billericay, Loughton and Witham as well as New Towns at Basildon and Harlow, and in return large numbers of commuters work in the capital. In varying ways, Essex has also served as the capital's playground: for royalty (notably Henry VIII, at Blackmore and Beaulieu (New Hall), Boreham) and nobility in the C16, and for East-Enders (by steamer to the seaside or railway to Epping Forest) in the C19 and C20. In the early Middle Ages, most of the county was royal forest, i.e. special laws applied to it governing how and by whom the land could be used. In the C14 this was restricted to a few royal manors – Hatfield Forest, Writtle Forest, and Kingswood Forest N of Colchester – and to a large area in the SW of the county known as Waltham Forest that comprised Hainault, Epping and Wintry. The last two (as well as Hatfield and Writtle, the latter mainly in Highwood) survive in something very like their medieval form, Wintry entirely and Epping largely within the modern county. The ownership of Epping Forest by the Corporation of London is another example of the symbiosis between Essex and the capital.

Now the SW border of the county is roughly the line of the M25, although some parts of Essex are to be found within it. Otherwise, the county boundary is as it always has been: watery. Much of the western boundary with Hertfordshire is formed by the Rivers Lea and Stort, and nearly all the northern boundary is formed by the River Stour; the southern boundary by the River Thames, and the eastern by the North Sea, where, in addition, the coast is penetrated by the estuaries of the Roach, Crouch, Blackwater, and Colne, as well as Hamford Water between Walton and Harwich. Indeed, Essex's coastline is longer than that of any other English county, and has been responsible for much of the county's character and wealth. Maldon and Harwich were prosperous ports, Brightlingsea a limb of the Cinque Port of Sandwich. Much of the trade was with Europe, including the export of wool from the sheep which grazed on the coastal marshland. This same marshland, protected by over 300 miles of sea wall, has contributed to the county's reputation for being flat, although, as with Norfolk, the perception of flatness is exaggerated. To be sure, Essex could hardly be considered hilly, still less mountainous, but in addition to the rolling countryside in the N of the county, Colchester, Loughton, Danbury, Maldon, Langdon Hills (Basildon), and Great Totham are all places where hills are an important feature.

The characteristic buildings of Essex are its medieval churches and timber-framed houses. The typical Essex church is small, its walls built of inferior materials, more often than not flint rubble, sometimes plastered. It might have a C16 brick tower or porch, but is more likely to have a timber belfry, either within the W wall or free-standing just beyond it, with a weatherboarded bell-stage and shingled, splay-foot (not broach) spire. The local style is one to which the Victorian restorers seem, on the whole, to have responded well. The timber-framed houses, described in more detail later, might be plastered or have their timbers exposed (only a few have brick nogging), and typically consist of a single-storey hall with a floor and brick chimney inserted in the C16, with one or two two-storey cross-wings, usually jettied. Smaller houses are, more often than not, weatherboarded, either painted white or (especially near the coast) tarred. These two building types are to be found in great numbers throughout the county. Grand churches are comparatively rare, as are grand houses. Grandeur in Essex is more commonly found in barns, Cressing Temple's and Coggeshall's especially. Essex would not be the first port of call for those interested in C18 or C19 buildings, although good examples are certainly to be found, and in spite of its resorts the seaside architecture is disappointing: Southend's pier is a notable exception, but more from an engineering than an architectural point of view, and although Frinton has much to offer it is hardly typical seaside. For the student of the C20, however,

Essex is an essential county to visit, with its important Modern
111 Movement housing at Braintree, Silver End, and East Tilbury;
for the New Towns of Harlow and Basildon; and for individual
112 buildings such as the Royal Corinthian Yacht Club at Burnham-
117 on-Crouch and Stansted Airport.

GEOLOGY

The highest point of the county is at Langley, in the far NW,
482 ft (147 metres) above sea level. From that point the ground
gradually slopes, fan-wise, to the S and E and SE, with occasional
protuberances such as Langdon Hill (374 ft; 114 metres),
Danbury (351 ft; 107 metres) and Beacon Hill, Great Totham
(272 ft; 83 metres). Geologically, this is explained by Essex's position on the eastern side of the London Basin, a great bed of chalk
laid down in the Cretaceous period which ended some 65 million
years ago. This chalk comes to the surface in the NW of the county
around Saffron Walden, dipping down to a depth of 360 ft (110
metres) below Chelmsford, emerging briefly at Purfleet and
Grays Thurrock (where chalk quarries were started in the C18,
and where the cement industry later developed), before finally
rising to form the North Downs in Kent. Below this chalk, at
some 1,300 ft (400 metres), is Devonian rock, and below that for-
mations of the Silurian and Devonian periods, laid down some
500 million years ago. Above the chalk are layers of sand and silts,
and above this London Clay.

What lies on the surface was determined by the changing
course of the River Thames and the Anglian ice sheet. About

Landscape regions of Essex

450,000 years ago the Thames lay N of Chelmsford and (joined by the Medway) flowed into the North Sea roughly where the Colne now does. The ice sheet then blocked its course and forced it southwards to its present position. Meanwhile the melting ice sheet left behind deposits of till in a series of terraces, while new rivers – Stour, Colne, Blackwater, Chelmer – and their tributaries laid down fluvial deposits and cut through the clay to the sand and gravel beneath. This resulted in quite distinct geological bands fanning out from the county's NW corner, with roughly the whole area NW of the A12 forming what is known as the Essex Till: thick deposits of boulder clays made fertile by chalk. SE of that is a mixed zone, typically of wooded hills to the SW (encompassing, for example, Epping, Great Warley, Danbury and Highwood) and former heathland (e.g. Tiptree) to the NE. Much of the woodland lies on the acid soils formed from the Bagshot and Claygate Beds, where layers of clay alternate with sand. The clay on the edge of these beds is particularly suitable for brickmaking, while along the rivers are considerable deposits of sand and gravel, the extraction of which has had an often dramatic impact on the landscape. Finally, there is the coastal zone, including the Dengie Peninsula and Tendring Plain, mostly on heavy London Clay but with marine and fluvial silts providing the basis for productive marshland.

What this means in terms of BUILDING MATERIALS is: no good natural stone. The most commonly encountered stone is Kentish Rag, seen mostly in churches near the Thames and along the coast (e.g. Little Wigborough) because it could be easily transported by water. Other stone, such as the Barnack limestone of Hedingham Castle, had a long way to travel, leading to the conclusion that the Colne must once have been navigable very much higher up than it is now. Reigate and Caen stone were also used, as was Tufa (e.g. Faulkbourne), the latter available locally. The most common material for churches throughout the county is FLINT and pebble rubble. Knapped flint and flushwork is relatively uncommon; it can be seen of course towards the Suffolk border, but also as far S as for instance St Osyth. Chalkland also produces CLUNCH, used for dressings and occasionally (e.g. Felsted and Saffron Walden churches) more extensively. Two particular materials are SEPTARIA and PUDDINGSTONE, both frequently found in church walls. The former are hardened nodules occurring in the London Clay (especially in NE Essex); used by the Romans as a building material, in Colchester it can be seen in the town walls, as well as the Castle. The dredging of septaria off Harwich – it was ground up to make stucco for Regency London – was responsible for severe coastal erosion. Puddingstone (also brown) is a conglomerate of flinty pebbles and small lumps of sandstone bound together by a natural cement of iron oxide (hence its alternative name of ferricrete). In the Middle Ages all these materials were freely mixed, and it seems certain that most such walls were originally rendered and perhaps (as at Holy Trinity, Bradwell) limewashed and painted in imitation of ashlar.

The other speciality of the county is BRICK. The lack of building stone encouraged the reuse of materials, and Late Anglo-Saxon and Norman church builders made particular use of tile-like Roman bricks, particularly for quoins and dressings but also as levelling courses and, very occasionally (Stondon Massey), for decoration. Pat Ryan has identified no fewer than 234 churches in Essex which incorporate Roman brick in their fabric. It was perhaps a shortage of Roman bricks that led, as early as the third quarter of the C12, to the making of bricks by the Cistercian monks of Coggeshall Abbey. These 'great bricks', as they are sometimes called, are found not just at the Abbey itself but also in a number of churches in the neighbourhood, suggesting that they were indeed made locally and not imported from the Continent, although it seems likely that the monks of Coggeshall benefited from the experience of other Cistercian houses. Similar bricks found at Waltham Abbey, on the other hand, were probably imported. They were of similar size but differed in quality and finish, and were probably later. The production of Coggeshall brick seems to have died out during the C13; later that century and into the C14 examples occur (e.g. at Lawford, Dengie and Purleigh) of a yellowish-white brick imported from the Low Countries (sometimes known as Flemish-type), closer in size and proportion to modern bricks. It is only in the late C14 and early C15 that red bricks, made locally from brick-earth rather than clay, start to be used for walling rather than for quoins and dressings; early examples are Maldon 57 Moot Hall, possibly *c.* 1424, and Faulkbourne Hall, *c.* 1439. The brick bridge at Pleshey Castle may even be late C14.

As far as roofing is concerned, clay tiles (pantiles on agricultural buildings) predominate.* Thatch is relatively common in villages in the NW of the county but is also occasionally found surprisingly far S, e.g. at Fobbing and Stifford. Slate is rarely found before the coming of the railways (but cf. e.g. Beaumont House).

The increasing use of brick towards the end of the C15 will be described later, as will the development of what is perhaps the county's single most important contribution to building history, the structural use of timber. First, however, it is necessary to go back to the beginnings of human history.

THE PREHISTORY OF ESSEX
by Nigel Brown

The county's variety of character described above contributed to the great diversity and success of prehistoric settlement in Essex. People have lived here for at least 450,000 years, of which 448,000 are prehistoric. For maybe 444,000 years the economic

---

*Pantiles are thought to have been introduced by Daniel Defoe, who had a brick and tile works at Tilbury in the 1690s.

base was not agriculture but hunter-gathering and, to hunter-gatherers, a landscape of estuaries, marshes, rivers and forest represented a world rich in resources and opportunities. The earliest evidence of human occupation in Essex is intimately connected with the foundations of the landscape itself. It is the sands and gravels deposited by the shifting course of the Thames which contain the earliest evidence of human activity. Deposits associated with an early course of the Thames at Clacton have yielded the tip of a wooden spear over 400,000 years old; this spear, recovered in 1911, remains the oldest wooden artefact ever found in Britain. Clacton has also given its name to the famous 'Clactonian' series of flint flake tools. It remains a matter of debate whether they represent a cultural expression of a particular human group, or are essentially just a subset of flint tools produced for a particular purpose. Most early flint tool assemblages are dominated by a large cutting or chopping tool known as a handaxe. Such objects are found widely and large groups have been recovered during quarrying in S and E Essex. From around 10,000 years ago during the MESOLITHIC period, the early part of the latest (and current) warm period, trees began to recolonize S Essex. Woodland spread across the landscape with significant breaks around the edges of lakes, streams and rivers, which provided good opportunities for people to hunt and gather wild food. The changing environment can be reconstructed from plant pollen and other evidence preserved in buried peats and alluvium. Such deposits have been exposed and recorded at many locations, particularly during quarrying in the Lea/Stort valley, with pollen indicating the spread first of pine forest and then mixed woodland of hazel and elm. Evidence from elsewhere indicates that later in the Mesolithic oak and lime trees dominated the Essex woodland.

The sea level was much lower in the Mesolithic than it is today, and the Thames at that time swung N to be joined by the Crouch and Blackwater rivers to form a broad estuarine complex. Extensive lowlands extending into what is now the North Sea would have been available for human occupation, but would have been progressively inundated during the Mesolithic. Important sites have been recorded in the inter-tidal zones of the upper Crouch and Blackwater estuaries, and these perhaps served as base camps from which the lower-lying areas to the E were exploited. Flint tools of this period are highly distinctive, consisting of very small blades called microliths, which could be hafted into wooden handles to form a wide variety of tools. Larger tools such as axes and maceheads were also made. The hills around Rayleigh and Thundersley in SE Essex and the high ground at Great Baddow in the Chelmer valley seem to have been particularly favoured areas for occupation, and large collections of Mesolithic flint tools were recovered during sand and gravel extraction in the early C20. Flint scatters also occur on the boulder clay uplands, indicating that these areas too were exploited. It is not difficult to envisage seasonal patterns of movement with particular locations visited at appropriate times of the year.

Evidence for settlement in Essex during the NEOLITHIC period (from *c.* 4000 B.C.), when farming was first introduced, is widespread. Extensive archaeological excavations on low-lying gravel terraces fringing the Blackwater estuary have revealed numerous scatters of pits and at least one substantial post-built structure, a rectangular building 39 ft 3 in by 65 ft 7 in (12 by 20 metres), which can lay claim to being the earliest Essex house. Some of the best-preserved traces of settlement is again found in the inter-tidal zone, where well-preserved evidence exists on the mudflats of what was once dry land. Artefact scatters indicate the presence of settlements, notably within the Blackwater estuary and the Jaywick/Clacton/Walton area. One site, at The Stumble (an area of mudflats in the Blackwater estuary), would originally have lain on dry land situated on the low-lying neck of a small promontory, between areas of higher ground represented by the present shore and Osea Island, with small watercourses to E and W flowing into the main estuary on the S. Pollen analysis of the soils points to a predominantly wooded landscape of lime, oak and hazel. Importantly, charred fruit stones, nuts and tubers of wild species are as common finds here as the abundant charred remains of crops. This may indicate continued reliance on foraging in woodland, rather than a complete and sudden switch to agriculture.

Major changes did occur, however, in the Neolithic. Most strikingly, this is the period when MONUMENTAL STRUCTURES, truly architectural in nature, began to be built. These included oval, earth-built burial mounds known as long barrows, together with massively elongated rectilinear enclosures of banks and ditches running for hundreds of metres known as 'Cursus' monuments. The largest, most complex and amongst the earliest of these new monumental constructions were causewayed enclosures. These last were major constructions of ditches and banks with many gaps, very roughly circular in form, sited on high spots in the landscape and clearly designed to define particular locations. The ditches often follow contours and seem designed to channel movement.

The nature of these developments may be briefly explored in the Chelmer valley/Blackwater estuary river system of central Essex. While Neolithic occupation appears to be widespread and fairly uniform within the river system, there is a marked variation in the distribution of these monuments, and oval or sub-rectangular long mortuary enclosures/barrows, together with some ring ditches, are widely distributed along the river system. Major monuments are known only from the Springfield area NW of Chelmsford. This area may have been selected as it was a major point of transition for people moving through the river system and up on to the boulder clay plateau or from there into the Chelmer valley. There may thus have been an opportunity for considerable gatherings of normally scattered groups of people in the Springfield area at particular times of the year. At Springfield Lyons a small causewayed enclosure was built on high ground overlooking a cropmark oval barrow enclosure situated close to the valley floor. Another major monument, the Spring-field Cursus, was constructed in the valley below Springfield Lyons and aligned on the oval barrow. The Cursus, as revealed by aerial photographs and extensive excavations in the early 1980s prior to housing development, was a rectilinear enclosure 2200 ft (670 metres) long and 130 ft (40 metres) wide with squared terminals and a circular setting of upright timbers at its eastern end. Together these two monuments cut across the neck of a spur of ground just above the Chelmer floodplain and marked by the 65 ft (20-metre) contour line within a broad meander of the river. The break in slope is not great but may have been significant. Despite the canalization of the Chelmer in the C18 and more recent drainage works, the river still floods each winter to the E of Chelmsford in the vicinity of the Cursus. Although now obscured by housing, the panoramic view of the Cursus and oval barrow from the causewayed enclosure at Springfield Lyons would have been dramatic in midwinter, with the rising sun reflected in the (often frozen) floodwater in the valley below. As winter flooding in the Neolithic would have been even more extensive than it is today, it seems likely that the Cursus and barrow would have formed a line of monumental earthworks cutting off an area of land surrounded on its three other sides by water.

By the MIDDLE BRONZE AGE (c. 1500 B.C.), settlement evidence in Essex is even more widespread and associated with the emergence of a fully agricultural economy. The most complete example of a Middle Bronze Age settlement yet revealed in Essex comes from the boulder clay area and was excavated at Stansted Airport. Here several post-built round-houses, set within small rectilinear enclosures defined by fences and ditches, lay close to a stream valley, which contained the remains of a round barrow. Round-houses are the dominant architectural form in Britain from the Bronze Age to the Roman period. A small number of rectangular buildings are also known from Essex. With the exception of a building excavated at Lofts Farm (Great Totham) which seems to have functioned as a 'long-house', with people occupying one end and animals the other, they appear to be confined to workshops, storehouses and shrines. Interestingly, the relatively few Neolithic houses known from Britain are rectangular, somewhat reminiscent of the long barrows, while there is a clear similarity between the round-houses of the Bronze Age and the round barrows of the period.

Many hundreds of ROUND BARROWS are known throughout Essex as ring ditches showing as cropmarks. A few survive as upstanding mounds, for example at Norsey Wood (Billericay), making them the earliest human structures still visible above ground in the county. Such barrows, in common with the earlier long barrows and other monuments, seem to have played a key role in forming boundaries and dividing up the landscape. Crop-mark evidence has been studied in detail in the Stour Valley, while at the opposite end of the county extensive excavations at Mucking have revealed a pattern of small round barrows marking

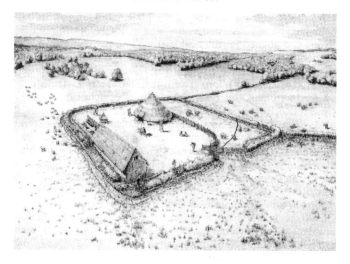

Lofts Farm, Great Totham.
Late Bronze Age enclosure as it might have appeared *c.* 800 B.C.

the boundaries of rectilinear fields. In NE Essex, highly distinctive barrow CEMETERIES of closely packed burial mounds were
constructed creating extensive burial landscapes of great complexity. Some of the best evidence comes from a series of excavations at Ardleigh where the eastern boundary of the cemetery
formed a major land division. Long, deep linear ditches with
large banks were also constructed in the Middle Bronze Age at
Ardleigh to form major land boundaries. Gaps in these ditches
and the eastern edge of the cemetery first established the course
of a trackway which has been traced as a cropmark for more than
a mile, and continued in use throughout the Iron Age and Roman
periods; indeed, its northern course is continued by a modern
road, Home Farm Lane.

This appearance of substantial, circular, ditched enclosures is
one of the most striking developments of the LATE BRONZE AGE
and such sites (usually between about 100 and 200 ft (30 and
60 metres) in diameter) are widely distributed across eastern
England. Their resemblance in form to Neolithic henge monuments is probably more than coincidence; it seems that the
builders of these enclosures deliberately chose an archaic form.
Essex is particularly rich in such enclosures; six have been extensively excavated or trial-trenched, and a number of others have
been provisionally identified from aerial photographs. They share
much in common, notably a circular form, substantial enclosure
ditches, and a similar range of artefacts and internal structures.
These clear similarities, however, mask a considerable variation
in detail – most striking for instance, when the plans of two of
the most extensively excavated examples, Mucking North Ring

and Springfield Lyons, are compared: each site appears to have its own particular history and pattern of use reflected in the arrangement of the internal layouts.

In common with the evidence from other circular enclosures, it is apparent that the Late Bronze Age occupants of Springfield Lyons were deeply involved in agriculture and other aspects of production. Artefacts recovered from the site include a large pottery assemblage, loom weights, spindle whorls and perforated clay slabs, while charred plant remains indicate that crop processing took place within the enclosure. The enclosure ditch contained the largest collection of clay mould fragments for casting bronzes ever recovered from a Bronze Age site in Britain. Weeds present in the plant remains indicate not only that the light soils of the gravel terrace were exploited, but that agricultural cultivation also extended on to the heavier clay soils and the damp conditions of the Chelmer valley floor. But there are also clear ceremonial or symbolic aspects to the Late Bronze Age site at Springfield Lyons. The decision to build there may have been connected to the existence of the 2,000-year-old Neolithic causewayed enclosure, the remains of which may still have been visible, and the Bronze Age enclosure has a highly unusual feature (unlike any of the other known Late Bronze Age circular enclosures) of numerous causeways, which appear to echo consciously the Neolithic site.

Furthermore, there is evidence that the Springfield Lyons enclosure was built to inherit rites and activities previously carried out on a Middle Bronze Age site 875 yds (800 metres) N, close to the A12 Boreham Interchange. Here a small rectangular structure (measuring 14 ft 9 in by 7 ft 2 in (4.5 by 2.2 metres)) has been interpreted as a shrine, in common with a similar building at Broads Green (Great Waltham), and partly by analogy with the better-preserved, waterlogged, remains of a shrine at Bargeroosterveld, Netherlands. It appears that the shrine was demolished and sealed in the Late Bronze Age, its posts removed, and the post-holes filled with a range of deposits. These included a pottery assemblage, comprising an unusual range of ceramics and fragments of a highly decorated, imported bowl, which can be dated to an early stage of the Late Bronze Age, and is contemporary with the earliest ceramics discovered at Springfield Lyons.

Although abandoned by the Early Iron Age, Springfield Lyons continued to provide a location for ritual deposition into the IRON AGE. It is during this period that the remains of buildings in Essex became prolific. Hundreds of round-houses have been excavated from the Middle and Late Iron Age sites throughout the county. These range from relatively isolated structures like an example excavated at Ardleigh, to concentrations of buildings forming, in effect, villages at, for example, Mucking, Little Waltham and St Osyth. The basic structure is a round-house built around a structure of earth-fast posts, with a more or less elaborate porch usually facing SE. The posts were generally surrounded by a gully, which often seems to have been a drainage feature partly intended to cope with run-off from the presumably thatched roofs; in some cases the perimeter gully seems to have been a foundation trench for the walls. Walls mostly appear to have been built of wattle and daub. Settlements tended to be unenclosed, but were sometimes surrounded by a ditch and bank, often of rather irregular form. The single house at Ardleigh had been set within a very small rectangular enclosure formed by a deep ditch, which must have given it a very striking appearance. In the Late Iron Age, much larger rectangular enclosures seem to have been used to similar dramatic effect. At Stansted Airport, excavations revealed a rectangular enclosure 262 by 262 ft (80 by 80 metres) surrounded with a substantial ditch and bank; round-houses were ranged around the internal side of the enclosure facing inwards towards a rectangular shrine. In the s of the county, at Rainham (now London Borough of Havering) and Orsett Cock, Late Iron Age rectangular enclosures defined by a triple series of banks and ditches have been excavated. The example at Orsett surrounded a single large round-house and must, like the earlier and smaller enclosed round-house at Ardleigh, have been an imposing and architecturally dramatic sight.

The banks and ditches of substantial Iron Age DEFENDED ENCLOSURES can be seen at a number of locations in Essex, e.g. at Prittlewell and Asheldham Camps, and most strikingly in the w of the county at Wallbury (Little Hallingbury), Ambresbury Banks (Epping Upland) and Loughton Camp, while at Uphall Camp, Ilford (now London Borough of Redbridge), parts of what may have been the largest such enclosure in England have been excavated. In the N of the county the remains of the huge system of defensive DYKES which surrounded the Late Iron Age settlement complex at Colchester, which was one of the most important Iron Age sites in southern Britain, are perhaps the most famous of upstanding prehistoric monuments in Essex. The ditches enclosed a number of religious, administrative and trading foci. A vivid reminder of Colchester's importance at this period are the recent excavations at Stanway of a series of Conquest-period burials of native chieftains, containing elaborate grave goods. The burials had been set within large rectangular ditched funerary enclosures. The establishment of a major Roman town at Colchester continuing the religious, administrative and trading functions of the Iron Age is by no means the only example of such continuity. A major Roman temple was built at Harlow, occupying the site of an Iron Age shrine, the focal point for depositions of coins which had itself been located next to a Middle Bronze Age cemetery.

ROMAN ESSEX
by James Kemble

The century between the visits of Julius Caesar to Britain in 55–54 B.C. and the invasion by a Roman army under the gener-

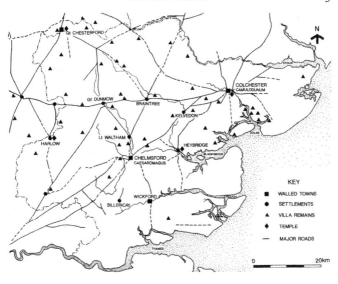

Roman Essex

alship of Aulus Plautius for Emperor Claudius in A.D. 43 had seen increasing contacts between the Continent and Britain. There is evidence of Roman goods such as bronze paterae and ewers from pre-Conquest sites at Pleshey, Rivenhall and Stansted. Some of the elite of the Trinovantes tribe (occupying what later became Essex) may already have been sympathetic to Roman merchandise and saw advantages in being part of the Roman world.

The capital of the Trinovantes tribe was the *oppidum* (fortified 'town') of Camulodunum, 'fort of the Celtic war-god Camulos'. According to coin-evidence this was already in existence by *c.* 20 B.C. and occupied some 10 sq. m., protected on the S by Roman River, on the N the River Colne and a hill-fort, and on the W by the series of earthen dykes referred to earlier, the last of which was constructed after the Roman Conquest. Although most of the *oppidum* was pastoral or under cultivation, concentrations of special activity have been identified in two areas: at Sheepen, NW of modern Colchester, are traces of industry and the coin-mint of the Trinovantian king Cunobelinus (Shakespeare's Cymbeline), while to the SW at Gosbecks (Stanway) was a ritual area and a large enclosure which may have been Cunobelinus' farmstead. Claudius with his army disarmed the Britons at Camulodunum and accepted surrenders, then returned to Rome leaving the army under Plautius' command. Legion XX set up its military base on a new site 2 m. NE of Gosbecks, protected by the Colne, where the army built a 49-acre fortress, which occupied the western part of the intramural part of present Colchester. It was protected by a V-shaped ditch 16 ft 6 in. (5 metres) wide and an earth rampart based on flat-laid timbers, and there is now evidence that the fortress and buildings within it were integrally planned in multiples of 50 and 100 Roman ft.

When the main military thrust had moved westwards and Colchester was no longer needed as an active military base after A.D. 49, the fortress buildings were adapted or replaced, and land to the E on a slightly different alignment was developed as a *colonia* for retired veterans. Surrounding land was confiscated from the British landowners and the *territorium* divided up for the benefit of the new citizens. A monumental double arch faced with tufa was built over the W gate in the A.D. 50s, later remod-

p. 259, 48 elled as the extant Balkerne Gate, a name perhaps deriving from Old English *balca*, a partition or bank. The former grid pattern of the town is approximately represented by High Street, Head Street/North Hill, East Stockwell Street/Lion Walk, and Maidenburgh Street, though the pattern was altered in later periods. The new-built town houses were mostly of wood. An excavated timber-framed example had ground-plates into which upright studs at 22 in. (56 cm.) intervals had been set, the intervening gaps filled with wattle. Another, near the Balkerne Gate, of simple wattle construction, had had stakes driven directly into the ground at *c.* 14 in. (35.5 cm.) intervals. The construction differences are explained in terms of the type of roof the walls were designed to carry, tiled for the former, thatch for the latter. In the eastern extension of the new town was built a huge temple dedicated to the emperor.

The revolt of the British tribes in A.D. 60–1 under Boudicca, Queen of the Iceni (Norfolk and N Suffolk), involved also the Trinovantes. Catching the Roman authorities off-guard with the legions fighting in Wales, the *colonia* was torched, the temple being the last defence of the beleaguered Romans. When order was eventually restored after the defeat of Boudicca's army, the 3,000-yd (2,750-metre) stone walls, which can still be seen surrounding the town, were built. Tentatively dated to *c.* A.D. 70, they enclosed 108 acres, with defences including six gates, two on the N, two on the S, and one each W and E. Remains of two, the W and NE, are still visible above ground.

Although the premier position of Colchester waned after the Boudiccan Revolt when the centre of administration moved to London, it is clear that the town attracted wealthy merchants and landowners into the C2. High-class town houses along North Street leading to the NW gate had elaborate mosaic floors with foliate and geometric designs. Another outside the NW gate had a mosaic of cupids, birds, animals, fruit and flowering branches. Recent excavations have revealed courtyards (one with a D-shaped ornamental pool faced with white mosaic), piped water supplies, and painted plaster walls.

The citizens enjoyed the amenities of a *circus*, an oval horse-chariot racing track, discovered to the S of the town in Abbey Fields. This is unique in Britain and may be the same one portrayed on the glass beaker found in 1870 in the western cemetery at Colchester (now in the British Museum). This shows four *quadrigae* racing around the central barrier at each end of which are three stone columns, and gives the names of the four charioteers.

S of the walled town was one of the several Roman cemeteries on which, in the early C4, was built an early Christian church. The native Britons continued to worship at their traditional site at Gosbecks (Stanway) and were allowed to build a new temple in the Roman style with a four-sided colonnaded portico or walkway. Close by was a theatre, designed for an audience of 5,000. The whole Gosbecks complex was overlooked by a small Roman fort built on rising ground to the W.

Forts, towns and villas

The Roman military would have needed to secure the major river crossings. This they did by building strategic FORTS. That at Great Chesterford, where the road westwards crosses the River Cam, may have been built in response to the Boudiccan revolt, and the fort here was protected by a double ditch 15ft (4.5 metres) wide and a timber rampart, in all enclosing about 24 acres. To the S, no doubt to trade with the soldiers, a civilian *vicus* or settlement grew up which, when the fort was dismantled, extended northwards into the fort area.

The main road westwards from Colchester, later called Stane Street, was probably in existence in the Iron Age. It led to settlements which developed into small Roman TOWNS: Coggeshall, Braintree, Great Dunmow. Braintree developed at the junction of Stane Street with a Roman road leading SW towards Little Waltham and NE towards Gosfield. Settlement in the Iron Age continued into the Roman period, with evidence of smithing and horse-tack manufacture. At Great Dunmow, where Stane Street crosses the River Chelmer, a Roman settlement of some 24 acres developed W of the junction of Stane Street with the road from Chelmsford to Radwinter. From a shrine have been recovered votives such as a pewter bowl, jewellery, coins and a bone comb dating to the C4. From here another Roman road led SW to Chigwell (possibly the site of Durolitum, the Roman staging post mentioned in the Antonine Itinerary, dated C2–3). Here has been found a hypocaust of a bath house dating to the C4. Excavations at Chelmsford, identified as Caesaromagus, have located the Roman town S of the River Can at Moulsham. Here an Iron Age farmstead was demolished to make way for a military fort, later replaced by a more substantial one defended by a ditch and bank occupying about 1½ acres. A *mansio* or travellers' inn, built *c.* A.D. 120, had rooms round a central courtyard, mosaic floors and a bath house. Along the main N–S road sprang up artisans' workshops, and about A.D. 325 an octagonal temple was constructed, probably dedicated to Mercury.

NE of Chelmsford, the Roman road leads to Witham. To the W of the entrance of the town is a large temple site (Ivy Chimneys). Developed from an Iron Age settlement, the Romano-British temple complex was built around a natural spring. A large square C3 timber temple with a double entrance to the E was replaced in the C4 by a rectangular one, and may have been the centre for Christian worship, as suggested by a tiled font-like basin and a chapel with tiled floor. Further NE is Kelvedon, Roman Canonium, where existed another *mansio* and, adjacent to it, a circular temple from where a chalk figurine was recovered (now in Chelmsford Museum). A major temple complex at Harlow was responsible for the prosperity of the town over several centuries, beginning as an Iron Age cult centre *c.* 50 B.C. Around A.D. 70–80 a Romano-British temple was built. At the beginning of the C3, a large courtyard was built in the area in front of the temple, entered through a gateway, and the whole complex was defined within a ditch 15 ft (4.5 metres) wide, in all enclosing 10 acres.

Over fifty VILLA sites have been identified in Essex. They range from richly ornamented mansions to working farmhouses, surrounded by estates. The lack of known villas on the coastal Dengie peninsula has been interpreted as this being an imperial estate gaining wealth from sheep-rearing and salt production. A mile off the main road at Rivenhall was one of several high-class villas, perhaps belonging to a Roman official or well-to-do Romano-Briton. The approach road leads to a courtyard villa, part dating from the late C1, which lay in the field E of the church. The building's N wing was at least 247 ft (75 metres) long, and part of a second contemporary building lies under the chancel. Walls were of Purbeck marble and mortared flint, plastered and painted with birds, veneered with red Egyptian porphyry, the floors of black and white tesserae. Cropmark and field surveys of villa sites at Pleshey and Chignall have shown central ranges with two side wings, part-surrounding a courtyard. The central location of the Pleshey villa to the group of parishes linked as the Easters renders it a candidate as the villa of a Roman estate of over 4,000 acres which persisted into Saxon times. Excavations at Chignall suggest it too had a significant estate attached, perhaps represented by the parishes of Chignall St James and Chignall Smealey. Many Essex churches containing Roman bricks in their walls (such as White Notley, Great Tey and Springfield) are evidence of a probable former Roman building nearby.

The Iron Age timber round-house (*see* above) had, by the early C1, largely been replaced by rectangular timber buildings. Those on timbers laid directly on the ground have seldom left much archaeological trace, and few outside the towns had a mortar construction or foundation. The majority of the Essex villas examined and known to have been of this construction were built from the late C1 to C3. A double-ditch-enclosed farm with a granary at Mucking was destroyed by fire in the later C2 and not rebuilt, while that at Boreham, dating from the C1 to C4, consisted of at least four buildings, including a thatched single-aisled timber farmhouse 95 by 52 ft 6 in. (29 by 16 metres), in which twelve aisle post-holes have been identified. Immediately adjacent were a tile-roofed bath house, a store, and wells. Occupation continued at the multi-phase farm at Little Oakley until at least the late C4. Aisled buildings have been identified at Gestingthorpe and Pebmarsh, where the farm had a tessellated floor and tiled roof and evidence of associated metalworking.

Three sites have been identified in Essex as WATER MILLS, at Ardleigh, Rivenhall and Great Chesterford. Not all were only engaged in milling flour, as the finding of a possible fulling trough and a trip hammer has shown. As in the Iron Age, salt production continued to be a major industry along the coast, where many 'Red Hills' mark the production sites and former shoreline. Here, industrial waste of clay salt pans, pedestals and burnt clay have left red-brown patch marks and mounds which were later used by sheep as refuges from rising water.

BURIAL STRUCTURES at the beginning of the Roman period continue those of the Iron Age tradition, the richest stratum of society having their cremated remains buried with displays of wealth in the mortuary box such as glass bowls, spears, and drinking vessels; a gaming board has been found at Stanway. The headstones from Colchester of a centurion of Legion XX and a cavalryman from Bulgaria are graphic records of military uniform and weaponry. Especially notable is the wheel tomb at West Mersea. From the C4, though pagan practices almost certainly continued, Christianity permeated more openly into Roman society. Inhumation burials sometimes were in stone coffins (such as at Chelmsford) but more usually of wood, and for the poorest no doubt just in a shroud. At Chignall was a cenotaph (apparently without a body) containing a glass cup of the C3–C4.

In the C3, a series of FORTS was built along the SE coast of Britain, purportedly to protect it from Saxon pirates. The Essex fort, Othona, has been identified at Bradwell-on-Sea. The E part has been lost to salt marsh; a fragment of the S wall survives, and the N and W walls are known from excavations. Much of the masonry was incorporated into the Saxon chapel built over the W gate c. 654, and a recent field survey has detected probable barrack blocks.

Increasing turbulence within the country in the late C3 into the C4 may have stimulated blocking of some of the gates at Colchester, widening of the town ditch and demolition of houses inside and outside the walls. Domestic problems in Rome, corruption within the army, weakening of the administration, barbarian encroachments, and increased raiding by Picts and Saxons have all been cited as causes of reduced prosperity. But villas clearly continued to be occupied in the late C4 into the C5. At Rivenhall, Saxons were occupying a disused Roman barn and were building anew, perhaps as estate workers under the native British owner. At Mucking, the evidence can be interpreted such that the new incumbent Saxons were employing British craftsmen who used Roman units of measurement in the construction of their new halls.

The departure of the Roman legions in the late C4 and early C5 left the British administration without adequate military backing. Decreasing links with the Mediterranean and the increasing influence of northern Europe resulted in new types of building construction. Central administration and control was replaced by more local initiatives, barter rather than a coinage economy. But for most of the land-dependent tenants outside the towns, the way of life probably altered little until wars, plagues and deteriorating weather in the middle of the C5 further disrupted an ailing economy.

THE MIDDLE AGES

The incoming East Saxons, from the late C6, gravitated naturally towards the districts which had been successfully farmed by the Romano-British agriculturalists, and in particular those along the river valleys. The main concentration of Early Saxon sites in Essex is thus to be found in the s of the county, along the N shore of the Thames (e.g. Mucking, Prittlewell, North Shoebury) and around the Blackwater (e.g. Heybridge and, inland, Springfield Lyons and Rivenhall). Excavations at Mucking, which was occupied on a shifting site from the early C5 to early C8, have revealed evidence of 53 post-hole buildings and 203 sunken huts, while at Springfield Lyons there were a large number of Early Saxon (C5–6) burials, as well as Late Saxon settlement. Post-Roman occupation is also apparent at Great Chesterford, where there was another large Early Saxon cemetery NW of the Roman town.

Of later Anglo-Saxon settlements, one of the most extensive to have been excavated was at Wicken Bonhunt, including a cemetery, where remains of timber-framed buildings and pottery indicate a high-status settlement of *c.* 700–850. The early years of the C10 in Essex were dominated by the driving out of the Vikings, who had invaded in the 860s and 870s. Edward the Elder built *burhs* at Witham (912), Maldon (916) and Newport (917), and that same year expelled the Danes from Colchester – the beginning of the revival of that town, which had been allowed to decay in the Early Saxon period. Witham and Newport did not develop as towns until after the Norman Conquest, but Maldon grew into a Saxon town to the E of the *burh*, around the present All Saints, with a royal mint (one of only three in the country) by 925. At the Conquest Maldon was second in importance only to Colchester, and they were the only boroughs in Essex.

Early Saxon churches

The earliest surviving SAXON BUILDINGS owe their existence to the re-introduction of Christianity in the C7. Sæberht, king of the East Saxons (†616 or 617) had been converted to Christianity by Mellitus (companion of St Augustine) in 604, but his pagan sons sent Mellitus back to Kent and it was St Cedd, a monk from Lindisfarne who came to Essex in 653, who achieved more lasting success. He was consecrated bishop of the East Saxons the following year, and established minsters at Bradwell-on-Sea and

Tilbury. Cedd's successor St Erkenwald (†693) became the first bishop of London, from which time Essex remained in the diocese of London until 1846.

Nothing remains of the minster at Tilbury, but St Cedd's Chapel of St Peter-on-the-Wall, built c. 654 over part of the wall 7 of the Roman fort of Othona, still stands. It consists almost entirely of Roman brick and other Roman materials. In type it belongs to the Kentish or South-East English group. It had originally an apse and a tripartite chancel arch or screen, and also probably porticus or side chambers on the l. and r. Also of the C7 is part of the N wall, including a doorway, of St Mary the Virgin, Prittlewell (Southend-on-Sea), which it is tempting to associate with the important burial chamber (possibly Sæberht's) discovered nearby in 2003. Other important C7 religious sites include St Osyth (said to have been founded as a nunnery before 683) and Hadstock (thought by some to have been founded as a monastery by St Botolph in 654).

Monastic foundations

The largest medieval churches of Essex were MONASTIC, ABBEY AND PRIORY CHURCHES, but although the county abounded in monastic foundations, surviving evidence is relatively scarce. Benedictine nuns were at Castle Hedingham (no remains) and Wix,★ Benedictine monks at St John's Colchester (only the gate- 36 house survives), Earls Colne, Hatfield Peverel, Hatfield Broad Oak, and Saffron Walden, Cluniac Benedictines at Prittlewell, Stansgate (Steeple), and Little Horkesley. But the most powerful order in the county were the Augustinians, canons not monks. St Botolph Colchester was their first house in England. It was followed by Little Dunmow (founded 1106), St Osyth (c. 1120), p. 672 and the smaller Berden, Bicknacre, Blackmore, Latton, Little Leighs (Leez), Thoby (Mountnessing), Thremhall (Stansted Mountfitchet), Tiptree, and (from 1177) Waltham. The newcomers amongst orders of the C12 were the Cistercian monks and the Premonstratensian canons, of the C13 the friars. Cistercian houses in Essex were Coggeshall (1148), and Tilty (1153); the Premonstratensians are represented by Beeleigh (c. 1180, which moved there from Great Parndon). Of Coggeshall and Tilty the *capellae extra muros* remain, of Beeleigh the chapter house and dormitory, of Prittlewell the refectory, of St Osyth one corridor apart from the early C16 abbot's mansion and the large gate- 37 house. The friars, whose role was to tend the sick and needy, have left no architectural remains, though it is known that the Franciscans and Crutched Friars had settlements at Colchester, the Carmelites at Maldon, and the Dominicans at Chelmsford. There were also alien houses at Panfield, Takeley, and West Mersea, the last founded before the Conquest, and of hospitals there are remains at Maldon (St Giles) and Newport (fragments only).

★The largest nunnery was Barking; see *The Buildings of England: London 5: East*, 118–20.

The grandest surviving monastic fragments are the complete
early C12 nave of Waltham Abbey, which by the C13 had become
one of the most important and prosperous abbeys in the country,
and the magnificent ruin of the nave of the Augustinian St
Botolph's Priory, Colchester, dedicated 1177. Both have massive
circular piers, but Waltham is much more richly decorated, while
St Botolph still has the grim bareness of the Early Norman style.
The w front of St Botolph is especially English in that its twin
towers are placed outside the aisles. The same was done at the
Benedictine Colne Priory, Earls Colne, which was begun about
1100–7. These buildings, however, have completely disappeared,
as have the huge E additions to Waltham Abbey, begun after 1177.

Eleventh- and twelfth-century churches

Besides Bradwell, the other standing SAXON CHURCHES of Essex
belong to the last fifty years before the Conquest, although it is
not always possible or indeed useful to distinguish between Late
Saxon and Early Norman, some churches (such as Hadstock,
Tollesbury, and White Notley) being best thought of as Saxo-
Norman. Most Saxon churches were no doubt of timber. Essex
was in the Middle Ages widely wooded, and if any one feature is
characteristic of the county as against all others right through to
the time of the Reformation, it is the importance of timber in
church architecture. So it is happily fitting that the only surviving medieval English timber church is in Essex, at Greensted. It
is built of oak logs split vertically in halves and set vertically. The
dating is a matter of some interest. Traditionally, it is assigned to
1013, because the body of St Edmund is thought to have rested
there in that year. Tree-ring dating of the nave timbers in 1995
established that the trees were felled after 1063, substantially later
than previously thought.

Of the undoubtedly pre-Conquest churches, there are
Inworth, Chickney, and Strethall (with a mid-C11 chancel arch),
the w towers of Holy Trinity Colchester (with a triangular head
to its doorway) and of Little Bardfield, and odd windows in a
few other places. Mention should also be made of Prior's Hall,
Widdington, a Late Saxon chapel converted to a dwelling in
1395–1400. The tower of Great Tey, originally a crossing tower,
seems in its lower stages to be Saxon rather than Norman, while
the crossing tower of Boreham probably started as the Saxon
chancel of that church. Saxon SCULPTURED STONES are
extremely rare, but include the fragment of a cross-shaft at
Saffron Walden, and fragments of grave covers at Great Canfield,
West Mersea, and White Notley.

The majority of surviving NORMAN CHURCHES in Essex are
of very simple plan, just a nave and chancel (Chipping Ongar
and South Shoebury, Southend-on-Sea), or a nave and apse
(Easthorpe), or a nave, narrower chancel, and apse (Great and
Little Braxted, Hadleigh, Pentlow, etc.). Langford is unique in
England for having a w apse, a German custom. Copford and
Great Clacton are almost unique for having had tunnel-vaulted

naves (but cf. Chepstow, Gwent), and the former is moreover distinguished by having nave, chancel and apse of equal width. All
these churches are small, and for parish churches with aisles there
seems to have been as yet little demand. Arcades or indications
of arcades remain at Blackmore and Great Tey. In other cases
where more space was desired, naves were made remarkably
wide. Such is the case at Great Clacton, Great Waltham, High
Easter, St Mary Maldon, and Southminster. The usual plan for
a larger Norman parish church, however, was cruciform: nave,
crossing, transepts, and chancel. In these cases the tower would
be placed above the crossing. An especially big example is Great
Tey, although the lower stages, as noted above, are probably
pre-Conquest. Others are, or were, Boreham (probably using the
Saxon chancel as its base), Fyfield, Great Easton, Hatfield
Peverel, Mount Bures, and Wakes Colne. The most impressive
Norman W tower is at Corringham, broad and massive in shape.
Others survive at Stambourne, Finchingfield, Felsted, and so on.
The W walls of Norman churches, where they are not hidden by
W towers, have occasionally a nice grouping of windows, including circular ones (Blackmore, Copford, Faulkbourne).

A speciality of the county are round towers, although there is
only a fraction of the number to be found in Norfolk and Suffolk.
Lamarsh, Great Leighs, and Broomfield are C12 examples, South
Ockendon C13, Bardfield Saling and Pentlow are as late as the 13
C14. The existence of former round towers has also been proved
at Arkesden, Birchanger, West Thurrock, and Wicken Bonhunt.
Textbooks explain their introduction by the absence of good local
building stone for corner-pieces, and that may well be true; for
if Norman builders used Roman bricks so extensively for quoins
and door and window surrounds, the reason was certainly that
they had nothing equally hard available. Their more extensive
presence in Norfolk, however, where stone and flint was also
widely used for the corners of square towers, suggests that stylistic considerations might equally have played a part, with parallels in other countries around the North Sea.*

Of Norman details not much need be said. There are no
especially spectacular doorways. What there is has occasionally
prettily carved columns with zigzag, spiral, or similar motifs
(Belchamp Otten, Elsenham, Great Clacton, Margaret Roding,
Middleton, South Ockendon). Lintels are often curved (Chigwell, High Ongar, Margaret Roding, Orsett, Stansted Mount 14
fitchet) and tympana often decorated with geometrical all-over
patterns such as diapers (Chigwell, Elsenham, Great Canfield,
High Ongar, Margaret Roding, South Weald, Stansted Mountfitchet). There is only one Norman tympanum in the whole
county which has figure carving, at Birchanger, and that has no
more than one humble and incompetently rendered little lamb.

An exceptionally ambitious parish church is Castle Heding 15
ham, which was under the special patronage of the de Veres up
at the castle. It is 125 ft (38 metres) in length and belongs to the

---

* Cf. *The Buildings of England: Norfolk* (1997–9), 43–4.

Transitional style of the second half of the C12. The nave is provided with aisles separated by alternating circular and octagonal piers; the chancel has a straight E end with a fine group of windows including a wheel window (which is a rarity in England). The tower stood at the W, but has been replaced.

The same alternation of circular and octagonal piers as at Castle Hedingham exists at East Tilbury and Felsted, continuing 16 in the C13 at Braintree. The remaining piers of Little Dunmow Priory make one regret the destruction of the rest of the late C12 work there.

Thirteenth-century churches

The C13 was not an age of great activity in Essex, except for the completion of the *novum opus* at Waltham Abbey. The church was consecrated in 1242. But no major work in the EARLY ENGLISH style survives in the county. Transepts exist or have existed at Berden, Great Chesterford, Great Sampford, and Newport. At St Osyth and Leez Priory they are provided with E aisles. Good Easter has a chancel of *c.* 1230–40 with much enrichment inside, 21 Berden an even richer chancel of *c.* 1270. WINDOWS at first were lancets, but by 1270 (Berden etc.) lancets are coupled, and pierced circles or cusped circles placed above them. Bar tracery does not occur so early. But by the early C14 it had developed into forms heralding in their wilfulness and illogicality the Decorated style to come (Gestingthorpe, Great Dunmow, Great Sampford). Clerestories occasionally have quatrefoil windows (Horndon-on-the-Hill). PIERS are usually circular and have moulded capitals, but stiff-leaf foliage occurs quite often and is occasionally of excellent quality (Berden, Stisted, etc.). Other pier shapes are rare (quatrefoil Saffron Walden, Wimbish; quatrefoil with four shafts in the diagonals Radwinter; circular with four attached shafts St Osyth; circular with eight attached shafts St Osyth). The double piscina at Barnston may in addition be noted. It is of the type of Jesus and St John's College chapels at Cambridge, i.e. with two intersected round arches. Another oddity is the arcade at Navestock, of wood plastered so that it looks like stone, a deceit perhaps more common than anyone yet realizes. Finally TOWERS. Here the only references necessary are to All Saints Maldon, which has that unique conceit, a triangular tower, and to Grays Thurrock with a C13 tower in transeptal position.

Fourteenth-century churches

The DECORATED STYLE can be seen in what Pevsner described as 'all its somewhat unhealthy luxuriance' in the chancel of 23, 24 Lawford, with its highly unusual tracery and its delicious foliage growing up inside the window surrounds, in the S aisle of All 22 Saints Maldon, and the chancel of Tilty. The surviving S chapel of Waltham Abbey is earlier and less *outré*, but has lovely double tracery in its straight-headed W windows. The surviving S chapel of Little Dunmow is later, hardly before 1360, and shows the deliberate mixing in of some Perp motifs in the window tracery. That circumscribes the extent in time of the Decorated in Essex. Now for details. PIERS are usually octagonal and capitals moulded. Sometimes the octagonal shape is continued upward above the capital so that the arches die into it. Frequent also are piers of quatrefoil section, with or without fillets on the shafts (Blackmore, Burnham, Danbury, Elmstead, Henham, St Leonard-at-the-Hythe Colchester, Lindsell, All Saints Maldon, Rickling). Sometimes between the foils of the quatrefoil there is a hollow (Hempstead consecrated 1365, Orsett) or a keeled shaft (Bardfield Saling, Little Maplestead, Shalford) or a filleted shaft (Finchingfield, Great Sampford, Thaxted). Sometimes the main attached shafts are polygonal instead of semicircular (Stebbing), sometimes the quatrefoil is replaced by a square with four attached semicircular shafts (Feering, Halstead, Witham). Quatrefoil windows, as they occurred already in the C13, are found in the C14 clerestories of Little Sampford and Sible Hedingham and the C14 porches of Great Bardfield and Stebbing. These two churches also possess what must be called the most spectacular pieces of interior stone DECORATION, rood screens filling with shafts, arches, and tracery the whole height of the chancel arch. Stebbing is earlier, c. 1340 (although one must be cautious, as most of the present detail is C19), Great Bardfield on the verge of Perp. As the same motif occurs at Trondheim in Norway, it must be assumed that it comes from some lost major work. Mention should also be made of the much-restored church of Little Maplestead. It belonged to the Knights Hospitaller and therefore had a circular nave.

Fifteenth-century churches

The PERPENDICULAR style corresponds to the period of greatest prosperity in East Anglia. As in Suffolk and Norfolk, the wool and cloth trades were the chief source of wealth. An Elizabethan statute speaks of the 'fair large towns of Essex inhabited of a long time with clothmakers'. Yet there are only three churches in the county which can stand up to a comparison with Long Melford and Lavenham in Suffolk or the best and grandest in Norfolk: Saffron Walden, nearly 200 ft (60 metres) long, Thaxted 183 ft (56 metres) long, and Dedham c. 170 ft (c. 50 metres) long. The rebuilding of Thaxted began first (c. 1340), and it remained the richest of all. Saffron Walden was begun c. 1450 and has its nearest parallels at Cambridge. Dedham of c. 1500 is wholly Suffolk in character. Similarly a church like Stansted Mountfitchet is of a Hertfordshire kind (see the 'spike' here and in other churches of the neighbourhood). East Anglian again are the smaller churches of Brightlingsea and Great Bromley. Great Bromley, like Dedham, has the very effective motif of twice as many clerestory as aisle windows. Window tracery of the Perp style in Essex is on the whole not rewarding. Dec motifs occasionally remain in use. A specially good group of Early Perp windows, straight-headed with varying tracery, belongs to the area of Great Bardfield, with Finchingfield, Wethersfield, and Shalford.

The proudest steeples are those of Thaxted, 181 ft (55 metres) high, and Saffron Walden (rebuilt). Thaxted employs a curious system to strengthen its buttressing. The buttresses are of the set-back type, but the angle of the tower is not visible, because the buttresses are connected diagonally by a canting of the angle itself. The same system, but with a straight diagonal, is to be found at Bocking, Great Bromley, Great Dunmow, and Little Sampford, i.e. nearly all churches with sizeable towers.

The most elaborate examples of FLUSHWORK, that typically East Anglian type of decoration, i.e. patterns formed by knapped flint and ashlar stone, are the gatehouses of St Osyth Priory and of St John's Abbey, Colchester. On churches it is to be found at Dedham, Ardleigh, Brightlingsea, and Chelmsford. Fingringhoe church makes use of alternating bands of flint and stone, and its doorway and the doorway of Ardleigh have figures of St Michael and the Dragon in the spandrels, Great Bromley St George and the Dragon. Thaxted, Brightlingsea, Great Bromley and others employ other means to enrich doorways. The richest PORCHES are those of Saffron Walden (one with a tierceron and one with a fan vault) and Dedham (panel-vaulted tower hall; cf. the N chapel at Pentlow). In the porches of Littlebury the projected fan vaults were never completed, or if they were, only fragments remain.

The greatest variety within the Perp style is met in the forms of PIERS. Generally speaking they tend to complexity and slenderness. The relative size of arches grows, and of supports decreases, so as to allow for the freest flow of space across, through nave and aisles. Slenderness of piers is often achieved by using a basic lozenge shape which appears at its thinnest when seen straight on from the nave. Fine mouldings of the sides add to the effect of slim verticality. Both elements are found to perfection at Saffron Walden. The lozenge shape at its simplest appears at Chelmsford Cathedral, with four attached shafts and no capitals at all at Little Sampford, with four attached shafts and concave sides at Dedham and St James Colchester, and so on. The octagon with concave sides is particularly characteristic of the desire for interpenetration of space. It can be seen at Prittlewell (Southend), Terling, etc. Another characteristic variety of piers is that in which semicircular shafts towards the nave are replaced by elongated semi-octagonal ones. This is the fashion adopted at St Peter Colchester, Great Waltham, Broxted, etc. To end this account a few piers must be recorded which are of materials other than stone. Shenfield has a Perp arcade of timber, as does Theydon Garnon, although later (1644). St Osyth parish church and Blackmore have Perp arcades completely of brick; see also the arcade to the chancel chapel at Ingatestone.

This brings us to the two most characteristic building materials of the late Middle Ages in Essex, timber and brick. Of the very many TIMBER PORCHES in Essex, the remarkable one at

Radwinter may be singled out for the C14 (although the upper storey is C19), Margaretting for the C15. In CHURCH ROOFS,* the skill of carpenters of more than local experience is most evident. The oldest church roofs are typically scissor-braced, with notched lap-joints (e.g. Coggeshall), though later on mortice-and-tenon joints were used in roofs of this type (e.g. Copford). Although church roofs may simply consist of seven-cant rafter trusses, they generally exhibit a great deal of variety, far more so than in domestic housing. Common to many of them is an arch at the principal truss formed by braces from the wall-pieces or eaves up to the collar. The intention, as in the domestic hall, was to create a space framed by arches, ideally without the visual dead weight of the tie-beam, though the omission of this risked the roof spreading and the walls leaning outwards. These roofs may be combined with familiar elements, such as crown-posts, or what in Essex terms are alien ones, such as side-purlins, king-posts, or ridge-pieces. Wall-plates, tie-beams and principals are generally moulded, and there may be pierced spandrel tracery. Moulding and carving becomes richer in the C15 and C16, in particular when applied to hammerbeam and flat camber beam roofs. Hammerbeam roofs are not as common in Essex as in Suffolk and Norfolk, Great Bromley and Gestingthorpe being the two most notable examples. Gestingthorpe bears the name of *Thomas Loveday*, one of the very few carpenters who can be identified as responsible for an Essex roof and who may also have built the hammerbeam roof at Castle Hedingham.[†] Camber-beam roofs are more numerous. They are flat, resembling floors in their construction. They bring the roof down to the level of the tie-beam, ensuring the walls are properly connected, particularly important in clerestories, and avoiding the impression of a dark void above the nave. In the more extravagant examples (e.g. Saffron Walden, Bocking), even the common rafters are moulded.

A notable feature of Essex churches are timber-framed BELFRIES AND BELL-TOWERS, of which there are more than a hundred. Some are small and largely concealed from inside the church, but many are imposing structures, supported on massive frames at the W end of the church, carried on tie-beams resting on the walls often reinforced by posts. From these beams a square tower, with saltire and sometimes arched bracing, rises through the middle of the roof, buttressed by the rafters which lean against it. At the top stage of the tower is the bell-chamber, which originally usually had traceried windows. From the top of the tower, there rises a timber spire, typically with a central mast with saltire-bracing between it and the rafters. However imposing belfries might seem, they were in effect built when resources did not permit the construction of a true tower. This is demonstrated

---

*Sections on church roofs and timber-framed belfries and bell-towers contributed by David Andrews.
[†] John Harvey also attributes to *Loveday* roofs at Stambourne, Steeple Bumpstead, Sturmer, and Wimbish.

St Peter and St Paul, Stondon Massey.
Isometric of belfry and spire

where a belfry has been superseded by a tower. Thus at Great
Clacton, the base of a belfry is preserved fossilized below the
rafters at the W end of the nave, left there when it was replaced
by the existing stone tower.

Nine Essex churches have structurally separate bell-towers
outside the stone W end of the church. These towers are thought
to give an insight into the construction of the now lost wooden
towers that stood on Norman mottes or at medieval castles. The
most magnificent is Blackmore (1400); the oldest is Navestock
(1365–91). Most belfries and bell-towers which have been dated
were built in about the first half of the C15. This may simply
reflect a peak in building activity, as they continued to be built
into the C16, presumably because timber was more readily available and economic than brick. That at Magdalen Laver was built
in 1534/35. Mundon's also probably dates from the C16.

BRICK was widely used for Perp churches in Essex. Those built entirely of brick are Berechurch, St Nicholas Chignall, East Horndon, Langdon Hills (Basildon) and Layer Marney. Of these East Horndon is the oldest, started between 1442 and 1476, the others early C16. But brick is encountered most commonly in porches and towers. Of porches, there are about twenty, all early C16 apart from Mount Bures, C15, where it is mixed with flint. The most elaborate have stepped gables (Colne Engaine, Pebmarsh) or stepped battlements (Feering, Rayleigh, Sandon). 32 About thirty churches have towers wholly or partly of brick, including three (Chelmsford late C15, Dedham *c.* 1494–1510, Thorrington *c.* 1483) that are faced with flint. The most magnificent, tall, often adorned with trefoiled corbel-friezes and stepped battlements, are probably those of Fryerning, Ingatestone, 30 Rochford, and Layer Marney. Dated towers are at Gestingthorpe *c.* 1498, Tilbury-juxta-Clare 1519, Theydon Garnon 1520, and Castle Hedingham 1616. The lower parts at Hedingham are no doubt earlier, but it is illuminating to realize that, except for the changing shape of bricks, the appearance of an early C17 tower in Essex is in no way different from one of the early C16. The long survival of Perp towers in brick is altogether a remarkable fact. The Early Tudor church builders for example liked to make their windows of brick as well, instead of dressing them with stone. An especially fine example is the clerestory of Great Baddow. At Layer Marney, however, the windows and hoodmoulds were plastered to imitate stone and terracotta. Brick mullions, brick arches to the individual lights of mullioned windows, and even brick tracery, most usually intersected under depressed, four-centred heads, occur often. In a chapel added to the church of Stapleford Abbotts the windows are for the first time of an arched Renaissance type. The date here is 1638. Other brick chapels added late and still in the Perp style can be seen at Ingatestone, C16 and early C17.

Medieval church furnishings and monuments

First FONTS. The raw decoration of the font at Little Maplestead suggests an C11 date. A good C12 example, circular with scrolls, etc., is at Belchamp Walter. But the most usual late C12 and C13 type is that provided in so many places and counties by the Purbeck quarries: a square bowl, rather flat, like a table top, and the sides decorated by shallow blank arcades, first with round then with pointed heads. A variety of this type adds interest by motifs of fleurs-de-lys, sun and moon, and a curious unexplained whorl (Abbess Roding, Fryerning, Little Laver). Not all these fonts come necessarily from Purbeck. Once the type was established it was imitated in the stones of other regions as well. Norton Mandeville for example has a font of Barnack stone of a design similar to a Purbeck type. The best C13 fonts in Essex are at Newport with gabled arches in bold relief and at Springfield with rich stiff-leaf foliage. Of *c.* 1300 is the handsome octagonal font of Roydon with four heads at the corners, men wearing hats with rolled-up brims. Perp fonts are more than can be counted, and most of them are octagonal with the standard decoration of quatrefoils framing shields or rosettes. One group at and near Dedham has figures or symbols of the Evangelists instead, but the standard of carving is low. The C15 font of Little Totham is exceptionally interesting, with its eight different tracery motifs. Of great rarity are the C15 oak font at Marks Tey, and the brick font of St Nicholas Chignall – not for nothing was the parish, formerly Chignall Smealey, also known as Brick Smealey.

FONT COVERS and font cases are effective pieces of decoration in a few churches. Takeley is perhaps the most sumptuous (though much restored). Others are at Thaxted and Littlebury, and also at Pentlow and at Fingringhoe and Great Horkesley (much repaired).

Essex SCREENS cannot compare with the screens of Suffolk and Norfolk.* A few (Foxearth, Great Yeldham, Stambourne) have painted figures on the dado as in East Anglia. But as far as the design of the screens themselves is concerned, one is hardly tempted to analyse it in detail. The richest screens are probably those of Finchingfield, Castle Hedingham, Henham, and Manuden, the oldest those with thin columns with shaft-rings instead of moulded mullions (Corringham, Magdalen Laver). They may belong to the earlier C14; of the late C14 is the screen of Bardfield Saling. The magnificent C14 stone screens of Stebbing and Great Bardfield have already been mentioned.

PULPITS are on the whole disappointing: there are only seven of pre-Reformation date in the county (Henham, High Roding, Leaden Roding, Rickling, Sandon, Takeley, Wendens Ambo), and not one of them is anything special. BENCHES and BENCH ENDS and STALLS and STALL ENDS also do not deserve much comment here. Several complete sets of benches are preserved, but they are plain (e.g. in the Bardfield area; also Hadstock, Stanford Rivers, Takeley, Wendens Ambo). Some have figures on the top of the ends (Belchamp St Paul, Danbury, Writtle), and a few stalls have misericords (Belchamp St Paul, Castle Hedingham). In N Essex is a small group of oak LECTERNS of the C15: Hadstock, Littlebury, Newport, and Ridgewell. Oak CHESTS are frequent in Essex churches, both of the dug-out and the iron-bound type. Of the former fourteen have been counted, usually undatable, of the latter eleven. By far the most interesting example is the later C13 altar chest at Newport, with external arcading and paintings inside the lid. Also of the C13 is the chest at Little Canfield with prettily ornamented short legs.

Of DOORS, the N door of Hadstock probably dates from just after the Norman Conquest. The N door of Little Totham incorporates timbers which may be as early as 1075, but probably did not assume their present form till fifty years after that. C12 and C13 doors with ornamental ironwork are not infrequent (C12

---

*The only screen in Essex to preserve the ribbed coving under the rood loft, at North Weald Bassett, is now at Crimplesham, Norfolk.

Black Notley, Castle Hedingham, Elmstead, Navestock, Willingale Spain; C13 Aldham, Bocking, St Peter Colchester, High Roding, Little Leighs, Margaret Roding). Typical of the C14 are doors with blank arched and traceried panels such as occur at St Giles Colchester, Finchingfield, Great Bardfield, and White Notley.

By far the best STAINED GLASS is that of the C12 and C13 at Rivenhall, and that is French and was bought only in the C19. 19, 20 Then there are small C13 and early C14 figures at St Mary & St Hugh Harlow, Lindsell, White Notley, Newport, and Stapleford Abbotts, and late C14 figures at Great Bardfield and Thaxted. At Sheering in the tracery lights is a complete little late C14 Coronation of the Virgin with angels. Of later glass the most noteworthy are the complete, if restored, Jesse window at Margaretting, the stories from Genesis at Thaxted, the panels of the story of St Katherine of the Norwich school at Clavering, and the kneeling members of the Mackwilliam family in the chancel of Stambourne which that family had given.

WALL PAINTING has much more to give in Essex than stained glass. Here any history of the art of England would be incomplete without at least two or three of the works in Essex village churches. First and foremost is Copford of *c.* 1125–30, once with 17 cycles all over the walls and no doubt also the vault. David Park* has drawn attention to similarities in facial types, draperies and backgrounds between these paintings and those in St Gabriel's Chapel, Canterbury Cathedral, shared also with the very fine head at Henham. The one seated apostle preserved at Little Easton also deserves mention as a contemporary piece of a similar style, related to work at Bury St Edmunds and St Albans. The C13 is represented by an extensive Passion Cycle at Little Tey, fragments of an interesting Doom at Vange, Basildon, and the exquisite seated Virgin at Great Canfield, near in style to 18 Matthew Paris (*c.* 1250). It is painted above the altar against the E wall of the church, between two windows – a rare and delightful composition. To the early C14 (*c.* 1325–30) belongs a group of wall paintings that may well be the work of a single travelling workshop: Belchamp Walter, East Hanningfield, Fairstead, and White Notley, those at East Hanningfield unfortunately mostly destroyed.† Also of the C14 are remarkable survivals at Bradwell, remains of a cycle at Wendens Ambo, *c.* 1330, and later in the century the St Christopher at Little Baddow, one of the best surviving in the country. The C15 is represented by the iconographically remarkable cycle at Little Easton, and the Doom at Waltham Abbey.

SCULPTURE is to be found mainly in the form of such small decorative figure-work as the numerous headstops of hoodmoulds, the delightful climbing and dancing jugglers and musicians in the window surrounds at Lawford, or the Virgin and 24 Child at Henham. The best free-standing pieces are at Fingring-

---

*Royal Archaeological Institute, *The Colchester Area* (1992), 31.
†Fragments in the Victoria and Albert Museum.

hoe, a Trinity Crucifix of *c.* 1390 and a late C15 or early C16 figure of St Margaret of Antioch, and a Madonna of *c.* 1380 at Waltham Abbey.

Of MONUMENTS a little more must be said. The earliest monuments are of knights and belong to the C13. That at Toppesfield is covered over and cannot be seen; others, a little later, are at Clavering and Faulkbourne. There follows the interesting group of oaken effigies at Danbury, Elmstead, Little Baddow, and Little Leighs. The dates go from the late C13 to the middle of the C14. Good cross-legged knights of *c.* 1300 are at Thorpe-le-Soken and Stansted Mountfitchet. Brasses and the technically similar incised stone slabs begin with the C14. The earliest stone slabs are to priests, at Bradwell and Middleton, both 1349. The latter, 7 ft (1.8 metres) long, is Flemish in style, as are some of the best BRASSES in the county. That of Ralph de Knevynton at Aveley, 1370 is a rare example of a brass that is actually of Flemish origin.

p. 236 It has a fine architectural surround, seen also at Chrishall, 1380.
p. 623 The earliest Essex brass is that of Sir William Fitzralph at Pebmarsh, engraved *c.* 1331–8. Other splendid examples are at Bowers Gifford, probably 1348, and the elegant small figures of 1347 in the head of a foliated cross at Wimbish. Also of importance are two small demi-figures of priests, at Corringham, *c.* 1340, and Stifford, 1378. The best of the later brasses is at Wivenhoe, 1507. The whole plate here is as large as 9 ft (2.8 metres). Of alabaster monuments the finest by far is that of the

39 Fitzwalters of Little Dunmow, a piece of sculpture of really high quality, a thing not frequent amongst English C15 funeral monuments. Of canopies over monuments the most sumptuous belong to the Dec style. They are at Shalford and Belchamp Walter (1324/5). Of the many tomb-chests under Perp canopies the following should be noted: the cenotaph of John Hawkwood at Sible Hedingham (1394?), the Bourchier tomb at Halstead

41 (1400), and the Webbe monument at Dedham (1506). The type remains the same when Renaissance ornament appears. The appearance of this can be dated almost precisely in Essex. It is connected with Lord Marney's rebuilding of his mansion at Layer Marney about 1520 and the monuments erected to him and his son after their deaths in 1523 and 1525.

Major medieval secular buildings

In the realm of medieval secular building it is only the major buildings that used stone, notably CASTLES. The Normans must have inherited from the Romans in some obscure way the respect

49 for Colchester. For here William erected a keep larger than any other in Europe, and built it, moreover, whether for symbolic or practical reasons, on the foundations of Temple of Claudius. It belongs to the type known as hall-keeps, i.e. the type of the White Tower in London, and had, likewise, a chapel with an apse projecting beyond the square walls and subdivisions of the main inner area into divers chambers. Of the more familiar type of the

50 tower-keep Castle Hedingham of *c.* 1142, the stronghold of the

de Veres, Earls of Oxford, is perhaps the most impressive example in the whole of England. The other castles of Essex are small (Saffron Walden for example) and mostly only surviving by their mounds or mottes (Pleshey, Chipping Ongar, Great Canfield, Great Easton, Rayleigh, Stansted Mountfitchet). Of LATE MEDIEVAL CASTLES only one stands, an impressive ruin: Hadleigh, which was rebuilt *c.* 1360–70 by Edward III.

Stone for domestic buildings, such as Little Chesterford Manor of the C13, is so rare as to be remarkable. Virtually every other house in Essex built before 1500, and the majority built before 1700, are timber-framed. (Prior's Hall, Widdington, mentioned earlier, is also stone, but was built as a chapel. There are known to have been six stone-built houses in Colchester, the last of which was demolished in 1886.) The earliest known house in the county – indeed one of the oldest surviving inhabited houses in the country – is Fyfield Hall, whose timber frame has been tree-ring dated 1167–85. It is discussed further below, but first we need to look in detail at the matter of timber framing, as it is the county's most important contribution to construction history.

TIMBER-FRAMED BUILDINGS *c.* 1200–1700
By David Andrews

Timber-framed buildings, whether black and white with the framing exposed, or weatherboarded, or most commonly plastered, make a significant contribution to the Essex landscape. Of the 14,000 or so listed buildings in the county, about 10,000 are timber-framed. Of these, more than one-third date from the C14 to the C17. They reflect the wealth and relatively dense population of the county in the later Middle Ages, a prosperity underpinned by good agricultural land, the proximity of the London market, and the wool and cloth trades. There is, however, a contrast between the towns and villages of the N and W, and those of the S and E, where the lower numbers of old houses are not simply a consequence of modern development, but also of this area being relatively less prosperous at the end of the Middle Ages. With the dearth of good building stone, and brick only becoming widely used for modest housing from the C18, timber remained in use until modern times. Even grand Georgian houses are sometimes timber-framed, as is some early C20 suburban housing.

The last fifty years have seen great progress in the study of timber-framed buildings, attributable not least to the influence of an Essex man, Cecil Hewett. A craftsman, Hewett brought the insights of a carpenter to the analysis of the buildings he saw around him. He developed the theory that carpentry and jointing techniques had evolved over time, and that they could be used for dating purposes. Fundamental to this research was his study of the two great barns at Cressing Temple which he argued were 51, 52 not C16, as had previously been thought, but instead were built by the Knights Templar in the C13. This argument was supported

by radiocarbon dates, and has since been confirmed by dendrochronology or tree-ring dating, which has made great progress
over the last twenty years.

The refinement of tree-ring dating has made a contribution to
the study of timber-framed buildings comparable to that of
Hewett. It has the potential to provide the felling date – and
hence the construction date, as timber was not seasoned – of the
timbers used in a building. This is dependent on the sapwood,
which includes the last rings that developed while the tree was
growing, being present on the timber analysed. If these final rings
have been removed by the carpenter in the process of converting
the tree to building timber, then an estimate, of the order of
10–50 years, has to be allowed for and added to the final date
obtained from the analysed timber.* At present tree-ring dating
generally works only on oak, the wood found in most Essex buildings earlier than the C17. Ash and elm were sometimes used in
the Middle Ages, and elm became common from the C17.

LATE SAXON AND EARLY MEDIEVAL TIMBER BUILDINGS
found on archaeological excavations are generally of EARTH-FAST
CONSTRUCTION. In other words, they were made with timbers
set in the ground, which appear as post-holes and slots when
excavated. Evidence from London shows that in this period a
variety of building techniques were current. They included stave
walling (comparable to the unique timber church at Greensted),
posts with wattle between them, posts surrounded by earth or
clay, and posts with horizontal boards set between them. One of
the more primitive ways of erecting a timber building is to use
trusses made from CRUCKS, forked or curved timbers, which may
be earth-fast or set on cills, and which rise from the sides of the
building to meet at the apex of the roof. Although widespread
throughout much of Britain, and believed from historical sources
to have existed in Essex, no such structures survive in the county
today.

Essex timber-framed buildings are instead BOX-FRAMED, a
technique which became widespread in the C12 and C13. This
form of construction is characterized by a rigid framework of
horizontal sole plates and top plates, with posts and studs rising
vertically between them and reinforced by braces, the sides being
connected by tie-beams. Unlike earth-fast buildings, so long as
the sole plates and the roofs were kept free of damp, box-framed
ones are capable of being maintained indefinitely, and as such
have become fossilized in our countryside, villages and towns.

If box-framed construction seems to have appeared fairly
suddenly in a fully developed form by the C13 without clear
antecedents, so does the PLAN OF THE MEDIEVAL HOUSE.
Central to it was the hall, a traditional communal living space
the ancestry of which extends back to Anglo-Saxon times or
beyond. This was single-storey, with an open hearth in the middle

---

*Tree-ring dates obtained for buildings mentioned in the text are given in brack-
ets. Where a date range is given, this is because sapwood rings are missing and an
estimate has been given to allow for this.

of it from which the smoke rose to the exposed and blackened rafters of the roof, where there might be a louvre to vent it. It was lit by tall windows, which might be contained in a projecting oriel. At their simplest, such windows consisted of diamond mullions above and below a transom, but more elaborate examples might have traceried heads. The hall was flanked at one end, the high end, by a parlour and private rooms, and at the other, the low end, by service rooms, typically a pantry, larder or buttery. At the low end of the hall, and often separated from it in later buildings by a spere-truss, was the cross-passage leading from the entrance door to another in the back of the house. Typically there were two doors in the side of the passage giving access to the rooms in the service end. The high and low ends, which were usually storeyed, were originally in-line, sharing the same roof as the hall, or they could be expressed as cross-wings at right angles to it, presenting a gable to the front which was often jettied. This basic pattern remained substantially unchanged until the C16 and C17, and was common to all but the poorest classes of housing.

The oldest known timber buildings in Essex (Greensted church apart) are AISLED HALLS, notably Fyfield Hall (1167–85) and Harlowbury, Old Harlow (1220–5), and the great C13 AISLED BARNS at Cressing Temple and Coggeshall. They are all built in the ARCHAIC CARPENTRY STYLE identified by Hewett, and are constructed of straight timbers of approximately square section; curved or arched bracing is absent. Their roof structures have passing braces or secondary rafters, long timbers at the main trusses set below the rafters, intersecting below the apex of the roof, and then running across the tie-beams, the main posts and out to the aisle-posts in the side walls, providing great transverse rigidity. The diagnostic carpentry joints are notched-lap and splayed scarf joints. These buildings were probably not constructed with continuous sole plates at the bottom of the walls, and the posts were either earth-fast or set on stones or timber pads: they were not in effect fully box-framed. The walls of these buildings may have been boarded rather than of the wattle and daub (i.e., clay tempered with straw applied to oak laths and hazel rods sprung between the studs) which is almost universal in surviving medieval timber-framed construction. Certainly the Cressing Wheat Barn (1257–80) had boarded walls, and the hall at Fyfield had boarded partitions at each end. The early cross-wing at Tiptofts, Wimbish (1287–1329), had double-boarded walls, and boards continued to be used in the walls of much later agricultural buildings, such as the Monks Barn at Netteswellbury, Harlow (1439–70).

The manor house at Harlowbury, the best-preserved early house in the county, comprises a two-bay hall, which may have had hipped ends. If so, it would have looked like a contemporary barn, such as those at Cressing. However, both here and at Fyfield, and indeed at other aisled halls, the arcade posts had carved capitals, reminiscent of the arcades of a church. Houses of this type continued to be built into the C14. Clavering Bury

(1304/5) is a good example. This too is a manor house. But this type of building can also be traced lower down the social scale, there being about twenty known SMALL AISLED HALLS in the county. These probably belonged to prosperous freehold or copyhold tenants. The best-preserved of these buildings, Songers in Boxted, is probably the oldest, dating to the first half of the C13. The rest seem to date from *c.* 1300–75, despite preserving elements of archaic carpentry. Some of these house were built of elm and ash as well as of oak, an interesting reflection of building practice in more modest housing at this relatively early period. Generally, elm did not begin to be used until the C17, when the availability of oak began to be seriously constrained.

Passing braces running across tie-beams, posts and aisles could impede the use of space if set low down, and being long timbers must have been difficult and expensive to obtain. Roofs of this type came to be superseded by CROWN-POST ROOFS, in which a post rises from the tie-beam to a collar-purlin which runs the full length of the building beneath the collars, notionally providing longitudinal rigidity to the structure. Crown-posts first appear in the C13, e.g. in the cross-wing at Tiptofts (1287–1329). Sometimes they are found in conjunction with archaic carpentry, as in a C14 outbuilding at Bocking Hall, which also had passing braces. Crown-posts became the standard Late Medieval roof of Essex houses, enjoying almost universal currency for about 250 years (except in churches, discussed earlier, which show great variety in roof construction). C14 crown-posts have moulded capitals and bases, and thick braces. Later ones are generally simpler (though they might be 'cross-quadrate', that is with fillets running down their sides) and have much thinner braces.

A classic example of an early aisled hall with a crown-post roof is that at Stanton's Farm, Black Notley, which must date to the first half of the C14. The posts of the central truss across the two-bay hall have moulded capitals. The hall was lit by an oriel window. In the wall of the low or service end facing on to the cross-passage, there is not just the usual pair of doors to the buttery and pantry, but a third central door between them which probably led to a kitchen.

The arcade posts of the central truss of the two-bay aisled hall were both a physical obstruction and a visual intrusion which medieval carpenters overcame by designing the central truss so that it encompassed the hall in a single span, thereby eliminating the posts. In so doing, they created some of the most original and impressive of our surviving timber houses. One method was to use BASE CRUCKS, forked posts in the sides of the hall to which the principal rafters were attached. These are more characteristic of the Midlands; only a handful of Essex examples have been recognized, of which two of the best-known are Wynter's Armourie, Magdalen Laver, and Crepping Hall, Wakes Colne (1301–37). A more curious but visually dramatic solution was to raise the arcade posts above a tie-beam set below the tops of the side walls, creating what is known as a RAISED-AISLE HALL. This type of construction is relatively common in Suffolk, but only a few such houses are known in Essex, Baythorne End, Birdbrook, and Fitzjohn's Farm, Great Waltham, being examples. A more radical solution, found at Normandy Hall, Wakes Colne (1368), was simply to omit the arcade posts altogether and support the tie-beam on the arcade plates. The HAMMERBEAM roof was of more enduring significance and widespread in East Anglia, if never common in domestic architecture: in this the tie-beam is omitted and the rafters supported by stub ties and arched braces. The hall (1282–1327) at Tiptofts is a fine early example.

The C14 buildings discussed above are high status, mostly manorial, and date from the transition between archaic and late medieval styles of carpentry. This transition also saw the abandonment of the aisled layout in houses, though not in barns, a development which had occurred by the first half of the C14. A manorial hall without aisles can be seen at Southchurch, Southend-on-Sea (1321–63), where another distinctive early feature, cusping on the arched braces, is also found. The braces rise to form a cusped pointed arch with the soffit of the cambered tie-beam, a dramatic centrepiece to the open hall.

The typical arrangement of the LATE MEDIEVAL HALL HOUSE is well illustrated lower down the social scale by Water Hall, Little Baddow, which probably dates from *c.* 1400. An in-line building (i.e., without cross-wings, the hall and the high and low ends being under a single roof), the cross-passage gives access to the two doors of the buttery and pantry, and a third to a stair to the first floor of the service end. The high end or parlour, however, did not have an upper storey, and like the hall was open to the roof. The hall has a cambered tie-beam with arched braces and a cross-quadrate crown-post. The stud walls have down or tension bracing, the invariable feature of Late Medieval Essex buildings and the successor to the arched bracing characteristic of C13 and C14 buildings.

By the C15, in-line houses as simple as Water Hall were probably exceptional amongst the more prosperous sections of society. Most manor and farmhouses of this date have one or two CROSS-WINGS, i.e., wings set at right angles to the hall. Cross-wings had appeared by the C13. One of the earliest is the service wing at Tiptofts (1296–1327), which is jettied to the front. The existence of an upper floor made the provision of a jetty (to maximize space, and doubtless also for aesthetic reasons) a possibility, depending on the direction in which the floor joists were laid. When the hall at Tiptofts, with its hammerbeam roof, was built a little later in the early C14, it was provided with a cross-wing at the high end too, making an unusually early H-plan house. It was more usual at this time for there to be one cross-wing, usually at the high end, as at Southchurch Hall (1321–63). A later and humbler example, but little different in general appearance (except that it is thatched and smaller) is Mashams, High Laver *p. 36* (1446). The development of the cross-wing saw the enthusiastic adoption of one of the most characteristic and popular features of Late Medieval and early modern architecture, the gable. The dominant form of the gable, and the massing created by its

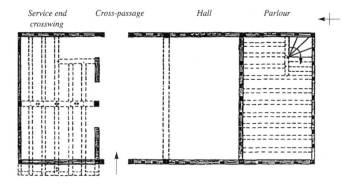

Service end   Cross-passage   Hall   Parlour
crosswing

Mashams, High Laver.
Plan

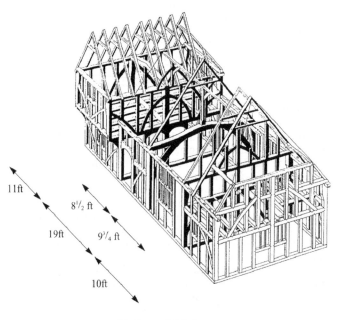

11ft

8¹/₂ ft

19ft

9³/₄ ft

10ft

Mashams, High Laver.
Isometric

repetition, transformed the front elevation of the hall house into a striking architectural composition. Analysis of the Late Medieval houses of Cressing parish has discovered four probable H-plan or double cross-wing houses, suggesting that this was the standard dwelling of the more prosperous yeoman of the C15.

Not that all these houses were entirely new. A cross-wing consti-
tuted a convenient and straightforward way of remodelling an
existing building, replacing the high or service ends, and providing extra space as well as an imposing façade. There are countless instances where this has taken place. An alternative way of
constructing a house of this format, jettied at each end of the
front elevation but without the gables and instead under a single
roof (and thereby doubtless achieving an economy) was the so-
called WEALDEN HOUSE, a much more widely distributed type
than its name suggests. More than twenty-five examples have
been identified in Essex, most of them C15. A good example is
to be seen at Nos. 29–35 The Street, Little Waltham.

MANOR HOUSES had a predictable suite of buildings comprising hall, chapel, chambers, lodgings, a court house, kitchen,
brew- or bakehouse, gatehouse, as well as the usual farmyard
complex of barns, granary, dovecote, stables and livestock sheds.
Many of these buildings were also shared by larger farms, which
like manors could be moated. Moated sites, which numbered in
excess of 800, are one of the most characteristic features of the
dispersed settlement of the Essex countryside. Southchurch Hall
is a fine example: it preserves the stone abutments for the timber
bridge which have been found in excavations in the moat. Today,
medieval ancillary and farmyard buildings are all rare, with the
exception of the barn, now sadly often converted to a dwelling.
A rare survival of a lodging range, with an open-sided passage at
the ground floor, can be found at Newland Hall, Roxwell.
Colville Hall, White Roding, still preserves much of the appearance of a late medieval manor and its appurtenances. Here John
Browne undertook a major reconstruction programme *c.* 1537–
50. The timber-framed H-plan manor house on a moated site is
accompanied by as many as eight buildings, including two barns,
a stable with a possible court hall at the first floor, a granary, a
chicken house, a cart lodge, and a brewhouse. A Tudor brick
gateway, with a moulded four-centred arch and finials above its
gabled surround, shows that the complex was formerly surrounded by walled enclosures.

The best surviving example of a detached KITCHEN is at Little
Braxted Hall (1398–1410). It is a tall square building, probably
linked to the manor house by a passage. Later converted to a
dovecote, it is now an office. A number of other buildings in the
county, typically three-bay with sooted roofs and sometimes with
a loft at one end, have been identified as kitchens. Medieval GRA-
NARIES are rare. A probable granary, a four-bay single-storey
building datable to the C14, exists at Grange Farm, Little
Dunmow. It had boarded walls. More common are the small
buildings on staddle stones which typically date from the C18 and
C19. However, the building type is older; the one on brick piers
at Colville Hall may date from the C16. MALTINGS were often to
be found on larger farms and in towns. The oldest known
example is the Boyes Croft maltings at Great Dunmow (1557–
80). They are long buildings with a low ground floor and a kiln
at one end, brick-built with a conical roof. The Granary (1623)

at Cressing Temple was originally a malting with a granary above at the first floor. In an arable county, livestock buildings are now rarest of all, but a number of rectangular buildings at both urban and rural sites, with doorways of more than average width, have been recognized as stables.

LATE MEDIEVAL BARNS are usually aisled and have crown-post roofs. Of five to seven bays, and often more than 100 ft (30 metres) long and 30 ft (9 metres) wide, they were the largest buildings in the countryside, larger than many churches, and monuments to a successful agricultural system and the wealth it generated for the great landowners. They are imposing, not simply for their size, but also because some of the manorial ones were built by carpenters who brought to their construction skills more often employed on grand houses and church roofs. Such an example is the Monks Barn, Netteswellbury, Harlow, which belonged to Waltham Abbey (1439–70). Curving passing braces rise from the transverse sole plates in the aisles and cross the posts on the way to the tie-beams, forming a huge arch at each truss. Instead of the ubiquitous crown-post, the roof is of side-purlin construction. But generally, the main variation in barns of this period is in the bracing used to tie the aisles to the main structure. This usually rises from the aisle ties to the arcade posts as at Prior's Hall, Widdington (1417–42), but may intersect both timbers in the manner of a passing brace. At the Lordship Barn, Writtle (1441–75), use is made of a Kentish-style raking shore rising from the transverse sole plate across the aisle tie and curving to meet the arcade post.

Building in towns and villages

In the TOWNS AND VILLAGES of medieval Essex, hall houses stood parallel to the street, with the entry to the cross-passage directly off it. They occupied a wide frontage, one that might typically be about 66 ft (20 metres) wide, serving a plot as large as half an acre or more. As there came to be more pressure on space in the towns and villages, so plots became subdivided. In this process, the standard hall-house plan underwent modification to adapt it to more cramped conditions and also to incorporate shops which had to be located on the street frontage. Typical responses were to turn the house through 90 degrees, so that it was at right angles to the street, usually with the shop at the front, the hall behind, and the parlour or service quarters to the rear; to have a shorter range on the frontage with another behind it, effectively a double-pile plan; to build upwards on three storeys instead of two; and to build smaller houses in terraced rows. In more substantial properties, some of these expedients could lead to courtyard layouts. Another process typical of town and village centres was encroachment on the street or marketplace, initially with lean-tos or pentices which could lead eventually to a full double-pile plan form.

Today, the most conspicuous surviving medieval feature of the main street of Essex towns and villages are GABLED CROSS-

WINGS. These suggest that in the more densely built-up centres, houses came to be laid out at right angles to the street. Such an impression is often misleading, the result of cross-wings having survived better than halls because they were two-storeyed and could easily be extended to the rear to include other accommodation, such as a kitchen. Where detailed examination of the frames of these cross-wings is possible, evidence for an adjacent hall can usually be found. There are, of course, exceptions: some cross-wings seem to have been built as separate units and their original character and function is now obscure. An example is No. 75 Bradford Street, Bocking, datable to the C14 by the traceried window in its flank. Cross-wings as independent units were favoured for priests' houses, as in the case of the old vicarages at Great Chesterford and Radwinter, or the W wing of All Saints' Vicarage, Maldon. One form of terraced housing was pairs of WEALDEN HOUSES, each unit comprising a cross-wing and a one-bay hall. Two C15 examples of these have been recognized on the S side of the High Street, Maldon, one in the former King's Head. The cross-wings had the cross-passage incorporated into them, a common space-saving device in urban buildings, shop windows adjacent to the entrance doors, and windows with traceried heads at the upstairs chamber.

SHOPS are easily recognizable as they have wide windows with arched heads located adjacent to doors. The windows were closed by shutters. An exceptionally large number of them survive at Saffron Walden (e.g. Cross Keys, the youth hostel in Myddylton Place), but they can also be seen in Thaxted, Braintree (Swan Inn, Bank Street), Colchester, Felsted (Old School House, formerly a guildhall) and elsewhere.

Timber-framed buildings of the sixteenth and seventeenth centuries

The late C15 and early C16 saw the passing of the single-storey hall open to the roof. Old hall houses gradually had upper floors inserted in them, and new houses were built in which the hall, though still recognizable as a focal element in the ground plan, had a first floor over it. The existence of a first floor throughout the building led to the development of the LONG-WALL JETTY HOUSE, in which a jetty runs the full length of the façade. Early examples are Moone Hall, Stambourne (1488–1515) and Cann Hall, Great Clacton (1511/12). These were of sub-manorial status, and remained loyal to the old format of the hall house inasmuch as they have a gable over the high or parlour end of the house. In towns, long-wall jetty houses became very common in the C16. The main streets of Colchester were lined with them, though few survive today (e.g. the Marquis of Granby, North Hill). Bradford Street, Bocking, preserves several examples, and had many more. Because of the provision for a large upstairs room, the GUILDHALLS erected by the religious guilds are typically long-wall jetty buildings. These late C15 or early C16 guildhalls are often to be found at the edge of churchyards, as at Clavering, Ashdon and Felsted (the Old School House). They are not to be confused with the MARKET HALLS which sometimes, as at Thaxted, are known as guildhalls. These were typically open at the ground floor for the use of the market, with large upstairs rooms which probably had a variety of public uses. Other examples can be found at Steeple Bumpstead and Horndon-on-the-Hill.

A popular feature of C16 and C17 houses, and one which implied an architectural composition distinct from the long-wall jetty house, was the display gable, inherited from the old cross-wings of hall houses and borrowed from the Tudor mansions of the later C16. These provided more light and space at the attic storey, with which houses were increasingly being provided. The former Woolpack Inn, Bradford Street, Bocking, has three gables, all in different styles. Two bear dates, 1590 and 1667, testimony to the long period of time in which they remained in fashion. Gables in a context where their presence could only have been dictated by fashion can be seen on the Granary at Cressing Temple (1623). This originally had four gables, rather than the existing two, and glazed windows; with a similar but now demolished stables parallel to it, it was designed to flank the approach to the Tudor mansion which once stood at the site.

There were changes too in carpentry technique in the C16. The long reign of the crown-post roof came to an end. From the middle of the century, it was generally superseded by the clasped-purlin roof, or sometimes by the queen post roof. Edge-halved scarf joints were replaced by face-halved ones. That most efficient of floor joist joints, the soffit tenon with diminished haunch, appeared at the very end of the C15 and became standard in the course of the C16. Narrow-section floor joists, in contrast to medieval ones which were laid horizontally, were in use by the middle of the C16, but did not become common in vernacular buildings until the early C17. The studs or vertical members in the timber frame, which had became increasingly close-set during the C15, now reached the stage where the studs and the gaps between them were of similar width. Such walls consisted largely of timber at a time when oak was probably becoming expensive: they are examples of conspicuous consumption, clearly designed to impress. Bracing patterns became less predictable: there was a return to arched bracing or even the use of serpentine bracing, but more general was the tendency to put the braces on the inside of the building.

From the C17, and sometimes before, timber buildings were plastered; this protected the frame and helped eliminate draughts. This plaster finish became a medium for decoration, the PARGETTING which is such a regional characteristic of Essex and Suffolk buildings. Most surviving examples are simple patterns such as zigzags or diaper work in rectangular frames, but more elaborate relief-moulded foliate patterns, strapwork or figures must once have been quite common. Most pargetting is C17. Notable examples are the foliate patterns covering Garrison House, Wivenhoe, the formal panels of the symmetrical façade of Crown House, Newport, and, most striking of all, the giant figures on the former Sun Inn at Saffron Walden, 1676.

Now that the frame was concealed, it could no longer contribute to the appearance of the house as an architectural composition. As a result, it became more important that carpentry should simply be efficient rather than impressive. These considerations, combined with a shortage of oak, manifest in the use of both elm and reused timber (almost unknown in medieval work), led to a decline in the appearance of the timber frame. Thinner timbers were used, and wall framing is characteristically primary braced, that is with long straight braces which interrupt the studs, a technique that permits effective use of short lengths of timber.

Other improvements included the introduction of GLASS WINDOWS. Medieval windows were typically made with diamond mullions and closed by sliding shutters. More sophisticated ones might have traceried heads. In the C16 and more particularly the C17, window glass was increasingly used in ordinary houses, cut to a lozenge shape or else to geometric patterns, and set in lead cames. The use of BRICK, which had been widespread amongst the higher levels of society from about the middle of the C15, began to permeate down the social scale. A few grander houses, such as St Aylotts (1500/1) and Littlebury Hall, Stanford Rivers, have ground floors of brick and were timber-framed above. Walls made with brick-nogging or infill between the studs of the timber frame were also considered an acceptable economic alternative to building entirely in brick (e.g. Monk's Barn, Newport, the stable at Colville Hall, White Roding, the lodging range at Newland Hall, Roxwell). But in ordinary housing, brick was used mainly for the plinth walls on which the timber frames rested, and for CHIMNEYS. The open hearth of the hall had sometimes been superseded by timber-framed stacks (e.g. at Chobbings Farm, Chignall, and Mashams, High Laver), usually recognizable today by gaps in the studwork of walls. The brick stack was a more enduring improvement which began to appear from the C15, though not becoming widespread at all levels of society until the late C16 and C17. Earlier examples appear as external features in the side walls of houses and often predate the insertion of an upper floor in the hall. A typical position for them was in the cross-passage at the low end of the hall. These stacks are large, often with hearths 6 ft (1.8 metres) or so wide, surmounted by a large timber lintel or bressumer, and they have diagonal or octagonal shafts above the roof.

The introduction of the chimney as a separate structural element within the house led to modifications in plan and layout. From the later C16, one-and-a-half-storey cottages were built with upper floors supported on clamps pegged to the studs in the wall. Plan form is no longer so predictable as in the past: stack position is variable, and often there is no cross-passage. Many two- and three-cell cottages of this sort, often with thatched roofs, were built in the C17 and C18, and in the N of the county are not rare today. Higher up the social scale, the LOBBY-ENTRY HOUSE appeared right at the end of the C16. In this, the entrance doorway leads into a lobby in front of the central stack; doors to either side give access to the 'hall' and the parlour. The space on the far side of the stack serves for a staircase. This plan form is typical of C17 farmhouses. A well preserved lobby-entry house is Rook Hall, Cressing, built from new, probably in 1674. It has a tall four-flue chimney with octagonal stacks and a central doorway in a symmetrical façade which reflects Renaissance and continental influences filtering down to a more vernacular level. From this type of house, it was but a short step to the development of the standard format of the smaller C18 house in which door, entrance hall and stairs remain in a central position, but the stacks are moved to the external flank walls.

MAJOR SECULAR BUILDINGS 1400–1660

The early use of BRICK in church architecture has already been noted, but the earliest use of brick in Essex for a major domestic building was at Old Thorndon Hall, where a licence to crenellate was granted in 1414. This house has been demolished, as has Heron Hall at nearby East Horndon, but here an early C15 brick granary remains, and the brick church dates from 1442. Of sur-57 viving houses, Faulkbourne with its mighty angle tower, its other towers, and its bay window with two little brick vaults on the two floors is as good an example of C15 brickwork as any. The encasing of Faulkbourne in brick began shortly after 1439, so that the house must range with Caister and the admittedly grander Tattershall and Herstmonceaux of the 1440s as one of the early examples of brick on a grand scale. The stair at Faulkbourne is very similar to that in the Moot Hall, Maldon, which may date from the 1420s. Other early brick buildings in Essex include Nether Hall, Roydon, 1460s, the late C15 chapel and cottage at Great Horkesley, and the charming garden wall with its angle turrets at Killigrews, Margaretting.

Brick is especially characteristic of buildings after 1500, and for the C16 it is hard to choose; there is so much to enjoy and admire, minor things such as the stair-turret with its crocketed pyramid roof at Jacobes, Brightlingsea, as well as major things 58 like Horham Hall of c. 1502–20. Although here only the hall range survives from that period, it makes a great show with its splendid bay window. The early years of the century saw some ambitious building activity at Beeleigh Abbey and St Osyth Priory, almost as if the abbots knew this was the last opportunity to make their mark, and in Essex as elsewhere the Dissolution gave rise to much new building, some of it spectacular. The well-named Sir Richard Rich is typical of the ruthless and ambitious *nouveaux riches* of Henry VIII's court, whose watchword was *occasio* 43 (see his monument in Felsted church), seizing whatever opportunity presented itself to despoil monastic property and enrich themselves. After 1536 Leez Priory was converted to become Rich's mansion. Its tall gatehouse is famous. The ranges were grouped round an outer and an inner courtyard without, it seems, regard for symmetry. Rich (who also probably rebuilt Rochford Hall after 1550) and his kind used the existing buildings as quarries without any sentimentality, or any romantic delight in ruins, and it is difficult now to visualize how they put up with new houses set amidst decaying old ones. Such certainly must have been the impression around the large, proud new ranges set up by Lord Darcy at St Osyth. They are not of brick, but of septaria and limestone and date from after 1553. Yet no Renaissance detail appears anywhere. The foremost brick MAN-SIONS OF THE MID-SIXTEENTH CENTURY in Essex are New Hall, Boreham, a courtyard house rebuilt by Henry VIII (of his *p. 157* time, however, chiefly the spectacular coat of arms inside remains; the rest is Elizabethan and later), Ingatestone Hall with its two courtyards and stepped gables, not yet symmetrically composed nor provided with Renaissance decoration, and Gosfield Hall with one courtyard and a façade made wholly symmetrical to the l. and the r. of the central gateway.

Of all the gatehouses of Essex, and indeed of England, the most ambitious, a showpiece of crazy height, is at Layer Marney.   56 This was begun by Lord Marney *c.* 1520, and it is here, as has already been said with reference to the church, that RENAIS-SANCE motifs first appear in the county. These are of terracotta, no doubt the work of Italian craftsmen, although probably made locally. The motifs are window mullions transformed into shafts with Renaissance candelabra in their sunk panels, ogee-arched window tops transformed into Renaissance scrolls and double scrolls, and cresting transformed into Renaissance shell-shapes. Immediately after, some bits of Renaissance ornament appeared in Abbot Vintoner's big oriel window at St Osyth (1527). A little later the fashion began to affect domestic panelling, which had, until then, been chiefly of the linenfold kind. Now roundels with heads or busts, foliage scrolls, candelabra, etc. appear: two examples are dated 1546, one at Elsenham Place (but originally from Beaufort House, Chelsea), the other from Beckingham Hall, Tolleshunt Major;* another fine example is at Tolleshunt D'Arcy Hall.

The full ELIZABETHAN style appears on a large scale at Hill Hall, Theydon Mount, chiefly of 1567–73, and New Hall,   60 Boreham, as remodelled after 1573. Both are still of the court-yard type, Hill Hall characterized by the unusual motif of attached colonnades in two orders above each other all round the courtyard, New Hall by the amazing show of seven identical bay windows all along the façade of what was then the inner side of the N range. The choice for special mention amongst medium-sized Elizabethan houses must be Moyns Park of *c.* 1575–93, which displays a symmetrical front with four gables and three polygonal bay windows of which the middle opens as a porch on the ground floor. Porters at Southend comes a little later, *c.* 1600, and, like Moyns, was planned round a great hall. Berden Hall,

---

* Beckingham Hall panelling now in the Victoria and Albert Museum.

although the dating is problematic (early C16, remodelled later in the century?) represents an early departure from this plan, with a passage or vestibule entrance leading to the stair, without a great hall in the old sense. Mid-C16 Clock House, Great Dunmow, has a similar compact plan, and shaped gables. Shaped gables also appear at about the same time at Great Graces, Little Baddow, and Woodham Mortimer Hall, but they survive in Essex to a surprisingly late date, as will be shown later. Another motif that seems to arrive in the county with Queen Elizabeth's reign is the pediment above a window or a door: examples are at 66 Roydon Hall, Ramsey, and Wix Abbey. Finally Bourne Mill, Colchester, of 1591, deserves notice as an oddity, with its fantastic shaped gables and obelisks; it was built as a fishing lodge.

By far the grandest JACOBEAN building of Essex, and one of 61 the biggest Jacobean mansions in England, was Audley End, *p. 96* which still adhered to the courtyard plan – a late example, since it was built in *c.* 1605–14. Like Hampton Court, it had an outer courtyard with lower buildings and a broad gatehouse and then an inner courtyard. The hall, however, was placed in the range between the two and not at the side or the far end of the inner courtyard. The outer courtyard and half the inner were pulled down in the C18. But even in its present dimensions it is on a splendid scale, and to show the lavishness of its owner it is all stone-faced, whereas the standard in Essex was brick with stone dressings, as Robert Cecil indeed did not mind using at the same time for his Hatfield mansion. The hall at Audley End is centrally placed, and to achieve external symmetry the bay window is placed illogically in the middle. Immense elaboration of strapwork, caryatids, and such Flemish C16 fantasies was also lavished 63 on the hall screen and some of the fireplaces. On the other hand, in such humbler buildings as the stables of Audley End and the remarkable almshouses (St Mark's College) – the best in Essex, grouped round two courtyards, which is an extremely unusual arrangement – horizontal mullioned windows with arched lights also still appear.

Among HOUSE FURNISHINGS, the finest Jacobean interiors 62 are without doubt at Langleys, Great Waltham, of a stupendous richness of plaster ornamentation. Good plasterwork is also found at Orsett Hall, but more characteristic of the county is the frequent occurrence of DOMESTIC WALL PAINTING. The most 67 famous and extensive example is Elizabethan, at Hill Hall, Theydon Mount, but at the end of the C16 and early C17 it pro- 65 liferates. The scheme at Clovile Hall, West Hanningfield, is unusual because it is dated (1615) and has grotesque work; more usual is imitative panelling (Rose and Crown, Ashdon), arcading (Sheepcotes Farm, Silver End), or Biblical texts (Feering House). STAIRCASES are few: the original ones at Audley End are rather cramped, that at Albyns, Stapleford Abbotts of *c.* 1620 was larger and at least as sumptuously decorated but survives only in part. Many others have the sturdy turned balusters familiar in houses of the Jacobean and Carolean periods.

POST-REFORMATION CHURCHES TO 1660

Churches of the mid C16 to mid C17 are rare in Essex, but those which survive show the persistence of medieval traditions after the Reformation. Ramsey and Chipping Ongar have roofs of the late C16 or early C17 which, though in details Jacobean, are basically Perp. Other examples of this 'Gothic Survival' evidenced by church towers have been mentioned. To these may here be added the wholly pre-Renaissance w tower of Waltham Abbey, 1556–8, and the little brick church of 1611–14 at Theydon Mount in the grounds of Hill Hall. The porch here has a shaped gable. The chancel at Ramsey on the other hand, dated 1597, has large transomed windows of an entirely Elizabethan domestic character. Also still essentially Gothic, in spite of its stepped gables, is the brick church at Woodham Walter, rebuilt 1562–3 and the only complete church in Essex from Elizabeth's reign. The coming of the classical style is marked – as stated already – by the introduction of arched windows in the brick N chapel of Stapleford Abbotts, which is dated 1638.

Elizabethan and Jacobean CHURCH MONUMENTS, however, are so frequent that selection must be arbitrary. The coming of the Renaissance has already been noted at Layer Marney church (1523). The tomb-lid and effigy here are of Catacleuse, a black Cornish stone, used also for the tomb of Prior Vyvyan at Bodmin in Cornwall, 1533, which is attributed to *Cornelius Harman*. Harman was responsible for the monument to Lord Audley at Saffron Walden, 1544, and probably also to that to the Earl of 42 Oxford at Castle Hedingham, 1539 – both in black touchstone, a similar material to Catacleuse. TOMB-CHESTS remain one of the usual types of monuments throughout the C16, see the alabaster tomb of the Earls of Sussex at Boreham, 1587–9, with recumbent effigies. Brasses on the other hand tend to disappear, although there is the exceptional, large brass plate to Archbishop p. 227 Harsnett at Chigwell, which dates from as late as 1631. The most popular new type is the hanging WALL MONUMENT with a kneeling figure or two kneeling figures facing each other across a prayer-desk. Of this there are examples all over the county. The most delightful is that of 1619 at Woodham Ferrers, where Cecilie Sandys kneels against an arbour carved in relief.

The most usual expensive monument is the direct continuation of the Perp canopy tomb. The tomb-chest is kept and the canopy has assumed a round-arched form usually with flanking columns, and achievements or obelisks instead of the former cresting. To this type belong the monuments of the Smiths of Hill Hall at Theydon Mount. The finest sculptural quality is reached in *Epiphanius Evesham*'s monument to Lord Rich at Felsted of 43 c. 1620. An equally sumptuous display is that for Sir Thomas Myddelton, Lord Mayor of London, 1631, at Stansted Mount- 47 fitchet. The figures on the tomb-chests are now more often reclining than recumbent, that is as a rule stiffly propped up on an elbow. This is still to be found as late as 1658 at Orsett and 1668 at Theydon Mount. Another attempt at achieving more variety

than the couples of the C15 lying side by side on a tomb-chest
had permitted is the odd custom of placing the husband on a
shelf behind and above his wife. This appears in the Denny monument at Waltham Abbey 1600 (by *Bartholomew Atye & Isaac
James*), Great Waltham 1611, St Osyth *c.* 1620, and Little Warley
as late as 1641.

Another fashionable Elizabethan type of major funeral monument is the six-poster. The Essex examples are at Borley (1599)
and Arkesden (1592). The effigy of Robert Wiseman (1641) at
Willingale Doe lies in a recess behind three columns – a halved
six-poster. Of special motifs or special types of the C16 little need
be said. Monuments at Gosfield of 1554 and 1567 are still entirely
Gothic in detail, but at Little Sampford in 1556 the strapwork,
termini pilasters, and so on of the new Netherlandish fashion
which was to replace the Italo-French fashion of the Early
Renaissance are already in command. The Mildmay monument
at Chelmsford, 1571, is of a type which seems wholly original. It
has steep triangular and rounded pediments and no effigy, only
kneeling figures in the base. New types appear about 1630, and
in a few monuments of that date a freedom of composition begins
to make itself felt which heralds the age after the Restoration.

A popular new type in Essex is the frontal demi-figure, e.g. at
Abbess Roding 1633, where angels hold a curtain open behind
the figure, Dedham 1636, Leigh-on-Sea (Southend) 1641, and
Fingringhoe 1655. Frontal busts also begin to appear, at Claver-
46 ing 1653 and 1658, and Hempstead 1657. This last, by *Edward
Marshall*, represents William Harvey and is an excellent likeness
as well as an excellent work of sculpture. At Writtle (1629) is a
monument by *Nicholas Stone*, the best English sculptor of his generation, which in poetic conception and delicacy of carving is far
above the current English standard. Its symbolism is matched by
the wholly emblematic monument to Dorcas Smyth at Toppesfield (1633) by *John Colt the Younger*. Seated whole figures also
appear now, although more rarely, e.g. at East Donyland 1613.
Finally there is the short craze for shrouded figures, caused, it
seems, by Stone's upright figure of John Donne in St Paul's
Cathedral. This is immediately reflected in the figure of Lady
Deane by *William Wright* at Great Maplestead (1634). Reclining
figures in shrouds are at Shenfield (1652) and Little Warley
(1658), both attributed to *Thomas Burman*. Other signed or
documented work can be found by *Thomas Cartwright the Elder*
(Purleigh 1659: tomb in churchyard; also Runwell 1692), *Epiphanius Evesham* (West Hanningfield, 1622), *Francis Grigs* (Braintree
1645, St Osyth 1640), and *Richard Stevens* (Boreham 1587–9).

Contemporary CHURCH FURNISHINGS need no more than a
sentence or two: the numerous pulpits of the earlier C17, the best
being perhaps that of Great Baddow 1639 (also Stondon Massey
1630, and Bardfield Saling), box pews at Little Warley, and the
panelling and chancel stalls at Messing. Also at Messing is rare
STAINED GLASS of the period, by *Abraham van Linge*; the
windows by *Baptista Sutton* at Little Easton were made for the
chapel at Easton Lodge, 1621. There are a few early ROYAL ARMS

of interest, including carved Tudor arms at Waltham Abbey and Middleton and Stuart arms at Messing, and a rare example of Commonwealth arms at Ramsey. Arms painted directly on to the wall survive at East Tilbury (C16) and Little Easton (1660), and in the tympana of the chancel arches at West Bergholt (James I) and Langdon Hills, Basildon (1660).

SECULAR BUILDINGS 1660–1830

Essex is not over-endowed with COUNTRY HOUSES. This is partly the result of losses in the C20: Essex suffered particularly badly in the orgy of demolition that took place in the 1950s; it has been suggested that it lost nearly a third of its country houses, a much higher proportion than, say, Suffolk (one in six) or Norfolk (one in eight).* Major post-war losses included Albyns (Stapleford Abbotts), Belhus (Aveley), Birch Hall, Easton Lodge (Little Easton), Langford Grove, Liston Hall, Marks Hall, Rolls Park (Chigwell), Shortgrove (Newport), and Weald Hall (South Weald). To that list must be added Copped Hall and Felix Hall p. 308 (Kelvedon), gutted by fire but surviving as ruins. Many factors contributed to this state of affairs, including the county's proximity to London on its unfashionable E side, making sites valuable for development. Often there was not the land to go with the houses to create self-supporting estates. In other cases (e.g. South Weald) landowners also had estates elsewhere, perhaps acquired by marriage, and preferred to have their main seat further from ever-encroaching London; they therefore abandoned their Essex estates, or kept the land but demolished the main house which, in a number of cases, had suffered as the result of military occupation during the Second World War. The result is that there are very few 'stately homes' in Essex; Belchamp Hall (Belchamp Walter), Ingatestone Hall, Langleys 76 (Great Waltham) and Terling Place are rare examples of houses 78 still occupied by descendants of their builders.

The same proximity to London which led to many houses falling out of favour in the C20 was also responsible for their construction in the first place. From the C16, Essex, a favourite haunt of Henry VIII (e.g. Boreham, Blackmore), was a popular destination for those who made their fortune at the Tudor court: Sir Thomas Audley (Audley End), Sir John Cutte (Horham Hall), Sir Henry Marney (Layer Marney), Sir William Petre (Ingatestone), Sir Richard Rich (Leez Priory and Rochford). In the C18, City merchants and bankers also looked eastwards: Benjamin Hoare, for example, spent a few years buying up land in and around Boreham, including the New Hall estate, before building Boreham House. The Tufnells of Langleys made their fortune in the City of London. The Strutts, on the other hand, had been successful local millers since the C17. Where Essex may have lost out to other counties, however, is in the absence of scenery of

* G. Worsley, *England's Lost Houses* (2002), 23.

the kind favoured later in the C18. Purfleet's cliffs and chalk quarries, surprisingly perhaps to modern eyes, enjoyed a brief reputation for dramatic scenery; Gainsborough (Auberies, Bulmer) and Constable (Dedham and the Stour Valley) found the landscape in the NE of the county eminently picturesque, although Constable also made a spirited painting of Hadleigh Castle. Generally, however, there was not enough excitement to satisfy a generation that was discovering, for the first time, the value of a good view. Three houses at Hatfield Peverel (Hatfield Priory, Hatfield Place, Crix), built in the second half of the C18, combine the advantages of proximity to London and Chelmsford with good views of the Ter and Chelmer valley.

In terms of design, Jacobean traditions were not immediately abandoned at the Restoration: straight gables occur even as late as Thorpe Hall, Thorpe Bay (Southend-on-Sea) in 1668, and as for shaped gables their longevity in Essex must be a record. Beaumont Hall is of *c.* 1675, Saling Hall, Great Saling, of 1699, while Old Riffhams, Little Baddow, may be as late as 1717. But in a more fashionable location, near the Cambridge and Newmarket road, Quendon Hall had given an example of the grand new Baroque of London by using giant pilasters all along the façade – curiously irregularly placed though they are. The date must be about 1680. Within about twenty years Orford House, Ugley, had been built nearby, an example of the nicely proportioned brick house that appears at this time: cf. Dynes Hall, Great Maplestead, rebuilt in 1689, which has a three-bay pediment and a staircase with sturdy twisted balusters.

The designers of these relatively sophisticated houses are unknown, although a case has been made* for *Henry Winstanley* as architect of Quendon Hall. He was clerk of works at Audley End (of which he made survey drawings), designed his own extraordinary house at Littlebury (known only from contemporary prints) and is best known for building the first Eddystone lighthouse. But in spite of being so close to London, the great names make only fleeting appearances in Essex. *Inigo Jones* probably worked at New Hall, Boreham, and *John Thorpe* at Audley End, as did *Vanbrugh*, but in more of a destructive than constructive capacity.

p. 96

The PALLADIANISM which was the expression of enlightened opposition against Vanbrugh's Baroque and which was to dominate English architecture of the C18 at its most representational fared better in Essex, perhaps as a result of the fame of Wanstead House (*see London 5: East*), the first major building in the Palladian style but, alas, no longer in existence. The full-blown Palladian type of country house must have wings or angle pavilions separated from the main block by colonnades or low connecting links. This type survives in Essex at Kelvedon Hall, Kelvedon Hatch (1743) and, much grander, at Thorndon Hall (1763–70) by *James Paine*. In other cases the pavilions are a later addition. Thus

p. 778

---

* By Alison Barnes, who suggests that he might also have designed Shortgrove Hall, Newport (dem.).

Hylands was built about 1726, but the wings were added later in the C18 and early C19; Blake Hall, Bobbingworth is also early C18 and had wings added in 1822 (by *Basevi*) and later, and Terling Place dates from 1770 with wings of 1810–14. The architect of the original Terling Place was *John Johnson*, a man of some merit, as can be seen in his charming Bradwell Lodge of 1781–6 and the Shire Hall, Chelmsford, to which we shall return later. He appears also at Boreham House, adding wings (later modified) to a house of 1726–33, probably designed by *Edward Shepherd*. The original house is in its restrained exterior and luxurious INTERIOR DEC-ORATION characteristic of the best Early Georgian of Essex. Langleys, Great Waltham is the other paramount example, rebuilt *c.* 1719. A third house with surprisingly exuberant interiors behind plain fronts is Gestingthorpe Hall of 1735. The universally current brick mansion of the period, nicely proportioned and of comfortable size, can perhaps best be seen in two houses at South Weald: Gilstead Hall of 1726 and Dytchleys of 1729. Inside such houses one usually finds some large and stately panelling and a staircase with gracefully twisted or varied balusters. C18 GOTHICK is rare in Essex. The principal surviving example is Colne Priory, Earls Colne, the exact date of which is not known. There is an interesting Gothick interior at Hutton Hall, similar to the lost interiors of Belhus, Aveley (dem. 1957), and the summerhouse at The Minories, Colchester, based on a design by *Batty Langley*, is a delight. In the same spirit, but Chinese in inspiration, is The Quarters at Alresford Hall, 1772 by *Richard Woods*, intended for lakeside banqueting. On a more austere note, three severely NEO-CLASSICAL houses of the 1820s: Stisted Hall by *Henry Hakewill*, Felix Hall as remodelled by *Thomas Hopper*, and Horkesley Hall, Little Horkesley, its architect regrettably unknown.

Parks and landscape

Any shortcomings in the natural landscape could, of course, be overcome by talented designers, two of whom – Richard Woods and Humphry Repton – were or became local men. *Richard Woods* was principally a land surveyor and landscape gardener, who moved to Essex in 1768 and in his later years lived at Ingrave as surveyor to Lord Petre. He was responsible for a dozen schemes in the county, including Brizes and Great Myles's at Kelvedon Hatch, Copford Hall, and above all Hatfield Priory (1765). Woods worked better at a smaller scale than his more famous contemporary, *Capability Brown*; this can be appreciated at Audley End and Thorndon Hall, where both worked. The other important Brown landscape is at Shortgrove Hall, Newport (1753). An earlier gardener, working in the more formal tradition that Brown supplanted, was *Adam Holt*, best known for Wanstead; ponds by him survive at Hedingham Castle (1726) and Coopersale House (1738). Of later landscape gardeners, *Humphry Repton* lived at Hare Street near Romford, then in Essex, and his name has been associated with twenty-seven properties within the present county boundaries, although only two

Red Books (for Hill Hall, Theydon Mount, and Stansted Hall, Stansted Mountfitchet, both 1791) are known. His work can be seen at Rivenhall Place (1789), Saling Grove, Great Saling (1791) and Hylands Park (*c*. 1797), but the best example is Riffhams, Danbury (1815–17), which demonstrates perfectly the smooth transition between the immediate formal surroundings of the house and the natural landscape beyond that was the aim of most such schemes. The house itself was probably designed with his son, *J. A. Repton*, who lived in Springfield after his father's death in 1818.

Smaller houses in the towns and villages

The fashion for decorating the façades of timber-framed houses with ever-increasing elaboration in the C17 has been noted above. Another form of embellishment was the enrichment of doorways by broad surrounds with segmental pediments, or by generously shaped shell-hoods such as can be seen at Wentworth House, Bocking, 1679, Manor House, South Shoebury (Southend-on-Sea), 1681, and Crown House, Newport, 1692. By the end of the C17, and especially in the C18, the fashion had changed to refronting in brick, often with a ruthless disregard for what lay behind, with old floor levels often not corresponding to new fenestration, and symmetry sometimes depending upon false windows. Manningtree and especially Witham provide many good examples of brick refronting, in many cases the only obvious indication of an older house behind the new front being a massive C16 brick chimneystack. Brick House, Margaret Roding, *c*. 1680–1700, is the unusual example of a timber-framed house with contemporary brick façade, of a type then being built in London. Of all-brick houses, the best are at Colchester (Hollytrees 1718–19) and Dedham (Grammar School and Shermans, 1730–1). Clarance House at Thaxted of 1715 also is of a town more than a country type, as is the delightful West Bergholt Hall.

True urban housing of the C18 is hardly to be found in Essex; Royal Terrace, Southend-on-Sea, of 1791–3, is exceptional. Mistley Thorn, developed in the early C18 and embellished by *Robert Adam* after 1774, feels more like a village than a small town, despite including terraced housing. Not least interesting aspect of Adam's involvement was the (unsuccessful) attempt to create a saltwater bathing establishment on the Stour. Equally improbable were the several SPAS established in Essex. Although Witham's (1736) lasted little more than ten years, it contributed to the town's prosperity, while Dovercourt's (1854) was an important component of what amounted to a new town. Hockley's, on the other hand (1838), left a pump room and hotel but nothing else by way of residential development. The other factor in Witham's C18 prosperity was its position halfway between London and Harwich; other places which benefited from the through traffic of coaches, and rebuilt or refronted accordingly, included Brentwood, Ingatestone, Chelmsford, and Colchester.

Public buildings

The Shire Hall at Chelmsford must of course have precedence, 77
a stone-faced, urbane building in the Adam style, by *John
Johnson*, 1789–91. Johnson was County Surveyor 1782–1812, and
although he lived in London can be considered the first Essex
architect of any consequence. His immediate predecessor in the
post, *William Hillyer*, has left the former House of Correction at
Newport, but otherwise he, like earlier surveyors, was occupied
mainly with bridges. Johnson worked on his fair share of these –
the stone bridge in Chelmsford, 1785–7, being the supreme
example – but as a result of his office he also gained a number
of commissions for private houses, although one of the best,
Langford Grove of 1785, has been demolished – one of the most
regrettable losses from Essex's small stock of Palladian country
houses. Johnson's immediate successor, *Robert Lugar*, son of a
Colchester carpenter, made less impression, although one bridge
for which he is known to have been responsible (at Witham, 1814)
is a very early example of the use of cast iron for such structures.
However, *Thomas Hopper* (Surveyor 1816–56) was prolific, like
Johnson picking up a number of private commissions (Terling
Place, Boreham House, Danbury Place, Wivenhoe Park) as well
as church work, although the latter was often undone later in the
C19. His major public building was Chelmsford Prison, built in
1822–8 but considerably altered within twenty years to take
account of the new style of prison regime introduced by *Joshua
Jebb* at Pentonville, and he also extended *M.G. Thompson*'s
County Hospital Colchester of 1819. Hopper's ability to design
in almost any style may account for much of his success.

At a more local level, TOWN HALLS were built at Saffron
Walden in 1761–2, quite plain and utilitarian, and Harwich in
1769, tall, narrow, not detached, and exactly like a wealthy
merchant's house. How small SCHOOLS were before the C19 can
best be seen at Brentwood and Chigwell, founded in 1568 and
1629 respectively, with purpose-built brick schoolrooms of about
that date. Both have Georgian buildings as well, as does Felsted
(by *John Johnson*), although here the school started in an existing Late Medieval building. There are no grander early schools
in Essex. ALMSHOUSES later than those of Audley End can be
seen here and there. Architecturally the only noteworthy piece is
the centre of Winsley's at Colchester of *c.* 1727, which has
markedly Vanbrughian features. The comparison between
Winnock's of 1678 and Kendall's of 1791 and 1803, also at Colchester, is instructive.

Early INDUSTRIAL BUILDINGS are to be found across the
county in the form of MILLS of one sort or another. Windmills
are an important feature of the landscape, something understood
by the County Council, which maintains post mills at Aythorpe 85, 86
Roding, Finchingfield, and Mountnessing, and the tower mill at
Stock. Other prominent windmills regularly open to the public
are to be found at Bocking, Rayleigh, Stansted Mountfitchet and
Thaxted. At their zenith, in the second quarter of the C19, there

were at least 285 windmills in Essex, of which 188 are known to
have been post mills, 63 smock mills, and 20 tower mills. In addition, there were at least a hundred water mills. A dozen or so of
these were tide mills, but only three survive: partially at Battlesbridge and Fingringhoe, but with a good example, restored by
84   the County Council, at Thorrington.
        Watermills, on the other hand, are plentiful, although mostly
converted to other uses; Alderford Mill, Sible Hedingham, C18
with complete machinery, is an exception, and is being restored
by the Council. Moulsham Mill and Springfield Mill, both in
Chelmsford, make typically pleasing groups with weatherboarded
4   mills and brick houses. More unusual is Townsford Mill, spanning the River Colne at Halstead. This was built in the late C18
as a corn mill, but in 1825 was converted to silk-throwing and
weaving by Samuel Courtauld. The Courtaulds were Huguenots
who worked first as goldsmiths in Spitalfields, East London,
moving into the silk industry in the C18. Their first mill was at
Pebmarsh, converted from a flour mill in 1799, followed in 1816
by a purpose-built mill at Bocking. This does not survive, but
Pound End Mill, Braintree, 1818, does. The Courtaulds' growing
business left an impressive legacy of later C19 and C20 buildings,
to which we shall return.
        The other main monument of early industrialization is the
Chelmer and Blackwater Navigation, 1793–7; the chief engineer
was *John Rennie*, with construction supervised by *Richard Coates*;
Robert Mylne was consulted for part at least of the work. The navigation runs for nearly 14 miles, from Springfield Basin, Chelmsford, to Heybridge Basin, and includes twelve locks and five
bridges; it avoided the expense of carting goods from Maldon to
Chelmsford via Danbury, and it is said that as a result the price
of coal in Chelmsford was halved. Equally important, although
not exclusively to Essex, were the Lea and Stort Navigations on
the western border of the county, the former dating back to 1581
but improved in 1770 and the C19, the latter conceived in 1759.
They provided the essential transport link for the Royal Gunpowder Mills at Waltham Abbey, and also for the many maltings
such as those at Sheering.

CHURCHES AND CHAPELS, 1700–1840

Not one Georgian church survives in Essex – at least not completely – which could be called a major work of architecture. The
reservation refers to *Robert Adam*'s church at Mistley of 1776, an
enlargement of a plain brick preaching house of 1735. Adam
added the two spectacular towers with their domes at the W and
p. 601 E ends and porticoes in the middle of the sides – an utterly
unorthodox and indeed ritually doubtful composition of which
only the towers remain. The only other church of interest is
68   Ingrave of 1734–6, in the Hawksmoor style, and here the interior,
never elaborate, was re-fitted in the C19. Otherwise there are a
number of plain rebuilt W towers (Toppesfield 1699, Terling 1732,

Bradwell-on-Sea 1743), a number of pretty cupolas set up on towers (Little Waltham 1679, Chelmsford 1749, and more in the Halstead–Bardfield area), the delicious c18 interior remodelling of Lambourne, and some unassuming brick naves (Kelvedon 69 Hatch 1753, Shellow Bowells 1754; others, e.g. Bradwell-on-Sea 1706, 'restored' in the c19).

These are in no essential way different from some of the early NONCONFORMIST CHAPELS of Essex, for example Little Baddow (originally Presbyterian), 1707–8. Other chapels were careful to be as unobtrusive as possible: Terling (Independent, 1752–3), Thorpe-le-Soken (Baptist, c. 1802) are essentially domestic in character. Only occasionally as at Harlow (Baptist, 1756), with its doorway with a big scrolly pediment, does something grander appear, although the Congregational Chapel of 1811 at Saffron Walden is already of the more ambitious and worldly c19 type with a portico. As usual, Friends' meeting houses are among the simplest such buildings, that at Stebbing 73 (1674) being the oldest surviving Nonconformist place of worship in Essex. That at Earls Colne is very similar and dates from the same year, but was probably rebuilt in 1733. The former meeting house of 1823–4 in Chelmsford, on the other hand, is considerably larger and more urban. By this time Nonconformists were less reticent, and *James Fenton* of Chelmsford established himself as a leading architect of chapels in Essex and beyond from 1830.

Fenton's pretty Congregational Chapel of 1833, at Felsted, is the only complete example of the GOTHICK STYLE in Essex churches and chapels. The octagonal chancel at Debden, 1792, 70 is perfectly of its time, combining the Romantic preoccupations with death – it sits above the Chiswell family mausoleum – and antiquarianism: the design was supplied by *John Carter*, and is based upon York Chapter House. (The same pattern inspired *George Mason* of Ipswich in 1838 at East Donyland, quite an interesting design of its date.) Debden's interior, with spindly vaulting, is surpassed in splendour by the interior of the chapel at Audley End, 1768–72, with fan-vaulted family pew. Both Debden and Audley End have contemporary stained glass. Finally, *John Johnson* restored and partly rebuilt Chelmsford church (the present cathedral) in 1801–3 to the original Perp design, but with piers and tracery of *Coade* stone. This artificial stone, made by *Coade & Seely* in Lambeth, is used also to good effect at Debden, not just in decorative details applied to the structure but also for the font of 1796; Johnson's font for Chelmsford, 1803, is now in Chelmsford Museum. Another Coade font is at Harwich, 1821; here *M. G. Thompson* introduced pinnacles in the same material, as he did also at Lexden. Harwich, incidentally, is unusual for having windows with cast-iron tracery.

Another Gothick font, with a miniature painting of the Baptism of Christ, is at Birdbrook (1793). Other noteworthy late c17 and c18 CHURCH FURNISHINGS are as follows: a number of fine pulpits of c. 1700 with garlands down the angles, for example at Thaxted, the screen at Roxwell made from the organ case of 1684 from Durham Cathedral, and a good early C18 reredos at Hatfield Broad Oak. Communion rails with twisted balusters are a very common Essex feature. Several earlier pulpits have wrought-iron hourglass stands attached to them; in most other counties they are rarer. Special mention must also be made of reused fittings from three of *Wren*'s City churches: the reredos from All Hallows the Great, Upper Thames Street, in a chapel at Halstead (and formerly also the font and font cover), the font from St Mary-le-Bow at Westcliff (Southend), and the pulpit from St Christopher-le-Stocks at Canewdon. Georgian box pews survive only at Elmstead and in the Black Chapel at North End, Great Waltham, which also retains its double-decker pulpit positioned centrally on one side of the nave. Another feature of Elmstead's charming interior is an unusual and decorative wrought-iron hatstand; the other good bit of C18 ironwork, gates at Little Easton, were made for Easton Lodge.

CHURCH MONUMENTS of *c*. 1660–*c*. 1830 deserve fuller treatment. The mid-C17 type with two demi-figures holding hands is still preserved in the Wyseman monument of 1684 at Great Canfield, though the two figures are now placed beneath a big segmental pediment. We have already seen the life-size bust, just like those in libraries etc., appearing in the 1650s, and these become increasingly popular, forming the centre of the composition. This appears in Essex in 1692 (monument at Arkesden by *Edward Pearce*) and reaches its acme in such monuments as those at Writtle of 1740 and Pleshey of 1758, the first signed and the second probably also by *Henry Cheere*. The reclining figure also goes on into the C18, getting in the course of the years more and more comfortable and less and less religious. Examples are at Little Sampford (1712), Steeple Bumpstead (1717 by *Thomas Stayner*), and Little Chesterford (1728 by *Cheere*). But the new, most ambitious and clearly least religious type of *c*. 1700 is that which has the figure of the deceased standing life-size in the middle, in the clothes he wore or in heroic Roman dress. The type can be called a Home Counties speciality, cf. for example such Hertfordshire monuments as those at Sawbridgeworth of 1689 and Knebworth of 1710. In Essex the grandest is the Maynard monument at Little Easton. Later versions of the type can be found in the same church (1746 by *Charles Stanley*), combining a standing figure with busts and relief medallions, and at Rettendon (1727 by *Samuel Chandler*). The same kind of arrogance appears in the life-size seated figures at St Mary-at-the-Walls Colchester (Rebow 1699), Gosfield (Knight 1733 by *Rysbrack*), and Faulkbourne (Bullock 1759). Of the type with large allegories there is only one example, but it is superlative: the Magens monument of 1766 at Brightlingsea. The Faulkbourne monument is by *Peter Scheemakers*, the Brightlingsea monument by the lesser-known *Nicholas Read*.

Other signed or documented works of before 1770 include those by *Thomas Adye* (Little Dunmow 1753), *Thomas Bellamy* (Stanford-le-Hope 1746), *Cheere* (Great Baddow 1753), *James Lovell* (Chelmsford 1756: big, without effigy), *J. Pickford & W.*

Atkinson (Birdbrook 1738, Steeple Bumpstead *c.* 1740), *Roubiliac* (Hempstead 1758: two profile medallions against obelisk) and Earls Colne 1761), *Henry Scheemakers* (Wicken Bonhunt 1731), *Peter Scheemakers* (Theydon Garnon 1739), *William Stanton* (Theydon Garnon 1683), *William Tyler* (Finchingfield 1766; also St Osyth 1773), and *William Winchester* (Stanford-le-Hope 1765: elaborate tomb in churchyard).

After 1770 signatures on funeral monuments become more and more the rule. *Wilton* appears at Lambourne in 1778, *Nollekens* at Chipping Ongar in 1776, *John Bacon* at Great Yeldham in 1799, and *Flaxman* at Lambourne in 1800 and Hatfield Broad Oak in 1816. The younger generation is represented by monuments by *John Bacon Jun.* (some in partnership with *Samuel Manning Sen.*), *Chantrey, Rossi,* and *Sir Richard Westmacott* (including three at Orsett). Still later, i.e. Early Victorian, come the works contributed to Essex churches by *Behnes, Baily,* and *J. Edwards.* As for minor names, all the successful monumental masons of London seem to have had Essex jobs (*Clarke* of Wigmore Street, *Edwin* and *Thomas Gaffin, George Garrard, John Hinchcliff, Kendrick* father and son, *J. F. Moore, Charles Regnart, Henry* and *Peter Rouw the Younger*), and in addition on the one hand firms so distant as *Reeves* and *Thomas King* of Bath and *Woodley* of Torquay, and on the other the local masons: *John Challis* of Braintree, *Joseph Dorman* of Chelmsford, *George* and *Henry Lufkin* of Colchester, *Charles Harding* of Ballingdon and *Edward Keogh* of Sudbury, Suffolk, and *William Vere* of Stratford – the last responsible for two particularly notable monuments, at Henham and Sutton. At Kirby-le-Soken is a monument in cast iron by *Coleman & Wallis* of Colchester (1832), who also made a number of sets of early C19 cast-iron ROYAL ARMS. Of the royal arms painted on canvas, two are signed: at Horndon-on-the-Hill by *William Waite* of Gravesend, 1715, and at Theydon Garnon by *Russell* of Chigwell, 1762, the former a reminder of the greater traffic that then existed between the N and S sides of the River Thames.

VICTORIAN ESSEX

During Victoria's reign the population of the county as it then was trebled, just passing one million in 1901, but the effects of this were felt mainly in those parts that now lie within Greater London. The other main area of growth was Southend, which barely existed as a separate place at the beginning of the reign. Southend and the other coastal resorts (Clacton, Frinton, and Walton), although initially supplied with visitors from London by paddle steamers – hence the need for piers – owed their great success to the RAILWAY, and it is no coincidence that the man largely responsible for developing Clacton and Walton, *Peter Bruff*, was first and foremost a railway engineer, who built the most impressive engineering achievement in Essex, the viaduct at Chappel (1847–9). The Eastern Counties Railway from London to Colchester (engineer, *John Braithwaite*) was the first 96 to penetrate Essex, 1837–43, with viaducts at Chelmsford and Lexden.* None of the original station buildings survive; among the earliest is Ingatestone (1846). The continuation northwards from Colchester was built by the Eastern Union Railway, engineered by Bruff, with station buildings mainly by the Ipswich architect *Frederick Barnes*. The EUR also built the Harwich line (1854) and the Marks Tey–Sudbury branch line, which includes the Chappel viaduct. Bruff was also responsible for the Tendring Hundred Railway (1863–7), from Colchester to Walton-on-the-Naze.

On the other side of the county, the line from Stratford to Newport was built by the Northern & Eastern Railway, continued by the ECR (whose engineer was *Robert Stephenson*) after 1844. This resulted in the fine tunnels at Littlebury and the stations at Audley End (Wendens Ambo) and Great Chesterford by *Sancton Wood* and *Francis Thompson*. All of these companies joined, with others, to form the Great Eastern Railway in 1862, which added lines from Loughton to Ongar and Bishops Stortford to Braintree (engineer, *Robert Sinclair*). Unusually for a medium-sized railway company, they appointed (in 1883) a staff architect, *W. N. Ashbee*, whose buildings can be seen at Southend Victoria, Rochford, and a number of other stations. A quite separate railway, terminating at Southend Central, was the London, Tilbury & Southend, founded in 1854, but this left few buildings of note and because of the mainly flat terrain was not called upon to execute any great feats of engineering. A curiosity and an example of something once commonplace but now extremely rare is the wooden viaduct at Wickham Bishops, on the Witham–Maldon branch line (1847–8).

Connected to the railways, physically and commercially, were the fortunes of the ports of Harwich and, from 1883, Parkeston, the latter developed by the Great Eastern Railway and soon superseding the former as the main point of embarkation for the continent. Tilbury Docks, opened in 1886, likewise depended for its success upon the railway, and took business (both passenger and cargo) from the London docks. A short distance downstream from Tilbury, an attempt had been made in 1836 to turn Shell Haven into a new dock for London (with *H. E. Kendall Sen.* as architect and *Francis Giles* and *Bewicke Blackburn* as engineers); only a small amount of work was done, and the dock did not prosper until it found a role unloading oil following restrictions on the shipping of hazardous materials up the river to London in the 1870s. It later became the site of an explosives factory and oil refinery (*see* Corringham).

Railways had a direct influence not just upon where buildings developed, but the manner in which they were built. The local availability of materials was no longer such an issue; brick and stone could be cheaply supplied from outside the county, and slate became a realistic alternative to thatch or tile. Church fur-

---

* This account is based on material kindly supplied by Peter Kay.

nishings and fittings, including stained glass, became readily obtainable from suppliers in London or Birmingham, while the employment of a London architect was no longer the prerogative of only the wealthiest landowners. Conversely, LOCAL ARCHITECTS whose activities would previously been confined to the immediate neighbourhood were able to open offices in London and establish a national reputation. The supreme example of this was *Frederic Chancellor*, who began his career working for *James Beadel & Son* in Chelmsford in 1846, set up his own firm in Chelmsford and London in 1860, and by 1896 had taken his son *F.W. Chancellor* into partnership. He was extremely prolific: over 730 works have been identified, 570 of which are in Essex, encompassing a wide range of building types. Latterly he was best known for churches, of which he built or restored over ninety, and nearly as many parsonages, but in his early days, with Beadel, he was known for farm buildings. In addition, there were many private houses, as well as commercial and public buildings. His pupils and assistants included *George Sherrin* (who, like Chancellor, had a successful London practice while continuing to live in Essex) and *Charles Pertwee* (who built much locally, including Nonconformist chapels, and was in partnership with his son *William Hart Pertwee*). Chancellor made his name by winning the competition for new buildings for Felsted School in 1854, although these are not so attractive as his National School in Church Street, Chelmsford, 1872 and 1885. Indeed he was often more successful working on a smaller scale: his churches at Creeksea (1878–9) and Steeple (1881–3) have a picturesque charm that is unusual. Ford End (1870–1), however, is perhaps his most successful new church, in spite of the loss of its chancel. Of his parsonages, those at Ford End (1870), Takeley (1874–5) and Purleigh (1883) are among the best. Pontlands Park, Great Baddow (1878–9) is his largest private house, although he also successfully enlarged Durwards Hall (now Kelvedon Park), Rivenhall, and, in partnership with his son, enlarged or restored Creeksea Place, Layer Marney, and Leez Priory. Again, with domestic work his smaller buildings are more pleasing, e.g. his estate cottages at Birch (*c.* 1860) and almshouses at Felsted (1878). 92

Churches and chapels

As far as CHURCHES are concerned, the C19 saw many changes in Essex as elsewhere, not least in terms of reorganization within the Church of England. Until 1846 Essex lay in the diocese of London, but in that year most of the county was transferred to Rochester (with the bishop's palace at Danbury). In 1877 Essex joined Hertfordshire to form the new diocese of St Albans, where it remained until the creation of the diocese of Chelmsford in 1913. There had been six other contenders for the see town (Colchester, West Ham, Woodford, Barking, Waltham Abbey, and Thaxted) but it was the centrally placed county town which won the day. More local in its consequences was the East Anglian

Earthquake of 1884, centred to the S of Colchester. In all, more than 1,200 buildings were reported damaged, over 400 in Colchester itself. Most of the damage was to houses, caused by falling chimneys, but some twenty churches were damaged, mainly by pinnacles etc. falling from towers. The most seriously affected were Great and Little Wigborough and Langenhoe; the latter was completely rebuilt.*

The cavalcade of STYLES imitated one after another takes place here as everywhere, the Neo-Norman fashion for instance affecting church design around 1840: St Botolph by *Mason*, 1836–7 and St James the Less (R.C.) by *Scoles*, 1837, both in Colchester, Holy Trinity Chelmsford by *J.A. Repton*, 1842–3, and St John Loughton by *Sydney Smirke*, 1845–6. The last was condemned by the ever-vigilant Ecclesiological Society as 'a most unsatisfactory production'; the Society advocated a return to what they considered to be true medieval values in all aspects of churchmanship and favoured the Gothic style, in particular that of the C13. Elsewhere in Essex they found much to praise, beginning with *R.C. Carpenter*, whose restoration (and in particular re-seating) of Hatfield Broad Oak in 1843 is very early work of its kind; although the next generation would probably have condemned his use of box pews, and would have gone further in removing C18 work. His restoration of Little Maplestead is also notable, completed after his death in 1855 by his partner *W. Slater*, who was himself responsible for restorations at Southchurch, Southend (1855–7), and Rochford (1862–3). Other favourites of the Society were *G.E. Street* (Hadleigh), *William White* (Great Maplestead and Little Baddow), and *R. J. Withers* (Panfield, Great Saling); mention must also be made of *Rev. J. H. Sperling*, a contributor to *The Ecclesiologist* who restored his own church at Wicken Bonhunt (1857–9) as well as building himself a rectory. *S.S. Teulon*'s new churches at Birch and Great Warley are surprisingly tame, his rogueishness more apparent in the almshouses at South Weald, where he also virtually rebuilt the church. *Gilbert Scott* designed only three new churches in Essex, of which St Nicholas Colchester was demolished in 1955: the others are Holy Trinity Halstead, 1843–4, immediately followed by Greenstead Green (both early works). More original is some of the work of *Henry Woodyer*, which includes one completely new church, Twinstead (1859–60), with decorative brickwork inside and out; while *William Burges*'s restoration of Waltham Abbey (1859–77), with its new E wall and nave ceiling painted by *E. J. Poynter*, is in a class of its own. Unusually for the time, Burges made no attempt to restore the church to its appearance as it might have been at a certain point in its history, but made a completely original and unmistakable contribution to the fabric.

A. W. Blomfield was just starting on his long career in the 1860s, and St John Colchester (1862–4) shows a youthful wilfulness that he was not to maintain. He soon turned to smoother, more correct and less robust forms, including many restorations. *Ewan*

*By F. Chancellor, 1886; dem. 1962.

Christian, who as architect to the Ecclesiastical Commissioners built a total of ninety new churches and restored over a thousand, is equally bland, although his rectory at Goldhanger (1851–2) is remarkable for its sheer size: as well as having nine bedrooms and the usual reception room, its basement contained a larder, dairy, beer, wine and ale cellars, potato store, and hot water apparatus. The sensitive and tactful fag-end of archaeologically faithful Gothicism is also shown in *James Brooks*'s All Saints Southend (1886–8 etc.) and *Bodley & Garner*'s at Epping (1889–91, 1907–9). The latest Victorian and Edwardian tendency to break away from imitation and revive once again originality is as a rule less noticeable in churches than in domestic work. But *E. C. Lee*'s churches at South Weald (1877–80) and Brentwood (1879–86) have some curious details and treatments of surfaces which herald the wilful things that E. S. Prior was soon to perpetrate. *W. D. Caröe*'s tower at Stansted Mountfitchet of 1894–5 introduces all kinds of Arts and Crafts or Art Nouveau motifs into his Perp, *Sir Charles Nicholson*'s early church at Westcliff (Southend-on-Sea; 1898–90) already shows some of his elegance in the handling of period elements, *Temple Moore* at Clacton-on-Sea 107 combines an earnest Perp exterior with an interior half round-arched and half pointed-arched, and *Charles Harrison Townsend* at Great Warley in 1902–4 adopts without qualms Voysey's domestic roughcasting and other motifs for church use. What matters here, however, is not the building but its contents and 103 decoration, for which the sculptor *William Reynolds-Stephens* was almost single-handedly responsible, creating an excellent example of the *Gesamtkunstwerk* (total work of art) associated with that period. The elaborate interior has become deservedly famous, but examples of Arts and Crafts work can be found elsewhere that are equally fine and perhaps more subtle: *C. R. Ashbee* working with *Caröe* at Horndon-on-the-Hill (1898–1904), *Charles Spooner*'s lectern at Holy Trinity, Halstead (1906) or *Harold Stabler*'s at Hatfield Heath (1911).

A completely different sort of church interior was that favoured by *Rev. Ernest Geldart*, rector of Little Braxted from 1881 to 1900, who had trained as an architect (in Waterhouse's office) and managed to combine the two careers. It is at Little Braxted that 102 he was able most effectively to demonstrate his artistic and religious creed, but Ardleigh and Rawreth also repay study. His output was not great, and comprises mostly restoration, minor additions, and fittings, but of 163 known projects 57 are in Essex. Priest-architects and craftsmen were something of a C19 phenomenon: besides Geldart (and Sperling, mentioned earlier), *H. J. Burrell* tried his hand at Littlebury, *John Escreet* at Hempstead, *William Gibbens* at Chignall Smealey, *G. W. Keightley* at Stambridge, *J. E. Long* at White Roding, *W. H. Lowder* at Southminster, *H. M. Milligan* at Althorne, and *Charles Lesingham Smith* at Little Canfield – with varying degrees of ambition and success.

Of FURNISHINGS other than those to be found in the churches already mentioned, stained glass of the C19 is ubiquitous and seldom rises above the ordinary. Comprehensive schemes are

rare, but glass by *Burlison & Grylls* at Great Bardfield, *Gibbs & Howard* at Radwinter, or *James Powell & Sons* at St John Loughton, show how glass can work well when it is part of an overall decorative scheme rather than an afterthought. Radwinter also includes the only known example of a window designed by *W. E. Nesfield*, who restored the church. Individual notable windows elsewhere include those by *Clayton & Bell* at Mistley, *Heaton, Butler & Bayne* at St Martin Colchester, *Henry Holiday* at Chelmsford Cathedral, Rettendon, and Stambridge, *Mary Lowndes* at Birch, Lamarsh, and West Mersea, *Powell & Sons* (designed by *Louis Davis*) at Kelvedon, and a few by *William Morris*. Of the last, windows at Frinton-on-Sea, Ingatestone (R.C.), Little Hallingbury, and Ugley include designs by *Burne-Jones*, who can, however, be seen at his best in the earlier
104 E window of Waltham Abbey (made by *Powell*) – as bold, vigorous and unsentimental as anything achieved in the C19. The only local maker was *Charles Clutterbuck* of Stratford, who belonged to the pictorial school that was out of favour by about 1850.

The ROMAN CATHOLIC CHURCH in Essex at the beginning of the C19 was represented by the Petres at Ingatestone Hall and the Wrights at Kelvedon Hall, with missions at Stock and Witham and the Canonesses of the Holy Sepulchre at New Hall, Boreham. Catholic Emancipation in 1829 encouraged the building of new, more visible churches: Brentwood and Colchester 1837, Chelmsford 1845, Witham 1853, Chipping Ongar 1869. The last two were by *D. C. Nicholls*, architect to William, 12th Lord Petre, who gave land or paid for a number of new churches, as well as commissioning the accomplished mortuary chapel by Pugin's pupil *W. W. Wardell* in the grounds of Thorndon Hall. The churches at Chelmsford and Colchester were by *J. J. Scoles*, whose son *A. J. C. Scoles* was a priest but designed or extended (in partnership with *George Raymond*) a number of churches and convent buildings. Another prominent R.C. architect was *F. W. Tasker*, a cousin of Countess Tasker of Middleton Hall, Shenfield (*see under* Brentwood School), who rivalled Lord Petre as a donor of church buildings. Tasker's best work is Our Lady of Light & St Osyth Clacton-on-Sea (1902–3), whose size and position make it the most prominent church in Clacton. The seaside towns generally, because of their capacity for convalescence and recuperation, were particularly well provided with churches and convents: at Westcliff (Southend-on-Sea) Our Lady Help of Christians and St Helen (by *T. Goodman*) was built in 1868–9, with Nazareth House (Home of Rest and sanatorium) opening nearby in 1873. Perhaps the best R.C. building of the C19 is the chapel of the Franciscan Convent at Bocking by *J. F. Bentley*, 1898–9, with high-quality sanctuary fittings.

NONCONFORMIST CHAPELS proliferated to an even greater extent during the C19, not just in the rapidly expanding resort towns but in practically every village, and increasingly in Gothic rather than classical style. *J. Fenton*, mentioned earlier, seems to have been among the first to move to Gothic (e.g. Billericay, 1837–8), while Lion Walk Congregational Chapel, Colchester by

F. Barnes, 1863, upset many by being indistinguishable externally
from an Anglican church; its spire (all that now remains) was
even, for a few years, the tallest in the town. *Charles Pertwee*
designed several Congregational chapels, the most ambitious
at Great Dunmow (Romanesque), 1869, and *Charles Bell*
designed a number for the Methodists in the Harlow area,
although his chapel there is outclassed by *R. Moffat Smith*'s of
1865, with its elaborate Venetian façade. Bell's best work is
perhaps the chapel at Steeple Bumpstead, 1883. The size of
some of the village chapels is surprising – *T.L. Banks*'s at Hat-   100
field Heath (1875–6), for example – but some of the smaller ones
have great charm, notably the 'tin tabernacle' at Old Heath,   101
Colchester, 1869.

CEMETERIES were opened, in Essex as elsewhere, as a result
of the 1853 Burial Act. They were usually the subject of a public
competition, and important components were, besides landscaping, provision of chapels (usually two: one C. of E., the other
Nonconformist, the former distinguished by having a bell), an
entrance lodge, and perhaps also a mortuary. The best examples
are at Braintree, Colchester, Halstead, and Saffron Walden, all
opened with four years of the Act.

Public buildings

The later C19 also saw the development of PUBLIC BUILDINGS
as a distinct building type, although what is most noticeable
about them as a group is that most now no longer fulfil their
original purpose. The principal exception is TOWN HALLS.
Edward Burgess's ostentatious but forgivable enlargement of
Saffron Walden Town Hall (1878–9) deserves an honourable
mention, but the palm must go to Colchester Town Hall by *John*   97
Belcher (1897–1902), a highly successful design that is quintes-
sentially Edwardian in its exuberant use of the Baroque. CORN
EXCHANGES, on the other hand, had a relatively short life, but a
few buildings remain, if only in part: *Laing*'s (1820) and
Brandon's (1845) at Colchester, *Tress*'s (1847–8) at Saffron
Walden, and *Chancellor*'s (1866) at Rochford (although not his
one for Chelmsford). The architect of the nice polychromatic
exchange at Halstead (1865) is unfortunately not known. It, like
Saffron Walden's, now houses the Public Library, as does the
Neoclassical exchange at Manningtree (1865). Purpose-built
LIBRARIES appear only later in the C19, such as *Chancellor*'s in
Chelmsford (1904–6, latterly part of Anglia Ruskin University)
and *H.T. Hare*'s in Southend-on-Sea (1905–6, now Central
Museum). The only purpose-built MUSEUM, on the other hand,
is that at Saffron Walden (1834), which although Neo-Tudor still
looks more like a private house. A similarly domestic look was
given to early POLICE STATIONS, designed by *Hopper* as County
Surveyor. Castle Hedingham and Great Dunmow (1842–3) were
among the first to be built and were intentionally domestic in
appearance, in case the new idea of a county police force failed
and the buildings needed to find another use. Once it became

apparent that the police were here to stay, Hopper adopted a
more distinctive Tudor Gothic style at Halstead (1851), followed
by Thorpe-le-Soken (1853) and others now demolished. *Henry
Stock*, Hopper's successor, continued in similar vein at Saffron
Walden (1884–6). Hopper's Chelmsford Prison has already been
mentioned.

C19 SCHOOLS are almost as numerous as churches, and for
most of the century were denominational, with sometimes rival
schools erected under the auspices of the British and Foreign
School Society (Evangelical and Nonconformist, founded 1808)
and the National Society (C. of E., founded 1811). Most of the
resulting buildings were cheap and simple; exceptions include the
British Schools at Harlow (Fawbert and Barnard's by *Robert
Abraham*, 1836) and Saffron Walden (1838). Both are sturdily
Tuscan. National Schools were almost exclusively Gothic and
ecclesiastical in style, very often designed by the same architect
employed to build or restore the parish church: thus *L.N.*
91 *Cottingham* at Great Chesterford (1845–9), *Gilbert Scott* at Greenstead Green (1844–5), *William Slater* at Southchurch, Southend-
on-Sea (1851), *G. E. Street* at Hadleigh (1854–5), and *William
White* at Great Maplestead (1862–3). Many more were designed
by local architects, including *G. E. Pritchett* and *George Perry*, both
of Bishop's Stortford. One architect who made a speciality of
school buildings was *Joseph Clarke*, architect to the Canterbury,
Oxford and Rochester diocesan boards of education. He published in 1852 *Schools and School Houses: a Series of Views, Plans,
and Details, for Rural Parishes*, which included his schools at
p. 704 Coggeshall, Coopersale, Foxearth, Leigh-on-Sea (Southend),
and Little Bentley. He was responsible for at least eight more
schools in Essex, as well as numerous churches, the best being
Farnham, 1858–9. As a result of the 1870 Education Act, schools
were erected by local boards; a particularly distinctive group is
to be found in Colchester by *Goodey & Cressall*, 1892–1903.
These seem to make a deliberate effort not to be churchy in style,
but favour the Domestic Revival or 'Queen Anne' style, of red
brick with big sash windows rather than small Gothic ones, and
embellished with gables and cupolas, the latter serving as bell-
cotes or ventilators.

Another aspect of C19 education was the re-foundation of a
number of schools that had started as GRAMMAR SCHOOLS in
the C16–17. Some continued as grammar schools, others became
public schools, but all required new buildings. Felsted, with new
buildings by *Chancellor* (1854 onwards), was one of the first,
followed by Brentwood (main building by *Chancellor & Son*,
1909–10) and Chigwell. Colchester and Chelmsford moved to
completely new sites, in 1853 (*H.W. Hayward*) and 1892 (*H.A.
Cheers*) respectively, both designed in the Neo-Tudor style which,
because of their Tudor origins, was favoured by many grammar
schools. Cheers also designed new buildings for Earls Colne
Grammar School (1897–8), but the best example of the type is
Newport (1875–8) by *Nesfield*, like a C17 manor house built round
a courtyard. At Saffron Walden, between 1877 and 1884, *Edward*

Burgess not only rebuilt the grammar school, but also designed the new Friends' School, and a teacher training college for the British and Foreign School Society, all supported financially by the Gibson family.

At the other end of the social spectrum were the schools and homes built by East London parishes and Poor-Law unions for pauper children, far outside the dense slums from which they sprang. In the later C19 these often took the form of 'cottage home villages', of which a good example survives (although converted to private housing) at Chipping Ongar, by *W.A. Finch* (1903–5), for Hackney Union. *Frank Baggallay*'s buildings for Stepney Union at North Stifford (1901) have mostly been demolished, as have *Holman & Goodrham*'s for Poplar Union at Hutton (1906). Here, however, the particularly fine dining hall that would not disgrace an Oxbridge college or inn of court, remains, and reflects the generosity of Poplar's Guardians under the progressive influence of George Lansbury. Another good building of this type is at Fyfield, built for the West Ham School Board by *J.T. Newman* in 1883–5 as an industrial school for persistent truants.

These late C19 buildings were of course making a deliberate attempt to provide something more enlightened and less institutional than the WORKHOUSE, where the destitute poor in need of parish relief could be compelled to reside and work. This type of residential institution became increasingly common in rural parishes from the beginning of the C18. Essex had numerous examples, either adapted from existing buildings or purpose-built, some of which can still be seen at Bocking, Maldon, and Witham. Their origins are by no means obvious in their wholly domestic façades, and they were converted to cottages after 1834 when the Poor Law Amendment Act led to the establishment of a national network of workhouses, intended primarily to deter idleness among the poor. Much thought and theorizing went into their design. Of fifteen workhouses built after 1834, ten are still substantially intact, three as hospitals (Bocking, Chelmsford, Maldon), three converted to housing (Billericay, Great Dunmow, Saffron Walden), and one a factory (Stanford Rivers). *Scott & Moffatt* were responsible for four, those at Tendring and Witham more austere than the elaborate Neo-Elizabethan Billericay and Neo-Jacobean Great Dunmow, which were among the most expensive of all the workhouses built at this time. Many workhouses were based on model designs prepared by the Poor Law Commission's architect, *Sampson Kempthorne*: thus Saffron Walden by *James Clephan* is based on Kempthorne's workhouse for 300 paupers, Lexden and Winstree at Stanway by *Foden & Henman* is a variation on the radial workhouse, here placed within an octagon, while Bocking by *W.T. Nash* is a rare example of a hexagon-plan workhouse with Y-plan main building.

The more fortunate needy were able to find accommodation in ALMSHOUSES, of which a few continued to be built in the C19, on a grand scale (by *Henry Harrison* and *William Nash*) at Saffron Walden, 1829–33. Here Lord Braybrooke's money enabled the construction of something more like the quadrangle of an Oxbridge college. On a homelier scale are almshouses at Ingatestone (1840), South Weald (*Teulon*, 1854), Felsted (*Chancellor*, 1878), Springfield (*Clarke*, 1878), Radwinter (*Temple Moore*, 1887) and Brentwood (*Barker & Kirk*, 1910).

HOSPITALS are rarer in the C19, for many years the only one being the Essex County Hospital at Colchester, founded in 1818, the original building by *M. G. Thompson*. Chelmsford had to wait until 1883 for its first proper hospital, the Essex and Chelmsford Infirmary and Dispensary designed jointly by *Chancellor* and *Pertwee*. Some smaller towns benefited from private generosity: the Courtaulds established cottage hospitals at Bocking (1871) and Halstead (1884), the latter designed by *Sherrin*, and at Saffron Walden the cost of *W. Beck*'s General Hospital (1864–6) was met by a legacy of W. G. Gibson. Some of the London hospitals built convalescent homes at the seaside, including a very large one at Clacton by *Young & Hall*, a specialist firm, for the Middlesex Hospital (1895–6), and a smaller one at Walton for the Poplar Hospital for Accidents (1909), while on the edge of Epping Forest, at High Beach, was a convalescent home for children recovering from TB by *T. W. Cutler*, 1895. This was built on the site of one of the houses that formed Dr Matthew Allen's lunatic asylum (where John Clare was incarcerated, 1837–41). Essex was well provided with public ASYLUMS: there was the vast
p. 175 Essex County Lunatic Asylum at Brentwood (*Kendall & Pope*, 1851–3), while at Colchester the Eastern Counties Asylum for Idiots was established in the former railway hotel by *Lewis Cubitt* (dem.). This was joined in 1910–13 by Severalls Hospital, elegantly designed by the county architect *F. Whitmore* and *W. H. Town* with 'Queen Anne'-style villas in spacious grounds, and laid out in the echelon plan that was widely used for Late Victorian mental institutions.

Country houses

If Essex is disappointing for its relative paucity of Georgian country houses, the same is even more true of the Victorian period; not so much because they have been demolished, as that few were built in the first place. We have mentioned already the country houses of *Hopper*, who made a smooth transition from Georgian to Victorian, in his case Tudor Gothic (Danbury 1832;
p. 552 Easton Lodge (Little Easton) 1847; Wivenhoe Park (University of Essex) 1846–53) or Italianate (Birch Hall 1843–8). The latter style was generally less popular, the other prime example being
88 *F. P. Cockerell*'s Down Hall (Hatfield Heath), of 1871–3. This is chiefly of interest for being constructed of poured and shuttered concrete, a method which was suited to Essex with its ready availability of cement and gravel. (Other early examples of concrete construction are a house at Grays by *Thomas Wonnacott*, 1872, and The Towers, Heybridge, by *C. Pertwee*, 1870–3, of which only outlying buildings remain.) Stone-built Tudor Gothic was
87 the more conventional choice: Hassobury (Farnham), by *P.C.*

Hardwick, and Gaynes Park (Theydon Garnon), were both built in that style in the late 1860s. In the 1870s, brick was used by *Richard Armstrong* for his Neo-Jacobean Stansted Hall (Stansted Mountfitchet), as it was by *W. G. Bartleet* for Holfield Grange (Coggeshall), in 1888. Although stylistically nondescript, Holfield Grange has the distinction of being remarkably unaltered. The greatest loss as far as C19 houses is concerned is *E. C. Lee*'s Berechurch Hall of 1881–2, in the 'domestic French Gothic' *p. 134* style; it cost over £25,000 and, unusually for the time, was lit by electricity throughout.

As for ESTATE BUILDINGS, there are a few examples of cottages built in a consistent style – e.g. at Stisted and Little Easton, *93* both very picturesquely. Particular mention should be made of the MODEL FARM BUILDINGS at Lawford Hall by *W. Lewis* *p. 524* *Baker*, 1871, which have survived virtually intact; Baker also designed the village school and, probably, other estate buildings.

Smaller houses

Both E.C. Lee (who owed many of his commissions to his uncle the brewer Octavius Coope of Romford) and W. G. Bartleet (of Brentwood) remained untouched by the Domestic Revival of 1870s. For this we need to look to more sophisticated London architects, such as *Norman Shaw*, whose lively Chigwell Hall, *89* 1875–6, exemplifies the spirit of the 'Queen Anne' movement. Two years later *W. E. Nesfield*, who in the 1860s had been young Shaw's slightly older partner, built Loughton Hall nearby in a very similar style. Nesfield had, as we have seen, a good connection in Essex; as well as restoring the church at Radwinter, he built a pretty row of shops and cottages there, and in Saffron Walden the remarkably original bank for Gibson, Tuke & Gibson. Of local architects, *Sherrin* designed in a highly successful Vernacular Domestic style, with much use of half-timbering and tile-hanging. His speciality was large houses for prosperous commuters (like himself) in Ingatestone and Fryerning, but he built *p. 505* one house on a larger scale (Tilehurst, Mountnessing, *c.* 1884) and was at home at the seaside (Alexandra Hotel, Dovercourt, 1902–3). It is also at the seaside – Frinton – that some of the best houses of the late C19 and early C20 are to be found: The Home- *94* stead by *C. F. A. Voysey*, 1905–6, is outstanding, with all the hallmarks of that architect – roughcast walls with horizontal windows, low picturesque roofs, sloping buttresses, and well-fitted interiors – combining to make a very pretty ensemble. But Frinton also has some very accomplished buildings by local architects, such as Brookmead by *Homer & Sharp*, 1903. A similar mix is to be found at Loughton, where Arts and Crafts houses by local men – *Edmond Egan* and *Horace White* – stand alongside those by *Baillie Scott* and *W. R. Lethaby*. Finally, *A. H. Mackmurdo* made his home on the borders of Great Totham and Wickham Bishops in the early years of the C20, and built a remarkable series of buildings in the area, including Great Ruffins (1904 *90* onwards).

Urban developments

Frinton is an example of a place that grew more or less from nothing at the end of the C19, laid out very simply along streets running back from the sea. Earlier in the century similar SEASIDE

p. 329 DEVELOPMENTS were planned and partially executed at Dovercourt, in the 1850s, and at Southend in the 1860s. The latter scheme (Clifftown) was designed by *Banks & Barry* and was carefully planned, with four classes of houses diminishing in size as they got further from the sea and closer to the railway, and laid out in such a way that all but fourth-class houses had a view, however glancing, of the sea. Inland, new quarters were created in Chelmsford by the construction of New London Road in the 1840s, and in Colchester along Lexden Road from the late 1830s onwards to the W of the town, and to the SE New Town from 1878, the latter by *J. F. Goodey*. Besides estate villages mentioned above, other planned schemes are mostly associated with industry, such as housing at Earls Colne around the Atlas Iron Works. The most prolific builders of houses for their workers – both factory and estate – were the Courtaulds. Some of these were designed by *John Birch* and used to illustrate his book *Country Architecture* (1874): two three-storey terraces at Halstead, and a row of five semi-detached houses at Bocking. The latter Birch acknowledged to be based upon cottages erected by Samuel Courtauld in the 1850s at Gosfield, 'reflecting much credit on the taste and liberality of that gentleman'. Also at
4 Halstead is a most attractive row of cottages along the riverside by *Sherrin*, 1882–3, with a communal dining room. At about this time Sherrin built a workmen's hall near the Courtauld factory at Bocking, as well as cottages near one of the family houses, Bocking Place. On a very much smaller scale, some interesting housing was built at Mayland by *Charles Holden*, 1906, for a 'farm labour colony' established by an American soap manufacturer and philanthropist, Joseph Fels.

ESSEX SINCE 1914

Churches

The sense of a continuing tradition is strong in many C20 churches, particularly in the work of three architects who had their roots in Essex: Sir Charles Nicholson, Stephen Dykes Bower, and Laurence King. *Nicholson* has already been mentioned for his early work, St Alban, Westcliff (Southend), which is more rugged than most of his later buildings, such as St Michael, Westcliff (begun 1926). He is at his most interesting when he moves away from the purely Gothic, as at Frinton, 1928–9, which uses Renaissance elements, and St Margaret, Leigh-on-Sea (Southend), 1930–1, although the credit for the Early Christian basilican form should probably go to his co-architect, *Graham Lloyd*. Many of his churches (and many others beside) include stained glass by his brother, *A.K. Nicholson*; for this, and other fittings at which Nicholson excelled, his home church of South Benfleet is the one to visit. *Dykes Bower*, similarly, is best seen at his local church, Quendon, when it comes to decoration; but his largest work was the partial rebuilding of Coggeshall, 1955–8, following bomb damage in 1940. *Laurence King* developed a bland style than can be seen in many churches, particularly as far as interiors are concerned (e.g. St Mary-at-Latton, Harlow), but occasionally surprises: his first church, St George, Brentwood (1933–4) is a rare example of a church with Art Deco styling. Of other architects, *Comper* is to be found, apart from fittings and minor additions, only at Southchurch, Southend, in 1906, but even here the chancel was added later (by *F.C. Eden*) and the building never completed. Few of the many C20 churches in Southend are memorable; exceptions include *Newberry & Fowler*'s all-brick St Andrew, Westcliff, 1934–5, and St Peter, Prittlewell by *Humphrys & Hurst*, 1963, built in contemporary style with all its fittings intact. St Paul, Clacton-on-Sea by *Roy Gould*, 1965–6, is similarly a period piece, with wonderful stained glass by *Rosemary Rutherford*. [108] [109]

The best contemporary designs are, not surprisingly, in the New Towns, and especially Harlow: St Paul by *Humphrys & Hurst*, 1956–9, with its *John Piper* mosaic, and Our Lady of Fatima by *Gerard Goalen*, with stained glass by *Dom Charles Norris*. Of ROMAN CATHOLIC CHURCHES, the latter is the most striking of the C20, although *Martin Evans*'s at Silver End (1966) and *James Boutwood*'s at Stansted Mountfitchet (2002) are both accomplished and interesting in their very different ways. The R.C. Cathedral at Brentwood by *Quinlan Terry* (1989–91) is a success on many levels, creating a truly cathedral-like space without being unduly large, at the centre of a group of buildings that have a sense of cohesion and enclosure – something which Chelmsford Cathedral, raised from the status of a parish church in 1913, has never managed to achieve, in spite of major reordering in 1983–4. [119]

NONCONFORMIST CHURCHES AND CHAPELS moved during the C20 from a peak of confident grandeur to an anonymous modernism. *George Baines*'s additions to the Crowstone Chapel at Westcliff-on-Sea, Southend (1924) created an enormous church that might be taken, on the outside, for Anglican. *William Hayne*, on the other hand, was much freer; his Free Church at Frinton (1911) has Art Nouveau elements, while Hutton (1913) blends with the exclusive houses on the surrounding private estate. Of post-war buildings, mention should be made of three: *Kenneth Cheeseman*'s Castle Methodist Church, Colchester (1970), which sits well in a sensitive location; *Paul V. Mauger*'s compact Friends' Meeting House in Chelmsford (1958); and the Methodist Church, Loughton (1986–7) by the *Goodrow Consultancy*, which shows how a modern church can be planned to relate to the community it seeks to serve. [106]

Redundancy in the second half of the C20 resulted in the demolition of surprisingly few churches: *Walter Tapper*'s magnificent but unfinished St Erkenwald, Southend-on-Sea, was the greatest loss (begun 1905, dem. 1995). Colchester is the only town in Essex with a large number of medieval churches, of which five have found alternative uses: two have been demolished, and two are now in the care of the Churches Conservation Trust. A number of churches have been converted to houses, including five, very successfully, by *Patrick Lorimer*: Chignall St James, Latchingdon, Pattiswick, and Shellow Bowells. The nave of St Michael Pitsea (Basildon) has been demolished, but its C16 tower spared in order to accommodate telecommunications equipment – a true monument to early C21 priorities. More widespread alterations have resulted from the adapting and extending of churches to accord with changing patterns of use, although internal reordering has, on the whole, been relatively unadventurous: apart from Chelmsford Cathedral, the interiors of very few churches have been radically altered, exceptions including Roydon (1969), Hawkwell (1995–6), and Great Baddow (1999). However, late C20 extensions to provide meeting rooms, kitchens, and other facilities, have had as great an impact upon church buildings as vestries and organ chambers did in the C19. Good examples include those at Stock (1989), Kelvedon (1993), Hatfield Peverel (1993), and Bulphan (1999–2000).

Secular buildings between the wars

The Courtaulds continued building into the C20, with housing in Halstead and surrounding villages, and generous village halls at Bocking, Colne Engaine and Blackmore End, all built to a high standard in an easily recognizable traditional Neo-Tudor style. It was on Braintree, however, that they lavished most attention, and in particular William Julien Courtauld, who paid not only for the hospital which bears his name, but also a recreation ground, the fountain and nearby buildings next to the church, and above all the Town Hall (1926–8). The architect for much of this, including the Town Hall, was *E. Vincent Harris*, who Courtauld later ensured was engaged to design the Council Chamber which he donated for the new County Hall in Chelmsford (1938). At Chelmsford, Harris worked with the County Architect, *John Stuart*, at Braintree with *John Sewell Courtauld*, W.J. Courtauld's brother, who practised for a time in partnership with E.S. and E.W. Coldwell; many of the other Courtauld buildings were by *Coldwell, Coldwell & Courtauld*, later *Coldwell & Nicholls*.

The other manufacturing firm to dominate Essex in the C20, and in very much the same geographical area, was Crittall's. As manufacturers of metal windows, their place in the history of the MODERN MOVEMENT is assured, and the buildings for which they (as both company and family) were responsible are arguably more important than the Courtaulds' because they were constantly innovating. The firm's original workshop in Braintree, bought by Francis Berrington Crittall in 1849, survives, but the first interesting buildings are family houses in Chelmsford: Southborough Lodge (originally New House), New London Road, by *C.H.B. Quennell*, 1908, followed in 1912 by White

House, Moulsham Street, by Quennell with *Charles & W.H. Pertwee*. Both mix traditional styles – Arts and Crafts in 1908 for W.F. Crittall, Neo-Georgian in 1912 for F. H. Crittall – with the firm's metal windows. Immediately after the First World War, W.F. Crittall worked with Quennell on a group of concrete houses in Clockhouse Way, Braintree, the first real Modern Movement houses in England, designed on a metric grid and with flat roofs. This became a precursor to the more extensive and famous planned village at Silver End, started in 1926. Quennell worked here also, designing F.H. Crittall's Neo-Georgian house, Manors, but the Modern Movement houses with which the village is really associated were by *Thomas Tait* and *Frederick* 111 *MacManus* of *Sir John Burnet & Partners*. As well as housing, the village included a very large village hall (by *C. Murray Hennell*), department store by *Messrs Joseph*, and a church converted from a barn by *W. F. Crittall* and the editor of *The Studio*, *C. G. Holme*.

A comparable scheme followed at East Tilbury for BATA, the Czech shoe company, in 1933. Here, factories, flat-roofed concrete houses and other buildings were designed by the company's architects, *František Gahura* and *Vladimir Kafik*. More traditional housing was built from 1934 by the Land Settlement Association, examples of which can be seen around Great Yeldham (by *Pakington & Enthoven*) and Lawford.

A different sort of Modern Movement development was planned at Frinton in 1934, under the overall direction of *Oliver* 110 *Hill*. Hill and local architects designed a few houses, and one street was given over to one-off houses by architects of national standing (*Percy Tubbs, Son & Duncan, Stanley Hall, Easton & Robertson, Frederick Etchells, Marshall Sisson*, and *E. Wamsley Lewis*), but the grander overall scheme was never realized. Individual Modern Movement houses elsewhere include Shipwrights, Hadleigh, by *Wells Coates* (1937), and at Chadwell St Mary one of the 'Sunspan' houses designed by *Wells Coates* and *David Pleydell-Bouverie* for the 'Ideal Home' exhibition of 1934. Away from Silver End, *Messrs Joseph* and *Sir Owen Williams* designed New Farm, Great Easton for W. F. Crittall (1934), and at Broxted *Ernö Goldfinger* and *Gerald Flower* built Hill Pasture in gardens laid out by the client *Humphrey Waterfield*, 1936–8 – a single-storey house more like an exhibition pavilion.

Of other Modern Movement buildings, the Royal Corinthian 112 Yacht Club at Burnham-on-Crouch by *Joseph Emberton* (1930–1) has achieved iconic status. The streamlined style was felt appropriate for waterfront buildings (*One Arup*'s Labworth Café, 113 Canvey Island, is another example), and also for transport: the Railway Station at Loughton by *J. Murray Easton* (1939–40) uses brick but is nonetheless firmly modern in both styling and construction, as is *Easton & Robertson*'s Bank of England Printing Works nearby, built 1953–6 but designed before the war. The South Essex Waterworks Co. (Abberton, Langham, Layer de la Haye, Tiptree) presumably felt that the style conveyed the right hygienic image for their company. The same is true of interwar HOSPITALS: Broomfield Hospital by *J. Stuart* (1935–40),

Southend Municipal Hospital, Rochford by *F. W. Smith* (*c.* 1933–9) and Runwell Hospital by *Elcock & Sutcliffe* (1934–7) all have a distinctly Modern feel.

Southend General Hospital, however, designed in 1927 by the leading architects in the field, *Adams, Holden & Pearson*, was more traditional, as were most PUBLIC BUILDINGS of the interwar years. *John Stuart*, County Architect from 1920 to 1945, demonstrates this better than anyone; his many schools, police stations and other public buildings seldom rise above a polite NEO-GEORGIAN, with the exception of County Hall, Chelmsford, mentioned earlier. *Sir Edwin Cooper*'s buildings for the Port of London Authority at Tilbury (1925–30) are typical of the period, as is Clacton's Town Hall by *Sir Brumwell Thomas* (1929–31). The prevailing tendency is illustrated by *Marshall Sisson*, a Modernist who won the competition for the new Colchester Public Library in 1936 with a Neo-Georgian design and never looked back.

Post-war domestic buildings

75   Sisson lived for a time at Shermans in Dedham, the town which was also home to *Raymond Erith*, the most accomplished classical architect of the mid C20, whose buildings range from modest
p. 435 farm cottages in Dedham and Lawford to Wivenhoe New Park, Greenstead (1962–4). His most sophisticated building is perhaps
118   Great House, Dedham (1937–8), of a stripped classicism reminiscent of Soane. The tradition is continued by his former partner
120   *Quinlan Terry*, whose country houses include Merks Hall, Great Dunmow (1982–6) and Badgers, Great Canfield (2000–3). The latter was one of the first houses in the country, and the only one in Essex, to be built under the so-called 'Gummer Clause' of Planning Policy Guidance Note 7, published in 1997, that permitted the construction on a green-field site of 'an isolated new house ... if it is clearly of the highest quality, is truly outstanding in terms of its architecture and landscape design, and would significantly enhance its immediate setting and wider surroundings' – requirements amply met at Great Canfield. Badgers is relatively plain, but Terry's buildings are on the whole more Baroque, more flamboyant than Erith's, which have a timeless quality. It is perhaps because of this that Terry's buildings provoke more extreme reactions among critics, of praise (for being traditional in design and construction) and condemnation (for being reactionary).

Post-war non-traditional houses are rare in Essex as elsewhere, but include four interesting and diverse examples from the 1960s: Ark House, Rochford, by *Yorke, Rosenberg & Mardall*, 1962 (for the owner of Keddie's department store in Southend, mentioned below); Shalford Hall, by *Edward Samuel & Partners*, 1967;
115   Grange Farm, Fingringhoe, by *Philip Pank*, and The Studio, Ulting, by *Richard & Su Rogers*, both 1968–9. The turn of the C21 produced a couple of interesting schemes of social housing, at Jaywick (Clacton) by *Pollard Thomas & Edwards* for the Guinness Trust, and at Tilbury by *Sergison Bates* for the New Islington and

Hackney Housing Association, while different approaches to eco-logical problems were taken in houses at Danbury (by *Paul Gladman*) and St Lawrence (by *Alison Brooks Architects*), both completed in 2004.

Building in Essex since 1945 is, however, dominated by the NEW TOWNS of Harlow and Basildon, established in 1947 and 1949 respectively – two of the eight New Towns built around London under the New Towns Act of 1946 to ease pressure on London and provide a replacement for housing destroyed during the Second World War but without adding to suburban sprawl. Both were based on existing villages, with the existing topography being more successfully preserved at Harlow than at Basil-don. Partly, this is because there was more at Basildon that needed replacing: the plotland developments of substandard buildings, often little more than shacks, had developed haphaz-ardly along unmade roads. Similar uncontrolled development had occurred at Jaywick, Clacton-on-Sea, after 1928: small houses never intended for year-round occupation. Jaywick still stands, but the Basildon plotlands were swept away with the same zeal as the East End slums from which many of the New Towns' residents originated. Another aim of the New Towns was to provide a sense of community that was so lacking in the large 'out-county' LCC housing estates at, for example, Debden (Loughton) and Billericay.

Of the two Essex New Towns, Harlow seems more successful, 114 largely due to the presiding genius of *Sir Frederick Gibberd* as architect-planner for the entire existence of the Harlow Devel-opment Corporation, 1947–80; Basildon had a succession of chief architects, none of whom quite had Gibberd's vision. On the other hand, Basildon produced some very innovative housing, particularly in its later stages, some by the Development Corporation's own architects under *Clive Plumb*, some by outside architects and in particular *Ahrends, Burton & Koralek*. Harlow's great strength is the integration not just of the existing roads and villages but the incorporation into the plan of the countryside (under *Sylvia Crowe*, who was also landscape consultant at Basil-don, but less happily), and owes much to the cohort of architects that Gibberd assembled to design particular areas, including *H. T. Cadbury-Brown*, *Fry, Drew & Partners*, *Richard Sheppard & Part-ners*, and *F. R. S. Yorke*. Above all there is a lightness of touch and a sense of humour at Harlow that is lacking at Basildon. Just how important Gibberd was is shown by the awfulness of the Church Langley estate built on the E side of Harlow in the 1990s, although the Newhall development to its N, begun in 1998, shows an encouraging new direction, with innovative housing by *Proctor Matthews Architects*, *PCKO* and others.

Nothing else on the scale of Harlow and Basildon has been attempted in Essex, but the county gained a third new town, South Woodham Ferrers, planned and largely built in the 1970s 121 under the auspices of the County Council. The chief interest of South Woodham Ferrers is as the embodiment of *A Design Guide for Residential Areas*, published by the Council in 1973 under the

Sketch of mews court.
'Essex Design Guide', 1973

county planner, *D. Jennings Smith* (team leader, *Melville Dunbar*, revised edition, edited by Alan Stones, expanded to include mixed-use areas, 1997). Known as the 'Essex Design Guide', this influential document laid down what was or was not acceptable and became more or less required reading for all developers of housing in the county. It achieved its purpose of banishing anonymous suburban housing, 'Anywhere' type houses as it called them, replacing them with houses laid out in a way that paid more attention to people and less to cars (the 'mews court' was particularly favoured), designed in a vernacular tradition using a mix of local materials – brick, plaster, weatherboarding, and so on. *David Ruffle* designed some of the early developments which successfully implemented the Guide's tenets, e.g. at Ingatestone and Brentwood, and the developers *Countryside Properties* have become particularly adept at designing new communities which seem to satisfy both the planners and house-buyers. Two of their largest schemes are Great Notley (1993 onwards) and Beaulieu Park, Springfield (1998–2002). While it is easy to find fault with such developments, for their tweeness and repetition, they are very much better than many of the alternatives, and Great Notley has the added advantage of including two fine public buildings, a primary school by *Allford Hall Monaghan Morris* (1998–9) and the Discovery Centre by *Penoyre & Prasad* (1999–2001). Chafford Hundred, West Thurrock (1988 onwards) is an example of the banal alternative, although this is redeemed by *Nicholas Hare*'s Chafford Hundred Campus (2000–1). Occasionally, as at Noak Bridge, Basildon, when the houses are all different and are made to look like houses and not like converted agricultural or industrial buildings, the result can be quite convincing.

Such residential growth was necessarily accompanied by RETAIL DEVELOPMENT. At Harlow and Basildon, neighbourhood shopping centres were an important and integral part of the design, and both South Woodham Ferrers and Great Notley also provided local facilities that help to create real communities rather than just dormitory suburbs. South Woodham Ferrers can claim the dubious distinction of being home to the first of the barn-style supermarkets (by *Holder & Mathias Partnership*, 1977–8) that sprang up across England in the 1980s and 1990s. Elsewhere, the trend has been towards out-of-town shopping: Lakeside, West Thurrock (1987–90) and Braintree's Freeport Designer Village (2000) are supreme examples. This new style of shopping had a disastrous effect upon many High Streets, Southend's among them: one victim was Keddie's Department Store, although its distinguished building by *Yorke, Rosenberg & Mardall*, 1960–4, remains, albeit altered. Many of the urban shopping centres built in the 1960s and 1970s (e.g. at Basildon, Brentwood, and Harlow) have been refurbished and extended in an attempt to win back customers.

Post-war public buildings

If pre-war public buildings were mainly traditional, the same cannot be said for many of those erected later in the century – with the interesting exception of the Neo-Georgian council offices in Brentwood by *John Brandon-Jones, Ashton & Broadbent* (1957). The major project in this respect was the University of Essex, for which the master plan, by *Kenneth Capon* of the *Architects Co-Partnership*, was prepared in 1962. Its deliberately urban feel, including tower blocks, seemed incongruous to many in its country-house setting of Wivenhoe Park, yet it works very well with the C18 landscape. Later buildings, particularly those built following the 1991 development plan by *Nicholas Hare Architects*, have maintained a high standard. Linked to the University is South East Essex College, Southend, with a building by *KSS Architects* (2001–4) that has dramatically changed the town's skyline. At Chelmsford, the development of Anglia Ruskin University's Rivermead Campus has resulted in some excellent contemporary buildings by *Wilkinson Eyre* (2001 onwards).

Large numbers of SCHOOLS were built in the post-war years under the direction of successive county architects: Harold Conolly, Ralph Crowe, and Alan Willis. *Conolly* developed an immediately recognizable style of continuous glazing and coloured panels, seen for example at Billericay (1965), and also employed outside architects, such as *Richard Sheppard & Partners* at Chigwell (1957–63). He also developed a simple standard branch LIBRARY design, with the prototype at Broomfield (1960–1), and good examples at Burnham-on-Crouch, Canvey Island, Loughton, and Sible Hedingham. *Crowe* inherited from Conolly a commitment to the SEAC (South East Architects

Consortium) system of modular system of construction, but was unhappy with its poor environmental performance and developed his own system (MCB), which used highly insulated concrete panels with flat roofs, flexible steel and reinforced concrete frame, and regular grid. Forty-nine primary schools were built using this system, the first at Elmstead in 1972. *Willis* continued to use the system after his appointment in 1976, but the decline in the number of projects made further use of MCB unviable and in any case the resulting buildings by then looked very out-of-date. The last years of the County Architect's Dept (which was phased out following the transfer of the county's Property Services Dept to *W. S. Atkins* in 1993) saw a greater variety of styles and innovative attempts to create buildings that were more energy-efficient, for example at Ravenscroft Primary School, Clacton (1981–2), Coggeshall (1983–6) and Mayland (1990). Tabor Science College, Bocking (1991–2) and Bishops Park College, Clacton (2003–5 by the *Architects Co-Partnership*) are, like Chafford Hundred mentioned above, notable for being multi-purpose, housing community as well as school facilities, and both have integral artwork, by *Michael Brennand-Wood* and others at Bocking and *Rob Olins* at Clacton.

Another late work of the *County Architect's Dept* was the extension of County Hall, Chelmsford, 1984–8, its use of atria influenced by new ideas in office planning to provide unencumbered open spaces. Such thinking, and the structural means to make it possible, is seen at its best in Essex's most famous C20 building, the High-Tech terminal at Stansted Airport by *Foster Associates* (1986–91), a beautifully elegant structure that makes the business of getting from road or rail to runway as simple as it can be. By inverting the usual arrangement of services and placing them below ground, it revolutionized airport planning and had the added benefit of reducing the prominence of the building within the landscape. It would be ironic if this addition to the county's stock of good buildings is followed by the total or partial damage of many more (including demolition of at least twenty-nine listed buildings, mostly in Takeley), not to mention destruction of some of the county's most attractive countryside, that would result from the construction of a second runway.

Conservation

Essex County Council, as well as encouraging sensitive new building through the Design Guide, was also active in promoting a better understanding of, and conservation of, Essex's historic buildings. The role of Cecil Hewett, centred on Cressing Temple, has been mentioned in connection with timber-framed buildings. Essex is particularly rich in medieval barns, and the Council published in 1979 *Historic Barns: a Planning Appraisal* in order to draw attention to their importance and to suggest ways of preserving those that had become redundant, preferably by finding alternative uses other than residential. A singular success was the restoration by the County Council of the C13 barn at

Coggeshall in 1983–5. The project architect, *James Boutwood*, had previously been architect for the Council's Revolving Fund, established in 1970, by which the County bought, restored and sold on historic buildings at risk. Buildings restored in this way included the Guildhall, Clavering and Garrison House, Wivenhoe. Another important restoration was that of Thaxted Guildhall, also by Boutwood, which was owned by the Council. Elsewhere, a notable achievement was the revival of the Dutch Quarter of Colchester by the Borough Council: the restoration of forty-two houses in the 1950s, followed by sensitive infilling in the 1970s and 80s. The Borough was building, consciously or not, upon the achievements of the Colchester Civic Society (established 1933) and its offshoot, the Colchester Improvement Trust, which restored a number of the town's buildings in the 1930s. Dedham was another town that was alert to the need to protect its built and natural heritage: the Dedham Vale Society, under the chairmanship of Raymond Erith, was formed in 1938. At both Thaxted and Saffron Walden the County Council were forward-looking in commissioning studies of the towns by *Donald Insall & Associates*, in 1966 and 1977–9 respectively.

The real threat to historic buildings and the landscape in general now comes less from neglect and ignorance than from over-development. The supposed need for ever more housing in SE England is hitting Essex as hard as its neighbouring counties. More housing means, in the C21, more shops, more schools, and above all more roads, because for most people the private car is the only form of daily transport to be contemplated. Cars have arguably done more to blight Essex than anything else – except, perhaps, for aeroplanes, which, because of Stansted Airport, have a devastating effect upon the NW corner of the county. Massive development proposed in the S of the county, as part of the Thames Gateway project, also looks set to have a considerable impact upon an area of Essex which, in spite of its poor image, still contains buildings and natural features of great importance. There can be little doubt that Essex will change as much in the next fifty years as it has since this book was first published in 1954.

WARFARE AND DEFENCE

A final word is needed on structures connected with warfare and defence since the Middle Ages. Because of its position, on the approach to London from the Continent, and because of its mostly flat coastline, Essex has always felt vulnerable to invasion and has been defended accordingly. The coast is in fact not very suitable for sea-borne invasion, consisting mainly of marsh and mudflats rather than beach, but aerial invasion proved to be a real threat in the C20, and Essex suffered much bomb damage during the Second World War: as well as many churches which lost their stained glass, Little Horkesley was completely destroyed, and Danbury and Navestock were badly damaged, as was New Hall, Boreham.

Henry VIII built blockhouses or bulwarks to defend the Thames, the Colne, and Harwich, but of these only a trace remains at East Mersea. Another survived until 1868 as part of Tilbury Fort, built 1670–83 by *Sir Bernard de Gomme* to defend against the French and Dutch. With its advanced design of moats
64 and earthworks and ornate gatehouse, this is the principal military monument in the county, but it is equally of interest for the way in which it has been updated over the centuries, right up to the Second World War, to cope with new threats and accommodate new weaponry. The next major threat was that posed by Napoleon at the end of C18, which resulted in the construction by the Royal Engineers of Martello Towers, mostly of stuccoed brick with stone dressings (the name comes from a Torre della Mortella on the island of Corsica which impressed the English in the campaign of 1794). The scheme was proposed by *Capt. W. H. Ford* and carried out by *Brig.-Gen. William Twiss.* Construction began along the S coast of England, 1805–8, followed by Essex and Suffolk, 1809–12. Those on the E coast were designed to carry heavier guns, so were more massively built and are cam-shaped rather than elliptical or circular. Eleven were built in Essex, of which six survive (at Clacton, St Osyth, and Walton). There were in addition four redoubts, three on the S coast and one at Harwich.

Continuing worries in the C19 resulted in the construction of
95 Coalhouse Fort, East Tilbury (site of another Henrician blockhouse) in 1847–55 and again in 1861–74. The latter structure survives largely intact, albeit with later modifications. The Redoubt at Harwich was remodelled at about the same time, while Beacon Hill Fort, Dovercourt, which had housed a battery during the Napoleonic Wars, was rebuilt from 1889 onwards. By this time, a new threat had been identified, that of an artillery assault upon London from an invading German army. To protect against this, in 1888 a defensive line was planned that ran from North Weald Bassett to Guildford in Surrey, via Tilbury. A redoubt was built at North Weald Bassett, but improvements in artillery soon made the scheme obsolete and the plan was scrapped in 1906. During the Second World War similar 'stop-lines' were formed, the most important of which was the General Headquarters Line. It ran N–S through Essex from Great Chesterford to Canvey Island via Chelmsford, and innumerable pillboxes remain, supplementing natural barriers such as rivers.

The coastal forts were upgraded during the First and Second World Wars, increasingly to protect against aerial attack. Relics of the First World War include buildings of an airfield, or 'flight station', at Stow Maries, and evidence of a naval base on Osea Island. The Second World War made a much greater impression, particularly upon the landscape by the construction of numerous airbases: one destroyed the park at Easton Lodge. Much can still be seen at Little Walden, North Weald, and Debden, the latter opened as a fighter station in 1937 and still in service. Of the many anti-aircraft sites, the best-preserved is at Lippitts Hill,

High Beach, while at East Tilbury and Burnham-on-Crouch are wonderfully sculptural concrete towers for controlling minefields in the rivers. The Cold War left two rather chilling monuments, the massive bunkers at Kelvedon Hatch and Mistley, of which little is to be seen above ground.

Behind the front line, extensive barracks remain at Colchester and Shoeburyness (South Shoebury, Southend). At Colchester the first permanent buildings were erected in 1862, and include some of the earliest surviving cavalry barracks in the country. The garrison church, 1856, is in theory demountable. The buildings at Shoeburyness date from 1847, but the most interesting element is the group of buildings known, because of its unique layout, as Horseshoe Barracks (1859). Shoeburyness, which housed the School of Gunnery whose successors still occupy Foulness Island, has been vacated by the army, Colchester is in the process of being so, but the best buildings are being preserved. Warley Barracks (Little Warley) fared less well; built from 1805 onwards, they closed in 1960 and were mostly demolished, with the important exception of the Italianate garrison church by *A.J. Green* and *Sir Matthew Digby Wyatt* (1855–7). Finally, the Royal Gunpowder Mills at Waltham Abbey, dating back to the C17 and taken over by the Board of Ordnance in 1787, supplied much of the armed forces' gunpowder and other explosives until 1943, continuing as a research establishment until 1991. From Waltham Abbey the gunpowder was taken by barge to the magazines at Purfleet, built in 1763–5, of which one (as well as the later proof house and clock tower) remains.

COUNTY SURVEYORS AND ARCHITECTS

Richard Porter, 1704–6, 1711–12
Edward Glascock, 1712–18
Edward Turner, 1718–19
John Sparrow, 1719–27
Thomas Pennystone, 1727–57

No permanent appointment until

William Hillyer, 1770–82
John Johnson, 1782–1812
Robert Lugar, 1812–16
Thomas Hopper, 1816–56
Henry Stock, 1856–1900
Frank Whitmore, 1900–14 (chief assistant, H.W. Mann)
G. Topham Forrest, 1914–19 (chief assistant, J.W. Spence)
John Stuart, 1920–45
Harold Conolly, 1945–66 (deputy county architect, 1942–45)
Ralph Crowe, 1966–76
Alan Willis, 1976–96 (Director of Property Services, 1990–96)

FURTHER READING

There are a number of COUNTY HISTORIES, foremost among them Philip Morant's *History and Antiquities of Essex*, 1768 (reprinted 1978). Later histories are based upon it, including Peter Muilman's *New and Complete History of the County of Essex* 'by a Gentleman', 1769–72, and Thomas Wright's *History and Topography of the County of Essex*, 1836, until we reach the *Victoria History of the Counties of England* ('VCH'), launched in 1899. The first Essex volume was published in 1903, covering natural history (including geology), early man, ancient earthworks, Anglo-Saxon remains, and the Essex Domesday. Vol. II, 1907, contains much general historical information that is still of great use, including sections on ecclesiastical history and religious houses, industries, schools, and tables of population. The planned section on Roman Essex did not appear until 1963, as a separate Vol. III. By then the topographical volumes were under way, of which ten have so far been published. These volumes follow the pre-1965 county boundaries (so include parts of Essex now in Greater London) and are based on the historic division of the county into hundreds. Vol. IV (1956) covers Ongar Hundred (Abbess Roding, Beauchamp Roding, Bobbingworth, Chigwell, Chipping Ongar, Fyfield, Greensted, High Laver, High Ongar, Kelvedon Hatch, Lambourne, Little Laver, Loughton, Magdalen Laver, Moreton, Navestock, North Weald Bassett, Norton Mandeville, Shelley, Stanford Rivers, Stapleford Abbotts, Stapleford Tawney, Stondon Massey, Theydon Bois, Theydon Garnon, and Theydon Mount); Vol. V (1966) includes Epping, Nazeing, and Waltham Abbey, as well as part of Becontree Hundred (now London, completed in Vol. VI, 1973). Chafford Hundred (including Great and Little Warley and South Ockendon) was started in Vol. VII (1978) and completed in Vol. VIII (1983) (Aveley, Brentwood, Childerditch, Grays Thurrock, South Weald, Stifford, West Thurrock), with Harlow Hundred (Great Hallingbury, Great Parndon, Harlow, Hatfield Broad Oak, Latton, Little Hallingbury, Little Parndon, Matching, Netteswell, Roydon, Sheering). Vol. IX (1994) brought a move to the E of the county, and was devoted to the Borough of Colchester (including Greenstead, Lexden, Mile End, and West Donyland), followed by Vol. X (2001) covering part of Lexden Hundred (Aldham, Birch, Boxted, Mount Bures, Chappel, Colne Engaine, Copford, Dedham, Earls Colne, East Donyland, Easthorpe, Fordham, Great & Little Horkesley, Langham, Stanway, Wakes Colne, West Bergholt, White Colne, Wivenhoe, Wormingford). Work is in progress on Tendring Hundred, including the seaside towns of Clacton, Frinton and Walton. Separate Bibliography volumes were published in 1959, 1987, and 2000, and provide references for the whole county, not just those places described in the published volumes.

Of the many single-volume histories, those by A.C. Edwards (1958, revised 1962) and Stan Jarvis (1993) may be mentioned. William Addison's *Essex Worthies* (1973) is an invaluable 'who's who' that includes mini-biographies of many of the owners and clients mentioned in these pages.

The EARLY HISTORY of Essex is covered by James Kemble's *Prehistoric and Roman Essex* (2001), which includes a gazetteer of sites, many of which are not included in this volume. The best overviews of basic data on the prehistory of Essex (indeed of the archaeology of Essex as a whole, including post-medieval and industrial archaeology) are *Archaeology in Essex to A.D. 1500* (ed. D.G. Buckley, 1980) and *The Archaeology of Essex* (ed. Owen Bedwin, 1996), while *The Archaeology of South Essex* by Nigel Brown and Roger Massey-Ryan (2004) provides a popular introduction. For the Roman period (in addition to VCH vol. III, mentioned earlier), the best work is *City of Victory* by Philip Crummy (1997), focusing on Colchester.

GUIDEBOOKS AND DIRECTORIES are of variable quality, but T.K. Cromwell's *Excursions in the County of Essex* (1818–19) is useful, while Norman Scarfe's *Shell Guide* of 1968 is every bit as individual as one would expect of that series. Of the directories, William White's *History, Gazetteer and Directory of Essex* of 1848 (2nd edn 1863) and the various Post Office Directories (Kelly's) often provide information about recently erected buildings that is otherwise elusive.

Of local PERIODICALS, which include much architectural as well as general historical information, the most important is the *Transactions of the Essex Archaeological Society* (now *Essex Archaeology and History*), published since 1858. Contributors, particularly in the C19, include several architects (notably Fred Chancellor) writing about churches and other buildings they had restored. The *Essex Review*, 1892–1957, and *Essex Journal* (1966 to date), are less academic but still invaluable, the former providing for many years quarterly reports of new work to churches etc.

For individual Essex BUILDINGS, the most important source is the four-volume Inventory published by the Royal Commission on Historical Monuments (England) between 1916 and 1923. Although they were concerned only with buildings erected up to 1714 (everything after that being described as 'modern'), and many of their conclusions have had to be revised in the light of later research, these volumes remain indispensable, especially for their plans of churches and selected secular buildings. The original survey notes and photographs are in the Commission's archive at Swindon and should be consulted by anyone needing more information about the condition of a building at the time of the survey.* The RCHME volumes have been supplemented but in no way superseded by the statutory lists of listed buildings, available in public libraries and also online. Descriptions for buildings in the Borough of Brentwood, Harwich, Maldon, and Saffron Walden, re-listed in the 1990s, are extremely full.

---

* One of the Commission's investigators was the young Mortimer Wheeler, whose account of working methods in his autobiography (*Still Digging*, 1955) makes it seem even more of an achievement that the series was completed.

Other sources are widely scattered. *The Colchester Area* (Proceedings of the 138th Summer Meeting of the Royal Archaeological Institute, 1992, ed. N.J.G. Pounds) gives brief accounts of a number of buildings, many based on recent research. The resources of the Essex Record Office, including building plans submitted for approval by the local authority, are seemingly endless, but more accessible than in the past thanks to a computerized catalogue. Of national sources for the C19 and C20, architectural journals are invaluable but hard work, lacking comprehensive indexes; *The Builder* is the best known, but others such as *Building News* and *British Architect* often provide better coverage of buildings outside London. Of great use are notes accompanying visits by the Georgian Group (*Houses of Mid-Essex*, 1999), the Victorian Society (*South-West Essex*, including Southend, 1978), and *The Superior Seaside* (Frinton and Walton), 1980), and in particular the Thirties (later Twentieth Century) Society (various, since 1989, including Braintree and Silver End, Frinton, and Harlow). For the C20, Charles McKean's *Architectural Guide to Cambridge and East Anglia since 1920* (1982) concentrates on the 1970s.

As far as the NATURAL ENVIRONMENT is concerned, John Hunter's *The Essex Landscape* (1999) provides an excellent survey, relating the landscape to the social and architectural history of the county (and has a useful bibliography). It is complemented by *The Essex Landscape: in Search of its History* (ed. Sarah Green, 1999). Oliver Rackham includes many Essex examples in his histories of woodland and the countryside, but his history of Hatfield Forest (*The Last Forest*, 1989) may be singled out. Raphael Medola and William White's *Report on the East Anglian Earthquake of April 22nd 1884* (1885) is a curiosity worth investigating. Gerald Lucy's *Essex Rock* (1999) provides a good introduction to the geology.

Information on BUILDING MATERIALS will be found in Alec Clifton-Taylor's *The Pattern of English Building* (4th edn, 1987). Of more local interest are Stephen Hart's *Flint Architecture of East Anglia* (2000) and, especially, *Brick in Essex* by Pat Ryan (two vols, 1996–9). TIMBER FRAMING is covered by three books by Cecil Hewett: *The Development of Carpentry 1200–1700* (1967), *English Historic Carpentry* (1980), and *Church Carpentry* (1982). These all draw extensively on Essex examples, as does *Regional Variation in Timber-Framed Building in England and Wales, down to 1550* (ed. D.D. Andrews and D.F. Stenning, 1998). *Historic Buildings in Essex*, a journal published by the Essex Historic Buildings Group since 1984, deals mainly with timber-framed buildings, and a number have also been written up in *Essex Archaeology and History* and *Vernacular Architecture*. The handbook compiled for the Vernacular Architecture Group's Spring Conference 2003 provides a convenient guide to nearly seventy buildings, mostly timber-framed, almost half of them in Maldon. Harry Forrester's *Timber-Framed Houses of Essex* (1959), still gives a useful, short introduction to the subject, even if much of the dating no longer holds good. Muriel Carrick's exhibition catalogue on *Essex*

Domestic Wall Paintings 14th–18th Century (1993) covers that important topic.

Histories of individual TOWNS are so numerous and uneven that only a few can be mentioned. One of the earliest was Morant's history of Colchester, first issued in 1748 and revised for inclusion in his history of the county. Vol. IX of the VCH is an exhaustive modern account of Colchester, but Andrew Phillips's short history of 2004 should not be overlooked. Chelmsford's history to 1888 has been thoroughly chronicled by Hilda Grieve (*The Sleepers and the Shadows*, two vols, 1988–94). There are good short histories of Southend by Ian Yearsley (2001) and Witham by Janet Gyford (2005). More particularly architectural are Chris Pond's *The Buildings of Loughton* (2003) and *The Buildings of Saffron Walden* by Martyn Everett and Donald Stewart (2003), which should be read in conjunction with Bruce Munro's article on 'Some Saffron Walden Buildings and their Architects' in *Saffron Walden Historical Journal*, vol. 3 (2003). Saffron Walden is also one of Alec Clifton-Taylor's *Six More English Towns* (1981). *Harlow: the Story of a New Town* (1980) by Frederick Gibberd and others is essential for an understanding of that town, and makes one wish something similar had been done for Basildon.

Twenty-one towns are described, pithily and with great insight, by David W. Lloyd in his *Historic Towns of East Anglia* (1989), and over thirty have been the subject of a series of Historic Town Assessment Reports compiled by Essex County Council.

Essex CHURCHES have been the subject of many books over the centuries, some of which have acquired historic interest in their own right. A.I. Suckling's *Memorials of the Antiquities and Architecture, Family History and Heraldry of the County of Essex* (1845), James Hadfield's *Ecclesiastical Architecture of the County of Essex from the Norman Era to the Sixteenth Century* (1848), and George Buckler's *Twenty-two of the Churches of Essex* (1856) provide an interesting record of many churches before they were restored. More recent and comprehensive surveys include *A Guide to Essex Churches* (ed. Christopher Starr, 1980) and *A Select Guide to Essex Churches and Chapels* (ed. John Fitch, 1996), the former thematic, the latter a gazetteer. The latter also includes a small number of R.C. and Nonconformist churches. R.C. churches are not well chronicled generally, although Stewart Foster's *History of the Diocese of Brentwood 1917–1992* (1994) provides the context. Nonconformist churches and chapels, on the other hand, have been comprehensively surveyed by Rosalind Kaye in her *Chapels in Essex* (1999), while a selection (mainly pre-1800) is to be found in Christopher Stell's *Inventory of Nonconformist Chapels and Meeting-Houses in Eastern England* (2002). *Lost Parish Churches of Essex* by Andrew Barham (2000) includes a number of reused churches as well as ruins and sites. Warwick Rodwell addresses the problems of redundant churches, as well as the archaeological investigation of 'living' ones, in *Historic Churches: a Wasting Asset* (1977).

As far as CHURCH FURNISHINGS AND FITTINGS are concerned, more than ninety churches have been (or are in the
process of being) recorded by NADFAS Church Recorders, their
inventories deposited in the Essex Record Office, at the National
Monuments Record, and elsewhere. Books on individual topics
abound, headed by Fred Chancellor's *The Ancient Sepulchral
Monuments of Essex* (1890). There are exhaustive works on the
county's church bells by C. Deedes and H.B. Walters (1909),
church chests by H. William Lewer and J. Charles Wall (1913),
church plate by G. Montagu Benton et al. (1926) and fonts and
font covers by W. Norman Paul (1986). *The Monumental Brasses
of Essex* by William Lack et al. (two vols, 2003) supersedes earlier
works on the subject. For monuments, one must still go to
Rupert Gunnis's *Dictionary of British Sculptors 1660–1851* (2nd
edn, 1964), although a revision is in progress. Adam White's
Ph.D. thesis, 'Church Monuments in Britain *c.* 1560–*c.* 1660'
(Courtauld Institute, 1992) and his 'Biographical Dictionary of
London Tomb Sculptors *c.* 1560–*c.* 1660' (*Walpole Society*, vol. 61
(1999)) fill some of the gaps and question earlier attributions.

A fair number of Essex's COUNTRY HOUSES (and gardens)
have been the subject of articles in *Country Life* since 1897, which
year also saw the publication of J.A. Rush's *Seats in Essex*. This
work, like many of the earlier *Country Life* articles, tends to be
more concerned with the history of the owners than the buildings.
Vol. III of *Burke's and Savills Guide to Country Houses* (1981; section
on Essex by John Kenworthy-Browne and Peter Reid) is comprehensive. Vol. II of Anthony Emery's *Greater Medieval Houses of
England and Wales 1300–1500* (2000) includes thirteen Essex buildings. Of books on individual houses, J.D. Williams's *Audley End:
the Restoration of 1762–1797* (1966) is particularly useful.

PARKS AND GARDENS have benefited enormously from recent
research, much of it carried out under the auspices of the Essex
Gardens Trust, who published *Paper Landscapes* in 2005 and are
preparing a biographical index of Essex garden and landscape
designers. In 2000 they published *A Gazetteer of Sites in Essex
Associated with Humphry Repton* (ed. Fiona Cowell and Georgina
Green), and an inventory of *Historic Designed Landscapes of Essex*,
supplementing English Heritage's *Register of Parks and Gardens
of Special Historic Interest*, is in progress (Epping District, 2006;
Braintree District, in draft; Uttlesford and Maldon in prepara-
tion). Publications on individual designers include 'Richard
Woods (?1716–93): a Preliminary Account' by Fiona Cowell in
Garden History, Vols 14–15 (1986–7). On the debit side, there is
Lost Gardens of Essex by Wendy Stubbings (2002).

Knowledge of other building types has been greatly expanded
in recent years, particularly by a series of books published by the
RCHME/English Heritage: on HOSPITALS (ed. Harriet Richardson, 1998), PRISONS (Allan Brodie et al., 2002), SHOPS (Kathryn
Morrison, 2003) and WORKHOUSES (Kathryn Morrison, 1999;
see also *Essex Workhouses* by John Drury, 2006), as well as books
by Wayne Cocroft et al. on Cold War buildings (2003) and the
manufacture of gunpowder and explosives (2000). Relating

specifically to Essex is a survey of *Buildings of the Radio Electronics Industry in Essex* (1999) by Cocroft and Adam Menuge, and a series of thematic surveys commissioned by Essex Council from 1995, including studies of buildings relating to the brewing, malt, lime, iron-founding, public water supply and textile industries, as well as Poor Law buildings and bridges and tollhouses. The County Council's periodical *Essex Education* is a good source for post-war SCHOOLS and LIBRARIES, especially the Special Building Supplements, 1955–63, while C.P. French's Ph.D. thesis 'Essex County Council Primary Schools (1973–1993): a Design Appraisal' (University of Greenwich, 1996) continues the story. The University of Essex is discussed in Stefan Muthesius, *The Post war University: Utopianist Campus and College* (2000). There are books on *The Cinemas of Essex* by Bob Grimwood (1995), and *Pigeon Cotes and Dove Houses of Essex* by D. Smith (1931). WINDMILLS are treated exhaustively by Kenneth G. Farries (five vols, 1981–88), WATER MILLS more selectively by Hervey Benham (1976). *Essex Spas and Mineral Waters* by Ronald & Ann Cowell (2001) deals with one of the more surprising aspects of Essex's social and architectural history.

INDUSTRIAL ARCHITECTURE in general is covered well by John Booker's account, *Essex and the Industrial Revolution* (1974); much of the information contained there is also to be found in gazetteer form in *The Batsford Guide to the Industrial Archaeology of East Anglia* by David Alderton and John Booker (1980). E.A. Labrum's *Civil Engineering Heritage: Eastern and Central England* (1994) covers a few Essex sites. Gordon Biddle's *Britain's Historic Railway Buildings* (2003) is similarly selective, Peter Kay's *Essex Railway Heritage* (2006) comprehensive.

The main source for information on ARCHITECTS is Howard Colvin's *Biographical Dictionary of British Architects 1600–1840* (3rd edn 1995; 4th edn in preparation). Relating to that period is Nancy Briggs's 'The Evolution of the Office of County Surveyor in Essex, 1700–1816' in *Architectural History*, Vol. 27 (1984). John Harvey's *English Mediaeval Architects* (1954) has little that relates directly to Essex, as is the case with A. Stuart Gray's *Edwardian Architecture* (1985). For the Victorian period, the British Architectural Library's *Directory of British Architects 1834–1914* (2001) includes many Essex architects (but does not list their works); these and others are also to be found in James Bettley's 'Checklist of Essex Architects 1834–1914' in *Essex Archaeology and History*, Vol. 24 (1993). Many Essex (and Suffolk) architects strayed over the county borders, so appear in Brown, Haward & Kindred's *Dictionary of Architects of Suffolk Buildings 1800–1914* (1991). There is too little on individual architects. For the C18, *John Johnson 1732–1814* by Nancy Briggs (1991). For the C19, theses by Brenda Watkin on William White's work in Essex and Anne Holden on Fred Chancellor (both A.A. Postgraduate Diploma in Building Conservation, 1994), and by James Bettley on Rev. Ernest Geldart (Ph.D., Courtauld Institute, 1999), as well as articles in *Essex Archaeology and History* on Chancellor by Holden (Vol. 26, 1995) and Geldart by Bettley (Vol. 31, 2000).

For the C20, *Raymond Erith, Architect* by his daughter Lucy Archer (1985) and *Raymond Erith: Progressive Classicist 1904–1973* (catalogue of an exhibition at the Soane Museum, 2004); and biographies of Quinlan Terry by Clive Aslet (1986) and David Watkin (2006).

An increasing amount of information is available online. Websites of particular relevance to Essex include:

seax.essexcc.gov.uk: Essex Record Office's online catalogue, including references for church faculties and building plans (including the archive of Chancellor & Son).

unlockingessex.essexcc.gov.uk: access to the Sites and Monuments Record for Essex, as well as other, mainly archaeological information.

www.imagesofengland.org.uk: descriptions of all listed buildings in England, including photographs for over 10,000 of those in Essex.

www.churchplansonline.org: the archive of the Incorporated Church Building Society, giving details (including plans) of many churches built and restored between 1818 and 1982.

ESSEX

ABBERTON

ST ANDREW. C14 nave, brick chancel, rebuilt in the C19, mid-C16 brick tower with blue bricks in diaper pattern. Thin buttresses, two-light bell-openings. Restored 1841, when a w gallery was erected, and 1865, when it was taken down.

ABBERTON MANOR, ¼ m. NNE. Early C18 brick, five bays and a pair of gables with semicircular windows. Early C19 extensions, and contemporary geometric staircase. C18 stableyard and the remains of an elegant garden.

ABBERTON RESERVOIR 1935–9 for the South Essex Waterworks Co., covering 1,300 acres. Modern Movement-style pump house (cf. Langham and Layer de la Haye).

ABBESS RODING

ST EDMUND. C14 nave, C15 chancel, w tower with spike 1866–7 (the date of restoration by *Robert Parris* for Capel Cure of Blake Hall, including new s porch and E window), N vestry later C19. Flint rubble, the original dressings of clunch. The nave roof has tie-beams on arched braces with a little tracery in the spandrels. Inside the chancel on the N side, a niche which was originally the opening into a closet recognizable on the outside. – FONT. Late C12, square, similar to Little Laver and Fryerning. Decorated on one side with a Norman foliage trail, on one with a trail of a rather unusual stylized shape, on the third with a disc, crescent, whorl and stars, and on the fourth with two flowers and three small roses. – REREDOS. Oak, crudely carved by *Isabel Capel-Cure*, 1938. – SCREEN. Late C15, with C19 cresting. Two-light divisions, the mullion carried up into the apex of the four-centred arch. Each light has an ogee arch with some panel tracery above. Brought from elsewhere and cut to fit. – PULPIT. With an uncommonly fine, generously large tester; C18. Adjacent wrought-iron HOURGLASS STAND, early C18. – STAINED GLASS. Chancel s, good C15 figures of a bishop and a female saint surrounded by tabernacle-work not in its original state. E window by *Powell & Sons*, c. 1867. – MONUMENTS. Sir Gamaliel Capell †1613, with the usual kneeling figures facing each other, the children kneeling in the 'predella'. – Mildred Capell, Lady Lucklyn †1633. Frontal demi-figure, head propped on elbow and a book in front of her, being crowned by two flying putti. Cherubs, seated on the outer volutes, hold back curtains. Attributed to *Edward Marshall* (GF).

ABBESS HALL. Late C16, timber-framed and plastered. Seven-bay barn of *c.* 1600, with brick nogging.

THE MANOR. Very large former rectory, 1859, for Laurence Capel-Cure, who began its 'Queen Anne'-style successor (Abbess House by *N.J. Dawson*) in 1912, completed by his son and succeeding rector.

ROOKWOOD HALL, ¾ m. WSW. Demolished. C15–C16 timber-framed BARNS, one of eight bays (tree-ring date 1539), the other of five. Rare hybrid construction, of crown-posts with collar-purlins and wind-braced side purlins. The smaller barn, originally floored and with high-level diamond-mullioned windows, may have been of domestic use or a malting.

ABRIDGE

4090

Lambourne

HOLY TRINITY. Small uninteresting chapel of ease, 1833, enlarged, with new W front, by *R. W. Edis* in 1877, chancel and vestries added by *Tooley & Foster*, 1930. Stock brick with red brick dressings. – STAINED GLASS. E window by *F. W. Cole* of *William Morris* of Westminster, 1954.

Quite a pretty group along the main road. On the N side of the Market Place, SW of the bridge across the Roding, 1777, RODING RESTAURANT, the r. hand part C15 with exposed timbers and jettied upper storey. Then (in a good position facing the traveller from the E) the Early Victorian BLUE BOAR. Painted brick, with quoins and a Tuscan porch. Around it remnants of various brewery buildings, and to the W the MALTSTER'S ARMS, C18, timber-framed and weatherboarded, originally two houses. Opposite the Blue Boar, THE COACH HOUSE, a C14 hall house. Low hall, brick-faced, and gabled and jettied cross-wing to the r. Cross-wing to the l. rebuilt in the early C20. A little further W, on the S side of London Road, the LOG CABIN CAFÉ, next to a late C19(?) house extravagantly embellished in Swiss style with heavy rustic window frames, half-timbered gables, decorative eaves, and niches with statues.

ALDHAM

9020

ST MARGARET. 1854–5 by *E.C. Hakewill*, replacing the medieval church (about ¾ m. WSW) and reusing its materials, with the addition of tower and spire in Bath stone. Very Victorian in the picturesque grouping, especially from the outside, and the wild overdoing of flint as the surfacing material. Even the low walls of the porch look cobbled. The porch timbers are the principal surviving medieval work; C14 with ogee-traceried side panels and a heavily bargeboarded gable, which also ends in an ogee. Chancel arch of 1854–5, on large carved corbels, as is the S arcade. From the old church, the arched recess framing the doorway to the N vestry, the roofs, and four DOORS, notably that to the tower which has a domed scutcheon with four foliated branches, iron, *c.* 1300. – STAINED GLASS. E and chancel N windows by *Ward*, 1855, good examples of bad Victorian designs. – MONUMENT. Rev. Philip Morant, Essex historian and rector †1770. Plain wall tablet on N side of chancel, gravestone on S side (by *Bremer* of Colchester), moved in 1855 and 1966 respectively.

ALDHAM HALL, ⅔ m. S. Timber-framed, mainly plastered but some brick nogging. Main N-facing range of two and one-and-a-half storeys incorporates an early C15 three-bay hall. Porch with C17 bargeboarding and pendant. One ground-floor room with late C16 panelling and overmantel. An L-plan wing (now a separate house) extends S and W of the main range, probably a detached C16 range joined to the house in the C17.

OLD BOURCHIERS HALL, ⅓ m. NNW. The main part is the brick NW wing, now painted, added *c.* 1700. Two storeys, with gambrel roof hipped at one end on a heavy modillion cornice. At right angles the remains of an earlier, timber-framed house, faced in brick *c.* 1800.

OLD RECTORY, ⅓ m. SW. By *E. Blore*, 1829–30. Gault brick, 'Elizabethan'.

FORDSTREET, 1¼ m. NNE on either side of the River Colne, has the greatest concentration of older houses.* The most prominent is THE OLD HOUSE, with much exposed timberwork and jetties. C15 hall and N cross-wing, C16 S cross-wing and taller two-storey extension on the N side. Remains of painted decoration in a first-floor room, *c.* 1600. Restored *c.* 1925 when a gabled lobby was added on the S side and a front door inserted in the N cross-wing.

ALPHAMSTONE

8030

ST BARNABAS. Rendered nave, lower flint chancel, and weatherboarded belfry. Much restored by *A.B. Jackson*, chancel in 1902–3, nave in 1909. One blocked Norman N window, completely plain C13 N doorway. The rest mostly C14, windows especially and SEDILIA, the latter reconstructed by Jackson from pieces found built into the S wall. Three seats and PISCINA with cusped pointed arches on detached shafts, framed in one. Low side chancel windows with original grilles and remains of shutters. GRAFFITO on the stonework of the S window reads: 'This chiancell was repayred wyth newe tymber by me Nycholas le Gryce, Parson, A. 1578'. Three-bay S arcade (also C14) with octagonal piers and double-chamfered arches. – FONT. Of the familiar Purbeck type, square, with five shallow

---

* For buildings on the N side of the river, *see* Fordham.

blank arches on each side, C12. Handsome, if modest, C17 COVER. Semi-globe with ribs crowned by a ball finial, with supporting scrolls added later. – S arcade SCREEN by *W. H. Wood* of Newcastle, 1918, as the rood screen for the House of Mercy, Great Maplestead, with ROOD FIGURES now separate. Installed here by *H. W. Pearce* (*Duncan Clark & Beckett*), 1960. – STAINED GLASS. E window by *A. O. Hemming & Co.*, 1919.

On the N side of the churchyard, which contains a number of sarsens, AMEN COTTAGE, thatched, late C17, and THE MANOR HOUSE, tiled, C15, a two-bay hall on the l. and two-storey parlour and solar wing to the r. A beam inside inscribed 'NG 1586' refers to alterations by Nicholas le Gryce (*see* above).

OLD RECTORY, Pebmarsh Road. Large and Picturesque with Gothick detail. C16, remodelled probably for Rev. Henry Hodges, rector from 1838.

ABBOT'S, ¾ m. SW. Timber-framed, clad with C19 flint and brick, with crenellations and Gothick sashes.

ALRESFORD

ST ANDREW AND ST PETER, St Andrew's Close. By *Bryan Thomas & Partners*, 1975–6. Barn-like. Steel A-frame, its ends projecting beyond the steep hipped slate roof with glazed gablets.

ST PETER. Preserved as a roofless ruin after a fire in 1971. C12, with Roman brick quoins on the NW corner of the nave and on the exterior of the W wall. C13 chancel, extended in the C14, when the nave was widened to the S. Chancel partially rebuilt in the C19 and a S vestry (dem.), S aisle and N porch added.

ALRESFORD HALL. Seven-bay, two-storey house of *c.* 1720 for Thomas Martin, a director of the East India Company and twice M.P. for Colchester. Brick with burnt headers and segment-headed windows. Later given slightly projecting pedimented wings and a central porch. Alterations by *J. W. Start*, 1909, including single-storey extension to r. of main front. Mid-C19 lodges, that to the W of flint and stock brick, that to the N weatherboarded, and both with decorated bargeboards.

Of most interest is THE QUARTERS, a 'Chinese Temple' erected for banqueting beside the lake S of the house.* Commissioned in 1772 from *Richard Woods* by Colonel Isaac Martin Rebow, a relative of the Martins, for whom Woods laid out the park at Wivenhoe (*see* UNIVERSITY OF ESSEX). An octagon with a veranda on the edge of the lake, linked by another room with a shallow loggia to an existing building. The trellised veranda, tent-like lead-covered roof and 'keyhole' windows are picturesque *chinoise* if not archaeologically correct. Sympathetically extended in 1951–2. At the head of the small lake a

---

*Painted by Constable in 1816 (now in the National Gallery of Victoria, Melbourne, Australia), who referred to it as a 'little fishing house'.

BRIDGE. Mainly brick, but the parapet on the temple side has matching trellising. To the N of The Quarters, a C18 cottage in similar style, and NE a square, brick C18 DOVECOTE. On the island in the lake to the S an early C19 ICE HOUSE.

In Ford Lane, N of the old church, the OLD SCHOOL HOUSE, dated 1846; flint and stock brick with decorated bargeboards, like the W lodge of Alresford Hall.

ROMAN VILLA, ½ m. S of the old church. Part of a corridor villa was excavated in 1884, when tessellated pavements and painted wall-plaster were found. Now built over.

ALTHORNE

ST ANDREW. Large flint and stone W tower, c. 1500, with diagonal buttresses. The battlements have a trellis pattern of ashlar against the flint ground. Above the W door, traces of an inscription which read: 'Orate pro animabus dominorum Johannis Wylson et Johannis Hyll quorum animabus propicietur deus amen'. They no doubt paid for the building of the tower. Embattled, flint, Perp nave, lower brick chancel early C16. New window tracery and other repairs by *Chancellor*, 1878, although the brick chancel arch seems to have been the design of the incumbent, *Rev. H.M. Milligan*, 1876. Fuller restoration 1884–5, the nave by *H.H. Langston*, the chancel by *E. I'Anson*. – FONT. Octagonal, Perp, with fleurons on the foot, panel tracery on the stem, and on the bowl figures of angels, saints, a baptism, the martyrdom of St Andrew, etc. Thoroughly bad figure carving. – BRASS to William Hyklott †1508 'which paide for the werkemanship of the walls of the church'. 18½-in. (47-cm.) figure.

ARDLEIGH

ST MARY THE VIRGIN. Striking W tower and S porch, both late C15. The tower is brick and flint and dark brown stone with two diagonal buttresses and pinnacled battlements of flint and brick decoration. The porch is extremely elaborate East Anglian work, all flint inlay and stone. Dec walls and battlements. Pinnacles with animals. Two figures of lions *couchant* as stops of the hoodmould of the doorway. In the spandrels of the doorway lively figures of St Michael and the Dragon. Above the doorway three niches. The inner doorway has Adam and Eve in the spandrels and also a niche above. Side openings of three lights with Perp tracery – the pattern identical with the aisles at Brightlingsea. The rest of the church by *William Butterfield*, 1882–3, said by him to have been a ruin, although the body of the church had been rebuilt in *c.* 1750 and the N aisle added in 1841. Only the W bay of the nave is original C14. Butterfield restored the chancel to its original length and added an organ chamber and vestry to the N and new S aisle. –

SCREENS. Chancel screen, base only, with late C15 tracery panels, much restored. Glazed oak tower screen by *Tim Venn*, 2003. – MOSAIC. Quatrefoils in chancel by *Alexander Gibbs*, 1883. – WALL PAINTINGS. Chancel arch (Crucifixion) by *Bell & Beckham*, 1890. Walls and ceiling of chancel by *Ernest Geldart*, executed by *Percy Bacon & Bros*, 1894–5, with figures of British saints etc. – SCULPTURE. Bronze statues of the Virgin and St Francis by *Ivor Roberts Jones*, 1958. – Virgin and Child by *Sara Wilkinson*, 2004. Limewood. – On S porch, St Mary the Virgin by *Earp, Son & Hobbs*, *c.* 1883. – STAINED GLASS. In chancel, S aisle and tower, by *Bell & Beckham*, 1886–92. S chancel chapel E window probably by *Geldart*, *c.* 1895. N aisle window by *Heaton, Butler & Bayne*, *c.* 1902. Nave W end, two windows of decorative quarries by *A. Gibbs*, 1883. – MONUMENT. Inside porch, Barbara and Henry Lufkin †1706 and 1721, marbled wooden panel with pilasters and broken curved pediment.

SEELY COURT (former vicarage), N of the church. C17 or earlier but of C18 appearance. Prominent cross-wings, built up in brick with parapets, painted and rendered, and three Venetian windows facing the church. Between the wings, a wide, central trellised porch, an unusual and delightful composition. Brick coachhouse and stables, with first-floor room reached by an outside stair, by *P. M. Beaumont*, 1911.

Immediately E of the church, ARDLEIGH COURT, a self-effacing late 1960s development of single-storey brick and timber houses built on the Swedish 'Stex' system. Opposite the church's W end, a nice row of cottages, including TUDOR COTTAGE and its neighbour with long-wall jetty, C16 or earlier, next to the C17 LION INN. On the S side of the main street the ANCIENT HOUSE, C15 with exposed timbers. Three ranges with gables to the street, the two on the l. jettied with herringbone nogging, the third underbuilt in brick. Some original windows, one of five lights in the return wall to the l. Inside, beams decorated with leaf trails. Restored in the 1930s by *Grace Faithfull Roper*.

Former STEAM MILL, Station Road. Mid C19. Four-storey main block, white brick, with pedimented gables on the returns. Windows with cast-iron glazing bars and lintels. Lower engine house at rear. To its r. the MILL HOUSE, also white brick.

ARKESDEN

ST MARY THE VIRGIN. Traces of a Norman round tower were found when the present W tower (of flint rubble, Caen stone dressings, and knapped flint panels) was built by *G.E. Pritchett* in 1855. At the same time the church was heavily restored. It consists of a C13 nave and chancel. To 1855 belong the clerestory, chancel arch, and hammerbeam roofs, with oversized corbels carved with figures of saints. The S arcade has circular piers, the N arcade octagonal piers. Both have arches with two slight chamfers. So they must both be C13, and not too late. – FONT. Square tapering bowl, possibly C12, the base C13. – Good display of encaustic TILES by *Minton* in the chancel, 1855. – STAINED GLASS. E window †1917 by *Heaton, Butler & Bayne*, who also did the S aisle window, 1928. – N aisle E by *W. Lawson (Faith Craft Works)*, 1929. – In W window, C16 heraldic glass re-set by *M.C. Farrar Bell*, 1968. – MONUMENTS. Brass to Richard Fox †1439. In armour, the figure 38 in. (96 cm.) long. – Effigy of a priest, thought to be John Croxby, vicar 1435–56. In a very low two-bay recess in the chancel N wall, which has three broad piers with figure niches. – Richard Cutte †1592 and wife. Large standing wall monument with two recumbent effigies, and the children (their heads missing) kneeling against arches on the front of the tomb-chest. The effigies under a heavy six-poster with odd short baluster columns, which have leaves growing up the lower thirds of their shafts. Straight top with inscription in the frieze, obelisks and achievements. Crudely repainted. – John Withers †1692 and wife. By *Edward Pearce*, a first-class work. Standing wall monument with an excellent stone relief of skulls and branches and higher up excellent marble busts. – Thomas Wolfe †1795 by *Hockley* of Saffron Walden. Plain marble tablet with inscription, one of many monuments to the Birch Wolfe family of Wood Hall. – Rev. W. Birch Wolfe †1864 and Marianne Birch Wolfe †1897. Mural brass by *W. Curtis & Sons*, Dublin. – On N side of churchyard, Allen Hurrell †1838. Large chest tomb with fluted nook-shafts and acroteria at each corner. Through the shorter sides protrude the ends of a sarcophagus.

The church stands at the top of a steeply sloping green, with thatched cottages stepping down the hill. Behind the church, THE OLD MALTINGS, C17 timber-framed with brick infilling and jettied gable at one end. Most of the village lies below the church along a little stream. Many good timber-framed houses, nicely varied, e.g. THE AXE AND COMPASSES, *c.* 1700, thatched, with a later C18 or early C19 brick front and canted bay windows, and THE OLD FORGE, early C18, weather-boarded, both on the S side. On the N side, SEXTONS contains remains of a late C16 or early C17 scheme of wall painting. To the NW, along Hampit Road, a former METHODIST CHAPEL by *Charles Bell*, 1887, brick with stock brick dressings, sympathetically extended and converted to a house.

WOOD HALL, ½ m. SSW. Of vaguely Queen Anne appearance, thanks to the roof with modillion cornice and dormers. 1652, according to a date carved inside, where there is also an imported early C16 beam, richly carved. Remodelled in the C18, and again in the late C19, whose additions (many removed in 1952) include the staircase, with high vaulted timber roof, and window with panels of C17 Flemish STAINED GLASS.

ASHDON

ALL SAINTS. Mostly C14, of flint rubble, but externally much renewed. The W tower has a W window of early C14 type, angle buttresses, high stepped battlements, and a spirelet. The S chancel chapel (Tyrrel Chapel), taller than the chancel and separated from it by a two-bay arcade with an early C14 circular pier and moulded arches, also has two early C14 windows. Again early C14, one window in the S aisle. Later, the arcades between nave and aisles, which have a broad polygonal shaft without capital towards the nave and finer polygonal shafts with capitals towards the (two-centred) arches. Similar chancel arch. C15 N porch, and early C16 S porch and clerestory (a will of 1527 refers to three of the clerestory windows), the porch and one window of brick. Chancel and S chapel roofs both early C14, the former with down-braced crown-posts. In the chapel the crown-post has four-way struts and the post itself is quatrefoil with moulded capital. General restoration by *John W. Alexander* of Middlesborough, 1883–9, including re-seating and new oak pulpit. Further restoration by *A.E. Richardson*, 1939, principally to the tower, but also including unblocking the E window of the S chapel. – PULPIT. In S chapel, upper part of old octagonal pulpit, dated 1578. – WALL PAINTING. Remains of a C14 figure of St Michael weighing souls (SE corner of nave). – STAINED GLASS. In a S aisle window some C14 and C15 glass in its original position, with fragments of medieval glass collected together from other windows. E window by *Clayton & Bell*, 1896. – MONUMENTS. Thomas Tyrrel and his wife Anne, big tomb-chest with three shields on intricately cusped panels, early C16; on back wall, coat of arms of Richard Tyrrel †1566. – Rev. Benedict Chapman, rector of Ashdon and master of Gonville and Caius College, Cambridge, †1852. Fine Neo-Gothic wall monument, with an ogee arch set in a two-centred arch, all richly decorated. – Rev. Edward Edward Hanson †1854, his curate. Also Neo-Gothic, but less ornate.

On the S side of the churchyard the late C15 GUILDHALL, converted to three dwellings in 1731 (now a single house). Exposed timbers on N side, with jettied upper storey, plastered on the S. Next to it the OLD VICARAGE, C18. NE of the church, ASHDON HALL, C19 brick, plastered and painted, round a C17 timber-framed core, with two gables on the N front. N of the church the former NATIONAL SCHOOL, now offices: flint with brick dressings, dated 1833.

The main part of the village lies N of the church down in the valley. At its centre, the ROSE AND CROWN INN has inside extensive early C17 wall paintings, chiefly imitative panelling with New Testament texts in the frieze. Next to it Nos. 1–4 MAIN ROAD, with C19 shopfront of square bay windows flanked by fluted Doric columns. N of the Inn the PRIMARY SCHOOL with a tall central gable surmounted by a bell-turret;

1878 with additions of 1972. Several nice houses along RAD-WINTER ROAD, including TUDOR CROFT, C16 or C17 with exposed timber-framing, and the brick BAPTIST CHAPEL, 1833.

WALTONS, 1¼ m. NE. The 'interesting house with a complex building history and a fine plain Georgian front of *c.* 1730' described by Pevsner was severely damaged by fire in 1954 and rebuilt for Edmund Vestey by *Ian Forbes*, 1958. Neo-Georgian, two storeys, with a curved façade of nine bays and in the centre of the concave garden front a three-bay arched loggia. SE of the house, WALTONS PARK COTTAGES, converted from the surviving early C17 brick wing of the old house, and C17 stables.

PLACE FARM FARMHOUSE, S of Waltons. Handsome C16 house on a half-H plan. Jettied upper storey with exposed timbers, gabled at each end. Fine original central chimneystack with five octagonal shafts grouped on a cruciform base.

WINDMILL, 1 m. NE. Weatherboarded post mill by *William Haylock*, carpenter, 1757, on a C19 brick round-house. Restoration began in 2001.

ROMAN VILLA, 1¼ m. NNW. The foundations of a building 52 ft (16 metres) long and 17 ft (5 metres) wide were discovered in 1852. The seven rooms of the building had floors of very coarse tesserae. Half of the structure was heated by a hypocaust system, and the whole may represent the bath building of an adjacent villa.*

ASHELDHAM

ST LAWRENCE. Converted to a youth centre, with prefabricated N addition, by *Patricia Stewart*, 1975–6, when excavations showed the nave and chancel to be Norman, with apsidal E end, rebuilt in the late C13 or early C14. Flint rubble. Solid-looking C14 W tower with diagonal buttresses and later battlements. The windows are either cusped lancets or have some little ogee detail. Chancel S window, S doorway (with headstops), and SEDILE form a group, their relationship obscured by internal partitions. Chancel E wall rebuilt in brick in the late C18, with E window and S porch added during restoration by *William Adams* of Maldon, 1866–7. Further N extension by *Purcell Miller Tritton*, 1989, when the interior was reordered.

ASHELDHAM HALL, N of the church. Two-storey C17 timber-framed house, to which a third storey and brick front were added *c.* 1830.

ASHELDHAM CAMP. Traces of an oval Iron Age fort, 600 yds W of the church. Banks and ditches discernible on the W, S, and E sides, with a mound on the E side of the enclosure.

---

*Bartlow Hills now in Cambridgeshire, following boundary changes in 1990.

ASHEN

St Augustine of Canterbury. One small lancet in the nave indicates a C13 origin. The w tower (restored by *F. W. Chancellor*, 1934–5) with diagonal buttresses and battlements was added *c.* 1400. The brick stair-turret with battlements on a trefoiled corbel-frieze, *c.* 1525, has a niche with SCULPTURE by *Malcolm Murduck*, 2003. Chancel by *J. L. Pearson*, designed 1853, executed 1857–8, knapped flint with bands of brick and stone, his first use of constructional polychromy. It sits uneasily with the flint-rubble walls of the nave, which Pearson planned to rebuild, but it was only restored (completed 1862) and extended e by a couple of feet. Simple C17 s porch. – DOOR in s doorway, with damaged early C14 ironwork. – A few C15 BENCHES, also a panel with carved inscription in Roman capitals, dated 1620: 'This hath bin the churching the mearring stoole and so it shall be still'. – STAINED GLASS. In chancel, by *Wailes*, including e window, 1862. – MONUMENTS. Brass of a knight and lady, *c.* 1440, probably John le Hunt and wife. The knight 20½ in. (51 cm.) – Luce Tallakarne †1610, an odd design (cf. Devereux Tallakarne at Helions Bumpstead) with termini caryatids and between them decoration with panels, a shield, and the inscription plates. – Stephen Piper †1721 and Dorothy Byatt †1752. Large, white marble, with lengthy inscriptions in classical surrounds.

Old Rectory, e of the church. Gault brick, three bays with a two-bay extension on the n side. Sash windows with cast-iron lintels, one dated 1835. Additions by *Pearson*, 1853, are no longer apparent.*

Street Farm, nw of the church. Early C16, with n cross-wing, original stair-tower in the rear angle, and continuous jetty to the front. Original hall, screen with blocked service doors, and parlour. Hall and parlour have moulded beams and joists, the hall also two original doorways and a door.

Ashen Hall, 700 yds ne. C18 timber-framed and plastered, a very attractive front with full-height canted bays and doorcase with attached columns and open pediment.

ASHINGDON

St Andrew. On a hill, widely held to be the site of the Battle of Assandun in 1016, following which a minster church was founded by King Canute; but cf. Hadstock. Present building mainly C14, of ragstone and flint rubble. Nave and chancel, with a small w tower about half the width of the nave. The tower has diagonal buttresses, a funny little saddleback roof with gablets, and CLOCK, 1910, with 'EDWARDVS VII REX' in place of numerals, but the V, VII and X correctly positioned. Brick s window in the nave C17 or C18, but the brick e wall of

*He also prepared unexecuted designs for the village school.

the chancel, as shown by the black diapering, is of *c.* 1500. This is also the date of the two-light brick window on the N side of the chancel, and may be the date of the relatively plain timber S porch. Evidence of earlier work is the Y-traceried window on the N side, usual for *c.* 1300. Similarly the original N respond of the chancel arch, trefoiled in plan with moulded capital. C14 to C15 roofs in nave and chancel. N vestry by *Sir Charles Nicholson*, 1921. – CHANCEL FITTINGS also by *Nicholson* (First World War memorial). – STAINED GLASS. E window by *A.K. Nicholson*, 1920, and probably also the small chancel S window of Stigand, later Archbishop of Canterbury. – Chancel N by *Powell & Sons*, 1952. – Nave S, 2003, including fragments of medieval glass. Nave N by *J.N. Lawson* (*Goddard & Gibbs*), 2004.

PRIMARY SCHOOL. 1870 by *J. Clarke*. Brick. Enlarged 1910, and *c.* 1985 by *Binns & Charles*.

ASHINGDON HALL, 250yds SW. C17 or C18 brick, with two shaped gables on the return wall. Early C19 four-bay, two-storey front, and late C20 rear additions.

AUDLEY END 5030

The largest of the Jacobean 'prodigy' houses, and even in its reduced form the most impressive country house in Essex. It occupies the site of the C12 Walden Abbey, granted in 1538 to Sir Thomas Audley (†1544) who converted part of the buildings to a residence. The estate passed via his daughter to Thomas Howard, 4th Duke of Norfolk, whose son Thomas distinguished himself against the Armada, was made Baron Howard of Walden in 1597, and in 1603 Earl of Suffolk and King James's Lord Chamberlain of the Household. Soon afterwards, *c.* 1605, he set about rebuilding. Howard told the king that Audley End cost £200,000, including furnishings; by comparison, Hatfield (1608–12) cost a mere £38,500.

Lord Suffolk was assisted in the design by his uncle, *Henry Howard, 1st Earl of Northampton*, and it seems that *Bernard Janssen* was employed to supervise the work, as he was at this time for Northampton's Northumberland House in the Strand, London. The new house followed very closely the outline of the old, being laid out as a court on the footprint of the abbey cloister.* The W range contained the Great Hall and the E range the Long Gallery, with State Apartments on the first floor of the N and S ranges, family apartments on the ground floor, and servants and lodgings on the second floor. Two wings projected from the E ends of the N and S ranges, containing the Council Chamber and Chapel respectively. Howard must then have decided that the house was not sufficiently grandiose, because he built an outer court on the W side; this was very much more elaborate in style, and it seems likely that the architect was *John Thorpe*. The use to

---

*Fragments of the abbey walls have been found within the walls of the present building.

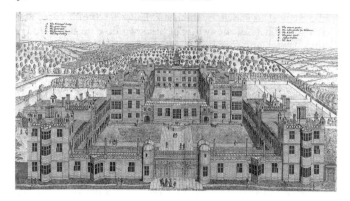

Audley End.
Henry Winstanley's 'General Prospect', *c.* 1676

which the rooms round the outer court were put is a matter of conjecture, but that might have been a secondary consideration: it was the architectural effect that really mattered. Work was largely complete by 1614. In that year Howard was appointed Lord Treasurer, but in 1619 was found guilty of embezzlement and retired to Audley End, where he died in 1626.

Building depleted the family's fortunes, a situation remedied by the sale of the house to Charles II in 1668. He took little interest in his new palace; no significant work was done to it, and it was returned to the family in 1701. During the C18 the house was reduced to its present extent, a half-H open on the E side, beginning after 1708 with the destruction of the outer court's N and S ranges by *Sir John Vanbrugh* for the 6th Earl of Suffolk. Demolition of the outer W range followed *c.* 1724–5, probably under the supervision of *Nicholas Dubois*, contemporary with the removal of the E wings (containing the Council Chamber and Chapel). Next fell the E range of the inner court, taken down after 1751 for Elizabeth, Countess of Portsmouth by *John Phillips* and *George Shakespear*, who appended single-storey pavilions to the exposed ends of the N and S ranges and connected these ranges with a ground floor behind the hall.

Lady Portsmouth's nephew, Sir John Griffin Griffin, who inherited in 1762, reversed this destructive process, commissioning *Robert Adam* and *Capability Brown* to improve the house and park respectively. Adam contributed to the variety of eyecatchers in Brown's landscape, but his main achievement was the creation of a suite of rooms on the ground floor of the S wing. At this time galleries were also created linking the N and S wings at first and second floor.

Sir John's schemes received new impetus in 1784 when his claim to the barony of Howard was recognized and he became Lord Howard de Walden; in 1788 he was created Baron Braybrooke. The N and S wings were enlarged to their present form by raising the 1750s single-storey E pavilions to three storeys, and on the first floor of the s wing State Apartments were created in anticipation (never realized) of a visit by King George III. For this second phase of building, which lasted until his death in 1797, Lord Braybrooke was sufficiently experienced to be considered his own architect, but he had some advice from *James Essex*, as well as being able to rely on a competent local carpenter and builder, *William Ivory*.

The final phase of significant alterations to house and estate, in the second quarter of the C19, was the responsibility of the 3rd Lord Braybrooke, a scholarly man who, like the 1st Lord, probably only needed an architect to put his own ideas into practice. He employed *Henry Harrison* to restore the Jacobean character of the house, especially of the interiors, which had been effaced in the C18; the antiquary *Henry Shaw* assisted with details. Apart from repairs and minor alterations in 1863–4 and rebuilding of part of the service wing by *William Butterfield* following a fire in 1881, no further significant structural alterations have been made to the house, which has been in state care since 1948.

EXTERIOR

Unlike earlier courtyard houses, Audley End was outward-looking, so the w (entrance) front has not suffered from the loss of the outer court. Lord Suffolk's ambition is still very evident, for although the house is built of brick, with limestone plinth and string courses, it was faced with stone, albeit originally clunch that was replaced with Chilmark and Ketton stone from the C18 onwards. The w front is symmetrical with three-storey towers flanking a lower centre range, containing the hall, which rises to the height of two storeys. At each end of this hall range are two-storey porches, built in the second 61 phase of Suffolk's building, an odd but not unique feature of houses of this date. They are the showpieces of the house, far more ornate than anything else and overcrowded with super-imposed orders of Ionic and Corinthian columns and curly strapwork. The columns, moreover, are of different coloured marbles and from them something of the character of the demolished outer court can be imagined. The doorways, however, belong to the first phase of building, their doors with carved wooden tympana representing War (s; its figure of Mars is a copy from an illustration by Virgil Solis, the C16 German printmaker) and Peace (N). The balustrades on the porches and hall were added after 1763, the date of the third storey that rises behind the hall range.

The sense of evenness is emphasized by the fenestration, with many-mullioned windows that have one or two transoms. The relative importance of the floors can be judged from the height of the windows; those on the first floor, which housed the main apartments, are tallest, apart from the full-height central window, with three transoms, that lights the Great Hall. The roof-line is punctuated by square angle turrets, which belong to the second phase of building; three on each side to

emphasize the angle blocks of the W front and two bigger ones
over the returning angles. They have pretty convex caps and
weathervanes in the form of pennants, lending a chivalric air
that was emphasized by garden walls continuing the line of the
front to N and S. Only part, on the S side, survives, but it has
a mock bastion that adds to the effect of fortification.

The other fronts show for the most part a uniformity of style.
The S front has along most of the ground floor a Doric arcade
that was originally an open loggia; it was enclosed in 1736.
Such features came into fashion just in the years when Audley
End was built (Hatfield, Knole, Cranbourne, Holland House,
Neville's Court at Trinity College, Cambridge). Before 1600
they had been rare (Burghley). The arcade on the E front,
however, is C18, and fronted a ground-floor passage built
by Lady Portsmouth c. 1752–3 to improve circulation, with
stonework reused from the demolished E range. The passage
was widened c. 1763–5, when the two upper galleries were
added, and enclosed in 1863–4 with tracery filling the arches.
The projecting wings are as remodelled in 1785 (mason, *John
Devall*), with full-height canted bays. The N front has projecting from it, at an angle, the kitchen offices of the 1760s, partly
rebuilt by *Butterfield* in 1882. Adam provided plans in 1762–3
but these are much plainer than what he proposed.

INTERIOR

In spite of the two porches, the N doorway appears to have served
always as the main entrance. The ENTRANCE HALL is separated from the Great Hall by a wooden screen. The stone
screen across the Entrance Hall itself seems to have been built
towards the end of Lord Suffolk's work, when the Great Hall
screen was altered to have a large central opening rather than
the more traditional two side openings. As well as reproducing
the form of a screens passage, the typical medieval and Tudor
arrangement for entry into a hall, there is evidence that this
follows almost exactly the layout of Lord Audley's house – a
remarkable continuity, especially as, by the C17, one might
expect the Great Hall to be on the opposite side of the inner
court.

The plan of the GREAT HALL is also influenced by the more
up-to-date desire for symmetry seen outside, with the bay
window placed at the centre of the room, opposite the fireplace, rather than at the dais end. The Hall's present appearance is the result of the 3rd Lord Braybrooke's restoration,
when much white paint applied in the C18 was removed. Dominating is the two-storey SCREEN, richly if a little coarsely
carved, with pairs of terminal figures on ornamented pedestals
and, on the upper part, strapwork and cresting in front of the
gallery. The appearance of perspective arches in the outer bays
is interesting in what is otherwise a somewhat old-fashioned
composition. The fireplace is similar in style even if not quite
so ornate. It was enlarged by *Henry Shaw*, who was quite happy

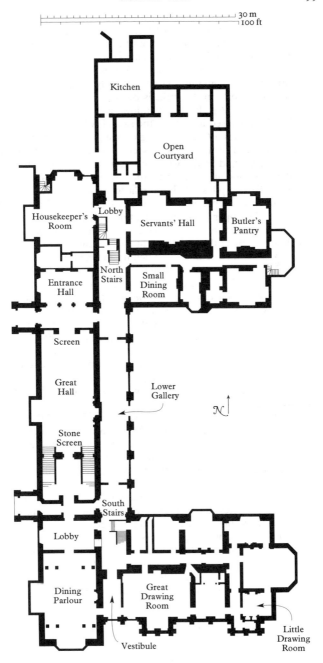

Audley End.
Plan of ground floor

to incorporate two *Coade* stone classical figures, repainted to
look like wood, from *Adam*'s Library (*see* below). The wooden
panelling was replaced in 1829 but the flat plaster ceiling with
timber beams is authentic. The main cross-beams rest on curly
brackets and have pretty pendants. Adorning the plaster panels
are medallions containing Howard family crests in relief; the
plaster strapwork on the walls is by *Joseph Rose*, for which he
was paid in 1764. In the window, a Neoclassical marble
pedestal, purchased in 1773 at the sale of Adam's own art collection, supports a *Coade* stone group supplied in 1772.

At the s end of the Hall is a second, stone, SCREEN of the
C18, as restrained as the wooden one is profuse: two storeys,
of three arches at each level, the lower ones separated by
coupled Tuscan pilasters; Ionic pilasters above. Starting from
the two outer arches is the staircase, in two straight parallel
flights to the upper landing, with a fine wrought-iron handrail.
Closer examination shows much of the composition is flawed:
the lower steps of the staircase cut awkwardly into the base of
the screen, while the doorways behind the central arches both
have Doric columns, an illiteracy that is explained by the fact
that they have been reused. It would seem that the lower part
of the screen is by *Vanbrugh*,[*] 1708, and that the staircase was
added by *Dubois c.* 1725; the Doric columns probably came
from the C17 Chapel that was demolished in that year. The
stucco upper part of the screen was remodelled by *Joseph Rose*
in 1763-4. Intriguingly, the space beyond the screen seems
always to have been intended as a second principal entrance,
from the s porch. The ceiling is Jacobean; but either no staircase was originally provided, or what was built was insuffi-
ciently impressive.

Most of the other interiors bear witness to the careful preservation of Jacobean features, and their revival, very evidently in
the plasterwork and chimneypieces. The main staircase leads
to the SALOON, formerly the Great Chamber of the Jacobean
state apartments in the s wing. It has an original ceiling, with
small closely spaced pendants, and whales, mermaids, sea-
monsters, etc., in the panels. The quatrefoil plaster frieze below
it probably dates from 1765-73, when the panelling was
installed. This incorporates carving salvaged from the demolished Long Gallery. Ionic pilasters, and round-headed recesses
filled with ancestral portraits by *Biagio Rebecca*, *Enoch Seeman*,
and others. Some of these were specially painted, others
extended to fit the panelling. Rebecca also decorated the chimneypiece, a confection of Jacobean and C18 elements with the
Earl of Suffolk's arms in the overmantel, all lavishly repainted
and gilded by *John Pither* in 1785 to celebrate the revival of the
barony of Howard de Walden and to provide a suitable room
for receiving King George III: the first of the suite of new state
apartments. The Jacobean apartments in the s wing were con-

---

[*] From as early as 1762 it was said that both screen and staircase were his work of
1721-2.

verted into bedrooms in 1736 and are now as remodelled in the 1820s. First the DRAWING ROOM, formed out of two rooms, with a Neo-Jacobean ceiling but an original chimney-piece that probably came from the N wing. The SOUTH LIBRARY has remnants of an original ceiling, the frieze on the E wall by *William Wilton*, 1753; chimneypiece by *Adam*, installed in the 1780s when this was the State Bedchamber. The main LIBRARY, housed in the 1785 addition to this wing's E end, has a genuine Jacobean chimneypiece, from the N wing, but the rest is due to *Henry Shaw*, who based his designs for the plasterwork on elements elsewhere in the house, and also modelled the library fittings, made by *Bennett & Hunt*, on the saloon panelling. Along the N side of the S range is the DINING ROOM, formed from two Jacobean rooms, retaining their original ceilings and friezes and with a matching pair of chimneypieces made up from old parts.

At the W end of the dining room are the SOUTH STAIRS, visually perhaps the most attractive feature of Audley End: narrow oblong well and narrow straight flights of stairs. The well is bordered by eight wooden posts in rows of two fours, reaching right up to the ceiling in pretty little obelisks. The balustrade has tapering square pillars instead of balusters. The stockade of decorated uprights is most successful. The date is of course that of the house, although it was much restored in the 1820s, when C18 white paint was stripped from it and the heraldic beasts added.

From the South Stairs the PICTURE GALLERY of *c.* 1763–5, with its thick mid-C19 chimneypiece, leads across to the N wing. At its N end, to the l., is the CHAPEL VESTIBULE, originally the music gallery behind the screen at the N end of the Great Hall. From 1725 it served the gallery of the new double-height chapel. This had been formed by removing most of the floor of the northern Great Chamber at this end of the W range. The floor was put back, however, in 1768–72 when the present CHAPEL was created at this level by *John Hobcroft*, a carpenter much employed at Audley End. Strawberry Hill Gothick at its prettiest; *James Essex* had some involvement with the work but apparently only after the design had been settled; the plasterwork is by *Joseph Rose*. It has a thin plaster vault (covering the original Jacobean ceiling) on thin quatrefoil shafts, passage aisles whose arches have gables with thin tracery, and a central crossing with a 'transept' projecting into the W bay window and a corresponding, shallower, recess containing the chaplain's raised Gothick SEAT and READING DESK. Carved in olive wood by *Sefferin Alken*, the chair based on one made for Croome Church, Worcs, by Hobcroft to *Adam*'s design. Behind, a half-size model of the MONUMENT in St Paul's Cathedral to Charles, 1st Marquess Cornwallis †1805, by *J.C.F. Rossi*. Given to the 3rd Lord Braybrooke in 1835; his wife was a daughter of the 2nd Marquess. The 'transept' has a Gothic-traceried false window with STAINED GLASS from Chicksands Priory, Beds. It originally contained the Offering

of the Easter Magi (1772, after *Van Dyck*), a companion to the
Last Supper in the (ritual) E window designed by *Rebecca*,
made in stained and painted glass by *William Peckitt* of York,
1771. Peckitt's glass was removed *c.* 1906 but reinstated in 1962
by *Dennis G. King*. Across the 'w' end is the family pew, a raised
platform complete with fan vaulting and fireplace.

The first floor of the N wing consists of the private apartment used by the 3rd Lord Braybrooke in the C19, adapted
from the State Apartments that originally mirrored those in the
s wing. Architecturally they are of lesser interest, but Jacobean
ceilings survive in the four western rooms, LADY BRAY-
BROOKE'S SITTING ROOM and the NEVILLE BEDROOM on
the s side, the HOWARD BEDROOM and SITTING ROOM on
the N side. The latter room also has a particularly good, but
restrained, Jacobean chimneypiece. The HOWARD BEDROOM
has a bed alcove, with Ionic pilasters, probably inserted *c.* 1736
and later widened. This now contains the most important piece
of furniture in the house, the State Bed, made by *Chipchase &
Lambert* in 1786 for the State Bedroom (now the South
Library). The curved cornice of the canopy adorned with a
baron's coronet, the Howard arms, and military trophies. The
two end rooms, the HOWARD and NEVILLE DRESSING
ROOMS, are in the additions of 1785, and have ceilings by *Rose*.

The NORTH STAIRS are part of the original house and
similar to the South Stair but less lively, a dog-leg with no well.
They lead to the LOWER GALLERY, which runs alongside the
Great Hall to the ground floor of the s wing, the subject of
many changes. When the first floor was converted to bedroom
apartments in 1736, the loggia on the ground floor was
enclosed and new public rooms formed. *Adam* was commissioned to remodel the suite in 1763 and the work was largely
completed by 1771. Much of his work was undone in the
1820s.[*] The LIBRARY at the E end of the wing was divided up
and the ceiling lowered to accommodate the new Library
above it. This is now the only room of the suite that has not
been restored to something like its original appearance, but in
it are *grisaille* panels by *G.B. Cipriani*, two of a set of six paid
for in 1771,[†] as well as a painted chimney-board by *Rebecca*
(1769, one of five), a single bookcase and mirror, and casts of
two of the four *Coade* stone figures modelled by *John Bacon
Sen.*[‡]

The remaining rooms, along the s side of the s wing, had
relatively low ceilings, and all Adam's skill as a designer was
needed to compensate for this, aided by *Rebecca*'s decorative
painting and *Rose*'s plasterwork. The first room (LITTLE
DRAWING ROOM) is the most elaborately decorated, with a
screened sofa-niche on the N wall. Much of the ornament here
is 'grotesque' or Pompeian in inspiration. The furniture, all but

---

[*] Work to restore this was begun in 1962 by the Ministry of Works and continued
by English Heritage.
[†] The other four are in Saffron Walden Museum.
[‡] The originals are on the fireplace of the Great Hall (*see* p. 100). Displayed in the
room are two benches made by *Hobcroft* for the Temple of Victory (*see* p. 104).

one piece of which survives, was supplied by *Gordon & Taitt* in 1771, as was that in the GREAT DRAWING ROOM. They also provided the pier glasses on the end walls, with frames carved by *John & William Robert Adair*; chimneypiece carved by *J.F. Moore*. The windows are fitted with copies of Venetian blinds installed in 1777. The VESTIBULE leads through to the DINING PARLOUR, with Jacobean bays of different sizes in its s and w walls. Adam overcame this irregularity by creating an inner space defined by two screens of columns. The view from the s window takes in a large urn on a pedestal. In the fireplace is another of Rebecca's chimney-boards. At the N end of the Dining Parlour is a LOBBY or ante-room that leads back to the Great Hall. The lobby was restored in 2005 to its form recorded in 1836, displaying tapestries supplied in 1766 by *Paul Saunders*. They have painted linen extensions added by 1797 for use in the dressing room to the State Bedroom.

PARK AND GARDENS

The setting of Audley End is substantially as laid out by *Capability Brown*, 1763–6, completed by *Joseph Hicks* after 1768. Brown swept away most of the earlier garden, except for the

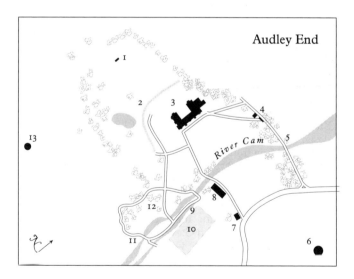

1	Temple of Concord	8	Stables
2	Ha-ha	9	Pond Garden
3	Parterre	10	Kitchen Garden
4	Lion Lodge	11	Tea House Bridge
5	Bridge	12	Elysian Garden and Cascade
6	Temple of Victory	13	Lady Portsmouth's Column
7	Cambridge Lodge		

Audley End.
Plan of park

MOUNT GARDEN s of the house. What remains of this is a raised walk, retained by early C17 brick walls.

Brown dammed the River Cam on the W side of the house to form a lake, and ha-has were built to provide an uninterrupted view beyond the river to Ring Hill, and also to enclose the garden on the N and E sides of the house, with open parkland beyond. Buildings were placed strategically:

BRIDGE over the Cam, SW of the house. 1763–4, by *Adam*, based on Palladio's bridge over the River Bacchiglione near Vicenza. Stone, of three arches, with medallions above each pier. Balustrade replaced *c.* 1781 by *Placido Columbani*.

TEMPLE OF VICTORY, Ring Hill, 1000 yds W of the house. Also by *Adam*, 1771–3, on the site of a C17 belvedere or hunting tower. Erected to commemorate the British successes in the Seven Years' War (1756–63). Circular, domed, surrounded by a twelve-bay Ionic colonnade. Paterae supplied by *Coade*, decorative plaster ceiling by *Joseph Rose*. Benches designed by Adam, made by *John Hobcroft*, now in the house. W of the Temple, RING COTTAGE, 1774, designed by an estate joiner, *John Mose*, in 1771, but as built perhaps designed by *William Shennan*. Originally a menagerie, with 'Keeping Room' (or aviary) at the E end and another room, probably a kitchen, at the W. The middle 'Tea Room' for visitors has a loggia of three Gothick arches. Picturesque bargeboards, porch and dormers, added *c.* 1840.

TEMPLE OF CONCORD, 400 yds E. 1790, by *R. W. F. Brettingham*, to commemorate George III's recovery from illness in 1789. Rectangular, with tall unfluted columns, grouped at the corners in clusters of three. Corinthian capitals and panels in the frieze on the N and S sides (design attributed to *Henry Tresham*) in *Coade* stone. Roofless since the 1960s.

LADY PORTSMOUTH'S COLUMN, 1000 yds NNE. 1773–4. Stone, surmounted by a vase, supplied by *Joseph Dixon*. The designer is unknown.

Following on from Brown, the ELYSIAN GARDEN, designed by *Richard Woods* in 1780 but amended in execution by *Placido Columbani*, 1781–3, was laid out along the banks of the Cam NW of the house. At the S end is Woods' CASCADE, at the N *Robert Adam*'s Palladian TEA HOUSE BRIDGE, 1782–3: an open summerhouse with Ionic columns on a single-span bridge. Most of the Elysian Garden was destroyed in the 1830s, when the formal PARTERRE was laid out on the E side of the house by *William Sawrey Gilpin*, 1832; restored, using the original planting plan, 1985–93. On the W bank of the Cam, between the river and the kitchen garden, the POND GARDEN, 1865 by *James Pulham & Son*, with two rectangular ponds and a large rockery of artificial stone, probably their speciality 'Pulhamite'.

The KITCHEN GARDEN, beyond the Pond Garden, was begun in the 1750s and restored in 1998–2000. The long W wall, heated with smoke flues, is signed by the bricklayer, *Richard Ward*, 1822. Along the N side the Vinery, *c.* 1811, replacing a greenhouse of 1774–6 by *John Hobcroft*. Behind it are the 'back sheds' with boiler house, mushroom house, bothy, etc. In the middle of the garden, The Orchard House, a greenhouse based on designs by *Thomas Rivers*, built in 1856, rebuilt 2001. In the SE corner, the Head Gardener's House, 1820s, remodelled 1875, brick with gables and decorative bargeboards. Glasshouses on its S side by *McKenzie & Moncur*, post-1877.

OTHER BUILDINGS

STABLES, WNW of the house. Early C17 brick E-plan range with gabled cross-wings, a large central gable, and gabled dormers. The windows on all three storeys are of three lights, all arched (cf. College of St Mark, below). Lantern above the centre. Similar N front. Archway with glazed pediment in the central bay and between the wings large canted bays.

LODGES. Mostly rebuilt in the first half of the C19 and, unless otherwise stated, brick, in various versions of Neo-Jacobean. The principal ones are (proceeding clockwise) LONDON LODGE, ½ m. SW, by *Thomas Rickman*, 1834; CAMBRIDGE LODGE, 1843; NORTHEND LODGE, ¾ m. NNW; SWAN LODGE, Bridge Street, Saffron Walden, is Tudor Gothic, flint with brick dressings, cast-iron lattice casements, and more part of the town than of the park; WALDEN LODGE, Abbey Lane, Saffron Walden, 1814, castellated; ICEHOUSE LODGE, 1827 by *Henry Harrison*, porch added by *J. C. Buckler*, archway by *Rickman*; and LION LODGE, 1846. Next to it LION GATE, now the main entrance, dated 1616. Originally a single archway, lower flanking gateways 1768, remodelled 1786 when the *Coade* stone lion and urns were added.

Estate COTTAGES include KEEPERS LODGE, ¾ m. WSW, originally two cottages, *c.* 1840, with shaped gables, and at NORTHEND, nearly 1 m. N, two semi-detached pairs and one row of three, 1873, with stock brick dressings. At DUCK STREET, 500 yds N of the house, C19 brick farm buildings, and HOME FARM COTTAGE, late C16 timber-framed and plastered, extended to the S in the early C17, with continuous jettied front.

AUDLEY END VILLAGE. Along the S side of Audley End Road, LION HOUSE, mid C18 with Gothick sashes, a canted N bay and picturesque W porch. It appears to be based on a design by *T. Lightoler* published in *The Gentleman and Farmer's Architect* (1762). Then ABBEY HOUSE, C17 timber-framed with a mostly C19 brick front to the road and two canted bays. But the windows to the r. of the bays belong to the large W wing added by *Philip Jebb* (interiors by *Dudley Poplack*), 1968–70, which has a three-bay pediment. Also on the S front, decorative C19 gables. To the E, HOME FARM HOUSE, C17 with a five-bay Georgian brick front. Then at right angles the charming VILLAGE STREET, two rows of mainly C18 timber-framed and plastered cottages, mostly single-storey with attics and

dormers, but incorporating some earlier structures, e.g. Nos.
1 and 3, on the E side, a C16 hall and cross-wing, and on the
W side No. 22, a four-bay medieval hall house.

The street leads to the COLLEGE OF ST MARK, almshouses
built by the Earl of Suffolk in the early C17. Excavations in
1993 showed that it stands on the site of a medieval building,
no doubt the hospital (1258) of Walden Abbey. Brick, and of
an uncommon completeness and plan. Two courtyards of ten
dwellings each, with the hall and chapel range separating them.
Mainly single-storey, apart from the W end of the central range.
Straight gables, and the only other external accent the two-
transomed chapel window of brick with all individual lights
arched (cf. the chapel at Hatfield House). The windows of the
dwellings also have arched lights. Dissolved in 1633, the college
gradually fell into disrepair. Restored for retired clergy by
Marshall Sisson, 1949–54, when the E end of the chapel, which
projects beyond the E wall of the courtyards, was rebuilt. Its
hammerbeam roof has one original truss. Further restoration
and conversion to residential youth centre by *Kay Pilsbury*,
1990–2. – In the former kitchen, a fireplace with carved
wooden surround of interesting C17 design, not *in situ*. – In the
chapel E window, many fragments of STAINED GLASS of
unknown provenance, some perhaps from Walden Abbey, reset
by *Dennis G. King*, *c*. 1951. Especially fine late C14 Virgin and
Child.

AVELEY
Thurrock U.A.

ST MICHAEL. Low W tower with angle buttresses and short spire
behind battlements, low flat-roofed N aisle, higher N chancel
chapel, all C13. Restoration by *Ewan Christian*, 1885–8, most
obvious in the large brick buttresses round the E end; windows
renewed. Roughly coursed ragstone and flint walls, the two-
storey SW extension by *Richard Burbidge*, 1994–6, toning in
well. Three-bay S arcade with broad piers of Greek cross-
section, C12. Fragments too of an earlier C12 building, e.g. part
of the arch of a window above the easternmost bay. The two E
bays have one-stepped arches, the W bay instead a double-
chamfered arch. In the E respond a C14 niche. The N arcade
has circular piers and double-chamfered arches, the tower a
single-chamfered arch. C15 N porch. C16 nave roof, with
painted figures in the spandrels of the easternmost bay. –
FONT. C12, the Purbeck type often met with: square bowl decorated with shallow blank round arches; five supports. – Pillar
PISCINA. C12. Sunk in S chancel wall and set in C14 trefoiled
recess.– PULPIT with tester, dated 1621. – SCREEN, formerly
between chancel and nave, now uncomfortably across the
tower arch, with some tracery and other early C15 woodwork.
– Carved oak REREDOS by *Christian*, 1893, and ALTAR with
painted panels by *Charles Holroyd* (N chapel, originally in

chancel). – STAINED GLASS. E window by *Holroyd*, 1896, probably made by *Heaton, Butler & Bayne*. Chancel s by *William
Morris*, 1875. Single light, St Michael and the Dragon, with
background of flowered quarries. – MONUMENTS. Important
brass to Ralph de Knevynton †1370; Flemish. 21-in. (53-cm.)
figure in armour, in rectangular plate with thin buttresses and
traceried spandrels. – Six sons and two daughters, *c.* 1520,
small figures from a brass probably of the Barrett family. – Elizabeth Bacon †1583, mural brass under Purbeck arch, almost
entirely covered by reredos. Figure of infant in swaddling
clothes, originally 6 in. (15 cm.), incomplete. – Nathaniell and
Elizabeth Bacon †1588. 11- and 10-in. (28- and 25-cm.) figures
of children. – Various wall monuments to members of the
Barrett and Barrett-Lennard family of Belhus, including
Thomas, Lord Dacre †1786, with draped urn.

UNITED REFORMED CHURCH, High Street. 1878 by *John
Sulman*. E.E. Stock brick, with minimal white brick decoration.

BELHUS, ¾ m. NNE. Only the footings survive of the brick courtyard house, dem. 1957, described as 'newly builded' in the will
of John Barrett (†1526).* Extensive alterations were made for
Horace Walpole's friend Lord Dacre, 1744–77, including work
to the park (much of it now a golf course), laid out by *Capability Brown*, 1753–63, with further work by *Richard Woods*,
1770–1. Visible remains include two wooded mounds N of the
site of the house, The Shrubbery (a woodland walk) to the w,
and the Long Pond (now bisected by the M25) to the NE. Near
the N tip of the Long Pond, a tall octagonal brick STENCH
PIPE, mid C19, like a Neo-Tudor chimney. Remains of the C18
wall of the kitchen garden can be seen in Irvine Gardens, South
Ockendon.

BRETTS, Romford Road, 1¼ m. NNW. Timber-framed, roughcast, the exterior giving away little of its possibly late C14
origins. Half-H plan. Of the C15 the blocked square-headed E
windows of the hall and a re-set doorway with four-centred
head. Most of the original frame and roof survives. Incomplete
moat.

SIR HENRY GURNETT PUB (formerly Kenningtons), Romford
Road, 1 m. NNW. Timber-framed manor house, originally an
aisled hall built between *c.* 1275 and 1310. Aisles removed later
in the C14 and the hall extended. Inside, the framing has been
revealed, including the first floor at the solar (W) end and the
crown-post roof.

AYTHORPE RODING *5010*

ST MARY THE VIRGIN. Nave and chancel C13, rendered walls
of flint rubble. C15 timber belfry with shingled splay-foot

---

*Various fittings survive, including an early C18 chimneypiece and some C17
panelling in Thurrock Museum, and C17 panelling in Valence House Museum,
Dagenham.

spire. Much renewed by *A.B. Jackson* (*Inman & Jackson*), 1896, including roofs, S porch, N vestry, and lychgate. – Nave BENCHES. Plain, C16, also fragments of the C17. – STAINED GLASS. By *H.J. Salisbury*, 1907.

AYTHORPE RODING HALL, SW of the church. Late C16 timber-framed, altered in the C18 with new roof and sashes. C17 farm buildings to SE.

AYTHORPE MANOR (former rectory), 1 m. ENE. By *G.E. Pritchett*, 1853. Brick with stock brick dressings. Gabled, with tall chimneys.

FRIAR'S GRANGE, 1¼ m. SE. Late C14, a grange of Tilty Abbey. Two-bay hall, its integral parlour/solar end (l.) and service end (r.), replaced with gabled wings in the late C16.

YEOMANS, 1¼ m. ENE. C14 or C15, thatched. Two-bay hall with integral parlour/solar end to the r. and service end to the l. Mid-C16 alterations included a timber-framed smoke-hood, with a later brick stack inside it.

Thatched cottages at KEERES GREEN, 1 m. SE, include JUDDS, a small early C14 hall house, floored and chimney inserted *c.* 1600, but otherwise largely unaltered.

85, 86 WINDMILL, ½ m. ESE. The largest remaining post mill in Essex, fully restored by *Vincent Pargeter*, 1975–82. Brick round-house and weatherboarded buck. Dated 1779.

6020   BARDFIELD SALING (OR LITTLE SALING)

ST PETER AND ST PAUL. C14, the chancel probably completed last. This was shortened *c.* 1700, remodelled in the C19, and again following bomb damage in the Second World War, when the E wall was rebuilt. Round W tower whose windows look early C14. Early to mid-C14 windows in the nave and chancel, but a quite marked difference in style between the S arcade and the chancel arch. The former has strong piers consisting of four main shafts and four keeled shafts in the diagonals, with moulded arches and headstops; the chancel arch has late C14-looking responds. Big ogee squint. Late C18 W gallery with chamber organ. Restored 1886, when the box PEWS were cut down to their present height. – PULPIT. Jacobean, the usual arched panels treated in perspective. The pilasters between of termini shape. Elaborate panelling round the base, of the same date. – SCREEN between nave and S aisle chapel. Contemporary with the chancel, that is of large and relatively plain forms, ogee arches and, above in niches, quatrefoils coming down to an ogee point. Strong framing. Set up as a reredos, 1886, and moved to its present position by *Duncan W. Clark* in 1948, incorporating Jacobean panelling in the base. As the reredos it framed STRAW DECORATION (plaiting), chiefly naturalistic vine trails with grapes, now mounted on W wall of S aisle. – WALL PAINTINGS. Consecration cross on N wall of nave, C14, and black-letter inscription in S aisle, C17 or early C18.

ARUNDELS, opposite the church. Mid C16, with some exposed
timbers. Hall with cross-wing to r. and lower extension to l.
ELMS FARM, ⅔ m. NE. Late C15. Solar cross-wing to r. with
exposed timbers and the upper storey jettied on curved
brackets. Larger cross-wing to l. a later rebuilding.

BARLING   *9080*

Barling Magna

ALL SAINTS. Stately battlemented W tower with recessed shingled spire and diagonal buttresses. Niches l. and r. and above
the W window, frieze of flint and stone chequer above the
window. Of ragstone rubble, and about the same date as the
early C15 tower at Little Wakering. Nave possibly C12. Higher
chancel, extended in the C15. Late Perp N aisle with two- and
three-light windows without tracery and concave-sided, relatively tall and slender octagonal arcade piers. Rood stairs in
the N wall. Restored and re-seated by *William Slater*, 1863–4.
– FONT. Perp, octagonal, with shields, quatrefoils, etc. –
PULPIT. Hexagonal, late C17. Back wall with a big odd-shaped
panel flanked by volutes and an unusually big sounding-board.
– SCULPTURE. Two headless alabaster figures, C15, one seated,
the other standing, only 12 and 15 in. (30 and 38 cm.) long;
probably part of a reredos. – STAINED GLASS. Nave S by *W.
Aikman*, 1937. – In churchyard, CHEST-TOMB of George Asser
†1674 and wife Susanna †1658, carved with skull and crossbones, hourglass, and acanthus leaves; also a number of good
C18 headstones.
BARLING HOUSE, ¼ m. SW. C18 timber-framed and plastered
three-bay N front with pedimented doorcase. Taller early C19
wing behind of stock brick, three-bay E front with arched
doorway and projecting eaves on brackets. To its W GLEBE
FARM (former vicarage). Mainly C17, with later small Gothic
casements.

BARNSTON   *6010*

ST ANDREW. Mostly flint, the E wall brick, and the W end timber-
framed, all rendered. Nave Norman with two N windows, one
S window, and a plain S doorway with one order of columns
with scallop capitals. Chancel E.E., originally apsidal, with one
N lancet window and a fine mid-C13 DOUBLE PISCINA of the
type of Jesus and St John's Colleges at Cambridge, that is with
intersected round arches. The shafts have stiff-leaf capitals. The
foliage runs on as a frieze behind the capitals towards the wall
and fills the spandrels of the arches as well. W steeple struck
by lightning in 1665 and replaced by a small wooden belfry
and pretty C18 cupola. W gallery with stairs that incorporate
three C16 splat-balusters. – FONT. Stone, octagonal, with

quatrefoiled panels and wooden cover, by *Cox & Son, c.* 1867.
– Other FITTINGS by *Ernest Beckwith* to designs by *F. W.*
Chancellor, 1941. Linenfold panels framed by classical pilasters
and cornices, a curious effect. – BARREL ORGAN, on W gallery.
By *Bevington & Son, c.* 1830, unusually large. – STAINED
GLASS. E window by *O'Connor,* 1857. – Chancel S by *Morris &*
Co., 1912, using a *Burne-Jones* design. Moved here *c.* 1946 from
St Cyprian's School, Eastbourne, Sussex. – Nave N by *E.R.*
Frampton, 1880. The window itself inserted 1857, a copy of that
on the S side, which includes a panel of C14 glass.

BARNSTON HALL, W of the church. Mainly mid C16, plastered,
with a rear wing added by *F. W. Chancellor,* 1920, with exposed
reused timbers. Attractive outbuildings include a late C15
square DOVECOTE, part plastered, part weatherboarded, with a
gabled section in the hipped roof providing access for the birds.
E of the church, BARNSTON LODGE, late C18 gault brick, its
elegance marred only by a too-prominent slate mansard roof.
Two storeys with attic and basement, the main front of five
bays. Three-bay pedimented centre, the door and flanking
windows in shallow arched recesses. Single-storey semicircular
extensions to r. and l. To its SE the OLD RECTORY, C17 timber-
framed and plastered with C18 alterations: tripartite sash
windows, and a glazed porch with pointed-arched heads.

BASILDON

Town Centre	111
The Neighbourhoods	111
Barstable	116
Chalvedon	117
Dunton	117
Felmore	118
Fryerns	118
Laindon	119
Langdon Hills	120
Lee Chapel North	121
Lee Chapel South	121
Nevendon	121
Noak Bridge	122
Pitsea	122
Vange	123
Industrial Areas	124

p. 112   Basildon was the largest of the New Towns conceived to absorb
the surplus population of post-war London. The designated area
covered 7,818 acres and was unusual in inheriting an indigenous
population of 25,000 from several existing settlements including
Laindon, Langdon Hills, Pitsea and Vange. But of 8,700
dwellings existing in 1949, a substantial number belonged to the
'plotlands' where some 5,500 substandard buildings, often little

more than shacks on narrow plots (20 ft by 160–180 ft), were strung out along nearly 80 miles of unmade roads. Their unregulated development had been encouraged by the opening of the railway between London, Barking and Pitsea in 1888, agricultural depression, and gratuities to returning soldiers after 1918 to buy or build cheap houses within commuting distance of London. Almost all were swept away in the rebuilding after 1949: a single example has survived complete into the C21 as a museum at Dunton (*see* p. 117).

The town lies between the London–Southend road (A127) to the N and the A13 and Tilbury–Southend railway in the S. Between these routes runs the London–Shoeburyness railway line, bisecting the town and with the Town Centre just to its N at the geographical centre encompassed by a ring road. Basildon's simple layout adheres closely to the ideals and principles of New Town planning, with industry reserved to an area in the N of the town close to the A127, and the town centre surrounded by self-contained residential neighbourhoods. Most have their own shopping centre, primary school, church, and playing field, but with pedestrian routes and cycleways linking the inner neighbourhoods to the shops and amenities of the town centre.

The Development Corporation's first chief architect and planner was *Noel Tweddell*, 1949–58, formerly Harlow's chief architect. He was succeeded by *Anthony B. Davies*, then *Douglas Galloway* (1964–79), and finally *John Byron*. *Sylvia Crowe* was landscape consultant, as at Harlow, until 1962. The Corporation was wound up in 1986. Basildon New Town was originally intended to house 50,000. This figure was increased with revised masterplans, the last (in 1977) setting it at 130,000. The population grew rapidly until the early 1990s but then flattened out. In 2001 it was just over 96,500.

A development plan for the town centre (by *DTZ* with *Alan Baxter & Associates* and *Maccreanor Lavington*), under discussion in 2006, has been prepared in anticipation of the wider development of Thames Gateway and to meet the needs of regeneration as a retail centre and as a place to live and work. It recognizes some of the centre's failings, including the way in which it is cut off from the neighbourhoods and the green space of Gloucester Park by the ring road, and the way in which the railway station formed no part of the original design.

TOWN CENTRE

The TOWN CENTRE, occupying a 65-acre site, was designed by the *Development Corporation*, with *Sir Basil Spence* as consultant. It was started in 1956, inaugurated in 1962, and in spite of some remodelling and extension is still surprisingly faithful to its original conception of a traffic-free pedestrian shopping precinct lying within an inner ring road for access to the rear of the shops and peripheral car parks (the generous provision of which seems farsighted for the late 1950s.) The original portion, remarkably well preserved, comprises the long and

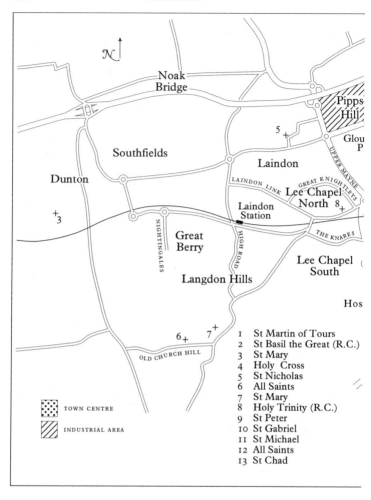

N

Noak
Bridge

Pipps
Hill

5

Glou
P

Southfields

Laindon

UPPER MAYNE

Dunton

LAINDON LINK

GREAT KNIGHTLEYS

Lee Chapel
North 8

+3

Laindon
Station

NIGHTINGALES

Great
Berry

HIGH ROAD

THE KNARES

Lee Chapel
South

Langdon Hills

Hos

6 7

OLD CHURCH HILL

1 St Martin of Tours
2 St Basil the Great (R.C.)
3 St Mary
4 Holy Cross
5 St Nicholas
6 All Saints
7 St Mary
8 Holy Trinity (R.C.)
9 St Peter
10 St Gabriel
11 St Michael
12 All Saints
13 St Chad

▓ TOWN CENTRE

▨ INDUSTRIAL AREA

spacious TOWN SQUARE, aligned E–W, with low buildings on
both sides, and the sunken EAST SQUARE at its E end. Where
they meet, the forceful BROOKE HOUSE, 1960–2, a fourteen-
storey tower of 84 flats standing on eight 27-ft-high reinforced
concrete V-shaped struts. All windows project triangularly in
plan. As well as being an important landmark for the New
Town, Brooke House was also valuable for keeping a significant high-density residential population at the town's heart, a
feature unique to Basildon among the New Towns. Coherence
is provided by exemplary hard landscaping of retaining walls,
steps etc., and in the main square a raised pool and sculpture,
Mother and Child by *Maurice Lambert*, 1962, and steel lollipop
clock by *Philip Harvey*. The deliberately asymmetrical treatment of the square's commercial buildings is also a major
visual asset. Town Square was refurbished *c.* 1997–8 by *Tibbalds*

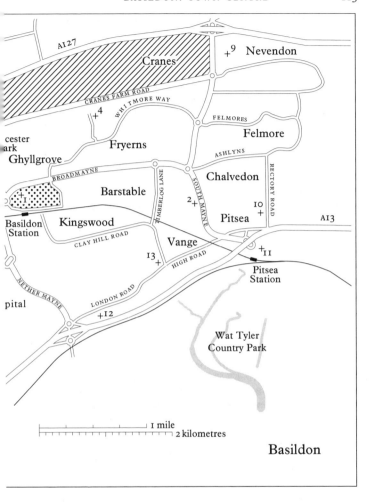

Basildon

Monro, with entrance arch at the w end and two free-standing, glazed pavilions.

Facing East Square, FREEDOM HOUSE, by *J. Seymour Harris & Partners*, 1958. Offices above two storeys of shops and a covered walkway which returns into EAST WALK, with the upper storey projecting on tapered supports to form an arcade. Wire and aluminium sculpture against a lozenge-pattern mosaic panel by *A.J. Poole* in the manner of Barbara Hepworth. Almost opposite, BARCLAYS, a large block with an upper storey faced in concrete panels and blind except for patterns of vertical openings, but with a curious cantilevered feature at first floor, of splayed plan with a curved front.

Tucked behind is EASTGATE SHOPPING CENTRE by *John Fairhead* of the Development Corporation with *Stanley Bragg Partnership*, 1981–5. Four levels along the main E–W axis, with barrel-vaulted glass roof and shiny, chrome-trimmed escalators. On the first upper level, a fantastical clock ('Pussiewillow III') by *Rowland Emett*, 1981, what he called 'a celestial cats'-cradle'. Off Town Square, open arcades lead s to MARKET SQUARE (completed first, in 1958, for a traditional street market) with two ranges of shops and offices, N and E, as the backdrop. The E range has sloping concrete canopies on thin columns which functioned also as shelters for the adjoining BUS STATION (*c.* 1960, rebuilt 1985–6, job architect *John Fairhead*). On the block's s face, a vast ceramic mural depicting Basildon's history.* Visible s across the ring road (Southernhay), the RAILWAY STATION, 1973–4 by the *Eastern Region Architect's Department* (*A. Boal*, architect, *H. Ormiston*, chief civil engineer, in association with the Corporation's architects, *George Garrard* and *Maurice Naunton*), and behind it the contemporary and depressing brick mass of TRAFFORD HOUSE (offices for the Ford Motor Co.) by *Sidney Kaye, Firmin & Partners*.

ST MARTIN'S SQUARE lies w of Town Square, and was completed last. The transition between the two is a mess and marks a decline in the mood and vision of the earlier parts, emphasized by the unappealing bulk of NORTHGATE HOUSE, 1970–1, with its modish feature of an external escalator to Town Square, and MARKS & SPENCER, which is a domineering presence on the E side of St Martin's Square. On its N side, the church of ST MARTIN OF TOURS. By *T.M. Cotton*, consecrated 1962, with its fibreglass SCULPTURE of the Risen Christ by *T. B. Huxley-Jones*, 1968. Of dark reddish-purple brick, tall, with nave and chancel in one. The w wall mainly glass, the side walls articulated by the concrete frame. Lady Chapel on s side, lower and facing s. Rather austere interior, with only an elongated cross on the windowless E wall, but softened with much-needed colour from STAINED GLASS by *Patrick Nuttgens*, 1987–90, in the low nave windows along both sides, and Lady Chapel.

The focal point of the square is now a 95-ft- (29-metre) high free-standing octagonal CAMPANILE opposite the church's w end. 1999 by *Douglas Galloway*, with engineers *Buro Happold*; executive architects, *Fletcher Priest*. Steel, fully glazed, the sides ending in little Neo-Gothic gables, behind which rises an elongated, copper-covered ogee dome. – In the garden on the church's N side, a small statue by *Peter Foster*, 1990, of St Martin and the beggar with whom he shared his cloak. In the square's NW corner, THE BASILDON CENTRE (council offices and library) and TOWNGATE THEATRE by *Renton Howard Wood Levin*, 1985–9. Buff brick with bands of darker brick (green glazed bricks on the theatre), the entrances set in large

---

*The earlier building also had a ceramic mural, of abstract design, by *William Gordon*, with tiles by *Carter & Co.* of Poole, 1958.

glazed sections, the theatre's emphasized by large green panels. The theatre has two auditoria, the main one with removable proscenium and semicircular galleries, and a studio. S, WESTGATE SHOPPING PARK, 1999, which borrows the buff-brick-and-green colour scheme of the theatre and adds round turrets. In the square, human sundial by *Tam Giles*, 1997, and Woodsman, carved on site by *David Chapple*, 1996.

On the w edge subways and pedestrian areas pass beneath the ring road at ROUNDACRE to the new neighbourhoods. Landscaping by *Wendy Taylor*, 1988–90, with sculpture in concrete and steel. Also by Taylor the 'compass bowl' at the underpass on the eastern edge of the centre (Southernhay/Long Riding).

Other public buildings

CROWN AND COUNTY COURTS, The Gore. By the *Property Services Agency*, 1989–95. Buff brick, with blue window frames etc. Public entrance across one corner, glazed to full height.

MAGISTRATES' COURT, Great Oaks. 1988–90 by *Howell Killick Partridge & Amis*. Two-tone brick, two storeys. Taller middle block with hipped roof with two pyramidal skylights; lower blocks in front of and behind this, each with round turrets at each end with conical skylights.

GLOUCESTER PARK. Started 1963–4, the design (by *Derek Lovejoy*) substantially modified over the years. SWIMMING POOL by *K. S. Cotton*, 1968. Walls of opaque glazing, with monopitch roof on the main pool hall.

THE NEIGHBOURHOODS

Although close to the Thames Estuary, the landscape surrounding the town centre is by no means flat, and much of the built-up area lies on the N slope of a ridge running sw from Langdon Hill, one of the highest points in Essex, to Pitsea in the E. Subsidiary spurs run through Laindon and through the site of the old hamlet of Basildon. On the tops of these hills are some of the old parish churches, and although they play only subsidiary roles in the neighbourhoods efforts were made to preserve views of them and to preserve such natural features as the southern slopes of Langdon Hills.

Because main drainage was immediately available, and to avoid disrupting residents in the existing settlements, redevelopment for the new neighbourhoods began at the eastern end of the designated area and proceeded westwards, providing an early build-up around the nascent town centre and eventually forming a physical link between the existing centres of Vange and Pitsea (E) and Laindon and Langdon Hills (w). About half the HOUSING was designed by the *Development Corporation*, but many private architects were appointed to individual schemes ensuring considerable variety of design.* The first houses (in Redgrave Road, Vange) were completed in 1951. Local stock brick predominates but, as at Harlow, uniformity was avoided by careful use of materials and different layouts. Most housing is two-storey, in short terraces, but enlivened by sometimes quirky use of tile-hanging and weatherboarding (both of various colours), panels of flint and cobbles, and little balconies that lend a 'Festival of Britain' air. SCHOOLS were the responsibility of successive County Architects, although some were delegated to private architects,† along with a number of the designs for SHOPS in neighbourhood centres.‡ They have inevitably suffered the vicissitudes of the late C20 and only the best examples are detailed here.

The development, as it moved from E to W, encapsulated evolving attitudes in planning, particularly towards the separation of pedestrian and vehicle routes. The early neighbourhoods of Fryerns, Barstable and parts of Vange had conventional, open 'new town' layouts, but at Kingswood and Lee Chapel South (S of the town centre) and Ghyllgrove (N) of the early 1960s, the gradual adoption of the rear-access principle can be seen; while Lee Chapel North and Laindon, NW of the centre, of the mid-1960s, have the first full-scale development of separate vehicle and pedestrian routes between all parts of the neighbourhood. In the later neighbourhoods, too, can be seen the result of the increased target of population which was planned for: the evolution of a notably more urban character derived from the use of bold and simple materials, from the sense of enclosure created by internal and external corner units to continue the line of a block or terrace unbroken, and the closing-up of distances between house fronts permitted by a segregated pedestrian circulation, and from the greater use of hard landscaping and textures to balance the soft landscaping. After that, Noak Bridge on the N side of the A127 provides a complete reversal of this process, and a return to a higgledy-piggledy village with cars once more in front of houses.

BARSTABLE

ST BASIL THE GREAT (R.C.), Luncies Road. By *A.J. Newton* of *Burles, Newton & Partners*, 1955–6. Quiet, dignified, and sensible. Buff brick, with the concrete frame exposed, and tall high-level windows. Lower entrance and Lady Chapel on S side, and (liturgical) SW tower with chapel (originally baptistery) in base.

---

*These included, in the early years, *Norman & Dawbarn*, *Clifford Culpin & Partners*, *Richard Sheppard & Partners*, *David du R. Aberdeen & Partners*, *Stanley Bragg*, *Basil Spence & Partners*, *William Crabtree* (later *Crabtree & Jarosz*), *Ralph Tubbs*, *Lionel Brett & Kenneth Boyd*, *Burles & Newton*, and *G. A. Jellicoe & Partners*.

†e.g. *The Austin-Smith, Salmon, Lord Partnership* (The Gore, Ghyllgrove), *Clifford Culpin & Partners* (Church Road, Fryerns), *Poulton & Freeman* (Clay Hill Road, Kingswood), and *Yorke, Rosenberg & Mardall* (Wickford Avenue, Chalvedon).

‡e.g. *Burles & Newton* at Fryerns and Barstable, and *William Crabtree and H. T. Cadbury-Brown* at Kingswood.

Light, spacious interior with wide alleys and large sanctuary. Including presbytery and (in Rippleside) ST TERESA'S PRIMARY SCHOOL.

BARSTABLE SCHOOL, Timberlog Lane. A robust design by *Yorke, Rosenberg & Mardall*, 1961–2, forms the core. Exposed, board-marked concrete frame with blue brick infill. Main block of three storeys, the bays separated by concrete columns detached from the glazing behind that rise the full height. Long, lower block at right angles with assembly hall, swimming pool, etc.

Some of the New Town's earliest housing is along LUNCIES ROAD, RIPPLESIDE and ELSENHAM CRESCENT: brick terraces intermingled with detached houses that have weatherboarded panels and little balconies. At the E end of Luncies Road a small centre is created by the R.C. church and school (*see* above), shops, and pub, THE WINGED HORSE, with pitched copper roof, concrete panels and green slate-hanging. To the W, right by the Town Centre, good use of varied materials in TINKLER SIDE and PINMILL: weatherboarding, flint, cobbles, etc., the façades further enlivened by balconies and oriels. The main NEIGHBOURHOOD CENTRE, by the *Development Corporation, c.* 1956, is on the corner of Timberlog Lane and Long Riding: shops, with flats and maisonettes over, brick and render; behind, workshops, 1961–2, faced in white brick. In LONG RIDING, a long crescent of three-storey terraced houses.

CHALVEDON

Off ASHLYNS (N side), housing by *Ahrends, Burton & Koralek*, 1974–80. One- and two-storey houses in terraces and courtyards. Brick and weatherboarding with asymmetric pitched roofs. Designed for high levels of energy conservation, with heating provided centrally and distributed via overhead ducts that form covered walkways.

GREAT CHALVEDON HALL, Tyefields. Early C16, T-plan, with W cross-wing. Three gables on the S front with C18 windows. Chimneystack with diagonal shafts. Bought by the Council in 1977 and converted into a community pub.

DUNTON

On the New Town's western edge, and not part of any neighbourhood.

ST MARY, Church Road. Rebuilt by *W.G. Bartleet*, 1873. Nave, chancel, and S porch. Dec, brick, with some surviving Tudor brick in the chancel N wall. C15 timbers reused for the W belfry, weatherboarded with shingled splay-foot spire. Now a house.

PLOTLANDS MUSEUM, ¾ m. SE. 'The Haven', a bungalow erected on one of three plots bought by Frederick Mills in 1933 and typical of its kind. Now in a nature reserve, but the grid of surrounding roads can still be discerned as well as remains of other houses. Visitor Centre by *Roderick Shelton*, opened 1996.

FELMORE

Along FELMORES, interesting timber-framed housing by the *Corporation* (job architects *C. Plumb, D. Brewster, R. V. Wilson*), 1976–80. Long L-plan terraces, each of twenty dwellings. The upper storeys (two or three, diminishing in height) have strongly contrasting bands of dark vertical boarding and bright red pantile roofs, creating a pagoda-like section.

To the E, the 1970s SHOPPING CENTRE, with two and three floors of flats above shops arranged round a nice little square, reached through an opening in the terrace supported on pilotis. On one side BRISCOE PRIMARY SCHOOL by *Stanley Bragg*, 1979. Low profile, white-rendered with shallow pantile roof. – N of the shopping centre, off DAVENANTS, a cluster of architecturally-named roads (Soane Street, Voysey Gardens, Stirling Place, etc.) with prefabricated starter homes by the *Development Corporation* (project leader, *Clive Plumb*), 1980–2.

FRYERNS

HOLY CROSS, Church Road. The old parish church of Basildon. A painted BOARD inside records that the parishioners restored 'their decayed and ruinous church' in 1702, the date on the WEATHERVANE. To this date belongs the brick of the N wall. Chancel also brick, rebuilt (according to an inscription, now illegible) in 1597, but much restored in 1880. Ragstone rubble nave C14, restored in 1888 by *Joseph Peacock*, who also repaired the plain C15 timber S porch. Unbuttressed mid-C15 W tower. Chancel roof with embattled purlins and wind-braces, 1597. – COMMUNION RAILS with twisted balusters quite substantial in girth; *c.* 1700.

N of Holy Cross, CRANES COURT (Basildon Foyer), single persons' housing by the *Development Corporation*, 1978–80. Brick, with cloister-like walkways, the blocks angled to give a sense of privacy and security. W of Church Road, close to the town centre, some good early examples of varied form and materials: a long curved terrace in THE GORE faced with knapped flint and coloured weatherboarding, also seen on houses in TANGHAM WALK, THE UPWAY etc., but set vertically and with cobbled flint facing.

Fryerns' main spine is WHITMORE WAY, with good early Corporation housing near the W end, at ORSETT END. Terrace along Whitmore Way with an opening supported on pilotis leading through to a square of cobble-faced houses with delicate little balconies. On the N side, the LIBRARY by *H. Conolly*, County Architect, *c.* 1963, and further E his JUNIOR SCHOOL, 1954, its chief accent the water tank. On the S side, the BAPTIST CHURCH by *E. J. Wood*, 1953–4, the New Town's first chapel. Pitched roof, aisles, and clerestory. W front faced

in random stone with recessed entrance. Extremely slender
flèche. Opposite, WHITMORE COURT by *Ahrends, Burton &
Koralek*, 1973–6. Flats and maisonettes, mainly for single or
elderly people, and day centre, in blocks of up to four storeys
arranged round s-facing courtyards. Light brown brick, with
rather heavy-looking concrete planting boxes at each level and
prominent handrails. Just beyond, the 1950s with domestic-
looking pub, the JOLLY FRIAR, by *Stewart & Hendry*, 1956–8.

LAINDON

Large and grim NEIGHBOURHOOD CENTRE of forty-seven
shops, with three-storey office block, pub, etc., *c.* 1964–5,
looking ready for redevelopment. On two levels, with pedestrians segregated from the traffic. In the precinct, Corbusier-
inspired funnels are excessively large in the confined space.
HEALTH CENTRE alongside by *Basildon Council* (chief architect, *K.S. Cotton*), 1971. Board-marked concrete on pilotis. –
To the s, strung out between Laindon Link and Laindon
Railway Station and along the railway, *Corporation* housing
(project architects *D. Brewster, J. Byron, M. Naunton, C. Plumb*)
of 1968–72. A large scheme of two-storey houses in a series of
linked courtyards (MELLOW PURGESS, HANDLEY GREEN),
with ground-floor archways and corner projections on pilotis,
on a pattern that repeats but provides changing vistas and so
never becomes boring. Across an open green space, SOMER-
COTES achieves similar effects with three-storey blocks of flats.

ST NICHOLAS stands on a steep eminence (Church Hill) above
the sea of housing. Small, of ragstone rubble and puddingstone
with a C15 timber belfry, darkly weatherboarded and crowned
by a shingled splay-foot spire. W of it an annexe, two storeys
and attic, probably the priest's house, later used as a school.
Early C17, timber-framed with plank-cladding of the type
found in New England, and brick N wall for a bread oven.
Inside the belfry one of the splendid sturdy Essex timber
constructions. In this case (cf. Horndon-on-the-Hill, Leaden
Roding, etc.) it is independently built inside the walls of the
nave. Moreover, it comprises two separate structures, an outer
frame carrying the turret and spire, an inner one the bells.
Nave C12 in origin, much rebuilt in the C14, the date also of
the s chapel and chancel. Two-bay s arcade with octagonal pier
and double-chamfered arches, but the s wall at least rebuilt by
Chancellor in his restoration of 1880–3. s porch timber, C15,
mostly rebuilt. However, the oddly primitive carvings in the
spandrels of the archway against the nave doorway are original, a beast pierced by a cross-shaft, a dragon, etc. C15 nave
and chancel roofs, the latter very fine with curved bracing,
traceried spandrels, and crested wall-plates. – FONT. Of the
Purbeck type, with shallow blank pointed arcades on each side;
C13. – BRASSES. Two brasses of priests, one 38 in. (96 cm.) long
of *c.* 1470, the other 13 in. (33 cm.), *c.* 1510.

LANGDON HILLS

ALL SAINTS, Old Church Hill. Closed in 1973; carefully converted to a house by *Colin Dollimore*, of *Trevor Dannatt & Partners*, with *Roger Coombs*. Nave and chancel early C16, brick with brick windows, the three-light E window with Perp panel tracery. The W wall, timber belfry and spire are rebuildings by *T. B. Crowest* of Billericay, 1841–2, who also inserted the W gallery. At the base of the walls are traces of an earlier, flint-rubble building, and inside is the indent of a late C13 BRASS. N chapel rebuilt in 1834 by *Roger Talbot* of Romford, but preserving the two-bay arcade with a thick short octagonal pier and round arches of 1621. The nave roof has two crown-posts, plastered over so that they resemble inside-out umbrellas. – TYMPANUM, i.e. plastered wall between upper parts of nave and chancel, resting on a tie-beam. Painted on it the ROYAL ARMS, dated 1660. – Pargetted inscription of 1666 above wall-plate on nave N side, and similar date (1621) in N arcade spandrel, with remains of decorative painting. – COMMUNION RAIL with turned balusters, dated 1686, conservative for its date – not yet of the Wren style.

ST MARY THE VIRGIN AND ALL SAINTS, High Road. By *William White*, 1876–7, replacing All Saints. An imposing sight, tall and very narrow, with W tower, standing immediately along the road, with the wooded hillside dropping sharply away on the N side, where aisle, transeptal organ chamber and vestry make a picturesque composition. E.E., faced with Kentish rag and with stone dressings, but the brick exposed internally on the window splays. The sense of height – with clerestory on the N side – is even more pronounced inside, especially as the nave is of only three bays. Restrained carving, e.g. to the SEDILIA, PISCINA, and CREDENCE. Figures of angels with outspread wings on the chancel roof, apparently reused. – STAINED GLASS. Including chancel S window by *Michael Buckley & Co.*, c. 1877, and a N aisle window †1922 by *A.L. Moore & Son*.

OLD RECTORY, Old Church Hill. 1875. Done by *White* for Rev. Euseby Digby Cleaver, before embarking on the church. Picturesquely asymmetrical Domestic Gothic, mainly red brick with some polychromy and tile-hung gables. The semicircular projection on the garden front contained, on the first floor, a chapel for Cleaver's R.C. wife. Interior largely unaltered, with original shutters etc.

The old church and rectory (now in Thurrock U.A.) are very prettily placed on the W slope of the hill, which isolates them from the New Town and from *Corporation* housing (design group leader, *Clive Plumb*) along the E side of the High Road, 1972–9. This hugs the northern face of the hillside and uses the change in levels to create varied and at times dramatic effects. Different housing types, up to four storeys, are arranged into little courtyards, connected by raised walkways. Brick, with some timber cladding, balconies and little stairways, all adding interest. Behind the rows along the High

Road, up to four storeys, lower terraces of houses, single-storey
at the front and two-storey behind. Across the High Road,
between Emanuel Road and Vowler Road, a private development of houses by *David Ruffle Associates* (project architect, *Joe
Hobbs*) for Countryside Properties, 1980, echoes the Corporation's scheme, also using brick and timber cladding. V-shaped
projections, one facet glazed and the other timbered, contain
cantilevered staircases.

w of Langdon Hills, along NIGHTINGALES, Great Berry, some
interesting housing by *Melville Dunbar Associates*, 1992–5.

LEE CHAPEL NORTH

MOST HOLY TRINITY (R.C.), Wickhay. 1979–80 by *Burles,
Newton & Co*. Dark brown brick, the walls relatively low, and
hipped slate roof with a sort of mansard turret glazed on the
w face to light the altar. Altogether rather ugly, although on
the (liturgical) w side is a nice secluded garden with presbytery
and hall.

Good NEIGHBOURHOOD CENTRE, Ballards Walk, *c.* 1964–7,
with ten shops, a pub, Methodist Church, and four-storey
block of maisonettes on pilotis. Behind the shops a little courtyard of sheltered housing, single-storey, faced with cobbles. To
the E, off Great Knightleys, BOYTONS, two-storey terraces in
black brick and cobbles with a large central square reached by
offset pedestrian roads, very formal and urban. SW of Great
Knightleys, in RAPHAELS and RISE PARK, housing (designed
for sale) by *Richard & Su Rogers*, the result of a competition
organized by the Corporation in 1971–3. Staggered two-storey
terraces.

LEE CHAPEL SOUTH

Off the s side of THE KNARES (Botelers, Gaynesford, Sporhams
and Fletchers), imaginative housing by *Tayler & Green*, 1960–3.
Detached square houses with pyramidal roofs, some in varying
shades of brick, others with coloured tile-hanging or weatherboarding. The latter type are set back behind screen walls with
garages at one end, not the usual open style general in New
Towns. Alongside the houses, three-storey terraces, again in a
variety of brick, with boxy timber oriels.

BASILDON UNIVERSITY HOSPITAL, Nether Mayne. 1967–73
by *Anthony B. Davies & Associates* in association with *W. G.
Plant*, architect to the North-East Metropolitan Regional
Hospital Board. Eight-storey administration tower, on a long
podium of up to four storeys with the changing level of the
sloping site.

NEVENDON

ST PETER, Church Lane. Small, of ragstone rubble. Chancel
with some renewed C13 lancets, nave with two C14 doorways.
C15 crown-post roofs. Little weatherboarded belfry on tie-

beams instead of posts. s vestry added during *Joseph Peacock*'s restoration, 1858–9. N porch by *Nicholson*, 1928. – REREDOS, PULPIT, PANELLING, etc. by the rector, *Alfred W. Hands*, made by *H. Cushman*, 1915 onwards. – STAINED GLASS. E window by *Rosemary Rutherford*, 1950.

NEVENDON HALL, N, is of brick with a carved date, 1833. Open porch on thin pillars. Otherwise there is no sense of any neighbourhood.

NEVENDON MANOR (formerly Little Bromfords), ¾ m. N. L-plan, with a smaller gabled and jettied wing that was probably the porch; late C16? Chimneystack with diagonal shafts. Remains of a moat.

NOAK BRIDGE

A late addition to the New Town and outside the main area, N of the A127. Its housing by the *Corporation* (project architects *Maurice Naunton* and *George Garrard*), 1975–81, is quite different from the rest of Basildon, indeed a seeming reversal of the post-war vision. The desired (and surprisingly convincing) effect is the random variety of a traditional English village, with no two houses alike unless they are in terraces. Plenty of Neo-vernacular features: weatherboarding, jetties, exposed timbers, brick, render, etc. The main focal points are a green near the western entrance and a square tucked away down COPPICE LANE, with a tall gabled building for shops, some modest brick cottages, and Primary School; nearby, the Village Hall. Just off the square, KENILWORTH COURT (sheltered housing) has lodge-like pavilions (linked by walkways), one hexagonal with an eccentric, rather Gothic-looking gabled roof. In 2000 Noak Bridge was designated a Conservation Area. Post-1981 development on the eastern half of the site is much more commonplace.

PITSEA

Much of Pitsea pre-dates the New Town. It had its own station from 1855, and a centre developed on the High Road between the Wars. On the BROADWAY, a good mock-Tudor group, well detailed with gables, oriels, etc. and varied half timbering: RAILWAY HOTEL, 1927, TUDOR CHAMBERS, 1929 and 1956, and ANNE BOLEYN MANSIONS, 1934. The latter joins BROADWAY CHAMBERS, 1959–64, an abrupt transition to curtain-walled Modernism but erected by the same family (Howard). Behind is the large and dreary SHOPPING CENTRE by the *Corporation*, 1975–7, with open market surrounded by blockwork ranges with set-back ground floor and slate mansards. Equally dour brick LEISURE CENTRE, *c.* 1985 by *Basildon Council* (job architect, *R. Field*). – Of the housing, that in PARKHURST ROAD, E, is most interesting, with single-storey terraces by *Leonard Manasseh*, 1967, facing narrow courts. Pale brick with square bays and recessed entrances.

In Rectory Road, St Gabriel of 1963–4 by *D. M. Corder*. Brick. Duodecagonal, with small w entrance block and vestries etc. on the NE and SE sides. Of the remaining sides, six are almost filled with coloured glass. Laminated timber-frame roof, with overhanging gables on each side rising as high as the centre, which is crowned by a tubular steel cross clad with fibreglass. Very spacious interior, with a shallow raised sanctuary curving across the three eastern sides. Central stone FONT by *John H. Macarthy*, also twelve-sided, tapered, with reliefs on a band of bronzed fibreglass.

The remains of medieval Pitsea, at the head of Pitsea Creek, are cut off by the A13 and railway, with the sad relic of St Michael on high ground with a dramatic panoramic view s down Holehaven Creek to the Thames and the Coryton oil refinery (*see* p. 311). The demolished nave of 1871 by *A. W. Blomfield* is marked out by stones and an altar; only the much-restored stone w tower of *c.* 1500 still stands. GAZEBO by *Gerald W. Barrett*, 2003, reusing old materials.

Pitsea Hall (now Cromwell Manor), ¼ m. sw. Timber-framed, *c.* 1600, the s front faced in stock brick in the C19 with two large bows added in the C20. On the N front the first floor is jettied, with exposed timbers, brick nogging, and original windows on the ground floor. Late C20 single-storey additions on the w side.

At Wat Tyler Country Park, Marsh Lane, two timber-framed houses from Coopers End, Takeley, demolished to make way for Stansted Airport *c.* 1987: Little Coopers Cottage, weatherboarded, a three-bay C15 hall house, with floor inserted and roof raised in the C16 or C17, and Blunt's Cottage, C16 hall house floored in the C17. Re-erected 1988 and 1990 respectively. Also Holly Cottage, C17, originally in Hockley Road, Rayleigh, re-erected 1985. – SCULPTURE. 'Seven' by *Robert Worley*, 2000–1, depicting the Peasants' Revolt. Also 'Progression' by *Michael Crondon*, 2001 (stainless steel), originally in Basildon Town Square.

VANGE

Like Pitsea, Vange began as a village on the escarpment of the Thames, on Vange Creek, and later expanded along the London Road.

All Saints. Small, on its own, with tiny w bell-turret. Nave and chancel of ragstone rubble with some flint and tufa. In the nave s wall remains of a Norman window, the chancel arch also Norman. Chancel extended in the C15, E wall rebuilt in the C18. Restored 1836–7 by *Thomas Sneezum*, who rebuilt the w wall and inserted the gallery on cast-iron columns. Further work, including re-seating, by *John Young*, 1896. Restored for the Churches Conservation Trust by *Alan Greening*, 2002–5. – FONT. Square bowl on five supports, one side with zigzag motif. C12–C13. Base 1881. – COMMUNION RAIL. With turned balusters, partly C17. – Fragments of C13 WALL PAINTING including, over the chancel arch, the figure of a resurrecting soul, indicating the presence of a Doom. – MONUMENTS. George Maule †1667, rector. Moulded marble frame and achievement. – His wife Mary †1659 and son Charles, less elaborate but with a verse beginning 'Reader, putt of thy shooes, thou treadst on Holy earth, / Where lyes the rarest Phoenix, and Her Onely Birth', and ends 'O let thy Cinders warme that Bed of dust for mee, / (The mournfull Husband) till I come to ly by Thee'. – NE is the PRIMARY SCHOOL, 1889 by *Young*, banded with red brick. Additions by *Stanley Bragg Partnership*, 2000–1.

The centre of post-war Vange is NE along Clay Hill Road.

ST CHAD. By *Humphrys & Hurst*, 1957–8. Brick, with some flint panels. High nave and chancel in one, low N aisle and transept-like organ chamber, W narthex linked by a canopy to the SW campanile, and NE vestries. Full-height strips of windows on the nave S and W walls, the upper parts unfortunately now boarded up. The interior is more appealing: light, with a cheerful painted scheme of blue and white. The blank E wall panelled, the overall design a large cross. Good contemporary FURNISHINGS and fittings, including utilitarian PISCINA. – STAINED GLASS. In baptistery, by *A.A. Burcombe* of Vange. – CHURCH HALL, W, by *R.D.C. Baxter*, 1931–2. Roughcast, undistinguished. – RECTORY, E, by *Wykeham Chancellor & Bragg*, 1958–60. – Nearby, BARDFIELD INFANT AND JUNIOR SCHOOL, with good timber-clad additions by *Stanley Bragg Partnership*, 2004–5.

In REDGRAVE ROAD, houses remarkable only for being the first to be completed in the New Town, in 1951. In THE KNOWLE, to the W, higher-income-group detached houses, developed in the early 1960s by the Corporation for sale. The houses are set informally around a landscaped cul-de-sac loop, connected to Clay Hill Road via Furlongs and Swan Mead. It was a pilot scheme for other housing of a similar type, developed as part of a policy to provide a more socially balanced population.

INDUSTRIAL AREAS

The 1951 Master Plan provided for three industrial areas to the N of the town, with the two main sites, Cranes and Pipps Hill, fronting the A127. The first factory at CRANES opened in 1952, where several early industrial buildings can still be seen, e.g. on the corner of Christopher Martin Road and Honywood Road. PIPPS HILL was laid out in the early 1960s (since redeveloped), the area between them entirely taken up by the Ford Motor Co.'s TRACTOR PLANT, then the largest in Europe, by *E.R. Collister & Associates*. First phase completed 1964; much enlarged (now CNH). An unrelieved block of about 400 by 625 ft (120 by 190 metres). incorporating the town's second major landmark: a huge 600,000-gallon WATER TOWER, a large, slightly squashed sphere balanced with elephantine circus grace on a slender tubular shaft.

SOUTHFIELDS, W of Laindon, was developed later, with HORNSBY SQUARE by the *Development Corporation* (*Clive Plumb* with *G.D. Gentry, D. Brewster, R.V. Wilson*), 1980–1, for small workshops and factory units. Figure-of-eight plan, for offices and public access round the outside, and deliveries on the inside. Similar development at SEAX CENTRE followed. To the N, Ford's DUNTON TECHNICAL CENTRE, the main four-storey building by *T.P. Bennett & Son*, 1966–7. Very long façade, broken down into twenty bays on the ground floor. At GLOUCESTER BUSINESS PARK, on the corner of Upper Mayne and St Nicholas Lane, IFDS HOUSE, a large office building by *Fitzroy Robinson*, 1999. Low-energy, with heavy stone cladding on the S side to add thermal mass, and a lake that provides water for cooling. On the N side, bright blue copper cladding.

BATTLESBRIDGE 7090
Rawreth and Rettendon

The BRIDGE across the Crouch is by *Henry Stock*, built by *William Webster*, 1872–3. Cast-iron centre span with gault brick side arches. The N side is dominated by the old GRANARY: late C19, four storeys, stock brick and black weatherboarding, towering over the BARGE INN, C17 or C18 with white weatherboarding. Among the buildings round the Green to the W, HAYBARN ANTIQUES, C16 with exposed timber framing, and GREAT COOPERS FARMHOUSE, timber-framed and dating to the C17, the latter moved here *c.* 1987 from Coopers End, Takeley. On the S side, a former C18 TIDE MILL, gault brick, three storeys and loft, with a lower red brick range rebuilt 1988, and upstream a former granary and drying kiln, early C19 brick, with pyramidal slate roof and timber cowl.

BEAUCHAMP RODING 5000

ST BOTOLPH. C14 nave and C15 chancel and W tower; flint rubble with some freestone and clunch dressings. The tower is quite tall and has diagonal buttresses and battlements. Soffit of chancel arch grooved to take the tympanum of former rood loft, the stair in a projection on the S side. Chancel roof with a tie-beam on arched braces. The beam rests on arched stone corbels. Restored 1870, when the S porch was added and W window inserted, and again in 1893. – PEWS. At the back of the nave, two rows of three stepped benches, probably C18, with steps that can be pulled out. – STAINED GLASS. *c.* 1850–72, including a two-light window by *Thomas Baillie & Co.*, none of it very good.

OLD RECTORY, School Lane. Timber-framed and plastered. Five-bay late C18 front range with older long back wing, possibly rebuilt following a report on its bad condition in 1618.

LONGBARNS, ¾ m. N. C15 and C17 house with some exposed
timbers. Many gables, one on the NW cross-wing with original
C17 bargeboards. Exterior remodelled c. 1840. To the N a group
of early C19 brick MODEL FARM BUILDINGS incorporating a
C17 timber-framed barn, now residential.

BEAUMONT-CUM-MOZE*

ST LEONARD AND ST MARY. All but rebuilt in 1853–4. Stone
rubble, the chancel rendered. Chancel restored 'under the
superintendence, and mainly at the cost of the incumbent',
W.R. Browell, according to *The Ecclesiologist*; this included
rebuilding the E wall (rebuilt again in 1950 by *E. Robbins Nixey*)
and adding a sacristy. Dec tracery, but on the N side one
window that is conspicuously Neo-Norman, presumably based
on evidence uncovered at the restoration. C14 chancel S
doorway. Nave and N aisle rebuilt by *E.C. Hakewill*, also the S
porch, reusing C15 wall-plates. Odd, diagonally placed bellcote,
the W corner resting on a central buttress. – STAINED GLASS.
Mostly of c. 1854. Nave S window by *Donald B. Taunton (John
Hardman Studios)*, 1961. – MONUMENTS. Samuel Dennis
†1852. Elaborate Gothic tablet with crockets and pinnacles by
M.W. Johnson. Corresponding tomb-chest in churchyard to S
of chancel. – In N aisle, simple Crimean War memorial, 1854–5.

BEAUMONT HALL. A remarkable and characteristic example of
Essex brick architecture of c. 1675, although some of the interior features suggest either that the house was remodelled at
this time, or that timbers were reused from an earlier house.
The core is a square, two-storey block with two shaped gables
on three of the sides. They have top pediments – segmental on
the entrance and garden fronts, triangular on the r. return.
Lower and quite irregular additions to the l and r., all with
gables and segmental pediments. Inside, small staircase with
twisted balusters, some C17 panelling installed in the C20 and
some *in situ* C18 panelling.†

BEAUMONT HOUSE, Chapel Lane. A high-quality double-pile
brick house, c. 1800. Five bays, with a central Doric portico.
Two storeys and a high attic floor with slate mansard. Geometric stair rising through all three storeys. Two ranges of contemporary outhouses: bakehouse and washhouse, coachhouse
and stable, with many original fittings.

BEAUMONT QUAY, ¾ m. SE. Built by Guy's Hospital, 1832, at
the head of an artificial navigation, reusing stone from old
London Bridge. Contemporary brick STORE and a circular
brick LIMEKILN, c. 1869–70, the latter a rare survival.

---

*Beaumont and Moze parishes were united in 1768, when St Mary, Moze, was
dem. Its site is next to Old Moze Hall, 1½ m. NE.
†The FOUNTAIN noted by Pevsner in 1954 was sold c. 1970.

BEELEIGH ABBEY

¾ m. NW of Maldon

Founded about 1180 for Premonstratensian canons, converted into a dwelling after the Dissolution. The fragment which one sees today is the E and SE parts of the buildings adjoining the cloister on the S side of the now vanished church, and chiefly the Chapter House and Calefactory below the Dorter. Their date is the first half of the C13;* the walls include a lot of puddingstone, with Reigate dressings. The CHAPTER HOUSE is naturally more elaborate and elegant than the Calefactory. It has three Purbeck marble piers of octagonal section along its centre line, dividing it into eight bays. The ribs have a deeply undercut filleted roll moulding, the space between them filled with chalk blocks. The second and fourth pairs of bays have their centres distinguished by bosses with stiff-leaf decoration. The entrance is as usual by a double door. The *trumeau* serves as a respond for the row of centre piers. It is semi-octagonal with three detached shafts and decorated with dogtooth. To the l. and r. of the entrance are two-light windows with a quatrefoil above. The only original outside window is a plain lancet.

The Chapter House is separated from the Calefactory by the PARLOUR, a small rectangular room with a barrel-vaulted roof. This has the remains of a medieval painted frieze with foliate scrollwork, and a window with stained glass by *John Hayward*, 1978. The Calefactory is, like the Chapter House, of eight bays with a row of middle supports of Purbeck marble, but these are circular, and the ribs are simply single-chamfered. There is a large fireplace with an elaborate C15 mantelpiece, perhaps made up of fragments of a tomb. In the windows are panels of stained glass of the C15, and further remains of wall painting, including a fine cockerel, possibly C16.

The CALEFACTORY was the undercroft to the DORTER (now the Library), which has an impressive roof made up of collar-beams and arched braces so as to form a wagon-vault of four-centred section. It has been tree-ring dated 1511–39, and was originally ceiled. On the W side of the Dorter was the FRATER, of which the beginning now remains; the roof here has been dated 1513, indicating considerable building activity only a few years before its Dissolution in 1536.† On the exterior this can be seen particularly on the E side, which has brick buttresses and two-light brick windows lighting the Dorter. On the ground floor large three-light C15 windows with one transom and Perp tracery. The r. hand gable corresponds to the Chapter House, the upper part of which was largely rebuilt in 1912–13 when the Abbey was restored by *Basil Ionides*. The l. hand gable corresponds to the Reredorter or lavatories, which in the original state projected from the Dorter.

---

* Reused timbers in the Tudor portion, perhaps from the church, have been tree-ring dated 1199–1214.

† When the monument to Viscount Bourchier, Earl of Essex †1483 was moved to St Mary, Little Easton.

After the Dissolution an addition was made to this narrow block on the w side, timber-framed with narrowly placed exposed uprights and brick nogging. The timbers here have been tree-ring dated to 1624. Of the former Frater range on the s side of the cloister only the E stump stands up with a passage and the site of a staircase. All this was incorporated in the post-Dissolution house, and the corner where this irregular piece meets the timber-framed gabled addition is a picturesque delight. On the w side is more evidence of work by Ionides, a rebuilt brick gable above the Chapter House, and a one-and-a-half-storey extension remodelled by *Purcell Miller Tritton* as part of their restoration of the house, 2001–5.

sw is a brick cottage with pargetting by *F. W. Chancellor*, 1919, partially reusing a brick outbuilding. It stands on the site of a s projection of the cloister's w range, and has medieval foundations. Excavations further w in 2001–4 revealed the foundations of a C15(?) timber-framed house, another C15 building that was perhaps a kitchen or brewhouse, and a Tudor brick clamp. Gardens on the E side of the house, laid out by Chancellor in 1930, with STATUE of the Abbey's founder, Robert Mantell.

MILL, N of the abbey. Remains of a large WATERMILL, rebuilt 1793–7, burnt down in 1875. It was five storeys high, the ground floor and basement of brick, the remainder of wood, and had twelve pairs of grinding stones. Two water-wheel chambers can still be seen, also two docking bays inside the mill for the lighters that would transport flour to Maldon Hythe. Next to it a STEAM MILL, 1845. Two storeys, mainly of stock brick, with semicircular arched recesses and iron windows. Original beam engine by *James Wentworth & Son* and 'Elephant' boiler, with much of the machinery of the five pairs of stones. Former MILL HOUSE to E (now Beeleigh Falls House). Mid-C19 gault brick with a tent-roofed veranda on decorated cast-iron supports.

8040

BELCHAMP OTTEN

St ETHELBERT AND ALL SAINTS. Norman nave; the s doorway has two orders of columns with beaded spiral bands, decorated scalloped capitals, and zigzag ornament in the arch. C13 chancel, largely rebuilt in the C14, when the s porch was added. C19 belfry reusing older timbers, including two C17 posts decorated with guilloche patterns. Early C19 BOX PEWS and tiny NW GALLERY. – FONT. C15, octagonal with quatrefoiled bowl and panelled stem. – PULPIT. Simple, with some blank arcading; *c.* 1600. – COMMUNION RAIL with twisted balusters, *c.* 1700.

8040

BELCHAMP ST PAUL

St ANDREW. The manor was granted in 930 to the Dean and Chapter of St Paul's Cathedral, who ensured that the church was of some consequence. Rebuilt following a visitation in 1458, completed by 1490, of flint rubble with dressings in limestone and clunch. Large w tower, restored by *W. D. Caröe* in 1901–3, with diagonal buttresses, five set-offs and battlements. Chancel with good roof with embattled wall-plates and E window of five lights and panel tracery. Two-bay N arcade, with octagonal piers and double-hollow-chamfered arches, and E of that a third opening with embattled capitals to the responds leading to a former transept, now a continuation of the N aisle; see also the change of the roof, low-pitched at the E end. Further E the N chancel aisle added to form a vestry during restoration by *A. W. Blomfield*, 1870–2. – FONT. Octagonal, with sunk panels decorated by saltire crosses, shields, etc. C15. – CHANCEL STALLS. Seats with misericords decorated by simple flower and leaf motifs. Traceried fronts and ends with poppyheads and good carved seated figures; *c.* 1500. – TOWER SCREEN. By *Terry Daniel*, 1999, with engraved glass panels by *Richard Bawden*. – STAINED GLASS. W window by *Pitman & Cuthbertson*, 1878. – MONUMENTS. Two brasses re-set in the same slab and disarranged, to William Golding †1587 and Elizabeth his wife †1591; figure of a man in armour, 2 ft (61 cm.) long, and smaller groups of children and figure of a woman. Possibly by *Garat Johnson*. – Tablets to various members of the Pemberton family, the earliest 1729, including Rev. Jeremy P. †1811 by *J. Challis* of Braintree (classical), Mrs Ursula P. †1834 by *Charles Harding* of Ballingdon (classical) and Rev. Edward P. †1859 by *Keogh* of Sudbury (Gothic).

PAUL'S HALL. Early C16, timber-framed with some brick nogging. Later C16 brick extension with original chimneystacks and a few original windows, part of what was once a much larger house. The rest seems to have been replaced in the C17 with the present N wing. Of greater interest the aisled sevenbay BARN SW of the house, documented in the archives of St Paul's Cathedral. Although partly rebuilt *c.* 1200, it incorporates a pair of free-standing posts from the original barn built two centuries earlier.

COMMUNITY HOUSE. By *Michael Tapper & J. Anthony Lewis*, 1961, with interiors by *David Hicks*. Similar to Birdbrook (q.v.), but larger, with tall cross-wings containing the village hall and two-storey caretaker's house.

SHEARING PLACE, ¾ m. NW. C18, with an early C19 gault brick façade, the central bay a pronounced bow with curved Tuscan doorcase and fanlight.

TURNERS, Church Street. Commonplace brick front masking remains of an aisled hall, tree-ring dated 1328/9.

BELCHAMP WALTER

8040

ST MARY. Chancel, nave, and w tower, the chancel much lower than the nave and, judging by its (renewed) lancet window, E.E. E wall rebuilt and chancel extended during restoration by Rev. J.M. St Clere Raymond, 1860, the architect perhaps *John*

J. Cole, who rebuilt the chancel arch, 1857–8. The strikingly high and broad nave dates from *c.* 1320, as indicated by the windows with intersected tracery with cusps. C14 S door with an elaborate rear frame unique in Essex and C15 timber S porch with pretty bargeboarding. C15 W tower with diagonal buttresses and battlements, high stair-turret, little bell-turret, and a very tall transomed three-light W window. – FONT. Circular, C12, the bowl damaged along the top. Decoration with beaded scrolls, leaves, etc. – Mosaic REREDOS, 1860. – PULPIT, 1865, and ALTAR, *c.* 1870, decorated with oil panels by *George Washington Brownlow*, who lived in the village. – STAINED GLASS. Various windows erected in the 1850s by J.M. St Clere Raymond to members of his family. Four-light nave N window by *William Wailes* to G.W. Brownlow †1876, celebrating the arts: Jubal holding a harp, David the score for a psalm, St Luke a paintbrush and palette, and St John the text of his gospel. – WALL PAINTING. In nave, an extensive scheme, c. 1325–30, including a very fine Virgin suckling the Child. Also on the N wall two tiers of paintings: on the upper tier scenes from the Passion; below, the Martyrdom of St Edmund, a rare Pelican in its Piety, and other doubtful subjects. On the S wall, a figure in a roundel, possibly St Sebastian, and what appears to be a Resurrection scene of Christ with three women.*

MONUMENTS. In nave, Sir John de Boutetourt †1324 or 1325, extremely ornate. Tomb-chest and effigy missing. A big cusped and sub-cusped arch flanked by thin buttresses, which must once have formed the opening to a structure that projected beyond the N wall: see the brickwork on the outside. Fleurons, leaf-branches, bossy leaves and shields serve to enrich the surfaces. Ogee details in the main arch and the cusping, but rather subdued. – In chancel, signed by *Robert Taylor Sen.* Large, with Roman pilasters, two seated cherubs, and more cherubs' heads. Erected by John Raymond †1720 listing members of his family; the sequence continued on the opposite wall, less grandly but charming in its own way, on a painted metal panel, started by J.M. St Clere Raymond in 1866. – MISCELLANEA. In the nave, a 'Tortoise' stove, and wooden candlebox and holder dated 1673.

BELCHAMP HALL. The estate was purchased by John Raymond in 1611 and the house rebuilt in 1720 by the John Raymond who died that year aged thirty-two. It seems highly likely that *Robert Taylor Sen.*, who was a master mason as well as a statuary (*see* Raymond monument, above), played some part in the new building. The emphasis is on the façade: nine bays and two storeys with giant pilasters at the angles and again two bays from the angles. The centre bay breaks forward slightly and has a pediment and a late C18 stone porch with Doric pilasters and urn finials. Stock brick, delicately shaded yellow and pink, with

76

---

*Pevsner recorded that the interior had been 'rather wildly painted in High Victorian days . . . probably by the same craftsman (or firm) who worked at Foxearth'. This has now been painted over.

pilasters, dressings and aprons of very fine and carefully rubbed Dutch red bricks. In the attic, behind a high parapet, three pedimental dormers, the central one semicircular, and at each end a prominent date, 1790, referring to alterations. Also dated, the canted bay on the s side, 1872, and outbuildings on the w, 1869. A short NW wing added in 1871 was removed by *Donald Insall*, 1966–7, leaving only an archway.

The C19 alterations were carried out by Rev. J.M. St Clere Raymond, who also installed various STAINED GLASS windows in the Hall, some incorporating old fragments, including a sequence of armorial windows on the ground floor recording the Raymond marriages. Two fine rooms on the ground floor, either side of the entrance hall, that on the r. now joined to the one behind it with pink scagliola columns inserted in place of the dividing wall, *c.* 1880. C17 panelling perhaps reused from the old house, parts of which may survive behind the front range. Simple dog-leg staircase, not nearly grand enough for the house.

On the s side of the house, a raised walk with a GARDEN HOUSE at each end, one in ruins, the other a sham ruined tower, with a pointed-arched door and stained-glass windows. ½ m. s of the house, a castellated flint FOLLY built as an eye-catcher, although no longer visible from the Hall, built by J.M. St Clere Raymond. N of the house, C18 STABLES, red brick with blue headers and painted weatherboarding, with lantern and circular windows; now offices. Two GATEWAYS, with massive piers of flint and rubble and incorporating reused carved masonry, those to the stables surmounted by the Raymond crest in painted iron. Similar piers act as boundary markers along the road. w of the house a thatched hexagonal LODGE, knapped flint with gault brick dressings, early to mid C19.

In the village, 1 m. w of the church, various brick and flint estate houses, one dated 1869, and including Rutland Cottage, where the artist G.W. Brownlow lived. At the central crossroads, THE OLD BAKEHOUSE, early C18, has nice early C19 cast-iron railings. In North Road the VILLAGE HALL, built as the school, by *W. R. Firmin*, a local man, 1872: brick with stone dressings and black brick diapers and bands, and prominent hipped gables with deep bargeboards.

MUNT HOUSE, N of the church. Early C18, with some exposed timbers and a later open porch with Doric columns and triglyphed frieze.

ST MARY HALL, 1¾ m. wsw. Late C16 H-plan house, with gabled cross-wings at each end. Late C15 kitchen wing to SE, almost detached, with heavy beams on the ground floor and original truss on the upper floor, consisting of tie-beam on arched braces, crown-post, and two-way struts.

EYSTON HALL, 1 m. NNE. Early C19 gault brick. Pedimented porch with small Tuscan columns *in antis*. Two-storey, five-bay garden front with pilaster strips and string band and central stucco porch with pairs of Tuscan columns.

BERDEN

St Nicholas. Cruciform. Flint rubble with clunch and lime-stone dressings. Norman nave, the only evidence two large blocked windows on the N and S sides close to the W wall. The C15 W tower cuts into them. Next in time comes the N transept with one C13 doorway. The S transept also is C13, but later, as proved by the arch towards the nave. Thin angle shafts and slight single chamfer in the arch. The S transept windows, however, are early C14, and the N transept arch was renewed at the same time. Contemporary with the S transept is the chancel with lancets as well as two-light windows with a cusped circle above. The E end of the chancel and the W wall of the S transept largely rebuilt by *J. Clarke* as part of his sensitive restoration of 1868; the E window is entirely new, but the two-light windows, although renewed externally, are original on the interior and lavishly enriched. They have shafts close to the window surface and stronger shafts in the rear arch. Both have stiff-leaf capitals, and stiff-leaf friezes connect the capitals along the arch jamb. The spandrels between the cusped lights and the circles also have stiff-leaf. All this seems to date the chancel *c.* 1270. S porch 1868. – PULPIT. Later C17, with geo-metrical patterns in the panels. – BRASSES. William Turnor †1473 and two wives (N transept), the figures only 12½ in. (31.5 cm.). – Ann, wife of Thomas Thompson, †1607: figures of a man in civilian dress and a woman, 33 in. (83 cm.), with smaller groups of nine sons and three daughters. In the style of the workshop of *Garat Johnson*, the main figures standing on circular hassocks.

Village Hall. National School by *T. S. Godwin*, 1857, sympa-thetically converted and extended. Simple Neo-Gothic brick with gault brick dressings. The village is small with a few nice houses along the road to Stocking Pelham, notably White House Farm, early C16 with gabled cross-wings, and Martin's Farm, mid C16, with jettied upper storey on curved brackets.

Berden Hall, S of the church.* Brick, with three straight gables to each side; short wings projecting at the back with large window lighting the staircase. Two storeys with attics and cellar. Probably early C16, timber-framed, cased in brick and the jetties underbuilt later the same century. Cross-windows seem to belong to cosmetic alterations in 1655 (date on rain-water heads). Good staircase (c. 1600?) to first floor, 6 ft (1.8 metres) wide, with square open well. The handrail has square openwork termini balusters and strapwork in the interstices.

NE of the house a two-storey brick GRANARY with straight gable, now a house. LODGE dated 1876, brick with white brick dressings, and COTTAGES in similar style along The Street, 1861 and 1864, all with the arms of Christ's

---

*I am grateful to Professor Andor Gomme and Alison Maguire for their analysis of the house.

Hospital, who acquired the Hall in 1860 and were the principal landowners.

BERDEN PRIORY, ½ m. NW. Possibly built in anticipation of Elizabeth I's visit in 1578, on the site of a C12 hospital or priory of Austin Canons.* Two storeys, with attics and cellar, and a short wing running N from the E end of the main S block. The jettied upper storey of the main block appears to have been built as one large room, well lit along the S side by five windows, three of which were originally oriels with small frieze windows on either side. The front door opens into a passage set between the hall and the parlour that leads to a stair-tower at the back, now incorporated into a rear extension. In the farmyard next to the house, a C17 weatherboarded WELL HOUSE, with a large open treadwheel in working order, and a GRANARY of the same date, the remaining building of a range of maltings. Brick farm buildings erected 1870 by Christ's Hospital.

FORTIFIED MOUND, ½ m. SE, known as 'The Crump'. 10 ft (3 metres) high, 123 ft (38 metres) in diameter. The origin is uncertain. A small ringwork about 500 yds to its NW was perhaps an earlier unsuccessful attempt at The Crump.

BERECHURCH

9020

ST MARGARET OF ANTIOCH, Stansted Road. 1968–72 by the *Tooley & Foster Partnership*, largely self-built by the vicar and parishioners. Square, with semicircular sanctuary at the SE corner. Dominant pyramidal copper roof (semicircular over the porch), carried on simple *glulam* portal frames. Triangular shaft over the sanctuary.

ST MICHAEL. Built as a chapel of ease to Holy Trinity, Colchester, a parish church from 1536. Closed in 1975, and partly converted to offices. Brick with stone dressings. Rebuilt *c*. 1500, reusing some C14 material from an earlier building, of which the W tower, with diagonal buttresses and battlements, survives. Nave and chancel all but rebuilt by *Charles Pertwee*, 1872. The AUDLEY CHAPEL (now in the care of the Churches Conservation Trust) has an E window of three lights, depressed pointed with intersected tracery, and much C16 brickwork. Structurally, the most interesting feature is the hammerbeam roof, with decorated purlins and wind-braces, and C17 shields bearing the arms of the Audleys. – Fine collection of MONU-MENTS, of which the most conspicuous is to Sir Henry Audley, erected 1648, during his lifetime. Stiffly reclining, in armour; kneeling figures of five children below. Big reredos background with inscription and segmental pediment. Black-and-white marble. Possibly by *Thomas Stanton*. – Robert Awdeley †1624. Marble tablet with hourglasses and skulls, draped shield and

---

*This entry is based on notes by Adrian Gibson.

Berechurch Hall

cherubs. Possibly by *Gerard Christmas*. – Sir Robert Smyth
†1802, large, grey and white marble, with urn in relief in a classical arch. – Charlotte White †1845, only child and heiress of
Sir G. H. Smyth of Berechurch Hall. By *J. Edwards*, 1848. She
lies on a couch, with two angels hovering near her. – Nicholas
Tomlinson †1847 and his wife Elizabeth †1839. Gothic, pinnacled and crocketed. By *J. Browne*, 1849. – Others include two
by *George Lufkin* of Colchester, *c.* 1835 and 1850.

BERECHURCH HALL. Dem. 1952. *E. C. Lee*'s most important
domestic building, for his uncle the brewer and M.P.
O.E. Coope, 1881–2. It cost over £25,000. The stables survive
(now STABLE HOUSE), brick with half-timbered gables and
central cupola. W of them a square, early C19 Gothick brick
DOVECOTE, now residential.

BERECHURCH DYKE. *See* Colchester.

6000   BERNERS RODING

CHURCH. Small, and derelict. Nave and chancel probably C14,
the walls mainly of flint rubble. Early C16 brick E and chancel
S windows. Nicely moulded wall-plates. S porch with C15 dwarf
brick walls and remains of C15 timberwork. Bay W of porch,
including belfry, dem.

BERNERS HALL. Early C16 with C19 brick front, partly moated.

7000   BICKNACRE
Woodham Ferrers and Bicknacre

BICKNACRE PRIORY. Founded *c.* 1175 by Maurice Fitz Geoffrey
for Augustinian canons, closed 1507. All that now remains is

one tall, lonely arch, consolidated in the C19 and again in 1997. It was the W arch of the crossing and is predominantly mid C13, although it appears to incorporate some C12 work; Reigate and Caen stone ashlar, combined with flint, pudding-stone, septaria, tufa, and bricks and tiles of various ages. Piers with big semicircular shafts. The low respond at the N end is re-set.

BRIDGE HOUSE, Moor Hall Lane, ½ m. N. 1976 by *Robert Hutson* for himself. Narrow frontage of white-painted brick and weatherboarding. Two simple, almost barn-like ranges, connected by a glazed passage bridging a small stream.

BILLERICAY

'A small decayed market town' in 1874 (Kelly's); the arrival of the railway in 1889 did something to reverse the decline. Several good houses testify to the town's former status, but they are mostly overwhelmed by uninspiring C20 replacements.

ST MARY MAGDALEN, at the angle of High Street and Chapel Street. A chapel of ease in the parish of Great Burstead until 1844. A very curious composition of late C15 brick W tower awkwardly fronting a large brick preaching box of c. 1780 with shallow apses to the N and E sides. The tower has set-back buttresses below and chamfered angles above continued in polygonal pinnacles. The battlements between these are stepped (cf. East Horndon), and rest on a trefoil-arched corbel-frieze. W window of two lights with Perp brick tracery. In the spandrels of the W doorway six glazed tiles from Manises, Valencia, of the same date as the tower, so probably built in from the first, but why is not known. The W ends of the aisles in the same style as the tower but of c. 1845, when the plain interior was remodelled with N, W and S galleries on thin cast-iron columns. The altar was originally on the N side, with a single gallery opposite.

CHRIST CHURCH, Perry Street. 1964 by *G. S. Amos* with *Trundle Foulkes & Co.* Functional, in pale brick with high-level windows. Low E tower with a high window that dramatically lights the sanctuary. Rows of small windows of coloured glass on the N wall.

EMMANUEL, Laindon Road. 1991–2 by *MEB Partnership*, partner-in-charge *John Marsh*. Octagonal, with walls of pale brick and thin windows at the angles, and a sort of gabled clerestory with a central lantern and short thin spire. Laminated timber joists support the roof. – STAINED GLASS. Engraved and enamelled panel 1992 by *Jenny Clark*, who also designed the glass CHANDELIER. – Church hall by *Mathews Serjeant Architects*, 2002–3.

ST JOHN, Outwood Common. *See* Perambulation.

HOLY REDEEMER (R.C.), Laindon Road. By *Edward Goldie* (*Goldie, Child & Goldie*), 1913–14, nave extension 1925–6.

Brown and red brick basilica with W narthex and bellcote.
Nave, lower aisles and apse.

UNITED REFORMED CHURCH. 1837–8 by *James Fenton*. Gault
brick, E.E.

MAYFLOWER HALL, Chapel Street. Rendered walls with brick
dressings and the impression of four pilasters supporting the
hipped end of a gableted roof at the front. By *E. Ford
Duncanson*, 1926–7, who also designed the modest SUN-
NYMEDE CHAPEL, Thynne Road, for the Congregational
Union, 1928.

POLICE STATION and POST OFFICE. *See* Perambulation.

MAYFLOWER HIGH SCHOOL, Stock Road. 1965, by the *County
Architect's Dept* (architects in charge, *Jack Sorrell* and *Paul
Markrow*). A good example of the Dept's characteristic style,
the walls mainly clad in coloured glass panels, here an attractive red with cream-coloured frames. Two-storey central block
with hall and gym, and projecting wings with single-storey
workshops and four-storey classroom block.

PERAMBULATION

Just N of the church, at the beginning of CHAPEL STREET, Nos.
3–5 (ST AUBYNS and THE NOOK), originally a single C16–C17
house, No. 3 the gabled and jettied cross-wing with exposed
timbers, No. 5 plastered with C18 sashes and doorcase with
open pediment. A little way down Chapel Street, on the W side,
No. 50 (OLD VICARAGE), Georgian brick with a gault brick
front, three bays with a wide pedimented doorcase on pairs of
pilasters. Adjoining St Aubyns on the N side THE CHEQUERS,
C16 timber-framed and plastered, and Nos. 38–40 HIGH
STREET, late C16 with C18 additions, weatherboarded. Opposite, No. 51 High Street (CRESCENT HOUSE), lying back from
the street, a three-bay, two-storey, Early Georgian house, brick,
rusticated brick quoins, the same quoining used to single out
the centre bay, a pediment over this, and a Tuscan porch. The
outer bays have tripartite sashes. Similar features to be found
on No. 43, fronting an earlier timber-framed building, but here
the outer bays project slightly, there is no pediment, and the
central upper window has a rusticated frame. No. 41 much
simpler, with a chequered brick front. Back on the E side, No.
24 has an early C19 stock brick front of three bays, the ground
floor windows set in round-headed recesses forming an arcade,
with No. 22 on its N side, C18 brick with a Tuscan doorcase
with open pediment and fanlight. A little further N No. 12 is
the gable of a C16 or C17 house with exposed timbers.

NORSEY ROAD then branches off to the NE, with a row of C18
brick cottages on the NW side and weatherboarded ones on the
SE, although Nos. 6–10 are formed from a late C14
in-line hall house of which the internal structure, including
crown-post roof, is largely complete. Beyond the railway, on
the NW side, GREY LADY PLACE, the former workhouse (now
flats), 1839–40 by *Scott & Moffatt*. Attractive (and expensive)

Neo-Elizabethan, brick with black diapers and stock brick and some stone dressings, on a more domestic scale than e.g. Great Dunmow. Three-storey central block with two gables and two-storey canted bays, flanked by two-storey wings and then projecting wings, first two-storey and then single-storey, enclosing a large courtyard. Small entrance lodge. Sympathetic new buildings by *Laing Homes*. About 600yds NNW, in LAKE MEADOWS, 'The Child in the Park' by *John Doubleday*, 2000, crouching bronze figure surrounded by flora and fauna.

Back now to the centre, and opposite the W front of St Mary, The Chantry and Nos. 57–59, an early C16 hall house with two gabled cross-wings, one with exposed timbers. Thought to be the home of Christopher Martin, churchwarden of Great Burstead and Governor of the Mayflower, where the Pilgrim Fathers assembled before embarking for America. On the same side, to the S, brick READING ROOM, 1886, with tile-hanging on the upper storey and a large half-hipped gable with gablet, then Nos. 75–79, formerly the White Lyon, early C16. Further S, No. 91, C16 with two gabled cross-wings, opposite the former town hall, now a restaurant, built 1830 as a market hall and school. Tall four-bay gabled brick front. Across Alma Link, No. 98, a five-bay Georgian brick house, joined on to a slightly later white-brick one, then No. 108, C17 with two gabled cross-wings and coach entrance.

BURGHSTEAD LODGE (Public Library and offices), near the S end on the W side, is the best house of Billericay; rainwater heads dated 1769. It lies back behind wrought-iron gates and railings. Five bays, two-and-a-half storeys, and a doorway with pediment on Tuscan pilasters. No. 146, on the E side, is much smaller, but especially delicate in the details of the doorway. The POST OFFICE (1938, opposite Burghstead Lodge) and POLICE STATION (about the same date, opposite No. 146) are both standard fare, Neo-Georgian of the *Office of Works* and *J. Stuart*, County Architect, respectively, but much politer to their older neighbours than most of what was built in the High Street in the second half of the C20.

Further from the centre, in LAINDON ROAD to the S, former GREAT BURSTEAD BOARD SCHOOLS, 1877–8 by *J. E. K. Cutts* (now arts centre, restaurant and offices). Brick, with black brick bands. Central E-plan schoolhouse set back with longer wings coming to the street front with triple lancets in the end walls.

E of the High Street, along VALLEY ROAD, first the CHANTRY ESTATE by *Paul Mauger & Partners*, c. 1952–3. Stock brick, a variety of semi-detached and terraced houses, with open-sided porches (some flat, some pedimented) on supports intended for training plants. Very generously landscaped. Further E, OUTWOOD COMMON ESTATE, c. 1959–63 by the Walthamstow Borough Architect, *F. G. Southgate*. Some of the earlier houses, along Greenway, Oak Green and Morris Avenue, are highly unusual: rows broken up by panels of vertical weatherboarding and different coloured brick, the roof and eaves line periodically interrupted by sections that start higher but come down to first-floor level, and asymmetric chimneys. Mediocre Community Centre and small square church (St John the Divine, 1967–8) with pyramidal roof.

EARTHWORKS. In Norsey Wood, 1 m. NW of St Mary Magdalen, an Iron Age bank and ditch circuit and two tumuli in which burial urns and Roman tiles have been found.

BIRCH

9010

The ecclesiastical parishes of Great and Little Birch were united in 1816, and before that for civil purposes.

St Peter, Great Birch. 1849–50 by *S. S. Teulon*, at the expense of Charles Gray Round of Birch Hall, on the site of a medieval church. A large church for a small village, with none of the offensive features so favoured by Teulon. Flint with Caen stone dressings. Quite a normal aisled interior, and an exterior ambitious, but not showy. Tall NW tower with stone broach spire, 110 ft (34 metres) high. Dec tracery.* – STAINED GLASS. E window by *Mary Lowndes*, 1908. Nave S and N windows by *Henry Holiday*, made by *Powell & Sons*, 1882 and 1884 respectively. – MONUMENTS. Oliver Simpson Bridges †1857 in the Massacre of Cawnpore. Marble wall monument with sword and other military impedimenta by *S. Manning Sen.*

Birch Castle, s of St Peter. Probably a motte and bailey. Only a short section of rampart and ditch remains.

Birch Hall. By *Hopper*, 1843–8, for C.G. Round, on the site of Little Birch Hall, itself an C18 rebuilding of the old manor house. Dem. 1954. It was a large and dignified Italianate villa, chaste and correct in the motifs. Something of its character can be deduced from the surviving section of the service wing and ancillary buildings: stables behind the house, and lodges to the NE and W, as well as a single-storey cottage on the road to Heckfordbridge, all late classical and stock brick. – In the grounds, St Mary the Virgin, Little Birch, a ruin since the C18. In the nave one can still recognize a plain C13 S doorway, one S window with Roman brick jambs and one much larger N window with one Roman brick jamb. Chancel rebuilt and W tower added in the C14. Rubble walls, the tower's brick upper part rebuilt in the C16 with brick stair-turret. – A number of good mid-C19 farm and other estate buildings, the best of which are Post Office Cottages, a terrace of four on Maldon Road by *Chancellor*, c. 1860. Brick with three large gables, the central one half-timbered. In similar style the Dower House w of St Peter's, originally two cottages.

In the village, opposite the w end of the church, the Primary School, opened 1847, stock brick with Tudor detailing, and

92

---

* *Teulon* also designed the rectory, 1859–60, ½ m. W of the church, destroyed by fire in 1986.

small, separate master's house (now LINDEN HOUSE), also Tudor but with pointed windows and doorway.

GATE HOUSE FARM, Birch Street. Strikingly positioned at the entrance to the village from the S. C16 with jettied cross-wings at each end and a large central porch of *c.* 1866.

BIRCHANGER 5020

ST MARY. Norman nave and E.E. chancel, formerly with a round tower. W bellcote by *G. E. Pritchett*, 1851, who also reroofed the nave. N aisle, with porch and vestry, by *Sir Arthur Blomfield & Sons*, 1898. The interesting thing about the church is the two Norman doorways, W (re-set and no doubt originally N) and S (discovered *c.* 1930). They are similar in decoration, but there is, as usual, a little more emphasis on the S. Abaci decorated with chip-carved saltire crosses, tympana with frieze of saltire crosses at the foot. On the S side in addition foliage scrolls along the extrados of the arch and – a feature unique in Essex although quite common in many other counties – figure carving in the tympanum: a lamb, small and placed oddly at a slight angle. – REREDOS of 1901 with later (?) ALTAR. A splendid piece, with much carved tracery, crocketed pinnacles etc., and painted panels depicting the Evangelists, angels, etc. – BENCHES. At the W end, seven, plain, with buttresses; restored. – STAINED GLASS. E window by *T. Willement*, the centre light 1848, two side lights 1857. – Four lancets by *Pitman & Cuthbertson*, 1877. – MONUMENTS. John Micklethwait †1799 by *Charles Manning*, and two by *Charles Randall*, to E.M. Bingham †1807 and Charles Hippuff †1815: usual draped urns etc. – Lt. J.S. Watney, killed in South Africa 1901. Brass by *A.L. Moore & Co.* with 13-in. (33-cm.) incised figure, an unusually early depiction of an officer in field uniform.

BIRDBROOK 7040

ST AUGUSTINE OF CANTERBURY. Nave and chancel have herringbone masonry in the N walls, indicating Early Norman. Inside the nave one blocked Norman window in the N and one in the S wall. The other windows chiefly C13 lancets belonging to a lengthening of the chancel to the E and the nave to the W. At the E end a group of three with individual hoodmoulds and two blank quatrefoils above and between them. At the W end also three lancets, the middle one placed much higher up. In the C15 an arch was struck across the nave to carry the belfry. Restoration by *Chancellor*, 1880–9, when the S wall of the chancel and S porch were rebuilt, a W gallery removed, and a new open nave roof and chancel arch built. – FONT. Thin octagonal piece with neatly decorated stem and bowl, a Gothick imitation given in 1763 by Thomas Walford of Whitleys. In the E panel a 4-in. (10-cm.) circular medallion with miniature of the Baptism of Christ, said to be by *Samuel Cooper*. – COMMUNION RAIL, with twisted balusters; *c.* 1700. – BAPTISTERY STALLS, formerly choir stalls, incorporating bits of the C15 screen; moved 1969. – PULPIT and LECTERN made for Long Melford (Suffolk) *c.* 1849 and brought here in 1884, as was probably the S clergy stall. N clergy stall made up from fragments in 1961. – The most striking feature of the church is WOODWORK by *H. & K. Mabbitt*, 1960–79, including nave seating, choir stalls (with integral organ console), chancel panelling, altar and other chancel furniture. Elegant and simple, enlivened with various flora and fauna. – SCULPTURE. Corbel head of Sir Winston Churchill on S doorway by *T. B. Huxley-Jones*. – ROYAL ARMS of 1816–37. Cast-iron, by *Coleman & Wallis* of Colchester. – STAINED GLASS. Mostly by *Powell & Sons*: nave S 1948, chancel windows (two signed by *Rupert Moore*) 1961–70, nave N 1966. The latter includes depictions of the church, old school, and Baythorne Hall. Lively Millennium window to W of S door by *Susan McCarthy (Auravisions)*, 2000. – MONUMENTS. Tablet in tower celebrates Martha Blewitt †1681, who had nine husbands, and Robert Hogan, who married his seventh wife in 1739. – John Pyke of Baythorne Park †1738. Sarcophagus. By *J. Pickford & W. Atkinson*. – James Walford †1743, put up *c.* 1790. Draped urn. By *Thomas King* of Bath. – Thomas Walford †1833. Mourning female leaning on urn. By *George Lufkin* of Colchester. – Joseph Cape †1866. Inscription in Perp surround. By *Keogh* of Sudbury.

COMMUNITY HOUSE. 1958 by *Michael Tapper & J. Anthony Lewis*, interior (e.g. light fittings) by *David Hicks*. An unusually lavish (for the C20) philanthropic venture by the Bryces of Moyns Park: hall, reading room, and caretaker's flat, carefully designed to fit into the village scene, with bowling green behind. Walls plastered, roof of Norfolk thatch. Cf. Belchamp St Paul.

A quiet village street. At the N end, beyond the church, BIRD-BROOK HALL, late C16 timber-framed and plastered, extended in the C18 and C19; near it a large aisled barn, weatherboarded, four bays late C14, extended by four bays in the C17. S of the church YEW TREE COTTAGE and the PLOUGH INN sit well together, the cottage thatched with applied Gothick ornament over the windows, both late C18 or early C19. Beyond the Community House, a lodge to Moyns Park (q.v.), and then the OLD SCHOOL HOUSE, 1873 by *F. Whitmore*. Flint with stock brick dressings. On the E side, the OLD RECTORY, rebuilt between 1791 and 1800. Stuccoed brick. Three-bay front with an elaborate, slightly later trellised porch.

At BAYTHORNE END, 1½ m. NE:

BAYTHORNE HALL. One of the earliest known examples of a hall house with contemporary jettied cross-wings. It is of *c.* 1300, about the same date as Tiptofts, Wimbish (q.v.), and perhaps by the same builder. Timbers exposed, with brick nogging on the side elevations. The raised-aisle hall was floored in the C16 and chimneystack inserted; also of that time the elaborately moulded timber ceiling in the solar (NE cross-wing). Original features include twin service doorways and a third doorway with two-centred heads. Octagonal crown-post with moulded cap and base over hall and heavily blackened roof timbers, simpler crown-posts in each cross-wing. Unobtrusive C20 rear additions.

BAYTHORNE PARK. Of seven bays and two storeys with a hipped roof and open cupola. Built in 1668 by George Pyke, whose father had purchased the estate, probably reusing timbers (as well as two overmantels and some panelling) from the previous house that stood near the River Stour. Sashed front and Tuscan porch 1801, the cupola probably renewed at the same time. Late C19 parapet with paired quatrefoils over the windows, which were given floating cornices supported on consoles. Also C19, a single-storey bay on the E front and a simple cast-iron S veranda. C18 W extension, also two storeys but lower; beyond that a stable block and cottages, 1969.

BAYTHORNE MILL, on the River Stour. C18 water mill, extended in the C19 and now a house. The main part brick, two storeys, with two attic storeys including two-storey lucam. C19 steam-engine house with chimney. Late C18 brick road BRIDGE of three round arches and contemporary cast-iron tie-plates.

BLACKMORE

6000

ST LAURENCE. Blackmore possesses one of the most impressive, if not the most impressive, of all English timber towers, built (according to tree-ring dating) in 1400. Outside it has on the ground floor lean-to roofs on three sides over a timber-framed base, the timbers exposed. Then a square part with vertical weatherboarding, then again lean-to roofs, the square bell-stage with horizontal weatherboarding, and finally a shingled splay-foot spire. Internally it has ten posts, the tower itself standing on the centre six. The arched braces for the cross-beams run N–S, between the second and the fourth pairs, while smaller and lower arched braces run E–W. Above these are two tiers of cross-struts. It is a most elaborate piece of carpentry and looks very powerful.

The church itself, mainly flint rubble, is Norman and had aisles from the beginning. The reason is that it was the church of the priory founded for Augustinian canons c. 1152–62. The W wall of the Norman church still exists behind the timber tower, with a doorway of three orders of columns with scalloped capitals. The arch is stepped and not otherwise moulded. Above are two large windows, and above these a circular window. The first bay of the nave on the N and S has a plain pier but colonettes placed in the angles. These also carry scalloped capitals. The arches are wholly unmoulded. A first pair of upper windows can also still be seen. The E parts of the priory church and all the monastic buildings have completely disappeared. There is no indication of a crossing. All that now tells of the monastery are two blocked pointed C13 doorways at the E end of the S aisle. One of them no doubt led into the cloister. The priory was dissolved as early as 1525, so that certain C16 alterations to the church may well be connected with the adjustments necessary when the church became parochial. The N aisle is early C14 (quatrefoil piers with many-moulded arches), but the S aisle clearly C16. The octagonal piers and the arches are of brick, as are the arches and responds to the aisle E chapel (that is the parochial chancel chapel). The half-timbered W end of the S aisle and the C17 dormers on the N, and C19 dormers on the S side, add a touch of irresponsible picturesqueness. Most of the N wall, E of the porch, rebuilt during restoration by *Chancellor*, 1896–1902.

STAINED GLASS. N aisle window by *A.L. Moore*, c. 1901. S aisle window by *Clayton & Bell*, 1914. – MONUMENTS. Brass to a civilian, c. 1420; lower half lost, what remains 10½ in. (27 cm.) high. – Thomas Smyth †1594 and wife. Recumbent plaster effigies, the heads on a rolled-up mat. The tomb-chest with decorated pilasters is not original, and the tomb is not complete. – Joanna Gibson †1746. Tented drapery with putti, scrolls etc.

JERICHO PRIORY, NE of the church. Square brick house, three storeys, on the site of what Morant calls one of Henry VIII's 'houses of pleasure'. Remodelled by Sir Jacob Ackworth, c. 1715–20. The windows and facing bricks of that date but the plan, with four square angle towers, not at all Georgian, cor-responding rather to a few mid-C16 brick houses such as Syon Park and Ince Castle (Cornwall). On the garden front deep plaster coving fills the recess between the tower arches.

Attractive green N of the church, with the most interesting houses along the E side of the street that connects the two. From the church, first LITTLE JERICHO, with projecting two-storey porch, possibly built as a vicarage c. 1600, then the OLD MANOR HOUSE, early C19 gault brick three-bay front at right angles to the street, the end wall brick with pedimented gable. Good wrought-iron gate and railings. Next LONGBEAM COTTAGE, the earliest house in the street, dating from the early C14 but with the front wall rebuilt c. 1600. Five bays with continuous jetty and exposed timbers on the upper storey. Next to it LITTLE JORDAN has a sashed front to Church Street but original early C17 windows on the return front in Bull Alley. Across the alley the BULL INN, originally two houses of the C15 and early C16, with much exposed timber-framing.

BLACKMORE END
Wethersfield

7030

ST MARY THE VIRGIN (Diocesan Furniture Store). 1866 by *C. Buckeridge*. Nave with E bellcote, chancel, and N vestry. Plain brick with minimal stone dressings to the cusped, single-light windows: 'we have not seen a better design for an unpretending cheap church' (*Ecclesiologist*). Bands and voussoirs of black brick inside, the PULPIT and especially the FONT austerely massive, of stone.

VILLAGE HALL. 1925. Neo-Tudor. Given by S.A. Courtauld, and of the quality that one would therefore expect. He also built, N of the Village Hall just off the main street, the terrace of three COTTAGES, 1939, with tile-hung upper storeys. Central two-storey gabled porch, and outer bays breaking forward with little porches in the angles.

OAST HOUSE, ¼ m. W. C18, conical and tiled. Converted to domestic use, the attached cottage rebuilt in the late C20. Another at GAINSFIELD FARM, ½ m. SSE. Unusual in Essex, but this area was noted for the growing of hops.

At LOWER GREEN, ½ m. WNW, LEALANDS FARM, C16 with an C18 cross-wing to the r. To its N, WRIGHT'S FARM, two-bay hall house with parlour and solar bay to the l. and cross-wing to the r. C16, but the wall-plate of the cross-wing has a scarf that suggests a C14 date, probably indicating rebuilding of an earlier structure. A little further N the ROUND HOUSE, in fact octagonal, *c.* 1800, timber-framed and plastered with thatched roof. More good timber-framed cottages at BRICK KILN GREEN, nearly 1 m. WNW of St Mary, including LITTLE THATCH, with exposed timbers, and LITTLEACRES, whose beams with lamb's-tongue stops and a crown-post date the house to *c.* 1570.

BLACK NOTLEY

ST PETER AND ST PAUL. Nave, chancel, and timber W belfry. Flint and pebble rubble, with diagonal brick buttresses to the chancel, one dated 1682. Norman windows and plain doorways. The belfry stands on eight posts forming a nave and aisles. The 'nave' has arched braces, the 'aisles' trellis-strutting in a N–S as well as a W–E direction. Restored by *A.W. Blomfield*, 1878–9, who added the N vestry, rebuilt the S porch, and provided most of the fittings, including the CHANCEL SCREEN, carved by *Polley* of Coggeshall. – DOOR. Some of the ironwork is C12. – Dug-out CHEST. 6 ft (1.8 metres) long, the lid part of the original trunk. – ROYAL ARMS. 1802, painted on canvas. Large and cheerful. – STAINED GLASS. E window designed by *Francis Stephens*, painted by *John Hayward*, 1952. – MONUMENTS. Floor slab in the chancel, partly covered, with Lombardic inscription to Sir Walter de Wydenal, rector 1296–1327. – In churchyard, by S door, John Ray †1706. Flaming obelisk on tall square pedestal.

MEETING ROOM. By *Terry Daniel*, 2002. Flint, with brick plinth and dressings, and half-hipped roof. Window by *Susan McCarthy* (*Auravisions*), reusing bomb-damaged fragments from the church (probably by *Heaton, Butler & Bayne*, 1879).

BLACK NOTLEY HALL forms an attractive backdrop to the church. C15, timber-framed and plastered, with an C18 front.

Behind C18 and C19 farm buildings a remarkably complete barn of *c.* 1400. Five bays, weatherboarded, with crown-post roof.

BLACK NOTLEY LODGE, ½ m. N.* Seems to be of *c.* 1700, but has gables on the side elevations with concave and convex forms entirely in the C17 tradition. Blue and red brick. Three-bay front, originally five, with C19 sashes in place of pairs of segment-headed windows, which can still be seen (mostly blank) on the sides. Rusticated stucco surround to the arched middle window, stucco string course and parapet, the latter with five panels.

RECTORY, ¼ m. NE. Timber-framed, probably C17, altered in the C18. Tall two-storey, three-bay front, rendered, with parapet and half-hipped roof.

STANTON'S FARM, ¾ m. SE. Documented 1305–6, and built shortly before. Two-bay aisled hall and service bay, of which the S aisle has been demolished; inserted floor removed 1970–1. The W end of the hall was lit by an oriel window on the N side, and the timbers of this bay are exposed, but the parlour-solar bay beyond it has gone. The roof truss rests on octagonal piers with moulded capitals, and at the low end are three doorways (rather than the usual two), with two-centred arches and carving in the spandrels. The E bay of the hall is almost filled with a C15 brick fireplace. C17 cross-wing at the E end, incorporating reused timbers, with exposed framing. Shallow C19 extension on the S front, largely obscuring an original external doorway. SE of the house a C17 weatherboarded aisled BARN. Eight bays, with two midstreys.

Of timber-framed houses in BAKER'S LANE, W of the church, CARD'S, *c.* 1500, has a virtually complete three-bay frame, and THE FRIARY, probably C15, a gabled and jettied cross-wing.

BOBBINGWORTH

ST GERMAIN. Unprepossessing exterior. White brick NW tower, 1841, containing the porch, by *Decimus Burton*, and white brick chancel, 1840, presumably also by him. Nave said to have been rebuilt in brick in 1680 and again in 1818, but the stone tracery is of 1902, by *Chancellor*, whose long involvement with the church included considerable internal alterations to the chancel, 1864. This remains an unaltered period piece: Bath stone chancel arch, carved oak stalls, encaustic tiles, timber roof, and STAINED GLASS by *Burlison & Grylls*, a good suite of five windows installed in 1866. Refixed C13 PISCINA in nave S wall, the only visible evidence of the possible age of the building. – FONT. Octagonal bowl with moulded shaft; C15. Replaced in 1770 but reinstated in 1936 after being discovered in Little Parndon churchyard. – PULPIT with attached reader's desk. The pulpit has simple early C17 decoration. – Nave PAN-

---

*Now in Braintree.

ELLING includes late C16 work. – BOX PEWS. 1864, some still labelled 'Blake Hall' and 'Blake Hall Farm'.

MONUMENTS. Many Cure memorials, including a double memorial erected by Capel Cure, *c.* 1805, to his first wife Elizabeth †1773 and his second wife Joanna †1804, by *Henry Rouw*, and to Capel Cure himself †1820 by *Peter Rouw the Younger*. In the churchyard a large chest tomb contains all three. – Capel and Frederica Cure, both †1878, by *G. Sinclair*, classical but with plenty of Renaissance detail that makes it more Victorian. – George and Ione Capel Cure †1943 and 1954, a simple surround to a C16 Istrian marble relief of the Madonna and Child, acquired in Mantua; school of *Tullio Lombardo*. – John Poole †1839, sarcophagus and urn with the serpent symbolizing eternity; by *Joseph Dorman* of Chelmsford. On the nave roof, a good group of painted HATCHMENTS of the Cure and Poole families.

BLAKE HALL. The manor dates back to the C12, but the old house was completely rebuilt by John Clarke after 1709. It was sold to Capel Cure in 1789 and remains in the family. Clarke's seven-bay, two-storey house, with colonnaded porch and central pediment, forms the core of the present building. The young *Basevi* remodelled it in 1822, one of the earliest commissions of his short career, but the extent of his work is not clear. The two bows on the E (garden) front may be his, as well as the N wing. The two rooms on the E front have elaborate and delicate cornices and are separated by a vaulted lobby and passage. But the house achieved its present form in the mid C19, when a third storey was added to the central block and the two-storey S wing built, containing a library and drawing room lit by tall round-headed windows. This wing was gutted in 1940 to form an RAF operations room; it remains unrestored, as a museum. Two beautiful Neo-Greek bookcases, pale oak with giltwood mounts, are now in the main house. The S wall of the C18 entrance hall was taken down and replaced by two Tuscan columns early in the C20 and a fine late C17 staircase installed, said to have come from Schomberg House, Pall Mall, London (*c.* 1698). It has balusters formed partly as slender Tuscan columns and carved tread ends.

N of the house a large BARN, part brick, part weatherboarded, with two half-hipped midstreys, and a date of 1642 on one of the timbers; walled garden of 1792. To the E, the park is separated from the garden by an C18 ha-ha; ice house S of the house. Grounds improved *c.* 1800, the land to the S laid out as parkland with curving drives replacing a straight avenue; associated with *Repton*, but undocumented. At the S entrance, a painted brick LODGE with projecting eaves and ornate bargeboards, dated 1860.

OLD RECTORY. Built by Rev. William Oliver, 1839, a large square three-storey house of gault brick.

NORTH WEALD MOBILISATION CENTRE. *See* North Weald Bassett.

ONGAR PARK. *See* Stanford Rivers.

BOCKING

Bocking adjoins Braintree, and only around the parish church is there any real sense of separate identity. Here Samuel Courtauld and his partner and cousin Peter Taylor acquired the mill in 1819 and developed what was to become the firm's principal factory. Most of Courtauld's buildings between the church and the River Pant have now gone, so that the church once more dominates.

CHURCHES

ST MARY. A large church for a prosperous village. C15, except for the C14 chancel. W tower with decorated base and doorway with decorated spandrels. The buttresses are most unusual: diagonal, but so broad that they have their own little buttresses placed so that it looks at first as if the tower had angle buttresses. Most of the lower stage is faced with ashlar, the rest (and the rest of the church) flint with ashlar dressings. Battle-

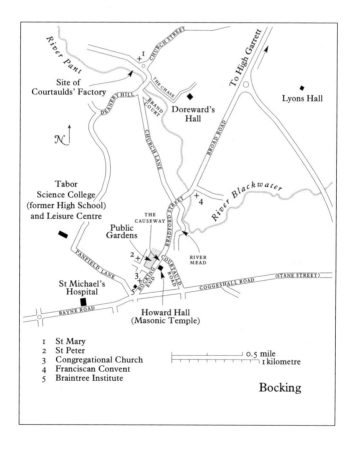

Bocking

1 St Mary
2 St Peter
3 Congregational Church
4 Franciscan Convent
5 Braintree Institute

0.5 mile
1 kilometre

ments and higher stair-turret. Nave and aisles parapeted, E parts embattled. S porch embattled with niches l. and r. of the doorway and two two-light windows on each side. Large three-light windows in aisles and N and S chapels. Wide four-bay nave with piers of the four-shafts-and-four-hollows type, with capitals only to the shafts. Two-light clerestory windows. Chancel chapels with piers of a complicated section with polygonal shafts and wave and hollow mouldings in the diagonals. Good roofs of the late C15 and early C16, all with carved decoration, especially the N aisle. Restoration of the nave roof formed part of work carried out by *F. Chancellor*, 1897, which also included rebuilding the chancel arch.

REREDOS and PANELLING given by S.A. Courtauld, 1913. – ROOD SCREEN. Central portion by *Chancellor & Son*, 1909, who also did the CHOIR STALLS. N portion, rood, and Majestas at W end of nave by *Sir Ninian Comper*, 1950–1; S portion 1955. – DOOR. Four vertical battens and between them rows of six scrolls each; *c.* 1300. – STAINED GLASS. E window 1913, probably by *Clayton & Bell*. Three-light chancel S by *N.W. Lavers*, designed by *Henry Stacy Marks*, 1858, large figures and colours with a deep glow. Two clerestory windows (chancel S) by *George Austin* of Canterbury, 1862. Tower window by *Lavers, Barraud & Westlake*, 1882. S aisle W by *W. G. Taylor*, 1883. – FUNERAL HELM (chancel). Late C16. – MONUMENTS. Brasses to John Doreward †1420 in plate armour and wife, 32-in. (81-cm.) figures (S aisle), and Oswald Fitch †1612, 26-in. (66-cm.) figure in long cloak and ruff (chancel). – Grisell Moore †1624, painted alabaster monument with kneeling figure, a common type. – Anne Nottidge †1799 and Thomas Nottidge †1816, elaborate coloured marble with Neoclassical motifs, both by *George Garrard*. – Joseph Green †1809 by *Peter Rouw the Younger*, white marble with urn and painted arms. – Josias Nottidge †1815 and wife, two urns beneath a weeping willow by *John Bacon Jun.* – Rev. Charles Wakeham †1822 by *Thomas Piper*. – In churchyard, in angle between chancel and S chapel, tomb of the Maysent family, with elaborate wrought-iron railing; early C18.

ST PETER, St Peter's Road. By *J.T. Micklethwaite & Somers Clarke*, 1896–7. Competent and sensitive. Nave and chancel only; side aisles and a SE tower planned but never carried out, as can be seen from the unfinished look of the vestry and organ chamber on the S side of the chancel and the unfinished brickwork on the N side, where there is a free-standing projecting wall that would have been the division between the N aisle and a Lady Chapel. Stock brick with red quoins and plinths, roughcast externally and plastered internally where finished, and a small amount of Casterton stone dressings. – SCREEN. Oak; by *F.W. Chancellor*, 1910, made by *Ernest Beckwith*. – SCULPTURE. Bronze relief of St Peter by *John Doubleday*, 1997. – STAINED GLASS. E window by *Kempe*, 1911. W window by *Leonard Walker*, 1926, making bold use of glass in marbled swirling patterns. – PARSONAGE by Chancellor, 1907–8, unexceptionable Neo-Georgian.

CONGREGATIONAL CHURCH, Bocking End. Originally 1707, which is to say early, but enlarged and considerably altered 1818, with further alterations, mainly internal, by *Charles Pertwee*, 1869. Broad domestic front in gault brick, five bays, with a door at each end and two rows of round-headed windows. Pyramidal slate roof rising to an octagonal lantern. Mid-C18 private burial enclosure behind, with high brick walls and arched entrance.

FRANCISCAN CONVENT (R.C.), Broad Road. Chapel and other conventual buildings added to an existing house by *J.F. Bentley*, 1898–9. Brick with stone dressings, the chapel Early Dec, a fine and original composition. Its w (liturgical E) end, facing the street, is accompanied by a polygonal turret and then a porch which is the public entrance. This leads into a long aisled s transept facing a N altar – a cross-axis, expressed externally at its N end, opposed to the main axis formed by the nave and sanctuary reserved for the nuns. The sanctuary fittings are as one would expect from Bentley, the ALTAR and REREDOS of Hopton Wood stone and Lancashire marble with *opus sectile*. – STAINED GLASS. Over N altar, by *Jones & Willis*, c. 1905. Also on N side, two-light window by *Shrigley & Hunt*. – SCULPTURE. In courtyard behind the chapel, stone bas-relief of St Francis by *Rosamund M.B. Fletcher*, 1953.

PUBLIC BUILDINGS

CAUSEWAY HOUSE, Bocking End. Braintree District Council offices by *Ley Colbeck & Partners*, 1979–81: brick, two storeys, with a third storey in the slate mansard.

Former COUNTY HIGH SCHOOL (council offices), Coggeshall Road. By *Chancellor & Son*, 1906. Subdued Baroque. Behind, the gymnasium (now Register Office), 1929 by *J. Stuart*, in similar style but considerably more lavish: paid for by William Julien Courtauld.

BRAINTREE INSTITUTE, Bocking End. By *Henry Stock*, 1863, as the Braintree and Bocking Literary and Mechanics' Institution, presented to the town by George Courtauld. Neat Italianate, white brick, with Bath stone dressings and discreet black and red brick decoration; altered and enlarged 1922.

HOWARD HALL, The Causeway. Masonic Temple, with first-floor dining hall, by *Sir John Burnet, Tait & Lorne* and *Douglas G. Armstrong*, 1933–4. In the modern style that was just then entering England, and in its emphasis on horizontals obviously under the influence of Dudok and the Dutch style of the 1920s. Its surprising presence is announced by gates with flanking walls of black glazed bricks. Symmetrical white façade with plinth and dressings of black glazed bricks, the side elevations relieved by a base of stock bricks and blue-tiled trim. Metal windows and entrance gates by *Crittall*; Temple furniture designed by *W. F. Crittall*, made by *Ernest Beckwith*.

VILLAGE HALL, Church Street. Given by Samuel Augustine Courtauld, 1926, and unusually large. Brick, with a lot of black carved oak and decorative leadwork in the familiar expensive Courtauld-Tudor style.

TABOR SCIENCE COLLEGE (former High School) and LEISURE CENTRE, Rayne Lane. 1991–2 by the *County Architect's Dept*, enlarged by *W.S. Atkins*, 1998–2000; project architect for both phases *Ian Fraser*. H-plan, plus two large sports halls in shared community use, and caretaker's house. Pale pinkish brick and blockwork with maroon panels and maroon and yellow detailing. Artwork, including external stainless steel sculpture by *David Watkins*, textile hangings by *Sally Freshwater*, and rope sculpture by *Michael Brennand-Wood* in the octagonal stair hall.

ST MICHAEL'S HOSPITAL, Rayne Road. 1836–8 by *W. T. Nash*, and a rare example of a hexagon-plan workhouse with Y-plan main building. Brick. Impressive yet domestic five-bay, three-storey entrance block at the foot of the Y, the central three bays projecting slightly, three storeys with round-headed windows on the ground and first floors, Tuscan porch and fanlight. Buildings in front by *F. Whitmore*, 1895–6.

Former COTTAGE HOSPITAL, No. 60 Broad Road. Tudor Gothic. Converted from cottages by Mrs George Courtauld, 1871, enlarged 1897, now residential.

BRAINTREE AND BOCKING PUBLIC GARDENS, The Causeway. Presented by Sydney Courtauld of Bocking Place, 1888, including keeper's lodge and bandstand; landscaping by *C. H. Bevan*, railings and other ironwork by *F. B. Crittall*. WAR MEMORIAL. (Portland stone obelisk) by *George Drinkwater*, 1926.

BRADFORD BRIDGE, over the River Blackwater. Early C20, with cast-iron dolphin lamp standards by *Macfarlane & Co.*, Glasgow.

PERAMBULATION

St Mary's churchyard is bound on two sides by a distinctive battlemented retaining wall, probably C15. To the s, a small open space with the 'Queen Anne' CHURCH HALL, 1884 by *G. Sherrin* as a workmen's hall and cottage for Samuel Courtauld & Co. (see the weathervane), on one side. Nearer the river JOHN DOREWARD'S ALMSHOUSES, a single-storey row of four, founded 1438, rebuilt 1869, with a further building dated 1924 (clearly a Courtauld benefaction) and extensive refurbishment and additions in 1995 Immediately NW of the church BOCKING HALL, built in at least four phases. The E range is earliest, *c.* 1530, jettied at the s end, with three gables: two are jettied, the central one has a Venetian window. The SW range appears to be a late C16 rebuilding. Three-bay rear wing, late C17, and another C17 extension to its w.

CHURCH STREET runs NNE, none of its older houses of special interest, with workers' housing, notably a row of five semi-detached 'mechanics' cottages' (Nos. 121–139) by *John Birch* for Samuel Courtauld & Co., 1872. Brick with stock brick dressings, decorative bargeboards and ornate glazing bars. At the top of the hill the WINDMILL, a weatherboarded post mill dating to 1721, moved to its present position *c.* 1830 when it received a round brick base. Further E, No. 257, HARRIOTTS, a decorative house of *c.* 1875 that must come from the same stable as the other Courtauld buildings in the neighbourhood.

Back at the river, a lane leads SE to DOREWARD'S HALL, an L-plan, timber-framed house which, for reasons unknown, was provided in 1572 (date-stone) with a brick SE front far too grand for it, perhaps the beginning of an ambitious rebuilding. This front is only one bay wide, with polygonal angle turrets. Between them a three-light one-transom ground-floor window with a steep pediment, a five-light one-transom first-floor window with a broader, lower pediment, and a steep gable with a three-light one-transom window – all very typical of the 1570s.

Once more back to the river and up CHURCH LANE. Just over the bridge, Nos. 190–210 was Bocking's Workhouse: adapted from a C16 or C17 two-storey, T-plan building, with the cross-wing making a pleasant courtyard at the rear. Restored 1988, with two rows of sympathetically detailed brick cottages (BRAND COURT) by *M.P. Brand Ltd.*

A short way uphill to the r., the OLD DEANERY (residential home). The first resident dean was James Calfhill, 1565, who had the existing rectory enlarged or rebuilt; what survives of the original building is uncertain, but the upper room at the northern end of the main building has a crown-post roof and the remains of a wall painting, wide vertical alternating stripes with a delicate floral-stem frieze. The main (E) elevation has four straight gables, the outer bays jettied. The brick S front, with a curvilinear gable, was probably added by Rev. Sir William Dawes, dean from 1698. *Hopper*'s refurbishment of 1835, which included encasing and rendering the exterior and adding a service wing, was mostly unpicked early in the C20. S front extended *c.* 1990, and further in 2001 to create an internal courtyard. SW of the house a square weatherboarded DOVECOTE, mid C17, with 135 nests.

Church Lane now runs SSE for ¾ mile. Half-way along, RESTING SEAT HOUSE, No. 125, probably a C17 or C18 lobby-entry house with a façade remodelled early in the C20, extended *c.* 1959 and converted to flats. Beside it and at right angles to the road, HILL MALTING, C18, timber-framed over a brick ground floor with gambrel roof. Further on, Nos. 35–37, TABOR HOUSE, picturesque early and late C16, with overhang and moulded bressumer, and fine chimneystacks. Malting at the far end of the outbuilding to its l., 1849. Opposite, BOLEYNS, late C18, with two bays and a central Venetian window, but based on a house begun by Joseph Saville in 1625.

BRADFORD STREET winds gently uphill from Bradford Bridge towards Braintree, presenting an almost uninterrupted sequence of good-quality houses, dating back to the early C13,

many refronted in the C17 or C18.* It was on the pilgrim route
to Bury St Edmunds, but it was the woollen cloth trade that
provided the wealth to build. BOCKING MILL, NW of the
bridge, is a highly picturesque agglomeration of white weatherboarding. It consisted originally of a single-storey six-bay
building, probably a fulling mill, constructed largely of softwood, so unlikely to predate the C18. Later adapted as a corn
mill. The Miller's House is a Regency recasting of an older
building, with remains of a C15 timber-framed structure. On
the same side, No. 173, DIAL HOUSE, with a carved date of
1603 that must mark alterations to an earlier structure: jettied
upper storey, partly filled below with two canted bays, and C18
sash windows. Further s, on the e side, RIVER MEAD by
Melville Dunbar & Associates, 1999, follows first the river and
then Bradford Street, mimicking its form and variety. Opposite the end of Church Lane, No. 114, TUDOR HOUSE, *c.* 1520,
jettied with carved bressumer and carriageway at the s end,
built for a Bocking clothier. No. 110 is unusual in the street as
being a new-built house of *c.* 1680–90 rather than a moderni-
zation of an older building. Nos. 106–108 was originally one
large late C16 three-bay house, extensively altered in the C18,
and in the C19 a brewery. No. 98, BADGERS, has pretty C19
bargeboards to the gable and a Gothic casement window.

Opposite, QUEEN'S MEADOW by *H.H. Jewell* for W.J. Courtauld, 1929: exposed brick plinth and dressings, otherwise
rendered, modest but good-quality. Down one side a pathway
through to a housing estate which runs between crinkle-
crankle walls that broaden out in an imaginative and enticing
way. Then come the best houses in Bradford Street all in a row.
First MAYSENT HOUSE, C15 behind an C18 façade of five bays
and two storeys. Pedimented doorcase on attached Roman
columns. Then WENTWORTH HOUSE, three gables, the s end
dating from the second half of the C14 and the two principal
bays mid C16. The big shell-hood over the door is perhaps associated with the rainwater head dated 1679. C18 walled garden
with two-storey summerhouse behind. MATTINGS has an
early C16 carved bressumer along the front and pargetting
above. Then Nos. 77–81 (former WOOLPACK INN), three
gables at different levels and projecting beyond the first-floor
overhang. Carved bressumer on the N bay dated 1590, the s
bay of the same date, but the central bay dated 1667. Across
Woolpack Lane, No. 75 has in its s wall a rare wooden window
frame of *c.* 1300, the arches having curved ogee heads and quatrefoil tracery. Nos. 67, 69 and 71 date from *c.* 1220 and the
size and quality of the timbers used suggest that the upper
floors were used as a wool hall.

Returning to the e side, No. 46 is a complete contrast, flamboyant Victorian Italianate, built as the Cardinal's Hat pub in

*This account relies heavily upon *Discovering Bradford Street* (Friends of Bradford
Street, 1977; undated 2nd edition), which gives a more exhaustive account than is
possible here.

1850. THE ANGEL (No. 36) originally C15 or C16, has a small gabled C16 staircase tower. Opposite, Nos. 43–45, sympathetic infill by *H.H. Jewell* for Mrs C.C. Courtauld, 1928. Further s, on the w side, GEORGIAN HOUSE, *c.* 1720 but with C17 work remaining in the rear wing, five bays and cartway with a doorway of Roman Doric pilasters, a triglyph frieze and a segmental pediment, and BRADFORD HOUSE, also Georgian, seven bays plus cartway, now filled with a shop, with a Venetian window over the arch. No. 11, THE OLD HOUSE, has fine panelling inside and early C17 monochrome wall painting on a ground-floor chimney-breast. Back on the E side, COURTAULD HOUSE, early C18, with five bays, segment-headed windows, and a pedimented doorcase on Roman pilasters.

Bradford Street now becomes THE CAUSEWAY, with Howard Hall (*see* above) on the E side and adjacent to it HIGH CEDARS, a Modern Movement house (flat roof, metal windows) that appears to have strayed from Silver End; perhaps built at the same time, and by the same architects, as the Hall. After St Peter's Road, BOCKING END follows, which is visually wholly part of Braintree and in fact, with its two best houses, leads right into the centre of the town. On the SE side, No. 2, C18, five bays, two storeys, with a doorway with Roman Doric pilasters and triglyph frieze. Then the WHITE HART, strategically placed opposite the end of Rayne Road, which formed the principal approach to the town from the w. Large, with timbers exposed, and although in its present form of the C17 contains timbers that have been tree-ring dated 1375. These appear to be the remains of an aisled hall. C20 pictorial tile panel by *Doulton* in the pediment over the main entrance.

The N side of COGGESHALL ROAD belongs to Bocking. E of the former County High School (*see* above) is the former COUNTY COURT, 1852, in *Charles Reeves*'s Italianate style. Single-storey front with heavily rusticated doorways, two storeys behind. Then what were the grounds of BOCKING PLACE, a large, irregular brick house by *Ernest Flint*, 1889, for Sydney Courtauld, now flats, with an entrance lodge in Courtauld Road. No. 19 is pretty mid-C19 Tudor Revival, and then Nos. 23–29, houses and cottages by *G. Sherrin* for S. Courtauld, 1883–4, with shutters and half-timbered gables. E of Courtauld Road, Nos. 91–101, a row of six Tudor-style brick cottages by *H. H. Jewell* for W. J. Courtauld, 1929, and behind them the RECREATION GROUND, given by Courtauld in 1926: entrance gates and groundsman's cottage by *E. Vincent Harris*, also the long, low sports pavilion with a loggia of eight brick columns and central clock turret.

HIGH GARRETT, 1¼ m. NE, along the Roman Road towards Gosfield, was a Courtauld stronghold, and contains many good estate cottages of the 1870s and 1880s, some with distinctive decorative lattice glazing. At the N end, FOLEY HOUSE, the residence of Samuel Courtauld, rebuilt 1885 for S.A. Courtauld, brick with tile-hanging and false half-timbering and stable block behind. The former SCHOOL was built by

Samuel and Ellen Courtauld in 1850, used also as a chapel ('United Christians') from 1853: brick with burnt headers and stone dressings, N porch with niche, roofed with hexagonal slates, and inside the most extravagantly carved roof, part-hammerbeam. To the S the HARE AND HOUNDS pub, brick front with three canted bays connected by a veranda and a tile-hung upper floor with a carved stone panel as the inn sign, remodelled by *Ernest Flint*, 1884.

FENNES, 1¼ m. N. Early C16 farmhouse extended in the late C18 and given an elegant entrance front in gault brick *c.* 1840: three bays, pilasters, tall sash windows, central pedimented break-forward with decorative frieze and a stucco Doric porch distyle *in antis*. In the garden a rustic Gothick SHELL HOUSE, early C19, flint with shell-encrusted interior, thatched, and sadly dilapidated; GARDEN HOUSE and LODGE of about the same date.

LYONS HALL, 1¼ m. ESE. Mainly timber-framed and roughcast, *c.* 1600; two storeys with gabled attics. Apart from some moulded and carved bargeboards and bressumers, extensively remodelled by *P. V. Mauger, c.* 1947, who removed outbuildings at the N end and a C18 wing; work by *Ronald Geary Associates, c.* 1990, included the addition of a ground-floor bay on the garden front. Elaborate C19 brick chimneystacks, probably by the same hand as those in Stisted village (q.v.). Inside, square newel post original to the house with panelled sides and a Composite capital beneath an abacus carved with animals.

EARTHWORK. Mill Hill, 1½ m. NNE. Low motte, about 110 ft (34 metres) in diameter, with moat.

BOREHAM   7000

ST ANDREW. The appearance from the street is most curious – more curious than beautiful. *Chancellor* worked on the church between 1868 and 1912 and resisted the temptation to smooth over the complexities of the building's irregular plan. Leading up to the S porch, a covered walk first erected *c.* 1843, rebuilt 1924 by *A. Y. Nutt*. The porch itself timber, with six arched openings on the W and E sides, but the W side blocked by the addition of a vestry, *c.* 1900, and the front faced in C19 white brick. The church has nave and aisles, the S aisle first narrow, and then, E of the porch, wider. This part refaced in bands of brick and flint, 1909. Then, set well back, is the sheer wall of the central tower. This seems to have started as the chancel of a Saxon church, the walls thickened and heightened by the Normans. It has a staircase in the thickness of the wall which projects into the interior, Norman windows on the ground floor to the N and S, and above them two-light windows with a middle shaft with block capitals. The bell-openings are similar but pointed. Tudor brick battlements, and low pyramidal roof. The chancel, as narrow as the tower, widens on the S into the Sussex Chapel, added in the late C16 but rebuilt, at half its original length and transept-wise, in 1860. On the N side of the chancel, looking like a porch, the Tyrell vault of *c.* 1804, rebuilt externally 1895.

Inside, the tower has a complete, very plain, E arch. Above the C14 W arch, which is off-centre to allow for the staircase behind it, can be seen the Roman brick voussoirs of the Saxon chancel arch. The nave and the narrower part of the S aisle are C13: see the W lancet of the S aisle, and the square chamfered arcade piers (also of the N arcade) and pointed, only slightly chamfered arches, no doubt cut out of the solid Norman nave walls. That nave may have been wider, for partly revealed in the E wall of the N aisle, in line with the arcade, is a Roman brick arch, which probably held a side altar. The S aisle has in its wider parts early C14 windows of two cusped lights with a cinquefoil in a circle above. The chancel is contemporary, as shown by the cusped lancets on the N and S. The N aisle windows are C15, large and plain, with panel tracery – three lights on the N, five lights on the W side. A five-light Perp window also at the nave's W end.

FONT. Early C14, hexagonal, no distinction of stem and bowl, each side with a gabled blank cusped arch filled with C19 glazed tiles. – LECTERN. By *Col. W. N. Tufnell* (cf. Ford End), with carved figures of the Evangelists. – SCREENS. Under the E tower arch and at the W end of the N aisle, both made up of fragments, the former moved to its present position in 1904. – STAINED GLASS. W window by *Lavers, Barraud & Westlake*, N aisle by *Ward & Hughes*, 1878, as are probably the two chancel N windows, †1858 and 1878. – MONUMENTS. In the Sussex Chapel, the first three Earls of Sussex †1542, 1567, and 1583. The work of *Richard Stevens* of Southwark, 1587–9, commissioned in accordance with the will of Thomas Radcliffe, 3rd Earl, who had been granted the manor of New Hall in 1573; it cost £266 13s. 4d. Alabaster. All three recumbent on one tomb-chest. – Alse Byng †1573. Brass. Female figure (13½ in.; 34 cm.) with group of one son and five daughters. Palimpsest, the reverse mid C15. – A large number of standard wall monuments, including four signed by *J. Ternouth*: Sarah, Lady Tyrell †1825, C.F. Bond †1829, Ann Rishton Ray †1831, and Arabella Carpenter Dowell †1841, the last attractively Gothick. – Anna Maria †1862 and her husband J. R. Spencer Phillips †1874 of Riffhams, Danbury (q.v.). Simple Classical, by *T. Gaffin.* – WAR MEMORIAL (nave S wall) by *A. Y. Nutt*, 1919–20.*

VILLAGE HALL, Main Road. By *Inkpen Downie*, 1993. Stock brick, breezeblocks and pantiles.

Boreham is a little too close to Chelmsford for comfort, but Church Road retains a villagey feel, with a small group of good timber-framed houses. Of these BOREHAM LODGE was refronted in brick with pilasters in the C18, but the OLD RECTORY, opposite, retains its late C15 jettied cross-wings with

---

*The Waltham Mausoleum of 1764 in the churchyard, based on the Tower of the Winds, was pulled down in 1944.

exposed timbers. E of the church, BOREHAM MANOR is C18 with open-pedimented doorcase and tall gabled W and S fronts. N of the church, on the old main road, CLOCKHOUSE, C16 or C17 with exposed timber framing and one jettied cross-wing, and the COCK INN, C17, timber-framed with a later brick front of three straight gables.

BOREHAM HOUSE, ½ m. SW. Built 1726–33 by Benjamin Hoare, a younger son of the banker, as the culmination of several purchases in Essex which included New Hall (*see* below). *Edward Shepherd* supervised the construction, and was in all likelihood responsible for the design; the mason was *Anthony Goud* of Springfield. It is ambitious, though not large. Brick, with stucco dressings. Only seven bays wide and two storeys high, the central three bays breaking forward with a pediment, with wings, originally carrying lanterns, and a straight pond or canal in front. Sir John Tyrell bought the house in 1796 and had alterations made by *John Johnson*, 1802–3, and in 1827–9 by *Thomas Hopper*, who altered the wings and created grand arched carriageways on the l. and r. with displays of coupled columns. Later C19 four-column Tuscan porte cochère. According to Morant, the house was 'adorned with fine marbles, and other valuable materials from New Hall'. There are two rooms of surprising splendour, the Entrance Hall and the Dining Room. They have pedimented doors, and in the Dining Room a fireplace on muscular terms, a kind of reredos of Venetian window shape with Victories lying on the arch, and superbly carved details. The date is clearly *c.* 1730. The staircase, lying immediately to the l. of the Entrance Hall, has a heavy cast-iron railing, belonging to *Hopper*'s alterations.

80

Hoare provided the house with a park, from the New Hall estate, with a walled kitchen garden SW of the house. His son Richard commissioned *Richard Woods* to lay out gardens SE of the house in the 1770s, the principal survivor of which is the lake, widened in the early C20.

NEW HALL
(School and former Convent of the Holy Sepulchre)

New Hall, one of the six manors of Boreham, was granted in 1062 to the Canons of Waltham Abbey and became the property of the Crown in 1450. The Earl of Ormond, who was licensed to fortify and crenellate in 1491, probably built the Tudor house of which traces can still be seen. It passed by inheritance to Thomas Boleyn, father of Anne, who sold to Henry VIII in 1516. *William Bolton* transformed the manor into a large quadrangular mansion, called Beaulieu, with gatehouse in the S range, the great hall in the E range, and chapel in the W range. Thomas Radcliffe, 3rd Earl of Sussex, was granted the house in 1573 and gave the N range its most distinctive architectural feature, the S façade with its canted bay windows. Further improvements were carried out after 1622 by George Villiers, Duke of Buckingham, but following confiscation during the Commonwealth, New Hall was granted

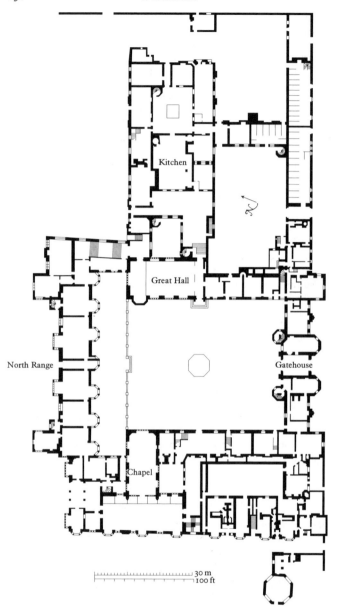

New Hall, Boreham.
Plan of the house between *c.* 1573 and 1738

New Hall, Boreham. South range of Henry VIII's mansion.
Engraving, 1786

to George Monck, 1st Duke of Albemarle. The widow of the 2nd
Duke married the Duke of Montagu, from whose son Benjamin
Hoare got possession in 1730. By then he was well advanced on
building Boreham House (*see* above) and sold New Hall in 1738
to John Olmius, 1st Lord Waltham, for £11,367. Olmius' creation
of a 'genteel residence' saw all but the quadrangle's N side demolished* and major remodelling of this range's interior. He used an
architect of some distinction, possibly *Henry Flitcroft*, who had
worked as surveyor for both Montagu and Hoare. The 2nd Lord
Waltham further improved the house before the Canonesses of
the Holy Sepulchre from Liège purchased the house in 1798.
They have adapted and extended the building up to the present
for community and school purposes, including much rebuilding
following severe bomb damage in 1943.

Approaching from the s by the long avenue, noted by John Evelyn
in 1656, one sees first the splendid s façade, remodelled by the   60
Earl of Sussex after 1573 (the l. portion rebuilt 1948): brick,
with stone dressings, with seven symmetrical bay windows, the
middle one containing the entrance with Roman Doric
columns and a frieze with Sussex emblems in the metopes.
Over the door, Elizabeth I's arms and glowing Latin tribute to
her. The façade is crowned by a parapet punctuated by short
piers with ball finials, probably added by George Monck; in
the parapet of the central bay a stone sundial with segmental
pediment and the date 1660. The front's end bays are squashed
uncomfortably into the corners against the short two-bay
return wings. These are in the same style, tidied up by Lord
Waltham in 1738 after demolition of the courtyard, the w wing

---

*The E window of the chapel went first to Copped Hall (q.v.) and is now at St
Margaret, Westminster. According to Morant, the Great Hall was 'translated' to
Witham as an assembly room for the spa established there in 1736.

given a canted bay to match the rest. Then comes the entrance
to the school block (1869–70) which has a two-bay w façade:
materials in keeping, less so its style, but filling its sw corner
another perfectly matching canted bay of 1923–5. A fine carved
stone dragon *passant* near this corner no doubt adorned some
part of Henry VIII's mansion. The e wing, with clock tower
and cupola added by the Canonesses, is continued by a two-
storey block for nuns' cells, built 1799–1800. It turns e and
forms the s side of the stableyard, largely built up by John
Olmius of reused Tudor bricks, still visible on the e range. Its
central archway reuses stonework from the main gateway to
Henry's mansion. On the w side of the yard are three Tudor
windows lighting the cellar. ne corner rebuilt 1952.

The much-altered n front preserves only two 1570s square
bays, the space between infilled and flanked by c18 shallow
canted staircase bays. On the l., projecting n, the single-storey
school refectory by *Chancellor*, 1872, and in the middle of the
n façade the convent refectory, a half-hexagon, by *Roff Marsh*,
1962–3, not sympathetic. On the r., major additions of 1923–5,
including gymnasium and theatre, probably by *Chancellor &
Son*. The courtyard is completed on the n and e by school
houses, 1968–9 by *Edward D. Mills & Partners*: three storeys,
with covered walk.

From the house's nw corner another schoolhouse, Campions, projects to the w; by *Roff Marsh*, 1962–3, extended by
K. A. Mitchell, 1983. To the s of this, Mores, by *Edward D. Mills
& Partners*, 1969–70, is the best of the additions, its façade of
alternating bays of brick and glass reading well as an extension
of the main s façade.

INTERIOR. The main entrance led into the double-height GREAT
HALL (now Chapel) created in 1738. On the n wall, set in a
frame of military trophies, the magnificent large coat of arms
of Henry VIII that formerly stood over the main gateway. It is
of stone, painted and gilded, as good as (and very similar to)
the carvings of Christ's and St John's College gateways and
King's College Chapel at Cambridge. The ceiling plasterwork
is of 1738, but with some of its more secular symbols, e.g.
Olmius' 'Black Boy' emblem, replaced by sacred ones. w
gallery *c.* 1800. The e end, with giant Corinthian columns
framing the altar, is probably part of alterations to the chapel
by *J.J. Scoles*, *c.* 1844.

n of the Great Hall, c18 additions to improve circulation,
including two staircases with a landing supported on slender
columns probably added by the 2nd Lord Waltham. e of the
chapel, in what would have been the ne corner of the former
quadrangle, are the earliest parts of the building. On the
ground floor, two Tudor doorways, and in the cellars two
ranges of octagonal brick piers and arches. A room on the
ground floor of the e wing contains two octagonal oak posts;
in the adjacent room more exposed woodwork and a single
baluster, apparently relics of the great staircase built for the
Duke of Buckingham, probably by *Inigo Jones*, 1622–3 (and

described by Evelyn as being 'of an extraordinarie widenesse'). Also in these rooms, but too out of place to be *in situ*, two fine chimneypieces in the manner of Batty Langley.

On the first floor, the room at the E end of the main front has late C17 panelling but the ceiling of its bay is decorated with late C16 plasterwork: the only surviving fragment of the Earl of Sussex's interior decoration. On the first floor of the E wing, the most remarkable room of all, John Olmius' bedroom, *c.* 1738, with plasterwork of the highest standard, and almost filled by the canopy of the bed, supported on two square Ionic columns with pilasters against the wall. Its entablature continues the frieze that runs round the room. Chimneypiece with shell decoration against the S wall, profile heads either side of the window in the W wall, and framed panels with swags of fruit and foliage, vases of flowers, etc. W of the chapel, the C18 Gothick interiors were mostly destroyed in 1943, but in the Library some doorcases and also a marble chimneypiece by *Henry Cheere* after a published design by *Batty Langley*, with a bucolic carving of a lovelorn shepherd.

Other buildings: RADCLIFFE WING (classrooms) by *K. A. Mitchell*, 1983. Single storey, terminating in an octagon with tall crown-like copper-covered roof.* – BEAULIEU, three-storey E-plan block by *Edward D. Mills & Partners*, 1966–7. – WALKFARES (classrooms), 1990–1 by *Barnsley Hewett & Mallinson*. Low brick walls and long tiled roof with almost continuous glazing in between. – E of the house a brick BARN, C18 but reusing Tudor bricks, restored in 1986 for use as the Diocesan Pastoral Centre.

Of the historic LANDSCAPE, the principal survivors (in addition to the avenue) are the Cedar Plot, W of the Hall, with trees planted by Olmius, and to the SW, S of a walled kitchen garden, the Wilderness, mentioned by Evelyn in 1656 and probably early C17 (*John Tradescant the Elder* was employed to supervise work on the grounds after 1622). On the W side of this the nuns' burial ground, with C19 brick walls and arched gateway. The 2nd Lord Waltham employed *Richard Woods* to make alterations to the gardens, *c.* 1767–8 and 1775–7, including the formation of a large pond on the N side, of which only a ditch remains.

BORLEY

8040

CHURCH. A topiary walk to the C15 brick porch is the most notable external feature. The nave, mostly rendered, may be C11: see the long-and-short work of the SW quoin. Chancel and W tower Late Perp, the tower with thin diagonal buttresses and stepped battlements. – STAINED GLASS. E window †1861, probably by *Hardman*; the chancel N and S windows go with

---

*Broadly following a proposed scheme by *Edward D. Mills & Partners*, *c.* 1970.

it. Nave s window †1892 by *E.R. Suffling*. – MONUMENTS. Sir
Edward and Frances Waldegrave †1561 and 1599. Tomb-chest
with recumbent effigies under a six-poster, and profiles of two
sons and three daughters. Clunch, painted in imitation of
marble. The columns have shaft-rings. Straight top with big
achievement. Waldegrave died while incarcerated in the Tower
of London (with his family and household) for saying mass at
Borley Hall. – Magdala Southcote née Waldegrave †1598, with
big kneeling figure, painted; not good. – Black marble floor
slab to Humphrey Burroughs †1757, rector of Borley and
Gainsborough's uncle.

BOWERS GIFFORD

7080

ST MARGARET. Quite on its own – apart, that is, from the railway
line to Southend. Its charm lies in the huge diagonal buttress
propping the small C14 w tower at the sw corner only, and the
tower's asymmetrically placed w windows. The tower top and
splay-foot spire shingled. Inside, this wooden upper part,
added in the C16, rests on unbraced posts with trellis-strutting.
Nave and chancel rebuilt in 1829, by *T. W. & C. Atkinson*, but
retaining some of the earlier fabric, which is mainly of coursed
ashlar. Further restorations in 1867–70 by *J. Peacock*, and 1910.
N nave vestry, 1923, and N chancel organ chamber, 1930, by
Sir Charles Nicholson, s porch rebuilt 1937. – CHANCEL
SCREEN and CHOIR STALLS by *Nicholson*, 1926. Seven narrow
lights with cusped heads, the central three forming the opening
and in the middle light a small, two-dimensional painted rood
group. – PEWS 1929–31. – PULPIT. Hexagonal, brought here
from Harrow School chapel in 1924; probably by *Sir Gilbert
Scott*, 1857. – FONT. Octagonal, early C16, with C17 pyramid
COVER. – STAINED GLASS. Good E window by *Lavers, Barraud
& Westlake*, 1868. Tower window by *C. Annys-Dhont* of Bruges,
1932. – BRASS. Figure of a knight, probably Sir John Gifford
†1348. The head not preserved, and what remains is 56½ in.
(143 cm.) tall. Shield with lovely fleur-de-lis and trail pattern.
Legs not crossed.
Former SCHOOL, London Road. 1846, enlarged by *George Wood*,
1892. Brick with gault brick dressings. Schoolroom to the l.
with high pointed window, entrance porch with bellcote in the
middle, and teacher's house to the r. with hoodmoulded
windows and cast-iron latticed casements.

BOXTED

9030

ST PETER. Norman w tower chiefly of puddingstone with generous use of mortar. Several exposed or blocked contemporary
windows. Completed early in the C16 in brick, with diagonal
buttresses, renewed top parts and battlements. The walls of the
rest of the church are a similar mix and the whole in its variety

of textures happens to look extremely lovely. Chancel with N
and S Perp windows. The rest much pulled about in the C17
and C18. Two dormer windows on the S side, one in the nave,
one (dated 1604) in the S aisle. Inside, more Norman evidence:
blocked windows in the nave (N side) above the rawly cut-
through arcade. The S arcade similar, but the arches higher.
Both probably C14, with an equally crude and irregular
clerestory. Chancel arch on plain imposts with one roll moulding. Above it, and on the W side, the Norman roof-line is
visible. Above this, two quaint little C14 E windows. W gallery
on cast-iron columns, 1836, by *Joseph Salmon* of Beaumont.
Restoration by *A. W. Blomfield*, 1870, including re-seating, but
not his proposed rebuilding of the arcades. Nave roof with
three crown-posts on tie-beams, chancel roof boarded with
painted decoration by *Howell & Bellion*, 1999: stars on a blue
ground, including the Hale-Bopp comet of 1998 and a total
eclipse of the sun in 1999. – REREDOS. 1924, by *W. H.R.
Blacking*, with panels painted by *Christopher Webb* and further
painted decoration by *W. Cales*. – PULPIT. 1882. Stone, including a sculpted group by *F. J. Williamson* of a mother and her
four children. – STAINED GLASS. E window by *Clayton & Bell*,
c. 1867. – MONUMENTS. Elizabeth, wife of Nathaniel Bacon
†1628, marble panel with an angel and a skeleton, probably
not in the original context. – Sir Richard Blackmore †1729,
without figures. – In churchyard, MAUSOLEUM of Arthur
Sidney Vesey †1890. Gothic, old-fashioned for its date, with
little marble columns to the W doorway and low trefoiled
arches along both sides. – Three good headstones S of the
chancel, 1714, 1720, and 1740.

METHODIST CHAPEL, Chapel Road. 1832. Brick, with round-
headed windows. Later C19 two-storey porch with pointed
windows.

BOXTED HALL, W of the church. Timber-framed, the plastered
N side looking early C19, the brick S side looking Georgian. Of
uncertain date, the oldest part perhaps rebuilt in the mid C15
but following a layout documented in 1325. W wing *c.* 1700. E
and W cross-wings extended S, 1922 and 1929–30, by *H.H.
Jewell*, who also built the racquets court E of the house. S end
of W cross-wing remodelled by *Miles Park* in the 1970s, including dreadful picture windows. Good BARNS and other farm
buildings N and E of the Hall, converted to residential use by
Plater Claiborne c. 2003–5.

E of the church a cluster of houses, the general appearance early
C19, including BOXTED HOUSE, *c.* 1815, gault brick front of
two storeys and three bays behind a smart entrance with cast-
iron gatepiers and railings, and the former VICARAGE, also
gault brick, 1836, extended by *Chancellor* in 1875.

BOXTED LODGE, Straight Road, ¾ m. S. Late C18, but with a
new E-facing front added in the C19, raised from two storeys
to three in 1888. Painted brick, four bays, with Tuscan portico.
Behind, mid-C19 red brick stables with water tower and cottage
added by *Erith* in the 1960s. Single-storey C19 LODGE.

CHESHUNTS, nearly ½ m. ENE. Late C17 or early C18 W range, probably timber-framed. Very smart early C19 E-facing two-storey range: gault brick, three bays of tripartite windows set in shallow segmental-arched recesses, and doorcase with Ionic columns.

CLIVES, ¼ m. NE. 1903 by *Nevinson & Newton*. Heavy-handed Queen Anne.

RIVERS HALL, ¾ m. E. Pretty L-plan house, on a partly moated site. Probably C16, but with pargetting that includes the date 1715 and fragments of a vine trail that originally extended all round the house at first-floor level. Two early C19 canted bays on the S front.

At Boxted Cross, ¾ m. SE, SONGERS, Cage Lane, the oldest known house in the county below manorial status, a two-bay open hall with a storied bay at one end. Extensive use of open notched lap-joints indicates a date in the first half of the C13. Extended E by two bays, probably in the C14, and floored in the late C16.

BRADFIELD

ST LAWRENCE. The nave and chancel are C13, and cemented. The W tower is C12 in origin, and out of alignment to the nave; it was added to the nave as it then existed, indicating an earlier building on the site. Most of the tower is a C15 rebuild, with the upper part (of brick) added early in the C18. In 1840 *Hopper* added the transepts and S vestry and restored the C14 S porch. Chancel alterations by Rev. L.G. Hayne, *c.* 1875, who rebuilt and enlarged the vestry, but the extent of this work is not clear following restoration by *Laurence King*, 1957–8.* – DOUBLE PISCINA on N side of chancel, C13 with dogtooth decoration, probably placed here by Hayne. – FONT. Octagonal, of Purbeck marble, C13, with two shallow blank pointed arches on each side of the bowl. – PULPIT. C18, with earlier panels of the C16 and C17, one being a relief of the Crucifixion. – STAINED GLASS. A very striking collection: three in N transept †1914 and 1917 by *Hardman*, one in S transept by *Morris & Co.*, 1919, and on the N side of the nave, two by *Rosemary Rutherford*, 1960. Weakest is the E window to Rev. Hayne †1883. – MONUMENTS. Brass to Joane Rysbye †1598, the figure nearly 3 ft (87 cm.), standing on a circular hassock after the style of the workshop of *Garat Johnson*. – Elizabeth Agassiz, by *Chantrey*, undated, with kneeling, mourning female figure. – Plainer tablets to William Thompson †1851 and Lewis Agassiz †1886 by *Henry Lufkin* of Colchester. – Capt. Frederick Carter †1854 following service in the Crimea. Gothic detailing with sword and shako, by *H.P. Peyman*. – WAR MEMORIAL by *Powell & Sons*, 1919. With *opus sectile* figure of St George.

METHODIST CHURCH. 1850. With pretty timber W belfry on brackets over deep eaves.

---

* Faculty granted in 2005 for extension on N side of tower by *G. Vale*.

BRADFIELD PLACE. Built as the vicarage, probably by Rev. Charles Umfreville †1774; separated from the churchyard by a crinkle-crankle wall.

BRADFIELD HALL. Dem. c. 1955. Between the site and Steam Mill Road, a mid-C19 brick building with round-arched windows, presumably the eponymous mill.

JACQUES HALL (special school), ⅔ m. ENE. Rebuilt probably in the 1870s, with a roof-line of Dutch gables. Mainly two storeys, with a taller water tower. Terracotta decoration, notably on the two-storey porch, which has garlanded columns, bucranium frieze, and sunflowers in panels. Extended by *Plater Inkpen Downie*, 1990. BARN to S (chequered brick and weather-boarding) adapted and extended as technology block by *Inkpen Downie*, 1995. Gabled LODGE.

BRADWELL

HOLY TRINITY. A small church, nave and chancel only, but of outstanding interest because its fabric remains essentially in its medieval state, with only minor restoration in 1905. Further partial restoration in the early 1950s enabled detailed examination of the structure. It belongs to the second quarter of the C12: see one window high up on the W side, one S window, the S doorway, the N windows and the N doorway, and parts of two E windows. The walls, of flint rubble, puddingstone, Roman brick, and other material, retain their original configuration of putlog holes, some with integral caps of medieval brick but more with thin oak caps, apparently a unique survival. This makes it possible to reconstruct the original scaffolding scheme. Analysis suggests construction took about five years, and that the church was fully plastered externally and, probably, limewashed and painted to simulate ashlar. Of still greater interest are the quoins and dressings of the doorways and windows, previously assumed to be of Roman brick, but now shown to be C12, and therefore extremely early – perhaps the earliest known post-Conquest bricks in the country. There may be a connection with the production of bricks at nearby Coggeshall Abbey, although Coggeshall bricks are not thought to have been produced until c. 1160. The roof was raised by about three feet in the early C14, when Dec windows were introduced (the sills raised in the C18, presumably when high pews were introduced); E and W and NW chancel windows Perp. C14 timber S porch ; the ogee tops of the side openings survive, but below them are C17 balusters, quite a pretty effect. The timber belfry in its present form probably dates from the C14, a rebuilding of an earlier free-standing structure that stood outside the W end.

The WALL PAINTINGS make Bradwell one of the essential churches to visit in Essex. Those of the C14 in particular are aesthetically of the highest quality, not at all rustic, like so much English church fresco-work. The most easily recognizable are in the nave, in the splays of a S window (Doubting

Thomas and St James the Great, with the Agnus Dei on the soffit) and in a N window (Throne of Mercy Trinity, i.e. God the Father enthroned, holding Christ crucified, and the Holy Spirit in the form of a dove; opposite, Noli me Tangere, with a Doom on the soffit). On the N wall near the W end a small head, undoubtedly that of a Christ Child originally carried by St Christopher. In the chancel, on the splays and soffit of one of the blocked Norman E windows, C13 architectural decoration, with masonry lines etc. C15 remains on the E wall: N, part of an angel supporting a cloth of honour, and S, part of an elaborate canopy.

SCREEN. C15, of single-light divisions with ogee tops and a little tracery; above the screen a solid panel that formed the E side of the former loft, remains of painting on its E face and two spyholes to enable those in the loft to observe the priest in the chancel. – FONT. Limestone, C12, originally square, cut down to octagonal presumably in the C16, when the brick base was made. Octagonal COVER, C17, with panelled sides and ball top. – TILES. Late C14 decorated floor tiles, re-set, at W end of nave and in SW corner of chancel. – STAINED GLASS. Some medieval glass in the N and S windows, rearranged. – MONUMENTS. Incised figure of a priest, only the lower half preserved; with inscription in Lombardic letters and the date 1349. – Anthony Maxey †1592 and his wife Dorothy †1602, erected by their son Sir Henry, alabaster, behind the altar. Two arched recesses flanked by blank columns carrying an entablature. In each recess kneels one couple at a prayer desk. – Sir William Maxey †1645, wife and sons, aedicule with scrolled pediment and achievement and a lengthy inscription. C17 HELM above. – Michael Nolan †1827, sarcophagus with draped urn by *William Hayward*.

GLAZENWOOD, 1 m. W. Plain brick, *c.* 1802, doubled in size after 1806 by Samuel Curtis, nurseryman and owner of the *Botanical Magazine*, who established a large nursery and arboretum. Remodelled by *Nicholas Jacob*, 1988–95, with orangery, and garaging in the style of a stable block. Extensive landscaping by *The Landscape Partnership*, including the creation of a lake and turfed amphitheatre.

The village is mainly strung out along the Coggeshall–Braintree road, about 1 m. NW. A half-timbered estate cottage, 1869, with the initials of Onley Savill-Onley, appears to have strayed from Stisted (q.v.). Behind BRIDGE HALL, a two-storey mid-C19 Gothic folly, of white brick with panels of knapped flint and clinker. Between the village and the church, PARK HOUSE, late C18 with a smart five-bay white-brick front and Tuscan porch.

BRADWELL-ON-SEA

Bradwell is really three sites: the Roman fort and St Peter's Chapel by the sea-wall to the E, Bradwell Waterside and the power station by the Blackwater Estuary to the W, and between them the main village with St Thomas (the parish church) and Bradwell Lodge.

The ROMAN FORT has been identified beyond much doubt as OTHONA, built on a natural promontory in the late C3, and one of a series of Saxon Shore forts constructed to guard against attacks by sea rovers. It was probably roughly square, but about half has been destroyed by the sea. Only one fragment of wall survives, part of the S side. Excavations have shown the W wall to have been 525 ft (163 metres) long, and of the N wall 290 ft (89 metres) are known. At the NW corner and in the W wall further S were horseshoe bastions. The walls were *c.* 13 ft (4 metres) thick and the fort was surrounded by a ditch at least 8 ft (2.5 metres) deep and 25 ft (8 metres) wide.

ST PETER-ON-THE-WALL stands astride the W wall of the fort, probably on the site of the gateway. It is in all probability the very church built by St Cedd *c.* 654. It consists now of nothing but the nave, but the existence of a W porch and an apsed chancel as wide as the nave has been ascertained. In addition there was probably a *porticus*, i.e. a side chamber, to either side of the chancel, just as in the earliest Saxon churches of Canterbury. The chancel was separated from the nave by a tall three-bay arcade, just as at Reculver and St Pancras Canterbury. In the responds of the l. and r. arches, Roman brick can be recognized. The church is almost entirely built of Roman materials, ashlar and septaria as well as brick. The W doorway is original apart from the lintel. Original also is the W window, of quite a generous size. The side windows high up have original splays and jambs. After a period of use as a barn, when large entrances were made in the N and S walls, the chapel was repaired by *C. R. Peers* of the *Office of Works* and re-consecrated in 1920. Roof renewed in 1947. Bare interior, with hanging painted CRUCIFIX by *Francis Stephens*, 1949, and stone ALTAR, 1985, incorporating stones from Lindisfarne, Iona and Lastingham, communities associated with St Cedd. The chapel lies alone except for one cottage a little to the S, exposed to the east winds of the North Sea, a moving sight.

ST THOMAS. Brick W tower of 1743, with arched windows, diagonal buttresses, and battlements, by *S. Anderson* and *T. Gough*. Timber S porch, late C14, with ogee-headed partitions on the E and W sides, from St Mary Magdalene, Shopland (dem. 1957). C14 chancel, nave rebuilt 1706, both restored by *Chancellor* in 1861–6. A curious detail is the remains of an early C16 brick gable at the E end of the nave. It rested on a trefoil-arched corbel-frieze. Another curious thing is the several C14 head-stops of former hoodmoulds now set in the S wall of the nave, and also the hoodmoulds of the C19 E window. W gallery, built or rebuilt by Chancellor, moved one bay E as part of alterations designed by *Hilary Brightman*, executed by *Tim Venn*, 2000–1, including the insertion of an upper floor. – FONT. C14, octagonal bowl, with four big ugly heads reaching up from the stem, as if their shoulders carried the bowl. – Indecipherable remnant of medieval WALL PAINTING over chancel arch. – STAINED GLASS. E window by *Burlison & Grylls* (*Harry Grylls*), 1927. One nave S window signed by *Heaton, Butler & Bayne*, who are recorded as having made several for the church. – BRASS. Margaret Wyott †1526. 18-in. (46-cm.) figure.

VILLAGE HALL. By *A.H. Mackmurdo*, 1932. Big, barn-like structure, roughcast, with large roof and arcading along the sides.

St Thomas stands on the corner of the main street, with a high stone MOUNTING BLOCK of 1755 by the S gate and in the SE corner of the churchyard the village LOCK-UP, 1817. Brick, square, the door surround formed of old stocks.

Attractive cottages along EAST END ROAD, and also in the HIGH STREET to the N, where there is one six-bay brick Georgian façade masking a C15 timber-framed house, WHITE LYONS, and further N NEW HALL, also timber-framed, probably C16, faced in brick in the C18.

79 BRADWELL LODGE, S of the church. A Tudor house, with exposed moulded beams, to which was added in 1781–6 a new S side, in a style clearly metropolitan. The architect was *John Johnson*, the client Rev. Henry Bate Dudley, an extremely able journalist, who purchased the advowson of Bradwell in 1781. The S front consists of a dining room and drawing room, and between them a small oval library, with round-headed windows, that projects beyond the S wall to form a single-storey bow. Behind the library is the staircase with wrought-iron railing in Johnson's favourite pattern. It opens to the N entrance hall, first conceived as a carriageway. Semicircular Doric portico by *Quinlan Terry*, 2005, who also added the modillion cornice to the S wing. To the r. of the portico, in the W wall of the S block, two niches containing *Coade* urns, either side of a Venetian window. On the roof an unusually spacious belvedere. Its four corners, with Doric pilasters, conceal the chimneys; the rest is almost entirely glazed, with bows at either end. Gainsborough, who painted Dudley and his wife, is said to have used it as a studio. High-quality interior decoration, the plasterwork using motifs found elsewhere in Johnson's houses.* The drawing room chimneypiece has seven small paintings in the style of Angelica Kauffmann; grisaille ceiling medallions by *Robert Smirke Sen.* The library in the old part of the house, formed from three rooms in the C19, contains two bookcases from Langford Grove (q.v.).

BRADWELL HALL, 1½ m. SW. Timber-framed, mainly C17, but with a roof structure similar to that found on aisled halls, smoke-blackened throughout, and datable to *c.* 1300. The constructional details resemble those at Fyfield Hall (q.v.). C14 crown-posts.

NUCLEAR POWER STATION. 1957–62 by *Maurice Bebb* for the Nuclear Power Group, and one of the first two nuclear power stations built under a programme inaugurated in 1955.† Two

---

* *Robert Adam*'s name has been invoked, but there is no evidence that he was involved.
† The other was at Berkeley, Glos.

large blocks, with fully glazed sections at either end, contained the two reactors, with the turbines housed in a long, lower block to the w. Closed 2002.*

BRAINTREE[†]

7020

CHURCHES AND PUBLIC BUILDINGS

ST MICHAEL THE ARCHANGEL, St Michael's Road. The principal feature is the tall shingled splay-foot spire on the C13 tower. This, like everything else, was restored after the church fell into appalling disrepair during a notorious church rates dispute from 1834 until 1853.[‡] By *J.L. Pearson*; an early work and somewhat ruthless. He began in 1859–60 with the tower and spire and rebuilding the N aisle. Now the oldest surviving part is the chancel E wall, the rest of the chancel restored by *Chancellor*, 1859–60. The s aisle is as restored in 1866–7 by Pearson, who added a N porch and replaced the C16 s porch, the early C16 clerestory, and all the windows (Dec), apart from two N windows of the late C14 N chapel, and those of the early

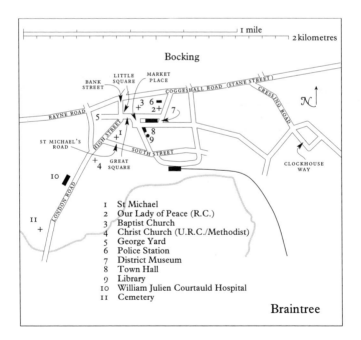

1 St Michael
2 Our Lady of Peace (R.C.)
3 Baptist Church
4 Christ Church (U.R.C./Methodist)
5 George Yard
6 Police Station
7 District Museum
8 Town Hall
9 Library
10 William Julien Courtauld Hospital
11 Cemetery

Braintree

---

* Demolition of the turbine hall planned to start in 2007, but the reactor halls will remain for at least a century.
† Although Braintree and Bocking now form a single district, the historic division has been maintained for this volume.
‡ Braintree had a large Nonconformist population, led by the Courtaulds.

C16 S chapel. Inside, the three-bay nave arcades are C13, with alternating circular and octagonal piers – alternating also across the nave. The arches have two slight quadrant hollows instead of chamfers. The two-bay S (Jesus) chapel has an early C16 pier. The section is of four main and four subsidiary shafts connected by deep hollows. Good early C16 roofs in the N and S chapels with carved bosses (including St Michael slaying the dragon, hidden by the organ). The aisles have pitched roofs of the 1860s – these and the nave roof the best of Pearson's work – also the date of the widened chancel arch and its refurnishing. The single-bay N chapel was widened in 1886 by *Geldart*, bringing it in line with the N aisle, to accommodate the organ. Choir vestry added at the W end of the N aisle, 1894.

STAINED GLASS. E window, *c.* 1869, three windows in S chapel, 1886 and 1921, and E window of N chapel, all by *Clayton & Bell*; the last a portrait of Charlotte S. Thomas †1889. S chapel, angel-musicians, by *Hardman*, *c.* 1880. – MONUMENTS. John Hawkins †1633 and his sons John and Abraham †1644, by *Francis Grigs*, 1645: marble, with central panel flanked by Doric pilasters carrying an enriched entablature, surmounted by two shields and cartouche of arms. – Three by *John Challis*, a local man: 1790–1820, with pleasant classical details.

ST MICHAEL'S CHURCH HOUSE (former vicarage) opposite the E end. 1855 by *Pearson*; an attempt at the vernacular, with black brick bands and diapers.

OUR LADY OF PEACE (R.C.), The Avenue. Airy, elegant design by *James O'Hanlon Hughes* and *W. E. F. Johns*, 1939. Brick. Free Perp; cruciform, with central flèche. Sadly, many of the original liturgical features by *Geoffrey Webb*, including the altar and baldacchino, have been removed during reordering. – STAINED GLASS. Two E windows by *Webb*, 1944–8. – Adjacent PRESBYTERY, 1953.

CHRIST CHURCH (U.R.C. and Methodist), London Road. 1832, classical, broad and bland, by *James Fenton*; remodelled internally (but retaining gallery) by *David Ferguson*, 1991. One window from the old Methodist chapel of 1868 (dem. 1988).

BAPTIST CHURCH, Blyth's Meadow. 1833. Classical, red brick with three-bay, pedimented gault brick front. Probably by *Fenton*.

TOWN HALL, Fairfield Road. 1926–8 by *E. Vincent Harris* and *J. S. Courtauld*, donated by W. J. Courtauld. Just right in size for a small but prosperous town. Neo-Georgian, two storeys, with a steep hipped roof and Baroque stone bell-turret, surmounted by a bronze figure of Truth by *Hermon Cawthra*. The interior, with its panelling, light fittings, contemporary furnishings etc., is virtually complete, and includes WALL PAINTINGS, 1929–30, by *Maurice Greiffenhagen* (Council Chamber) and *Henry Rushbury* (Chairman's Room). STAINED GLASS on main stair by *George Kruger Gray*, 1927.

POLICE STATION, Avenue Road. 1989 by the *County Architect's Dept* (project architect, *Graham Beighton*), and very unobtrusive (cf. Colchester). Pentagonal plan, to accommodate existing large trees on the site, creating an interesting internal space with courtyard.

DISTRICT MUSEUM, Manor Street. Spikily detailed Gothic former Board School, given by the Courtaulds in 1862; infants' building by *J. W. Clark*, 1897. Statue of the C17 naturalist John Ray by *Faith Winter*, 1986.

PUBLIC LIBRARY, Fairfield Road. Next to the Town Hall, but totally, and successfully, different: circular plan, in brick, glass and concrete, with a dome. By *Alan Willis*, County Architect, and *Rick Broadley* of *W.S. Atkins Property Services*, 1996–7.

LEISURE CENTRE. See Tabor Science College, Bocking.

WILLIAM JULIEN COURTAULD HOSPITAL, London Road. 1920–1 by *Coldwell & Nicholls*, who also did staff houses, 1923 and 1926, and maternity unit, 1936–7. Appropriately cottagey style, mainly single storey. Simple timber and brick summerhouse by *Frank Roscoe*, *c.* 1931, with flat lead roof.

CEMETERY, London Road. Opened 1856. Double chapel by *John Johnson* of Bury St Edmunds, who also designed a lodge, rebuilt in the 1950s. Brick with Caen stone dressings and short stone spire over the central porch. Landscaping by *William Davidson*.*

PERAMBULATION

Various schemes apparently designed to frustrate the motorist and appease pedestrians make Braintree seem more complicated than it really is. But the layout has always been irregular, and there is no real centre, so the TOWN HALL is a good place to start, as a reminder of just how much the town owes to the Courtaulds. George Courtauld established his silk business at Pebmarsh in 1799, moving to Braintree in 1809. The family's mark is everywhere, including the DRINKING FOUNTAIN, 1882; opposite the Town Hall, CORNER HOUSE, with W. J. Courtauld's initials, 1929, and probably by *E. Vincent Harris*. s of the Town Hall, in Fairfield Road, first the former POST OFFICE, 1933, a typical *Office of Works* production (*D. N. Dyke*), then the former EMBASSY CINEMA, 1935, by *Kemp & Tasker*, making a bold statement without being too rude to its more conventional neighbours. Now a pub, but with much of the interior (by *Mollo & Egan*) preserved.

The old heart of Braintree lies N and W of here. Market Place leads at the top into the funnel-shaped GREAT SQUARE, its E end dominated by the CONSTITUTIONAL CLUB. Broad Georgian brick front, with keystones to the windows, but dating back to the C16 and with much C17 panelling and other woodwork inside. Behind lies SAINSBURY'S, 1983 by *J. Sainsbury Architects & Engineers Dept* with *Kirby Adair Newson Partnership*, keeping with the scale and complexity of the townscape, partly through its use of traditional materials: mostly faced

* Information from Sarah Green.

with yellow brick with red dressings but with some black weatherboarding. Eight sculpted panels in terracotta-coloured concrete by *Steven Sykes* illustrate the story of shopping and trading in Braintree. Behind it loom two polygonal brick WATER TOWERS, 1880 and 1928, which dominate views of the town from the S.

An intricate neighbourhood of little lanes and openings N of Great Square leads through LITTLE SQUARE, containing the MANOR HOUSE, late C16 with two jettied upper storeys, carved brackets and fascias with plaster decoration, into BANK STREET. The best building here is the SWAN INN, long and varied, with exposed timberwork, at a point where the street widens into a kind of subsidiary marketplace. The southern side of the Swan presents a relatively complete frontage of C16 buildings that began as a range of covered market stalls and a small shop. Carriage arch dated 1590. At the top of Bank Street a staggered crossroads: BARCLAYS looks down Coggeshall Road to the E, as the White Hart (*see* Bocking) looks W along Rayne Road. Mid C19. Five-bay, two-and-a-half-storey front of gault brick with two two-bay pediments. Two entrances: Greek Doric on Bank Street, Ionic on Rayne Road.

At the S end of Bank Street, just before the High Street, a broad, rather clumsy house of seven bays with three-bay pediment – brick, with white brick quoins, bands etc., and glazing in octagonal panes of the type favoured by *Sir Robert Taylor* – a 1753 refacing of a C15 house with jettied rear. It forms the entrance to GEORGE YARD SHOPPING CENTRE by *Stanley Bragg & Partners*, 1988–90. Traditional construction, using numerous types of bricks, incorporating the original workshops (heavily restored) where F.H. Crittall started making metal windows in the 1880s. Whatever its own merits, George Yard has further reduced the status of the HIGH STREET as the main thoroughfare. Some good timber-framed buildings remain, e.g. Nos. 100–106 with jettied upper storeys, and No. 77, its C15 or C16 origins more apparent in the yard behind than in its attractive C18 front. Opposite Bank Street, the former HORN HOTEL, rebuilt in the C18, with the central carriageway flanked by bay windows. At the S end, where it meets St Michael's Road, the High Street widens out into an open space created by W. J. Courtauld in 1937, allowing a view of the W end of the church and designed to improve the entrance to the town from London. The centrepiece is a pretty bronze FOUNTAIN by *John Hodge*, 1936, with a boy, a huge shell, and fishes, seals etc. The single-storey building opposite, on the S side of St Michael's Road, was designed by *Vincent Harris* as almshouses, the larger building (LEAHURST) at right angles to it (added in 1939) as a home for district nurses. Lettering and the figure of a nurse by *Eric Gill*. Neo-Georgian with tall chimneys and Dutch gables, pale brick with Portland stone dressings. Individually good but the overall effect, against the background of Braintree, not entirely successful.

LONDON ROAD, S, starts with BLANDFORD HOUSE, *c.* 1700 with a shell-hood on carved brackets, then after Christ Church (*see* above) a row of C18 timber-framed cottages (Nos. 23–33) and some good early C19 stuccoed villas, mostly semi-detached but one (No. 41) rather grander, with elliptical ground-floor bows.

SOUTH STREET, E, has several early C19 silk spinning mills (now in other use), including on the N side Courtauld's Pound End Mill, 1818, and on the S side the mid-C19 New Mills: long low buildings with continuous glazing separated by weatherboarding. Nos. 118–120 and 141–145 South Street are mid-C19 weavers' cottages, two-storey stock brick, with single-storey lean-to loom rooms at the sides.

Further E, in CRESSING ROAD and CLOCKHOUSE WAY, a group of concrete 'cottages' designed by *C. H. B. Quennell* and *W. F. Crittall* and erected by the Unit Construction Co. for the Crittall Manufacturing Co., 1918–20.* A pioneering attempt to provide cheap housing using modern materials and methods, and the first example in England of the International Modern style. Mostly semi-detached; the plans conform to a metric grid, two concrete blocks making one unit. Floors and (flat) roofs were cast in reinforced concrete, with Crittall's unit steel casement windows. The contemporary claim that 'the colour and surface of the concrete slabs is little inferior in aesthetic appearance to that of good freestone'† now seems extravagant, and all but one pair of houses have been rendered or painted, but the spirit of the enterprise survives, an important precursor to Silver End (q.v.).

On the S edge of the town, BRAINTREE FREEPORT DESIGNER VILLAGE, 2000, where the Essex Design Guide and shopping come together in a grotesque parody of a 'village' that epitomizes the triumph of commerce over culture at the end of the C20.

BLACK NOTLEY LODGE, Notley Road. *See* Black Notley.

BRENTWOOD

No record of Brentwood exists before 1176, and most of what is now the town was, until 1873, part of the parish of South Weald. Nonetheless the settlement soon acquired importance because of its position at a crossroads of the London–Colchester road and a pilgrim route from N Essex towards Canterbury. A licence to build a chapel was granted in 1221, and to hold a market and fair in 1227. In the C18 it was a busy coaching town, and the arrival of the railway in 1840 further stimulated growth.

---

* Crittall's Manor Works, now demolished, were in Coggeshall Road.
† *The Architect*, 26 December 1919.

CATHEDRAL CHURCH OF ST MARY AND ST HELEN (R.C.)*
Ingrave Road

119   1989–91 by *Quinlan Terry*, incorporating a church of 1860–1 by
G.R. Blount. A surprisingly homogeneous complex, given its dis-
parate components, which successfully creates a sense of place.

The first church (then chapel) of St Helen stands N of the present
cathedral. 1836–7 by *Henry Flower*: a yellow brick Gothick
preaching box with pepperpot turrets; S aisle *c.* 1845. A school
from 1861 (and later a parish hall), when it was superseded by
Blount's building. This is Dec, of Kentish rag with a curious
polygonal SW tower with stumpy spire ('of that assertive ugli-
ness which is characteristic of much church work of the sixties',
wrote Pevsner in 1954). Aisled nave and chancel with flanking
chapels and NE sacristy. In 1972–4 *A.J. Newton* of *Burles,
Newton & Partners* removed the N wall and N arcade and
extended the church to the N, before a new bishop, Thomas
McMahon, decided upon an ambitious rebuilding on the site
of this work.

Like Blount's church, *Terry*'s cathedral is built principally of
Kentish ragstone, but there the similarity ends. It is classical,
its inspiration taken from the early Italian Renaissance fused
with the English Baroque of Wren. The main N front consists
of nine bays separated by Doric pilasters, with five-bay returns
joining up with Blount's church. The classical elements are in
smooth Portland stone to contrast with the ragstone. The N
front's central bay has a semicircular Doric portico and two of
the flanking bays have pediments. Round-headed windows,
with Venetian windows in the E and W walls. Set back behind
a balustrade is a clerestory of yellow brick with a pyramidal
slate roof and domed octagonal lantern. Inside, the effect is
that of a Florentine *cortile*, with aisles on the E, N, and W separated from the central double-height rectangular space by a
Tuscan arcade (with pronounced entasis) that is continued
on the S side where it meets Blount's nave. The interior is
extremely light, spacious, and airy, with Portland stone floor
and walls predominantly white but with stone-coloured arcade
and entablature. The arcade spandrels, reminiscent of the
Foundling Hospital in Florence, have STATIONS OF THE
CROSS, terracotta roundels by *Raphael Maklouf*. Central ALTAR
with AMBO on N side and BISHOP'S CHAIR – inspired by one
at San Miniato al Monte, Florence – on the S, of Nabrasina
stone, by *Terry*. Large cruciform FONT also on N side. Behind
the Bishop's Chair are the nave and S aisle (including four-bay
Gothic S arcade, with circular piers) of Blount's church. Choir
stalls in the old nave and at the W end the ORGAN, from St
Mary-at-the-Walls, Colchester, 1881, given a classical case by
Terry. – Blessed Sacrament Chapel (old chancel), with painted
decoration of 1911 and STAINED GLASS by *Mayer & Co.*

---

* The Roman Catholic diocese of Brentwood was formed in 1917, having previously
been part of the archdiocese of Westminster.

The new cathedral forms the S side of a courtyard with the 1837 church on the N side and on the W the original priest's house of 1836, in white brick with pilasters and decorative eaves, embellished by *Terry* with central Tuscan porch and Gothick sashes. CATHEDRAL HOUSE, S of the Cathedral, brings a change of mood. The core is the former Convent of the Sisters of Mercy by *F. W. Tasker*, 1873, also Kentish ragstone, but more rugged than Blount's church; additional offices by *Laurence King*, 1982, and new entrance by *Terry*. Former chapel now Choir School, extended by *Terry* in 2001.

ST GEORGE THE MARTYR, Ongar Road. 1933–4 by *Laurence King*,[*] his first church, with *Crowe & Careless*. Brick basilica with Art Deco styling. Apsidal E end, curved on the inside, polygonal on the outside, flanked by vestry and sacristy on the N side and Lady Chapel on the S, both also polygonal and projecting beyond the sanctuary. No E window, but an external pulpit of Portland stone with canopy on fluted columns; on the wall, a crucifix carved by *Lestocq de Castelnau-Bucher*. The five-bay nave, with tall thin metal-framed windows, was to have been three bays longer, with a W tower; W wall completed by *White & Mileson*, 1994–5, with a SCULPTURE of the Risen Christ by *John Doubleday*. Inside, low N and S arcades with round arches, passage aisle, and a wide chancel arch. Walls of brick and painted render, the ferro-concrete roof structure clearly expressed, with brick pilasters between the metal windows. Massive Hornton stone ALTARS and FONT. – STATIONS OF THE CROSS. By *Faith Craft Works*, installed in the 1950s, but in keeping with other Art Deco fittings.

ST THOMAS OF CANTERBURY, St Thomas Road. 1879–86 by *E. C. Lee*.[†] His *magnum opus*, large and serious. The total cost was over £22,000, of which his uncle O. E. Coope (the brewer) gave £2000 and Rev. Charles Belli £6000. The main part was finished in 1883: nave, N and S aisles, chancel with N chapel, S vestry and organ chamber, and W gallery. The NW tower, with porch in its base, and tall shingled splay-footed spire with four pinnacles and lucarnes, added 1886. The interior is E.E., competent but rather dull, but the outside has certain mannerisms which are reminiscent of such a younger man as E.S. Prior. At the W end are two stair-turrets linked by an open gallery, semicircular in plan, a motif repeated at the base of the tower. These, together with semicircular buttresses elsewhere, give the exterior a curiously primeval flavour, especially as the Westwood stone dressings have weathered badly. Walls of flint, some roughly knapped, some pebble. Richly sculpted W doorway, the carving by *Earp & Son*. Chancel, including REREDOS of 1896,

---

[*] King was a native of Brentwood, educated at Brentwood School, and designed the town's coat of arms.
[†] It replaced a church of 1835 by *James Savage*, whose tower fell. Lee originally planned to keep the chancel (by *J. Clarke*, 1856), but as work progressed this was abandoned.

redecorated by *Laurence King*, 1958. – STATIONS OF THE CROSS. 1904 by *Mayer & Co*. From the R.C. Cathedral. – STAINED GLASS. E, W and N and S aisle windows by *A.O. Hemming & Co.*, *c.* 1884–1908. Lancet by N door by *John Hayward*, 1983, to Laurence King †1981. – Parish hall and offices. 1988 by *Laurence King & Partners*. Flint and slate.

UNITED REFORMED CHURCH, New Road. 1847. Typical, with its broad stuccoed front with big pediment, square piers on the ground floor forming a loggia, and arched windows above. Interior rebuilt and subdivided 1982.

SION COMMUNITY (R.C.), Sawyers Hall Lane. 1974–6 by *Burles, Newton & Partners* (project architect, *Len Greaves*), as the Convent of the Sisters of Mercy. A complex roof-line and zigzag walls to the residential wings create an almost Gothic effect. Walls of load-bearing pale brown brick and slate roofs, climbing the slope to the CHAPEL. This contains a complete scheme of STAINED GLASS by *Patrick Reyntiens*. Abstract organic shapes in muted colours, apart from a brighter splash in the panel above the shrine of Our Lady opposite the altar. Windows to the internal courtyard by *Goddard & Gibbs*, reusing C19 glass. – SCULPTURE. On external wall of chapel, open metalwork figures of the Virgin and Christ by *Sean Crampton*.

PUBLIC BUILDINGS

TOWN HALL, Ingrave Road. 1957 by *John Brandon-Jones, Ashton & Broadbent*. Long, three storeys, in the Neo-Georgian manner learnt by Brandon-Jones in the 1930s from C. Cowles-Voysey. Matching extension at the S end by *Brandon-Jones & Andrew Thorne*, 1983–4. Load-bearing red brick with pantile roof. Very old-fashioned, but Brentwood's councillors spent their money wisely.

POLICE STATION, London Road. 1937 by *J. Stuart*, County Architect, and one of the rare occasions when he achieved something a little out of the ordinary. Mostly Neo-Georgian. Two blocks at right angles joined by a quadrant colonnade of giant square columns with plain capitals.

COUNTY HIGH SCHOOL. By *J. Stuart*, 1926–7. Neo-Tudor. Brick with stone dressings, stone frontispiece in the middle of the long façade, and projecting wings with straight gables and canted bays at either end. Enlarged 1935–6 and 1975.

COMMUNITY HOSPITAL, Crescent Drive. 1933–4 by *Hugo R. Bird*. T-plan, two storeys with dormers in the mansard roof. Vaguely Neo-Georgian, the effect spoilt by rough stock brick with red brick dressings.

HIGH WOOD HOSPITAL, Geary Road. Built as the Metropolitan Asylums Board Ophthalmic School by *C. & W. Henman*, 1899–1903, on the 'cottage home' system. Domestically scaled buildings arranged round two greens. Five groups of three cottages for children, two school buildings, and administration block. Brick, mostly two storeys, architecturally unpretentious.

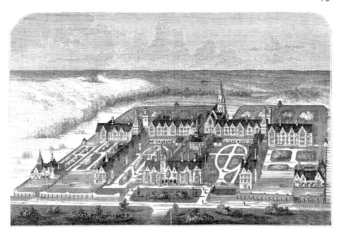

Essex County Lunatic Asylum, Brentwood.
Aerial perspective, 1857

Former WARLEY HOSPITAL, Warley Hill. By *H.E. Kendall* (*Kendall & Pope*), 1851–3, as the Essex County Lunatic Asylum. Neo-Tudor brick with black diapers. The original main block survives, with its steep gables and curious central tower, as well as the water tower (now Tower House), 1885, and Lodge House and Chapel, 1889. The rest of the site has been developed for housing since 2000.

RAILWAY BRIDGE, Seven Arches Road. By *John Braithwaite*, 1842–3. Brick, with wide elliptical central arch and three narrow round-headed arches to either side.

BRENTWOOD SCHOOL
Ingrave Road

Founded as a boys' grammar school in 1558 by Sir Antony Browne of Weald Hall, South Weald. Refounded in 1851. The oldest part is OLD BIG SCHOOL, Ingrave Road, 1568. A single schoolroom, originally only one storey. Only the outer brick walls and a doorway survive. Foundation stone inside, as well as a C16 timber fire-surround and panelling from Weald Hall (dem. 1950). Other panelling from Mitre House, Shenfield Road. On top of it a dormitory of 1854. To the N, SCHOOL HOUSE, built in 1773: five bays, with a canted bay added in 1864, joined to Old Big School by a gabled block of 1926. N of School House, BARNARDS HOUSE, purchased *c.* 1926. Early C18 five-bay front, red brick with burnt headers, with a C17 timber-framed core.

s of Old Big School, 1860s additions, including the CHAPEL. By *W. G. Bartleet*, 1867–8, E.E., brick with stone dressings and a bell-turret and flèche at the W end. N and S aisles added 1924–5. REREDOS 1916, donated by Evelyn Heseltine of Great Warley, chairman of the governors. The sanctuary's decorative embellishment is reminiscent of Townsend's St Mary the Virgin, Great Warley (q.v.), from where originated the N aisle's STAINED GLASS lancets, also given by Heseltine. Faith, Hope, and Charity by *Reginald Hallward*, *c.* 1904. E window (First World War memorial) by *A. K. Nicholson*, more crowded and satisfying than his later glass. – W window by *Percy Bacon & Bros*, 1910. – Second World War MEMORIAL at W end by *Laurence King*, 1949.

S of the chapel, set back from the road, is MAIN SCHOOL, 1909–10 by *Chancellor & Son*. Brick, mostly Neo-Tudor style but in the middle an ungainly projecting clock tower topped with a cupola. Finally, in this stretch along Ingrave Road, OTWAY HOUSE, built as the vicarage for the new parish of Brentwood by *W. G. Bartleet*, 1877–8, and typical of its date: bands of black brick and pointed arches over the ground-floor windows. Extended 1928 as a boarding house.

Behind the Ingrave Road front, to the r. of Main School, the former gymnasium (now CCF HEADQUARTERS) by *John Young*, 1890, moved here in 1908 to make way for Chancellor's building. Main School was extended in a matching (if simpler) style in 1924 with a N wing and, on the E side, the MEMORIAL HALL by *R. T. Barker & A. H. Kirk*, tucked in unobtrusively to its rear. This backs on to the E quadrangle, closed on its N side by the BEAN LIBRARY, 1929. On the quadrangle's E side a stone mounting block and obelisk from Weald Hall, and beyond it, facing the playing fields, the WAR MEMORIAL PAVILION by *Laurence King*, 1954; weatherboarded gables and clock turret. N of the Pavilion, the HARDY AMIES DESIGN CENTRE by *Hollins*, 1999, brick with a stone arcade on the ground floor and a large gabled, glazed cross-wing. Between this building and Old Big School to the W, a garden with open-air STAGE that incorporates stone balls and other fragments salvaged from Weald Hall. N of the Design Centre, WEALD HALL by *Tooley & Foster*, 1947–8, has panelling from Weald Hall and a copy of a large painting of the Tudor house attributed to *William van der Hagen*, *c.* 1720.

MIDDLETON HALL, Middleton Hall Lane. The preparatory school since 1949. C18 brick with incongruous Jacobean-style additions of 1898–1900 for Countess Tasker, perhaps the work of her cousin *F. W. Tasker*: stone frontispiece and bay on the entrance front, and extension to the rear of brick with stone dressings. W of the house, beyond the HIGGS BUILDING by *Hollins*, 1995–6, a C18 WALLED GARDEN, three of its walls a zigzag crinkle-crankle.

PERAMBULATION

A perambulation of the town requires little more than a brisk walk up and down the High Street, where the interesting buildings are too far apart and too much interrupted by C20 commercial premises to be visually rewarding. The C14 ruins of ST THOMAS'S CHAPEL, founded 1221, are a good place to start. All that remains is some W and N walling of the nave and the stump of the NW tower, forming the centrepiece of an open space. Behind it the BAYTREE CENTRE by *T.P. Bennett & Son*, 1973–7 (refurbished 2003–5 by *Bernard Engle*), the sort of precinct development from which most Essex towns were mercifully spared. It leads through to NEW ROAD, with the former County Court building on the W side, *c.* 1848. Probably by *Charles Reeves*, County Court Surveyor. Gault brick with stone and stucco dressings. Single-storey entrance block with royal arms; behind it the higher courtroom. New Road leads down to Coptfold Road, and on the corner of this and Library Hill is the former Police Station (now nursery school), designed in 1844 by *Hopper*, opened 1851, extended later in the C19. Brick, with gault brick dressings on the original portion.

Back to the HIGH STREET, and immediately in front of the W end of St Thomas's Chapel a small brick house of *c.* 1700, No. 44, two storeys with a parapet partially concealing a hipped mansard roof. Two-storey canted bay to the l. Opposite, an idiosyncratic 1930s Neo-Tudor rebuilding of the LION AND LAMB inn (now W.H. Smith). Arched doorways either side of a large arched window and above that an oriel. To its r., Nos. 63–65, the cross-wing of a C15 house, extended to the rear in the early C16, with an early C17 range parallel to the street replacing the original hall. W of the Chapel, on the S side, Nos. 60–64, three gables to the street. Nos. 60–62, *c.* 1400, probably represent the remains of a hall to the r. and cross-wing to the l., separated by a passageway (leading to South Street) cut through part of the cross-wing, with an original blocked doorway leading back into the hall. In No. 62, an octagonal crown-post, probably not *in situ*. No. 64 is early C16, and may represent a rebuilding of the W end of the hall. On the N side again, the former WHITE HART HOTEL has a C20 Neo-Georgian brick front of ten bays, with a carriageway leading through to a coaching yard. Its W range, *c.* 1500, survives in remarkably good condition, the original jettied long gallery easily recognizable with its row of low arched openings. Inside this range, the timber framing indicates that it was built with two large chambers on each floor, possibly intended for pilgrims on their way to Canterbury. Traces of painted decoration were discovered in 1986.

Further W, beyond King's Road, on the N side Nos. 163–169, a brewery of *c.* 1820 converted to a terrace of three-storey town houses *c.* 1890. After this, High Street becomes LONDON ROAD, with the Police Station (*see* above) on the S side and on the N a complete and welcome contrast, OFFICES for BT by *Arup Associates*, 1997–2000.* Three storeys, but seeming lower

---

* On the site of St Faith's Hospital, built as Shoreditch Industrial School by *T.E. Knightley*, 1854.

from the road because it sits slightly beyond the crest of a hill
and is extremely long and meandering. Glazed external walls
reveal internal walls of brick and glass.

Now back to St Thomas's Chapel for the remainder of the
HIGH STREET. On the s side, on the corner of St Thomas
Road, the POST OFFICE, 1939–41, a typically good Neo-
Georgian job by the *Office of Works*. Nine bays to the High
Street, ten to St Thomas Road, of which the outer bays at each
end are set back slightly, each bay separated by vestigial
pilasters of brick fluting. Further E, No. 12, Georgian brick,
five bays, two storeys with Roman Doric porch. Next Ingrave
Road is reached, and on the far side WILSON'S CORNER
(former department store), a wonderfully brash piece of commercial architecture of 1889, rebuilt to the original design following a fire in 1909. Straight gables topped with little
segmental pediments, and a corner clock tower.

SHENFIELD ROAD continues the High Street E, and the char-
acter changes noticeably, with a wide green verge on the s side.
At the beginning of this a granite obelisk MEMORIAL to
William Hunter, the Protestant martyr who was burnt at
Brentwood in 1555. Erected (hardly coincidentally) in 1861, the
year that the Roman Catholics opened their new church in
Ingrave Road. Then come three houses belonging to Brentwood School (*see* above). First NEWNUM HOUSE, late C19
'Queen Anne' front, with two-storey bow window beneath a
projecting gable that has in it a small Venetian window. Behind
this a timber-framed building dating back to *c.* 1600. To its l.,
RODEN HOUSE, a fine display of C18 brickwork, with burnt
headers, the pattern mostly continued through various alterations and additions. Built before 1717, with additions dated
on a rainwater head 1724. Main block of five bays and on the
l. a two-bay wing with Dutch gable. Two large two-storey bow
windows on the garden front. Behind and to the side an early
C19 brick coachhouse with a hexagonal louvre and cupola.
Finally MITRE HOUSE, timber-framed and plastered with
exposed false framing, dating to the C15. Hall range with floor
inserted in the C16, cross-wings to l. and r., and C17 additions.
Restored and extended by *George S. W. Tappen*, 1883.

Opposite, OLD HOUSE (Brentwood Arts and Community
Centre), formerly two buildings, the Red Lion Inn with two-
storey bow and single-storey canted bay, and Shenfield Villa,
of six bays. Both have C18 brick fronts, but the villa has remains
of medieval timber framing. Further E, on the same side, THE
HERMITAGE (County Council offices), two-storey, five-bay
house of *c.* 1800 with a single-bay addition to the r. Behind it,
BRENTWOOD THEATRE by the *Tooley & Foster Partnership*,
1993, industrial in appearance apart from a curved entrance
canopy on giant columns. On the s side, SHEN PLACE
ALMSHOUSES by *R. T. Barker & A.H. Kirk*, 1910, paid for by
Evelyn Heseltine. Six houses round a courtyard open to the
road. Neo-Tudor, brick with timber framing and pargetting in
the gables, heavily carved bargeboards, and tall chimneys.

Further E, a nicely designed cross on an island, the First World War MEMORIAL by *A.E. Hill*, 1921.

BRENTWOOD PLACE, Sawyers Hall Lane. By *David Ruffle Associates* for Countryside Properties, 1975–9. The archetypal 'Essex Design Guide' scheme. Sixty-four houses grouped in mews courts either side of the spinal road, in varying combinations of brick, render, weatherboarding (black and white) and tile-hanging.

MERRYMEAD, Sawyers Hall Lane. 1912 by *Hugo R. Bird*. A large and expensive Neo-Georgian house. Two storeys with attics in the hipped roof, the main house of ten bays with bows on the S (garden) and W fronts, the latter with a tiled half-dome. Servants' wing to the E and beyond that a separate garage block and pair of cottages, both well detailed, the garages more Arts and Crafts. Formal gardens with a long, curved wall down the E side.

BRIGHTLINGSEA   *0010*

ALL SAINTS. A town church, yet away from the little town. Its situation is not as illogical as might first appear: the high ground overlooks Alresford Creek to the N which was once a harbour. Like Dedham, a grand example of the East Anglian Perp type on Essex soil. Yet there is ample evidence of a building earlier than those prosperous years. In the S aisle wall W of the doorway a round-headed recess with Roman brickwork, probably the remaining doorway of an Early Norman church whose nave S wall would have been here. After this follows the chancel. Here, on the N side, one blocked C13 lancet window, another on the S side opposite. The nave S doorway also C13 and simple. Moreover, the E parts of the S and N arcades (octagonal piers and double-chamfered arches) belong to the C13 or to c. 1300. Then, however, the Perp style began its enlarging and remodelling. The W tower, completed in the 1490s (restored 1886, following the 1884 earthquake), is big and sturdy with a base decorated by shields in quatrefoils. Diagonal buttresses of an unusual section enriched by niches. Four-light W window, two-light window on the second stage, three-light bell-opening with one transom. Battlements pierced and decorated; crocketed pinnacles. The existing nave was lengthened to join it. The S vestry was added c. 1518, the N chapel (for the Beriffe family) c. 1521. The S chapel and S porch seem contemporary. Finally c. 1530 the N aisle was reconstructed. Much flushwork decoration. S porch with carved battlements. Diagonal buttresses with niches. Doorway with fleurons and crosses in the voussoirs. One niche above. Three-light side openings. S aisle plastered, with flint battlements. Three-light windows with Perp tracery. The N chapel tracery is like that of the S aisle, the N aisle tracery simpler and later.

The arcades inside the W half of the nave, i.e. the work of *c.* 1500, have piers of an odd section: basically lozenge-shaped, with attached shafts towards the arches (with capitals), a thin polygonal shaft to the nave, and recessed parts in the diagonals (all this without capitals). Many niches scattered in the interior: in one of the C13 N piers, in the C13 S window in the chancel, in the E wall of the N chapel. The clerestory fell in 1814 and was not rebuilt – a great pity. The nave roof was rebuilt the following year. Restorations of 1874 and 1878–9, including new chancel arch, by *Charles Pertwee*, brother of the vicar.

FONT. Perp, octagonal, with traceried stem and, on the bowl, quatrefoils with roses. Traces of colour found and renewed. – DUMMY BOARDS. Life-size painted figures of Moses and Aaron, early C18. Intended to stand either side of the altar. – SCULPTURE. Celestial Mary by *John Doubleday*, 1981. – A frieze of TILES round the nave records parishioners who have died at sea. Started by Rev. Arthur Pertwee, 1885, and back-dated to 1872 when he became vicar. The earliest, with decorative lettering, designed by *Rev. Ernest Geldart*, made by *Cox, Sons, Buckley & Co.* – STAINED GLASS. E window by *Heaton, Butler & Bayne*, 1881. N aisle, figure of St Paul, *c.* 1850, from Prior Crauden's Chapel, Ely, repaired by *A.L. Wilkinson* and installed by *Dennis G. King*, 1961. – N chapel E by *Caroline Swash*, 1982. – S aisle, heraldic, by *Jane Gray*, 1987.

A fine collection of BRASSES of the Beriffe family, wool merchants who contributed to the rebuilding of the church. In N chapel, John †1496 and wife (24-in. (61-cm.) figures), with five sons and four daughters and merchant's mark; indents of two other wives and more children. – John †1521 and two wives (28-in. (71-cm.) figures) and children, with merchant's mark. – Alice †1536 and daughter (22-in. (56-cm.) figures). Palimpsests, reusing the brasses of two priests, early C15, standing on a shafted bracket. – William †1578, including an inscription commemorating his father John †1542 (18-in. (46-cm.) figure including the head, now missing). In N aisle, Mary †1505 (24½-in. (62-cm.) figure) and children and Margaret †1514 (28-in. (71-cm.) figure). In nave, William †1525 and wife (38-in. (96-cm.) figure).

72   In the chancel a sumptuous marble MONUMENT to Nicolas Magens †1764 by *Nicholas Read*. Magens, born in the Duchy of Holstein in 1697, grew rich in London as an importer and in the insurance business. No effigy, concentrating instead on the source of his wealth. At the centre is a globe. To its l. the Angel of the Resurrection leaning against bales of goods and holding a large scrolled parchment with inscription. To the r. a putto on a gigantic cornucopia from which flow fruit and coins. Projecting beyond the main composition the stern of a ship and an anchor. A host of cherubs in swirling clouds above. Massive black ledger stone in the chancel floor with deep-cut coat of arms. – Later monuments insignificant by comparison, but including Magens Dorrien Magens †1849 by *R. Physick* and his wife Henrietta Cecilia †1829 by *H. Hopper*, the former with draped urn.

ST JAMES, Victoria Place. By *William Mason*, 1834–6. Lancet style, with a quirky tower and porch at the (liturgical) SW corner of the nave that contracts after two storeys to an octagonal lantern and spire. It might be 'elegant' and 'graceful', as described at the time, were it not built (like the rest of the church) of white brick. Side galleries added to existing W gallery 1866. Chancel and vestries by *Roy Gould*, 1957–8. No E window, instead a wooden SCULPTURE of Christus Rex by *Donald Simpson*, 1962.

NEW CHURCH (New Jerusalem Church), Queen Street. 1867–8 by *E. C. Gosling*. Classical façade, stock brick with red brick dressings, cornice and open pediment, red brick behind.

UNITED CHURCH (Wesleyan), Chapel Road. 1843. Brick, three-bay front with central gablet and pointed-arched windows (cf. Great Bentley). Internal fittings largely unaltered.

COLNE COMMUNITY SCHOOL, Church Road. 1935–6 by *J. Stuart*, County Architect, with an Art Deco feel untypical of his work.

The town's best buildings are to be found in the HIGH STREET, the most remarkable JACOBES, the house of the Beriffe family of wool merchants. C15 hall house with two gabled wings projecting towards the street. They are about the same size and have exposed timbers. Roof with tie-beams and crown-posts. The rare feature is a polygonal brick stair-turret in one of the re-entrant angles. It has battlements and a small crocketed conical roof on brick trefoil friezes (cf. Faulkbourne), and is of *c.* 1500, when the hall was floored; Early Tudor ceiling with moulded and carved beams. Opposite, a nice Georgian brick house, No. 51, with an Early Victorian porch of elaborate cast-iron trellis-work, probably by *Wallis* of Colchester. Further E, Nos. 80–86, originally a hall house with cross-wings at each end, dating to the C16, with a C17 extension on the l. Exposed timbers on upper floor. In JOHN STREET, former Independent Chapel by *Horace Darken*, 1865, now in commercial use.

By the Creek, in COPPERAS ROAD, the former Anchor Hotel (now flats), 1901 by *G.H. Page*. An overblown affair in best Edwardian style: ground floor of Kentish rag and two timber-framed upper floors, with large octagonal cupola. In WATERSIDE, a number of C19 sail lofts and other buildings associated with the port, including a warehouse of *c.* 1809 known as the CINQUE PORT WRECK HOUSE. Brick, part rendered, four bays by two with a pattern of elliptical arches separated by pilasters.

At the W end of the Promenade, BATEMAN'S FOLLY, *c.* 1880, a gently leaning octagonal tower, 25 ft (8 metres) high with pointed windows, once used as a lighthouse.

Near MOVERONS FARM, ½ m. WSW of All Saints, Early Neolithic pottery has been found in a ditched and banked enclosure about 75 ft (23 metres) in diameter. Nearby, a Middle Bronze Age cemetery, and a ROMAN VILLA, never properly excavated. Remains of a Roman house or houses with mosaic pavements were found at Well Street in the C19.

BROOMFIELD

Broomfield is now joined on to the N side of Chelmsford, but has managed to maintain its separate character, especially round Church Green.

ST MARY. Norman round tower with much Roman brick. Low, with later shingled splay-foot spire. Unmoulded round-headed tower arch. Norman also both nave and chancel, with Roman brick quoins on the S side. Chancel lengthened and given its large E window in the C15. Restored by *Chancellor*, 1869–70, who rebuilt the N aisle and S porch, added the N vestry, and re-roofed the nave. Later work by Chancellor includes the REREDOS, 1880, made by *Wray & Fuller* of Chelmsford, and SEDILIA, CREDENCE, and LYCHGATE, 1893. St Leonard's Hall, attached to the N side of the vestry, by *Tim Venn*, 1996–7, is rendered but has flint plinth and buttresses and reuses some of Chancellor's stonework for the windows. Its slight splay echoes the misalignment of nave and chancel. – FONT. Square, of Purbeck marble, C13 with three shallow blank pointed arches on each side and (an exception) angle shafts. – PRAYER DESK. Carving by *Gwynneth Holt*.[*] – WALL PAINTING. In base of tower, fresco by *Rosemary Rutherford*, daughter of the vicar, 1941, assisted by her brother *John*. – STAINED GLASS. Four chancel windows by *Rutherford*, 1950, 1952 (made by *Nicholsons*), 1956 (made by *Spear Studios*) and 1966. N chapel E by *G.E.R. Smith*, 1953. Nave S (two) by *Powell & Sons*, 1948. – MONUMENTS. Brass of Thomas Huntleye †1613. Only one figure survives, probably that of his daughter Ann, but is not visible. – Two large marble tablets, Thomas Manwood †1650 and family of Priors and Thomas Pocklington †1769, heir of the Manwoods. Both have pediments with shields of arms, the older monument more elaborate with flaming lamps, drapery, etc.

PUBLIC LIBRARY, Main Road. A very neat design by the *County Architect's Dept* (architect in charge, *D. A. Stanhope*), 1960–1, intended as a prototype for a standard library in rural areas. Flat-roofed, with continuous clerestory, but the walls and fascia have traditional weatherboarding.

KING EDWARD VI GRAMMAR SCHOOL SPORTS PAVILION, Woodhouse Lane. By *J. P. Hiner & Associates*, *c.* 1977. Pale brown brick and weatherboarding. Overhanging upper storey, glazed on three sides.

BROOMFIELD HOSPITAL. In the grounds of Broomfield Court, a Neo-Jacobean house dated 1904. It became the Nurses' Home for the TB hospital for 300 patients by *J. Stuart*, the County Architect, 1935–40. Symmetrical layout, with a wide, S-facing ward block, in pale brick with generous glazing and

---

[*]The sculptors Gwynneth Holt (1909–95) and her husband Thomas Bayliss Huxley-Jones (1908–68) lived in Broomfield and are buried in the churchyard.

broad, cantilevered sun balconies running its length. Central block with semicircular pavilions at each end, originally with long angled wings (dem.) terminating in brick stair-towers with glass-block panels. The treatment block and main entrance formed the s side of a central square (sundial by *Nancy Coulson*, 1994), with recreation hall on the w side (with later first-floor lecture room), patients' dining room on the N, and administration block (dem.) on the E, linked by curved colonnades. Flat-roofed matron's house (now offices) to the NW. On the site of the E range, the Accident and Emergency and Out-Patients' Dept, part of large additions in the 1980s and 1990s by *George Trew Dunn Beckles Willson Bowes*, later *George Trew Dunn Partnership*. A major new building by *Llewelyn Davies Yeang* with *The Bouygues Consortium* (P.F.I.), partly on the site of Stuart's E wing, is due for completion in 2008.

FARLEIGH HOSPICE, NE of Broomfield Hospital. By *Mathews Serjeant Architects*, 2004–5. Traditional style and materials: yellow brick and black weatherboarding.

The church faces on to the triangular GREEN, with a number of nice houses round, notably BROMFIELDS and THE VINERIES on the N side. Originally a single dwelling, with some exposed timbers in the gables of the cross-wings. C16, altered in the C17 and later. On the s side, a development of twelve houses by *Raymond Ball* of *John S. Wood Chartered Surveyors*, *c.* 1975, sticking to the tenets of the Essex Design Guide. Where Church Green meets Main Road, on the s corner the KINGS ARMS, C16 or C17, with exposed timber framing.

In MAIN ROAD, nearly opposite the Kings Arms, Nos. 252 and 252a (THE WELL HOUSE), late C16 with cross-wings at either end, that on the l. smaller but jettied. Towards Chelmsford, two large early C19 houses, both gault brick. On the E side, BROOMFIELD PLACE (County Council offices), five bays, two storeys, with Greek Doric portico *in antis* and to the r. a single-storey wing with three-bay blind arcade. Octagonal LODGE, originally single-storey. On the w side, BROOKLANDS, *c.* 1827. Five-bay entrance front with giant pilasters at each end and to either side of the stuccoed Tuscan porch.* Opposite Broomfield Place, THE ANGEL, C15 hall house, one remaining cross-wing at the N end with a large canted bay added to the ground floor.

PRIORS, ¾ m. sw. Interesting C16 brick house, with original brick windows and an original two-storey canted bay window. Next to this three plastered gables, two original (timber-framed), one late C20, projecting from the main block. Very tall chimneystack with four octagonal shafts. Good staircase of *c.* 1600 and two rooms with C16 panelling.

---

* *Alfred Waterhouse* made unspecified alterations and additions for W. Christie-Miller, 1896.

BROXTED

ST MARY. C13 nave and chancel, of flint and pebble rubble, and
C15 N aisle. Weatherboarded belfry, on four posts of which two
rest on corbels, with squat, shingled, splay-foot spire, rebuilt
by *J. Clarke* as part of his restoration in 1874–6, which also
involved rebuilding the W wall and the chancel's S wall. The
chancel has original lancets, the nave two early C16 brick
windows. The N arcade piers have an elongated semi-polygonal
shaft without capital towards the nave and normal semi-polygonal shafts towards the arches, which are double-chamfered.
W of the arcade in the C13 wall a tall ogee-headed niche with
a small vault; statue by *Francis Stephens*. – PULPIT. With elaborate Elizabethan arabesque ornament. – REREDOS, TESTER,
portable FONT and STATUE of John the Baptist at E end of N
aisle by *Stephens*, 1961, under the direction of *Laurence King*.
– STAINED GLASS. Nave S by *Chance & Co.*, 1853, who were
perhaps also responsible for the chancel lancets of 1845. N aisle
E by *Stephens* with *Gordon Beningfield*, 1963. At W end, two
striking windows by *John K. Clark*, 1993, one predominantly
grey, the other predominantly blue, symbolizing captivity and
freedom respectively. – MONUMENTS. Thomas Bush †1791. By
Hugh Hunter. Elegant composition of coloured marbles, with
wreath, covered urn, lamps etc. – W. P. Mellen †1953. Nicely
carved inscription by *Hugh L. Powell*.

CHURCH HALL (now Whitehall Hotel), on E side of churchyard.
Late C16 with picturesque façades, front and back, of four
gables of different sizes and heights. Sympathetic E extension,
1987, and further extensions to the W to link up with a C17
brewhouse and an early C15 nine-bay aisled barn, both now
incorporated in the hotel.

OLD VICARAGE, 300 yds SW. By *Richard Armstrong*, 1870. Brick.
Unadventurous Gothic Revival, with straight gables and a little
porch with half a gable leaning against the side of a projecting
wing. To the E, BRICK HOUSE, early C18 with open segmental pediment on Ionic columns.

HILL PASTURE, 300 yds NE. By *Ernö Goldfinger* with *Gerald
Flower*, 1936–8, for *Humphrey Waterfield*, painter and garden
designer, who laid out the garden (begun in 1936 on a bare
four-acre site) as a series of rooms. The house as built was a
modest, single-storey, flat-roofed, brick pavilion, with large
living room and studio, dining area, kitchen, bathroom, and
bedroom. The approach is through a courtyard, divided into
inner and outer areas by a covered walk (reconstructed by *John
Winter* during restoration, 1996–2005). Upper storey added
1957, with a two-storey wing to the NW, based on designs by
Flower – changes which Goldfinger deplored. Small bungalow
(The Studio) S of the house by *Winter*, 2000. Black corrugated
steel sheeting. N of the house a brick summerhouse by *Richard
Tyler*, 1974, a memorial to Waterfield.

HORHAM HALL. *See* p. 496.

BUCKHURST HILL

St John the Baptist. In an unexpectedly pretty setting for a suburban church, on a narrow hilltop strip of Epping Forest next to a pond. Dec, of brick faced with Kentish rag, with sw tower with four pinnacles and recessed spire that rises above the surrounding trees. By *Jonathan Savill* of Chigwell, 1837, but of this little remains. N aisle, chancel, N chapel, and choir vestry by *G. Smith & G. B. Williams*, 1864, s aisle by *Joseph Tanner*, 1869–70, extended by *T. E. C. Streatfeild*, 1878–9, who also designed the tower and w wall of the nave. w front completed 1892 by the addition of a narthex and baptistery, the latter incorporated into a meeting room together with part of the N aisle, 1987. Chancel enlarged and clergy vestry added by *J.O. Scott*, 1896–7, and further alterations made to the nave, including the addition of a clerestory and new w window, by *Milne & Hall*. Instrumental in much of this was Nathanael Powell, churchwarden 1855–94 and partner in the firm of James Powell & Sons, but in spite of this connection the interior is generally disappointing. Reordered 1980, when the SCREEN of 1933 (by *F. E. Howard* for *A.R. Mowbray & Co.*) was moved E to enclose the sanctuary rather than the chancel. – FONT. Given by Mrs Nathanael Powell, 1865. Stone and marble, with four roundels of opaque glass by *Powell & Sons*, painted by *Miss Shepherd*. – WALL PAINTING. In lunette over w door, fresco by *B. Playne*, 1937. – STAINED GLASS. Extensive scheme by *Powell & Sons*, including N aisle (Road to Emmaus) by *Ada Currey*, 1893, E window to Nathanael Powell †1906, and N chapel E designed by *J. W. Brown*, 1917. N aisle †1962 by *Carl Edwards*. – MONUMENTS. In churchyard, on N side of church, tomb of Nathanael Powell and others, with opaque glass roundel by *Powell & Sons*.

St Elisabeth, Chestnut Avenue. 1938 by *R.C. Foster*, extended by him 1960. Neo-Tudor, designed to double as a community centre. More like a village hall than a church.

St James (United Reformed), Palmerston Road. The Gothic stone tower of *Edmond Egan*'s Congregational chapel of 1873 still stands, a landmark that vies with the spire of St John's, now attached to undistinguished flats. The present church is in the former hall, upgraded in 1987.

Public Library, Queen's Road. Former Baptist chapel, 1866. Brick with stone dressings, the windows vaguely Neo-Tudor, including a large oriel over the main entrance.

Primary School, High Road. 1838, next to St John's, and in similar style, so probably also by *Savill*; extended by *Tanner*, 1865.

The STATION was rebuilt in 1891–2, probably by *W. N. Ashbee*, but the Eastern Counties Railway had arrived in 1856 and development dates from shortly after. The names of the nearby streets say it all – Queen's Road, Prince's Road, Victoria Road, Salisbury Road, and Palmerston Road – but the architecture is generally undistinguished. Two houses designed by architects for their own occupation: FAIRSTEAD, Roebuck Lane, by *Herbert Tooley*, *c.* 1895, and ELCOT, No. 79 Russell Road, by *Arthur Needham Wilson*, 1906. Both have tile-hanging; Tooley's house brick, Wilson's roughcast. Also in Roebuck Lane, by Tooley, the former FOREST HOSPITAL, 1909–12, roughcast, Arts and Crafts, and probably originally quite picturesque.

BULMER

ST ANDREW. Mainly flint and pebble rubble. The emphasis lies on the early C14 chancel, unusually long, with a band inside going all the way round, rising and falling to accommodate the S doorway, windows, sedilia, and piscina. The SEDILIA and paired CREDENCE and PISCINA have cusped arches on detached shafts. The chancel roof is much later, *c.* 1500, and has collar-beams on braces with a little tracery in the spandrels. The braces rest on angel figures. N arcade, also C14, with octagonal piers and double-chamfered arches. Battlemented C15 W tower with diagonal buttresses; some flint and stone chequerwork at the base. *Chancellor* restored the chancel, 1883, and nave, 1891. Most of the window tracery is his, as well as the nave roof and N vestry. – FONT. Octagonal, C15; tracery on the stem, and on the bowl panels with angels, shields, and a green man. – PULPIT. C18; panelling and a little inlay. – STAINED GLASS. E window by *Lavers, Barraud & Westlake*, 1883. N aisle E, 1955, and three porch windows to the Minter family †1942, 1957 and 1968, by *Muriel Cooper*, beautifully drawn and coloured. – MONUMENT. Robert and Frances Mary Andrews †1806 and 1780 of Auberies, the Mr and Mrs Andrews who were the subject of Gainsborough's painting. Standard marble wall monument with coat of arms.

AUBERIES. The Andrews' house was rebuilt after 1806. Five bays, two storeys, of rendered brick, with a three-storey addition by *Henry Harrison* for Col. Augustus Meyrick, *c.* 1835. Eight-bay orangery beyond. Two-storey porch with two pairs of Roman Doric columns. Gault brick STABLES W of the house, with brick coachhouse and grooms' quarters added by *Chancellor*, 1889.[*] ENTRANCE SCREEN with wrought-iron gates to the S. The setting is more important than the house, parkland rather than the farmland that the Andrews knew:[†] a largely unaltered landscape in the manner of *Repton*, who engraved it for *The Polite Repository* in 1811. A classical BATH HOUSE at one end of the lake has disappeared but a two-storey C19 brick bathing tower survives.

A few nice houses in the village, prominent among them THE DOWER HOUSE, early C19 brick with a later C19 porch and

---

[*] Estate cottages in Church Road, SW of Auberies, probably also by *Chancellor*, 1885.
[†] The oak beneath which they posed for their portrait in about 1748 is still standing.

two-storey canted bay, and GRIGGS FARMHOUSE, C17 with exposed timber frame.

BUTLER'S HALL FARM, 1¾ m. SSE. Some exposed timbers. C15 or C16 gabled cross-wing, formerly jettied, to which an L-plan house was added on the S side, *c.* 1600. Further C17 N addition.

BULPHAN

6080

ST MARY. The main interest of the church lies in its timberwork: the tower, the porch, the screen, all *c.* 1500. The exterior does not prepare one for this. The tower's base has vertical weatherboarding, but the upper part ornamental tile-hanging from *T. E. C. Streatfeild's* restoration of 1874–5, when the N vestry was added and the nave walls (mainly knapped flint) rebuilt. The large clock came later, to mark the 1897 Jubilee. The tower stands internally on six posts forming a nave and aisles. The aisles are divided horizontally by cross-beams with diagonal braces, and braces spring from the aisles too. The centre has beams on big braces springing from the 'arcade' posts. Streatfeild inserted a brick plinth beneath the timbers on the S side, removed a W gallery, opened up the W window and inserted two windows N and S. The S porch has ornate bargeboarding with tracery decoration, the carving's quality suggesting a London carpenter. Inside, the prevailing atmosphere is Victorian, including painted texts over window arches etc., despite major work by *David Ferguson*, 1999–2000. Chancel restored 1866. – SCREEN. C15, uncommonly rich. Two side openings and doorway. Each side opening is of two lights under one arch with the mullion rising up into the apex of the arch, and cusped tracery. All spandrels have blank tracery panelling. The carving on the E side is more elaborate; the W side would have been hidden by the loft. – STAINED GLASS. E window (central light) by *Cox & Sons*, 1866; sidelights added *c.* 1879 and 1891. Single-light window (Virgin and Child) by S door by *Kempe*, 1907.

PARISH ROOM. By *Ferguson*, 1999–2000, a model of what such buildings should be. Free-standing, so not interfering with the church fabric, but close enough to it, and of similar materials (timber cladding on a brick plinth, tiled roof), to read as one.

BRANDON HALL (former rectory), 300 yds W. Early C16 timber-framed core, extended early C18 and late C19. Brick. Three storeys, double pile, each range gabled, and with corner chimney turrets. Pointed arched windows, some Gothic tracery.

YE OLDE PLOUGH HOUSE MOTEL, ½ m. NE. In the grounds a C15 hall house (formerly Appleton's Farm) with gabled and jettied cross-wings and some exposed timbers. Crown-post roof. Also two stone archways from *C.M. Shiner's* Library, Grays Thurrock, 1903 (dem. 1971).

BURES HAMLET*

Several nice houses, the most prominent SECRETARIES FARM-HOUSE on the corner of Station Hill and Water Lane. Good Georgian brick front with pedimented doorway and a Venetian window above. Behind this a large hall house, rendered, dating back to the C14, with C18 and C19 extensions. N of the house an early C19 brick coachhouse and stable block and a C17 weatherboarded barn. PARSONAGE HALL, Colne Road, has two jettied gable ends facing the road. That on the r. is the end of a C15 cross-wing (extended early C16) of a hall that extended to the l., replaced in the late C16 by the parallel range. Some original glazing and stair with solid treads, and early C17 panelling. Former MALTINGS, Station Hill, dated 1851 (housing since *c*. 1984). Brick with gault brick dressings. Three storeys, with two-storey cross-wings and square kiln behind.

BURNHAM-ON-CROUCH

ST MARY THE VIRGIN. Not a church type of South Essex. Nave and chancel, and aisles and chancel chapels, without any structural divisions, so a total of nine bays, even if the slightly lower arches of the last three bays indicate that they belong to the chancel. Yet the church, which is mostly of roughly coursed flint, is not as big as all this sounds. The piers are not high, the arches not wide. The main view is from the s – seven three-light Perp windows with four-centred arches and a variety of panel tracery a little more imaginative than the common run of South Essex. Slight differences again between nave and chancel. The aisle and chapel are embattled, as is the s porch, which is decorated with shields. The N windows of the church are C14, those of the aisle earlier than those of the chapel. The aisle windows go with the ragstone-rubble w tower, which must be early to mid C14, as indicated by the ogee-reticulated w window. Above it a tall foliate cross in flint flushwork. Angle buttresses. The upper part with the battlements was rebuilt following storm damage in 1702, and it may be that the w window was given its oddly shaped top at the same time. The church's N side is definitely the back, although it has a pretty, early C16 brick porch with a stepped gable, for the benefit of BURNHAM HALL, a C17 timber-framed and plastered manor house that lies on this side beyond a moat.

The church's interior is characterized by the contrast of the long arcades with the long smooth plastered barrel vault built after a fire in 1774. It is broken only by simple dormer windows, three on each side, and a fine CANDELABRUM of twelve branches in two tiers. The s arcade has C14 filleted quatrefoil piers, reused in the C15, when the bases were made to fit the length of the piers, and the capitals and moulded arches

---

*The village of Bures St Mary, including the parish church, lies in Suffolk.

were added. The N arcade has octagonal piers with double-chamfered arches. Restored *c.* 1871–9 by *Charles Read*, a local man, the evidence mainly to be found in fittings. – FONT, *c.* 1200, square bowl on five supports, Purbeck marble, undecorated. – PULPIT. 1877, designed and made by *J. Forsyth*. Unusually fancy, of Caen stone with marble panels and shafts, and figures of Christ, St Peter and St Paul under elaborate ogee canopies. – Contemporary LECTERN with wooden base and desk, brass stem and fittings. – STAINED GLASS. E window 1874, S chapel E 1881 by *Clayton & Bell*, N chapel E 1884 by *Jones & Willis*. Another N window (to Abraham and Elizabeth Clay) by *Cox & Sons*, 1879. – BRASS. Charming seated figure of the Virgin and Child, *c.* 1500, only 5½ in. (14 cm.) high. Found when the church green was ploughed up in 1977.

ST CUTHBERT (R.C.), Western Road. Church and presbytery, 1911–12, by *Gordon Smart*. Brick. E.E., with polygonal apse. Lady Chapel and porch added 1966–7 as part of reordering. – STAINED GLASS. One window signed by *T. M. Westlake*, 1923, another by *C. Massen*, 1978.

BAPTIST CHURCH, High Street. By *Searle & Hayes*, 1904. Brick with rendered panels and 'patent stone' dressings, looking more like a hall or small theatre than a church.

Former PRIMITIVE METHODIST CHAPEL, Albert Road. 1865, with distinctive polychrome front of red, black, and white brick.

LIBRARY, Station Road. By the *County Architect's Dept.* (architect in charge, *J. E. C. Brand*), 1960–1. A small version of the standard 1960s Essex branch library, with panels of glazing and brick and continuous clerestory.

ST PETER'S HIGH SCHOOL, Southminster Road. By *Johns, Slater & Haward*, completed 1962. As well as the usual predominance of glazing, some brick and timber cladding.

Former COTTAGE HOSPITAL, Albert Road. By *Eric P. W. Cooper*, *c.* 1937. Neo-Georgian, with prominent dormers. Now housing.

PERAMBULATION. It is Burnham's riverfront that really matters; its chief attraction one terrace of low houses along THE QUAY. The centre is the WHITE HART HOTEL, a little higher than the others, with a porch on carved brackets. C18 brick, six windows wide including two large bays. The other houses are also of brick, some rendered, of no composition, but very pleasant. The one to the E of the hotel has a rainwater head dated 1781. Further along, to the W, some good weatherboarding at No. 1, and also beside the White Hart in Shore Road. Further W still BURNHAM SAILING CLUB, a modest timber clubhouse with pantile roof by *Eric P. W. Cooper*, *c.* 1937, with later additions.

Towards the sea, a note of a very different kind, the ROYAL CORINTHIAN YACHT CLUB, 1930–1 by *Joseph Emberton*. One of the most famous, and earliest, buildings of the Modern Movement in England, its position and function making it an appropriate epitome of the stylistic similarities between sleek 112 white structures and ocean liners. It was commissioned by the club's commodore, Philip Benson, an advertising man who knew Emberton from his work designing exhibition stands. Three principal storeys, sheer towards the land but stepped back along the riverfront to provide tiers of balconies with nautical, inward-curving railings. The ground floor provided facilities for both sexes, the first floor for men only, with members' bedrooms on the second floor and 'race box' above that on the flat roof. The river front is almost totally glazed with Crittall windows that wrap round the corners and narrow to horizontal slits on the side and rear elevations, and follow the line of the stairs on the E wall. Steel frame construction, the walls of cement-rendered hollow brick. Some good external detailing, e.g. the lettering and lamp by the landward entrance, but very plain interiors. To its W the former clubhouse, weatherboarded with slate roof, and between the two the OTTER HUT, 2001–2 by *Bailey Lewis* as their own office. Single-storey, traditional weatherboarding and slate at the landward end, then walls of glass and blue enamelled glass with portholes beneath a curved copper roof jutting out towards the river.

The broad HIGH STREET seems almost of secondary importance, its buildings mostly modest in scale. The chief accent is the CLOCK TOWER, built in 1877 in front of what was then the Charity School, now St Mary's House. Octagonal tower, three storeys of brick with black brick quoins and diapering and Tudoresque hoodmoulds, then a stuccoed clock stage and finally an open cupola with ogee-shaped roof. School 'restored and enlarged' 1863, also in red and black brick, and gables with carved bargeboards; alongside a pair of houses. Almost opposite, No. 30 has a nice C18 brick front with wide windows flanking a narrower central bay with pedimented doorcase. At this point the street narrows; a little W, backing on to the river, Nos. 15, 17 and the Cabin Dairy, C18 and early C19, make an attractive timber-framed, plastered and weatherboarded group. Towards the E end, No. 83 (Creel Cottage) is particularly appealing: one weatherboarded storey with dormers in the mansard roof. Opposite, an attempt at a more urban scale: No. 70, dated 1848, stock brick with a gault brick front of two-and-a-half storeys with Ionic portico *in antis*.

CHERRY GARDEN, London Road, ½ m. W. Brick house, perhaps *c.* 1670. Two wings with straight gables and between them a two-storey projecting porch with Dutch gable. Spoilt by a large plastered E extension of *c.* 1980.

MINEFIELD CONTROL TOWER, about 4 m. ESE. Second World War observation post. Concrete, two storeys surmounted by a pyramidal firing post, a bizarre and rare survival.

BUTTSBURY

Stock

ST MARY. Small and alone. Squat W tower, the upper part (and the S porch) weatherboarded. C14 nave of only two bays with two aisles, wider than it is long. The aisles' Dec E windows look uncomfortably large, as if reused. Typical late Perp nave arcades, composite, with the centre parts to the nave carried on into the arches without the capitals and the side parts concave-sided semi-octagonal. Chancel also C14 (see the PISCINA and blocked N doorway) but much altered in the C18 and in 1876, the date of the E window. C15 crown-post roofs in nave and chancel. – DOORS. The N and S doors are both old, that on the N more interesting. C11, altered and elaborate ironwork added in the mid C12. – Fragment of a C15 Doom PAINTING, on wood. Cross nimbus and part of Christ's head, flanked by the heads of angels, one holding a spear and the other a nail. Discovered after removal of the nave's plaster ceiling, 1977.

CANEWDON

8090

ST NICHOLAS. An unusually stately church for such an out-of-the-way place. Massive, tall W tower of elephant-grey dressed ragstone. Four stages, with angle buttresses and battlements with stone and flint chequer. W doorway with decorated spandrels. Three-light W window and below it three panels with shields of arms. Niches l. and r. of the doorway and in the W faces of the buttresses. All this must be C15. Of the same time the S front of the nave and broad three-light windows with coarse panel tracery (renewed), and the S porch with battlements of stone and flint chequer, an outer and an inner doorway with shields in the spandrels, and two-light N and S windows. The rest mostly C14, see the three-light intersected tracery in a N aisle window and the W bays of the N arcade with octagonal piers and hoodmoulds on defaced corbels. Late C15 E pier. Chancel largely rebuilt by *W. Hargreaves Raffles*, 1893–4. Nave roof with four large tie-beams, one dated 1698; crown-posts with four-way struts. – FONT. From St Mary Magdalene, Shopland (dem. 1957). Early C13. Square bowl on five supports. Decoration on one side with interleaved arches, on another with trefoiled arches, on the other two incised fleurs-de-lys etc. – PULPIT. From *Wren*'s St Christopher le Stocks, City of London, 1670–6 (dem. 1782). Hexagonal, carved with garlands and cherubs' heads. – PEWS. Installed 1989–90. From St Peter upon Cornhill, another City church, perhaps part of *J.D. Wyatt*'s restoration, 1872. Good quality, with low doors. – S DOOR. C15, with trellis-framing, hinged down the middle as well as at the side. – COMMANDMENTS BOARD, on chancel E wall, presumably contemporary with the large Charities Board in N aisle, 1818. – STAINED GLASS. E window, 1924, and N aisle (war memorial), 1919, by *Percy Bacon*.

S of the church the former VICARAGE, 1758, the N front with porch and crowstepped gable all C19 additions.* By the churchyard's E entrance a small weatherboarded LOCK-UP, restored 1983. Stocks and whipping-post inside dated 1775.

---

* Canewdon Hall, 1807, has been demolished.

THE ALGIERS, High Street. C18 timber-framed and weather-boarded house and shop with high mansard roof.

LAMBOURNE HALL, 1 m. ESE. Late C13 two-bay hall, the E cross-wing built not long after. Main chimneystack inserted in the late C15. In the C17 the cross-wing was raised under a mansard roof and a two-storey porch, originally jettied, added to the S front.

CANVEY ISLAND

7080

Canvey Island was reclaimed under an agreement of 1622 between the landowners, principally Sir Henry Appleton, and Joas Croppenburgh, 'a Dutchman skilled in the making of dikes'.* It seems likely that the work might already have been completed by the date of the agreement, which allowed Croppenburgh one-third of the reclaimed land. Further impetus to the development of the island was provided by the opening of the railway station at Benfleet, just across the creek to the N, in 1855. Between the wars Canvey Island was the fastest-growing resort in the country, with a bridge replacing a causeway over Benfleet Creek in 1930–1, but much of the resulting housing had to be rebuilt after the disastrous floods of 1953. The whole island E of the main access road is given over to seaside and suburban development, much of it bungalows.

Former ST KATHERINE, Canvey Road (heritage centre). 1875 by F. G. Lee. The Dutch built a chapel on the site, rebuilt as an Anglican church in 1712, and again in 1845. Timber-framed, because of the boggy soil, and originally weatherboarded, but plastered in the 1930s. Nave and chancel with transepts, and S porch reused from the 1845 church. Bellcote and flèche over the crossing originally taller.[†]

ST NICHOLAS, Long Road. By *Stanley Bragg & Associates*, 1960. A-frame, the eaves about 6 ft (1.8 metres) off the ground. Six triangular dormers. Wooden relief SCULPTURE on E wall, 1981, depicting Canvey Island, the Thames, and sea-wall. – HALL to W by *R.C. Foyster*, 1964, with link to church by *Tim Venn*, 1987.

OUR LADY OF CANVEY AND THE ENGLISH MARTYRS (R.C.), Long Road. 1938 by *E. E. Lawrence* of Canvey Island, and very odd-looking; was it meant to be Dutch? W tower with diagonal buttresses that slope inwards up the full height, and short splay-foot spire. This originally had green glazed tiles, as on the nave. Brick, painted white. Presbytery by *A. J. Newton* (*Burles & Newton*), 1952.

PUBLIC LIBRARY, High Street. 1960, by the *County Architect's Dept.* (architect in charge, *K. W. Benoy*). Single-storey, brick, with clerestory window beneath flat roof, the entrance marked by a projecting canopy supported on thin columns.

---

* Morant.
[†] School, 1873, and vicarage, 1876, S of the church, also by *Lee*; dem.

CASTLE VIEW SCHOOL, Meppel Avenue. 1979–81 by the *County Architect's Dept.* (project architect, *David Schreiber*). Lightweight pavilion blocks floating on concrete rafts, connected by circulation areas which have large expanses of sloping glazing incorporating solar panels. Detached sports hall.

The island's earliest surviving buildings are two cottages, both called DUTCH COTTAGE, erected for Dutch workmen, one in Canvey Road (now a museum) dated 1618, the other in Haven Road dated 1621 (cf. Rayleigh). Octagonal, timber-framed, faced in brick, the former plastered, the latter painted. Single storey with attics, and circular thatched roof with central chimney. The Museum has pretty Gothic casements. In Haven Road, overlooking Hole Haven, the LOBSTER SMACK, mainly C18 and C19, and nearby a row of late C19 coastguard COTTAGES – all timber-framed and weatherboarded.

Canvey Island's development as a resort in the 1930s was centred further E on Furtherwick Road, of which the principal monument stands on the sea wall: the LABWORTH CAFÉ, 113 1932–3, the only building designed by *Ove Arup*. Reinforced concrete, circular, with continuous windows, and flat roof. Below the café, facing the water and with straight wings extending to either side, open shelters (now glazed). Arup was then chief engineer for *Christiani & Nielsen*, and the café formed part of sea defences they were constructing.

CASTLE HEDINGHAM   7030

HEDINGHAM CASTLE. It is understandable that the castle gave its name to the village. It dominates it and all the country round. This was one of the mightiest and most famous castles of East Anglia, built by, and belonging to, one of the most powerful families of Norman England, the de Veres, Earls of Oxford. It stands to this day as an ideal picture of a keep – on a mount, high above old trees, with two of its square corner turrets still rising up to nearly 100 ft (31 metres). It is, moreover, probably the best-preserved of all tower-keeps of England. In proportion, style, and detail that of Rochester is its nearest relation, and the two may well be the work of the same architect or *ingeniator*, as the designer of fortifications was called.

The KEEP stands on a mount which represents the inner 50 bailey. It was built by Aubrey de Vere, probably to celebrate his creation as Earl of Oxford in 1142 and to provide a suitably impressive setting for ceremonial occasions. The walls are of ashlar in Barnack stone that is still remarkably crisp, and all have putlog holes. Attached to the W side was a forebuilding – perhaps containing the prison – of which only rough walling remains. The outlines of its roofs can be seen on the W wall of the keep. At ground-floor level, inaccessible from outside, were stores. The staircase to the main entrance ran up inside the forebuilding parallel with the W wall of the keep. It led to a doorway with thick columns with scalloped capitals and an arch dominated by zigzag ornament. Through this doorway the large first-floor room or Lower Hall was reached. This has a segmental arch across from E to W, the central portion rebuilt, and a fireplace in the S wall with a zigzag arch. The windows are shafted inside and out. Outside they are of course very small, but inside they are set in tall arched recesses. In the thickness of the wall are divers narrow chambers or recesses. One of these, in the NE angle, can be identified as a garderobe. The main staircase is in the NW angle.

On the second floor lies the Upper Hall, 38 by 31 ft (12 by 9.5 metres) in size by 27 ft (8.5 metres) in height, but originally (*see* below) open to the roof, a height of 33 ft (10 metres). It is surrounded by a gallery at about half its height. Across the Hall, again from E to W, a large arch is struck. It rests on responds with angle shafts and in the middle on heavy demi-columns each carrying extremely heavy two-scalloped capitals. The arch moulding is of two rolls with a small ridge between. The fireplace has again a zigzag arch, and the windows here also have zigzag decoration in the arches. The gallery openings are as large towards the Hall as the window recesses, but plainer. To the outside shafted twin openings correspond to them, as against the single opening below. The entrance from the staircase to the gallery is enriched by some pretty beaded spiral fluting.

The third floor is lower and simpler, and there was originally no room at this level but just a pyramidal roof concealed behind the high parapet, as for example at the White Tower in London. The present top floor may have been formed as part of late C15 alterations, but all the internal timberwork, including floors, was destroyed by fire in 1918 (replaced *c.* 1921). The windows on this floor were never fitted with glazing or shutters but are, on the outside, the most elaborate of all, single openings set in wide arches with bold zigzag decoration designed to be seen and admired from afar. Above this were the battlements, of which nothing remains. Of the four much taller angle turrets only two survive, and these also are now deprived of their battlements.

None of the other buildings of the medieval castle survive, although much remains of the earthworks of both the inner bailey and the outer bailey to the E, mostly wooded. Excavations by *Chancellor* in 1868 showed that the GREAT HALL stood SW of the keep and had a vaulted undercroft and a bay window. The CHAPEL was immediately to the S of the keep. Considerable new building was undertaken by the 13th Earl of Oxford in the late C15, including a brick GATEHOUSE, of which the two bases of the octagonal angle turrets can be seen beyond the position of the curtain wall to the S. Also of this date is the handsome brick BRIDGE across the moat to the E of the keep, with four four-centred arches. The retaining walls of the moat on the N side of the bridge seem to be the remains of a TENNIS COURT that was recorded in this position in the early C17. The wall on the E side of the moat has been incorporated in C18 brick STABLES.

The castle was bought by Sir William Ashurst in 1713, who built a new HOUSE in the outer bailey. Horace Walpole thought it, in 1748, 'a trumpery new house . . . in the bad taste of architecture that came between the charming venerable gothic and pure architecture'. The rainwater heads are dated 1719, the year of Sir William's death. Principal range of seven bays, two storeys and attics and vaulted cellars. Brick with stone dressings and stone parapet with wooden balusters. Ionic stone doorcase on the S front. Handsome, spacious contemporary staircase with wrought-iron railing. On the E side, set back, a separate seven-bay range with three-bay pediment, the remodelling of an existing building. The two ranges are connected by a late C19 entrance porch and corridor which has, on the E side, a bow staircase. The layout of the garden was undertaken or completed by Sir William's son Robert, whose initials and the date 1720 are picked out in black headers on the red brick octagonal DOVECOTE SE of the house. It has a square lantern with gaps at the bottom of the glazing to allow the pigeons to enter, but too narrow for birds of prey. Fishponds S of the house were joined up to form a canal, and in 1726 *Adam Holt* was employed to form an octagonal basin at the N end and plant an avenue flanking the canal.

ST NICHOLAS. The brick W tower is dated 1616, on a stone plaque naming 'the master builder of this stepell' as *Robart [sic] Archer*, but seems to be substantially of the early C16. It is impressively high when you stand near it, but suffers from the position of the whole village centre in a dip. The tower is built entirely in the Tudor style, with diagonal buttresses, a higher stair-turret (with a small C18 cupola), stepped battlements, and (obelisk) pinnacles. Above the five-light W window is a frieze of shields referring to the 13th Earl of Oxford †1513, e.g. a chain of state, because he was Lord Great Chamberlain. Also of brick are the battlements on the nave and aisles, and the clerestory windows. Above the latter a frieze with de Vere emblems, alternate boars and mullets. Early C16 also the S porch. The windows of the church are mostly Perp, except for the chancel, and all renewed by *Woodyer* during his restoration of 1870–2.

In spite of all this external appearance and the dominance of the tower, the church, once it is entered, reveals itself as one of the most important and, of its period, the most ambitiously designed in Essex. A complete Late Norman parish church, the nave and chancel 125 ft (38.5 metres) long. The six-bay nave arcades rest on alternatingly circular and octagonal piers with splendidly carved leaf capitals, mostly of crocket-like leaves, but in one case also of real crockets on the French Early Gothic pattern. That dates the nave not earlier than *c.* 1180, as do the complex mouldings of the arches. The tall tower arch has semicircular responds and must have led into a tower of substantial size. The triple-chamfered arch, however, is Tudor, if not

1616. The s as well as n doorway belong to the Late Norman building. They have columns with volute and waterleaf capitals and round arches.

The long chancel is even more of a showpiece. First externally. The e end has an exceptionally impressive design, which does not seem to have been decided upon at once. The ground floor has two shallow buttresses or pilaster-strips ending at the sill level of the windows. There are three small lancets shafted outside and inside and above them a large wheel window with eight columns as spokes. This is a rare motif in Norman England (Barfreston, Peterborough). On the s side is a doorway with one order of colonettes with thin long volute capitals and two-dimensional zigzag work in the (round) arches. The s and n windows are shafted like those at the e end. Internally a whole order of blank arches on shafts runs round the windows, a large arch for each window and also a narrower and less high one for each interval. Here also all the arches are round. The chancel arch makes a special display of three-dimensional zigzag and similar motifs and very thin long nook-shafts. Can it be earlier than *c.* 1190?

The late medieval alterations and additions are minor and have been mentioned – with one exception: the double-hammerbeam roof of the nave which, as a crowning motif, is worthy of the Norman columns. It is one of only four roofs of such type in Essex, and is attributed by John Harvey to *Thomas Loveday*, who was living in Castle Hedingham when he made his will in 1535. *Woodyer* added the n organ chamber, and the too-perfect stepped SEDILIA and PISCINA. Many of the internal arches received his characteristic scalloped edges, mostly since covered up.

CHANCEL STALLS. On the s side with misericords, e.g. a fox carrying off a priest, and man's face and two leopards' heads, etc. – SCREEN. One of the most ornate in a county poor in worthwhile screens. One-light divisions, each with a heavily cusped and crocketed ogee head and much panel tracery above. *c.* 1400, restored by *Woodyer*, who added the gates and a floriated cross, the latter since removed. – FONT. 1863, Neo-Norman. Square stone with coloured marble inlays, massive central stem and four columns with leaf capitals. – STOUP. Norman, with ornamental carving of a beast's head and foliage (s aisle). – CUPBOARD (under the tower). Made from C17 panels. – DOORS. In the n and two s doorways, late C12, with long iron battens with long thin scrolls. – SCULPTURE. Obscure demi-figure, perhaps of a woman praying; small; probably C12 (s wall s aisle). – PAINTING. Fragment of plaster with the head of a bishop or king, diaper background, preserved in a glass case at the w end. Early C14. – MOSAIC and *opus sectile* panel, 1883 (s aisle e wall). By *James Powell & Sons*, designed by *Charles Hardgrave*. – STAINED GLASS. Three e lancets by *Hardman & Co.*, 1870, and presumably the remaining chancel windows also. w window by *Geldart*, 1892–9, made by *Percy Bacon & Bros*. s aisle s also by Bacon,

1910. N aisle N by *J. Wippell & Co.*, 1927. – MONUMENTS. John, 15th Earl of Oxford †1539 and wife. Tomb-chest, of black touchstone. Along the side the kneeling figures of four daughters. On the opposite side four sons, not visible, as the monument, which was originally placed in the middle of the choir, now stands against the wall. On the lid the kneeling figures of the earl and his lady under some drapery gathered up, and above a coat of arms, all very deeply carved. Only minor details are in the new Renaissance taste. The monument is probably by *Cornelius Harman*, to whom we owe the Audley Monument at Saffron Walden (1544, q.v.). The other de Veres were buried at Earls Colne Priory. – Daniel Sandford †1779. By *William Pinder*. Open pediment on attached Corinthian columns, white on grey marble. – CHURCHYARD CROSS. C12 shaft and plinth, with carved decoration and bosses on the chamfered edges. Incorporated into a war memorial by *P. M. Johnston*, 1921, with the addition of a wooden wheel-cross.

UNITED REFORMED CHURCH (Presbyterian/Independent). 1842, probably by *Fenton*. Gault brick front and sides. Two tiers of windows, the upper ones with round heads. The central five bays of the front break forward with pediment. Horseshoe gallery and box pews. In front, paving in black and white pebbles, dated 1868. Behind, former SCHOOL, red brick with stock brick dressings, 1853.

POLICE STATION, Queen Street. By *Hopper*, 1843, contractor *H.H. Hayward*. Plain brick, essentially domestic.

CEMETERY, Sheepcot Road. Opened 1884. LYCHGATE by *Chancellor*, 1908.

POOLE'S BRIDGE, ⅓ m. SW, over River Colne. By *Robert Poole*, surveyor, 1736, enlarged 1819. Three arches, brick with stone copings.

THE VILLAGE. Although the Castle dominates visually, its enclosures have disappeared and left no obvious physical mark on what was in the Middle Ages a small town, and is now a village, one moreover that is throughout pleasant to look at. What there is of unsightly developments lies half a mile to the W along the A1017. Close to this there was a Benedictine nunnery founded in 1191 (*see* Nunnery Farm, below). The village is a triangle with Bayley Street to the N, St James Street to the S, and Crown Street to the W. The pattern is repeated right in the centre by the small triangular opening E of the churchyard, FALCON SQUARE. On the N side FALCON HOUSE (formerly Falcon Inn), early C16, two ranges, each jettied with carved brackets, with exposed timbers. Inside, C17 wall paintings on the ground floor, heavy arcading with pendant motif. To the l., the cottages of CHURCH PONDS facing the N side of the church, to the r. a vista closed by the YOUTH HOSTEL, C16 with an unexceptionable C19 gabled façade. Opposite, by contrast, FALCON HOUSE, gault brick, dated 1849. Five bays, with paired pilasters at each end and two more either side of the entrance bay. To its r., at the bottom of King Street, a Georgian brick house of five bays and doorcase with open pediment. To the S of this another, unfortunately painted, seven bays wide with parapet. This links up with St James Street and Queen Street, with at the corner of St JAMES STREET a particularly pretty half-timbered house, now a restaurant (THE OLD MOOT HOUSE), C15. More timber-framed houses along St James Street to the E, and on the N side BANK HOUSE, C16 with a Georgian brick front, to which Eric Ravilious moved from Great Bardfield in 1934.

Back in QUEEN STREET, but looking E along St James Street, the WHEATSHEAF, C16, with long-wall jetty supported on iron columns. After a bend in the road the OLD VICARAGE, the best classical brick house: five bays, three storeys, stucco bands and quoins, Ionic pedimented doorcase, Venetian window above, and semi-elliptical window above that. It must be Early Georgian. To its r., TRINITY HALL, early C18 timber-framed and panel-pargetted, with a later C18 brick rear façade. Behind Trinity Hall, off Sheepcot Road, THE MEADOW, a large brick and stucco house with Crittall windows by F.W. Chancellor, 1923–4. S of Sheepcot Road, opposite the United Reformed Church (see above), SHEEPCOTE, C17 timber-framed and plastered but with many later additions. Gabled cross-wing to the l., and to the r. a forward cross-wing that has double gables with carved bargeboards.

KIRBY HALL, 1¼ m. NNW. C16 timber-framed with some brick facing. Three-gabled front. C18 outhouse of diapered brick to r.

NUNNERY FARM, ⅓ m. W. Two C16 front ranges, of which one is jettied, and a later wing to the rear, probably C17. Good farm buildings, including a large C17 or C18 BARN along the street, clad with brick and weatherboarding.

CHADWELL ST MARY
Thurrock U.A.

ST MARY. Norman nave with S doorway. Above the C15 N doorway, C12 tympanum with rosettes and saltire crosses. Chancel C14 with original roof. W tower of c. 1500 with diagonal buttresses at the foot, W doorway with original DOOR, and little ogee-headed niche to its r. The difference in the Norman and the C15 flintwork is worth noting. Restoration by C.E. Powell, c. 1889–93, who added the S vestry. – SEDILIA. Made from C17 carved panels. – STAINED GLASS. Mostly 1886–7, except chancel S by G.E.R. Smith (A.K. Nicholson Stained Glass Studios), 1952–4. – Churchyard: some nicely carved C18 HEADSTONES, and large standing stone to Kadzuo Yamazaki †1899, a Japanese seaman killed in an accident at Tilbury Dock. Finished on one side only, with English and Japanese inscription.

SLEEPERS FARM, W of the church. C15 thatched house, timber-framed and plastered, with gabled and jettied cross-wing to l.

SUNSPAN, Sandy Lane, ⅓ m. SE. One of the few built examples of the flat-roofed prototype 'Sunspan' house by Wells Coates and *David Pleydell-Bouverie* shown at the 1934 'Ideal Home' exhibition. White-painted rendered brick. Compact square plan with two rounded corners, one containing the curved front door. The living room on the opposite corner looks towards the River Thames.

CHAPPEL

8020

ST BARNABAS. Formerly a chapel of St Barnabas, Great Tey, whence the dedication and the name of the village. Recorded in 1285. Nave and chancel in one, mainly of flint rubble, and belfry with very pointed little weatherboarded spire. The E window and one S window are early C14: two lights cusped under one pointed head, with a cusped quatrefoil in the head. C18 S porch, N vestry by *H.W. Pearce* (*Duncan Clark & Beckett*), 1959. The interior equally simple, with plain C18 W gallery. Seating probably dates from a restoration in 1860–1. Restoration by *Duncan Clark & Beckett*, 1936–7, exposed the C14 roof; chancel reordered by *W. D. Caröe* at the same time. – PULPIT and READING DESK. Incorporating C17 panels.

PRIMARY SCHOOL. 1871, by the vicar, *J. P. Britton*. Brick with bargeboarded gables. Sensitively extended by the *County Architect's Dept* (project architect, *C.P. French*), 1976–7.

Some attractive houses immediately round the church, in particular BRIDGEWICK HALL to the E. Timber-framed hall house floored and enlarged *c.* 1600, remodelled in the late C17. Plastered five-bay front of the 1820s with central semicircular porch. The first-floor sashes are squeezed up to accommodate plaster reliefs, the Four Seasons (rectangular) and roundels of Night and Day after *Thorvaldsen*. One Gothick window. To the r., RAYNHAM HOUSE, with exposed timber framing. Mostly *c.* 1600 but with a mid-C14 N wing. W of the church, VIADUCT FARM, C16 timber-framed, but with an early C19 gault brick front. Five generously spaced bays, Gothick window over the central porch, and large ornamental chimney off-centre.

The village is dominated visually by the VIADUCT, rightly described in White's 1848 *Directory* as 'stupendous'. Built in 1847–9 to carry the Colchester, Stour Valley, Sudbury & Halstead Railway over the River Colne 80 ft (25 metres) below. Engineer, *Peter Bruff*, contractor, *George Wythes*. Thirty-two arches, 1,136 ft (350 metres) long, constructed of locally made bricks, rather than timber as originally intended. 96

CHAPPEL STATION. *See* Wakes Colne.

OLD VICARAGE, ½ m. ESE. By *Joseph Grimes*, builder, 1869–70. Domestic Gothic, with decorative black brickwork. Grimes was sufficiently competent to be trusted also with church restorations.

CHELMSFORD

Cathedral   201
Churches   206
Public Buildings   208
Industrial Buildings   213
Perambulations
    1. The Town Centre   214
    2. New Street and the Anglia Ruskin
           University campus   217
    3. North-west beyond the railway   219
    4. Springfield Road   220
    5. Moulsham Street and New London Road   221

Charles Dickens found Chelmsford 'the dullest and most stupid spot on the face of the earth', a judgement with which many would still agree. Although the county town, it falls far short of Colchester in historic and architectural interest; even the town's official guide (*c.* 1936) began by saying that 'most of Chelmsford's ancient buildings have been demolished by the great progress of the place in modern times', and Pevsner's observation in 1954 that 'the centre has remained singularly unaffected by the coarser and louder forms of commercialisation' is no longer true. The town possesses one very good building – the Shire Hall – and a cathedral that is in essence still the large parish church of a prosperous market town. Neither can match the sense of authority and civic pomp that is conveyed by Colchester's Castle and Town Hall. In spite of all that, however, the persistent tourist will find many individual buildings of interest.

p. 202 Chelmsford lies at an important point on the Roman road from Colchester to London where it crosses two rivers, the Can and the Chelmer, just before their confluence.* The Roman town (Caesaromagus) was on the s side of the Can, dating from the CI A.D. The area of settlement, approximately 850 ft (260 metres) square, is roughly defined by Moulsham Street and Manor Road to w and e, Parkway and Hamlet Street to n and s. A fort was built after the invasion in A.D. 43 and in *c.* 120 a *mansio*, or hostel for travellers, its position still discernible by a slight rise in Roman Road. An octagonal temple was built just outside the fort to the NE in about A.D. 325, but after 400 the town declined. The bridge over the Can collapsed and was not rebuilt for 700 years.

The centre of activity shifted after the Norman Conquest to the N side of the Can, although a Dominican friary, of which nothing remains, was built in the C13 on a site between Parkway and the river. In the same century the parish church was built at the upper end of the High Street, and the Walkers' map of 1591 shows the basic shape of the High Street much as it is today, widening towards the top with houses beginning to form a middle row that would eventually separate Tindal

---

* Chelmer is a back-formation from Chelmsford.

Street from the High Street. The first major changes to the town's layout occurred in the 1840s, with the development of New London Road and the arrival of the railway. Industry soon followed, with the founding of Crompton & Co. (electrical engineers) in 1878, the Hoffmann Manufacturing Co. (ball bearings) in 1898 and Marconi's Wireless Telegraph Co. in 1899.

The population rose from 2,858 in 1801 to 12,627 in 1901, and through the C20 growth was rapid. The council made a tentative start on housing before the First World War, continued in the 1930s with the Boarded Barns and Springfield Park estates, and after the Second World War at Melbourne Park. In the last quarter of the C20 major housing developments in Springfield (q.v.) – North Springfield, Chelmer Village, and Beaulieu Park – brought the population of Chelmsford and its immediate built-up area to nearly 100,000. Industrial development after the Second World War took place mainly to the SW of the town, along Waterhouse Lane and Westway, with factories for Marconi, Britvic, and the English Electric Valve Co. (the latter incorporating a weatherboarded barn of *c.* 1600, converted for use as a social club).

A comprehensive scheme for redeveloping the town centre, drawn up under the direction of *Anthony Minoprio* and published in 1945, would have obliterated the historic street plan, and fortunately none of it was carried out. The most intrusive developments were a new inner ring road, Parkway, 1965–8, and the High Chelmer Shopping Precinct, 1972, which destroyed one side of Tindal Street and included the demolition of *Chancellor*'s Corn Exchange, but N and E of the centre efforts have been made to improve the landscaping of the riverside, providing a green link to the University's Rivermead Campus and suburban areas beyond. Development continues at a rapid pace, with considerable changes planned or under way on the site of the University's Central Campus and the bus station,★ on the S side of Duke Street either side of the railway.

CATHEDRAL CHURCH OF ST MARY THE VIRGIN, ST PETER AND ST CEDD

A diocese for the county of Essex was created in 1913 and Chelmsford had been chosen as its see town in 1908. How to turn St Mary's, the parish church, into a cathedral, was a problem that has still not been entirely solved. Perhaps Liverpool and Guildford were wiser to build new temples. At Chelmsford it was decided to expand the existing building. *Chancellor & Son*'s proposals of 1908, for extending the chancel and building vestries and an octagonal chapter house on the N side, were superseded in 1920 by an extremely ambitious, but also unrealized, scheme by *Sir Charles Nicholson*, who planned to retain the church as a

★ Mixed development by *DLA Architecture* under construction in 2005–7.

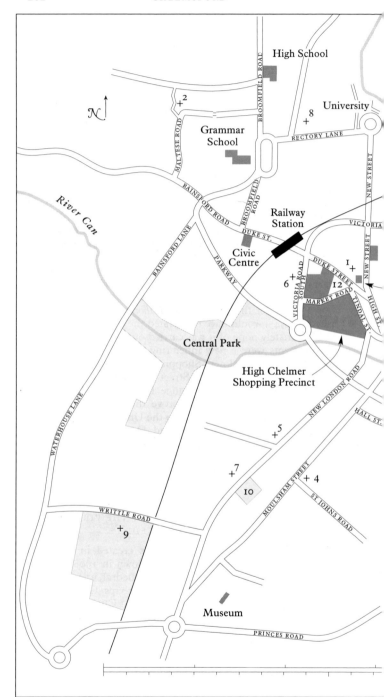

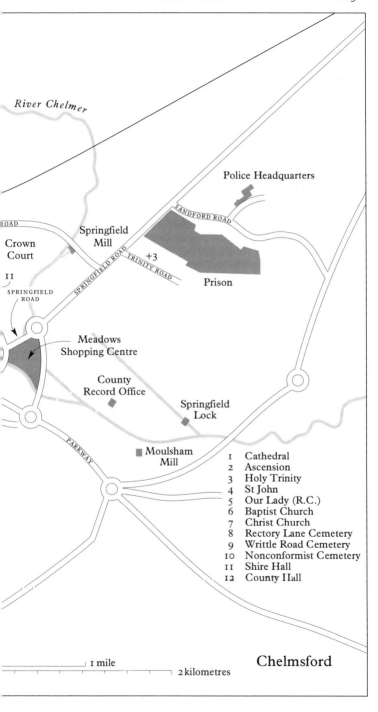

River Chelmer

Police Headquarters

SANDFORD ROAD

Springfield
Mill

Crown
Court

SPRINGFIELD ROAD

TRINITY ROAD

+3

Prison

11

SPRINGFIELD
ROAD

Meadows
Shopping Centre

County
Record Office

Springfield
Lock

PARKWAY

Moulsham
Mill

1 Cathedral
2 Ascension
3 Holy Trinity
4 St John
5 Our Lady (R.C.)
6 Baptist Church
7 Christ Church
8 Rectory Lane Cemetery
9 Writtle Road Cemetery
10 Nonconformist Cemetery
11 Shire Hall
12 County Hall

1 mile

2 kilometres

Chelmsford

s aisle to the new cathedral and balance its w tower with a second.* In the end only modest additions were built.

The church was entirely rebuilt in the C15, mainly of flint rubble, comprising nave and aisles, chancel and chapels, w tower and s porch. The commanding late C15 tower, of brick faced with stone, has angle buttresses on the E, set back on the W. The battlements are decorated with flushwork and carry eight small pinnacles. Carved emblems along the string course by *T.B. Huxley-Jones*, 1959. The charming open lantern is of 1749, when the needle spire was also rebuilt (by *George Gainge*, joiner, with plumbers *John Blatch* and *Edmund Mason*). w doorway with two-centred arch under an ogee label and shields within quatrefoils in the spandrels. The spectacular two-storey s PORCH has a great display of flushwork, among the best in Essex, that is continued along the battlements of the s aisle. Inside, the panelled ceiling reuses pieces of wooden tracery. To its E the bays of the s AISLE are ashlar-faced, as is the s side of the clerestory, showing those parts rebuilt by *J. Johnson*, 1800–3, following the collapse of the nave. The E and N walls of his clerestory are of stock brick. The CHANCEL and s CHAPEL were restored by *Chancellor*, 1862 (new s windows and s door); chancel clerestory by *A.W. Blomfield*, 1877–8. Figure of St Peter on the SE corner of the s chapel by *Huxley-Jones*, 1960. The two eastern bays of the chancel, slightly higher, by *Nicholson*, 1926–8, with very characteristic buttressing with plain detailing. The E window, enlarged from three to five lights by Blomfield, is reused. Also by Nicholson the N block of vestries etc., 1929, that originally also contained the chapter house.† All this work is distinguished from the C19 additions by the greater use of pebbles, tilework and unknapped flint. Two storeys, apart from the NE corner, which was raised to two storeys in matching style by *Andrew Murdoch* of *Fitzroy Robinson*, 2003–4. The vestries lead off the N transept, added by *Chancellor* in 1873 together with the outer N aisle.

The INTERIOR, transformed by reordering in 1983–4 by *Robert Potter*,‡ is somewhat cold and austere, with white limestone floors, but the space is more cathedral-like. The broad nave has only four bays, but these are wide, with thin arcade piers. Aisles embrace both the chancel and the tower, whose tall arch is multi-moulded. *Chancellor*'s outer N aisle carries on in similar style but with bolder capitals. *Johnson* rebuilt the late C15 nave arcades with their characteristic lozenge shape and their mouldings. Sufficient stonework survived for the N arcade

26

---

* Cf. Nicholson's contemporary scheme for Sheffield.

† For the present chapter house, *see* p. 216.

‡ Many FURNISHINGS were lost in the process: marble FONT by *G.E. Street*, 1869, marble PULPIT by *F. Chancellor*, 1873, HIGH ALTAR by *F.W. Chancellor*, 1931, COMMUNION RAIL, *c.* 1675, from Holland, BISHOP'S THRONE by *Nicholson*, 1921, PROVOST'S STALL by *F.W. Chancellor*, carved by *E. Beckwith*, 1936, and s chapel SCREEN by *F.W. Chancellor*, 1919, in memory of F. Chancellor. Street's font replaced one of 1803 by *Coade*, now in Chelmsford Museum.

but on the s side *Coade* stone is used above the original bases, also for the tracery of two s aisle windows E of the porch and of the clerestory windows. Johnson also designed the nave's prettily ribbed, coved Tudor Gothic ceiling (painted and gilded in 1961), with draped female figures between the windows standing on cherubs' heads. The nave aisle roofs, ceiled by Johnson, were replaced in 1899, their design based on the C15 westernmost principals in each aisle. Above the s door, a little stone balcony with traceried lights gives access to the upper floor of the porch, part of its restoration by *Chancellor* in 1882. Chancel arcades early C15, three bays on the s side with depressed arches but on the N side an unusual round arch divided into two pointed arches with openwork panel tracery in the spandrels. The thin pier has four shafts and four hollows in the diagonals. Open timber chancel roof painted and gilded by *S.E. Dykes Bower*, 1957.

FURNISHINGS mostly date from 1983–4. – MAIN ALTAR, at w end of chancel, and FONT, by *Robert Potter*. Both slate, the font a shallow round bowl on tripod support by *Alan Evans*. – BISHOP'S CHAIR or cathedra by *John Skelton*, against the E wall. Behind it a patchwork HANGING by *Beryl Dean*. – In the Mildmay Chapel, ALTAR FRONTAL designed and woven by *Philip Sanderson* on the theme of St Cedd, 2004, and Cathedral BANNER by *Beryl Dean*, 1960. – AMBOS to either side of chancel arch by *Giuseppe Lund*. Steel and bronze. – Also by *Lund*, the SCREENS to the chapels of St Cedd (NW) and St Peter (SW) of rough, tapering steel spikes. – SCULPTURE. St Cedd's Chapel: Christus by *T. B. Huxley-Jones*, cast posthumously in 1968; Mother and Child (bas relief) by *Peter Eugene Ball*, *c.* 2000; Christ the Healer (bronze plaque) by *Georg Ehrlich*. – St Peter's Chapel: The Bombed Child by *Ehrlich*. – Chancel arch: Christus Rex by *Ball*, 2000. – ORGANS. By *N.P. Mander Ltd*: the nave organ (1994) by *Stephen Bicknell* with case based on the work of Dr Arthur Hill, chancel organ (1995) by *Bicknell* and *Didier Grassin*, with decorative painting by *Donald Smith*. – PAINTING. The Tree of Life by *Mark Cazalet*, 2004, in the blocked tracery of a N transept window.

STAINED GLASS. E window by *Clayton & Bell*, 1859, enlarged 1878. Also by them the two two-light s windows of the former s chapel, 1863 (w) and 1881 (E). Small three-light window in gable of s aisle by *Britten & Gilson*, 1900, designed by *Mrs Rogers*, wife of the headmaster of the Grammar School. s aisle, w of porch, by *Henry Holiday*, 1905 6, made by *Lowndes & Drury*. – In St Peter's Chapel, engraved figure of St Peter by *John Hutton* in s window, 1969, w window by *A.K. Nicholson* (First World War memorial). – Clerestory windows: chancel, angels by *A.O. Hemming*, 1906–7; nave (four only of incomplete scheme) by *A.K. Nicholson*, after 1927. – In s porch, heraldic glass by *Edward Woore*, 1953. – Mildmay Chapel (N aisle) E window by *A.K. Nicholson Stained Glass Studios* (*G.E.R. Smith*), one of several replacements after bomb damage, 1950–1.

MONUMENTS. N Transept: Thomas and Avice Mildmay †1566 and 1557, erected 1571. Standing wall monument of curious shape. Base divided into three panels by colonettes, with kneeling figures of Avice at the head of seven daughters and Thomas at the head of eight sons. Above the entablature three enriched pediments, two triangular and one semicircular, and then a big ogee top with strapwork decoration and epitaph. Repainted. – Mildmay Chapel: Earl Fitzwalter (Benjamin Mildmay) †1756. Large standing wall monument with an over-sized urn in the centre flanked by Corinthian columns, and big cherubs standing to the l. and r. Signed by *James Lovell.* – Chancel: J. E. Watts-Ditchfield †1923, first bishop of Chelmsford. Life-size statue in niche by *John Walker.* – S chancel chapel: Matthew Rudd †1615. Small mural incised slab. Attributed to *Francis Grigs* (GF). – Mary Marsh †1757. Of various marbles with an urn and fine Rococo decoration. Erected by her executor and sole legatee John Olmius of New Hall, Boreham. Attributed to *Henry Cheere.* – J. P. Tindal †1797 on board HMS *Monarch,* which is shown in relief at the base with flags, cannons, etc. – Nave, W end: Evelyn, Lady Rayleigh †1934. By *C. d'O. Pilkington Jackson,* informally modelled and coloured. – Outer N aisle: Robert Bownd †1696, with Ionic columns, flaming urn, and fine flower garlands. Attributed to *William Stanton* (GF).

The CHURCHYARD is laid out as a lawn with a sprinkling of interesting tombs, including a triangular monument to three women killed in a fire in 1808. – To SE, John Wallinger of Hare Hall †1767. Large sarcophagus with tapering sides on scrolly feet, lid with armorial cartouches and urn. – At the SE entrance to the churchyard, beside the Shire Hall, wrought-iron GATES by *John Johnson,* 1792.

CHURCHES

ASCENSION, Maltese Road. 1961–2 by *Laurence King,* and less traditional than one might expect from him. Pale brown brick with stone S porch, and copper-covered asymmetric pitched roof with its apex (crowned by a cross) at the meeting of nave and chancel. Small N chapel (Lady Chapel) and vestries. Large windows, mainly clerestory. Sanctuary refitted and decorated by *Anthony Delarue,* 2000. – STAINED GLASS. Sanctuary window, abstract, by *John Hayward,* 1963. In Lady Chapel, four panels by *J. N. Lawson* of *Goddard & Gibbs,* 2000.

ST ANDREW, Melbourne Avenue. 1958–9 by *Robert Potter & Richard Hare.* Brick, with artificial stone dressings. Nave and shallow chancel, with full-height windows. W gallery, and narrow aisles formed by slender columns. Vestries on S side linking to vicarage.

HOLY TRINITY, Trinity Road, Springfield. Neo-Norman by *J. A. Repton,* 1842–3. The date corresponds to the height of the fashion for Norman Revival, especially ill-advised where, as here, the material is white brick. Tall round-headed windows.

Angle turrets to the façade and w bellcote. Elaborate decora-
tion. No aisles, no galleries, and only the shallowest of
chancels. – Good MODEL of the interior of the church by *Fred
Spalding Jun.*, 1882, showing various fittings and decoration
now dispersed. – STAINED GLASS. The surviving top only of a
N window by *T. Willement*, 1844. Triple E window and one nave
S of similar date and style. – Also by *Repton* (who lived in
Springfield until his death in 1860) the small brick SCHOOL-
ROOM (now part of church hall), 1844. 'Elizabethan' with
gabled ends.

ST JOHN THE EVANGELIST, Moulsham Street. 1836–7. *J. W.
Wild*'s design, executed by a local architect, *Stephen Webb*. White
brick with stone, in the lancet style, and originally only nave
and shallow chancel. Chancel enlarged by *J. Clarke*, 1851, with
the addition of N and S transepts, N and S chancel aisles, and
S vestry. Further additions by *Chancellor*, for which he stuck to
the thin pinnacled Gothic that was not to his normal taste:
N (choir) vestry 1873–4, W tower and additional bay to nave
1882. W half of nave walled off and floor inserted in phases,
1996–2005. – STAINED GLASS. E and N transept lancets by
Clayton & Bell, after 1879. – Two flamboyant nave windows by
Kempe, 1902. – In the tower, S window by *W. B. Simpson &
Sons*, 1883. N lancet perhaps reused from the chancel, for which
three lancets were supplied by *Hudson* of Pentonville in 1851.
– MONUMENT. Henry Guy †1859. By *J. M. Lockyer*, an unusual
and decorative piece. Large mural tablet of Sicilian marble
inlaid with black and coloured marble, with lettering inside a
Gothic archway and other decoration.

BLESSED SACRAMENT (R.C.), Melbourne Avenue. By *H.B.
Towner*, 1961–2, with presbytery, 1965. Nave and low side
aisles. Brick, with aluminium roof. Pre-cast concrete framework of 'Arcline' rafters. Reordered by *Williams & Winkley*,
1984. Previous church (now hall) to w by *O'Neill & Fordham*,
1953.

OUR LADY IMMACULATE (R.C.), New London Road. 1846–7
by *J. J. Scoles*. Late E.E. Flint, with stone dressings. Nave,
chancel, aisles, S porch, and bellcote over chancel arch. N
extension, 1973, and further reordering 1988–90. – FONT and
AMBO. By *Stephen Scully*, 1990. Stone. – Byzantine-style
hanging CRUCIFIX by *William Gordon*, 1988. – SCULPTURE.
Wooden figure of Our Lady by *Gwynneth Holt*, 1957, with base
by *Nancy Coulson*, 1994. – On S porch, Our Lady by *Michael
Lindsey Clark*. – STAINED GLASS. E window and three others
by *Wailes*, one dated 1851.

BAPTIST CHURCH, Victoria Road South. 1908–9 by *W. Hayne*.
Brick with stone dressings in free Perp. Gabled front with
porches to l. and r., that on the r. extended upwards to a tower
with pyramidal roof. Interior reconstructed to form two levels,
with new gabled entrance on N side, by *The Fairhursts Design
Group*, 1999–2000.

CHRIST CHURCH (United Reformed Church), New London
Road. 1970–1 by *John Finch & Associates*. On a sloping site,

with sanctuary at street level, and hall and other rooms below. Brick, with vertical bands of glass lighting the tall sanctuary, which is an irregular octagon with gallery. Fittings designed by the architect, including COMMUNION TABLE, PULPIT and LECTERN. Exposed pipework of ORGAN, by *Cedric Arnold & Hyatt*, on stepped platform.

EBENEZER STRICT BAPTIST CHAPEL, New London Road. By *J. Fenton*, 1847–8. E.E. Gault brick.

ELIM CHRISTIAN CENTRE, Hall Street. 1978–9 by *Richard Ferguson Associates*. Uninspiring exterior, except for a remarkable splay-foot slate spire that appears to have been cleft down the middle, the two halves held apart by a cross. The exposed inner faces glazed, lighting the worship area.

FRIENDS' MEETING HOUSE, Rainsford Road. By *Paul V. Mauger*, 1958. Stock brick, with a pattern of projecting headers. Square double-height meeting room with pyramidal roof.

Former FRIENDS' MEETING HOUSE, Duke Street, *see* Perambulation 1.

METHODIST CHURCH, Hall Street. 1863, by *Thomas Moss Sen.*, built by *Thomas Moss Jun.* E.E., stock brick, and very plain.

TRINITY METHODIST CHURCH, Rainsford Road. By *Cubitt Nichols*, 1961. Pale brown brick, two storeys, with hall over worship area, and narrow, full-height windows. Three-storey annex, fully glazed, with some engraved glass panels. Sculpted stone panels, with another (by *Nancy Coulson*, 1984) on a separate hall to the E.

RECTORY LANE CEMETERY (church cemetery, closed 1918). Entrance gateway and lodge by *Chancellor*, 1859. Kentish rag with Bath stone dressings. Mildmay family memorial chapel (Dec, with bell-turret and STAINED GLASS by *Clayton & Bell*) and vault, also by Chancellor, destroyed in an air raid in 1943.

WRITTLE ROAD CEMETERY (municipal cemetery) and CHELMSFORD CREMATORIUM. Cemetery laid out by *C. Pertwee*, 1886. Stone entrance building, including chapel and lodge, with triple-arched gateway in half-timbered gable. Crematorium, 1961, grey brick with stone dressings and stone panels with carved figures of St Cedd and St Helena. – MONUMENT. Robert Cook †1908, 'the pioneer of Essex athletics'. Headstone carved with figures of sportsmen, bicycle, cricket stumps and other sporting equipment, masonic emblems, etc.

NONCONFORMIST CEMETERY, New London Road. Opened 1846, laid out by *J. Fenton*.

PUBLIC BUILDINGS

77   SHIRE HALL, Tindal Square. 1789–91 by *John Johnson*, the County Surveyor. Chelmsford's best and most prominent building, thoroughly civilized, far more important visually than the Cathedral. Plans for rebuilding the old Sessions House had been prepared by *William Hillyer* in 1779, but not carried out. It is only five bays wide, but generously spaced and with a front of good Portland stone; the rest of white Suffolk brick. The

three middle bays project slightly and have arched entrances, originally open. The whole ground floor is rusticated. Above, in the middle, four attached giant columns with Adam capitals. The windows between them have pediments. The outer windows are tripartite and segment-headed. Then above the middle windows three *Coade* relief plaques (Mercy, Wisdom, and Justice), modelled by *John Bacon Sen.*, and a pediment. *Coade* stone also the capitals, balusters, etc. To either side, lower wings set well back, originally single storey. That on the l. was raised in 1851, that on the r. rebuilt 1903–6 with a new E façade in white brick with stone pilasters and dressings, a coarser version of Johnson's detailing. This was done as part of improvements by *F. Whitmore*, including a tunnel under New Street to his Police Station (*see* Perambulation 1).

Johnson's interior arrangements broadly followed those of James Adam's Shire Hall at Hertford (1767–9), with an open, piazza-like market hall on the ground floor, County Room (assembly room) above it, and Crown and Nisi Prius Courts at the back of the building. Only the County Room survives in anything like its original state, running across the whole front, with barrel-vaulted ceiling (replaced in replica in 1936), and Adamesque plaster decoration. Chimneypieces at either end with carved panels by *Charles Rossi*, and three female figures in niches (originally four), possibly by *Bacon*, that held two-light lustres. The rest of the interior was reconstructed by *J. Stuart*, 1935–6, with new entrance hall, staircase, and courts. The detailing is contemporary (e.g. full-height Crittall window lighting the staircase on the N elevation, the walls of the entrance hall faced with marble with Deco detail), but the loss of the courtroom fittings, and of the columned market hall, now seems regrettable. In the entrance hall, a *Coade* stone naiad that formed part of a conduit by *Johnson*, 1791, which stood W of Shire Hall until rebuilt in 1814.★

COUNTY HALL, of several dates and by successive County Architects, occupies a large site bounded by Duke Street, Threadneedle Street, Market Road, and Victoria Road South. The earliest part is on Duke Street, a three-storey block of 1908 by *F. Whitmore*. Free Edwardian classical, brick with stone dressings, with off-centre entrance under an open pediment. The plan may have been to extend it E to form a symmetrical front, but instead it butts up against *J. Stuart*'s imposing five-storey extension. Built in phases, 1929–38, of artificial Portland stone on a granite plinth, it is not a success and the whole composition seems to crave a better site. Neoclassical motifs are handled loosely and without distinction, and a grand entrance is lacking where it turns the corner into Threadneedle Street. In the middle of this long frontage is a triumphal balcony, but it overlooks nothing of importance.

But this is redeemed by the Council Chamber and its associated Lobby, Committee Room, and Chairman's Room, the

★ For its replacement, *see* Tower Gardens, below.

cost of which was met by W.J. Courtauld, who here did for the
county what he had previously done for Braintree and brought
in *Vincent Harris* to design this most important part of the
building. The result is lavish: walls faced with Doulting stone,
Scagliola columns in the Lobby, and leather doors to the
Chamber which is fitted with oak seating made by *J.P. White
& Son* of the *Pyghtle Works*. Two windows of heraldic STAINED
GLASS by *George Kruger Gray* in the Lobby, and a series of
PAINTINGS illustrating aspects of Essex history: in the Lobby,
by *A. K. Lawrence* and *Neville Lewis*, in the Council Chamber
by *Colin Gill*, *B. Fleetwood-Walker*, *A. Thompson*, and *R. Lyon*.
On the end walls of the Chamber, seven portraits of famous
Essex men and women by *Henry Rushbury*, and two large
county maps, with coats of arms, also by Rushbury.

The Threedneadle Street frontage has a return along what
was originally King Edward's Avenue, the line of which has
been cleverly preserved as a public thoroughfare in the extensions of 1984–8 by *Alan Willis*, who created a glass-fronted
atrium between the older buildings and a new block along
Market Road. Within, the atrium has between three and five
storeys of offices on three sides, the entrance wall hung with a
STAINED GLASS SCULPTURE by *Alex Beleschenko* in the form
of suspended sails or banners. The block towards Market
Road, faced in reconstituted Portland stone, is of four storeys
(with a fifth storey set back), with shops on the ground floor
set back behind columns and an entrance to the CENTRAL
LIBRARY and 'Public Square', contained within a second, six-
storey atrium. On Victoria Road South, a three-storey block
has continuous glazing set back between broad bands of reconstituted stone. At the centre of the complex, buildings of
1959–65 by *H. Conolly*, including one of nine storeys, that fortunately have no presence on the street.

CIVIC CENTRE, Duke Street. The core is the former Library and
Civic Suite by *Cordingley & McIntyre*, 1933–5. Two-storeyed,
symmetrical, brick Neo-Georgian with a stone entrance in the
centre and good staircase inside. In front, WAR MEMORIAL by
the Borough Engineer, *E.J. Miles*, 1923. Stone obelisk. Extensions by *Jackson & Edmonds*, 1962. Brick, up to five storeys,
very bland. The contemporary CIVIC THEATRE, facing Fairfield Road, is slightly more interesting, with the angular wavy
roof echoed in the entrance canopy. Adjoining is the CRAMP-
HORN THEATRE (studio theatre and theatre workshop) by
Michael Hart, *John Lambie* and *Sarah Woolley* of *Sheppard
Robson*, 1981. Brick, with glass-fronted foyer.

CROWN COURT, New Street. By the *Property Services Agency*,
1981–2. Brown brick, with dark windows set between little projections, giving it a fortress-like appearance. Only three storeys,
but it feels much bigger, gloomy and oppressive.

POLICE STATION, New Street. 1969–71 by the *County Architect's
Dept.* (project architect, *Bert Mabane*). Divisional headquarters, designed for 275 personnel. Five storeys, with the main

entrance at upper ground level on a raised podium. The next two floors of offices overhang and are supported on pilotis.

POLICE HEADQUARTERS, Springfield Road. By *Clare & Ross*, won in competition in 1900, completed 1902. Edwardian Free Style, brick with stone dressings, adorned with cupolas, gables with segmental pediments, bays, etc. Main buildings flanked by separate chief constable's house and recruits' accommodation, with stable block and gatehouse. Extensions by the *County Architect's Dept.*, including five-storey, octagonal building (concrete), 1975–8 (architect in charge, *W. G. Apps*), on s side. To the N, hexagonal command and control centre, 1993, brick with copper roof rising to a lantern, and further out the cadet school, 1969, six storeys, pale brown brick.

PRISON, Springfield Road. 1822–8 by *Hopper*. Originally designed on the 'silent' system, with seven cell blocks radiating from a central octagon containing the governor's house, chapel, and turnkey's room. Altered 1845–8, by Hopper with *Joshua Jebb*, to the 'separate' system of solitary confinement on the model of Jebb's Pentonville. One wing was demolished, two wings enlarged, individual cells enlarged, and a separate governor's house built in the W corner of the prison between the inner and outer walls. Central block rebuilt by *Taylor & Hunt*, 1979–80, following fire damage. Hospital block 1901, and healthcare centre by *Aedas AHR*, 2003–4.

Hopper's outer brick wall is 20 ft (6 metres) high and 420 ft (129 metres) long to Springfield Road (later extended to the SW), with stone buttresses like Tuscan pilasters and rusticated stone bastions at the corners with loopholes. The return along Sandford Road has brick buttresses, semicircular with conical tops. At the E corner of the site, outside the wall in Sandford Road, the chaplain's house (now offices), part of the 1845–8 alterations. Stuccoed, three storeys, three bays. The original sombre entrance with heavy rustication and massive Tuscan pilasters was replaced in 1973.

COUNTY RECORD OFFICE, Wharf Road. 1997–9 by *W. S. Atkins*. Public search room on the first floor, with tall glazed W wall, beneath an upswept roof. To the N a two-storey range of offices etc., to the E the windowless three-storey repository, and glazed single-storey entrance, all flat-roofed. Repository of white brick, the remainder rendered, with string courses of dark engineering brick. – In the atrium, beside the stairs, 'Timeline', an interactive SCULPTURE by *Michael Condron*, 2002. Also a statue of Marconi by *Stephen Hicklin*, 2003.

CHELMSFORD MUSEUM (Oaklands), Moulsham Street. Italianate house with low square tower by *C. Pertwee*, 1865, for his brother-in-law Frederick Wells, a brewer; acquired by the Borough Council in 1929. White brick with carved stone dressings, particularly on the two canted bays. Unfortunate black brick SW extension by the Borough Engineer for the Essex Regiment Museum, 1972–3, on the site of servants' quarters demolished in the 1920s, and a better extension in recycled white brick, *c.* 1995 (project architect, *Geoff Eaton*). In front, a CANNON captured at Sebastopol in 1855, presented to the town in 1858. It formerly stood in front of Shire Hall. – LODGE, Rothesay Avenue. Single-storey, random rubble with brick dressings, and a fancy gable.

MELBOURNE PARK ATHLETICS CENTRE. Indoor athletics training centre by *Peter Emptage Associates*, 2001–2.

RIVERSIDE LEISURE CENTRE, Waterloo Lane. Mostly of 1963–5 by *E.P. Allen*, Borough Engineer (architect in charge, *J.R. Bishop*), enlarged by addition of ice rink and other facilities, 1987, under a big barrel roof. Inside, a very jolly ceramic mural, 'Serendipity', by *Lisa Hawker*, as part of refurbishment by *Peter Emptage Associates*, 1995–6. The open-air swimming bath, by the Borough Engineer, *Cuthbert Brown*, opened 1906.

ANGLIA RUSKIN UNIVERSITY, Bishops Hall Lane. *See* Perambulation 2.

CHELMSFORD COLLEGE, Moulsham Street. The main building is Dovedale, formerly Hamlet House, built for Henry Guy, *c.* 1845; alterations by *Chancellor & Son*, 1905–8. Gault brick, five-bay front with two pedimented gables and porch.

KING EDWARD VI GRAMMAR SCHOOL, Broomfield Road. By *H. A. Cheers*, 1891–2, won in competition in 1889. Neo-Tudor, brick with stone dressings. Two storeys and attics with dormers, with Assembly Hall (now Library; STAINED GLASS by *Heaton, Butler & Bayne*, *c.* 1904) to the r., and Headmaster's House to the l. Apart from the Gymnasium of 1894, various extensions were demolished in 1935–7, for new classrooms round two brick cloisters. Also Neo-Tudor, and probably by the County Architect, *J. Stuart*. Later C20 additions include Hall and classrooms, 1962–3, in *H. Conolly*'s standard style, Music School by *Frankham Consultancy Group*, 2001, with a striking curved, blue-painted entrance and stair-tower, and Learning Development Centre by *Lyster Grillet & Harding*, 2003–4, with external metal stairs and gallery.* – SPORTS PAVILION, *see* Broomfield.

COUNTY HIGH SCHOOL FOR GIRLS, Broomfield Road. 1906–7 by *Chancellor & Son*. Brick with stone dressings, and rather severe. Two storeys, with quoins, straight gables at either end of the long front, and doorcase with open pediment. Louvred turret with little leaded dome. N and S extensions by *H.W. Mann*, 1914–16.

PRIMARY SCHOOL, Trinity Road, Springfield. 1909–11, by *W. H. Pertwee*. Free Style, very large, brick with stone dressings.

OAKLANDS INFANT SCHOOL, Vicarage Road. By the *County Architect's Dept* (architect in charge, *Jack Sorrell*), *c.* 1967. Single storey, pale brick with glazed and coloured panels and some horizontal boarding.

CHELMSFORD AND ESSEX CENTRE (formerly Essex and Chelmsford Infirmary and Dispensary), New London Road.

---

*Proposed Sixth Form Centre by *Stanton Williams* for projected completion in 2008.

1882–3 by *F. Chancellor* and *C. Pertwee*. Stock brick with stone dressings. Two storeys. Three-bay central block, two canted bays and Dutch gables, and flanking wings. Considerably extended 1908–9 by *Keith Young* (*Young & Hall*) with *W. H. Pertwee*.

St John's Hospital, Wood Street. *William Thorold*'s workhouse of 1837–8 was rebuilt by *F. Chancellor* following a fire in 1886. Brick, two and three storeys. In the middle of one range, former hall or chapel with little cupola and flèche. Many later additions, including infirmary and nurses' home s of the main buildings by *Tooley & Foster*, 1926, the latter with half-timbered gables.

Central Park. Laid out by *F. Whitmore*, opened in 1894. The lake had been excavated in 1842 to provide earth for the railway embankment.

Tower Gardens, Roxwell Road, contains the former conduit of 1814 by *George Wray*. Rotunda with Doric columns and small dome. It originally stood near the Shire Hall, eventually moved here in 1940.

Industrial Buildings

Moulsham Mill, Parkway. Rebuilt 1712, with further work in 1756. Fine Georgian brick mill house of five bays and two-and-a-half storeys, the central bay breaking forward slightly. Impressive pedimented doorcase with Corinthian pilasters. Four-storey mill behind, one range C18 timber-framed and weatherboarded, the other stock brick, 1891 by *Henry Simon* of Manchester. Sandwiched between the mill and the house, a C16 timber-framed cottage.

Springfield Mill (now Riverside Inn), Victoria Road. C18 timber-framed and weatherboarded. Three storeys, with central lucam. The mill house at the s e end has a five-bay front at right angles to the street of blue-brick header bond with red brick dressings and parapet, and chequered brick return along the street.

Railway. The Eastern Counties Railway (engineer, *John Braithwaite*) reached Chelmsford in 1843. The station, opened that year, was rebuilt in 1856, 1898–9, and again in 1987–8. Of more interest is the line itself, on embankments linked by three viaducts and two bridges, 1841–2. The viaducts are of eighteen, forty-eight, and three arches.

Springfield Lock, off Navigation Road. The first lock on the Chelmer & Blackwater Navigation, opened 1797 (*see* Introduction, p. 52). At the foot of the cut that leads up to the basin and wharf. Just below the lock, a brick bridge.

By-pass. 1930–2, on the s e side of the town, from Widford to Springfield. Concrete bridge over the Chelmer, of one main span and two side arches, with stripped classical detailing including obelisk lamp standards, approached by a long raised section on stilts to allow for flooding of the meadows.

1. The town centre

The centre of the town is TINDAL SQUARE, in front of the Shire
Hall, with its statue of Chief Justice Tindal (seated) by *E.H.
Baily*, 1850–1, the base by *Chancellor*. Its surrounding buildings, although each different, give the space a unity that could
be more easily appreciated if it were rid of its traffic. Opposite
the Shire Hall, HSBC, 1919, mainly stone with a little brick
on the upper floor, and a little clock turret on the corner.
Forming a w extension to it is the stone former National
Provincial Bank by *Palmer & Holden*, the bank's surveyors, with
Pertwee & Howard of Chelmsford. Three bays with giant
attached Corinthian columns and balustrade with urns. On the
square's E side the former Post Office (No. 1 High Street), 1908
by *H.N. Hawks* of the *Office of Works*. Portland stone ground
floor, two upper floors of brick with panels of carved brick
and pedimented half-dormers. Then No. 2, BARCLAYS, by
A.C. Blomfield, 1905. Five bays, brick. Rusticated ground floor
with pedimented stone doorways, giant Ionic pilasters on the
next two floors, slate roof with dormers above deep modillion
cornice on brackets.

The rest of the HIGH STREET has few buildings of individual merit, but with the conspicuous exception of Cater House
at the far end it has managed to preserve its scale. What has
spoilt it most of all is pedestrianization (1993–4), to be precise
the wall-to-wall paving that has such a damaging visual effect.
Things start well, however, with the SARACEN'S HEAD,
c. 1720, five bays, three storeys, with quoins and rusticated
ground floor. Later porch. Opposite, No. 96, *c.* 1800, gault
brick, three bays and three storeys with attics. Greek Doric
porch and slightly tapering first-floor windows. No. 91, also
three bays and three storeys, is timber-framed with a brick
front and is jettied on the N side along Crown Passage. Surprisingly, it seems to be of one build, *c.* 1725. Back on the E
side, Nos. 16 and 17 have a nice front with two upper floors of
grey gault brick, the windows set in tall segment-headed
recesses.

The w side of the High Street originated as a line of buildings which grew up in the middle of the triangular marketplace
at the top of the High Street and separated it from Tindal
Street. Where the streets rejoin is a little open space, with
LLOYDS TSB by *Clare & Ross*, 1902 (brick and stone, but
modest compared with those banks higher up the street) on its
own island. New London Road branches off to the SE, and the
angle between this and Tindal Street is now filled by the mis-
erable HIGH CHELMER SHOPPING PRECINCT, 1969–72,
which debouches into the High Street at this point.

Continuing down the High Street, just two buildings stand
out. On the E side, MANSION HOUSE (No. 26), built in 1755
for Dr Benjamin Pugh, is five bays. The ground and first floors
have been rendered, but above that are two floors of brick. The

central bay breaks forward and has on the second floor a window with brick pilasters carrying Corinthian capitals of stone and a brick pediment. Opposite, *Aukett*'s W.H. Smith and H&M, 2001–2, with glass boxes projecting from the stone-clad façade. Thereafter, the dispiriting commercial architecture reaches a nadir with the MEADOWS SHOPPING CENTRE, completed 1992, entered through a tall pseudo-classical portico. CATER HOUSE, 1960–1, just before the River Can, is another monument of its age. Two storeys along the High Street with a further seven storeys set back on a podium. The narrower s elevation is enlivened by concrete reliefs, part of the dismal view up and down the River Can, where the High Street ends. The only elegant note is provided by MOULSHAM BRIDGE (also known as Stone Bridge), built across the Can by *Johnson*, 1785–7. Portland stone, with balusters and paterae of *Coade* stone. Single span with a boldly curved parapet.

Before the river is reached, SPRINGFIELD ROAD branches off the High Street to the E. On the NW side is the former Gray's Brewery, whose attractive C18 and C19 stock brick buildings (including kiln) were converted to shops (principally Habitat) by *John Clark Associates* (project architect, *Meir Berk*), c. 1985. The scheme included the whole block of buildings back to the corner of the High Street. Then the road crosses the River Chelmer, and here more recent developments, including MEADOWS II shopping centre, opened 1994, are much more brash, but have opened up the riverside, with a new open space, BACKNANG SQUARE.

MOULSHAM STREET starts on the river's s side. The only building of interest is THE REGENT on the E side of 1913, by *Francis Burdett Ward*, an early 'ciné-variety' house for both film and stage performances, now a bar. Two-storey plastered front with recessed balustrade balcony with composite pilasters, swags, etc. Interior with decorative Rococo plasterwork. Foyer remodelled by *A.E. Wiseman*, 1935. At the corner of Baddow Road, 'Guardian Figures' by *James Davis*, 1999, seated stone figures of a Roman centurion and Dominican monk.

Moulsham Street is interrupted by Parkway, and it is better to walk w to NEW LONDON ROAD (*see* Perambulation 5 for Moulsham Street and New London Road s of Parkway), which has on the corner the GEMINI CENTRE (former Chelmsford Rural District Council offices), 1938 and good Neo-Georgian. Further up, on both sides, some gault brick terraces of the 1840s, leading up to the former CHELMSFORD INSTITUTE, 1841, white brick with giant Tuscan pilasters and window surrounds of stone. Rebuilt as offices behind the façade, 1975. Then comes the River Can, crossed by a bridge of 1890 (replacing *Fenton*'s of 1839) with delicate cast-iron balustrade. On the N side of the river, the upper part of Central Park (*see* Public Buildings) to the W, MARKS & SPENCER by *Monro & Partners*, c. 1970, faced in pale brick and with a gently curving wall along the river, to the E. New London Road leads back to the High Street, past the rear of *Aukett*'s building seen in the

High Street, but differently treated with panels of brick, a pub
with wavy rendered panels, and bus shelters.

The tour now continues N of Tindal Square along NEW STREET,
along the E side of the Shire Hall and churchyard. It was new
in the early Middle Ages – not an ancient thoroughfare, but
created to provide access to the bishop's hall and mill to the
N. No. 1, dated 1906, is a good corner building of brick with
stone dressings, but it is outdone by the former Police Station,
on the opposite corner of Waterloo Lane, by *Whitmore*, 1903–6,
contemporary with his alterations to the Shire Hall (*see* above).
Stock brick but with extensive stone dressings, the entrance set
in a two-storey bow, and with a hexagonal Free Baroque turret
on the corner. Some good houses face the Cathedral. First,
MAYNETREES, Nos. 55–57, a medieval house bought by
Edward Gepp in 1786 and remodelled by him. It has a gault
brick front of five broad bays with a central motif of Greek
Doric columns flanked by one-bay pediments. Fine rooms
overlooking the garden including one with curved end walls.
Then, set back from the street, GUY HARLINGS, built by John
Comyns between 1716 and 1721, but refronted by Dr John
Badeley after 1785 in gault brick. Seven bays, two storeys, with
pedimented doorcase, and a two-storey canted bay on the
garden front. Early C16 linenfold panelling in the Hall with
frieze of carved heads, probably reused from an earlier house.
On the N side large additions by *Maguire & Murray* (project
architects, *Rajindar Singh* and *Jennifer Edwards*), 1978–9. A
strikingly early piece of Neo-vernacular, with jettied front and
gables, but quirky in its details, e.g. the supports with decorative patterns and the spacing of the windows. Lower range
beyond a courtyard with a pantiled cloister walk on the garden
side. In the garden, figure of St Francis by *Catharni Stern*,
c. 1997.

The churchyard on the W side of the street provides a welcome
open space in the middle of the town, but there is little sense
of a cathedral close. Along the N side, CHURCH STREET has
the former National School by *Chancellor*: single-storey classroom, 1872, in red brick with black diapers, and two-storey
addition of 1885, in Queen Anne style, with an oriel, half-timbered gables, and panels of moulded brick decoration. The rest
of Church Street is very out of keeping, beginning with a
hugely over-scaled office development (No. 1) in pale beige
brick, and on the corner of Cottage Place the undistinguished
Cathedral CHAPTER HOUSE, 1989–90 by *Jerram Falkus Construction Ltd*.

Neo-Georgian pastiche faces the W end of the Cathedral on
Church Lane, which leads on to DUKE STREET. This has a
few minor older frontages, but is dominated by County Hall
(*see* Public Buildings) along its S side. Beyond that a nice pair
of late C18 houses (Nos. 72 and 73), plastered, with tripartite
windows and doorcases side-by-side with half-columns and
swags and urns in the entablature. Then Nos. 68–70, a terrace
of three houses, early C19 white brick, the ground-floor

windows and doorways set in round-arched recesses, and on
the corner of Victoria Road South No. 66 by *Beadel, Son &
Chancellor* for the Essex Provident Society, 1853. Rusticated
ground floor of red brick with rusticated stone entrance, and
two floors of stock brick with Italianate eaves. W of Victoria
Road South, the former FRIENDS' MEETING HOUSE of
1823–4 by *John Collis* of Moulsham. Gault brick. Sides of five
tall round-arched windows, pedimented front with two blank
arches and a wide porch on four sturdy Greek Doric columns.
For Duke Street W of here, *see* Perambulation 3.

VICTORIA ROAD SOUTH was formed after 1875. The E side is
occupied by County Hall (*see* Public Buildings), but the W side
has the Baptist Church of 1908–9 (*see* Churches), harmoniz-
ing well with its neighbour, the town's former library, science
and art school, and museum (FREDERIC CHANCELLOR
BUILDING) of 1904–6 by *Chancellor*, Neo-Tudor mixed with
Baroque motifs. In 2005, this is part of Anglia Ruskin University's Central Campus, along with the former School of Technology (EAST BUILDING) that lies behind it. By *J. Stuart*,
County Architect, 1931, in a darker brick with stone dressings
and good Art Deco detail, including a stained-glass window to
the stairwell. The rest of the campus is scheduled for redevelopment in a mixed scheme by the *Richard Rogers Partnership*
and *Countryside Properties*, for the area between Duke Street
and Central Park, with a land bridge over Parkway.

MARKET STREET leads from Victoria Road South back to Tindal
Square with a grisly succession of developments on its S side,
from the ugly concrete MULTI-STOREY CAR PARK by *Noel
Tweddell & Park*, 1969–70, with ground-floor covered market,
to the banal CHANCELLOR HALL by *Kenneth Wakeford, Jerram
& Harris*, 1971–2; hardly a building with which Chancellor
would wish to have his name associated.* The N side has the
far more successful approach to County Hall and Central
Library (*see* Public Buildings) described above.

The remaining perambulations describe the area beyond the
inner ring road and railway.

2. New Street and the Anglia Ruskin University campus

The area N of the railway was developed at the end of the C19
for industry and associated housing, but it is increasingly post-
industrial at the beginning of the C21. The major monument
here is the former MARCONI'S offices and workshops (New
Street, W side) by *Dunn & Watson*, 1912[†] – the first purpose-
built radio factory in the world, from which the first official
British sound broadcast was made in 1920. Stock brick with
Portland stone dressings in Edwardian Baroque style, the

---

* It is close to the site of *Chancellor*'s Corn Exchange of 1857, demolished in 1969
to make way for the High Chelmer Shopping Precinct.
[†] In 2005, Selex Communications, but due to be vacated.

central bay heavily quoined with balcony and tall window over the entrance, open segmental pediment, and domed clock turret. Behind it, best seen from Glebe Road to the w, is a taller streamlined concrete building with Crittall windows by *W. W. Wood*,[*] *c.* 1935, and at the back of the site EASTWOOD HOUSE (now BAE Systems), by *Sipson Gray Associates*, 1992–4. Yellow and red brick, partly striped, with Postmodern elements.

Further N, the E side of the road is dominated by the remains of the former Hoffmann's ball-bearings factory (GLOBE HOUSE), now flats and offices. 1897–8 by *W. Ralph Low*, extended 1910–11. Stock brick with brick dressings. To the street, a four-storey office block with Baroque doorway and pedimented gable fronts a five-storey factory building. The main part of forty-two bays stretches E down Hoffmanns Way, as far as the still active CHELMER MILLS, 1899–1901 by *Chancellor & Son* for W. H. Marriage & Sons. Stock brick with red brick dressings, mostly of four storeys, with a distinctive tower (containing silos and water tank) of which one face is dusted with flour. Mechanical engineers *Woodhouse & Mitchell*, contractors for silos *Henry Simon*.

Further industrial buildings occupied the site to the N, cleared since 1992 for ANGLIA RUSKIN UNIVERSITY,[†] to supersede the Central Campus in Victoria Street South (*see* Perambulation 1). The first building on Rivermead Campus, completed in 1993–4, was QUEEN'S BUILDING by *ECD Partnership*. Pale brown brick, four storeys with chamfered corners, with low energy use achieved by passive solar heating, natural ventilation, and relatively small windows. Set back at right angles to it, SAWYERS BUILDING, by the same firm, completed 1999, has long runs of glazing shaded by horizontal fins. Outside the entrance, 'Harmony' by *John Reveler*, 1998 (steel, stone, and concrete).

Buildings of the C21 have been far bolder, and have given the campus a proper entrance with the MICHAEL A. ASHCROFT BUILDING, 2001–3, the first part of a master plan by *Wilkinson Eyre*, comprising a four-storey block clad in grey terracotta tiles, with a glazed, energy-efficient double-layer S front. Above the entrance, seemingly miraculously, floats a 150-seat raked auditorium, its curved form expressed externally and its walls sheathed in stainless steel, resting on four slender columns that allow views through to the riverside greenery beyond. The purity of glass, grey, and silver is delightfully undermined externally by *Martin Richman*'s strips of applied film that changes colour according to the viewpoint and ambient light, and internally by bold use of colour, e.g. shades of blue and violet in the auditorium. At the rear, the building

---

[*] He was principal of the Technical College at this time.
[†] Formerly Anglia Polytechnic University; a merger of the Essex Institute of Higher Education and the Cambridge College of Arts and Technology.

encloses the back of the Queen's Building with a glazed entrance hall and café.

To the N of Ashcroft, Wilkinson Eyre plan two main teaching blocks for completion in 2008, part of a crescent of buildings following the line of the Chelmer. Already completed, in 2003–5, is TINDAL, of four storeys, with student facilities on three floors and Vice-Chancellor's suite on the top, with walls faced with oak strips and in which the storey-height windows are set somewhat randomly. The end wall is rendered, lime green, with more green, maroon, and other strong colours inside. A slightly different green is used on the single-storey sports centre (MILDMAY) at the far end of the site, contrasting with the grey cladding of its lower offshoot.

Set off on the SW corner of the campus is RIVERMEAD GATE by *David Ruffle Architects*, c. 1997. Pale brick, two and four storeys with shops on the ground floor, medical centre on the first floor, and commercial space above that. Pyramidal roof with a central 'roof terminal' with monopitch roof providing passive stack ventilation. Permanent tent-like awning over the shop windows. Behind it, the STUDENT VILLAGE by *Countryside Properties*, 1994, scarcely distinguishable from speculative housing of a dull sort, and designed to be easily convertible to flats.

The eastern boundary of the campus is the River Chelmer, with the former BISHOP'S HALL MILL, of which some machinery survives over the leet. Timber-framed mill house with C18 gault brick front. A riverside walk provides a route back to the town centre, which can also be reached via RECTORY LANE (on its S side, almost opposite the cemetery, a block of brick cottages by *Chancellor*, 1882, with tall central chimney) and Broomfield Road.

3. North-west beyond the railway

The opening of the Railway Station in 1843 led to the development of the area to its NW. Off Duke Street on the N side is WELLS STREET, with an interesting, varied group of buildings of c. 1900 along its E side from the corner up to the CHELMSFORD STAR CO-OPERATIVE STORES, 1895, probably by *C. Pertwee*; stock brick with red brick dressings, at the corner with RAILWAY STREET. Across is TOWNFIELD STREET, with modest C19 terraced housing on its W side, once typical but now rare following much clearance. At one end a domestic-scale pub, THE ROYAL STEAMER, at the other the WHITE HORSE, later C19, gabled. It faces a two-storey car park by the *Alex Gordon Partnership*, 1988, faced in brick and showing that a car park need not be unneighbourly. Railway Street leads to Broomfield Road and back to Duke Street, which continues as RAINSFORD ROAD. On its N side, COVAL HALL, now offices. Two-storey, seven-bay E front of painted brick, and on the S side three parallel ranges, one with a two-storey canted bay, and a tetrastyle portico squeezed into an angle. It appears C18, but the core is C17 or earlier.

Parkway now intervenes, and our tour returns to the station. The keen tourist can continue on to the road's far side for the Friends' Meeting House (*see* Churches). On the S side of Rainsford Road, at right angles to it, CRITCHETT TERRACE, a pretty stuccoed development of the mid C19. Then on the N side a picturesque lodge, single-storey painted brick with low-pitched slate roof and casements with Gothic tracery. This was the gatehouse to COVAL LODGE, mainly single-storey, stuccoed brick, with tall decorative chimneys, in Valletta Close off MALTESE ROAD. In Maltese Road, MALTESE COTTAGE, similarly picturesque but with thatched roof, and No. 47 (Congresbury), 1909 by *F. W. Chancellor* for himself. Brick, with pedimented gables, but otherwise rather plain.

The tour can be further extended along BROOMFIELD ROAD. On the E side, the JOHN HENRY KEENE MEMORIAL HOMES by *A.E. Wiseman*, 1933. Pairs of single-storey brick almshouses round a very large quadrangle, with a gabled, round-arched entrance gateway. Opposite, No. 85, built as the lodge house to the Friends' Cemetery by *Chancellor*, 1855, an early work while still a partner in the firm of *Beadel, Son & Chancellor*. A little two-storey Italianate villa, of stock brick with stone dressings, round-headed windows, projecting eaves with exposed rafters and corner brackets. Off Broomfield Road to the W, the BOARDED BARNS ESTATE, built by *Chelmsford Borough Council* in the 1930s, 1,090 homes with shopping centre and school. The main spines are Kings Road and North Avenue. It continues to the N and W as MELBOURNE PARK, 1946–8 and 1952–3, with a fifteen-storey residential block in Melbourne Avenue, MELBOURNE COURT, by the *Borough Engineer's Department*, completed 1962.

4. Springfield Road

Originally part of the through route from London to Colchester. Something of its former status can still be discerned and, once past the 1980s hideousness of Tesco and Iceland, one reaches survivors of a more elegant age, in what was the parish of Springfield but had already, in the C19, become a suburb of Chelmsford. On the NW side, two large early to mid-C19 gault brick houses (Nos. 73–75), similar in character, one with round-headed windows on the ground floor, the other with Ionic porch. Then No. 79, MACKMURDO HOUSE,* by *J. Fenton* for himself, *c.* 1834. Gault brick, two storeys and five bays. In the pedimented centre bay an Ionic portico *in antis*. Nos. 83–91 are a terrace of gault brick three-storey houses, four dated 1814 and a fifth added later to the S end. On the SE side, in NAVIGATION ROAD, KENMORE HOUSE, mid C19, three

---

*Offices of the Rural Community Council of Essex, of which the architect A.H. Mackmurdo was founding secretary, 1929.

bays and two storeys of painted brick, has deep eaves on brackets and an open timber porch.

The next stretch of Springfield Road is dominated by RIVERS HOUSE, 1959–62 by *E.R. Collister & Associates*, a seven-storey office slab on a two-storey podium, remodelled in the 1990s. Thereafter the buildings of interest are strung out over ¾ m. On the NW side, just after the Prison (*see* Public Buildings), RANDULPH TERRACE (Nos. 269–289), built in 1842 of local white brick. Much altered, but the pattern can still be seen of roof heights getting higher towards the middle house, which has a third storey and a gable like an open pediment. Further out, on the same side, LATIMER HOUSE, Llewellyn Close, a development of sheltered housing by *Richard Ferguson Associates* (project architect, *D. Ferguson*), 1979. Brick, the blocks arranged irregularly with monopitch roofs in all directions. The characteristic buildings of Springfield Road are, however, large, later C19 brick houses, including No. 240 (formerly OAKLANDS), 1889, and TYRELLS, 1888, both by *Chancellor*. The former has a semi-octagonal corner turret and door with large shell-hood, the latter half-timbered gables, the largest of which sits on top of a two-storey canted bay. Finally, WHITTLES HALL (No. 347), an interesting house of the 1860s that might be early *Chancellor*. Domestic Gothic, stock brick with dressings (including bands and relieving arches) of yellow and red brick, with gables (one half-hipped) and massive chimneys. Just a little further on is Springfield Green, the centre of 'old' Springfield (q.v.).

5. *South of Parkway: Moulsham Street and New London Road*

Moulsham was a separate village in the Middle Ages, a hamlet of Chelmsford that became an ecclesiastical parish in 1838. Moulsham Hall, the C16 seat of the Mildmay family rebuilt to designs by *Giacomo Leoni* in 1728–45, was demolished in 1809; it stood about ½ m. SSE of St John's. MOULSHAM LODGE, just over ½ m. SE of St John's in Moulsham Chase, is now surrounded by housing. Five bays, two storeys and attics with three dormers. Blue brick in header bond with gauged red brick dressings. Doorcase with flat hood and frieze that sweeps up in a graceful curve. Moulsham, or at any rate Moulsham Street, has regained something of a separate identity since the construction of Parkway in 1965–8 cut it off from the rest of the town.

The perambulation starts on the S side of Parkway (for Moulsham Street and New London Road N of Parkway, *see* Perambulation 1). But before venturing down Moulsham Street, a short diversion along HALL STREET leads at the far end to a former FACTORY built by John Hall of Coggeshall as a silk mill, 1858, acquired by the Courtaulds in 1865, and then by Marconi in 1899 for his first wireless factory. Now offices. Two storeys, main façade of four bays separated by pilasters. Contemporary three-bay, two-storey house on W side and

two free-standing C19 industrial buildings. In MOULSHAM
STREET, on the SE side, Nos. 40–41, C16 with jettied front, and
to the rear a wing also jettied and with exposed studs. Another
jettied front to No. 44, of similar age. Opposite, THE BAY
HORSE, late C17 timber-framed and plastered with weatherboarding on the ground floor and sham timbers above. Further
S, opposite Hamlet Road, a nice row of buildings, C16 to C18,
including one with gambrel roof and weatherboarding. Then
on the E side, just before St John's, ST JOHN'S COURT, former
National School by *Chancellor*, 1860–1, with additional building by *C. Pertwee*, 1885. Gothic. Stock brick with stone dressings and bands of red and black brick, quite delicately handled.
Opposite, down ANCHOR STREET, a former generating station
built for R.E.B. Crompton, 1890, which supplied the town's
electricity until 1931. Five bays of full-height round-headed
windows and off-centre arched entrance doorway, and three
bays of two-storey offices, with ball-finialled parapet and segmental pediments.

In ST JOHN'S ROAD, alongside the church, two two-storey Early
Victorian villas, painted brick; No. 48 with parapet and bays
with curved ends, No. 50 with Roman Doric doorcase with
open pediment, dated 1843. Then on the corner of Mildmay
Road a quite different sort of villa, or *cottage orné*, that cannot
be more than ten years later: gault brick with fish-scale slate
roof, gables with shaped and pierced bargeboards, a window
with hoodmould and latticed casements, assorted chimneystacks round, octagonal, and twisted. The next-door house,
in Mildmay Road, appears to have been built in similar spirit,
but much altered.

Back in Moulsham Street, and further S on the W side a row of
six ALMSHOUSES founded by Thomas Mildmay of Moulsham
Hall in 1565, rebuilt by William Mildmay in 1758. Brick, twelve
bays and two storeys with a four-bay pediment and segment-
headed windows. On the E side, Chelmsford College and
Chelmsford Museum (*see* Public Buildings).

Moulsham Street meets New London Road at an acute
angle, where stands THE WHITE HOUSE, 1912 by *Charles &
W.H. Pertwee* with *C.H.B. Quennell* for W.F. Crittall. Two storeys
and five bays, of which the central bay is wider, steps forward,
and has an open pediment, and with quoins; so a sort of Neo-
Georgian, but of painted brick and with Crittall windows –
altogether very advanced for its date.

NEW LONDON ROAD was laid out from 1839 by a consortium
of local Nonconformists: John Copland, his son Edward, his
son-in-law the architect James Fenton, Thomas Greenwood of
Sparrow's Bank, and W.C. Wells of the Duke Street Brewery.
Buildings soon followed, including a large Independent chapel
(by *Fenton*, 1839–40, dem.). The initial development, completed by the end of 1842, is characterized by two-storey semi-
detached and terraced houses of gault brick (or stock brick
with gault brick fronts), many of them by *Fenton*. The southernmost houses on the W side are later. First, MOULSHAM

GRANGE, dated 1907 in the Tudor Gothic style of fifty years earlier, then HIGHFIELDS and FARLEIGH by *Chancellor*. The former 1882, extended 1893, with a lot of moulded brick decoration and a heavy stone porch, the latter 1858, relatively early in Chancellor's career and rather more interesting. Gault brick with bands of stock brick and stone dressings. High gables, and on the entrance front two ground-floor bays connected by a three-bay arcade to form a portico *in antis*, with balustrade above.

The houses associated with mid-C19 New London Road start N of the junction with Moulsham Street, on the W side: Nos. 206–8 (Osborne Terrace), and No. 200, a four-bay house (originally Falcon Cottage), 1843, the ground-floor windows and doorway in segmented arches. On the NW corner of Writtle Road, SOUTH LODGE HOTEL (originally Orchard Lodge), 1841–2, more Picturesque than classical with bargeboarded gables. Insensitive red brick additions. Down WRITTLE ROAD, W of the railway, the two-storey office block of the former Crompton & Co.'s Arc Works, an electrical lighting factory of 1896, by *John Slater*. Stock brick with red brick dressings, the long street frontage interrupted by two three-bay gables. The remainder of the factory site developed for housing in 2002 by *Fairview Homes*.

Back in New London Road, N of Writtle Road, some larger, later C19 houses, e.g. on the E side No. 201, dated 1878. On the opposite corner of Southborough Road, SOUTHBOROUGH LODGE (originally New House, for F. H. Crittall) provides a complete contrast: 1908 by the ever-versatile *C.H.B. Quennell*, here in Arts and Crafts mood: roughcast over brick, leaded windows with dark frames (but at the rear one of Crittall's metal 'V' windows), a variety of large and small bays, and two large and extravagantly shaped gables. Contemporary four-car garage. Inside, contemporary panelling and other woodwork.

N of the cemetery, more terraces and semi-detached houses of the 1840s, but then on the W side the largest houses of the initial development: first, on the corner of New Writtle Street, LAUREL GROVE (now the Chelmsford Club), 1845–8 by *Fenton* for himself. The usual gault brick, but with stucco surrounds to the windows, floating cornices on consoles, and an impressive tetrastyle Corinthian portico. Billiard room added by *Chancellor*, 1897–8. Entrance lodge and outbuildings along New Writtle Street.

On the opposite corner, BELLEFIELD, 1841–2 by *Fenton* for his brother-in-law Edward Copland; later the home of Frederic Chancellor. Two pedimented gables, shallow bows below them, and portico with square piers. Lower flanking wings and at the back a pretty two-storey bow with first-floor veranda. Next to it THORNWOOD HOUSE, 1848 by *Fenton* for his other brother-in-law John Copland Jun., and rather grander: two-and-a-half storeys, three bays with pedimented windows on the ground floor and another on the first floor over the tetrastyle Corinthian portico with balcony. Both Bellefield and Thorn-

wood House restored 1991–2 and converted to offices as part
of COUNTY SQUARE, with additional blocks of offices and flats
that borrow elements of the older houses. Bronze STATUE of
Graham Gooch ('The Cricketer') by *John Doubleday*, 1992.
Finally the Essex and Chelmsford Centre (*see* Public Buildings), and *Fenton*'s Baptist Chapel (*see* Churches), before
Parkway is reached.

WRITTLE WICK (Family Centre), Chignall Road. C16 or C17
timber-framed, part plastered, part faced in gault brick. To this
G. Sherrin added, *c.* 1884, a parallel range of red brick with
stone dressings and half-timbered upper storey. Canted bay to
the l., broad gabled wing to the r., with veranda and balcony
between them, and r. of the gabled wing a polygonal belvedere
tower. He also added a porch that extends to the street.

LODGE FARM, Goat Hall Lane. *See* Galleywood.

CHICKNEY

ST MARY THE VIRGIN. A quaint flint and pebble-rubble church,
with hardly a right angle to be found. Saxon nave with two
double-splayed windows. Chancel with small E.E. lancets. The
chancel arch is about 100 years later, although rebuilt in the
restoration of 1858–9. Its exceedingly curious imposts may be
based on the C14 originals. Pretty two-light squint to the l. of
the arch. Early C14 W tower with three two-light windows in
the W face, and a square shingled spire. Now vested in the
Churches Conservation Trust. – ALTAR. Remarkably for
1858–9, the ancient mensa or altar slab, removed and buried
at the Reformation, was brought back into use. Mounted on a
wooden base painted to look like stone, with arched panels in
front. – PRIEST'S STALL and DESK. 1858; extravagant Gothic
carving. Nave BENCHES of the same date, but plain. – FONT.
Late C14 with buttressed stem and bowl with deep crocketed
ogee arches with shields in the spandrels. – FONT COVER. 1858.
Pyramidal, with embattled foot, and crockets.

NEW CHICKNEY HALL. 1935 by *A. Bensly Whittingham*. Brick,
Neo-Georgian but for two large shaped gables. Lower service
wing with a Swedish-looking copper-covered clock turret.

SIBLEY'S FARM, 1¼ m. WNW. With gables and jettied cross-
wings. The W cross-wing C14, the rest rebuilt in the second
quarter of the C16, including staircase tower with original
newel stair. Two-storey main range includes hall with original
screens, and a number of original windows and doors. Remains
of wall painting in a ground-floor room of the E cross-wing. In
front of the house, a timber-framed DOVECOTE, part plastered,
part weatherboarded, converted in the C16 from a small C15 or
earlier gatehouse. Large weatherboarded aisled BARN behind
the house, three late C16 bays with two bays added in 1683.

CHIGNALL

Civil parish formed in 1888 from the parishes of Chignall St James and Chignall Smealey.

ST JAMES. C13 or C14 nave and chancel of flint rubble, with three early C16 brick windows. On the nave's N side the rood stair-turret projects like a massive buttress; the stairs later served the pulpit. Much restored 1865: s porch rebuilt, N vestry and w bellcote added. Redundant, 1981; converted to a private house by *Patrick Lorimer, c.* 1989.

Next to the church, a nice row of C18 weatherboarded cottages.

Former SCHOOL, ⅔ m. NNW. By *Beadel, Son & Chancellor*, 1849. Schoolroom and master's house, brick with stock brick dressings, now two houses.

BRICKBARNS FARM, 1 m. SE. Early C17 timber-framed farmhouse with small central gable. C18 brick barn combined with a dovecote, the gable ends having double walls with nesting holes.

BROOMWOOD, 1¼ m. E. Built by *Fred Rowntree* for Miller Christy, the Essex historian and naturalist (and fellow Quaker), 1912–13, in 'the Elizabethan style of about the year 1550' (*Essex Naturalist*). Half-timbered, mostly with brick nogging, gabled. Chimneystack copied from Priors, Broomfield (q.v.), Christy's previous home.

CHOBBINGS FARM, 1 m. E. The farmhouse was originally the kitchen block or open hall for a larger house. Late C14, with timber-framed chimneystack, extended in the C17. Square weatherboarded granary, mid C17, and barn, late C16 or C17 but with sections of late C14 timber framing, whose sooted rafters prove that it was formerly a house. Converted back into a house in the late C20.

STEVENS FARM, ¼ m. N. Unusually large covered yard by *Beadel, Son & Chancellor*, 1852. Stock brick with red brick dressings. Converted to houses by *Hibbs & Walsh Associates*, 2001.

ST NICHOLAS, Chignall Smealey. An all-brick church of the early C16, partially decorated with blue brick diapers; N aisle and vestry added by *J. Clarke*, 1847. The view from the E is especially picturesque with three gables of different heights. The w tower is not tall, with diagonal buttresses, battlements, and brick windows. Brick windows in nave and chancel as well, the E window renewed. Two-bay brick arcade, octagonal pier and four-centred arches. *Rev. William Gibbens* restored the interior, 1894, removing plaster from the walls. Further restoration, including rebuilding of s porch, 1904, probably by *A. Y. Nutt*. – Even the FONT is brick (cf. Potter Heigham, Norfolk), octagonal and quite undecorated, except for the moulding between stem and bowl. Until 1904 it was plastered. – SCREEN. Plain, one-light divisions with ogee arches. – PULPIT. Nice plain C17. – STAINED GLASS. In E and w windows, 1904.

Former RECTORY, E of the church, by *Chancellor*, 1868. Brick.

CHIGWELL

Dickens called Chigwell 'such an out of the way rural place', and in spite of its proximity to London it has managed, in its historic centre at least, to retain its individual character. The best buildings are to be found at the top of the hill that leads up from Woodford Bridge (*London 5: East*), centred on the parish church and Chigwell School, but a number of fine houses survive lower down the High Road, surrounded by the C20 suburban sprawl that followed the arrival of the railway in 1903. Buckhurst Hill and Chigwell Row (qq.v.) are described separately.

CHURCHES

St Mary, High Road. From the s, one still sees a typical, small Essex village church, of nave (rendered), chancel (flint rubble), tiled roof and weatherboarded spire with splay-foot copper-covered spire, and C19 s porch. From any other angle, however, the true situation becomes apparent, because the church was enlarged to more than twice its size in 1886–7, when *A. W. Blomfield* replaced the C15 N aisle with a new nave and chancel, the old nave and chancel becoming the s aisle and s chapel (Lady Chapel). The original church was Norman and still has its s doorway with one order of rather tall columns, scallop capitals, a curved lintel, an arch with zigzag decoration, and a tympanum with carved diaper ornament, little squares, divided into two triangles. C15 N arcade with piers of the familiar four-shafts-four-hollows profile. Splendid C15 roof with tie-beams, crown-posts, and four-way struts, three bays, the C15 belfry forming a fourth. The belfry rests on eight posts, two against the N and two against the s wall, the remaining four inserted later to support the spire and forming a square in between. The usual arched braces connect the wall-posts with the square. Beams along the N and s sides of the square, and cross-strutting.

The old church was restored in 1854 by *F. T. Dollman*, who presumably added the arch at the entrance to what is now the Lady Chapel to create a larger chancel that incorporated the eastern bay of the N arcade. Following Blomfield's additions, which included also the two-storey N vestry, the chancel was decorated by *G. F. Bodley*, 1896, of which date the painted ceiling and alabaster REREDOS survive; two painted panels of angels, formerly on the E wall, moved to the W wall as part of alterations by *Higgins & Thomerson*, 1968; ceiling repainted by *Campbell, Smith & Co.*★ – PULPIT also by *Bodley*. – In s aisle, good collection of HATCHMENTS, seventeen between 1656 (which is very early) and 1872; also ROYAL ARMS of George II. – In vestry, C18 wooden wall CUPBOARD to hold bread as dole for poor parishioners.

★ Bodley's reredos replaced one of 1868 by *S. S. Teulon*, executed by *Earp*.

St Mary, Chigwell.
Brass to Archbishop Samuel Harsnett †1631

STAINED GLASS. E window, 1887, and E window of nave, 1902, by *Kempe*. Pulpit window by *Burlison & Grylls*, 1896. Also in the nave, two windows by *Powell & Sons* (*J. H. Hogan*), 1943, and two by *Goddard & Gibbs*, 1962 and 1972, the former designed by *A.E. Buss*, the latter by *J. N. Lawson*, painted by *F.W. Smith*. – In S aisle, western window by *William Morris & Co.* of Westminster, 1948, middle window by *Frederick W. Cole*, 1960, including a depiction of the King's Head (*see* Perambulations); eastern window (Lady Chapel) by *A.L. Wilkinson*, *c.* 1961. Engraved glass window by *Jennifer Conway*, 2002–3. –

p. 227 MONUMENTS. Brass to Samuel Harsnett, Archbishop of York, †1631, bearded with cope and mitre.* Frontal figure about life-size (6 ft; 1.8 metres) mounted on the wall and in excellent condition. Probably designed by *Edward Marshall*. – Thomas Colshill †1595 and wife Mary †1599, small, with the usual kneeling figures facing each other. – George Scott of Woolston Hall †1683 and his wife Elizabeth †1705, black-and-white marble tablet with Corinthian columns, broken pediment and shields of arms. – Many C18 and C19 wall tablets, including John Thomas Kilpatrick †1791 with a mourning female leaning on a column and pointing at his name. – In churchyard, S of Lady Chapel, William Browne †1653, brick table tomb with base, corner pilasters and slab of stone. – CHURCH HALL W of church by *Frederick E. To*, 1989: brick, square, with pagoda-like slate roof.

ST WINIFRED, Manor Road, Grange Hill. 1934 by *Higgins & Thomerson*. Simple rendered nave, chancel and N vestry, green slate roof. Short square concrete NE tower. – STAINED GLASS. Small one-light E window, high up, by *Goddard & Gibbs*, 1963.

CONVENT OF THE SACRED HEART (R.C.), High Road. The former manor house. Georgian, of yellow brick, with iron railings and gateways of unusual quality, but the façade sadly altered by institutional additions since 1896. Inside, a fine graceful original staircase and one ground-floor room with elaborate late C19 doorcases and other decoration. Chapel by *Leonard Stokes*, 1910–11, Neo-Georgian and tunnel-vaulted. Sisters' choir extended *c.* 1925 and the whole chapel reordered 1968–70, including STAINED GLASS by *Earley* of Dublin. Attached to the Convent, ST JOHN'S SCHOOL. Sixth-form block by *Sefre Architects*, 1999–2000. Postmodern, with a pediment-like gabled entrance and corner turret. Polished concrete blocks, in stripes of green and red. Mosaic by *Larrisa Acharya*. Double-height atrium, part-Florentine, part-Moorish.

PUBLIC BUILDINGS

CHIGWELL SCHOOL. Founded by Samuel Harsnett, who purchased land for the site in 1619. The school was functioning

---

*He was born in Colchester in 1561, was vicar of Chigwell 1597 and later archdeacon of Essex and rector of Shenfield; bishop of Chichester, 1609, Norwich, 1619, and archbishop of York, 1628.

by 1623, but formally founded in 1629. The original school-room (Big School, now SWALLOW LIBRARY) survives. Brick, the roof with tie-beams and queenposts, and at least two original four-light mullioned windows; bust of Harsnett by *Ada Palmer*, 1887. C19 porch; there were originally two entrances, as the schoolroom was divided for teaching Latin and English. At the E end, with C18 Venetian windows, was the Latin Master's (i.e. headmaster's) house, probably based on an existing building, but remodelled; three-bay S wing added shortly after 1775, with a large pedimented Doric doorcase and contemporary interior fittings. Opposite, HARSNETTS, a lobby-entrance house of *c.* 1600 purchased by Harsnett in 1627, with C18 and C19 additions. Expansion after 1867 saw the English school given a separate building in the garden of Harsnetts (dated 1868, now a private house), and additions to the back of the Latin Master's house. Three-storey Neo-Gothic brick block to its E added by *F.T. Dollman*, 1873, as a boarding house and dining hall. CHURCH HOUSE, on the corner of Roding Lane, a C17 timber-framed house with C18 additions, was purchased in 1876.

NE of this nucleus lie the C20 buildings, all red brick and broadly sympathetic. Added to Dollman's building is a DINING HALL by *Herbert Tooley*, 1910–11; collegiate-style with dais and oriel at one end and heraldic stained glass; extended 1936–7 when the SWALLOW ROOM was built by *Tooley & Foster*, with furniture by *E. H. S. Walde*, the headmaster. Free-standing CHAPEL, Tudor detailing (e.g. 2-in. (5-cm.) bricks and rectangular hoodmould) with apsidal E end, by *Tooley & Foster*, 1923–4, as a First World War memorial; sacristy added 1955. Some fittings designed by *Walde*, including sanctuary lamp; CRUCIFIX by *Joseph Mayer* of Oberammergau. STAINED GLASS. Two apse windows by *Reginald Hallward*, c. 1924; two nave windows, N and S, by *Paul Quail*, 1976; another nave window and chancel N by *Gerald W. Slowman*, 2000. Further NE, the very distinguished NEW HALL (Tercentenary Hall), also *Tooley & Foster*, 1929, with a nicely detailed stone doorway set between brick pilasters. The extension to this is the BROWNING BUILDING, 1992, one of a number of buildings designed by *Feilden & Mawson*, including the WALDE MUSIC SCHOOL, 1962 (extended by *Barnsley Hewett & Mallinson*, 2001). DRAMA CENTRE by *Arts Team @ RHWL*, 2003.

ST JOHN'S SCHOOL. *See* CONVENT OF THE SACRED HEART.

WEST HATCH HIGH SCHOOL, High Road. 1957–63 by *Richard Sheppard & Partners* with *H. Conolly*, County Architect. Four storeys with continuous glazing on all sides.

CHIGWELL HALL (Metropolitan Police Sports Club), W of the church. By *Norman Shaw*, 1875–6, for Alfred Savill, whose connection with Shaw was both personal and professional: his brother Walter was a partner in the Shaw Savill shipping line, and in 1862 Alfred had been the contractor for one of Shaw's earliest buildings, a warehouse in East London (dem.). Chigwell Hall is Shaw's only Essex house, and an especially good one, surprising in its freshness, and looking as if it might well be twenty-five years later. Brick ground floor, projecting tile-hung upper floor, and coved eaves. The s front has an asymmetrical bay window, three slightly projecting windows on the first floor and then three more windows in the broad gables above. The entrance is at the side, with a flat wooden hood over the doorway. It is not a large house, but is well planned round a central, top-lit hall. Orangery added to the s, 1994–5. On the High Road, a LODGE survives from Belmont Hall, 1810, destroyed by fire 1973.

PERAMBULATION

A walk along the HIGH ROAD can start at the SW end by the Convent (*see* above). On the NW side, next to West Hatch School, GREAT HATCH (renamed Cedar Park), a large early C19 stock brick house with stucco dressings and a Doric porch, now divided. Across Luxborough Lane, LITTLE HATCH, Regency, stuccoed brick with a slate roof and two short wings enclosing a recessed Doric entrance porch. Further N, FLINT COTTAGE, early C19 with a later C19 extension, panels of flint set in stock brick with red brick dressings. Almost opposite, CHIGWELL LODGE, late C18 stock brick, two storeys with attics and dormers. Five-bay front with central Doric doorcase with open pediment and fanlight. Back on the NW side, OAK COTTAGE, a small C18 stock brick house with a conspicuously elaborate doorcase: two engaged Corinthian columns with a swept-up architrave beneath a depressed segmental pediment. Then comes the railway, and the C20 intervenes in an undistinguished manner; but to the E, in HAINAULT ROAD, two interesting rows of three mid-C19 cottages, Nos. 44–48 and 50–54, stock brick, entered via a tiled veranda between cross-wings. Next to them ELCES, C17 lobby-entrance house, timber-framed with a stock brick façade.

Returning to the High Road, Chigwell Hall (*see* Public Buildings) lies on the NW side, and on the SE side two good Georgian houses, first BROOK HOUSE, with C19 and C20 additions, stock brick with red brick dressings, of five bays and two-and-a-half storeys. Then GRANGE COURT (Chigwell School), rebuilt 1774, stock brick with red brick and stucco dressings, three storeys, five bays with single-storey wings (one raised to two storeys). On the entrance front, four-column Doric portico and the window above it with architrave and segmental pediment. Elaborate garden front, with two-storey canted bays and a two-storey central feature with a pedimented window flanked by draped urns over a round-headed doorway. Alterations by *Lutyens* for the Hon. Cecil Baring, 1915. Further N, opposite the parish church, is the KING'S HEAD, the model for The Maypole in Dickens' *Barnaby Rudge* and aptly described by him as 'an old building, with more gable ends than a lazy man would care to count on a sunny day'. C17, three storeys with jettied upper floors, weatherboarded on the ground floor and exposed timbers above; two first-floor oriels, one above.

Various additions, including a large one with another gable of
1901, the overall composition very picturesque.

At this point Chigwell School (*see* Public Buildings) dominates the scene. Next to the main school buildings, on the NW
side, the very modest brick COULSON'S ALMSHOUSES,
founded 1559, according to a stone placed here during rebuilding in 1858 by the vicar, *Rev. W. S. H. Meadows*. Then a pretty
row of houses and cottages, mostly C18, a mixture of brick and
weatherboarding, that help justify Chigwell's claim to have
remained a village. Beyond them HAYLANDS, a plain two-
storey rendered house of *c.* 1800, and HAINAULT HOUSE,
rebuilt *c.* 1870, stock brick with stone dressings: porch, veranda,
and two-storey bay, square below and canted above on the main
elevation, canted two-storey bay on the S elevation and two-
storey bow on the N. Then CHRISTIES, No. 81 High Road, and
PROCTORS and DICKENS COTTAGE, Nos. 83–85, two pairs of
C18 houses, both timber-framed, the former plastered (with a
cistern dated 1762), the latter mainly weatherboarded.

Further N on the same side, TAILOURS, an impressive early
C18 house of plum brick with red dressings; central door with
flat hood on elaborately carved brackets. C18 wrought-iron railings and gate with arched overthrow. Finally, on the E side,
what remains of ROLLS PARK, the seat of the Harveys, which
dated back to *c.* 1600 and was demolished 1951–3. Behind a
substantial C17 red brick wall are the former STABLES, now a
house: C18 stock brick, nine bays each with a shallow round-
arched recess, single storey and a square open cupola.*

FOREST HOUSE, Vicarage Lane, 1 m. SE. Elegant late C18 stock
brick, five bays and three storeys with a two-storey C19 extension to the l. of the entrance front. On the garden front, two-
storey cast-iron veranda with tented copper canopy, *c.* 1805.
Next to the house, an octagonal DAIRY with slate roof, originally thatched, sunk floor, glazed tiles and marble shelf. N of
the house the former coachhouse and stables, now converted
to dwellings, and to the S two houses by *Robin Hiscott*, 1970,
stock brick with little cupolas in an idiosyncratic Neo-
Georgian style, complementing the main house and
outbuildings.

PETTITS HALL, Pudding Lane, 1 m. NE. 1905, in the Neo-
Georgian style of that time, with canted bays and heavy dentilled cornice. It took the name of a late medieval hall house,
which became the lodge, altered and renamed PATSALLS.

TURNOURS HALL, Gravel Lane, 1¾ m. NE. C17, but completely
Victorianized *c.* 1871 while the residence of the artist *Ada
Palmer*. Elaborate Tudor Gothic, including cloisters and
chapel. A C16 barn was partially converted as Palmer's
STUDIO, now a separate house.

WOOLSTON HALL, Abridge Road, 1¼ m. NNE. Timber-framed
and plastered, *c.* 1600, L-plan, the main front in particular

---

*The grand staircase, possibly by *Thomas Kinward*, was moved to Hinchingbrooke
House (Cambs).

remodelled in the C18. Extending SW, a good brick wall, then wrought-iron railings with gates and elaborate overthrow.

CHIGWELL ROW

ALL SAINTS. 1865–7 by *J. P. Seddon*. Brick faced with Bargate stone and Bath stone dressings. The style is C13. Tall nave with clerestory and narrow, lean-to aisles; NW tower 1903, but without the planned spire. Chancel and N vestry added after 1919, the chancel of just one bay, where Seddon had intended a two-bay chancel with N and S vestries beyond wide N and S transepts; the shallowness spoils the proportions of the nave. Low three-bay W porch with wheel window above. Arcades with thickly carved stiff-leaf capitals, the carving by *E. Clarke & Son*. – REREDOS. By *W. H. R. Blacking*, 1924. Oak, with painted saints and shields. – STAINED GLASS. E window *c.* 1923 in the style of *Anning Bell*. S aisle window of Simeon and Anne, signed by *H. G. Murray* of *Belham & Co*. and designed by *Seddon*, 1897. N aisle, two by *A. L. Moore*, *c.* 1891 and 1893. Clerestory by *Clayton & Bell*, 1867.

Former VICARAGE, SE of the church, by *Seddon*, 1867. Stock brick, a lot of pointed-arched windows, and not pretty.

Across the Green NW of the church, HAINAULT HALL, late C18, five bays with three-bay pediment, stock brick with dressings of red brick and stone. To its W, the small UNITED REFORMED CHURCH, white brick with arched windows. 1804 with a Victorian front. Behind it CLARE HALL, a modest late C18 three-bay house of stock brick. On the S side of the road WOODVIEW, formerly Woodlands, rambling brick house by *W. G. Bartleet*, *c.* 1880.

At the E edge of the village, SHEEPCOTES, a smart three-storey stock brick villa of *c.* 1800. Attractive three-bay garden front, originally the entrance front, with two-storey canted bays on each return. Timber-framed service wing. A painted iron COAL TAX POST, *c.* 1861, just by the gate, reminds one how close to London this rural spot is.

CHILDERDITCH
Brentwood

ALL SAINTS AND ST FAITH. By *D. C. Nicholls* and *Fred Johnstone*, 1869. E.E., of Kentish rag and Bath stone. On the site of the old church, with some fittings reused. – FONT. Octagonal bowl with quatrefoil panels. Early C16. – MONUMENT. Sarah Wheeler †1762. White marble with a small figure of Father Time set in the scrolled pediment.

HILLCREST, ¼ m. NNE. By *H. E. Kendall Jun.*, 1841–2, as the vicarage. Brick, the upper floor with exposed timbers and gables. Also by Kendall the tiny former NATIONAL SCHOOL, 1844, on the corner of Childerditch Lane and Childerditch Street. Red brick with white dressings. Enlarged 1891; a house since 1912. The few houses are in Childerditch Lane, the best at the far end: WOODLANDS, a modest weatherboarded and plastered hall house with one mid-C16 cross-wing; and ROSEBROOK, the oldest part of which, *c.* 1500, was originally the cross-wing of a now demolished hall, altered and extended in the C17 and C20.

CHIPPING ONGAR
5000
Ongar

ST MARTIN OF TOURS. Uncommonly complete Norman village church. Nave and chancel, both with characteristic masonry, brick quoins, and small windows, as well as two plain chancel doorways. The bricks seem to be very early medieval examples (cf. Bradwell), which would place the church in the C12 rather than C11. The E end is altered, but traces, especially inside, prove that there were originally six windows in two rows of three, and at the W end similarly three small windows where now there is only one. Belfry probably C15. Nice W gallery on two Tuscan columns erected by 1749, the dormers inserted 1752–3. S aisle by *C.C. Rolfe*, 1883–4, and W porch, 1888. Chancel roof with arched braces supporting collar-beams and additional arched braces carried to a pendant hanging from the collar-beam. In its present form of 1643, but incorporating an earlier structure dating back to the C13. The nave roof is simple, with arched braces on headstops and tracery between the braces and tie-beams. Crown-posts in addition. The S aisle roof has angels carved by *Harry Hems*. – FONT. C14, found and erected on a new base in 1963. Square, with corner pillars and two cusped panels on each face. – PULPIT. Panels with diamond-cut frames and thin strapwork, *c.* 1600. – COMMUNION RAIL. With twisted balusters, *c.* 1700. – STAINED GLASS. E window by *Leonard Walker*, 1929; also single-light window in S aisle, a ferocious-looking St George. S aisle E by *Heaton, Butler & Bayne*, 1885. S aisle (True Vine) by *Powell & Sons*, 1925. Chancel N by *Horace Wilkinson*, 1935, also S aisle (St Martin). Two nave N windows by *Francis Stephens*, assisted by *Gordon Beningfield*, 1963. – MONUMENTS. Nicholas Alexander †1714, epitaph with two cherubs' heads at the foot. It might be by *Edward Stanton*. – Mrs Sarah Mitford | 1776. By *Nollekens*. Epitaph with the usual obelisk and two cherubs against it and an urn between them; one stands, the other sits and sobs.

ST HELEN (R.C.). 1868–9 by *D.C. Nicholls*. E.E., brick, with a bell-turret and little more. Sanctuary at W end by *Birchall Scott, c.* 1973, when the orientation of the church was reversed. – STAINED GLASS. Nave S window to Rev. Thomas Byles who died on the *Titanic*, 1912.

UNITED REFORMED CHURCH (Congregational). 1833 by *James Medland*. White brick with big pediment. Internal alterations by *I.C. Gilbert*, 1870, who also added school and lecture rooms, 1865, but these were largely rebuilt following a fire in 1919.*

CEMETERY. 1866, with Anglican and Nonconformist chapels by *I.C. Gilbert & Fothergill Watson*. Stock brick with red brick dressings, and exceptionally plain, but (unusually) semi-detached.

BUDWORTH HALL. Public hall and meeting rooms by *Fothergill Watson*, 1886. Brick with a large, squat tower, fancifully described by Kelly's as being 'in the Elizabethan style'.

PUBLIC LIBRARY. By *Mark Harris*, 1996. Red and stock brick, single-storey, large pyramidal roof broken by a clerestory halfway up and topped with a little louvre.

PERAMBULATION. The centre of Ongar lies within the earthworks of the Norman CASTLE, with the High Street running more or less through the middle. NE of the church and hidden from the High Street is the motte, 50 ft (15.5 metres) high and 230 ft (71 metres) in diameter. Inner bailey to the W. Across part of the earthwork of the inner bailey, CASTLE HOUSE, built by William Morice in the mid C16 and remodelled *c.* 1840. Plastered, the ground floor probably brick, two upper floors timber-framed. Three gables on the front, originally wider, with single-storey crenellated extensions to either side, that on the r. probably the base of a staircase wing. On the mound, fragments of an C18 garden building associated with the house. E of the motte, a pair of cottages by *J.E.M. MacGregor*, 1936, of traditional form with pitched pantile roof and overhanging first floor, but constructed of 'Heraklith' slabs in a reinforced concrete frame. Between Castle House and the church, WHITE HOUSE, late C16, timber-framed, with a gault brick front of *c.* 1835.

The town centre is the market-like widening of the HIGH STREET, with a timber-framed house at the corner of the lane that leads up to the church, scrolly brackets supporting the jetty and the date 1642 carved on a lintel. Nearly opposite, a three-bay timber-framed building (KISMET INDIAN RESTAU-RANT), originally the early C17 market house and open on the ground floor. Adjoining it to the r. the KING'S INN, brick with burnt headers, dated 1697. Five windows on the first floor, two wide windows on the ground floor either side of the carriage-way. To the l., GREYLANDS, No. 159, by *T. M. Baynes*, 1843, gault brick with rusticated stucco ground floor and Tuscan porch. Next to it, a house of *c.* 1600, now shops, with a front of three gables and central stack of eight octagonal chimneys. Still on the W side, set back from the street, Nos. 113 and 117 have Gothick windows, *c.* 1800.

Further s, on the e side, LIVINGSTONE COTTAGES, a row of six in front of the United Reformed Church, with a passageway through the middle. Back towards the centre, No. 114 has a five-bay front and a rather fanciful arched porch; timber-

* Medland's sister had married in 1825 the son of the minister, Isaac Taylor. Gilbert was Taylor's grandson.

framed and plastered, *c.* 1780. On the corner of Castle Street, ESSEX HOUSE, built as council offices, 1896. In CASTLE STREET, No. 10, brick, dated 1809, and on the N side, adjoining the churchyard, the former Matthews' MILL by *Robert H. Browne*, 1912; brick, three storeys, now offices.

Back in the High Street, and N of the church, ONGAR HOUSE, No. 212, timber-framed with a five-bay early C19 front of gault brick, the third storey added in 1952. Opposite, down Banson's Lane, HEALTH CENTRE by *John Amor*, 1976, steel and glass pavilion, raised on a steel framework originally open, now filled in. Continuing N, on the W side of the High Street, CENTRAL HOUSE is the former grammar school, opened 1811, seven bays with two two-bay wings, probably by *T.M. Baynes*. Stuccoed, the central section timber-framed, top floor and central pediment added later in the C19. Opposite, HERMITAGE COTTAGES, mid C19, timber-framed, the first floor plastered, the ground floor weatherboarded and with Gothick windows. In the middle a recessed entrance, doors to the two cottages to either side and a passageway between. On the same side, on the corner of Shakletons, the OLD RECTORY, timber-framed and rendered, the small N wing C17, the main five-bay block early C18. Back on the W side, in BANSONS WAY, brick cottages built for staff of the Great Eastern Railway, 1892 and 1912, and then the STATION itself, 1865, brick with stock brick dressings, all to standard G.E.R. designs.

On the northern edge of the town, GREAT STONY PARK, converted in 1998 from 'cottage homes' for 300 children by *W.A. Finch*, 1903–5, for Hackney Board of Guardians. Twelve blocks spaciously arranged in a large oval round a central lawn, brick with upper floors plastered or half-timbered, and with plenty of variety. Single-storey school to the s, 1907 (now Arts and Education Centre).

CHRISHALL   *4030*

HOLY TRINITY. Quite large, mainly of pebble rubble, restored by *J. Clarke*, 1867–9, and *F. C. Penrose*, 1876–8. Clarke rebuilt the chancel arch, clerestory, and C16 N porch, and replaced the nave and s aisle roofs. Penrose restored the chancel, with new hammerbeam roof, and added the N vestry. The oldest parts are C13: the responds of the chancel arch and of an arch at the E end of the N arcade. The rest Perp: the diagonal buttresses and the flint and stone chequered battlements of the W tower (restored 1914, when the spirelet was taken down), the battlements nearly all round the church (not N aisle), and most of the windows, and also the aisle arcades. These have an elongated semi-polygonal section without capitals and only towards the arches small semi-polygonal shafts with capitals. – REREDOS. 1889, stone, now painted. Probably by *Jones & Willis*, who sign the accompanying plaque. – FONT. Plain, of *c.* 1300. – PAINTING. Large copy by *Philip Reinagle* of *Rubens'*

Holy Trinity, Chrishall.
Brass to Sir John de la Pole and wife Joan, *c.* 1380

'Adoration of the Magi' (1624) at Antwerp. – STAINED GLASS.
N aisle E by *Shrigley & Hunt*, 1947. S aisle E by *Goddard &
Gibbs*, 1993, reusing glass by *H.J. Salisbury* from St Peter, Dun-
stable, Beds. – MONUMENTS. Effigy of a lady in a recess (S
aisle) with depressed segmental arch and battlements; late C14.
– Brass to Sir John de la Pole and wife Joan, *c.* 1380. Figures
5 ft (1.5 metres) tall, under a tripartite arch with thin side buttresses, an uncommonly important and satisfying piece. –
Unidentified brasses to a lady, *c.* 1450 (13 in. (33 cm.) long),
and to a civilian and wife, *c.* 1480 (18½ in. (47 cm.) long; good).
– Elizabeth Bankes †1754. Nicely lettered inscription: 'Beauty
& Sense, in vain to these you trust; Both Sense & Beauty must
be laid in Dust.'
CHISWICK HALL, ¾ m. S. H-plan, *c.* 1600, with gabled wings,
those on the SE side jettied, with a third, gabled staircase wing
on the NW side. Moat on three sides, and fishpond to the S.
EARTHWORK, 70 yds NE. Medieval mound, about 120 ft (37
metres) in diameter, surrounded by a ditch. Two ponds 200
yds further E seem to be the remains of another ditch or moat.

CLACTON-ON-SEA

1010

The discovery of Clacton as a seaside resort came later than that
of Walton, earlier than that of Frinton, but the same man was
connected with all three – Peter Bruff – and it is at Clacton that
he made the greatest impact. He purchased land in 1864, drew
up a scheme for laying out the town in 1870, the pier opened in
1871, and the Royal Hotel in 1872. The arrival of the railway in
1882 ensured the resort's continued success. Of the three resorts
it is the largest, and the brashest.

CHURCHES

The two Anglican churches are situated in residential areas either
side of the town centre, St James to the SW, St Paul to the NE.
The other denominations are to be found between them, much
more advantageously sited.
ST JAMES, Beatrice Road. 1912–13 by *Temple Moore*. The exterior looks earnest, Perp and a little grim, the walls rendered.
The nave is unfinished, and was to have been two bays longer,
with a W tower. Although detrimental, this serves to accentu-
ate the austerity of the interior, which is one of the most surprising in Essex. The eye is immediately drawn to the high
altar, raised fifteen steps above the level of the nave, and the
very large and lavish REREDOS by *Leslie Moore*, 1932 (largely
using Temple Moore's design). Nave arcades with two very
large pointed arches on the plainest piers. Most original is the
chancel, where the two sides are treated as if different periods 107
had been at work. The S side Early Christian, as it were, with
plain round arches, and a gallery; the N side pointed, with
opposing rhythms, and a sort of triforium. Then a Dec window

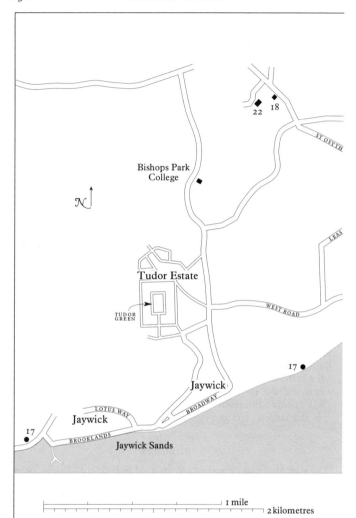

1	St Paul	13	Clacton Centre
2	St James	14	St Helena Hospice
3	Our Lady of Light and	15	Clacton and District Hospital
	St Osyth (R.C.)	16	Oulton Hall
4	Baptist Church	17	Martello Tower
5	Methodist Church	18	St Clare's R.C. Primary School
6	Christ Church URC	19	County High School
7	Masonic Temple	20	Holland Park Primary School
8	St Michael's Convent	21	Windsor School
9	Town Hall	22	Ravenscroft Primary School
10	Middlesex Court	23	West Cliff Theatre
11	Moot Hall	24	Royal Hotel
12	Police Station		

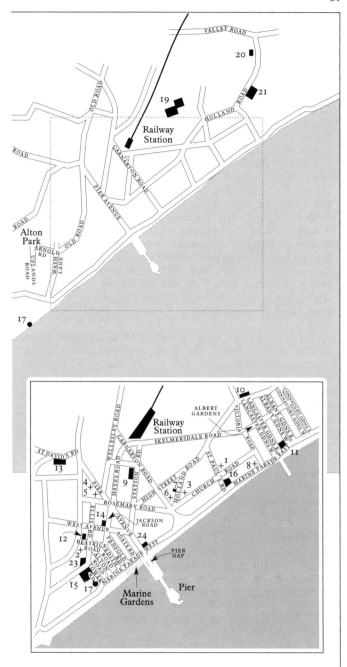

Clacton-on-Sea

on either side of the sanctuary, and joining it all together a Perp clerestory, two-light windows along the sides and a three-light over the altar. All the detail very severe, and only the sparsest bits of brick to relieve the whiteness of the plastered walls. N and S chancel chapels (Lady Chapel and Children's Chapel), with vestries beneath the sanctuary. Church rooms and choir vestry on S side by *Leslie Moore*, 1924. – STAINED GLASS. Lady Chapel, four windows by *W. C. Langsford*, 1918; also Children's Chapel E and S aisle. Children's Chapel S by *Robert J. Newbery*, 1932. N aisle by *A.K. Nicholson*, 1957. – MONUMENT. Calvary (First World War memorial) on outside of E wall by *Temple Moore*, 1921, sculpture by *Alfred Southwick*.

108 ST PAUL, Church Road. By *Roy Gould*, 1965–6, replacing a building of 1875 by *George Gard Pye*.* Nave with shallow chancel, and S aisle screened off as a Lady Chapel, and SW bell-tower. Brick-faced, with portal frames exposed internally. The interior
109 is dominated by the STAINED GLASS E window by *Rosemary Rutherford*, installed by *Goddard & Gibbs*, filling the E wall of the sanctuary: *dalle de verre* in vivid colours that move through the spectrum, but red, blue, and purple predominate. Other panels of stained glass from the old church re-set by *Kent Blaxill & Co.* to Rutherford's design, the colours of the new glass carefully co-ordinated. – CHURCH HALL by *Gould*, 1978–9.

OUR LADY OF LIGHT AND ST OSYTH (R.C.), Church Road. 1902–3 by *F. W. Tasker*. The most prominent church in the town. Neo-Norman, nave with low circular piers, transepts with crossing tower, apse with narrow ambulatory and vestries beyond the E end: quite an uncommon type of design around 1900. Rock-faced exterior of Kentish rag with Ketton stone dressings. W front with three stepped round-headed lancets and square angle turrets. Reordering of sanctuary with new stone furnishings by *David Rackham Partnership*, 1998. – STAINED GLASS. By *Jones & Willis*: ambulatory windows *c.* 1903, two nave windows 1925.

BAPTIST CHURCH, Pier Avenue. By *W. Hayne*, 1928. Byzantine, brick, with a monumental quality, and the sort of quirkiness one expects from Hayne.

CHRIST CHURCH (United Reformed Church), Carnarvon Road. 1886–7 by *T. H. Baker*. Brick with stone dressings. Nave with slender tower, originally with a spire, at the liturgical NW corner. Canted N transept, larger S transept added 1890, lecture hall and classrooms at E end 1901. – STAINED GLASS. In N transept, by *Abbott & Co.*, 1949 and 1951.

METHODIST CHURCH (Wesleyan), Pier Avenue. By *Charles Bell*, 1877. E.E., Kentish rag with Bath stone dressings. E wheel window and small NE steeple.

Former FRANCISCAN CONVENT (R.C.), Church Road. Now housing. Opened 1897; school by *Sherrin*, 1898, extended

*The old church was built of cement concrete, using sand from the beach, with shingle-dashing. Vicarage by *R. W. K. Goddard*, 1890, also dem.

1904, and chapel by *A.J.C. Scoles & C. Raymond*, 1908. Stock brick with red brick dressings. Grim.

ST MICHAEL'S CONVENT (R.C.) AND CARE HOME, Marine Parade East. Opened 1908, converted from existing houses by *Hinsley & Co*. Behind, large red brick CHAPEL, 1936, with high parabolic ceiling and altar set in a semicircular canopy of striped green and white marble.

PUBLIC BUILDINGS

TOWN HALL, Station Road. 1929–31 by *Sir A. Brumwell Thomas*, replacing the old Town Hall in the High Street by *J.W. Chapman* (*see* Perambulation). In the conventional Neo-Georgian regarded as suitable for such buildings at this date. Brown brick with stone dressings. Recessed central tetrastyle portico and pediment with giant Composite columns. Behind this, and rising above the wings to either side, the PRINCES THEATRE, to the l. the mayor's parlour and other offices, to the r. a matching wing originally for the Public Library.

POLICE STATION, Beatrice Road. By the *County Architect's Dept*, 1993–7, with a panache appropriate for a seaside town and more than a hint of the Modern style of the 1930s.

COLVIN MEMORIAL TEMPLE (Masonic), Holland Road. 1937 by *E. Robbins Nixey*. Chunky, with a little decoration including two round windows set in Star-of-David patterns of black brick. Incongruous blind tetrastyle stone portico.

BISHOPS PARK COLLEGE, Jaywick Lane. By the *Architects Co-Partnership*, 2003–5. Brick and render. Two storeys, with a square core round an atrium. At three of the corners, pavilions with curved glazed walls and dramatic projecting roofs on Y-shaped supports. The pavilions are rendered in different colours – one for each of the semi-autonomous schools within the college. Within each pavilion another central space with smaller atrium. On the fourth corner, multi-purpose community facilities. Integrated artwork by *Rob Olins*.

CLACTON CENTRE, St Osyth Road. Former Board School, 1893–4 by *T.H. Baker*, enlarged by him 1899: brick, single-storey, two large and two small straight gables, large central bell-turret and smaller ventilation turrets. Also by Baker, HOLLAND PARK PRIMARY SCHOOL, Holland Road, 1902–3, with shaped gables.

COUNTY HIGH SCHOOL, Walton Road. 1928 by *J. Stuart*, County Architect, and uncommonly large: two storeys, brick with stone dressings and rusticated brick quoins. Courtyard plan, with a recessed central entrance framed by giant columns.

RAVENSCROFT PRIMARY SCHOOL, Nayland Drive. By the *County Architect's Dept* (project architect, *Barrie Page*), 1981–2. Solar-passive design with heat pumps using ground water from bore holes.

ST CLARE'S R.C. PRIMARY SCHOOL, Cloes Lane. Colourful classroom block by *Cottrell & Vermeulen*, c. 1998. Sandy-coloured walls with blue vertical stripes and portholes.

WINDSOR SCHOOL, Holland Road. By *Fred Rowntree*, 1911–12,
originally the Ogilvie Children's Home. Neo-Georgian, a pair
of long two-storey blocks linked by a dining hall, the s-facing
block with verandas and open-air classrooms.

CLACTON AND DISTRICT HOSPITAL, Freeland Road. The
nucleus is *J. W. Martin*'s Cottage Hospital, 1898–9, brick with
half-timbered gables and a little oriel over the entrance. Wings
by *Arthur Sykes*, 1926, and many further additions.

ST HELENA HOSPICE, Jackson Road. A striking, curved, corner
building by *Purcell Miller Tritton*, 2001–2. To the street brick,
with red cedar boarding on the upper storey beneath a sweeping slate roof. Behind, rooms arranged round an enclosed and
private courtyard.

RAILWAY STATION. Rebuilt 1929. Heavy brick and stone
Neo-Georgian.

MARTELLO TOWERS. 1809–12 (*see* Introduction, p. 76). Three
SW of the pier, the first low and broad at the corner of Tower
Road, the second in Hastings Avenue, the third on the golf
course. The first tower is unusual in being set in a brick-lined
moat; there was formerly a glacis and outer battery.

PERAMBULATION

A walk along the seafront, plunging inland where necessary,
should start at the PIER: 1870–1, extended 1890–3 with PAVIL-
ION by *Kinniple & Jaffrey*, now largely concealed by cladding.
Entrance buildings *c.* 1922–32, with Art Deco touches. The
pier is approached by Pier Gap, the BRIDGE across it by *Daniel
J. Bowe*, the Council's surveyor, 1914. To either side, the
MARINE GARDENS, those to the NE laid out 1899, those to
the SW 1911. Attractive cast-iron lamp standards, 1912. Bowe
replanned the gardens in 1921, including Garden of Remembrance with memorial by *Charles Hartwell*, 1924. Restored by
The Landscape Partnership, 1999, including a stainless-steel
pergola. The PROMENADE itself dates from the construction
of the sea-wall by *Charles W. Whitaker*, 1880, with further work
by *T. A. Cressy*, 1889.

The character of the buildings along the front is varied, the
most distinctive feature being a few short terraces with shaped
gables, mainly NE of the pier. Only a short stretch to the SW,
leading to the Martello Tower (*see* above); beside it, in TOWER
ROAD, a row of red brick COASTGUARD COTTAGES, 1888. At
the top of Tower Road the WEST CLIFF THEATRE, rebuilt by
G.H.B. Gould, 1928.

PIER AVENUE, the spine of the town, retains a late C19 brashness, with first-floor balconies, some enclosed, and garish
shopfronts. Inland, on the corner of STATION ROAD,
NATWEST BANK by *T.H. Baker*, 1898–9, brick with stone
dressings but restrained by comparison with its neighbour,
BANK CHAMBERS, 1900, with panels of decorative plasterwork. On the opposite corner, LLOYDS BANK, 1922, single-
storey, stone, and classical. Station Road leads N into the

commercial centre; at the corner of the HIGH STREET and ROSEMARY ROAD is BARCLAYS BANK, a rebuilding following bomb damage of part of the old Town Hall of 1893–4 by *J. W. Chapman*. The Operetta House that formed part of this group can be seen along Rosemary Road. Brick with terracotta dressings. Between High Street and Station Road, CLACTON ARCADE, a development of shops and offices by *G.H.B. Gould*, 1920s commercial classical. Also by Gould, in Station Road, HURLINGHAM CHAMBERS, built as his own office in 1924, and at the far end of Pier Avenue where it joins Old Road, the CENTURY CINEMA (now Flicks), 1935–6, with an Art Deco painted entrance on the corner, brick behind.

MARINE PARADE NE of the Pier starts with the ROYAL HOTEL, 1872: plain, long, painted, with a thick iron veranda on the first floor. A good terrace of gabled houses in BEACH ROAD, then comes CARNARVON ROAD, approached by curved terraces and island gardens, Clacton's grandest public space.* On the corner of CHURCH ROAD, the OLD LIFEBOAT HOUSE by the R.N.L.I.'s architect *C. H. Cooke*, 1878, brick with a pedimented entrance and short ogee-capped tower; now a pub and lacking its original charm. Back in Marine Parade, a pair of large hotels, both now converted to flats, at the entrance to Vista Road. First THE GRAND, 1892–7 by *Smith, Son & Gale*: a busy façade of gables, canted bays and corner turrets linked by balconies, and an early example of steel box-frame construction with a brick skin. On the opposite corner THE TOWERS, 1891–2 by *W. A. Finch*, extended 1894 and later: stock brick with stone dressings, more picturesquely arranged than The Grand with decorative bargeboards etc.

Further on, at the corner of St Paul's Road, OULTON HALL by *Alan H. Devereux*, 1935; now flats, built as a sort of super guest house with rooms for 250: four storeys, H-plan, in a rather plain version of Art Deco with square clock tower. Then Russell Road, and at the far end, in SKELMERSDALE ROAD, HOLLAND HOUSE, built for Thomas Lilley of Lilley & Skinner. At the front the original portion by *J. W. Chapman*, 1891, rendered, recessed balconies to the ground and first floors, and a polygonal corner turret with lead ogee cap. To this *Arthur Sykes* made a considerable extension in 1908, including a veranda with giant columns. Converted to flats by *G.H.B. Gould*, 1938–9. Large entrance gates at the corner of Holland Road. Along HOLLAND ROAD, on the N side, MIDDLESEX COURT (flats), built as the Middlesex Hospital Convalescent Home by *Young & Hall*, 1895–6: large, brick with some half-timbering and two-storey verandas.†

---

* A clock and outlook tower was designed for the site by *T.H. Baker*, 1889, but not executed.

† Other convalescent homes, in which Clacton once abounded, include the Essex Convalescent Home, Coppins Road, by *F. Chancellor*, 1884, the Passmore Edwards Holiday Home, Marine Parade, by *Charles Bell* and *T. A. Cressy*, 1898–9, and the Reckitt Convalescent Home, Holland Road, by *H.E. Mathews*, 1908–9; all demolished save the lodge of the Essex Convalescent Home.

One more building to notice on Marine Parade, on the corner of Albany Gardens West: MOOT HALL, a C15 timber-framed farmhouse with brick nogging, moved here from Hawstead, Suffolk, in 1911 by *J. A. Scheuermann* for a London builder, J.H. Gill. It acquired in the process a symmetry not originally its own, as well as some additional chimneystacks and windows. Pleasant leafy streets with central gardens – Lancaster Gardens, Albany Gardens, Connaught Gardens – before Clacton merges into Holland-on-Sea (q.v.).

ALTON PARK at the opposite end of the town, sw of Wash Lane, was planned as a garden village by *Pepler & Allen*, 1911, although the scheme was only partially executed. The best houses are to be found in Arnold Road and Uplands Road.

JAYWICK, 1½ m. sw of St James. Jay Wick Farm was bought by F.C. Stedman in 1928 and developed by him as a cheap and cheerful resort for day-trippers. Roads were laid out by *G.H.B. Gould*, who also provided standard designs for chalets and bungalows. Two distinct areas along the front, the better half with streets (named after flowers) running off Broadway. E of that, BROOKLANDS, the roads named after makes of motor car. The chalets here are now occupied all year, which was not the original intention, the result little better than a shanty town. But in LOTUS WAY, on the edge of Brooklands, is a distinctive development of forty houses and bungalows by *Pollard Thomas & Edwards* for the Guinness Trust, 1999–2000. Prefabricated with cedar cladding and monopitch shingle roofs. A little way inland a third area, the TUDOR ESTATE, intended as a more up-market development for year-round occupation, but only one or two houses – e.g. on the N side of Tudor Green – live up to the name, with half-timbering, brick nogging, and other Neo-Tudor details. Known by some as West Clacton to make the distinction from Jaywick even clearer.

CLAVERING

ST MARY AND ST CLEMENT. Of pebble rubble, all Perp and all embattled. Restored in 1863–5, by *J. Clarke*, and 1893–4, when all the walls, except the N aisle, were refaced. The W tower has angle buttresses, the aisles and clerestory three-light windows. Inside, the N and S arcades have curiously detailed tall, slim, lozenge-shaped piers. They have a thin demi-shaft on a semi-polygonal base and towards the (four-centred) arches semi-polygonal shafts. The roofs are all original, low-pitched, and have some original head corbels, with carved figures of angels on the intermediate rafters. The nave roof has tie-beams. – FONT. Octagonal, of Purbeck marble, with two shallow blank pointed arches to each side; *c.* 1200, the stem and base C19. – PULPIT. Early C17, with two tiers of the typical short, broad, flatly ornamented arches. Stem, with hexagonal moulded base, reused from a C15 LECTERN. – BENCHES. C15, with traceried ends, in the aisles. – SCREEN, with broad, tall, one-light openings, cusped and crocketed ogee heads and panel tracery above. Some colouring and the outlines of figures of saints remain on the panels. – STAINED GLASS. Much of the C15 in the N windows; probably Norwich school. – Fragments also in the tracery of the S aisle E window, the rest by *E.R. Suffling*, 1893. – EFFIGY of a knight in chain-mail with coif and mail-coat reaching nearly to the knees. Purbeck marble, early C13.

BRASSES. Songar and wife, *c.* 1480 (female figure 17 in. (43 cm.), male originally larger but top half missing). – Three daughters, *c.* 1520 (5½ in. (14 cm.) figures), all that remains of a brass to Joan Smith and her two husbands. – Ursula Welbore of Pond's †1591, with kneeling figures of her husband Thomas and children. – Joan Day †1593, with husband (20 in. (51 cm.) figures). – Four sons and three daughters, *c.* 1530. – MONUMENTS. John Smith, vicar of Clavering †1616. Small marble tablet with columns and kneeling figure. – At the W end of the N aisle, a pleasing group to the family of Haynes Barlee †1696. His own monument, erected 1747, has an elegant frontal bust with decoration of a cool and classical style. – His parents, John †1633 and Mary †1643, and grandparents William †*c.* 1610 and Elizabeth †*c.* 1619. Black marble tablet, the inscription inlaid in alabaster within the outlines of two urns. It formerly had a surround. Attributed to *Edward Marshall* (GF). – Haynes' first wife Margaret †1653 and second wife Mary †1658. Almost identical, with frontal busts in oval niches between columns, except Margaret has small kneeling figures of her surviving children and seven skulls on coffins for children who predeceased her. Attributed to *Joshua Marshall* (AW). – Haynes' son William †1683. Stained-glass panel with inscription and shield of arms.

CHRISTIAN CENTRE (former Congregational Chapel), Stortford Road. By *Sulman & Rhodes*, 1872. White brick with bands and arches of red and black, and stone plate tracery, 'of Early French character'. Galleried interior, reordered by *The Kenneth Mark Practice*, *c.* 2000, with a small (liturgical) NE extension.

The parish church's setting, and in particular the approach to it from the SW, is very attractive. It is set back from Pelham Road to the S and joined to it by Church Walk. At the entrance to the churchyard, THE OLD GUILDHALL, early C16 with jettied front and N return and, at the corner, a dragon post with moulded capital. Single-storey early C19 extension to S. Restored by *James Boutwood*, Assistant County Architect, *c.* 1984. Then, on the corner of Church Walk and Pelham Road, THE OLD HOUSE, timber-framed, dating to the C15. Chequered brick S range added *c.* 1690; the roof of the older part, which had been refronted *c.* 1600, raised to match. Remarkable interior, with a large painting on the staircase wall depicting two scenes from the biblical story of Jephthah's daughter, and first-floor rooms with elaborately carved panelling and three painted panels, as well as another painted panel in an attic room, C17–18. Staircase with twisted balusters to the first floor and half-balusters on the wall of the next flight.

w of Church Walk, on the N side of PELHAM ROAD, PIERCEWEBS, Late Georgian brick. Three bays, with two shallow bows on the ground floor, tall windows on the first, and dormers almost hidden by a deep parapet. Beyond it THE OLD VICARAGE, 1822, a posthumous work of *James Lewis*. Painted brick, the first floor set back behind the ground floor. On the N side of the church is the site of the mid-C11(?) CLAVERING CASTLE, trapezoidal with a moat 75 ft (23 metres) wide and 18 ft (5.5 metres) deep. Beyond, an extensive system of earthworks, in part to contain the River Stort. E of the castle, THE BURY, a handsome house with three C17 gables on the S front. Within the centre gable a fourth smaller gable jettied over the front door. At the back the roof descends to the level of the ground-floor windows, indicating that this was originally an aisled hall house, of which much of the framing is visible internally; tree-ring dated 1304. Continuing E, a track leads to MIDDLE STREET, with good thatched houses on both sides and, at the bottom, a ford across the Stort.

Most of the village is spread out along the main road towards Newport, with thatched houses at THE DRUCE, ⅓ m. E of the church. HILL GREEN, ¾ m. NE, boasts a thatched CRICKET PAVILION converted from a hut from RAF Debden, 1950, next to the METHODIST CHURCH, 1877, brick with stock brick dressings, and a 'wheel' PUMP by *Charles Lack & Sons* of Cottenham, 1917.

POND'S MANOR, ¼ m. E. Early C16. Exposed close-set timber framing and brick nogging. Gabled and jettied E front with moulded bressumer.

WINDMILLS, about ¾ m. NW. Two tower mills, both with aluminium caps and no sails: the S 1757, the N and larger 1811.

8020

COGGESHALL

Coggeshall, wrote Morant, 'is a pretty large and populous Town [which] owes its existence to the Abbey', of which the principal remains lie S of the River Blackwater: fragments of the abbey buildings, and Grange Barn. The town's continuing prosperity was due to the cloth trade, which flourished from the C15 to the end of the C17. Evidence of this is found mainly N of the river, not only the parish church and the town's most famous house, Paycocke's, but also the exceptional number of timber-framed buildings, with very little to detract from the overall effect. Great Coggeshall (N) and Little Coggeshall (S) were formerly two parishes.

ABBEY

Founded by King Stephen in 1140; it became Cistercian in 1148. Dissolved in 1538; the church was demolished within three years, and the cloister soon after. No traces of either remain above ground, but limited excavation and aerial photography show that the church was large, with an internal length of about 210 ft (65 metres). Excavation of part of the cloister to

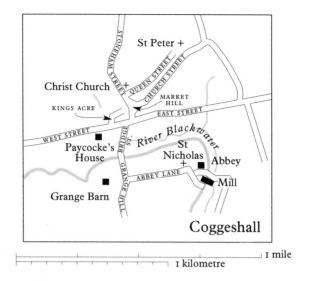

the s yielded typical mid-C12 stone capitals and bases and a
slender shaft with spiral grooves and nail-head projections. As
early as 1518 Sir John Sharpe occupied a mansion in part of
the complex, having exclusive use of one of the church's
chapels, and much of the present house seems to have been
formed from the remaining monastic buildings. This was built
probably *c.* 1570 and complete by 1581, when it was acquired
by Richard Benyan, husband of Anne Paycocke. The house has
a two-storey porch on the w front and a fine n chimneystack
with four shafts. This partly served a fireplace, now on the
outside wall, which is all that remains of Sir John Sharpe's
house. Inside, the hall has a good late C16 screen with Doric
pilasters, reinstated in its correct position (with additional
woodwork) in 2001. The room above has panelling of the same
style. In the e wing the top of a brick arch and a circular C12
brick pier, part of one of four bays of the abbey infirmary.

The main group of surviving medieval buildings lies to the
s, along the River Blackwater, and what is chiefly remarkable
about them is the use of C12 brick dressings – and brick which
is definitely not Roman. It is very early, as medieval brickwork
goes. Some of it at least was plastered in imitation of stone,
and traces of painting survive that represent ashlar lines. s of
the porch are visible indications of the dormitory undercroft.
This must date from *c.* 1180, but the vaulting is early C13. A
fine C13 doorway (blocked) led from the dormitory into a completely preserved corridor. This is two-storeyed and has single-
chamfered ribs and arches to the e. The details of the vaulting
are again early C13. At the s end of the corridor was the
ABBOT'S LODGING. It has lancets with round heads inside.
The upper floor, with a niche in the e wall and piscina near it,
must have been a chapel. se of this, but not aligned with it, a

detached building that was most probably a GUESTHOUSE. It also has lancets, and a round-headed doorway in the N wall. Inside, below the windows, are recesses, fourteen in all, like sedilia. Both this building and the Abbot's Lodging are of *c.* 1190, their roofs raised and replaced in the late C16.

The CHAPEL OF ST NICHOLAS, about 100 yds W of the abbey church, was the gate chapel or *capella extra portas* of the abbey (cf. Tilty). A plain rectangle, with lancets, those on the N side quite regularly arranged. The date must be about 1225. It was partially restored in 1863–4, when a barn entrance on the S side was removed and new S door inserted, and again in 1896–7 by *Bodley & Garner*, when it was re-roofed. Brick SEDILIA and PISCINA with traces of plasterwork and painting were, surprisingly, not restored, and are crudely propped up with C19 brick. – STAINED GLASS. E window by *Burlison & Grylls*, 1897.

The picture at the back of the house with the C16 and the medieval buildings, the River Blackwater, and the ABBEY MILL, is of great charm. The weatherboarded water mill, downstream of the abbey, was rebuilt in the mid C18. A row of long windows indicates its use, from 1820, as a silk-throwing mill. Converted to corn-grinding 1839–40, the machinery still in working order. Brick extension and chimney for steam engine, 1857. MILL HOUSE, W, dates back to the C15. Timber-framed, part plastered, part weatherboarded, with four-bay brick front of *c.* 1820. Four bays, doorway with semi-elliptical arch and fanlight and C20 semicircular porch.

GRANGE BARN, 600 yds W of the abbey, was built in the third quarter of the C13. Weatherboarded, with a huge tiled roof, hipped with gablets at each end and two hipped mid-streys. Six bays and aisles. The crown-post roof dates from a C14 rebuilding, but many of the original joints and timbers, including the principal upright posts, survive. Restored 1983–5 by *James Boutwood* of the *County Architect's Dept.* S of the barn, GRANGE FARM, timber-framed and plastered, *c.* 1600, altered and extended in the C18 and C19. Three storeys and a tall hipped roof, sash windows, and a front door with fluted pilasters that have carved heads in place of capitals. E of the barn, No. 15 GRANGE HILL, late C14, is probably of monastic origin. Restorations and weatherboarded extension to rear by *James Blackie*, 1977–8.

THE TOWN

ST PETER-AD-VINCULA. A large church (over 120 ft (37 metres) long) built to one plan in the C15: W tower, S porch, nave and wide aisles, chancel and equally wide chapels that are as long as the chancel. Nave and chancel under one roof, but with a chancel arch to separate them, and short solid walls projecting inwards from the E end to separate altar spaces from each other. Restored by *E. Christian*, *c.* 1851–69, and the N wall, W tower, and roof rebuilt by *Dykes Bower*, 1955–8, following bomb damage in the Second World War. The tower has diagonal buttresses and battlements, like its predecessor, but not the spire that Dykes Bower planned. The rest of the church also embattled, including the two-storey s porch with tierceron vault and bosses. Aisle walls flint rubble, E parts ashlar-faced with a frieze of shields at the base and below the E window a cusped recess. The nave and chancel N and S arcades are of tall slender piers with four attached shafts with concave sides running on into the arches without capitals. Four-centred arches. Clerestory windows and large aisle windows of three lights. Renewed E window of seven lights, E windows of the chapels of four lights – all with Perp panel tracery. Large two-storey extension on nave N side by *David Whymark*, 2001–2, its entrance from the church marked by two low standing stones with lettering by *Gary Breeze*.

REREDOS. 1880, in memory of W. J. Dampier, vicar 1841–76, perhaps by his son *E. J. Dampier*. Stone figures in elaborate alabaster canopies. – In N chapel, by *F. E. Howard* and the *Warham Guild*, *c.* 1929. Small carved and painted wooden figures in decorated frame. – PULPIT, 1871, CHOIR STALLS and COMMUNION RAIL by *W. B. Polley*. The opening in the rail is flanked by life-sized kneeling figures of angels. – FONT. C13. Round bowl with shallow arcade of trefoiled arches. Brought here from Pattiswick, 1851, when the base was added. – STAINED GLASS. E window by *Clayton & Bell*, 1866. – S chapel S by *Lavers, Barraud & Westlake*, 1888. – W windows of N and S aisles †1903 and 1908 by *Heaton, Butler & Bayne*. – Many other C19 windows destroyed in 1940. – Two windows by *Leonard Evetts*: N chapel N, 1974, and N aisle N, 1975. – MONUMENTS. N chapel, brasses of John Paycocke †1533 and wife with indent of brass of the Virgin above, 36-in. (91-cm.) figures, and Thomas Paycocke †1580, 27-in. (68.5-cm.) figure. – On wall, smaller figures of two ladies, *c.* 1490, and of a civilian and lady, *c.* 1520. – Thomas Aylet †1638. Lozenge-shaped brass plate with inscription and achievement. – S chapel, Mary Honywood †1620, monument with kneeling figure. Attributed to *William Wright* (AW). The inscription says that Mrs Honywood left four generations of descendants, '16 of her owne body' and 367 in all. Moved here from Markshall in 1933. – In chancel floor, two lozenge-shaped brasses by *Hart & Son*, *c.* 1860, marking entrances to the vaults of Henry Skingley †1793 and Henry Skingley †1832. – LYCHGATE. 1880 by *E. J. Dampier*. C15 style.

CHRIST CHURCH, Stoneham Street. Former Independent chapel, 1710. Timber-framed and plastered. Four-bay gabled front, and side walls with two tiers of four windows. Enlarged 1834, probably the date of the wide porch with Greek Doric columns *in antis*. Apsed E end, with two-storey vestry, 1865. Interior refitted in 1882 by *C. Pertwee*, now subdivided. To the E, former BRITISH SCHOOL, *c.* 1841. Gault brick. Two storeys, six bays, with corner and central pilasters. Pyramid roof with lantern. Classrooms and lecture room to the E by *Pertwee*, 1890. Stock brick with white brick arches and bands. Gabled S front with triple round-arched window on first floor.

PUBLIC LIBRARY, Stoneham Street. Former Friends' Meeting
House, 1878, probably by *William Doubleday*. Gault brick, and
chapel-like. Gabled front with tall round-headed doorway and
windows and a round ventilator above.

PRIMARY SCHOOL, Church Green. By the *County Architect's
Dept* (project architect, *Barrie Page*), 1983–6. The impression
is that it consists almost entirely of roof: low-pitched, pantiled,
broken by areas of glazing, rising to a lantern.

PERAMBULATION

The town lies along the old Braintree–Colchester road (West
Street and East Street, part of Roman Stane Street), with Bridge
Street joining more or less at right angles from the s. But instead
of continuing directly across the main road, towards the church,
there is a break – good for the eye, and good for traffic – with a
little triangular marketplace to the N acting as a collecting point
towards which Stoneham Street and Church Street converge.
The church is at the top of Church Street, on the NE edge of the
town centre. The centre must have shifted away from the church
when the abbey granted a market charter in 1256.

The WOOLPACK INN, SW of the church, provides an appropriately picturesque start. The earliest part is the lower gabled
cross-wing (r.), late C14. The wing behind, with hipped roof
and gablet, was added *c.* 1400, as was another wing at the rear
to the l. The main jettied cross-wing to the l., and the open
hall between the cross-wings, were built in the mid C15: hall
floored in the C16, and given oriel windows. On the ground
floor of the l. cross-wing are two original shop windows with
four-centred arched heads, and a blocked narrow doorway.

A little way down CHURCH STREET, on the other side from
the Woolpack, COGGESHALL HOUSE, C16 timber-framed,
refronted in 1897 by G.F. Beaumont, solicitor and historian.
His architect was *P. M. Beaumont* (probably his brother), with
carving by *W. B. Polley*. Brick ground floor with Tudor-style
stone windows and doorways. Carved bressumer. Half-
timbered first floor with three square oriels that rise through
the eaves as gabled dormers with carved bargeboards and
finials. Then a three-bay timber-framed and plastered house,
No. 80: C17, the front range added *c.* 1800. Pedimented Roman
Doric doorcase and above it a round-headed window with
Gothick tracery. C20 belvedere on roof. Next to it No. 76, a
five-bay Georgian brick front, C17 timber-framed and plastered
behind.

Back on the NW side, No. 61, COCKRELLS, restored 1922,
when the C17 timbers were exposed. More exposed timbers on
Nos. 49–55, *c.* 1565–70. Full-length jetties with original carved
bressumers, and on No. 55 an early C19 butcher's shopfront.
More carved bressumers opposite, that on Nos. 52–54 a late
C19 copy with a date of 1565, probably an accurate copy of the
original and the date of the timber-framed structure behind
the brick front. The bressumer on the house to the r. is also

late C19 in C16 style, but the building is *c.* 1560, with a pretty weatherboarded range at right angles along Albert Place.

Opposite Albert Place, Nos. 45–47: No. 47 two bays of an early C14 three-bay hall, set back from the street by the width of its missing s aisle, No. 45 its cross-wing, probably C16. On the same side, LONDON HOUSE, Nos. 37–39, has a painted brick front of *c.* 1700, with five original tall sashes on the first floor. Opposite, No. 40, C14 or C15 with exposed timbers: one-bay hall with two-bay cross-wing, incorporating a cross-passage, to the r. Further down on the same side the CONSERVATIVE CLUB, late C17 timber-framed and plastered, much altered in the late C19. Brick-faced ground floor with two canted bays, two jettied upper stories, pargetted, with three first-floor oriels. Variety is provided by No. 10, which has an early C18 façade of blue bricks with red dressings with an unusually high first floor. Nos. 5–7, opposite, was a single house, the main range *c.* 1600, cross-wing to the r. late C15, both jettied with exposed timbers.

Church Street now opens out into MARKET HILL, its focal point the charmingly eccentric CLOCK TOWER of 1787 (restored 1887). Hexagonal, with horizontal weatherboarding, domed roof and cupola. It is attached to a cottage dating back to the C14. Nice buildings on all three sides of the marketplace, nearly all timber-framed and plastered. To the s the eye is drawn to the WHITE HART HOTEL, the centre with a C18 sashed and plastered façade, its C15 origins apparent from the rear. Gabled buildings with exposed timbers to l. and r. now part of the hotel. To the r. of the hotel, BRIDGE STREET, where one notices first FOUNDRY HOUSE, C16, remodelled in the C18, with two two-storey canted bays, and cast-iron railings that join up with the balustrade of the early C19 SHORT BRIDGE across Back Ditch, which follows the River Blackwater's original course before it was diverted by the abbey's monks. The river's new course is crossed by LONG BRIDGE, to the s, rebuilt 1705 and widened in 1912, but with C13 Coggeshall brickwork on the w side. Between the two bridges, set back from the street, early C19 brick and weatherboarded buildings of the former LITTLE COGGESHALL BREWERY, including chimney, now converted to houses. Then BRIDGE HOUSE, C18 with an early C19 gault brick front. Main part of three bays, stone doorcase with attached fluted columns, and stone lintels to the windows inscribed to imitate gauged bricks. On the n side of Long Bridge, RIVERSIDE MALTINGS, now houses, late C16 timber-framed and plastered, including conical kiln.

We return to the centre and WEST STREET. On its s side, immediately after the junction with Bridge Street, Nos. 1–3, the service bay and hall of a long-jetty house, *c.* 1500, with No. 5 the r. cross-wing of an earlier house which Nos. 1–3 replaced. Next the CRICKETERS, a late C18 brick façade but behind that the remains of the town's late C14 timber-framed shambles or market hall. On the n side, behind a varied row with some C18 and C19 fronts, KINGS ACRE, housing by *Melville Dunbar Associates*, *c.* 1989–90, combining the Essex Design Guide vernacular with C19 industrial motifs to evoke the site's former use. THE MILL HOUSE, early C19 gault brick, was restored by the firm for their own offices. At the entrance to Kings Acre, No. 20 West Street, early C17, much restored in the C20, with exposed timbers, brick nogging on the ground floor, and jettied upper storey.

53   PAYCOCKE'S, a little further w on the s side, was rebuilt early in the C16 (tree-ring date of 1509) by the chief clothier of the town, Thomas Paycocke. It is one of the most attractive half-timbered houses of England, regardless of the fact that much of its façade has been restored. This was done by *P.M. Beaumont* for Noel Buxton, who bought the house in 1904; the local woodcarver *E. Beckwith* played a more prominent role in the restoration than one would normally expect of a craftsman. The façade consists of five bays, and was originally of three storeys (cf. the Conservative Club, Church Street); the top floor was taken down *c.* 1588 (the tree-ring date of the present roof timbers). Narrowly placed timber studs with brick infill; the diagonally arranged bricks are original, the horizontal ones C20. At the e end, a carriageway decorated by two little figures l. and r. and original doors with linenfold panelling. Then, to the r., a blocked doorway and then the first of two five-light oriel windows added in 1904–10, but apparently correctly. There follows a three-light window that was also originally an oriel. All have transoms. There are two more doorways, one on the r. now blocked, the other more or less central and with a door with original linenfold panelling, but not in its original position. This has small carved figures l. and r. by Beckwith. The jettied upper floor has a richly carved bressumer, with a carved frieze bearing Paycocke's initials and merchant's mark. Five unevenly spaced oriels to the upper floor, again of 1904–10, some of five, some of four lights. Above can be seen the jetty plate and sawn-off beams and joists of the third storey; all the carved decoration at this level is by Beckwith. The rear elevation is completely irregular, with a jettied extension of *c.* 1570 and various other additions, including a C18 stair-tower.

Inside, several rooms with moulded and carved beams, and several original fireplaces, although much of the more detailed carving is probably Beckwith's. The room on the e side of the hall has in addition excellent linenfold panelling, as well as three decorated panels. This room was originally the same size as the one on the other side of the hall, but was extended into the carriageway within about fifteen years of the house's construction. Staircase of 1905, replacing a C18 one.

On the w side of Paycocke's is THE FLEECE, with long-wall jetty. The main range is early C17, with a C15 cross-wing to the r. from an earlier hall house. Then Nos. 31–35, originally a C15 hall house, with the framing of the upper part of the hall exposed and blocked windows filled with late C19 trefoiled ogee tracery. Opposite, the former school and teacher's house of Sir Robert Hitcham's Free School, now offices. 1858 by *J. Clarke*. Red and black brick with stone dressings, with Gothic windows with plate tracery but gables and chimneys more in the Elizabethan style.

About 500 yds w of Paycocke's, Nos. 104–112, a row of C16 and C17 houses mainly with exposed timbers, and then Nos. 114–116, seven-bay Georgian brick with an impressive pedimented doorcase. Beside this the brick buildings of a disused isinglass factory, *c.* 1853–75, being converted to housing in 2004. Main building of three storeys and ten bays.

It is now necessary to return to the White Hart Hotel for the start of EAST STREET. On the s side, Nos. 6 and 6A, the front range late C14 with cross-wing to the r. and various extensions to the rear. Then No. 8, C15 and C17 with C20 shopfront and first-floor oriels, the front plastered and other elevations weather-boarded. Many of the C20 features, especially of the interior, may be attributed to *E. Beckwith*, who purchased the house in 1899 and had his workshop on the first floor. Then an attractive assortment of houses on both sides of the street, some with exposed timbers and carved bressumers, including Nos. 32–34 dated 1585. This originally joined up with the house to its r. (No. 18), restored *c.* 1978 by the *County Architect's Dept* (project architect, *James Boutwood*). More unusual is No. 42, early C16 with long-wall jetty, the plaster inscribed to imitate stone, rusticated below the jetty, ashlared above. Beyond it to the E LAKES MEADOW, sheltered housing by *Melville Dunbar Associates*, *c.* 1990, that blends immaculately with the streetscape. No. 39, opposite, is C18 with Baroque pargetting motifs dated 1902. Pargetting is an art which kept traditions alive long, and one has to be careful not to be deceived. Still on the N side, No. 59, C18 timber-framed and plastered with a pedimented doorcase, C19 canted bays, and on the first floor a round-headed window flanked by Venetian windows. E of this the recreation ground, with First World War MEMORIAL by *L.J. Watts*, square stone column with bronze figure of Victory, opposite WATERSIDE (No. 66A) by *Alan Willis* for his own occupation, 1984. A little further E on the s side No. 68, a large late C18 timber-framed and plastered house. Five-bay sashed front with pedimented doorcase, smaller doorcase on the return wall with round-headed window above.

An alley on the N side of the recreation ground leads back to Church Street, but STONEHAM STREET, on the N side of the marketplace, remains to be considered. It starts strongly with the three gables of BAUMANN'S BRASSERIE, Nos. 1–6, on the E side. C15 hall house with gabled cross wings to l. and r. and a false gable between them. Houses with exposed timbers further to the N, No. 14 particularly conspicuous, the 'high end' cross-wing of an early C15 hall house. Beyond Christ Church and the Library (*see* above), ROYAL OAK COTTAGE, No. 38, early C17 timber-framed, plastered and weatherboarded, with two-storey jettied porch. Opposite, SCHOOL MEWS, a conversion by *Lexden Restorations* and *Mark Perkins*, 1997, of the former National School buildings. Probably by *J. Clarke*, *c.* 1845–7, with a two-storey Tudor Gothic block of *c.* 1875.

From Stoneham Street, QUEEN STREET runs beside Christ
Church. Beyond its school buildings (described above),
WISTARIA HOUSE is early C19 with a gault brick façade, pedimented doorcase, and cast-iron railings. On the corner of
Vane Street, Nos. 47–51 is early C17, but contains two remarkable fireplaces with elaborately carved overmantels of *c.* 1700,
one with 'memento mori' text and cherubs holding swags.
Beyond, after a nice row of early C18 cottages, ALMSHOUSES,
c. 1795, single-storey with attics, at the entrance to the
churchyard.

COGGESHALL HALL, 1½ m. SSE.* Late C16, timber-framed and
plastered, with some weatherboarding. Long-wall jetty, the
bressumer carved with grotesque figures. Tall concertina chimneystack. C18 extension to l. and C19 brick cross-wing to r.
Semicircular brick service tower at the rear by *G. Vale*, 1990.

HOLFIELD GRANGE, 1½ m. WNW. The most complete Victorian
country house in Essex, rebuilt by *W. G. Bartleet*, 1888, for
Osgood Hanbury. Not particularly attractive. The style, with
large bargeboarded gables, gabled dormers, and many more
smaller gables on the lower E (service) wing, might be called
a simplified Elizabethan, but the brick is C19 and industrial in
its hardness, and large plate-glass windows impart a blank
look. Inside, the principal rooms are half-panelled, and one
completely so with panelling from the C18 house which this
replaced. Stableyard NE of the house, entrance lodge, part tile-
hung (with C18 ice house beside it) to the NW; across the lane
another lodge and C18 kitchen garden, and along the lane an
C18 ha-ha with retaining wall of thirty concave bays. C18 brick
dovecote SE of the house, with pyramidal roof and open cupola
with ogee roof topped with a lead pigeon. PARK LODGE,
600 yds NE, also 1888.

HOUCHIN'S FARM, 1¼ m. ENE. Three-storey house of *c.* 1590,
with lower N service range. Main range of five bays with central
stack. Both upper floors jettied on the S and W fronts, with
moulded fascias and two carved grotesques at the SW corner.
Original panelling and carved overmantel in E ground-floor
room. The top floor consists of two large storage lofts, probably
associated with the cloth-making industry.

MARKSHALL. *See* p. 592

COLCHESTER

See also BERECHURCH, GREENSTEAD, LEXDEN, MILE END

Introduction	255
Camulodunum	255
Roman Colchester	256
Medieval and later Colchester	261
Churches	263
St Botolph's Priory	271

* Partly in the parish of Feering.

St John's Abbey   272
Castle   272
Public Buildings   276
Colchester Garrison   281
Perambulations   282
    Town Centre
        1. High Street   282
        2. North of the High Street:
            a. The Dutch Quarter   286
            b. North Hill   288
        3. South of the High Street: Head Street, Queen
            Street, and the area between   290
        4. West of the High Street: Balkerne Gardens to
            Crouch Street   293
    Outer Colchester and Suburbs
        5. East Hill and East Street   294
        6. West: Lexden Road   296
        7. South and East: New Town, The Hythe, and St
            John's Green   298
Dykes   301

INTRODUCTION

Colchester's claim to fame is that it is Britain's oldest recorded town. Historically and architecturally it is the most important town in Essex, yet neither is it the county town, nor does it have a cathedral. Those honours went to Chelmsford, although Colchester managed to ensure that the University of Essex (q.v.) was built on its eastern boundary in the 1960s. The town owes both its rise and its fall to its location. It was the Romans' first *colonia*, but its lack of a good port nearby meant that it soon lost out to Londinium. In recent times, Colchester's position in the county's NE corner, rather than its centre, has counted against it, although this – and its distance from London – has helped to preserve its character. The old town lies on a hill, with the Roman walls embracing its top and the High Street running along its brow; two streets, North Hill and East Hill, run down to and then cross the River Colne which curves round the town on its N and E sides. The highest point is occupied not, as one might expect, by the Castle, but by the 'Jumbo' water tower.

p. 256

Camulodunum

Camulodunum, originally an Iron Age fortified settlement and later protected by a complex of dykes (*see* p. 301), was the capital of Cunobelinus (†c. A.D. 40). Most of it lay on the area between the River Colne to the N and Roman River to the S, with its main centres – agricultural and industrial respectively – at Gosbecks, about 2 m. SW of the present town centre (*see* Stanway), and at Sheepen, near the River Colne, in the NW.

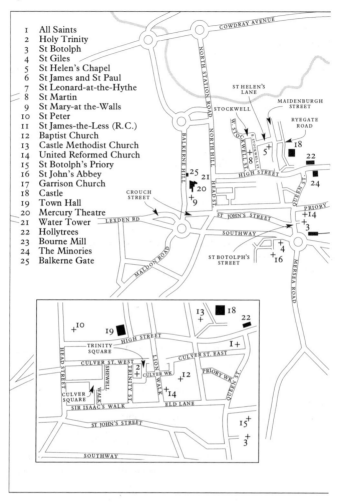

1   All Saints
2   Holy Trinity
3   St Botolph
4   St Giles
5   St Helen's Chapel
6   St James and St Paul
7   St Leonard-at-the-Hythe
8   St Martin
9   St Mary-at-the-Walls
10 St Peter
11 St James-the-Less (R.C.)
12 Baptist Church
13 Castle Methodist Church
14 United Reformed Church
15 St Botolph's Priory
16 St John's Abbey
17 Garrison Church
18 Castle
19 Town Hall
20 Mercury Theatre
21 Water Tower
22 Hollytrees
23 Bourne Mill
24 The Minories
25 Balkerne Gate

Roman Colchester

p. 258 The visitor to Colchester at once notices the remains of the Roman city, which occupied a space of 108 acres and was oblong in shape. The core of the town is still defined by its wall, most of which is still visible, as well as the very impressive remains of the p. 259 great W gate, known as the Balkerne Gate. Following the invasion under Emperor Claudius in A.D. 43, a legionary fortress was established on part of the area now bounded by the city wall, and quite separate from the existing settlement of Camulodunum. Within a few years the fortress acquired the status of *colonia*, the foremost type of Roman town, and was probably known as Colonia Victricensis, 'Colony of the Victorious'. The basic layout

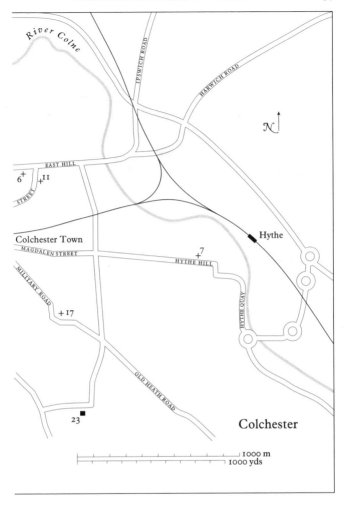

was retained and many military buildings adapted for civilian use. The Temple of Claudius and a theatre were built E of the fortress. In A.D. 60–1, the town was sacked by Boudicca and razed to the ground; when it was rebuilt, along almost the same lines, massive walls were erected to prevent future attacks. The WALLS were probably built *c*. A.D. 65–80; this makes them remarkably early, but the date is supported by excavations. They are nearly 9 ft (2.8 metres) thick, and must have been nearly 20 ft (6 metres) high including battlements; considerable lengths are still 15 ft (4.6 metres) high. They were constructed of alternate layers of septaria and mortar faced with coursed septaria and bands of Roman brick, and rest on foundations about 4 ft (1.2 metres)

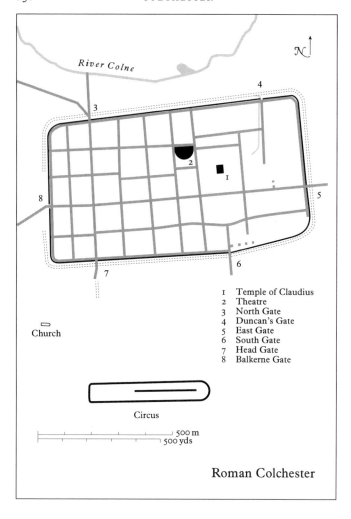

River Colne

N

4

3

2

1

8

5

6

7

1   Temple of Claudius
2   Theatre
3   North Gate
4   Duncan's Gate
5   East Gate
6   South Gate
7   Head Gate
8   Balkerne Gate

Church

Circus

500 m
500 yds

Roman Colchester

deep that are also formed of layers of septaria and mortar. The early rampart was at least 25 ft (7.7 metres) wide, and the face of the wall covered by it is very finely finished, with every joint marked out by the trowel. Of six gates (North Gate, Duncan's Gate, East Gate, South Gate, Head Gate, and Balkerne Gate), two (Balkerne Gate and Duncan's Gate) are still visible. Between the gates were rectangular towers set against the inside of the wall. Eight are known, and it is likely that there was one at the end of each street, and at each corner: one corner tower (NE) has been discovered. The Balkerne Gate and the position of the E gate give the main axial line of the Roman city, the *cardo maximus*. A secondary axis runs between North Gate and Head Gate, in the line of North Hill and Head Street.

Balkerne Gate, Colchester.
Reconstruction

The most complete sections of wall can be seen along Balkerne Hill, in Castle Park, and behind Priory Street and Vineyard Street. The latter two sections also have four semicircular bastions, of which there were originally eight, added between 1381 and *c.* 1413. The entrance to the underground service area of the Culver Centre, on the N side of St John's Street, cuts though the wall, where a section of it can be seen. The only significant gap is in the SW corner, where the wall was damaged in the siege of 1648.

BALKERNE GATE, the main gate, was the W entrance from London and Verulamium, and one of the largest and most impressive town gates in Roman Britain. 107 ft (33 metres) wide, it projects 30 ft (9 metres) in front of the wall. It began as a monumental arch, built in tufa, *c.* A.D. 50, with two archways 17 ft (5.2 metres) wide for wheeled traffic. When the town walls were built it was incorporated in them, with towers of an unusual quadrant-shaped plan containing two smaller pedestrian archways to either side. The original arch was not designed as a defensive structure, and apparently towards the end of the C3 it was dismantled and blocked up, although the pedestrian gateway on the S side was probably left open. This gateway is still standing, the N tower 20 ft (6 metres) high.

DUNCAN'S GATE. In the N wall (Castle Park). A single portal, 11 ft (3.4 metres) wide, built as part of the walls, and may have been blocked at about the same time as Balkerne Gate. Surviving fallen masonry suggests it had an upper storey of Roman brick with round-headed windows.

TEMPLE OF CLAUDIUS. The largest classical temple known in Britain, probably built after Claudius' death in A.D. 54, and rebuilt or completed after the Boudiccan revolt. It stood within a large precinct, approximately 535 by 425 ft (165 by 131 metres), that included, in the middle of its S side, a monumental arch flanked by arcaded screens. Only the temple's substructure is visible, on which was built the Norman castle (*see* p. 272), whose walls contain much Roman brick and stone. This area has the appearance of vaults, but is in fact the underside of the Roman foundations. Trenches dug in the sandy soil took foundations for the temple's outside walls, while another, shallower trench ran in parallel under the middle of the building to support the floor. The soil between these trenches was smoothed into curves, over which wooden shuttering (the marks of which can be seen) was placed and the foundations of stone and mortar built on top. The 'vaults' were formed in the late C17, when John Wheeley quarried beneath the castle to extract the sand. The size and position of the foundations makes it possible to deduce that the temple measured about 115 by 80 ft (35 by 25 metres) and had an octastyle pronaos with colonnades of ten or eleven columns down each side.

THEATRE. On the NW side of the Temple, and perhaps the theatre mentioned by Tacitus. Semicircular, with its straight side on the N, roughly along the line of St Helen's Lane. Foundations of the curved walls can be seen at No. 73 Maidenburgh Street, with its continuation marked out in the surface of the road. Remains of the NE corner of the theatre form the base of part of the wall of St Helen's Chapel (*see* p. 265).

CHURCH. Next to the Police Station, Southway. Small rectangular structure, *c.* 330, with an E apse added about fifty years later and further enlarged *c.* 400. The foundations and some low walls are visible, excavated 1976–88. Associated with an extensive cemetery along Butt Road, probably originally pagan, but Christian from the C4.

CIRCUS. The only known example in Britain, discovered in 2000 about ¼ m. s of the town wall. Orientated E–W, about 490 yds (452 metres) long and 76 yds (70 metres) wide, with one semicircular end, and built of Kentish greensand. Probably C2.

In Castle Park, a group of HOUSES was excavated in 1920, of which an area of paving (four panels of plain red tesserae) remains exposed. A Roman street, a seven-roomed house, and a large double building of courtyard type were discovered. E of the Castle, a massive-walled Romano-British building was excavated in 1927–8 and 1954. It contained a room with a thick concrete floor which was 8 ft (2.5 metres) below the level of the floors of the adjoining rooms. It had been deliberately demolished, probably in the C4, and its purpose is not known. One theory is that it was a Mithraeum, dedicated to the worship of Mithras, but the presence of a large arched drain on one side and a spring which rises in the main chamber suggests that it was connected with a system of waterworks.

Remains of a large C2 house were found in the early C20 during construction of the Sixth Form College, North Hill. Excavations there from 2003 revealed further buildings, including a *mansio* and a semi-sunken room that was probably a bath house or possibly a *nymphaeum*, or shrine to the nymphs. The latter is exceptionally well preserved, with tessellated floor and painted plaster walls. Large parts of Colchester have been excavated, not least the areas now covered by the Culver Square and Lion Walk precincts in the 1970s and 1980s. Mosaics found at sites in Middleborough, North Hill, North Station Road, Culver Street, and Lion Walk are now in the Castle Museum. This also contains a large collection of tombstones, dedication stones and statues.

Medieval and later Colchester

There is little evidence of Anglo-Saxon occupation – three houses have so far been discovered, in Lion Walk and Culver Street – but the construction of the Norman Castle, followed by the foundation of St Botolph's Priory and St John's Abbey late in the C11, reaffirmed Colchester's importance. There were eight medieval churches within the walls, and three more only a short distance beyond.* The Greyfriars and Crutched Friars had establishments. A moot hall was built in the C12 on a site still occupied by the Town Hall; the carving of its s doorway has been shown to have come from the same workshop as the w doorway of Rochester Cathedral, *c.* 1160. A C12 stone-built house in Foundry Yard, on the N side of the High Street, stood until 1886.

Although by the end of the C14 Chelmsford had become the county's administrative centre, Colchester remained in many respects the principal town of Essex. It recovered relatively quickly from the effects of the Black Death largely on the strength of its growing cloth industry, which attracted a steady stream of immigrants. There was considerable trade across the North Sea, particularly with Hanseatic merchants, and by 1500 there were five mills on the River Colne. The Roman walls continued to define the limits of the town – Rye Gate was added to the N side, and bastions erected in the late C14 and early C15 to strengthen the SW section – but there was also extra-mural development, particularly to the E and SE along the roads to Greenstead and the Hythe, Colchester's port. This began in the mid C12, quite separately from the town, when the port moved upstream from the old hythe (Old Heath), but was not significantly built up until the C14. In 1377 Colchester was the eighth largest provincial town in England, with 2,951 people paying poll tax (suggesting a total population of 4,500–5,000).

After a period of contraction at the beginning of the C16, the cloth trade boomed later, helped by the arrival of Dutch and Flemish immigrants who introduced the 'bays and says' (i.e. baize and serge) for which the town became famous and which sustained its prosperity throughout the C17. The area in which many of the clothworkers lived, N of the High Street, is now known as the Dutch Quarter. In 1648, Parliamentarians besieged the town and did much damage to its buildings, some of which – St Botolph's Priory, the tower of St Martin – have never been repaired. Daniel Defoe noted in 1722 that the town 'still mourns in the ruins of a civil war', with its 'battered walls, breaches in the turrets, and ruined churches'. In the C18, however, Colchester profited from its position on the London–Harwich road and diversified in trade and industry as the centre for the surrounding rural area. Several substantial town houses were built, notably Hollytrees and East Hill House, as well as many lesser but equally elegant examples in North Hill, East Hill, and West Stockwell Street.

---

* Two of the intramural churches, St Runwald and St Nicholas, both in the High Street, were dem. in 1878 and 1955 respectively; St Mary Magdalen, outside, in 1990.

Colchester grew steadily but not spectacularly during the C19. The population rose from 11,520 in 1801 to 38,373 in 1901. The railway reached Colchester from London in 1843 and by 1854 was linked to Ipswich, Norwich, and Harwich. By the time Victoria came to the throne, Colchester could boast a theatre and a hospital, the Castle had been partially restored and its grounds beautified, most of the medieval churches had been repaired and a number of Nonconformist chapels and meeting houses newly built. The building of a few large houses along Lexden Road, and in Lexden itself, marked the first real development of new residential areas beyond the Roman walls. The formation of the garrison wrought major change. Barracks were built during the Napoleonic Wars; the present buildings date from 1856, and include some of the earliest surviving cavalry barracks in Britain. By 1901 the principal occupations in the town were building and engineering, with the latter taking first place in the first half of the C20: Paxman's engineering works off Hythe Hill employed nearly 1,000 people by 1915. Other important industries were footwear, clothing, brewing and milling, with Marriage's mills at the foot of East Hill providing one of the town's landmarks.

The new building that accompanied this growth was significant but not overwhelming. The main areas of development were in the area of Lexden and Maldon Roads to the w and New Town in the SE, and churches were built to meet the needs of the new suburbs, including All Saints, Shrub End, St John the Evangelist, Ipswich Road, and St Paul, Belle Vue Road (the latter, by *J. Clarke*, 1869, now demolished). By the beginning of the C20 Colchester had acquired its most enduring landmarks, the 'Jumbo' water tower and the Victoria Tower of the town hall, opened 1902. This was the grandest and most complete expression of Colchester's pride both in its present status and its past glories, an affirmation that even if it was not officially the county town, it deserved to be.

Colchester grew in the C20 at much the same rate as it had in the C19, but in 1974 the borough was enlarged, bringing the population to 155,794 in 2001. Most of the housing that accompanied this growth was on the s side, with large municipal as well as private estates in Lexden, Shrub End and Old Heath. The largest post-war developments were to the NE at Greenstead, where 2,800 homes were built between 1955 and 1985, and at High Woods, w of Ipswich Road, with about 4,000 houses.

The historic centre of Colchester has suffered mixed fortunes. The value of the Dutch Quarter was early recognized by the borough, which began restoring houses there in 1958, and followed this after 1977 with an impressive scheme of infilling gaps left by clearance of buildings deemed beyond restoration. The rebuilding, in the vernacular style advocated by the Essex Design Guide, represented a dramatic change in attitude to regeneration. By this time, however, the High Street had lost two prominent buildings – St Nicholas and The Cups pub, both replaced by the most mediocre commercial architecture. Another unwelcome intrusion was the Telephone Exchange of 1968–9, between West Stockwell Street and North Hill. On a larger scale was the Town Centre Plan of 1969, which resulted in some of the most radical changes to the town ever made, including the construction of a new inner relief road (Southway, 1973–4, and Balkerne Hill, 1976–7) and the development of pedestrian shopping precincts in previously cleared areas around Lion Walk (1976) and Culver Street (1988). Despite demolition of some historic buildings and changes to the street pattern, on the whole these schemes were to the advantage of the town, and enabled the large-scale archaeological investigation which led to a complete reappraisal of town's origins and early development. Cars were now banished to a string of multi-storey car parks, which as a group are the least successful and most intrusive buildings of the period. Industry moved away from the centre, with the Severalls industrial estate developed to the N of the town in the 1970s (*see* Mile End), joined in 1990 by a business park off Severalls Lane. The University of Essex at Wivenhoe Park (*see* p. 797), begun in 1962, office buildings in the area around Middleborough, and the new District General Hospital were also significant new landmarks for the town.

CHURCHES

GARRISON CHURCH OF ST ALBAN THE MARTYR, Military Road. *See* p. 281.

ALL SAINTS, High Street. Natural History Museum since 1957. In an impressive position, its fine W tower of flint, with diagonal buttresses and flint and ashlar decoration of the battlements, nicely closing the view E down the High Street. Big three-light bell-openings. Tower rebuilt *c.* 1500 but retaining its C14 tower arch. Early C14 chancel and mid-C15 N aisle, but the arcade belongs to the restoration by *H. W. Hayward*, 1854–5, when he also refaced the S wall. N wall repaired 1859. – STAINED GLASS. E window *c.* 1869. Five N windows by *Ward & Hughes*, 1861. Tower window by *Kempe*, 1905. All *in situ* but not visible inside. – MONUMENTS. Stone tablet with crocketed ogee top and indents of unidentified brasses; *c.* 1500. Originally in St Runwald (dem. 1878). – Samuel Great †1706 and wife Susan †1722. Bulbous marble tablet with cherub's head and cartouche. Both from St Nicholas (dem. 1955).

ALL SAINTS, Shrub End. By *G. R. French*, 1844–5, to serve the growing suburban population of Stanway and Lexden. Hard red brick with Caen stone dressings. Nave, chancel, and low tower with splay-foot spire over the N porch; organ chamber added 1883, S choir vestry 1958, and the nave extended W in 1982. Plain exterior enlivened only by the carved label stops along the N side, those at the W end portraits of Queen Elizabeth II and Prince Philip. – REREDOS. Expensive memorial to Edward Coope Fulcher †1880, of marble and gold mosaic by *John Hardman & Co.* – STAINED GLASS. E window, 1879. On S side of nave, to John Smith Dolby, first incumbent, by *Cox & Sons*, 1878, and to Edith M.M. Scarman †1930 by *Powell*

& Sons. – MONUMENTS. T. J. Turner of Little Olivers, Stanway, †1866. By *L. J. Watts.**

HOLY TRINITY, Trinity Street. Closed 1953, a museum from 1974, now closed again, a regrettable waste of an interesting building in such a central location. The W tower is the only Anglo-Saxon (pre-Conquest) monument of Colchester. Built with plenty of Roman bricks, and crowned by a low pyramid roof. The oldest part is the E wall and arch into the nave, with odd capitals of the responds in three steps of brick, without any mouldings. The tower itself is slightly later, its small W doorway with triangular head a wholly Saxon feature. Saxon upper windows, the bell-openings developed as twin windows but not separated by a turned shaft or colonette as usual. On the sides below that stage traces of a blank arcade. Nave rebuilt in the C14 and the chancel built or rebuilt; S arcade and aisle and S porch added in late C15, the S chapel later in the same century. Vestry added at E end of chancel and S aisle, 1840, church re-seated and repaired *c.* 1854, N aisle and N chapel by *G. E. Laing,* 1864–6. – STAINED GLASS. In tracery of E window, probably the remains of a window by *William Warrington, c.* 1856. – MONUMENTS. William Gilberd †1603. Marble and alabaster tablet with thirteen shields of arms and pilasters supporting a cornice on which stand two obelisks either side of an achievement.

ST BARNABAS, Old Heath Road. 1955, and of interest only for its fittings. – PULPIT. 1893, from *Scott*'s St Nicholas (1875–6; dem. 1955). Octagonal. Portland and Caen stone, with trac-eried panels of alabaster separated by columns with marble shafts. – STALLS. Also from St Nicholas, 1875–6. – Brass eagle LECTERN. Early C20. From St Giles. – STAINED GLASS. Two E windows by *Benjamin Finn,* 2000.

ST BOTOLPH, St Botolph's Street. 1836–7 by *William Mason* of Ipswich. The nave of the Priory (*see* p. 271) was used as a parish church until it was destroyed in the 1648 siege. The present church lies immediately S of the ruins and was therefore built, with the curious assertiveness that belongs to the Victorian age, in the Norman style and yet bigger than what was still stand-ing of the old priory. White brick, with a massive W tower with pointed turrets, plenty of Norman ornament, and a broad inte-rior with coarse Norman columns in two tiers, the upper one at the level of the usual galleries of that time. The gallery railings are decorated with intersected arches. Groin-vaulted aisles and tunnel-vaulted nave. Straight E end with only the shallowest of chancels, also usual for that time, but no longer acceptable by 1882 when the church was 'restored' by *E. J. Dampier.* A deeper chancel was formed by taking down one bay of the gallery on either side at the E end, and introducing low screen walls and open iron screens to the N and S as well as a chancel screen (ironwork by *A. G. Mumford*). Additional seats were provided in the W gallery, formerly occupied by the organ, which was moved to the N side of the chancel.

*Parsonage to the W, 1847, by *H.H. Hayward & Son,* dem. 2003.

Reordered in the 1970s when the chancel screen, pulpit, choir stalls and nave seating were removed. SE extension by *Tim Venn*, 1996–2001. – STAINED GLASS. E window by *J.B. Capronnier* of Brussels, 1882–3. Four windows in S aisle and one in N aisle by *Clayton & Bell*, *c.* 1886–93. Window in S aisle commemorating Archbishop Harsnett by *Powell & Sons*, *c.* 1928. – MONUMENT. William Hawkins †1843, with life-size allegorical figure of Hope. By *J. Edwards* of London, 1854.

CHRIST CHURCH, Ireton Road (C. of E. and U. R. C.). By *Bryan Thomas & Partners*, 1977–8. Brick, square, with a pyramidal slate roof and E-facing top window like the cowl on an oast house.

ST GILES, St John's Place. Closed 1953. Now Masonic Hall. Founded between 1133 and 1171, built in the monastic cemetery of St John's Abbey (*see* p. 272). One C12 window, blocked, survives in the S wall to the W of the porch; a blocked lancet, C13, in the S wall of the chancel. N aisle added in the C14, N chapel *c.* 1500. Also early C16 the brick S porch and the W tower, timber-framed and weatherboarded, but the latter was probably rebuilt as part of extensive alterations by *Joseph Parkins*, 1819. This included remodelling the interior with W, N and S galleries beneath a flat ceiling, removing the distinction between the nave and N aisle. Re-seated by *H.W. Hayward*, 1859, and the E end restored by *Sir Arthur Blomfield & Sons*, 1907: chancel arch replaced, N arcade restored, S chapel or vestry (now kitchen) and S chancel arcade added, and the E and N walls refaced externally with flint and buttressed. Converted for its present use by *C.M.H. Barritt*, 1972–6, including the insertion of a mezzanine floor at the W end of the nave with lodge room on upper level, and single-storey additions on the N and W sides of the nave. – DOOR, N doorway. C14 with rich tracery.

ST HELEN'S CHAPEL (now Greek Orthodox), Maidenburgh Street. C12 or earlier, built on the corner of the Roman theatre (*see* p. 260), remains of which are visible along the base of the N and E walls. Single cell, of stone rubble with bands of brick and two C13 lancets. In secular use from the mid C16 and as a Quaker meeting house in the C18; the E and W windows belong to the restoration by *Butterfield*, 1884–6, as a chapter house for Colchester rural deanery.

ST JAMES AND ST PAUL, East Hill. Formerly St James the Great. The chancel and its chapels, high up above the rise of East Hill into High Street, are the best Perp work in Colchester. The rest is of less importance. The NW angle of the nave with its Roman bricks is proof of Norman origin. The W tower may be C13 (see one upper window) altered in the C14. Diagonal buttresses and battlements. The odd little spire was added by *S.S. Teulon*, 1870–1. He rebuilt the N aisle, N porch and N arcade, restored the S aisle, replaced the S aisle and clerestory windows, and enlarged the W door and tower arch. On the S side a very visible and very horrible vestry by *Duncan W. Clark*, 1953. Roughcast concrete. It was intended to be temporary, a dreadful warning against all such proposals. Most of the church is of rubble with ashlar dressings, but the N and S chapels and the chancel E end are faced with knapped flint, with flushwork at the base of the walls. The N chapel in addition, as it faces the street, has a parapet decorated with a frieze of diapers, mostly renewed.

Internally the chancel is splendidly tall with a five-light E window and tall N and S arcades. Lozenge-shaped piers with four slim shafts and four long shallow diagonal hollows. The two chapels have large three-light windows and ceilings with prettily carved beams. The nave arcades are more curious but less impressive. They are of four different varieties, in chronological order SE (two bays, octagonal pier, arches with one concave and one convex moulding; c. 1300), NE (two bays, octagonal pier, arches with two hollow chamfers; mid C14), then SW and NW differing only in minor features (C15 piers with, towards the nave, as their central motif, thin polygonal shafts without capitals).

PULPIT. By *H. & K. Mabbitt*, 1951. Oak. – S chapel SCREEN. By *T. G. Jackson*, 1899–1900. – PICTURES. Adoration of the Shepherds by *George Carter*, 1778, painted as an altarpiece. Last Supper by *James Archer*, 1855. – STAINED GLASS. In S chapel, by *Warrington*, 1843. – MONUMENTS. Brasses of John Maynard †1569 and Alice Maynard †1584, 21½-in. (54 cm.) and 18½-in. (46 cm.) figures, the latter palimpsest. – Arthur Winsley †1727. Standing wall monument with reclining figure in informal dress.

ST JOHN THE EVANGELIST, Ipswich Road. A new church for a new parish, by *A. W. Blomfield*, 1862–3, and still with the grit which he possessed in his youth. Red brick with yellow and black bricks and Ancaster stone dressings; the style is Early Dec. Nave, chancel, and N transept. Small and low projection at the W end, originally the baptistery, with timber porches l. and r., and above it a circular bellcote with a conical roof and a kind of open lantern with thick short black columns. This building now forms the northern cross-wing of a much larger church by the *Falconer Partnership* (partner-in-charge, *J. E. Thatcher*), 1988, which works well with Blomfield's rather than just putting up with it. Similar materials but with walls and roof in inverse proportion, so that there is a huge expanse of red tiling above a relatively low wall of striped brickwork. Pyramidal roof with lantern and squat splay-foot spire. Old nave now a meeting room with mezzanine floor inserted towards the W end; chancel (which retains its original fittings, including coloured marble REREDOS by *Henry Lufkin*) screened off as a chapel. On the S side of the nave a lobby leads into the C20 church, square with a slightly raised sanctuary at the S end. Lit by corner windows and lantern. Main entrance and church offices on E side. – STAINED GLASS. In original chancel, E window and four others by *Heaton, Butler & Bayne*, 1863; N side of original nave, Good Shepherd by *Horace Wilkinson*, c. 1919, and Light of the World by *Heaton, Butler & Bayne*, c. 1927.

Immediately N of the church the former VICARAGE, brick, presumably by Blomfield, c. 1863.

St Leonard-at-the-Hythe, Hythe Hill. The Hythe's parish church, redundant since 1985 (now vested in the Churches Conservation Trust, for whom it was repaired by *John Burton* of *Purcell Miller Tritton*). It lies close to the street, with only a small churchyard. Impressive but much restored in the C19. The N side is the most rewarding: N aisle *c.* 1330, N chapel *c.* 1500. The N arcades show these dates clearly too. The piers of the Dec style are quatrefoil, as usual, the C15 piers of four shafts and four hollows in the diagonals. The arch mouldings differ too. The C15 type appears in the s arcade, the w bay of the N arcade, and both chapels. Early C16 hammerbeam roof in the nave. C15 s porch with room over, rebuilt incorporating older work, but it is uncertain to which of the many C19 restorations it belongs. Repairs were carried out in 1839, and in 1848 the chancel roof was replaced. *H. W. Hayward* was responsible for a partial restoration in 1863,* with further work (including re-seating) by *W. A. Moy*, 1865–6. Following the 1884 earthquake the upper part of the C14 tower was rebuilt by *Walter Scargill*, 1888, a competent job (executed by *L. J. Watts*) with flushwork parapet, the main part of the tower faced with rubble, like most of the rest of the church. On the s face of the tower, surprisingly low down, is a stone clock face of *c.* 1500 with niche above to hold the jacks. – FONT. Octagonal, Perp, with shields and quatrefoils and big leaves. From East Donyland (q.v.), 1840, replacing a brick font of 1662. – CHOIR STALLS. 1849, by *Henry Ringham* of Ipswich. – SCREEN with rood. 1904 by *Jones & Willis*. Were they also responsible for the WALL PAINTING over the chancel arch, 1901, the only surviving part of an extensive decorative scheme? – Good collection of STAINED GLASS by *Heaton, Butler & Bayne* in the Lady Chapel and aisles, *c.* 1902–20. – MONUMENT. William Hawkins †1812. By *George Lufkin*.

St Martin, West Stockwell Street. Redundant since 1953 (now vested in the Churches Conservation Trust).† The NW angle of a C12 N aisle, narrower than the present aisle, reveals a church of that date. The w tower also Norman but a little later. It was built with much use of Roman bricks, amongst a mixture of limestone, cobblestones, septaria and flint. The tower's upper part was destroyed during the 1648 siege and has never been restored; it was repaired and roofed in 1768, but looks very picturesque. The chancel follows next; early C14, as can at once be seen from the E window, of three lights with ogee-reticulated tracery, the s doorway, and the PISCINA inside, both with richly crocketed ogee heads. The way in which the SEDILIA are subdivided into two by bringing down the mullion of a two-light window in a double curve is also characteristic of the Dec style. But perhaps the most impressive early C14 feature is one roof truss across the chancel which possesses moulded wall-posts, arched braces with elaborate foiled tracery, an

---

*When he also built the rectory further up Hythe Hill, dem. 2003.
†FONT in St Lawrence, East Donyland (q.v.).

embattled tie-beam, an octagonal crown-post with capital, and four-way struts. *Sir Gilbert Scott* was so taken with it on a visit in 1876 that he restored the chancel roof at his own expense. Early Perp transepts with tall windows and panels tracery, and Early Perp N and S arcades with octagonal piers and double-hollow-chamfered arches. The S porch is attributed to the early or mid C17, perhaps on the strength of the amusing side windows with balusters instead of mullions. General restorations by *E. J. Dampier*, 1882–3, and *E. Geldart*, 1891, who took down the W gallery, opened up the tower arch, and re-floored the nave and chancel. A temporary N vestry was built that still stands, with an internal window from the chancel and door incorporating late C17 panels carved with garlands. Of Geldart's interior decoration and fittings, little survives. – WALL PAINTING. Over chancel arch, remains of an early C16 Doom: figures from Hell on S side, with demons tormenting the damned, and the blessed on the N. The figures are German in style, perhaps based on prints. – Two decorative plaques of glazed TILES by *Geldart*, 1891–2, recording his restoration and commemorating the partial destruction of the tower. – STAINED GLASS. One window only, in the S transept, but an exceptionally good one: six miracles of Christ by *Heaton, Butler & Bayne*, 1865, and characteristic of the early work of *Robert Bayne*. – MONUMENT. A number of tablets remain inside, including one by *Lufkin* to Mrs Ann Dennis, 1793, but none of them special. – In the churchyard, S of the porch, big, heavy, Neo-Greek sarcophagus to William Sparling †1816.

ST MARY-AT-THE-WALLS, Church Street. Closed 1978, now an arts centre. Big Late Perp W tower with diagonal buttresses and at the base a frieze of shields. Upper parts brick, 1729; the very top of 1911 by *S. Gambier Parry*. The rest of the church had been ruined in the siege of 1648, was first rebuilt by *John Price* 1713–14, and again (in brick) by *A. W. Blomfield*, 1871–2. Long nave with circular piers with elaborately and naturalistically carved capitals; this and the carving over the S porch door by *Earp*. Circular clerestory windows. Shallow chancel with straight E end, N vestry and organ chamber, and S transept for children's seating. Apse added to S transept as war memorial chapel, 1922. NE vestry by *Duncan Clark & Beckett*, 1936. Elaborate marble and painted decoration of the chancel by *Parry*, begun 1907, continued by his assistant *George R. Phillips*, 1925, with paintings by *F. A. Jackson*. – PULPIT. 1871–2, designed by *Albert Hartshorne*, executed by *L. J. Watts*. Finely carved with coloured marble inlays. – STAINED GLASS. E window by *Heaton, Butler & Bayne*, 1903. – Nave N and S windows by *William Morris & Co.* of Westminster, 1929, with new tracery by *G. R. Phillips*. – MONUMENT. John Rebow †1699, erected by Sir Isaac Rebow M.P. †1726. Whole figure, seated, very well carved, with inscriptions on flanking panels like a marble triptych.

ST PETER, North Hill. Medieval origins – in 1066 this was the richest church recorded in the county – but now curiously nondescript as a result of remodelling in 1758 and partial C19 restorations. What one mainly sees from the street is the square red brick w tower of 1758. The upper part has white brick quoins and white brick battlements. To the street on a coarse bracket a clock in a stone case by *C.F. Hayward*, 1866. White brick battlements on the aisles, which have arched windows also of 1758, when the medieval central tower, damaged by earthquake in 1692, was taken down and the nave extended into the chancel. Walls of mixed rubble with septaria, brick and ragstone. Inside, only a few reminders of the medieval church. C15 arcades with piers with demi-columns to the aisle arches but a slim demi-polygonal shaft to the nave, and a single C15 window at the E end of the N aisle. Behind the arcades, galleries on Tuscan columns, the N (and probably also W organ gallery) 1791, the s 1815. Below the N vestry a BONE-HOLE of *c.* 1520 with a brick vault with single-chamfered arches and ribs, used by *Hayward* as a heating chamber as part of his restoration and re-seating, 1857–9. Further restoration by *King & Lister*, 1895–6, when the clerestory was added, with a new roof, and the chancel arch replaced. – PULPIT. Fine late C17 piece with richly moulded frames of the panels and garlands of fruit down the angles; cherubs' heads at the top of these. Restored and placed on new pedestal 1859, with additional carving by *Richard Ellisdon*. – Heavy Neo-Gothic FONT, 1859 by *Hayward*, executed by *Earp*. – COMMUNION RAIL with twisted balusters, of same date as pulpit, now used for tower staircase. – DOOR in s doorway with large iron scrolls. Ironwork attributed to *Thomas of Leighton* (Buzzard), *c.* 1300. – MONUMENTS. Five brass plates with kneeling figures and inscriptions, 1509–1610. – Martin Basill †1623 and wife, with the usual kneeling figures, quite large; the figures set against a blank arch; columns l. and r. – George Sayer †1577 and wives, smaller and broader, also with kneeling figures, but with three columns and a straight entablature. Attributed to *Garat Johnson* (GF). – Brass plate to the Sears family by *C.L. Bly*, 1830. – Memorial to the Protestant martyrs of Colchester by *William Bremer*, 1843. – Samuel Carr †1854 by *George Lufkin*: large, plain and serious.

ST STEPHEN, Canterbury Road. Simple brick building, 1904–6 by *C.E. Butcher*, adapted as a community hall for the octagonal church built on its s side by *Purcell Miller Tritton*, 2001–2. Brick with bands of reconstituted stone, recessed clerestory, slate roof and lantern. Mottled brown brick and timber ceiling inside. – STAINED GLASS. Between main church and St Mary Magdalen Chapel, the former E window of St Mary Magdalen, Magdalen Street,* by *Lavers, Barraud & Westlake*, *c.* 1870.

ST JAMES THE LESS (R.C.), Priory Street. By *J. J. Scoles*. 1837, white brick, in the Norman style; the same year, same material, and same style, that is, as nearby St Botolph. Sanctuary enlarged and N aisle added 1904, s aisle 1907, by *C.E. Butcher*.

* Church by *F. Barnes*, 1852–4, dem. 1990.

Wide interior with Norman columns, clerestory, chancel arch
and apse, reordered 1987. Exterior without tower, but with the
typical turrets of the (Gothic) Commissioners' churches of the
early C19. Attached presbytery on s side, also white brick, with
round-headed windows. – STAINED GLASS. Four apse
windows by *Lavers & Westlake*, 1904. Central apse window by
Heaton, Butler & Bayne, from the Church of St Leonard,
Leicester, and two lancets in N chapel by *A. W. N. Pugin* from
a redundant church in Derbyshire, installed 1987.

CARDINAL BOURNE INSTITUTE, s of the presbytery: red
brick, vaguely Neo-Norman, by *Scoles & Raymond*, 1911.

BAPTIST CHURCH, Eld Lane. 1834 by *John Penrice*. Classical.
White brick front with three-bay central pediment above three
arched windows. 'Restored' 1883 by *F. E. Morris*, rear vestries
etc. by *J. F. Goodey*, 1889. Building on l. by *W. T. Cressall*, 1923,
linked to the main building by *K. C. White & Partners*, 1977,
and balanced on the r. by *Michael Woods*, 1991, both unmistakably of their time but incorporating classical elements to
create a coherent façade. Largely unaltered interior with galleries on iron columns.

CASTLE METHODIST CHURCH, Maidenburgh Street. 1970 by
Kenneth Cheeseman. Low, with flat copper roof supported on
concrete columns that start inside and continue outside in
front of the recessed clerestory. – PULPIT. From which Wesley
preached in Colchester's first Methodist chapel, 1759, also in
Maidenburgh Street. – STAINED GLASS and decorative hessian
FRIEZE by *Carol Rose*. Glazed entrance screen incorporates
panels dating from the remodelling by *Goodey & Cressall*, 1900,
of the old Culver Street chapel of 1836.

CONGREGATIONAL CHAPEL, East Stockwell Street. Now
offices. 1816–17, brick, with a classical façade of 1836. Three
bays wide beneath a pediment. Entrance with short Tuscan
columns *in antis*. Behind, in St Helen's Lane, Sabbath Schools
added 1867, also now offices.

CONGREGATIONAL CHAPEL, Headgate, Chapel Street North.
Now Headgate Theatre. 1844 by *W. F. Poulton*. White brick with
stone dressings. Three-bay pediment supported by pilasters
over round-headed windows. Schoolroom to s added by *Baker
& May*, 1903. Screen-printed glass window in foyer by *Gay
Hutchings*, 2002.

101 CONGREGATIONAL CHURCH, Old Heath. 1869. Good example
of a tin tabernacle, with pointed windows and little false
buttresses.

FIRST CHURCH OF CHRIST SCIENTIST, Trinity Street. 1975–7
by *Bryan K. Thomas*. Octagonal auditorium set back behind
reading room and Sunday School.

METHODIST CHURCH, Wimpole Road. By *Goodey & Cressall*,
1903–4. Gothic; brick with stone dressings. NW tower with
spire and matching hall and schools on s side.

FRIENDS' MEETING HOUSE, Church Street (formerly St
Mary's House). Two-storey, gault brick house of 1802–3; three
bays with two-storey bow windows either side of entrance
and one-bay extension on E side. Converted 1974 by *Bryan*

Thomas, who rebuilt the garden front and added a single-storey hexagonal meeting room.

UNITED REFORMED CHURCH (Independent), Lion Walk. 1984–6 by *David Roberts*, replacing *F. Barnes*'s Congregational Church of 1863 but retaining the spire. Kentish rag with Caen stone dressings, 125 ft (38.5 metre) high, and when new the most conspicuous landmark in Colchester; the top section rebuilt 1885 by *Roger Smith & Gale* following the 1884 earthquake. Roberts's church is octagonal, two-storey, with shops on the ground floor. Bands of ragstone with angle buttresses of reconstituted stone and tile-hung upper storey. Octagonal lantern. – STAINED GLASS. Three panels from the 1863 church reused internally. – To the N, hall and meeting rooms also by *Roberts*, 1973–6 as part of the Lion Walk development (*see* Perambulation 3).

CEMETERY, Mersea Road. By *Law & Edwards*, 1855–6, with landscaping by *B. R. Cant*. Two similar Dec ragstone chapels, one Episcopal, one Nonconformist, with large porte cochères. – MONUMENTS. Stone obelisk, with three bands of vermiculated rustication, by *James Deane*. Erected in the High Street, 1760, and painted with mileages to London and other towns; removed 1858, and re-erected as monument to Mary Ann Swire †1859. – Standard *Blomfield* 'Cross of Sacrifice'.

ST BOTOLPH'S PRIORY

The most important and impressive ecclesiastical monument of Colchester; the ruin of a Norman church of considerable size. St Botolph's was founded late in the C11 as a house of secular canons and refounded *c.* 1100 as the first British house of Augustinian canons. The church was rebuilt and dedicated in 1177. What remains is a ruin, and the ruin only of the W front and seven bays of the nave (108 ft (33 metres) long), with narrow N and S aisles. Excavations in 1991 revealed the plan of the demolished chancel and transepts and also a crypt or undercroft beneath the S transept. The church was built of rubble with plenty of Roman bricks, used in the walls as well as more consistently for dressings. The W front is broad; the two towers stand outside the aisles, not identical incidentally either in size or in shape. There are three portals; the middle one of four orders of columns, the capitals with finely intertwined scrolls or decorated scallops (badly preserved), the arches with much zigzag. Above the portals, but with the middle one cutting into it, two tiers of intersected arches without capitals. The principal W window was circular, and the earliest major round window in England. The façade must date from after the mid C12. Nothing survives of the upper parts of the towers.

Inside the façade a passage, carried on a tunnel vault, runs on the first floor from one tower to the other, open to the nave. The nave has mighty circular piers (5 ft 8 in. (1.7 metres) in diameter). They have no proper capitals and support a gallery with unsubdivided openings as large as the arcade. The arches are single-stepped and unmoulded on both floors. Flat pilaster strips stand on the circular piers to divide the bays of the gallery from each other. The aisles were groin-vaulted. C14 windows in the N aisle, one with Dec tracery. The building is immensely impressive as a ruin, but the grim severity which the absence of all surface embellishments gives may have been a quality of the church even when it was new. It would share this quality with the contemporary Benedictine St Albans and to a certain degree with all Early Norman buildings. To the s of the church, foundations of the N wall of cloister. The priory was dissolved in 1536 and the nave and aisles were used as a parish church until damaged in the 1648 siege.

ST JOHN'S ABBEY

36   Of the Benedictine abbey founded by Eudo Dapifer in 1096 and dissolved in 1538, the most significant survival is the N GATE-HOUSE, dating probably from the C15. It is a splendid piece of display, characteristically more ornate to the outer world than to the abbey precincts. Flint outer façade with a great deal of flushwork decoration, chiefly shafts and blank crocketed arches. Tall carriageway with four-centred head and tall niches above and to the l. and r. Below the r. niche the entrance for pedestrians, also with four-centred head. Two two-light upper windows and battlements. Flanking polygonal angle turrets with big crocketed pinnacles. No flushwork on the other side and only one wide gateway with a much simpler arch mould-ing. Inside the gateway is a star-shaped lierne vault. Extensively restored in the C19, on one occasion by *Major-General Montagu* of the Royal Engineers; this included replacing details of the upper storey damaged when the gatehouse was stormed by Parliamentary troops in 1648. E of the gatehouse are the N and E walls of a C15 porter's lodge. Parts of the original C12 precinct wall survive along Mersea Road, Napier Road and Flagstaff Road, as well as reused fragments.

CASTLE

49   Colchester Castle is the largest Norman keep in existence. It measures 110 ft (34 metres) by 151 ft 6 in. (46.5 metres), about one-third larger than the White Tower in London. Both belong to the small group of so-called hall keeps, much broader than the more usual tower keeps and not so high in proportion, and both were built on the orders of William the Conqueror, that at Colchester probably by Eudo Dapifer, to whom the castle was granted by Henry I in 1101. The traditional date of con-struction, derived from the C13 'Colchester Chronicle', is 1076, although it is not known whether this refers to the start of work or the completion of a first phase. There is insufficient evidence to conclude which is earlier, the White Tower or Colchester Castle, but there are striking similarities, in particular an apse projecting at the SE corner housing a chapel. This form seems

to be based on earlier castles in Normandy, notably Ivry-la-Bataille, *c.* 1000.

The castle was maintained throughout the medieval period, although it only once saw serious action, when King John retook it from an occupying French force in 1216. During the C14 and C15 it was used mainly as a gaol, and by *c.* 1600 it was no longer defensible. It was alienated by the Crown in 1629 and by 1637 parts of the hall roof had fallen in. In 1683 it was sold to John Wheeley for demolition. He removed considerable quantities of building materials and also much of the sand on which the castle is built, thus revealing the so-called 'vaults' (see p. 259); however, Wheeley was defeated by more solid masonry, and in 1705 the castle was purchased by Sir Isaac Rebow M.P. In 1727 it came into the ownership of Charles Gray, who treated it as a somewhat Brobdingnagian garden ornament in the grounds of his house, Hollytrees (see p. 285). He employed *James Deane* to carry out various alterations, 1746–67, and also strengthened the foundations which had been undermined by Wheeley. The E side of the castle was used as a county prison (enlarged and improved by *John Johnson*, 1787–8), until it was superseded in 1835. On Gray's death in 1782 the castle passed to James Round, who carried out further work, but the Round family sold it to the borough in 1920 as a war memorial. Since 1855 the castle had housed the collections of the Essex Archaeological Society and these were amalgamated with those of the corporation in 1926 to form the basis of the present museum. The castle 'vaults' were reinforced in 1931, and in 1934–5 the keep was roofed in steel over a concrete frame and a bridge built to the main entrance. Extensive restoration by *Purcell Miller Tritton & Partners* in the 1980s.

The castle's dimensions and indeed its location are largely dictated by the foundations on which it sits: the podium of the Roman Temple of Claudius (*see* p. 259). This means that the castle does not occupy a logical site – such as the highest ground – from the defensive point of view. The reasons for reusing the old podium were not only practical but probably also symbolic: the new rulers were taking advantage of the solid foundation already present and asserting their status as the inheritors of Rome.

EXTERIOR. The N, E and W walls of the castle clasp the podium, while the S block extends beyond it, over the space occupied by the temple steps. This extension contains the well, which it would have been difficult to sink through the podium. The entrance lies on this side at ground-floor level (albeit higher than the level of the ground itself), a remarkable exception, and it may be that the main entrance was originally intended to be on the N side. It seems likely that there was a major change of plan during construction, perhaps because of the lack of good building stone, and it is still not certain how high the castle was. It is now of two storeys, but considerable quantities of masonry were removed by Wheeley in the late C17, including (according to Morant) 'the tops of the towers and walls', which might refer to an additional storey. Comparisons with the White Tower suggest the possibility of an additional two storeys, planned if not actually built, although this – because of Colchester's larger floor area – would have resulted in a castle of very great size.

The construction is largely of rubble and septaria with many Roman bricks, the walls articulated by broad flat buttresses. The plinth, over 15 ft (4.5 metres) high, was faced with ashlar, of which only parts now survive. In the E and W walls and the SW turret traces remain of temporary crenellation indicating that the castle was built in two stages. The S doorway has two orders of columns with typical Early Norman capitals (upright leaves and little volutes) and an arch with several roll mouldings. Traces of a large stone forebuilding, all part of the complex entrance to the keep, were exposed in 1932. Inside the doorway to the l., in the largest of the angle towers, is the main stair, a spiral with a rising tunnel vault. To the r. are the well and then two thick walls forming small chambers, the 'Lucas' vault and sub-crypt, the latter subdivided to form prison cells in 1727. Steps lead down to the 'vaults' formed by the construction of the Roman podium.

The GROUND FLOOR was originally three rooms, but now only two. The surviving dividing wall has much herringbone masonry with the use of Roman bricks. There are no fireplaces or garderobes, and only the narrowest of slit windows. On the FIRST FLOOR the space is divided in the same way as the ground floor, but in addition there is a small chamber in the NE tower, another in the SW tower next to the main stair, and in the NW tower a second, smaller, spiral stair starts. The first floor contained rooms of great importance, although how they were used is a matter of conjecture. The larger area may have been the Great Hall, the smaller private apartments. Four large fireplaces with rounded arches and double flues leading to holes in the walls survive, two in each of the W and E walls. They are among the earliest known. In the E wall, about halfway down, is a garderobe with a tunnel-vaulted lobby. Two more are in the NW tower, flanking the smaller spiral stair that starts at this level. Next to it in the N wall is a blocked postern doorway, a very unusual feature. Along the S side is Charles Gray's library, 1754–5 by *Deane*, with two large windows either side of a fireplace, and on the N side an arcaded passage of brick and stone. In the apsidal SE corner is the chapel undercroft, a low vaulted room with the very exceptional feature of two pairs of apsed side chapels forming in their vaults groins with the main vault (cf. Copford). Two large windows in the S wall also inserted by *Deane*, 1754–5.

Of the SECOND FLOOR hardly anything remains except for the lower courses of the chapel apse, showing that it had flat inner pilasters in line with those on the exterior. On the S side of the apse is a small chamber with its own apsidal E end. The floor of the chapel is crazy paving of Roman brick laid by *Deane* for Gray. His also is the continuation of the main staircase to

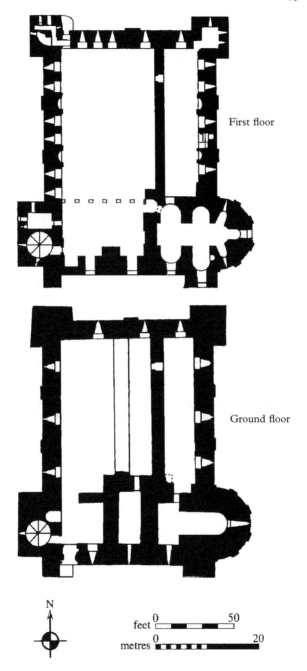

First floor

Ground floor

N

feet 0 50

metres 0 20

Colchester Castle.
Plans of ground and first floors

the top of the walls, 1760, roofed over with a brick dome, and
the top of the NE tower, 1767, with curious pyramidal finials
of stepped brick. The timber and glass roof of the chapel was
added in 1988–9 as part of a restoration of the area by *Purcell
Miller Tritton & Partners*. W of the chapel, along the S wall, is a
passage or walkway that may have continued round the W and
N walls, forming a gallery in a double-height Great Hall, but
there is insufficient evidence, documentary or archaeological,
to be sure about the form of the castle at this level.

The outer bailey originally extended as far N as the Roman
town wall, and the inner bailey made it necessary, S of the castle,
for the High Street to bend a little. One of these baileys – it is
not known which – was constructed 1172–3. Near the SE corner
of the keep are the foundations of an apsidal chapel, probably
Late Saxon, retained when the keep was built. A Great Hall and
apartments, possibly those of the sheriff and constable, stood
between this chapel and the southern bailey wall.

CASTLE PARK (*see also* Roman Colchester, p. 260). The castle
grounds were landscaped by Charles Gray of Hollytrees,
1728–9, including the creation of a raised terrace on the N side
of the castle ending in a wooden SUMMERHOUSE in the form
of a tetrastyle Greek temple, 1731. In 1747 he rebuilt a rotunda,
30 yds E of the castle, using *James Deane* as architect, of which
now only an ARCHWAY survives, a mixture of stone, flint,
Roman tiles and C18 brick. The Round family sold the grounds
to the borough in 1892 for the creation of a public park, laid
out by *Backhouse & Co.* of York, in the form of a parkland landscape rather than municipal garden. Wrought-iron entrance
gates from Museum Street made by *Barnards* of Norwich.
Similar entrance off Middle Mill Road. N of the castle, octagonal BANDSTAND with pagoda-like roof on cast-iron columns
by *Walter Macfarlane & Co.*, 1894.

PUBLIC BUILDINGS

97 TOWN HALL, High Street. 1897–1902, won in competition by
John Belcher, and a supreme example of Edwardian Baroque.
The materials are, as one would expect, red brick and Portland stone.* It cost about £55,000, of which £12,000 was sub-
scribed by local benefactors. James Paxman of Stisted Hall
(q.v.) donated the Victoria Tower (specified in the competition
conditions to commemorate the Diamond Jubilee), estimated
at £4,000. The result was a triumphant expression of Colchester's civic pride, the embodiment of the borough's history
and tradition. Belcher designed in the exuberant display style
of *c.* 1900–10 with more braggadocio than anyone, and the
Town Hall is proof of that. But the way in which he placed his
exceedingly high tower – 162 ft (50 metres) – in exactly the spot

---

*The original moot hall on this site had been replaced in 1843–5 by *Brandon &
Blore*.

where the High Street narrows, as one walks towards the w, is excellent according to any standard, and the scale is excellent too. The tower is slender and square, and ends in a Borrominesque flourish – two stages of stone columns, big curved pediments on the lower, concavely curved sides between the columns on the upper. Seated allegorical figures are also present, carved in Portland stone by *L. J. Watts*, representing the four main activities of the town: engineering, military defence, agriculture and fishery. The crowning bronze figure is St Helena, patron saint of Colchester, and below her four ravens, designed by *F. Carruthers Gould*, symbol of the portreeve who administered the town's medieval port. The main façade has three pairs of gigantic giant columns, each carrying an open pediment. These are segmental, triangular, segmental. The Composite capitals are enriched with local produce: ears of wheat, roses, and oyster shells. All the details on the brackets of the main balcony swell and bulge. In niches at third-floor level are six statues of historical figures associated with Colchester, also by *Watts*: Eudo Dapifer, Thomas Lord Audley, William Gilberd, Archbishop Samuel Harsnett and (on the West Stockwell Street elevation) King Edward the Elder and Boudicca. Stone lamp standards mark the main entrance in the High Street and the side entrance (to the magistrates' courts) in West Stockwell Street. Cast-iron gates to main entrance by *Starkie Gardner & Co.*, with stone figures over doorway by *Fabbrucci* and *McCrossan*.

After the extravagance of the exterior, the INTERIOR does not disappoint, starting strongly with the marble staircase by *Farmer & Brindley*. The plan is vertical, with public offices and law courts on the raised ground floor. On the staircase itself, seated statue of Queen Victoria by *L. J. Watts*, who also made the memorial to the Colchester martyrs on the top landing. Also carved wooden figures, *c.* 1719, of a boy and girl from the demolished Bluecoat School, Culver Street. On the first floor is the mayoral suite of three rooms that can be opened into one, and the COUNCIL CHAMBER. The latter has a ceiling painted by *Charles Edward Baskett* and his son *Charles Henry Baskett*, incorporating chronograms composed by Rev. Cecil Deedes. Mayoral chair made by *A. W. Arrowsmith & Co.* of Bond Street. Also on this floor the N COMMITTEE ROOM: fireplace with oak surround carved by *W.R. Simkin* of Colchester, using oak from the old Town Hall, and tiles painted by *W. Gurney Benham*. On the top floor is the spatial climax of the building, the MOOT HALL, with more giant Composite columns and a barrel ceiling. – STAINED GLASS. On first landing of main stair, by *Clayton & Bell*. At w end of first-floor corridor, in council chamber, and in moot hall, by *James Powell & Sons*. Windows on upper landing 1922, probably also by Powell's.

POLICE STATION, Southway. 1988–9 by the *County Architect's Dept* (project architect, *Graham Beighton*). Square, with the corners cut off, round an internal garden. Three storeys, built into the side of the hill, and inconspicuous, but the main front has presence, with small windows in the ground floor to lend an air of strength.

FIRE STATION, Cowdray Avenue. 1937 by the Borough Engineer, *Harold Collins*. Dark brick, functional but nicely detailed.

Former PUBLIC LIBRARY, West Stockwell Street. 1893–4 by *Brightwen Binyon*. Picturesque Neo-Jacobean, brick with dark timberwork and pargetting. Two parallel ranges with gables to the street, the larger with a tall oriel lighting the reading room, and an open pediment within the gable supported by terms. Inside, large bas-relief representing Queen Victoria opening the Great Exhibition, 1851, by *G. Oldofredi* of Milan; commissioned and donated by James Paxman, the local engineer, who is depicted as a young man in the crowd.

Former PUBLIC LIBRARY, Shewell Walk. *See* p. 291.

PUBLIC LIBRARY, Trinity Square. *See* p. 291.

NATURAL HISTORY MUSEUM, High Street. *See* CHURCHES, All Saints.

HEADGATE THEATRE. *See* Churches, Congregational Chapel.

MERCURY THEATRE, Balkerne Gardens. 1970–2 by *Norman Downie Associates*. Brick on steel frame with reinforced concrete columns and beams, with hexagonal, slate-hung, tiered fly tower. The irregular plan grows from the hexagonal stage, which projects into the auditorium (a larger hexagon, stretched) functioning both as traditional proscenium and 'semi-thrust'. Glazed foyer wraps round the auditorium, with a bar in the corner over the entrance. Bronze figure of Mercury (after *Giambologna*) on the roof. Offices, workshops, restaurant etc. added round the edge. Windows high up under the projecting eaves, more hexagons. Yellow brick and glass extension (workshops and paint rooms) by *Stanley Bragg Partnership*, 1997–8.

COLCHESTER NORTH STATION. 1895–6, by *John Wilson*, Great Eastern Railway chief engineer, and *W. N. Ashbee*. Ironwork by *Handyside & Henderson*, Derby.

COLCHESTER TOWN STATION. Originally St Botolph's, 1866–7, refurbished and renamed 1991. Lower, early C19 house adjoins.

COLCHESTER INSTITUTE, Sheepen Road. By *H. Conolly*, County Architect, as the North-East Essex Technical College and School of Art. Four-storey block with single-storey workshops 1954; reinforced concrete with brick and hardwood facing. A cantilevered administration area provides covered space over main entrance which has a SCULPTURE ('Constellation') by *Franta Belsky*. Five-storey block to w, 1959, faced with aggregate panels and Portland stone. To the s, four-storey octagonal Learning Resources Centre by the *County Architect's Dept*, 1987–9, including galleried library on three levels and attached three-storey teaching block, pale brown fair-faced concrete. Catering and hospitality building, NE, by *Lambert Scott & Innes*, 2000–2, provides a dramatic contrast to the 1959 building, with staircases behind large corner windows, and concrete block walls with timber below the eaves of the curved, powder-coated, eggshell-blue steel roofs.

COUNTY HIGH SCHOOL FOR GIRLS, Norman Way. 1957–8 by *H. Conolly*, in his usual style.

HIGH SCHOOL, Wellesley Road. By *E. E. May*, *c.* 1902. Watered-down Queen Anne with large Venetian windows set in pedimented gables.

ROYAL GRAMMAR SCHOOL, Lexden Road. 1852–3 by *H. W. Hayward*. Tudor style in red and blue brick. Considerably extended in similar style by *Newman, Jacques & Round*, 1908–9. Further extensions and alterations by *John Young* in association with the County Architect, *H. Conolly*, 1958–9 and 1963–4. Good classroom block by *Latham Architects*, 2000, two storeys with verandas and purple-painted railings. – STAINED GLASS. War memorial window in library by *Francis H. Spear*, 1951; heraldic.

SIXTH FORM COLLEGE, North Hill. 1908–9 by *Cheers & Smith* of Blackburn, as the Secondary Girls' School & Technical Institute. Edwardian classical. Large, red brick, with stone dressings that merge between the window arches and quoins to form bands, and open pedimented gables. Extended to more than double its original size by the *County Architect's Dept*, 1985–6, and *Roff Marsh Partnership*, 1995–6, the latter including a four-storey concave glazed entrance. IT building also by Roff Marsh, 2003–4.

BRINKLEY GROVE PRIMARY SCHOOL, Highwoods. 1999 by *Stanley Bragg Partnership*. Two adjoining open octagons, the larger round a courtyard, the smaller round a hall; brick and slate with lots of structural timber inside.

ROACH VALE PRIMARY SCHOOL, Roach Vale. 1977 by the *County Architect's Dept* (project architects, *Malcolm Johnson, Peter Page* and *K. J. Spiers*, consulting engineers *Chamberlain & Partners*). Flat-roofed, system-built with concrete panels and round-cornered doors and windows, a good example of its date.

BOARD SCHOOLS. Colchester School Board was formed in 1892 and disbanded in 1903. Their architects were *Goodey & Cressall*, whose distinctive style is easily recognized: red brick with classical detailing, gables of all shapes and sizes, and usually incorporating a tower. Their first was NORTH STREET SCHOOL, John Harper Street, 1893–4, and others include Barrack Street (now WILSON MARRIAGE CENTRE and Adult Community College), 1894–6, with decorative plasterwork panels in the gables, ST JOHN'S GREEN PRIMARY SCHOOL, St John's Green, 1898, and ST GEORGE'S NEW TOWN JUNIOR SCHOOL, Canterbury Road, 1903.

DISTRICT GENERAL HOSPITAL, Turner Road. Main block 1981–5 by *Percy Thomas Partnership*. Three storeys, concrete frame, clad with concrete panels and lime-green glass curtain walling. Internal courtyards, with contemporary SCULPTURE by *Bruce Gernand, Paul de Monchaux*, and *John Foster*. Tubular steel figures outside main entrance by *Michael Condron*, 2000, with seating by *Nicola Henshaw*. SW of the main building, ELMSTEAD DAY UNIT by *The Design Buro*, 1992–3, single-storey, brick-clad with shallow-pitched slate roof, extended by *The Devereux Partnership*, 1995–7. STAINED GLASS panel by *Deborah Lowe*, 1996, and more figures by *Michael Condron*. W of the main block, CONSTABLE WING by *Alex Gordon Partnership*, 1996–7, three and four storeys, red and yellow brick, with SCULPTURE by *Rachel Fenner* and internal mosaic panels by *Tessa Bleecker* and *Cleo Mussi*. GAINSBOROUGH WING N of the main block by *Frank Gibberd Partnership*, 1998–2000, similar to the Constable Wing. Mosaic panels by *Cleo Mussi* and stained glass by *Kate Baden Fuller*.

ESSEX COUNTY HOSPITAL, Lexden Road. Founded 1818, the oldest part built the following year by *M.G. Thompson*; Ionic portico added 1825 by *William Lay*. Gault brick, still Late Georgian in style. Wings added by *Thomas Hopper*, 1839, and extensive alterations by *T.H. Wyatt*, 1879–80, including the addition of a third storey to the central block and diagonal sanitary blocks at either end of Hopper's wings. New block to the SW by *Goodey & Cressall*, 1897–8, extended by *Duncan Clark & Beckett* (nurses' home), 1932, the latter with nice Art Deco detailing. Out-patients' department at NE corner of site by *W.T. Cressall* and *Duncan Clark*, 1924–6. Radiotherapy block at NW corner by *W.G. Plant*, 1964, concrete frame with brick and block cladding, with ceramic motifs on entrance wall by *Hedy Fromings* and copper sculpture on N wall by *Peter Fagan*.

Former SEVERALLS HOSPITAL, Boxted Road (County Lunatic Asylum). 1910–13 by *F. Whitmore* and *W.H. Town*. 'Queen Anne' brick with Art Nouveau elements. The accepted echelon plan for mental hospitals, with a large central hall, wards and administrative offices connected by walkways to detached villa-style wards in park-like grounds. Asymmetrically placed water tower, and separate chapel with lancet windows. Later additions include nurses' home, 1928, and four ward blocks, 1937. Closed 1997.

TURNER VILLAGE HOSPITAL, Turner Road. 1933–5, Neo-Georgian brick, by *J. Stuart* as an outpost of the Royal Eastern Counties Institution.* Central row of administration blocks, with a water tower at the far end and a quadrant of eight villas to the N; planned S quadrant not built. Largely disused.

48 WATER TOWER, Balkerne Gardens. 1882–3, by *Charles Clegg*, Borough Surveyor and Engineer, and soon nicknamed 'Jumbo' because of its bulk; it has an elephant as its weathervane.† The tower is 105 ft (32 metres) high, and before the building of the Town Hall would have been even more prominent. Its design was no doubt meant to be in the Roman spirit. Four massive red brick piers with splayed bases joined by large round-headed arches support a platform, corbelled out to support the

---

*The Institution's main building was the former railway hotel by *Lewis Cubitt*, 1842–4 (dem. 1985).
†Jumbo was the elephant sold by London Zoo to Barnum's Circus in 1882.

iron tank. Pyramid roof of bright green copper and little lantern to finish the assertive composition.

PUMPING STATION, Balkerne Hill. 1894 by *J. Mackworth Wood*, engineer, in a Roman Italianate style sympathetic to the Jumbo water tower, which it served. Red brick with reconstituted stone dressings. Converted to offices 1988. Adjoining it to the W, ROWAN HOUSE by *Pick Everard Keay & Gimson* for the Anglia Water Authority, 1985: seven octagons with pyramidal roofs round an inner courtyard, three storeys, pale brown brick with bands of continuous glazing.

COLCHESTER GARRISON*

Troops were billetted in Colchester from the late C17. Nothing remains of the first barracks, built in 1794 s of Barrack Street. A temporary camp of demountable huts was erected in 1855–6, between Mersea Road and Military Road, but the first permanent buildings, including provision for cavalry, were erected in 1862, following the purchase of St John's Abbey gardens and farm in 1860. These now constitute the last surviving example of the new layout of cavalry barracks developed at Aldershot in the 1850s, with blocks in parallel rather than arranged round a central parade ground.

GARRISON CHURCH OF ST ALBAN THE MARTYR, Military Road. 1856. Timber-framed and weatherboarded, with exposed cast-iron brackets supporting iron trusses. Plain exterior with round-arched windows and W bellcote. – ALTAR RAILS, PULPIT, CHOIR STALLS and PEWS. By *A. W. N. Pugin*, 1849, originally for St Mary, West Tofts, Norfolk. Elaborately carved with poppyheads, arms and symbols of the Sutton family etc. – ALTAR. By *Rev. Alfred Malim, c.* 1885, for the Garrison Church, Shoeburyness. Heavily carved. – REREDOS, Lady Chapel. By *Robert Thompson*, 1957, for the Garrison Church, Catterick, moved here 1980.

NAPIER ROAD. Two pairs of houses erected for commanding officers of the artillery barracks, 1868. Stock brick with rusticated quoins and deep eaves. Plainer blocks along Flagstaff Road 1874–80. Good wooden CRICKET PAVILION on s side of Napier Road, *c.* 1895.

LE CATEAU BARRACKS, Circular Road North. Designed for the Royal Artillery, mostly 1873–5, under *C.B. Ewart R.E.*, Deputy Director of Works at the War Office. Of the C19 buildings, the two-storey Officers' Quarters, two-storey Sergeants' Mess, single-storey Adult School (1884), and two (of six) blocks of stables and barrack rooms survive: red brick with stock brick dressings. The Officers' Quarters is of twenty-six bays, of which

---

*In 2006, the Garrison is the subject of a development plan that will see almost all the older part of the site, closest to the town, vacated and redeveloped as housing, retaining a number of the older buildings. Construction of the new garrison by *W.S. Atkins*, to the s of Abbey Field, began in 2004.

the central four step forward with a taller gable and round-headed windows on the first floor. The stables have most of their fittings intact, with tall cast-iron columns separating the stalls and supporting jack arches. Although men still slept over the stables, the high ceiling of the stables and concrete floor of the living quarters were a considerable improvement in terms of hygiene and accommodation. In the NW corner of the site an octagonal brick WATER TOWER, 1878, with bath house on the ground floor.

CAVALRY BARRACKS, SW of Le Cateau Barracks, now bisected by Circular Road West. 1861–3. *Capt. Douglas Galton R.E.*, Assistant Inspector-General of Fortifications, was at least partly responsible for the design, which includes the large, rectangular Riding School, with office and viewing gallery at one end and complex roof trusses with wrought-iron ties and paired struts. Other surviving buildings from the original barracks include three blocks of troops' stables with soldiers' quarters over, two further blocks of soldiers' quarters, officers' quarters, and single-storey stables.

GOOJERAT BARRACKS, Circular Road West. Rebuilt 1970–5, except for the GARRISON THEATRE, *c.* 1898.

REED HALL, ½ m. SW, was purchased in 1904, a small, elegant gault brick house of *c.* 1825: three bays, two storeys, hipped slate roof. On the ground floor, tall sash windows either side of the front door. Semicircular porch on two slender columns.

KIRKEE and McMUNN BARRACKS, next to Reed Hall. Dated 1938. Officers' Mess in very accomplished Neo-Georgian, with central Portland stone porch with four pairs of Tuscan columns. Two-bay corner towers at each end and then angled flanking wings connected to the main block by stone colonnades.

GYMNASIUM, Circular Road South. 1864. Brick, with tall round-headed windows.

MEEANEE and HYDERABAD BARRACKS, Mersea Road. Brick Officers' Quarters, 1898 and 1904.

PERAMBULATIONS

TOWN CENTRE

1. High Street

The HIGH STREET is the spine of the town. In a town the size of Colchester it can hardly be perfect, and the skyline on both sides is jagged and untidy, but there are plenty of individual buildings of note. The main visual accents are the 'Jumbo' water tower at the W end and the Town Hall in the centre. Seen together from the E, they make a pleasing combination.

From W to E, the street starts strongly on the N side with No. 157, built as the CORN EXCHANGE by *David Laing*, 1820 (later Essex and Suffolk Fire Office, now shops and offices). Greek Revival, originally two storeys, a third (with pediment and clock) added later. Nine bays with Greek Doric colonnade (of painted iron, cast by *Joseph Wallis*) over the pavement. This was replaced as the Corn Exchange in 1845 by the building adjoining to the r. (now the CO-OPERATIVE BANK), by *J.R. Brandon*, a single-storey, five-bay sandstone front with central three-bay Ionic portico *in antis* and rusticated outer bays. Closed 1884, this became the Albert School of Art and Science, enlarged 1896 by *H. Goodyear*, Borough Surveyor, and reconstructed internally 1925–6 by *Duncan W. Clark* as the Albert Hall and Art Gallery.* Behind No. 156, ST GEORGE'S HALL, 1851, brick with apsidal ends and tall arched windows.

The s side gets off to a gentler start, e.g. Nos. 1–2, simple 'Free Georgian' originally for Boots the Chemist by their house architect, *Percy J. Bartlett*, 1936. Between first- and second-floor windows stone panels carved with chemists' jars etc. Nothing then until No. 11, C17 with a Late Georgian front of five bays and three storeys and a two-storey central bow window with arches and columns.† No. 12 is pompous C20 classical bank architecture, probably interwar; three bays wide but with a deep entablature and balustrade supported by attached Corinthian columns. Beside it No. 14, good commercial High Victorian Venetian of *c.* 1870, seems very restrained. No. 17, originally the Capital & Counties Bank by *Baker & May* dated 1901, breaks the skyline with a flamboyant scrolled pediment. No. 21 has a Late Georgian gault brick front with an elaborate pedimented tripartite central window on the first floor, and No. 22 a segmental bow window with decorated entablature and pretty, thin glazing bars. Then a run of C20 banks: NATWEST, *c.* 1904 by *W. Campbell Jones*, Free Style with richly coloured bands of dark stone, the ground floor probably a later alteration; HSBC, a clean 1950s design with projecting mullions; and LLOYDS TSB, dated 1926, stone, stripped Wrenaissance. On the corner of Pelham's Lane BURTON'S, 1936 in their house style, giant attached columns, square with Art-Deco-ish composite capitals.

Meanwhile on the N side WILLIAMS & GRIFFIN'S department store of the 1960s and GREYTOWN HOUSE of *c.* 1975 provide a depressing prelude to the absolute highlight of the Town Hall (*see* Public Buildings). On the E side of West Stock- 97 well Street, ANGEL COURT, 1988–90, Borough Council offices, modern glazed entrance and atrium behind a pastiche vernacular façade. Looming over it THE HIPPODROME (formerly Grand Theatre), 1903–5, begun by *J. W. Start*, completed by *Ben Kirk* of *Kirk & Kirk*, contractors: red brick with stone and stucco dressings in a poor Edwardian Baroque. Interior remodelled by *Stanley Bragg Partnership*, 1987. Its neighbour,

---

*Figures representing ancient and modern agriculture now on St Mary's car park, Balkerne Hill.
†Painted panels of *c.* 1690–1710 from a room at No. 11B, now demolished, are stored with Colchester Museums.

the BAY AND SAY (now After Office Hours) pub by *G.H. Page*
for the Colchester Brewing Co., 1904, has a three-bay ashlar
façade with Baroque features, e.g. slightly Mannerist pediments, combined with Art Nouveau decoration to the ground-
floor windows.

Opposite, Nos. 35–37 are dated 1879, refurbished 1983 but
retaining Gothic windows. To its l., the upper floor has oriel
windows and rainwater heads adorned with gryphons. To the
r., No. 38, MARKS & SPENCER, Art Deco with lotus columns.
Then comes the remarkable RED LION HOTEL, early C16
with exposed timbers. Three storeys, the upper floors jettied
and rich in original detail, with bands of traceried panels below
the sill line at first and second floor. Shafts with carved capitals
and moulded bases separate the bays, with a moulded bressumer to the eaves supported on brackets. Two blocked original window openings. First recorded in 1515 as the New Inn
or White Lion (the badge of the Howards). Its planning does
not correspond to contemporary inns, e.g. the White Hart,
Brentwood. The front is of four bays, one with a bay window
at the first floor above a carriage arch with carved spandrels
depicting St George and the Dragon and figures in canopied
niches. The other bays were originally independent three-
storey units, perhaps shops, but with moulded ceilings and fireplaces on the ground floor that appear to preclude normal
commercial use. The earliest part, however, lies behind the
street and at right angles to it: a two-bay, two-storey hall, probably part of a town house for John Howard, Lord Howard, who
built a number of houses in Colchester in 1481 or 1482. The
ground floor still has its moulded beams, and on the upper
floor is a more important chamber, with elaborate crown-post
roof. Various C18 and C19 alterations and additions, mostly
now removed; rainwater head in courtyard dated 1716. Refurbished by *Dunthorne Parker*, 1987–8; the hotel now occupies
the upper floors, with shops below.

Back on High Street's N side, a little further downhill, the
GEORGE HOTEL provides a contrast: early C18 front of five
bays, with a cast-iron balcony running the length of the first
floor. Originally C15 with cross-wings and cellars. Exposed
timber framing to George Street, and visible inside, on this
side, remains of two C15 shop windows. On the first floor, a
detached panel of C16 wall painting: bold swirls of foliage and
flowers, two with putti springing from them. After the hotel,
at the corner of Museum Street, Nos. 105 and 106, picturesque
C17 with shops on the ground floor and jettied upper storey.
Now comes a noticeable bend in the street, where it had to
accommodate the bailey of the Castle.

Returning to the S side of the High Street, Nos. 45–47 are
of C16 origin, but with C14 cellars. Projecting upper storey at
the rear with C17 pargetting of strapwork and foliage. On the
corner of St Nicholas Street, ST NICHOLAS HOUSE, brick and
nondescript, built 1957 on the site of Scott's church (dem.
1955). Part of the churchyard, including gravestones, survives

behind in Culver Street East. On the E corner of St Nicholas Street, 'Queen Anne' of 1890, two high gables with decorative plasterwork and little oriels facing N and W. Then a long Late Georgian plastered front to No. 63, with canted oriel window, and PARK HOUSE with bow oriel window, before the contrast of No. 66, red brick with black diapers, the former rectory of All Saints by *H. W. Hayward*, 1858.

Opposite All Saints (*see* Churches) the street broadens out with COWDRAY CRESCENT forming an opening towards the Castle. Laid out 1922–6 by *Duncan W. Clark* with gates, railings, and lampposts, as a setting for the town's somewhat florid WAR MEMORIAL. Portland stone, with bronze figures by *H.C. Fehr*, who also sculpted the lions on the flanking piers. To open out in this place was a good idea, as until then the Castle had not been visually part of the town at all, but it breaks the continuity of the street entirely, and, more serious, makes HOLLYTREES, the town's best C18 house, appear isolated, whereas it should be part of the general street scene, like all the other Georgian houses. Hollytrees was built for Elizabeth Cornelisen in 1718–19 on the site of an earlier house. Brick, with rubbed bricks for the trimmings. It has three storeys and five bays of segment-headed windows. The doorcase has Roman pilasters, a straight entablature on lusciously carved brackets, and a frieze rising to a point in the middle, in a fashion typical of the time of George I. In 1748 Charles Gray employed *James Deane* to add the set-back W wing: the main window to the street with raised brick surround and pediment, rusticated ground floor with three-bay arcade to the garden and Venetian window above. Balancing single-storey arcade on the E side, no more than a screen. C18 railings and gate. Purchased for the Borough by Viscount Cowdray, and opened as a museum 1929 following internal alterations by *Duncan Clark & Beckett*. The principal original interior is the entrance hall, with dog-leg stair with twisted balusters. In a ground-floor room, formed from two *c.* 1880, a C17 ceiling from a house in the High Street (dem. 1959). Refurbished 2000–1 by *Purcell Miller Tritton*, who created a new entrance through the W arcade. Against the E wall, C18 tombstones from the demolished church at Markshall. Formal gardens including rectangular fishpond laid out by *R. W. Wallace* after 1922.

Nos. 67–72, facing Hollytrees, form a suitable, quiet Georgian background to the house, although most are of C17 origin and refronted in brick There follows THE MINORIES (art gallery), a C16 timber-framed house remodelled in 1776 for Thomas Boggis. Five bays, with central Doric porch supporting a canted two-storey bay. Venetian window on the garden elevation, and a rather ramshackle single-storey C19 service wing. Gently curving open-string staircase. Extended into No. 73 with timber and glass additions at the rear, 1976. In the garden a large, E-facing Gothick SUMMERHOUSE by 83 *James Deane*, *c.* 1745: semicircular, with a battlemented screen front and an opening of three arches, apparently inspired by

Batty Langley's 'umbrello . . . to terminate a walk'.* The walk
in question was in the grounds of EAST HILL HOUSE, from
which the summerhouse was unforgivably separated by the
construction of a road to the bus station and car park in
1971–2.† The house is especially fine; early C18 of seven bays
with segmental pediment on the central Tuscan doorcase. Two
three-storey canted bays on the garden front. Third storey
added by George Wegg *c.* 1742, who also laid out the grounds
behind the house, extending S to the Roman wall. The wall
along the street incorporates stone rustications, probably by
Deane. E of the house, a drinking fountain dated 1864.

Across from The Minories, No. 83 (GATE HOUSE) and No.
84 (EAST LODGE), an excellent house, probably of the C16 but
refronted for William and Susan Boys in 1680, the date on a
jetty bracket. Plastered, with imitation rustication, and four
symmetrical gables with curved oriels under. In the centre an
oval window. Next to it No. 85, WINSLEY HOUSE, late C17,
timber-framed and plastered, with a row of carved brackets to
the cornice, but transformed by the insertion of Georgian
Gothick sashes with plaster hoodmoulds and arched heads to
the front door and carriage arch. Then HILLCREST, three-
storey, three-bay late C18 brick house, and GREY FRIARS
(adult community college), whose centre, dated 1755, has two
two-storey canted bays either side of the doorcase with
pediment and attached Ionic columns. Above this a Venetian
window and then another pediment in the deep parapet. Two
overpowering wings by *St Aubyn & Wadling*, 1904, when the
building was in use as a convent. Garden front, 1780, has
Venetian windows on both floors flanking an elaborate canted
bay, classical on the ground floor and Gothic on the first.
Finally ALL SAINTS' HOUSE, C18 brick with a two-storey
canted bay on the E front. For the continuation of High Street
W, see Perambulation 5.

2. North of the High Street:

2a. The Dutch Quarter

The DUTCH QUARTER, in the angle between the High Street
and North Hill, contains perhaps the most attractive and architecturally rewarding streets in Colchester. They are narrow, not
straight, and relatively unspoilt. First, running N down the E
side of the Town Hall, is WEST STOCKWELL STREET. On the
W side, the former public library (*see* Public Buildings), and
the churchyard of the medieval St Runwald (dem. 1878).‡ On
the l. at the corner with St Runwald Street, VICTORIA

---

* *Ancient architecture restored and improved* (1741).
† The bus station is to be redeveloped, with a new arts building by *Rafael Viñoly*
between East Hill House and the Roman wall due to open in 2008. The view of
the summerhouse will be restored.
‡ Arcade reused in St Albright, Stanway, and some of the rubble used to build two
houses in Maldon Road (*see* p. 297).

CHAMBERS, good mid-C19 commercial architecture (J.F. Goodey and W.T. Cressall had their offices here): stock brick, with arched windows to the offices on the first floor and the ground floor almost entirely glazed. Opposite, Nos. 3–6, late C15, with two gables to the front, exposed close studding, the upper storey jettied on brackets with demi-figures of angels. Original screens passage doorway, on the r. of which lay the hall, window tracery with cusped heads, and several surviving doorways inside. Further down, Nos. 8–9, a five-bay early C18 house subdivided with adjoining doorcases, one very much larger than the other. Opposite St Martin (*see* Churches), ST MARTIN'S HOUSE, built for Dr Richard Daniell and probably designed by *James Deane*, dated 1733. Rusticated doorcase, and heavy wooden cornice projecting beyond the end walls. At the rear, Tuscan columns support a first-floor garden room with Venetian windows. Some good plasterwork over the staircase. Added on to its N side is a former Telephone Exchange, well-mannered *Office of Works* Neo-Georgian of 1928, behind it to the r. a less-well-mannered six-storey manager's office, 1965, and behind that Colchester's principal eyesore, the downright rude eight-storey TELEPHONE EXCHANGE erected 1968–9 using Crown immunity to override local opposition. Thus did public architecture decline in the course of the C20.

Domesticity resumes with No. 62, *c.* 1600 with a late C18 front, plastered with plain Tuscan doorcase and curved iron balconies on the first floor, and Nos. 59–60, a single mid-C18 house for Samuel Wall, divided probably in the C19. Giant angle pilasters and at its centre, below a three-bay pediment, two doorways. Between them two Venetian windows above each other; the lower one looks C19. Across the road again, N of St Martin's churchyard, COLCHESTER TOWNHOUSE, a youth club by *Sir Guy Dawber, Fox & Robinson*, 1969, in hard and uninviting brick and concrete. Next downhill, Nos. 11–12, unassuming C18 red brick, and No. 13, C17, timber-framed and plastered; Tudor Gothic doorway. Nos. 14–17 are good 1980s infill (*see* below). Opposite, No. 56, at the corner of Walter's Yard, C16, with two gables and jettied upper storey that steps down the hill to Nos. 53–55, C15 with cross-wings (the N wing rebuilt in the C17), again jettied. Restored 1958, when the lost gable of the S wing was reinstated.

The street now turns to the l. Finally, on the E side, the STOCKWELL ARMS, C15 but over-restored. Straight ahead, closing the view, timber-framed and plastered Nos. 19–21, incorporated into the scheme for forty-seven vernacular-style houses and flats by the Borough Architect, *Ken Bell* (job architect *Russell W. Rose*), begun in 1977. Some of these are along the N and E sides of West Stockwell Street, the remainder in courtyards created to the rear: WAT TYLER WALK and JOHN BALL WALK. Some of the detailing looks a little mean, with narrow door- and window-frames comparing unfavourably to those seen on its older neighbours, but overall the result is impressive, with deeply projecting upper storeys, gables and steeply pitched roofs on the right scale providing appropriate rhythm to the street. Colour contributes to the effect too, pastel shades but varied. The layout also incorporates an especially picturesque group (Nos. 29–31) with three gables and two jetties on brackets. This was among forty-two houses restored in 1958 by *J. S. Orchard*, Borough Engineer.

E now along STOCKWELL STREET, with cottages on its S side, to EAST STOCKWELL STREET, of similar character to its western counterpart. Climbing uphill on the W side, No. 30, PEAKE'S HOUSE. Exposed close studding with jettied upper storey and gable with moulded bressumer. The l. half is the surviving portion of a mid- to late C14 hall house, of which the service end and screens passage stood further to the l. but were demolished in 1935. The hall itself was rebuilt or remodelled *c.* 1550 as a three-storey house, linked in the early C17 to the separate building to its r., of *c.* 1500, by a brick chimneystack. Restored for the Landmark Trust by *Peregrine Bryant Architects*, 1995. Further up on the same side, Nos. 37 and 38, a picturesque C16 house with S gable and projecting upper storey. Then in the corner of the churchyard, a small former church school, 1847, now a house: red brick with unusual black brick patterns round the windows, like picture frames. On the churchyard's S side, STOCKWELL HOUSE, C17 with early C18 red brick six-bay front. Pedimented doorcase. On the N side a canted first-floor oriel beneath a Venetian attic window.

The street's E side is dominated by the former Congregational Chapel (*see* Churches) and then to the S of St Helen's Lane a row of C18 houses. On the corner of William's Walk No. 7, THE GABLES, C17 with C18 alterations and additions; gable at the W end and projecting upper storey. E along ST HELEN'S LANE, the former National School (S side) by *H. W. Hayward*, 1860–1, brick with stone dressings, and on the corner of Maidenburgh Street St Helen's Chapel (*see* Churches).

MAIDENBURGH STREET has a good row of houses (Nos. 15–26) down the E side, of which No. 23 has the upper storey projecting at two levels; restored 1958. (For the remains of the Roman theatre at No. 73, *see* p. 260.) At the S end of the street, more infill by the Borough Architect, 1984–5. At the bottom of the hill, opposite the entrance to Castle Park (*see* p. 276), the street becomes MIDDLE MILL ROAD, with Nos. 3–5 on the corner, C18 brick and weatherboarded cottages with pedimented doorways. The High Street can be regained via RYEGATE ROAD, with the Museum Resource Centre on the W side, originally Daniell's Brewery but reconstructed as the Arclight Works after 1921.

2b. North Hill

The view up the High Street is closed by No. 67 WEST HILL, now the Post Office, an extravagant Mock Tudor display with three gables and exposed timbers. From here NORTH HILL drops away sharply, with houses on both sides stepping down the hill, always a nice effect. Opposite St Peter (*see* Churches)

No. 60, dating from 1650 but with a Georgian brick front, stately, with two symmetrical two-storey canted bays and a Tuscan doorcase beneath a Venetian window and pediment. No. 59 has a Gothick doorcase, with composite shafts instead of columns, and a pediment decorated with tracery. Another good Georgian doorcase on No. 58, Ionic with open pediment. No. 57 by contrast is C17, jettied, timber-framed and plastered. Restored by *Roff Marsh*, 1964, as his own office. On the E side Nos. 4–5 (with little iron balconies to the windows, iron window heads, and the date 1809) and 8 are Georgian.

The best timber-framed houses come lower down. Behind the frontage of Nos. 13–15 is a range at right angles datable by its carpentry to the early C15: long-wall jetty with framing exposed and original double window with cinquefoil-headed lights. Inside, on first floor, late C16 or early C17 wall painting: *trompe l'œil* frieze of a geometric motif giving the secondary impression of rafter stop ends over imitative panelling. No. 18 is late C16 with a Late Georgian gault brick front. Painted black-letter inscriptions in principal ground-floor room. Nos. 19–20 again Georgian, with one Venetian window. Near the bottom the MARQUIS OF GRANBY, *c.* 1525. Heavily restored by *T. H. Baker*, 1913–14, but with exceedingly good, very richly carved interior detail in the E wing. The main ceiling beam with foliage, animals, dragons, etc. rests on brackets with very well characterized figures. Also in this room a painted bas-relief plaster panel by *J. Hearn* depicting the mythical origin of the Colchester Oyster Feast, based on a design by *W. Gurney Benham*, *c.* 1914. The passageway from the street contains two doorways, probably once leading from the screens passage to the offices – wooden surrounds with leaf carvings in the spandrels. On the W side, No. 47, C18 plastered front and C17 rear range with original mullioned windows and carved grotesques supporting the jetty. Early C17 wall painting on ground floor.

MIDDLEBOROUGH, at the foot of the hill, has a portion of the Roman wall, rebuilt in the Middle Ages, forming part of No. 1. Beyond it the C20 makes its mark in a none-too-subtle manner with new roads encircling the bastions of the ROYAL INSURANCE (now Royal London) offices by *Cruickshank & Seward*, 1979–82: brick, of irregular shape round two court-yards, with towers adding to its castle-like appearance. In its shadow, BRIDGE HOUSE, now a pub, a pretty picture by the river: C17, whitewashed, gabled to the street, and with recessed oval brick panels between the S front's Gothick windows. Across the river, on the l., the former CASTLE INN, and on the r., very attractively sited, RIVERSIDE COTTAGES, C17 with exposed timber-framing. NORTH BRIDGE itself, over the River Colne, 1843, is of cast iron by *Richard Coleman*, three arches; widened 1903 by *Herbert Goodyear*, Borough Engineer.

Beyond the bridge, NORTH STATION ROAD is of less interest. On the W side, the former RAILWAY MISSION by *William Willett*, 1896, stock brick with red dressings, and the curious-

looking VICTORIA INN, recognizably C17 with its hipped roof
and cornice but the brickwork rendered and panelled in the
C19. On the E side, No. 27 is the jettied cross-wing of a C15
house, the hall rebuilt in the C17 and C18 now forming No. 25.
For buildings N of the railway line, *see* Mile End.

3. South of the High Street: Head Street, Queen Street, and the area between

HEAD STREET runs S from the top of the High Street's W end.
At first all the interest is on the W side, e.g. No. 21, on the
corner of Church Street, early C16 with projecting upper floor
and original moulded bressumer running along the N side,
rebuilt 1834 following a fire. Nos. 33–35 comprise the former
Post Office of 1872–4, four-storey brick with Gothic detailing,
with a large, seven-bay addition of 1934–6 by *D. N. Dyke* in the
unmistakable Neo-Georgian of the *Office of Works*, a good
example of the genre. Doors with Gibbs surrounds at either
end, giant brick pilasters rising through two of the three storeys
and stone urns on the parapet. Now the ODEON, rebuilt
behind by *Stephen Limbrick Associates*, 2001–2. Then Nos.
37–39, late C18 brick front of five bays with a central semicircular Doric porch that continues as a two-storey bow. Next to
it No. 41, late C18 gault brick upper floor, with a shallow bow
over the r. half and a deeper one on the l. over the entrance to
HEADGATE COURT (formerly King's Head Yard). On the far
side, the former King's Head Inn, now offices. C16 or C17, two
storeys, timber-framed and plastered. Main front late C17, five
bays with sashes and central doorcase. Lower wing on N side
of courtyard of same date.

On the E side, S of Culver Street West, the Culver Centre
(*see* below), which lies partly behind the over-restored façade
of Nos. 44–52 (Woolworths), all that remains of a fine three-
storey brick house of 1763–5, seven bays with a three-bay
central pediment. Replacement ground floor using C18 motifs
but not in keeping. To its S a three-bay, two-storey addition,
and then No. 54, early C17 with a brick front of 1774: five bays
with eared central window over a heavy doorcase with open
pediment head and semicircular fanlight. Across the yard,
REBOW'S HOUSE, the house of Sir Isaac Rebow, M.P. and
Recorder of Colchester. Built *c.* 1697, with medieval cellar,
divided in the C18 when it was refronted and given a central
oriel. Two gables at the rear with jettied first floor supported
on carved brackets.

In SIR ISAAC'S WALK, No. 17 forms part of Rebow's House.
Nos. 12–14 have a coved plaster eaves cornice dated 1711.
Further E, on the N side but set back behind a handsome front
garden, No. 11, an interesting early C18 house with a central
bow window of a curve that is more than a semicircle and
crowned by a concave roof *à la chinoise*. After Trinity Street, a
row of single-storey ALMSHOUSES, now shops, rebuilt 1897
and 1905 by *C. E. Butcher* for Lady D'Arcy's Charity. On the

s side, Nos. 6, 6a and 6b are built on the old town wall and incorporate SCHEREGATE, with steps s down to St John's Street. The buildings are C17 (one dated 1692), and form a very attractive group; restored by *Ronald Geary*, 1966–7. E of Scheregate Sir Isaac's Walk becomes ELD LANE, with the Baptist Church (*see* Churches) set back from the street on the N side. On the s side VINEYARD STEPS, 1976 and 1996, leads through to the Roman wall.

The area between here and the High Street saw major change in the late C20. From w to E, first the CULVER CENTRE, 1985–8, by *Sheppard Robson*, a new square linked by staggered streets to Culver Street West (via Shewell Walk, formerly Shewell Road), Sir Isaac's Walk and, through Woolworths, to Head Street. Big, brash Postmodern of the booming 1980s, but varied and on the whole agreeable. Services all underground, entered from St John's Street. In Shewell Walk the Neo-Georgian central block of the former Public Library by *Marshall Sisson*, 1936–9, has been retained. The l. wing was demolished in 1987, the r. wing never built. Everything else is new, as is most of CULVER STREET WEST. Here most of the buildings lead through to the High Street, including NEXT by the *John Brunton Partnership*, 1988–9.

Then comes TRINITY STREET, running N–S. Largely unspoilt, with good houses on both sides. At the N end is Holy Trinity (*see* Churches), and a good view beyond the tower of the upper part of the Town Hall. On the w side No. 6, a seven-bay C17 timber-framed house with an C18 brick front. TYMPERLEYS (Clock Museum) lies back at right angles to the street, reached by an archway in No. 7. Late C15 two-bay house, extended westwards *c.* 1580 and stair-turret added *c.* 1680. Timber-framed, with framing exposed on the front, the projecting upper storey plastered, brick nogging on the ground floor. Inside, original moulded ceiling beams and staircase with late C17 twisted balusters. Restored and altered by *R. J. Page*, 1956. At Trinity Street's s end, where it meets Sir Isaac's Walk, the CLARENCE INN, C16 but much restored, jettied on two sides. E of Trinity Street's N end is the LION WALK CENTRE, 1974–6 by *Frederick Gibberd & Partners* in association with *Stanley Bragg & Associates*, including the PUBLIC LIBRARY, Trinity Square, 1980. Its main E–W thoroughfare is CULVER WALK, connecting on the N via the courtyard of the Red Lion Hotel to the High Street and on the E side to Culver Street East. In the middle it opens out where it meets LION WALK, which runs s to Eld Lane. Stylistically somewhat heavy-handed, slipping between the two stools of International Modern and Neo-Vernacular revival. Brick with box-like projections above first-floor level with slate tile-hanging. Concrete and mosaic sculptural panels at entrance to BHS by *Henry & Joyce Collins*, 1976.

In CULVER STREET EAST, the surviving façade of the Co-operative Society's store by *Goodey & Cressall*, *c.* 1914, brick with stone dressings, the upper storey divided by pilasters with a central oriel beneath a shaped gable set in a straight gable. Its stone-faced extension is dated 1926. Further along Culver Street East, two substantial C18 town houses face All Saints (*see* Churches), five bays each. No. 3, dated 1743, has blue brick chequer and an oval window in the centre of the upper storey; No. 1, an impressive arched doorcase with attached Corinthian columns and fanlight.

QUEEN STREET, leading s, has less of importance, but the early C14 cross-wing of Nos. 7–9 at the N end has a jettied upper floor and below it evidence of a medieval shop window, the earliest known in Colchester. s of the bus station, No. 37, mid-C18, considerably altered in the C20: three storeys, red and blue brick, with vestigial pilasters and pediment over the central first-floor window. Garden front with central three-bay pediment above first floor broken to take the top-floor window, which has its own little pediment. Opposite, PRIORY WALK, the redevelopment of a 1920s arcade leading through to Long Wyre Street; 1968 by *Stanley Bragg & Associates*, who refurbished it 1989–90 with arched entrances that link visually with the Norman arches of St Botolph's Priory nearby. Of the shops in Priory Walk, Sainsbury's best preserves its 1960s character, with concrete sculptural panels by *Henry & Joyce Collins*. Queen Street continues as ST BOTOLPH'S STREET, with the ruins of the Priory (*see* p. 271) and St Botolph's Church (*see* Churches) on the E side. A short way down PRIORY STREET, on its s side, are the former British Schools of 1852, brick with three tall gabled windows overlooking the street, and tiled roof with black diaper pattern. On the N side of the roundabout at the bottom, FAGIN'S BAR, late C19 pub, three storeys with rusticated brick quoins and open segmental pediment over the central first-floor window, and a projecting gable with decorative bargeboards and false half-timbering.

Back w now along Osborne Street to the E end of ST JOHN'S STREET, where the SCHEREGATE HOTEL sustains the picturesque tone set by Scheregate. C18 timber-framed and plastered, with Gothic hoodmoulded windows and porch. Effort has been taken on the N side of the street to continue the character of Sir Isaac's Walk, even if this verges on tweeness: of the row of C17 shops and houses that form Nos. 41–46, No. 45 is now 'St John's Wynd', an echo of Scheregate. No. 47 was demolished to make way for the underground service entrance to Culver Square in 1985, which involved cutting though a 35-ft (8-metre) section of the Roman wall; part of this was rebuilt in 1987. All this care does not prepare one for the s side and for the fortress-like, tile-hung shopping centre and car park built originally for Tesco by *Gordon White & Hood, c.* 1977. Cream-coloured giant tetrastyle Doric porticoes linked by a metal arcade have been added to the St John's Street front in a desperate attempt to jolly it up, but the true character of the beast can still be appreciated from Southway. Also on the s side, and perhaps equally startling in its day, the former PLAY-HOUSE, 1928–9 by *John Fairweather*, now a pub, converted by

Tuffin, Ferraby & Taylor, 1993–4. Brick with stone dressings and just enough Art Deco detailing to make it interesting. Back on the N side, a large commercial block fronting on to Headgate that extends back down both St John's Street and Sir Isaac's Walk, 1909 by *Goodey & Cressall*, and on the s corner, along the E side of Headgate, auction rooms (now a restaurant) by *J. F. Goodey*, 1891, two storeys with five large arched windows stepping down the hill.

4. West of the High Street: Balkerne Gardens to Crouch Street

The closing of the Roman Balkerne Gate, apparently in the late C3 (*see* p. 259) resulted in the area W of High Street becoming something of a backwater, which it remains to this day. It is reached by BALKERNE LANE, physically and visually separated by the buildings facing the W end of the High Street. Off the N side of Balkerne Lane, in BALKERNE CLOSE, TUDOR COTTAGE, C16, with exposed timbers on the upper floor front, brick infill below. Straight ahead is PROVIDENT PLACE, almshouses built round a large garden for the Colchester Provident Asylum. On the N side, a long two-storey, gault brick range. Round-headed ground-floor windows, some in arched recesses. Originally twelve bays, 1836, of which the middle four break forward slightly with a two-bay pediment. Eight-bay extension by *G. G. Pye*, 1879, and a further four-bay extension in the C20 that destroyed the symmetry. On the garden's W side, cottage-style Alice Twyman House, late C19 grey brick with fish-scale roof. C20 buildings of less interest. At the far end of Balkerne Lane, the C18 HOLE-IN-THE-WALL pub, over the N carriageway of the Balkerne Gate. Enlarged 1843 to provide a view of the newly opened railway.

   s of Balkerne Lane is an open space with a curious assemblage of buildings: the 'Jumbo' water tower, Mercury Theatre, Friends' Meeting House, and St Mary-at-the-Walls (*see* under Churches and Public Buildings). CHURCH STREET runs off from the SE corner. On the s side No. 8, the Old Court Coffee House, formerly County Court Offices, *c.* 1802: single-storey stucco front of five bays brick with a shallow tetrastyle portico *in antis* and recessed clerestory. Opposite, No. 3, early C19 red brick, the façade with gault brick first floor and the ground floor rendered with banded rustication. On the s side of St Mary's churchyard, in CHURCH WALK, CHARLES MAY HOUSE, formerly St Mary's Cottage: Gothick *cottage orné* (although not as *orné* as it once was), 1823.

Church Walk leads through to the s end of Head Street, with the start of CROUCH STREET a few yards further on. Crouch Street was, at least until the building of the by-pass in the 1930s, the main road into Colchester from London, and this is reflected in its buildings. The first section, W as far as Balkerne Hill, is still very much part of the town. On the SW corner with Headgate, the BULL HOTEL, C18 and C19 front, but evidence of an earlier coaching inn behind. Also on the s side, the former ODEON, 1931 by *Cecil Masey*: vaguely Spanish, with an early example of an 'atmospheric' interior. Then Nos. 20 and 22, mid C18 for John Cole, merchant. Brick with painted quoins, bands and cornice, five bays and two-and-a-half storeys with the middle bay slightly projected and the central window arched. The flow is now interrupted by BALKERNE HILL, created 1976–81, with on its W side a large three-storey CAR PARK by the *Borough Architect*, 1981, in the Romano-military style favoured at that time. Life-size figures representing agriculture originally decorated *Brandon*'s Corn Exchange of 1845 (*see* Perambulation 1). Beyond Balkerne Hill, the interest is all on the N side, a most attractive row, mostly with shops on the ground floor. The exceptions, all of gault brick, are No. 55, Late Georgian with two shallow bows, the early C19 KING'S ARMS, and further W No. 107, CROUCHED FRIARS, *c.* 1776 by *William Phillips* with C19 additions, and finally WELLINGTON PLACE, a terrace of four houses dated 1837.

Off the N side of Crouch Street, in RAWSTORN ROAD, ST MARY'S HALL by *J. W. Start*, 1899, brick with Bath stone dressings, quite elaborate, with two tall W windows rising through the eaves into dormers with half-hipped roofs.

5. East Hill and East Street

EAST HILL is the continuation of the High Street. It begins with the Church of St James and St Paul (*see* Churches) on the S side. On the N side, No. 86, Greek Revival of 1817–18 for Rev. John Saville, two-storey, five-bay stucco front, but the central bay very wide with a tripartite window on the first floor over a heavy Greek Doric porch. Downhill No. 82, Early Georgian of seven bays, with segment-headed windows and central doorcase with Corinthian columns. On the S side, C18 timber-framed, Nos. 6 and 7 on the corner with exposed timbers along Priory Street, then Nos. 9 and 10, four-bay Early Georgian town houses, extended after 1775, with two doorways side by side in the centre, the l. one impressive with Roman Doric pilasters and a broad segmental pediment. No. 15 has an C18 front with a very attractive two-storey canted bay window, with arched heads to the windows and decorated entablature. By contrast Nos. 16 and 17 are early C16, with exposed timbers, upper floor projecting on brackets, and at the E end a good C16 door with lozenge shapes in each of its twelve panels.

Returning to East Hill's N side, No. 78, doctors' surgery by *John Burrell* and *Matthew Hartley* of *Care Design Group*, 1993, stock brick central block with two plastered jettied cross-wings, competent pastiche. Next to it but set back from the road, No. 76, the RECTORY of St James and St Paul, by *Teulon*, 1859, but not at his most exciting. Brick with some black diapers, small-scale and domestic. Then the buildings of the former Eagle

Brewery, 1882–8 by *H. Stopes*, whose family founded it in 1828. Italianate, red and white brick with some stone dressings. Two-storey block at No. 75 with three arched bays linked by a later addition to the main office building, which rises to three and four storeys. Brewhouse behind, up to six storeys, now flats. Further downhill, No. 73, early C19 stucco front to an earlier building, two storeys, the doorway with recessed fluted columns carrying Empire capitals, and adjoining it Nos. 71 and 72, originally a C17 or earlier structure, the front again early C19 but this time gault brick with label mouldings over the windows and a small central pediment. Opposite, a very pleasing row of houses, Nos. 25–42, mainly C17 and C18, with just that degree of variety in form and colour to give added interest. Nos. 38 and 39 form a C16 house with cross-wing at the E end and projecting upper storey, with C17 extensions to the rear along Rosebery Avenue. More timber-framing on the other side of Rosebery Avenue, conspicuous at Nos. 40 to 51, C16 with exposed timbers. Finally, back on the N side, No. 55, an intrusive but welcome example of High Victorian brickwork, with a steep decorative tiled roof, built as the parish orphanage, 1871.

At the foot of the hill the street broadens out into a green with EAST BAY along its S side. On the corner of Brook Street Nos. 1 and 2, a C15 cross-wing to the E and the main block rebuilt in the C17. At the other end of the row the entrance to BERRYFIELD COTTAGES, single-storey terrace of twelve red brick Arts and Crafts almshouses, 1895–6 by *G.H. Page*, refurbished and extended by *Duncan Clark & Beckett*, 2002–4. Tucked away between here and the river, C18 BAY COTTAGE, exceedingly picturesque timber-framed and plastered, and EAST BAY HOUSE, a double house of c. 1780. N front of four plus two bays with ground-floor bow window, four-bay E front with two more bows, one two-storey. Ionic doorcases. EAST BRIDGE itself, over the River Colne, 1802, five arches of brick, the carriageway widened 1928 by *Harold Collins*, Borough Engineer, but retaining the original structure including stone piers and iron railings. Across the bridge, to the l., the former EAST MILLS of Marriage & Sons. The mill, recorded in 1311, was purchased by Edward Marriage in 1840. Rebuilt 1885–95 mainly in stock brick, dwarfing the original small Georgian miller's house on the E side. Mostly by *J.F. Goodey*, but with additions by *Brightwen Binyon*, 1893–5, to whom are due some of the more picturesque elements. Large tower with pyramidal slate roof and hoist lofts, one timber-framed with brick nogging. Closed 1976, now flats. At its gate the OLD SIEGE HOUSE, Nos. 73–75 East Street, a good timber-framed building, early C16. Purchased by Marriage in 1902 and restored by *Brown & Burgess*, 1905, who exposed the timbers and revealed bullet holes (marked on the street front) from the 1648 siege. L-plan, with jettied upper storey on two sides and carved corner post. Inside, original moulded ceiling beams and panelling.

EAST STREET continues with timber-framed houses on both
sides. On the S, Nos. 11–12, C16 with projecting upper storey,
restored by Colchester Civic Society in 1936, and Nos. 24–25,
of C15 origin with cross-wing at the W end. Nos. 21–23 have an
Early Georgian plastered front with a Gibbs surround to the
door and Venetian window above. Opposite, Nos. 60–66, with
a row of four gables. Timber-framed and plastered, most of the
first floor jettied. The first gable to the l., over a tall archway, is
C15, as is the next; the third belongs to the oldest part of the
building, mid C14, the cross-wing at the high end of an open
hall that was replaced in the mid C17 by the fourth gable and
the range to the r. Restoration by *Roy Grimwade*, 2004–5,
revealed original mouldings and a traceried window in the C14
part. E of Ipswich Road Nos. 29–33, C16 but with alterations
dated 1692 in a plaster oval wreath: jettied first floor along the
whole front, six sashes on the upper floor. Another picturesque
group leading up to No. 41 on the corner of Moorside, C17 with
exposed timbers and jettied first floor. Restored *c.* 1962, by
Grace Faithfull Roper, who had done the same in 1937–9 for the
ROSE AND CROWN HOTEL opposite, originally an early C14
aisled hall house with E and W cross-wings, the upper storey of
the hall inserted in the mid C16. C18 and C19 alterations largely
removed during Roper's heavy restoration; she exposed all the
existing timbers and brought in more from elsewhere. EAST-
GATE JUNCTION SIGNAL BOX, 1924, a non-standard design,
anticipates Roper's work with its half-timbering.

6. West: Lexden Road

For those who wish to see how the prosperous citizens of C19
Colchester housed themselves, LEXDEN ROAD and the roads
leading off it to the S in the angle formed with Maldon Road
is the place to look, and the effect – large houses on generous
plots – is almost unspoilt, for a distance of about ½ m. W of
the County Hospital (*see* Public Buildings). From the E end,
the tone is set by No. 19, gault brick, two storeys, five-bay front
with large central Doric porch. 1837, probably by *H.H.
Hayward* for Thomas Catchpool, a local ironfounder. Then
Hayward's contemporary ST MARY'S TERRACE EAST, Nos.
21–31, three storeys, each end of the eleven-bay front breaking
forward beneath a pediment. ST MARY'S TERRACE WEST
(Nos. 33–51) came twelve years earlier, five pairs of large semi-
detached gault brick houses set well back from the road. The
next point of interest on the N side is THE TURRETS, No. 89:
1817–18 for Francis Smythies, town clerk, attributed to *Robert
Lugar*, a plastered fantasy with battlements and turrets, sited
at the edge of the high ground overlooking Lexden village.
Now part of ST MARY'S SCHOOL, based in a late C19 house.
Additions include arts block and classrooms by *Laurie Wood
Architects*, 2001–2. More early C19 gault brick houses at No. 93
and Nos. 95–97, the latter with a porch supported on impos-
sibly slender cast-iron columns.

The S side exhibits less restraint and more variety. OXFORD HOUSE SCHOOL, on the corner of Oxford Road, is a riot of High Victorian Gothic, with pointed windows, turrets, and gables with decorative bargeboards, dated 1877. In OXFORD ROAD itself some less extreme examples of the same style (Oxford Lodge, Merton Lodge), but then comes No. 6, a sort of Queen Anne with gables of every variety and an octagonal corner turret, but in stock brick rather than the expected red. On the opposite side, No. 3 is by *George Lee*, builder, 1878, No. 5 by *J. F. Goodey*, 1888, and Nos. 7–9 by *Goodey & Cressall*, 1893, variations on the villa theme with turrets, bay windows and half-timbering. Off Oxford Road, in GRAY ROAD, an ordinary brick terrace house given a Dutch gable and the name MAISONETTE in 1878, and in CREFFIELD ROAD No. 25, more Dutch gables but on a grander scale. Oxford Road and Creffield Road were developed on land sold by C.G. Round in 1876 and 1878. Creffield Road leads to WELLESLEY ROAD which, as Blatch Street, was the first of these streets to be laid out S of Lexden Road, from 1865; it included an elongated square in the middle, of which much remains. On the W side of Wellesley Road are the buildings of the High School (*see* Public Buildings), and at the N end WELLESLEY HOUSE, conventional Queen Anne Revival.

MALDON ROAD contains houses one or two steps down the social scale from those just seen. Few individual houses of note: THE CLOISTERS and ST RUNWALD'S, on opposite corners of SALISBURY AVENUE, built largely from the rubble of St Runwald, High Street (dem. 1878). ½ m. further on, No. 155 stands out: house and studio in the manner of Voysey, 1899 by *Alick Horsnell* for C.H. Baskett, assistant master at Colchester School of Art. Back to Lexden Road, and after the Royal Grammar School (*see* Public Buildings), which harmonizes with the road's domestic character, is No. 14, WEST-FIELDS, a mid-C19 two-storey villa, grey brick with yellow brick dressings, classical (large ground-floor Venetian window with vermiculated rustication set in a semicircular arch) yet unmistakably Victorian. Then three more roads leading off to the S, Beverley Road, West Lodge Road, and The Avenue, the last of these laid out by 1868 by *H.W. Hayward*, who bankrupted himself in the process. They in turn lead to Cambridge Road and Victoria Road, laid out in the late 1870s by a local builder, *Walter Chambers*. In BEVERLEY ROAD, BEVERLEY TERRACE is red brick with stock brick dressings and black diapers, decorative bargeboards and gables etc. No. 16, opposite, is stock brick, Italianate with a square tower after the manner of Osborne House: 1874–5 by *George Gard Pye* for Charles Davey of Davey, Paxman & Co. At the beginning of CAMBRIDGE ROAD, THE HOLLIES, stock brick, dated 1878. THE AVENUE has similar contrasts: at each end, large red brick houses with Dutch gables, that at the N end (No. 26 Lexden Road) dated 1885; in between, sedate stock brick terraces and villas; but Nos. 10–12 are High Victorian

Gothic, probably by the same architect as Nos. 2–4 Lexden Road.

VINT CRESCENT, W of The Avenue, is surprising; six two-storey blocks of flats looking like semi-detached houses, by *D.C. Wadhwa*, 1937. Rendered, with metal windows and Art Deco doors, little balconies, and roofs of green glazed pantiles. Beyond, SOVEREIGN CRESCENT, 1997–8 by *Mark Perkins Partnership* for Lexden Restorations Ltd: classic three-storey town houses, each two bays wide, stock brick with rusticated stucco ground floor and slate roofs. For the continuation of Lexden Road westwards, *see* Lexden.

7. *South and East: New Town, The Hythe, and St John's Green*

The SE quadrant of extra-mural Colchester consists principally of the parishes of St Giles and St Botolph (known also as West Donyland) and of St Leonard-at-the-Hythe (known as Hythe or The Hythe). West Donyland includes the Colchester Garrison (*see* above), and its southern portion also comprises Berechurch (*see* p. 133). Hythe is dominated by James Paxman's ironworks, on the S side of Hythe Hill, and between the two is New Town, developed from 1878.

From Colchester Town Station (*see* Public Buildings), MILITARY ROAD leads SE, where one immediately encounters KENDALL'S ALMSHOUSES on the NE side and WINNOCK'S ALMSHOUSES on the SW. The latter are the older, dated 1678, a range of six, and a good example of brickwork of the period. Low, broad proportions, with a pediment and two superimposed orders of which the upper oddly dies into the wall like buttresses. Restored 1990. Kendall's are two ranges side by side, 1791 and 1803, each of four bays and two storeys, and each with a small pediment. To both have been added single-storey, red brick dwellings, 1914–34, all in the same style with gabled fronts, many donated and probably designed by the builders, *George Dobson & Son.*

WINNOCK ROAD leads E. NEW TOWN HOUSE (No. 2), 1882, marks the start of New Town, begun in 1878. 293 houses had been built by 1885. The developer was *J. F. Goodey*, who lived at the large NEW TOWN LODGE on the corner of New Town Road, which displays much of the pre-cast concrete detailing in which he specialized. On the opposite corner, ASHFORD LODGE, smaller and plainer in stock brick but with similar detailing. Good semi-detached houses of the same period in the continuation eastwards of Winnock Road, also semi-detached 'cottages' in Winsley Road dated 1881, but the best and largest houses are in the southern part of NEW TOWN ROAD, e.g. GLADSTONE LODGE on the corner of Gladstone Road. Smaller terraced houses in the northern streets running S from Barrack Street indicate the developers' intention of creating a social mix. Goodey and his partner *W. T. Cressall* also designed the Wesleyan Methodist Church in WIMPOLE ROAD (*see* Churches). Off Winnock Road, GOODEY CLOSE, housing for Colchester District Council by *P. Andrew Borges & Associates*, 1976–7: mixed development of houses, flats and bungalows using brick, render and black weatherboarding.

At the S end of New Town Road we are back in MILITARY ROAD, and on the S side a row of five ornamental Gothic villas, Nos. 77–89, mid C19, red brick with black diapers, steep pitched roofs with decorative slates and curved bargeboards on the gables. Originally named Camp Villas and intended for army officers. In OLD HEATH ROAD, Military Road's continuation, are WINSLEY'S ALMSHOUSES, established according to Arthur Winsley's will (proved 1727) in an existing late C16 brick farmhouse. This was given a remarkably freely treated frontispiece, rendered and painted, the sides of which are polygonal shafts like medieval turrets, the crowning motif a pediment on two curves as in the Dutch gables of about 1630. The upper floor, fitted up as a chapel, contains a small-scale copy of Winsley's monument in St James and St Paul, East Hill (*see* Churches). Wings jut forward on both sides to create an open courtyard, made steadily deeper by successive additions from 1808 to 1954. These are broadly in keeping, apart from those of 1906–7 (Nos. 5–6) which break the accepted skyline with gables; the culprits were *George Dobson & Son*. A new square of seventeen almshouses was built to the E along Old Heath Road, 1933–8, by *Duncan Clark & Beckett* (Nos. 41–57), and another square of ten SW of the original buildings, 1936, by *F. Stanley Daniell* (Nos. 78–87). Further buildings of 1968 and 1975.

Beyond Winsley's Almshouses, Old Heath Road drops down to the valley of a stream that runs E to the River Colne and powered three mills. First, on the W side of Old Heath Road, CANNOCK MILL, rebuilt 1845: weatherboarded, three storeys with hoist loft, the stock brick mill house looking down on it. Upstream, reached via BOURNE ROAD, is BOURNE MILL, a 66 delightful piece of Late Elizabethan playfulness. Built 1591 as a fishing lodge by Thomas Lucas, of reused freestone rubble and brick, as well as septaria; there is also flint galletting. It has mullioned windows and two wildly oversized gable ends of the utmost exuberance. They go up in convex and concave curves and carry four pairs of obelisks, with an octagonal chimney-shaft at the apex. It was originally two storeys, with one large room looking out over the pond. After 1833 it was converted to a flour mill; another floor was inserted, the roof was raised to a steeper pitch and dormer windows and weatherboarded hoist loft added. Given to The National Trust in 1936, who restored the machinery. C19 miller's cottage on E side. Downstream of Cannock Mill, DISTILLERY LANE leads to the site of Hull Mill, with an appealingly rambling late C19 house, MAITLANDS, on the N side of the pond, and on the E side HULL HOUSE, probably a former mill house, dating back to the C16.

Distillery Lane comes out near the S end of HYTHE QUAY, once Colchester's port, first used in the C12 but not much developed until the C14. Now a mixture of light industry, disused warehouses and warehouse-style housing that is not as picturesque as such mixtures sometimes are: the balance between decay and regeneration is not (yet) quite right. The old river crossing at the N end of the quay has been by-passed by main roads leading to out-of-town shopping centres, notably TESCO supermarket by *Biscoe & Stanton* at the N end on the corner of Greenstead Road. Pavilions and other decorative features give some character to what would otherwise be a bleak corner. More interesting is the B&Q WAREHOUSE on the E side of Colne Causeway by *Dawe & Geddes Architects*, 2000–1, a refreshing piece of contemporary design. (For University Quays, E of here, *see* University of Essex, p. 800). Staying on the W side of the river, offices and laboratories for RMC in WHITEHALL ROAD s of Distillery Lane. By *Ray Mellor Associates*, 1966–7: three storeys, reinforced concrete columns and slabs faced with ceramic tiles, and three rows of continuous windows with black frames.

Back in Hythe Quay, a fine five-bay house at the N end, Nos. 6–8, *c.* 1720, of vitrified bricks with red brick dressings. Then the road turns E up HYTHE HILL, where the best houses are. On the N side, closing the view up Hythe Quay, No. 100, formerly The Swan pub, C18 brick with a hipped roof behind a parapet and a rounded corner at the E end. An attractive row on the S side: one house with a jettied front, the next weatherboarded, another with exposed timbers. In the wall between Nos. 88 and 87 a good C19 cast-iron drinking fountain, and on the corner of Maudlyn Road No. 80, formerly the Queen's Head Inn, C16 with jettied upper storey but much altered. Returning to the N side, Nos. 126 and 127, another former inn (The Dolphin), dating back to the C17 but much restored, with exposed timbers. Then comes St Leonard (*see* Churches) and on the W side of the churchyard Nos. 133–133B, timber-framed, white and crooked, with a gabled overhang just at the churchyard corner. Opposite the church, Nos. 61 and 62, Georgian brick, plastered, with a pediment on pilasters with fancy decoration and a Venetian window above. On the N side again, No. 143, Georgian brick, of three bays with two Venetian windows on the ground floor. Off the S side of Hythe Hill, STANDARD ROAD leads to the former Standard ironworks, opened 1873, part of the company (Davey, Paxman & Co.) established by James Paxman in 1865.* On the W side of St Leonard's Road a row of C19 workers' cottages, and on the S side the former St Leonard's National School, now houses: brick with stone dressings by *E. Swansborough*, 1869.

After Port Lane, Hythe Hill becomes BARRACK STREET, continued as MAGDALEN STREET. The main interest here is the former Board School on the N side (*see* Public Buildings), and

---

*Their early products included cast-iron railings, a rare surviving example of which can be seen at No. 21 Portland Road, off Mersea Road.

at the w end good views N towards St Botolph's Church and Priory.

We are now back at Colchester Town Station (*see* Public Buildings), from which Southway runs w, providing an almost impenetrable barrier on the s side of inner Colchester, truncating a number of old streets and isolating St Giles (*see* Churches) and St John's Green, to the latter's advantage. SOUTHWAY itself, 1973–4, has only two buildings of any sensitivity: at the w end the Police Station (*see* Public Buildings) and on the N side, on the corner of Stanwell Street, Essex County Council offices, 1983–5, by the *County Architect's Dept* (project architect, *Graham Beighton*). Light buff brick. In the underpasses, sculptural mosaic panels by *Henry & Joyce Collins*, 1973–4.

On the E side of ST JOHN'S GREEN, No. 31, GIMBER COTTAGE, prettily Gothick and dated 1823. Nos. 35–49 form an island of late c18 and early c19 cottages, an attractive mix of brick, render, tiles and pantiles. The w side is dominated by the Primary School (*see* Public Buildings) and on its N side a small brick parish room for St Giles by *C.E. Butcher*, 1903. On the s side, ABBEY HOUSE, *c.* 1825, gault brick with projecting Ionic porch.

DYKES

Camulodunum, which covered an area about ten square miles, was protected by an extensive system of dykes, the largest such group in Britain. The earthworks were begun by the British, probably before the end of the c1 B.C., and were extended in the early Roman period, and for the last time in the aftermath of the Boudiccan revolt. The dykes varied in size but each consisted of a V-shaped ditch, up to 13 ft (4 metres) deep, with a bank behind it, and most faced w.

The outermost dyke, which is probably the latest (early Roman), is the most impressive. This is GRYME'S DYKE, 3 m. long. 'Gryme' is the Devil, to whom in Christian times were attributed many ancient edifices whose origin and purpose had been forgotten. It runs roughly N–S from the River Colne to Roman River and the best surviving stretch is between London Road and Stanway Green. N of here at the spot now occupied by the former gravel pit known as 'King Coel's Kitchen', the Roman roads from Cambridge and London once converged to cross the Dyke. E of (i.e. behind) Gryme's Dyke run the remnants of the TRIPLE DYKE, also early Roman, visible on the E side of Straight Road, Lexden, N of Heath Road. Behind the Triple Dyke lies a great barrow called 'The Mount', excavated in 1910, when it was found to have been rifled in antiquity, and behind that in turn is LEXDEN DYKE, which runs through Lexden Park to Bluebottle Grove. It is continued to the N of the River Colne by MOAT FARM DYKE, both sections ½ m. long. Many pre-Roman graves have been found in the vicinity of Lexden Dyke. The most famous is the great barrow, lying within the ditch itself, known as the LEXDEN TUMULUS. This was excavated in 1924, and yielded up a marvellous treasure, now displayed in Colchester Castle Museum. The objects of bronze, all damaged or broken in antiquity, included a table, a pedestal, a figurine of Cupid, and models of a boar, a griffin, and a bull. There were fragments of chain-mail with a leather undergarment and traces of very fine gold tissue. A notable find was a striking silver portrait-disc of the Emperor Augustus, with the head cut from a *denarius* of 18–16 B.C. It seems likely that the burial dates from the late CI B.C. and may be that of one of the British kings at Camulodunum, Addedomaros.

Returning to Gryme's Dyke, at Stanway Green it makes two sharp right-angled turns before proceeding S to Roman River. Reinforcing this portion is a barely traceable section of ditch, OLIVER'S DYKE and LAYER DYKE, running through Oliver's Thicks, crossing Roman River and continuing through Chest Wood in the direction of Layer de la Haye. Behind this lies the settlement at Gosbecks Park, at Stanway (q.v.). This settlement was further protected along its N flank by HEATH FARM DYKE, the earliest of the dykes and dating from the end of the CI B.C. It is relatively small, about 10 ft (3 metres) from the bottom of the ditch to the top of the bank, but over 2 m. long. A shorter dyke, PRETTYGATE DYKE, lay to its N.

1½ m. SE of the S end of Lexden Dyke begins the relatively unexplored BERECHURCH DYKE, which runs from Monkwick for nearly 2 m. to meet Roman River. A peculiarity of this dyke is that the ditch lies on the E and not on the W side of the vallum, as it does in the other dykes.

A further dyke, now entirely destroyed, was discovered by excavation in 1930. This is the SHEEPEN DYKE, lying within the large area of land subjected to extensive excavation in the 1930s and again in 1970. Moulds for bronze coins of Cunobelinus have been found, indicating the presence of a British mint, as well as other metalworking tools. The area was burnt during the Boudiccan revolt but four Romano-British temples have been found as well as evidence of extensive manufacturing and commercial activity. This includes a series of C2 kilns, among them the one designed specifically for the manufacture of Samian ware, the only one yet to be recognized in Britain. The manufactory was in operation between A.D. 160 and 200.

COLD NORTON

8000

ST STEPHEN. Rebuilt 1855 by *G.E. Pritchett*. Dec. Nave, chancel, and small N vestry, Kentish rag with Caen stone dressings, and a timber S porch in the local tradition.* Good roof, with wall-

---

* Pevsner wrote in 1954 (but not in 1965): 'with a bellcote quite out of keeping with the style of this part of Essex. But what did the High Victorians care?'

posts resting on corbels carved as crouching figures of the Apostles, looking very large in the small chancel. – BRASS. To a Lady, *c.* 1520. 18-in. (47-cm.) figure.

THATCHED COTTAGE, Stow Road. Former National School, 1842. Single storey, painted brick, three sashed windows and gabled porch.

COLNE ENGAINE

ST ANDREW. The W tower with diagonal buttresses is C14 below, mainly flint and stone rubble, and brick above, *c.* 1500, with battlements on a trefoiled corbel frieze and polygonal pinnacles. On the E face of the parapet the de Vere mullet. 40,000 bricks were ordered under the will of John Draper, 1496. The surplus rebuilt the S porch, which has stepped battlements, but retains its C15 roof and bargeboards. Bronze STATUE by *Mrs A.C. Stewart*, 1938. Norman nave, see the W quoins and N and S traces of windows. Much Roman brick reused. Early C13 chancel doorway and blocked lancet. Restored 1872–3 by *E. Swansborough*, who replaced the furnishings and fittings and added a N vestry and organ chamber. – STAINED GLASS. Chancel N by *A.O. Hemming & Co.*, 1919. Chancel S by *Alan Younger*, 1961, a vigorous, modern design, in contrast to the more traditional window of the same year by *Arthur F. Erridge* (nave S; another by *Reginald Bell* of *Clayton & Bell*, 1936). – MONUMENT. Philip Hills of Colne Park †1830. By *Hutchinson* of Colchester. – Unusual LYCHGATE, 1897, with hexagonal tiled roof and two passages either side of a substantial resting place for the coffin.

VILLAGE HALL and caretaker's house, S of the church. 1921, a Courtauld donation and all that that implies in terms of quality. Neo-Tudor brick and half-timbering.

Former SCHOOL, Brook Street, W of the church. Now a house. 1847. Pebble walls with gault brick and limestone dressings, shallow-pitched slate roof, and tall octagonal chimneys. Opposite, a row of four cottages (almshouses?), probably C18, timber-framed with C19 brick refacing. Gabled porches, doubled in the middle of the row, and lean-to dormers in the gambrel roof.

COLNE PARK, 1¼ m. E. Built for M. R. Hills by 1774 and remodelled by his heir Philip Hills, who added the stable block to the NE and entrance lodge to the SE. House downgraded to servants' quarters in the C19 when a new house (dem. 1956) was built to the S. The old house restored and extended 1971, remodelled internally in the 1990s. Gault brick. Two storeys, five-bay centre with wings set back to either side, and three-bay pediment on Tuscan pilasters; at the back a ground-floor Venetian window. Stable block with pedimented gables, wooden clock turret, and cupola, the lodge a tetrastyle Tuscan portico and gateway with cast-iron gates and railings. In the park N of the house a limestone Ionic COLUMN with copper urn by *Soane*, 1791. Erected by Philip Hills in memory of M. R. Hills.

KNIGHT'S FARM, ¾ m. w. C17 timber-framed house, enlarged in the C18, with a six-bay gault brick front of *c.* 1826, later extended by two bays. Extensions of 1936 and 1947, the latter by *A.S.G. Butler*, who remodelled and extended the stables, adding a clock turret and cupola, and built staff cottages.

MAYFLOWER HOUSE, 1 m. SSW. Early C17 timber-framed and plastered lobby-entrance house, similar to the earliest houses in New England where Essex carpenters were active.

OVERSHOT MILL, ¾ m. ESE. C17 fulling mill, converted or rebuilt for corn in the late C18. Timber-framed and weatherboarded, including lucam, with brick ground floor. Converted into a house in the 1970s. Early C17 timber-framed and plastered MILL HOUSE to the w.

4000

COOPERSALE
Epping

ST ALBAN. Built 1852 by Miss Archer-Houblon of Coopersale House, who also paid for the parish room, vicarage, and school. E.E., of flint rubble. Probably by *Clarke*, who designed the school. Nave, chancel, s porch and N vestry (enlarged 1957). A N aisle was anticipated – see the stone arcading. – STAINED GLASS. E window (triple lancets) †1865. Nave N lancets by *Powell & Sons*, 1953, and *Rupert Moore* of *Whitefriars*, 1968.

OLD RECTORY, NW of the church. By *William White*, 1857. Mainly stock brick, with bands of black and red, the result 'more whimsical than effective' (*Ecclesiologist*). Also whimsical the little gables with fanciful half-timbering.

Former PARISH ROOM (now school), opposite the church. 1882. Small, extreme (and late) example of High Victorian polychromy, in stock, red and black, brick with stone dressings. N and E gables have paired windows in an arched recessed panel infilled with nailhead brick and with a quatrefoil opening.

Former SCHOOL (now house), ¾ m. s. By *J. Clarke*, 1850. Diapered brick and (an extravagant touch) carved oak bargeboards on the mistress's house. Enlarged 1879.

COOPERSALE HOUSE, ¼ m. WSW. Until 1920, much larger than now. Altered by *John Redgrave* for John Archer, 1763–4, when the main nine-bay façade, now of two storeys, was of three, with a five-bay pediment instead of the present three-bay open one. One bay survives of the three-bay NE wing, built *c.* 1670–80 and remodelled by Redgrave. Garden laid out by *Adam Holt*, 1738, which included a large polygonal pond s of the house. *Capability Brown*'s 1774 scheme for landscaping, if executed, has not survived.

COOPERSALE STREET, below Coopersale House, is an attractive little settlement with the THEYDON OAK pub at its centre, C18 weatherboarded, and opposite Nos. 24–26, late C16 or early C17 with a chunky pedimented Doric doorcase, and a C16 six-bay weatherboarded barn to the N. To the S, COOPERSALE LODGE, mid C15, extended in the C16 and C18. Gabled cross-wings, both with crown-post roofs, and C16 stair-tower with original stair. Just beyond it, the lodge to Gaynes Park, Theydon Garnon (q.v.).

COPFORD

9020

ST MICHAEL AND ALL ANGELS. The most remarkable Norman parish church in Essex, chiefly because of its wall paintings, but also architecturally. It was built *c.* 1125–30, probably as a chapel by the bishops of London, who held the parish from before the Conquest. What makes it of exceptional architectural interest is that the body of the church – three-bay nave, one-bay chancel – was originally vaulted, probably with groins. The springers are still clearly visible, while the apse, separated by an arch on the plainest of responds, has its complete semi-spherical vault. Norman vaults in parish churches are exceedingly rare in England; the closest parallels – structurally and geographically – are the undercroft of the chapel in Colchester Castle and Great Clacton parish church. The surviving upper windows of the nave, cut into by later arches on the S side, are shafted inside and out and quite large in size. In particular the lower W window (now C14, recognizable inside) is surprisingly spacious. Above it is a smaller Norman window flanked by two odd blocked (or blank) circles or oculi. Two doorways on the N side; the one into the nave has two orders of columns with primitive capitals and in the arch two roll mouldings. The apse is articulated by broad flat buttresses (cf. Colchester Castle). These, and all the Norman detail, are heavily fortified with Roman bricks; the walls otherwise are of rubble. The addition of the S aisle apparently proceeded gradually. First an E bay was thrown out, as a kind of transept. This still has Transitional characteristics. The arch is pointed. The responds have angle shafts. The second bay is interesting in its own way. The responds and the arch are triple-chamfered and entirely of brick, and only the outer order uses Roman bricks. The inner orders have home-made or imported bricks, and yet the date seems to be no later than 1300. So we have here bricks amongst the earliest medieval ones in England (cf. Coggeshall Abbey). The westernmost arch was inserted in the late C14 or early C15 when the aisle was extended, the S porch added, and the timber belfry erected. The arch on the chancel's S side was ruthlessly inserted during restoration by *Woodyer*, 1879–84, who created a vestry and organ chamber by continuing the S aisle eastwards. In the process wall paintings were lost, as they were on the N side of the nave where the square pulpit window was renewed. Part of the W wall was rebuilt, a W gallery taken down and the early C15 screen supporting it returned to its original position as CHANCEL SCREEN. The mosaic floor in the chancel and round the pulpit is *opus criminale* (i.e. made by female convicts). s porch rebuilt, having been badly restored by *Ebbetts & Cobb* of Colchester in 1878.

17   The WALL PAINTINGS are by far the most important in Essex. They are contemporary with the building, and are comparable with contemporary paintings in St Gabriel's Chapel, Canterbury Cathedral. Originally no doubt the whole church, inclusive of the vault, was painted, and the iconography, which is quite unlike that found in parish churches, strengthens the suggestion that this was a bishop's chapel. What remains has been heavily restored, especially the apse, whose paintings were discovered during repairs by *Slater & Carpenter* in 1871–2 and overpainted by *Daniel Bell*. Here we see Christ in circular Glory surrounded by angels, with apostles below and Signs of the Zodiac in the soffit of the arch. Ornamental designs in the windows, zigzag bands, Greek key or crenellated bands, diapers of bands, etc. – all shaded. On the chancel N wall remains of a miracle, then in the nave the Raising of Jairus's Daughter. w, remains of David or Samson and the Lion. Flanking the NW window, full-length figures of knights, that on the w original, the E a C19 copy. More armed figures on the w wall, as well as arches with architectural motifs and a seated figure on a throne. On the s wall near the E end two angels apparently with heart and chalice, relating to the Eucharist. Other scenes, including the Woman of Samaria and Abraham pointing to a ram caught in a thicket, are recorded. Visitation of Shepherds over arch to apse by *Clayton & Bell*, 1886; also the figure of Queen Matilda (copied from Rochester Cathedral) above arch on s side of chancel.

        FONT. Of the usual square Purbeck type of *c.* 1200, with four shallow blank arches on each side. Marble base, 1878, by *Ebbetts & Cobb*, made by *Cox & Sons*. – PULPIT. Large, octagonal, elaborately carved oak, 1886, by 'Mr. Peters' of Antwerp, probably *Hendrik Peeters* or his son *Pierre*. – BENCHES and CHOIR STALLS. By *H. & K. Mabbitt*, 1951–6, elegant and restrained. – DOOR. N doorway, original, moved from the s doorway *c.* 1878 when the ironwork of the hinges was renewed. – CHEST. Rectangular, iron-bound, assigned to the C14. – STAINED GLASS. Apse N window by *Daniel Bell*, 1872. w window by *Clayton & Bell*, 1886.

COPFORD HALL, N of the church. The house forms an admirable picture with the church on the r. and the stables with their lantern on the l. With the lawns and trees it is almost the *beau ideal* of what to the foreigner is an English landscape scene. A plain, stately Georgian front – brick, with sparing stone dressings, seven bays, two-and-a-half storeys, hipped roof behind parapet. Tuscan porch added 1919. The garden front of two (taller) storeys, with two canted bays. It is in fact the result of the remodelling or rebuilding in various stages during the C18 and early C19 of an early C17 house built for Alan Mountjoy (†1625), of which a timber-framed wall with mural painting has been found. Similarly the stables, white brick with red dressings, are built round an earlier timber-framed structure, and are connected to a former farmhouse that lies close to the N side of the house.

Entrance hall with screen of Ionic columns. Narrow staircase that curves elegantly at the base, the ceiling over it in three shallow-domed compartments with elaborate plasterwork. Two rooms in the SE corner have fireplaces with painted decoration in the style of *Angelica Kauffmann*. Ugly extensions to the N by *F.W. Chancellor*, 1919, and *Miles Park*, 1969–70. Grounds landscaped by *Richard Woods* from 1784 for John Haynes Harrison. Woods's scheme included, as well as planting, a series of pools based on existing ponds, fed by a cascade emerging from a grotesque arch. Classical BOATHOUSE, with flint quoins and a Venetian window opening on to a balcony over the water, shown on a survey of 1766.

The parish borders to the N on LONDON ROAD (Roman Stane Street), which has some attractive houses, among them COPFORD PLACE, late C17 brick refaced *c.* 1800 in gault brick to create a new entrance front with jagged *Coade* stone chimney pots. On the same side of the road, to its W, OLD MILL HOUSE, brick, of three bays with white brick giant pilasters, early C18 with C19 additions. On the S side, further W, COPFORD LODGE, a clumsy-looking early C19 gault brick villa with Ionic portico.

COPPED HALL
Epping Upland

4000

Well known as the ruin visible from the M25 between Waltham Abbey and Epping. Built close to the site of an earlier house (*see* below) in 1753–8 for Sir John Conyers by *John Sanderson*, although the amateurs *Thomas Prowse* and especially *Sir Roger Newdigate*, Conyers's brother-in-law, seem to have been responsible for the design. Conyers himself is known to have had some ability as an architect. *James Wyatt* carried out internal alterations and decoration for John Conyers II, 1775–7, and probably also designed the lodges S of the house. In 1869 the estate was purchased by George Wythes, whose fortune came from railways. His grandson, E.J. Wythes, made extravagant alterations and additions to the house and gardens *c.* 1895–1901, designed by *C.E. Kempe* although the architectural work was probably managed by *William Tale* of Kempe's office, and some of the work was also delegated to Kempe's cousin *Walter E. Tower*. Gutted by fire in 1917, the remainder stripped after the estate was sold in 1952, but partial restoration by *Alan Cox* has taken place since 1995.

Sanderson's house was austere, of white brick with Portland stone dressings. Three storeys, seven bays, with central three-bay pediment breaking forward, and modillioned cornice. Round-arched rusticated doorway, and quoins on the ground floor only. *Kempe* added the balustrade and heavy, stone-

p. 308

Copped Hall.
Elevation of John Sanderson's house

capped chimneys, embellished the doorway, and built to the r.
a four-bay service wing. To l. and r. a blind arcaded screen wall
based on a design by Sanderson. The w (garden) front was
originally even simpler, with no surrounds to the windows, but
Kempe added these and balustrade, and faced the central three
bays and pediment in stone, with giant Ionic pilasters and in
the tympanum carved figures and a sundial. On this side the
outer two bays of the service wing are also stone-faced, with
Ionic pilasters. This provides a suitable backdrop to the formal
GARDENS which Kempe laid out on the w side of the house,
consisting of a raised walk that runs directly w from the centre
of the house with parterres to either side. The basic structure
survives, and two small stone Neo-Jacobean pavilions, but the
balustrading, obelisks, fountains, statues and other ornaments
with which the garden was crammed have all been removed or
destroyed. On the s side of the house, part of a screen wall with
blind arcading, niches, and attached Ionic columns, behind
which stood a winter garden, connected to the house by a
glazed corridor.

Practically nothing survives of the interior, which included
fireplaces from the Tudor house and STAINED GLASS by
Kempe. The destruction of wall coverings has shown that stone
from the Tudor house was reused, and has also revealed niches
and other features concealed by Kempe's alterations. Fine
brick vaulting in the cellars and double-height kitchen.

To the N of the house, C18 STABLES and other outbuildings,
remodelled *c.* 1895 with a lead-covered clock tower and bellcote, converted to residential use 1996–7. On the w side of
these, but visually part of the garden, the RECREATION
HOUSE by *Hoare & Wheeler*, 1904–5. Roughcast with brick and
stone dressings, the pilastered s front facing the garden with
Venetian window set in a segmental pediment. Racquets court
with internal balcony and Jacobean-style staircase. To the NW,
the foundations of the Tudor house have been excavated. This
may have dated back to the C12, but was rebuilt by Sir Thomas
Heneage in 1564–8. It seems that he retained the hall from the
earlier house. His mansion is well documented, notably in
detailed drawings prepared by *Newdigate*. It consisted of three-
storey ranges on three sides of a courtyard, with a single-storey
loggia on the N side that was rebuilt by *Edmund Kinsman*,

c. 1630, for Lionel Cranfield, Earl of Middlesex.* Other alterations were carried out by *Nicholas Stone*, 1638–9. Conyers, who inherited in 1742, may have contemplated restoring the Tudor house, but by 1748 had started demolishing it. On the N side of the site a fragment of old house remains standing, a brick pier from the loggia. Tudor outbuildings to the E adapted as farm buildings in the C19 (one dated 1891), and there are also remains of an C18 ice house. W of the old house, the KITCHEN GARDEN, contemporary with Sanderson's house. Brick wall with blue-brick lozenges, pilasters, and two gateways with wrought-iron gates with overthrows.

The PARK was in existence in the C13 and was enlarged at various times then and later. *Capability Brown* received a small payment for work at Copped Hall and may have advised John Conyers II after 1775; ornamental lake below the house to the E, with clumps of trees beyond it to the SE.

LODGES, Crown Hill, ⅔ m. S. Probably by *Wyatt*, *c.* 1775. Pair of two-storey lodges, stock brick with stone dressings, flanking wrought-iron carriage and pedestrian gates, rear extensions *c.* 1895. Single window in arched recess with pediment and short, lower screen walls with niches to l. and r. *Coade* stone plaques and urns.

LODGE, High Road, 1 m. ESE. Brick with half-timbered and roughcast upper floor, *c.* 1895. Along the High Road towards Epping, a number of estate cottages in similar style.

WOOD HOUSE, ¾ m. E. Built for his wife's uncle by E. J. Wythes, 1897–1900, and to which he moved after the 1917 fire destroyed Copped Hall; by *Walter E. Tower*, assisted by *William Tate*. On a sloping site, the show front towards the garden of four storeys with four full-height gabled bay windows, deep eaves, and elaborate pargetting, inspired by Sparrowe's House, Ipswich. (Equally elaborate Neo-Jacobean plasterwork inside, and a chimneypiece dated 1607 with the Conyers arms. – STAINED GLASS by *Kempe*, including a series of roundels (The Round of Life) in the manner of Kate Greenaway or Walter Crane, 1898, and heraldic glass, 1902–6. – GARDEN HOUSE and pergola by *Hoare & Wheeler*, 1904.)

CORNISH HALL END
Finchingfield

6030

ST JOHN THE EVANGELIST. 1840 I by *J. D. Morgan* (*Webb & Morgan*). Brick, with white dressings. Lancet style with W porch, and W angle turrets (originally pinnacled). Alterations by *Chancellor & Son*, 1910–11, who replaced Morgan's W bell-turret with a bell-tower inside the W wall, and extended the E end to provide enlarged chancel, vestry and sacristy. –

---

* A plan by *John Thorpe* of 'Copthall' in the Soane Museum may represent an unexecuted scheme for Lord Middlesex.

STAINED GLASS. E window by *Holiday*, 1911, not one of his best.

OLD VICARAGE, E of the church. 1846. Brick, with prominent gables.

Former SCHOOL, now village hall and house, 100yds NW. After the manner of the church, but too late to be by Morgan. Paid for by G. W. Gent of Moyns Park, 1847, rebuilt 1871.

SHORE HALL, 1 m. WNW. Late C16 timber-framed and plastered. Garden front of three gables, the middle one dated 1619. Weatherboarded barn on the N connected to the house by a wing built over a pond, 1965 by *Alan Bloomfield*. Garden by *Kenneth Midgley*, 1952.

CORRINGHAM
7080
Thurrock U.A.

ST MARY. The tower is one of the most important Early Norman monuments in Essex, without buttresses, and with two tiers of flat blank arches below the parapet. The middle one of the upper row on each side is pierced, has a colonette set in, and serves as a bell-opening. Pyramid roof. The whole is in its severity and clarity extremely impressive. Also late C11 part of the chancel S wall, where the ragstone and flint are laid herringbone fashion. Inside, the tower arch is small and has the plainest imposts. N aisle, N chapel, and most of the chancel are C14, see the two-bay aisle arcade (octagonal piers, double-chamfered arches) and several Dec windows. But the E window belongs to *Scott*'s restoration of 1843–4, as does the S porch; tower restored in 1864, and N aisle (by *William White*) in 1875.

N chapel SCREEN. An early example of timber screens in Essex; first half of the C14. Five lights to one side of the opening and three to the other, with thin columns with shaft-rings as mullions and intersected ogee-cusped arches. Plain straight moulded top beam. – STATUE. Our Lady by *Martin Travers*, 1939. – STAINED GLASS. In E window, reused from various windows damaged in the Second World War; only the central panel, *c.* 1848, *in situ*. – N aisle by *A. K. Nicholson* (designed by *G. E. R. Smith*), 1928. Nave S, *c.* 1999, and N chapel E, 2003, by *Susan McCarthy* (*Auravisions*). – MONUMENTS. Brasses to Richard de Beltoun, *c.* 1340, demi-figure of a priest, and a civilian, *c.* 1450, reset. Both 13 in. (33 cm.).

The area immediately round the church has miraculously preserved its character. THE BULL is timber-framed, mainly rebuilt in the C17 but with a C15 gabled cross-wing. S of the church, CORRINGHAM HALL, early C18 with a chequered brick front and dormers in the gambrel roof. To the N, opposite Fobbing Road, the old SCHOOL. 1840, Neo-Elizabethan. Perhaps by *H. E. Kendall Jun.*, who in 1841 built the rectory (dem.) in the same style.

Modern Corringham consists of C20 housing to the NW of the church, and oil storage depots and refineries along the Thames to the SE. Here an explosives factory was opened in 1895 by Kynoch & Co. who built a model village named Kynochtown, 2½ m. SE, renamed CORYTON when it was taken over by the oil company Cory Bros.* Only the name has survived expansion of the oil refinery (now BP). Further extensive development along the river towards London as a container port is planned.

CREEKSEA
Burnham-on-Crouch

9090

ALL SAINTS. 1878–9 by *Chancellor*, who here, as at Steeple, indulges in the most curious surface effects of stone, with bits of flint, brick, and tile, mostly reused from the church he was replacing. N and S windows with cusped lights beneath flat heads, elaborate carving in the spandrels, and inner arcades to the nave windows. – FONT. C15, octagonal, carvings of a serpent and a cross-saltire. – BRASS. Sir Arthur Herris †1631. No figure, but the inscription reads:

> If any prying man, heere after come,
> That knowes not, who's the tenant of this tomb,
> Wee'l tell him freely, as our sighes giue leaue,
> One, whose religious brest to GOD did cleaue,
> One that to men iust offices discharg'd
> And to the pinched soule his hart inlarg'd,
> One, that though laid in dust of breath bereft,
> Like dying Roses sweet distillments left
> And moulders hoping, from this stone god may
> Raise vp a child to Abraham, one day.

CREEKSEA HALL, E of the church. Two-storey, three-bay Georgian brick, with a later addition at the E end. At the back a C16 wing with exposed timbers.

CREEKSEA PLACE, ½ m. SSE. Dated 1569 (rainwater head on N side), but it is not easy now to discern this sizeable Early Elizabethan mansion. The original approach was from the E, where the pretty gabled gateway survives, and the walls of an enclosed garden or outer courtyard. The range opposite the gateway was built 1901 by *Chancellor & Son*, but stands on the foundations of the Elizabethan E wing. Through this a narrow inner courtyard was reached. Of the W range of this courtyard only some of the footings can be seen, and it is uncertain whether there ever was a S range, or only an enclosing wall. In the NE angle of the courtyard is the original staircase wing with newel stair. The N range, which perhaps contained the Hall, is mostly intact, with the addition of a gabled bay in 1901 and an unsympathetic small extension by *F.W. Chancellor*, 1918, both

---

* The Air-Life Thermofin Catalytic Cracking Unit, which Pevsner found 'thrilling aesthetically', like 'abstract sculpture', has been replaced.

on the N side. The original windows are of brick with mullions and transoms, but there is no recognizable composition. To the W a much lower range with brick windows and dormers in the roof. Some rooms have C16 or C17 panelling. Entrance Lodge, gateway, bridge and an extension of the outer courtyard walls also by Chancellor & Son. Their client was William Rome, whose money came from oysters.

CRESSING

ALL SAINTS. Nave, short chancel, and stunted W belfry with shingled splay-foot spire. The belfry is supported on four posts braced with timbers (tree-ring dated 1388–1410) that form a broad shallow arch. Walls mainly flint rubble, more mortar than flint in the nave, which must be Norman or replace a Norman nave – see one re-set bit of zigzag work above the N doorway. Excavations have revealed the foundations of an earlier Norman or Saxon church, with apsidal E end. The present chancel is of the early C13, with much Roman brick, and has two N lancets. In addition some C14 and C15 windows; those of the C14 have a characteristic Essex motif of tracery. White brick N vestry, 1823, E wall rebuilt 1833, the whole church restored and refitted in 1868 by *Chancellor*. C15 nave roof of unusual construction, with four tie-beams set on wall-pieces and arched braces. Above the tie-beams are timber arches joined to the principal rafters with tracery panels between them. – MONUMENTS. Anne Smith of Cressing Temple †1607 and husband Henry, with the usual two kneeling figures. Below, kneeling daughter and baby in a cradle. – Brass of Dorcas Musgrave †1610. Seated figure, 20½ in. (52 cm.), with infant in swaddling clothes.

PRIMARY SCHOOL, Tye Green. 1901–2 by *Clare & Ross*, with detached house for headmistress to S. Brick, gabled to front and side. Enlarged 1996–7.

ROOK HALL, 300 yds NNW. Three-bay, two-storey lobby-entry house, timber-framed and plastered, with central stack of four tall chimneys, and rusticated plastered doorcase with pediment. Probably built 1674. Late Medieval rear range.

BULFORD MILL, 1¼ m. W. C19 water mill, now a house. Three storeys of brick, fourth storey and attic, with hoist loft, weatherboarded. Single-storey engine house with cast-iron windows. Across the road, BULFORD MILL HOUSE, early C19 gault brick front range of three bays, central doorway with Tuscan columns and fanlight; C16 or earlier timber-framed and plastered range behind.

CRESSING TEMPLE
1 m. S of the church

An exceptionally attractive group of farm buildings, farmhouse, and garden wall scattered over a partially moated site. The early date of the buildings has made Cressing Temple famous, and

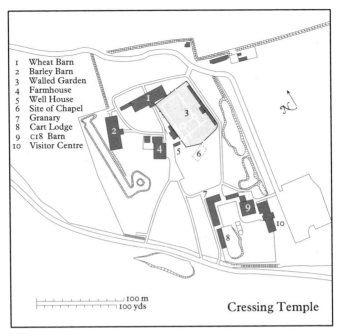

1 Wheat Barn
2 Barley Barn
3 Walled Garden
4 Farmhouse
5 Well House
6 Site of Chapel
7 Granary
8 Cart Lodge
9 C18 Barn
10 Visitor Centre

100 m
100 yds

Cressing Temple

since it was acquired by Essex County Council in 1987 has become the centre for the study of vernacular buildings in Essex.

There is archaeological evidence of an Iron Age settlement at Cressing Temple, which later formed part of the royal manor of Witham. In 1137 Cressing was granted by Matilda, wife of King Stephen, to the Knights Templar; they received Witham ten years later. At the suppression of the order in 1312 Cressing went to the Hospitallers. In 1515 parts of the estate were leased to John Edmondes, then in 1539 to Sir John Smyth. The Hospitallers were suppressed the following year; the Smyths, who changed their name to Nevill, held the estate until 1657, building a large house of which only the walled garden, parts of the farmhouse, and the granary remain. Later owners included Herman Olmius of Great Leighs and his descendants, from 1703 to 1882; it became a tenanted farm and the Great House was demolished, replaced by the more modest farmhouse.

The oldest building is the BARLEY BARN on the W side of the complex, part plastered, part weatherboarded. Tree-ring dating shows that it was built between 1205 and 1235. It is aisled, of five bays with half-bays at each end. It is now about 118 ft (36 metres) long and 45 ft (14 metres) wide, smaller than it was originally as a result of rebuilding of the side walls in c. 1420. The crown-post roof is part of C16 alterations, and in

the late C17 or early C18 the E wall was rebuilt and the midstrey inserted. The WHEAT BARN stands more or less at right
angles to it and was built between 1257 and 1280. It has been
altered less than the Barley Barn. Five bays, 130 ft (40 metres)
long and 39 ft (12 metres) wide. The walls were originally
boarded, rebuilt with close studding c. 1420, with brick
nogging inserted probably in the late C16. Early C15 midstrey.

Abutting the eastern half of the Wheat Barn is the brick N
wall of the WALLED GARDEN, built in the second half of the
C16 as a pleasure garden for the great house that lay to its S.
The wall is mostly original, including some of the coping, apart
from a large part of the E side that was rebuilt in the C19. Laid
out and planted in the manner of a Tudor garden 1994–5,
including a handsome Tudor-style brick FOUNTAIN. W of the
Garden, the FARMHOUSE, L-plan, timber-framed and plastered. Its external features, including sash windows and Tuscan
portico, are mainly C18 and C19. The northern wing, tree-ring
dated 1603, was probably built as a granary. The S cross-wing
was originally separate, built c. 1620 at the rear of the Tudor
mansion, extended c. 1800, with C19 additions (including bakehouse) to N and W. Between the garden and the Farmhouse,
a WELL HOUSE, c. 1920, a barn in miniature; the well, lined
with Reigate stone, is the Templars'. To its E, the foundations
of the Templars' chapel, excavated 1978–81, are marked out in
the grass.

THE GRANARY extends towards the S of the complex, in
front of the site of the great house, whose approach it originally flanked; a similar (demolished) building stood to the W.
Plastered and weatherboarded, with some modern brick
nogging. Two storeys, ten bays, dated 1623 (confirmed by tree-
ring dating) but reusing timbers from a building of c. 1420.
Two gables (originally four) on the W side; built as a malting,
with the kiln in a brick building at the NE corner (now toilets).
To its S an eight-bay CART LODGE, c. 1800, and E an C18 aisled
barn, mostly rebuilt. This adjoins the VISITOR CENTRE, 1997
by the *County Architect's Dept* (project architect, *Graham
Beighton*). Suitably barn-like, with the entrance in the form of
a midstrey, but the walls (especially the N end) mostly glazed.

DANBURY

ST JOHN THE BAPTIST. The church and its churchyard lie within
a roughly oval, poorly preserved EARTHWORK, the remains of
an Iron Age or Saxon hill-fort. This can best be appreciated to
the S of the church, where there is some visible evidence and
a fine view that shows just how commanding a defensive position this was.

The church itself is remarkably roomy. Nave and aisles
together are wider than they are long. Chancel, S chancel
chapel and N vestry form one straight E end. The oldest part
is the N aisle wall with cusped two-light windows with a qua-

trefoil in the spandrel. This must be *c.* 1300. The rest is essentially C14. W tower with diagonal buttresses, a W door with niches to the l. and r., a W window with two ogee lights and a quatrefoil in the spandrel, and a later recessed, rather tall, shingled spire, largely rebuilt after being struck by lightning in 1749/50. The walls mainly of stone rubble, including a lot of puddingstone, with stone dressings and, round the W door, tile and flint decoratively combined. *R.C. Hussey* carried out some restoration work in 1847–8 that included replacing the chancel arch, but the major changes were left to *G.G. Scott*, 1866–7. He rebuilt the S aisle (rebuilt in brick in 1776), and extended it eastwards to form a S chancel aisle; what remains is entirely puddingstone, seldom seen undiluted in this way. Scott also added the N porch. The E wall and SE corner of the church were damaged by a bomb in 1944 and rebuilt in 1951–2 by *E.P. Archer* and *Andrew Carden* of *Carden & Godfrey*, reordered with the S aisle as chapel and the S chancel aisle as choir vestry.

Inside, three-bay C14 arcades with typical quatrefoil piers and double-hollow-chamfered arches (on the N side dying into a vertical continuation of the pier). The N aisle has its original early C14 trussed rafter roof, boarded over later in the E parts with ribs resting on oak head corbels. Squint from N aisle to chancel, and small squint-like window from vestry to chancel. – COMMUNION RAIL of 1632, with turned balusters, re-used in the C19 as a balustrade to the ringers' gallery. – BENCHES. Four in the nave with poppyheads and various beasts on the shoulders, C15, restored by *Scott*, the remainder in similar vein by him and others since, making a fine display. – PULPIT also by *Scott*, 1868. – SCULPTURE. White alabaster relief of the Annunciation. The surviving panel of a reredos erected in memory of T.L. Claughton, Bishop of St Albans, 1894.* – MONUMENTS. In low recesses in the N and S aisle three oak effigies of knights, probably of the St Clere family who built the church. All are cross-legged, the N aisle ones late C13, the S aisle very early C14, but each remarkably different in attitude and mood; not at all shopwork. The earlier ones have their hand on the sword, but one of the two is bent more lyrically than the other. The younger one is in an attitude of prayer. – In tower, Rev. George Wither †1605, alabaster tablet with strapwork etc. and a lengthy inscription. – STAINED GLASS. E window by *Carl Edwards* (*Edwards & Powell*), 1954–5. – Vestry, figure of St Luke from Danbury Palace chapel, moved 1951.

UNITED REFORMED CHURCH (Congregational), Little Baddow Road. 1937 by *F. W. Lawrence*. Brick, with round-headed lancet windows, and very small. Nave and E vestry (no chancel) under a half-hipped roof with gablets, with flat-roofed W porch and transepts all ending in canted bays.

DANBURY PARK. The Danbury Place estate was purchased by John Round in 1830; it had belonged to Sir Walter Mildmay, Chancellor of the Exchequer under Henry VIII, who is said to

---

* Replacing one by *Hussey* that was then presented to Great Sampford (q.v.).

have built a seat there, but the house was deemed too dilapidated to preserve and plans for rebuilding were prepared by *Hopper*. Round's wife *Susan Constantia Round* has been credited with the design but her role may be exaggerated. The house, which was ready for occupation in 1832 but not completed until 1834, is of brick, its style perhaps influenced by Mildmay's, and it certainly contains all the characteristic motifs of Tudor architecture: square and polygonal towers, stepped gables with pinnacles at the apex, mullioned and transomed and Perp windows, all freely arranged, without any noticeable principle other than picturesqueness, although the effect has been diminished by the removal of the pinnacles. Some materials from the old house were reused, including the library chimneypiece. Interior decorations by *George Morant & Son*. At the same time the park was remodelled, with an 'American Garden' laid out NW of the main lake. N LODGE on the Chelmsford road, which was diverted away from the house in 1834. ICE HOUSE, W of the lakes. Shown on an 1829 estate map.

In 1845 Round sold the house to the Ecclesiastical Commissioners for the Bishop of Rochester's residence when Essex became part of that diocese. A chapel was added in 1850. Danbury Palace (as it was then known) returned to private hands in 1892. A conference centre from 1972, with a SW range added 1974 by the *County Architect's Dept* (project architect, *Graham Beighton*). This bends round to connect up with the old stable block and creates an enclosed space that is both modest and does not impinge visually upon the house.*

The parish church is set back from the main road on the S side of a small green. On the W side, the OLD RECTORY, C18 red and blue brick with cement quoins. Three storeys, three bays, and off-centre pedimented doorway. C19 alterations and additions (e.g. by *Chancellor*, 1879). On the E side, FRETTONS, early C16 hall house with later C16 and C17 additions, faced with brick in the C18. Good group of chimneystacks, early and late C16. Opposite the entrance to the green, on the N side of the main road, THE GRIFFIN, timber-framed and roughcast with gabled cross-wings, one with exposed timbers. Hall house, built soon after 1500, an inn since 1744. Almost opposite, LINGWOOD HOUSE has an C18 brick front divided into two unequal sections by pilasters. Pedimented doorcase with fluted pilasters. W, on the same side, MILLINGTON HOUSE, dated 1719. Painted brick, five bays with segment-headed first-floor windows. Then RECTORY FARM HOUSE, early C19 with distinctive windows with semicircular heads and cast-iron latticed casements, a form repeated on other (unplastered) brick buildings W towards Well Lane, and also on ST CLERE's HALL, ½ m. beyond. Before that point is reached the road opens out on the N side at ELM GREEN, with views down to the Chelmer Valley, a good setting for the WAR MEMORIAL by *Sir Reginald Blomfield*, 1921: his 'Cross of Sacrifice' with bronze sword.

* Conference centre closed 2004; likely to be converted to housing.

EVES CORNER, ¼ m. E of the church, forms an almost separate village centre, a pretty scene of cottages and shops round a green with pond. Some large houses in the vicinity, particularly where the village merges into the surrounding commons and woodland, of a character that is more Surrey than Essex. In MAYES LANE, S of Eves Corner, MAYESFIELD, 1912–14 by F.W. Chancellor, part rendered and part tile-hung, with Crittall windows, dormers, and clusters of tall diamond chimneys. Extended by Chancellor, 1933, who in 1932 built the smaller GREENACRE to the N. Further S, in COPT HILL, HERONSFIELD, c. 1931, by E.P. Archer of Dudley Newman, Elliott & Archer. Brick, with some tile-hanging on the entrance front, and tall diamond chimneys, but otherwise nearer to Queen Anne, especially on the garden front. At the junction of Maldon Road with Copt Hill, HILL HOUSE, Georgian brick of five bays with three-bay pediment that just breaks forward. N of Eves Corner, by contrast, No. 2 LITTLE BADDOW ROAD by Gn²design (Paul Gladman) with Peter Ross of Arup Engineering, 2004. A demonstration house for a sustainable modular construction system. Fully demountable post-and-beam timber frame on concrete pads. Varied cladding, including stainless steel and oak. Garage made from rammed earth excavated for the foundations, with sedum roof.

RIFFHAMS, ¾ m. NW. 1815–17, for J.R. Spencer Phillips of Old Riffhams, Little Baddow (q.v.). Repton advised on its position and the park layout; a sketch of the view from the new house, dated 1815, is signed by H. & J. A. Repton. Did the son design the house for the location specified by his father? Two storeys, gault brick with cement cornice and end pilasters. Pilasters between the bays on the entrance (E) front, of three bays with Tuscan portico in antis, three further bays set slightly back, and a one-bay later C19 extension. Five bay garden (S) front and on the first bay of the W front a segmental bow with lean-to veranda. Inside, shallow-domed hall and fan vaulting over the staircase. Stables etc. to the N, and kitchen garden to the W. Greek Revival gatepiers to main entrance. Across the lane to the N the Cedar Park, some trees contemporary with the house. The main part of the park lies to the S on both sides of a valley, with two lakes at the bottom formed by damming a stream, and views towards Danbury Church, all to be seen from the pleasure grounds closer to the house. It is, on a relatively small scale, a near-perfect embodiment of the harmony between architecture and tamed nature that Repton strove for.

SLOUGH HOUSE, 2 m. SE. Timber-framed and plastered, c. 1500, with central hall, gabled cross-wings, and fine chimneys with polygonal shafts at the N and S ends.

DEBDEN

5030

ST MARY THE VIRGIN AND ALL SAINTS. C13 arcades of four bays with circular piers with moulded capitals and moulded arches. On the s side the first two capitals are enriched by upright leaves. The s aisle windows are Dec; C14 also the s porch. N aisle rebuilt in the C15, and the chancel in 1733, on the site of a crossing tower that fell (in two stages) in 1698 and 1717. But the real interest is connected with Richard Muilman Trench Chiswell, son of the 'gentleman historian' of Essex, Peter Muilman, who changed his name upon inheriting the Debden estate of his uncle Richard Chiswell in 1772. *James Essex* prepared a design for encasing the whole church, 1782–4, and his is probably the w front, which manages to slip an open pediment into the Gothic composition, as well as the various pinnacles and battlements on the nave and porch. w steeple by 'the ingenious Mr Essex' erected posthumously in 1786 (replaced in 1930), in which year Chiswell turned to *Richard Holland* for the design of the FONT, made by *B. De Carle* of *Coade*'s 'lithodipyra', as an inscription records. Octagonal, in an elaborate and crisp Neo-Perp, with foiled panels; against the stem minute figures of the Cardinal Virtues and Christian Graces, derived from Reynolds's w window of New College, Oxford.

In 1792 *Holland* rebuilt the chancel, from a design provided by the antiquary *John Carter*. It is octagonal, on the pattern of such a chapter house as York, connected with the church by a broad passage, and higher than the nave with the Chiswell burial chamber beneath. The material is white brick with stone dressings, and all the detail of the tracery is of papery thinness. The chancel has a ribbed plaster vault, the passage timber arches with thin pendants. Inside and outside are medallions, roundels and shields of arms of *Coade* stone, one dated 1793. At the E end Chiswell placed MONUMENTS to his uncle, Richard Chiswell †1772, and his parents Mary and Peter Muilman, †1785 and 1790, both by *Thomas King* of Bath; coloured marbles, one with a draped urn, the other with a female figure leaning against an urn. Against the s wall (opposite the position of the family pew), his own monument (†1797), probably also designed by *Carter*. Elaborate sandstone tomb-chest with foiled decoration in the style of the C15 under a sumptuous arch in the style of *c.* 1300. – STAINED GLASS. s aisle by *James Pearson*, 1793, with the arms of Chiswell, Muilman, and Trench. Originally the E window, the present one by *Gibbs & Howard*, 1882. – N meeting room and vestry by *Purcell Miller Tritton & Partners*, 2000, in stripped Gothick.

The church stands all on its own by a made lake in the landscaped grounds, now overgrown, of DEBDEN HALL. Remodelled by *Henry Holland* for R.M.T. Chiswell, 1795, dem. 1936. Large former STABLE BLOCK, late C17 brick, two storeys, NW of church, and walls of kitchen garden to SE. At DEBDEN HALL FARM, 300yds N, a range of C18 outbuildings, including a large square entrance pavilion dated 1782. NEWPORT LODGE, ½ m. N. Windows with pointed arches and, in a little gable over the door, a trefoil.

The VILLAGE consists of little more than one street with a number of attractive cottages, some thatched. At the centre the WHITE HART INN, C17 timber-framed and plastered with a cross-wing to the l. and a C19 extension beyond it. Opposite, the SCHOOL and teacher's house, 1852. Good Tudor Gothic. Small rear extension by *Alan Willis*, County Architect, 1977–8, and a larger one by *Martindales*, 2001–2, with diapered brickwork reflecting the original school and a hall in the style of an Essex barn. N of the school THE OLD WINDMILL, converted to a house in 1957. Tower mill, red brick, with stone dated 1796 and others bearing Chiswell family arms. No sails.

BRICK HOUSE FARM, ¾ m. NW. Late C15 Wealden house. Two-bay open hall floored *c.* 1700. Crown-post roof. C17 brick wing projecting to the S.

DEBDEN MANOR, ¾ m. NNE. 1796 by *Richard Holland* as the rectory. Large, white brick, with slate mansard roof.

NEW AMBERDEN HALL, 1¾ m. SSE. Brick house of *c.* 1670, Five bays, two storeys and attics. Central doorway with fanlight and flat hood. Cf. Thistley Hall, Widdington, ½ m. NW.

DEDHAM   0030

Dedham is easily the most attractive small town in Essex, something that has long been appreciated by both residents and visitors. Its character derives initially from the prosperity it attained from cloth working. The industry was established by the mid C13, developed rapidly in the later C14, and peaked in the C15. Prosperity came to an end in the mid C17, and in 1642 a petition was delivered to the King for help for the depressed condition of the town. But in the C18 Dedham revived as a genteel small town (its Assembly Rooms opened *c.* 1745), and in the C19 the painter John Constable, born at East Bergholt just over the River Stour in Suffolk but educated at Dedham Grammar School, did much to draw attention to the natural beauty of the town's surroundings and make it a tourist destination. The importance of preserving both the natural and architectural heritage was recognized relatively early, and the Dedham Vale Society was formed in 1938 with Raymond Erith as its founding chairman. 'There is nothing at Dedham to hurt the eye', wrote Pevsner in 1954, and it remains true, but the effect has not been achieved without effort.

ST MARY THE VIRGIN. One of the most prosperous Perp churches of Essex, the visible proof of the flourishing cloth trade of the town, of which the church is the principal witness. The chief donors were the Webbes, whose initials and merchants' marks appear in the tracery of the passageway under the tower. The church is the rebuilding of an earlier structure, of which fragments remain at the W end; the (re-set) S doorway is C14 and within the S porch is some masonry from the former S wall aisle. But otherwise all is of the late C15 and early C16, starting with the chancel. The nave was begun *c.* 1491 and John

Gurdon bequeathed money for the N aisle in 1504. Money was left for the building of the steeple in 1494–5, 1504–5, 1505–6, and a further £20 towards finishing the steeple in 1510. In 1519 Stephen Denton left £100 'for the battlyment of the steeple'. So the tower and the whole church were probably complete by about 1520 – built it appears at one go and without change of plan. It stands along the main street, but its S side still faces the fields. It has a long nave with clerestory, a long chancel, two tall porches (the N two-storeyed, the S originally so), and a W tower about 130 ft (40 metres) high. The length of the church is about 170 ft (52 metres). The whole building is more Suffolk than Essex in style.

The W tower of brick faced with knapped flint has big polygonal clasping buttresses* with much stone dressing, a very large four-light W window, three-light bell-openings, battlements with flushwork decoration, and tall crocketed pinnacles. The ground floor of the tower forms a passageway from N to S. It has a depressed pointed vault entirely panelled with tracery, quatrefoils, roses and portcullis, etc. The aisles have three-light windows with depressed pointed heads, the chancel taller two-centred windows – of five lights at the E end, of three on the sides. The wall on the N side is treated as the show side. The base, for example, has flushwork panels, and the parapet battlements. The N porch uses flushwork for base, buttresses, and battlements. The doorway has lions *couchant* on the l. and r., tracery in the spandrels, and niches l. and r. of the upper window. The S side is more restrained, and has prominent brick buttresses added in 1717.

The inside is airy and clear, six bays of identical slender piers with a section of thin shafts with capitals and broad shallow diagonal hollows without capitals. The roof, of low pitch, rests on shafts rising from the capitals as well as the apexes of the arches; for there are twice as many clerestory windows as arcade arches. These arches are four-centred. The chancel roof has angels carved by *Aileen Kent*, and the nave roof shields, all added in 1960. Church restored by *J. M. Roberts*, 1861–2, who removed part of a W gallery and uncovered the PISCINA in the chancel. Further work in the chancel by *Woodyer*, 1879–80, who designed the REREDOS, SEDILIA and STALLS, as well as the PULPIT. In 1906–9 the chancel was again restored, by *T.G. Jackson*, who opened up four of the windows that had been blocked in the C18 and laid the black-and-white marble flooring. At the back of the W gallery, behind the organ, a round-headed DOORWAY to the ringing chamber by *Erith*, 1963.

FONT. Octagonal, with the symbols of the Evangelists and angels, the figures thoroughly defaced. Discovered during the restoration by Roberts and set on a C14 pier base found at the same time. – DOOR in N doorway. With tracery panelling and one band of small figures in niches. – SCREEN. At W end of N aisle, 1916, by *W. D. Caröe*, to form choir vestry. Panel by N

* Cf. Great St Mary, Cambridge, and Saffron Walden.

door carved with names of vicars and lecturers also by Caröe. – PAINTING. The Ascension, by *Constable*. Painted as an altarpiece for Manningtree, 1821–2, installed here 2001. – STAINED GLASS. Seven chancel windows by *Kempe* or *Kempe & Co.*, E 1902, N and S 1907–9. S aisle E by *Warrington*, 1865, and in S wall, from E to W, *William Wailes* †1863, *Powell & Sons c.* 1848 (Ascension) and *c.* 1850 (Good Shepherd), and Charity, Faith, and Hope, by *W. G. von Glehn*, 1909. N aisle E window by *Clayton & Bell*, 1890, and another by them in N wall (Raising of Lazarus), *c.* 1870. Over the Webbe monument, the Sherman window has fragments of late C16 and C17 glass in the tracery, the lower part designed by *Raymond Erith*, 1965, incorporating C18 and C19 coloured glass. S aisle W also reglazed by Erith, and three more based on his design.

MONUMENTS. The chief monument is to Thomas Webbe 41 †1506, erected by his son John Webbe. It is in the N aisle, built up to reach into the window space, but probably not in its original position. Given its form, and Webbe's role in rebuilding the church, the chancel would be the expected place for it. It is a proud but not an imaginative piece. The decoration is copious but all too much a repetition of quatrefoil friezes, large and small, and with and without shields. The tomb-chest has two of them, one with the Webbe initials. The back of the depressed pointed recess has more, the soffit of the recess yet more. Above the recess a framed stone panel with the indents of Thomas Webbe and his family. Battlements and pinnacles above. – Edmund Chapman †1602. Alabaster and marble tablet with broken pediment and arms. – John Rogers †1636, frontal demi-figure in a niche, the ornament of the gristly kind fashionable in the second third of the C17. – William Burkitt †1703. White marble tablet, draped, with elaborate surround. Signed by *Thorne*, who is apparently otherwise unrecorded. – Rev. T. G. Taylor †1818. Austerely classical tablet with lengthy Latin inscription, and a female figure weeping over his urn. By *William Whitelaw*. – Lady Pilkington †1841. By *Robert De Carle*. Gothick. – A number of other tablets by local masons, e.g. W. Boyfield †1829 by *Watts* but probably dating from his daughter Charlotte †1877, and Rev. R.M. Miller †1839 by *G. Lufkin*. – Rev. G. Taylor †1871, elaborate brass inscription by *Jones & Willis*. – In churchyard, SW of the church, headstone of his parents by *R. Erith*, 1948, and SE of the church, of Erith himself †1973 by *Quinlan Terry*, carved by *W. J. Curtis*.

ASSEMBLY ROOMS, High Street. Opened by 1745. Pedimented front, with four pilasters, with wings to either side each with open pediments. Timber-framed and rendered. The main room has a shallow-arched ceiling and gallery at one end. Restored 1908 for use as village hall.

WATERWORKS. Pumping station W of Westgate House, High Street. 1947 by *R.J. Page*, with *Erith* as consultant. Main building with five round-headed windows and subsidiary pavilion-like buildings, in Suffolk white brick, based on Soane's lodges at Tendring Hall, Suffolk.

PERAMBULATION

The Town consists chiefly of the one High Street with Mill Lane branching off to the mill stream and the River Stour. Oppo-site Mill Lane, and E of the church, ROYAL SQUARE, a small open space that is the obvious place to begin a perambulation. In the middle of the square, the First World War MEMORIAL, 1921 by *W. D. Caröe*. On the E side, the former GRAMMAR SCHOOL, a group of two stately Early Georgian brick houses, the one on the E (WELL HOUSE) a little later and dated 1732 by an inscription. This is of white brick with red brick dress-ings, five bays by four, and has a doorway towards the street, on pilasters with a segmental pediment, an arched niche above it, and arched ground-floor windows. The same type of doorway is the entrance to the other house, which is distin-guished by giant angle pilasters. Both houses have brick para-pets decorated by sunk oblong panels. On the opposite side of the High Street, every building deserves a separate glance, although not one is of high individual merit. On the corner of Mill Lane, the MARLBOROUGH HEAD, C14, with exposed timber framing on the upper storey, and also C14 the adjoin-ing house to the r. (LOOM HOUSE), given a formal quoined front, but still plastered, in the C18. The next house C17 with a C18 brick front, five bays, the next (GOULD HOUSE) also five bays but painted brick and with a Diocletian window on the second floor. Then DALEBROOK HOUSE, timber-framed with gault brick front and Doric portico of 1811, *Raymond Erith*'s home to which he made internal alterations in 1936; BROOK HOUSE, late C15 or early C16 timber-framed and plastered with a gable at the W end; and finally No. 1 High Street, also timber-framed and plastered, C18.

Back on the S side, LINDSAY HOUSE is the former manse, 1739. It was contemporary with the Independent chapel, replaced in 1871–2 by the former CONGREGATIONAL CHURCH (converted to an art and craft centre, 1984).* By *Sulman & Rhodes*. E.E., brick with stone dressings and some black brick decoration. Liturgical NW tower with a slate steeple that is not much more than pyramidal.

Beyond the Congregational Church, the High Street con-tinues as BROOK STREET, and round the corner to the S FROG MEADOW, 1966–80, seven houses in an C18 vernacular classi-cal style, a mixture of brick and roughcast. No. 1 was built by *Erith* for his sister, 1966–7, Nos. 2 and 3 also by *Erith*, 1969 and 1972. The remainder by *Quinlan Terry*: No. 4, 1977, echoing C18 houses opposite with their mansard roofs, and Nos. 5–7, 1979–80, a symmetrical composition with Palladian pavilions flanking a five-bay house with a *trompe l'œil* niche and urn over the front door painted by Terry. On the opposite corner, set back, DEDHAM HALL, timber-framed with a low cross-wing of *c.* 1500, the hall range rebuilt in the early C17.

---

* Pevsner's advice in 1954 was to get the Congregational Church over quickly: 'After that one has nothing to fear.'

Continuing s along Brook Street one soon reaches a group of buildings on three sides of a garden known as WHITMORE PLACE, C16 timber-framed cottages adapted for use as the workhouse *c.* 1725 and enlarged 1730. On the s side of the garden two blocks faced in brick, the N range with a shaped gable to the street, the s range dated 1725 and with pedimented windows on the upper floor. Returned to domestic use in 1838. Opposite, MARY BARFIELD'S ALMSHOUSES, 1834, 'restored' 1893: brick, with pretty bargeboards to gables and porches, and further up the road (Crown Street), STEPHEN DUNTON'S ALMSHOUSES, plain brick, rebuilt 1806. But to return to Whitmore Place, for behind lies SOUTHFIELDS, the most important medieval house in Dedham, quite on its own. Built *c.* 1500 as a rich clothier's house, including round a courtyard his own living quarters, probably on the s side, and the offices and warehouse. Some of the timbers are exposed – more now than in, say, 1923, when photographed by *Country Life*, due to various C20 restorations, including one in 1935 in which *Grace Faithfull Roper* played a part. At the SW angle facing s is an extremely handsome gable with two overhangs on brackets. To the W the room on the ground floor has a bay window leaning against a brick chimney. The main feature of the N side is the carriageway with a gable over. It lies exactly in the middle of the side. Inside the courtyard there is an original porch on the W side, and an original door on the E. Divided into cottages by 1841.

From Southfields a path leads N past DRIFT COTTAGE, single-storey brick with pantile roof by *Erith*, 1973–4, and so back to Royal Square. N into Mill Lane, which leads down to the MILL by the River Stour. Rebuilt in brick after a fire in 1908, converted to flats in 1987. In MILL LANE, on the E side, MILL HOUSE, *c.* 1500. Open hall with crown-post roof, chamber block and porch added *c.* 1630. On the W side OCTAGON HOUSE, C19 painted stucco, in fact only three sides of an octagon facing the road, a rectangular block behind. The low cottage next to it, MEADOW COTTAGE, may date back to the C17 but was almost entirely rebuilt *c.* 1935, using old timbers, by *Grace Faithfull Roper* for herself. To what extent she acted as architect remains unclear, but her work here and elsewhere is typical of the period.

Now, at last, for the main part of the HIGH STREET to the W of Royal Square. It begins with the church on the s side, and opposite SHERMANS, the most self-consciously architectural building in the town. The house was bequeathed to the town by Edmund Sherman in 1601 for the English or Writing School, a counterpart to the Grammar School described above, and was refronted in 1730–1. The same masons were obviously responsible for both buildings, but Shermans is narrower in its front and more compact; two storeys, three bays, giant angle pilasters, a doorway with pediment on Corinthian pilasters, arched windows in broad frames l. and r., an arched niche in an aedicule above the door pediment, and a parapet with sunk panels curving up in the middle to allow space for a sundial – a lively, somewhat restless composition. In the niche, an urn by *Quinlan Terry* with an inscription commemorating its last private owner, the architect Marshall Sisson, who bequeathed the house to The National Trust in 1978.[*]

To the r. of Shermans, IVY HOUSE, five bays, two storeys, brick fronted but with a timber-framed range behind dated 1767 on plasterwork, and to the r. of that a C15 or C16 timber-framed house, part fronted in brick, with a gable on the r. and, along the return down Mill Lane, a jettied upper storey. C17 decorative plaster ceiling in a room over the teashop. To the l. of Shermans, a C17 house with painted brick front, shops on the ground floor, and then THE SUN, early C16, converted to a tavern by 1667, and with Georgian features including quoins, cornice, and a canted bay. At the E end a carriageway leads through to the yard, which retains its C17 covered external staircase. Next to The Sun, THE MERCHANT WEAVER'S HOUSE with overhang, Georgianized windows, and a big square chimneystack on the roof. On the r. return remains of C17 pargetting, a very elaborate scheme apparently based on a design of 1638 by *Borromini*. Then a picturesque four-gabled front, SHAKESPEARE HOUSE, *c.* 1500 enlarged in the C17.

On High Street's S side, immediately W of the church, the VICARAGE, 1815 by *M. G. Thompson*, extended 1841 and later in the C19: painted brick, with some battlements, hoodmoulds and buttresses to lend a Gothic air. Beyond it, several more timber-framed cottages, and also off to the N in PRINCEL LANE. After this, three large houses near the W entrance to the High Street. On the S side, set back from the street, DEDHAM HOUSE, a plain three-bay villa of gault brick dating from *c.* 1830, Erith's home from 1945 to 1973. On the N side, GREAT HOUSE, 1937–8 by *Erith* for his parents-in-law, to replace a Georgian-fronted house destroyed by fire. White Suffolk brick with slate roof. Three bays, three storeys; central Ionic doorcase with lunette above and windows with shutters to either side. It is a very stripped, Soanean sort of classicism, Soane's influence also apparent in the entrance hall's shallow vaulting. All internal fittings, including fireplaces, were designed by Erith and have survived. Next to it, WESTGATE HOUSE, true Georgian, with two storeys and a doorway with open pediment on brackets. Conservatory at the rear by *Erith*, 1937, and at right angles an attached house in similar style designed by Erith in 1973, built posthumously 1974–5; alterations by *Ronald Geary*, 2004–5. Below the house, on the River Stour, a brick and stucco BOATHOUSE, also by Erith, 1939, in the form of a tetrastyle Ionic temple.

Beyond the town centre, several large houses, many sited to take advantage of views over Dedham Vale and the River Stour, and mostly C19, either new or the remodelling of earlier, humbler buildings.

CASTLE HOUSE (Sir Alfred Munnings Museum), Castle Hill, ½ m. SSE. Late C15 front range, and S range added in the late C16 or early C17, all timber-framed and plastered. Early C19 additions on the N side, rendered brick, including the drawing room with large bow. A circular room with domed ceiling was formed in the existing S range. Some later C19 decoration, including hoodmoulds and Gothic detailing in the staircase hall. Home of the painter Sir Alfred Munnings, 1919–59; his studio, S of the house, a prefabricated timber building by *Boulton & Paul*, extended in brick and thatched. E of Castle House, in East Lane, KNIGHTS MANOR, early C17 timber-framed with exposed timbers, T-plan with a central chimneystack with four octagonal shafts, another of the houses restored by *Grace Faithfull Roper* in the 1930s. Also in East Lane, DAIRYFIELD COTTAGES by *Erith*, 1956–7, very plain brick, and SAMUEL BARKER'S ALMSHOUSES, 1863, brick with stock brick dressings and a veranda between two gabled cross-wings.

DALETHORPE, Stratford Road, ¾ m. W. A complex house, divided in three since 1950, and dating back to the early C16. At its core is a hall house with two cross-wings. Remodelled *c.* 1740, with a new staircase, and *c.* 1831 a two-storey E wing was added, including new entrance hall, and the E and S fronts remodelled and rendered. Opposite, MILSOMS (originally Dedham Lodge, now a hotel), stock brick Italianate villa of 1868, with C20 additions of varying quality. ¼ m. E of here, MAISON TALBOOTH (originally Hillands, also a hotel), 1850, rendered, with gables on all sides (some with decorative bargeboards) and gabled porch, well placed for the view across the valley to Stratford St Mary Church, Suffolk.

THE GROVE, Grove Hill ¾ m. SSW. By *David Laing*, *c.* 1811, for Stephen Tessier, although less interesting than the design published by Laing in 1818. Gault brick. Seven-bay, two-storey W front to the road with Ionic portico, and S front with two large bows.

LOWER LUFKINS, Bargate Lane, 1½ m. SE. By *Erith*, 1952–3. Small brick cottage, one end with canted sides like a half-hexagon.

LOWER PARK, 300 yds S. Close to the centre of the town but quite separate. C18 gault brick, with a three-bay entrance (E) front with central pedimented bay breaking slightly forward, enlarged early in the C19 (two large canted bays on the S front) and again after 1896, reduced by *Erith* on the N side 1964–5. Early C19 former COACH HOUSE to the S, two storeys with central archway, now blocked.

STOUR HOUSE, 1¼ m. SE. 1868. Large, of dark red brick, in a style perhaps fondly imagined to be Elizabethan. Straight gables with raised brick to suggest bargeboards and pendants. In the middle of the W front a square tower with gables on all four faces, topped with a sort of wrought-iron gazebo. Stable block in similar style. On the N side of the house a fine free-standing conservatory, with transepts, clerestory, and central turret, the timber structure supported by spiral columns and other cast ironwork by *Steven Bros & Co.*

LE TALBOOTH, Gun Hill, 1 m. w. C16 timber-framed house, now a restaurant, jettied on three sides, restored and extended by *Grace Faithfull Roper* as refreshment rooms, 1937. Various further extensions in similar style, with exposed timbers, 1960–88, and a larger, less harmonious extension by *Stanley Bragg & Associates*, 1973–4, semi-underground with platform roof.

DENGIE

9000

ST JAMES. C14 nave and chancel, the walls a remarkable variety of colour: septaria, flint, pebble, and, unusually, C14 yellow brick. C14 windows, those of the nave with ogee detail, those of the chancel with a very peculiar tracery pattern. Restored by *J. Clarke*, 1849–50, who provided the good nave BENCHES with low doors. His also the stone bellcote, supported by carved corbels of two lions and a man, and S porch. Nave roof restored and N vestry added by *P. M. Beaumont*, 1909–10. – REREDOS and SEDILIA. Stone, designed and carved by the rector, *E.J. Warmington*, 1878–80, with three painted panels by *Miss Warmington*. Two single sedilia, one each side of the chancel, each with its own credence, elaborately canopied. – STAINED GLASS. E window by *John Hall & Son*, 1921. – BRASS. 15-in. (38-cm.) figure of a lady, five sons and three daughters, *c.* 1520, not *in situ*.

DENGIE MANOR, W of the church. Early C18 brick front range, rebuilt *c.* 1820–30, added on to a C17 or earlier timber-framed building. C18 walled garden with crinkle-crankle walls.

DODDINGHURST

5090

ALL SAINTS. Flint, the nave and chancel virtually rebuilt by *J.P. St Aubyn*, 1886–7; N vestry and organ chamber added. Much of the nave's N wall is original C13, also the S doorway with one order of colonettes and a moulded arch with dogtooth ornament. Uncommonly large early C16 timber S porch, each side having ten arched openings. Timber W belfry with small, shingled, splay-foot spire. The bell-stage has vertical boarding. It stands on six posts with rather shallow arched braces and much diagonal trellis-strutting. The bell-frame appears to be integral with its construction. Probably C15, the date of the nave roof, which has tie-beams, crown-posts, and four-way struts. – FONT. Late C14, octagonal, with quatrefoils round the bowl and traceried panels on the pedestal. – ROOD. Figures probably German, early C16. – STAINED GLASS. All by *A.O. Hemming & Co.*, 1886–7.

Former Priest's House (now CHURCH HALL). Early C16 timber-framed and weatherboarded.

BARFIELD FARM, ⅓ m. NNW. Early C17 with exposed close studding on the N front. Thought originally to have been a hunting
lodge or standing. One storey removed when it became a farm.

DAYS FARM, 1½ m. S. C16 and early C17, part plastered, part
weatherboarded, and some exposed timbers. In a first-floor
room, painted black-letter Biblical texts.

DOVERCOURT
Harwich

2030

Dovercourt is the mother parish of Harwich, although the latter
has been administratively and strategically more important since
the C14. The church and most of the older buildings are at Upper
Dovercourt, in the western part of the parish. In the eastern part
are the C19 development and commercial activity so noticeably
absent from Harwich.

ALL SAINTS. Perp W tower, the lower part with diagonal
buttresses and plastered, the upper part rebuilt in brick in the
early C19 and battlemented. Nave and chancel pebbledashed.
Norman nave, with one N and one S window. Chancel early
C14, see the renewed N and S windows. A little more elaborate
and slightly later N and S nave windows. The tracery here is
flowing. C14 crown-post roof in the nave, the posts octagonal
with 'crown' capitals. Brick S porch with reused C14 stone
archway. Restored 1897–8 by *J.E.K. & J.P. Cutts*.* A number
of blocked windows were opened up and the ceiling removed.
Visually over-large N extension in red and yellow brick, 1987.
– FONT. Octagonal, C14, with cusped panels of tracery (intersected and other), quatrefoils, etc. – ROOD BEAM. Medieval,
but dated 1615. This must refer to the carving, with vine scroll.
– ORGAN. Of the 1890s, with a little painted decoration and
two small carved figures of angels. COMMANDMENT BOARDS
probably of the same date. – POOR BOX. Plain, square, iron-
bound, dated 1589. – ROYAL ARMS of 1816–37. Cast iron, by
Coleman & Wallis of Colchester. – STAINED GLASS. Eleven
windows with glass by *E.R. Suffling*, *c.* 1898–1900, who donated
the chancel S window. – Small nave S window in C12 opening
by *William Morris* of Westminster, 1958. – W window of
Munich glass, donated in 1899 by Kaiser Wilhelm II in
memory of German soldiers who died of fever following the
Walcheren Expedition of 1809. The British dead are commemorated by a LYCHGATE by the *Cutts*, given by Queen
Victoria. – BRASS to a Civilian, *c.* 1430, the figure about 25 in.
(63 cm.).

CENTRAL CHURCH (Methodist and U.R.C., originally
Wesleyan), Main Road. 1904–5 by *W. J. Jolley*. Dec. Brick with
stone dressings. Extended 2002.

---

* St Augustine, Hill Road, Lower Dovercourt, by *J.E.K. Cutts*, 1883–4, enlarged 1888,
has been demolished.

OUR LADY QUEEN OF HEAVEN (R.C.), Fronks Road. By *R.A. Boxall*, 1955. Brick. It replaced *E. W. Pugin*'s church in Harwich, 1869, damaged in the 1953 flood.

CEMETERY, Main Road. 1855. Brick Neo-Gothic lodge and chapels by *C.H. Edwards*. The Anglican chapel has a little bell-turret.

MAGISTRATES' COURT, Main Road. Built as Hill Schools by *Brown & Burgess*, 1913–4. Edwardian Baroque, two storeys with rusticated ground floor, pedimented first-floor windows, and little domes on the projecting wings.

KINGSWAY HALL (now arts centre and community hall). Mission hall, given by R. J. Bagshaw in 1874. Italianate, stuccoed, with tall slender W tower. W narthex and shallow chancel.

HARWICH SCHOOL, Hall Lane. 1957–8 by *Johns, Slater & Haward* in collaboration with *H. Conolly*, County Architect. Up to three storeys. Sixth Form Centre N of the main school converted from THE GRANGE, a large mock-timber-framed house by *H. Steward-Watling*, 1911.

MAYFLOWER PRIMARY SCHOOL and ADULT COMMUNITY CENTRE (former Harwich County High School), Main Road. 1909–10 by *Brown & Burgess*. Queen Anne, with narrow tall sash windows, dormers, and ventilation turrets. Headmaster's house 1911 by the same architects.

ALL SAINTS' PRIMARY SCHOOL, Main Road. By *J. W. Start*, 1894. Brick, single-storey. Extended 1992.

FRYATT HOSPITAL AND MAYFLOWER MEDICAL CENTRE, Main Road. By *Nightingale Associates*, 2004–5. Mainly two storeys, with buff brick and timber cladding.

WATER TOWER, Fronks Road. 1903. Round corrugated metal tank with conical roof on an open steelwork tower.

PERAMBULATION. Most of the older buildings are at UPPER DOVERCOURT near All Saints. Opposite, OLD TIMBERS (No. 519 Main Road), timber-framed with an early C19 three-bay brick front, and to the E a terrace of five cottages, early C16 timber-framed with rendered brick front and gambrel roof. 250 yds E, POUND FARM, C17 timber-framed and plastered, partly encased in brick in the C19. DOVERCOURT HALL, ⅔ m. SE, has a late C17 range with exposed timbers and early C17 plastered cross-wing.

LOWER DOVERCOURT, between Upper Dovercourt and Harwich, was developed by John Bagshaw, M.P. for Harwich. In 1845 he built Cliff House (dem. 1909), whose grounds contained a chalybeate spring. In 1854 he opened a spa to coincide with the opening of the railway to Harwich, with a Tudor-style Spa House by the beach below his house (also dem.), and Orwell Terrace at right angles to the shore on the SW side of the spa grounds. A plan was drawn up for a formal layout of streets to the SW centred on Kingsway, which to the N of the High Street curved round to the railway station. Bagshaw's architect was *W.H. Lindsey*, although *Horace Darken*, a local architect, seems to have been involved with individual buildings, and further development was planned in

'New Town', Dovercourt.
Garden and Principal Fronts of £650 houses

the 1860s by *James Butterworth* of Ipswich for Bagshaw's son, R.J. Bagshaw.

ORWELL TERRACE is the main surviving element, a row of thirteen three-storey houses with attics and basements in the typical prosperous style of 1850s London. The garden front is just as important as the street front, with all the unsightly service quarters safely below ground. At the N end is a slightly larger house (a similar house at the S end collapsed in 1994) and beyond it another house, attached but in different style, probably later. In the gardens (CLIFF PARK, opened 1911) a small, octagonal, thatched garden building, faced with clinker, with ogee-headed door and windows, formerly in the garden of Cliff House. Bagshaw also built the Undercliff Walk, 1858.

CLIFF HOTEL, Marine Parade, marks the southern extremity of Bagshaw's development. Three and four storeys, mainly painted but with one portion of brick with stock brick dressings that links it stylistically to the cheaper housing erected by the Bagshaws, examples of which can be seen in Cliff Road and, N of the High Street, in Victoria Street, as well as to the RAILWAY STATION of 1854 (probably by *F. Barnes*), and the Queen's Hotel in the High Street. There was a further spate of development in the early years of the C20, notably around the crossroads of KINGSWAY and HIGH STREET. Two corner buildings of 1902, both with turret and spire: the Co-Operative Society (SW) has at the rear what was originally a concert hall; LLOYDS BANK (NE) has coupled Corinthian columns, strapwork balustrades, and elaborate shaped gables with pinnacles. In Kingsway, S, BARCLAYS BANK, more refined. Queen Anne with Ionic pilasters. Looking down Kingsway from Marine Parade, a marble STATUE of Queen Victoria, 1904, and on the corner the former ALEXANDRA HOTEL, 1902–3 by *Sherrin* (now a retirement home), in a more informal, cosier, and picturesque style than the Cliff Hotel's. Amenities included a 500-seat concert hall, now dem.

In FRONKS ROAD, ¼ m. sw of Cliff Hotel, Nos. 35–41, mid-C19 row of Trinity House cottages. Rendered brick with gables and gabled porches.

TOWER HOTEL, Main Road, ¼ m. sw of Kingsway. Built 1885 as a private house. Osborne-Italianate with a four-storey tower at one corner. Converted and extended 1982–4.

LIGHTHOUSES. Leading lights, 1863, to replace those at Harwich, and in use until 1917. Probably by *James Walker*, consulting engineer to Trinity House. On cast-iron circular legs, the upper light having six legs and the lower four.

BEACON HILL FORT. Occupying a spur at the sw end of Harwich Harbour and commanding the entrance to it and the rivers. In use in the Napoleonic Wars, but the present battery built from 1889 and considerably enlarged and fortified in the First World War and remodelled in the Second, with concrete gun emplacements, battery observation post, pillboxes, etc.

7090

DOWNHAM

ST MARGARET. Big sturdy brick w tower of *c.* 1500. Diaper pattern of vitrified headers. Diagonal buttresses. Battlements. Nave and chancel rebuilt by *G.E. Street*, 1871, in Kentish rag, but with a few reused windows. N vestry, with some quirky detailing, 1909 by *S. Gambier Parry*, who was churchwarden. Gutted by fire, 1977, and rebuilt with a simplified interior. Small N extension, 1987. – REREDOS. Five stone arches with marble panels and red marble cross, belonging to *Street*'s rebuilding. – STAINED GLASS. E window, 2000, and nave N, 1988, by *Jane Gray*. Chancel S by *Valerie Green*, 1992. – MONUMENT. In w tower, Sarah †1692 and Benjamin Disbrowe †1708. Slabs from a chest-tomb with deep carvings of skulls and other emblems of mortality. – On the churchyard's N boundary, a small shelter for the rector's carriage and horse during services, probably C18 but with C19 ecclesiastical decoration. Beyond, an octagonal C18 brick DOVECOTE with cupola from Downham Hall, moved here 1991.

WOODLEIGH, School Road. By *R.V. Wilson & Clive Plumb*, *c.* 1976, then both working for Basildon Development Corporation. Pitched roof supported at the corners on free-standing steel columns, the house below it an independent structure. Separate garage a smaller version of the same.

8020

EARLS COLNE

ST ANDREW. The most rewarding part is the big w tower, with diagonal buttresses and three-light bell openings. Begun *c.* 1460, it has battlements with flushwork decoration dated 1534 and the arms and mullets of the de Veres. Brick E face, as is the top part of the stair-turret, but the rest of the tower is of flint rubble with stone dressings. On top of the turret an iron openwork 'corona' for the weathervane, probably early C18. The body of the large church is almost square, with N and S aisle and chapels, S porch, and only a shallow projecting sanctuary. Little medieval work survives: the sanctuary walls, but without original features, the S aisle with C14 windows, and the S arcade with octagonal piers. S chapel by *William & Richard Ward*, 1838, then in 1863–4 *H. W. Hayward* restored the lot and added the N aisle and N chapel, removing the N vestry and W gallery added by *Abraham Rayner* ('an experienced architect of Halstead') in 1835. Chancel walls and ceiling nicely stencilled, originally more extensive, and surprisingly late (1924). – REREDOS. By *J.H. Hakewill*, 1875. Stone, with *Salviati* mosaic of the Last Supper. – CHOIR STALLS. 1896. – PEWS. All the seating in the nave and aisles by *Duncan Clark & Beckett*, 1931, as a memorial to Reuben and Elizabeth Hunt, the ends carved (by *Bryan Saunders*) with symbols of their personal and professional interests. – STAINED GLASS. E window 1864, and in the S chapel two Jubilee windows of 1897, but by different makers. S aisle by *Clayton & Bell*, 1897, and *Heaton, Butler & Bayne*, 1922; N aisle by *Christopher Webb*, 1947. – MONUMENTS. Roger Harlakenden †1602/3 and four wives, the usual type of wall monument, painted alabaster, with kneeling figures. – George Cressener †1722. By *Horsnaile*. Lengthy inscription set in a frame of Composite pilasters and open segmental pediment, with painted and gilded shields. Funeral HELM on top. – John Wale of Colne Priory †1761. Tablet by *Roubiliac* with relief of Mercury and Justice. – T.H. Blackall †1903. By *G. Maile & Son*, with an expensive-looking Gothic surround. – On exterior S wall of tower, Abraham Plastow †1836, servant and gamekeeper 'of humble station, yet of sterling worth, . . . to all our Village dear!' – LYCHGATES. 1910 and 1912, one or both by *E. Beckwith*.

BAPTIST CHURCH. 1860, by *Mr Moore* of London. Very large and urban-looking, to cater for the ironworks behind it. Brick. Façade with a row of five doors, above that four narrow windows, and above them a large wheel window. Above the round-headed doors and windows, black brick string courses which are pointed, the combined effect vaguely Saracenic. Central gable with decorated brick verges Rear schoolroom added 1899.

FRIENDS' MEETING HOUSE. 1674, rebuilt in the early C18 (brick in N wall dated 1733). Square, with pyramidal roof. Additions by *Alan Bragg*, 1986.

COLNE PRIORY. The present house, built by John Wale, dates from 1736. Originally plain Georgian brick, by 1770 it had battlements, Gothick windows, and two symmetrical castellated bay windows and a tripartite central window with ogee tops. Extended in similar vein for H.H. Carwardine in 1825, with further alterations and additions later in the C19 and C20. The house partly occupies the site of a Benedictine priory, founded from Abingdon about 1100–7 by Aubrey de Vere. Hardly anything survives above ground, but excavations have shown that the church had nave and aisles of six bays, two w towers standing outside the aisle ends as at St Botolph Colchester, crossing and transepts, and chancel with chancel chapels. There were five staggered apses (transepts, chancel aisles, chancel). Later in the C12 the chancel and its aisles were slightly enlarged and provided with square ends. The nave was rebuilt in the mid C14, probably following the collapse of the central tower. Later still, in the C15, the s chancel aisle was rebuilt on a much larger scale (as in the C14 at Little Dunmow). The cloister and the apsed chapter house have also been traced. Of the tombs of the de Veres, Earls of Oxford, many were destroyed in 1736. Three tomb-chests with effigies which had been taken to the parish church were displayed by Carwardine in his remodelled house in 1825, but taken to St Stephen's Chapel near Bures (Suffolk) in 1935.

PERAMBULATION

Earls Colne falls into two separate parts: the High Street, running w from the church, and Holt Street at the bottom of Church Hill leading to the River Colne. First the HIGH STREET, which starts promisingly on the s side with Nos. 122 and 124 with two jettied gables, the date 1674 carved on one bressumer. Nos. 112 and 114, mid C16, have a long-wall jetty to the street, the bressumer carved with the de Vere mullet, and exposed timbers on the upper floor. Opposite the church's N side, COLNE PLACE, three-bay, six-storey, early C19 gault brick, and then THE CASTLE pub. Behind the plaster front two cross-wings, the l. late C14, the r. mid C16, and the middle range c. 1600. Wall painting in a ground-floor room of 'memento mori' text with appropriate symbols flanked by heraldic lions beneath garlands.*

In YORK ROAD, off the High Street to the s, the former GRAMMAR SCHOOL, a C16 foundation. Closed 1975. Remaining buildings converted to private houses. By the road the Headmaster's House and Boarding House, 1897–8 by *H.A. Cheers*. Exuberant brick with stone dressings and a busy roofline with half-timbered gables, dormers, and a turret with weathervane on top of a tall spike. Set back from the road, single-storey buildings in similar style, including classroom block by *J. W. Clark*, 1892–3, and additional classrooms and new main entrance by *Chancellor & Son*, 1903–4, the latter with a short tower, cupola and flagpole, almost a miniature version of their building for Brentwood School (q.v.). Opposite, the VILLAGE HALL by *P. M. Beaumont*, 1912. Brick, Neo-Tudor,

---

* The text and garlands are almost identical to those on an overmantel at 49 Queen Street, Coggeshall, according to Muriel Carrick.

dominated by a large half-timbered gable above a two-storey oriel with brick nogging, diamond-paned windows. Hood-moulded doorways to r. and l.

After the junction with York Road and Queen's Road, the street broadens, with on the s side a row of ten cottages, 1859–60, projecting from the centre of which is the gabled Institute (now PUBLIC LIBRARY). This and the semi-octagonal end pavilions are of red brick, the cottages of stock, each with contrasting dressings. On the High Street's N side, mainly late medieval timber-framed houses, including Nos. 17–19, whose brick front conceals the remains of a C14 aisled hall, the front aisle now missing, with a late C15 cross-wing to the r.

Before the High Street broadens out further into a green comes FOUNDRY LANE and the ATLAS IRON WORKS of Reuben Hunt & Co. Founded by 1856, and the most important influence on the town after the de Veres. Closed in 1988, most of the site has been redeveloped, but some of the best industrial buildings have been converted to residential and commercial use by *Jeremy Smith* for *East Anglian Renovations* with some infill, completed 2005. These include four main ranges of the original foundry, 1869–72, of stock brick, the end walls with round-headed doors and windows set in arched recesses of red brick. Behind them, the water tower, steel tank on two-storey stock brick base, 1885 (now MUSEUM), and further back the pump house (now SURGERY). Additional housing by *Wimpey*. Steel SCULPTURE of Atlas and benches by *Paul Margetts*. Along the road, brick stable and ancillary buildings of 1886–94. Opposite, two terraces of workers' houses, Hibernia Cottages and Belle Vue Cottages, 1872 and 1876. Brick with stock brick dressings, but otherwise quite plain. More housing round the corner in HAYHOUSE ROAD, 1899. Back at the junction with the High Street, Reuben Hunt's own house (now flats), TILL-WICKS, 1876, dour stock brick with lots of gables and decorative bargeboards. In BURROWS ROAD, almost opposite on the N side of the High Street, a row of five almshouses built by Hunt, 1909, as well as two pairs of brick cottages dated 1835, built for H.H. Carwardine of Colne Priory.

W of Foundry Lane, the Baptist Church (*see* above) dominates the scene, and beyond it more foundry workers' housing, but here 'Garden City'-style semi-detached villas of *c.* 1905–12. On the corner of Station Road, a picturesque LODGE, originally to the plain COLNE HOUSE, built for Mrs Mary Gee, *c.* 1840. Opposite the lodge, thatched cottages with Gothic windows, built by Mrs Gee at about the same time. ¼ m. along Station Road, MEADOW CROFT, 1912 by *P. M. Beaumont* for Arthur Hunt. Large house, lodge and outbuildings in that mixture of red brick, roughcast and false half-timbering that Sherrin, for example, handled so much better.

Now E of the church. At the bottom of Church Hill, on a green at the junction of Coggeshall Road and Upper Holt Street, a cast-iron PUMP erected in 1853 'in thankful commemoration in the absence of cholera for the common use of the people and to provoke them to cleanliness'. Octagonal, with traceried panels and ogee-domed cap. Some nice houses along UPPER HOLT STREET, notably No. 9, recorded as recently built in 1683. Timber-framed, plaster front and weatherboarded sides, and tiled gambrel roof. Front remodelled in the early C19, with two canted bays on the ground floor and a decorative wrought-iron porch. Further E, PRIORY COTTAGE, almshouses on three sides of a quadrangle, built by H. H. Carwardine of Colne Priory, 1843. Stock brick, the gabled porches probably later. Finally PRIORY CLOSE, c. 1670, flint and brick rubble with brick dressings, and a stock brick extension of c. 1840.

CHALKNEY MILL, 1 m. ESE. Early C18 weatherboarded water mill (now residential). Miller's house at one end with plastered front and large sashes.

COLNEFORD HOUSE. See White Colne.

EAST DONYLAND

ST LAWRENCE. 1837–8 by *William Mason* of Ipswich. Quite remarkably original. Octagonal, of white brick, in the lancet style, said to be inspired by York Minster's chapter house. Groups of five stepped lancets on three sides, two sides blank, entrances on two others, and three lancets on the E side, which also has a very shallow gabled chancel. W gallery cutting across a third of the interior, the vestries beneath formed by *L.J. Selby*, 1937–9, during reordering which included the PULPIT and other fittings by *H. & K. Mabbitt*. Further reordering by *S.E. Dykes Bower*, 1967–70, included the installation of the FONT, from St Martin, Colchester: C14, octagonal, with recesses in the stone crowned by three-dimensional ogee arches. – MONUMENT. Elizabeth Marshall †1613. Frontally seated woman, full-length, flanked by obelisks. Below, one kneeling daughter and two babies in cradles. Long inscription which reads as follows:

Clotho	In tender armes thy tickle rocke I beare
	Wherein consists of life, this Hemispher
	Frayle Flyeinge Fadeinge, Fickle sliperye
	Certayne in nothing but uncertantye

Lachsis	From of thy rocke her slender thred I pull
	When scarce begun but yt my spoale is full
	Thus tyme begetts bringes forth & with her haste
	Makes after tyme, tymes former workes to waste

Atropos	I with my Knife have cutt that thred in twayne
	And loosde that knott, not to be knitt agayne
	What two wer one my knife hath both opposd
	In heaven her soule in earth her corpes inclosde

The verses are attributed to Gilbert Longe, then vicar of East Donyland. – BRASSES to Nicholas Marshall †1621 and his wife Mary Gray †1627, 20-in. (51-cm.) figures.

MARINER'S CHAPEL, Chapel Street. 1850, painted brick in rat-trap bond, two storeys. Later C19 gabled porch.

The medieval church stood next to East Donyland Hall (*see* below), but was rebuilt in Rowhedge, the then growing part of the parish by the Colne. The quayside here is unpretentiously picturesque, but overwhelmed by late C20 and early C21 heritage-style houses. Streets to the W have rows of modest C19 and early C20 houses, with some C19 weatherboarded boat stores or sail lofts in CHURCH STREET and TAYLOR'S ROAD. Below the church, the former SCHOOL by *Joseph Grimes*, 1862, additions by *George Lufkin, c.* 1893. In REGENT STREET the Co-op, *c.* 1900, with deep canopy over the pavement and former public reading room on first floor, an early example of a purpose-built rural Co-operative Stores. Further up the street the former PRIMITIVE METHODIST CHAPEL, now a house, by *S. Wilson-Webb*, 1913. Brick with stone dressings. Off Parkfield Street, WATER TOWER, 1902. Campanile-style with Romanesque detailing (cf. Wivenhoe).

EAST DONYLAND HALL, ½ m. SW. Early C17, partly moated. Purchased in 1730 by *David Gansel* of Leyton, an amateur architect, who encased it in brick, creating a stately seven-bay façade with rusticated quoins; its size exaggerated by the narrow windows and a deep parapet with false windows. This hid the attic storey until it was lowered *c.* 1943, revealing dormers, when single-storey bays were also added at either end. Facing the entrance, three low pedimented ranges of outbuildings, arranged slightly fanwise, each with a smart, broken-pedimented doorcase echoing the house's. They form an element of the park laid out by Gansel, of which many splendid cedars survive. NE of the outbuildings a ruined brick DOVECOTE or gazebo.

EAST HANNINGFIELD   7000

ALL SAINTS. By *Henry Stone*, 1884–5. The medieval church, S of East Hanningfield Hall, was gutted by fire in 1883. No visible remains.* Its replacement, in the centre of the village, is of stock brick faced with Kentish rag and Carr stone, artfully interspersed with red tiles, and Bath stone dressings. Timber W bellturret. Rather mechanical carving of font, reredos, pulpit etc. by *J. Frampton*. – STAINED GLASS. By *A.O. Hemming, c.* 1900–1.

Pleasant village centre (THE TYE) with a green on the E side of the road and a few pretty houses. At the S end of the green, RAILS FARM, C16 with gabled cross-wing, and a few yards to its S WILLIS FARM, of similar date, with two-storey porch. Late C16 or early C17 wall painting includes imitative panelling in two first-floor rooms. At the green's N end, the OLD RECTORY, brick with stepped gables, mostly by *Chancellor*, 1898.

---

*Fragments of early C14 WALL PAINTING in Victoria and Albert Museum.

Off BACK LANE, old persons' flats and houses by *James Gowan*, 1978, commissioned by Chelmsford Borough Council in a rare moment of adventure. Arranged in two-storey terraces following the conventional 'Radburn' layout, wilfully defying the Essex Design Guide. Rhythm is the striking feature – monopitch roofs, alternately high and low at the street front, with round chimneys in between, and large round windows made from standard sections of sewer pipe – emphasized by colour: red and yellow brick, white render, and brown Roman tiles.

6080

EAST HORNDON
Brentwood

ALL SAINTS. Brick church, once gloriously sited, on a hill with wide views to the s, but now on the N side of the busy A127, with EAST HORNDON HALL (C16 timber-framed, brick-clad with many additions) on the s side. Made redundant in 1970 after years of neglect but now in the care of the Churches Conservation Trust. This has not prevented vandalism and the loss of most of the interior fittings.* The exterior remains unspoilt, with its eminently picturesque short C17 W tower with thick diagonal buttresses, continued in polygonal angles and polygonal pinnacles. The battlements between these are stepped. Large arched windows as bell-openings, with raised frames. The church was rebuilt following the grant of the advowson to Sir Thomas Tyrell in 1442. It has – an unusual feature – N and s transepts. Charming group of s porch and s transept under one sloping roof leading up to a gable, and then projecting s chapel, added after 1510. Inside, this chapel is separated from the chancel by a two-bay arcade with a pier of four demi-shafts and four diagonal hollows, and moulded arches. In the chancel N wall a deep recess, with brick-panelled back and sides and ribbed vault, contains the MONUMENT of Sir Thomas Tyrell †1476 and his wife, but of the brasses only part of the inscription remains. Excellent roofs, flat-ceiled in the s chapel, pitched and ceiled with panels separated by bosses in the chancel, open with tie-beams and crown-posts in the nave. The narrow transepts are divided into two storeys, the upper floor on the s side having an original brick fireplace, indicating its use as a room. Later used as galleries, with early C17 balustrades. Extensive repairs by *Bodley*, 1898–1908. The most visible sign is the E window. Further restoration by *Laurence King*, 1972–3, including rebuilding the s arcade. – MONUMENTS. Lady Tyrell †1422, large incised limestone slab with figure in horned head-dress under canopy with figures of nine children up the l. and r. shafts. An object of great rarity and beauty. – Unknown family, *c.* 1520, in recess in s transept.

---

*Font removed to Great Wakering, 1969. Monument to Sir John Tyrell †1766 by *Nollekens* now in the Victoria and Albert Museum.

Altar tomb with quatrefoil decoration. Indents of brasses against the back wall show that they were praying to the Trinity. – Opposite W door, group of three headstones to members of the Freman family †1801, 1818 and 1831. Similar carvings on each, with draped figure leaning on an urn.

HERONGATE, 1 m. NNW, was the main centre of population, with a few nice houses spread out along Brentwood Road, including FRIARS, early C19 gault brick, and HERON COTTAGE, C18 timber-framed and weatherboarded. More weatherboarding in CRICKETER'S LANE, parallel to Brentwood Road on the E side, notably No. 27, late C17, with one large and one smaller two-storey canted bay and an Ionic doorcase. Originally one house with No. 25, clad in brick in the early C19. To the N, MAXES (No. 59), recorded in 1733 and enlarged shortly before 1791 by *Richard Woods*, then Lord Petre's surveyor. Canted bays added in the late C19 or early C20. Tudoresque windows.

HERON HALL, 1½ m. NNE. An interesting group of brick buildings, the oldest an early C15 granary. Remodelled in the C17 when the house, stables, and a two-storey building that may have served both as granary and manorial court hall were built, probably by John Tyrell †1675. They stand beside the moat of the seat of the Tyrells, demolished 1788.

EASTHORPE

9020

ST MARY THE VIRGIN. Nicely placed with Easthorpe Hall a little to the W. Small church with nave and chancel under one roof, of mixed materials with Roman brick in the dressings. Slender timber W belfry. Essentially Norman – see the W window high up, and several N and S windows and indications of windows as well as plain doorways. The Norman church had an apse, of which the beginning is exposed on the S side. The chancel is a C13 alteration. It has good SEDILIA with two pointed trefoiled arches on shafts and three widely stepped lancet windows with internal dogtooth ornamentation. Some C14 windows were inserted to give more light. In addition there is a curious quatrefoil low side window leading to a recess in the S wall. Restoration by *F. W. Chancellor*, 1910–11, including new roof and rebuilding of C15 S porch. – WALL PAINTING. Mid-C13 figures in the splays of a S window: Resurrection and Angels. – STAINED GLASS. Christ preaching, German or Swiss, *c.* 1530 (S window).

EASTHORPE HALL. H-plan, E wing C16, central three-bay hall range rebuilt in C17, W wing also C17. C18 alterations including the fitting of much heavily moulded panelling. C17 barn behind.

WELL COTTAGE, opposite the church. Over-restored late C15 hall house with crown-post roof and two-storey E wing jettied on two sides. Exposed timbers.

ST MARY'S GRANGE, ¼ m. E of the church, until 1929 the rectory. Large two-storey hall range, probably built after 1637, with C15 W cross-wing. Timber-framed and plastered, with C18 and C19 brick additions to the E and N.

EAST MERSEA

St Edmund King and Martyr. Big stone Perp W tower with diagonal buttresses, battlements, and higher stair-turret. At the base a little flushwork decoration, also some flushwork crosses higher up. Of the same time most of the church – see the tracery of the windows. However, three were replaced in the C18 by big bare pointed openings, with simple wooden tracery. Perp N arcade of four bays with tall two-centred arches and piers of a section in which four deeply undercut attached shafts are connected by deep hollows. The chancel arch and the arch from the chancel to the N chapel are of the same type. NICHE, chancel N wall. Crocketed ogee arch not *in situ*; probably from a nave window splay. – FONT. Octagonal, C15, with uncommonly pretty blank arches. – PULPIT. Early C17, still with its tester and HOURGLASS STAND. Panelled sides with lozenges. Perched high up on the S wall; there were high pews in the church until 1912, one reused as screen at the N aisle's W end. – SCULPTURE. Wooden figures of St Edmund and St Mary the Virgin by *H. & K. Mabbitt*, *c.* 1960. – STAINED GLASS. E window by *T. F. Curtis* (*Ward & Hughes*) to E. A. L. Barlow †1914, but erected after the war. – Roundels and other fragments of Flemish glass from Topsham, Devon. – MONUMENT. Lt.-Col. Edward Bellamie Esq. Citizen and Fishmonger †1656. Achievement of arms, painted on board. – Sarah Wrench †1848. Grave by N wall of chancel with mort safe, i.e. an iron cage to deter body-snatchers, with inscription on cast-iron plate.

The church shares a moated site with EAST MERSEA HALL, a timber-framed and plastered house dating back to the early C16. GLEBE HOUSE, 250 yds N, replaced a rectory by *G.E. Street*, 1859–60 (dem. 1924), of which the coachhouse remains; Street also built the National School to the W, now church hall and shop.

BLOCKHOUSE, about 1¼ m. ENE. 1547, with moat and drawbridge. Some fragments visible but mostly demolished or built into the sea-wall.

EAST TILBURY
Thurrock U.A.

St Catherine. On the N escarpment of the Thames, close to the river. The most interesting feature is the four-bay N arcade with alternating circular and octagonal piers, square capitals of scallops with angle volutes, and unmoulded pointed arches. The E respond shows waterleaf, the aisle outer walls two lancets. All this must belong to the later decades of the C12.

Evidence of the Norman church which was enlarged by this aisle is one blocked window above the fourth arcade arch. The chancel is a good piece of E.E. building; three stepped E lancets, also N and S lancets. On the N side one two-light window of *c.* 1300. The nave S side shows evidence inside and out of a former arcade. It is said that this and the W tower – which to judge by the blocked tower arch must have been C13 – fell victim to the Dutch raid of 1667. Good original C14 windows in the repaired S wall. Most of the church is flint and stone rubble, except for the two-storey SW vestry which is of very rugged, coursed Kentish rag. This was to have been the base of a tower begun in 1917 by men of the London Electrical Engineers under *Captain C. W. C. Kaye*, the stone probably taken from part of Coalhouse Fort (*see* below). Wooden W belfry taken down during restoration by *George Patrick*, 1906. – PULPIT. Usual early C17 type. Hexagonal, each panel arcaded with fluted pilasters at the corners. – ROYAL ARMS. Three sets. One painted over the chancel arch, C16, very faded. Two on canvas, both of George III, one from West Tilbury. – STAINED GLASS. E lancets by *Charles Evans & Co.*, 1905. W window by *Auravisions*, 2000. – MONUMENT. Henry Knight †1721. Large stone tomb-chest, its carving beautifully preserved: skull and crossbones and hourglass on one panel, seven cherubs' heads on another.

RECTORY, opposite the church. 1835. Stock brick. Originally two bays square, later extended. The eaves of the garden front's gable form an open pediment with a Diocletian window.

COALHOUSE FORT, S of the church. East Tilbury lies at a strategic point on the Thames. A blockhouse was built in 1539–40 but nothing survives of this, nor of the artillery battery constructed in 1799. In 1847 work started on a fort, part of a general improvement of coastal defences, completed in 1855, but developments in armaments soon rendered it obsolete and it was replaced by the present structure in 1861–74. *Colonel W. F. D. Jervois* and *Captain H. T. Siborne* were responsible for at least part of the design; later stages were supervised by *Colonel Charles Gordon*. Facing the river, a semicircular casemated work, with a battery extending NW at one end to form a J, defended by an inner dry ditch and wide outer wet ditch. Magazines below the gun emplacements, each emplacement with its own separate cartridge store and shell store. On the landward side the enclosure is completed by the gateway and barracks. Stock brick, faced with granite and Kentish rag, and concrete roofs. Altered to accommodate different guns by 1903 and during the First and Second World Wars. Concrete emplacements were added on the roof and the river front earthed up to reduce the fort's profile, filling up the dry ditch and covering the original gun embrasures (now partly excavated). On the NE side of the fort a Second World War MINEFIELD CONTROL TOWER, three concrete cubes like a piece of abstract sculpture, and by the river a hexagonal RADAR TOWER. Between river and fort the QUICK-FIRER BATTERY, 95

with four concrete gun emplacements, 1893. ¼ m. N, EAST
TILBURY BATTERY, 1890–1, which accommodated six guns
in deep concrete-lined pits, and was designed to be virtually
invisible. At Bowaters Farm, ¾ m. WNW, a large ANTI-
AIRCRAFT BATTERY, first requisitioned 1939, expanded
1945–6 and 1950. Eight concrete emplacements and brick
barracks.

BATA ESTATE, 1 m. NW. Planned factory village for the British
Bata Shoe Co., begun in 1933 by *František Gahura* and
Vladimir Kafik, the company's architects, on the pattern of
their buildings in Zlin (Moravia, now Czech Republic). Comparisons with the earlier Silver End (q.v.) are obvious, but Bata
is less leafy – more 'City' than 'Garden' – and there is less
variety of design. The factory buildings (now in other use)
came first, two of five storeys each (although twelve were
planned, three of which would have been of ten storeys), and
a similar administration block, each thirteen bays by three.
They follow the Zlin modular construction system of exposed
reinforced concrete columns with brick infill and large *Crittall*
windows. The steel frame was arc-welded (rather than bolted
or riveted), a method then almost unknown in England. To one
side of the administration block, a bronze STATUE of the
company's founder, Thomas Bata, by *Hermon Cawthra*, 1955,
who was also responsible for the Second World War MEMOR-
IAL in the park opposite.

On the N side of the factory BATA AVENUE, the first street
to be built: sixteen pairs of semi-detached houses for workers
(many of whom were Czech) and two larger hostel blocks. Flat-
roofed, with shallow projecting cornice. Front and side walls
of concrete, the rear wall and internal walls apparently of brick
faced in concrete. The staggered layout cleverly gives the
impression that there is only half the number of actual houses.
STANFORD HOUSE, opposite, was originally the Community
House, or company hotel, opened 1936. The same basic construction as the factories, also thirteen bays wide and five
storeys, with shops on the ground floor. Upper floors converted to flats by *David Belsom*, 1982. To the r. the bunker-like
VILLAGE HALL, originally cinema, 1938. Behind Stanford
House, a RECREATION CENTRE, coffee bar and shops by *Katz
& Vaughan*, 1957. Single-storey, with exposed steel frame with
brick infill. N of Stanford House, more flat-roofed houses built
later in the 1930s and 1940s (Coronation Avenue etc.): brick,
mostly now painted or rendered, with recessed first-floor balconies, some with integral garages. More company houses with
pitched roofs, the last in Princess Margaret Road, 1959–66 by
A. Marcanik.

ROMANO-BRITISH HUTS, 1½ m. SW. Remains have been examined on the Thames foreshore below high-tide level. They consisted essentially of an outer ring of stones and an inner ring
of stakes. The largest was 20 ft (6 metres) in diameter. Pottery
suggests a mid-CI date. The SOLDIERS' GRAVES, W of the
churchyard, is an artificial scarp ½ m. long, of unknown origin.

EIGHT ASH GREEN

ALL SAINTS. 1898 by *Chancellor & Son*. Plain, brick, Gothic, with bellcote. W narthex added *c*. 1971.

FIDDLERS FOLLY, ½ m. NW. One of the first local authority schemes to follow the Essex Design Guide. 100 dwellings for Colchester Borough Council by *Peter Barefoot & Partners* with *Ken Bell*, Borough Architect, 1978. Brick with black weatherboarding, flat-roofed dormers, pantiles, some roofs monopitch.

HOUSE ON THE HEATH, Fordham Heath, ½ m. NNE. By *Bryan Thomas*, *c*. 1970. Single-storey, of pale brown brick with large windows and flat roof. The main living room, facing the view N, has one glass wall with glazing bars that are continuations of the roof beams.

ELMDON

ST NICHOLAS. C15 W tower, with angle buttresses and battlements, 'effectually restored from its dilapidated state and improved' in 1847, as recorded on a plaque inside. Nave and aisles rebuilt 1852 by *James Barr*, the chancel 1879–80, the S chapel 1905. All in flint, but with prominent stone dressings on the chapel and tiles used like Roman bricks to add interest. Good carving, e.g. label stops and other heads. Dec tracery. N and S arcades with octagonal piers. – SCULPTURE. 'Madonna of the Lily' by *Allan Howes*. Marble. Exhibited at the R.A. in 1932. – STAINED GLASS. E window by *Clayton & Bell*, 1911. S chapel E, panels of C17 glass from Wenden Lofts (q.v.), removed from there in 1958. – MONUMENTS. – Brass of William Lucas and wife, *c*. 1460; 15-in. (38-cm.) and 14-in. (35.5-cm.) figures, with group of daughters (from Wenden Lofts; in tower). – Brass of John Cooke †1532, two wives, and two groups of children; the main figure 29 in. (73.5 cm.) – Brass of Thomas Crawley †1559 and two wives: only the two small groups of children survive. – Tomb-chest, probably of Sir Thomas Meade †1585. Three decorated quatrefoils and shields, under depressed arch, with quatrefoil decoration inside, quatrefoil frieze over, and cresting. Large coat of arms against the back wall of the recess.

The church is well positioned on high ground above a little green, on the village's N side. Opposite, the OLD VICARAGE. Late Georgian with a tall thin doorcase. Fluted pilasters and a little hood on carved brackets resting on little heads. E along Ickleton Road, FARTHING GREEN, *c*. 1600, with gabled and jettied cross-wings, the remains of ornamental pargetting, and gabled porch. Then CHURCH FARM, *c*. 1625, on whose staircase wall is the painted figure of a woman carrying a candle and warming pan. On the N side CHURCH COTTAGE, C17 or C18, thatched, and the former NATIONAL SCHOOL by *James Walter* of Cambridge, 1844. White brick.

Along the HIGH STREET, running s from the church, more interesting houses include THE BANGLES, C16, and HILL FARM, perhaps C15, both with some exposed timbers. At the top of the hill, PIGGOTTS, early C16 moated manor house. N and s cross-wings, jettied with exposed timbers. Addition on E side with external brick chimneystack dated 1665.

EARTHWORK, ¼ m. NNW. Fortified mount, 165 ft (51 metres) in diameter, with rampart and dry ditch.

ELMSTEAD

ST ANN AND ST LAURENCE. The N side should be examined first. It has a display of a doorway and some windows giving a complete chronology of the church, from the Norman doorway with Roman brick surround by way of the two-light windows with Y-tracery (*c.* 1300) in the chancel, to the C14 and C15. The chronology is completed by the all-too-visible, unattractive brick N extension by *R. S. Nickson*, 1983, linked to the church by a glazed cloister that partially obscures the Norman doorway. The church itself, essentially C14, is covered with a depressing C20 render and its charms lie mainly within. Tower over the s porch no higher than the nave roof; w window like those in the chancel. The best architectural feature is the s chapel, again early C14: probably the chantry established by Sir Thomas de Weston in 1329. Its two-bay arcade has a quatre-foil pier and an arch of two quadrant mouldings and in addition wall shafts and wall arches against the s wall. Contemporary PISCINA on demi-shafts. Also early C14 the SEDILIA and PISCINA in the chancel. The cusped arches have hoodmoulds resting on heads of exceptionally fine quality and gratifyingly unrestored. The E window unfortunately was reduced in size in 1821, see the outside; the stone tracery probably dates from a restoration of 1897. It must originally have given the chancel great breadth and dignity, although the absence of choir stalls and stained glass means that it still feels uncommonly light and spacious. Unusual features in the church are the quatrefoil squint s of the chancel arch, uncovered in 1897, and the three low side windows, one in the chancel and two in the chapel.

PULPIT. C18, originally a three-decker, but broken up and moved to the s side of the chancel arch and then back to the N side in 1897. Tester, backboard and clerk's desk reinstated by *H. & K. Mabbitt*, 1956. – DOOR. Norman, with C12 ironwork, from N doorway. Now displayed on w wall. – COMMUNION RAILS. On three sides of the altar, in the Laudian manner; mid C17 with C18 balusters. – BOX PEWS. Installed *c.* 1819–21. Until 1956 also in the chancel. Not of the highest quality, but a rare survival and (with the wall paintings) responsible for the interior's very special character. W GALLERY, on two very slim iron columns, of about the same date. – HAT STAND, attached to a pew. Wrought iron, cruciform, with highly scrolly decoration; late C18. – ROYAL ARMS. Painted, on board, and unusually large. Dated 1749. – Several WALL PAINTINGS, some pre-Reformation and including a Wheel of Fortune, were discovered in 1958 and covered over again. There remain three medieval dedication crosses, on the N and W walls of the nave, and a splendid sequence of painted panels with Biblical texts, dating from the C17 but overpainted since. Another panel added to commemorate Rev. Ron Smith, rector 1986–96. – STAINED GLASS. In low side windows, fragments from the old E window, early C14. In chapel E window, pieces of C17 glass (one dated 1617) from St Michael and All Angels, Manningtree (dem.). – BRASSES. Head only, 2 in. (5 cm.), c. 1425–50 (chapel W wall). – Two hands holding a heart inscribed 'Credo' and a scroll inscribed 'videre Bona domini' ('I believe verily to see the goodness of the Lord'); c. 1500. – MONUMENTS. Oak effigy of a cross-legged Knight, possibly Sir Thomas Weston †1354; the armour of c. 1345–60. His head rests on a lion and his feet on a skirted figure, possibly a woman. – Painted wooden boards in chancel to Rev. Thomas Martin †1672 and his son William †1664, with imaginative spelling that adds to their poignancy. – In churchyard, group of four headstones, 1818–37, each with a pair of cast-iron winged cherubs. Nearby, a metal monument on stone base, a variety of Greek cross *fleurée*, 1861.

ELMSTEAD HALL, W of the church. Surprisingly broad and tall for a timber-framed house of the C15 and C16. Central hall with cross-wings to r. and l., the centre of five bays, the gabled wings of two; two storeys and a very high roof. Two blocked windows with moulded mullions and transoms; the front is sashed. A C16 grotesque wall painting (found in the 1930s) has been covered over.

The church and hall now constitute Elmstead. The main centre, properly Elmstead Market, lies 1 m. S along the Colchester road. Another church (St Paul) was built in School Road in 1908 by *J.E.K. & J.P. Cutts*, extended 1928, now a house; simple brick with stone dressings.

MARKET FIELD SCHOOL, School Road. 1972, by the *County Architect's Dept*, the first primary school to be built using the Council's own modular component system (M.C.B.), with lightweight pre-cast concrete walls.

BETH CHATTO GARDENS, ½ m. SE of the village centre. By *Beth Chatto*, begun in 1960, on a five-acre site, and based round a stream dammed to form a series of ponds. House by *Bryan Thomas*, c. 1960. Painted brick. Single-storey, split-level, with a single dormer interrupting the long expanse of roof.

ELSENHAM 5020

ST MARY THE VIRGIN. Norman windows in nave (N and S) and chancel (N). Unbuttressed early C15 W tower, battlemented, more flint than brick. In the nave on the S side a three-light mid-C16 brick window and an early C16 porch, more brick than flint, with brick doorway, niche, and two-light side openings. But inside the porch is the best piece of Norman decoration, a doorway with zigzag-carved columns, oddly decorated capitals (do they mean Sun and Moon?), a tympanum with chip-carved stars and tiers of saltire crosses, and the extrados of the arch with another two strips of saltires. Inside, against the tympanum, a reused COFFIN LID of the same early date, with a rough cross and bands of saltires. The chancel arch also is Norman and has, like the doorway, columns with zigzag carvings and two bands of saltires in the extrados of the arch. In the chancel a C13 addition, a DOUBLE PISCINA with a shaft carrying a stiff-leaf capital and arches with dogtooth decoration. Small, porch-like white brick N vestry, mid C19. – PULPIT. Early C17 stem, the pulpit itself later but still with strapwork and arabesque motifs. – STAINED GLASS. E window by *Heaton, Butler & Bayne*: centre panel 1927, side panels 1935. – MONUMENTS. On N wall of chancel, indent of brass of William Barlee †1520 or 1521 and wife. Kneeling figures in panel with ogee head, and band of cresting above.[*] – Mural brasses of Anne Field †1615 and Alice Tuer †1619, with inscription and kneeling figures. – Arthur Heath †1833 by *M. W. Johnson*. Draped urn. Several similar monuments to the Rush family of Elsenham Hall.

ELSENHAM HALL (now flats). Late Georgian brick, castellated, with a three-bay cemented Tudor porch between two projecting wings. Late C19 additions by Sir Walter Gilbey, including NE wing. Gilbey also built a large stud farm 500 yds W of the house, with stock brick stables etc.

ELSENHAM PLACE, ⅓ m. N. C16, H-plan, much restored in the late 1930s. Two symmetrical wings, jettied and gabled, plastered. Timber frame exposed at the rear: one jettied cross-wing to the l., and a shorter cross-wing to the r. with a mainly brick wing extending beyond it, the surviving part of an earlier house. Inside, woodwork from The Close, High Street, Saffron Walden (dismantled 1934), originally at Beaufort House, Chelsea. It includes panelling, a chimneypiece with fluted pilasters, and two doors with re-set panels of arabesques, strapwork, and heads in roundels, one dated 1546 (cf. Beckingham Hall, Tolleshunt Major). L-plan range of C17 and C18 barns W of the house, and C17 dovecote with pyramid roof and open cupola.

The VILLAGE lacks any real focus. Between the church and the High Street, the OLD VICARAGE, Regency stucco, with gabled wings on the N side and two two-storey bows on the S. The only feature of the HIGH STREET is the GILBEY MEMORIAL, a large octagonal canopy for the village pump, erected 1896 by Sir Walter Gilbey. Ogee dome, once gilded, with ball finial, on bulbous wooden columns. Base of brown glazed

---

[*] Fragments of the inscription preserved in Saffron Walden Museum.

bricks. In ROBIN HOOD ROAD, s off the High Street, WELLS COTTAGES, C17 timber-framed and plastered with thatched roof. At FULLERS END, ⅓ m. WSW, several attractive cottages, mostly thatched, and also at TYE GREEN, 1 m. s, centred on TYE GREEN FARM, C17 brick with two gables.

EPPING

See also COOPERSALE

4000

ST JOHN THE BAPTIST. The medieval church was at Epping Upland (q.v.). The town had a chapel, rebuilt in 1832 by *S. M. Hubert* and enlarged by *Hopper* in 1849. When it came to building a new parish church, in 1889, the authorities were wise in their choice of architects. They went to *Bodley & Garner*, and got a church of remarkable dignity if not striking originality. Bath stone. Nave, chancel and s aisle 1889–91, N aisle and s porch 1908, tower 1907–9. The latter is the outstanding feature, broad and strong with two large bell-openings on each side and three big battlements. Angle buttresses with, halfway up, figures of saints in little canopies. It stands at the street corner with only a low link to the s chapel, with the great Dec chancel window facing the High Street. It is all very serious, and no light relief is permitted. The motifs inside, e.g. the arcade piers and arches, are in a correct East Anglian C14 tradition. Much trouble was taken over the furnishings, including large triptych REREDOS by *Bodley & Hare*, 1909; ROOD SCREEN also by *Bodley*, with loft and figures; PULPIT, 1889, rebuilt 1914; and ORGAN CASE, 1892. – STAINED GLASS. Seven-light E window, and E window of s chapel, by *Burlison & Grylls*, 1890. – Two s windows of s chapel, 1902, and w window of s aisle, 1904, by *Kempe*. – N aisle window by *Gamon & Humphry*, c. 1909.

METHODIST CHURCH, High Street. 1887 by *Charles Bell*. Brick. Gabled front with three arched windows and the beginnings of an octagonal turret.

FRIENDS' MEETING HOUSE, Hemnall Street. By *W. Beck*, 1850. Stock brick. Entrance remodelled c. 1957, with the door set in a large round-headed window.

CIVIC CENTRE OFFICES (Epping Forest District Council), High Street. By *Richard Reid Architects*, 1985–90. Large, Postmodern, but of the right scale for its setting. Three prominent features break up the long, mainly brick façade into an agreeable composition. First, and most welcome, a square brick tower to echo the town's water tower and church, broached to octagonal upper stages, its base and cap of reconstituted stone. This material, as well as a simulated-stone render, is used to distinguish the two other principal components: the three-storey Council Chamber, with its apsidal end jutting out towards the street, and the Members' Room at the far end, with large, yellow-framed windows. Between the Council Chamber and the tower an archway spanning the discreet public entrance and flight of steps up to a more ceremonial entrance. s of the tower, a mid-C19 stock brick villa incorporated into the offices; existing offices run NW. Inside, a narrow atrium with boldly striped blockwork walls, and very nicely finished Council Chamber.

ADULT COMMUNITY COLLEGE, St John's Road. Former National School by *G.E. Pritchett*, 1860–1. Stock brick with stone dressings. Two wings with straight gables, and separate teacher's house behind.

ST MARGARET'S HOSPITAL, The Plain. The Epping Union Workhouse was erected in 1837 by *Vulliamy*. Only a brick former laundry remains, Elizabethan-style with stock brick quoins and diamond-latticed windows. Additional buildings by *Herbert Tooley*, including Birchwood House, 1911–12. Neo-Georgian brick, two storeys with dormers in the hipped roof and canted gables on the s side. P.F.I. community hospital by *Murphy Philipps*, 2005–7.

The town has, thanks largely to the *cordon sanitaire* provided by Epping Forest, managed to preserve its individuality as a small roadside town and avoid being swallowed up by suburban London. Most of the interest is along the main thoroughfare, long and generally quite broad. The best houses are at the s end at the Forest's edge, where the High Street is still called HIGH ROAD. WINCHELSEA HOUSE, *c.* 1700, is of five bays with modillion cornice and hipped roof. Tuscan porch. EPPING PLACE, also of brick but four bays and lower, seems to have been built later in the C18 as an extension.

The HIGH STREET's beginning is marked by the castellated Gothic WATER TOWER of 1872 by *Thomas Hawksley*. Red brick with polychrome dressings to the pointed windows. 90 ft (28 metres) with higher stair-turret. The street remains wide with deep grass verges, the buildings set well back. Then comes St John the Baptist (*see* above), with a row of weatherboarded cottages (Nos. 5–17) in ST JOHN'S ROAD opposite its s porch, late C18 or early C19 and unusually carefully detailed. Beyond the church, on the corner where the road widens again into the old marketplace, BARCLAYS BANK by *J. H. Taylor*, *c.* 1932, 'Queen Anne' with a very wide entrance beneath a large semicircular canopy on brackets. But the High Street's buildings are mostly disappointing. The THATCHED HOUSE HOTEL towards the N end makes a bold statement with canted bays and C19 gabled porches, but of the COCK HOTEL only the long stock brick façade of *c.* 1800, with its wide doorway, survives, the earlier timber-framed building behind subdivided. Next to it the POLICE STATION, 1938, with magistrates' court behind, dignified Neo-Georgian no doubt by *J. Stuart*, County Architect, and then the former POST OFFICE, stock brick with round-headed arches on the ground floor, of similar date. On the opposite side a good weatherboarded building of the C17 (No. 269), and before the Civic Offices (*see* above) are reached, a late C18 brick house of seven bays and three storeys with C20 shopfronts. Then the road widens out to a large green, eventually dividing where it meets the northernmost part of Epping Forest.

EPPING FOREST covers an area of just over 6,000 acres, a crescent shape that extends about twelve miles from Epping in the N to Wanstead in the S. It consists of two surviving parts of 60,000-acre medieval Waltham Forest: Epping Forest proper, and Wintry Forest, now known as the Lower Forest, NE of Epping. The third part, Hainault Forest, was ploughed up in the mid C19 (*see London 5: East*). It is important to remember that royal forests were hunting grounds, not exclusively wooded, and the wooded areas of present-day Epping Forest represent roughly the full extent of the medieval woodland. It is of great antiquity: the area has been wooded since the last Ice Age, and analysis of pollen samples shows that there has been continuous woodland cover since at least 3000 B.C. After about A.D. 850 the composition of the woodland changed from small-leaved lime to the present mix of beech, oak, and hornbeam, trees which were managed through pollarding (or lopping) of the upper branches as a source of fuel, while the lower branches were browsed by the king's deer. The land also provided grazing for commoners' cattle. This state of affairs was threatened by private enclosure in the C18 and C19 and, following the disafforestation of Hainault in 1851, steps were taken by the Commons Preservation Society, encouraged by Edward North Buxton, to preserve Epping. That resulted in the Act of 1878, which placed the Forest in the care of the Corporation of London. It was declared open to the public by Queen Victoria in 1882. Lopping ceased (cf. Lopping Hall, Loughton), which changed the character of the woodland, but some pollarding has been reintroduced on a experimental basis in recent years.

In the Forest are two earthworks, Ambresbury Banks (*see* Epping Upland) and Loughton Camp (*see* Loughton). The other principal structure associated with the Forest is The Warren (*see* Loughton).

EPPING UPLAND

4000

The rural part of the ancient parish of Epping. The main settlement is at Epping Green, ¾ m. NW of the church.

ALL SAINTS. Until 1889, Epping parish church. Nave and chancel in one, over-restored by *James Brooks*, 1876–8. Unattractive pebbledashed walls, relieved on the N side by a deep doorway faced with knapped flint. There is no safe indication of a date, but the fact that the windows have all been renewed as lancets indicates a C13 origin for the church. This is corroborated by the nave PISCINA (the church was perhaps lengthened to the E later), which is original and clearly E.E. C15 S porch. Late C16 W tower of brick with diagonal buttresses and battlements. Brooks added the N vestry and organ chamber, separated from the chancel by a two-bay arcade. – ALTAR and REREDOS. 1913 by *Harry Hems*, the former carved with a relief of the Last Supper; panelling added 1925. – COMMUNION RAIL. Of Roman Doric colonettes, probably late C18. – BENCHES. Five with poppyheads in the nave, early C16. – Wooden COLLECTING BOX. Dated 1626. – STAINED GLASS. w window by *N.H.J. Westlake*, 1878. – s windows by *Gamon & Humphry* (†1865 and 1875, but looking C20; St Fillan and St Etheldreda), *Goddard & Gibbs* (†1982; St Stephen), and *Ian Carthy* (1998; St David and St Margaret). – MONUMENTS. Brass of Thomas Palmer, Professor of Common Law at Cambridge, †1621, the figure 29 in. (73.5 cm.) long. – Rev. Edward Conyers †1822. Tablet with sarcophagus. By *S. Manning Sen.*

EPPING GREEN CHAPEL (Union Chapel). 1862 by *J. Tarring*. Stock brick with red brick dressings. Gabled front with rose window over small porch. Its predecessor of 1834 survives as BRIAR COTTAGE, part of a row of painted brick cottages 50 yds NE, distinguished by its hoodmoulded windows.

WALTON, immediately E of the church. Former vicarage. Irregular, plastered and painted, at least partly rebuilt by Rev. Edward Conyers after 1779. C19 s range with large bow at the E end. Its replacement ½ m. NW by *T.G. Hart*, 1913.

TAKELEY MANOR, 300 yds E. C16 or earlier, timber-framed and weatherboarded with four-bay Georgian brick front. Elaborately carved fireplace, and remains of floral wall paintings in an upper room; C17.

AMBRESBURY BANKS, 2¾ m. s. Iron Age hill-fort, in the highest part of Epping Forest. Roughly rectangular, enclosing nearly 12 acres. Of univallate construction, the rampart still surviving to a height of 7 ft (2 metres) in places; ditch 22 ft (7 metres) wide and 10 ft (3 metres) deep. The defences are broken by entrances on the w and SE. The w is of simple type and contemporary with the building of the fort; the SE inturned entrance is medieval.

COPPED HALL and WOOD HOUSE. *See* p. 307.

7010

FAIRSTEAD

ST MARY. Nave, chancel and w tower with shingled splay-foot spire. Norman nave, with Roman brick quoins and small original windows, one in the N, one in the s wall, also the remains of a s doorway – all with Roman brick dressings. Norman also the plain, broad chancel arch. Tower added *c.* 1200, with much use of Roman but also of Coggeshall brick. Lancets and w doorway with one renewed order of E.E. columns. Chancel Norman, extended in the C13, with restored lancets. The group of three at the E end is unusual in that they are stepped not only at the top but also at the foot. SEDILIA and PISCINA are original, but not especially ornate. C15 timber N porch. Tower and nave restored by *E. Geldart*, 1890, when a

W gallery was removed, the tower arch opened up, and wall paintings discovered. Further restoration by *F.W. Chancellor*, 1939–40, when the TOWER SCREEN was erected. – REREDOS. Of stone, fragmentary, at the NE end of the nave. What remains is part of the ribbed soffit of *c.* 1500. – BENCHES. Fourteen in the nave, straight-topped ends with linenfold decoration, early C16. – CHEST. Dug-out, heavily iron-bound, C13 or C14, in the nave. – WALL PAINTINGS. Above the chancel arch, and the church's most important feature. They date from *c.* 1325–30 and are related stylistically to those at Belchamp Walter and White Notley (qq.v.). Four tiers increasing in size as the eye moves upwards. The lowest has small scenes, in the second one recognizes the Crowning with Thorns, the Mocking, the Scourging, Christ before Pilate, and the Carrying of the Cross. Above this the Last Supper and the Betrayal, and in the top tier the Entry into Jerusalem. Elsewhere, C14 figures of St Christopher, shepherds, and a grotesque head; consecration crosses; and black-letter bidding prayer for King James I.

FARNHAM

ST MARY THE VIRGIN. Rebuilt by *J. Clarke*, 1858–9; it cost over £5,000. Robert Gosling of Hassobury contributed £4,000, and the rector, W. J. Copeland, the remainder. Early Dec. Battlemented W tower, with pyramidal roof, and S porch loosely based on those of the old church. Nave, N aisle, and N chancel aisle (organ chamber and vestry). The chancel is separated from the nave by a low stone wall, with integral lectern and pulpit. Of Ancaster stone, with various coloured marbles and serpentine; crisply carved foliage by *Farmer*, the exterior faced with a mixture of stones, mostly flint. – REREDOS. Carved by *Farmer*; panels of mosaic and *opus sectile* by *James Powell & Sons* added 1890. – PRIEST'S STALL by *John Pym*, 1957. – FONT. Mosaic base and cover by *Geldart*, 1909. – STAINED GLASS. N chancel aisle E, early C17 (?) figure of St Basil the Great purchased in Ghent and placed in the old church's E window in 1827. E window, *c.* 1869, chancel S *c.* 1880, and two N aisle windows, 1908 and 1923, by *John Hardman & Co.* – MONUMENTS. Several from the old church refixed in the tower, including Rev. William Greenhill †1849 by *T. Gaffin*.

HASSOBURY, ¼ m. NE. The estate was leased by the Gosling [87] banking family in 1746 and purchased in 1773. The new mansion for Robert Gosling by *P.C. Hardwick*, 1866–70, replaced an Elizabethan manor house. It cost about £50,000; the builders were Cubitt & Co. The style is a romantic sort of Tudor, with gables and pinnacles asymmetrically disposed and a good deal of external carving, but the use of hard grey ragstone facing suppresses any gaiety. Two LODGES in similar vein. Nothing remains of the formal gardens by *Robert Marnock*, but the parkland setting is largely unspoilt, with fine views from the terrace. Converted by the *English Heritage*

Property Co. into ten units, 1997–2000, with additional buildings NW of the house, all quite sympathetically managed. On
the edge of this development a six-bay weatherboarded BARN.
Five bays of *c.* 1300, extended and refurbished *c.* 1500, with
two large mid-C18 gabled midstreys.

WALKERS FARM HOUSE, ½ m. WSW. Manor house of *c.* 1560,
attractively framed by farm buildings, including a five-bay C17
cart lodge. Ground floor of W front faced in brick in the C17.
Large gables at each end and a gabled two-storey porch leading
into the screens passage, with former kitchen to the l. and great
hall and solar to the r. C16 and C17 panelling. Surviving section
of wide moat to the E.

The church stands in the middle of fields between the village and
Hassobury. In the village, THRIMLEY HOUSE, built as the
rectory by *Samuel Ware* for William Greenhill, 1826, school by
G.E. Pritchett, 1855, extended 1892, and parish room, 1904, by
Arthur Needham Wilson. A number of picturesque timber-
framed C17 houses at HAZEL END, 1¾ m. SE of the church.

7010   FAULKBOURNE

ST GERMANUS. In the park of Faulkbourne Hall, to which the
early C17 brick S porch and, probably, one brick S window are
architecturally related. Nave and chancel mostly of flint rubble,
with some Roman bricks and unusually extensive use of tufa
for dressings. Nave and chancel Norman, as can be seen from
the N and S windows and also the three W windows. The upper
one of these is original, with two circular openings l. and r. (cf.
Copford). On the S side a good Norman doorway with one
order of extremely odd columns, semi-polygonal, with capitals
with roughly indicated crosses, and bases made of the same
sort of capitals upside down. The chancel was extended eastwards in the second half of the C13 and the timber bell-turret
added in the C15; wrought-iron weathervane dated 1701. The
brick S vestry probably dates from *A. W. Blomfield*'s restoration,
1885–6. – BENCHES, a few, *c.* 1500, in the chancel. – PULPIT.
By *S. Gambier Parry*, 1905. – MONUMENTS. Mid-C13 effigy in
Purbeck marble of a knight: flat-topped helm, kite-shaped
shield and long surcoat, and illegible traces of Lombardic
inscription. – Brass of Henry Fortescue †1576; 36-in. (92-cm.)
figure in armour with smaller groups of his children. – Brass
of Mary Darrell †1598. 23-in. (58-cm.) figure. – Josiah Bullock
†1753. Ornate marble affair with Corinthian pilasters, an open
segmental pediment, topped with a flaming urn, and cherubs'
heads at the foot. – Hannah Bullock †1759. By *Peter Scheemakers*. Excellent seated female figure before a grey obelisk. – Rev.
John Harrison †1797. By *John Challis* of Braintree. – John
Bullock †1809 and his wife Elizabeth †1793. In the Neo-Greek
taste. Big standing female figure leaning mournfully against a
tomb that bears a double portrait medallion. – STAINED
GLASS. Nave N by *Morris & Co.*, 1920.

FAULKBOURNE HALL.* The most impressive C15 brick mansion in Essex, as early in its beginnings as Herstmonceux, Tattershall, and Caister. The property was acquired before 1426 by Sir John Montgomery, a Welshman who had served in France under Richard Duke of York. There was then a timber-framed house on the site, which Montgomery encased in brick, having received licence to crenellate in 1439. After his death in 1449, the house was further aggrandized by Sir Thomas (†1495) to form three sides of a courtyard entered from the s. It is still in appearance half castle and half mansion, a character emphasized by C17 and early C19 embellishments for the Bullock family, which imposed a symmetry probably absent from the C16 house.

The earliest part is the E range, which retains some timber-framed internal walls of the house remodelled by Sir John. He added the two canted bays of unequal size, which have battlements on trefoiled corbel friezes; this distinctive motif occurs also in the other C15 parts of the façades, and makes clear that, while declaring Sir John's status, the crenellations are decorative rather than defensive. The N front, probably completed by Sir Thomas, is the main show side: a *tour de force* of brickwork, with no stone to be seen. It has a big square tower with corner bartizans and a polygonal stair-turret, rather French- than English-looking. The spiral stair in the turret is also of brick with a rising brick tunnel vault, similar to the one in the Moot Hall, Maldon (q.v.). Off-centre in this range is another two-storey canted bay. This would be in the middle of a symmetrical façade if it were not for the tower, so was the tower originally meant to be smaller, of the type that balances it at the NW corner of this range, with its curious crocketed brick spire? On the upper floor W of the canted bay is an oriel window. A rainwater head on this part is dated 1637, the year in which Sir Edward Bullock roofed in the courtyard and built the main staircase with its turned balusters. Later in the C17 the W wing was entirely rebuilt, terminating in an angle tower matching that at the NW corner, but the present appearance of this front, now the entrance side, is as extended by Jonathan Bullock, who inherited in 1832. He left that date, and his initials, on two rainwater heads on the addition (containing a drawing room) that made the W range as long as the E. Bullock tidied up the existing frontage, to make it symmetrical, and added the turreted porch between the towers. A rainwater head, re-set on the side of the porch, is dated 1666, and two more of 1693 were formerly on the SE wing but are no longer *in situ*. During this period the E range was extended s, with sash windows on the first floor and, in spite of this late date, two straight gables. The SE corner is the only part, save some utilitarian C19 additions hidden between the E and W wings, that makes no attempt to match the C15 work.

57

*This account owes much to research by Andor Gomme and Alison Maguire.

The layout of the C15 house is uncertain. Anthony Emery has argued that there must have been a great hall on the W side, with private apartments in the N range. But the N range has at its W end a main room (later the dining room; now sub-divided) whose moulded ceiling beams may be evidence that Faulkbourne is an early example of a house – like St Aylotts – with a single-storey hall, its screens passage at the E end in line with the canted bay of the N front, which has a very pretty brick lierne vault on the ground floor. It seems less likely that this was the dais end of the hall, because it is nearest the kitchen.

Jonathan Bullock (†1860) also built the stables (clock dated 1844) and, ¼ m. SE, the former RECTORY and WARREN HOUSE, all in keeping and the rectory particularly splendid with elaborate brick Tudoresque chimneys. The two lodges also date from this time, but the gardener's cottage, by the church, is 1899, the year after the house was purchased by C.W. Parker. No village to speak of, but a few nice cottages in the street to the N.

8020

FEERING

ALL SAINTS. C14 N aisle and chancel, C15 W tower, both of flint and septaria rubble, although the western part of the chancel's N wall may survive from a late C12 or early C13 structure. Between chancel and tower lie the early C16 nave and S porch, which are of brick, diapered on the porch, and the most interesting feature of the church. Three- to five-light windows, a little brick and flint decoration, battlements on trefoiled corbel-friezes. Stepped battlements on the porch, which has a star-like tierceron vault (cf. St Peter-ad-Vincula, Coggeshall). Chancel and N aisle windows simply Dec. N arcade on square piers with four demi-shafts (cf. Witham), arch with two quadrant mouldings. Restored by G.G. Scott, 1844–9, including new chancel arch, S doorway, and tiny N vestry; also the PULPIT, which incorporates older carved woodwork, and very good SEATING, the chancel's made by John Barleyman & Son of Feering. Nave roof C17, the tie-beams ornamented with carving and pendants. – ALTAR. In Lady Chapel (N aisle), stone, 1961, incorporating fragments from Coggeshall Abbey, Walsingham Abbey, Colne Priory and Westminster Abbey. – SCULPTURE. In Lady Chapel, Our Lady and Holy Child, alabaster, Nottingham school, c. 1400, found near Colne Priory. Restored with heads added by Patrick Elmes, 1961. The half statue, possibly of St Anne, belongs with it. – In niche of porch, Our Lady and Holy Child, brick-clay relief by Mary Stella Ling, 1985. – STAINED GLASS. Original C14 tabernacles in situ in a N aisle window, with other fragments of C16 and later glass. Fragments of C15 glass in a chancel S window. E window by Thomas Wilmshurst, c. 1847, a typical pictorial piece, brightly coloured. – MONUMENT. Tomb-recess in the N wall, shafted and with ogee head, late C14.

The VILLAGE has two centres of interest, separated by the railway. The church and surroundings still have a villagey feel, with cottages and a large green to the S. In Coggeshall Road the old SCHOOL, 1846, with two large crowstepped gables and diapered brickwork, and a plainer extension. N of the church, DRUMMONDS (former vicarage). Plastered front of four narrow gables, 1844–50; brick gabled cross-wing added 1883. Single-storey additions for The Spastics Society (now SCOPE) by *Dennis E. Pugh Associates*, 1967–8; external walls of concrete masonry blockwork, and flat roofs. Might the school and vicarage be by *Scott*?

The most interesting buildings are to be found ¾ m. SW along FEERING HILL, which leads up from the River Blackwater (for the bridge, see Kelvedon). On the NW side is a former mansion now divided into three (Sun Inn, Sun Cottage, and Feering House). At the E end, an early C15 three-bay hall, now part of FEERING HOUSE. Behind this a C16 two-storey cross-wing, on the first floor of which are late C16 wall paintings showing scrolling stems with leaves, fruit and flowers, comparable to but more colourful than those at the Cricket Pavilion, Felsted School (q.v.), and a text from Tyndale's Bible. On the hall's l. is a two-storey rebuilding of another hall, connected with the mid-C15 gabled cross-wing to its l. Next SUN COTTAGE, C15 extended in the C16, with continuous jetty and porch. Remains of a crudely painted C17 arcaded scheme in the attic. Finally the triple-gabled SUN INN, early C16, altered in the late C16 and C20, with exposed timbers. Across the rear elevation, an original gallery, the studding partly exposed internally, that connected with the adjacent buildings.

FEERINGBURY, 1 m. NW. Timber-framed and plastered house with two gables at the front, that on the r. jettied over a C19 canted bay window. Originally a C13 aisled hall, on the evidence of the roof timbers; r. cross-wing rebuilt in the C15 with crown-post roof, hall floored in the C16 and aisles removed, and l. cross-wing rebuilt *c.* 1600. C19 extension to rear, as well as porch and other Neo-Gothic touches of *c.* 1878. C15 timber-framed and weatherboarded outbuilding SE of the house, probably originally a chapel. Galvanized steel GAZEBO, 1990, and circular BENCH, 2000, by *Ben Coode-Adams*.

PRESTED HALL, nearly 1 m. SE. Timber-framed and plastered house, of which the oldest visible part is on the W side, with two gables and a lower narrow gable between them, and a date of 1527 in the plaster, although the origins of the house are older. Considerably enlarged in 1934, with a new gabled entrance front to the N, and a small free-standing chapel with apsidal E end to the N.* Now a hotel and sports club.

SOUTH COTTAGE, Old Road, ¾ m. NE. Two terraced brick cottages of *c.* 1832, knocked together and extended by *Nicholls Associates*, 1977, for *Cliff Nicholls*. Single-storey flat-roofed extensions on two sides of the house, with a courtyard and

* Stained-glass window now at Messing.

walkway leading to a two-storey studio with monopitch roof. Predominantly glass, with black-stained timber and some brick.

COGGESHALL HALL and HOUCHIN'S FARM. *See* Coggeshall.

FELSTED

HOLY CROSS. A sizeable, prosperous town church, excellently placed away from the main street and separated from it by a range of low houses with a gateway through (*see* below). Unbuttressed Norman W tower with battlements, restored by *F.W. Chancellor*, 1914–15. Octagonal cupola and weathervane added in 1700; the mechanism of the CLOCK is dated 1701, by *John Fordham* of Dunmow. W doorway of two orders of columns with defaced capitals, zigzag decoration in the arches. The rest of the church exterior mostly C14, much renewed. Exceptions are the C15 S porch and N vestry and the Riche Chapel, S of the chancel, built by the 3rd Lord Rich †1619 in accordance with his father's will, proved 1581. Faced with clunch ashlar on the S side, thought to come from Leez Priory, E wall of brick. The rest of the church flint rubble with tile and brick. Earlier evidence inside. S doorway with waterleaf capitals of the later C12, S arcade of the same date, with short sturdy circular and octagonal piers. Capitals decorated with upright leaves, single-stepped pointed arches. Round tower arch. C14 N arcade of octagonal piers with double-chamfered arches. The scalloped edges formed in the plaster are due to *Woodyer*, who restored the church in 1874–8,* removing an early C18 W gallery (built for the school), and S gallery by *Joseph Young* of 1828. To compensate, the S aisle was extended (and given new windows) to join up with the Riche Chapel, but became the organ chamber in 1933. – ALTAR TOMB, chancel N side. C14, the pre-Reformation altar of the Trinity Chapel (S aisle), removed by Woodyer and restored. Recess with crocketed ogee arch, the shafts flanked by projecting buttresses with embattled tops and finials. – *Woodyer*'s rather brutal FURNISHINGS include the ALTAR, alabaster REREDOS (for which the E window was reduced), PULPIT, LECTERN (with eagle carved by *W.B. Polley*), and SCREEN. – FONT. Norman. Large, circular, with human heads connecting the circular with an upper square part, and much weathered. Neo-Norman base by Woodyer; COVER made by *Polley*. – TOWER SCREEN. By *F.W. Chancellor*, 1938, carved by *E. Beckwith*. – POOR BOX. Iron-bound and studded; late C16?

MONUMENTS. Brasses to Cristina Bray †1420, half-length figure (12 in. (30 cm.)), and to a Knight in plate armour, 24-in. (62-cm.) figure, dated 1414. – Richard, 1st Lord Rich †1567 and his son Robert †1581. Erected according to the will of

---

*The same motif can be seen at Castle Hedingham and Copford.

Robert, 3rd Lord Rich, 1st Earl of Warwick †1619, and squeezed into a corner of the Riche Chapel. Attributed to *Epiphanius Evesham* (cf. the Earl of Warwick's monument at Snarford, Lincs). Richard Rich (or Riche), born in 1500 in the City of London and great-grandson of a London mercer, had risen, by means of ability and absence of scruples, to be made Lord Chancellor in 1548. Big standing wall monument with the 1st Lord Rich comfortably reclining and looking back at his son, who is kneeling on the ground by the side facing a prayer-desk attached by a generous scroll to the monument. Behind are two coats of arms and three reliefs of groups of standing figures, with all the lyrical intensity of which Evesham was capable: Lord Rich with Fortitude and Justice, Lord Rich with Hope and Charity, and Lord Rich with Truth (?) and Wisdom. One looks in vain for Lord Rich with Intolerance and *Occasio*. The monument is flanked by two tall bronze columns carrying a pediment, topped off with the gilded wooden figure of Fame blowing a trumpet. – Ann Walker †1712, *trompe l'œil* drapery in white marble with painted inscription. – Anne Edwards †1849. By *H. Downes*, severely classical. – In churchyard, by N aisle, three headstones with skull and crossbones and four footstones to members of the Bigg family †1664, 1676, 1679 and 1687.

FELSTED SCHOOL

Founded by Lord Rich in 1564 but reconstituted in 1851 and expanded into a full-blown public school with buildings to match by *F. Chancellor* following a competition in 1854: an important commission that helped make his name. Further significant development took place between the Wars, mostly in rather municipal Neo-Georgian, and again after 1964.

A tour begins with OLD SCHOOL HOUSE in Braintree Road, timber-framed and plastered with jettied upper floor of *c.* 1500. Previously the Trinity Guildhall; a passage through it connects the street with the churchyard. This once had a row of four single-room shops, whose original shutters survive on the W side. Its neighbour to the E is the former headmaster's house. At the corner of Stebbing Road New School House (now INGRAM'S CLOSE) by *John Johnson*, 1799–1802. Outwardly domestic, in brick of three storeys and five bays with the central three projecting slightly forward. Much more functional within. Then, set back from the main road, comes the Victorian school. The buildings still appear incongruous in their setting, and must have looked even more so when new – the High Victorian scholastic style at its least attractive. *Chancellor* completed the first phase in 1867, with the Headmaster's House at the W end, the Second Master's (dated 1860) at the other, and the main eight-bay range of school accommodation (with water tower) in between. Mostly of three storeys, red brick with some blue decoration and detailing, stone dressings and slate roofs. The overall effect is gloomy, mainly due to the barrack-like central block; only the domestic buildings at either end show something of the charm that Chancellor was able to achieve when working on a smaller scale. Alterations and additions at the NW corner by *Chetwood & Grant*, 1937 (*H.J. Chetwood* and *T.F.W. Grant*, both Old Felstedians).

W of the main building the free-standing CHAPEL of 1873, also by Chancellor, in the same materials, but less rugged in style; transepts added by *A.E. Munby*, 1926. Remodelled 1964 by *Dykes Bower*; he completely rebuilt the E and W ends, with a second pair of higher transepts and a flèche over the new crossing, and redesigned the interior, including a W screen with stalls that incorporates part of the War Memorial screen by *Frank O. Salisbury*, 1921. *Chancellor* and his son *F.W. Chancellor* continued to add to the school buildings, including a gymnasium (1883), swimming bath (1894–6), and science laboratory (1899), E of the main building. To the NW *Chancellor* built an infirmary, *c.* 1879, extended in 1894 and again in 1934–5 by *H.J. Chetwood* (now Gepp's and Deacon's, boarding houses).

JUNIOR SCHOOL (Felsted Preparatory School) on the S side of Braintree Road, 1894–5 by *Chancellor*, considerably extended 1934–5 by *Chetwood* and again in 1994 and 1997 by *Tooley & Foster*. Courtauld Centre by *Cowper Griffith Associates*, 2003. On the N side of the road, almost opposite, ELWYN HOUSE by *Reginald Blomfield*, 1900, a return to the elegance of Johnson, and characteristic Blomfield: brick with Portland stone dressings, a five-bay, two-storey façade with projecting wings, dormers in the slate roof, and a large central window with broken segmental pediment and urn. Facing it, FOLLY-FIELD HOUSE, 1928–9 by *A.E. Munby*, too large to be elegant, and municipal in style. Munby had taught science at the school before taking up architecture.

The first major addition to the main buildings was a CLASS-ROOM BLOCK to the E with distinctive Dutch gables by *Sir Arthur Blomfield & Sons*, 1902–3. GRIGNON HALL, 1909–10, was rebuilt after a fire in 1931 by *Chetwood & Grant*, architects of the MEMORIAL BUILDINGS of 1923–4, which adjoin Blomfield's block to the E. Behind, in a separate building, a single-storey ARMOURY. All this is in the style of Follyfield House, although Grignon Hall has Tudor windows in addition to its hipped roof and dainty lantern. Also by *Chetwood* the Science Block to the E, given by S.A. Courtauld, and the STEPHENSON MEMORIAL GATES, 1938. The SCIENCE BLOCK, originally also the art school, is still in brick with stone dressings but in an appropriately Modern, stripped classical style. Good stone relief depicting Pegasus carrying Bellerophon towards the sun.

S of the chapel is the single-storey MUSIC SCHOOL by *Tooley & Foster*, 1964, NW STOCKS'S HOUSE by *TFP Architects* (project architect, *Michael Foster*), 1977–9, its zigzag plan following the site boundary and helping to reduce its apparent size. Otherwise of traditional form and construction, brick with blue Staffordshire cappings and pitched roofs. N of the main building the LORD RICHE HALL (dining hall, with staff common rooms in a 'cross-wing' at the W end) by *Nicholas Hare Architects*, 1989, which picks up motifs from existing buildings – brick, slate, gables – and combines them with the form of the traditional Essex barn. A very simple-looking composition of triangles on rectangles, resulting from the absence of eaves. Less conspicuous but equally successful is the CROMWELL CENTRE by *Ian Steen Associates*, 1999, neatly inserted into a yard at the E end of the main building, which extends the covered walk with an enclosed cloister.

CRICKET PAVILION. Converted by *Chetwood & Grant*, 1933, from a mid-C16 house, retaining its heavily beamed interior. On the first floor some late C16 wall paintings. It originally formed the N side of a group of buildings known as Queen's Square, and had a central hall with solar at one end and buttery at the other. Further E along Braintree Road GARNETTS, now a school house, C16, a very picturesque grouping with roofs of different heights, projecting wings and upper storeys, and a two-storey jettied porch. Imaginatively extended to the E in a contemporary version of Essex vernacular by *Attfield & Jones*, 1983, brick, plaster and black weatherboarding, with a new block to the N by *Tooley & Foster*, 2002. W of the chapel, N of Holy Cross, THE BURY, H-plan, the N wing early C15 extended in the C16, the S wing possibly earlier, two-storey gabled porch and C19 fenestration. One large room upstairs in the S wing with barrel-vaulted ceiling.

VILLAGE

In spite of the large church and the presence of the school, Felsted remains a village. N of Holy Cross, BURY FARM has a weatherboarded C16 barn with an intact frame of high quality, with two gabled midstreys on the S side, and a ten-bay queen-post roof. S of the church, opposite Old School House (*see* Felsted School), GEORGE BOOTE'S HOUSE (now a restaurant), as described on the bressumer, and dated 1596; tall gable at the junction of Braintree Road and Chelmsford Road, and supporting the projecting upper storey a dragon bracket in the form of a carved female figure with cloven hooves. The adjoining house in Chelmsford Road is older, early C15, a hall house with cross-wing to the r. and stair-turret to the l. E of George Boote's House, on the S side of Braintree Road, ANDREW'S, the former vicarage; early C16 with early C18 additions. On the N side, after Stebbing Road, the former CONGREGATIONAL CHAPEL by *James Fenton*, 1833, a pretty Gothick confection with a gault brick façade, red brick behind; the church (U.R.C.) now occupies the former schoolroom in Stebbing Road, rebuilt 1923. E of the chapel, ALMSHOUSES built around an open courtyard. Founded 1565 by Lord Rich, rebuilt by *Chancellor* in 1878 and refurbished in 1997 by *Ratcliffe & Burridge*, on both occasions following a fire. Much use of decorative brickwork. Continuing E, THE CHEQUERS, dated 1901, by *Charles & W. H. Pertwee*, part brick and part plastered, with welcoming timber verandas. Back on the S side, E of Follyfield House, THE FOLLY, C15 with gabled and jettied porch and cross-wing to r.

On the edge of the village in this direction CHAFFIX FARM, the centre range C16 with two wings extending N, that on the W C15. Early C17 wall paintings in two of the upper rooms.

Returning to Chelmsford Road, a number of enjoyable houses to the S, including FELSTED PLACE (E side), C17, remodelled *c.* 1720, concealed behind a tile-hung front, and FELSTED HOUSE (W), C15 with a C17 kitchen wing to the N and an C18 front. Further S, at CAUSEWAY END, GLAND-FIELD'S FARM, timber-framed and plastered hall house with three gables, the two outer jettied and the central one dated 1565. Next to it MILLBANKS, with a carved inscription similar to that on George Boote's House (*see* above). Dated 1598, although most of the house is probably C15.

HARTFORD END, 1½ m. SSE: RIDLEY'S BREWERY, by the River Chelmer. Established by T. D. Ridley in 1842, as picturesque an agglomeration of brick and weatherboarding as a working industrial building can be.* Keystone over the round-headed window of the main brewhouse dated 1843, with various C20 additions, including a two-storey gabled administration block by *John Finch Partnership*, 1990, stock brick with bands of stone and blue-framed windows set in three gables. Behind are two pairs of workers' houses, *c.* 1897, and then the MILL of which the brewery was originally just an offshoot: the mill and bridge *c.* 1780, brick with some weatherboarding, attached house early C19, plastered brick. Exterior sluice by *Whitmore & Binyon* of Wickham Market, 1881.

FELSTED MILL, 1100 yds SW. Rebuilt 1858, converted to a house in the 1960s. Brick, four storeys, three by five bays, the bays on the long side separated by brick pilasters, and weather-boarded hoist loft. It perches precariously between the river and the road; a little to the N pretty, single-storey MILL COTTAGE, weatherboarded and thatched, and opposite MILL HOUSE, Georgian brick with tent canopy porch. Regular four-bay front to the road, but the other elevations more muddled, suggesting an earlier core.

COCK GREEN, 1¼ m. ESE. Former steam mill, now a house; late C19. Brick with weatherboarded gabled hoist loft, and small-paned iron windows with segmental brick arches.

GATEHOUSE FARM, Gransmore Green, 1¾ m. NE. The interest is the unusual roof construction of the two-bay single-storey hall, which is spanned by a low tie-beam that supports two octagonal queenposts with moulded capitals and bases, a design without parallel for its early C14 date – suggested through comparison of the mouldings (half-rolls and frontal fillets) with examples at St Alban's Cathedral and Navestock

---

* Closed 2006.

Church. The first-floor stairwell uses soffit tenons, a method introduced at Winchester Cathedral in 1307–9. The original kitchen wing, to the l., retains its crown-post roof and one service door with four-centred head. Late C20 three-bay extension in place of the solar wing.

HELPESTONS MANOR, Hollow Road. Modest three-bay, two-storey Early Victorian house on a moated site with a C16 outbuilding. The window on the W side, inserted in 1915, is the reused stone tower screen of St Giles Cripplegate, London, erected as part of that church's restoration by *Edmund Woodthorpe*, 1858–69.

LEIGHS LODGE, 2 m. ESE. C17 house, timber-framed and plastered, two storeys and a large hipped, gambrel roof. Semicircular two-storey porch with open-pedimented doorcase. W of the house an unusually long late C17 BARN: eleven bays (159 ft; 50 metres), with three half-hipped midstreys on one side.

QUAKER MOUNT, Bannister Green, 1½ m. E. Quaint thatched cottage, probably C17. Next to it a small MOUND, perhaps the base for a windmill, possibly a low motte, used as a Quaker burial ground 1657–1732.

LEEZ PRIORY *See* p. 531.

FINCHINGFIELD

6030

Finchingfield is more often illustrated in journals and calendars than any other village in Essex, and rightly so. It is the picture-book village of a completeness not often found. The church lies on a hill. Its little cupola on the square tower is an accent which is lovable and a little funny. The street runs down and bends towards a bridge and a duck pond, with a triangular green beyond. The houses around the green are of all heights and styles and do not all stand on the same level. A windmill, complete with sails, can just be seen, balancing the church.

ST JOHN THE BAPTIST. Norman tower, originally unbuttressed, though the one C19 diagonal buttress no doubt adds punch and the cupola grace.* W doorway of three orders of columns with scalloped capitals and decorated zigzag arches. Defaced heads at the top of the inner jamb-like crockets. The tympanum has been removed. The tower arch towards the nave is low and completely plain. To its l. and r., inside the tower, blank arcading continued along half the N and S sides of the tower. What was its purpose? Was it connected with former altars? The chancel arch, the two-bay N chancel arcade, and the five-bay S nave arcade belong to the C13 (octagonal piers, double-chamfered arches). A little later, early C14, the more handsome N arcade with four major and four minor shafts, all with fillets, and complex arch mouldings. The W bay alone is

* C18 cupola rebuilt in 1966.

different. It has a characteristically Perp pier, similar to that of
the s chapel. The window tracery is mostly of the same date,
say the last third of the C14, and of interesting shapes. The cross
of figures of eight, which one meets so often in Essex C14
tracery, is prominent. The chancel has an unusual and successful feature, a clerestory. Straight-headed windows of intersected pointed and cusped arches. The nave clerestory is C15.
It is like the rest of flint rubble, the typical material of this part
of Essex, with brick battlements. In the s chapel's s wall, a C16
brick doorway with four-centred arch; above it a moulded
brick panel containing four shields. Flat-pitched nave and
chancel roofs on stone corbels, with carved dates 1561 and 1635
respectively. Stone s porch, 1865–6, added during restoration
(which also included re-seating) by *Henry Stock*, son of the
vicar and patron.

FONT. Octagonal with quatrefoils and shields, late C14, on
C19 stem and base. – SCREENS. The s aisle screen is the earlier,
of the same date as the aisle; see the Dec details inside the
Early Perp panels. The early C15 rood screen is one of the most
elaborate in Essex, with tall divisions with big crocketed ogee
heads and much fine panel tracery; restored (with coving)
1972. – S DOOR. C14 with much tracery, also Christ crucified,
a pelican, a dove, etc. – ORGAN. 1896 by *A. T. Miller* of Cambridge, the case safely attributable to *Geldart*. Painted on the
pipes are letters of the notes each plays; in the middle a trum-
peting angel. – ROYAL ARMS. 1660. Very large, painted on
canvas.

MONUMENTS. John Berners and wife Elizabeth †1523,
tomb-chest with Purbeck marble top and brass effigies (31-in.
(79-cm.) and 30-in. (76-cm.) figures). The tomb-chest elaborately decorated with shields of arms in traceried panels separated by bedesmen in canopied niches. – William Kempe †1628
and wife Philip [*sic*], erected 1652. Tablet with inscription on
an oval plate and handsome scrolls and flower bunches. – John
Marshall †1760. Coloured marbles, with urn, prettily done. –
Thomas Marriott †1766. Large monument, coloured marbles,
with bust. Signed by *W. Tyler*. – Anne Marriott †1720, erected
by her granddaughter. By *R. Westmacott*, 1811. Large Greek
female figure and urn, with a verse by *A. Pope*. – In the Kempe
(N) Chapel, many monuments of the Ruggles-Brise family of
Spains Hall (q.v.), including Thomas Ruggles †1813 by *P. Rouw
the Younger* and John Ruggles-Brise †1852 by *R. Brown*, both
severely classical, and mural brass to C.E. Ruggles-Brise †1888
by *Geldart*, made by *Cox, Sons, Buckley & Co.* – In churchyard,
sw of church, A. J. A. Symons of Brick House †1941. Tall headstone with bronze portrait medallion and shelves holding
carved representations of his published work.

UNITED REFORMED CHURCH (former Congregational
Chapel). 1779, rear extended 1820, the whole raised (and
presumably refronted) about ten years later. Brick, with stucco
front. Three tall, round-headed windows beneath a pediment,
recessed entrance with Tuscan portico. Inside, hidden by a

false ceiling, a horseshoe gallery and upper side galleries with cast-iron railings.

PRIMARY SCHOOL, Vicarage Road. 1854–6 by *Allen, Snooke & Stock*. Brick, with shaped gables and matching bell-turret.

The village lies mostly w of the church, but to its E, in Vicarage Road, CABBACHES, C15 hall house, with gabled cross-wings to l. and r., that on the r. added in the mid C16 when the hall was floored. Below the church on the s side the OLD PARSONAGE, also C15, hall and two cross-wings. Roof of the hall and r. cross-wing rebuilt and raised in the C17. On the gabled l. cross-wing, late C16 bargeboards carved with grotesque heads. Late C16 staircase with square newels and finials.

Along the N side of the churchyard, as an excellent beginning to exploration of the village, the former GUILDHALL of *c.* 1500, with long jetties on both sides. Endowed by Sir Robert Kempe of Spains Hall, 1658, as a school and almshouses. Now flats, meeting room, and library. Near the w end a gateway through from the churchyard to Church Hill. Across the street the RED LION, early C16 long-jetty house encased in brick and looking altogether C19. Late C16 and early C19 extensions to the rear. Downhill, on the l., BRICK HOUSE, C17 with a seven-bay Georgian front with pedimented doorcase, and BRIDGE HOUSE, *c.* 1600, timber-framed and plastered, with two gables and massive chimneystack of four octagonal shafts. These houses look N along THE CAUSEWAY towards Duck End. On the E side, a nice row of cottages. On the w side, SPRINGMEDE, very similar to Bridge House, and then STREET FARM, C16 with an early C19 front of sash windows and gabled porch, and a good range of farm buildings. Then comes DUCK END, with thatched cottages on both sides of the road, and behind them on the r. the windmill (*see* below). Just outside the village the ROUND HOUSE, a late C18 two-storey hexagonal model cottage with thatched roof lying a little higher, built by the squire of Spains Hall.

Now back to the bridge and the large green on the w side of the brook. At the top of the green the well-named PROSPECT HOUSE, early C19, plastered, with two gables and Tuscan porch, and FINCHINGFIELD HOUSE, with five gables, that on the l. an addition of 1929. The rest is a C16 hall house, with cross-wings to l. and r. of a two-bay hall, the front C19 with decorative bargeboards, porch in the same style, and hoodmoulded windows. On the N side, a memorable row begins by the bridge with THE MANSE, 1810. Three bays, three storeys, plastered. Then follows THE FOX, *c.* 1500, but with Gothick windows, then a cottage set back with a late C16 chimneystack with octagonal shafts, and so on to SUNNYSIDE HOUSE, early C16 with cross-wing to the r. Finally the OLD SCHOOL HOUSE, 1865, pushing out in front of the chapel (*see* above) to which it should have been subordinate. Brick, inexplicably described by *The Builder* as mixed Gothic and Byzantine in style. Narrow front to the street with porch and Gothic windows.

WINDMILL. Post mill, the smallest remaining in Essex. Weatherboarded, mid C18, on a brick round-house built round the
substructure in 1840. Restored by Essex County Council in
the 1980s.

FINGRINGHOE

0020

ST ANDREW (originally dedicated to St Ouen). Norman nave,
see the quoins on the N side and one blocked window, all with
much Roman brick. Tower, S aisle, and chancel C14. The tower
has bands of stone and brick, flint and stone chequerwork at
the base, added brick buttresses, and a parapet but not battlements. Flint S porch with battlements of stone and flint
chequer. In the spandrels, St Michael and the Dragon, and
bronze figure of Virgin Mary by *Gerald Laing*, *c.* 1980. Embattled S aisle. White and airy interior. The S arcade is no more
than a cutting of pointed arches through the Norman S wall.
C15 nave roof with four bosses with carved heads. Minimal
restoration by *E.J. Dampier*, 1894, including removal of W
gallery. – FONT COVER. C15. Tall, octagonal, of wood, much
repaired. Buttresses with pinnacles at the angles. Plain panels
between ending in traceried heads. Plain second stage. Top
stage with openwork ogee ribs carrying a finial. – DOOR. In S
doorway, traceried, C14, badly preserved.

WALL PAINTINGS. Revealed by the earthquake of 1884, and
much still visible, although only faintly. The best are on the
piers of the S arcade: Our Lady and Holy Child, Christ of Pity,
and St Michael and Our Lady. C15. Other paintings have been
covered over again but watercolours of 1885 are displayed. –
SCULPTURE. Trinity Crucifix, *c.* 1390. Seated figure of God the
Father holding Christ on the Cross. Discovered 1965 in a
walled-up piscina in the S aisle. – St Margaret of Antioch, C15
or early C16. Limestone, painted and gilded. Gracefully carved
standing figure in a niche, holding the cross with which she
slays the dragon. Discovered 1968, reversed and plastered up
in the E reveal of a nave N window. – ROYAL ARMS. Carved and
painted. Given by Joseph Keeling of Fingringhoe Hall, 1763.
– STAINED GLASS. E window *c.* 1901. The only discordant note
in the church. In a nave S window, single diamond quarry of
clear glass engraved by *Laurence Whistler*, 1991. – MONU-
MENTS. Brass to John Alleyn, *c.* 1610. 12½-in. (30-cm.) figure,
with the tiny figure of his daughter. – George Frere †1655.
Good frontal demi-figure, hand on a skull. In a round niche
framed by a wreath. Curly segmental pediment on top. Marble,
with painted coats of arms. No doubt the work of a good sculptor of the day. – Hester Keeling †1756. Marble tablet with
cherub's head and open pediment. By *Benjamin Palmer*.

Much of the charm of the church lies in its setting, above Roman
River with views to the E, and the little pond with oak tree
below to the W, and further W THE WHALEBONE pub,
recorded in 1735 but refurbished in the early C19. Opposite the

church, FINGRINGHOE HALL, mid C17 and Georgian, rebuilt by *Alfred Lester* on a smaller scale following a fire in 1975, reusing the old bricks. Five bays, two storeys, with single-storey bay to r. and original surviving one-and-a-half storey wing to rear. Original Georgian doorway reused, its Corinthian pilasters carrying a frieze rising to a point in the centre, and segmental pediment. – Square two-storey brick DOVECOTE, late C18; pointed window openings, pyramidal roof and louvre. Garden room on ground floor with domed ceiling and niches; ice house below.

TIDE MILL, below the church across Roman River, converted to housing 1996–2001. Late C18 or early C19, timber-framed and weatherboarded, two storeys rising to three at the apex of the slate roof. Beside it, later C19 four-storey, five-bay granary, stock brick with red pilasters and window arches.

FINGRINGHOE WICK NATURE RESERVE, 1¼ m. SE. Visitor centre by *P. Andrew Borges & Associates*, 1975. Part brick, part weatherboarded, with pantile roof, single-storey with observation tower. Built around the skeleton of a C17 barn.

THE GRANGE, Abberton Road, 1¼ m. SW. Georgian brick, five bays with two canted bays on the ground floor and arched window over a doorcase with open pediment. Behind it, GRANGE FARM by *Philip Pank* of *Howard & Pank*, 1968–9, for his mother: single-storey, flat-roofed, brick but with a large amount of glass and dark-stained timber. E of The Grange, KINGSLAND, C18 brick with a later rendered front: five bays, central open pediment, and open-pedimented doorcase. To the S, GUN HOUSE, C15 with one cross-wing at the S end and jettied upper storey with moulded bressumer at the N end.

FOBBING

Thurrock U.A.

ST MICHAEL. In the N wall one blocked Late Anglo-Saxon window, in the chancel N wall one small C13 lancet. The rest is C14 and C15, restored 1904–6 by *C.H. Fowler*. Mainly ragstone, with some flint, septaria, and dressings of Reigate stone. C15 the big W tower, battlemented, with higher SE stair-turret and diagonal buttresses, C14 the S aisle, as wide as the nave and separated from it by an arcade with octagonal piers and double-chamfered arches. C14 also the chancel and S chapel (C20 arcade pier). The timber S porch is typical C15 Essex work, with nice carving in the spandrels: the head of a king, and a man holding open the jaws of a dragon. Original C15 roofs inside chancel and chancel chapel, nave and aisle. – FONT. C13, Purbeck marble, octagonal, with shallow blank trefoil-arched arcades; two panels to each side. – PULPIT. Plain C18. – BENCHES in S aisle. Five with traceried bench ends, *c.* 1500, two with shaped tops and finials, *c.* 1600. – N DOOR. C14, with two large C and strap hinges across the whole width. – SCULPTURE. Virgin and Child, headless, only about 10 in.

(25 cm.) high, C15? (S chapel). – STAINED GLASS. Chancel S by *T. F. Curtis, Ward & Hughes*, 1906. Nave N by *G. Maile & Son*, 1948. – MONUMENT. Tablet with inscription in Lombardic characters, *c.* 1340, translating as 'For the love of Jesus Christ pray for the soul of him who lies here a Paternoster and Ave. His name was Thomas de Crawedene'.

The church stands proudly just where the land drops down to the marshes, where there was until 1953 a navigable creek and wharf. N of the church, PELL HOUSE (former rectory), late C17 chequered brick with large C19 extensions, also red and black brick but diapered. Also chequered the C18 front of PROSBUS HALL opposite; C16 rear wing.

Several handsome timber-framed houses further N along High Road, especially WHEELER'S HOUSE (E side), a C15 Wealden house; COPELAND HOUSE (W side) retains its C14 timber frame, a two-bay former open hall with a rare example of A-frame construction between the cross-passage and service bay. On the same side, FISHER'S COTTAGE, C15 with jettied cross-wings, mostly plastered but with some black weatherboarding and thatched roof like a big hat.

PEASANTS' REVOLT MONUMENT, Recreation Ground. 1990 by *Ben Coode-Adams*. Galvanized steel triumphal arch. Bas-relief and cut-out panels depict events of 1381.

FORD END
Great Waltham

ST JOHN THE EVANGELIST. By *Chancellor*, 1870–1, and one of his most original churches. Tower with spire with an oddly broken outline, at the E end of the S aisle, adorned by large figures of the Evangelists at the angles just below the belfry. S aisle covered by the same big roof as the nave. Low one-light S aisle windows. The porch is of an unusual timber construction, not following medieval precedent; *The Builder* called it 'constructional in its design'. The main uprights lean towards the centre and are in fact straight braces. Exposed brickwork inside; stone is used sparingly. The octagonal apse subsided and was rebuilt to similar design by *A. Y. Nutt*, 1892–3, but with buttresses added and an organ recess on the N side. This new apse was demolished to floor level in 1984–5. – PULPIT, LECTERN and CHOIR STALLS carved by *Col. W. N. Tufnell* of Langleys, Great Waltham, 1869.

OLD VICARAGE, NE, by *Chancellor*, 1870. Brick, Gothic well on the way to Queen Anne.

PRIMARY SCHOOL, S, by *Whitmore*, 1873, with master's house, extended 1881. Brick, used decoratively. Stumpy tower between school and house originally with spire.

St John the Evangelist, Ford End.
Perspective, 1874

FORDHAM

9020

ALL SAINTS. Mostly C14, when the chancel was rebuilt, with cusped windows of two lights under one pointed arch, and N and S aisles added. The arcades have octagonal piers and double-chamfered arches. Walls mainly of rubble but with marked bands of coursed flint and brick on the aisles and S porch. W face of tower rebuilt in brick following the fall of the spire in 1796, and the top rebuilt in stock brick in the C19. Restoration by *Joseph Grimes*, 1861, who removed plaster from the chancel's exterior and fitted up the base of the tower as a vestry. This was remodelled with a classical screen and small gallery by *Quinlan Terry*, 2001. – ROYAL ARMS. Hanoverian, painted cast iron, by *Joseph Wallis*. – MONUMENT. John Pulley, Captain of H.M.S. *Launceston*, †1715. Impressive marble wall monument to the rector's son, erected 1719. Above the inscription a bust, below it a bas-relief of warships.

FORDHAM HALL, sw of the church. Timber-framed and plastered, *c.* 1500, with jettied cross-wings at either end of an unusually long front. Almost in the middle, a large Late Georgian canted bay window, generously glazed. Towards the road a big weatherboarded BARN, *c.* 1800.

PRIMARY SCHOOL, s of the church. Flint, with bold brick diapers. 1849. Additions include two black weatherboarded classrooms with slate roofs, 2002.

Opposite the church OAK HOUSE, originally two mid-C17 houses, the first at the N end followed by a taller one that was extended s in the C19. On the N side of the churchyard the THREE HORSESHOES, C16, timber-framed and plastered. ¾ m. further N, MOAT HALL, mid-C18 and Georgian in style but incorporating an earlier structure. Much of the moat survives. Continuing N, CHAPEL HOUSE is the former chapel (converted *c.* 1983) of the Countess of Huntingdon's Connexion, 1790: rendered (formerly weatherboarded), hipped roof, with large sashed side windows and at the front two C19 hood-moulded windows and gabled porch.

ARCHENDINES FARM, 1 m. NNE. Five-bay Georgian painted brick front, rebuilt by *Raymond Erith*, 1968–9, with further additions by *Quinlan Terry*, 1975.

At FORDSTREET, ⅔ m. sw, two medieval farmhouses. BARNARDS FARM, *c.* 1400, has a single jettied cross-wing and crown-posts in the hall and solar. WASH FARM consists probably of the chamber wing of a medieval house with C18 red brick additions. The earlier portion has an unusually well-preserved queenpost roof of raised-aisle construction, a method normally associated with Norfolk and Suffolk. By the River Colne, the SHOULDER OF MUTTON, attractively weatherboarded with gabled cross-wings, the frame datable to the C14. *See also* Aldham.

0090

FOULNESS*

ST MARY THE VIRGIN, ST THOMAS AND ALL SAINTS. 1850–3 by *J.C. & William Hambley*, replacing a church of 1550. Surprisingly large for such an out-of-the-way place. Nave, N and s aisle, chancel, and a tower-cum-porch with splay-foot spire on the s side. E.E., in very rugged ragstone. – MONUMENTS. In the churchyard, s of the church. Headstones of Jonas Allen †1698, Richard Archer †1738, and Mary Thornbarrow †1769. Carved with skull and crossbones etc. – First World War memorial by *Percy F. Smith*, Southend. Stone. Unusual design of a ball, draped with swags, on a tapering square column carved with a sword and a rifle.

The army opened a firing range in 1849, established the School of Gunnery ten years later, and in 1915 purchased the whole

---

*In 2006 the island is a restricted area.

island, building a bridge, central road, and several semi-detached weatherboarded COTTAGES (by *F.C. Stredder*) in 1921–3. Other military structures include a replica section of the ATLANTIC WALL, constructed before the 1944 Normandy landings to test the strength of the German defences, and buildings erected from 1947 for the Atomic Weapons Research Establishment.

A number of attractive, mainly timber-framed and weather-boarded buildings at the two remaining centres of population, Churchend and Courtsend. At CHURCHEND, by the church, the GEORGE AND DRAGON, C17, originally three cottages, and the former RECTORY, rebuilt 1846 in gault brick. At COURTS-END, 1¼ m. ENE, the former KINGS HEAD pub: C19 range of plastered brick attached to a cottage of *c.* 1560. Opposite, SIGNAL HOUSE, single-storey, built *c.* 1800 as one of a line of coastal stations that relayed messages by semaphore during the Napoleonic Wars. NW, RIDGEMARSH FARM, *c.* 1700, plastered brick, incorporating an earlier building.

FOXEARTH

ST PETER AND ST PAUL. The main effect is Victorian, although the chancel is of *c.* 1340, with a three-light E window with flowing tracery, and the N arcade may be of the same date: slim octagonal piers and double-chamfered arches. Perp N windows, the S windows renewed or new. Rev. John Foster was the High Church rector from 1845 until 1892, and devoted much time, money, and energy to the fabric, mostly commemorating his own family. S porch added 1848. W tower by *Woodyer*, 1862. Large and square, with unusual bell-openings (fine tall cusped lancets in a row on each side). Knapped flint with Bath stone dressings. The loss of its splay-foot spire makes it look like a water tower. *J. Clarke* also worked on the church, *c.* 1884–5, but what he did is unclear. Richly decorated interior, with C19 WALL PAINTINGS in the chancel and on the tympanum over the rood beam; at the base of the tower tiles and mosaics, as well as exceptionally colourful chancel FLOOR TILES, and painted panels on the ALTAR and PULPIT. Nave and chancel roofs both of *c.* 1340, that in the chancel hammerbeam with carved angels, restored, painted and gilded, perhaps by Clarke. – SCREEN. Early C16 lower part, with over-restored figures of saints; C19 upper part. – Elaborate eagle LECTERN with brass candleholders; probably by *Henry Ringham*, who did other woodcarving. – ORGAN CASE. Painted panels by *Henrietta Fricker*, 1880–4, 'in the style of Fra Angelico', according to a Latin inscription. – STAINED GLASS. W window by *Hardman*. The rest by *Clutterbuck*, including two nave S windows dated 1853 and 1854 with initials 'J.F.', presumably indicating Foster's patronage. Central panels removed in the C20. – MONUMENT. In churchyard, E of chancel, to four children †1858, reusing a medieval crocketed pinnacle.

SCHOOL (now closed). By *Clarke*, 1847. Coursed flint with stone dressings. Chapel-like schoolroom and gabled teacher's house.

FOXEARTH HALL. Late C13 hall, r. cross-wing of *c*. 1500, C19 l. cross-wing, both jettied. On the first floor the roof construction of the hall, with tie-beams and crown-posts.

FOXEARTH HOUSE (former rectory), S of the church. Seven-bay, two-storey brick house of 1702 with doorway adorned by fluted pilasters and pediment. Picturesque C19 LODGE.

FRATING

OLD CHURCH HOUSE, Church Road. Former church, declared redundant 1976 and converted *c*. 1981. The mid-C14 W tower had already been demolished. Mainly puddingstone and rubble. The nave has a Norman window with Roman brick surround on the S side, and a Dec window which is repeated similarly on the N side. Chancel windows of *c*. 1300. Plain timber-framed S porch on flint base. Restored by *H.H. Hayward*, 1857, who introduced additional nave windows and STAINED GLASS by *Powell*; and in 1872 by *C. F. Hayward*, who restored the tower, rebuilt the chancel arch, provided a new open timber roof, and extended the N chapel westwards to create a N aisle.

FRATING HALL, N. C16 timber-framed, with C18 and C19 brick facing and extensions. On the E side, a C16 brick gateway and garden wall.

BISHOP'S HOUSE, ⅓ m. SE. Large, of gault brick and slate roof; two storeys, the six-bay garden front with two slightly projecting wings. Built as the rectory by Richard Duffield, *c*. 1832, and 'encompassed by beautiful grounds, laid out and planted with great taste' (*White's Directory*, 1848).

FRINTON-ON-SEA

Frinton's population in 1861 was 29. The railway to Walton opened in 1867 but Frinton did not have its own station (by *W. N. Ashbee*) until 1888, following pressure from the Marine & General Land Co. who had previously developed Clacton. However, development did not prosper until the estate came into the hands of Sir Richard P. Cooper in the late 1890s. By 1901 the population had jumped to 644, reaching 3,032 in 1921. Frinton's reputation was built upon its exclusive, genteel character, still very much in evidence.

ST MARY THE VIRGIN. The medieval parish church, of which the nave, probably C14, is only 25 ft (8 metres) long. The chancel blew down in 1703. Nave restored 1868 by *Henry Stone*, whose father was churchwarden; he added the present chancel in 1879 and in 1894 extended the nave, nearly doubling its length. This extension was removed by *Beresford Pite*,

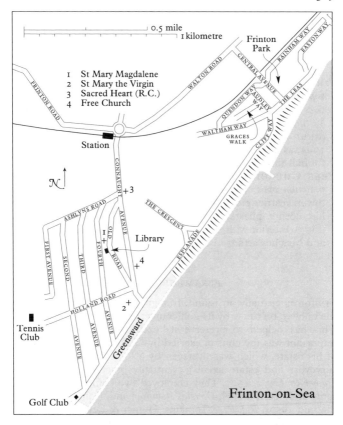

0.5 mile
1 kilometre

Frinton
Park

1 St Mary Magdalene
2 St Mary the Virgin
3 Sacred Heart (R.C.)
4 Free Church

WALTON ROAD

CENTRAL AVENUE

RAINHAM WAY

EASTON WAY

FRINTON ROAD

QUENDON WAY

AUDLEY WAY

THE LEAS

Station

WALTHAM WAY

GRACES WALK

CLIFF WAY

CONNAUGHT AVENUE

N

+3

ASHLYNS ROAD

THE CRESCENT

FIRST AVENUE

SECOND AVENUE

THIRD AVENUE

FOURTH AVENUE

OLD ROAD

1 +

Library

+4

ESPLANADE

HOLLAND ROAD

AVENUE

AVENUE

2 +

Greensward

Tennis
Club

Golf Club

Frinton-on-Sea

1911, whose temporary nave was demolished following the opening of St Mary Magdalene (*see* below). Septaria and flint, with s porch of brick, early C16 but rebuilt by *Stone* in 1879. – STAINED GLASS. W window given by Peter Bruff in memory of his mother, 1879. In the E window four panels of *Morris* glass, designed by *Burne-Jones*, *c.* 1862 and obviously still in the early style of the firm, before the peacock blues and greens began to dominate.

ST MARY MAGDALENE, Old Road. 1928–9 by *Nicholson*. Perp exterior, without the planned NW tower. Flint and bands of brick. s aisle flat-roofed and embattled. Inside not at all Perp. Italian cruciform piers with round arches, a Renaissance effect, although the s chancel aisle is separated from the s aisle by two arches with a single round column. Prettily painted ceilings, blue with stars, as usual in Nicholson's churches. N vestry now partly absorbed into a sprawling extension by *Gould Grimwade Shirborn Partnership*, 1988–9. This also connects with the flat-roofed, concrete CHURCH HALL by *Gilbert C. Roberts*, 1933.

WOODWORK. Nice carving of childhood scenes on the screen to the children's area, W end of S aisle. – STAINED GLASS. E window by *A.K. Nicholson Studios*, 1934. S aisle †1947 by *Charles E. Moore*, depicting the old and new churches. Another by *Moore* in the N aisle. S aisle †1950 by *Christopher Webb*; also by *Webb* the W window in the children's area, 1952. S window in children's area by *A.L.Wilkinson*, 1964. In N aisle, two by *Whitefriars Stained Glass Studios*, 1962, one by *Francis W. Skeat*, 1969, another †1986 by *Paul Quail*.

SACRED HEART (R.C.), Connaught Avenue. By *William Hayne*, 1904, as a public hall. Brick, with stucco imitating very fanciful half-timbering.

106 FREE CHURCH, Connaught Avenue. By *William Hayne*, his *magnum opus*. The body of the church 1911, (liturgical) SW tower, vestries etc. 1935. Brick with stone dressings. The tower has corner pilasters, slightly battered, topped with a little dome. Interior with striking exposed roof timbers, raked floor and benches arranged in an arc.

PERAMBULATION

Frinton is virtually an island, triangular, bounded on the N by the railway, on the W by its golf course, and on the SE by the sea. This has helped to preserve its exclusive character. Equally important was the control exerted by Cooper over development of his estate, which was overseen by a local firm of architects, surveyors and estate agents, eventually practising as *Tomkins, Homer & Ley*, c. 1907. They employed two competent and versatile architects, first *A. Douglas Robinson* and, from c. 1930 until the mid 1950s, *R.J. Page*. Tomkins, Homer & Ley, together with the equally prolific but less interesting *William Hayne*, erected the majority of Frinton's buildings up to the mid 1930s, most of them essentially Edwardian in character.

The main thoroughfare is CONNAUGHT AVENUE, which runs from the station to the Esplanade, with St Mary the Virgin at its S end. Few individual buildings of merit. On the r., going S, No. 115, Neo-Tudor estate office with exposed timbers of limed oak, 1920s, then the brick POST OFFICE, 1912–13 by *Hayne*, and BARCLAYS BANK, Neo-Georgian, apparently by *Tomkins, Homer & Ley*, 1909, although the two upper floors in brick with giant Ionic pilasters are almost identical to *A.C. Blomfield*'s Chelmsford branch of 1905. Opposite, on the corner of Harold Grove, NATWEST, also very decent Neo-Georgian, by *Campbell Jones, Sons & Smithers*, 1924, and PEACOCKS, a streamlined shop by *Page*, 1936, brick with metal windows. Immediately W of Connaught Avenue, OLD ROAD, a relic of old Frinton with a five-bay Georgian brick farmhouse, extended by three bays in the 1930s and since 1989 the LIBRARY.

Between Connaught Avenue and open country to the W are First, Second, Third, and Fourth Avenues, containing the best of

Frinton's characteristic houses. They are mostly large, and in large gardens, and a surprising number are still intact. FOURTH AVENUE contains some of the earliest buildings, with small houses at the N end (Nos. 72–78) and bungalows at Nos. 22–26 built before Frinton had found its own character. EARLY-WOOD (No. 44) was the home of *Beresford Pite* from *c.* 1895, a small brick farmhouse to which he made various alterations and additions, 1904–21. In THIRD AVENUE, some later houses, including No. 85, Neo-Tudor by *Page*, 1929, and in contrast No. 48, 1935, also by *Page* but in what Osbert Lancaster called the 'Pseudish' style, with rendered walls, Dutch gable, and green glazed pantiles. No. 73, THE LONG HOUSE, with fine chimneys, by *Douglas Robinson*, 1925, extended (in traditional style) by *Oliver Hill*, 1928–9.

FIRST AVENUE, developed last, contains only one house of interest: MEADOW BROOK, Neo-Tudor by *Page* for Mrs Tomkins, 1934. It is reached by ASHLYN'S ROAD which includes No. 30, a good example of 1937, white stucco with round-headed metal windows on the ground floor.

The best houses are to be found in SECOND AVENUE, between Holland Road and the Esplanade, with Frinton's two social centres at either end: the TENNIS CLUB off Holland Road, its thatched clubhouse with Crittall windows by *Tomkins, Homer & Ley*, *c.* 1920, and the GOLF CLUB: clubhouse by *Homer & Sharp*, 1903–5, with a curious cupola'd entrance, remodelled and extended by *Page*, 1933. In Second Avenue itself, Nos. 5 and 7 by *Harrington & Ley*, *c.* 1904, altered and extended since but in the characteristic seaside villa style with half-timbered gables and a polygonal corner turret to No. 5. BROOKMEAD (No. 27), 1903 by *Homer & Sharp*, stands out for its sophisticated, irregular composition, with gable, dormers and prominent chimneys, the walls mostly rendered but in places the render deliberately fallen away to reveal the bricks beneath.

On the corner of Holland Road, THE HOMESTEAD, 1905–6 94 by *Voysey*. The client was S.C. Turner, general manager of the Essex & Suffolk Equitable Insurance Society, whose head office was in Colchester. It is in Voysey's unmistakable, homely and sensitively proportioned and detailed style. The house should be looked at from the corner so that the difference of levels comes out. L-plan, with a large parlour occupying most of the Second Avenue front and an octagonal dining room at the corner. Most of the return along Holland Avenue is a service wing. Walls of roughcast brick, stone window dressings, red tiles on edge round the entrance arch, and roofs of green slate. The interior is fully fitted with original doors, cupboards, staircase etc.

In HOLLAND ROAD, No. 29, MARYLAND, the largest of Frinton's houses, Tudor Vernacular by *Douglas Robinson*, *c.* 1912, now flats. Back in Second Avenue, N of Holland Road, IVANHOE (No. 47), 1912–13, also by *Robinson*, rendered with tall chimneys and stepped gables, and FLEMISH HOUSE

(No. 59), a Neo-Tudor bungalow with oak framing, brick nogging and leaded lights by *Hayne*, 1924. Originally thatched, with narrow eyebrow dormers.

THE ESPLANADE is dominated by the former GRAND HOTEL, now flats, on the corner of Fourth Avenue: 1896, extended 1936, rounded where it turns the corner with double-height veranda and turret. This feature is echoed by the circular SHELTER on the GREENSWARD that lies between the Esplanade and the sea. A few large villas s of the Grand Hotel, most now hotels or flats, but to the N FRINTON COURT, Frinton's only tower block and an unwarranted intrusion. Private flats by *Ronald Ward & Partners*, *c.* 1966. Twelve storeys, cruciform.

Less of interest N of Connaught Avenue: a few good houses in THE CRESCENT, including CORNERS by *Baker & May*, 1904, a cosy-looking house with roughcast walls and long, sweeping roof, ASTELL LODGE by *Tomkins, Homer & Ley*, 1912 although dated 1882, roughcast with brick dressings and chimneys, and No. 27, Neo-Georgian brick by *Page*, 1933. In RAGLAN ROAD, NELMES COTTAGE (No. 3), good Neo-Tudor, the exposed timbers stripped rather than blackened; by *Page*, 1934. On the corner of Raglan Road, FRINTON LODGE of 1985–6 by *Cound Page* sits happily alongside its older neighbours. Three storeys with a turreted corner echoing its Edwardian neighbour.

Edwardian Frinton stops at the Esplanade's N end. Beyond is FRINTON PARK, 200 acres bought in 1934 by the South Coast Property Investment Co., who set up the Frinton Park Estate Co. with *Oliver Hill* as consultant architect. Hill drew up plans to include a large hotel, three churches, shops, and over a thousand houses. The resident architect was *J. T. Shelton*, and Hill also recruited 'the cream of our younger designers in the contemporary style' to contribute individual designs, including Serge Chermayeff, Wells Coates, Maxwell Fry, Frederick Gibberd, Raymond McGrath, and Tecton. Little was carried out before Hill resigned in 1935. The company collapsed the following year and *Tomkins, Homer & Ley* were appointed agents, their architect *R. J. Page* demonstrating his versatility by designing in the Modern Movement style rather than his habitual Neo-Tudor. Houses built by Hill, or under his direction, have some characteristic Modern Movement features, e.g. flat roofs, metal windows (mostly replaced); the construction was of concrete block or brick, rendered and painted. Many have one curved wall, and most have a balcony with metal railings.

CLIFF WAY is the Esplanade's continuation. Nos. 3 and 5 are by *Page* to *Hill* designs, 1936. THE ROUND HOUSE (No. 7) was designed by Hill as the estate office, 1934, completed by *Tomkins, Homer & Ley*, 1935, later converted to a house. Inside, mosaic map of the planned estate by *Clifford & Rosemary Ellis*. Round the corner in WALTHAM WAY, several houses, some Modern, built after the company's collapse. Across Audley Way, THE LEAS, by Hill, who designed Nos. 1,

3 and 4 AUDLEY WAY (at least one executed by Page, 1935–6).
Off Audley Way to the l., GRACES WALK, mostly by *Shelton* in
a variety of forms; No. 10 was unfinished and adapted as a
bungalow. Across the top of Audley Way, Nos. 55 and 57
QUENDON WAY, both by Hill, the former the best-preserved
of his houses.

At the N end of Quendon Way is CENTRAL AVENUE, leading
over the railway to FRINTON PARK COURT, the intended
shopping centre of the estate; only two bays were built of an
intended circus. Back at the seaside, No. 16 WARLEY WAY
is another exceptionally well-preserved *Hill* house. Finally
EASTON WAY, N of Warley Way. Nos. 1 and 2 are by Hill, the
remainder by other architects he selected: No. 10, with curved
staircase tower, by *Percy Tubbs, Son & Duncan*; No. 12 by
Stanley Hall, Easton & Robertson; Nos. 14 and 19 by *Frederick
Etchells*; and No. 23 by *E. Wamsley Lewis*. The company's managing director said of the uncompromising No. 21, by *Marshall
Sisson*, that it 'has an unfortunate exterior . . . [and will] be difficult to sell'.

ELM TREE CLOSE, Elm Tree Avenue. Residential home, 1985–6,
by *Barrie Page* of the *County Architect's Dept*. Interesting clus-
tering of bungalows round a central communal area, linked by
enclosed walkways. Brick, now rendered, with slate roofs.

FRYERNING   *6000*

Ingatestone and Fryerning

ST MARY. Small, with early C16 brick tower, with blue brick dia-   30
pering, stepped battlements on a pointed-arched corbel-frieze,
and brick pinnacles. Early Norman nave of coursed puddingstone and Roman bricks, with four original windows (and
another blocked one) and plain N and S doorways. Restored by
Chancellor, 1869–70, including new chancel arch, chancel roof,
seating, and the removal of a W gallery and external rendering. – FONT. Big square bowl carved with a vine and the sun,
moon, and stars (cf. Abbess Roding and Little Laver); *c.* 1200.
– Brass LECTERN with low screen by *Jones & Willis*, 1902. –
ROOD BEAM. First World War memorial, with figures by
William P. Gough. – MONUMENTS. Palimpsest brass (in vestry),
22 in. (56 cm.). Woman of *c.* 1460 on one side, on the other
Mary Gedge, widow of Leonard Berners †1563. A fragment of
his foot survives – Rev. Richard Stubbs |1810. By *T. Tyley*,
Bristol. Inscription on a scroll draped over the Bible. – William
Gordon Coesvelt of St Leonards †1844 and his son †1839.
Identical austere but expensive-looking tablets with sarcophagi
by the *Westminster Marble Co.* – Edgar Disney of The Hyde,
Ingatestone, †1881. Bas-relief profile by *Edgar Boehm*, set in a
Romanesque arch. – Family monument on N side of church-
yard, stone column on a massive plinth, erected for John
Disney †1816. – STAINED GLASS. E window and chancel S
(Abraham and Melchizedek) by *Lavers, Barraud & Westlake*,

c. 1880. Another chancel s by *Lavers & Barraud, c.* 1865. – Chancel N and heraldic glass in w window by *T. Willement,* 1851. – Nave N by *Penelope Neave,* 1985, to Airey Neave M.P. assassinated in 1979. – Nave s (Millennium window) by *Lisa Z. Morgan,* made by *Tony Sandles,* 2000, its imagery inspired by the font. Small s window by *Ian Carthy,* 2005. – GATEWAY to burial ground s of church, 1901, large for a country churchyard. Brick, with half-timbering in the gables, and lean-to sheds either side of the carriageway.

FRYERNING HALL, NE of the church. Early C15 two-storey main range facing the church with an early C16 cross-wing to the l. and later rear additions. Farm buildings include a C16 DOVE-COTE, converted to a granary in the C18, and an eight-bay aisled BARN, once longer. This has structural features which suggest a late C13 origin.

BARN MEAD, formerly The Tiles, ⅔ m. WNW. 1870 by *Sherrin,* brick and tile-hanging, but lacking some of his later panache: it was his first job in the area (cf. Ingatestone).

LYNDSAY HALL, ¾ m. NW. Timber-framed and plastered, the exposed timbers mostly added 1900. Main range and cross-wing to r. late C16, l. cross-wing C15. Considerably altered and extended by *Tooley & Foster,* 1927.

ST LEONARDS, ⅞ m. NW. For W.G. Coesvelt, *c.* 1804. Gault brick. On the garden's show front (s) two wide bays project, with a cast-iron canopied balcony between and canopies also over the French windows of the two bays, all on lattice-work stanchions. Entrance front (E) with central pedimented bay. Remodelled by *Walter A. Belshaw* for William J. Squire, *c.* 1939, mainly restoring the N façade. (In the central room of the garden front a bas-relief of Cupid and Psyche by *John Deare,* brought from Italy by Coesvelt.)

FYFIELD

ST NICHOLAS. An interesting but unattractive exterior. Norman nave and crossing tower, the tower, with its curious weather-boarded top, partly rebuilt in brick, probably 1817 by *J.B. Papworth,* who repaired the church and added the wooden spire. The rest of the church flint rubble, mostly rendered. Narrow early C13 N arcade with circular piers and double-chamfered arches. The capitals are neither round nor square. s arcade, mid C13, with octagonal piers and double-hollow-chamfered arches. The chancel belongs to the Dec style of the early C14. The E window, renewed externally in 1875, has an inner surround with original carving: alternating roses and four-leaved flowers on the splays, various heads on beasts on the rere-arch. Hoodmould on headstops. SEDILIA with polygonal Purbeck marble shafts between the seats, cusped arches, and big, rather bad headstops. Between two of the arches three balls, the symbol of St Nicholas. E of the sedilia, also with cusped arches, not a double piscina, but a PISCINA and CRE-

DENCE. The blocked E window of the N aisle deserves notice, because of the pretty diagonally placed NICHE to its l.: C15 work. In the first half of the C19 the N aisle was extended to form a vestry (organ chamber after 1901).

Restoration and re-seating by *Stephen Webb* of Chelmsford, 1852–3, and a more thorough restoration in 1892–3 by *C.H.M. Mileham*. Tower arches rebuilt, and a stone window and doorway at the W end replaced C18 timberwork. Chancel fitted with seats and reredos, the oak for which came from St Paul's, Knightsbridge. – FONT. Square, of Purbeck marble, late C12, with the familiar motif of a row of (six) shallow blank round-headed arches on two sides, and on the two others a fleur-de-lys and two quatrefoil leaves. – STAINED GLASS. E window, 1901, good Arts and Crafts with some Art Nouveau detailing.

FYFIELD HALL, N of the church, looks like an unexceptional early C16 timber-framed house with C19 fenestration, but is built round a two-bay aisled hall, of which the S aisle has been lost. Analysis of the roof structure, which is largely intact, shows the oak was felled 1167–85, with additional oak for a remodelling in 1391–1416. Visible timbers inside include one of the N arcade posts, octagonal with pyramidal stops. The lower three-bay E wing is perhaps C15. Parallel N range with long-wall jetty added late C15, cross-wing at the NW corner *c.* 1600, and balancing cross-wing at the NE in the C17 or C18. The hall was floored in the C16 or C17 and the S aisle removed. Sash windows and canted bays *c.* 1886. C16 weatherboarded DOVECOTE.

The village centre is the junction of the Ongar–Dunmow road with Queen Street. The mid-C17 QUEEN'S HEAD is the principal building, followed by a row of pretty village houses running S towards the C19 water mill. N, on the W side, BRIDGE HOUSE has a very small late C14 open hall whose frame and crown-post roof survive, floored in the late C16.

ELMBRIDGE HALL, Ongar Road. 1883–5 by *J. T. Newman* for the West Ham School Board, as an industrial school for persistent truants; now housing. Board School 'Queen Anne' come to the country: stock brick with red dressings, two storeys, tall sash windows, Dutch gables, hipped roof surmounted by a clock turret and weathervane.

LAMPETTS, ¾ m. NW. Early C14 aisled hall, of which both aisles survive. Two-bay hall with original frame and ornate octagonal crown-posts. E wing late C14 with similar crown-post roof. Hall floored in C16 and W wing added early C18. Early C17 ten-bay aisled barn beside house.

GALLEYWOOD   6000

ST MICHAEL AND ALL ANGELS. On the high ground of Galleywood Common, and encircled by Chelmsford's racecourse, which flourished between 1759 and 1935. 1872–3 by *J. P. St Aubyn*; it cost £6,300, paid for by Arthur Pryor of Hylands (cf.

Widford). 'Early Dec'; nave, chancel, aisles, transepts (N for organ chamber, S for vestry), S porch, and W tower and spire, overall height 131 ft (40 metres). Octagonal broach spire, of stone, originally with crocketed pinnacles; the rest stock brick with stone dressings, bands and voussoirs of red brick, and more elaborate red brick patterns inside. Fine open timber roofs in nave and chancel. – REREDOS. *Opus sectile* panel by *H. Burrow* of *Powell & Sons*, 1874, with tile panels and mosaic roundels on E wall. – STAINED GLASS. E window by *Clayton & Bell*.

THRIFTWOOD SCHOOL, Slades Lane. 1975–6 by the *County Architect's Dept* (project architect, *Derek Kemp*). White block-work with dark wood trim, and shallow-pitched slate roof, set very low in the landscape.

LITTLE SIR HUGHES, 2¼ m. ESE. Early C18. Timber-framed and plastered, with a surprisingly formal front. Two wide, two-storey canted bays and central, heavily rusticated and pedimented doorcase. Modillion cornice and deep hipped roof with a single dormer on three sides.

LODGE FARM, Goat Hall Lane, ⅔ m. WSW.* Unremarkable exterior concealing a complete timber frame of a four-bay house, dated to *c.* 1280–1330. Open two-bay hall in the centre, the end bays floored. Roof with two crown-posts.

SEABRIGHTS BARN, 1 m. NE. Now a pub. Eight bays, weather-boarded, with crown-post roof, *c.* 1520; midstrey on S side added a little later.

GESTINGTHORPE

ST MARY. The church is small in comparison with the tower. This was added after 1498 (when 40s. was bequeathed by William Carter for its construction) to a church partly Norman, partly C14, and partly C15. The chancel has a blocked C13 N window; the others early C14. The five-light E window is especially interesting. The tracery is of a rare (early) variety of reticulation, where the net pattern is arrived at by simply placing arches on top of the apexes of other arches. The SEDILIA have simple ogee arches, although much of their stonework dates from the restoration by *A. B. Jackson*, 1893–4, who rebuilt the nave S arcade and added the organ chamber at the S aisle's E end. The W tower is of brick with blue brick diapering. It has angle buttresses, stepped battlements on a corbel table of trefoiled arches, and short pinnacles. The W doorway and the W window are also of brick. Bell-openings of three lights with one transom and depressed pointed heads with intersecting tracery. Soon after the tower was built, the nave received a roof uncommonly splendid for Essex. It is of the double-hammerbeam type of which there are only a few examples in the county. It is carved with the names of Thomas

33

---

* In Borough of Chelmsford.

Loveda(y), Peter Barnard, and their wives Alys and Marget: probably the donors, although John Harvey attributed the design to *Loveday*.*

FONT. Octagonal, Perp, with traceried stem and a bowl decorated by shields and the symbols of the four Evangelists. – SCREEN. By *Jackson*, made by *E. Beckwith*, 1907, incorporating two bays of C15 woodwork. With one-light divisions. The heads are quite richly decorated: crocketed ogee arches and panel tracery above them. – On W wall, PAINTINGS of Moses and Aaron, *c.* 1700. – STAINED GLASS. Chancel N and S by *Lavers, Barraud & Westlake*, 1878 and †1876. Chancel S †1917 and two nave N windows by *Heaton, Butler & Bayne*, 1898 and 1900, the second incorporating a seated Virgin, probably late C15, much restored. – MONUMENTS. John Sparrow †1626, alabaster, with small kneeling figure. Attributed to *William Wright* (GF). – John Elliston †1741. By *Thomas Scott Jun.* Large marble tablet with inscription and modest architectural surround. – LYCHGATE. 1914, by *Jackson* and *Beckwith*.

GESTINGTHORPE HALL.† Chiefly of 1735, for John Elliston; the date and his initials appear in the brickwork of the N wall. Inside, timber framing and brickwork from an earlier house, probably early C17, as well as panelling. Seven-bay, two-storey front with a three-storey centre topped by a late C19 pediment. The windows l. of the projecting centre are false, the true floor levels shown by the windows on the return. Pedimented doorcase on Ionic demi-columns. At the far end of the Entrance Hall a two-storey screen with Ionic columns below and plain piers above. It screens the staircase, which has very finely twisted balusters. Stair window with late C19 armorial STAINED GLASS. But the showpiece is the Drawing Room, one-and-a-half storeys high, splendidly decorated *c.* 1740 with stucco ceiling, an extremely ornate fireplace, and pedimented door surrounds. Rocaille as well as naturalistic flower decoration. Rear additions of 1891 and 1914, neither particularly sympathetic, both probably by *A.B. Jackson*. The earlier is Queen Anne Revival, the later built as a memorial to Captain L.E.G. Oates, the 'very gallant gentleman' who died in Antarctica in 1912 and whose family lived at the Hall. Staircase by *Beckwith*. Good C19 outbuildings, stables, and walled kitchen garden, and two concrete SCULPTURES by *Harold Brown*, 1963.

HILL FARM, ¾ m. ENE. House by *F. Chancellor*, 1884: brick with half-timbered gables. Outbuildings include what appears to have been a C14 guildhall, with crown-post roof and remains of mullioned windows, re-erected in the C16.

THE MOAT, 1 m. S. Late C14 farmhouse, half-H plan with gabled cross-wings. Altered in the C16, with staircase and internal doors of that date, and later. E of the house a three-storey DOVECOTE, early C17.

*Lay Subsidy rolls of 1523–4 show Loveday assessed under Gestingthorpe (Harvey, *English Medieval Architects*).
† Known until the C19 as Over Hall.

81

GOLDHANGER

ST PETER. The N side of the church shows its CII origin: one chancel window, the nave E angle, and one nave window. Much reuse of Roman brick among flint, septaria and puddingstone. CI4 S aisle mostly flint, but also incorporating Roman bricks. CI5 W tower with diagonal buttresses, stone rubble with some flint and stone decoration, and late CI5 S chapel. Considerable alterations *c.* 1790, before which there were three gables in the roof of the S aisle. Restored 1853–4 by Rev. C.B. Leigh: most of the windows were renewed, the chancel arch and S arcade were rebuilt, and new FURNISHINGS introduced. The BENCHES have low, pew-like doors, the PULPIT and STALLS elaborately carved panels. The architect was presumably *Ewan Christian* – cf. the rectory.* Late CI4 crown-post roof to nave, mounted on wall pieces with carved heads, and very carefully done with every timber chamfered. – STAINED GLASS. In the chancel and nave, contemporary with the restoration; in S chapel, two windows by *Heaton, Butler & Bayne* to Priscilla Leigh †1858, typical of their date. – MONUMENT. S chapel, tomb-chest of Thomas Heigham †1531 and three wives. Base of Purbeck marble with panels on the sides containing shield, black cover plate with brass of a woman (15 in. (38 cm.)) and two indents. Later inserted brass inscription to Anthony Heyham †1540 and wife.

Attractive village centre where Church Street, Head Street and Fish Street converge. On Head Street's S side, set back behind houses, the former WESLEYAN CHAPEL, with pretty Gothic sashes, dated 1839.

GOLDHANGER HOUSE, 400 yds N. 1851–2 by *Christian*, as the rectory, for Rev. C.B. Leigh. On the scale of a small country house, in the 'true Tudor domestic Gothic style'. Diapered brick, with Caen stone dressings, and impressively tall chimneys. To the S, its modest replacement by *Laurence King, c.* 1948, rendered, with metal windows and pantiles; extended 2003–4.

FOLLY FAUNTS HOUSE, Little Totham Road. CI8 painted brick façade of three bays, the windows set in round-headed recesses. Almost entirely rebuilt behind in 1930 by *A.L. McMullen*, retaining a single-storey extension with mansard roof of *c.* 1700.

GOOD EASTER

ST ANDREW. Nave and chancel, flint rubble with some stone, and clunch dressings; belfry with vertical weatherboarding and a tall thin shingled spire. The belfry rests on four posts with arched braces to the E and W as well as the N and S. The nave

* Also St Bartholomew, Wickham Bishops, erected in memory of Leigh's father, patron of Goldhanger.

is of the C13, the chancel also, but a little later. The evidence
is not easily understood. Early C13 W window, original internally. In the nave's E wall two blank half-arches of the same
date. They must at first, in their complete form, have flanked
a narrower, probably Norman, chancel. Then the chancel was
rebuilt and widened. That also, on the evidence of the SEDILIA
and PISCINA, cannot have been later than c. 1240. The piscina
has typical shafts, the sedilia and some blank wall arcading on
the chancel's N side have an odd alternation of arches continued below without any capitals, and arches carried on
capitals ending in (Cistercian) corbels instead of shafts. The S
arcade is a little later. One circular and one octagonal shaft,
moulded capitals and only slight double-chamfered arches.
The third pier is the same, but rests on a square base and was
probably reconstructed as part of an enlargement of the S aisle
in the C14. Its arches are properly double-chamfered, the westernmost one and its respond rebuilt after 1885. C15 S porch.
Nave restored 1877–8 by *S.C. McMurdie*, following a lightning
strike, the chancel 1879–81 by *E. Geldart*. His is the REREDOS
and the decoration of the piscina, the only surviving part of a
larger scheme of decorative painting. Nave badly damaged by
fire in 1885, restored by *Chancellor*, including new tower and
spire, new W wall, and new S aisle roof. – HELM. Probably late
C16. With separate wooden crest. – STAINED GLASS. Bits of the
C14 and C15 in two S aisle windows; one of these by *G.J. Hunt*,
1930. E window by *H.J. Salisbury*, 1897. – BRASS to Margaret
Norrington †1610. 18-in. (46-cm.) figure.

Immediately NW, the former RECTORY by *McMurdie & Wagstaffe*,
1870. Not very inspired. Beyond it, the more cheerful FAL-
CONER'S HALL, mid-C19 brick, with a range of BARNS. One
contains five posts with Norman-style capitals, most likely
reused when the barns were built in their present position,
perhaps at the beginning of the C17.

GOSFIELD

7030

ST CATHERINE. C15 and C16, apart from the C19 S porch and
small N vestry. Of the C15 are the W tower, with diagonal buttresses and a large transomed W window, and the chancel E
window of four lights with an embattled transom and much
panel tracery. Nave and tower of flint and pebble rubble, as
well as part of the E wall. But the most interesting parts are
brick: the N chapel and the chancel's S side, with large, very
domestic-looking Perp windows, straight-headed, of four lights
with a transom and arched heads to all lights. These parts are
as late as c. 1560, added by Sir John Wentworth of Gosfield
Hall, and as at the Hall the dressings are of rendered brick.
The N chapel arcade has a pier with a lozenge-shaped chamfered section and four-centred arches. The N chapel's E wall
has along the plinth part of a C16 diapered band of brick and
plaster, and, above the window, black and yellow plasterwork

of lozenges in squares stepping up.* The position of this decoration suggests that the chapel roof was subsequently raised, but
not later than 1735–6, the date of the remarkable adaptation
of the chapel's w end by Anna Knight, widow of John Knight
of Gosfield Hall. The chapel's westernmost bay was taken over
and the w wall rebuilt slightly further out, to create a square
room for a private pew over a burial vault. Venetian window to
the w, and to the e an internal Venetian doorway reached by a
double flight of six steps.

Inside, a sort of balcony with shutters opens into the nave.
And the congregation could see, behind the arch of this
theatre-box, against the room's N wall, the large and magnificent MONUMENT to John Knight †1733 and his widow †1756.
It is by *Rysbrack*, probably begun by *Guelfi*, with verse epitaph
by *Alexander Pope*. The two white marble figures are seated,
with an urn between them. The sculptural quality is high. The
chapel has a handsome plaster ceiling too. – In the N chapel,
large tomb-chests of Purbeck marble with black marble tops
to Sir Hugh Rich †1554 and Sir John Wentworth †1567. The
one has on the chest elaborate quatrefoil, etc. panels, the other
blank arcading that originally held brass shields – all the motifs
still entirely Gothic, suggesting that the tombs were reused. –
A third and earlier tomb-chest, also with quatrefoil decoration,
on the chancel's s side; in the slab the brass of Thomas Rolf
†1440, 39-in. (99-cm.) figure in the robes of a Serjeant-at-Law.
– James Goodeve Sparrow of Gosfield Place †1838. Tall marble
wall monument with drapery, by *John Soward & Son*. – Basil
Sparrow †1880. Elaborate mural brass, mounted on marble,
by *Hart, Son, Peard & Co*. – BENCH ENDS in the chancel, with
poppyheads, probably late C16. – PANELLING with Early
Renaissance decoration in a style frequently found in houses,
c. 1550, along the back of the chancel seats. – WALL PAINT-
INGS. In nave, Commandments, Creed, and other texts, one
in a surround decorated with birds, foliage, a winged cherub's
head, etc. Perhaps late C17. – STAINED GLASS. e and four s
windows by *Clayton & Bell*, 1880–*c*. 1917. Tower window by
John Hardman & Co., 1922. e window of N chapel, 1980, and
nave N (armorial), 1987, by *Goddard & Gibbs*.

The church lies ½ m. outside the village to the w. On the s side
of the road leading to it, HIGHGATES, originally a single
house, early C15, with former open hall and two jettied cross-
wings, that on the r. with a lean-to porch enclosing the jetty
(visible inside). At the back of this is a stair-tower which has
an original mullioned window with surviving shutter. On the
r., to the front, a three-storey parlour block, with every late C16
comfort: glazed windows, plastered ceilings, and fireplaces. On
the corner with the main street, THE KING'S HEAD, C16, with
exposed timbers, the front remodelled in the C18 with sashed
bay windows and, over one of them, a Venetian window.

---

*The central latticed device noted by Pevsner in 1965 is no longer visible.

Opposite, and s along the street, many other good houses, but the village's character comes from the buildings erected by Samuel Courtauld during his ownership of Gosfield Hall. On the N side of the turning to the Hall, the SCHOOL, dated 1858, plastered, with three gables and imitation timber framing. It originally served also as a lecture hall. Opposite, of about the same date, PARK COTTAGES, four pairs, each with three gables, ground floor brick with stock brick dressings, the upper floor rendered with batten decoration. Iron casements with ornate glazing bars. Then, s, three more pairs but all brick (one in its original state), followed by the READING & COFFEE ROOM. Red brick with black and stock brick dressings, false half-timbering in the gables, and over the elaborate doorway the exhortation 'So live that you may live'. Finally, brick cottages dated 1875: *John Birch* is the likely architect (cf. Bocking), although not of the earlier buildings. Attached to the right hand pair a communal BAKEHOUSE. Single-storey, square, the tiled roof rising to a louvre finished off with a little pyramidal spire.

Further s, but still on the E side, GOSFIELD COTTAGE, mid C19, has a flat canopy on iron columns with trellis decoration that runs from the front door to the gate, and joins up with trellis-work railings that run across the whole frontage, including carriageway gates. Further on, DIAL HOUSE and DIAL COTTAGE, originally one house. C16. Handsome front with two gabled cross-wings, that on the l. jettied, and some exposed timbers. Chimneystack at the l. side of the central block, with an arched window recess at the base. Spiral shaft rebuilt in the C19, and below it a sundial. Finally, at the bottom of the hill, SPARROWS, C16 with much of the timber frame exposed.

GOSFIELD PLACE, ¾ m. ESE. Nothing remains of the house itself, remodelled by *Richard Elsam c.* 1800 and rebuilt *c.* 1865 for Basil Sparrow (dem. 1920s). *Repton* drew the house for Cromwell's *Excursions through Essex* (1819) and may have had a hand in landscaping the park for James Goodeve Sparrow, *c.* 1811. Large lake, N of the house, crossed by a single-span BRIDGE of bar-stayed cantilever design, the stays suspended from four cast-iron towers. Decorative cast-iron balustrades, now mostly missing. Probably *c.* 1865. At the park's W entrance, by Gosfield Bridge, a COTTAGE by *Frank Roscoe* for W. J. Courtauld, 1937, on the site of an earlier lodge. Rendered, with hipped roof of glazed black pantiles.

GOSFIELD SCHOOL, Halstead Road. Early to mid-C19 house (Cut Hedge, home of George Courtauld III), with later C19 extensions. The main block has a pedimented Tuscan porch between two-storey bows, and deep eaves on moulded brackets. To the l. former stables, converted to school use by *Alan Bragg*, 1984, and at the back an octagonal well house (cf. Gosfield Hall).

GOSFIELD HALL

Built by Sir John Wentworth, who inherited the estate in 1539 and died in 1567. Quadrangular, and although not crenellated, still

essentially a defensible house, with a single entrance on the
W front and no windows on the ground floor. In its substance,
the original mansion is still there, although three of the
four fronts have been rebuilt and the fourth has been much
restored. The result is most unusual, because although the
inner faces of the quadrangle have an architectural unity,
the outer faces might be four different houses. The owners
who left their mark were Sir Thomas Millington, 1691–1704;
John Knight, 1715–33; Robert Nugent, who married Knight's
widow in 1737, was created Earl Nugent in 1776 and died in
1788; and Samuel Courtauld, 1854–81. Converted to flats,
1959.

The W FRONT remains an exceedingly impressive Tudor
façade, in spite of early C19 projections at the ends. The material is brick with occasional blue diapering, the dressings of
plastered brick. The Tudor design was completely symmetrical, with a central entrance with four-centred arch, a six-light
window with one transom above (all lights arched – just as in
Gosfield church), a gable above, and a later cupola. To l. and
r. of this gable are chimneystacks with polygonal shafts. Then
follow recessed bays also with six-light windows, and then
again gabled bays with the same windows. Only the upper
storey has these large windows. Below, the walls are closed,
apart from two in the outer bays added by Courtauld. Attic
timbers have been tree-ring dated 1547–83. The gateway leads
through the quadrangle, entirely of red and blue brick and with
similar windows, but on the ground floor as well. The inner
faces of the W and S fronts retain their original appearance,
although the S face is largely rebuilt, but the central portions
of the E and N faces have been raised to accommodate the
changes made to them which are so apparent on the exterior.

The E FRONT was rebuilt by Sir Thomas Millington, whose
arms appear over the courtyard door. Much blue brickwork
with the red, and two angle projections of three bays' width
and three bays' depth. Dentilled cornice and dormers with
alternate straight and segmental pediments. Three more bays
either side of the central five bays, but this is altogether different, with the tall segment-headed windows and splendid big
doorway (segmental pediment on fluted pilasters rising against
a rusticated background; the frieze above the pilasters rising to
a point in the middle) of the Grand Salon. In place of the attic,
a full-height third storey with 'Tudor' windows to match those
on the W front, probably the work that *Sanderson Miller* is
recorded as doing for Nugent in 1755, but looking later.

On the S FRONT, the five outer bays with dentilled cornice
appear of the same date as the E front, but the central seven
bays are later, probably for Nugent, and the whole front is stuccoed apart from the W end, which is part of the C19 addition
to the W front. The central portion is rusticated on the ground
floor, the first-floor windows have heavy voussoirs, and the
middle three bays project as a pedimented centrepiece, with
arches below and Doric pilasters above.

The N FRONT, also stuccoed, is part of John Knight's early C18 alterations. Similar to the S and W fronts, in that there are seven bays of two-and-a-half storeys either side of a raised seven-bay centre, which contains the Ballroom on the first floor. The centre is rusticated, with two doorways with segmental pediments, and the tall upper storey embellished by giant Corinthian pilasters.

Inside, the C16 LONG GALLERY on the first floor of the W wing is virtually intact, with linenfold panelling, described by Horace Walpole in 1748 as 'a bad narrow room'. Of the later interiors, the GRAND SALON on the E front is the most impressive. Painted panelling, and full-height sash windows. Marble chimneypiece supported by carved figures of mermen, two each side facing each other with their tails entwined. Painted ceiling, the central oval (Minerva attended by the Arts) by *Sir James Thornhill*, surrounding grisaille medallions *c.* 1820. On the N front, the BALLROOM has a C19 painted ceiling. Dark wood-graining here and in the LIBRARY on the S front, the latter entirely C19 in character, but with a reused C17 stone chimneypiece with Ionic columns and carved frieze. Over it, a DRAWING ROOM with Rococo decoration.

NW of the house, an octagonal, open-sided structure housing a wooden horse or donkey gin connected to a pump in the nearby octagonal brick WELL HOUSE. Early C19, the original machinery intact. Further N, the old STABLES, now a school. C18 brick, round three sides of a yard with a wall across the fourth. Opposite, KEEPER'S LODGE, brick with gables and applied battens, *c.* 1860 (cf. the village's Reading & Coffee Room). W of the stables, the brick walls of the C16 WALLED GARDEN. One surviving LODGE, early C19 brick, with recessed arches on three sides, now extended to form part of a house.

Nugent laid out the PARK, of which the main survival is the splendid lake, about ½ m. long but originally nearly twice that length.

GRAYS THURROCK (OR GRAYS)

Thurrock U.A.

Grays is now a substantial town, since 1998 the main centre of Thurrock Unitary Authority. Although a port since the C13, there is now little sense of being on the water; the parish church and riverside lie S of the railway (opened 1854), while the C19 growth of the town was to the N along the E–W highway.

ST PETER AND ST PAUL. A gloomy-looking church, the mainly flint-rubble exterior almost entirely C19. Chancel, transepts and S wall of nave as restored by *F. C. Cope & C. Eales*, 1846, when the S porch and vestry were added and the tower (over the N transept) rebuilt with squat broach spire. Stone dressings replaced with Portland cement. Nave extended westwards and N aisle added by *Henry Stock*, 1867. N vestry by *J.C.*

Stoneham, 1929–30, S vestry extended by *N. F. Cachemaille-Day*, 1937. N porch 1958, incorporating the original C12 N doorway, removed in 1867 but preserved elsewhere. More signs of medieval fabric inside. C12 crossing with round W and E arches, almost entirely rebuilt; the base of the N transeptal tower (fitted up as Lady Chapel by Cachemaille-Day, 1937) C13 with double-chamfered arch and similar blank N and E arches; S transept shorter, with work of *c.* 1300 towards the crossing, originally a chapel (piscina in S wall), now organ chamber. The S doorway may also be C13. Chancel remodelled 1908 with bold black-and-white marble floor and brass COMMUNION RAIL. – REREDOS and CHOIR STALLS. First World War memorial, good-quality carving. – SCREEN. Former chancel screen, now across N side of crossing. Perp, plain. – FONT. Perp, octagonal, with quatrefoil panels. – CHAIRS. Two good later C17 armchairs. – HELM. Late C16. With gauntlet and short sword. – Some medieval TILES in S vestry, not *in situ*. – STAINED GLASS. E window 1870. Lady Chapel lancets by *G. Maile & Son* (St Michael designed by *Frederick M. Baker*, 1939, Gabriel and Raphael by *Arthur S. Walker*, 1954). Five large windows by *Philippa Heskett*, 1973–80, in nave and N aisle. An outstanding group, each different in colouring and massing. – MONUMENTS. Brass of two wives and six daughters (husband and son missing), *c.* 1510; 13-in. (33-cm.) figures, now mounted on wall. – Mrs Sarah Button †1781. Minimal decoration, but the inscription very attractively laid out and lettered. – Anne Cox †1796. Seated female leaning against an urn. By *C. Regnart.* – Richard Wheeler and boys of the Forest Gate School who died when the training ship *Goliath* was destroyed by fire, 1875. Tablet with anchor, rope, and two little sailor boys. By *Druitt*, Mile End Road.

ALL SAINTS, John Street (now Thurrock Christian Fellowship All Saints Centre). By *Sir Charles Nicholson*, 1927. Nave, chancel, S aisle, and W bellcote. Perp, brick with stone dressings. Divided internally, partially reusing SCREENS by *Cyril E. Power* (*Faith Craft Works*), 1944.* – STAINED GLASS. E window by *Heaton, Butler & Bayne*, 1930. S chapel S by *Terence D. Randall* (*Faith Craft Works*), 1948.

ST JOHN THE EVANGELIST, North Grays. *See* Little Thurrock.

ST THOMAS OF CANTERBURY (R.C.), East Thurrock Road. 1886 by *F. H. Pownall.* E.E. Stock brick with red brick and stone dressings. A large town church, one uninterrupted space, with school (now closed) beneath.

BAPTIST CHURCH, Orsett Road. By *Charles Cobham*, 1893. Unusually elaborate brick façade with stone dressings, and a joyfully incorrect composition. E.E. central recessed doorway, the carved arch resting on paired colonettes, and above a pair of windows and then a straight gable. Lower sides with curved gable ends, the overall effect like a shaped gable.

---

* Some fittings now in St Clement, West Thurrock.

METHODIST CHURCH, Lodge Lane. 1938–9 by *Smee & Houchin*. Brick, in a very pared-down Gothic.

MAGISTRATES' COURTS, London Road. 1929 by *C.M. Shiner*, originally also the Police Station. Brick and stone dressings, with rusticated quoins that provide a Vanbrughian quality. Main three-storey building of nine bays, flanked by tall single-storey windowless pavilions with a single arched recess. Behind, off Quarry Hill, DIVISIONAL POLICE HEADQUARTERS by the *County Architect's Dept* (project architect, *Owen Legerton*), 1976–9. Four storeys, brick-faced.

CENTRAL LIBRARY, THAMESIDE THEATRE, and LOCAL HISTORY MUSEUM, Orsett Road. By *Thurrock U.D.C. Architect's Dept* (chief architect *D.C.W. Vane*, succeeding *H.K. Brown*), designed 1966, built 1968–72.* Brutal, clad partly with pre-cast concrete units and partly with dark stock brick. Three-storey podium block with museum on first floor and traditional proscenium theatre on third floor. No fly tower, but a four-storey tower block set back from the front. Interior relieved by carvings in red brick of scenes from the Canterbury Tales etc.

ADULT EDUCATION CENTRE, Bridge Road. Board School Queen Anne of 1897–8 by *C. M. Shiner*.

GRAYS SCHOOL, Hathaway Road. 1931 by *J. Stuart*, County Architect. Brown brick with stone dressings and large Georgian-style windows. Mainly single-storey, with later additions.

A PERAMBULATION need not take long. The HIGH STREET s of the parish church was demolished in 1970, redeveloped with housing by *Frederick Gibberd & Partners* (project architect, *D. Roberts*), mostly completed 1977. 802 dwellings. Five tower blocks and long three-storey terraces, the latter of pink brick with white weatherboarding and pink panels. The 1930s Neo-Georgian WHITE HART is marooned, but good of its kind. What is left of the High Street runs northwards from the parish church, its beginning marked by a stainless-steel SCULPTURE by *Ray Smith*, 1993, representing a Thames barge. The usual late C19 and early C20 mix of shops; behind those on the r. two covered shopping centres, the first (with multi-storey car park) opened 1975, refurbished 1992. On the l., in George Street, the STATE CINEMA by *F. G. M. Chancellor* of *Frank Matcham & Co.*, 1938, a well-preserved 'super cinema' in brown brick and faience.† Squat tower at one corner, the name in the frieze beneath the overhanging flat roof. Circular entrance lobby with large open staircase. Many original fittings, including a Crompton Theatre Organ. Close by, an OBELISK with bronze reliefs by *Trupti Patel*, 1995, and opposite, the POST OFFICE, *c.* 1930, stock brick with three carved heads on keystones. On the High Street's E side, along CLARENCE ROAD, another

---

*On the site of the Carnegie Free Library by *C.M. Shiner*, 1903, the porch from which was re-erected in the grounds of Ye Olde Plough House Motel, Bulphan (q.v.).
†Another 'super cinema' by Chancellor, The Regal, New Road (1930), has been demolished.

SCULPTURE, based on the tiller and rudder of a boat, by *Jon Mills*, 1995. At the top of the High Street, stone First World War MEMORIAL by *A. Cox*, 1921, a covered urn on an obelisk. Across London Road, in QUARRY HILL, the former RITZ CINEMA (Mecca Bingo) by *E. Hamilton Parke*, 1939–40. Stock brick with tower, and streamlined double-height foyer block abutting a blank façade with brick pilasters topped by shelf-like concrete projections. Good internal plasterwork, possibly by *Eugene Mollo*.

In COLLEGE AVENUE, ⅓ m. NE of the war memorial, THE DELL (No. 25, now a convent). By *Thomas Wonnacott*, prominently dated 1872 on one of its gables. Shuttered concrete, rendered and whitewashed.

CHAFFORD HUNDRED. *See* West Thurrock.

7000   GREAT BADDOW

ST MARY THE VIRGIN. A splendid exterior, thanks chiefly to the Early Tudor brick clerestory with its stepped battlements on a trefoiled corbel frieze and brick pinnacles. W tower and aisles C14, of flint rubble, the tower with angle buttresses only at the foot, battlements, and a tall leaded spire, the aisles with Dec windows (mostly renewed). S doorway also C14, see the keeled columns and keeled roll moulding; S porch C17 brick. Aisle battlements, added in brick when the clerestory was built, continue along the brick S and N chapels. The chancel's large dormer windows were rebuilt during repairs and alterations by *C. & W.H. Pertwee*, 1892–1903, which included rebuilding the N vestry. The three-bay aisle arcades give evidence of an earlier church. They are E.E. The N arcade came first: one circular pier, the other octagonal. W respond on a head corbel. Arches only slightly double-chamfered. The S arcade has circular piers and normal double-chamfered arches. Reordered 1999 by *Gerald W. Barrett*, with two small N extensions.

PULPIT. The best of its date in the county. 1639, but entirely Jacobean. Complete with a big tester on a tall narrow back panel up the wall. The motif of the panels of the pulpit itself is little aedicules on columns. In the centres false perspectives. Strapwork along the sides of the back panels and on top of the tester. – ROYAL ARMS. 1660, painted board, in a frame with broken pediment. On the backboard, now mounted separately, verses from Romans. – STAINED GLASS. E window by *H. Hughes* (*Ward & Hughes*), 1876. – MONUMENTS. – Brass of Jane Paschall †1614, the figure nearly 3 ft (90 cm.) long. – Hellen Sydnor †1651. Black and white marble, with good lettering. – Monument to the Gwyn sisters, Amy and Margaret, and Ann Hester Antrim, 'spinster belov'd by them as a sister', erected 1753. By *Sir Henry Cheere*. Big, with the usual grey obelisk, a cherub in front of it, leaning on a draped oval medallion with the portraits of the two sisters. Rocaille and foliage at the foot. – Simple LYCHGATE by *Comper*, 1930.

White's 1848 Directory described Great Baddow as 'one of the handsomest villages in Essex', but THE VINEYARDS shopping centre, with flats and offices, by *Stanley Bragg & Associates*, 1966–8,[*] has confirmed it as a suburb of Chelmsford. Wealthy Chelmsforders built houses in the village from Georgian days. The best are along CHURCH STREET. Opposite the S front of the church, the OLD VICARAGE: brick, *c.* 1725, five bays by three, two storeys and attics, with curved parapets on all sides and pedimented doorcase. E of the church (N side), two C17 timber-framed houses with early C19 five-bay gault brick fronts, the grander (BADDOW PLACE), with stucco parapet and pilasters and Tuscan porch. Then a complete contrast with a nine-bay, three-storey former BREWERY, now offices, 1868, only two bays deep at the W end. Polychromatic, mainly stock brick. Round-headed windows on the ground floor set in pointed arches. Additions by *George Scamell*, 1878. Bottling stores opposite, rebuilt 1989 reusing medallion portraits of King Edward VII and Queen Alexandra, 1902. E of the brewery BADDOW COURT, early C19 gault brick, commands the entrance to the village, the five-bay SE front with central pedimented bay, and an unusual corner oriel looking down towards the church. A little further E, on the S side, PITT PLACE, C18 painted brick, five bays with parapet and S wing with Ionic porch.

BADDOW HOUSE, now flats, stands SW of the church between Vicarage Land and Galleywood Road. C18 brick, three storeys with five-bay E front, three windows on the W front with Tuscan Doric pedimented porch. Segment-headed windows, those on the ground floor of the entrance front set in arched recesses. Lower C19 additions. Down the churchyard's W side, the HIGH STREET, with a nice row along the far side including the WHITE HORSE and Nos. 66–68, C15 or C16 and jettied along the whole front. Ceiling in a first-floor room painted with leaves, flowers, etc. Opposite, an Early Victorian warehouse, converted to offices by *TFP Architects, c.* 1977. White brick, two storeys and cellars, with two bays of windows set in semicircular arches, and central loading doors. Further N, on the W side, ROTHMANS (No. 22), altered and mostly refaced in white brick in the late C18 or early C19, but with C17 internal features. At the N end an early C19 white brick house, two storeys, the ground-floor windows set in arched recesses. Ionic porch. A few more good houses along MALDON ROAD, facing The Vineyards, including JEFFERY'S HOUSE, timber-framed with a three-bay Georgian brick front. On its W side the VILLAGE HALL, built as a schoolroom for Jeffery's School (endowed 1731) by *Chancellor*, 1865, with three gabled dormers; adapted by *Lester H. Sacré*, 1913–14. A little E, No. 27 contains a late C14 first-floor hall.

---

[*]Replacing a house of 1740, altered in the 1760s and again in 1907 by its architect-owner, *Arnold Mitchell*.

BAE Systems, West Hanningfield Road. Built as the Marconi Research Centre, 1937–9 (by *W.W. Wood*?; cf. Chelmsford). Wide, two-storey brick front, with a very 1930s entrance, and additional buildings behind by *Taylor & Collister*, 1957–8. In the grounds a 360-ft (111-metre) transmitter tower of lattice steel construction, erected in 1937 at Canewdon as part of an early warning radar system; moved here in the 1950s.

Pontlands Park, ½ m. se. By *Chancellor*, 1878–9, for Joseph Foster. Brick with stone dressings. Not large, but with the full range of accommodation then expected in a country house. Now a hotel, much extended.

Little Sir Hughes. *See* Galleywood.

Barnes Mill Lock. *See* Springfield.

6030

GREAT BARDFIELD

A large village, pretty without being self-consciously picturesque. Its character is captured well in *Life in an English Village* (1949), illustrated with lithographs by Edward Bawden, who (with Eric Ravilious) had been attracted to Bardfield in 1925. Other artists followed, including Michael Rothenstein, Kenneth Rowntree, and John Aldridge. The colony of 'Bardfield Artists' flourished until Aldridge's death in 1983.

St Mary the Virgin. Late c12 chancel and w tower without buttresses. Small lancets and a small, pretty, recessed spire of the c18. Apart from a bleakly rendered n vestry (1956, extended 1984), the rest is all later c14, with the surprising feature of large, straight-headed three-light windows with curiously High Gothic tracery, i.e. no specifically Dec or Perp motifs, but a development from the classic moment of Geometrical tracery. Such windows fill the n and s aisle walls and also appear in the chancel (many renewed). The s porch has in addition very pretty openings on the e side. They look earlier than the larger windows, and it is quite possible that the porch as well as the s aisle and chancel masonry are earlier than the straight-headed windows. The openings in the porch consist of one two-light Dec window flanked by small quatrefoil windows (cf. Stebbing). Four-bay arcades inside with late c14 piers of four polygonal shafts connected by deep hollows with four slim circular shafts in the diagonals. Moulded arches; headstops. Richly carved and painted tie-beams in the chancel, dated 1618 and with the initials and motto of Edward Bendlowes.

Also late c14 is the most prominent and famous feature of the church, the stone SCREEN between nave and chancel. It is tripartite and, with its openings and tracery, fills the chancel arch completely. The idea probably came to Great Bardfield from Stebbing (q.v.), but how it came to Stebbing we do not know.[*] That Bardfield is later than Stebbing is obvious. Both,

---

[*] The connection (if any) with another such screen in the cathedral at Trondheim, Norway, has yet to be satisfactorily explained.

it is true, share the luxuriance of design, the rich cusping and crocketing and the delight in ogee arches, although much of the detail at Stebbing is C19. But at Bardfield the two main dividing shafts or mullions run straight up into the arch, an unmistakable sign of the Perp style. Also the arch responds are decidedly first half of the century at Stebbing, second half of the century at Bardfield. The rood figures are a reconstruction of 1896–7 and due to *Bodley*.

REREDOS. Oak, partly gilded, with a central carved alabaster relief. No doubt by *Bodley*, as it is designed in conjunction with the E window. – PULPIT. Polygonal, and slightly tapering, with buttresses at the angles and tracery between. By *Bodley*, made by *Rattee & Kett*, 1872; sounding-board added. – ORGAN CASE. 1866–7, with stencilled motifs. *Bodley* seems likely. – N and S aisle SIDE ALTARS. By *Laurence King*, 1953. Stone, that in the S aisle incorporating pieces from St Peter-on-the-Wall, Bradwell. – TOWER SCREEN. With engraved glass panels by *Richard Bawden* in memory of his parents, 2003. – S DOOR. Late C14, with much tracery. – Two HELMS. Early C17. – STAINED GLASS. A fine collection by *Burlison & Grylls*, the earliest the E window (attributed) designed by *Bodley*, 1869–70, the latest 1949. Eight in all. Two in the N aisle incorporate late C14 fragments, including complete figures. – Small tower window early *Clayton & Bell*, single-light chancel N by *Goddard & Gibbs*, 1990. Three-light chancel N, and E windows of N and S aisles, by unidentified makers, 1870s. – MONUMENTS. Low Purbeck tomb-chest with frieze of small quatrefoils and brass to Alienor, wife of William Bendlowes †1584. 17½-in. (45-cm.) figure. The tomb-chest is no doubt older. It also served as sedilia. – Thomas Stebbing †1832. Classical. By *Downes*. – LYCHGATE. By *E. Beckwith*, 1929–30.

In the picture of Great Bardfield the church has no part. It lies away at the SE end close to the C16 HALL to its S. S of the Hall a big early C14 weatherboarded BARN. NW of the church YORK HOUSE (former vicarage), mid-C19 painted brick with Neo-Tudor porch, hoodmoulds, and battlements.

The village proper starts 100 yds N at the bottom of BROOK STREET. This, like the other streets, is gently sloping and gently curving. By the stream a square brick FOUNTAIN with ball finial, 1860. The most striking houses visually are on the N side. Nos. 6, 7, and 8 have C19 applied framing, carved bargeboards, and cast-iron Gothic casements, but the hall is C15 with l. cross wing of the same date and r. cross-wing *c.* 1570. To the W, on the corner of Crown Street, SERJEANT BENDLOWES' COTTAGE, thatched and with some exposed timbers. Early C17, now joined to an early C18 cottage at right angles to the street. Opposite, WHITE HART (formerly an inn), early C15 open hall house. Exposed timbers to the hall, r. cross-wing completely underbuilt, l. cross-wing jettied and partially underbuilt by a bay window. Rear wing of *c.* 1600 now a separate house. On the same side to the W, THE FIRS, C15, the E part showing evidence of having been a medieval shop.

Brick House, Great Bardfield.
Drawing, by Edward Bawden

Now the street broadens out into a triangular Green, with
the FRIENDS' MEETING HOUSE on the N side. 1804,
extended 1848. Plastered walls, large sash windows, and
hipped roof, overlooking its humble and secluded graveyard.
The HIGH STREET curves away to the SW. Opposite Brook
Street is BANK HOUSE, modest early C19 plastered brick, but
the rear wing is late C15 with jettied upper storey, probably the
Guildhall mentioned in C16 documents. On the same side, to
the SW, the most prominent building in this stretch, BRICK
HOUSE, rented by Bawden and Ravilious in 1925 and
Bawden's home until 1970. Early C18, five bays and two-and-
a-half storeys, with chequered brickwork and a large pedimented doorcase. Then on the SW corner of Bell Lane,
GOBIONS (formerly Durham House), a late C14 hall house
with exposed timbers of which the three-bay open hall survives. It was floored in the C16 but the carved heads on the
ends of the false hammerbeam central truss can still be seen
inside. Black-letter moral text in white on tie-beam of a first-
floor room. The building has no right angles.

Opposite is the funny TOWN HALL of 1859, looking exactly
like a Nonconformist chapel, but placed back behind pollarded
lime trees, rather like in a French town. Red brick with black
dressings, and in the end wall four tall round-headed windows,
with three round windows in the gable, all with cast-iron
glazing bars. To the SW, on the same side, BARDFIELD

COTTAGE MUSEUM, single storey, thatched, built as an almshouse under the will of William Bendlowes †1584. Opposite, OAK COTTAGES, apparently C19 brick but with part of the underlying C17 timber framing and plasterwork (and a painted date, 1600) exposed in an arch.

Back on the SE side, PLACE HOUSE, home of William Bendlowes in the C16 and of John Aldridge in the C20. Mostly plastered, but part of the l. return wall jettied, and below the jetty exposed timbers with brick nogging. On the corner a carved bracket with the initials 'WB' and date 1564 to mark alterations by Bendlowes. The front has two C18 sashes, a C19 bay window, and a C18 doorway with Roman Doric half-columns, and the r. return is brick with a C16 window of three round-headed lights. C18 and C19 farm buildings behind, and to the SW CHAPEL COTTAGE, also C16. Plastered front, part timber-framed but mostly brick, and original three-light window of plastered brick. Further SW, in DUNMOW ROAD, SOUTH LODGE, gault brick, dated 1829, and a nice row of late C18 or early C19 thatched cottages.

VINE STREET is the continuation NE of the High Street. One house of note, on the NW side: THE GABLES, a late C14 hall house with contemporary cross-wings, both underbuilt. Side jetty apparently C20. Vine Street curves l. into BRIDGE STREET, with BEAM COTTAGE and CAGE COTTAGE on the l. Thatched, c. 1600, with a single (earlier?) cross-wing. To the r., the village CAGE or lock-up, brick and flint rubble, 1816, and CAGE HOUSE behind it, early C17. More good timber-framed houses at BRIDGE END, on the far side of the River Pant; the BRIDGE itself brick, of two arches, 1782–4.

GIBRALTAR MILL, Mill Road, ¼ m. NE. Brick tower mill, recorded in 1707. Converted to a house but returned to its original use and heightened in 1751. Converted again in 1958, the house part rebuilt 2001. N of the windmill was the water mill, burnt down in 1993, but the smart Georgian MILL HOUSE remains.

GREAT LODGE, 1½ m. SE. A house of c. 1622 was demolished by Edward Stephenson in 1729. Part of the stables became the present house, which was connected to a great brick barn, forming a U. The connecting range was demolished in the C20, leaving the barn and an L-plan house. Barn of seven bays, with kingpost roof, early C17 or possibly late C16. House also brick, with irregular fenestration including one blocked window in a gable with brick pediment, and a moulded brick string course, partly plastered with strapwork. Garden by *Rosemary Alexander*, who lived here in the 1980s.

GREAT PITLEY FARM, Beslyns Road, 1¾ m. NW. C16 with long-wall jetty, now underbuilt, and single cross-wing to l. Poly-chrome wall paintings, including a frieze of foliage, fruits, and flowers.

GREAT BENTLEY

ST MARY THE VIRGIN. Nave, chancel, W tower, and S extension. The N side shows clearly that nave and chancel are Norman. The puddingstone is laid diagonally and bedded in excessive amounts of mortar. Three Norman windows on the N side, two on the S. N doorway with responds and a scroll each. Arch extrados with trellis decoration. S doorway with one order of slightly decorated scalloped capitals, gabled lintel with two tiers of rosettes, and voussoirs with zigzag. Chancel extended E in the early C14; in the E wall inside, two charming niches with rosettes in the jambs, ogee tops, and leaf sprigs in the spandrels. W tower later C14, with diagonal buttresses, W doorway with fleurons, three-light W window, later battlements. Restoration of 1871–4, begun by *Horace Darken* and completed, after a dispute, by the contractor *Joseph Grimes*, included the removal of a W gallery, new E window and chancel arch. W gallery replaced 1960, by *H.F. Clarke*. Unsympathetic vestry room on S side by *E.D. Mills & Partners*, 1987, taking up an unreasonable amount of the otherwise garden-like churchyard. – MOSAIC over internal door by *Andrew Fawcett*. – FONT. C15, octagonal, with trefoils and shields; simple. – TILES. Nine slip-tiles of *c.* 1300; red, with pattern including a stag and a greyhound. – STAINED GLASS. Nave S by *A.L.Wilkinson*, 1961. – MONUMENTS. F.H. Thompson †1862 at Montego Bay, Jamaica. Draped sarcophagus with tropical foliage. By *T. H. Hart.* – Peter Thompson †1865 by *Sanders* of Euston Road, still in the traditions of 1800.

The village GREEN of Great Bentley is the largest in Essex, so large that it is almost a common. It covers 45 acres and was statutorily preserved in 1812. Whatever houses border on it seem small, seen across that great expanse, and there are in any case few of any age that are larger than cottages. One tongue reaches into the green, and two islands are in it, one with a white Early Victorian villa and the dark trees of its garden, the other with the brick METHODIST CHURCH of 1843 (three-bay front with central gablet and pointed-arched windows; cf. Brightlingsea) and other later brick buildings. The best houses are on the SW side, towards the church.

PRIMARY SCHOOL, Plough Road. 1897 by *J. W. Start*. Brick, in 'the modern Queen Anne style'. Single storey with projecting wings. Elaborate doorway. Schoolmaster's house to the r.

At Aingers Green, 1 m. SE, the OLD SCHOOL HOUSE, built as a mission chapel and infant school by *E. Geldart* with *J.R.Vining*, 1887. Single storey, with bellcote and prominent chimneystack.

GREAT BRAXTED

ALL SAINTS. A picturesque little church, above the lake of Braxted Park. The best view is from the W, showing the C13 tower partially rebuilt in 1883–4 by *E. Geldart* with W buttresses and gabled bellcote, behind which is attached the timber belfry and spire – a very curious composition. The mix of materials adds to the picturesqueness: septaria, flint, freestone, clunch, and bricks. Some of the bricks are Roman – e.g. those set herringbone-wise in the walls of the chancel – but others, in the quoins of the tower and chancel, are of Coggeshall type, early CI3. Of that date a s and a N lancet and the tower arch towards the nave without any break between jambs and voussoirs. The rest principally Norman, see one N window of the nave (widened) and one of the chancel. The chancel was originally apsed. Its present E end is CI3 and has lancets, at the E end a group of three. The s porch is CI5 with a crown-post roof on carved corbels. Brick N transept added 1761, as the Du Cane family pew, with their vault beneath. To its w a CI9 vestry, enlarged by *David Whymark*, 2004–6. – REREDOS. 1919. Designed by *Geldart*, executed by *Samuel Marshall* of Coggeshall, with figures by *Nathaniel Hitch*. At the same time early CI7 PANELLING was installed in the sanctuary. – CHOIR STALLS and N transept PEWS by *Geldart*, 1893; probably also the DESK, 1890. – STAINED GLASS. Large window in N transept by *Warrington*, 1844. – E lancets by *Percy Bacon & Bros* to Sir Charles Du Cane †1889, probably designed by *Geldart*. – MONUMENTS. Robert Aylett †1654. Inscription tablet, and l. and r. of it two tablets with shields and two roundels with skulls, bones, an hourglass and a shovel (in tower). – In N transept, Du Cane family monuments, including Peter †1803 by *J. Moore*, and a mural brass to Sir Charles †1889 by *Cox & Buckley*. – Rev. J.M. Wallace †1828. By *Brown* of Colchester. Plain, with urn.

BRAXTED PARK. The estate was purchased in 1751 by Peter Du Cane, a director of the Bank of England and the East India Co. Exposed timber framing inside the house, and its general plan, suggest that he thoroughly remodelled the existing CI7 house rather than rebuilt. Having consulted Isaac Ware and the otherwise unknown Thomas James, Du Cane appointed *Robert Taylor*, who had redecorated his house in St James's Square, London. Contracts were signed in 1752 and the mason, *John Malcott* (who had been apprenticed to Robert Taylor Sen.), was employed 1754–9. Brick, two storeys and attics, half-H plan, facing s. Centre range of nine bays, with two-bay wings projecting five bays forward. Of the wings' inward-facing bays, three on the first floor and two on the ground floor have niches rather than windows. Porch with attached Roman Doric columns. On the nine-bay w front, towards the lake, a broad two-storey canted bay. All rather plain, except for the windows, with Taylor's characteristic octagonal panes. Peter Du Cane II, who inherited in 1803, employed *John Johnson* to make additions in 1804–6, consisting chiefly of a new N front, thirteen bays wide, the ground-floor windows in the form of an arcade. Part of the N wall of Taylor's building, including a window (now internal), was retained behind. Johnson's sash windows are conventional in appearance but have exceedingly thin metal (possibly copper) glazing bars. At the E end of the N front a four-bay C18 ORANGERY with round-headed windows. Inside, the Entrance Hall has vaulted arcades at either end. The greater part of the W wing is occupied by the Saloon, with an Adam-style ceiling of *c.* 1950 by *Clark & Fenn.* Staircase with serpentine metal balustrade by Johnson.

On the E side of the house, an C18 STABLE BLOCK with two-storey arched, pedimented gateway, and pedimented three-bay coachhouse on the E side with domed bellcote. Later court-yard E of this, and N of that a walled kitchen garden, mid C18, enlarged in the early C19. The garden N and E of the house is enclosed by a ha-ha.

Peter Du Cane I was responsible for much planting in the surrounding PARK, notably turning the single approach avenue from the S into a triple one, the drive finishing with a circle in front of the house, laid out in 1762 by *Thomas Potter.* Other avenues radiating from the house were removed by his son, who also combined ponds on the S side of the house to form the lake. At its W end is a LODGE and cave or ICE HOUSE, for-merly surmounted by a summerhouse. Peter Du Cane III, who inherited in 1822, enlarged the park, and enclosed it with an impressive brick wall, 4½ m. in circumference.* Datestones mark its progress, 1825–34. Three principal entrances, with rather plain lodges. Kelvedon Lodge, in the NW corner, has massive stone gatepiers incorporating cast-iron pedestrian gates. A few houses near the church were demolished and replacements built at Bung Row, an existing settlement 1 m. SE which remains the village centre. These probably include the two terraces of brick cottages at right angles to the street: two storeys, four bays each with a little gables and hoodmoulds over the windows. Du Cane acquired the parsonage and glebe in 1833 and built a new rectory (now GLEBE HOUSE) just outside the park's N boundary.

PUNDICTS LODGE, on the eastern edge of Braxted Park. Late Medieval timber-framed with three gables. Large additions to l. and r. of the last quarter of the C20, including a jettied cross-wing and two-storey porch, all with exposed timbers, and looking more like interwar work.

KELVEDON HALL, 1 m. NE. Late C17. Attractive painted brick front of Venetian windows on the ground and first floor, between them a pedimented doorcase and sash window. Hipped roof with three dormers.

GREAT BROMLEY

ST GEORGE. A fine sight, proud and compact; entirely in the East Anglian style. Big W tower, tall nave with tall clerestory of closely set windows, short chancel. The late C15 tower is the

---

* *Henry Harrison* is recorded as working for Peter Du Cane III, but it is not known what this amounted to.

most spectacular piece, although the extensive use of puddingstone locates it firmly in Essex. It starts at the base with a quatrefoil frieze. The buttresses are clasping but continue higher up as a combination of diagonal and angle buttresses. w doorway with fleurons in the jamb and arch mouldings, hoodmould on a griffin and an angel. Five-light w window with panel tracery, three-light bell-openings with one transom. Stepped battlements and crocketed pinnacles. The s porch is all flushwork-panelled. It has a parapet at the front, the more usual battlements on the sides. Niche above the doorway (figure by *H. & K. Mabbitt*, 1956), St George and the Dragon in the spandrels, standing figures as stops – one now missing, the other damaged – and three-light side openings.

The s doorway has fleurons in one order and a foliage trail in the other, both in jambs and voussoirs. Above, two re-set spandrel figures: Adam and Eve (cf. Ardleigh). The s chapel is also singled out as something special, by flushwork panelling at the base, and there is more flushwork on the clerestory. Three-light windows in the aisles, with Perp panel tracery, the patterns different on the N and s sides. N doorway minor, yet with three orders of fleurons in jambs and voussoirs. Two-light windows with one transom in the chancel (the E window dates from the restoration of the chancel and sanctuary in 1867). The clerestory windows of two lights are oddly not in line with the arcades below. There are seven windows to three bays. The s arcade is C14, the N arcade C15. Both have octagonal piers, but the proportions differ characteristically. The s piers have capitals generously decorated with leaves. The westernmost instead uses figures of angels, lions, a head with tongue out, and a dragon and a frog biting him. The nave is covered by one of the most magnificent roofs of Essex, a double-hammerbeam (cf. Castle Hedingham, Gestingthorpe), of which the two E bays have polychrome decoration.

PISCINA. C14, with a mask over the drain, and emblems of the Passion carved on two sides. Discovered buried and now mounted on a wooden stand. – REREDOS and panelling of sanctuary. By *Cecil G. Hare* (*Bodley & Hare*), 1931–2. – FONT. 1932, by *Duncan Clark & Beckett*. Octagonal, with traceried panels, and elaborate oak cover. – W and N DOORS. Both elaborately traceried; *c.* 1500. – PEWS. 1856, made by *Henry Ringham* of Ipswich. Low, but still with doors. – SCULPTURE. Stone figure, probably St John the Evangelist, *c.* 1500. – St George and the Dragon. Bronze. By *Shirley Morrison*, 2002. – STAINED GLASS. E window by *A.K. Nicholson Stained Glass Studios*, 1953. s aisle, 1871 (Faith, Charity, and Hope), probably by *Clayton & Bell*. N aisle by *Harvey & Ashby*, 1904. w window has decorative glazing by *Mark Bowden & Co.* of Bristol, 1858.– MONUMENTS. Brass to William Byschopton †1432. Figure of a priest, 37½ in. (96 cm.), under an ogee canopy, crocketed and originally pinnacled. – A number of tablets by *John Bacon Jun.* and *S. Manning Sen.*, the best by *Bacon*, 1815, to Captain William Hanson †1813, killed in the

Peninsula War, with kneeling figure of a grieving brother officer. – In the churchyard, N of the church, monument of the Alston family of Great Bromley Hall, *c.* 1857. Square, of three decreasing stages, the topmost in the form of an open domed lantern containing a lotus bud.

PRIMARY SCHOOL. 1862, by *H. W. Hayward*, with various additions, the largest and most recent in 2002. Brick with stone dressings.

COPLEY DENE, ½ m. s. C18 brick, two storeys with parapet and attics. Two-storey canted bays to either side of the pedimented front door. Built as the rectory.

RADAR TRANSMITTER TOWER, ¾ m. s. Second World War, steel, about 360 ft (111 metres) high.

GREAT BURSTEAD

A parish once more important than it now appears, which until 1844 included Billericay. Now the tables are turned and it feels like little more than an appendage to the town.

ST MARY MADGALENE. Low C14 ragstone w tower with angle buttresses and tall shingled spire behind battlements. Nave, chancel, and s chapel, of mixed rubble, and s aisle with separate pitched roof. The nave is Norman, as witnessed by one small window on the N side. The rest C14–C15. N doorway with head corbels and the Annunciation in the spandrels; N porch of heavy timber. Inside, the s aisle arcade has octagonal piers and double-chamfered arches. Two-bay s chapel arcade with composite pier and hollow-chamfered arches. Various C19 and early C20 restorations including one of 1885–92 by *W. J. Wood*. Small w extension, 1998. Four separate crown-post roofs, C15 and C16. – BENCHES, s aisle, C15. – CHEST. Dug-out type, bound with iron, C12–C13. – WALL PAINTINGS. An extensive scheme, discovered in 1989, over the s wall of the chapel and aisle. The oldest date to *c.* 1320–30, and include the trials, tribulations and death of St Catherine of Alexandria; the Annunciation, Nativity, and Adoration of the Magi; Weighing of Souls; Christ with Doubting Thomas; and the Three Living and Three Dead. – STAINED GLASS. Two windows in the s aisle have fragments of early C14 glass, some *in situ*, including the arms of Grey of Wilton. s aisle window †1869, three Pre-Raphaelite Marys. E window, 1928, and s chapel E, 1909, by *Kempe & Co.* s chapel s by *Matthew Lloyd-Winder*, 2003. – MONUMENTS. Ursula Cooke †1705 'of that mercyless distemper the Small Pox'. Ornate tablet with shield at the top and cherub's head at the bottom. – Joseph Fishpoole †1703, erected 1762. Similar, but with coloured marbles. – Felton Nevill †1780, with three cherubs. – In the churchyard, N and s of the church, an unusual number of good early headstones, many elaborately carved; the earliest 1664 and 1665.

Opposite the church, GLASS BOTTLE COTTAGE, C17 or C18 timber-framed and plastered, formerly two cottages, and GOBIONS FARMHOUSE, late C16 or early C17, mostly faced in brick but with exposed timbers on the gabled cross-wing.

GATWICK HOUSE, 1 m. N. Handsome tuck-pointed brick front, rainwater heads dated 1767. Five bays, two storeys and attics, Tuscan doorcase with open pediments and fanlight. Behind the front range a parallel range of *c.* 1745. C19 rear additions.

EARTHWORKS, Norsey Wood. *See* Billericay.

GREAT CANFIELD

5010

ST MARY THE VIRGIN. Distinctive weatherboarded W belfry with copper-covered battlements and recessed shingled spire. The framing is C15, as is the embattled S porch. Otherwise essentially Norman, of flint rubble with dressings of Barnack stone, many of the Norman features exposed by *Chancellor* in his restoration of 1872–6. Norman nave and chancel N windows. In addition a plain N doorway with columns with carved zigzag pattern, and a more ornate S doorway with ornamented capitals (the l. one with a bearded face and two birds pecking at it), a tympanum with flat concentric zigzag decoration probably representing the Sun, roll mouldings, and a billet moulding. The remarkable feature of the church starts with the Norman chancel arch, which has one order of columns with scalloped capitals and arch with an outer billet moulding. The abacus of the S respond is a reused Anglo-Scandinavian (mid C11) burial slab of the Ringerike style. Above this a round opening probably inserted by Chancellor. Through the arch one sees, at the E end of the straight-headed chancel, three round arches. Those to the l. and r. contain small windows, that in the middle must always have been connected with some form of reredos. It enshrines a WALL PAINTING of the Virgin and Child seated which is one of the best C13 representations of the subject in the whole country, full of tenderness. It is drawn in red, with some yellow. Other colours have disappeared. The ornamental borders and other decoration around, also in the adjoining windows, is mostly of stiff-leaf type. The date must be *c.* 1250 (cf. the Matthew Paris manuscripts). It was hidden behind the Wyseman monument (*see* below) until that was moved to the nave in 1888.

18

REREDOS, CHOIR STALLS, PULPIT and FONT belong to *Chancellor*'s restoration; woodcarving by *Polley* of Coggeshall. – HELM. Mid C16, of Italianate design. – STAINED GLASS. In nave: S lancet by *Brian D.L. Thomas*, 1970; two-light S by *Heaton, Butler & Bayne*, 1874; W by *Clayton & Bell*, 1896; N (heraldic) by *M.C. Farrar Bell*, 1980. – BRASSES. Lady, *c.* 1530, the figure nearly 17 in. (43 cm.). – John Wyseman †1558 (in armour) and wife, both figures kneeling, with four sons and six daughters behind; the main figures about 13 ½ in. (35 cm.)

–Thomas Fytche of High Easter †1558 (in armour). 21-in. (53-
cm.) figure. Three sons mounted separately, wife and daughters missing. – MONUMENT. Sir William Wyseman †1684 and
wife Anne, attributed to *Thomas Stanton* (AW). Demi-figures
holding hands, below an open segmental pediment. Good. –
Also floor slab in the chancel floor. Black marble with arms
and 'Anne/Lady Wyseman/1662', boldly cut.

CASTLE, SE of the church. Of the motte-and-bailey type. Mentioned in 1214. The mount is 45 ft (14 metres) high and at the
foot 275 ft (85 metres) across. The bailey can be seen S of the
mount, and an outer bailey S to SW of the church.

The church's setting is very attractive, with the castle mount
behind it and the River Roding nearby. Opposite the W front,
cottages that give little indication of being C17 and timber-
framed following remodelling with tile-hanging for the Maryon
Wilson family (the smaller pair in 1901), principal landowners, vicars and rectors for much of the C19 and C20. Further
examples are scattered about the parish (e.g. PECKERS, 1½ m.
NW), as well as new-built estate cottages in similar style. SW of
the church, in the outer bailey, THE HALL, an L-plan timber-
framed and plastered house of the C16 and C17, extended in
the C19 and C20. Less altered is THE MALTINGS, NW of the
church: hall with integral service end to the r., cross-wing to
the l.

BADGERS, ½ m. ENE. By *Quinlan Terry*, 2000–3. Neo-Palladian,
without any superfluous embellishment. Brick with stone
dressings, two storeys, attics and basement. Entrance front of
eleven bays, of which the centre three break forward slightly
and have a modillioned pediment. Round window in the tympanum, and a round-arched window over the Roman Doric
porch. The garden front is similarly treated but with three
windows instead of four either side of the centre, and an
enclosed three-bay loggia with attached Doric columns and
pilasters. Simple three-bay garages, pool-house etc. SE and SW
of the house, as well as a single-storey cottage that alone has
stone dressings; between them, formal gardens by *Arne
Maynard.*

At BACON END, ¾ m. NE of the church, some good thatched
houses, including FOXLEYS, an aisled hall of *c.* 1300 with
smoke-blackened rafters, altered in the C16 and later. Further
N, at BACON END GREEN, nice weatherboarded farm buildings, some thatched, C16–C17.

At GREEN STREET, 1¼ m. NW, CHAMPNEYS, an early C17
lobby-entrance house with thatched roof and C19 cast-iron
casement windows, those on the ground floor with Gothic
tracery to go with the Gothic front door – an attractive
combination.

SALKYNS, 2 m. NW. Good late C16 farmhouse, originally of four
bays, extended to the S in the C20. Original clasped purlin roof,
half-hipped at the N end.

GREAT CHESTERFORD

ALL SAINTS. Visually unsatisfactory, mainly the result of two C19 restorations, the second unfinished. The most unified view is from the NE, mostly flint rubble. Much cement on the S side, also on the W tower, rebuilt 1790, raised in 1841–2 and given pinnacles etc. by *L.N. Cottingham*,* who also rebuilt the chancel arch. Much of his work was undone by *Sir Arthur Blomfield & Sons* in 1891. They demolished a N porch and NE vestry, but their replacements never materialized, nor did plans to restore the nave to its original length and rebuild the tower on its original site further W. Chancel C13, shown by one original lancet on the N side. Nave originally C13 (aisle arcades with octagonal piers, but re-cut), the W parts of the nave and aisles C15. – STAINED GLASS. E window †1910 and others in chancel and S aisle, *c.* 1906–20, by *Heaton, Butler & Bayne*. – BRASSES. 18-in. (45.5-cm.) figure of a woman, with the indent of her husband. S chapel floor. Possibly William and Agnes Holden †1532. – John Howard †1600, aged twelve days. In swaddling clothes. 7¼ in. (18 cm.), partly covered.

CONGREGATIONAL CHURCH, Carmel Street. 1841. Stock brick. Taller, later C19 front with bold red dressings.

PRIMARY SCHOOL, School Street. 1845–9 by *Cottingham*, completed by *N. J. Cottingham*. Gothic, knapped flint with limestone dressings and decorative roof tiles. Originally T-plan, the master's house, distinguished by dormers and tall, diagonal chimneystacks, forming the stem. Balanced by a S wing, 1875.

Several attractive timber-framed houses in the village, the most interesting the OLD VICARAGE, on the NE side of the churchyard. Late C15, of cross-wing form, the upper storey jettied on two sides with a carved post at the corner. Pargetted panels on the E side, dated 1672. S of the church, BISHOPS HOUSE, early C18 brick but with overwhelming gault brick additions of the 1830s forming a ten-bay front. Picturesque entrance LODGE, with panel-pargetting dated 1841, for Rev. Lord Charles Amelius Hervey. Conceivably by *Cottingham*.

CHESTERFORD HOUSE, High Street. Gault brick refronting with C19 Gothic porch, two two-storey canted bays, and Gothic arches to the window casements. Austere red brick garden front, probably later C19.

THE CROWN HOUSE, Newmarket Road. Mainly C18 red brick. Three-bay, three-storey block with end pilasters and open pediment. Canted first-floor oriel with small pediment, round-headed window above it, and semicircular window in main pediment. Single bay to the l. with stone Tuscan doorcase, and lower two-bay block to the l. of that with two-storey canted bay. Stands on site of the Roman town's E gate (*see* below).

KING'S MILL, SW of the church. Large late C19 steam mill (now flats). Four storeys. Seven-bay stock brick range, joined and at right angles to a six-bay red brick range, with a further

---

* His relation R.M.J. Cottingham was a local farmer and churchwarden.

three-bay addition. Red brick mill house and other associated buildings.

RAILWAY STATION. By *Sancton Wood* and *Francis Thompson*, *c.* 1845. Gault brick. With stucco architraves, otherwise quite plain. Now offices.

ROMAN FORT AND TOWN. The site lies NW, between Newmarket Road and the Cam (which formed its western defences), and N of an earlier, Late Iron Age settlement. The fort, probably built in response to the Boudiccan Revolt of A.D. 60–1, covered an area of about 24½ acres. The walls of the later town, still visible in the C18, were obliterated by quarrying for road-making material. The walled town was roughly oval, 36¼ acres in area, and may be dated to the C4. It was strengthened by an external ditch (difficult to detect from the ground but clearly visible on aerial photographs). Most of the internal buildings appear to have been of timber, but in the N part of the town the foundations of two stone-built houses were found. In a second enclosure, SW, excavations have revealed foundations of a Roman wall, particularly along the N side of the churchyard.

1010

GREAT CLACTON

ST JOHN THE BAPTIST. A Norman church and quite remarkable for what was a small village. This is due to the patronage of Richard de Belmeis, bishop of London 1108–28, founder of St Osyth's Priory, who enclosed a park at Clacton. The church must always have been very impressive in size, tall and wide, as the proportions of the chancel arch prove. The broad flat outer buttresses are also remarkable. They and their counterpart pilaster responds inside indicate that the nave was once vaulted, like Copford (q.v.), which also was under the control of the bishops of London. The windows too seem to be correct, at least in their unusual size. S doorway with two orders of columns and two roll mouldings in the arch; all renewed. N doorway of similar design, but two of the columns decorated with carved diaper (or star) and spiral motifs. Chancel rebuilt in the C14, W tower in the C15, replacing a belfry, the tie-beams of which were kept. The W tower has angle buttresses and a three-light W window. It was not completed; the wooden belfry and short octagonal spire date from 1810, battlements replaced by a balustrade in 1913. Restoration by *E.C. Hakewill*, 1865–6, who rebuilt the E wall, introducing three Norman-style windows, and added a two-bay N chancel aisle. All the window detail is his, as is the septaria of the walls, previously rendered. Further restoration, including re-flooring, by *Gerald W. Barrett*, 1997–2000. – C15 FONT. Octagonal, with three seated figures and two angles holding shields; defaced.

The 'village' now forms the northern part of Clacton-on-Sea (q.v.), but a few buildings remain to indicate its former character. At the churchyard's SW corner ST JOHN'S HOUSE, C18

brick with later plastered façade. Central Greek Doric porch
and to its r. a doorway with Doric pilasters. s of the church the
SHIP INN, C16 with exposed timbers although so altered and
restored as to look like a C20 imitation, and w of the church
the QUEEN'S HEAD, C16 or earlier with C18 alterations and
additions, including an unusually generous two-storey bow.
Adjoining the pub, in North Road, THE PLOUGH, *c.* 1700,
once its brewery. E of the church, in Nightingale Way,
SODBURY HOUSE by *J. O. Smith*, 1892, 'Queen Anne' with tall
chimneys and a rooftop belvedere.

CANN HALL, Constable Avenue, ¾ m. WNW. Built for St Osyth's
Priory, probably in 1512 (tree-ring dating). Two storeys, with
a continuous jetty. Two-bay single-storey hall, with service end
to the r. and parlour to the l., the hall and parlour heated by
a shared stack. Behind, and joined in the C18 to the cross-wing
that projects from the parlour, what was originally a free-
standing building, possibly a kitchen.

GREAT DUNMOW

6020

Dunmow (as it is usually known) has two quite separate parts:
the market town, where Stane Street meets another Roman road
leading s to Chelmsford, and Church End, ½ m. N.

ST MARY THE VIRGIN. A large town church, in spite of its rural
setting. Flint rubble, restored in 1907, when *R. Creed* removed
render from all but the chancel walls. The chancel is earlier
than the rest, early C14, as the windows clearly show. Thin
tracery with cusped lancet lights, foiled circles, spheric triangles, and no ogee arches: these motifs are a safe indication
of date. The five-light E window (renewed 1891) is unusually
sumptuous. Chancel arch on triple-shafted responds. Inner
nook-shafts to the windows. SEDILIA with polygonal shafts.
DOUBLE PISCINA. C15 w tower with angle buttresses connected by a chamfer, an uncommon form (cf. Little Sampford), battlements and polygonal embattled pinnacles. Above
the w doorway a frieze of shields. Three-light w window and
large straight-headed three-light bell-openings. The s side all
embattled, with two-storey porch with a higher stair-turret.
Niches l. and r. of the doorway. The later C15 s chapel projects
a little to the s beyond the s aisle. The N side also embattled.
Aisle windows renewed as part of *G.E. Street*'s restoration of
1872–3, which also involved reseating and removal of earlier
C19 galleries. Only the s doorway proves that the s aisle was in
fact built as early as the chancel. It has a handsome arch with
roll mouldings with fillets and a hoodmould ending in big
scrolls. The wide four-bay arcades inside are C15. They have
piers of the familiar four-shaft-four-hollow moulding with no
capitals over the hollows, and two-centred arches. The fact that
the w tower has E buttresses projecting into the nave shows
that it was built before the nave joined up with it. The vestry
on its N side was added in 1889. The most attractive feature of

the interior is the wooden balcony extending from the upper storey of the porch into the S aisle. It is of late C15 date and served the guild chapel behind it.

FONT. 1847. Designed by *Mr Smart*, executed by *W. Ollett*. – STAINED GLASS. Many fragments of medieval glass in a S aisle window and in the tracery of other windows. A N aisle window (St Mark and St Luke) was said in 1873 to be a restoration of old glass by *James Bell*, who had been Street's assistant, but it appears mostly new. – Small figures of Saints on purple panels, C18, Dutch, in two S aisle windows. – E window centre light 1891, side lights 1913. – Chancel S by *Clayton & Bell*, 1864, chancel N †1913 by *E.R. Frampton* and 1951 by *Pilgrim Wetton*, made by *Lowndes & Drury*. – S aisle E also by *Wetton*, 1958, made by *Luxford*. S window †1871 by *Clayton & Bell*. – N aisle by *Lewis F. Day*, 1906, made by *Walter J. Pearce*, still strikingly modern. – MONUMENTS. Brass to William Glascock †1579 and wife Philippa; only her figure survives, 17 in. (43 cm.). – Elizabeth Vassall †1652, with the small figure of a woman. – Sir John Swynnerton Dyer of Newton Hall †1701. With Ionic columns and achievement of arms. – William Beaumont †1729 and his parents, by *Stanton & Horsnaile*. Corinthian pilasters, segmental pediment open and broken, with achievement of arms, flaming lamps and urns, cherub's head, etc. – Dame Ann Henniker †1792 and her husband John, Lord Henniker †1803. Two similar monuments, with cherubs sitting on a sarcophagus holding back drapes that frame their arms, by *Coade*. – Sir George Beaumont †1762 and his wife Rachel †1814. By *J.C.F. Rossi*, in the Grecian style. – John Pepper †1822 by *George Lupton*. Another cherub. – Charlotte Henniker †1852 by *Reeves* of Bath. Draped urn. – In churchyard, S of the tower, a large chest-tomb by *Druitt* (George Wade †1839 and others). Also an early C19 coffin-shaped tomb with headstone and footstone, all with Gothick detailing. – N of the church, Thomas and Louisa Gibbons †1891. Wooden post carved with emblems of craft and industry, with a shallow ogee copper-covered dome supported on brackets with cusped tracery and frieze.

UNITED REFORMED CHURCH, New Street. 1869 by *C. Pertwee* at his most ambitious. Romanesque. Brick with stock brick dressings. Gabled W front with three-bay arched loggia and triple-arched window above, and gabled stair-towers each side. Apsidal E end with vestries on the ground floor and organ above. Horseshoe gallery, the balustrade still visible but with a false ceiling behind it. Plain, separate brick school by *Thomas Gibbon*, 1864, enlarged by Pertwee.

FRIENDS' MEETING HOUSE, New Street. 1833. Brick, with hipped roof. Central doorway, two large sash windows to either side, and recessed panels between them.

POLICE STATION, Stortford Road. 1842–3, the first purpose-built police station in Essex. Brick, and still domestic in appearance. Built by *H.H. Hayward*, presumably to *Hopper*'s design.

PUBLIC LIBRARY AND YOUTH CENTRE, North Street. By *G. G. Scott Jun.*, 1867–8, as the National School.* Brick, with stone dressings; Gothic, but the main entrance has a Tudoresque stone doorway with flat ogee arch.

PRIMARY SCHOOL, Stortford Road. By *Stanley Bragg Architects*, 2004–5. Four linked blocks, light-brown brick and timber cladding.

PERAMBULATION

A perambulation is quite strung out, because of the church's relative remoteness from the town. White's description of Church End in 1848 as a 'sylvan suburb' still holds true. The church's neighbours are attractive, e.g. the former vicarage opposite the W door: mid C16 with exposed timbers and pargetting. A pleasant and varied row also along the E side of CHURCH STREET, with sympathetic late C20 houses on the W side. Church Street continues S, with CHURCH END running E over a BRIDGE by *Henry Stock*, 1881–2, with cast-iron balustrade. Along Church Street's E side, the ANGEL AND HARP, C17 timber-framed and plastered with C18 door and windows. Where the road bends to the r. PORTERS YARD, a complex group of three houses, originally an H-plan hall house of the C14 and C15, with two-storey cross-wings. Joined on the S side a C17 house, with a pair of semi-detached cottages also part of the group.

At the top of the hill one sees CLOCK HOUSE, on The Causeway. Three-storey timber-framed and plastered house of the mid C16 with a stately, symmetrical, brick front range which cannot be much later. It is only three bays wide, and the proportions of the front form an approximate square to the tops of the gables. These are shaped, two on the front and larger ones on each side. Square clock turret, said to be contemporary, with an octagonal bell-cupola. The façade windows are of three and four lights and transomed, although on the second floor the upper half of the windows (here pedimented) is false. Porch with Doric pilasters and semicircular arch. Lower C19 rear extensions. C20 brick gateway mimicking the form of the porch and gables, replacing the C18 wrought-iron gateway now at Warwick House, Easton Lodge, Little Easton (q.v.). Sir George Beaumont, one of the founders of the National Gallery, was born at the house in 1753.

S of Clock House, THE LIMES, timber-framed and plastered with three display gables to the road. These and other elements – staircase tower, chimneystacks – are C17, but a rear cross-wing has C16 or earlier framing. Little of interest then until The Causeway's S end, where the road forks. A few nice houses along THE DOWNS, to the r., including Nos. 6 and 7 on the N side, with raised ground floor reached by steps to a timber veranda. Early C19 timber-framed and plastered, with gabled central bay and varied fenestration, including round-headed

---

* The vicar, William Langston Scott, was his uncle.

and Serlian windows. But NORTH STREET, to the l., is the more important, beginning with BROOK HOUSE (E side), early C16 timber-framed and plastered with imitation exposed framing in the cross-wing gables. Fine late C18 doorcase with open pediment and ogee architrave in the tympanum. Further s, the KING'S HEAD, C15 with gabled N cross-wing, jettied on brackets. Opposite, the former National School (*see* Public Library, above), and then DOCTOR'S POND, where Lionel Lukin, inventor of the first lifeboat in 1784, is said to have undertaken experiments with model boats. Now the street rises and curves gently; on the l. a row of C16 cottages (Nos. 20–24) at right angles to the road. Attached to No. 13, a little brick shop with pointed windows, weatherboarded to the rear and until 1843 the lock-up.

After another slight bend the road widens into MARKET PLACE, with three chief points of interest – The Star (N), the Old Town Hall (SE), and the Saracen's Head Hotel (on the s side of the High Street, *see* below) – and a very satisfactory sense of enclosure with good if unexceptional buildings. The OLD TOWN HALL is C15, with close-studded timbers on the ground floor and teetering upper storeys. Much altered in 1855 when the first floor was raised for a meeting room. Big oriel window, and above it a jettied gable and then a bell-cupola. Along its s side, in White Street, BOYES CROFT, C17 with two gabled cross-wings (converted to flats, with additional new housing, *c.* 1967), and behind it former MALTINGS, restored by *Kay Pilsbury Architects*, 1998–2000, as a museum and meeting room. The structure is remarkably complete, and dates to *c.* 1565. Seven-bay, two-storey timber-framed and plastered range containing the germinating floor; brick drying kiln at the E end with conical roof added *c.* 1780. At the w end the steeping pit, *c.* 1780, with weatherboarded store over it *c.* 1833, and a separate C19 drying kiln and store w of that.

From Market Place's s end, the High Street leads SE and Stortford Road w. STORTFORD ROAD should be explored first, beginning with THE CHESTNUTS, a large C16 and C18 timber-framed house (now offices) whose outbuildings form a yard on the w side. On the street's s side an interesting row, jettied with a nice variety of oriels and inserted shopfronts, including No. 19 (Old Forge Cottage), said to be formed from a C13 cross-wing. Another good shopfront on the N side, SWEETLAND'S butchers with C19 canopy on wrought-iron brackets and carriageway through to yard with slaughterhouse etc., the basic timber-framed structure C16. Then a change, with the Police Station (*see* above) on the s side, and on the N the E.T. FOAKES MEMORIAL HALL by *A. E. Wiseman*, 1934, with additions by *P. J. Rayner*, 1994. Brick, with panels of plaster and low-sweeping tiled roof: a complete contrast to its Modern neighbour of 1935, PERKINS GARAGE, painted brick with flat roof, metal windows and curved corners. Just beyond it, a row of timber-framed houses of which one (No. 20) has a splendidly out-size pedimented doorcase with Roman Doric columns and

rosettes in the metopes. About 300 yds further on, THREAD-
ERS GREEN, a group of C16 and C17 thatched cottages set back
from the road, and the QUEEN VICTORIA pub, also thatched.
Now back to the HIGH STREET, for the SARACEN'S HEAD
HOTEL: smart seven-bay plastered front of the C18 with a big
doorcase with broken pediment. Early C17 painted decoration
in a first-floor room. On the same side to the S No. 12, late
C18, with steps up to a front door in an elaborate surround
with cast-iron fanlight. No. 15, opposite, is jettied over an alley
at its S end with exposed dragon post, the timbers tree-ring
dated 1381–1407. Remodelled in the C19, but the N end has a
crown-post roof with soot-blackened timbers. Back on the W
side, Nos. 20–24 still discernible as a late C14 H-plan hall
house; No. 28 also timber-framed but with an early C19 brick
front and Tuscan portico. Opposite, a cast-iron PUMP in Tudor
Gothic style, and then the BOAR'S HEAD, with two gables to
the street, mainly C16 but with C14 parts. On the W side again,
the DUNMOW CLUB, *c.* 1886, dull, worthy and vaguely Italianate with portico on square Tuscan piers. The street widens
a little where New Street runs off to the S. On an island at the
junction the WAR MEMORIAL by *Basil Oliver*, 1921, an unusual
design like a triangular obelisk. Above the base the sides are
concave, with lettering by *Eric Gill*, carved by his apprentice
Joseph Cribb; at the top a cross carved in relief on each of the
three sides, beneath a little curved canopy. Behind, the POST
OFFICE, 1938, typically well-mannered *Office of Works* Neo-
Georgian. Doorcase with scrolly architrave. Set back a little on
the opposite side, THE DUNMOW INN, also decent Neo-
Georgian, by *Campbell F. Cargill, c.* 1940. One canted bay and
pedimented doorcase.

Nearly ½ m. further S, on Chelmsford Road, THE CLOSE, formerly the WORKHOUSE, by *Scott & Moffatt*, 1838–40, with
later C19 additions by *F. Chancellor* and *R. Creed*. One of the
most expensive and ostentatious of the New Poor Law workhouses, it cost about £10,000. Neo-Jacobean. Brick, with black
diapering and gault dressings. Gatehouse with chapel and
boardroom rather too close in front of the main three- and
four-storey U-plan range. Long symmetrical façade, the
central section with two three-storey bays, straight gables, and
ogee-capped cupola. At the rear, terraces of staff houses by
Chancellor.

Opposite The Close, ONGAR ROAD, with the KICKING DICKEY
pub on the W side, early C19 with cast-iron Gothic casements.
In LUKIN'S DRIVE, off Ongar Road to the N, 'Design Guide'
housing by *David Ruffle Architects, c.* 1990: the approved mix
of brick, plaster, and black weatherboarding.

BIGODS, 1 m. N of the church. Unappealing C19 stock brick front,
but straight gables and a chimneystack give a clue to its
early C16 origins. Alterations and additions by *Chancellor*,
1898–1901, for the technical school established here by Lady
Warwick (of Easton Lodge). SW, an Elizabethan SUMMER-
HOUSE. Two storeys, with stuccoed pilastered doorway, and

shaped gables. Blocked transom-and-mullion windows. Much of the garden wall, including blocked gateway, also survives.

120 MERKS HALL, ¾ m. E. By *Quinlan Terry*, 1982–6, for Richard Wallis. Classical country house in the C17 tradition of e.g. Roger Pratt's Coleshill House. Brick with stone dressings. Five bays, two storeys and attics with dormers, belvedere (the balustrades of which contain the chimneys) and lantern with little domed roof and finial. Central three bays of the N (entrance) in stone, rusticated and pedimented, with superimposed orders of Doric and Ionic pilasters (cf. Erith & Terry's Kings Walden Bury, Herts); round-headed windows, set in canted reveals at first floor to give an impression of depth. Urns on the pediment. The composition of the S (garden) front is similar, but all brick. On the E front, one Palladian window on the first floor. Large central hall rising to octagonal dome and lantern, with imperial staircase.

NEWTON HALL, ¾ m. W. Rebuilt 1858 for Sir Brydges Henniker by *E.B. Lamb*, and, as one might expect from that architect, of no great beauty. Crowstep gables are the favoured motif, used without restraint, on later additions as well as the original building. Brick. Between two large gables on the three-storey entrance (S) front, a little lantern with splay-foot spire. Three gables on the garden front. Lower wings W and E, the latter joined to the multi-gabled service range. Beyond it a stableyard with a crenellated wall between two gables. Now flats.

WINDMILL, ¼ m. SE. Brick tower mill, 1822, with only its domed cap intact. Joined to the former mill house in 1907.

GREAT EASTON

ST JOHN AND ST GILES. Nave and chancel of flint and pebble rubble. The nave is Norman, see the S doorway with one order of columns (scalloped capitals). The E half of the nave has noticeably thicker walls, an indication that originally it carried a crossing tower. One C16 two-light brick window in the N wall. The chancel is E.E., with lancets. The tower is a jumble when seen from W, the W wall carried up in brick to support a bell-turret of *c.* 1800, the turret replaced by a short tower in 1928 by *F.W. Chancellor* in a darker brick with black diapers and a low pyramidal roof. The rest of the church restored by *R. Creed*, 1899, who replaced the roofs and built a new chancel arch with ROOD BEAM and figures. – ALTAR and REREDOS. Also 1899, with painted panels including figures of the apostles in side-pieces extending right across the chancel like the wings of a triptych, only much wider. – STAINED GLASS. Chancel: E window and three others by *Clayton & Bell*, 1897, a fifth added *c.* 1909. – Nave N by *Carl Edwards*, 1976. – MONUMENT. Mrs Anne Meade †1758, by *Joseph Pasco*. Hatchment in a cartouche at the bottom, two little urns above the inscription, and then a stele.

EASTON HALL, SE of the church. Timber-framed and plastered, single-storey hall range to the E and two-storey cross-wing to the W, C15 and C16. – Large BARN, dating back to the C14, with two gabled midstreys and dormers on the W side. SE of the house the remains of a MOTTE AND BAILEY. The motte is 21 ft (6.5 metres) high and 130 ft (40 metres) across at the base. The ditch is 45 ft (14 metres) wide. The bailey lay to the S.

The village centre lies W of the church, a very attractive group of houses along The Endway, including ESSEX HOUSE, a mid-C16 long-wall jetty house with exposed timbers, STONE COTTAGE of flint with brick dressings dated 1822, and some estate cottages of Easton Lodge, one dated 1860. At the street's W end, by the River Chelmer, BRIDGEFOOT, a remarkably unspoilt C14 hall house with gabled cross-wing to the W and in-line parlour to the E, altered to give the impression of a second cross-wing. C16 rear service wing. Original traceried bargeboards. Across the river, CROYS GRANGE, late C16 but remodelled with mid-C19 gables, porch, false exposed timber framing, and the Maynard badge. E of the church, on the corner of the Dunmow–Thaxted road, P. & A. Wood's CAR SHOWROOM by *Stephen Mattick*, 1995. In the Essex vernacular style. T-plan, with a clock turret at the crossing of the tiled roof, a Venetian window in the main projecting gable, and carriage arch to one side. Inside, a galleried showroom on two storeys with the slope of the ground. The cars are Rolls Royces and Bentleys, the building of commensurate quality.

BLAMSTER'S HALL, I m. NNE. C16 timber-framed house remodelled in the early C19, when it was encased in brick and given a nice part-trellised porch. Good cast-iron railings with at one end a polygonal SUMMERHOUSE with pointed roof, of gault brick, flint and clinker.

NEW FARM, ¾ m. SE. 1934, by *Messrs Joseph* for *W. F. Crittall*, who was responsible for much of the design of the house, its interior, and gardens. In the Modern Cubist style, although the layout, particularly the symmetrical garden front, and the continued provision for servants, remains traditional. So too the materials: brick, surprisingly painted pink, the Crittall windows and other metalwork originally painted emerald green. The entrance front's striking feature is the central polygonal three-storey tower, with ground-floor porch and staircase landings above, composed of Crittall windows. The top section leads only to the flat roof and water tanks. Across three bays of the five-bay garden front a cantilevered concrete balcony, inset with glass discs to light the terrace below, by *Sir Owen Williams*. On the house's E side a single-storey block added after Crittall's death in 1956, and on the E side of the entrance courtyard an original range of garages and studio, with wooden doors and weatherboarding, another traditional element. Largely unaltered interiors, including staircase with red enamelled handrail and glass balls on the newels. Metal doorframes, skirtings, and picture rails. Many rooms still have their original Chinese wallpaper. Furniture made for the house by *E.W. Beckwith* has mostly been dispersed.

w of the house a c16 thatched and weatherboarded BARN (now a house) moved by Crittall from Clare, Suffolk. Beyond it a single-storey pantiled cottage built by Crittall. Another barn SE of the house came from Writtle.

At DUTON HILL, 1 m. NNW, THE WARRENS, late c16 timber-framed, although externally only the central chimneystack with four octagonal shafts indicates the true age. Otherwise it appears to be of *c.* 1905, with false half-timbering and bay windows. Inside a good early c17 staircase with pilaster balusters, probably not *in situ*, and a wall-post dated 1632. A little w, ELIZABETH'S COTTAGE, a small hall house of *c.* 1500. Two-bay hall with in-line parlour and service or solar bay; later inserted floor and dormers. Most of the original framing survives.

At LITTLE CAMBRIDGE, 1¼ m. NE, THATCHED COTTAGE was originally an open aisled hall house, possibly c14.

GREAT HALLINGBURY

ST GILES. Virtually rebuilt by *G.E. Pritchett*, 1873–4, for J.A. Houblon of Hallingbury Place; flint rubble with stone dressings. Otherwise, externally, only a single Norman window on the s side close to the w end, and the c15 w tower with thin diagonal buttresses and battlements. Pritchett added the tall shingled spire, as well as the N aisle, continued alongside the chancel. The detailing is good, with richly and naturalistically carved capitals to the arcade, hammerbeam roof, and screen-like stone arches to l. and r. of the chancel arch. But the arch itself provides the real surprise, for it is Early Norman or Late Saxon and all but complete, built up entirely of Roman bricks, with imposts of unmoulded stepped bricks. Ecclesiologists will be interested in the extremely rare feature of a PISCINA high up on the r., apparently to serve the rood loft. – REREDOS. 1874. Alabaster, elaborately carved (by *Rattee & Kett*) with symbols of the Evangelists, angels etc. Wings of Ancaster stone added 1889, apparently based on the reredos in Beverley Minster, Yorks. – WALL PAINTING. Naturalistic vine and pomegranates, covering the E wall, *c.* 1896. – FUNERAL HELM. Early c17. Also a copy of another, early c16.* – STAINED GLASS. E window by *Clayton & Bell*, 1891, and probably also the eastern nave s window. – Nave s (St George and St Giles), 1917, and w window †1926 by *James Powell & Sons.* – MONUMENTS. In w tower, inscribed brass commemorating the Morleys of Hallingbury Place, erected by Henry Parker, Lord Morley, 1556. Above, a small marble niche containing a figure of Death. – Susannah Houblon Newton †1837. By

---

* Original in the Victoria and Albert Museum.

Ternouth. Gothic. – G. B. A. Houblon †1913. Pictorial tile panel in the manner of *Powells*.

HALLINGBURY PLACE, ¾ m. SE. The seat, from 1729 to 1923, of the Houblon family. The early C16 house, remodelled and enlarged for Jacob Houblon by *John Redgrave* in 1771–3, was demolished in 1924. CLOCK HOUSE survives, converted from late C16 brick stables and forming one side of a large walled garden. To its E a timber-framed and plastered C18 granary on staddle-stones. Formal water garden, N, part of an extensive scheme by *Robert Wallace, c.* 1909. At the entrances to the estate, EAST LODGE, dated 1867, brick with panels of flint and false half-timbering on the upper floor, and WEST LODGE, similar date, diapered brick with stone dressings, probably by *G.E. Pritchett. Capability Brown* drew up a scheme for improvements to the park in 1772, but it cannot be said how much of the surviving landscape – including a lake to the N of the site of the house – is due to him. Jacob Houblon treated Hatfield Forest as an extension of the park, the two joined in 1857 (*see* Hatfield Broad Oak).

The VILLAGE lies mostly NW of the park near the church. HALLINGBURY HALL, SW of the church, has a brick front of *c.* 1813 with a pretty tented porch on ornamental pillars. Timber-framed and plastered rear ranges, late C16 and C17. NE of the church the former SCHOOL, 1851. Neo-Jacobean, diapered brick with three gabled cross-wings, like almshouses in form and appearance. *G.E. Pritchett* is the probable architect, perhaps also of estate cottages in the village. Beyond the school, GLEBE HOUSE, built as the rectory, 1878. Roughcast, rather Scottish Baronial with slate roof and a square corner turret. Of the older houses, TUDOR COTTAGE, opposite Glebe House, is prominent. C15 with exposed timber framing, joined by a single-storey (C19?) range to CENTURIES, dated 1673.

On the park's S side, WOODSIDE GREEN, common land with a variety of attractive cottages and farm buildings on the W.

WALLBURY CAMP. *See* Little Hallingbury.

GREAT HENNY   8030

ST MARY. Long nave and chancel without division; W tower. The lower parts of the tower are Norman, the diagonal buttresses C15 or later, the shingled broach spire early C18. The rest of the church is C14, flint rubble, except for one Early Tudor brick window in the S side and the absolutely plain brick S porch. Restored 1860, when the N transept and vestry were added. The main points of interest are the DOUBLE PISCINA with cusped pointed arches on detached shafts, and the nave roof with tie-beams on shallow arched braces, and queenposts. Corbels with figures carrying musical instruments. – STAINED GLASS. E window by *Hardman*, 1860. Chancel S to Laura Barnardiston †1871. Good. – BRASS. William Fyscher and wife, *c.* 1530, with children; small figures, the parents only 10 in. (25 cm.). – LYCHGATE. 1917 by *E. Beckwith*.

GREAT HOLLAND

ALL SAINTS. By *A. W. Blomfield*, 1866, except the mighty brick W tower of *c.* 1600. This has polygonal clasping buttresses and a higher polygonal stair-turret. Tower and turret are embattled. W doorway with many mouldings in the arch. Large four-light brick window with panel tracery. Blomfield shows himself here, in 1866, already tamed. No longer the challenging Butterfield-ian crudities of his first years; he is now competently and dully E.E. with circular piers and geometrical tracery. Nave and lower chancel, N aisle; flint with stone dressings. N vestry 1918. – STAINED GLASS. E window by *Ward & Hughes*, *c.* 1866. N aisle windows *c.* 1918 by *Heaton, Butler & Bayne*, also credited with a reredos and nave S windows at the time of the rebuilding, but little survives of either. – MONUMENT. H.G. Rice †1821, by *John Hinchcliff*. With kneeling, mourning female figure.

METHODIST CHURCH. 1927–9 by *W. H. Wrightson*. T-plan, with a very slender copper-covered spire at the crossing. Rendered walls, brick dressings, and battered buttresses.

VILLAGE HALL. By *W. Hayne*, 1909, extended 1914. Roughcast.

OLD RECTORY. Four-bay timber-framed range with a prominent Regency addition with recessed porch and deep eaves – probably the design for Rev. H. Rice exhibited by *William Brooks* at the R.A., 1812.

GREAT HORKESLEY

ALL SAINTS. The nave has Norman SW quoins, and inside above the tower arch is a C12 window of the original nave. The tower is C13 or early C14, unbuttressed with some small lancets. The rest is Perp, with big three-light windows with panel tracery of usual patterns. The battlements oddly enough are of Roman brick. Otherwise the walls are rendered. Handsome C15 S porch, its 1918 restoration rather too loudly proclaimed: timber with traceried sidelights and bargeboarded gable. C15 three-bay N arcade on thin piers with a section of four main shafts and four slimmer shafts without capitals in the diagonals. The arches (and also the C19 chancel arch) are decorated with fleurons (cf. e.g. St Peter, Sudbury, Suffolk). Hoodmoulds with headstops. Roof on big head corbels, one wall-post carved with a figure holding a shield. Sensitively restored by *C. J. Blomfield & Morgan*, 1928–9. – REREDOS. Mid-C19 Commandments, Creed and Lord's Prayer painted on metal by *R.B. Hardy* of Colchester. – PULPIT. Early C17, with arched as well as moulded panels. From St Margaret, Ipswich. – FONT COVER. Of tall, pinnacled Gothic form (cf. Sudbury), but mostly C19.

– Some good C19 STAINED GLASS, including N chapel by *William Wailes*, 1855. N aisle W window to two sons of the rector †1870 includes portraits of the boys in the tracery, one in bed, one kneeling. – MONUMENT. Rev. John Cock †1796. Usual tablet and urn, but nicely done by *Thomas King & Sons* of Bath.

ST JOHN, The Causeway. Private chapel built by J.L. Green of Terrace Hall (*see* below), 1837. Gault brick front and sides with Gothic openings, rounded corners and high parapet; plain red brick rear. Central porch added probably later in the C19, chancel 1925. Set back from the road with two single-storey LODGES, one circular, of gault brick, dated 1833, the other octagonal, chequered red and white brick, a little later.

CHAPEL COTTAGE, 1 m. SSE. Late C15. Originally a combined chapel and two-storey priest's house, whose upper storey projected into the chapel's W end. Diapered brick with blue brick blind arcading to the plinth. Large blocked E window; small niche above. N doorway now inside a late C19 or C20 single-storey extension. Very steep stepped gables. Probably the chantry chapel of St Mary referred to in a document of 1491; converted into a cottage at the Reformation.

OLD SCHOOL, School Lane, 1½ m. SSE. 1873. Brick, with stepped gables and niche in imitation of the old chapel (*see* above). Detached teacher's house in the same style. Schoolroom imaginatively and successfully extended as offices by *Rolfe Judd*, 1998. Brick, D-plan, with irregular fenestration.

THE CHANTRY, NE of the church. Stuccoed former rectory, with Doric portico *in antis* on the three-bay S front, large bow to the W, and deep eaves. Probably built in 1808 for Rev. Philip Yorke, whose family gave Sir John Soane several commissions. *Raymond Erith* made this connection when designing the modest roughcast LODGE, 1938, but one of Soane's pupils seems more likely for the main house.

THE GROVE, ⅔ m. SSE. C16 timber-framed, but with early C19 plaster quoins, Tudoresque windows with hoodmoulds, and flat porch on square columns. E of the crossroads, OLD WHITE HOUSE, C14 with two jettied cross-wings. Further E along Church Road, BAYTREES and BAYTREES HOUSE, both probably C15, with jettied cross-wings and exposed timbers.

HORKESLEY HALL (Littlegarth School), ¾ m. NE. Timber-framed core, C17 or C18, rendered, with a C19 extension of painted brick to the r. of the six-bay, two-storey entrance front. Remodelled at the end of the C18, perhaps following designs by *William Hillyer* for Samuel Gibbs, but *Soane* was paid for minor decorative work in 1786. One room has a marble chimneypiece and Adam-style ceiling, but the interiors mostly date from *c.* 1900.

TERRACE HALL, 2¼ m. SSE. 1837 for J.L. Green, extended 1928. Two-storey, five-bay gault brick house. Windows in arched recesses with a cast-iron rosette in each, and shallow bows on each return wall. Porch with two square pilasters and two Ionic columns. Unexpected things happen above the eaves: a single, central, gault brick dormer with finial, the window again set in a round arch but the dormer itself a pointed arch, and two sets of ornamental chimneys. – Circular two-storey LODGE, with encircling and projecting roof veranda, dated 1835.

PITCHBURY RAMPARTS. Early Iron Age hill-fort, 2 m. S of the church. Only the N end of the oval camp survives, but this is well preserved in a wood. There is a double rampart and a ditch, the ramparts 10 ft (3 metres) high and the ditch 60 yds (55 metres) wide, originally enclosing an area of about 5 acres. The double rampart is an unusual feature in Iron Age camps in East England (cf. Wallbury, Little Hallingbury). The attempt of early antiquaries to identify Pitchbury Ramparts as an outpost of the system of dykes round Colchester (*see* p. 301) has now been definitely disproved, but the true purpose of the enclosure remains uncertain. Evidence from excavations in 1933 and 1973 suggests a date of the CI B.C., but produced no signs of extensive occupation.

GREAT LEIGHS
Great and Little Leighs

7010

13   ST MARY. Mainly flint rubble. Norman round tower with small windows, restored by *Chancellor* in 1882, who rebuilt the splay-foot shingled spire, octagonal with four lucarnes. W doorway with zigzag ornament in the arch. Nave also Norman (two N windows, one S window, and the outer order only of an arch over the C14 S doorway). Chancel with renewed two-light windows of the early C14. The four-light E window has very elongated reticulated tracery. The interior of the chancel is gen-
25   erously decorated. A large recess in the N wall with an arch on short shafts flanked by thin buttresses that extend upwards to pinnacles as tall as the arch itself. The arch is cusped and sub-cusped and gabled. In the spandrel of the gable an extremely good spray of leaves in deeply undercut carving. The leaves are already bossy or knobbly, but much of the naturalism of *c.* 1300 is still preserved. The SEDILIA and PISCINA arches opposite have ogee heads, but the style is otherwise very similar. The seats are separated from each other by buttresses, not by shafts. Recess and sedilia much restored by Chancellor in 1866–7, when the chancel roof was replaced and the white brick N vestry added. W gallery 1720, with panelled and balustraded front. Base of tower neatly fitted with kitchen, meeting room etc. by *Peter Messenger*, 1995–6. – FONT. Perp, octagonal. Stem with tracery, bowl with quatrefoils carrying fleurons and shields. – BENCHES. Eight in the nave with straight-topped, traceried ends. Late C15. – Small BARREL ORGAN, early C19. – STAINED GLASS. A little of the C14 *in situ* in the chancel N windows; other fragments from the E window made up into a fire-screen (now in vestry). – E window 1884 by *E. R. Frampton*, made by *Clayton & Bell*. Three chancel S windows

also by *Clayton & Bell*. – Chancel N 1889 by *Powell & Sons*, drawn by *Charles Hardgrave*. – MONUMENTS to three rectors. Brass to Ralph Strelley †1414. Demi-figure in prayer. Originally about 13 in. (33 cm.), but the head replaced from a brass of *c.* 1370. – Rev. William Harby †1823. Classical marble tablet by *Joseph Dorman* of Chelmsford. – Rev. William Kay †1886. By *William White*. Mural brass in painted and gilded marble and onyx frame.

LYONS HALL, W of the church. Conspicuous late C19 extensions, grey brick with half-timbered gable facing the church. Behind this a mid-C15 range with gabled cross-wings, faced in grey brick earlier in the C19. Estate cottages S of the Hall, and a round timber pump shelter with conical thatched roof.

OLD RECTORY, ¾ m. N. 1869, for Rev. William Kay. Large, stock brick with stone dressings. A little further N, GRAYSTONES, the National School of 1847–8. Picturesquely irregular Tudor Gothic, the schoolroom at an oblique angle to the teacher's house.

The centre of population is round the crossroads over 1 m. NW of the church. On the E side of the main road, HIGHWAYS by *Clare & Ross*, illustrated in their *Ideal Homes for the People*, 1900. Additions by *F.W. Chancellor*, 1925–9. Behind the main road on the E side, No. 39 CASTLE CLOSE, 1976–7 by *Clive Plumb* for himself, and self-built. Single-storey, L-plan, two walls of full-height sloping glazing, rear walls of brick. Monopitch roof, and no load-bearing internal walls. In SCHOOL LANE, W of the main road, the former British School, 1845, and teacher's house, 1885. Brick, with stock brick dressings.

GOODMAN'S FARM, ½ m. W. C15 hall house with jettied and gabled cross-wings. C17 chimneystack at one end with two diagonal shafts.

LAWNS FARM, 1 m. S. L-plan, timber-framed and plastered. The older part is the mid-C16 front range (tree-ring dated 1538–52), at right angles to the road, with long-wall jetty, the roof hipped with gablet at the W end. The rear range is about a century later. Above the entrance, an original window with ovolo mullions.

GREAT MAPLESTEAD

7030

ST GILES. Sturdy, unbuttressed Norman W tower with later battlements, and Norman apse, complete with its three windows. The chancel, however, is E.E. (one N window with a low side window beneath, and remains of a second N window). C14 S aisle with the typical octagonal piers continued with a vertical piece which dies into the double-chamfered arch. The W end and part of the tower repaired in brick following a lightning strike in 1612. Walls otherwise of flint. The C14 S transept was adapted to make a chapel for the Deane family of Dynes Hall in the C17. S porch and N vestry 1849–50, N aisle and N transept by *William White*, 1861, who was also responsible for decorating the chancel, 1866, of which vestiges remain in the window reveals and on the ceiling. – FONT. Perp, octagonal, with traceried stem. Remains of colour found in 1930. The panels were bright blue with yellow diapering, and the shields on the bowl had painted Emblems of the Passion with alternating borders of green and yellow, and red and yellow. – PAINTING. Copy of 'Lo Spasimo di Sicilia' by *Raphael*, given by Henry Sperling of Dynes Hall in 1800.

MONUMENTS. Sir John Deane of Dynes Hall †1625. Reclining painted figure stiffly propped up on one elbow, columns l. and r. supporting a shallow segmental arch. Between the columns against the back wall kneel the children. Attributed to *William Wright*. – Anne Lady Deane †1633, erected by her son Sir Dru Deane in 1634. Reclining effigy of her son rolled towards us with arms crossed. The painted figure is propped up on a folded-up mat. Behind him stands most impressive and ghostly the figure of the lady in her shroud. She looks up and raises one hand. In the coffered arch carved angels. The arch is broken open in the middle, and there a crown appears, held by two figures sitting on top of the arch. The monument rests on three short Ionic columns. It is documented as the work of *William Wright* of Charing Cross (AW), one of a series of such macabre monuments the most familiar of which is Nicholas Stone's Donne in St Paul's Cathedral. They are all of the 1630s; there was a decided fashion for them at that moment. The inscription says:

> Her shape was rare: her beauty exquisit.
> Her wytt accurate: her judgmt singular.
> Her entertaymt harty: her conversation lovely.
> Her harte mercifull: her hand helpful.
> Her courses modest: her discourses wise.
> Her charity heavenly: her amity constant.
> Her practise holy: her religion pure.
> Hew vowes lawfull: her meditations divine.
> Her faith unfaygnd: her hope stable.
> Her prayers devout: her devotions diurnall.
> Her dayes short: her life everlasting.

Both monuments restored 1964 by *Beryl Hardman* and *François Angello-del-Cauchferta*.

SCHOOL and schoolmaster's house, 1862–3, and former VIC-ARAGE, 1860, N of the church, by *White*, the former red brick with Caen stone dressings, the latter yellow brick, both modestly polychromed. *The Ecclesiologist* liked the vicarage, designed with White's 'usual extraordinary cheapness, and his usual picturesqueness, arising from the natural irregularity of the ground plan'.

BARRETT'S HALL, ½ m. SSW. C15 timber-framed and plastered, with C18 gault brick front range. Two storeys, three bays, the central bay breaking forward with pediment and Roman Doric porch. Opposite, remnants of the DIOCESAN HOUSE

OF MERCY for Fallen Women, 1866–8, by *Woodyer*, with an additional wing by *Henry Law*, demolished *c.* 1960.[*] Surviving former COACHHOUSE, its rainwater heads dated 1866 but incorporating an older timber-framed structure. WIMBLES, N, was the warden's lodge, and before that the rectory. C16, with gabled cross-wings and C19 canted bays, porch, and decorative eaves and bargeboards.

CHELMSHOE HOUSE, ½ m. NNW. Early C18 brick. Doorway with Gibbs surround. C18 brick DOVECOTE to NE.

DYNES HALL, 1 m. S. Part of the house built by William Deane, who purchased the estate in 1575, forms the W wing; original timber framing visible inside. The rest mostly demolished in 1689 and replaced by Sir Mark Guyon of Coggeshall, although this was incomplete on his death in 1690; the old part seems to have been refronted at the same time, so that the whole front is of red and blue brick chequer. The C16 part of three bays and three storeys, the C17 part of seven bays and two storeys and attics with three-bay pediment, dormers behind parapet, and hipped roof. Rubbed brick quoins and raised brick frames to the windows. Late C17 staircase with heavy twisted balusters.[†] Alterations and additions by *John Young* for Charles Sperling, 1883. He tried to make the W wing look more like the main house, although the result is closer to Queen Anne Revival, with pedimented dormers rising through the old parapet. Young also added an upper floor to the back of the W wing, various shaped gables, and a drawing room at the NE corner. To this was added a sun-room and conservatory by *Alan Bragg*, 1984. Young's plate-glass windows replaced in the C20 with pretty Gothick tracery. Brick STABLES NW of the house, 1770, with wooden clock tower and cupola on the central range; two gabled wings enclosing the yard.

HULL'S MILL, 1¼ m. SW. Unusually large C19 water mill. Painted brick ground floor and three weatherboarded upper floors. Converted to a house in the 1960s. C16 mill house across the lane.

GREAT NOTLEY   7020

Begun in 1993, Great Notley Garden Village by *Countryside Properties* comprises *c.* 2,000 homes on a 465-acre greenfield site, incorporating some existing housing along the W side of the B1053. It is an attempt to create the sort of village that planners and developers believe most people would like to live in, and they are probably right. What distinguishes Great Notley among contemporary large-scale developments is the infrastructure – shops, schools, public buildings – necessary to create a real community, rather than just a dormitory. Given Braintree's proximity, it would have been easy not to have bothered.

[*] Chancel screen from the chapel now in St Barnabas, Alphamstone (q.v.).
[†] Some C16 panelling now in All Saints, Springfield (q.v.).

The layout is deliberately irregular, but although it is based around three 'hamlets' – Notley Green in the S, Oaklands Manor in the middle, and Panners Farm to the N – these have tended to merge into one confusing maze of winding roads, frequently punctuated by roundabouts and other traffic-calming features. The best approach is from the S, by the village ponds, leading to GREAT NOTLEY AVENUE, the only really formal part of the village, with a long straight road leading up to the 6-acre green. At the avenue's S end an open shelter like, say, a market hall, but with no apparent function except to house a bronze SCULPTURE, 'Mrs Hedges', by *Siobhan Coppinger*, 1995. On the green's N side the VILLAGE HALL, 1996. Brick, hipped roofs with gablets, the main roof with a decorative metalwork cresting by *Gary Thrussell*. Inside, ceramic floor by *Kitty Connolly* and *Jason Boatswain*, and timber wall panel by *Anne Wesley*. To the l., THE OVAL pub, 2002. Essex vernacular, the main part resembling a timber-framed and plastered farmhouse, with a weatherboarded 'extension'. To the W of the green, the shopping centre, dominated by a very large barn-like TESCO, 1996.

N of the green and shopping centre is THE MANOR HOUSE, complete with 'Regency' lodges. Stock brick with rendered ground floor. Three storeys, seven bays, the central three breaking forward and with pediment. Deep eaves. Flat Ionic portico. It is in fact three houses – suggesting a converted C18 country house, perhaps, its grounds filled with Neo-Georgian boxes. This may be taking realism too far. Other houses in a variety of styles and materials, mostly Essex vernacular – brick, flint, render – and the more expensive ones, particularly as one moves N into the Panners Farm area, individually quite attractive. But the impact of, say, a Tudor-style mews, with stepped gables, diamond chimneys, and gateway, is reduced by having an identical structure opposite. Good use of natural features – ponds, trees, including newly planted semi-mature trees – to create some genuinely villagey corners, but too much is assembled from a limited range of standard designs.

The village has two exceptional public buildings:

NOTLEY GREEN PRIMARY SCHOOL, Blickling Road. 1998–9 by *Allford Hall Monaghan Morris*. Single-storey, on a highly original triangular plan, with classrooms along one edge and all other accommodation arranged round a central court. Blockwork internal walls, load-bearing timber external stud walls insulated with recycled newspaper and clad with cedar. Sedum roof. Extended by *Bryant Harvey Partnership*, 2003–4.

123 DISCOVERY CENTRE, Great Notley Country Park. By *Penoyre & Prasad*, 1999–2001, similar to their Millennium Centre, Dagenham (*see London 5: East*). Multi-purpose building, designed as a model of sustainability, including a wind turbine for electricity generation, solar panels for water heating, rainwater collection, and reed-bed sewage disposal. Built on an artificial mound, facing S. Two storeys on the S side, mainly glazed, with a monopitch roof angled for the solar panels. Four

storeys on the N side. Constructed of sand-coloured breeze blocks, with a high proportion of recycled materials, and Douglas fir cladding. 'TermoDeck' flooring, i.e. concrete floors with hollow cores to allow circulation of air for ventilation and heating. NW of the Discovery Centre, GREAT NOTLEY BOWL, a grass amphitheatre, and at the top of the man-made hill 'The Bird' by *Jonathan Clark*, metal SCULPTURE with a wing-span of 13 ft (4 metres).

GREAT OAKLEY
1020

ALL SAINTS. Prettily sited in a sloping churchyard, so that what one sees first is the W tower with weatherboarded upper stage and pyramidal roof, rebuilt far short of its original height in 1766. Brick W face. Long aisleless C12 nave (N wall: one Norman window and traces of a second, besides a mid-C16 three-light brick window), and long, lower early C14 chancel, all of pebble and flint rubble. The chancel E window, however, is Early Perp, of four lights with panel tracery. The chancel arch also is late C14 in style. Inside the chancel a charming small N doorway (blocked) with heads and angels in jambs and voussoirs, and a DOUBLE PISCINA under an ogee arch. Restored 1880, when galleries were removed, and in 1909 by *Chancellor & Son*. – FONT. C12, of Purbeck marble. Square, with five round-headed panels on each face. – REREDOS. 1889, by *E. Geldart*, with a rather badly drawn crucifixion. – STAINED GLASS. E window, 1900, crammed with figures: forty-two saints, four evangelists, and four archangels. Probably by *Clayton & Bell*.

SE of the church, the OLD RECTORY, 1834–5 by *Thomas Rickman*. Neo-Tudor, but with sash windows. Two-storey porch with Perp doorway, battlements and diagonal buttresses. St John's College, Cambridge, where Rickman had just built New Court, were patrons of the living.

HOUBRIDGE HALL, ¾ m. WSW. C16 timber-framed, extended in the C18, with mid-C19 gault brick entrance and garden fronts, three and five bays respectively. Large windows with cast-iron lintels. Above a blocked window over the entrance a reused shell-hood. Across the road, BROOKLANDS, late C18 with Gothick features, but so over-restored that it has lost all its character. Octagonal LODGE and landscaped grounds with large lake.

GREAT SALING
6020

ST JAMES THE GREAT. Flint rubble with stone dressings. Late C14 W tower, with thin diagonal buttresses and battlements. Restored by *R.J. Withers*, 1857–8 and 1864. He rebuilt the chancel, N vestry and organ chamber, and S porch, and left nothing untouched in the nave. Chancel fittings also by

Withers, including the REREDOS, singled out for praise by *The Ecclesiologist*. It uses encaustic tiles of the sort normally seen on the floor, with stone carving by *Earp*. – FONT. Octagonal, with tracery panels. Early C15. – STAINED GLASS. E window and chancel s contemporary with the restoration. Nave s †1883 by *Clayton & Bell*. – MONUMENTS. Two large monuments hidden away at the restoration. Elizabeth Yeldham †1786. Seated female, resting on the pedestal of a closed urn. By *Charles Harris*. Now in nave. – Bartlet Shedden †1823. Standing wall monument with full-sized kneeling female in front of a tomb, in a plain archway with four-centred head. By *Theakston*. In vestry. – Catharine Goodrich †1821. Also by *Theakston*, but smaller, and Gothick, so allowed to remain *in situ*.

SALING HALL. Timber-framed, *c.* 1570, but refaced on the s façade and the w and e. Red and blue chequerwork, timber cross-windows. On the main front two plus five plus two windows, and on the side parts two symmetrical shaped gables consisting of double-curved pieces and segmental tops (cf. Beaumont Hall). The date is 1699, late for choosing shaped gables. Inside, late C16 panelling. Main staircase with twisted balusters, and enclosed secondary staircase with balustrade of plain bars set fret-wise, both *c.* 1699. Two front doors of *c.* 1795, when the house was shared by two sisters. Walled garden on w side (brick wall dated 1698), this and the grounds beyond laid out by Lady (Isabel) Carlyle, 1936–59, developed and extended by Hugh Johnson from 1971. – Classical garden TEMPLE OF PISCES with tetrastyle Tuscan portico by *A.D.C. Ross*, 1988, with carved relief of fishes in the pediment and lettering by *D. Kindersley*.

The church lies sw of the Hall, visually a part of the garden, as is the late C17 HALL FARM immediately s of the church. s of that the OLD VICARAGE by *Withers*, 1858. Domestic Gothic, patterned in black brick. Separate coach house.

SALING GROVE.* Built by John Yeldham, 1754, altered and extended by William Fowke after 1827. Brick, mostly rendered in a depressing grey. Three-bay N portico. Mid-C19 gault brick E extension with clock tower. Large mid-C19 brick stables including covered yard and carriage house (now converted). N lodge and gardener's cottage to E in similar style. Gault brick W lodge, railings, and gates, *c.* 1800. Gardens, pleasure grounds, and park laid out by *Repton*. Commissioned by Yeldham in 1790, Red Book (whereabouts unknown) dated 1791, and completed by Yeldham's death in 1795.

6030   GREAT SAMPFORD

ST MICHAEL. Flint rubble, with dressings of limestone and clunch. Battlemented w tower with angle buttresses, 're-inforced and renewed' by *Sir Charles Nicholson & T.J. Rushton*,

---

* Access refused in 2003.

1938–9. But the dominant feature is the s chapel, the transept of a former, larger church (now screened off as vestry). It is later C13, proved by the two two-light E windows with a separated sexfoiled circular window above. The two pointed windows each have two pointed trefoiled lights and an unencircled quatrefoil above. Large bricked-up s window, below which is a C14 recess with a crocketed gable and deep niches l. and r., also with crocketed gables. The rest is all of the first half of the C14, the chancel unusually lavish. It can hardly be later than 1320, as the ogee arches occur only very secondarily in the s side windows. Very large E window, of five lights with a large circle as the central tracery motif. In the circle are four smaller circles with quatrefoils arranged in two tiers, and not cross-wise. Niches in the E and s buttresses, also one below the E window. Inside, seats under deep cusped pointed arches run all along the N and s sides, and all windows are shafted. Chancel restored in 1874, the dated rainwater heads the trademark of *Ewan Christian*. The N aisle is contemporary with the chancel, shown by the windows, and the arcade of quatrefoil piers with very thin shafts in the diagonals (cf. Thaxted) and double-chamfered, two-centred arches. Characteristically later s arcade, with octagonal piers, and arches starting with short vertical pieces dying into them. Nice arch from the s aisle into the s chapel. The capitals have bossy leaves, with a lively variety of figures among them, including human faces, an owl, and a snail. Original roofs, apart from the s aisle. – REREDOS. Four alabaster panels, with crocketed gables, carved with the Lord's Prayer etc. By *R.C. Hussey*, 1847–8, for Danbury (q.v.), where James Hadfield opined that 'a finer piece of workmanship has not been executed since the Reformation'. Moved here 1894. – Original s DOOR, with elaborate saltire-bracing on the inside. – Above N arcade, two large fragments of medieval WALL PAINTING, one representing the Seven Deadly Sins in the form of a diagrammatic tree, the other (perhaps) St Christopher. Discovered in 1979.

BAPTIST CHURCH. 1875. Plastered front, painted a startling yellow. Two tiers of three round-headed openings. Brick rear, as is the schoolroom to the l., 1903, the architect named as *Steyning*. Manse to r., 1889. Two bargeboarded gables and trellised porch, the (blue) plastered walls framed in stock brick.

PRIMARY SCHOOL. By *C. Pertwee*, 1876. Brick with stone and stock brick dressings. Porch on the r., feature gable near the l. end with turret behind. Sympathetic extension by *Jonathan Green* of *W. S. Atkins*, 1997, to provide combined school hall, village hall and other community facilities. To the r., former teacher's house. Beyond, the smaller mid-C19 school, with bargeboarded gables. Now a house.

The village centre is along two roads that meet at a T-junction by the church. Several pretty houses, some thatched. On the corner opposite the church's E end, MANOR HOUSE, C16 or C17 timber-framed and plastered, with a long front gabled at each end facing the church and a three-bay Georgian return at the s end. Along the High Street, N of the church, a single-storey row of C17 thatched cottages. Further N, on the W side, STOW FARMHOUSE, late C16 with a cross-wing at the s end and two tall chimneystacks. Opposite, THE CORN MILL, the octagonal brick base of a smock mill, thatched and converted to a house. S of the church, CHURCH COTTAGES, a C15 hall house. N and S cross-wings, the s jettied with a canted ground-floor bay. Also on the ground floor a former shop window, C18 or early C19 bow oriel.

TINDON MANOR, Tindon End, 1¾ m. ESE. Picturesque, timber-framed and plastered, with a plausible date of 1684 carved inside. Bargeboarded gables l. and r. of the main range, and then on the r. a mid-C19 addition, also gabled, but taller, with a double-height canted bay with Gothic glazing bars. On the road to Tindon End, a number of good timber-framed farm-houses, including GIFFORDS, with an original chimneystack dated 1626 and C19 Gothic casements, and BYEBALLS, early C17 with jettied front. Wall painting in a ground-floor room, repeated geometric forms enclosing flowers, and fragments of a painted scheme on the first floor. At right angles to the main house an outhouse that was the original house on the site, probably C14. Four bays, of which the central two were an open hall with sooted crown-post roof.

GREAT TEY

ST BARNABAS. In Norman times this must have been a magnificent church, and one would like to know the reasons for this display in this particular place. The crossing tower is one of the proudest pieces of Norman architecture in Essex. The nave had aisles, and there were no doubt a chancel and transepts. As it is, the chancel and transepts have only C14 features and the nave, which was of about the same length as the chancel, was pulled down in 1829 and replaced with a short annex by *James Beadel* (of Witham). This has porches either side of a vestry. In the S porch one circular pier of the Norman nave is still recognizable, with a low capital with angle volutes. The tower is of four stages, the three lower stages, with Roman brick quoins, different from the topmost and most likely pre-Conquest. The lowest stage must have communicated with the roofs. The second has on each side small coupled groups of three arches, the third two large windows, and the fourth the bell-openings with a colonnette and side windows. There is a circular stair-turret higher than the tower. The battlements are later.

Inside, the plain E and W arches are preserved. The C14 chancel is also a fine piece of work, with a very large five-light E window with flowing tracery, and two designs of Dec motifs in the tracery of the two-light N and S windows. The N transept N and S transept S windows are of the same date. So are the (much restored) SEDILIA: three arches on shafts with knobbly foliage in the spandrels. *James Brooks* restored the church 1896–7, principally strengthening the tower; chancel reopened 1902 with new furnishings (including REREDOS) and STAINED GLASS E window. – FONT. Octagonal, Perp, with shields in circles or quatrefoils. – PULPIT. Plain, C17, with decorated lozenge-shaped centres of the panels. – BENCH ENDS. Four, C15, with traceried panels and poppyheads and the figure of a bagpiper, used in the Reader's Desk. Three more, one with panelling on one side, used in a seat by the S transept. – CHEST. Painted iron, on wheels, unique in Essex. Thought to be Flemish, Dutch, or possibly German, and probably C17, but its origin and purpose uncertain. – ROYAL ARMS. In S porch, Charles II, painted on canvas. On Beadel's W gallery, George IV, cast iron, by *Coleman & Wallis* of Colchester. – MONU-MENTS. Several C19 marble tablets, the best by *J. S. Farley* to Rev. J.B. Storry †1854: scroll with overhanging foliage and a single fallen bloom. – LYCHGATE (First World War memorial) by *E. Beckwith.*

The church, in the middle of a large churchyard, dominates the village centre. Opposite the E end, THE BARN, converted by *Geoffrey Smith*, 1951, for himself; exposed timbers inside and out, many brought from elsewhere but all structural and in the best Arts and Crafts tradition. In the garden, some fragments from the demolished nave. The barn belonged to the moated RECTORY, behind. By *C.F. Hayward*, 1854–6, incorporating an older building: brick with black diapers and stone dressings, gables with decorated bargeboards. Surprisingly pretty and comparatively modest for its date. The rectory was a sinecure, so there was a vicar as well; the OLD VICARAGE lies N in Chappel Road, gault brick, early C19, three bays with Tuscan porch, and a crinkle-crankle garden wall. A little further N, on the corner of Moor Road, the modest brick OLD SCHOOL and SCHOOL HOUSE by *G. Sergeant*, 1871–2.

Of the nice houses along THE STREET, on the N side of churchyard, COB COTTAGE, C15, has a jettied cross-wing. E of GREAT YARD COTTAGE, C15 or C16, a row of four half-tim-bered cottages built for his workers by Reuben Hunt of Earls Colne, 1903.

WALCOTT'S HALL, Coggeshall Road, ¾ m. SW. Elegant gault brick front, dated 1823, of five bays separated by pilasters and central Ionic portico. C18 red brick behind.

In Buckley's Lane, ¾ m. further SW, BUCKLER'S FARM, early C19 gault brick, five bays, two storeys, with off-centre Tuscan porch; alterations by *Geary & Black, c.* 1992 onwards. Attrac-tive C18 and C19 outbuildings. Opposite, GULL'S FARM, modest C15 timber-framed house, originally an open hall. The roof shows evidence of two cross-wings of an H-plan house of some importance.

GREAT TOTHAM

ST PETER. The usual attractive mixture of rubble, puddingstone and brick, with timber belfry and splay-foot spire. Mainly C14, but the chancel's SE quoins possibly C13. C15 roofs. N aisle and S porch by *J. Clarke*, 1878–9, who also rebuilt the tower. Vestry and organ chamber by *E. Geldart*, 1882, also the transeptal pew (for Sir Claude Champion de Crespigny of Champion Lodge) on the chancel's S side. Chancel decoration by *William D. Key* and *Campbell Smith & Co.*, 1973. N extension by *Carden & Godfrey*, 1990. – WALL PAINTING. Indistinct remains in the NE corner of the nave, probably C15. – STAINED GLASS. E window by *Geldart*, 1882, made by *Cox, Sons, Buckley & Co.*; main nave S window by *Powell & Sons*, c. 1913; N aisle by *Jones & Willis*, c. 1900; N extension, 1995, by *Rowland & Surinder Warboys*. – MONUMENTS. Brass to Elizabeth Coke †1606 and daughter. 29-in. (74-cm.) and 24-in. (61-cm.) figures (under choir stalls). – In churchyard, Eliza Mackmurdo †1941, wooden (replica of original), by her husband *A.H. Mackmurdo*.

THE BARN FREE EVANGELICAL CHURCH, Prince of Wales Road. A notably early example of a barn conversion, 1822.

UNITED REFORMED CHURCH (Congregational), Chapel Road. By *C. Pertwee*, 1871, alongside an Evangelical Arminian Chapel of 1830 (now vestry and schoolroom) that was refaced in red and yellow brick to match the new building.

HONYWOOD SCHOOL, Hall Road. 1857, built by W.P. Honywood of Marks Hall (q.v.), then the lay rector. Modestly Gothic.

WILLIE ALMSHOUSES, School Road. 1855. Brick group of six, arranged in an L with their back to the road and former schoolroom at the corner. Refurbished, with discreet extensions, by *Tim Venn*, 1992–4.

The village is scattered with the church, HALL (C17 and c. 1825) and former VICARAGE (rebuilt 1757 but considerably altered 1877 onwards, including a two-storey jettied porch) at its geographical centre. Some larger houses on BEACON HILL 1¼ m. N, taking advantage of views over the Blackwater estuary:

MOUNTAINS, originally C15 or C16, extended in the C18 and in 1897 by *E. Geldart*. Remodelled c. 1921 by *S. Gambier Parry* for the Hon. Lady Du Cane, formerly of Braxted Park, incorporating items (e.g. panelling) said to come from there. She created a famous Japanese garden in a valley S of the house. Sympathetic but contemporary additions by *Plater Claiborne*, 2000. Parry also remodelled the more cottage-like BEACON HILL HOUSE nearby for Ella Du Cane, 1906.

90 Most remarkable is GREAT RUFFINS, by *A.H. Mackmurdo* for himself; construction started in 1904. It is surprisingly Italianate, considering that architect's earlier style, and would look at home by Lake Garda. Big middle tower with octagonal lantern (steel-framed, covered with zinc) and symmetrical side lanterns on the façade l. and r. Mackmurdo intended the house to be seen from the extensive gardens laid out to the S c. 1903, before building began; the 80-ft (25-metre) façade here is

dominated by the central drawing room ('studio' on original plan), 32 ft (10 metres) long, with five tall windows to the terrace. Flanking bays which jut forward like the prow of a ship. Upstairs, beneath the lanterns, a billiard room and music or book room, each 22 ft (7 metres) square and panelled to the ceiling in mahogany. It is fun, but for all its symmetry has the air of a building assembled from blocks that do not quite fit together, and the comparison of it to a South American railway station is not altogether unfair. Mackmurdo never lived in the house. The outbreak of war in 1914 halted progress, and in 1920 Mackmurdo, in financial difficulties, sold the house and retreated to a cottage (MACKMURDO'S) he had built on the corner of Goat Lodge Road. Great Ruffins was to have been the centrepiece of a considerable establishment, all to Mackmurdo's designs. Opposite Great Ruffins is BEACONS, 1902–3, with a lantern and good gardener's lodge (now BEACON COTTAGE, extended 2004). See also Wickham Bishops.

Mackmurdo interested himself in social problems in rural areas and was founding secretary of the Rural Community Council for Essex in 1929, one of whose objects was the provision of village halls. His is the VILLAGE HALL, Maldon Road, 1929–30. Just above the purely functional, although sketch designs* dated 1906–9 show plans for a grander elaborate Baroque front. See also Bradwell-on-Sea and Southminster.

TOTHAM LODGE (nursing home), Broad Street Green Road, ½ m. SW of St Peter. By H.C. Boyes, c. 1877. Originally Woodlands, renamed Champion Lodge by Sir Claude Champion de Crespigny. In no way lovely. Brick with tile-hung upper storeys and some decorative details approximating to the Queen Anne style.

At LOFTS FARM, 1¼ m. SSE, was a double-ditched Bronze Age *p. 9*
enclosure (c. 800–700 B.C.), about 150 ft (46 metres) square. Excavations have revealed that it contained an oval building of about 30 ft (9 metres) in diameter, and in one corner a rectangular longhouse.

GREAT WAKERING 9080

ST NICHOLAS. At the E end of the village, looking down the long High Street that just avoids being absolutely straight. The church's most singular feature is the two-storey C15 W porch added to the Norman W tower, all in ragstone rubble. This is an Early Saxon motif, and one wonders why it was introduced here. Older foundations, or simply some obstacle in the way of a two-storey S porch? The nave is Early Norman, shown by one blocked N window and the more interesting blocked W window. This proves that the W tower, though in its lower stage with the flat broad pilaster buttresses also clearly Norman, must be later than the nave. Its arch into the nave has the

---

*At the William Morris Gallery, Walthamstow.

simplest imposts and one step, unfortunately obscured by the organ. The tower's upper parts are later Norman, and the neat boarded broach spire C15 or later. Early C15 W door now covered by the porch. In the chancel S wall two C13 lancets, in the nave N wall one two-light window with Y-tracery, cusped, of a type characteristic of *c.* 1300. Nave roof with tie-beams, octagonal crown-posts with moulded capitals and four-way struts – copied in the N chapel, added 1843 by *T.B. Crowest* of Billericay. General restoration and re-seating by *W. J. Wood*, *c.* 1883–91, and further repairs by *A.B. Jackson*, 1905. – FONT. From East Horndon. Square, of *c.* 1200, with flat sunk decoration of interlaced arcading on two sides, and foliated crosses on the others. – WALL PAINTINGS. On the splay of a nave N window, remains of a sophisticated late C14 Annunciation. Also an C18 panel of text. – CREED AND COMMANDMENT BOARDS. C18, nicely painted, with pretty cherubs' heads (w wall). – STAINED GLASS. E window by *G.E.R. Smith* (*A.K. Nicholson Stained Glass Studios*), 1958. Chancel S by *F.C. Eden* with *George Daniels*, 1936. – MONUMENTS. John Roberts †1820. Signed by *Peter Rouw the Younger*, 'Modeller to His Majesty'. – Elizabeth Peart †1832 by *T. Gaffin*. Inscription in oval wreath.

METHODIST CHURCH. 1906 by *C. Cooke*. Fancy front of red brick with plenty of stone dressings, E.E. windows and little turrets. Strictly utilitarian stock brick behind.

UNITED REFORMED CHURCH (Congregational). By *C. Pertwee*, 1889. Stock brick with red dressings and round-headed windows.

GREAT WALTHAM

One of the largest parishes in the county comprising, in addition to the village itself, the hamlets of Ford End (q.v.), Howe Street, Littley Green and North End (q.v.).

ST MARY AND ST LAWRENCE. Quite a large church with a substantial W tower, originally Norman, but strengthened with brick buttresses. Upper half rebuilt with battlements and a new stair-turret by *A. Y. Nutt*, 1892. Plain Norman tower arch. The nave and chancel are also Norman: see the quoins of Roman brick in the nave, and traces of Norman work, also with Roman bricks, at the E end; otherwise mainly of flint and pebble-rubble. The nave is remarkably wide for a Norman village church. S aisle added in the C14, but rebuilt *c.* 1525, when the clerestory and S porch were added; chancel clerestory mid C17. Perp S arcade with three bays and piers having demi-shafts towards the arches and a polygonal shaft without capital towards the nave. Restoration by *Chancellor*, 1862–3, including rebuilding of S porch and parapet of S aisle, new N vestry, removal of W gallery of 1834, re-seating of nave, and new hammerbeam chancel roof. In 1874–5 he added the N aisle and an upper floor to the N vestry as organ chamber, extended 1890.

N aisle door by *Nutt*; further work in the 1890s, probably also by him: TOWER SCREEN, 1893; new chancel arch with a niche above it containing a FIGURE of the Virgin and Child, CHOIR STALLS and PULPIT, 1894; and S porch partially rebuilt with figures added in niches, 1899. Carved panels from the old pulpit, *c.* 1600, reused for cupboard in vestry. – REREDOS. Stone, with a relief depicting the Ascension and figures of saints, 1884, when *Chancellor*'s reredos of 1862–3 was moved to the S aisle. – FONT. In S porch, plain square bowl, C12, discovered during reflooring in 1961–2. – BENCHES. Ten with traceried, straight-headed ends, mid C15, and others incorporating old work, repaired by *Chancellor*. – STAINED GLASS. S aisle W, seven shields, late C14. – Seven windows by *O'Connor*, 1850–66, most to members of the Tufnell family: E, three chancel S, S aisle E and two S aisle S. – N aisle N by *Ion Pace*, *c.* 1894; also the tower window, and probably the four pretty clerestory windows on the nave's S side. – BRASSES. 18-in. (45.5-cm.) figure of a civilian, *c.* 1580. – Thomas Wyseman, wife and three children, 1580 (main figures 18½ in. (47 cm.)). – Richard Everard of Langleys †1617 and his wife Clemence †1611. 27-in. (68-cm.) figures. – MONUMENTS. Standing wall monument for Sir Anthony Everard, son of Richard and Clemence, †1614 and his first wife Anne †1609, erected by Sir Anthony in 1611. Stiffly reclining alabaster figures on two shelves – Sir Anthony above and slightly behind his wife – between pilasters carrying stone inscription tablets. Large coffered arch above two small arched windows in the back wall, the glass of which is largely original. Small figures of children on small tomb-chests on the ground in front. Originally against the N wall of the nave; painting and gilding restored by *Campbell Smith & Co.* during refurbishment of the N aisle by *Dykes Bower*, 1957–9. – Hugh Everard †1703, marble tablet with a bas-relief of the sinking ship in which he met his end. – Peter Curgenven †1729, another white marble tablet with an even longer inscription describing his death following an operation. – Richard Sobell †1738 and others, erected in accordance with the will of Richard Tyson M.D. †1784, coloured marbles with white marble draped urn.

LYCHGATE. By *E. Beckwith*, 1920, as a war memorial, with accompanying oak board in the church. – In churchyard, N of church, Hugh Western †1934, a simple stone slab with inscription by *Eric Gill*, 1935.

LANGLEYS

Samuel Tufnell bought Langleys in 1710 from Sir Richard Everard, whose family acquired the estate in two stages in 1515 and 1529. Samuel, a City man of great business acumen as well as taste and sensibility, sat in Parliament for both Maldon and Colchester, and lived for some years in Antwerp as one of the plenipotentiaries attached to the Congress of Antwerp. In 1718 *Thomas Michener* and *John Legg* were paid £47 and £27

respectively for two brick architraves, and in 1720 the execu-
tors of *Captain Edward Tufnell* (†1719), resident mason and
architect to Westminster Abbey, were paid £117 13s., the
balance of a larger sum, for work here; but other documents
suggest that Samuel was to some extent his own architect.

The house is of brick, large and essentially straightforward,
H-plan and incorporating in the N wing much of a preceding
house of *c.* 1620; parts of the windows are false to accommodate floor levels that do not correspond to the façade. The W
(entrance) front is thirteen bays wide, of which the two outer
bays on each side belong to the wings projecting by three bays.
On the E (garden) side the rhythm is the same but the projection of the wings is slight, only one bay of blind windows. Two-
and-a-half storeys, with hipped roofs hidden behind a parapet
with sunk panels. Rainwater heads dated 1719. The three
centre bays of the entrance front were brought forward by John
Jolliffe Tufnell II to form an entrance hall; the idea probably
came from *C.R. Cockerell*, who visited in 1827. When this was
done the trim of the doorway, windows above, and top pediment were preserved and re-set. The doorway has a broad segmental pediment resting, very oddly, on Corinthian pilasters
as well as two thin brackets. The first-floor window is connected to the pediment and has in addition the big ears typical
of *c.* 1720, i.e. volutes coming down by its side and hung with
thick garlands. The central window in the second floor is again
connected with the window below and has a raised surround,
also typical of *c.* 1720. On the garden side all this is repeated
almost identically, but with a less rich doorway and without
the Tufnell arms in the top pediment. At the house's S end considerable additions were made in the C19, including servants'
hall and conservatory by *Chancellor*, 1864–5, but much of this
was removed and the remainder simplified after the Second
World War.

The most remarkable INTERIOR ensembles are without
doubt the two rooms of *c.* 1620 at the E end of the N wing, the
OLD DINING ROOM on the ground floor and the LIBRARY
above. They display plasterwork which Pevsner rightly considered 'of an exuberance not exceeded anywhere in the country'.
The Library ceiling is of barrel type, the Dining Room's flat.
Both have patterns made by broad bands. The bands are
adorned with fine trails of foliage, the spaces between them
with strapwork cartouches and coats of arms, etc. As the rooms
are not high, the effect is almost oppressively rich. The fireplaces in both rooms are yet more ornate. The Library's has in
the overmantel the Five Senses, full-bosomed allegorical
figures, seated around a panel that depicts Tobias and the Fish;
in the Dining Room Peace and Plenty face each other. The
mantelshelves rest on elaborate termini caryatids. In addition
the lunettes of the end walls of the Library have a seated figure
each: Doctrina, and an angel with the Tufnell coat of arms. This
last is one instance of the way in which Samuel adapted the
existing room to suit his new house, and it is an interesting

reflection on his taste that he went to such pains to preserve what he found. Not only did he not destroy it, but he seems to have restored and altered it in a style intended to be Neo-Jacobean. The C18 work is noticeable in the pieces put in to reduce the size of the fireplace openings, also the decoration of the ceiling does not line up with windows and the decoration of the walls, as it would if it had all been designed as a piece.

Samuel's own period appears at its grandest in the SALOON, the principal apartment on the garden side. Until the alterations of *c.* 1827 it was entered directly from the front entrance. It is two-storeyed, and decorated by heavy fluted Corinthian giant pilasters and a towering chimneypiece. *Isaac Mansfield* was paid £85 for the plastering in 1718. The grandeur is diminished by an irregularity in the laying out, for which there is no obvious explanation: at the N end there is an extra quarter bay with a bit of pilaster that disappears into the wall. N of the Saloon, the White and Yellow Drawing Rooms, as well as the best bedroom on the first floor, were decorated by William Tufnell, 1797–8; the windows in the centre of the garden front were lowered, and given thinner glazing bars, at about the same time.

S of the house is a detached LAUNDRY, a functional building designed to be seen. Three middle bays projecting slightly with a pediment. Brick with rusticated quoins. Weathervane dated 1720. NE of the house are STABLES, C17 with a Dutch gable, altered 1865 by *Chancellor* who *c.* 1870 built the NORTH LODGE as a coachman's cottage: picturesque brick, half-timbering and tile-hanging. SOUTH LODGE, Chelmsford Road, is to an amusing degree a miniature version of the house itself, and like it was built by Samuel Tufnell. One storey with parapet and only a door and two windows, but the door has Ionic pilasters, the windows have ears, and the top-heavy pediment across all three bays repeats the coat of arms and motto found on the house. Two-storey C19 rear extension, invisible from the front. WEST and EAST LODGES *c.* 1965 and *c.* 1985 by *Eric Logan* and *Graham Jones* respectively, sympathetic but simpler.

The GARDENS were laid out by *Charles Bridgeman*, for which he received £50 3s. 7d. and £106 3s. 7d. in 1719. William Tufnell consulted *Repton* who may have made alterations to the park *c.* 1803–7. Terrace and parterre laid out by *James Howe*, 1864.

PERAMBULATION

Langley's grounds are the background to the village, whose main street bends attractively round the churchyard's s side. The first thing one sees is not characteristic: HATCHFIELDS, a housing estate that includes some striking houses by *Clifford Culpin & Partners*, *c.* 1964. The most conspicuous are monopitch, brick, some painted white, and in a staggered formation emphasizing their profile. Once past them, everything is much more what one would expect, e.g. BADYNGHAMS, E of the church (formerly, and spuriously, known as The Guildhall), with exposed timbers and close studding and four fine twin-shafted chimneystacks, *c.* 1600. Originally H-plan; only the E wings survive. Two-storey porch in the courtyard. Across the road the CHURCH HOUSEN, a terrace of four almshouses and two schoolteachers' houses by *A.Y. Nutt*, 1896–7: brick with tile-hanging, and not as quaint as the name suggests. On the churchyard's S side THE OLD COTTAGE, a single-storey medieval hall, C15 or earlier, with a single two-storey cross-wing, jettied towards the church which it originally faced. The similar CHURCH GATE LODGE, W, likewise built to face the church, has a street façade of C19 brick with burnt headers. W of the church, across the road, the VICARAGE, C18 brick with additions of 1873 (now GLEBE HOUSE) by *Chancellor.*

Off the main street: In BARRACK LANE, W, WISEMANS, with some exposed timbers. W cross-wing late C14 (roof with octagonal crown-post), hall and jettied E cross-wing *c.* 1500. In SOUTH STREET, THE OLD SCHOOL HOUSE, 1891, stock brick with steep slate roof and three gabled dormers. The central dormer, flush with the front wall, incorporates panels with Latin inscription from Ecclesiastes: 'In the morning sow thy seed, and in the evening withhold not thine hand'. Built for the headmaster, John Sydes, and his family of thirteen children. Opposite, the PRIMARY SCHOOL, 1847, by *Charles Dyer:* 'Elizabethan', stock brick, enlarged by *Chancellor*, 1874. Low pyramidal W block by the *County Architect's Dept* (project architect, *Ian Fraser*), 1980–1.

At HOWE STREET, ¾ m. NNE, WALTHAM HOUSE. Brick, early C18, with steep gabled roof and three dormers behind the parapet. Lower projecting wings, that on the r. built round a mid-C16 timber-framed house. Behind the main block, on the S side, a late C18 range, with lower hipped roof, reusing the original front (N) door. Orangery added 2001–2.

Across the Chelmer (BRIDGE by *Whitmore*, 1871; attractive cast-iron balustrade by *Coleman & Morton* of Chelmsford), in LUCK'S LANE, a pair of almshouses built by L.G. Howe of Waltham House, 1935: single-storey, with almost Rococo pargetting, tall hipped roof and even taller brick chimneystacks. In the main street, TUDOR HOUSE, C15 hall house with two gabled cross-wings and jettied upper storeys, the framing exposed. Doorway inside dated 1623 and an original C15 roof truss with arched braces and crown-post. On the village's NW edge the GREEN MAN INN, timber-framed and plastered, the main part brick-faced with sashes. Inside is revealed its origin as a C14 hall house: roof with crown-post and four-way struts.

FITZJOHN'S FARM, 1¼ m. WNW. Fine four-gabled W front with C16 carved bargeboards. Large two-bay raised-aisle hall, C14, the S cross-wing of the same date, the N cross-wing C16. Hall floored later in the C16. Much of the original smoke-blackened roof structure survives. E of the house a five-bay BARN, also C14, converted to a house *c.* 1979–80.

HILL HOUSE, 1¼m. NNE. C16 with exposed timbers and jettied cross-wings. Rear staircase tower and several original window openings.

HYDE HALL, 1½m. NE. Timber-framed and plastered house of *c.* 1600, with projecting four-gabled front and gabled two-storey porch. Very prettily situated with part of the moat remaining on the SW side and brick garden wall.

LITTLEY PARK, 2½m. N. Littley Park was a medieval deerpark of about 420 acres, expanded N by Sir Richard Rich to include land that had belonged to Leez Priory (q.v.). LITTLEYPARK FARMHOUSE, roughly in the centre, probably incorporates the hunting lodge, a two-storey timber-framed structure of six bays; this part of the building has a crown-post roof, probably *c.* 1470. At right angles to this a one-and-a-half-storey three-bay extension, *c.* 1585. In the C17 the main block was extended four bays to the N using old timbers, perhaps when the building became a farmhouse.

GREAT WARLEY

Brentwood*

CHRIST CHURCH, Warley Hill. 1853–5 by *Teulon*, a chapel of ease for the populous northern part of the parish. E.E., of red brick interlaced with black (although mostly faded), and stone dressings. W tower with battlements, corner pinnacles and machicolations. W gallery, taken down in 1956. S aisle by *John Young*, 1877, who in 1891 replaced Teulon's apse with a chancel, chancel aisle and vestry. Another vestry formed at the W end of the S aisle, 1960, and the chancel successfully reordered by *Tim Venn*, 1990: screen moved one bay to the E with an altar to the W. – STAINED GLASS. E window by *Jones & Willis*, 1905. S aisle E by *Young & Marten*, builders' merchants of Stratford, 1899. CHURCH HALL by *Len Radley*, 1985. – Former VICARAGE to the S, 1853 by *Teulon*, an irregular, gabled, picturesque composition of red and black brick; to the N was a small SCHOOL, 1854–5 (dem. 1975).

ST MARY THE VIRGIN.[†] 1902–4 by *Charles Harrison Townsend* for Evelyn Heseltine as a memorial to his brother Arnold †1897. Modestly pretty exterior, embedded in trees, roughcast and buttressed à la Voysey. The basic form, with apsidal E end, S chapel and timber W belfry, derived, at Heseltine's request, from Woodyer's St Peter's, Hascombe, Surrey. The initial approach, however, was to the sculptor *William Reynolds-Stephens*, who had overall artistic responsibility, and Townsend did little more than provide a shell; even the layout of the

---

*The southern tip of the parish, including the site of the old church, is now in the London Borough of Havering.

[†]The old parish church, which stood 1 m. SSE, was restored by *Teulon* 1858–60 but by 1892 was largely disused. Pevsner described the W tower with 'its gracelessly fanciful W window', but that was demolished *c.* 1966.

grounds is said to have been by Reynolds-Stephens. Only the Art Nouveau rainwater heads, and the w window's heart-shaped tracery, provide a hint of what lies within. It was predicted at the time that the church would become famous for its interior, and so it has proved. It is a supreme exemplar of Arts and Crafts workmanship, overlaid with motifs from that most un-English of styles, Art Nouveau. Its detailing is highly symbolic; in the words of the *Explanatory Memorandum* published at the time, 'the primary object . . . has been to lead the thoughts of the worshipper onward through [the] decorations to the glorified and risen Christ, whose form in the centre of the reredos is the keystone of the whole'. The interior's colour is derived mainly from the carefully graduated ceiling decoration: aluminium in the sanctuary, with a decoration of vines and red grapes; walnut with aluminium ribs in the choir; walnut with green ribs and oxidized floral ornament in the tunnel-vaulted nave. The bases of the nave ribs have panels with lilies. In the s chapel the ceiling was originally walnut and green only; painted panels by *Reginald Hallward* were added later. Walnut panelling in the nave, marble in the sanctuary and at the w end.

FITTINGS. All designed and largely executed by *Reynolds-Stephens*, unless otherwise stated. – REREDOS. Figure of Christ in oxidized silver on copper against mother-of-pearl background, gilt metal panels at sides with brass groups of trees and coloured marbles. – REREDOS in s chapel, 'The Gateway to Life', added as a First World War memorial: marble bas-relief of Christ in the Tomb with angels. – FONT. Marble, with two standing angels and cover of copper-bronze with blue mother-of-pearl inlays. – PULPIT. In the form of three broad copper crosses, backed by marble, supported by bronze trees, inlaid with mother-of-pearl. – LECTERN. Wrought oxidized copper on black marble base with brass book-rest. – CHANCEL SCREEN. In the form of flowering fruit trees, each tree bearing an angel; brass with mother-of-pearl flowers and cast ruby-glass fruits and oxidized silver figures on green and black marble base. – SCREEN to s chapel. Walnut and pewter, with stylized poppies that are the most conspicuously Art Nouveau forms of the interior. – ALTAR RAIL. Brass Crown of Thorns and oxidized copper rail with base and panels of green and grey marble. – ORGAN CASE. Hammered steel with bas-relief copper panels of scenes from the Benedicite. – BISHOP'S CHAIR and settle-like SEDILIA in walnut and pewter. – Galvanized-iron ELECTROLIERS with enamel panels. – STALLS AND PEWS: designed less excessively by *Townsend*. – PAINTING over N door to vestry: 'Pilgrim dreams that the angels of God come to him with heavenly food', originally installed on the s side of the choir to cover the three lancets after the removal of Hallward's glass; attributed to *Louis Davis*. – STAINED GLASS. Only some of the original stained glass remains. Apse and sanctuary windows by *Reynolds-Stephens*. Three lancets in choir by *Lawrence Lee* with *Janet Christo-*

pherson, 1971; original glass by *Hallward* now in Brentwood School chapel (q.v.). In the nave, six two-light windows and W rose window originally by *Heywood Sumner*, of which only the W window (restored following bomb damage) survives. The rest destroyed in 1940, as well as the seven small baptistery windows by *Louis Davis*. Their replacements, on the N side, from the E: two two-light windows, probably by *A.K. Nicholson*; single-light by *Luxford Stained Glass Studios* (*C.C. Powell*), 1953, and single-light by *Powell & Sons*, 1946; two-light window by *Wippell Mowbray*, 1975. On the S side, two-light window by *Powell & Sons*, 1956, and another by *Susan McCarthy* (*Auravisions*), 2002, from designs by *Sumner*. Baptistery windows by *J.H. Hogan* (*Powell & Sons*), 1946. S chapel window by *Morris & Co*, 1931, using *Burne-Jones* designs, as a memorial to Evelyn Heseltine †1930, replacing original by *Reynolds-Stephens*. – MONUMENT. In vestry, effigy of Gyles Fleming †1623, from the old church; painted alabaster bust. – LYCHGATE. By *Townsend*, 1903, with carved fruit and texts by *Eric Gill*. – SUNDIAL in churchyard, W of the church, by *Nancy Coulson*, 1991, with lettering by *Lesley Williams*.

HOLY CROSS AND ALL SAINTS (R.C.), Warley Hill. 1881 by *F. W. Tasker*, cousin of the donor, Countess Tasker of Middleton Hall, Brentwood. Faced with Kentish rag, with Ancaster dressings. Porch added 1884, N aisle 1886. – REREDOS, ALTAR, and external Calvary group. Stone, carved by *Earp*. – STAINED GLASS. E windows by *J.N. Lawson* (*Goddard & Gibbs*), 1986.

CEMETERY, Lorne Road. CHAPEL and GATES by *T.E. Knightley*, *c*. 1860.

WARLEY HOSPITAL. *See* Brentwood.

The village centre is Warley Green, with a cluster of nice houses, the most prominent WALLETS, gabled and with exposed timbers. N cross-wing and probably also the hall early C16, S cross-wing *c*. 1600. TWO DOOR COTTAGE opposite (No. 2 Great Warley Street), has a N cross-wing dated to the C13, with a later medieval hall to its r.

A surprising number of large houses along the main road that runs N–S through the village. N of the Green, WARLEY LEA, said to have been altered by *Lutyens*, *c*. 1894, and WARLEY PLACE, purchased by Frederick Willmott in 1875, famous as the home of his daughter Ellen, who created celebrated gardens there up to 1914. The house, probably rebuilt by *James Gandon c*. 1777, was doubled in size by F. Willmott, but demolished in 1939 and very little can now be seen apart from two LODGES, the S one a picturesque affair, originally thatched. The gardens now a nature reserve, including a walled garden, the foundations of glasshouses, a boating lake, and the remains of an artificial cave with glass roof for growing filmy ferns.

DE ROUGEMONT MANOR (hotel), formerly Goldings, the home of Evelyn Heseltine, much altered and extended. Heseltine bought it in 1881, employing *Ralph Nevill* to make alterations and additions, *c*. 1884–1905. Nevill's estate buildings

include a double cottage and row of four (dated 1883) on the
E side of the road and a lodge and cottage (1887) on the W:
the cottages brick with half-timbered upper storeys and ornamental plastering, the ground floor of the lodge concrete, with
pebbledash. More estate cottages in BIRD LANE, as well as the
old SCHOOL, 1843, enlarged 1870, with teacher's house of
1862; flint with red dressings. SE of Goldings, FAIRSTEAD
HALL, a large house with lodge and stables on the road. Neo-
Jacobean brick by *J. L. Pearson*, 1889, for the rector, H. Roberson Bailey.* New rectory opposite St Mary's by *Guy Dawber*,
1904, also brick (now GREAT WARLEY PLACE). Although on
a much more modest scale it was nonetheless provided with a
lodge cottage, also by Dawber, 1903.

PUMPING STATION, 600 yds SE. For the South Essex Waterworks
Co., to supply Brentwood. Main pump house, 1882, stock
brick with red dressings, with tall round-headed windows. Two
other brick buildings, one dated 1886.

GREAT WIGBOROUGH
Great and Little Wigborough

ST STEPHEN. Standing on a hilltop. Of mixed rubble and septaria. Badly damaged in the 1884 earthquake; W tower (with
battlements and corner pinnacles) rebuilt by *J. Clarke*, 1885–6,
the chancel in 1889–93 by *F. W. S. Bowles*, who also restored
the C14 nave. The latter work included the nave's hammerbeam
roof, and the chancel arch. S doorway mid C15, S porch rebuilt
1903. S vestry by *E. Geldart*, 1895. – Also by Geldart the
CHANCEL SCREEN and FONT COVER, 1894. – FONT. Octagonal, Perp, bowl with panels filled by shields in quatrefoils,
roses, a heart, and feathers. – STAINED GLASS. E window by
Hardman, c. 1892. Nave N (Faith, Hope, and Charity) by *F. C.
Eden* with *George Daniels*, 1929.

THE HYDE. Early to mid-C15 hall house, the hall partly open to
the roof, with a cross-quadrate crown-post. Gabled cross-
wings at each end, the W one mid C16. Some exposed timbers,
otherwise plastered or clad in C20 brick. Much restored
c. 1920, and extended W, incorporating fragments from elsewhere, e.g. gargoyles on the W chimneystack from Little Wigborough church. Late C17 wrought-iron gates with brick piers.

MOULSHAMS MANOR. C14 hall house, with exposed timbers.
Part of the screen survives, and a doorway with ogee head. C17
plastered W wing at right angles. Restored by *Bailey & Walker*,
1954, who introduced the early C18 staircase with turned balusters. Alterations and additions by *R. Geary*, including gable and
bay with Gothick windows on N front. Two-storey bay on W
front 2004.

*Wooden mission church in the grounds, 1892, re-erected as St James, Baildon,
(Yorkshire West Riding).

GREAT YELDHAM

St Andrew. A busy composition from the SE, with a cluster of vestry, chapel and porch all projecting on the S side of the mid-C14 Perp nave and chancel, with the tower behind. The mighty porch began later in the C14 as a tower, which for reasons not convincingly explained was added to the nave's S side, near the W end. It has angle buttresses and a big S doorway enriched by an ogee canopy and two niches l. and r., but was not continued and was later given a stepped brick gable as a piece of decoration. Instead, late in the C15, a more normal W tower was erected, also with angle buttresses. It has bell-openings of three lights with one transom, stepped battlements with pinnacles and, between them, in the middle of each side, a smallish figure of an angel. *Chancellor* was responsible for the general restoration of 1884, which included renewing the mid-C14 N aisle's arcade and windows, new nave and chancel roofs, and re-seating. – PULPIT. Elizabethan, with two tiers of blank arches with plaited decoration on each panel. – SCREEN. One-light divisions with ogee tops and a little tracery above them. On the r. side the dado is painted with saints, in the East Anglian manner. The quality of the paintings is low and one of the four figures has been completely effaced; the others represent SS Ursula, Eloi and Edmund. – REREDOS and PANELLING. By *Seely & Paget*, 1952–3, made by *H. & K. Mabbitt*. – BRASS. Plate with arched top to Richard Symonds †1627 and wife. 8-in. (20-cm.) kneeling figures, with children. – MONUMENTS. Gregory Lewis Way of Spencer Farm †1799 by *J. Bacon Sen.*, closed urn and inscription on a stele. – Similar Way family monuments by *S. Manning Sen.*, *c.* 1833 and 1835. – STAINED GLASS. E window by *Butterfield*, made by *Hardman*, 1854–61. Chancel NW (St Andrew) by *Gamon & Humphry* to Catharine Way †1902. Porch N, 1924, and S transept N, 1926, by *Wippell & Co.* – LYCHGATE by *E. Geldart*, 1894.

Yeldham Hall, S of the church. Broad, low timber-framed house of *c.* 1500 with C17 wing, attractively sited below the church amidst farm buildings and large ponds. Detached DOVECOTE, weatherboarded and plastered, its prominent tiled roof with open gablets.

Old Rectory, NW of the church. C15 with cross-wings at each end and C19 additions. In the SW wing an exceptionally fine first-floor timber ceiling with arched braces and moulded beams, the spandrels carved with foliage and shields bearing various badges. Early C17 wall painting in a ground-floor room depicts three rows of niches each containing plants, beneath a frieze of fruit and foliage; once part of a larger scheme.

Applegates, Church Road. L-plan timber-framed house with a late C16 or C17 five-bay range, probably the building (later a school) said by Morant to have been 'anciently used and appropriated for dressing a Dinner for poor folk when married'; the three-bay N extension may have been built as a marriage feast room (cf. Matching). Extension on S side 2001–2.

THE CHANGE, Church Road. Timber-framed, mainly C16, with gables. Along the road, a crinkle-crankle wall 150 yds long (in two sections) by *John Whitehead & Associates*, *c.* 1968–72.

WHITE HART INN, Poole Street. Timber-framed, *c.* 1500, half-H plan with wings extending to the W, made rectangular by alterations and additions in the C17 and later.

SPAYNES HALL, ½ m. SE. C16 timber-framed and plastered, with many gables, but much of the detailing – bargeboards, brackets, porch, etc. – of the late C19 or early C20.

SPENCERS, ½ m. N. Built by Viscountess Bateman (née Lady Anne Spencer †1769). Stucco refronting *c.* 1810, with a Greek Doric porch *in antis* and a bay on the garden front that had little Regency balconies and shutters. Large walled garden, including an C18 timber GLASSHOUSE, with small overlapping panes. The park contains oaks which are considerably older than the house, and BROOK FARM, on the park's eastern edge, dates back to *c.* 1400.

Along STAMBOURNE ROAD, TILBURY ROAD and RIDGEWELL ROAD, and also at Little Yeldham and Tilbury-juxta-Clare, several small brick cottages with distinctive half-hipped slate roofs built by the Land Settlement Association, founded in 1934 to provide smallholdings for unemployed industrial workers. Most of the houses on the Great Yeldham Estate (three basic types) by *Pakington & Enthoven*.

GREENSTEAD

ST ANDREW. Thin W tower of *c.* 1600, with two- and three-light arched windows without any arches to the lights or any tracery; brick with diaper and other patterns. C18 W window. Nave and chancel Norman, structurally undivided, of mixed rubble, rendered. Chancel and nave E end refaced in the late C18. S aisle of Kentish rag added by *G. Sergeant*, 1856–7, with repairs and other alterations following the 1884 earthquake by *E.J. Dampier*. Chancel reordered and S aisle W end screened off with upper room by *Tim Venn*, 1995–6.

WIVENHOE NEW PARK. 1962–4 by *Raymond Erith*, for Mr and Mrs Charles Gooch, to replace their former home, Wivenhoe Park, when that became the nucleus of the University of Essex (q.v.). An interpretation of the simple Palladian farmhouse villa, seven bays wide, the middle three forming a two-tier arcaded loggia whose upper openings (now glazed) appear above the cornice in an attic storey with pediment. To each side are single-storey wings, with garaging on one side and domestic offices on the other, the total length being 174 ft (54 metres). The house, intended to be both a family home and a centre for the estate, is grand yet economical; built of a pale red brick with minimal stone dressings, and pantile roof. The arrangement of the rooms matches the exterior: on the ground floor, four main rooms opening off a central hall, with an inconspicuous but elegant staircase which has a rising barrel-

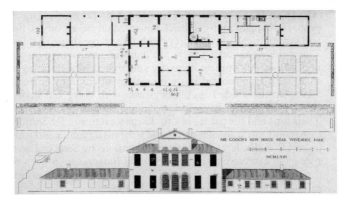

Wivenhoe New Park, Greenstead.
Linocut, 1963

vaulted ceiling. Erith's plans for a garden on the s side of the house were not executed, leaving it somewhat exposed – an effect since softened by planting.

GREENSTEAD GREEN

8020

Originally a hamlet of Halstead.

ST JAMES. 1844–5 by *G.G. Scott (Scott & Moffatt)*, following on from Holy Trinity, Halstead (q.v.). Dec; coursed flint and pebbles with stone dressings. Nave, chancel and N vestry. W tower with diagonal buttresses, octagonal bell-chamber, and spire of gault brick, the change from square to octagon marked by crocketed pinnacles supporting miniature flying buttresses. – REREDOS. By *Sir Arthur Blomfield*, 1893. Stone, with mosaic and *opus sectile* panels by *Powell & Sons*. – PULPIT. Stone, with carved figures of Christ and the Evangelists, reached by a staircase in the wall (also the original arrangement at Halstead). – CHANCEL SCREEN. By *William White*, 1888. – STAINED GLASS. E window by *Powell & Sons*, 1949.

Also by *Scott*, of the same date and the same materials, the VICARAGE, N side of the church, and SCHOOL across the road; both now private houses.

VILLAGE HALL. Former lecture room, with flanking cottages, by *James Fenton*, 1858. Gables with pierced bargeboards, and five stepped lancets to the hall.

GLADFEN HALL, ¾ m. WSW. C16 timber-framed and plastered, remodelled in the early C19 with a Tuscan doorcase and large sashes of twenty-eight panes. Rear stair-tower containing an early C19 spiral staircase, and a C17 wing sensitively extended *c.* 1995–6 by *Geary & Black* and continued by a single-storey weatherboarded, then brick-and-flint range to form a courtyard.

STANSTEAD HALL, ⅓ m. NE. The s (kitchen) range of a larger, probably U-plan, mid-C16 brick house. Main (N) elevation, flat and symmetrical, of two storeys with three large shaped gables. The windows are of 2, 3 : 3, 3 : 3, 2 lights and transomed on the upper floor. All window lights are still arched. The doorway is small with four-centred head, no display of columns or pediment. On the s side big chimneystacks with polygonal shafts. On the E a central bay window flanked by polygonal turrets. Their tops and the gable are C19. Large s extension for Samuel Courtauld, 1913; smaller one to the N for his daughter and son-in-law, R. A. Butler, 1934. Internal alterations by *Seely & Paget*, 1960, and extensive restoration by *Alan Bragg*, *c.* 1986–91. s of the moat, a C16 weatherboarded BARN, eight bays with aisles, extended by five bays probably in the C18.

5000

GREENSTED

Ongar

ST ANDREW. The church is famous all over England as the only survival – and what an unlikely survival – of a log church. Dating this remarkable building has proved problematic. Tradition has it that the body of St Edmund rested here on its way from London to Bury in 1013, but tree-ring dating gives a felling date for the logs after 1063, probably before 1100. Even so it remains the oldest wooden church, indeed the oldest standing wooden building, in the country. The nave is built of oak logs split vertically in halves and set vertically in an oak sill. The present sill and the brick plinth belong to the restoration of 1842–9 by *T.H. Wyatt*. The nave roof belongs to a further restoration in 1892 by *Chancellor*, replacing one by Wyatt. Wyatt also rebuilt the dormers, increasing their number from three to six, as well as the timber s porch and chancel E wall. The chancel itself is of brick, early C16 (one s window and the s doorway), but the lower courses are of flint rubble, presumably the remains of an earlier structure. The w tower is also entirely of timber, in the Essex tradition, and is probably C18 – it is not shown on a print of 1748. It has the usual internal construction, is externally weatherboarded and painted white, and carries a shingled splay-foot spire. Wyatt added the traceried window. – FONT. Of oak, shaped with a hand adze, 1987; by *Sir Hugh Casson*, made by *Russell Thomas*. – PULPIT. Oak, octagonal, dated 1698. – PILLAR PISCINA. Octagonal bowl and moulded rim, probably late C15. – PAINTING. Small arched panel of the Martyrdom of St Edmund, *c.* 1500. – STAINED GLASS. In w window, head of a man, *c.* 1500. Re-set, perhaps when the other windows, by *Lavers, Barraud & Westlake*, were installed, including the E window to William Smith †1871, and two of the dormers dated 1873 and 1876. – MONUMENT. Jone Wood †1585. Alabaster tablet with enriched pilasters, cresting and arms.

GREENSTED HALL (now divided). The core of the house is thought to be a medieval hall, rebuilt by Alexander Cleeve at about the same time he presented the pulpit to the church; there are dates of 1695 and 1698, renewed but probably reliable. Inside, a staircase and panelling of this period. Extensively altered by P.J. Budworth, 1875, when the E front was rebuilt, although its door dates from the 1950s. To the W a C17 brewhouse, converted to a house in 1950.

HADLEIGH

ST JAMES THE LESS. A complete little Norman church, essentially unaltered, but unfortunately located on an island in the A13. The E end is apsed. A chancel preceded the apse, a nave the chancel. The only later additions are a C16 weatherboarded W belfry, resting inside on a free-standing four-post structure, C18 weatherboarded S porch, and NW vestry by *Nicholson*, 1927,[*] banded with red tiles and with tiled battlements. Only a few windows are not original: nave N one C13 lancet, chancel S one two-light Dec window, nave N and S two-light Perp windows. Impressively simple interior. Two low blank arches flank the chancel arch, each with C15 circular foiled squints. Niche on splay of SE window with damaged tabernacle work and traces of painting. Restored by *G. E. Street*, 1855–6, including new roofs; his furnishings do not survive. W organ gallery, 1968. – FONT. Made up of various parts, the columns and base by *Street*. The best is the lower part of the bowl with stiff-leaf growing diagonally; C13. – WALL PAINTINGS. Very remarkable fragments. In the nave NE lancet demi-figure of St Thomas of Canterbury of *c.* 1200, in the window W of this an Angel with outspread wings. – STAINED GLASS. Three apse windows by *Hardman*, 1855. Chancel S and nave N by *Cox, Sons, Buckley & Co.*, 1891 and 1885 respectively, designed by *E. Geldart* in his richest style.

ST BARNABAS, Church Road. 1957–8 by *R. W. Hurst* (*Humphrys & Hurst*). Low stock brick walls with continuous glazing and high pantiled roofs. Nave and chancel E gables also glazed, with coloured glass. W wall all window apart from a slightly projecting baptistery. SW porch and tall slender brick bell-tower. – Good contemporary chancel FURNISHINGS and FONT. – STAINED GLASS. Nave N and S windows by *F. W. Skeat*, 1964.

ST THOMAS MORE (R.C.), High Street. 1982 by *Kenneth Cheeseman*. Monopitch, the end wall brick, main wall and semicircular protuberances roughcast. Clerestory and other windows with STAINED GLASS, also by Cheeseman.

SANDCASTLES NURSERY, London Road. The core is the former National School by *Street*, 1854–5, with pointed windows

---

[*] The beginnings of an unexecuted scheme to enlarge the church to the W, with the nave becoming a new chancel.

(extended 1895 and 1909). Brick, now painted. Street's rectory, 1855–6, was demolished in 1937.

HADLEIGH CASTLE is by far the most important later medieval castle in the county. It was built originally for Hubert de Burgh, Chief Justiciar to King John; licence granted 1230, probably mostly complete by 1239. It was largely neglected after its forced surrender to Henry III and virtually rebuilt *c.* 1360–70 by Edward III, who spent £2,287 on it and made it one of his favoured residences. But the castle's importance declined from the late C14 and it was largely demolished after sale to Lord Rich in 1551. The chief residential parts, to the S, have been entirely obliterated by a landslide. What survives is the W, N and E curtain wall, but not to any impressive height, the wall and one outer turret of the barbican on the N side, and four circular towers, all open towards the bailey. The highest, famous from Constable's painting of 1829, is the SE tower. Here three storeys can still be recognized with windows and chimney flues. The tower N of this has two storeys remaining. The whole castle is of irregular oblong shape, and visually a little disappointing after the high hopes raised by Constable's interpretation.

SHIPWRIGHTS, No. 241 Benfleet Road. By *Wells Coates*, 1937, as a weekend house for John Wyborne, an engineer for Ekco of Southend (q.v., Prittlewell). One of only two individual houses by Coates, the other being at Esher (Surrey); both were influenced by Le Corbusier's Villa Savoye. *Patrick Gwynne*, then working for Coates, had a close hand in both. White-painted rendered brick on a concrete-encased steel frame, with flat roof. Most of the ground floor was originally open (now infilled), with main accommodation on the upper floor supported on pilotis. Long horizontal window. Roof shelter with curved wooden roof on tubular steel supports.

HADSTOCK

5040

ST BOTOLPH. The church has a strong claim, probably stronger than Ashingdon's (q.v.), to be the minster church founded by King Canute following the Battle of Assandun in 1016. Certainly that would explain such a large church in this location. The visible evidence is C11, but excavations in 1973–4 showed it to be the rebuilding of an earlier Saxon church, possibly C7, supporting the suggestion that this was the site of a monastery founded by St Botolph in 654. The earlier church consisted of a nave and transepts and, perhaps, an apsidal chancel. Saxon transepts are a rarity (cf. e.g. Dover). The foundations remain of a crossing tower added in the C11. To this later period belong the double-splayed windows of the nave (with original wooden frames) and the N doorway with one order of columns, a square abacus, an inner roll moulding of the arch and an outer band, quite distant from it (cf. Strethall). The roll moulding indicates a date after 1060, supported by tree-ring dating of the DOOR itself. This has plain oak boards and three long undecorated straps riveted through to circular wooden bars at the back. The straps terminate in split curls. It was formerly covered with cowhide (not, as legend states, human skin). The capitals, abaci, and the band around the arch are decorated with an irregular pattern of diagonal lines which may signify leaves. It is not, however, in its original position, but probably stood further W, and was moved to line up with the S doorway when that was inserted in the early C13. The W door has reused strap hinges similar to those on the N door, perhaps from the N transept.

Inside, the evidence is even more interesting. It concerns the arches towards the two transepts. These were rebuilt in the C13, following the collapse of the tower, but the old stonework was reused. The arch on the S side is complete to the abaci. Of that on the N side only the bases survive. The rest is C14. The C11 jambs have one order of colonettes at the angle towards the crossing and a quite unskilled abacus. The capitals of the colonettes are decorated with the same sketchy leaf pattern as the N doorway, a shape very similar to the Norman one-scallop. The N transept has an early C14 N window (replacing a doorway) with flowing tracery, but outside long-and-short work can be seen. On the gable of the S transept is a fine C14 finial cross, carved from a single piece of Barnack stone. Small E.E. S doorway with stiff-leaf capitals. The W tower was added in the C15, see its tall arch towards the nave, the flint and stone decoration at the base, and the diagonal buttresses. Until the late C18 it had an octagonal timber spire, the supporting timbers for which remain inside. The Saxon chancel was probably rebuilt in the C14, but this was replaced in 1790 by a shallow polygonal apse, which in turn was rebuilt by *Butterfield*, 1881–7, with S vestry and organ chamber. On the exterior he uses flint and stone decoration to link to the tower, and inside the chancel arch follows closely the two transept arches, but otherwise the addition is unsympathetic and the interior has an unfinished air, as if awaiting decoration and stained glass. It includes tiled flooring, stone reredos, altar rails, choir stalls and pulpit.

SCREEN (to S transept). C15, damaged, with broad single-light divisions, ogee arch inside pointed arch, with quatrefoil and other motifs between the two. Carving in one of the spandrels of fox and geese. – LECTERN. Good, C15, wooden, on octagonal concave sided base. – BENCHES. Throughout the nave, C15, plain, many renewed in the C19, probably by Butterfield. – MILLENNIUM CROSS. Stainless steel and bronze. By *Donald Stewart*, 2000.

Immediately E of the church the former school, now VILLAGE HALL, 1871, by *R.R. Rowe* of Cambridge: stock brick with red dressings and other decoration, and two large windows with elaborate glazing bars. On the S the former RECTORY, 1873, brick. On the N side the churchyard slopes down towards the Green, connected by CHURCH PATH, in which is BEAM

ENDS, a charming C15 house with jettied s end. On the s side of THE GREEN, HADSTOCK HALL, *c.* 1600, altered in the C18 and later, with exposed timber framing. E of here, an attractive row of houses leads uphill. On the N side of Bartlow Road, HILL FARM, C15 with two large gabled and jettied cross-wings. The original hall screen survives inside.

ROMAN VILLA, 1¼ m. NNE, on the s bank of the Granta. Discovered in 1826 and partially excavated over the following thirty years. Part of a winged corridor villa, incorporating a bath suite, was uncovered. Several mosaic pavements were found, including one that was removed and relaid at Audley End.

HALSTEAD

See also GREENSTEAD GREEN

The town lies across the River Colne with the High Street running up the hill to the N and Trinity Street up the hill to the s. The two parish churches, St Andrew and Holy Trinity, face each other across the valley. Along the Colne are relics of Halstead's former industrial past: Courtauld's mills, Portway's ironworks and the Colne Valley Railway, all now closed and redeveloped.

ST ANDREW, Parsonage Street. Of flint rubble with Caen stone dressings, much renewed. Restored 1849–52, the chancel by *H.W. Hayward*, the nave by *J. Clarke*, who also rebuilt the w tower further out into the churchyard. Also by Clarke the organ chamber on the chancel's N side, 1882. The chancel itself is pretty well deprived of medieval detail, with the E wall and most of the N wall rebuilt. The rest mostly C14, porches and vestry C15. s aisle windows Dec, N aisle Perp. Inside, C14 six-bay arcades, with square piers with four demi-shafts and double-chamfered arches. The chancel roof, whose date (1413) is known from documents, is hidden behind boarding. – FONT. Octagonal, Perp, with motifs of shields and flowers. – REREDOS, 1893, and chancel decoration, completed 1899, by *Sir Arthur Blomfield*, executed by *Percy Bacon & Bros.* – Nave ALTAR. Wooden cube, installed during reordering by *Purcell Miller Tritton*, 1999–2000, with carved panel by *Jonathan Fearnhead*, 2002. – Tower SCREEN by *H. Munro Cautley*, 1948. STATIONS OF THE CROSS. Wood, by *Fearnhead*, 2001.

STAINED GLASS. Mostly by *James Powell & Sons*, including E window 1905, replacing one of *c.* 1850 by *Clutterbuck*; s aisle s, 1891, in a style showing clearly the influence of Burne-Jones in design if not in colour; and three clerestory windows, part of an incomplete scheme designed by *Charles Hardgrave*. s aisle E by *W. B. Simpson & Sons.* – MONUMENTS. Effigies, probably John Bourchier †1328 and his wife Helen, each under a separate canopy on thin shafts. The tomb-chest with weepers and shields and the diapered panels behind belong to the tomb of Robert, 1st Lord Bourchier, †1349. – Effigies of Robert and his wife Margaret lie on the adjacent tomb-chest, made for John, 2nd Lord Bourchier †1400 and his second wife Elizabeth, which is richly decorated with quatrefoils carrying shields. Tall canopy of a chaste, rather frigid design, again with frieze of shields, and ending in a cresting with small shields. Higher angle shafts. – Brass to Bartholomew, 3rd Lord Bourchier †1409 and two wives. Three figures, the largest Lord Bourchier in armour, 44 in. (112 cm.). – Elizabeth Watson †1604. Brass plate with kneeling figure, 11 in. (28 cm.) in her hat, and six children. – Sir Samuel Tryon †1626. Slate tablet in a surround of coloured marbles, with Corinthian columns, military trophies, etc. – Samuel Fiske †1718, who paid for rebuilding the spire in 1717. Inscription on copper by *Jos. Nutting*, including a poem by *Matthew Prior*. – Rev. John Manistre †1826. Large tablet with particulars of bequest, by *Slythe & Lufkin*. Similar tablet, even larger, in N aisle, detailing the bequest of Elizabeth Holmes †1783.

HOLY TRINITY, Trinity Street. By *Scott & Moffatt*, 1843–4. Still 98 in the lancet style, but already with a bold steeple with broach spire standing by the side of the S aisle close to the W end. The hastily-built spire had to be rebuilt twice, just before and within a year after consecration. Flint-faced brick walls, spire and dressings of gault brick. N organ chamber added by Scott, 1876. Alternating circular and octagonal piers inside; square capitals decorated in early C13 style. Clerestory and wheel window above lancets at E end.* – CHOIR STALLS, 1913, SCREENS (war memorial chapel), 1922, and PRIEST'S STALL, 1931, by *Duncan W. Clark*, carved by *Kenneth Mabbitt* and *Samuel Marshall*. – LECTERN. By *Charles Spooner*, 1906. Four wooden shafts with two curved iron candle-holders. – STAINED GLASS. W window by *Clutterbuck*, 1851, restored and re-set by *Lowndes & Drury*, 1913: typical elongated medallion shapes and glowing colours. E window by *Burlison & Grylls*, 1887. S aisle E by *J. C. N. Bewsey*, 1922. Three in S aisle by *A.K. Nicholson*, 1931–2. – Contemporary SCHOOL building on N side of churchyard; vicarage by *William White*, 1854, demolished.

ST FRANCIS OF ASSISI (R.C.), Colchester Road. By *O'Neill & Fordham*, 1954–5, the principal donor Dr Richard Courtauld. Brick, T-plan, with transepts just W of a very shallow sanctuary, and short square W tower. Reordered by *Broadbent, Hastings, Reid & New*, 1987. – SCULPTURE. Stone bas-relief by *Philip Lindsey Clark*. – STAINED GLASS. E window (lunette) by *Rosemary Rutherford*, 1955. S chapel E by *Goddard & Gibbs* (*J.N. Lawson*), 1970–2. Nave N, 1979, and four sanctuary windows, 1995, also by *Goddard & Gibbs*. Nave S (two) by *E.A.H. Archer*, 1993–6.

Former UNITED REFORMED CHURCH, Parsonage Street. By *F. Barnes*, 1865–6. Kentish rag with Caen stone dressings. An

---

* David Andrews points out the similarity between this and the E end of St Nicholas Castle Hedingham.

ambitious, lifeless building with fussy tracery. Now converted to flats and deprived of its spire. Adjacent school building 1894, with Gothic detailing.

POLICE STATION, Trinity Street. By *Hopper*, 1851, and the prototype for a series by him in Tudor Gothic style. Brick with stock brick dressings, straight gables of varying sizes, and tall diamond chimneys. Including magistrates' court, now closed.

PUBLIC LIBRARY, Bridge Street. Former Corn Exchange, 1865. Gault brick, with exuberant red and black brick dressings and some carved stone, notably a circular panel in the pedimented end wall.

RICHARD DE CLARE PRIMARY SCHOOL, Factory Lane East. 1909–10 by *Goodey & Cressall*, but without the panache of their Colchester schools. Single storey, brick with stone dressings.

HOSPITAL, Hedingham Road. 1883–4 by *Sherrin*, in his characteristic half-timbered style, paid for by George Courtauld. Out-patients' block in similar style added in his memory by his daughter, Dr Elizabeth Courtauld, by *W.T. Cressall*, 1920–1.

PUBLIC PARK, Trinity Street. Opened 1901. Landscaping by *T.W. Sanders*. Octagonal bandstand.

CEMETERY, Colchester Road. Opened 1856. Large Gothic entrance lodge and gateway, flint with stone dressings. No chapel, but a small mortuary by *R.M. Phipson* of Ipswich. Landscaping by *William Davidson*.

PERAMBULATION

The town's focal point is the crossroads at the top of the High Street, here known as MARKET HILL, marked by a stone drinking FOUNTAIN given by George Courtauld in 1887. The Courtaulds' influence upon the buildings of Halstead was even greater than at Bocking (q.v.). Samuel Courtauld started manufacturing silk in Halstead in 1825 and numerous houses, public buildings and other monuments to the family's patronage remain.

From Market Hill, HEDINGHAM ROAD leads NNE ¾ m. towards The Howe, home of S.A. Courtauld until 1953. He ensured that the buildings seen on the way to his house were pleasing to the eye, and replaced old cottages with new houses: dated from 1920 to 1929, mainly semi-detached, brick or plastered with false half-timbering. One group is named after Jane Austen's novels (Sense and Sensibility etc., some off to the r. in MILL CHASE). Probably by *E.W. Coldwell* of *Coldwell, Coldwell & Courtauld*. Then comes the Hospital (*see* above) and the HOMES OF REST by *E.W. Coldwell*, 1923, on the site of the workhouse: five single-storey blocks, four houses in each, linked round three sides of a large garden, with a central common room in the middle block. Neo-Tudor brick, with tall chimneys. On the corner of BOX MILL LANE a former SCHOOL, built 1861 for Edward Hornor of The Howe, followed by Courtauld houses in the lane. Opposite, WASH FARM, mid C16, with original chimneystack, jettied upper floor and two large C17 gabled dormers. Finally THE HOWE itself, two storeys of gault brick, three bays with Doric portico and dentilled eaves, built 1825 for Edward May.

Back to the centre, for the continuation N of the High Street along HEAD STREET. Several nice houses, those nearer the church timber-framed and plastered, gault or stock brick further out, the best perhaps No. 93: five bays, two storeys, with corner pilasters and Tuscan porch. Behind it, old forge buildings dated 1886, gault brick and weatherboarding. Set back on the W side, in FINSBURY PLACE, a terrace of mid-C19 weavers' cottages with characteristic elongated top-floor windows. Just before No. 49 Head Street, THE CHASE, also set back, a hall house of *c.* 1500, now incorporating an adjoining cottage of *c.* 1600. Then in MILL CHASE the octagonal brick base of a SMOCK MILL of 1790, surrounded by former mill buildings, now houses. On the E side, Nos. 32–38, C17 timber-framed and plastered cottages, restored by the *County Architect's Dept*, 1978–9. Further out, off COLNE ROAD, two drum-like brick WATER TOWERS, the larger and later by *Jabez Church*, engineer, 1889; converted to a house in 2003.

Along the N side of St Andrew's churchyard, COLCHESTER ROAD runs ESE, with RED HOUSE opposite the church's E end. Built by Edward Barron after 1773, five bays with a two-bay projection at one end. Brick front and side, but the rear and Broom Hill elevation timber-framed, the latter dated 1899 in the plaster. Next to it the former offices of the Halstead Union by *E. W. Coldwell*, 1923, brick with stone porch. Opposite, THE WOODMAN pub, brick with half-timbered upper floor, also by Coldwell, 1931–2. More Courtauld houses in Colchester Road and Mallows Field, off it to the S, 1927–9 and 1935. Further along Colchester Road, ½ m. from the church, KING'S HOUSE, built 1937–8 by *Basil Oliver* as the King's Head pub. Local white brick, originally thatched, but rebuilt after a fire in 1962 by *Russell Walker* with tile roof. Fireplace with glazed tiles by *Heather Perry* of Essex subjects.

Along the S side of St Andrew's churchyard, PARSONAGE STREET runs SE before turning sharply to the r. On the same side as the church a terrace of four houses, Nos. 1–7, flint pebbles with stock brick dressings but embellished with carved stone heads plausibly said to have been salvaged from the pre-1850 church tower. Opposite, Neo-Tudor brick CHURCH HALL, 1924, largely paid for by S.A. Courtauld. After the corner, on the l. WEAVERS ROW, a substantially unaltered mid-C19 terrace of twelve houses: brick, workrooms on the first floor with original large, small-paned windows, and attics in mansard roof.

Finally MARKET HILL and the broad HIGH STREET, with a good mix of buildings stepping nicely downhill. Across the top, looking down, a row of shops by *C. F. Hayward*, 1862, with lively Gothic polychromatic brickwork above plate-glass windows. The better houses are on the NW side, and not always what they appear to be. Nos. 18–20 have an C18 façade, three-

storey canted bays either side of a Venetian window and pediment, but behind is a late C16 timber frame. Fragments of C17
wall painting in a first-floor room. The grandest is PRE-
MABERG HOUSE (Nos. 22–24), late C18, built for James Scarlett. Distinguished by a pedimented bay, breaking slightly
forward, with carved stone arms in the pediment, a Venetian
window on the first floor and a Diocletian window on the
second. Two bays to either side and a further two bays, set
slightly back, but on the l. only. A double porch across two of
the central feature's three bays provides a further distressing
lack of symmetry. Next to it No. 26 (Whispers Restaurant), its
undistinguished exterior giving no clue to what lies beneath.
Originally a College or Chantry House founded under the will
of Bartholomew Lord Bourchier in 1412. Most of the hall,
which was set back from the present street line, survives intact,
with part of its hammerbeam roof visible on the first floor.
No. 32 is of *c.* 1800, painted brick with a Venetian window over
a Tuscan porch. Then No. 34, the former GRAMMAR SCHOOL
by *C.F. Hayward*, 1862, in a rather gloomy brick, next to BAR-
CLAYS BANK, a more original exercise in Ruskinian polychromy (cf. the Public Library) – although behind the façade
the building is timber-framed, probably C17. On the corner of
Chapel Street, the former POST OFFICE, 1895, brick, with the
Royal Arms prominently placed in a high gable.

Less of note on the street's SE side. Near the top, the WHITE
HART INN, C15 hall with cross-wings; plastered front with C16
bargeboards but an overall appearance that is closer to the C19,
and exposed timbers to the rear. Lower down, Nos. 41–43, C16,
have at the l. end a high timber-framed gateway that formerly
led through to cottages in Gate House Yard, of which one
remains. At the bottom of the High Street, Halstead's industrial past makes itself felt. Off to the l., FACTORY LANE EAST,
sixteen three-storey brick houses in two terraces by *John Birch*
for Samuel Courtauld & Co., 1872. Decorative glazing bars (cf.
Bocking). The top floors provided lodgings during the week
for workers from surrounding villages. Beyond the terrace, in
VICARAGE MEADOW, early 1920s semi-detached company
houses, in a Garden Suburb style that pre-dates the fully developed 'Courtauld Tudor' style. On the s side of Factory Lane
were Courtauld's mills, closed 1982 and the site mainly redeveloped. Two ancillary brick buildings remain, dated 1904 and
1912, and a twenty-bay C19 brick range, now part of Weavers
Court Shopping Centre, along the river's N bank. The principal monument, however, is TOWNSFORD MILL across the
river itself, long, three-storeyed, white and weatherboarded,
with impressive uninterrupted bands of windows on two floors.
Built as a water-powered corn mill in the late C18, converted
to silk-throwing and weaving by Samuel Courtauld in 1825.
Adjoining mill house at s end. Along the river's s side, THE
CAUSEWAY, with more workers' housing, 1882–3 by *Sherrin*:
ten cottages with a communal dining room (now British
Legion hall) at the factory end and a semi-detached pair, brick

with Dutch gables that would not look out of place in Bedford Park.

s of the river the High Street becomes BRIDGE STREET with a sharp turn to the r. and the half-timbered BULL HOTEL looking back up the hill: C16, Georgianized, then restored in the early C20 by *E. W. Coldwell*. At the other end of the street the former CO-OPERATIVE SOCIETY building, 1867, with stepped gable and symbolic relief of a beehive. Extended 1924 and 1957. Here the corner turns into TRINITY STREET, crossing the line of the former railway, with the public park (*see* above) on the l. To the r., along Butler Road, were Portway's ironworks, including the foundry where Tortoise stoves were made. Opposite Kings Road, the former SAVOY CINEMA, 1916, a wildly incorrect confection of classical motifs including two open pediments and pilasters with vaguely Corinthian capitals, and then the BRITISH WORKMAN'S TEMPERANCE HALL, 1876, now flats. Round-arched first-floor windows. Behind here, ironically, was Adams' brewery, of which a few buildings remain, including the unusual feature of a CHAPEL (used also as a meeting room; now museum store). 1883, rebuilt and enlarged 1902 to accommodate fragments from *Wren*'s All Hallows the Great, London, 1677–83 (dem. 1896).* REREDOS with Corinthian pilasters and broken pediment and, supporting the chancel arch, two fine Corinthian columns and pilasters that also formed part of the original reredos. Above the arch, a carved stone cherub's head with wings. Four-bay brick nave with large sash windows set in arched recesses, and N and S entrance porches. Amid the former brewery, TRINITY HOUSE, C17 timber-framed, with Late Georgian gault brick front. Off New Street, which runs SE opposite Trinity House, BROOK PLACE, with more weavers' cottages.

Beyond Holy Trinity (*see* above) CHAPEL HILL leads off to the r. On the S side, the best-looking timber-framed house in the town, Nos. 7–13, dated by its carpentry to the mid C13: hall, floored *c.* 1600, two cross-wings, that on the r. jettied, that on the l. underbuilt with a C19 shop, and a narrower two-storey wing to the r., probably originally stables. ¼ m. further on, at CROWBRIDGE FARM, a pair of cottages dated 1866: red brick with black headers, gables with bargeboards, patterned tile roof with decorative slate ridges, and windows with small diamond panes.

ASHFORD LODGE, 1½ m. NE. Large Neo-Georgian brick rebuild for Col E.F. Hoblyn, *c.* 1924, by *Coldwell, Coldwell & Courtauld*.

BLUEBRIDGE HOUSE, 1 m. SE. Five-bay front of red and blue brick, with a stone plaque giving the date (1714), the name of the owner (John Morley), and the arms of the Butchers' Company. The windows still straight-headed. Later C18 doorway; porch with open pediment. Staircase with twisted

---

*A member of the Adams family worked for the City of London Brewing Co., which purchased the site of All Hallows. The font and font cover noted by Pevsner in 1954 are now in the Chapel Royal, Hampton Court Palace.

balusters. Other interior features, including timber framing, are of the C17. Good wrought-iron railings and gate, including elaborate overthrow with Morley's initials.

OAKLANDS, 1 m. WNW. By *C.F. Hayward*, *c.* 1872. Local yellowish white brick with stone dressings. Garden front with two gabled bays, one square, the other canted.

PENNY POT, 2 m. SW. By *J.S. Courtauld*, *c.* 1907–10, for W.J. Courtauld. Neo-Georgian, but with a picturesque irregularity, especially on the garden front.

SLOE HOUSE, ¾ m. ENE. Probably by *Richard Elsam*, for Charles Hanbury; not the design published in his *Rural Architecture* (1803), but with a double-height, three-bay bow window on the garden front similar to that on his remodelling of Gosfield Place (dem.).[*] Stuccoed brick. One bay either side of the bow, extended to the N later in the C19, when a cast-iron veranda was added to the entrance front. Entrance hall with Soanean vaulted ceiling.

STANSTEAD HALL. *See* Greenstead Green.

4000

HARLOW

Introduction	446
Town Centre	451
The Neighbourhoods:	
Mark Hall North, Mark Hall South, Netteswell	454
Little Parndon and Hare Street	458
Brays Grove, Latton Bush, Tye Green	460
Passmores, Great Parndon, Kingsmoor, Stewards	462
Industrial Areas: Temple Fields and Pinnacles	464
Katherines and Sumners	465
Church Langley	465
Old Harlow	466
Potter Street	471
Gibberd Garden	471

INTRODUCTION

p. 448 Harlow is now synonymous with the New Town set up in 1947, but the area it covers comprised five ancient parishes: Great Parndon, Harlow, Latton,[†] Little Parndon, and Netteswell, with a combined population of some 4,500. Their churches and other buildings have been absorbed, although some remain quite separate and retain their own character. The names of the villages were borrowed for some of the New Town's neighbourhood areas, but these do not correspond to the old village boundaries.

Harlow was the second New Town to be designated (after Stevenage), but fewer difficulties were encountered at the initial

---

[*] Both houses are illustrated in Cromwell's *Excursions in the County of Essex* (1819).
[†] For Latton Priory, *see* North Weald Bassett.

stages than elsewhere and Harlow was thus the first realization of the ideals of post-war reconstruction. *Frederick Gibberd* was appointed to prepare the master plan in 1947 and remained the town's architect-planner until the winding up of the Harlow Development Corporation in 1980. He made his home there (*see* p. 471) – an unusual case of cordiality in such situations, and a circumstance which must have contributed to the town's success. The original plan, approved in 1949, was for 60,000 inhabitants, to provide housing for overspill population from London and in particular from those areas which had suffered from bombing during the Second World War. Gibberd wanted the residential areas to feel like a town, rather than a series of villages, and strove for a compact layout in each area, but the officially approved low densities of 30–50 people per acre made this difficult to achieve. By 1952, however, it proved possible to raise the population figure to 80,000 without departing from the original design. Further expansions were proposed in the 1970s, up to as much as 150,000, but these were rejected and by 1980 the population was a little short of 80,000. It declined in the 1980s and 1990s but by 2001 had recovered to just under 79,000.

The designated area for the town, 6,320 acres, was predominantly rural, with four villages and a market town too small to form the nucleus of the new town centre. The plan imposed was semicircular, with the railway (the Liverpool Street–Norwich line), the River Stort, and the proposed Norwich motorway (M11) forming the baseline on which were sited the two main industrial estates, Temple Fields on the E and Pinnacles on the W, with the railway station in the centre between them. The fact that in 1964 the M11 was relocated to the E of the town was one of the few things that spoilt Gibberd's master plan, and resulted in an unplanned increase in traffic across the town; it opened to London in 1977, and Cambridge in 1979, but never reached Norwich. Although links with London remained strong, Harlow was not to be, like the interwar LCC out-county estates, a dormitory for commuters. The industrial areas provided local employment, and from the early 1960s the government encouraged business (e.g. Longman's, Pitney Bowes, and Gilbey) to relocate there.

S of the railway station (*see* p. 465) was the central area, rising up to the town's highest point, with housing grouped in four neighbourhood clusters within the semicircle. Each cluster had its major neighbourhood centre (Town Centre, The Stow, Bush Fair, Staple Tye) with church, library, community centre, health centre, and light industrial areas. An irregular grid of new roads both separated and linked the different areas, with the old A11 (now A414, and until the construction of the M11, the main access and through-road for the town) to the E, and leading off it to the W, from S to N, Southern Way, Second Avenue, and Edinburgh Way. Each neighbourhood area, typically of 200 dwellings, was connected by a central spine route, with linking roads given names beginning with the first letters of the neighbourhood (e.g. Mardyke Road and Momples Road in Mark Hall) with the

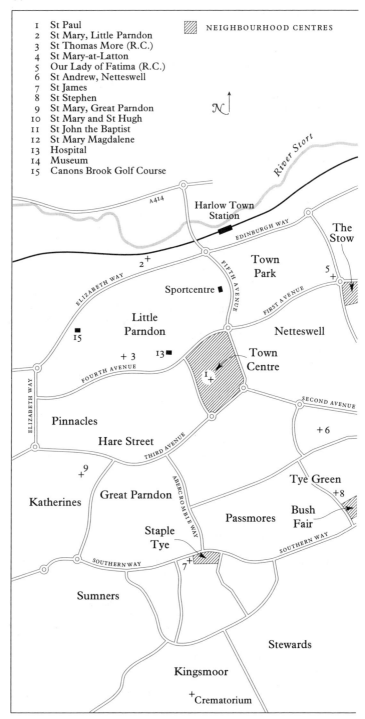

1 St Paul
2 St Mary, Little Parndon
3 St Thomas More (R.C.)
4 St Mary-at-Latton
5 Our Lady of Fatima (R.C.)
6 St Andrew, Netteswell
7 St James
8 St Stephen
9 St Mary, Great Parndon
10 St Mary and St Hugh
11 St John the Baptist
12 St Mary Magdalene
13 Hospital
14 Museum
15 Canons Brook Golf Course

NEIGHBOURHOOD CENTRES

River Stort

N

A414

Harlow Town Station

EDINBURGH WAY

The Stow

2

Town Park

FIFTH AVENUE

5

ELIZABETH WAY

Sportcentre

FIRST AVENUE

Little Parndon

Netteswell

15

FOURTH AVENUE

3

13

Town Centre

1

ELIZABETH WAY

SECOND AVENUE

Pinnacles

Hare Street

6

THIRD AVENUE

9

ABERCROMBIE WAY

Tye Green

8

Katherines

Great Parndon

Passmores

Bush Fair

Staple Tye

SOUTHERN WAY

7

SOUTHERN WAY

Sumners

Stewards

Kingsmoor

Crematorium

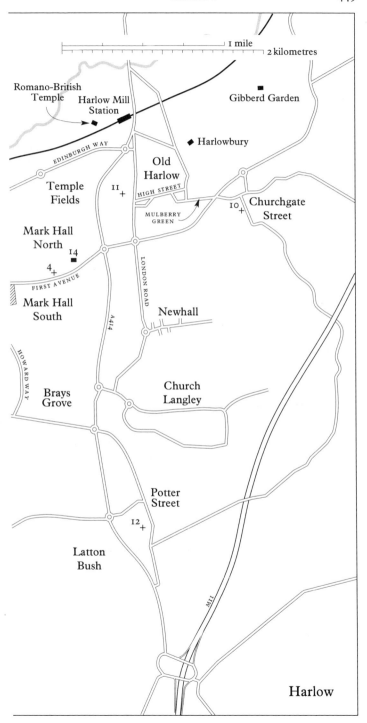

1 mile
2 kilometres

Romano-British
Temple

Harlow Mill
Station

Gibberd Garden

♦ Harlowbury

EDINBURGH WAY

Old
Harlow

Temple
Fields

11 +

HIGH STREET

10 + Churchgate
Street

MULBERRY
GREEN

Mark Hall
North

14 ■

LONDON ROAD

4 +

FIRST AVENUE

Mark Hall
South

Newhall

A414

HOWARD WAY

Brays
Grove

Church
Langley

Potter
Street

12 +

Latton
Bush

M11

Harlow

intention of aiding orientation for tenants. The neighbourhoods were meant to be sufficiently compact for residents to be within ten minutes' walk of the neighbourhood centre, and for most people longer journeys would be by bicycle. Many existing lanes were preserved as footpaths and cycle tracks, with the result that the topography of the former villages can still be discerned.

Most of the HOUSING was by the *Harlow Development Corporation Design Group*, led by Gibberd; the executive architect for most of the Corporation's life was *Victor Hamnett* (1949–73), with chief architects *Noel Tweddell* (1947–9) and *Alex McCowan* (1973–80). Two-storey housing, much of it terraced and most of it in stock brick, predominates, but there is nonetheless great variety in form and layout, with a mixture of houses, maisonettes, and flats within each neighbourhood, and buildings of varying heights. Moreover, from the outset other architects were invited to design individual areas, thus adding greatly to the interest of what might otherwise have become very monotonous. Many of those invited to contribute designs were young, with roots in the pre-war avant-garde around the MARS group, Tecton, etc. But at Harlow they showed the influence of Scandinavian models, rather than the Modernism of Le Corbusier which inspired other younger British architects of the post-war period, and this is one of the factors which have contributed to Harlow's success.

Of other factors, the most important must be the guiding mind of one man, Gibberd, who was able to impose a uniformity of thought upon the whole undertaking. He brought to the job not just vision, but also a sense of humour and humanity. There is a 'Festival of Britain' lightness of touch about much of Harlow, exemplified in the naming of the pubs: all are named after moths or butterflies, and the signs originally depicted the insect on one side, and a play on its name on the other. Humanity and attention to detail are also demonstrated by the siting of sculpture, mostly contemporary and mostly outside, of which over sixty pieces can be found across the whole town. This was managed by the Harlow Art Trust, set up in 1953, whose members included Gibberd and Patricia Fox-Edwards, later Gibberd's second wife. Only a selection can be noted here.*

Another important aspect of the New Town is the way in which the countryside comes right into the centre, with 'tongues' of green and carefully preserved vistas towards open country (*Sylvia Crowe* acted as landscape consultant). This is something which is in danger of being eroded; planning permission was granted in 2005 for a new Leisure Centre (by *Saunders Architects*) on the s side of the junction of Second and Third Avenue, interrupting the open view from the Civic Centre. It will replace the town's original Sportcentre and playing fields, releasing a 27-acre site N of Hammarskjold Road for housing.

The greenness did not find universal favour, particularly among those critics who did not feel that Harlow was urban

---

* Fully catalogued in *Sculpture in Harlow*, ed. Danielle Olsen (2005).

enough. J.M. Richards wrote of 'inhabitants marooned in a desert of grass verges and concrete', and Pevsner, in 1954, while approving the 'happy look' of urban types of building in a green rural setting, deplored the emphasis on a green setting for every house, leading to lower densities, that was insisted upon by the authorities. Ironically, it is that green setting which most people wanted (and which, in the case of the early residents especially, distinguished their new houses from the flats and terraced houses they had left behind in London), although the most recent development at Newhall is distinctly urban in character.

Other shortcomings of Harlow are more the result of general changes than intrinsic failures of planning. The decline in manufacturing industry as the town's chief employer has resulted in greater numbers commuting to work elsewhere. The expansion of car ownership has meant that walkable (or cyclable) distances are no longer as important as they once were, and people are prepared to drive further to work and shop. This has contributed to a decline in the neighbourhood centres with their small shops; Church Langley, with its single large supermarket, is a striking example of the new pattern of shopping, while the southern part of the Town Centre, after going through a period of sharp decline that is still evident in West Square, has been radically remodelled to cater for changing tastes.

TOWN CENTRE

ST PAUL, Playhouse Square. 1956–9 by *Humphrys & Hurst* (principally *Derrick Humphrys*, following Hurst's death in 1958). The main church of the new town, and the first building to be completed in the Civic Square. In view of its importance, Gibberd suggested that it should be of brick to distinguish it from the concrete of the civic buildings; that chosen is brown. But there are also large expanses of window with thin concrete tracery in lozenge patterns, so that from many angles one can see right through the building. Traditional plan: nave, shallow sanctuary, transepts, and S chapel, with vestries etc. beyond the E end. Copper flèche over the crossing. A short, detached SW bell-tower has a flying cornice and open-air pulpit with colourful mosaic frontal (small splashes of coloured mosaic on the main structure also). The main feature of the airy, light interior is the E wall, entirely covered by a MOSAIC of the Risen Christ at Emmaus by *John Piper*, the figures vividly delineated in colour against a black background. All the traditional FURNISHINGS are present (pulpit, lectern, font, piscina, sedilia, pews) in an economical contemporary style by Hurst with PROCESSIONAL CROSS by *John Skelton*. In the choir gallery (N transept) a PAINTING of the Crucifixion by *Zdzislaw Ruszkowski*. Organ (S transept) in a rectilinear case. Most of the glass is clear, apart from slits of coloured glass round the W and S doors. – SCULPTURE. Madonna and Child. Carved and painted stone. Probably Italian, C16, with a replacement C18 head.

PERAMBULATION

The principal building of the town centre is now the CIVIC CENTRE by *Benoy*, 2002–4, which lies across the site of Gibberd's Civic Square. Although a Civic Hall was planned for by Gibberd, his Town Hall tower (1958–9) stood off to the E side of the square. Its successor is only four storeys, but monumental, with a sinuous aluminium roof and a projecting white-rendered box at the W end providing a quasi-formal entrance and housing the Council Chamber at first-floor level behind a screen of giant louvres. Ribbon windows in pale brown blockwork mark three floors of offices, with shops on the ground floor. Inside the foyer, *Henry Moore*'s 'Family Group', 1954, commissioned for the Civic Square by Harlow Art Trust and one of Moore's first major public works, on a theme entirely appropriate to the optimism of the New Town. The centre provides the backdrop for the WATER GARDENS by *Frederick Gibberd & Partners*, originally constructed in 1960–3, but reconstructed to a reduced form in 2003. They descend in steps from a long canal with a blue mosaic retaining wall into which are set seven 'lion's head' fountains by *William Mitchell*,* which pour into a lower canal. At this level smaller square lily ponds between yew-hedge compartments. Much attention is given to public SCULPTURE including two major pieces, *Henry Moore*'s 'Upright Motive No. 2', 1955–6, and *Rodin*'s 'Eve' of 1882. Other bronzes by *Hebe Comerford* ('Bird', 1985), *Elisabeth Frink* ('Boar', 1970, replacing a concrete version of 1957 originally sited in Bush Fair neighbourhood centre).

The view S from Civic Square was originally enhanced by landscaping by *Sylvia Crowe*, designed to conceal the busy Third Avenue to the S; much of this land was soon taken for car parking (now double-decked) and the dignity of this space has further diminished with the construction of large retail sheds on the E and W sides (ASDA, etc.). The other great benefit, a view to the S across open country, is threatened by construction of a new Leisure Centre.

Remodelling for the Civic Centre has unfortunately turned PLAYHOUSE SQUARE into a backwater that is an inappropriate setting for the town centre's other major building, St Paul's Church (*see* above). Next to it the PLAYHOUSE THEATRE, 1969–71 by *T. Hinchliffe*, chief architect, Harlow Urban District Council. Clad in precast aggregate panels but with a glazed projecting front through which one can see the concrete stairs and lobbies etc. Main auditorium with proscenium arch, and studio theatre. Inside, SCULPTURE includes a marble fountain figure, *c.* A.D. 180, and a stone head, both Roman.

Facing the theatre, OCCASIO HOUSE (Harlow Foyer, young people's flats etc.), 2001 by *Levitt Bernstein Associates* (concept

---

* Mitchell acted as consultant for the reconstruction and two of his large concrete reliefs, 1961 and 1963, were salvaged in the redevelopment and re-erected on the rear of the Civic Centre and Asda supermarket.

architects, *Wilkinson Eyre*). Curved, six storeys. Timber volu-metric units prefabricated off-site, with aluminium rain-screen. s of this is COLLEGE SQUARE, ill-named since the demolition of *Gibberd*'s Technical College in the late 1990s and its replacement with characterless housing.* Looking forlornly towards its site, 'The Philosopher' by *Keith Godwin*, 1961–2. Behind, Essex County Council offices, including register office, by *Mike Woods* of *Essex Property Services Dept*, 1993, mainly of red and grey blockwork in stripes.

A new square has been created on the E side of the Civic Centre but its backdrop is only the mediocre LIBRARY, 1964 by *H. Conolly*, County Architect (project architect, *D.A. Stanhope*), extended 1979–80, one of several buildings which clutter the approach to BROAD WALK, the main pedestrian shopping precinct of the early New Town, completed in phases from 1958. Its muddled appearance is not an asset but Gibberd's vision is clearer here now than elsewhere, notably the promi-nence given to a bronze SCULPTURE by *Lynn Chadwick* ('Trigon', 1961). Halfway along, an OBELISK by *Gibberd*, con-crete faced in Portland stone, erected 1980 to commemorate the building of the New Town. Shops of mixed heights on both sides, tallest at the s end, originally for Woolworth's (E side, by *Halpern & Partners*, c. 1966–7, concrete-clad) and the Co-op (w side). The blocks at the N end, beyond Little Walk and East Walk (through to the BUS STATION and grisly TERMINUS HOUSE, 1968–70, nine storeys over a three-storey car park) were completed first: on the E (with crazy-paved panels in the upper storey and overlapping canopies) by *Seymour Harris & Partners* and on the w side by *Kenneth Wakeford, Jerram & Harris*.

Both of the northern ranges on Broad Walk face the MARKET SQUARE of 1955, and the w block in particular is closely in sympathy with the architecture around Gibberd's earlier Market Square at Lansbury with flats above shops and windows in concrete surrounds. The 'Festival of Britain' spirit is evoked strongly in other ways, e.g. the conspicuous clock on *Gibberd*'s ADAMS HOUSE (E side) against a tiled background of blue and white vertical stripes and the placing in the square of 'Meat Porters' by *Ralph Brown*, 1959, one of the most pow-erful of the works commissioned by the Harlow Art Trust. But the standard of design of the other blocks is rather feeble, with the possible exception of THE ROWS (NW) with its upper terrace of shops. Crude permanent sheds for market traders seem a long way from Gibberd's original conception of open stalls.

WEST GATE leads out of the square, past the HARLOW ADVICE CENTRE, 1978 by *HDC Design Group*, a concrete cube with circular windows projecting over the pavement on columns. Then comes WEST SQUARE, a bleak backwater surrounded by

---

* It contained a mural by *John Piper*, acquired from the Festival of Britain.

taller offices, and s to WEST WALK, a small court with *F. E. McWilliam*'s 1956 bronze 'Portrait Figure' of Elisabeth Frink, in beatnik dress. Finally the HARVEY CENTRE, a double-height covered shopping mall which occupies much of the central area behind other buildings so with little external presence. By *Gibberd*, 1979–82, refurbished by *Leslie Jones Architects*, 1995. A normal shopping street was originally planned for the site, a good example of Gibberd modifying plans to changing fashion. Inside, 'High Flying' by *Antanas Brazdys* (stainless steel, 1977; Brazdys' 'Solo Flight', 1982, now on the s side of First Avenue, was originally sited in the atrium), and, on the first floor of BHS, a wood wall sculpture by *Henry & Joyce Collins*, 1982.

At the periphery of the shopping area are a few civic buildings: in the SE corner on SOUTH GATE, the very dull POLICE STATION, 1957, and MAGISTRATES' COURTS, 1959, by *Gibberd* with *H. Conolly*. N of Fourth Avenue, equally unmemorable FIRE STATION by *Conolly*, 1957, and TELEPHONE EXCHANGE. Between the two, SAINSBURY'S by *Terry Farrell & Co.*, 1992–4,* set into a dip but announcing its presence with three white rendered rooftop cubes echoed by little pavilions at the pedestrian entrances. Two entrances in blue enamelled cylinders. N of this the site of the SPORTCENTRE by *Gibberd & Partners* (partner in charge, *G. T. Goalen*), 1963–4.[†]

THE NEIGHBOURHOODS

MARK HALL NORTH, MARK HALL SOUTH, NETTESWELL

ST MARY-AT-LATTON, The Gowers. Norman nave and chancel – see the arch over the s doorway and window beside it, both with Roman bricks. Also in the s wall, which is mainly flint rubble, a C16 brick doorway that must have led to the rood-loft staircase. N chapel of brick with two-light stone windows, added shortly before 1466 by Sir Peter Arderne. Late C16 W tower with diagonal buttresses, three-light W window, and battlements. The church's N side refaced in brick, *c.* 1800, with general restorations in 1848–50, 1873, and 1888. The appearance of the interior, including ROOD BEAM and CANOPY over the altar, is as restored by *Laurence King* in 1964–5 following a fire; he added the stock brick N vestry, 1973–4. – WALL PAINTING. Scant remains of a late C15 cycle (N chapel). – STAINED GLASS. E window 1864, W window (*Clayton & Bell*?) *c.* 1883. Nave s by *Holiday*, 1913. – MONUMENTS. Sir Peter Arderne of Mark Hall †1467, Chief Baron of the Exchequer, and his wife Katherine. Tomb-chest with three large panels

---

*Replacing Gilbey's Head Office and Bottling Plant by *Peter Falconer & Partners* with *Alexander Gibson* of the *Design Research Unit*, 1962–3. This was demolished in spite of being the first of the New Town's buildings to be listed.
[†]Due to be redeveloped.

with quatrefoils and shields. Heavy canopy of three arches. Fleuron frieze and crenellations. Brasses on the lid, over 3 ft (90 cm.) long. Set in an arched recess between chancel and N chapel, with an iron grille in the opening. – Other brasses to Richard Harper and wife, *c.* 1490 (28-in. (71-cm.) and 26-in. (66-cm.) figures, with children), Emanuell Wollaye and wife, engraved *c.* 1600 before their deaths and the dates not filled in (figures about 30 in. (76 cm.)), and Frances Franklin †1604, 3-ft (90-cm.) figure in boldly ornamented dress, with son and daughter. – James Altham †1583 and wife. Monument with the usual kneeling figures. Children kneeling below. – Sir Edward Altham †1632, erected 1640. Attributed to *Thomas Stanton* (GF). Black and white marble, with inscription between Corinthian pilasters, open segmental pediment, and flanking figures of angels. – Rev. Stephen Lushington †1751. Half-urn, on a little shelf with Rococo cartouche, an unusual design. – Frances Elizabeth Campbell †1818 by *George Garrard*. No effigy; cherub's head at the foot.

OUR LADY OF FATIMA (R.C.), Howard Way. The most significant church of the New Town and one of the first churches in England to be influenced by the Liturgical Movement. By *Gerard Goalen*, designed 1953–4, built 1958–60.[*] T-plan, with a slender 84-ft (26-metre) copper-covered wooden spire over the crossing, and nave and transepts of equal length. These have brick-clad ends inset with wheel windows but glazed sides providing the interior's outstanding feature: brilliantly coloured *dalle de verre* STAINED GLASS by *Dom Charles Norris* of Buckfast Abbey, assisted by *Paulinus Angold* and *Jerome Gladman*. The figurative scheme depicts Our Lady of Fatima and Mary in the Old and New Testaments. The reinforced concrete frame is exposed inside forming a vault over the central ALTAR. Pierced mosaic screen behind holding a terracotta SCULPTURE of Christ by *Daphne Hardy Henrion*. – Our Lady of Fatima, terracotta, by *Mrs Scott Pitcher*. – St Augustine of Hippo, bronze, by *Philomena Davies*, *c.* 1980. – STATIONS OF THE CROSS by *Mrs Foord-Kelsey*. Hopton Wood stone, in the style of Eric Gill.

ST ANDREW (Methodist), The Stow. By *Paul Mauger & Partners*, 1952–4, paid for by fervent Methodist and film-maker J. Arthur Rank. Pale brown brick with patterns of projecting headers. Intended as the hall for an unbuilt church, which would have occupied the E side of a courtyard. This has classrooms, hall and cloister walks.

TOWN PARK, between First Avenue and Edinburgh Way. Designed without formal boundaries, and covering over 160 acres. The existing hamlet of Netteswell Cross, with pub and old houses, was incorporated in the design. SCULPTURE by *Ernest Adsetts*, 1950, *Hilary Frew*, 1965, *Jesse Watkins*, 1973.

[*] Goalen was in partnership with Gibberd by the time the church was under construction.

The neighbourhoods group around THE STOW, the first of the neighbourhood centres, opened in 1952. *Gibberd* began the design in 1949 and strove for an intricate layout, urban in character with three-storey buildings for flats above shops and a Z-shaped plan to create a sense of enclosure. Splashes of colour – e.g. a wall of yellow tiles, columns with bands of brown and green tiles – enliven the architecture. The centre incorporates a pub, library, and separate buildings on The Stow's W arm for Health Centre (NUFFIELD HOUSE, by *Booth & Ledeboer* (now Dental Centre); extension by *AHA Architecture*, 2005), and Methodist Church (*see above*). Set off from the precinct's S end is MOOT HOUSE, Latton's mid-C19 former vicarage, co-opted as the Community Centre. Stock brick, two storeys, main block of three bays with Tuscan porch and lower three-bay extension. In front, a dreary square with 'Chiron' by *Mary Spencer Watson* 1953, the Corporation's first commissioned SCULPTURE and partly carved on site.

The neighbourhoods centred on The Stow are much the most rewarding visually. MARK HALL NORTH, N of First Avenue and W of Howard Way, was the first built, and illustrates the planning theory followed for the rest of the town, in particular the excellent use of landscaping to provide definition between each of the three distinct housing groups. A prominent position is given at the edge of First Avenue to St Mary-at-Latton (*see above*) but the neighbourhood's true heart is N on MUSGRAVE ROAD, with its small group of shops, pub, and TANYS DELL PRIMARY SCHOOL (by *Richard Sheppard & Partners*, 1952), a terrace of three two-storey blocks stepping downhill.

Uphill E, early housing by *Gibberd* in MARK HALL MOORS, BROOMFIELD, and STACKFIELD, 1950–4, with a varied use of brick and weatherboarding. In this resolutely two-storey milieu is *Gibberd*'s THE LAWN of 1950–1, the first residential tower in Britain and evidence of Gibberd's enthusiasm for mixed development at Harlow from the outset. Ten storeys, with a butterfly-plan giving all the flats S-facing balconies. Gibberd wanted it to be four or five storeys higher, but feared public opposition, and set it among mature trees. Beside it a long three-storey block for larger flats.

S of here, partly shrouded by a wooded belt, are the remains of MARK HALL, the principal house of Latton parish (dem. 1960 after a fire in 1947). This was the medieval seat of Sir Peter Arderne, the Althams, and in the C19 the Arkwrights (descendants of the inventor). Late C18 STABLES (with domed cupola) and other many-gabled outbuildings converted for the MUSEUM OF HARLOW 1981–2 by *Anglian Architects* (project architect, *Raymond Hooper*), who inserted a glass gallery on one side of the inner courtyard. Part of the WALLED GARDENS survive. Well-head by *Jane Ackroyd*, 1988, and a stone seat by *Ernest Adsetts*, 1948–9, with animals supporting a top slab, renewed by *Paul Mason*, 1978. The mid-C19 NORTH LODGE is on Fesants Croft. Clusters of tall octagonal chimneystacks.

NW of the church, the landscape undulates and in this area are two groups by *Fry, Drew & Partners*, 1950–3. THE CHANTRY comprises terraces of houses sitting very comfortably in the landscape, on the edge of grassy slopes below St Mary-at-Latton; they have flat fronts, of coloured render, and shallow monopitch roofs – all very Swedish. At TANYS DELL, N of Mowbray Road, the main block is a staggered composition of four-storey flats with ground-floor voids on pilotis. Further to the w similar housing at GLEBELANDS, by *HDC Design Group*, 1950–4, with staggered brick terraces and flats: in front of Glebe House (Nos. 46–55) is *Barbara Hepworth*'s celebrated 'Contrapuntal Forms', abstract figures in blue limestone, originally commissioned for the Festival of Britain and an early instance of the post-war vogue for incorporating contemporary art into public housing. Behind was a children's wild area laid out by *Sylvia Crowe*, but sadly robbed of its original character. In the neighbourhood's SW corner STORT TOWER by *E.C.P. Monson*, 1962–4, Y-plan with fluted concrete balconies.

w of Howard Way, ranged along FIRST AVENUE, come a string of major buildings, starting with Our Lady of Fatima (*see* above) and ST ALBAN'S R.C. PRIMARY SCHOOL by *R.A. Boxall*, 1956, with eyecatching prefabricated modular NURSERY by *Cottrell & Vermeulen* with *Portakabin*, c. 1998. Yellow walls, steel frame and tented awnings. Next, BURNT MILL COMPREHENSIVE SCHOOL, 1961 by *H. Conolly*, County Architect. Substantial, curtain-walled blocks of mixed heights with a swooping-roofed hall and the strange counterpoint of a prominent brick chimney. Finally, the SWIMMING POOL, 1960–1 by the U.D.C (*T. Hinchliffe*). 110 ft (34-metre) basin under a curved roof. Also at Mark Hall North, but separated from the rest of it by the A414, MARK HALL SCHOOL by *Richard Sheppard & Partners*, 1954, with two four-storey and other lower blocks. The New Town's first secondary school.

The spacious, low-density development at Mark Hall North led Gibberd and the *HDC Design Group* to encourage a more urban environment in the next neighbourhood, MARK HALL SOUTH, s of First Avenue. The results can be seen at ORCHARD CROFT, E of The Stow, of 1951–4. Street façades are much longer and continuous and turn the corners by means of blocks of flats, and the spaces between buildings are much smaller. Front gardens are absent from this phase, in favour of open grass lawns. On the N side blocks of flats angled towards St Mary, the intended view now largely obscured by trees; and on Mardyke Road three-storey terrace houses, some with integral garages – an important concession at this period to growing car ownership. E is COOKS SPINNEY, 1951–2 by *H.T. Cadbury-Brown* (who also designed the SPINNEY JUNIOR AND INFANT SCHOOL s of Mardyke Road), CHURCHFIELD, 1951–4 by *Richard Sheppard & Partners* and LADYSHOT, SE, 1951–4 by *F.R.S. Yorke*, all variations on denser arrangements of two-storey stock brick terraces and proving the inherent difficulty of avoiding monotony over a large area. Yorke designed the COMMON ROOM (for tenants) in MOMPLES ROAD, timber-clad and raised on piers, with alternative access by a ramp of earth (intended for the elderly; now overgrown); beside it, 'Sheep Shearer' by *Ralph Brown*, bronze, 1955.

Rather more responsive to landscape is QUARRY SPRING, long curved four-storey maisonette blocks (encouraged by Gibberd as architecturally and spatially more economical than terraces but unpopular with tenants and Corporation) by *Norman & Dawbarn*, 1953–4, overlooking a disused quarry and defining the neighbourhood's southern boundary. Providing focus, a point block (PENNYMEAD TOWER, 1959–61).

At PURFOOTS GREEN, SE of Quarry Spring, COPPINS, C14 timber-framed hall house with one jettied cross-wing and some exposed timbers. Outbuildings include a C19 sawpit shed. S of it SCHOOL HOUSE, 1830, gault brick, square, cottages of similar style and date, and then a house and CLOCK TOWER of 1864, built by Joseph Arkwright of Mark Hall. Stock brick. Four-storey tower with short broach spire and weathervane.

The third neighbourhood in the cluster is NETTESWELL, SW of The Stow, which follows the Mark Hall South pattern. Subsumed within the housing are a few older buildings associated with C18 Netteswell, including, in MANSTON ROAD, the former RECTORY (Shaftesbury Society). Brick, three bays, two storeys and attics, built between 1766 and 1771. Tuscan doorcase with open pediment. Additions by *Chancellor*, 1874–5, including open timber porch on W side. In SCHOOL LANE, running N–S through the neighbourhood, is a former SCHOOL (now Nexus House) built in 1777. Plain brick house with an inscription noting its original endowment by William Martin.

The housing is not especially interesting other than in minor details, e.g. PITTMANS FIELDS by *H.T. Cadbury-Brown*, 1953–4, with bronze 'Donkey' by *Willi Soukop*, cast 1955, and THE DASHES by *Gerald Lacoste*, 1952–4, with splayed projections for porches and stores. At the neighbourhood's western edge, on Velizy Avenue, HUGHS TOWER by *HDC Design Group*, 1955–6, marks the eastern entrance to the Town Centre. NETTESWELL TOWER, N of First Avenue, by *Harlow District Council* and *Wimpey Construction*, 1986, shows the residential tower returning to favour; twelve storeys, brick with a curved terrace at its foot. Further N, LEAH MANNING DAY CENTRE, Park Lane. By *Harlow District Council*, 1980, with Portland stone relief panel by *Christopher Dean*. Single-storey, brick, with pantile roof. It lies on the edge of TOWN PARK (*see* above).

LITTLE PARNDON AND HARE STREET

ST MARY. *See* below.

ST THOMAS MORE, Hodings Road (R.C.). By *Burles, Newton & Partners*, 1964–5. A-frame, with brick porch and aisles, so only at the E end is it apparent that the steeply pitched roof comes to within a foot of the ground. The end walls project like a ship's bow, with a 'clerestory' below the eaves at the W end. Short detached bell-tower.

PRINCESS ALEXANDRA HOSPITAL, Hamstel Road. By *Easton & Robertson, Cusdin, Preston & Smith*, in three phases, 1958–66. Cross-shaped centre with a five- to six-storey E–W block and lower arms. Kent Wing, NE, by *Percy Thomas Partnership*, 1996, and Jenny Ackroyd Centre (with new main entrance) by *Tangram Architects & Designers*, 2003–4. – PARNDON HALL (Education Centre, NW), 1867, was built for L.W. Arkwright of Mark Hall, very possibly by *J. Clarke*. Italianate, two storeys, of brick and stone. Broad front with three bays of tripartite windows, the centre recessed with an arcaded ground floor loggia and round-headed windows above. Inside, a remarkable group of contemporary painted doors and ceilings, attributed to *Elizabeth Arkwright*, but in a variety of styles.

Former YWCA ALEXANDRA RESIDENTIAL CLUB, Hamstel Road and Fourth Avenue. By *Elsworth Sykes & Partners* (partner-in-charge *Michael James*), 1968–9. Mainly seven storeys, but with an extra floor (with boxy oriel) to emphasize the corner.

The two small neighbourhoods are separated by Fourth Avenue but contiguous with the town centre. The spine of Little Parndon is HODINGS ROAD. On its S side, HESTER HOUSE (sheltered housing). Built as Little Parndon's rectory, 1881, by *Chancellor*. Brick, and rather dull. Garden front of four bays and cross-wing with pedimented gable and canted bay. Further E, MORLEY GROVE by *Gibberd*, five-storey flats, 1961–2, and groups of three-storey terraces, 1965–7, some of the densest housing in the town; the terraces have alternate white and brown weatherboarding, and bold coloured doors. Similar density was earlier achieved by Gibberd in THE HORNBEAMS, 1956–9, and RIVERMILL, 1959–61, where the dwellings are either drawn together into a series of enclosed, rectangular spaces, each of a different colour and linked by narrow alleys, or are in exceptionally long terraces.

There is a comparatively small sub-centre at COLT HATCH by *William Crabtree & Wladyslaw Jarosz*, with SPRING HILLS housing (four-storey maisonettes, 1955–7, and a nine-storey slab, 1963–5) in the background. By the shops, 'Iceni' by *Anthony Hawken*, 1995. UPPER PARK, W of the hospital, by the HDC Design Group, 1955–7, was the first area of houses developed by the Corporation for sale.

At HARE STREET the specially noteworthy design is NORTHBROOKS, 1955–7 by *Powell & Moya*, second phase by *Cecil Handisyde*: box-like terraces (flat roofs were generally barred by the Corporation) in parallel series, with narrow footpath access, climb the hill to four-storey blocks set at right angles, a compact, geometric building mass superbly set in the landscape.

CANONS BROOK GOLF COURSE, Elizabeth Way. 1963–4 by *Henry Cotton*. The clubhouse incorporates a nine-bay brick

BARN of *c.* 1500, aisled along the W side, and a C17 brick
gateway. They belonged to the manor house Canons, rebuilt
very plainly in the early C19.

N of the neighbourhood, in Parndon Mill Lane by the River Stort,
are the remains of Little Parndon village, quite distinct from
the New Town developments:

ST MARY. Small, rebuilt by *J. Clarke*, 1867–8. E.E., of flint
rubble, very neatly laid. Nave, apsidal chancel, N vestry, S
porch, and timber-framed W belfry with brick-nogging. Complete contemporary FURNISHINGS, including benches with
brass candle standards, and STAINED GLASS in the apse. From
the old church, late C14 PILLAR PISCINA with octagonal shaft.
and MONUMENTS including Bridget Woodley †1756. Especially interesting is the headstone of her West Indian slave,
Hester Woodley †1767 (now inside). Expensively carved with
skull, hourglass, etc., and a lengthy inscription explaining
whose property she was. – Edward Parson †1780 and family.
Large tablet by *J. Forsyth*.

PARNDON MILL (Arts Centre), 200 yds NW. Four storeys, of
white brick, rebuilt in 1862 following a fire. Segment-headed
cast-iron windows, and two lucams. The mill house, S, is three
storeys and five bays with porch. Probably mid C16, refronted
and the third storey added in the C18, further remodelled
probably 1862.

BRAYS GROVE, LATTON BUSH, TYE GREEN

ST ANDREW, Netteswellbury. The parish church of Netteswell
but separated from the neighbourhood of that name (*see* above)
by Second Avenue. Now Harlow Study Centre. Nave and
chancel in one, C13, of flint rubble, and C15 belfry. Belfry with
four arched bell-openings in a row on each side and short
splay-foot spire. It stands on two posts with arched braces. The
chancel has lancets, and a DOUBLE PISCINA separated by a
Purbeck marble shaft. Other windows are Perp insertions. On
the S wall near the W end a replica of a brick panel (original
inside tower), which has the arms of Abbot Rose of Waltham
(i.e. 1497–1500). To what does this allude? Possibly the S porch,
though it was rebuilt as part of *Chancellor*'s thorough restoration of 1875. He also added the NW vestry. Conversion in
1988–9 by *Purcell Miller Tritton & Partners*, who inserted a free-
standing gallery on four metal columns toward the nave's W
end. Of the surviving fittings: FONT. Plain, octagonal, C13. –
STAINED GLASS. Various fragments, mainly C15, including
symbols of the Evangelists and figures of St Mary Cleophas
and St Mary Salome. E window by *Ada Currey*, 1891. –
MONUMENTS. Brasses to Thomas Laurence †1522 and wife
Alice (24-in. (61-cm.) figures, with children), and to John Bannister †1607, wife Elizabeth, with three sons and a daughter in
swaddling clothes (22-in. (56-cm.) figures). – William Martin
†1717. By *William Palmer*, *c.* 1729. Large marble monument

1. High Easter, St Mary the Virgin, from the south-east (p. 490)
2. Tollesbury Fleet (p. 1)

3. Finchingfield (p. 359)
4. Halstead, The Causeway, cottages by George Sherrin, 1882–3, and part of Townsford Mill, late C18 (p. 444)

5. Wivenhoe, from the south side of the River Colne (p. 852)
6. Colchester, West Stockwell Street (p. 286)

7. Bradwell-on-Sea, St Peter-on-the-Wall, *c.* 654 (p. 165)
8. Colchester, Holy Trinity, west doorway, Saxon (p. 264)
9. Hadstock, St Botolph, south transept with C11 stonework and C15 screen (p. 439)

10. Colchester, St Botolph's Priory ruins, dedicated 1177 (p. 271)
11. Hadleigh, St James the Less, Norman (p. 437)

12. Waltham Abbey, Holy Cross and St Lawrence, second quarter of the C12 (p. 808)

13. Great Leighs, St Mary, Norman round tower with spire by F. Chancellor, 1882 (p. 412)

14. High Ongar, St Mary, Norman south doorway (p. 492)

15. Castle Hedingham, St Nicholas, nave north arcade, late C12 (p. 195)

16. Little Dunmow, St Mary, north arcade c. 1200, east window and south side c. 1360 (p. 548)

13	15
14	16

17. Copford, St
    Michael and
    All Angels, apse,
    wall paintings
    c. 1125–30, partly
    overpainted by
    Daniel Bell, 1871–2
    (p. 306)
18. Great Canfield,
    St Mary the Virgin,
    wall painting,
    c. 1250 (p. 397)
19. Rivenhall, St Mary
    and All Saints,
    stained glass, Virgin
    and Child,
    c. 1170–80 (p. 644)
20. Rivenhall, St Mary
    and All Saints,
    stained glass, knight
    in armour, mid C13
    (p. 644)
21. Berden, St
    Nicholas, chancel
    south window,
    c. 1270 (p. 132)

| 17 | 19 20 |
| 18 | 21 |

22. Tilty, St Mary the Virgin, chancel, c. 1330 (p. 787)
23. Lawford, St Mary, south side of chancel, early C14 (p. 522)
24. Lawford, St Mary, detail of a chancel north window, early C14 (p. 523)
25. Great Leighs, St Mary, detail of recess in north wall, c. 1300 (p. 412)

26. Chelmsford,
    Cathedral, porch, C15
    (p. 204)
27. Saffron Walden,
    St Mary the Virgin,
    south aisle,
    c. 1450–1525 (p. 656)
28. Thaxted, St John the
    Baptist, nave arcades
    c. 1340, clerestory
    c. 1510 (p. 764)
29. St Osyth, St Peter and
    St Paul, nave south
    arcade, c. 1527 (p. 675)

| 26 | 28 |
| 27 | 29 |

30. Fryerning, St Mary, brick tower, early C16 (p. 373)
31. Margaretting, St Margaret, timber north porch, C15 (p. 591)
32. Pebmarsh, St John the Baptist, brick south porch, early C16 (p. 622)
33. Gestingthorpe, St Mary, double-hammerbeam roof attributed to Thomas Loveday, c. 1525 (p. 376)

34. Takeley, Holy Trinity, font cover, C15 (p. 758)
35. Stebbing, St Mary the Virgin, stone rood screen, mid C14, restored by Henry Woodyer, 1884 (p. 745)
36. Colchester, St John's Abbey, gatehouse, probably C15 (p. 272)
37. St Osyth's Priory, gatehouse, late C15 (p. 672)

| 34 | 36 |
| 35 | 37 |

38. Ingatestone, St Edmund and St Mary, monument to Sir William Petre
    †1572 and his wife Anne, effigies attributed to Cornelius Cure (p. 502)
39. Little Dunmow, St Mary, monument to Walter and Elizabeth Fitzwalter
    †1432 and 1464 (p. 549)
40. Hatfield Broad Oak, St Mary the Virgin, headstop, late C14 (p. 477)
41. Dedham, St Mary the Virgin, monument to Thomas Webbe †1506 (p. 321)

42. Saffron Walden, St Mary the Virgin, monument to Thomas Lord Audley, Lord Chancellor †1544, by Cornelius Harman (p. 657)
43. Felsted, Holy Cross, monument to Richard, 1st Lord Rich †1567 and his son Robert †1581, attributed to Epiphanius Evesham, *c.* 1620 (p. 354)
44. Stambourne, St Peter and St Thomas, Mackwilliam arms, early C16 (p. 731)

45. Ingatestone,
    St Edmund and
    St Mary, monument
    to Captain John
    Troughton †1621,
    attributed to
    Maximilian Colt
    (p. 502)
46. Hempstead, St
    Andrew, monument
    to William Harvey
    †1657 by Edward
    Marshall (p. 485)
47. Stansted
    Mountfitchet, St
    Mary, monument to
    Sir Thomas
    Myddelton, late
    Lord Mayor of
    London †1631
    (p. 738)

48. Colchester, Balkerne Gate, *c.* A.D. 50, and 'Jumbo' water tower by
   Charles Clegg, 1882–3 (pp. 259, 280)
49. Colchester Castle, late C11 (p. 272)
50. Castle Hedingham, the keep, *c.* 1142 (p. 193)

<table>
<tr><td>48</td><td rowspan="2">50</td></tr>
<tr><td>49</td></tr>
</table>

51. Cressing Temple, Wheat Barn, *c.* 1257–80 (p. 314)
52. Cressing Temple, Barley Barn, *c.* 1205–35 (p. 313)
53. Coggeshall, Paycocke's, early C16 (p. 252)
54. Thaxted, Guildhall, third quarter of the C15 (p. 766)
55. Newport, Crown House, late C16 or early C17, with pargetting and shell-hood of 1692 (p. 613)

51 | 54
52 | 55
53 |

56. Layer Marney Tower, *c.* 1520–5 (p. 527)
57. Faulkbourne Hall, east range remodelled after 1439, north-east tower after 1495 (p. 351)
58. Horham Hall, early C16 (p. 796)
59. Spains Hall, *c.* 1585 (p. 726)

60. Boreham, New
    Hall, north range,
    after 1573 (p. 157)
61. Audley End, north
    porch, *c.* 1605–14
    (p. 97)
62. Great Waltham,
    Langleys, library,
    c. 1620 (p. 426)
63. Audley End, Great
    Hall, screen,
    c. 1614 (p. 98)

60	62
61	63

64. Tilbury Fort, Water Gate, 1683 (p. 784)
65. West Hanningfield, Clovile Hall, wall paintings of 1615 (p. 821)
66. Colchester, Bourne Mill, 1591 (p. 299)
67. Theydon Mount, Hill Hall, wall paintings of c. 1570 (p. 776)

64 | 66
65 | 67

68. Ingrave, St Nicholas, 1734–6 (p. 508)
69. Lambourne, St Mary and All Saints, interior remodelled in the first
    quarter of the C18 (p. 516)
70. Debden, St Mary the Virgin and All Saints, chancel by John Carter and
    Richard Holland, 1792 (p. 318)

71. Rettendon, All Saints, monument to Edmund Humphrey †1727
   by Samuel Chandler (p. 640)
72. Brightlingsea, All Saints, monument to Nicolas Magens †1764
   by Nicholas Read (p. 180)
73. Stebbing, former Friends' Meeting House, 1674 (p. 746)
74. North End, Black Chapel, C14, interior refitted in the early C19 (p. 614)

71	73
72	74

75. Dedham, Shermans, refronted 1730–1 (p. 323)
76. Belchamp Walter, Belchamp Hall, 1720 (p. 130)
77. Chelmsford, Shire Hall, by John Johnson, 1789–91 (p. 208)
78. Terling Place, by John Johnson, 1770–7, south front remodelled by Thomas Hopper, 1818–21 (p. 761)
79. Bradwell-on-Sea, Bradwell Lodge, south front by John Johnson, 1781–6 (p. 166)

75	77
76	78
	79

80. Boreham House, Dining Room, 1726–33 (p. 155)
81. Gestingthorpe Hall, Drawing Room, *c.* 1740 (p. 377)
82. Alresford Hall, The Quarters, by Richard Woods, 1772 (p. 88)
83. Colchester, The Minories, summerhouse by James Deane, *c.* 1745 (p. 285)

| 80 | 82 |
| 81 | 83 |

84. Thorrington, tide mill, 1831 (p. 781)
85. Aythorpe Roding, post mill, 1779 (p. 108)
86. Aythorpe Roding, post mill, 1779 (p. 108)

84
85 | 86

87. Farnham, Hassobury, by P.C. Hardwick, 1866–70 (p. 349)
88. Hatfield Heath, Down Hall, by F.P. Cockerell, 1871–3 (p. 480)
89. Chigwell Hall, by Norman Shaw, 1875–6 (p. 229)
90. Great Totham, Great Ruffins, by A.H. Mackmurdo, 1904 onwards (p. 422)

<table>
<tr><td>87</td><td>89</td></tr>
<tr><td>88</td><td>90</td></tr>
</table>

91. Great Chesterford, primary school, by L.N. Cottingham, 1845–9 (p. 399)
92. Birch, Post Office Cottages, by F. Chancellor, *c.* 1860 (p. 138)

| 91 | 93 |
| 92 | 94 |

93. Little Easton, Church Row, 1895 (p. 551)
94. Frinton-on-Sea, Second Avenue, The Homestead, by C.F.A. Voysey, 1905–6 (p. 371)

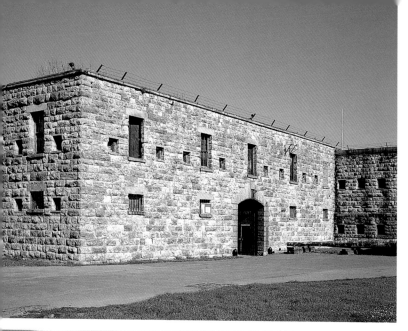

95. East Tilbury, Coalhouse Fort, 1861–74 (p. 339)
96. Chappel, viaduct, by Peter Bruff, 1847–9 (p. 199)
97. Colchester, Town Hall, by John Belcher, 1897–1902 (p. 276)

98. Halstead, Holy Trinity, by Scott & Moffatt, 1843–4 (p. 441)
99. Twinstead, St John the Evangelist, by Henry Woodyer, 1859–60 (p. 794)
100. Hatfield Heath, United Reformed Church, by T. Lewis Banks, 1875–6 (p. 480)
101. Colchester, Old Heath, Congregational Church, 1869 (p. 270)

98	100
99	101

102. Little Braxted, St Nicholas, interior decorated by Rev. Ernest Geldart, 1881–6 (p. 541)
103. Great Warley, St Mary the Virgin, by Charles Harrison Townsend, 1902–4, fittings and decoration by William Reynolds-Stephens (p. 430)
104. Waltham Abbey, Holy Cross and St Lawrence, part of east window by Edward Burne-Jones, 1861 (p. 810)
105. Radwinter, St Mary the Virgin, reredos, c. 1510, wings added by Temple Moore, c. 1888 (p. 632)

| 102 | 104 |
| 103 | 105 |

106. Frinton-on-Sea, Free Church, by W. Hayne, 1911 and 1935 (p. 370)

107. Clacton-on-Sea, St James, by Temple Moore, 1912–13 (p. 237)

108. Clacton-on-Sea, St Paul, by Roy Gould, 1965–6 (p. 240)

109. Clacton-on-Sea, St Paul, east window by Rosemary Rutherford, 1965–6 (p. 240)

| 106 | 108 |
| 107 | 109 |

110. Frinton-on-Sea, Cliff Way, The Round House, by Oliver Hill, 1934–5 (p. 372)
111. Silver End, Silver Street, housing by Frederick MacManus, 1927–8 (p. 688)
112. Burnham-on-Crouch, Royal Corinthian Yacht Club, by Joseph Emberton, 1930–1 (p. 189)
113. Canvey Island, Labworth Café, by Ove Arup, 1932–3 (p. 193)

110	112
111	113

114. Harlow, The Lawn, by Frederick Gibberd, 1950–1 (p. 456)
115. Ulting, The Studio, by Richard & Su Rogers, 1968–9 (p. 796)
116. University of Essex, by Kenneth Capon of the Architects Co-Partnership, 1962 onwards (p. 797)
117. Stansted Airport, by Foster Associates, 1986–91 (p. 735)

114 | 116
115 | 117

118. Dedham, Great House, by Raymond Erith, 1937–8 (p. 324)

119. Brentwood, Roman Catholic Cathedral, by Quinlan Terry, 1989–1
(p. 172)

120. Great Dunmow, Merks Hall, by Quinlan Terry, 1982–6 (p. 406)

121. South Woodham Ferrers, Queen Elizabeth II Square, by Holder &
Mathias Partnership and others, 1981 onwards (p. 725)

122. Purfleet, Queen Elizabeth II Bridge, by Sir William Halcrow & Partners and others, 1988–91 (p. 629)
123. Great Notley, Discovery Centre, by Penoyre & Prasad, 1999–2001 (p. 416)

with shield of arms in broken segmental pediment, and cherub's head.*

w of the churchyard, BARNS restored by *Purcell Miller Tritton & Partners*, 1988–9, with sympathetic additions, and sheltered housing by *W.J. Linford* of Harlow District Council. MONKS BARN, tree-ring dated 1439–*c.* 1470, is six bays, aisled, clad with vertical boards. For the rectory, *see* p. 458.

ST STEPHEN, Tawneys Road. By *Tooley & Foster*. Hall, 1957, with church at the N end, 1962, forming a T with short square tower over the entrance, with open copper flèche and cross. Brick, with concrete framing the windows and outlining the balustrade. Sanctuary against the N wall with altar, pulpit and lectern grouped on a dais beneath a canopy. Central FONT of Doulting stone.

LUTHERAN CHURCH OF THE REDEEMER, Tawneys Road. 1964–7 by *Maguire & Murray*. White-painted blockwork, low with a shallow dome, in a walled compound, with a bungalow.

FRIENDS' MEETING HOUSE, Church Leys. By *Norman Frith*, 1962. Brick, on a pebble-faced plinth. Flat roof, with clerestory to the meeting room.

The SE neighbourhood cluster has its centre at BUSH FAIR, its Z-shaped design similar to The Stow but with a more spacious feel. It too has pub, church (Lutheran, *see* above), health centre (KEATS HOUSE by *Booth & Ledeboer*, with Grecian Urn SCULPTURE by *Angela Godfrey*, 2000), and lively octagonal TYE GREEN LIBRARY by *HDC Design Group*. In the precinct, 'Six Cubes' by *Shelley Fausett*, 1972.[†]

The individual neighbourhoods follow the previous pattern. NE is BRAYS GROVE, including housing by *Ralph Tubbs* at GREAT BRAYS and HIGHFIELD, 1955–7, and at LITTLE BRAYS by *David du R. Aberdeen*, 1956–7. In the neighbourhood's SE corner, on Southern Way, BRAYS GROVE SECONDARY SCHOOL by *Yorke, Rosenberg & Mardall*, 1956, two to four storeys of stock brick with blue panels.

LATTON BUSH, s of Southern Way, has an interesting design of 412 houses (UPPER MEALINES and PEAR TREE MEAD, as well as shops at CLIFTON HATCH) grouped in small squares, by the *Architects Co-Partnership*, 1959–61. To the w of these, SPINNING WHEEL MEAD, LITTLE PYNCHONS and WHARLEY HOOK by *Booth & Poulson*, 1959–61, with cedar shingle cladding. On the southern boundary, RADBURN CLOSE, an experimental layout by *HDC Design Group*, 1960–2, on the principle of segregating vehicles from pedestrians with houses facing greens and service courts for garages behind.

The third neighbourhood, TYE GREEN, lies NW of Bush Fair, and includes housing by the *HDC Design Group*, HOOKFIELD, 1956–9, and WATERHOUSE MOOR, 1958–60, and in

---

* The superb monument attributed to *Sir Robert Taylor*, erected by William Martin's widow Mary to her brother Robert Crosse †1741 and nephew Thomas Crosse †1732, is now in the Victoria and Albert Museum.
† Originally commissioned for this site was Elisabeth Frink's 'Boar', 1957.

the NW of the neighbourhood WESTFIELD and BUSHEY CROFT, 1958–9, by *Sir John Burnet, Tait & Partners*.

PASSMORES, GREAT PARNDON, KINGSMOOR, STEWARDS

ST MARY, Great Parndon. *See* below.

ST JAMES with ST LUKE (C. of E., R.C., and Methodist), Perry Road. 1967–8 by *Gerard Goalen*. Small, square, of multi-coloured brick, with narrow corner windows and octagonal roof with lantern. Brick exposed inside, as well as reinforced concrete beams etc. Small baptistery against the liturgical s wall, with narrow side windows, and FONT with marble bowl on concrete base. Vestries etc. on W side with later hall to N. RECTORY, 1969–70, with monopitch roof and lean-to extension at the front for garage, entrance, and study.

CREMATORIUM, Parndon Wood. 1960–1 by *A. W. R. Webb*, Harlow U.D.C's engineer and surveyor, and *T. Hinchliffe*, chief assistant architect. Light brown brick, the main chapel and small circular remembrance chapel faced with reconstructed Portland stone slabs. Lawn-style CEMETERY in an undulating valley laid out by *Gibberd* and *Webb*.

The original neighbourhood centre of STAPLE TYE, although the last of the three to be built (*c.* 1967), has been redeveloped, but associated buildings remain: the Health Centre (LISTER HOUSE by *D. Dyer* of *Mauger, Gavin & Associates*), and GREAT PARNDON LIBRARY. Across Parnall Road from the Library, 'Echo' by *Antanas Brazdys* (stainless steel, 1970). As far as housing is concerned, this cluster marked a further stage in design development, with increased density and changes to housing standards as an outcome of the Parker Morris Report. These changes were seen as improvements at the time, but more refurbishment and redevelopment seems to have been necessary in this quarter than in any other. Nonetheless the genuine variety of housing achieved here still seems exciting, bringing relief after wearisome two-storey, stock brick development.

Such relief is quickly found in PASSMORES, E of the shopping centre, at BISHOPSFIELD and CHARTERS CROSS, won in competition in 1961 and executed with one of his competitors (as *Neylan & Ungless*), 1963–6. Both are made up of courtyard houses, those at Bishopsfield on a hillside radiating from a piazza at the top which has flats in a semicircle around it. The great achievement here is the exploitation of the sloping site, so houses have both a view and privacy. Cars were banished to parking areas beneath the housing, so that roads could be dispensed with in favour of alleyways. It was quickly nicknamed 'the Casbah', and on a sunny day the narrow alleyways ascending the hill between the houses do indeed have an eastern Mediterranean feel. In one of the little squares that punctuate the alleys, 'City' by *Gerda Rubinstein* (bronze, 1970), unfortunately damaged.

To the N, off Tendring Road, OLD ORCHARD by *Clifford Culpin*, 1962–4, won in a competition promoted by *Ideal Home* and the RIBA. Two groups in culs-de-sac, some arranged in staggered courts, in distinctive white brick with white weatherboarding. Culpin also designed the adjacent COPPICE HATCH. On Tendring Road's N side WILLOWFIELD by *R.T. Kennedy* for the *HDC Design Group*, 1962–4. Two-storey terraces with little projecting weatherboarded rooms on slender columns, and at the corners of the street small squares of two-storey houses with a storey of flats above. N of this in open space, PASSMORES. House recorded in 1623, the brick front added 1727. Pedimented doorcase and to the l. of it a canted bay. Weatherboarded outbuildings. Formerly Harlow Museum; now empty.

GREAT PARNDON neighbourhood, W, includes some good housing by *James Cubitt & Partners* at HOLLYFIELD, 1963–5, with two carved standing stones by *Menashe Kadishman*, 1965. Cubitt's terraces mainly of the usual stock brick but with sections of red brick that bear no relation to the breaks between the individual houses. Hollyfield leads into SHAWBRIDGE by *Eric Lyons & Partners*, 1962–4, quite startling for its use of black brick. The houses are particularly uncompromising cubes, with windows small and far apart, but the overall effect very smart.

KINGSMOOR neighbourhood lies S of Southern Way, SW of Staple Tye with BROCKLES MEAD by *Leonard Manasseh & Partners*, 1965–8, providing an interesting variety of dwellings within a compact rectangular layout: courts of houses with monopitch roofs, terraces, small three-storey blocks of flats, and at the highest point a long three-storey quadrant of flats over garages. To the S, MOORFIELD by *Clifford Culpin & Partners*, 1966–9, flats top-heavy with overhanging, tile-hung top storeys and orange panels on the lower floors, but behind them terraces of housing opening on to secluded courtyards, garages quite separate. Below the flats SHERARDS HATCH by *G.T. Goalen*, shops and a pub, completed 1969. On the W side of Paringdon Road, THE MAPLES, 1966–8, 173 houses by the *Canadian Central Mortgage & Housing Group* to advertise Canadian construction methods: timber-framed, clad in brick and timber.

The neighbourhood took its name from KINGSMOOR HOUSE (Family Centre) on the N side of Paringdon Road. Stuccoed, much altered and extended, and difficult to unpick although the core seems to be C18. *T.G. Hart* of Epping worked on the house in the late C19 or early C20. Three-bay centre on the E front with a C20 Neoclassical porch, and projecting wings. Five-bay S front with central single-storey canted bay with ogee roof, and on the W front two two-storey bows added in the 1930s with an Ionic loggia between.

The fourth neighbourhood, STEWARDS, SE of Staple Tye, was dominated by the troubled scheme of system-built flats and bungalows of CLARKHILL, FERNHILL, and WOODHILL by *Associated Architects & Consultants* (senior partners, *John Bickerdike* and *Bill Allen*), 1966–7, using storey-height concrete panels. Largely redeveloped 1996–9 by *AD Architects* who also refurbished BERECROFT, in the SW corner of the neighbourhood, another experimental design (with concrete walls and asbestos panels) by the *National Building Agency*, 1968–72. More successful was LONG BANKS, by *Patricia Thorman* and *Geoffrey Brimilcombe* of *HDC Design Group*, 1965–7, exceptionally compact and dense (twenty-three dwellings per acre), based on culs-de-sac branching off a single spine road. – PETERSWOOD INFANT SCHOOL and PARINGDON JUNIOR SCHOOL, Paringdon Road, by *The Austin-Smith, Salmon, Lord Partnership*, 1963–6.

Separated from the rest of Great Parndon by Katherine's Way, a group of older buildings of the village from which that neighbourhood took its name.

ST MARY, Peldon Road. Flint rubble and brick. Mainly C15, including the unbuttressed W tower. Nave and chancel in one, and N vestry. S transept probably C17, N transept 1913. N porch by *C.H. Lindsey-Smith*, 1975–6. Restoration (mainly internal) by *J. Clarke*, 1855–6. – FONT. Perp, octagonal, with traceried stem and a bowl decorated by quatrefoils carrying roses. Carved wooden cover by *Bertram Bishop*, c. 1911. – Good late C19 REREDOS with tiles, mosaic, and coloured glass. – BENCHES. A few with poppyheads, C15 or early C16. – STAINED GLASS. Chancel S (1901) and N (1911). Unusual and attractive pieces by *T. F. Curtis, Ward & Hughes* to Queen Victoria and King Edward VII, with portraits of both. N transept by *Powell & Sons*, 1923. Nave S by *June Armstrong*, 1978, for Queen Elizabeth's Jubilee. – MONUMENTS. Brass to Rowland Rampston †1598. 19-in. (49-cm.) figure. – Robert Milward †1763. Marble, with fluted pilasters and open pediment, and cherub's head.

The CHURCH HALL, 200 yds NE, was built as a village club by *J. Clarke*, 1856. 'Attached will be a smoking-shed, and every inducement to attract the labourer from the beer-shop' (*The Builder*). School from 1860 with teacher's house (in rat-trap bond) added 1861; further additions 1882 and 1897.

KATHERINES, E of the church. The main part C17, remodelled in the C18. The E end is lower and earlier, and the underside of the floorboards of the first floor are painted with a tile motif based on large central flowers, late C16 or early C17.

INDUSTRIAL AREAS: TEMPLE FIELDS AND PINNACLES

TEMPLE FIELDS was the first of the two industrial areas to be developed, and many of the original buildings, to standard designs by *HDC Design Group*, can be seen, e.g. along Edinburgh Way, Central Road, and River Way: stock brick offices fronting production areas. W of Temple Fields, by Harlow Town Station, was *Gibberd*'s building for the publishers Longman Green, 1966–9, replaced (for Addison Wesley Longman, now Pearson) by *Conran Roche* (later *CD Partnership*), 1992–5. Five-and-a-half storeys, with three atria that act as stacks to provide natural ventilation. Concrete, exposed internally, with external limestone cladding and expanses of glass.

HARLOW TOWN STATION was an overdue addition to the developing New Town in 1959–60; by *Paul Hamilton*, with *John Bicknell* and *Ian Fraser*, of the *British Railways Eastern Region Architect's Department*. Low, crisp and entirely ungimmicky. Double-height booking hall linked to a bridge across the lines. Light grey brick with plywood fascias. The principal vertical accents are three concrete lift towers, the strong horizontals provided by flat roofs cantilevered in steps over the booking hall and stairs. By the same architects, good SIGNAL BOX (disused) at Harlow Mill, 1959. Brick, with fibreglass 'sunbreaker' roof over the glass box.

Development of PINNACLES, on the western edge of the New Town, began in 1958, and the Pitney Bowes building in Elizabeth Way became one of the symbols of the town's success: 1962–3 by *HDC Design Group* with *Fuller, Hall & Foulsham*. Four storeys of offices, mainly aluminium and glass curtain walling with stock brick end walls, and factory behind. Refitted and partially reclad by *DGI International, c.* 1994–5.

S of Fourth Avenue, NEW FRONTIERS SCIENCE PARK, 1994–7 by *The Hillier Group* with *Amec Design & Management*. Two large laboratory buildings, linked to form an H, with bluegreen cladding. Internal artwork includes a stained and sculpted glass screen by *Graham Jones*. The complex continues on the S side of Third Avenue, incorporating former divisional headquarters of BP by *Wilson, Mason & Partners*, 1967.

KATHERINES AND SUMNERS

Town expansion (taking the target population to 90,000) was approved in 1972–4 and two new neighbourhoods were formed on the town's W side. They consist mostly of housing by the HDC, 1973–80, but include 116 dwellings at PEACOCKS, Katherines, by *H. T. Cadbury-Brown & Partners*, 1976–9.

CHURCH LANGLEY

On the E of the town, NE of Potter Street. The main post-Corporation development of 3,500 homes built 1992–2006. Standard developers' fare, with no individual identity, demonstrating better than anything else how important Gibberd's overall vision and guiding hand was for the rest of the town. Tellingly, the neighbourhood centre is dominated by TESCO by *Saunders Partnership, c.* 1994, extended 2002, in supermarket-vernacular style with clock turret and little broach spire. The Harlow tradition has been maintained with a bronze SCULPTURE by *John Mills*, 1992. Interesting PRIMARY SCHOOL by the *County Architect's Dept*, 1993, like a terrace of houses with monopitch roofs.

To the N of Church Langley, however, something altogether more exciting is happening at NEWHALL, where the

landowners have retained some control over what is being
built. The master plan by *Roger Evans Associates* received
approval in 1998, with the first phase of development by
Barratt Homes with *Roger Evans*. *Proctor Matthews Architects*
and Copthorn Homes were appointed in 2001 for the next
phase of eighty-two dwellings, on the N side of THE CHASE.
The development is sophisticated, attractive, and above all
varied in terms of building heights, layout, and materials,
which include gabions and thatch. The third phase of seventy-
four dwellings by *PCKO* and *CALA*, under construction in
2005, is equally varied, although more gimmicky; the chief
landmark is a six-storey copper-clad tower shaped like a sail-
less post mill. Planning permission granted in 2005 for a four-
storey timber-clad residential and commercial building by
ORMS, with further proposed developments by *ECD Architects*
and *Richard Murphy Architects*.

OLD HARLOW

ST MARY AND ST HUGH, Churchgate Street. The medieval
parish church, but the only indication is one Norman window
in the nave N wall, revealed during *Woodyer*'s complete restoration of 1872–3. Nave, transepts (S transept restored by *William
White*, 1857–8) and chancel of flint rubble with stone dressings, and crossing tower with tall shingled broach spire. Crossing towers are unusual in Essex, and this may have been part
of the original C12 church, or added with the transepts in the
C13. Largely destroyed by fire in 1708, it was replaced by a W
tower, which Woodyer removed. The chancel and original N
vestry were added in the late C14; between N transept and
vestry Woodyer's organ chamber. Timber S porch and lychgate
1883, N (choir) vestry by *Charles S. Adye*, 1894, and N extension by *Ron Williams* and *B. Gooding*, 1988. Chancel ceiling decorated by *Harland & Fisher*. – FURNISHINGS 1872–3.
REREDOS. Crucifixion, flanked by high reliefs of the Entry into
Jerusalem and the Way of the Cross. Caen stone, carved by
T. Nicholls. – FONT. Octagonal, with panelled sides, and outstanding, tall oak and wrought-iron COVER. – BENCHES. In
nave, the ends nicely shaped with flowing tendrils. – STAINED
GLASS. In the N vestry, a small C14 figure of the Virgin seated,
c. 12 in. (30 cm.) long. Salvaged from the 1708 fire, as were fragments of C14–C17 glass that make up the large N transept
window: mainly heraldic but including scenes from the life of
Solomon dated 1563. Heads of King Charles I and Queen
Anne probably postdate 1708. Of this date also the S transept
E window. – Ten windows by *Hardman*, 1857–93, including in
the N wall of the nave one to J.W. Perry Watlington* †1882,
who funded much of Woodyer's restoration; to its E another to
him by *Powell & Sons*, designed by *George Parlby*. – BRASSES.

---

* Of Moor Hall, Matching (q.v.).

St Mary and St Hugh, Harlow.
Brass to W. Newman †1602

An uncommonly large number collected in the N transept. Especially noteworthy: Knight and Lady *c.* 1430 (his figure 19 in. (48 cm.)); civilian, probably Robert Druncaster †1490, and wife (17½ in. (45 cm.)); Thomas Aylmer †1518 and wife (10 in. (25 cm.), with children); William Newman †1602, plate with standing figure and figure of Death either side of inscription: VERITAS MIHI DULCIOR VITA; Richard Bugges †1636 and two wives (39 in. (99 cm.)). – MONUMENTS. Alexander Stafford †1652 and wife. Large kneeling figures facing each other, of a type rather out of date in 1650. C19 surround. – John Wright †1659, Stafford's executor. Wooden tablet with painted inscription and small figures of Faith, Hope, and Charity on top. – Peter Gunning, bishop of Chichester and Ely †1684. Inscription by *I.T.* on painted board with flanking terminal figures. – Edward Taylor †1695. Wooden tablet with painted inscription. – Anthony Parkin †1827. Gothic stone tablet by *C.H. Smith*. – J.P. Watlington †1862. Infant on a cushion by *W. Theed*, on a window ledge in the S transept, with contemporary stained glass (possibly by *Lavers & Barraud*).

PARISH ROOM (Church Office) by *Woodyer*, 1872, converted by *Mike Allen*, 1992. Small, single-storey, but with four tall straight gables, the walls alternately banded in red brick and knapped flint.

Former ST JOHN THE BAPTIST, High Street. Now Arts and Recreation Centre. 1839–40 by *Thomas Smith*. Yellow brick, in the lancet style. No aisles. Battlemented W tower, shallow chancel. Redundant, 1979; converted 1986 by *E. William Palmer & Partners*, who added a 'N aisle'. S of the churchyard, ST JOHN'S HOUSE, former school etc., with heraldic STAINED GLASS by *Roy E. Youngs*, 1970. – SCULPTURE. E of entrance, 'Help' by *F. E. McWilliam*, 1977 (bronze).

BAPTIST CHURCH, Fore Street. 1865, by *R. Moffat Smith* of Manchester. Stock brick (of finest quality on the front) with stone dressings. Impressive three-bay front, the higher centre with pediment (quatrefoil window in the tympanum), balustrades to either side; heavy, square porch, windows with Venetian Gothic tracery, rusticated pilasters, ball finials, etc. Unaltered interior with gallery on three sides. It cost about £2,000. The METHODIST CHURCH by *Charles Bell*, 1886, at High Street's far end (brick, E.E.) cost £620.

FAWBERT AND BARNARD'S PRIMARY SCHOOL, London Road. 1836, 'from the very elegant and chaste designs of *Robert Abraham*' (*Architectural Magazine*). Symmetrical, the two-storey master's house with Tuscan porch flanked by single-storey schoolrooms with round-headed windows. Projecting two-bay schoolrooms, in similar style, added 1892 and 1897. Technical Instruction block of 1912, its ground-floor windows set in high arched recesses, the upper floor with continuous glazing below the eaves.

PERAMBULATION. Gibberd did not wish Old Harlow to remain a distinct village, but it is possible to be quite unaware of the New Town, particularly in CHURCHGATE STREET, dominated by the spire of St Mary and St Hugh. S of the lychgate, the STAFFORD ALMSHOUSES with exposed timbers, dated 1630, and then the QUEEN'S HEAD, early C16 with long-wall jettied front. Then the street curves gently down past C18 and C19 cottages to the CHURCHGATE HOTEL. Formerly The Chantry, early C17. Three-storey front with three gables, the central one on a projecting porch, the outer ones jettied over two-storey canted bays. Sadly altered, including additions by *D. W. Harris*, c. 1972.

To the N of the lychgate, a group of four ALMSHOUSES, 1867, stock brick with red brick dressings, windows in arches with stone columns, and tile-hanging in the gables. Then GODSAFE, mid C16 with close-studded timbers and jettied, restored and enlarged by *Woodyer* for an infant school and teacher's house, 1874–5. Its neighbour is the former CHURCHGATE SCHOOL by *G. E. Pritchett*, 1850, for J.W. Perry Watlington. A grand ragstone affair set back from the street. T-plan, originally one very tall storey. E front with skinny windows, two hefty chimneystacks and gabled porch. Perky roof lantern. Separate teacher's house on the street. Opposite, No. 15, c. 1600, has its timbers exposed on the side wall, but a plastered C18 front with two two-storey canted bays. Finally, No. 1 is C16 but with C17 and later alterations, including coved eaves, a large porch with fluted pilasters, and Venetian window.

Now SHEERING ROAD is reached. ¼ m. E, HIGH HOUSE, dated 1876 on rainwater heads of the same design as *Woodyer*'s Godsafe and the church. Originally a pair of C16 cottages, apparently subjected to a very thorough restoration. Delightful hipped roof with gablets, dormer, and central chimneystack. Back W, almost opposite Churchgate Street, MILLHURST. Stately early C19 plastered front to a C18 house of three storeys and five bays of windows with floating cornices. Corinthian porch with tripartite sash above and Diocletian window at the top. A little further W, Nos. 13–15, tiny former almshouses (originally four), 1716, provided in the will of Francis Reeve of Huberts (i.e. Hubbard's) Hall for 'fower poore widdowes'.

Old Harlow is abruptly divided in two by Gilden Way, created for the New Town, but w of this is MULBERRY GREEN. Visually the best spot of Old Harlow, marred only by the ruinous MULBERRY GREEN HOUSE, gutted by fire in 2000. Its fine late C18 front has two-storey bows flanking a first-floor Venetian window above a delicate doorcase with open pediment, unconventional Corinthian capitals, and elaborate fanlight. Lower additions l. and r. At right angles, facing w, the curious, two-storey HILL HOUSE, Georgian in its windows, but with square three-storey stair-towers at the ends suggesting a C16 date for the concealed timber frame. Lower down the Green, the GREEN MAN, C17 with a Venetian window over the carriageway.

At Mulberry Green's w end, a double bend leads into High Street; on the first bend, a small stock brick FIRE STATION, built by J.W. Perry Watlington in 1870 and still in use. In the HIGH STREET, two smart houses: MARIGOLDS, late C18 gault brick of five bays and two storeys to which were added in the C19 a wide canted bay and, at the w end, a pedimented entrance; and THE WAYRE, late C18 or early C19 stock brick, five bays with ground-floor windows set in arches and a Tuscan doorcase with open pediment. Opposite, a late C18 thatched cottage and behind it, on the corner of St John's Avenue and Bury Road, chapel-like VICTORIA HALL, 1887–8.

After The Wayre, High Street was pedestrianized, comprehensively restored and infilled by *Frederick Gibberd & Partners* (partner-in-charge, *John Graham*), 1963–70. Marking the entrance are two residential 'pavilions', with upper floors projecting over the pavement supported on square columns. Among the older buildings, No. 34, C17 with two canted bays, and No. 2, at the w end, a nine-bay Georgian plastered front to an older timber-framed house. Good doorcase with open pediment on thin pilasters. Adamesque decoration in the tympanum. Opposite No. 34, 'Kore', bronze figure by *Betty Rea*, 1963.

High Street's redevelopment also encompassed Fore Street, w of London Road/Station Road, and Market Street. FORE STREET is narrow at first, with THE GABLES on the s corner and the former GEORGE HOTEL on the n: the one C15 with two jettied cross-wings and higher hall range, and exposed timbers on the e cross-wing, the other *c.* 1800, three storeys of plastered and painted brick with fronts of two and three bays. Just beyond The George, the MARQUIS OF GRANBY, its rear (to Market Street) clearly a Late Medieval timber-framed building, mostly weatherboarded. Then there is a widening with Fore Street on the s and MARKET STREET on the n, where Gibberd removed an island block that encroached upon the medieval market place. Both street frontages are pleasantly varied in scale and date. In the middle of Market Street THE CROWN, Late Medieval with cross-wing to the l. and to the r.

a three-storey wing, originally a separate house, that has on the ground floor floral wall paintings of *c.* 1740 imitating wallpaper. Set back on the N and S sides behind the street frontage are the Baptist Church and St John (*see* above). Between Market Street and St John, former MALTINGS, three-storey stock brick of *c.* 1900 with pyramidal slate-roofed kiln at the W end, converted by *Gibberd & Partners* as part of a campus for the Memorial University of Newfoundland, 1968–70.

S of the crossroads, along LONDON ROAD, Fawbert and Barnard's Primary School (*see* above), then the early C19 EAST LODGE to Mark Hall (*see* p. 456). Tetrastyle Doric portico with slender columns. C20 additions. E off London Road CHIP-PINGFIELD, the first substantial development by the *HDC Design Group*, 1950–1, of 120 houses in terraces.* Already the 'house style' was set: stock brick with pantiles, picture windows, simple flat porches and side doors as well as front doors.

FELTIMORES, ½ m. SE of St Mary. Gault brick with stone dress-ings, of the third quarter of the C19, with decorative barge-boards and octagonal chimneys, and various additions. MODEL FARM BUILDINGS, E, of similar date, with a prominent two-storey stock brick range. Built for J.W. Perry Watlington of Moor Hall (*see* p. 595).

HARLOWBURY, Old Road, ½ m. NNW. Manor house, with stock brick of *c.* 1860 encasing the house built by the Abbot of Bury St Edmunds from timbers felled in 1220–5. The well-preserved two-bay hall was originally aisled, its E end replaced by a four-bay cross-wing in the late C14. To this a long-jettied wing was added in the C15. There is evidence that the hall continued to the W. SW, a detached CHAPEL, late C12, of flint rubble. Orig-inal windows survive on three sides and N doorway (columns with waterleaf capitals). Crown-post roof of *c.* 1300. Floor inserted in the mid C16 and an upper platform in the C19, for use as a granary. Restored 1982–6 by *Joyce Jones*, who retained part of the inserted floor.

HILLINGDON HOUSE (St Nicholas School), Hobbs Cross Road. Large Edwardian Baroque house of 1908. Entrance front with two open pedimented gables and curved portico between with two paired Tuscan columns. Similar portico on the return, with a Venetian window above, and a long, rather featureless garden front. A more homely Arts and Crafts STABLE, with archway and clock turret, and entrance lodge.

HUBBARD'S HALL, 1,100 yds S. Large early C15 hall, of similar size to Harlowbury, of which it was a dependent manor. N cross-wing of *c.* 1600, S cross-wing a little later. Faced in brick in the C17 or C18, with straight gables on the cross-wings, and a second cross-wing (weatherboarded) added S. Wings at either

---

*Design published in 1948 under the name of the then Chief Architect, *Noel Tweddell*.

end, and new entrance on the N side, by *Clough Williams-Ellis*, 1934. His parts, and the whole of the E front, roughcast.

ROMANO-BRITISH TEMPLE. The site lies on a small hill 250 yds w of Harlow Mill railway station. The temple, excavated in 1927, consisted of a square shrine with sides measuring 18 ft 9 in. (5.8 metres) internally, standing within an enclosure 48 ft 6 in. (15 metres) square (marked out with paving). Access to the shrine was from the SE. The walls had been plastered internally and perhaps externally as well. It dates from *c.* A.D. 80, but coins dating from *c.* 50 B.C. to A.D. 40 show that this had previously been an Iron Age sanctuary. Additions were made *c.* A.D. 200. It was surrounded by an earthwork which probably marked the boundary of the temple precincts. At the NW end of the hill was a hollow 180 ft (55 metres) in diameter which might have marked the site of a THEATRE, which is frequently associated with such temples.

POTTER STREET

A former hamlet, S of Old Harlow, on the old London Road.

ST MARY MAGDALENE, Church Road. Perp, faced with flint rubble. Originally by *Thomas Smith*, 1833–4, but replaced by *Ewan Christian* in three phases from E to W in 1888, 1892–3 and 1894–5, finishing with the battlemented tower and spire, carved with heads of W.E. Gladstone and the vicar, Henry Ewell. – STAINED GLASS. E window by *Jones & Willis*, probably 1888. The crude pictorial chancel S window must have been reused from the original building. W window by *H. Wilkinson*, 1942. – Former PARSONAGE (Magdalene House, S side of Harlow Common). Also by *Smith*, enlarged by *George Perry*, 1864. Stock brick, with a plain three-bay front with gabled cross-wing to the r.

BAPTIST CHURCH. 1756. The usual plain little brick rectangle, but adorned by a doorway quite exceptionally fine. Scrolly open pediment on brackets, the scrolls expressed in lush foliage. Gallery on Tuscan columns. Enlarged in the early C19 and in 1970.

PRENTICE PLACE (shopping centre) by the HDC, 1954–5, with large areas of housing, including flats and maisonettes, by *Hening & Chitty*, 1952–5.

GIBBERD GARDEN
Marsh Lane

In 1956 *Gibberd* purchased 'a semi-bungalow of nondescript design' in the Green Belt E of Old Harlow with the intention of creating a landscaped garden. The house, built in 1907, was remodelled over the years, including the addition of full-height living room at the W end, but was always secondary to the garden. This occupies a five-acre site sloping NE down to Pincey Brook, and incorporates formal vistas, principally the Lime Walk, and a wild garden along the river, begun in 1962.

Below the house a two-storey concrete GAZEBO built by a previous owner, its thatched roof replaced by Gibberd with a concrete pyramid. By the river a primitive rendered PUMP HOUSE by Gibberd, who also designed the moated CASTLE, in the garden's NE corner, a mound contained by terraces of elm logs. In the NW corner is a TEMPLE using pieces salvaged from Coutts' Bank in the Strand, London, which Gibberd remodelled in 1973: two giant Corinthian columns and four swagged urns by *J. Macvicar Anderson*, 1903. Other architectural fragments include a FONT and FINIAL CROSS from St John the Baptist, Old Harlow, a font from a church in Leamington Spa, and a capital from University College, Oxford, used as a planter. After his second marriage in 1972, Gibberd embellished the garden with more than eighty pieces of mainly contemporary sculpture, including work by *Antanas Brazdys*, *Christopher Dean*, and *Gerda Rubinstein*. Rubinstein's works include the concrete tondo of Gibberd at his desk and Patricia, Lady Gibberd, weeding. Two murals of enamel on steel, by *Stefan Knapp*, were trials for Gibberd's No. 3 Passenger Building at Heathrow Airport.

HARWICH

Harwich's significance as a port, positioned on the tip of a peninsula at the mouth of the rivers Orwell and Stour, was confirmed by its status as a free borough from 1318, with further charters culminating in that of 1604. Its parliamentary representatives included Samuel Pepys and Sir Anthony Deane, both Admiralty officials, reflecting the importance of the naval dockyard in the C17 and C18. Harwich developed as a passenger port for the Continent in the C19, stimulated by the arrival of the railway in 1854, and aided by the construction of a large breakwater (begun 1846) to prevent the harbour silting up. Much of Harwich's business was lost to Parkeston after 1883, and later C19 growth centred on Dovercourt (q.v.). The town still feels slightly run-down, but ameliorated since the 1960s by some good restoration of buildings by the County and Borough Councils, and largely sympathetic infilling.

ST NICHOLAS. Rebuilt 1820–2 by *M. G. Thompson* of Dedham. Gothic of the lean Commissioners' type. Suffolk white brick with stone dressings, *Coade* stone pinnacles, and cast-iron window frames. Tall W tower with octagonal spire behind battlements, full-height castellated porches to l. and r. High, stately interior, nave and aisles with arcades of very thin cast-iron piers and galleries on three sides, the W gallery occupied by a fine contemporary ORGAN by *Flight & Robson*. High up to either side of the pipes another tier of galleries with latticed iron fronts. Sham but elegant groined vault, continued into the chancel, which is as high as the nave but polygonal and quite shallow. It has only one tier of large windows, against two in

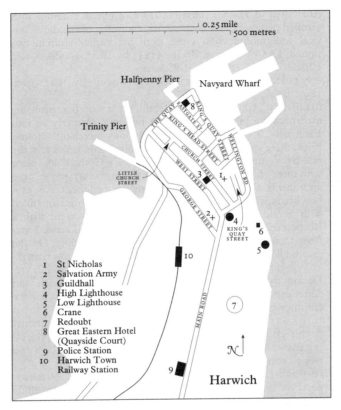

1 St Nicholas
2 Salvation Army
3 Guildhall
4 High Lighthouse
5 Low Lighthouse
6 Crane
7 Redoubt
8 Great Eastern Hotel
   (Quayside Court)
9 Police Station
10 Harwich Town
   Railway Station

Harwich

the aisles. – Three FONTS, the oldest early C13, octagonal, of Purbeck marble. Of the usual type with two shallow blank arches to each side. Movable *Coade* stone font, 1821, its pedestal similar to the arcade columns' heads round the rim of the bowl. The third given in 1873. – PEWS. In nave and galleries, all contemporary and largely intact, including mayor's pew in the nave set at right angles. – PAINTING. Moses giving the Law, the figure of Aaron apparently copied from Poussin's 'Adoration of the Golden Calf'. Altarpiece supplied for £40 in 1700 by *William Paris*, who may have done the lettering of the Commandments. – Large collection of C17 Delft TILES from a house in West Street. – STAINED GLASS. In the chancel, contemporary heraldic glass with decorative borders. – Three-light N aisle windows by *Henry Holiday*, 1922, and *William Morris & Co.*, *c.* 1930; S aisle, by *G.B. Cooper-Abbs* of *J. Wippell & Co.*, 1934, and *Goddard & Gibbs*, 1955. – MONUMENTS. Sir William Clarke †1666.

Attributed to *Thomas Burman* (GF). Corinthian columns with scrolled pediment and bust. – A large number of standard classical wall monuments, some from the earlier church, two signed: Lt Col Cyprian Bridge †1843 by *W.M. Gardener*, and Charles Bridge †1843 by *R.W. Sievier*.

SALVATION ARMY CITADEL, George Street. By *W.G. Scott*, 1892. Brick, like a toy fort.

GUILDHALL, Church Street. Rebuilt in 1769, but probably incorporating fabric of a late C17 building, formerly an inn. Externally, it is entirely like an ambitious merchant's house: brick, three storeys, with full-height canted bays l. and r. of the one-bay centre. This has to one's surprise a Gothick doorpiece with three-shafted supports (with shaft-rings) carrying an ogee arch inside a broken Georgian triangular pediment. Above it two blank windows, the first with segmental pediment (filled with heraldic STAINED GLASS in 1891), the second with a Rococo triple-curved pediment framing the royal arms. First-floor Council Chamber with C18 and C19 panelling. On the ground floor is a former cell, its walls lined with planks remarkably graffitied with warships, fishing boats, a windmill, etc. Dating from the 1770s, in part the work of French and American prisoners-of-war. Crude WALL PAINTING on the chimney-breast.

POLICE STATION, Main Road. 1913–15 by *F. Whitmore*, County Architect. Dark red brick and terracotta. Two slightly projecting bays with straight pediments, four bays between them and two to either side.

HIGH and LOW LIGHTHOUSES. 1817–18 by *D. A. Alexander*, surveyor to Trinity House, supervised by *J. Rennie*, consulting engineer. Leading lights, which when aligned guided ships into the harbour. High Lighthouse, s end of West Street, about 90 ft (28 metres), nine-sided, stock brick with stone dressings. Low Lighthouse by the beach, about 45 ft (14 metres), ten-sided, of the same materials but painted white, and with a little canopy added for shelter on the sea side. Both have pretty, tent-like roofs. After the channels shifted, they were superseded by Dovercourt's lighthouses (*see* p. 330).

THE REDOUBT. 1807–9, part of the chain of defences that included the Martello Towers, but one of only four redoubts, the others (at Dungeness, Hythe, and Eastbourne) all on the s coast. They were armed with ten guns. Circular tower, 200 ft (62 metres) in diameter, of brick with granite and limestone embrasures etc., within a 20-ft (6-metre) deep dry moat. Remodelled 1861–3.

PERAMBULATION

Harwich is a pleasant place to walk round. It has four main streets, more or less parallel, running N–S – a planned medieval town – with the quay at the top. The town wall lay across the s end, a fragment of which can be seen in the wall along the churchyard's s side. WEST STREET is broader and straighter

than the others and mainly Georgian, e.g. on the NE side
BRIDEWELL HOUSE (formerly the House of Correction), red
brick with gault brick quoins, and further up on the other side
Nos. 31–32, timber-framed and plastered, and No. 39, timber-
framed with rendered brick front and pedimented doorcase
with Corinthian capitals and masks. By contrast Nos. 35–36,
mid-C19 red and black brick with a stone cornice on a corbel
table with triangular arches and grotesque heads. Opposite, a
large development of local authority housing by *Fitzroy Robinson*, 1973, running right through (along Currents Lane) to
Church Street. Brick ground floor, two further storeys with
tile-hanging and white weatherboarded bays. It connects with
MAYFLOWER HOUSE, Church Street, also for Harwich
Borough Council, by *Bryan Thomas*, 1989, which has a slender
North-German-looking tower with crowstepped gables.

CHURCH STREET, which twists very slightly, is altogether varied,
starting at the S end with No. 5 (Foresters), mid C16 with
jettied front. N of the church, the Guildhall (*see* above) and the
THREE CUPS face each other, the latter early C16 L-plan, faced
in Georgian brick and the seven-bay street front rendered.
Staircase of *c.* 1700 with twisted balusters. Higher up, on the
SW side, Nos. 18–18A with two gables, dated 1698 in the plaster,
and No. 57, nearly opposite, the surviving gable (of three) of
a C16 house. The best houses are towards the top: Nos. 34–35
(SW side) are mid to late C16, timber-framed with four-bay
Georgian brick front, Nos. 42–42A (opposite) five-bay Georgian brick. Both have fine doorcases, No. 42 with Ionic
pilasters, fretwork frieze, and pediment. Between West Street
and Church Street, LITTLE CHURCH STREET has two early
C19 three-storey cottages, timber-framed and weatherboarded
with slate roofs.

KING'S HEAD STREET runs out of the NE corner of the churchyard, and in that corner is the OLD VICARAGE, black-banded
brick, by *George Gard Pye*, 1873. The more interesting houses,
again, are further up: No. 13, C17 with two jettied upper
storeys; No. 14, Old Swan House, early C17 with earlier cross-
wings. The l. cross-wing is late C15 and has inside a contemporary wall painting showing a seated man with horn and taper
and text; the r. cross-wing probably mid C16. Carved jetty bressumer. Opposite, former METHODIST CHAPEL, 1821, now a
workshop. Square, with pyramidal pantiled roof, and plastered
front with two tall pointed recesses. Back on the SW side, No.
16, five-bay Georgian brick with pedimented doorcase, and
near the top No. 21, mid C16 with jettied first floor and two
gables, reputedly the home of Christopher Jones, master of the
Mayflower. In MARKET STREET, between King's Head Street
and Church Street, a good C19 shopfront with tile picture by
Carter & Co., Poole.

KING'S QUAY STREET is perhaps the most rewarding. It is cut
in two by the churchyard, on whose S side are the most impressive houses, with a view across the Green to the sea. Nos.
29–30, *c.* 1820, three bays, three storeys and attics, gault brick

with rendered ground floor and absurdly big ironwork trim –
cast-iron railings and wrought-iron lantern-holders. Although
apparently a single large house, in fact designed as two
dwellings, with a secondary side entrance. Nos. 31–32, described
as newly built in 1813, are of the same dimensions, but with
two full-height bows. Further s, Government House, now flats,
five-bay Georgian brick, wide doorway with Diocletian window
above. *Robert Adam* designed a house for this site in 1778, but
this is not it. On the Green, the old treadwheel CRANE from
the Navyard. Late C18 or early C19, with mid-C18 wheelhouse.*

N of the churchyard, the ELECTRIC PALACE CINEMA, 1911
by *H.R. Hooper*, a rare surviving example (including interior)
of an early purpose-built cinema, reopened 1981 after restoration. Exuberant front with plasterwork wreaths, swags, etc.
combined with Art Nouveau lettering and Mackintosh-style
balustrades. On the same side, Nos. 42–45, the former Free
School and master's house, founded by Sir Humphrey Parsons
in 1724. Brick front, rendered and painted, eleven bays in all.
Opposite, former bank premises, 1908. Flemish Gothic, brick
with stone dressings. Between this group and the sea, the old
Lifeboat House, 1876, and Angelgate, a square of coastguards'
housing (fifteen cottages and officer's house) by *Horace
Darken*, 1858. Brick, with white brick dressings. On the sea-
wall, Navigation House, overlooking the harbour, built for the
Harwich Haven Authority, 1974. Three storeys, with control
room in glazed top storey.

Towards the top of King's Quay Street, NAVAL HOUSE, Late
Georgian brick, and a nice varied row opposite; then where the
street narrows THE GLOBE, C17 and jettied on two sides, and
a C19 weatherboarded building with decorative gable, formerly
the Angel Inn, brings one to THE QUAY and a row of waterfront buildings vying for attention. After the relatively modest
Angel comes the PIER HOTEL, *c.* 1875, festively painted, three
storeys with an octagonal belvedere perched on the slope of
the roof. Then Quayside Court, built in 1864–5 as the GREAT
EASTERN HOTEL by *Thomas Allom* – a white elephant, if ever
there was one. Now flats, it never recovered from the opening
of Parkeston Quay (p. 635), with its own hotel, in 1883; closed
1922, and from 1952 to 1974 the Town Hall. Five storeys,
yellow brick with stone dressings (including a row of busts of
famous people associated with the town), exhibiting what was
called at the time the 'free Italian or mixed style', and making
heavy use of rustication, consoles, and other clutter. It has
none of the charm either of the Pier Hotel or of the timber
buildings on the HALFPENNY PIER opposite: 1851–4, octagonal booking office rebuilt in the 1890s. Next the offices of the
Harwich Haven Authority, 1974, brick with bands of inward-
sloping windows, and the more conventional brick Trinity
House building by *J.P. Bowen*, engineer in chief, 1951–2. New

---

*A crane of this type was erected at the yard in 1667.

OFFICES AND BUOY MAINTENANCE SHED for Trinity House by *Milsom Architects*, 2004–5, at the W end of the Quay. Three-storey office block, faced in stone cladding, brick, and coloured render, with a prominent bow front. On the NW corner, beyond Trinity Pier, the former TRAIN FERRY BERTH with gantry. Made in 1916 for the War Office at Richborough (Kent); moved here in 1923. Two 42-ft (13-metre) steel towers with high-level machinery.

HATFIELD BROAD OAK   5010

ST MARY THE VIRGIN. The second Aubrey de Vere founded a Benedictine priory at Hatfield in about 1135. The present church consists of the parts of the priory church W of the crossing. Of the parts further E nothing remains but the two W crossing piers, with demi-shafts and one waterleaf capital of *c.* 1175. The present church's N wall also is C12, but the only ornamental feature surviving on the outside, two arches of a blank arcade, is a C15 enrichment. The fact that the N aisle windows are placed so high is connected with the existence of the cloister on that side. In 1378, in a quarrel between the priory and the village, the cloister and parts of the walls were damaged, and afterwards the nave and aisles must have been rebuilt. It is this state that we now see inside, five-bay arcades with piers of the common four-shaft-four-hollow section with no capitals above the hollows. Two-centred arches and extremely good small headstops for the hoodmoulds. Externally it is rather the C15 that dominates. To this belong most of the windows, the S porch, which has a doorway with tracery spandrels, battlements, pinnacles, and three-light side openings with panel tracery, the S turret to the former rood loft, the S chapel with a very large five-light window with panel tracery, and the big W tower with angle buttresses, stepped battlements, higher stair-turret, W doorway with tracery spandrels, three-light W window, and three-light transomed straight-headed bell-openings. The clerestory windows are, it seems, original late C14 work. The whole exterior is of pebble rubble, partly covered with cement, except for the choir vestry of late C17 chequered brick on the N side. Restored by *R. C. Carpenter*, 1843 – his first restoration of a medieval church. His are the roofs, in the nave particularly handsome with tie-beams and panelling to cover the rafters. He also enlarged what is now the clergy vestry at the S aisle's E end, added in 1708 to house the parish library of about 300 volumes of the C15–C18. W end sensitively reordered by *Kay Pilsbury*, 1999–2003.

REREDOS and CHANCEL PANELLING. Probably 1708, and quite sumptuous. Ascribed to *John Woodward*, who, *c.* 1725, worked in Trinity College, Cambridge, the church's patron. Two panels are hinged, concealing the doorway and window (secured by a C15 IRON GRILLE) of a former vestry, with priest's chamber above. – SETTLE (S chapel). Of the same date and the same courtly style, with openwork foliage scrolls. – COMMUNION RAIL with sturdy twisted balusters, the bulbous foot surrounded by growing-up leaves. Again belonging to the same set of woodwork, as do four carved SYMBOLS OF THE EVANGELISTS, now mounted as pew ends. – SCREENS. To N chapel, C15, of simply traceried one-light divisions. Former chancel screen, now at W end, by *H. G. Ibberson*, 1905, also very simple and light, with carving by *F. A. Markham*. – PULPIT, CHANCEL STALLS, and PEWS. By *Carpenter*. Very fine work, and at an interesting moment from the ecclesiological point of view: the nave seating in Gothic style, with the poppyheads then fashionable, yet old-fashioned box pews with doors. Interesting also that no attempt was made to interfere with the chancel's C18 woodwork. – LITANY DESK. The base is the kneeling figure of priest, about 30 in. (76 cm.) tall, of *c.* 1400. It was originally part of a hammerbeam truss in the chancel. – CANDELABRA. Gorgeous C18 piece, purchased in 1780. Brass, with thirty-six branches in three tiers. – STAINED GLASS. E window *c.* 1843, designed by *William Whewell*, master of Trinity College, Cambridge. S aisle windows by *Holiday* for *Powell*, *c.* 1887, and *Hardman*, 1895. N aisle W by *Shrigley & Hunt*, *c.* 1913.

MONUMENTS. Effigy of Robert de Vere, third earl of Oxford †1221, cross-legged, sword-handling, very defaced. It is thought to have been commissioned by his great-grandson, the sixth earl, *c.* 1315. Placed in the chancel in 1891. – Brass to a Lady, *c.* 1395. Head only. – N aisle and chapel: Sir John Barrington †1691. Standing wall monument with two rather coarsely carved putti and an urn between them. Attributed to *Grinling Gibbons* (GF). – Sir Charles Barrington †1788 by *J. F. Moore*. Marbles of various colours, with oval relief of mourning female figure and urn, and much ornament. – William Selwin of Down Hall, erected 1800. By *Thomas Cooke*. Another mourning female figure, and a weeping willow. – Lady Ibbetson of Down Hall †1816 by *Flaxman*, with two almost horizontally floating angels above the inscription. – Mary Leveson Gower †1861, and a double monument to Sir John Selwin Bt †1869 and Isabella Selwin †1858, both by *M. W. Johnson*, justifying Gunnis's description of him as 'prolific but dull'. – S aisle and chapel: Sarah Chamberlayne †1742 and Richard Chamberlayne †1758, identical monuments with profiles in oval medallions in front of the usual obelisks. – Stanes Chamberlayne †1782, characteristically more classical in all the ornamental details; the portrait medallion is here at the foot, standing putti and urn higher up. – Mary Chamberlayne †1819 and Stanes Chamberlayne †1834. Matching monuments by *Bacon & Manning*. – Thomas Lowndes †1840. Inscription, including verses composed by Lowndes, engraved on brass by *J. Browne*, 1841, in a stone frame.

ST JOHN THE EVANGELIST, Bush End. 1856–8 by *J. Clarke*. E.E., on a tiny scale with short W tower with pyramidal roof. – STAINED GLASS. Three chancel lancets, including one donated by Clarke. – S of the church the former PARSONAGE, the front range added by *R.W. Drew*, 1867, and the former SCHOOL and teacher's house by *G.E. Pritchett*, 1877. Both brick, the latter with black diapering.

PRIMARY SCHOOL. By *R. George Suter*, 1861, extended 1869 by *Chancellor*. Enlarged 1966, including a shallow-domed hall.

An attractive village, with St Mary's set back N of the High Street. Joining the large churchyard to the High Street, brick-fronted CHURCH COTTAGE of 1708 and ALMSHOUSES. The HIGH STREET mainly Georgian in appearance. On the S side CHALKES, 1837–41 by *William Cheffins* as the rectory, the top storey by *Chancellor*, 1874. Brick, E-plan, with hoodmoulded windows and three straight gables. To its W, BRICK HOUSE, timber-framed, has a brick front with two bows and Gothick windows. N side dominated by the COCK INN and adjoining buildings, a long Georgian brick front with medieval timber-framed houses behind. These continue round the corner to the OLD COURT HOUSE, looking down Feathers Hill, C14 with a four-bay brick front of *c.* 1800. On the opposite corner THE PRIORY, *c.* 1600, faced in C18 brick. A pretty row closes the view W along the High Street, notably an early C15 gable with exposed timbers over a carriageway (part of RUNDLE HOUSE), which marks the beginning of CAGE END, running S at right angles to the High Street. Several good timber-framed houses along here, some plastered, some weather-boarded, the grandest TOWN FARM with three jettied gables. Two-bay hall with high-quality framing, probably late C14, with C15 and later additions.

A few more nice cottages at BROAD STREET GREEN, at the E end of the High Street, and along DUNMOW ROAD cottages by *Chancellor* for G.A. Lowndes of Barrington Hall, 1872. Stock brick with bands of red brick and broad gables.

BARRINGTON HALL, ¾ m. NNW. Built for J.S. Barrington, *c.* 1735–40, by *John Sanderson*, the builder probably his cousin *Joseph Sanderson*. Remodelled 1863 by *Edward Browning* of Stamford for G.A. Lowndes in a heavy Neo-Jacobean style. Shaped gables, balustrades, bays, and no symmetry. Inside, a grand galleried entrance hall, and some C18 plasterwork. The service wing, and coach house beyond it, survive in something like their C18 form.

HATFIELD FOREST. A rare example of what Essex's royal forest looked like in the Middle Ages. Wood-pasture, a mix of grass-land, coppice woods, pollarded hornbeams, and oaks, to support deer and cattle as well as providing firewood and timber. A rabbit warren was added in the C17. Jacob Houblon of Hallingbury Place (*see* Great Hallingbury) owned the forest in the C18 and in 1746 formed the lake (originally larger) and built a small cottage (rebuilt 1940s) beside it, to which was added *c.* 1757–9 THE SHELL HOUSE. Timber-framed, faced with flint, slag, and shells, with pediment. Lake further improved by *Capability Brown*, 1757–62. FOREST LODGE, SW of the lake, C16 with long-wall jettied front. Just outside the

present boundary, FOREST COTTAGE incorporates part of a
very small aisled hall, tree-ring dated 1360. Floor inserted in
1634. The forest was acquired for The National Trust by the
conservationist (Edward North Buxton in 1923, cf. Epping).

PORTINGBURY HILLS, 2½ m. NNW. Low four-sided mound in
the N part of Hatfield Forest, about 100 ft (31 metres) in diameter, surrounded by a ditch and with other irregular earthworks. Probably a farmstead or other settlement; excavations
in 1964–5 yielded Iron Age pottery.

HATFIELD HEATH

5010

HOLY TRINITY. 1856–9 by *J. Clarke*. E.E., of flint rubble with
stone dressings. S porch in the base of a three-stage, splay-foot
tower. S aisle, extended E for organ chamber by *G.E. Pritchett*,
1882–3; vestry W of tower by *F.W. Chancellor*, 1934. – LECTERN.
Fine Arts and Crafts of 1911 by *Harold Stabler*. Wrought iron,
with inscription on embossed brass panel, and openwork
scrolls and foliage on the book-stand. – STAINED GLASS. By
Powell & Sons the E window, 1910, designed by *Read*, and a
nave N window, 1911, designed by *Coakes* and *Penwarden*.
Another N window by *A.L. Wilkinson*, 1952.

100 UNITED REFORMED CHURCH (Congregational). By *T. Lewis
Banks*, 1875–6. Impressive gabled W front, with large Dec
window (contemporary STAINED GLASS), and a dumpy
octagonal flèche. Unusually splendid and unaltered interior,
with gallery on three sides supported on slender Corinthian
columns, a fine roof, pulpit and organ at the E end. Vestries
and first-floor schoolroom at the rear. Hall on N side, 1984–5.

DOWN HALL, 1¼ m. S. Purchased in 1720 by Edward Harley,
Earl of Oxford, who gave it to the poet and diplomat Matthew
Prior. Before his death in 1721 Prior commissioned a new
house from *James Gibbs* (unexecuted), and gardens by *Charles
Bridgeman*, whom Harley continued to employ until 1726. His
formal garden, NW of the house, is covered by woodland. The
88 house is now as rebuilt 1871–3 by *F.P. Cockerell* for Sir Henry
Selwin-Ibbetson (later Lord Rookwood). Sumptuous Italian
style. Mainly two storeys, with a colonnaded loggia on the
garden front between three-storey pavilions. Lower service
wing at right angles to the entrance front. Walls of poured and
shuttered concrete (for which *Charles Drake* acted as consultant), with stone dressings, and panels of ornate sgraffito decoration by *Francis Wormleighton* and *W. Wise* in the South
Kensington manner. NE of the service wing a square game
larder with open arcaded sides and pyramidal roof. A hotel
since 1986, with bleak and overwhelming additions trying to
be in keeping.

John Birch designed several cottages and other estate buildings in the 1860s. These might include two pairs of *cottages
ornés* on the E side of Hatfield Heath, both of similar basic
design with bargeboarded gables. One has false timber framing

to the upper storey, the other canted bays and diamond-paned leaded lights.

LEA HALL, ½ m. NE. Moated house dating to the C15 with exposed timbers. In the garden, various architectural fragments brought from Yorkshire, *c.* 1931. These include the C14 tracery of a window from St Augustine, Hedon, removed during *G.E. Street*'s restoration of 1868–77, and a round stone arch said to have come from Hull Citadel by *Martin Beckman*, 1681–3 (dem. 1864).

HATFIELD PEVEREL

7010

ST ANDREW. Hatfield Peverel possessed a Benedictine priory, founded in the reign of Henry I using a pre-existing college of canons. The present church is the nave of the cruciform priory church, with a C15 N aisle, and a S aisle of 1873 by *G.E. Street*, to whose restoration the building owes much of its present appearance. The E wall of the present chancel is the W arch of the former central tower, plain and clearly of the early C12, with some wall stumps of the N and S walls; the vestries' E wall is all that remains of the S transept. Of the C12 nave the W wall survives, with a doorway with one order of columns with scalloped capitals and zigzag in the arch voussoirs. Street removed two small W towers. The S wall of the nave is also original (C13 lancet), from the W end to the point where the S aisle adjoins, as is one upper window of the nave's N wall (now above the N arcade). The N arcade of octagonal piers with double-chamfered arches is ascribed to the C15. In the N wall a re-set early C14 window and one of the C15; the others are C19. The brick battlements and the stair-turret halfway along the N side are of *c.* 1500. NE bell-turret by Street, who also rebuilt the N porch of 1826 added by *Hopper* and converted to vestries a small, mid-C16 two-storey building on the chancel's S side.* – CHURCH HALL by *Purcell Miller Tritton & Partners*, 1993, a thoughtful design, ambitious in scale and well detailed.

SCREEN (N arcade, E bay). Perp, with panel tracery. – BENCH ENDS. Three in chancel, poppyheads and heads of a king, queen, etc. – STAINED GLASS. Small fragments of the C14 and C15 in N windows, larger pieces of the C16–C18, largely foreign, in S windows, collected by John Wright of Hatfield Priory; repaired by *Clayton & Bell*, 1873. E window, 1875; N aisle by *Lavers, Barraud & Westlake*, 1875; S aisle by *Heaton, Butler & Bayne*, 1893; W window by *Kempe*, 1895. – MONUMENTS. Chancel: tomb-chest of blue marble with very fine, elaborate quatrefoil decoration. – On a N window sill, effigy of a man in civilian clothes holding his heart in his hands, *c.* 1300, badly preserved. – Several good C18 and C19 tablets, e.g. Arthur Dabbs †1750, with Rococo cartouche surrounded by flower

---

* *Hopper* also designed a vicarage, 1824–6 (dem.).

and putti-heads; George Lovibond †1817 by *W. & C. Thompson*
with mourning female figure, his wife Martha †1828 and their
daughter Harriet Catherine †1818 by *Coulman*; G.B.M.
Lovibond †1870, elaborate Gothic surround by *C. Raymond
Smith*, and a simpler Gothic affair by *Wray* of Chelmsford to
Sarah Ann Raven †1870. – Three excellent brass Puginian
Gothic CORONAE LUCIS, *c.* 1875 and 1882.

METHODIST CHURCH, The Street. 1874, by *J.C. Lewis* of
Woodford. Ugly Gothic, red and black brick, with steeple.

The village lies along the old main road and the Maldon
Road branching off it, where are the LOVIBOND ALMSHOUSES,
1820, renovated and extended by *Tim Venn*, 1991–2: a row of
four, white brick, low, but with high chimneys that have
recessed Gothic panels echoing the windows. Deep wooden
porches with benches. Nearly opposite, the SALVATION ARMY
HALL, 1895 by *E. Geldart* as the parish room, brick with black
diapering, much altered and extended.

The village's proximity to Chelmsford, combined with the
views it afforded of the Ter and Chelmer valley, led to the construction of three large houses in the late C18:

HATFIELD PRIORY, next to the church, was built for John
Wright of Witham, Master of the Guild of Coachmakers. He
acquired the estate *c.* 1765, including the remains of the original priory, erecting his new house *c.* 1769–71 100yds to the S,
and raised on a little knoll. Two storeys over a basement, in
white brick. Exterior plain to the point of austerity, relieved
only by a small triangular pediment over the entrance door and
the curved brick cornice. Each elevation of five bays, with
shallow three-bay projections on the two principal elevations.
It has been attributed to *Robert Taylor*, but Wright is described
on his memorial in the church as being 'architecturae, picturae
aliarumque artium liberalium plusquam mediocriter sciens' –
having more than ordinary knowledge of architecture, painting and the other liberal arts – and it seems equally likely that
he directed a competent local builder.

The interior comes as a surprise, because the fittings – doorcases, window architraves and chimneypieces – are 1730s, possibly from *Leoni*'s Thorndon Hall (q.v.) of 1733–42 (dem.
1763). The Entrance Hall is exceptional; here Wright assembled a careful display of symbolic images. The overmantel is a
relief, signed by *Laurent Delvaux*, of the Sacrifice of Diana,
dating from the 1720s. Three brackets supported busts by
Pietro Torrigiano of Henry VII, Henry VIII and Bishop Fisher★
from the Holbein Gate at Whitehall Palace, demolished in
1759; Wright had them repaired by *John Flaxman*, then a boy
working in his father's shop. Opposite the entrance, plaster
reliefs of three kings celebrated for upholding civil liberties:
Alfred, flanked by George II and William III, surrounded with

---

★ Now in the Victoria and Albert Museum, Metropolitan Museum of Art, New York,
and the Getty Museum, respectively.

garlands of husks; around Alfred six shields display the Wright arms. The kitchens and double-height servants' hall, together with other domestic offices, were in the basement. On the piano nobile, the Drawing Room and Dining Room still serve their original functions; the library is now a kitchen and a new library has been created in the former Dressing Room. Wright seems to have planned the PARK before starting work on the house; a scheme by *Richard Woods*, prepared in 1765, survives much as planned, with two linked ponds N of the house. Gothick temple S of the house constructed in 1986 using fragments of a garden building from Wardour House, Wiltshire, designed by Woods in 1768; 'Ice House' E of the house, 1998, by *Ben Pentreath* in the spirit of Woods.

HATFIELD PLACE lies NW, on the main road; by *John Johnson* for Colonel John Tyrell, 1791–5. Like Hatfield Priory, of white brick, but three bays only, with rusticated ground floor and *Coade* stone dressings, e.g. keystones of Pomona and Flora (dated 1791) at ground floor, and at first floor four pairs of pilasters with floriated capitals supporting a frieze with paterae. The design closely follows Johnson's Holcombe House, Mill Hill, Middlesex, of 1775. Completely plain garden elevation. Additions made by W. M. Tufnell between 1855 and 1874 – the porch, single-storey ballroom, and cast-iron veranda at the rear – and a large two-storey rebuilding of the kitchen wing by *Sherrin*, 1905, detract from the house's elegance.

Inside, Johnson's striking oval staircase hall, with geometric stair and honeysuckle scroll balusters, leads to a lobby with three small female medallions surrounded by scrollwork. The main rooms, on the garden front, are the Drawing Room and Dining Parlour; in the latter, three large medallions, two with female figures (cf. Holcombe House) and the third with Apollo; in the Drawing Room, a frieze with sphinx, urn, dolphin and pillar motifs, also identical to one at Holcombe House.

CRIX, a little W along the main road, is also of the 1790s but in two phases, as is clear from the brickwork. The client was Samuel Shaen, a Chelmsford solicitor. Large (six bays, three storeys, with a broad Adamish doorway) but plain, with no unnecessary decoration and, unlike its neighbours, of red brick. 1920s bow window on the garden elevation. A pleasing stable block adjoins to the W.

BERWICK PLACE, 1½ m. NW of the church. Two-storey white brick house by *Hopper*, c. 1830, for Abraham Johnson. Three-bay entrance front with recessed porch and five-bay garden front, extended later in the C19 and again in the C20. SW, across the valley, TOPPINGHOE HALL, the remains of a much larger house, mostly timber-framed but incorporating one gabled brick wall with stone windows, late C16, and another separate end wall, free-standing with nothing behind.

8090

HAWKWELL

St Mary. c14 nave and chancel; the low side window on the s side of the chancel is original. c15 belfry and weatherboarded splay-foot spire on four oak posts with cross-beams supported by arched braces. Moderate restoration by *William White*, 1875, with new s porch, the fittings sadly swept away in a reordering of 1995–6. The positive gain is the two-storey N aisle by *David Ferguson*, incorporating meeting rooms etc., a near-perfect match of style and materials. – STAINED GLASS. Mostly *c.* 1860, but central panel of E window by *Jones & Willis* (First World War memorial).

Old Rectory, ⅔m. wsw. Three-bay, two-storey stuccoed house of 1831, enlarged 1858.

8000

HAZELEIGH

Hazeleigh Hall. Timber-framed and plastered, *c.* 1570, incorporating an earlier structure. Two storeys and attics, six bays with two full dormers irregularly spaced. One original window in the gable of the l. return, which has exposed studwork, but mostly refenestrated in the late c19, when a gabled porch was added. – St Nicholas (dem. 1922) stood to its w.

6040

HELIONS BUMPSTEAD

St Andrew. Brick w tower dated 1812, with pointed windows, hefty buttresses and battlements. Mid-c13 chancel with some renewed lancets, plastered; the nave older, probably Norman, of flint rubble, with limestone and clunch dressings. Mid-c14 s aisle arcade with massive octagonal piers and double-chamfered arches, but the aisle itself demolished in the late c18 and rebuilt (mostly in brick) in 1834. s porch of 1956 replacing that of 1834. Restoration by *C.C. Winmill*, 1932, included removal of box pews and w gallery, the front of the latter reused on BENCHES and the octagonal PULPIT, with ogee-domed tester. His CHOIR STALLS particularly fine, late-flowering Arts and Crafts, incorporating late c15 traceried panels. Other woodwork (including the small ORGAN by *J.W. Walker*, 1851) painted cream, giving an c18 Gothick air. – FONT. Perp, octagonal, with traceried stem and the usual quatrefoils along the bowl. – MONUMENTS. Devereux Tallakarne †1627 and wife, of unusual design, similar to the Tallakarne monument at Ashen (q.v.). No figures. Inscription and ornamental panels between termini and caryatids. Tall obelisks and shield on top. – William Gardener †1667 and wife Margaret †1683. Marble tablet with Ionic pilasters, scrolled pediment and shield.

Boblow House, ¾m. s. One of the Hospitallers' more important Essex manor houses, the centre of an estate estimated at

150 acres. The present building appears to be a C17 parlour
wing added to a now-vanished house: two storeys with two
rooms on each floor, all heated, the fireplaces with carved pedimented surrounds, and glazed windows.

PARSONAGE HOUSE, ½ m. NE. Mid C16, with exposed timbers
and some brick-nogging, and four very good brick fireplaces,
with pilasters, moulded capitals and bases. One has an unexpectedly sophisticated terracotta frieze of Renaissance ornament, tritons, scrolls etc. Garden room and swimming pool
pavilion, 1996, garage and flat 2000–1, by *Charles Morris*,
meticulously detailed and sympathetic additions.

HEMPSTEAD

6030

ST ANDREW. Consecrated 1365 as a chapel of ease to Great
Sampford. Of that date the nave and aisles. The arcades have
quatrefoil piers with slight sharp hollows in the diagonals and
two-centred arches with a two-quadrant moulding. Chancel
probably C15, with rebuilt early C16 brick E end. Also brick its
N extension, *c.* 1655, for Sir Eliab Harvey, providing a schoolroom (E, now vestry) and Harvey family chapel (W) and a
burial vault (extended beneath the chancel in 1766). The C15
W tower fell in 1882, bringing with it half the nave and part of
the S aisle. Nave subsequently restored 1886–8 by *Samuel
Knight*, who designed the S porch with woodcarving by the
curate, *John Escreet* (he also made the PULPIT, READING DESK
and LECTERN). Tower rebuilt 1933–4 by *Sir Charles Nicholson*,
completed by *Stanley Bragg*, 1959–61. – BRASSES to a Civilian
and wife, *c.* 1475, figures about 19 in. (48 cm.), to a Civilian,
c. 1480, 24 in. (62 cm.), and to a Civilian and wife, *c.* 1530, 15
in. (38 cm.) – Thomas Huntingdon †1498 (27-in. (68.5-cm.)
figure) and wife Margaret. – MONUMENTS. William Harvey
†1657, chief physician to Charles I and discoverer of the circulation of the blood. By *Edward Marshall*. Frontal bust of outstanding workmanship in a restrained Baroque surround, and
said to be a striking likeness. In 1883 Harvey's remains were
moved from the vault and placed in the massive white marble
sarcophagus (by *G. Maile & Son*) that now occupies most of
the space in Harvey's chapel. – Eliab Harvey †1661, and
descendants. A suitably impressive wall monument of black
marble within a white marble architrave, surmounted by
broken segmental pediment. Cartouches of arms. – Sir William
Harvey †1719. Standing wall monument with a big arched
niche containing a low broad urn on a fat column. No figure.
– William and Mary Harvey †1742 and 1761, erected by her in
1758. By *Roubiliac*. Standing wall monument with the usual
grey obelisk, and in front two draped profile medallions. –
Admiral Sir Eliab Harvey †1830, commander of the *Temeraire*
at Trafalgar. Spiky crocketed Gothic, by *Humphrey Hopper*. The
vault contains a remarkable collection of C17 lead COFFINS,
some anthropomorphic, with modelled faces.

LITTLE BULLS FARM, 2 m. NE. Small early C17 thatched farmhouse, with later rear addition. Two elevations of the main
block have exposed timber framing with brick-nogging.

HENHAM

ST MARY THE VIRGIN. Chancel mainly C13, with some lancets
and a plain S doorway, but on the E wall outside remains of a
blind round-headed arcade with simple roll mouldings which
look late C11. The rest mostly C14 (except for the large embattled C15 S porch), including the W tower with diagonal buttresses (also into the nave, where squinches are necessary to
underpin the buttresses). Later brick battlements, and recessed
lead 'spike' of Herts type. C14 four-bay arcades, with quatrefoil piers, moulded capitals, and double-chamfered arches. The
earlier S arcade has sturdier piers of *c.* 1300, when the aisle was
added. It incorporated a late C12 S transept, to which belong
the two semi-octagonal responds at the S aisle's E end. The N
arcade has a similar irregularity: a piece of the C13 nave wall,
containing the rood-loft staircase, was left standing at its E end.
The capital of the arcade's middle pier has a delightful enrichment, a tiny carved demi-figure of the Virgin, very simply
dressed with rather Baroque folds and two censing angels l.
and r. of her. Their style seems to be *c.* 1500. On the pier's
opposite face is a laughing devil. Unobtrusive restorations in
1897, 1911 (tower, by *W. G. Horseman*) and 1939 (*W. Weir*).
   FONT. Octagonal, C15, with shields: seven heraldic, one with
symbols of the Passion. – SCREEN. C15. Especially sumptuous,
as Essex screens go, single-light divisions with ogee heads and
elaborate panel tracery above. – PULPIT. C15 with C17 book-
rest. Hexagonal, two panels to each side and a buttress between
them. – LECTERN. Adapted from a reading desk. C17 guilloche
ornament and an acorn knob l. and r. of the top. – WALL
PAINTING. On E wall, very fine head of a king or emperor, C12,
partially uncovered in 1988. Similar in style to paintings in St
Gabriel's Chapel, Canterbury Cathedral (cf. Copford). –
STAINED GLASS. Fragments of C15 glass in the E window and
in the chancel N wall. C16 heraldic glass in S wall. S aisle W
†1856 by *Swaine, Bourne & Son*, Birmingham. – MONUMENTS.
Thomas Kirbie †1603. Slate floor slab inlaid with white
marble; incised figure in civilian dress. – Samuel Feake,
Chairman of the East India Company, †1757 and family. By
William Vere of Stratford, 1790. Very purely Neoclassical, with
an urn (carved with an East Indiaman in full sail) against an
obelisk. The urn's base projecting triangularly – a design quite
out of the ordinary run.
The church, village green, and thatched cottages (including, N,
   LONG YARDS, home of C.C. Winmill, who is buried in the
   churchyard) make a pretty scene. Many attractive houses,
   several thatched, along Church Street, High Street (especially

The Row, which runs behind and parallel to the High Street), Crow Street, and round Woodend Green at the E end of the High Street. In Crow Street, a typical BOARD SCHOOL, 1875 by *George Perry* (enlarged 1883 and later), with bell-turret. Opposite, the Congregational Chapel's school house, now a private house and much altered: chapel (dem.) and school house both 1864 by *Jasper Cowell*, native of Henham.

PLEDGDON HALL, ¾ m. SE. Probably a medieval hall house, with W cross-wing, altered and extended in the C17 and C20. Large C17 barns on either side of the yard in front.

PENNINGTON HALL, I m. S. C17, L-plan, with exposed studding in one gable. E of the house a square DOVECOTE. Flint and brick ground floor, timber-framed upper floor, pyramidal roof with open cupola.

HEYBRIDGE

8000

ST ANDREW. Almost completely Norman, with nave, chancel, and impressive, slightly later W tower. Flint rubble, septaria and puddingstone, with limestone dressings. Only the E end of the chancel (with its five-light window) is Perp. The tower was laid out very broad, but its original height can only be guessed at, because in the middle of the C15 it collapsed into the nave. Sir Henry Bourchier was instrumental in rebuilding that took place later in the century, leaving the shortened tower with a pyramidal roof. Original NW stair-turret, and C15 W doorway beneath the original C12 arch. Nave and chancel have on the N side three original windows and one doorway, on the S side two doorways and two blocked but still noticeable windows. Inside the nave the splays of the Norman clerestory windows also exist, not in line with the lower windows. The chancel roof has at the E end a hammerbeam truss, sign of its Perp origin, W of that tie-beams with crown-posts. Similar nave roof, with monograms by which it can be dated *c.* 1518. Re-seated by *Ewan Christian*, 1885, who also restored the tower and porch. – COMMUNION RAIL with twisted balusters, *c.* 1700, the work of a local craftsman, *John Junols*. – S DOOR with ornamental iron hinges, *c.* 1100. – STAINED GLASS. Female saint, late C13, and C14 fragments (chancel N). Nave S, The Calling of St Andrew by *Benjamin Finn*, 2002. – MONUMENTS. Brass of John Whitacres †1627. 14-in. (35.5-cm.) figure. – Thomas Freshwater †1638 and wife. Big, with kneeling figures opposite each other. Corinthian columns. Attributed to *Thomas Stanton* (GF). – Julines Hering †1775 of Heybridge Hall.* Elaborate affair in coloured marbles. – Eleanor Incledon †1823, 'a native of Jamaica' and servant of Mr and Mrs Hering of Heybridge Hall. Simple but elegant white marble, by *Carr*.

---

*Heybridge Hall, which incorporated an early C14 open hall, was destroyed by fire in 1997.

PLANTATION HALL (community hall), Colchester Road. 1998–9 by *Inkpen Downie*. In two shades of yellow brick, two rectangular blocks with hipped roofs, one higher than the other, the corners emphasized by sloping, buttress-like projections.

ELMS FARM, ½ m. w. The site of a major archaeological excavation, 1993–5, in advance of housing development. Evidence was found of a small Neolithic farmstead, Bronze Age ring ditch, burial mound and beaker pit, and a substantial settlement during the Late Iron Age and Roman period, including a temple precinct, the temple itself rebuilt in the mid C2. The village appears to have been abandoned by the C5 or C6.

Heybridge owes its existence to its location on the River Blackwater, but its modern form was determined by the Chelmer and Blackwater Navigation, opened 1797 (*see* Introduction, p. 52), to whose banks William Bentall moved *c.* 1815 the ironworks he had established at Goldhanger in 1808. Its principal monument is the vast stock brick WAREHOUSE, four storeys high and seventeen bays along the canal; 1863, still classical in its mood, the bays separated by pilasters and the three-bay ends with open-pedimented gables. NE, on the corner of Colchester Road and Goldhanger Road, stood THE TOWERS, a large Italianate house by *C. Pertwee* for E. H. Bentall, 1870–3, chiefly remarkable for its concrete construction. Only the entrance lodge, gates and some boundary walls remain. 500 yds along Colchester Road, WOODFIELD COTTAGES, three terraces of workers' cottages, forty in all, built by Bentall in 1873 and also in concrete. Single-storey, originally flat-roofed, with outhouses across the roadway.

At HEYBRIDGE BASIN, 1½ m. SE, a settlement grew up round the sea LOCK where the Navigation debouches into the Blackwater Estuary. The waterfront scene, with weatherboarded cottages, brick lock-keeper's house, pub, and boats' masts, is attractive without having been consciously prettified.

ST GEORGE, little more than a hut, was originally the sergeants' mess of Goldhanger Airfield, re-erected here in 1920. Two good STAINED GLASS windows, by *A.A. Orr*, 1930, and *Andrew Fawcett*, 2001. The UNITED REFORMED CHURCH of 1850 is weatherboarded, and charming in its simplicity.

SALTCOTE MALTINGS, ½ m. NNE of St George. 1893–5 by *Chancellor*, stock brick with red dressings, slate roof and three pyramidal kilns, and originally with three malting floors. Converted to houses, *c.* 1997. Surrounding houses by *Plater Inkpen Vale & Downie*, in the vernacular idiom – stock brick, weatherboarding, slate roofs – but modern.

HIGH BEACH
Waltham Abbey

HOLY INNOCENTS. 1873 by *A. W. Blomfield*, replacing a church of 1835–6 by *S.M. Hubert* on a different site. Built at the expense of T.C. Baring of Wallsgrove House, on high ground entirely surrounded by Epping Forest. Stone, E.E. NW tower with angle buttresses and tall broach spire with lucarnes and gargoyles. Nave, transepts, and apsidal chancel. Chancel raised behind a low wall with stone PULPIT on the N side. – In N transept, ALTAR with carved and painted wooden REREDOS, CROSS and CANDLESTICKS by *Francis Stephens*. – STAINED GLASS. In transepts, by *Mayer & Co.*, *c.* 1897. Most of the S transept window and other C19 glass destroyed in the Second World War. – Three E lancets by *James Powell & Sons*, 1948.

High Beach (or Beech) is a popular destination for visitors to Epping Forest and it was here that Queen Victoria declared the Forest open to the public in 1882. But before that it had already attracted prosperous residents. N of the church, ARABIN HOUSE, built (or rebuilt, and originally Beech House) for Richard Arabin by *F. O. Bedford*, 1848. Stucco, three bays and three storeys, with various later additions. W of the church, WALLSGROVE HOUSE, early C19 stucco. Five-bay front with tetrastyle Doric portico and at the outer corners a group of three giant Doric columns. The only older house of any size is MANOR HOUSE, WNW of the church, now divided in three. Late C17 chequered brick with three shaped gables. C18 rear extension, gabled extension by *Vulliamy*, 1845, to the l., and to the r. a less sympathetic addition dated 1875, when the gabled porch was also added.

BEECH HILL PARK, ¾ m. NNW. Large mid-C19 Elizabethan-style house, demolished soon after 1945. The stable block survives, now three houses. Brick with stone dressings, shaped gables, and a slender clock tower with stone bellcote and flèche.

HIGH BEECH HALL, ¼ m. SW. By *T. W. Cutler*, *c.* 1897, as the vicarage. Brick, with tile-hung upper storey, and a wing with half-timbered jettied upper storey over a canted bay. Also by *Cutler*, ¼ m. further S, SUNTRAP FOREST EDUCATION CENTRE, built 1895 as a convalescent home for children recovering from TB. Brick and roughcast. Two wings splayed to catch the sun, one with canted end, with (originally) a ward and dining hall on the ground floor and dormitories above. Entrance in the angle and kitchens etc. behind.

LIPPITTSHILL LODGE, ¾ m. SSW. Three-bay, three-storey stucco house, *c.* 1824, once part of the lunatic asylum where the poet John Clare was a patient, 1837–41. (In the grounds a semi-underground GROTTO or catacombs built in the 1880s with stones from Chelmsford prison.)

(LIPPITTS HILL CAMP (Metropolitan Police), ¾ m. SW. An unusually well-preserved Second World War anti-aircraft site, with gun emplacements and magazine, built 1939–40, from 1944 to 1948 a prisoner-of-war camp. Inside the main gate, SCULPTURE of a seated man by *Rudi Weber*, a German prisoner, carved in 1946 from concrete. The site also includes a Cold War anti-aircraft operations room, a two-storey concrete bunker similar to Mistley (q.v.).)

HIGH EASTER

1 ST MARY THE VIRGIN. Wide and large Norman nave and Norman chancel. The quoins of Roman brick are unmistakable; also some Roman bricks used herringbone fashion in the walling, which is otherwise of flint rubble. Remains of the Norman chancel arch. Plain Norman s doorway. Nave heightened in brick early in the C16 and given three-light clerestory windows and battlements; the line of the older, steeper roof can be seen on the tower's E face. There are also two windows in the E wall above the chancel arch. Unusually impressive roof, of flat pitch, with numerous carved bosses and tie-beams on braces whose tracery incorporates the rebus (a five-barred gate) of the donor, Sir Geoffrey Gate. C14 N aisle with two-light windows with an octofoiled circle over two ogee heads. The four-bay arcade has octagonal piers and double-hollow-chamfered arches. C15 W tower with diagonal buttresses, a little chequer flushwork along the base, and a doorway with the demi-figure of an angel in the apex and obscure carvings in the spandrels, probably two men on the N side and a winged beast on the S. Three-light W window, two-light, transomed bell-openings, battlements, and taller, embattled stair-turret. Early C16 embattled brick porch. Restored by *Chancellor*, 1864–5, including removal of W gallery, re-seating, rebuilding of C15 N vestry, and renewal of windows. – FONT. Octagonal, Perp, with symbols of the Evangelists and four shields. – SCREENS. Two parclose screens at E end of N aisle, *c.* 1400. – CHEST. Iron-bound, late C14. – Stone MORTAR, found embedded in the chancel wall, 1968. Probably C14 or C15, with two large pouring lips. Perhaps used for the manufacture of leading for stained-glass windows. – STAINED GLASS. In two nave S windows, fragments of C14 glass. – E window by *Martin Travers*, 1931. – Two N aisle N windows (and perhaps others) by *Heaton, Butler & Bayne*, 1868.

UNITED REFORMED CHURCH. Built 1893 as the Manning Prentice Memorial School for the Congregational chapel, provocatively sited close to the parish church's SE end. Decorative brick. The vaguely classical chapel (now THE CHANTRY), dated 1847, on The Street's N side, has been stylishly converted to a house.

The approach to the parish church from the village is charming, a narrow passage between two timber-framed and gabled houses, C15 and C16. Opposite, the former COCK AND BELL inn, with timber framing exposed on the front and N side. H-plan, with jettied cross-wings; the N cross-wing and hall *c.* 1400, the S wing C16. SW of the church, HIGH EASTERBURY, a large timber-framed and plastered house with a late C16 gabled cross-wing at its E end. The hall was originally aisled and the W end appears to incorporate remains of a solar, dated by its construction to the C13 or C14. S of here, the OLD MILL, an eccentric C20 conversion of the round-house and trestle of a post mill; beam inside dated 1799. Next to it the early C17 MILL HOUSE has dovecotes in the gable ends.

N of the church, in School Lane, the surprisingly elaborate OLD SCHOOL HOUSE (former National School), *c.* 1850, with diapered brickwork and stone dressings, single-storey, with a two-storey teacher's house at the N end followed by a three-storey tower. Perhaps by *Kendall & Pope*, who designed the OLD VICARAGE (now divided) at The Street's E end, 1849–50, for Rev. Edward Gepp, vicar 1849–1903. Tudor Gothic with battlements. It cost £850 plus £150 for stables. W wing by *Chancellor*, 1887.

PENTLOW END, 1m. N. Late C14 weatherboarded hall, with a late C16 brick cross-wing, now plastered. Over-restored, but with original brick mullioned windows and brick fireplaces.

STAGDEN CROSS HOUSE, 1m. E. C16 timber-framed house with two brick chimneystacks, of two and four octagonal shafts. C20 E extension.

HIGH LAVER

5000

ALL SAINTS. Norman nave of flint rubble with E quoins of Roman brick and one original N window; other windows C14, mostly renewed. E.E. chancel with renewed lancets, at the E end a group of three. C14 W tower with Dec two-light window, but much renewed in brick in the C18. Battlements and short recessed spire. C14 also the broad four-centred chancel arch on responds which run up into the arch without capitals. Restored by *Chancellor*, 1863–5, who added the S porch. – FONT. Octagonal, Perp, with traceried stem; bowl with quatrefoils carrying shields. – C18 CHARITY BOARD recording 'A. BENEFACTOR. Whose name by some misfortune, or neglect is now unknown'. – MONUMENTS. Brass of Edward Sulyard, wife and children, *c.* 1495, the main figures about 18½ in. (47.5 cm.) – Damaris Cudworth †1695. White marble tablet with nicely lettered inscription. – Rev. Samuel Lowe †1709, 'to himself Frugal to his friends Bountiful'. Broken segmental pediment, cartouche with arms, winged cherubs and skull. – Rev. Richard Budworth †1805. Elegant oval with draped urn. Large stone tomb-chest in churchyard N of chancel. – Rev. Philip Budworth †1861. Marble quatrefoil with inscription on inset brass cross and coats of arms. By *Moring*. – John Locke, the philosopher, †1704 lies buried at High Laver. Standing outside against the nave S wall is his brick tomb with stone slab, but the tablet with Latin inscription composed by him was moved to the inner S wall in 1932. Locke lived at Otes, the manor house (dem. 1922), as paying guest of Sir Francis and Lady Masham; a group of Masham tombs lies E of the chancel.

ST EDMUND and SCHOOL. *See* Matching Green, Matching.

HIGH LAVER HOUSE, ⅓ m. SSE. Former rectory, 1864. Brick, gabled, two and three storeys. Perhaps by *Pritchett*, who designed the school.

MASHAMS, 1,000 yds WNW. Small thatched hall house, with exposed timbers, tree-ring dated 1446. Gabled service-end *p. 36* cross-wing to the l. with underbuilt jetty, in-line parlour/solar end to the r. A timber-framed chimney was inserted in the C16, which survives with a later brick chimney built inside it. Hall floored in the C17 and another chimneystack inserted, blocking the screens passage and the original s entrance.

5000

HIGH ONGAR

14 ST MARY. The exterior is dominated by the white brick s tower with porch, an unfortunate addition by *Edward Swansborough*, 1858, that conceals one of the most ornate Norman doorways in Essex. This has one order of columns, a curved lintel with zigzag, a tympanum with three strips of rosettes, also curved, an arch with zigzag, and a hoodmould with saltire crosses, etc. Norman also the N doorway and several windows. The chancel, barely separated from the nave, belongs to the E.E. period, see some lancets. The three tall lancets are C19 externally, but their internal aspect with detached shafts is original. Chancel restored 1883 and the N vestry and w gallery added (by *Chancellor*) in 1885. Reordering in 1993 removed all the furnishings noted by Pevsner in 1965, except the mid-C17 COMMUNION RAIL, with its few heavy balusters. The interior is consequently rather bland, apart from the good nave roof with five tie-beams, each with an octagonal crown-post with capitals and four-way struts. – Heavy stone FONT by *Swansborough*. – STAINED GLASS. In the E window's outer lancets, arms of Jane Seymour and Henry VIII, therefore *c.* 1536. Central lancet, chancel s and nave N windows by *Lavers, Barraud & Westlake*, 1895–1903. – MONUMENTS. Brass to a civilian, *c.* 1510; 18-in. (46-cm.) figure, now wall-mounted. – Richard Stane †1714. Large, with Corinthian pilasters, flaming urns, cresting and arms. – Two tablets with urns by the younger *John Bacon*, 1801 and 1806. – Rev. Edward Earle †1820, an elaborate monument in the shape of a sarcophagus, signed by *Woodley* of St Mary Church, Torquay.

PRIMARY SCHOOL. 1867, with teacher's house, enlarged 1887. Red brick banded with black and very steeply pitched tile roofs, an interesting composition for its time. The architect was *Swansborough*, which compensates for what he did to the church.

E of the church, part-weatherboarded cottages, originally a single hall house, C15, with cross-wings and large C16 chimneystack. Further E the FORESTER'S ARMS, late C18 painted brick with an elaborate C19 pedimented door surround. On the street's s side, BLACKSMITHS COTTAGES, a row of three, late C17, part timber-framed and part brick with recessed arched doors. Opposite the church's s side, SANUK (formerly Three Horseshoes Inn), the exposed mid-C17 timber framing with visible carpenter's marks.

MULBERRY HOUSE (conference centre), 400 yds WNW. 1767, for Edward Earle; the rectory from 1788. Brick, two-and-a-half storeys, square but with five windows and pedimented Doric porch on the entrance front and only three windows on the other sides. Contemporary stables and cottage. Various alterations and extensions since 1979.

HIGH RODING

ALL SAINTS. Flint rubble. C13 nave and chancel, the DOORS with early C13 ironwork, but S porch of c. 1400. Restored by *G.E. Pritchett*, 1853–4. E and W walls rebuilt, N vestry added, and also the W bellcote, replacing a spire struck by lightning in 1832. Pritchett's also the open timber roof, with wall-posts resting on characteristically large carved figures and emblems of saints, and seating with poppyheads. – FONT. Octagonal, Perp, surprisingly large, with quatrefoils with shields. – PULPIT with traceried panels of c. 1500. – STAINED GLASS. Small bits in several windows, mostly C14.

A varied village street ¾ m. NE, a mix of hall houses and cottages, some thatched, some weatherboarded; conspicuous at the S end the BLACK LION with exposed timbers, a C15 hall house with two cross-wings. In the middle, THE OLD SCHOOL, red brick with stock brick dressings, 1861, with a clock and bell-turret added for the Diamond Jubilee, 1897.

PORTERS, nearly 1 m. ENE. An unusually well-preserved manor house of c. 1400, altered in the C16 but very little since. Two-bay hall with integral service wing to the l. and jettied cross-wing to the r. Floor and chimneystack inserted in the C16 and staircase tower added at the rear; windows (including ground-floor oriel in the cross-wing, with pedimented oriel on the first floor) altered c. 1600. Crown-post roof with smoke-blackened timbers over hall.

HIGHWOOD

ST PAUL. Built 1840–2 by *Stephen Webb* of Moulsham as a chapel of ease to Writtle (formally separated from the main parish in 1875). E.E., brick with minimal stone dressings, W bellcote and porch. E end remodelled by *C. Hodgson Fowler*, 1890–1, for choir and raised sanctuary. – PULPIT. C18, from Writtle. – STAINED GLASS. E window by *Heaton, Butler & Bayne*, 1894. – MONUMENTS. In churchyard, W. T. Strutt †1850. Pedestal with pediments and corner acroteria. Signed by *Joseph Dorman* of Chelmsford.

Opposite the church's W end, in Wyse's Road, the OLD VIC-ARAGE: brick, with a gabled bay at one end of the garden front, contemporary with the church and presumably by *Webb*. PRIMARY SCHOOL, ¼ m. SE, also by *Webb*, 1835, with house by *W. E. MacCarthy*, 1866. MacCarthy also built the former school at Radley Green, 1½ m. NW. 1870–1, enlarged 1910. Bands of white brick.

WRITTLE PARK. The principal seats of the Petre family were first
Ingatestone Hall and then Thorndon Hall (qq.v.), but in 1603
Sir John Petre took the title Baron Petre of Writtle, his father
having been granted the manor in 1554. The manor's S part
consisted mainly of royal forest, with two deerparks, Horsfrith
Park and Writtle Park. The outlines of the latter are still discernible and the house lies near the centre. Brick, with some
timber framing visible inside. Two storeys, originally a U-plan
house of three C16 ranges with crowstepped gables. The two
principal elevations (SE and SW), of seven bays, were refronted
in the C18. The C19 NW range completed the square, with the
courtyard roofed over. N of the house, a circular DOVECOTE,
probably the last in Essex; C18 brick, possibly on a C16
foundation.

HORSFRITH PARK FARM, 1½ m. W. C17 timber-framed, altered
in the C18 and C19. Mainly plastered, but the S front faced in
brick with three crowstepped gables. S of the house a six-bay
timber-framed building, now a house, thought to be a maltings built for Sir John Petre, c. 1588.

BIRCH SPRING, 1¾ m. SW. Four-sided enclosure occupying
about 1½ acres, surrounded by a ditch and bank. Late Iron
Age pottery has been found.

HOCKLEY

ST PETER AND ST PAUL. Away from the village on a hilltop.
Short, unusual C14 W tower with big bulky angle buttresses at
the foot and then changing from the square into an irregular
octagon, as if something much larger was originally intended.
Small recessed shingled spire. The big cusped, ogee-headed W
doorway probably dates from the restoration of 1842–3. The
rest of the church C13, of mixed rubble, with N vestry added
1854, extended in the C20. Nave and low, narrow N aisle
separated by a four-bay arcade on round piers with stiff-leaf
capitals (upright leaves) and one-stepped, slightly single-
chamfered arches. Original aisle windows small. The nave roof
is ascribed to the C14. It has tie-beams and crown-posts with
moulded capitals. Inside the tower a wooden belfry frame. –
FONT. Uncommonly big, octagonal, C13, of the Purbeck type,
with shallow blank pointed arches, the stem cut down. Carved
and painted wooden cover by *Siegfried Pietzch*, 1973. – PULPIT.
Carved by *A.S. Tawke*, 1926, who also did the wooden WAR
MEMORIAL, 1919. – SCULPTURE. Rood figures, Stations of the
Cross and other statues by *Anton Dapré* of Austria, mid C20.
– STAINED GLASS. C15 quarries in N aisle E window.

METHODIST CHURCH, Main Road. 1906, by *Greenhalgh &
Brockbank*. Late Gothic.

In 1838 a salubrious spring was discovered at Hockley, and so in
1842–3 in Spa Road a PUMP ROOM was built. It was designed
by *James Lockyer*. It is a modest building as Pump Rooms go,
but of course of quite a different order from what the village

knew until then. Tall arched windows, Tuscan pilasters, and a heavy somewhat restless parapet with a small pediment on the return. It is typical 1840s, in a chaste yet formal mood. Attached to it on the l. a late C19 brick house. The spa did not prosper and the Pump Room was later used as a Baptist Chapel. Of the same date, and also by Lockyer, the SPA HOTEL at the fork of Spa Road and the main road. Two-storeyed with quoins and upper arched windows.

OLD VICARAGE, NE of the church. Gault brick, three bays with central doorway and pediment on Ionic columns. Front rooms added c. 1820 to an existing farmhouse.

PLUMBEROW MOUNT, nearly 1 m. ENE. The mound is 76 ft (23 metres) in diameter and 14 ft (4 metres) high. Excavations in 1913 revealed a core of clay covered by a capping of gravelly earth. Roman and Early Saxon pottery was found on top of the clay core, suggesting a Roman origin, but the function of the mound is uncertain.

HOLLAND-ON-SEA

2010

Little more than a residential suburb of Clacton.

ST BARTHOLOMEW. 1971–2 by *Roy Gould*. Square nave formed round an octagonal steel frame, the beams of which meet in a central octagon and continue above the roof to form a slender open bellcote. Brick, with brightly painted eaves accentuating the crown-like form of the roof. Small projecting sanctuary, and meeting rooms at the W end.

METHODIST CHURCH, Kings Avenue. By *Basil & David Hatcher*, 1968–9. Pale brown brick, with a bold copper roof in the form of an irregular, truncated pyramid with a window to light the altar. The previous church, now hall, by *G.H.B. Gould*, 1925, has rendered walls with brick dressings and half-hipped roof.

The most prominent secular buildings are the KINGSCLIFF HOTEL, Kings Parade, 1931 and 1935, and inland THE ROARING DONKEY pub, Frinton Road, 1934, both by *Basil Oliver* for Greene King. The hotel (with *Naish & Mitchell*) is respectable Neo-Georgian, with rendered, painted walls and pantiles; the single-storey pub has more of the air of a road-house. In MADEIRA ROAD, a small characterful house (No. 76) by *F.G. Vincent-Brown*, c. 1922. Brick, mainly rendered, with a balcony facing the sea.*

LITTLE HOLLAND HALL, ¾ m. E. Timber-framed, probably C16 with C17 additions, faced with brick in the C18 and C19. Converted for use as a nursing home, with additional buildings in the grounds, 1987–9. SE are remains of the medieval parish CHURCH of Little Holland. C11 or C12, rebuilt and extended

---

* A Modern Movement house in Haven Avenue by *Ronald H. Franks*, 1934, appears to have been demolished.

c. 1200, demolished in the mid C17. Only the outline of the walls and a few stones visible.

HORHAM HALL
2 m. SW of Thaxted

58 One of the two or three finest pre-Reformation brick mansions in Essex. Built by Sir John Cutte, Treasurer of the Household of Henry VIII, incorporating a timber-framed house built by Richard Large and occupied by 1451. Cutte acquired the manor in 1502, acquired Thaxted manor in 1514, and died in 1520, leaving the house unfinished. The estate was sold by Cutte's great-grandson in 1599 and purchased soon after by Sir William Smith of Hill Hall, Theydon Mount (q.v.); his descendant Sir Edward Bowyer-Smith restored the house in 1841–4, and further work was carried out by Sir George Binney in 1958.

The C16 mansion seems to have been an H-plan, but the house consists now of one range facing E. The main façade is entirely irregular and eminently picturesque, an effect increased by the variety of shades of colour in the brickwork and its busy stone dressings. The hall lies in the traditional place and is approached, as usual, by a porch leading into the screens passage. The porch is two-storeyed and has a doorway with a four-centred arch. The windows of the hall lie high up except for the magnificent large canted bay window which extends with three transoms and a front of six lights right to the parapet and its (renewed) battlements. It is the showpiece of the house. The individual lights are arched and cusped, and along the top runs a glazed frieze of quatrefoils. To the r. of the bay window the façade is continued by an odd skewed two-storey bay of later Tudor date, which occupies the inner angle with the N wing. This wing formerly extended further out,* where probably lay the chapel, and also to the W, where it touched the moat (whose N and W sides still exist). Both of its fronts now have stepped gables, the W one dated 1844. Of the balancing S range nothing now remains. There was probably a link of some kind between the two wings, with a gatehouse on the E side of a courtyard opposite the entrance. At the façade's N end is the staircase tower, with a datestone near the bottom, 1572 (top part *c.* 1610–20).

The l. bay of the main façade has a low straight gable and original canted bay window. It is of brick, a refronting *c.* 1575 of the mid-C15 timber-framed house. Set back to the S and at an angle of forty-five degrees a kitchen block of *c.* 1660, remodelled by *Walter Ison*, 1958, and divided into two storeys with a Venetian window on the S side's upper floor. Outside Ison created a small courtyard and, beyond, a swimming pool with pavilions of timber and copper tent-like roofs.

---

* Shown in an early C18 painting.

Inside, the hall has a plinth with an ogee frieze which runs right into and along the bay window. The bay window (as well as the other hall windows) has tracery-panelled reveals. The hall has a coved and panelled ceiling hiding the timber roof, but in its middle a louvre opening communicating with the charming lantern on the roof which, as the fireplace is original, can only ever have been decorative, rather than a means of allowing smoke to escape. The screens at the s end appear to be original, and there is some original stained glass in the bay. An ante-room opens off the w side of the N dais while a doorway at its E end leads through passages in the skewed bay into a straight passage along the front of the N wing and so to the staircase tower, which has a solid square newel surrounded by the stair rising in three flights from storey to storey (cf. St Osyth). In the N wing itself, three rooms on the ground floor: an ante-room opening off the N side of the dais end of the hall, two rooms on the ground floor and a chamber on the first floor with a coved and panelled ceiling similar to that in the hall. The staircase to the cellars is thought to be the position of the main stair before 1572.

At the lower end of the hall, the layout of rooms is more complex and has been subjected to numerous alterations. At the front on the ground floor is a room (now the dining room) where a wall-post and bracket can be seen, part of the original jettying of the C15 house. Remains of Elizabethan black-and-white wall painting depicting dense foliage inhabited by a mythical bird and half-masks, below a guilloche frieze, probably done soon after the jetty was filled in. In the window, original glass (re-set) with the initials and emblem of John and Elisabeth Cutte. Above it the four-bay solar of the C15 house, with open ceiling and tie-beams with crown-posts. The ground-floor room of the C17 kitchen wing was fitted out by *Ison* with C18 panelling from The Sun Inn in the Strand, London, bombed in the Second World War.

HORNDON-ON-THE-HILL   6080
Thurrock U.A.

St Peter and St Paul. Primarily E.E., but with a harmonious Arts and Crafts interior of 1898–1904 by *C.R. Ashbee* (nave) and *W.D. Caröe* (*Christian & Caröe*, chancel and N chapel). C13 the four-bay nave arcades and the remains of a clerestory (with quatrefoil windows) above, and the N chapel arcade. The N aisle's arcade seems to have come first: two circular piers and one octagonal, and capitals with crockets and flat stiff-leaf. The voussoirs of one of the arches are decorated with rosettes, a most uncommon motif. The s arcade is nearly identical, except that the capitals are undecorated. The E responds, however, have upright leaves which look as if they might have been re-tooled in the C15. The N chapel arcade has an octagonal pier with moulded capitals. The arches are double-chamfered, whereas most of the arches of the nave arcades are of one step with one chamfer. C13 S doorway with two orders of colonettes (one keeled), and many-moulded voussoirs. Timber bell-turret with shingled spire erected *c.* 1500. Its independent construction, on four sturdy posts with cross-beams and carved braces, was restored and opened to the nave by Ashbee. An interesting feature is that the N and S beams cantilever out to the E and support struts for the superstructure. Trellis-strutting above the cross-beams. Chancel and nave roofs partly original C15, their later ceilings removed by Ashbee. One alteration is that dormer windows have been set into the nave roof on both sides, probably in the C16. The effect on the N side is particularly striking, with a very large expanse of tiled roof resting on a low wall of ragstone and flint rubble. This, and much of the S wall, rebuilt 1898–1904. Timber S porch dates from the C15 but has more of 1903.

LECTERN. By *Ashbee*, made by the *Guild of Handicraft*, 1898. Stem of eight octagonal columns on an octagonal base, then an octagonal drum with copper panels, alternate panels set with ovals of blue-green enamel. On top of that a copper hemisphere, out of which rises an oak shaft supporting the latticework double book-rest. – CHOIR STALLS. By *Caröe*, with traceried panels and castellated ends, a form repeated in simpler style in the nave BENCHES. At the end of alternate benches, painted candleholders on tall staves. – PANELLING of the sanctuary, 1903, presumably by *Caröe*, with Art Nouveau motifs found also on a PRAYER DESK and CUPBOARD. – Simple oak FRONTAL CHEST probably by *Ashbee*, who designed three frontals. – FONT. C14, square bowl with some panelling; on square stem. – ROYAL ARMS. 1715 by *William Waite* of Gravesend. Large and splendid. – STAINED GLASS. Fragments of C15 glass in E window. – Chancel S (David and Solomon) by *Percy Bacon & Brothers*, 1904. – S aisle S (Samuel and Anna) by *Cox, Sons, Buckley & Co.*, 1887, as is probably the next window (Magnificat). – At W end of N aisle, single quarry by *Ashbee*, made by *Christopher Whall*, 1901, depicting the church. – MONUMENT. Daniel Caldwell †1634 and wife. With inscription and two black columns; figures of angels with scrolls stand outside these. Attributed to *William Wright* (GF). The inscription reads:

> Take gentle marble to thy trust,
> And keep unmixt this sacred dust;
> Grow moist sometimes, that I may see
> Thou weepst in sympathy with me,
> And when by him I here shall sleepe,
> My ashes allso safely keep,
> And from rude hands preserve us both, untill
> We rise to SION MOUNT from HORNDON HILL.

Horndon-on-the-Hill is aptly named, and improved by the exclusion of through traffic. The church lies behind and to the W of the High Road, at the centre of which is the OLD MARKET HALL, probably late C16. Restored 1969–70 by *John Graham* (*Graham & Baldwin*). Open ground floor, upper floor supported on massive oak posts with exposed timber framing. Opposite, HIGH HOUSE. Brick with burnt headers, dated 1728, with a wide bay at the S end with carriage arch and original wooden gates curving down to the centre. HILL HOUSE, adjoining, is late C17, brick, with coved eaves cornice. A little further S, THE BELL has timbers exposed on its jettied N elevation. Mainly C15, but the S cross-wing may be late C14. Gabled carriage arch and then an addition, probably C18, with jettied first floor.

ARDEN HALL, ½ m. NE. Three-storey, five-bay Georgian chequered brick, probably the remodelling of an earlier house. Behind it a timber-framed and plastered outbuilding, formerly a C15 hall house, now bereft of its service end. Square C17 brick dovecote.

GREAT MALGRAVES, 1 m. N. C16. Cross-wings at each end with hipped roofs. Pair of Arts and Crafts cottages at the entrance by *Ernest Runtz & Co.*, c. 1900–1. Roughcast, with brick plinth, wide gable with oriel window, half-timbering, and tapering chimneys.

SAFFRON GARDENS, ¾ m. SSW. C16, with two small bays added to the S front in the C18. Walled garden of late C16 brick in two compartments.

HUTTON
Brentwood

6090

ALL SAINTS. A small church, rebuilt 1873 by *G.E. Street*, and not one of his masterpieces. E.E., flint with Bath stone dressings. Nave and aisles on the old foundations, extended chancel with N vestry and S chapel. Large S choir vestry 1959. Of the medieval church the nave arcades with quatrefoil piers, moulded capitals, and arches of one wave and one hollow-chamfer mouldings survive – typical C14 work. The chancel arch and nave roof with two crown-posts belong to the same date, as does the timber N porch. The bell-turret, with its dumpy splay-foot spire, is also medieval, but probably C15. It stands on six posts, and has tall braces from N and S and trellis-strutting from E to W. – PULPIT, LECTERN etc. Metalwork in the typical *Street* style. – FONT. Round, of polished marble, on a solid base with four attached colonettes. Tall wooden COVER, 1893. – REREDOS, now at W end, by *Bodley & Garner*, 1898, made by *Thomas Martin* of Victoria Street, with panels painted by *Sister Catherine Ruth* of All Saints, Margaret Street, London. Richly carved, painted and gilded. – ROOD BEAM, with carved oak figures. 1917. – STAINED GLASS. Nearly all of 1873, and no doubt by *Clayton & Bell*. – MONUMENTS. 16-in. (41-cm.) brass of a man in armour, c. 1525, his wife, and children. – Thomas Cory †1656. Segmental pediment with skull and achievement of arms.

HUTTON AND SHENFIELD UNION CHURCH, Roundwood Avenue. Domestic Arts and Crafts by *William Hayne*, 1913, chiming perfectly with the comfortable houses of Hutton Mount, with big half-timbered gables at the (liturgical) w end and transepts. Slightly tapering sw tower with short octagonal spire behind battlements. Hall 1937, offices etc. by *Michael Buckingham*, 1992.

HUTTON HALL. An interesting C17 brick house on an older moated site. Two storeys and attics, with a seven-bay front with three symmetrical straight gables. Three similar gables at the back and a long, lower, C19 service wing. Windows altered in the first quarter of the C18, the central one on the first floor with basal scrolls and below it a large doorcase with Ionic columns, pilasters and open segmental pediment. Panelled entrance hall with a central timber Ionic column and ornate C17 wooden chimneypiece, probably Flemish and a later import. Staircase with twisted balusters of varying shapes. The most striking room has painted Gothick panelling similar to that executed by Lightoler under Sanderson Miller's direction at Belhus, Aveley (q.v.), in the 1750s.

The area known as HUTTON VILLAGE has one Georgian brick-fronted house (Hutton Lodge) with a C17 timber-framed core, a few cottages, and the former National School, dated 1840, with large windows with cast-iron Gothic tracery. But most of Hutton has been swallowed up by housing: expensive at the beginning and end of the C20 (e.g. Hutton Mount), in between large estates built by London County Council (completed 1955), Brentwood Urban District Council (1963), and East Ham Borough Council (1963). Prominent among this, in RAYLEIGH ROAD, the former POPLAR UNION TRAINING SCHOOL for poor children in the care of the Poplar Board of Guardians. Under the progressive influence of George Lansbury they provided a 100-acre 'cottage home village' in the best surroundings the rates could stand. Most of the buildings, by *Holman & Goodrham*, 1906, have been demolished. The notable exception is POPLARS HALL, Poplar Drive, the former boys' dining hall. Very ornate Baroque, with Dutch gables, two tiers of dormers and central domed clock turret with large weather-vane. Tall, round-headed windows with Gibbs surrounds between brick Ionic pilasters and a decorative brick frieze of poplar trees, figure of St Leonard, etc. Hammerbeam roof inside. On Rayleigh Road: a LODGE and the former SCHOOL (now Mid Essex Adult Community College), with simpler Dutch gables and cupola, T-plan with large assembly hall.

6000

HYLANDS
Writtle

Built for Sir John Comyns, who purchased the estate in 1726. His house was of brick, two-and-a-half storeys high and seven bays wide, with a three-bay central pediment. In 1797 it was bought by a Dutch merchant, Cornelius Kortwright, for whom *Repton* prepared a Red Book (now lost) proposing alterations to the house and park, after which the house was stuccoed and given its giant Ionic s portico, N canted bays, and a single-storey E wing with a three-bay Ionic colonnade. The balancing w wing followed after the house was purchased by P.C. Labouchere in 1815. He employed *William Atkinson*, 1819–25, but apparently only for greenhouses and other garden buildings which have not survived. Additions by *J.B. Papworth*, 1842–8 (including a third storey to the house and second storeys to the two wings) were removed during restoration in 1986–7 by *Esmond Abraham*, Chelmsford Borough Architect. The Borough had acquired the estate in 1966, principally for the sake of the park; the house fell into disrepair and came close to being demolished. The appearance of the restored s front is close to that of J.P. Neale's engraving of 1819, except that the w wing has a doorway added by *Chancellor & Son*, 1908. On the return wall of the E wing is a cement relief of Ceres, the design copied from one by *J. Bacon Sen.*, originally manufactured in *Coade* stone.

The INTERIOR was extensively restored, 1994–2005, after serious neglect. In the ENTRANCE HALL, with arcaded walls, four plaster reliefs (roundels) by *B. Thorvaldsen* of Night and Day, the original models executed in 1815. The DINING ROOM, part of the original house, has an Ionic screen. Beyond it, in the w wing, the BANQUETING ROOM, the house's most striking interior, part of the 1840s alterations but redecorated in 1859. Very French-looking Neo-Baroque. E of the Entrance Hall, at the foot of the GRAND STAIR (the principal surviving part of *Papworth*'s alterations), a frieze of The Triumphal Entry of Alexander the Great into Jerusalem, a copy of Thorvaldsen's 1812 marble original by his pupil *Pietro Galli*, begun 1822.* In the E wing, the SALOON leads through to the elaborately decorated DRAWING ROOM and more sober LIBRARY.

The extent to which *Repton*'s proposals for the PARK were carried out is uncertain, but during Kortright's ownership the park was extended NE up to the River Wid and a serpentine lake formed between the house and the river. The kitchen garden SE of the house, by the London Road, was part of *Atkinson*'s improvements, in an extension of the park by Labouchere. W of the house is the brick STABLEYARD with clock turret on the E side, and w of that an early C19 COTTAGE, faced in flint with rustic woodwork on the corners, originally thatched.

---

* *Thorvaldsen's* statue of Venus with the Apple awarded by Paris formerly stood in the Entrance Hall; there is now a plaster copy.

6090

INGATESTONE

Ingatestone and Fryerning

Ingatestone is a large village with quite a prosperous High Street, and far more prosperous Late Victorian and Edwardian houses of Londoners, especially round the railway station and towards Mill Green, an outlying part of the parish beyond Fryerning (for which *see* p. 373).

ST EDMUND AND ST MARY. A truly magnificent brick W tower with black diapers. Late C15 or early C16. Tall, with angle buttresses, a three-light brick window with Perp panel tracery, and two-light windows in two tiers above it. Stepped battlements on a corbel frieze. Behind the tower the small and shortish N wall of the nave, obviously Norman, of puddingstone and Roman brick. The projecting N chapel is C17 brick, as is the chancel's E wall. S aisle of stone rubble, *c.* 1300, and S chapel built (or rebuilt) in brick by William Petre in 1556. Three-light E window with a transom and two- and three-light S windows.

Inside, the impression is somewhat disappointing after the glory of the tower. Three-bay S arcade with short piers of the well-known Perp four-shaft-four-hollow section, and double-chamfered arches. Nave roof with tie-beams, octagonal crown-posts with capitals and four-way struts, restored by *Chancellor*, 1866–7, who also rebuilt the chancel and aisle roofs as part of a general restoration. Incongruous brick organ chamber on N side of chancel, 1905, and vestries of 1974 (by *Carden & Godfrey*) no better.

Carved stone PULPIT and FONT by *Chancellor*, 1866–7. – Early C18 iron HOURGLASS STAND, fixed to the wall. – ROYAL ARMS of 1673. Painted, on wood. – STAINED GLASS. E window and others in the nave and S aisle, of the last quarter of the C19. – S chapel E, 1923, cheerfully coloured by comparison. – MONUMENTS. Between chancel and S chapel the alabaster tomb-chest of Sir William Petre †1572 and his wife Anne, with recumbent effigies on rolled-up mats. Very fine quality. The tomb-chest with shell-headed panels separated by columns. The effigies are attributed to *Cornelius Cure*, Crown Mason, although the tomb-chest itself is not his style and has been attributed to *William Cure Sen.* (AW). – In the chapel itself Robert Petre †1593, monument with the usual kneeling figure; between columns of touchstone. – Also Captain John Troughton †1621, with an outstandingly good portrait bust in an oval niche. Relief, in an informal demi-profile. Attributed to *Maximilian Colt* (GF). – N chapel: John, Lord Petre, †1613 and wife Mary. Standing wall monument of triptych composition. Under a coffered arch in the centre, and on a higher step, two kneeling figures. In the wings, two more kneeling figures: William, 2nd Lord Petre, who erected the monument and the chapel, and his wife Katherine †1624. The parts are separated by black columns. The whole is straight-topped with obelisks and achievements. On the base in relief nice figures of kneeling children. Attributed to *William Cure Jun.* (AW).

St John the Evangelist and St Erconwald (R.C.), Roman Road. 1931–2 by *Frank Sherrin*, superseding the chapel at Ingatestone Hall (*see* below), and in the style of the Hall, i.e. Tudor brick. Nave with w gallery and undifferentiated chancel, and presbytery on s side. – STAINED GLASS. From Ingatestone Hall: nave s, two windows at w end by *John Hardman & Co.*, 1870s, and nave n by *Morris & Co.*, 1907, from cartoons by *Burne-Jones*. Chancel windows also by Morris, 1934–5, using designs by *Burne-Jones* and *J.H. Dearle*. Nave s by *Reginald Hallward*, 1931, characteristic in its use of slab glass and bright colours, pink and purple, contrasting with the overall green of the Morris windows.

United Reformed Church (Congregational), High Street. 1840 by *J. Fenton*. Broad gault brick front with plenty of lancets, red brick behind. Internal alterations and new school building by *C. Pertwee*, 1876–7. Further alterations including new entrances by *D. Ferguson*, 1985.

Fire Station, High Street. By *Alan Willis*, County Architect (job architect, *John Ferguson*), 1976. Small and self-effacing, with low brick walls and slate platform roof.

Railway Station, Station Lane. 1846, in a friendly Neo-Tudor to complement Ingatestone Hall. Possibly by *H.A. Hunt*. Brick with erratic diaperwork and windows with nice cast-iron tracery. Up-platform buildings by *W. N. Ashbee*, 1884–5.

The High Street, formerly part of the Great Essex Road, has no house of independent value. In aggregate its Georgian brick and its fewer c16 and c17 timber-framed houses form a generally happy picture. Some pleasing vistas, with the church tower rising above old houses, remain, and a view of the church has been opened up from the street. But s of the church, where the High Street meets the Market Place, the effect of demolition and replacement in the 1960s and 1970s is deplorable.* Here The Chequers (shops and offices, 1968–9) dominates, of interest only for its large two-storey ceramic mural by *Philippa Threlfall*. But there is an assortment of nice houses to the nw, and at the far end of Market Place Chapel Croft, a development of ten houses by *David Ruffle Associates* for Countryside Properties, 1977–8, a textbook example of an Essex Design Guide scheme in brick, render, and weatherboarding.

sw of the Market Place, on the High Street's nw side, No. 98, a four-bay, two-storey early c18 house. Blue brick with red brick dressings, pedimented doorcase, and two pedimented dormers in the hipped roof. Opposite, No. 51 (Hammonds Restaurant), early c16, then an early c19 shop with cartway, and then The Bell, dating back to the early c15, with a continuous jetty. A little further sw the Ginge Petre Almshouses, built in 1840 by William, 11th Lord Petre, to

---

* Demolitions include the Spread Eagle, 1963, noted by Pevsner in 1954 for its Early Victorian lettering.

replace those in Stock Lane (*see* below). Neo-Tudor with black diaper-work and gault brick dressings. Three ranges round a court, with a chapel in the middle of the centre range. Probably designed by Lord Petre's agent, *Joseph Coverdale*, whose initials are carved on a brick.

STATION LANE is the place to study the domestic work of *George Sherrin*. In 1882 he leased several sites on the Petre estate to build houses for prosperous commuters, including himself. Completed *c.* 1884, each is large, mostly different variations on 'Old English' picturesque, with gables, false half-timbering, and tile-hanging. At the lane's N end, ARDTULLY (now a nursing home), then FAIRWINDS (originally The Chantry), then RED HOUSE (Queen Anne Revival, with a large ogee-roofed porch), and finally THE GATE HOUSE, Sherrin's own house, now flats. Across the railway line, in HALL LANE, two more houses, NEWLANDS and LONGHOLT.

In ROMAN ROAD, the continuation S of the High Street, ST ETHELBURGA'S, 1913, by *Frank Sherrin*, George's son, for his mother, in his more conservative Neo-Tudor. Between here and the R.C. church TOR BRYAN, distinctive housing by *Design Planning Associates*, 1966–72, carefully landscaped. Detached houses, with flat or shallow-pitched roofs, predominantly in pink brick.*

Now back to the church, and the remainder of the High Street to the NE, which has some nice C18 timber-framed cottages near the end of the village with steep steps up to the front doors. COMMUNITY CENTRE (SE side) built as the Working Men's Club by *G. Sherrin*, 1888, brick and roughcast with a little cupola, much extended.

In STOCK LANE, leading off the High Street to the SE, former ALMSHOUSES founded by Sir William Petre in 1557 in order to qualify for exoneration by Pope Paul IV from any suspicion of having plundered Church property at the Dissolution of the monasteries. Plain, single-storey, brick. Seven of the original ten were demolished for the railway line, beyond which lies a large house, FAIRACRES, *c.* 1920 by *F. Sherrin* for himself, and a smaller one, MARYCOT, both Neo-Tudor.

THE HYDE, ½ m. N. Demolished following a fire in 1965. 1719, altered by *Sir William Chambers* in 1761 for Thomas Brand (later Thomas Brand Hollis), who had a famous collection of classical statues and other works of art.

TRUELOVES, 1 m. WSW. By *William White*, 1859.[†] 'Very picturesque Pointed' (*Ecclesiologist*): polychromatic brickwork and patterned slate roof. Mainly two storeys with attics and one- and two-storey service wing to rear. Open porch on low thick marble shafts supporting a gabled upper storey with oriel. Minor late C19 alterations, more extensively altered and extended in the C20 for a children's home. Large STABLE

---

*On the site of a house enlarged by *G. Sherrin*.
[†]White also designed a school in the village, 1858–60 (dem.).

Lightoaks, Ingatestone

BLOCK in same style, and a small detached outbuilding, perhaps a dairy or laundry, simpler and probably late C19.

MILL GREEN and the houses on the way to it, about 1¼ m. NW of the parish church, form a quite distinct part of Ingatestone, separated from the village by the by-pass. The eponymous WINDMILL is a post mill, rebuilt 1759 by *Robert Barker*, millwright, on an existing base and circular brick round-house. Traditional weatherboarded body of 1959, extensively repaired in 1989–90 and 2001 by *Vincent Pargeter*. Most of the machinery is original and capable of working. The mill stands in the grounds of MILLHURST, by *G. Sherrin*, 1906, much altered; but opposite, LIGHTOAKS, *c.* 1884–5, has his usual picturesque combination of brick and half-timbered gables. A little further NW, MILL GREEN PARK, started as a *cottage orné* for Charles Grant by *H.E. Kendall Jun.*, 1845: brick on the ground floor, timber-framed above, and many gables with elaborate bargeboards.* Nothing of the ornateness survives. Extension after 1877 and considerable remodelling *c.* 1937. SW, in Beggar Hill, DELAMAS, a large early C20 brick house with shaped gables, and a bay on the garden front with corbel frieze borrowed from Fryerning church tower. Now flats.

Of the older houses, of which there are a number along Back Lane to the S of Mill Green, the most prominent is HUSKARDS. Five-bay brick block of 1735 (rainwater heads), two storeys and attics, and to the r. a single-bay wing set back. It appears that there was originally a similar wing to the l., but this is masked by an extension dated 1878, with a shaped gable and large ground-floor bow window. L. of that another extension, 1906, that runs all down the side of the house, with gables

*Included in Kendall's *Villa and Cottage Architecture* (1868), where it is said that a similar house was built at Childerditch – perhaps a reference to the vicarage.

at either end, also shaped but of a different pattern from that of 1878. Good wrought-iron gates and railings to the front, and another gate in the garden wall to the rear. Partly moated, and on the site of a Tudor house. Converted to flats, 1981.

INGATESTONE HALL

Ingatestone was a manor of the nunnery of Barking. In 1539 it came into the hands of William Petre, son of a wealthy tanner in Devon, lawyer and protégé of Thomas Cromwell, busy in the commissions for the Dissolution of the monasteries. Knighted in 1543, Petre was appointed Secretary of State by Henry VIII, a post he managed to hold through the reigns of Edward VI, Mary, and Elizabeth, in spite of his unwavering adherence to the Catholic faith. He was also Chancellor of the Order of the Garter. Only ill health forced him to retire, in 1566.

There was a house on the site but no trace has been found. Sir William Petre's house is of brick and was externally complete by 1548, although interior work seems to have gone on to *c.* 1560. Robert, 9th Lord Petre, resided at Ingatestone in 1764–70 while Thorndon Hall, by then the principal family seat, was being rebuilt, and made considerable alterations. For most of the C19 the house was divided into apartments, but in 1919–22 Lady Rasch, widow of Lionel, 16th Lord Petre, restored the Tudor character of the house with the assistance of a retired architect, *W. T. Wood.* Further work was carried out in 1935–7 by her son Joseph, 17th Lord Petre.

The original form of the house is known from a survey plan by *Thomas Larke,* 1566, which shows a base court, a middle court, and an inner court, aligned W–E. What remains is chiefly the inner court, though shorn of its W range, which contained the Great Hall and lay between the middle court and inner court. It was pulled down in the 1770s. One enters by a GATEWAY, part of the surviving W range of the base court, remodelled in the C18 with a pretty single-handed clock and bellcote. The other surviving buildings of this and the base court's N range are timber-framed, mostly plastered and sashed, partly exposed on the gateway, showing on the inner face how the C18 sashes were inserted into the old framework. The carpentry of the W range, which incorporates a three-bay court hall, suggests that this might pre-date William Petre's ownership, although by only a few years.

The remaining three ranges of the main house are still entirely lacking in the systematization which is characteristic of the Elizabethan style and already existed in some of the leading buildings before her time. On the other hand the mullioned and transomed windows have the Elizabethan form without arches to the tops of the lights; some on the W side of the E range are original, although many are of the 1920s. In another respect, also, the house was advanced: it had a piped water supply and flushing drains; Larke's survey shows that the bedchambers each had 'a little room within' provided with a 'close stool'. Water from natural springs was collected in a circular CISTERN, latterly pumped to a tank in a tower at the NE corner of the house (apparently added in the C19). This water supply system remained in use until 1998.

The most striking external features are the stepped gables, particularly along the S front, where they combine with the many chimneystacks, some of which are original, to create a picturesquely irregular façade. The effect is heightened by the shallow projections that were added on this side later in the C16. Their purpose may have been to conceal the construction of two PRIEST HOLES, one of which was discovered in 1855 and another after the First World War.

Internally, the only room which survives in anything like its original form is the LONG GALLERY on the first floor of the E range. It originally had a coved ceiling, and in the middle of the E side was an opening (now blocked) into a family pew above the CHAPEL. The chapel itself was demolished in 1959 except for a single bay on the ground floor.* Otherwise the layout of the house is mainly as reconstructed by Lady Rasch and her son. In 1936–7 a new main entrance was created in the middle of the E range to the STONE HALL formed out of several small rooms, perhaps to compensate for the missing Great Hall; the fireplace came from the Long Gallery. Lady Rasch created the DRAWING ROOM in the S range, inadvertently destroying the original screens passage through the centre of the range between the garden and inner court. Beyond it was the original kitchen wing, so the linenfold panelling in the DINING ROOM here, like much of the panelling elsewhere in the house, must have been reused. One first-floor room, at the S end of the Long Gallery, remains in its C18 state, so that there is a solitary sash window on the E elevation. A further idea of the C18 appearance of the house is provided by the wing added by the 9th Lord Petre on the NE side of the N wing. The N wing itself, now offices, has one first-floor room with good mid-C16 panelling, probably re-set.

The GARDENS, clearly shown on Larke's survey of 1566 and a map by *John Walker* of 1605, included a stew pond, parterres and banqueting house. The pond survives, and also much of the garden wall. W of the Hall is a former BARN with C13 or early C14 timbers but rebuilt in the C16, and NW of the Hall another BARN, late C16, also timber-framed. The unusually large and fine brick GRANARY was built by Sir William Petre. Two storeys with crowstep gables. The brickwork is in a special form of Flemish stretcher bond, identical to that used for Woodham Walter church. At the drive's W end, a pair of mid-C19 Neo-Tudor lodge COTTAGES.

---

*Rebuilt *c.* 1660, enlarged 1852 and again in 1862–3 (by *D.C. Nicholls*); served as the R.C. parish church until 1932 (*see* St Erconwald, above).

INGRAVE

Brentwood

68 ST NICHOLAS. The most remarkable C18 church in Essex. Erected in 1734–6 by the 8th Lord Petre, to replace the parish churches of Ingrave and West Horndon. The architect is unknown. It has been suggested* that Lord Petre might have designed it himself, and *Leoni* was at this time remodelling old Thorndon Hall (q.v.). The church stands in a hexagonal churchyard, with wrought-iron railings and gates on the W side, and its massive brick W tower is widened by N and S polygonal turrets. These geometric shapes seem to relate to the contemporary landscaping by Lord Petre at Thorndon Hall. The turrets rise above the tower parapet, on its arched corbelfrieze.[†] Big inscription plate. The result has been likened, not unfairly, to a water tower. The rest is more elegant, the interior quite plain. Nave with central entrances from N and S; round-arched windows. Narrower chancel with arch on very thick imposts. N and S vestries. Collegiate-style stalls replaced with benches by *J. Clarke*, 1854, when the church was considered 'a most wretched specimen of the age'. – FONT. Perp, octagonal, with quatrefoil panels. From old Ingrave church. – PULPIT. Panelled, probably *c.* 1735. – C19 chamber ORGAN, from Thorndon Hall. – STAINED GLASS. E window by *E.R. Frampton*, 1894, designed to harmonize with the chancel decoration (now painted over) by *Reginald Hallward*, 1893. – MONUMENTS. Brasses from West Horndon: Margaret Wake †1466, wearing a butterfly headdress, 37½-in. (95-cm.) figure. – Sir Richard Fitzlewes †1528 and his four wives, the main figure 36 in. (90 cm.). – On N side of church, chest-tomb of Martha Manley †1816, wife of *Robert Manley* of Brentwood, stonemason, who may be assumed to have made it; he also is commemorated, †1849.

INWORTH

Messing-cum-Inworth

ALL SAINTS. Ambitious brick W tower and S porch, competently if not sensitively done. The date is 1876–7, the architect *J. Clarke*. The rest is Late Saxon or Early Norman with the chancel E end of the later C14. The two C11 windows in the N and S chancel walls are memorable. They have the equal outside and inside splays typical of their date. The masonry – stone, flint, puddingstone, and Roman brick – should also be studied. C11 also the low and narrow chancel arch inside. To its sides and in the adjoining nave N and S walls C13 blank arches (cf. South Shoebury, Southend-on-Sea). The ones by

---

* By George Clutton.
[†] Which perhaps gave rise to the otherwise inexplicable description of the church, in Kelly's Directory, as being 'in the Lombardo-Gothic style'.

the side of the chancel arch are pierced by large squints. Above the chancel arch remains of WALL PAINTINGS, *c.* 1300, in two tiers, depicting scenes from the life of St Nicholas. – Chancel SCREEN, *c.* 1500, three bays. – BENCH in the nave with uncommonly carved back panels, about the same date. – TILES. In chancel, C13 and C14 ornamented slip-tiles. – STAINED GLASS. C14–C15 fragments in small S chancel window. E window by *James Powell & Sons (J.H. Hogan)*, 1946. – MONUMENTS. Frances Wix †1851, by *Henry Lufkin*. Large, Gothic. – Her husband, Rev. Samuel Wix †1861 by *E.G. Papworth*, also white marble, in the form of an open book.

OLD RECTORY, W of the church. Rebuilt 1862–3 by *A. E. Browne*, and lacking in charm.

INWORTH HALL. Late C18. Seven-bay gault brick façade with central Tuscan porch beneath a round-headed window. C19 conservatory.

KELVEDON

8010

Kelvedon has been identified as the site of Roman CANONIUM, one of the staging posts on the London–Colchester road, itself developed on the site of a Late Iron Age settlement. The enclosure lay SE of the High Street and was bisected by a road that more or less continued the line of the Roman road as it enters Kelvedon from the SW. The Roman settlement appears to have been started in the mid to late C1, to have been enclosed by a ditch in the C2, and to have declined by the late C3, after which it returned to agricultural use. No structures visible above ground, but excavations have revealed the site of a temple, a kiln, rubbish pits, and cemeteries outside the enclosure.

ST MARY THE VIRGIN. The NW angle of the nave, with Roman brick quoins, is evidently Norman. Nothing else of the period is visible. Nave and aisles belong to the C13, see especially the arcades. They have circular piers, except for one N pier with a four-shaft-four-hollow section. The capitals are partly moulded, partly with some stiff-leaf and crocket decoration. The arches are of many mouldings. C14 chancel, and W tower with diagonal buttresses, battlements, and recessed, shingled spire. Also embattled the two aisles. The N chapel (organ chamber) is early C16, brick with a stepped gable and four-light window with intersected tracery applied to a four-centred head. Between chancel and vestry a C14 window and a C14 doorway made out of the head of a two-light window. S chapel added 1841–2, reusing the chancel windows, S porch rebuilt, and the nave roof, early C15 with carved bosses and half-figures, opened up; the architect for this said to be *Hopper*. Further restoration by *A. W. Blomfield*, 1876–7, mainly in the chancel (new roof and five-light E window with reticulated tracery), but also including refacing most of the exterior in flint. Large but appropriate N extension by *Alan Stones*, 1993. – ALTAR (N chapel). By *Edward Beckwith*, 1964. – SCREEN (s chapel). By *C.J. Blomfield*, made by *Ernest Beckwith*, 1922. – STAINED GLASS. E window by *Burlison & Grylls*, 1877, w by *Lavers & Westlake*, 1896. – s chapel E by *Powell*, designed by *Louis Davis*, 1898; first s window also by *Powell*, 1938. The earlier window, belated Pre-Raphaelite, is infinitely the more powerful. Second s window by *Clayton & Bell*, 1859. – MONUMENTS. To the Abdy family of Felix Hall, especially Sir Thomas †1685 with inscription on a draped marble curtain (by *William Stanton?*), and Sir Anthony †1704 (by *Edward Stanton*).

ST MARY IMMACULATE AND THE HOLY ARCHANGELS (R.C.), Church Street. 1891 by *C.T. Thorn*. Enlarged by *Sherrin*, 1909, when the presbytery was also added. Brick with stone dressings, Perp tracery. – STAINED GLASS. Several windows by *Lavers & Westlake*, 1892.

UNITED REFORMED CHURCH (former Congregational Chapel), High Street. 1853. Brick, with gault brick dressings. Front with pedimented gable, pilasters, and four round-arched windows. Schools in same style by *C. Pertwee*, 1879–80, who also remodelled the galleried interior, 1900–1.

PUBLIC LIBRARY and MUSEUM, Maldon Road. Former school, dated 1743 in plasterwork inside. Brick, with C19 porch, extension to r., and Gothic windows. Lower weatherboarded extensions to the l. School founded *c.* 1635 by Thomas Aylett; to the N THE OLD SCHOOL HOUSE, C15, timber-framed and plastered.

PERAMBULATION

The parish church lies next to the railway at the NW corner of the little town, to which it is joined by CHURCH STREET. On the s side of the churchyard lying back from the street, the OLD VICARAGE, Georgian with C19 additions, mainly plastered but with some gault brick. Across the street, LAWN COTTAGE, Georgian, and FULLERTHORNE, Late Medieval with a Georgian front, then RED HOUSE, with a fine C18 front: five bays, brick, with white brick giant pilasters, three-bay pediment, and Ionic doorway. The house behind is timber-framed, of complex plan, the earliest part a hall, originally aisled, facing SW, probably not later than the mid C13. Additions include a C16 wing to the l. of the hall range and an early C19 ballroom to the rear. On the SW side again MARLER'S COTTAGES, a block of four single-storey almshouses by *Chancellor & Son*, 1899–1900. Three little half-timbered gables. Back on the NE side, just before the High Street, OLD TIMBERS, C15 and early C16 with exposed framing, and then on the corner, but mostly along the High Street, KNIGHTS TEMPLAR TERRACE. Stock brick front, 1873, concealing a large early C16 timber-framed building, apparent at the rear; thought to have been built by the Abbot of Westminster as a provincial mansion. In a first-floor room at No. 5 painted wooden panelling, with delicate lozenge motifs and radiating arabesques; more painting in No. 3, including decorated arcading with pendants.

Church Street meets the High Street at ST MARY'S SQUARE, and the way in which the High Street does not start in line with the Roman road from the SW but only after a quite noticeable kink is one of those accidents of town planning that make all the difference to the character of a place. ST MARY'S HOUSE, closing the view from the SW, is thought to have been originally a C15 public building, perhaps a market hall, converted to a house in the C16, with later alterations and additions. Central gabled bay with C18 Corinthian portico. The view back down the High Street is similarly closed, by the long, Tudoresque building of the OLD CONVENT and orphanage, 1890, enlarged by *Sherrin*. The HIGH STREET itself avoids being straight, and the general impression is of a great variety of skyline and more of gables than of Georgian brick cubes. A noteworthy group of timber-framed and plastered houses near the S end, on the SE side, including GRANGEWOOD, early C18, five bays with segmental pedimented doorcase, and to its r. Nos. 4–8, C15 or C16 with two gabled cross-wings, the whole front jettied, now part of a residential home with single-storey rear additions by *Dennis E. Pugh*, c. 1964. No. 16, l. of Grangewood, is late C16 with a C18 doorcase, sash windows and two two-storey canted bays, and then Nos. 26–30, C15 two-bay hall house with gabled and jettied cross-wings. Opposite, an attractive row, with OAKLAND COTTAGE, dating back to the C14, its full-length jetty and fascia dated 1685; its N end is a C15 house with a good broad doorway of *c.* 1700 and a C19 brick cross-wing, originally a butcher's shop, with curved canopy. Then BRIMPTON HOUSE, early C19 gault brick, and opposite, on the corner of Easterford Road, the MASONIC HALL, 1894–5 by *F. Whitmore*, extended 1933. Single-storey, brick, with Ionic pilasters, cornice and parapet.

The street now becomes more diverse, with false half-timbering on the LABOUR CLUB, formerly the workhouse, early C17 with C18 and later additions, and also on THE INSTITUTE, mainly brick, by *P. M. Beaumont*, 1911. This is opposite the United Reformed Church (*see* above), which stands back from the street's NW side, as does the former BRADDY'S three-storey warehouse and workshop. C19, weatherboarded, with continuous rows of windows and a semicircular window in the gable; restored and converted to housing, complemented by new build on the High Street, 1986–7. Then a nice group: ORMONDE HOUSE and, set back, ORMONDE LODGE. The former C16 or early C17, timber-framed with a C18 brick front of a deep panelled parapet and fluted Doric doorcase in front of a deep arched and rusticated recess; the latter all brick and a little later.

After that a stretch of less interest until DOUCECROFT SCHOOL, No. 163, late C18 brick, and opposite it WHITE HOUSE, C17 timber-framed and plastered with an C18 or early C19 five-bay sashed front. Then, on the corner of Orchard Road, Nos. 148–150. The front range a C14 hall house (divided), with gabled and jettied cross-wings, and C18

addition to the r. To the rear of the l. (service) cross-wing a
five-bay C16 extension, a two-storey range that leads to an
aisled structure, of uncertain purpose, possibly an inn. Another
good hall house at Nos. 156–160, C14, with C19 canted bays
and a bow oriel window. Opposite, behind Nos. 203–205, the
former FRIENDS' MEETING HOUSE, 1802: brick, four bays,
hipped roof, with large segment-headed windows and an oval
window above the entrance. Finally, back on the SE side, No.
178, BRIDGE HOUSE, five-bay Georgian brick with pedimented doorcase and three dormers, and No. 180, early C15
hall house with two gabled cross-wings, a small gabled dormer,
and a fourth gable at an angle turning the corner into Swan
Street. All the gables have C19 bargeboards and finials.

SWAN STREET, turning E, was formerly the line of the main road,
before the BRIDGE over the Blackwater to Feering was built in
1788 (one wide arch, brick with stone dressings); brick arches
of its predecessor, probably C17, visible a little way downstream
on the N side. Swan Street has attractive timber-framed and
plastered houses facing the river, notably THE OLD BRIDGE
HOUSE, C17 with an C18 two-storey canted bay, and No. 3
(SWAN HOUSE), with a first-floor oriel. For Easterford Mill,
see below.

BRIDGEFOOT HOUSE, ½ m. SE of St Mary. Complex timber-
framed house, mainly plastered, principally comprising a two-
bay hall and cross-wing, late C16, with a lower C15 cross-wing
to the r. Beyond the cross-wings are C17 and C18 extensions.
The hall has a contemporary screen, *ex situ*, and panelling, and
rooms in the l. cross-wing have panelling and painted texts on
chimney-breasts.

FELIX HALL, ¾ m. NW. The delightfully preserved and inhabited ruin of a seven-bay house begun *c.* 1710 for Sir Anthony-
Thomas Abdy, to which wings were added *c.* 1750. Grandiose
Neoclassical improvements were made for C.C. Western of
Rivenhall Place *c.* 1825 by *Hopper*, who stuccoed the house,
embellished the NW front with Giant Doric pilasters and
attached columns, and gave the SE front a noble Ionic tetrastyle
portico, based on the Temple of Fortuna Virilis, Rome. The
wings have gone, taken down in 1939 by Geoffrey Houghton-
Brown, and a year later the remainder was gutted by fire.
Houghton-Brown roofed over the northern portion at first-
floor level, and the same was done to the southern portion by
Milner Gray (with architectural input by colleagues in the
Design Research Unit) after 1953, leaving the main entrance hall
behind the portico open to the sky as a courtyard between two
flat-roofed, two-storey wings within the shell. Houghton-
Brown also converted the mid-C18 rear service wing (now THE
ORANGERY) and stables (now CLOCK HOUSE) in 1939. Both
have six bays of windows set in arched recesses (with some of
the additional windows of Clock House reused from the main
house). Clock House has a central pedimented bay, originally
the carriage entrance, with an octagonal timber clock tower,
copper dome, and domed bell-turret. *Repton* was consulted

about improvements to the park in 1793, immediately after Western purchased the estate; the winding approach may be due to him.

EASTERFORD MILL, Swan Street. Two-storey C18 weatherboarded water mill, with hoist loft, its machinery intact and restored. Three-bay timber-framed and plastered mill house attached, with large sashes and a window with arched head over the front door.

GREY'S MILL, Maldon Road. Water and steam mill, rebuilt following a fire in 1858. Painted brick, and windows with cast-iron lintels and casements. Four storeys and loft, five bays with corner pilasters and two further pilasters. Gabled ends of three bays with Diocletian windows to the loft. Single-storey engine house to the SE added shortly afterwards, with tall windows with semicircular heads. Facing the mill, the former mill house and office. All now converted to domestic use.

KELVEDON HATCH

5090

ST NICHOLAS. 1894–5 by *J. T. Newman*, who lived in the village. Ostensibly E.E., but Goodhart-Rendel thought it 'rather in the cricket pavilion style'. Brick with oddly stunted apse, and half-timbered dormers in the hammerbeam roof. SW tower over entrance porch with shingled splay-foot spire. – PULPIT, LECTERN, CHANCEL SCREEN and FONT COVER. Elaborate wrought-iron work, 1895–8. – STAINED GLASS. Striking E window, 1977, insipid nave windows, *c.* 1966 onwards by *F. W. Skeat* and others, the most recent by *Judy Hill*, 1999. – MONUMENTS. Some from the old church.

OLD ST NICHOLAS, next to Kelvedon Hall. Ruinous. 1753, brick, but in general shape keeping to the Essex tradition. Nave and lower chancel, and belfry. Arched and circular windows, with Venetian windows originally at either end. Restored by *J. Clarke*, 1873, but in disrepair from the 1890s.

KELVEDON HALL. The manor was purchased by John Wright in 1538 and the house rebuilt in brick by his descendant John Wright (†1751). Rainwater heads dated 1743. Seven bays wide, with in addition on the entrance side quadrants connecting to pavilions of three-bay length, each with a turret and ogee-domed cupola, and on the garden side three-bay pavilions in line with the façade. Both façades are very plain. The main doorway alone is distinguished by a pediment on attached Roman Doric columns. Porch on garden front added *c.* 1780. Restored by *Wellesley & Wills* for Henry 'Chips' Channon M.P., 1937–8.

Inside, the ENTRANCE HALL and the STAIRCASE are in their original state, with pediments over the doors. The staircase walls are stuccoed with hanging garlands, trophies, etc. depicting War, Music and the Chase, and the stair railing is of wrought iron. The other best rooms were redecorated in Adam style *c.* 1780, especially the dining room and drawing room. In one of the pavilions towards the garden is the former ORATORY (the Wrights were Roman Catholic) with a segmental vault, attached columns on the slightly apsed altar side, and pilasters opposite. This later work was for John Wright (†1792) and a plan in the house by *John Tasker* suggests that he was responsible. In the STUDY a painted ceiling, probably by Italian workmen. Oratory restored by *Sir John Oakley*, *c.* 1932. Octagonal bathroom off the former Oratory decorated by *John Churchill*, who also painted a panel over the door of the late C18 orangery. Much of the interior redecorated by *David Hicks*, *c.* 1965; he inserted the tight staircase with Chinoiserie balustrade. – Neo-Austrian-Baroque bathing pavilion s of the house by *W.W. Kellner*, 1938, and C18 stable block to NW. Neoclassical stuccoed entrance LODGES, linked by an archway, by *Wellesley & Wills*.

BRIZES (Peniel Academy), Ongar Road, 400yds s of St Nicholas. Nine-bay, two-and-a-half-storey brick house with Tuscan tetrastyle porch and three-bay pediment. Probably built (or substantially altered) for William Dolby, following an advantageous marriage in 1770; a rainwater head (not *in situ*) dated 1722 with initials of Richard Glascock probably refers to earlier work. Entrance hall with a Venetian screen to separate the room from the imperial staircase. Its window incorporates C17 STAINED GLASS roundels of soldiers with muskets etc. Grounds laid out for Dolby by *Richard Woods*, 1788.

GREAT MYLES'S, 1½ m. N. Demolished after a fire in 1837, but the late C18 brick STABLES survive. Their central three bays break forward slightly and rise to an octagonal wooden lantern and cupola. Park laid out by *Richard Woods* for John Luther, 1771, forming a lake by damming a tributary of the Roding; graceful brick bridge with stone cappings and keystones, a single span with sweeping walls.

HATCH FARM, Ongar Road, opposite St Nicholas. Mid C16, but with a prominent cluster of early C17 brick chimneystacks, and two C18 brick façades, of five and three bays, with dormers in the hipped roof.

Former NUCLEAR BUNKER, Kelvedon Hall Lane, ½ m. NW. One of four 'R4' bunkers purpose-built by the Air Ministry as Sector Operations Centre for the Metropolitan Sector, *c.* 1951–3 (engineers, *Mott Hay & Anderson*). Built into a hill, the only visible parts the guardhouse, disguised (unconvincingly) as a bungalow, a small ventilation hatch and emergency exit, and radio mast. Below is a 27,000 sq. ft (2,600 sq. metre) complex on three levels. 10-ft (3-metre) thick reinforced concrete walls, within a wire-mesh Faraday cage. Adapted in 1961 as a seat of regional government. Now a museum.

2020

KIRBY-LE-SOKEN

ST MICHAEL. Surprisingly big and important-looking w tower. Knapped flint with a quatrefoil frieze at the base, massive diagonal buttresses, tall two-light bell-openings with one transom, and battlements with flint and stone chequer decoration. C15, as is the N doorway. 'Improved after the fashion of the day' by *Joseph Parkins*, 1833, restored by *Henry Stone*, the vicar's son-in-law: chancel rebuilt 1870, nave restored 1872, including new arcades, new S aisle and organ chamber on S side of chancel, and N porch. Much septaria in the walls. – STAINED GLASS by *Messrs Francis* of London included in Stone's restoration, probably the E window and S aisle (Nativity), since re-set. Chancel N (Annunciation and Nativity) by *Alexander Gibbs*, similar date, also probably the N aisle (Crucifixion). N aisle E, 1936, and S aisle W, 1948, by *Townshend & Howson*. S aisle (St Michael), 1960, and chancel N (St Osyth etc.), 1962 by *A.L. Wilkinson*. Two windows in N and S aisles, 1969–70, and chancel S by *Rupert Moore* (*Whitefriars Stained Glass Studios*). – MONUMENT. On E wall outside, Richard and Mary Savage †1816 and 1832. Large cast-iron plaque by *Coleman & Wallis*, Colchester, with four-centred arched head and side-shafts, enclosed by railings.

EVANGELICAL (Primitive Methodist), The Street. 1926, by *G.H.B. Gould*. Brick, nicely detailed.

PRIMARY SCHOOL, Kirby Cross, ¾ m. S. 1900. Brick, tall windows with half-hipped gables and an open bell-turret, typical of *C.E. Butcher*'s work.

SW of the church the OLD VICARAGE, 1824, possibly by *Joseph Parkins*: gault brick, three bays with central Doric porch. Beyond it KIRBY HALL, red brick, *c.* 1700. Central doorcase with fluted pilasters and open pediment.

Opposite the church, the RED LION, C16, and a scattering of cottages. Further W, in Walton Road, LOW BARN, 1924 by *Searle & Searle*, in the Arts and Crafts tradition with two gables and a dormer; reused brick and tiles. At the edge of the village, DEVEREUX FARM, 1950–1 by *Raymond Erith*, extended to his design 1973–5 by *R. Geary*. It has the appearance of a timber-framed farmhouse modernized in the C18 with stucco, Gothick windows and a trellis porch (but retaining two stone-mullioned windows); in fact rendered brick with concrete floors.

LAMARSH

8030

HOLY INNOCENTS. Round tower, rendered, with Norman windows. Mostly of flint rubble apart from one timber-framed section, only visible inside, the result of repairs following a lightning strike in 1797. The octagonal splayed spire with dormers belongs to the restoration of 1865–9 by *A.W. Blomfield*, and looks it. Nave and short chancel in one, mostly C14, except the chancel E lancets which belong to Blomfield's rebuilding of the E wall. Late C16 brick S porch, with recesses in the SE and SW internal angles. The painted text over the S door is probably C18. – SCREEN. Of ten bays including two-bay doorway, two traceried panels to each bay; C15. – STAINED

GLASS. E lancets by *Mary Lowndes*, the central one 1895, two side ones †1896 and 1913.

LAMARSH HALL, N of the church. Close-studded S front, the two jettied bays to the l. C14, extended to the rear in the late C16 and to the r. in the early C17.

OLD RECTORY, opposite the church. 1909 by *R. M. F. Huddart*, a pupil and assistant of Lutyens. Brick, with black diapers on the upper storey of the garden front, and a string course that forms triangular and segmental pediments over the ground-floor windows. Two canted bays on the E front. W extension by *Quinlan Terry*, 1985.

SHRUBS FARM, ⅔ m. S. Three-bay timber-framed and plastered farmhouse, 1843 with decorative verges and eaves but otherwise C18 in appearance. Rear three-bay extension by *Raymond Erith* for his nephew Robert Erith, 1972, further extended by *R. Geary*, 1988, to make a five-bay garden front with central bow window.

₄₀₉₀

LAMBOURNE

ST MARY AND ALL SAINTS. Of quite exceptional charm. It consists of C12 nave, a chancel rebuilt in the C13, and C15 weatherboarded W belfry crowned by a leaded splay-foot spire. The exterior and interior were remodelled boldly, naively, and very successfully in the Early Georgian age. Single Norman windows on both sides, and Norman doorways, both blocked: plain on the S, on the N more elaborate, with one order of columns (without shafts), an arch decorated by zigzag, and a fragmentary tympanum diapered with carved stars. Other windows C18, pointed in the nave, arched in the chancel. Internally the chancel windows (those on the N lost to a shallow organ chamber, added 1889) have Gothic ogee mouldings. The W doorway with a canopy on carved brackets and oval window above is dated 1726, the W gallery inside 1704–5 (given by William Walker of Bishops Hall). This hides much of the belfry superstructure. But more unusual and ingenious is the way in which the C15 roof construction was hidden. The tie-beams are plastered and have Greek-key friezes along their undersides, and one crown-post with its four-way struts is clothed in rich acanthus leaves. Low and broad chancel arch, of segmental form, resting on thick coupled brackets.

FONT. C18, with baluster stem. – CHANCEL STALLS. 1889, reusing fine early C18 openwork foliage carving. – PULPIT. Jacobean. – SCULPTURE. On E wall, five fibreglass figures or motifs by *T.B. Huxley-Jones*, 1963. – WALL PAINTINGS. On nave S wall, upper half of a large high-quality figure of St Christopher. C14, painted over a mid-C14 version, partially renovated late C15. – Further W, a fragment of post-Reformation painting, part of a frame for texts. – Either side of the E

window, fragments of a classical scheme, probably early C18.*
Two pediments, perhaps the top of a frame for painted Commandments etc. – STAINED GLASS. Fine small panels of Swiss
glass, dated 1623–37. Brought from Basle in 1817, re-set 1959.
– E window by *A.K. Nicholson*, 1931.

MONUMENTS. Brass to Robert Barfott †1546 and wife, with
children; 18½-in. (47-cm.) figures. Palimpsest, with parts of
seven brasses on the reverse, late C14 to early C16. – Thomas
Winniffe †1654, rector, later Dean of St Paul's and Bishop of
Lincoln. Black-and-white marble tablet with Corinthian
pilasters, broken segmental pediment and shields. Attributed
to *Thomas Burman* (GF). – Many C18 and C19 monuments,
mostly to members of the Lockwood family, the most ambitious that of John Lockwood, erected 1778. Largish figure of
Hope with an anchor and an urn. By *Joseph Wilton*, a reduced
version of his monument to the Earl of Bath in Westminster
Abbey. – Rev. Robert Tooke †1776. By *John Peck* of Bishop's
Stortford. – Lady Rous †1794. Figure of Faith, addressing a
classical monument with urn. Now at the W end, originally
above the altar blocking the E window. – Matilda Lockwood
Maydwell †1800. Marble block on the sloping shelf of a S
window, with a decorated lamp. By *Flaxman*. – George Lockwood †1854 in the Charge of the Light Brigade. By *A. Gatley*,
1860, with relief of an angel at the last trump.

The attractiveness of the church, whose white paint, weatherboarding, and Georgian features on the W front give it a New-
England air, is enhanced by its setting, with LAMBOURNE
HALL facing it. C16 timber-framed and plastered, with five
bays of sash windows and Doric porch. Cross-wing to r.
1937. Some panelling from Marks Hall (dem. 1950, q.v.).† C16
brick wall with bee boles and late C16 weatherboarded granary
to SE.

LAMBOURNE PLACE (former rectory), ⅔ m. NNE. C17 timber-
framed house, faced with brick *c.* 1740. Show front of seven
bays and two storeys with a high parapet concealing dormers.
Rusticated quoins and window surrounds, quoins also for the
slightly projecting pedimented three-bay centre. Doorway with
pediment on consoles (said to come from Dews Hall, *see*
below), arched window above. Good, graceful contemporary
staircase.

BISHOPS HALL, ½ m. SSE. The seat of the Lockwood family was
first Dews Hall, demolished *c.* 1840, then Bishops Hall, which
had been rebuilt in the early C18 but was demolished 1936,
when the present house was built nearby. Sprawling Neo-
Tudor, with gables and half-timbering. On the S front, carved
stone Lockwood arms from the old house, and inside reused

---

* The painting must pre-date the classical wooden reredos noted by Pevsner in 1954,
removed the following year.
† Some of Lambourne Hall's original panelling, dated 1571, was removed in 1917
and is now in the Lady Lever Art Galley, Port Sunlight.

C17 panelling. Entrance lodge with Gothick windows and rustic veranda.

LANGFORD

ST GILES. From the NE the church looks entirely of the date of its restoration: 1880–2 by *Edward Browning*. It is only when one walks round that one sees a Norman apse, complete with three small windows. The impression is confusing, because an apse in England is only expected at the E end, and here we have a W apse – indeed the only one surviving, although it is known that Abingdon about the year 680 had a church with apses at both ends. Langford originally had an E apse as well. The type is in all probability to be derived from Carolingian and Ottonian Germany, where apses at both ends were quite frequent, though not, it is true, for village churches. Thus, even internationally speaking, Langford was a great exception, and it is much to be regretted that the E apse did not survive the late Middle Ages. It was taken down in the C14 or C15 and a square extension added to the chancel. It is surprising, perhaps, that Browning did not reinstate it. As it is, he further disoriented the visitor by adding a bell-turret on the chancel's N side, replacing a conventional Essex W belfry, as well as the N aisle, vestry, and S porch. Apart from the apse the only Norman evidence is the plain S doorway. – REREDOS. By *Gerald Cogswell*, 1928. Elaborately carved with two angels in low relief, brightly painted in silver, red and blue. – SCULPTURE. Clay figure of St Francis by *Catharni Stern*, c. 1998. – STAINED GLASS. E window by *Percy Bacon & Bros*, designed by *E. Geldart*, c. 1895. Nave S, eastern window by *Kempe*, 1918; another to Mary Jane Byron †1909, the patron responsible for the restoration, including a depiction of the church.

W of the church, LANGFORD MILL, rebuilt by *Chancellor*, 1879; four storeys, the lower two in red brick, the others in stock brick with red dressings. The MILL HOUSE, now a hotel, has a C19 front, but was probably built at the same time as the previous mill, 1776. Also by Chancellor the former SCHOOL, E of the church: brick with a bellcote at the W end and master's house at the other, 1874; closed 1922.

MUSEUM OF POWER. Built by the Southend Waterworks Co., 1927, as a pumping station to supply Southend-on-Sea. The water was extracted from the Rivers Chelmer and Blackwater and held in two thirty-million-gallon reservoirs before being treated and pumped to Prittlewell, about 14 miles away. Three 'inverted vertical' triple-expansion steam pumping engines supplied the power, of which one remains *in situ*, made by the *Lilleshall Co. Ltd*, 1931. Stock brick buildings with concrete block dressings in imitation of stone and a chapel-like 'E end' with a pair of triple round-headed windows, each set in a larger round arch. The engineers were *Edward C. Bilham* and *T. & C. Hawksley*. Superseded 1963, following which the 150-ft (46-metre) hexagonal chimney was demolished.

LANGFORD GROVE. Mostly demolished in 1953.* It was a very handsome house of white brick by *John Johnson* for Nicholas Wescomb, 1782. Main block of five bays and two-and-a-half storeys, with single-storey connecting passages and then three-bay pedimented outer pavilions. The W pavilion remains with its connecting passage, the latter raised to two storeys with the new brickwork incorporating a keystone with a bearded head, probably the one that was originally over the front door. NE, the COACH HOUSE, a three-storey pedimented central block flanked by two-storey wings with pyramidal roofs. This served to conceal from the house some existing farm buildings: these include a C16 weatherboarded barn, now a house (HOME FARM). Surviving features of the park include a long octagonal WALLED GARDEN E of the coachhouse and to the W of the main house a TEMPLE, red and gault brick with two stone Tuscan columns and end piers, and a BRIDGE with attached weir, also gault brick, with knapped flint voussoirs and stone caps. The temple, now lacking its pediment, can be seen in two gouaches of the house, park and lake by *Thomas Sandby*.†

LANGFORD HALL, N of the church. Mostly late C17 brick, but with a delightful S front of 1748 that has black brick quoins. The middle three bays (of seven, although to the r. there is only one window where symmetry requires two) break forward slightly, with a fine central Roman Doric doorcase.

LANGFORD LOCK and BRIDGE, ½ m. S. The most accessible of the parish's three locks and two bridges of the Chelmer and Blackwater Navigation, opened 1797 (*see* Introduction, p. 52). Brick with stone copings.

LANGHAM

ST MARY THE VIRGIN. Norman nave, now only recognizable by the NE quoins of Roman bricks; otherwise mainly of rubble and flint. The one small N window looks all new but may be renewed correctly. Nave extended to meet the C13 W tower, which has diagonal buttresses added in the C14, and brick battlements with crocketed pinnacles, but cusped lancets. C14 S aisle with low six-bay arcade of octagonal piers and double-chamfered arches. The aisle windows are also C14, the E of an unusual variety: straight-headed, of five lights with slender ogee heads. In the S wall a recess with three heads, two as label stops, one as keystone in the apex. Also in the C14 the chancel was extended (using much puddingstone), and presumably at this time the chancel arch was widened to the S with the S wall splayed to meet up with the E end of the S aisle, resulting in a disconcerting asymmetry. Restored and re-seated by *H. W. Hayward*, 1862–3, when N and S porches were added. W gallery,

---

* Bookcases reused at Bradwell Lodge, Bradwell-on-Sea (q.v.).
† Photographs in Essex Record Office.

including ORGAN CASE, by *Nicholas Jacob*, 1997–8. – BENCH ENDS. With poppyheads, two with angel figures, C16, reused in chancel stalls by *Hayward*. – In the floor, and probably dating from 1862–3, a METAL PLATE forming part of 'Mitchells Patent Reverbrating Smoke Consumeing Hypocaust for warming Churches' [*sic*]. – STAINED GLASS. E window, chancel N, and tower window by *Mayer & Co.*, 1883–4. – MONUMENT. Margaret Eleanor Maude †1833, draped sarcophagus with a female figure drifting heavenwards. By *John Bacon Jun.* and *Samuel Manning Sen.* – In churchyard, S of tower, headstones of Joseph Downes †1714 and his wife Deborah †1725, and their daughters †1725 and 1730, carved with cupids' heads, skulls, hourglass etc.

The church lies away from the village, near Langham Hall. In the churchyard's NW corner a low, gault brick SCHOOL-ROOM built by Rev. J.T. Hurlock, 1832: 'designed for the daily instruction of poor girls of this parish, . . . and for the reception of the poor and infirm between the services on the Sabbath', according to the cast-iron notice. A similar plate in the church porch, probably originally made for nearby Gun Hill, reads:

> The dumb animals humble petition.
> Rest, drivers rest, on this steep hill
> Dumb beasts, pray use, with all good will
> Goad not, scourge not, with thonged whips
> Let not, one curse, escape your lips.
> "God sees and hears."

On the churchyards's N side, CHURCH FARM, the subject of Constable's painting 'The Glebe Farm' (1830). C15, with gabled two-storey porch and a large jettied and gabled cross-wing to its r.

LANGHAM HALL. Plain, six-bay, two-storey stuccoed house, pedimented centre projecting slightly with Diocletian window. Probably built for Jacob Hinde after his marriage in 1756. Remodelled and extended *c.* 1900, when the Greek Doric porch was added and C16 panelling introduced from Valley House (*see* below). Gardens by *Percy Cane*, *c.* 1930, including terrace, semicircular rose garden, herbaceous walk, and glade. Early C19 classical EAST LODGE on Gun Hill, ½ m. ESE, single-storey with the shallow slate roof extending to form a veranda on thin Tuscan columns. Massive iron gates by *Bayliss & Co.*

VALLEY HOUSE, 1 m. WNW. Early C16, timber-framed and plastered, remodelled and partly rebuilt in brick later in the century. The main addition was the rear staircase wing, with mullioned and transomed windows and a well stair uncommonly ornate for its small scale. Symmetrical balusters and newel posts with strapwork ornament, although the principal post, decorated with a demi-figure, has been lost. Other terms and carvings reused in the C19 porch on the S front. Brick buttresses, very substantial against the staircase wing, probably added after the 1884 earthquake. New N entrance part of alterations by *Gerald Shenstone & Partners*, *c.* 1980.

The village covers a large area S of the church and Hall, with no real centre. GLEBE HOUSE, ½ m. SSE of the church, built as the rectory in 1847: gault brick, the entrance front of three bays with Ionic portico, the garden front with two-storey canted bay. Lower service wing of painted brick. 1 m. SSE, LANGFORD HALL, C16, jettied on the front and at the l. end with dragon beam. ⅓ m. SW, WHALEBONE HOUSE, gault brick, with rain-water heads dated 1801, and further on THE OLD HOUSE, with a hall and jettied E cross-wing probably of *c.* 1400 and C16 W cross-wing. A first-floor room has painted decorative arcading of *c.* 1600. More extensive painting in HILL FARM, 1¼ m. SW, including the date 1566.

WATERWORKS. 1932–3, for the South Essex Waterworks Co. (cf. Layer de la Haye). Buildings in the Modern Movement style. S of the main site a row of staff houses.

LANGLEY

4030

ST JOHN THE EVANGELIST. Pebble-rubble nave, chancel, and unbuttressed C14 W tower with pyramid roof. Restored and re-seated by *Ewen Christian*, 1884–5, who rebuilt the S porch, nave S wall, and upper part of the tower, renewed the pebble facing, and added the N vestry. The nave is C12, see the single window in the N wall, although the restored S doorway has, in the arch, one roll moulding and one keeled roll moulding. Mid-C16 brick chancel, also one brick window in the nave S wall. Nave roof late C15, double hammerbeam. – STAINED GLASS. In E window, royal (Stuart) arms, late C17. – Nave N by *Hugh Easton*, 1935.

The church lies in the part of Langley known as Upper Green, next to LANGLEY HALL, C17 with exposed timbers and single-storey C18 addition to W. SE of the church, on the edge of the Green, former SCHOOL by *G.E. Pritchett*, 1856, and E of that the BAPTIST CHURCH, 1828, rebuilt 1892 by *Butcher & Abrams*. Both brick with stock brick dressings, the school much more attractive without being much more elaborate. S of the church, the OLD VICARAGE by *Frederic Hammond*, 1876–9. White brick with red dressings, and rather suburban.

Lower Green, ½ m. SW, has a few good thatched cottages, including BROOMS, C18, with a notice warning beggars that they will be 'punish'd as the law directs'. Opposite, THE BULL, C19 brick with iron lattice casements. Simple METHODIST CHURCH, 1862, enlarged 1871, brick with stock brick dressings on the front and black diapers on the sides.

RUMBERRY HILL, ¾ m. ESE. Large round barrow, 120 ft (37 metres) in diameter and 8 ft (2.5 metres) high. Excavations in the C19 produced fragments of Roman brick, glass, and Samian ware.

8000
LATCHINGDON

CHRIST CHURCH. 1856 by *J.P. St Aubyn*. Nave and chancel, of Kentish rag and Bath stone, with bell-turret and shingled spire atop steep-sided roofs. – STAINED GLASS. Two windows from 1856, E window *c.* 1864, good of their kind. Chancel N and S by *Morris & Co.*, 1889 (*Bowman* and *J.H. Dearle*) and 1895 (*Walters*).

ST MICHAEL. The old parish church, 1 m. S, converted to a house by *Patrick Lorimer* of *ARP Architects*, *c.* 1976. Nave and S porch only, C14; the chancel (rebuilt 1815) was demolished after 1856. Kentish ragstone rubble with some brick, notably part of the N wall which has a four-light brick window of 1618, still with the lights ending in four-centred arches. W wall faced with brick in late C18.*

LATCHINGDON HALL, E of St Michael. By *Ewan Christian*, 1850, as the rectory. Brick with stock brick dressings, gabled, gaunt.

TYLE HALL, ⅓ m. E of St Michael. Timber-framed and plastered house of *c.* 1500, moated, with two cross-wings originally jettied and gabled but now underbuilt and with hipped roofs. Large, uncompromising late C19 brick extension.

OLD POLICE HOUSE, The Street. 1842. Plain domestic Late Georgian by *Hopper*, the first divisional headquarters building for Essex, with magistrates' court and living accommodation for a superintendent and two constables.

0030
LAWFORD

ST MARY. The early C14 chancel is one of the most splendid monuments of its date in Essex. It is four bays long, divided by buttresses into pairs of two. The buttresses between and the diagonal buttresses at the E end have niches, no doubt for statuettes, a preparation for the show to come. The walls also are showy, whitish-yellow brick and flint and stone in bands and chequered. The large three-light N and S windows have eight different tracery patterns of which at least five are quite unusual and must probably be credited to the imagination of this particular master mason. The E window is unfortunately renewed, part of *Sharpe & Paley's* restoration of the chancel in 1853, and inside the REREDOS underneath it (by *C.F. Hayward*, 1884, with carving by *Earp*), by trying to outdo the magnificence of the medieval stonework in alabaster and naturalistic carving, is another blemish. It needed all the Victorian self-confidence not to restrain oneself in the presence of so much
23   ornamental carving as the chancel displays. The windows are shafted and up to the voussoirs run thick bands of bossy foliage. Between the pairs is a buttress outside, and inside a narrow blank arch with a tall concave-sided gable flanked by

---

*Ten panels from the medieval ROOD SCREEN, painted with figures of saints, now in Chelmsford Museum.

thin buttresses. In the third window from the W on the N side one detects owls in the leaves, on the S side squirrels. Moreover the easternmost N window has instead of foliage two chains of little men. They dance, wrestle, play musical instruments, hold each other by their feet. It is all full of indomitable exuberance. On the S side the priest's door, SEDILIA and PISCINA make a similar display, five ogee arches separated by triple shafts, the front part of which is square and diapered, while the side parts are the usual demi-shafts. The spandrels again are full of figures, their heads broken off by vandals. Some are angels making music on the portable organ, psaltery, gittern, organistrum (hurdy-gurdy), and harp. The chancel arch and stalls are of 1853, the floor and a general restoration of the walls and roof 1887–9. 24

As for the rest of the church, nave, S porch, and W tower are also C14, but seem in their details (especially the nave S windows, restored 1930) later than the chancel. The S porch has on the sides the remains of tracery. The W tower is a bewildering mix of materials, much repaired in brick, with the remains of flushwork where the knapped flint is set in frames of puddingstone. The tower arch is early C16 brick, reopened with the addition of carved corbels in 1864, which is also the date of the W window. N aisle by *John Lewis*, 1826, with a gallery inserted in 1841 (taken down 1961, part of its panelling reused on the organ gallery). The N arcade, however, probably belongs to 1864. Church hall, vestry and offices on N side by *Tim Venn*, 1991, harmonious in form and materials. – FONT. C18 on baluster stem. – STAINED GLASS. Minor fragments of tabernacles and leaves in chancel windows, *in situ*. E window by *A.K. Nicholson Stained Glass Studios*, 1952. W window 1864, geometrical. – MONUMENTS. Edward Waldegrave of Lawford Hall †1584, and wife, the usual kneeling figures facing each other. – Edward Green of Lawford Hall †1814, tablet surmounted by sarcophagus. By *T. Elliot* of Hull. – Rev. Henry Green †1844 and Thomas Nunn of Lawford House †1837, both by *Henry Lufkin*, plain marble tablets. – Rev. E.K. Green †1902. Brass plaque by *H.B. Sale Ltd*, Birmingham.

LAWFORD HALL. A large half-H plan timber-framed mansion of 1583, for Edward Waldegrave. The main show front does not reveal that, for it was faced with brick and entirely Georgianized for Edward Green *c.* 1756. The new S front has a five-bay centre and two-bay wings projecting a little. In the middle a three-bay pediment with lunette, the dentilled cornice not stone, as first appears, but white brick. Parapet with stone capping and balls, and hipped roof. The entrance hall belongs to that date, too, the walls divided by pilasters, and the W front also was given a symmetrical brick face with a range of six sash windows between the chimneystacks at either end. But behind, where the wings project considerably more, the Elizabethan character is almost unchanged. The wings are gabled, their upper storeys jettied with moulded bressumers. Moulded eaves cornices supported on cast-iron brackets. In the re-entrant angles two stair-turrets, that on the r. the main stair with heraldic STAINED GLASS, dated 1596 and 1599, inserted by F.M. Nichols in the C19. Some original windows are also preserved, that at the end of the w wing of five lights with one transom. Two original chimneystacks with octagonal shafts. Rainwater heads dated 1866 mark the acquisition of the house by Nichols, those of 1949 alterations on the courtyard side by *Marshall Sisson* for Sir Philip Nichols. Internal alterations to w wing by *Erith & Terry* for Francis Nichols, 1973.

C18 STABLE BLOCK S of house at right angles to main front, two storeys and eight bays, the central two-bay pediment added as part of alterations by *Sisson*. Small GARAGE to l. by *Raymond Erith*, 1958. – MODEL FARM N of the house by *W. Lewis Baker*, 1871, with *J.L. Baker* of Hargrave Kimbolton, agricultural engineer. Brick with black diapers, carved stone panels with initials, dates, and improving mottoes. Two open yards either side of a three-bay covered yard, with stables, feed-houses and an apsidal barn across the top. Three-storey bailiff's house, dairy and farm kitchen with stepped gables and dormers. Cottage by the farm and lodge sw of the Hall in similar vein and presumably also by W.L. Baker.

Church and hall lie nearly ½ m. N of the Harwich Road. Some nice cottages tucked away on the lane (Church Hill) leading to them, as well as the brick OLD RECTORY of 1757, and a small former schoolroom, 1848. On the s side of the main road (Wignall Street) the former SCHOOL by *W.L. Baker*, 1872–3; brick with black diapers, suggesting that he also designed the adjacent cottages, and perhaps the row of four ALMSHOUSES, the front set back behind a veranda, endowed by Mrs Cox of Lawford Place (†1867). On the N side, on the corner of Church Hill, the OGILVIE HALL, 1909 by *Raymond C. Wrinch*. Roughcast with half-timbered gables. w of Church Hill, opposite Dedham Road, a pair of farmworkers' cottages by *Erith* for Sir Philip Nichols of Lawford Hall, 1956–7, good plain brick with sash windows and pedimented doorcases on a generous scale.

Lawford Hall.
Model farm

ALDHAMS, Bromley Road, 1 m. SSE. Small early C18 cottage, more than quadrupled by *Robert Kirk*, 1933–4, in a convincing pastiche. Kirk, then working in *Maurice Webb*'s office, intended it for Webb's brother, hence the spider's web in the elaborately carved doorcase. Two massive brick chimneystacks at either end of the entrance front.

LAWFORD HOUSE, Bromley Road, ¾ m. SSE. Rear range mid C17, timber-framed faced with brick; front range of gault brick, late C18, seven bays with central porch on fluted columns.

LAWFORD PLACE, Wignall Street, ½ m. SE. For George Bridges of Mistley, *c.* 1790. Plastered brick with a Greek Doric colonnade of six sturdy columns. Gutted by fire, 1999.

STATION HOUSE, ½ m. NE. Built as the Railway Tavern, 1846, for what soon became known as Manningtree Station. Two pedimented pavilions, two storeys with Venetian windows on the first floor, either side of a square central block that rises another half-storey capped with a pyramidal roof. Main station building by *W. N. Ashbee*, 1900.

MOUND, ½ m. WNW. Bronze Age burial mound (round barrow).

LAYER BRETON 9010

ST MARY THE VIRGIN. By *R. T. Barker* (*Barker & Kirk*), 1922–3, and reminiscent of its medieval predecessor (dem. 1915), which stood opposite Layer Breton Hall. Brick, with stone dressings, and Perp windows. Nave and chancel in one, and an oversized white weatherboarded W belfry. Inside, an interesting piece of SCULPTURE: Tondo of the Virgin seated on the ground and playing with the Child; Italian Mannerist. – Also a C16 carving of Abraham and Isaac, from St Peter, Birch. – STAINED GLASS. E window by *Clayton & Bell*, 1926.

LAYER BRETON HALL, ¾ m. SSE. Georgian brick, three bays square. On the E front, a pilastered doorcase, and three dormers in the hipped roof. On the S front, a much grander doorcase, with attached columns, pediment, and fanlight.

SHALOM HALL, ½ m. SSE. Former rectory by *J.B. Watson*, *c.* 1840. Painted brick.

LAYER DE LA HAYE 9020

ST JOHN THE BAPTIST. Mostly C14, including the battlemented W tower, but the nave has a Norman SE angle and the chancel a Norman N window. Good timber N porch with C14 gable – see the bargeboards. S side and S arcade all part of a restoration by *G. Sergeant*, 1849–50. – MONUMENT. Thomas Tey †1543 and wife. Straight-headed Purbeck marble recess on N side of chancel with curves down to the jambs. Quatrefoils in the coving, quatrefoil frieze above, and cresting. Originally held brass of two kneeling figures and inscription. – In churchyard, near N door, Lt-Gen. John Brown †1763. Obelisk, supported by consoles and decorated with swags. – Memorial by *Jamie Sargeant*, 1997. 6-ft (1.8-metre) standing stone with bas-relief of St John baptizing Christ.

BLIND KNIGHTS, ¾ m. E. One bay of an early C14 hall, with contemporary gabled and jettied cross-wing to the l. and then an early C15 extension with long-wall jetty. Cross-wing and extension to the r., *c.* 1972. N of the house a six-bay weatherboarded BARN, dating back to the C13.

MALTING GREEN HOUSE, ¾ m. NE. Early C18 brick. Two storeys, five bays, the windows with segmental heads. Gabled, timber-framed wing to r. C19 Tudor Gothic outbuildings.

WATERWORKS. Treatment works of the South Essex Waterworks Co., *c.* 1935, in the Modern Movement style. Employees' housing on S side of site. Cf. Langham.

LAYER MARNEY

9010

The Marneys had held Layer Marney from the C12, but they did not reach prominence until the time of Sir Henry (1456/7–1523). He became a Privy Councillor of Henry VII and Henry VIII, Captain of the King's Bodyguard, Sheriff of Essex, and finally Keeper of the Privy Seal. Only six weeks before his death he was created Baron Marney. His son John succeeded him but died two years later, in 1525. The line was then extinct.

It is not known when Henry Marney began to rebuild the church and house, but the latter can hardly be earlier than *c.* 1520, for reasons given later. Henry left money in his will for completion of the Marney chapel, while John stipulated that he was to be buried in the new N aisle.

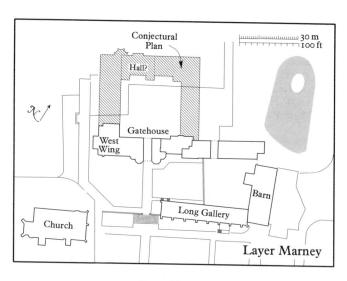

Layer Marney.
Plan, including conjectural extent of planned house

LAYER MARNEY TOWER. It is understandable that the house became known as Layer Marney Tower, for Henry Marney's showpiece is a gatehouse with four towers, higher than any of the other Tudor mansions that had preceded his. These gatehouses were the ambition of the age. They were no longer needed for fortification and reached fantastic heights of display, especially in the brick counties of the E. Tattershall of the 1440s may still have had some military considerations, even if they were secondary. At Oxburgh in 1482 they can hardly have played a part any longer. And the gatehouses of St James's Palace and Hampton Court, of Christ's and St John's Colleges and then of Trinity College at Cambridge, or Lupton's Tower at Eton, are all for the purpose of chivalric display only. From the size of the gatehouse one can presume that the house itself was intended to be on a grand scale. It was to be to the N of the gatehouse, but was barely begun before the first and second Lords Marney died. The date when Henry Marney started is not preserved, but because of the use of terracotta in Italian forms (*see* below) it can hardly have been before 1520. Quite evidently the gatehouse was hurried up at once and then a beginning made on the ranges to the W and E of it. That to the W remains, as well as part of the E, and outbuildings to the S. The brickwork is diapered, with moulded plinths and string courses, and bands of cusped panelling. Remains of plastering on the mouldings suggest that it may have been treated in the same way as the church (*see* below).

Very little seems to have been done to the house thereafter. Already dilapidated, it was further damaged by the 1884 earthquake. Additions were made by the Peache family in the C19, but the present form of the house owes most to Walter De Zoete, for whom *Chancellor & Son* made considerable changes in 1904–12. Further work has been done by the Charringtons, including restoration and internal alterations by *Henry Freeland* since c. 1995.

The three-storey GATEHOUSE is flanked by higher turrets, 56 the inner ones (to the N) of seven windows above each other, the outer ones of eight, flanked by further ones of seven. The inner turrets (for stairs) are square but the outer ones polygonal, and it is on the outer face that most of the display is to be found. The tops of the turrets are decorated in the accepted way by a trefoiled corbel-frieze. But above this, instead of battlements, little semicircular shell-gables with dolphins on them – an Italian Quattrocento motif, executed in the newly fashionable Italian material, terracotta (cf. Henry Marney's tomb, below), probably made locally. This had been introduced into England by Italian craftsmen a little before 1510, and was a way of achieving decorative effects otherwise only possible with stone. Behind the frieze appear the Tudor chimneys of pre-Italian twisted shapes. Between the turrets is the gateway and on the first and second floors two large rooms with wide windows to N and S. The windows appear at first to be straightforward five-light Perp windows with ogee-arched heads and one transom. But in looking at them carefully one discovers that the mullions and transoms are of terracotta decorated with the typical candelabra forms of the Italian Early Renaissance, and the ogee tops consist of Renaissance scrolls and counter-scrolls. The same windows repeat, on a smaller scale, on the upper floor of the W WING, again on both the N and S sides. They must have been meant to be the beginning of a type of fenestration, large, wide, and regular, then still very unusual, but not unique, since at just this time windows of a similar general shape were put in at Sutton Place in Surrey. But at Layer Marney any regularity which must have been intended was defeated by the short time available before the deaths of the Marneys. The gable to the S is in fact different in the brick-work and probably somewhat later. The wing finishes on the W side with a stepped gable. In the NW corner is a three-storey gabled addition of 1900.

The INTERIOR fittings are mainly Edwardian but in the W wing two first-floor rooms have interesting ceilings. One of them must be one of the earliest in the country with polygo-nal panels of various sizes made into a pattern (cf. Wolsey's rooms at Hampton Court). The fireplaces are probably early C20 imports. One, in the NW addition, appears to be early C16. It has ornamented pilasters, brackets, and an ornamental frieze, all of a purity extremely rare in England. Elsewhere an overmantel incorporating early C17 woodwork including terms, and a C17 marble fireplace, no doubt the work of a Fleming. It has demi-caryatids, carrying Ionic capitals. They are white against black terms.

The E WING also ends with a stepped gable. It is joined to the gateway by a three-bay block by *Chancellor & Son*, who also inserted the carriageway further E. The windows on this range are simple, of the straight-headed medieval type with individual lights arched, apart from one three-light transomed window in a gable. Part of the range was converted to stables by De Zoete (stalls and fittings by the *St Pancras Ironwork Co.*), the remainder restored by *Freeland* with new internal stairs.

S of the main buildings is the so-called LONG GALLERY. It is contemporary with the house and was built as stables. It has stepped gables at each end, that at the W by *Chancellor & Son*, who *c.* 1910 converted the building into a gallery and ante-room, in the course of which the upper floor (for storage and dormitories) was removed. Some original windows to both storeys survive, but the three large windows are part of the Chancellors' conversion, as is the broad oak staircase (return flights and gallery by *Freeland*). Impressive roof of twelve bays with three tie-beams, of similar construction to that in the E wing. The tie-beams carry (or did originally) thirteen queen-posts, the collar-beams above them four. The rafters are strengthened by ogee-shaped wind-braces. It is possible that another similar range was intended to be built to the W, so that the two would flank the approach to the gateway (cf. Leez Priory), or it may have been intended to form part of an outer courtyard. But it is disconcerting that the Long Gallery is not parallel to the main buildings.

Between the Long Gallery and the E wing, a mid-C15 weatherboarded BARN with some reused C13 timbers.

The formal GARDENS S and W of the house were mainly laid out by De Zoete, who also built the TEA HOUSE, 1910 by *Chancellor & Son* (converted and extended by *Freeland*, 1999–2000), 300 yds. SE on the axis of the gatehouse. S of the Long Gallery, SWIMMING POOL HOUSE by *Corinne Wilson*, *c.* 1970. Octagonal, with tented copper roof. ENTRANCE LODGE (N) by *Chancellor & Son*, with stepped gables.

ST MARY THE VIRGIN, SW of the gatehouse and contemporary with it. Brick, the W tower with blue diapering. The rest of the brickwork retains fragments of plastering. Most of this was added later, but it seems that the plastering round the windows was original and intended to imitate stone. Unusually, the plaster of the hoodmoulds was painted to imitate the terracotta that adorns the house. So the church, as built, would have appeared to be of brick, with stone windows, and terracotta hoodmoulds. The tower is of a type frequent in Essex (cf. Ingatestone, Rochford, St Osyth, etc.) with diagonal stone-dressed buttresses, battlements, and polygonal stair-turret. Three-light W window with a depressed head and an odd variety of intersected tracery as favoured 200 years before. Two-light bell openings with a transom. S porch and S chancel porch (a rare addition) with stepped battlements. The windows all with four-centred heads, and in the nave of brick. Five-light E window with renewed Perp panel tracery. At the W end of the N aisle a priest's chamber with a chimney which adds to the W view of the church an element of surprise. The N aisle's E end forms a chantry chapel of the Marneys and also has a fireplace. The arcade piers inside as well as the tower arch have semi-octagonal shafts and hollows in the diagonals. The roof has tie-beams, but above the rood screen the tie-beam is enriched by braces and braces up to the collar-beam – a hammerbeam effect without hammerbeam. Chancel and N aisle E end restored by *C. F. Hayward*, 1870–1,[*] the nave by *Chancellor & Son*, 1911. The Chancellors' work included reopening two bricked-up arches of the N arcade.

PULPIT. Made up of C16 and C17 woodwork (including mid-C17 tester). – SCREENS. The rood screen, restored by *Hayward*, has one-light sections with ogee arches and a little panel tracery above. The Marney chapel screen (which stood E of the tomb of John, 2nd Lord Marney, until 1911) is severely plain, only straight lines, its two-light sections separated by iron mullions. – BENCHES in nave with some linenfold and early C17 panelling. – CHEST. Very long, iron-bound, C14 or C15. – SCULPTURE. In niche of S porch, Virgin and Child by *John Shuffleton*, *c.* 1970. – WALL PAINTING. Large C16 figure of St

---

[*] Including carved REREDOS by *Thomas Earp*, partly gilt, since replaced.

Christopher, curiously rustic for a place so intimately connected with the taste of the court. It includes an early depiction of an angler. – STAINED GLASS. Figure of St Peter, early
C16, and four heraldic medallions, in N chapel E window.
Chancel s by *William de Morgan*, 1870, a rare example of his
work in this medium. Also by him the four roundels and vesica
in the E window, remains of a larger scheme. Nave s †1915
probably by *James Powell & Sons*.

MONUMENTS. Sir William Marney †1414. Alabaster effigy,
on a tomb-chest with elaborately cusped quatrefoils and
shields. He wears bascinet, camail, and hip-belt, as was the
fashion. Moved here from the chancel in 1870. Round the
tomb six oak posts with zigzag carving topped with leopards
holding shields with the Marney crest, made for the tomb of
John, 2nd Lord Marney. – Henry, 1st Lord Marney †1523.
Between chancel and Marney chapel. The composition of
tomb-chest, recumbent effigy, and canopy above is in the Perp
taste, but the detail is all of the Early Renaissance. What is
more, it is executed in terracotta, a material favoured by the
Italians at the Court (cf. above). The tomb-chest has panels
with shields separated by balusters. The lid and the beautifully
carved effigy are of Catacleuse, a black Cornish stone, and
Marney – like his son – rests his head not on his helm, in the
English fashion, but on a cushion. This, and the modelling of
the face, suggest foreign craftsmen. The canopy has balusters
and Renaissance foliage, but they are not used in a Renaissance spirit. The angle pilasters, for example, clearly suffer
from a Gothic hangover, and the canopy has pendants for
which the designer does not mind using Composite capitals.
On the canopy four semicircular pediments or gables or acroteria – a predominantly Venetian motif. – John, 2nd Lord
Marney †1525, clearly by the same hands. The effigy of the
young man has all the characteristics of his father's. The tomb-
chest is simpler, but also terracotta and also with balusters. The
monument is organically connected to the w with a chantry
altar placed at right angles to it. The decoration is again the
same. – Robert Cammocke of Duke's †1585 (chancel s wall).
Tomb-chest on which stand two short Doric columns supporting an entablature. – Nicholas Corsellis †1674, a London
merchant who had purchased the estate in 1667. Elegant, in
grey and white marble with classical detailing. Surmounted by
a similar monument to Sir Caesar Child †1753 and his sister
Frances Corsellis †1759. – Thomas Hermitage St John Boys
†1897, by *Matthews & Co. (Gawthorp)*. Mural brass, showing
the boy (who died at Rio de Janeiro) kneeling in prayer beside
his bunk, beneath a depiction of his ship. – In SE corner of
churchyard, large chest-tomb of Amy Chambers †1752, the
sides carved in deep relief with pilasters, swags, drapery, etc.
(in N aisle until 1911).

DUKE'S, ½ m. NNE. The gabled w wing is the surviving E wing
of a C16 U-plan house. Diapered brick with brick windows of
five transomed lights on ground and first floors. E of this a

three-bay C17 range, timber-framed and faced in brick within
a few years. Coved eaves and three dormers. Early C19 Tuscan
porch. Some original early C17 panelling, and a late C16
roundel of stained glass with the Tudor rose and initials E.R.

LEADEN RODING   5010

ST MICHAEL AND ALL ANGELS. Nave, chancel, and belfry. The
early C16 belfry is weatherboarded with shingled splay-foot
spire. It rests on posts with thin, low braces and cross-strutting to the l. and r. Nave and chancel Norman (s doorway with
odd capitals of four thin stone slabs on top of each other),
mainly of flint rubble, the windows much renewed. Restored
by *Chancellor & Son*, 1907–8: part of s wall rebuilt, s porch and
N vestry added. The nave roof simple, of trussed rafters, with
low tie-beams. – PULPIT. C15 with traceried panels and quatrefoils at their foot. – COMMUNION RAIL. C17, with sparsely
placed heavy balusters. – ORGAN. Late C19, by *G. M. Holdich*.
Unusually ornate carved case and polychromatic pipes. –
MONUMENT. Rev. Thomas Parkes †1864. By *John Eaton* of
Ashton-under-Lyne. Simple Gothic.
LEADEN HALL, N of the church (now three houses). Two blocks
at right angles forming a 'unit system' group, i.e. for separate
households working the same land. The earlier block a hall
house of *c.* 1400 with two-storey parlour/solar end to the N and
service cross-wing to the s. Adjacent two-storey house early
C16. Weatherboarded BARNS W of the house; the larger (eight
bays) is late C17 and of imported Baltic pine, an early use.

LEEZ PRIORY   7010

1¾ m. NW of Little Leighs*

The Priory of Little Leighs was founded by Augustinian Canons
late in the C12. Excavations, of which much is exposed, have
revealed the PLAN. The church had transepts with E aisles, a   *p. 532*
chancel, and a much longer Lady Chapel instead of a N chancel
aisle. It lay s of the cloister, which had on its N side the refectory and to the E several chambers including the chapter house
which projected eastward. Fragments of the bases of the piers
of the crossing tower survive, trefoiled in section and filleted.
Many Purbeck shafts have been excavated, and also some early
C13 capitals, etc. The E parts of the church can be dated by
them; the Lady Chapel was added about 1300 or a little later
(cf. Waltham Abbey, Little Dunmow).

The house was dissolved in 1536 and granted to Sir Richard
Rich. He pulled most of it down and built himself a mansion
in its place. Of this significant portions remain upright, but the

---

*Divided between the civil parishes of Felsted and Great and Little Leighs.

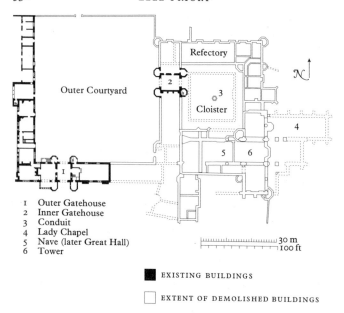

1 Outer Gatehouse
2 Inner Gatehouse
3 Conduit
4 Lady Chapel
5 Nave (later Great Hall)
6 Tower

30 m
100 ft

■ EXISTING BUILDINGS

☐ EXTENT OF DEMOLISHED BUILDINGS

Leez Priory.
Plan, including outline of demolished portions

greater part was razed in 1753 after it was bought by Guy's
Hospital, so one must be careful not to confuse the visible
foundations of the C16 house with those of the medieval
buildings.
Rich's house was built entirely of brick, ornamented with blue
brick diapers and other patterns, including chequerwork. It
consisted of outer and inner courtyards. The inner courtyard
was created from the priory cloister, and Rich built his gatehouse in its w range, not only reusing the foundations but
retaining and refacing some of its walls. This arrangement
would be just like Hampton Court, except that the main
gateway into the inner courtyard was at right angles to, instead
of in axis with, the inner gateway. The main living quarters lay
round the inner courtyard. The Great Hall occupied the s side,
where the nave would have been originally. There were two
spiral stair-turrets at the NE and SE corners of the courtyard,
and to the outer world polygonal turrets at the corners
and buttresses, chimneys, and bays breaking the frontages
irregularly.
    The surviving parts, all restored by *Chancellor & Son*,
1908–15, for M.E. Hughes Hughes, are the Inner Gatehouse
and parts of the w and s ranges of the outer courtyard, including the OUTER GATEHOUSE in the s range. It is flanked by
polygonal turrets with angle pilaster-strips and two trefoiled
corbel-friezes. The top is all embattled. The main window is of

three lights with a transom. The adjoining quarters are two-storeyed, the w range a little lower than the s. The windows and battlements l. of the Gatehouse are the Chancellors', as are the chimneystack and two small windows in the s range's E wall, but more of the original fenestration survives on the w range's inner (E) face. The windows are mullioned or mullioned and transomed, of two and more lights, and the individual lights are still arched – the pattern followed in the restoration. In the middle of the w range, but not in line with the Inner Gatehouse, is a gabled cross-wing which contained a subsidiary gateway. It led into the walled kitchen garden, which contains the lowest of a series of fishponds along the River Ter. On the pond's N side is a c16 two-storey brick cottage called the FISHING HUT, and behind it a three-storey brick WATER TOWER by *F. W. Chancellor*, 1935, with pitched roof and angle buttresses.

The INNER GATEHOUSE now stands alone like a tower. It is considerably more ornate than the Outer Gatehouse. It is one storey higher and has two main rooms between the octagonal battlemented turrets, both with four-light transomed windows and both with original fireplaces. The doorway has the Tudor rose and the French fleur-de-lys in the spandrels. The tower rooms were fitted with panelling by *E. Beckwith*, 1914, since removed but partly reused in an upper room at the E end of the s range. In the inner courtyard a Gothic CONDUIT, made up from stone fragments of the monastic buildings, the stepped base and finial part of the Chancellors' restoration.

Two c16 brick BARNS remain to the s of the s range. They have queenpost roofs, and the plastered walls inside the eastern barn are inscribed with a large number of witch-warding symbols. Probably originally built as stables with lodgings, but the floors were removed and timber-framed midstreys added in the c18. They frame the approach to the Outer Gatehouse from the park which Rich created to the s (*see* Littley Park, Great Waltham).

LEXDEN

9020

ST LEONARD. Rebuilt 1820–1 by *M. G. Thompson*. Cemented, Neo-E.E., but the window tracery Neo-Perp. Nave with w gallery, shallow chancel, w tower with a very funny spire, N and s porches (the N with *Coade* stone pinnacles): all very unecclesiological, so in 1892–4 a deeper chancel was added by *J. C. Traylen*, comprising choir, sanctuary and N chapel, and on the s side an ambulatory, containing the organ, ready for a planned s aisle that was never built. The chancel higher than the nave, with clerestory; Early Perp (supposedly based on Sherborne Abbey), of local flint with Box stone dressings, and bands of Bath stone and alabaster on the E wall inside. The nave ceiling had been removed two years previously and an open roof constructed, but still very shallow; further work in

1897, including re-seating, to Traylen's design, supervised by *Baker & May*. The rector, *J.H. Lester*, designed and carved much of the woodwork (e.g. bench ends, altar and other chancel fittings). No attempt seems to have been made to harmonize the two parts of the building. – STAINED GLASS. E window, 1893, and N chapel E, 1920, by *Heaton, Butler & Bayne*. In N aisle and nave, an impressive collection of windows installed 1946–67, including six by *Whitefriars* and one by *Geoffrey Webb*. – SCULPTURE. Figures of St Leonard and St Mark by *Mark Bridges*, 2001–2 (chancel arch). – MONUMENTS. Richard Hewett †1771. Exceedingly good standing wall monument, without effigy, from the old church. Not signed, but attributed to *Richard Hayward* (GF). Big plinth with rich Neoclassical ornamentation. Inscription plate held by two genii. Large urn high up with a scene in relief. – Fanny Eliza Hume †1852. Profile portrait within a wreath of flowers and foliage. – GARDEN OF REST. 1950 by *Bailey & Walker*. Brick walls, a trim garden, and an open-air altar. Behind it, CHURCH HALL by *Ivor H. Morgan*, 1969–70. Stylish entrance but otherwise utilitarian.

ST TERESA OF LISIEUX (R.C.), Clairmont Road. The original church, now hall, by *T.H.B. Scott*, 1936–7. Brick. Short w tower with nice stone bas-relief of the Virgin and Child. Replacement church to the (liturgical) s by *J.H. Dabrowski*, 1971. Mostly brick, with rows of glazed gables down each side and exposed concrete frame inside. Gabled lantern over sanctuary. – SCULPTURE. Risen Christ by *Tita Madden*, c. 1977, over entrance. – STAINED GLASS. In E wall, two full-height windows by monks of Buckfast Abbey, 1983.

JESUS CHRIST OF LATTER DAY SAINTS, Straight Road. 1964 by *Graham & Baldwin*. Large A-frame with chapel and hall in-line; pale brown brick with a panel of stone at the W end, but mostly roof.

LEXDEN PARK, E of St Leonard. Large Italianate house with tower. Said to have a nucleus of 1825–6 (by *David Laing*), but now essentially of c. 1850–60. Converted into flats, 1995, with vaguely Neo-Georgian additions that make the original house look very drab. Remaining parkland, now public, to the s.

Several elegant houses along LEXDEN ROAD, notably on the N side SPRING HOUSE (No. 191), plain two-storey, three-bay early C19 gault brick with cast-iron railings by *Richard Coleman*, and HILL HOUSE (No. 183), with Regency bows and deep eaves; between them JACQUELINE COURT (no. 185), C17 with an early C19 brick front, and WEAVERS (No. 187), with Late Medieval cross-wing, the rest of the house rebuilt in the early C17 with continuous jetty. E of Hill House, No. 1 GRANGE ROAD by *E. E. May*, 1909, as the rectory: brick, with gables, loggias, and panels of decorative strapwork. In the same manner, on a larger scale, LEXDEN GRANGE (No. 127 Lexden Road), vernacular revival, an irregular composition of bays, gables, half-timbering etc. (For the continuation eastwards of Lexden Road, *see* Colchester, Perambulation 6, p. 296.)

s of St Leonard, SPRING LANE leads to THE OLD
RECTORY of 1814, with nice Gothic windows and porch;
behind houses on the lane's w side, former SCHOOL buildings,
originally of 1842. w of Spring Lane, CHURCH HOUSE (No.
197 Lexden Road), C16 hall house with gabled cross-wings, the
larger one jettied. On the s side of Lexden Road, MANOR
HOUSE (No. 134), dating back to the early C17, with C18 additions; enlarged and remodelled 1837. Further w, good groups
of older cottages, notably Nos. 162–164, C15, restored 1935. In
Heath Road, HEATH LODGE, a large Gothic house of c. 1860
with diapered brickwork, fancy chimneys, gables, etc. Additions by *Goodey & Cressall*, 1908.

SEVEN ARCHES VIADUCT. By *John Braithwaite*, engineer of the
Eastern Counties Railway, 1842. Brick.

LEXDEN DYKE AND TUMULUS. *See* Colchester, Dykes.

LINDSELL

6020

ST MARY THE VIRGIN. Small and compact, of pebble rubble
with – unusually – brick dressings. The tower moreover is an
unusual position, at the sw corner. It is late C16, with a diagonal buttress and battlements. The nave reveals a Norman
building. Chancel arch round-headed, on the simplest imposts.
Large pointed squint arch s of it. Two-bay s aisle, E of the
tower, with a quatrefoil pier and two quadrant mouldings in
the arches, i.e. early C14. The later tower cuts into the arcade,
its base converted into a vestry during restoration in 1863.
s porch probably added at the same time. In 1926 traces of an
ANCHORITE'S CELL were discovered N of the chancel N wall
with a small hatch into the chancel as its only opening. – FONT.
C15, octagonal, with quatrefoils and shields; the stem panelled
and buttressed. – STAINED GLASS. In E window, C13–C16 fragments; especially noteworthy a C13 figure of a bearded saint
and a C14 figure of St John the Evangelist. Arranged by *A.K.
Nicholson*, 1929. – BRASS. Thomas Fytche †1514, his wife
Agnes, and children, the main figures about 16 in. (41 cm.).
Thomas and Agnes are also depicted in the E window.

One of the church's attractive features is the approach through
the yard of LINDSELL HALL. C15 with two jettied, gabled
cross-wings, facing an extensive range of farm buildings,
including a large barn, now converted. More nice timber-
framed houses along the road to the s, including the OLD
VICARAGE, C15 or earlier, with one gabled and jettied
cross-wing.

GLEBE HOUSE, 400 yds NW. 1866–7 by *F. Barnes*, as the vicarage.
Brick, with shaped gables, an uncommon motif for that date.
100 yds further, the former SCHOOL and teacher's house,
1876–7, by *S.C. Parmenter*. Stock brick with bands of red.

LISTON

CHURCH. Nave and chancel Norman: see the masonry at the E end, and the plain, blocked N doorway. Chancel widened in the C13, but all the windows are renewed. W tower, not too big, early C16, of brick with blue diapers, diagonal buttresses, three-light brick W window, and stepped battlements on a trefoiled corbel frieze. Higher stair-turret. S (mortuary) chapel, S porch and N vestry added by *Woodyer*, 1867, who also restored the chancel. The additions are in flint, like the rest of the church, squared and coursed on the chapel. Inside, Woodyer provided a wooden CHANCEL SCREEN, carved stone REREDOS, and decoration of the E wall that includes painted figures and a mosaic frieze punctuated with large round knobs of red glass. More wall painting in the chapel – with an elaborate tiled floor including a raised cross – and stained glass. Decorated plaster tympanum in chancel arch dated 1701, presumably when the nave was ceiled. – FONT. Octagonal, Perp, traceried stem, and bowl with cusped panels and shields. – COMMANDMENT BOARDS. In tower. C18, painted on wood, signed by *P. Richold*, Melford. – STAINED GLASS. E window 1864, probably by *Hardman*. Chancel S by *Powell & Sons*, designed by *Henry Holiday*, 1873. Nave S by *Lavers, Barraud & Westlake*, 1869. Nave N, 1932, and W window, 1927, by *C.E. Kempe & Co.*; the nave window incorporates in the tracery several small C15 figures. – MONUMENTS. Dr Poley Clopton †1730, founder of the Clopton Asylum at Bury St Edmunds. Large marble wall monument, with a scrolled pediment on which sit cherubs either side of his achievement. – John and Elizabeth Campbell of Liston Hall †1826 and 1838. Marble tablet by *H. Hopper*. – R.B. and H.B. Thornhill †1857, their wives, children and nurses, variously 'cruelly massacred' at Cawnpore and 'ruthlessly murdered' at Seetapore; marble tablet placed inside a C15 nave piscina.

LISTON HALL. The mid-C18 brick house was largely rebuilt by *Woodyer* following a fire in 1870; dem. 1951. It had four corner pavilions, connected by quadrants; two, the SE and NW, survive, but the former is much altered and the latter alone retains its quadrant. Additions by *Doug Bowen*, 2001, including as it were a sub-pavilion – single-bay, single-storey – at the end of the quadrant on the corner of the site of the main house, a nice conceit. C19 stables to the N.

GLEBE HOUSE (former rectory), ¼ m. S. Five-bay brick front, *c.* 1800, but behind, at right angles, a range datable by its framing to the C14, and including a contemporary brick chimneystack.

LISTON MILL, ¼ m. ENE. Pretty weatherboarded mill house, timber-framed, late C18. The mill itself dem. 1887.

LITTLE BADDOW

ST MARY THE VIRGIN. C14 W tower with angle buttresses on one side, a diagonal buttress on the other, W doorway with niche, two-light Early Dec W window and battlements. Very wide nave which seems somewhat lop-sided, because it consists of a Norman nave of which the N wall with a plain doorway remains, and an early C14 S wall pushed so far to the S as if an aisle had been intended. This S part has a Dec two-light E window and inside two low recesses, designed to form one group with the PISCINA. This is typical Dec, with richly crocketed ogee arches. In the recesses stand two very low tomb-chests with quatrefoil decoration and oak EFFIGIES, a man and a woman, of *c.* 1340–50. The man lies straight, the woman slightly and very tenderly bent. The figure of the woman especially is of uncommonly fine quality. The architect of the church also appreciated sculpture. There are small heads used as label stops and otherwise. Restrained restoration by *William White*, 1858. – FONT. 1858. Octagonal. Also a large circular trough with four handles, probably a MORTAR for mixing lead, resting on a mill-wheel. – WALL PAINTING. One of the best surviving depictions of St Christopher in England, richly coloured; late C14. Also on N wall, the figure of a devil. – STAINED GLASS. St Michael and the Dragon; also several fragments; all *c.* 1400 (E window). – MONUMENTS. Henry Mildmay of Graces †1639. Attributed to *John & Matthias Christmas* (AW). Standing wall monument with reclining figure, propped on elbow, between black columns which carry a broken segmental pediment. Above him trophies and oval inscription plate. Large figures of two wives below, kneeling either side of a prayer desk. – Mary Mildmay †1715. Oval, with ornamental border, shield at the top and skull at the bottom.

UNITED REFORMED CHURCH (Presbyterian, later Congregational). 1707–8. Plain gabled brick rectangle. Arched cross-windows with a second transom at the foot of the arch, and in addition oval windows in the N gable and W wall. Interior refitted by *C. Pertwee*, 1888, with benches and pulpit. Schoolroom, now vestry, at S end, 1907. Late C18 MANSE, roughcast, attached to NW corner, and to the SE the HISTORY CENTRE by *Anne E. Smith*, 2002–3. Rendered, with triangular oriels on the long walls.

MEMORIAL HALL, North Hill. 1960, by *Graham & Baldwin*, with *Patricia Stewart* and *Peter Page*. Brick, with portal frame exposed inside. Lower N entrance block with distinctive butterfly roof.

The main centre is along NORTH HILL, ¾ m. E of the church. At the bottom, COLERAINES, C17 timber-framed and plastered with an C18 front of blue brick with red dressings. Segment-headed windows. ¼ m. S, on the corner of Tofts Chase, WALTER'S COTTAGE, C18 painted brick. Three bays, with a round-headed window over the central Tuscan porch. Glazed garden room to l. by *Patricia Stewart*, 1998. At the top of the hill the road becomes THE RIDGE, with larger C20 houses set back in woodland in an expensively suburban sort of way. THATCHED COTTAGE, on the corner of Riffhams Chase, was probably built at the same time as Riffhams,

Danbury (q.v.), i.e. 1815, in the manner of *Repton*. Single storey, with C20 additions.

In COLAM LANE, off North Hill to the W, THE OLD RECTORY by *William White*, 1858. Much variety of materials and roof-line windows. *The Ecclesiologist* wondered whether 'simplicity and cottage-like effect' had not been carried too far. Next door, WOODLANDS by *K.M.B. Cross*, c. 1936, Neo-Georgian.

In SPRING ELMS LANE, off North Hill to the E, BIRCH-WOOD (formerly Greville) HOUSE, by *K.M.B. Cross* for himself, 1934, and interesting to see the grand style in which a successful architect of that time lived. Neo-Georgian, brick, with a nine-bay garden front that is almost as much window as wall. Projecting loggia with tent-canopy copper roof, now glazed in. Stone semicircular Tuscan porch (and fewer windows) on N side. ¼ m. E (in Woodham Walter) SYLVAN COTTAGE, also by Cross, c. 1936, originally thatched.

In PARSONAGE LANE, off North Hill to the W and S of Colam Lane, RYEFIELD HOUSE, another architect's home: *Rolf Rothermel*, c. 1970. Single-storey, H-plan, and flat-roofed with a small pyramidal skylight over the central living area. Steel frame, with full-height windows and brick infill.

LITTLE BADDOW HALL, opposite the church. Central part C14 or C15, extended to the N in the C16, with stack of diagonal chimneyshafts. Much of the framing exposed. S cross-wing rebuilt in the late C19 or early C20.

CUCKOOS, 600 yds SE. C17, the upper storey jettied at the W end with exposed timbers. Until 1630 Thomas Hooker kept a school here assisted by John Elliot, both early dissenters and pioneers of New England.

GREAT GRACES, 1 m. S. A fine brick group with C17 or C18 weatherboarded barn. The present house is probably the E wing of a larger house. At the N end of the W front is a slightly projecting wing with straight gable; the S front has a big shaped gable and, partly covered, blocked mullioned and transomed brick windows, plastered to resemble stone. The date may be c. 1560. Inside, a staircase of c. 1600 and much panelling. Two other buildings, now houses, have straight gables. C18 brick wall along the lane with a small pavilion at the S end.

OLD RIFFHAMS, 1¼ m. SE. The manor of Riffhams is documented from 1422, but the present building appears to be mid C16, considerably altered early in the C18. H-plan, on a sloping site, so that the ground floor on the S (road) side is the first floor on the N (garden) side. The C16 work is visible on the N front: a two-storey gabled porch with brick ground floor and exposed timber frame above, with a very small upper oriel, also gabled. To its r. a chimneystack with three octagonal shafts. Between the two a small area of plastered wall, all that escaped the encasing of the house in brick probably after 1717, when the house changed hands. Of this date, segment-headed windows, rusticated quoins, a broad doorway on Tuscan pilasters, yet still small shaped gables. These sit on a high

parapet, particularly noticeable on the s side where the greatest effort was made to achieve symmetry; in the parapet – and
elsewhere – are blind windows, some with dormers behind. On
the w front the parapet steps down towards the central chimneystack. One room inside has early C17 panelling and a large
fireplace with four-centred arch.

WATER HALL, ½ m. ssw. Remarkably well-preserved in-line hall
house, dating from c. 1400, with a later extension at the E end.
Part plastered, but mainly weatherboarded. Original external
doorways at either end of the cross-passage, and internal doorways to the service rooms and stair. Crown-post roof. Hall
floored, but its large transomed window on the s side, with
diamond mullions, is exposed.

LITTLE BADDOW LOCK AND PAPER MILL LOCK, 600 yds NW
and 1 m. NE respectively. On the Chelmer and Blackwater
Navigation, opened 1797 (see Introduction, p. 52). Brick with
granite copings. At Paper Mill Lock, an agreeable assortment
of unpretentious canal-side buildings.

LITTLE BARDFIELD   6030

ST KATHARINE. Late Anglo-Saxon w tower, unbuttressed, with
arched openings on three floors. Later recessed pyramid roof.
The nave masonry – mainly flint rubble – is of the same character as that of the tower. One Saxon s and one N window,
double splayed. C14 chancel, restored by *Bodley*, 1865–6, when
he added the s chancel aisle. s porch C15, restored 1894 by
Richard Creed,* who added the niche and figure of St
Katharine. Nave roof C14 with crown-posts on moulded tie-
beams, chancel roof boarded with carved bosses and angels by
Creed, 1907. – REREDOS. By *Bodley*, 1866. Alabaster, part
gilded, said to be an exact copy of one uncovered during the
restoration. – CHOIR STALLS and low SCREEN also by *Bodley*.
– ROOD FIGURES by *Creed*, 1909. – SCULPTURE. St Katharine
by *Igor Livi*, 2005. Painted and gilded limewood. – ORGAN.
Made for Jesus College, Cambridge, 1688, probably by *Renatus
Harris*; moved to All Saints', Cambridge, 1790, and to Little
Bardfield in 1866. Fine oak case with open-work foliage scrolls
and cherub's head. – STAINED GLASS. E window and single
light in s chancel aisle by *Clayton & Bell*, 1866. Nave s by
Shrigley & Hunt to Richard Creed †1914. w window †1857 by
Wailes. – BRASSES. Three, mural, designed by *Creed*: R.B.
Creed †1875, with copper relief of mother and child. – Rev.
R.H. White †1905, with 10½ in. (7 cm.) figure of priest in vest-
ments. – R. Creed †1911, with relief of rood figures, 'erected
by his friends and fellow-pupils in the office of the late G.F.
Bodley R.A.'.

LITTLE BARDFIELD HALL, immediately w. Symmetrical front
with two large gables and full-height gabled porch, all jettied

* Creed lived at Little Bardfield Hall from c. 1882 until his death in 1914.

and delightfully pargetted. The back is irregular but also has jettied gables, pargetting etc. A rainwater head says 1634. In one room is a fireplace dated 1580. Another room upstairs has C16 panelling and the staircase to the attic is also C16, with splat balusters. But the antiquary has to be careful. *A. V. Heal*[*] restored the house in 1919–20 and before that it had a flat Georgian brick façade. Much was introduced into the interior that did not originally belong, and there have been further internal alterations since. The genuine C16 part of the house is the l. hand portion of the front, extended to the r. (and refronted) in the C18, with further extensions at the rear in the C19. Single-storey extension on E side by Heal. On two sides of the garden an unusually long crinkle-crankle wall, C18 and C19 brick.

A few nice timber-framed cottages in the village street E of the church, and a row of ALMSHOUSES, 1774. Brick, single-storey with attics and dormers. At the W end of the row a former school, part of the original foundation, rebuilt 1871, with conical bellcote.

CHEQUERS, ¾ m. ENE. Handsome house, nicely positioned at a fork in the road, with a carved date 1609. Two-storey gabled and jettied porch and three gabled dormers. C20 gabled cross-wing to r. Across the lane to the N the OLD RECTORY, five-bay Georgian brick with C19 additions. W of Chequers, WAINSFORD'S FARM, C16 with a C19 painted brick façade with decorated bargeboards to the gables. Two more timber-framed houses with later brick fronts in the lane running NW from Chequers towards Little Sampford: MOOR HALL, with a late C19 three-storey brick addition, and HILL HALL, very pretty mid C19 with bargeboarded gables and porch, Gothic windows etc.

LITTLE BENTLEY

ST MARY THE VIRGIN. Chancel C13: see the three stepped E lancets and one each in the N and S walls. N aisle Early Perp, but heightened and lengthened in brick early in the C16, when much other renewing and adding went on: e.g. the S porch, with diagonal buttresses and battlements and three-light side openings, now blocked. The nave S wall has a brick parapet and one (renewed) three-light brick window. Early C15 battlemented W tower, an attractive mixture of stone, flint, and brick, the W door with shields in the spandrels and large three-light W window. Inside, to one's surprise, one sees that the nave must be Norman; for it has a N arcade cut roughly through the wall early in the C13. Arches with one slight chamfer on circular piers with minimum capitals. Restored 1868, when most

---

[*] Heal had trained in Bodley's office, worked as assistant in Creed's office, and was in partnership with Cecil G. Hare, Bodley's former partner, 1919–24.

of the STAINED GLASS was installed, some windows incorporating fragments of C15 and C17 glass. Fine C16 hammerbeam roof, six bays, with defaced angels. – FONT. Octagonal, plain, only one shield on the E front (Pyrton arms). – BENCH ENDS. Some few with poppyheads. – CHEST. Very impressive, large C15 piece, iron-bound and closely studded, with semi-cylindrical lid. – MONUMENTS. Brass to Sir William Pyrton †1490, wife and children. Lower part of his figure missing, but c. 35 in. (90 cm.). – Mrs Elizabeth Lidgould †1726 and Mrs Jane Spencer †1741. Stone, carved with drapery and three cherubs' heads.

By the W door, former NATIONAL SCHOOL by *J. Clarke*, 1848. Neo-Tudor brick with burnt headers. To the S, a pretty octagonal thatched LODGE of Little Bentley Hall. The HALL itself modest, early C19, but on its S side a garden wall remains from the Baynings' great Jacobean house.

METHODIST CHAPEL. 1874. Open-pedimented gable and round-arched window over small porch. Round-arched side windows, separated by pilasters. Disused.

LITTLE BRAXTED

8010

ST NICHOLAS. *Ernest Geldart* was rector of Little Braxted, 102 1881–1900, and here he was able to give free rein to his belief that 'God's house ought to be the finest . . . and . . . most beautiful house in a parish'. It is much as he left it. Norman, very small, with a semicircular apse, which has one original window. Two C13 lancets in the W wall and another reused in the N aisle. *Ewan Christian* restored the fabric in 1856, and the exterior gives little hint of what lies within. Geldart wasted no time in adapting the church to suit his own tastes and his own brand of High Churchmanship. In 1881 he introduced new choir seating and a PISCINA which he carved himself. In 1883 he installed stained glass in the chancel, and the following year came the major alterations: new N aisle and vestry, FONT, more choir stalls, low chancel SCREEN, ALTAR and REREDOS, the last framing the E window (paintings added 1886). The interior was completely decorated with stencil-work and pictures in 1885, together with further stained glass. Much of the PAINTING was done with his own hands; the fittings and STAINED GLASS were made by *Cox, Sons, Buckley & Co.* (E and nave S windows), the small window of St Nicholas (chancel N) by *Ward & Hughes*. Practically no surface was left unadorned, and the combination of pictures, texts and symbolic devices spells out Geldart's theological as well as his artistic creed. Paintings restored by *Donald Smith*, the brocade and raffia wall coverings by *Rachel Ricketts*, 1989–92. – STAINED GLASS. Chancel S by *James Powell & Sons*, 1856. Stamped quarries, 'York Chapter House' pattern. – BRASS to William Roberts †1518, 19-in. (48-cm.) figure, with two wives, and small kneeling children below.

LITTLE BRAXTED HALL, W of the church. C15 or earlier but with numerous additions. Timber-framed, faced with brick. C16 garden wall with square summerhouse in SW angle. Good brick farm buildings (now offices) by *Chancellor*, 1870. N of the house, in a moated enclosure, is a detached former kitchen, which served a now-vanished manor house. Tree-ring dated 1398–1410. Just below, a MILL over the Blackwater with adjoining Late Georgian brick house, the weatherboarded water mill rebuilt after a fire in 1990.

The main village lies 1½ m. SE at the top of the hill; halfway up, the former SCHOOL, *c.* 1853, extended 1890 by *Geldart*. On the S side of a small green, BRAXTED PLACE, the rectory from 1869 to 1980: chequered brick, six bays, mainly Queen Anne but with later additions, principally the CHAPEL on the E side by *Geldart*, 1896, with characteristic internal decoration; enlarged 1932. E of Braxted Place, HEATH HOUSE, Braxted Road. Low two-storey range, timber-framed and plastered, C17 or C18, and a larger gabled cross-wing on the r., with Tudor-style timbers and carved bargeboards and bressumer, dated 1905. Rear additions, 1936.

BEACON COTTAGE. *See* Great Totham.

0020

LITTLE BROMLEY

ST MARY THE VIRGIN. Largely puddingstone. Nave and chancel in one. The nave is Norman, see one N and two S windows, and the roof timbers at the E end suggest that there may originally have been an apse. The chancel belongs to *c.* 1300, E window of three lights with intersected tracery, N and S cusped lancets. Plain brick and timber C16 S porch. Of the same time the completion in brick of the C15 W tower. Diagonal buttresses, three-light W window. Unobtrusively restored and re-seated by *T.G. Jackson*, 1884–5. – FONT. Octagonal, stem with buttresses, bowl with the four symbols of the Evangelists and four rosettes. Early C16. The carving is very primitive. – COMMUNION RAILS, *c.* 1700, with twisted balusters. – ROYAL ARMS of 1816–37. Cast iron, by *Coleman & Wallis* of Colchester. – STAINED GLASS. Three-light nave N window by *A.L. Ward* for *A.R. Mowbray & Co.*, 1933, including figure of Sir Christopher Wren. – MONUMENTS. Rev. Thomas Newman Jun. †1829 by *Henry Lufkin*, Rev. Thomas Newman Sen. †1837 and Joseph Page †1854 by *George Lufkin*. Classical, with the usual urns, sarcophagus etc.

6090

LITTLE BURSTEAD

ST MARY THE VIRGIN. 'Stands obscurely', wrote Morant, but in a commanding position overlooking rolling country. Free-standing timber belfry, C14, on six posts with beams on braces; shingled splay-foot spire. Walls mainly rendered, but containing much puddingstone; SE corner of the nave of C16 brick with black diapers. C13 nave and chancel, with one small lancet in the nave N wall. Early C16 brick windows in the chancel, three-light with Perp panel tracery at the E end, two-light on the S side. The nave roof is C15 and has tie-beams on the braces and crown-posts. The braces rest on corbels carved with (defaced) angels. The chancel roof, a little later, has braces connected with the tie-beams by tracery. Timber tympanum above the tie-beam at the chancel entrance. C19 S porch and N vestry; W gallery 1880, re-seating 1888, small N extension 1990. – Remains of the lower part of the S side of C15 CHANCEL SCREEN, with original painting, built into the wall. – STAINED GLASS. In nave N wall, C17 heraldic glass, with fragments of C15 border, and another window with nine panels of C17 glass, probably Flemish. – E window by *Clayton & Bell*, c. 1890. – MONUMENTS. Good group of ledger stones to members of the Walton family, C17–C18, some with inset brass inscriptions. – R. H. J. Johnson †1915. Bronze, with raised lettering, shields etc., by *F. Ransom*, 1916.

HOPE HOUSE, ⅓ m. NNW. Early C19 brick. Three storeys, with wide overhanging eaves. Five bays, the centre stuccoed with pilasters. Large picturesque late C19 additions, with tile-hanging, and half-timbered octagonal turret.

STOCKWELL HALL, ½ m. NNW. Timber-framed, late C16 or early C17, with contemporary panelling and fireplaces. Plastered, Georgianized front of six bays, with two small and one large gabled dormer. At the S end, in the gable, a large clock face with bellcote. The figures of the clock were originally made of blackened bones.

HATCHES HOUSE, ⅔ m. NW. C16. In the main room of the jettied cross-wing, two doors of c. 1545, each with six panels with heads in roundels, cupids, and foliage, rustically carved. Four similar panels incorporated in an overmantel.

LITTLEBURY

5040

HOLY TRINITY. Chancel of 1873–5 by *Edward Barr*, who had restored the nave and aisles in 1870–1. This included replacing all the windows, except that in the W tower; he also added two small baptistery windows, W of the S door. The roof was raised and round clerestory windows inserted. The tower can be dated to the early C14 by its window, which has flowing tracery. It has half-angle buttresses, because both aisles extend nearly as far W as the tower, a feature very uncommon in Essex. The S doorway must be re-set. With its waterleaf capitals on two orders of columns and its two roll mouldings of which the outer is keeled, it cannot be later than the late C12. Here we may well have the date too of what originally was a S transept – see the E bay of the S arcade – and it is most probably that of the N arcade as well, with circular piers and one-step arches with one slight chamfer. The S arcade in its W parts is later.

The details here tally with the tower arch, i.e. correspond in date to the Dec style. The most ambitious pieces, at least in their conception, are the two porches. Bequests for building (or rebuilding) the s porch were made in wills of 1504 and 1505, and both can be dated to the first decade of the C16. They were given entrance arches much taller than usual, two-centred, with large two-light openings at the sides. What is more, the porches were fan vaulted, as at Saffron Walden, or were meant to have fan vaults, although only fragments remain. To this impressive church, Barr added a chancel, with N vestry and organ chamber, of appropriate grandeur, in the same materials – predominantly flint – but in E.E. style, with three E lancets. The budget, to judge by the amount of carving inside and out, must have been generous (the cost was borne by Lord Braybrooke).

REREDOS. 1874. Stone, carved with reliefs of the Last Supper, Ascension, etc., in crocketed canopies. More good stone-carving on the CREDENCE, SEDILIA, and PULPIT. – LECTERN. On a concave hexagonal base, with buttressed stem, C15, the book-rest not original. – FONT. Square bowl, late C13, in an early C16 CASE (cf. Thaxted). Square, with linenfold panelling and a pyramidal canopy with niches, gables, buttresses, crockets, and finial. – CHANCEL SCREEN. Low, wrought-iron, on stone base, with gates, c. 1873–5. – SCREEN to N chapel. With much pretty inlay work and other ornamental details in the Neo-Early-Renaissance taste; 1911, designed and carved by *Rev. H.J. Burrell*, who probably also made the ALMS BOX at the w end. – DOOR (N doorway). Late C15. On one horizontal batten two shears as the only decoration, referring no doubt to the source of income of the donor. – WALL PAINTING over chancel arch. Rood figures, 1881. – In vestry, a former REREDOS, three painted wooden panels with figures of kneeling angels, similar in style. – STAINED GLASS. E window 1874 by *Clayton & Bell*, who probably also did a number of the others. Tower window by *Mayer & Co.*, about the same date. – BRASSES, none *in situ*. Civilian, c. 1480 (19-in. (48-cm.) figure); Priest, c. 1510 (18½ in. (47 cm.)); Civilian and wife, c. 1510 (25 in. (64 cm.)); Jane Bradbury †1578 (24½ in. (62 cm.)); and Anne Byrd †1624 (20½ in. (52 cm.)).

ST PETER, Littlebury Green. 1885, by *Messrs C. Kent*, of corrugated iron, painted green, and a gem of its type. Tiny w porch and bellcote, and shallow chancel. Pointed windows, transfer-printed in poor but charming imitation of stained glass. Unspoilt interior, walls and ceilings lined with pine boards.

Holy Trinity stands on the s side of the village, and a short circular walk takes in several good houses and cottages, mostly timber-framed and plastered and many thatched. Opposite the church's w end, GRANTA HOUSE, early C19 rebuilding of a C16 house. H-plan, brick with stuccoed walls, and two pedimented wings on the E front with deep eaves. To its r. the former SCHOOL, 1865 by *Barr*, brick with little arches over the windows, gables, etc., and good wrought-iron railings. Further

N, where the High Street widens at the junction with Strethall Road, THE GATEHOUSE, C16. Single-storey hall with exposed timbers and two-storey cross-wings.

A little further on, on the same side, PARRISHES, C17 with jettied upper storey, and opposite FLINT COTTAGE, dated 1843. Then comes WALDEN ROAD, running E, with BAKERS ROW on the S side: two jettied and gabled cross-wings, C16 or earlier, the central hall floored in the C17. An upstairs room has remains of an intricately patterned wall painting. To the E, on the N side, No. 3 and FOLLY COTTAGE, late C16 with a jettied and gabled cross-wing to the r.; No. 3 has a late C16 wall painting on the ground floor. Before the bridge, MID-SUMMER HOUSE, *c.* 1600, with exposed timbers. Opposite, MILL LANE leads back to the church, past KINGS MILL: late C18 weatherboarded mill with mansard roof, and three-storey plastered mill house with a single large bow.*

BRIDGE, over the River Cam. Single-span, cast-iron, by *Henry Stock*, 1858, one of the first to be built by him as County Surveyor. Roadway and parapets rebuilt.

LITTLEBURY and AUDLEY END RAILWAY TUNNELS, ¼ m. SE and ¾ m. SSE. On the Eastern Counties Railway, engineer *R. Stephenson*, 1845. Brick and stone portals, probably designed by *Sancton Wood*; the keystone of the Audley End tunnel's S portal is carved with the Braybrooke arms.

RING HILL, ¾ m. S. Early Iron Age encampment, well sited. There is a wide ditch and an internal rampart enclosing an area of 10½ acres. The original entrance is unidentified. Now in the park of Audley End; for Ring Cottage and *Adam*'s Temple of Victory, as well as other estate buildings in the parish of Littlebury, *see* p. 104.

LITTLE CANFIELD

5020

ALL SAINTS. The general impression and much of the detail are due to *Rev. Charles Lesingham Smith*, rector 1839–78, who restored the church in two phases, 1847 and 1856–8. It amounted to rebuilding, and although Smith is credited with having been his own architect, only the S porch and the MONUMENT to his mother Mary †1856 (elaborate Gothic recess with three pendant arches, executed by *W. Jago* of Great Dunmow) can be ascribed to him with any certainty. The 1847 work, which seems to have included the NW tower and spire, as well as rebuilding the nave W wall and chancel S wall, was superintended by *William Ollett Jun.*; that of 1856–8 by *C. H. Cooke*, who published drawings of the elaborate canopied priest's door (with carving by *Jacquet* of Vauxhall Bridge Road). The nave was C12, the chancel C14, but little of the original remains, apart from the Norman S doorway with one order of columns

---

*Reusing materials from *Henry Winstanley*'s house of 1677 (dem. 1778).

(one-scallop capitals) and two two-light Dec windows in the nave. The N vestry above a burial vault was added in 1757 by James Wyatt of Little Canfield Hall: brick, but coated in cement (like the rest of the church, which is of rubble construction) and lancets by Smith. – FONT. Stone, octagonal, with quatrefoils in recessed panels, by *Ollett*, 1847. – REREDOS. Four stone panels with cusped and crocketed ogee tops, painted with the Ten Commandments, Lord's Prayer and Creed, probably 1847. – SCREEN. With four-light sections ending in interlaced cusped arches, C14. – CHEST. C13. Broad boards as feet. In the front of the feet semicircles are cut out and little colonettes put in instead, as an attempt at decorative enrichment. – STAINED GLASS. Three chancel windows by *Clutterbuck*, 1858. – BRASSES. William Fytche †1578, figure missing, with figures of wives Elizabeth and Ann, each about 23 in. (59 cm.), and groups of children. – Ann Pudsey, William Fytche's widow, †1593; 28-in. (71.5-cm.) figure, with 11½-in. (29-cm.) figure of a son.

CANFIELD MOAT, ½ m. E. By *Rev. C. L. Smith*, 1839, as the rectory. Mainly white brick, in the Elizabethan style. New entrance hall and staircase 1934, further extended 1990. Lodge dated 1864.

LITTLE CANFIELD HALL, ⅔ m. N. Timber-framed, C16, but the front mainly C19, with two square bay windows and little gables with the Maynard crest in plasterwork. Late C14 aisled BARN, SW, five bays with gabled midstrey.

Between church and hall, some nice houses along Stortford Road: N side, HALL COTTAGE, mid C15, with a very large brick chimney added at the W end in the late C16; S side, BLATCHES, early C16 with gabled cross-wings, and some C16 and C17 thatched cottages.

STONE HALL. *See* Easton Lodge, Little Easton.

LITTLE CHESTERFORD

ST MARY THE VIRGIN. Long nave and long chancel of the C13 under one roof. But the E window is late C14, indicating a possible rebuilding of the chancel. Lancets on the N and S sides, and an over-restored double PISCINA; also two nave piscinas. Restored and refitted by *James Barr*, 1855, who added the W bellcote and S vestry. – SCREEN. Plain, C15, with two-light divisions. – MONUMENTS. Brasses of George Langham †1462 and widow Isabel. 28-in. (72-cm.) figure of Isabel; only the upper part of George survives, in armour. – James Walsingham †1728, in a recess added to the chancel S wall. By *Henry Cheere*, one of his earliest works, but already very accomplished. Standing wall monument, with a comfortably reclining figure in Roman toga, his hand resting nonchalantly on a skull.

LITTLE CHESTERFORD MANOR, W of the church. That rare survival, an early C13 manor house. To that time belongs the E wing. The walls are very thick, of flint rubble, plastered, with some clunch dressings visible inside; remnants of medieval, hand-cut, crested ridge tiles. Two surviving doorways with moulded two-centred arches in the W wall, and in the N wall two small straight-headed windows with round rere-arches. On the upper floor two windows of four lights and one transom inserted in the Elizabethan period (as well as a fireplace), but one has remains of keeled shafts to the opening similar to the moulding of the doorways. Also upstairs an external doorway and the entrance to a vanished garderobe. There was probably an external stairway, but it is unclear whether this wing was free-standing or had a timber-framed hall attached to its W. The hall in the middle of the present building belongs to the end of the C13 or early C14. It must have been subdivided horizontally in the C16. Originally it went through to the roof, and was aisled, although only the S aisle remains. This has three posts, the centre one quatrefoil with fillets. Curved braces spring from them towards the opposite wall, forming high two-centred arches. At the back of the spere post is a groove for a wooden screen in the aisle. Crown-post roof, with evidence of a wooden louvre. The two-storey solar wing on the W is probably C15; after it was added the stone wing was downgraded to the service end.

The VILLAGE consists principally of the High Street, running E from the church. By the church the former school (now VILLAGE HALL), and further E the former reading room (now house), both 1862. Brick with stock brick dressings. Opposite the Village Hall, OLD COTTAGE, C16 hall house, later floored, the cross-passage blocked by a fireplace but with the frame of the original front door exposed. More timber-framed and plastered houses towards the main road, including KINGS FARM and THE MALTINGS, both with gabled and jettied cross-wings.

CHESTERFORD PARK, 1½ m. ENE. Farmhouse, 1840, considerably enlarged 1856; brick, mostly painted. Neo-Jacobean front range added by Lord Inchcape, 1913–14. Large porch with attached columns, cresting, etc., and a corbelled oriel. Offices since 1952, with various ancillary buildings for scientific research, including two-storey laboratory by *Fitzroy Robinson Partnership*, 1977–9, and Central Facilities Building by *Barber Casanovas Ruffles*, 2003–4. S of the house, EMANUEL COTTAGE, 1856, with flint N front.

LITTLE CLACTON

ST JAMES THE GREAT. In the chancel a tiny Norman N window; also a C13 double PISCINA with two moulded two-centred heads. Timber S porch, sturdy and unadorned, much renewed, probably C14, as are the windows and N and S doors. One large C16 brick window in the nave N wall. The C15 weatherboarded belfry stands on four posts with tie-beams and curved braces. N extension by *Purcell Miller Tritton*, 1993, brick on flint plinth.

– FONT. Purbeck marble, square, late C12, on four C20 pillars.
– PULPIT, CHOIR STALLS and PEWS, the latter with doors, by
H. & K. Mabbitt, 1952–63. Limed oak. – ROYAL ARMS. Painted,
on wood, 1726. – STAINED GLASS. E window by *Charles E.
Moore*, 1945. Nave S by *William Morris & Co*. of Westminster,
1928.

LITTLE DUNMOW

6020

ST MARY. A priory of Augustinian Canons was founded here in
1106 by Geoffrey Baynard. The church, dedicated by his
mother two years earlier, had a nave, N (and probably also S)
aisle, crossing tower, transepts, chancel, and two chancel aisles
or chapels, the plan ascertained by excavation in 1914. All that
is now above ground is the S or Lady Chapel, used as the parish
church, and as restored by *Chancellor*, 1872–3. He rebuilt the
N wall further out, and added the N vestry and a silly, chimney-
like NW turret, using for its base the stump of the SE corner of
the C12 crossing tower. The result is curiously unbalanced, but
one of interest wherever one looks, and in addition of great
architectural beauty in parts. For a parish church it is long and
narrow. Inside the N wall is the chancel arcade of the priory
16   church, five bays of magnificent thick-set solid piers of about
1200. They consist of four major and four minor shafts, alternatingly keeled. Capitals crocketed or with stylized upright
leaves, not yet of the stiff-leaf type. Richly moulded arches. To
their E, visible from outside, a shafted, blocked C13 window
with shaft-rings and below it blank intersected arcading. That
of course belonged to the priory chancel, and the arcading may
be the remains of sedilia. In the church's W wall, the joint of
the opening from the former S transept into the chapel, and in
addition three niches. These are part of the extremely opulent
remodelling of the chapel which took place *c.* 1360. Its chief
glory is the set of five splendid windows, that at the E end of
five lights and the four S windows a rhythmic alternation of
three and four lights, and at the same time of two-centred,
four-centred, two-centred, four-centred arches. In addition,
whether or not a conscious device, the E window and three of
the S windows have tracery of the flowing type, but the remaining S window is entirely Perp.

Inside, below and between the windows, a charming blank
arcade with leaves and animals – a ram, a pig, a squirrel, a cow.
This is continued below the E window, with human figures,
joining up with the REREDOS, uncovered in 1872, and much
defaced. – CHAIR in the chancel. C15, made up of part of a C13
stall with tracery on one side, a trefoil frieze on the back, and
shafts in front of the arms. – PULPIT. Part of Chancellor's
restoration, reusing C15 Flemish traceried panels. Other traceried panel-heads also incorporated in the COMMUNION
RAILS and PRAYER DESK. – WALL PAINTING. One bay of
N wall with inscriptions, *trompe l'œil* drapes etc., framing a

stained-glass window, as First World War memorial. By *Florence Burnett*, executed by *W. Perry Leach & Sons*, 1920. – Collection of medieval floor TILES, some formerly at Bourchier's Farm, Little Dunmow, and perhaps originally in the priory church (N wall by sanctuary step). – MONUMENTS. Walter and Elizabeth Fitzwalter †1432 and 1464. Alabaster effigies on a tomb-chest decorated with shields. The two effigies are of the highest quality available, faces which in their remote dignity have a direct appeal rare in English C15 funeral sculpture. – Unknown woman, on a tomb-chest. The effigy is early, the tomb-chest late, C15; of lesser quality. – Sir James Hallet or Hallett †1753, by *Thomas Adye*. Obelisk with seated female figure holding a portrait medallion.

PRIORY PLACE, W of the church, within the precinct of the priory. It may have been the guesthouse. Aisled hall with two cross-wings, one jettied, with exposed saltire-bracing in the gables. Early C14, according to Cecil Hewett.

The village, N of the church, has several good medieval timber-framed houses: MONKS HALL, N side of Grange Lane, with two jettied cross-wings, exposed timbers, and weatherboarding in the gables; ROSE FARM, E side of The Street, one jettied cross-wing and weatherboarded ground floor; and a little further S KINGS BARN, thatched, single cross-wing. On the corner of Brook Street, IVY HOUSE, also timber-framed, with C20 pargetting, but early C17 and the plan quite modern, i.e. rectangular with no cross-wings. Two storeys with attics, pitched roof, and large central chimneystack. More nice houses N of Grange Lane, and among them a tall and elaborate cast-iron PUMP, by *Warners* of Cripplegate, London, commemorating the 1887 Jubilee. Further N, the OLD SCHOOL HOUSE by *Chancellor*, 1870–1. A broad gabled bay for the schoolroom with slate bell-turret behind, then a smaller gable over a two-storey bay for the teacher's house. N extension by *Simon Ward*, *c.* 1997, for himself. Alternate courses of red and yellow brick, a witty echo of Chancellor.

GRANGE FARM, 300 yds WNW. C17, with large C18 wings towards the road. Thatched four-bay GRANARY, with crown-post roof, the central post moulded. Studs grooved to take planking, of which some survives. Probably C15.

BRICK HOUSE, ½ m. S. Late C16 or early C17, and a fine example. Two storeys and attics, half-H plan, with the main entrance between the wings on the W front, and a lower service block at the E end of the N wing. Straight gables, including a display gable over the entrance.

LITTLE EASTON

6020

The manor and estates of Little Easton, held in the Middle Ages by the Bourchiers, were granted to Henry Maynard, Lord Burleigh's private secretary, in 1590; he was knighted in 1603. The village's principal buildings of interest lie close to the church, many of them associated with the patronage of Frances Maynard, Countess of Warwick, her family and friends.

ST MARY. The nave's Norman origin is visible only in scanty fragments of two N windows. The rest, as it appears to the eye, is essentially Perp and C15, in flint rubble, except for the N chancel aisle (part now the American Chapel), added by *J. Clarke*, 1879–81. The W tower has diagonal buttresses and a W doorway with shields in the spandrels. The chancel has a four-light window with panel tracery. In the C15 Bourchier (S) Chapel, which is as wide as the nave, are large windows, those on the S side having apparently been converted first in the C18 into plain arched shapes and then in 1857 into their present preposterous Neo-Norman shape. The pier of the two-bay arcade towards the chancel has semi-polygonal main shafts and circular shafts in the diagonals. – GRADINE and CHOIR STALLS. 1899 by *G.H. Pryer*, Easton Lodge estate carpenter. – SCREEN to Bourchier Chapel. Wrought iron, early C18. Originally a gate of Easton Lodge. – WALL PAINTINGS. Splendid figure of a seated apostle, *c.* 1130, with one of the Labours of the Months below; no doubt the surviving one of twelve. True fresco, using lead pigments; the black underpaint for the flesh has been compared by *Professor Tristram* (who restored the paintings in 1934, and made the framed copies displayed below them) to St Albans, the style to the Bible of Bury St Edmunds. – Stories from the Passion of Christ in two tiers, late C14. The scenes represented are Last Supper, Agony in the Garden, Betrayal, Christ before Pilate, Christ crowned with Thorns, Christ carrying the Cross, Crucifixion, Deposition, Entombment. The iconography is North Italian. – Also painted on nave wall, ROYAL ARMS, 1660. – STAINED GLASS. E window †1865 probably by *Clayton & Bell*. – In the Bourchier Chapel, six panels depicting the Life of Christ, made for the chapel added to Easton Lodge in 1621, and attributed by M. Archer to *Baptista Sutton*. Placed here in 1857. – In the American Chapel, two windows by *Phillips Stained Glass Studio*, Cleveland, Ohio (*Douglas Phillips*, assisted by *Mona Clark*, *Ben Parsons*, and *Bill Greenberg*), 1990, commemorating the USAAF Bomb Group based at the airfield in the park of Easton Lodge.

MONUMENTS. Brass to Robert Fyn, priest, praying; *c.* 1420; the figure 19 in. (48 cm.) long. – On N side of the chancel, monument to Lady Bourchier, *c.* 1400. Tomb-chest with three cusped panels carrying shields. Tall cusped ogee arch between thin buttresses with finials. Six shields in the spandrels. On the tomb-chest a small effigy of a C13 knight, only 2 ft (60 cm.) long. – Between chancel and Bourchier Chapel, Viscount Bourchier, Earl of Essex †1483 and wife, moved from Beeleigh Abbey (q.v.) at the Dissolution. Purbeck marble tomb-chest, panelled and traceried, with brasses on top, the figures 4 ft (1.2 metres) long. The brasses retain some of their enamelling. Large heavy straight-topped canopy, tripartite, with richly cusped vault. – In the Bourchier Chapel, Sir Henry Maynard †1610 and wife. Alabaster monument with two reclining effigies on a tomb-chest with large kneeling figures of children. The sculptural value high. – Lady Maynard †1613, reclining figure. – William, Lord Maynard †1640 and wife Anne †1647, erected some fifty years later. Large standing wall monument with life-size standing figures in Roman costume, an urn between them. The type is one familiar from *Grinling Gibbons*, and the attribution to him carries more weight than the other, to Pearce (GF). – William, 2nd Lord Maynard †1696 and family, erected 1746; by *Charles Stanley*. Also a large standing wall monument, opposite the last. Lord Maynard in the middle in a musing attitude leaning on an urn, with the portrait of his wife. Other members of the family as busts or relief-medallions. Big relief below with figures of Justice (blindfold), Charity, Fortitude, etc. – Bust of Frances, Countess of Warwick †1938. Shown in her heyday by *Sir Edgar Boehm*, 1890. – In nave, Francis, 5th Earl of Warwick †1924. Profile portrait by *S. W. Ward Willis*. – Dame Ellen Terry †1928. Richly modelled bronze panel set with semi-precious stones, with brass and enamel plaques, by *Alfred Gilbert*. – Rev. Jack Filby †2000. Bronze bust by *Austin Bennett*.

MANOR HOUSE, N of St Mary. The core is C17, with two gables and tall chimneystack, and had been remodelled in the C19, but the rest is a theatrical composition by the actor and impresario Basil Dean, who married Lady Warwick's daughter Mercy in 1925. Dean's initial campaign, 1925–7, was intended to take the house back to a purer state; the porch was rebuilt, the staircase replaced, beams exposed, etc., under the direction of the intriguing *Marquis d'Oisy*. Further work, however, was increasingly grand and elaborate. A six-bay C18-style block was added to the E, joining up with a C17 timber-framed cottage; the link to the main house (two overlapping circles, one a stair-tower) cleverly devised by *A. V. Heal*. He also added a music room on the W side of the house. In the cellar, Dean had a cocktail bar decorated with murals by *Teddy Craig*, of which a fragment survives.

Behind the house a brick and flint service courtyard, and across a roadway to the E a pair of plastered cottages, converted in 1938 from workshops and incorporating a C18 granary, connected by C20 weatherboarded outbuildings to a C16 plastered and weatherboarded BARN. Converted to a theatre before 1913 by Lady Warwick; performers include Ellen Terry and H.G. Wells. The overall effect is charming, with gateways, walls reusing old materials (including some from Easton Lodge), and compartmented gardens leading down to a lake, and with more than a touch of Hollywood (or Pinewood).

Opposite the church's s side, CHURCH ROW, six highly pic- 93 turesque former almshouses built by Lady Warwick, 1895. Brick, pebbledash and timber framing. Gabled, with veranda, and a low wall with cast-iron railings by the *Hope Foundry Co.* Opposite the w end, CHURCH LODGE, a C17 timber-framed and plastered cottage, with C19 veranda and decorative bargeboards.

EASTON GLEBE, ⅓ m. NW. Former rectory, from *c.* 1911 to 1928 the home of H.G. Wells. The mid-C18 brick front with pedimented Ionic doorcase probably hides an older structure. Extended by *A. Winter Rose*, 1915, with bows on two sides; on the E bow the windows fold completely open. NW of the house a BARN dated in the plaster 1746 (now a house), and on the garden wall a MONUMENT to Wells's gardener, Henry Grout †1925, with lettering by *Eric Gill*.

ROUND HOUSE, ¾ m. NNW. Small round brick tower, crenellated, with turrets, and single-storey wings with stepped gables, hoodmoulded windows, and other folly-like features. C19.

EASTON LODGE
¾ m WNW

Sir Henry Maynard built a mansion ¾ m. WNW of the church, to which a W wing and chapel were added in 1621, but it burnt down in 1847 and was rebuilt by *Hopper*. In 1884 extensive alterations and additions were made by *William Young*, including the remodelling of the Jacobean W wing, for Frances Maynard, later Countess of Warwick (†1938). In 1902 she employed *Harold Peto* to design the gardens and in 1918, after a fire, had the W wing remodelled by *Philip Tilden* as the 'Great Room', double-height with sleeping gallery at one end, in which she lived. The main house was demolished in 1950 and the gardens gradually restored from 1971.

The house's site is discernible, with a terrace on its SW side. At the NW end of the terrace is the C17 W wing (now WARWICK HOUSE) as remodelled first by *Young* and then by *Tilden*. Brick with stone dressings and at the S end a shaped gable and large

Easton Lodge, Little Easton.
Engraving, 1768

bay window. On its w side a late C17 brick DOVECOTE, square with pyramidal roof and octagonal lantern (now display area and offices). In the garden behind it, four stone finials from Knightsbridge Barracks, London, by *T. H. Wyatt*, 1880 (dem. 1966). On the N side of Warwick House, a cobbled courtyard with fountain by *Peto*. At the SE end of the terrace, a PAVIL-ION, probably by *Tilden*, *c.* 1920. Brick with stone dressings and hipped tiled roof, the main opening in the form of a Venet-ian window. S of the house, C18 wrought-iron gates and over-throw from Clock House, Great Dunmow (q.v.).

NE of the site of the main house, the ITALIAN GARDEN, the most impressive of *Peto*'s designs for Lady Warwick: a sunken garden with stone balustrading and a rectangular pool 100 ft (30 metres) long. Beyond, a grove of pleached lime trees with the remains of a thatched TREE HOUSE by Peto, designed to sit above the treetops like a cottage in the middle of a lawn. NW of the Italian Garden, the glade leading down to a lake was laid out by Peto as a JAPANESE GARDEN, originally with a timber tea house by the lake. At the SW end of the glade, looking down it and built against the kitchen garden wall, the SHELLEY PAVILION, formerly the porch to Maresfield Park, Sussex (*B.D. Wyatt*, 1816; dem. 1921).

NW of Warwick House, the former stable yard, with a terrace of six cottages, 1896, in the same picturesque style as the almshouses opposite the church (*see* above). Behind them a tall, plain, brick WATER TOWER, 1902, and GARDENER'S COTTAGE by *A.V. Heal*, late 1920s. On the NE side, a timber-framed and plastered house, built in the C17 as servants' quar-ters. Much altered in the C20, by *Tilden* among others.

About 400 yds NE of the site of the main house, THE OLD LAUNDRY, now a house, probably part of *Young*'s alterations and additions of 1884: brick, with two large ventilator louvres on the roof.

The PARK was, by the C18, laid out with radiating avenues in a *patte-d'oie*, but all this was swept away in 1942–3 by the USAAF airfield. At STONE HALL, just outside the park 1 m. s of the house, Lady Warwick laid out a garden and transformed the timber-framed cottage into a folly incorporating old stone-and timberwork (C14 windows may have come from Little Canfield church).

1¾ m. SE of the house, on Stortford Road, a C17 brick GATE-HOUSE. Central carriageway with four-centred arch, flanking lodges with arched windows and doorways.

LITTLE HALLINGBURY

ST MARY THE VIRGIN. Flint rubble, with some tile and Roman brick. Timber-framed w belfry with slender recessed shingled spire by *G.E. Pritchett*, 1901, following its predecessor of 1712. Pritchett (whose father was vicar, 1835–49) restored the church and added the N aisle in 1853, and added the s vestry and organ chamber in 1898. Vestry extended by *Purcell Miller Tritton*, *c.* 1996. Inside, Pritchett's work includes the chancel arch, hammerbeam roof in the chancel, and Neo-Norman FONT. Of original Norman, perhaps Late Saxon, work, the plain s doorway with Roman bricks. C13 chancel with renewed lancets. Interesting C14 s porch with unusual tracery of squashed ogee arches and squashed arches and squashed circles with ogee tops and bottoms. – STAINED GLASS. E window by *A.E. Buss* (*Goddard & Gibbs*), 1948; also nave s single-light. – Chancel s, 1898, and w window (St Etheldreda, founder of Ely Cathedral, and Alan de Walsingham, builder of Ely's octagon) to G.E. Pritchett, 1913 by *James Powell & Sons*, the earlier one probably designed by *W. Aikman*. – N aisle E †1894 by *Percy Bacon & Bros*, N wall E †1905 also by *Bacon*, and w by *Morris & Co.*, 1908, with *Burne-Jones* figure painted by *Titcomb*, border and inscription by *Watson*. – E of the church, a group of C19 HEAD-STONES of the Pritchett family, including a longitudinal wooden grave marker, and a similar marker, in stone, for G.E. Pritchett †1912.

PRIMARY SCHOOL. 1869 by *Pritchett*, enlarged 1884 and 1975. Flint rubble with stock brick dressings, not a particularly attractive combination.

Pretty group opposite the church of MALTINGS COTTAGES, C17 brick, behind a little pond, MALTINGS FARM, C16 with symmetrical gabled cross-wings, and behind them a C17 thatched BARN, now a house. On the churchyard's E side, the former RECTORY, C18 brick, 'restored' 1866, no doubt by *Pritchett*, but still essentially Georgian in character.

GASTON HOUSE, ⅓ m. SW. Brick, *c.* 1730. Five bays, two-and-a-half storeys, with Doric porch. Later C18 service wing to l. and similar extension to r., 1979. – Palladian former STABLES. Brick, with stone dressings and pantiles. Two-storey centre with pedimented gables, flanked by single-storey aisles with lean-to roofs that give the semblance of a lower broken pediment.

HALLINGBURY MILL, ½ m. SW. 1874. Three storeys, with vertical weatherboarding, and front and rear lucams. Fully restored machinery.

WALLBURY CAMP, ¾ m. NW. Early Iron Age hill-fort, well sited on a spur overlooking the Stort valley. The fort is pear-shaped, covering 31 acres. The ditch is 50 to 70 ft (15 to 22 metres) wide, and there is a double rampart 7 ft (2.1 metres) high, a most unusual feature in monuments of this class in Eastern England. There were originally two entrances.

LITTLE HENNY

THE RYES. By *Robert Lugar* for Nathaniel Barnadiston, the design exhibited at the R.A. in 1809. Then called The Ryes Lodge, it was carefully sited: 'the entrance . . . from the public road is carried through a broad plantation, and the view, even before the house is reached, bursts upon the sight with the most pleasing effect of rural beauty.'* Gault brick and stucco, with slate roof and deep eaves with paired brackets. Entrance front with (originally) two bays with pedimented gables and, in the recessed central bay, a Doric portico with two pairs of columns. On the garden front, to the r., a two-storey semicircular bay. Service wing set back to the l. and into the re-entrant angle *E.F. Bisshopp* inserted an addition for Col. Nathaniel Barnadiston, 1884. One of Lugar's gables was lost but the style is in keeping. Lugar's principal reception rooms were retained, although his staircase was replaced by a new staircase hall. Former STABLE and COACH HOUSE to the W.

In the garden, SE, the ruins of the parish CHURCH. Low walls only. Probably C12, destroyed by fire *c.* 1600.

LITTLE HORKESLEY

ST PETER AND ST PAUL. The medieval church was almost completely destroyed by a bomb in 1940 but rebuilt in Perp style by *Duncan Clark*, 1957–8, completed after his death by *Marshall Sisson*. Nave, chancel, battlemented W tower, S aisle, rendered walls with stone dressings, and a brick S porch, closely following the form of the old church. Light, spacious interior. – STAINED GLASS. E window, 1961, and S aisle E (Lady Chapel), 1963, by *Hugh Powell*. – MONUMENTS. Salvaged, incredibly, from the old church. Three oak effigies, probably of Robert Horkesley †1295, his son William and William's wife Emma, both †1332. Both knights have their legs crossed, their feet resting on lions; the lady's feet on two small dogs. – Sir Robert Swynborne †1391 and his son Sir Thomas †1412. Low tomb-chest with brasses of two men in armour under triple-arched canopies. 69-in. (1.7-metre) figures. – Part of the side of a tomb-chest, late C15, Purbeck marble with cusped panelling enclosing shields with rivets of former brasses. – Brass to Katherine Leventhorp †1502. 19-in. (48-cm.) figure in a shroud. – Brasses of Bridget Marney †1549, wife of William Findern (incorrectly named as Thomas) †1523 and John, 2nd Lord Marney †1525. 27-in. (68-cm.) figures of lady in pedimental headdress and husbands in armour. Palimpsest with the figure of a shrouded lady on the reverse, *c.* 1490.

The centre of the village, NE of the church, is marked by an unusual First World War MEMORIAL with a very slender wooden cross on stone base, opposite THE BEEHIVE pub by *Mitchell & Houghton*, 1954, rebuilt following damage by the bomb that destroyed the church. Inn sign by *Basil Oliver*, a skep on a post. The rest of the village has a large number of high-quality houses relative to its size.

HORKESLEY HALL, SW of the church. Surprisingly sophisticated for such a rural location; *c.* 1828, on the site of an C18 house.

*Lugar's *Plans and Views*, 1823.

The client was Rev. J.C. Blair-Warren, squire and perpetual curate of Little Horkesley from 1829. Unfortunately no architect is recorded. Two storeys, gault brick and stone. Five-bay N (entrance) front with a giant tetrastyle Ionic portico (porte cochère) beneath anthemion and palmette frieze, and three-bay E front with central two-storey bow. S front of five bays, the central three breaking forward slightly; the central window has pairs of attached columns, Greek Doric, also found inside. At right angles, W of the entrance, a stucco Greek Doric archway with gault brick stables to either side. Two ponds below the house to the S, probably part of C18 landscaping, and kitchen garden to the W.

OLD HALL FARM, W of the church. C16, with exposed timbers on the E elevation, and brick extension to the W of c. 1700. Full-height N stair-tower.

THE PRIORY, NE of the church. The surviving wing of a Cluniac priory founded c. 1127. The E wall is probably the end wall of a C14 priest's house, the remainder early C16, with a C17 or C18 wing to the N.

HOLTS, 1 m. SW. Timber-framed and plastered with a two-storey, five-bay Early Georgian front. Pedimented doorcase with attached Ionic columns, the window above it with scrolls at the base. Parapet cornice with unusual Gothic arcading in the moulding. C15 hall and cross-wing.

LOWER DAIRY FARM, ¾ m. NE. Exposed timbers. Cross-wing to the r. ending in a fine gable with carved bressumers, dated 1601.

OLD JOSSELYNS, ½ m. NE. A delightful house dating back to c. 1500, all the timberwork exposed. The oldest part is the cross-wing facing the road that continues the long-wall jetty of the early C17 range to its r. Windows of four and five lights with one transom, placed in projecting frames almost like oriels. The hall stood to the l. of the central cross-wing but what is there now is probably a C17 replacement, followed by a C17 wing. By the early C20 it had been divided into cottages, but was returned to a single house by *Reginald Blomfield*, c. 1908. N wing added 1923, gabled S wing (drawing room) with carved bressumers 1928, all carefully done. The back with two big chimneystacks is equally attractive. First-floor room with remains of Late Elizabethan stencilled decoration.

JOSCELYNS, next to Old Josselyns. 1969–70 by *Erith & Terry*. A miniature French château approached by a short avenue of pollarded limes. Five-bay stone ground floor with round-headed windows. Slate mansard with dormers and low pavilions with steep roofs.

WESTWOOD PARK, 1¼ m. S. Brick, with a rainwater head dated 1692, but almost entirely rebuilt for W.J.M. Hill, c. 1906–13. Neo-Jacobean, with large shaped gables and two-storey porch. Lavishly panelled interior. Two LODGES by *Erith*, 1938, in similar style.

LITTLE LAVER

St Mary the Virgin. Flint rubble, mostly of 1872 by *J. Goldicutt Turner*. He restored the C14 nave and chancel and added the s porch, N vestry and organ chamber, and apsidal sanctuary. The E windows have an inner arcade screen. – REREDOS and sanctuary walls of carved stone and alabaster, 1886, incorporating a C14 PISCINA. – FONT. Square, *c.* 1200, of the Abbess Roding and Fryerning type, but re-cut in 1872. On one side three fleurs-de-lys, on another a trail of stylized foliage, on another two four-petalled flowers or rather quatre-foils with rose centres, on the fourth the sun, moon, a whorl, two roses, and two stars.

Little Laver Grange, to be precise its early C19 gabled w wing, faces the church's E end. Beyond that a timber-framed and plastered range, C15 or earlier, its chimneystack dated 1587.

Little Laver Hall, ½ m. NNE. Mid C19, painted brick and stucco, with hoodmoulded windows. s and E wings added 1930. Pretty thatched lodge with rustic porch.

White Lodge, nearly ½ m. s. Built as the rectory, 1831.

LITTLE LEIGHS

Great and Little Leighs

St John the Evangelist. Nave and chancel of flint rubble, weatherboarded w belfry with shingled splay-footed spire. The nave is C12, the chancel C13; it can be observed that the C12 laid the stones coursed, the C13 did not. One Norman window each in the N and s walls, and part of the arch of a third on s wall inside. No original chancel windows, but an original C13 doorway in the nave, with one order of columns and a roll moulding with fillet. In the chancel N wall an early C14 recess with ogee arch, cusped and sub-cusped, thin buttresses by the sides, and a big finial. In the spandrels oak, roses, heads etc. – the leaves already bossy. Restored 1895 by *A.Y. Nutt*, who rebuilt the E wall, reinstated the w window, and added the s porch and N vestry. – FONT. Octagonal bowl on eight shafts round a central stem, with worn figures of animals as bases. C13, with tracery on the panels of the bowl added in the C14. – PULPIT. 1895, with C16 and C17 linenfold and incised panels reused from old pews. Other woodwork reused as panelling in the vestry. – Also of 1895 the CHANCEL SCREEN and stone REREDOS. – BENCHES. Ten in the nave of a plain design, with a kind of vertical reeding on the ends. Early C16. – SOUTH DOOR. Late C13 or early C14, with two strap hinges with scrolled branches. – STAINED GLASS. E and w windows 1895, probably by *Ion Pace*. – Nave N by *G.E.R. Smith* (*A.K. Nicholson Stained Glass Studios*), 1951. – MONUMENTS. In chancel recess, the oak effigy of a priest, *c.* 1300, of a startling and moving simplicity. In mass vestments, with two animals, prob-ably dogs, at his feet, and two defaced angels supporting his head. Traces of gesso and blue and red paint hint at how it might once have looked. – Herman Olmius †1726. Inscription on *trompe l'œil* drapery, broken scrolly pediment above, winged cherub's head below. Accompanying HATCHMENT. – George Welstead †1796. With mourning female figure leaning on an urn.

LITTLE LEIGHS HALL, ½ m. NNW. C15 or earlier, extended in the C17. The taller S wing, *c.* 1750, has some moulded beams that may have been reused from Leez Priory (q.v.).

OLD RECTORY, ¼ m. N. 1851, for Rev. John Green, in the Tudor-Gothic style favoured by *Hopper*.

LAVENDER LEEZ, 1 m. N. 1920s, by *Fred Rowntree* with his sons *Douglas W. & Colin Rowntree*. Lutyensesque touches, e.g. low sweeping roofs, the entrance set in a low round arch, and two-storey bows.

LITTLE LEIGHS PRIORY. *See* Leez Priory.

₈₀₃₀

LITTLE MAPLESTEAD

ST JOHN THE BAPTIST. Those who believe in texture and the handiwork of the medieval mason will not be pleased by Little Maplestead. Most of what one sees is from the restoration of 1851–7 started under *R.C. Carpenter* and completed by *W. Slater* after Carpenter's death in 1855. But those who are looking for design and composition can still enjoy the noble rotunda which takes the place of the nave. Little Maplestead was the church of a Commandery or Preceptory of the Knights Hospitallers and as such was built (as the Templars had done before) on the pattern of the Church of the Holy Sepulchre at Jerusalem, that is as a circular building. There are only five circular churches left in England, the late C12 Temple Church in London being the most famous. The others are at Ludlow Castle, Northampton, and Cambridge, all Norman. Little Maplestead was built as late as *c.* 1335, but replaced an earlier building on the site that must have been built soon after the village was granted to the Hospitallers in 1185–6. The piers of the rotunda are trefoil with sharply V-shaped shafts separating the columns. The arches have two quadrant mouldings. The windows are of two lights and also of a typical early C14 form. The chancel is contemporary with the rotunda and has an apse. The C14 W doorway, with its rich fleuron decoration, is original, and is illustrated in William Wallen's book on the church published in 1836; it was restored by Carpenter, who also 'renewed' the corbels of the arches round the outside wall of the rotunda. Carpenter replaced the timber porch, refaced the external walls, renewed windows and buttresses, and provided new roofs, with a series of little dormer ventilators on the aisle roof. The wooden belfry was rebuilt. A large S vestry was planned but never built; the present vestry was to be the passage connecting the new vestry to the chancel. – FONT. C11, originally square, cut down at some point to make an irregular octagon. Very raw decoration: a saltire cross, two arches, a composition of two volutes. – STAINED GLASS. A complete scheme, presumably 1851–7.

LITTLE MAPLESTEAD HALL. Brick-faced, of C19 appearance, but built in the C17 reusing many C14 timbers.

LITTLE OAKLEY   *2020*

ST MARY. Outside the village, and sitting high up behind fields overlooking the marshes and coast. Converted to a house in 1976, the walls rendered. The nave is Norman. The W tower, begun *c.* 1500, was once a landmark; gradual restoration of the church by *J.E.K. & J.P. Cutts*, 1895–1902, included rebuilding it, but they did not get any higher than the nave roof. Remains of flushwork in the moulded plinth. The W doorway has shields in the spandrels, a hoodmould resting on two lions couchant, fleurons in jambs and voussoirs, shields of arms of Vere and Howard in the spandrels, a frieze of small shields above, and then the three-light W window. The chancel of *c.* 1330 is what really matters, and although the effect is damaged by an inserted floor, the essentials remain. Three-light window with reticulated tracery and inside, two niches l. and r., with very steep canopies with crockets and finials. PISCINA of the same character. Its steep gable is flanked by thin tall decorative buttresses. N and S windows of two lights of three different simple kinds of Dec tracery. The priest's door on the S side is placed in the middle of a buttress which widens porch-wise to take it (cf. Burnham-on-Crouch).

LITTLE OAKLEY HALL, E of the church. Early C19 gault brick front, gabled cross-wings flanking a three-bay centre.

LITTLE SAMPFORD   *6030*

ST MARY THE VIRGIN. Small, but relatively long, of flint and stone rubble. C14 W tower of the type exemplified by Great Dunmow, that is with set-back buttresses, but the angles between them chamfered, carried on polygonally towards the top and provided with polygonal flat-topped pinnacles (spirelets added later). Battlements, and late C17 lead spike. Also C14 the nave with clerestory (quatrefoil windows) and the N aisle. The arcade has piers of an exceptional form: lozenge with four attached shafts. No capitals at all. The tower arch is of a similar design. The chancel is later, probably C15, see its broad five-light E window. Early C16 brick window near the W end of the S side, and C17 brick S porch. N vestry 1862, and an unobtrusive restoration in 1908. Roofs of very shallow pitch, that in the nave dated 1682. – SCREEN with broad single-light divisions with segmental arches and a little panel tracery above. – BENCHES. Quite plain, in the nave. Early C16. – STAINED GLASS. Fragments of tabernacles in E window. – N aisle E †1964 by *F.L. Luxford*. – MONUMENTS. Large cartouche on N side of chancel with pilasters and strapwork: 'Lo in this tumbe combyned are thes toe bereft of lyfe / Sur Edward Grene a famus knyghte and Margerye hys wyfe'. She died in 1520, he in 1556. No figures. The monument is repeated on the S side, but without inscription. – William Twedy †1605 and wife. Small wall monument with the usual kneeling figures. – Bridget Peck †1712, attributed to *Thomas Stayner* (GF). Standing wall monument with the lady (aged 31) comfortably reclining. She holds her book in her hand which she has just laid down.* –William Savage †1736 and others. Greek Revival tablet by *R. Westmacott*, 1806.

LITTLE SAMPFORD HALL, N of the church. Rebuilt 1926 – see the harsh brick on the NE front. But the SE front and an outbuilding have shaped gables inspired by those of the C16–C17 house and reuse old white bricks.

TEWES, ¾ m. W. Small late C15 manor house, restored in the 1920s, when the two-storey porch and SW bay were added. Some original high-level windows on the main front, which is jettied, as well as inserted sashes. Small C17 NW wing. In two ground-floor rooms finely carved beams and wall-plates.

8020

LITTLE TEY

ST JAMES THE LESS. C12 nave and apsidal chancel in one, and timber belfry with pyramid roof. Walls of flint rubble with limestone dressings and conspicuous puddingstone quoins. Several small Norman windows, and S doorway with a tympanum decorated with Norman lozenge diapering. Roof at E end gabled, rather than rounded as at Copford or Little Braxted. – WALL PAINTINGS. In the apse, an extensive C13 Passion cycle, with fragments indicating a C14 repainting. In the nave, remains of other C13 work, and a fine C14 Virgin and Child; on N wall, fragmentary St Christopher and part of the Three Living and Three Dead.

6070

LITTLE THURROCK
Thurrock U.A.

ST MARY THE VIRGIN. Norman nave and chancel arch (rebuilt except for the slightly decorated abaci of the responds). Plain Norman S doorway. C14 chancel, with SEDILIA separated by shafts with moulded capitals; pointed arches, hoodmoulds; the whole framed. W end by *F. Franey*, 1883–4, who added the little square tower with bands of flint of stone, and inside a pretty triple arch separating the tower part from the nave. The rest of the church restored by him 1878–9, when the early C13 RECESS

---

*The upper part of the monument, with Corinthian pilasters, inscription on *trompe l'œil* drapery, cherubs' heads, garlands, etc., was stolen in 1993.

in the s wall was uncovered. Shallow N organ chamber, 1909.
– REREDOS. Nicely painted panels, late C19, framed with
tracery that incorporates C15 work; from Kempston, Beds.
Now against W wall, together with COMMANDMENT BOARDS
by *J. Sanders* of Orsett, 1837. – PULPIT. Dated 1700; plain
panels; the Jacobean tradition at last completely gone. –
STAINED GLASS. E window by *A. E. Buss* of *Goddard & Gibbs*,
1966. – MONUMENT. Thomas Green †1808. Above the tablet
an attached fluted column with flaming urn and a shield
propped up against it.

St JOHN THE EVANGELIST, Victoria Avenue. Chancel, E vestries
and bellcote by *W. E. Ellery Anderson*, 1932–3, very traditional
for that date. E.E., brick with stone dressings. White brick nave
by *D.M. Corder*, 1964–5, the walls fanning out slightly from the
chancel arch with zigzag windows à la Coventry Cathedral. The
two parts work better together inside than on the outside.
Narthex by *Geoffrey Vale*, 2006. – STAINED GLASS. E window,
1947, and three chancel s, 1956, by *R. M. De Montmorency*.

THURROCK AND BASILDON COLLEGE (Woodview Campus).
By *H. Conolly*, County Architect, 1954–60. Six-storey classroom block, with lower blocks either side and workshops
behind. Portland stone and green slate cladding on the main
entrance and administration block, coloured and insulated
glass panels on the classrooms.

PALMER'S COLLEGE, Chadwell Road. 1931 by *J. Stuart*, County
Architect, at his most monumental Neo-Georgian. Main block
with hipped roof, five tall round-headed windows separated by
Giant Ionic pilasters and three-bay pediment.

Former SCHOOL, next to St Mary. By *Elmslie & Franey*, 1872.
What mainly survives is the teacher's house, now pebbledashed. Corner clock turret with shingled pagoda-like roof.

DENEHOLES, Hangman's Wood, ½ m. E of St John. Shafts about
4 ft (1.2 metres) wide and up to about 100 ft (30 metres) deep,
with chambers at the bottom. Of uncertain age and purpose,
but probably medieval chalkpits. Over seventy have been found
in the area.

LITTLE TOTHAM 8010

ALL SAINTS. Good Late Norman s doorway of two orders of
columns decorated with certain unusual motifs. The columns
for instance have square blocks with rosettes round their
waists – rather a low waist-line, about one-third up. The voussoirs combine roll mouldings with a kind of three-dimensional
double-saltire frieze. One frieze runs parallel, one at right
angles to the door opening. Earlier Norman N doorway, quite
plain, rebuilt perhaps in the C16. C13 lancets in nave and
chancel. Handsome E end with three stepped lancets. Early in
the C16 a big W tower was added, of squared flints; w door
dated 1527. But the enterprise was stopped and the tower later
finished in timber, weatherboarded, with a pyramid roof. The

rest of the church rendered, with a simple weatherboarded C19 s porch, and balancing N extension by *David Ferguson*, 2001. Inside, original roofs with low tie-beams. Unobtrusive restoration by *E. Geldart*, 1883 – see the floor tiles. – FONT. Perp, octagonal, the bowl decorated with tracery. Unusually interesting, because the carver apparently used what were to him eight current tracery motifs. They are indeed such as one sees frequently in church windows. But although the date is no doubt C15, the Dec motifs of cusped intersection and of ogee reticulation are still there. Otherwise the motifs are those of three- and four-light panel tracery and the Perp type with straightened reticulation, both with and without transom. – PULPIT. Incorporating bits of the C17. – DOORS. Original s door. Tree-ring dating has shown the timbers of the N door to belong to the last quarter of the C11, so they may be reused; mid-C12 ironwork, a large C-hinge and barbed strap. – Early C19 chamber ORGAN with Gothick cresting. – STAINED GLASS. E window †1916 by *Heaton, Butler & Bayne*. – MONUMENT. Sir John Samms †1606 and wife Isabell †1633. Standing wall monument in the Jacobean tradition, marble, with two large kneeling figures opposite each other by a prayer desk. Each figure against an arched niche. Below, a deep arched recess with the equally large figure of their son Sir Garrard †1630.

LITTLE TOTHAM HALL, NW of the church. C15, mostly rebuilt in the C19 and later. At the NE end a late C16 addition partly of brick, with angle pilasters and a blocked doorway with four-centred arch.

NODROG, Moors Farm Chase, ½ m. N. By *P. Andrew Borges & Associates*, 1976–7. Three A-framed bays linked together to form a single dwelling.

LITTLE WAKERING
9080

Barling Magna

ST MARY THE VIRGIN. The proud ragstone W tower was contributed by Bishop Wakering of Norwich (1416–25). It has big diagonal buttresses, a W doorway with the arms of the Bishop and the Countess of Stafford, a three-light window with panel tracery, niches to l. and r., battlements with stone and flint chequerwork, and a rather tall recessed spire. Nave and chancel, of mixed rubble, are much earlier – see their tiny Norman N windows. Inside, the nave N wall has a fine early C13 recess with one order of colonettes and an arch with a keeled roll moulding. The rood-stair doorways and the stairs themselves are preserved. Restoration of chancel, 1878, and nave, 1884, by *W. J. Wood*; further restoration by *C.C. Winmill* and *William Weir*, 1935–6. – WALL PAINTING. On the splays of the chancel N window, remains of a Nativity and the figure of a bishop, possibly St Denis; *c.* 1200. – ROYAL ARMS. 1769, painted on board, in frame with arched head. – STAINED GLASS. Nave N by *Rosemary Smith Marriott*, 1937, with a very lively St Michael.

LITTLE WAKERING HALL. C15. Cross-wings to l. and r., the latter jettied to the front and side with dragon beam. Hall floored 1599 (date on a beam bracket) and panelling put into several rooms; newel stair with solid treads and moulded balusters. In the hall a sumptuous fireplace of *c.* 1730 with caryatids in profile carrying baskets. C16 brick outbuilding and garden wall.

LITTLE WALDEN
Saffron Walden

5040

St John. 1894 by *E. Burgess*. E.E., brick, with stone dressings. Chapel-like, with timber w porch and bellcote.

Cinder Hall, ¾ m. ssw. Small folly of *c.* 1820, with battlements, corner bartizan, corbelled oriel, and so on. Mainly flint cobble but with decorative panels of cinders or clinker. Restored and enlarged by *The Kenneth Mark Practice*, *c.* 1981–2, in the same materials and the same spirit.

LITTLE WALTHAM

7010

St Martin. Norman nave, mainly of flint and pebble rubble, with s doorway (one order of columns, one-scallop capitals, roll moulding) and one s window. Chancel Perp, w tower also Perp but much repaired in brick in the C16 or C17. Behind the battlements a minute cupola with weathervane dated 1679. N aisle, organ chamber and vestry, and s porch by *Chancellor*, 1883–4, who also carried out a general restoration, including re-roofing. – Reredos. Stone, C19, but with inserted bas-relief figures of the Evangelists, 1953, beautifully carved by *Joseph Cribb*. – Pulpit. By *Chancellor*, 1892. Stone, large and round. – Chest. Dug-out, 7ft (2.1 metres) long, heavily bound with iron; C13 or C14. – Stained Glass. e window by *Lawrence Lee*, 1951, incorporating fragments of older glass in the tracery and borders, and with a view of Little Waltham church, rectory etc. as background to the Crucifixion. Heraldic glass in N aisle also by Lee, 1952. – Nave s (Ascension) and w window by *A.O. Hemming & Co.*, 1884, under the direction of *E.J. Dampier*. Two-light chancel s and N aisle w windows probably also by Hemming. – Engraved glass screen in tower arch by *Jennifer Conway*, 1982. – Brass to John Maltoun †1447, in armour, the figure 38 in. (96 cm.). – In churchyard, N of church, The Barn (church hall), 1994 by *Nicholas Jacob* of *Purcell Miller Tritton*. Black weatherboarding on brick plinth, hipped roof with gablet at one end, appropriately modest.

United Reformed Church (Congregational), The Street. 1803. Stuccoed brick, painted white, with corner pilasters, plinth, cornice, and raised window surrounds painted black.

Two doors in front, with small windows above and large round-headed window between, and two tiers of three windows along the sides.

St Martin stands on a slight hill, with LITTLE WALTHAM HALL, C18 and C19 painted brick, opposite its S side, and on its W the OLD RECTORY, C17 but much altered in the C18 and C19 and encased in gault brick. N and S fronts each have two gables, the W front a five-bay façade with parapet and bracketed cornice. The main part of the village lies 500 yds NW, along THE STREET, part of the old road from Chelmsford to Braintree where it crosses the Chelmer. THE WHITE HART makes a suitably bold statement at the NW end of the village, C18 painted brick refronted in the C19 with three canted bay windows. Then a pleasingly varied row on the E side, ending with No. 106, dated 1811, gault brick with stuccoed arches to the doorway and two flanking windows. Opposite, KNIGHTS, Georgian brick, three bays, two storeys with parapet, standing back from the road. The street continues to wind attractively down the slope with several nice houses, some thatched, particularly round the junction with Brook Hill. At the bottom, WINCKFORD CLOSE, 'village' houses by *Countryside Properties*, 1998–9. Another gentle curve up the other side from Winckford Bridge, with Nos. 29–35 on the N side, a Wealden house, probably C15, the r. wing jettied. Finally FOXTONS (No. 23) C18 timber-framed and plastered with gabled cross-wing.

Opposite the end of The Street, on the W side of the main road, LITTLE WALTHAM LODGE, mid-C19 gault brick with parapet and stuccoed quoins, cornice and raised window surrounds. Two two-storey canted bays on the NE front with central Ionic doorcase, a single large canted bay on the SW front with Doric portico. Some good houses along the main road at BLASFORD HILL, ½ m. S, including TUDOR COTTAGE, C15 thatched hall house with jettied N cross-wing, and THORLEY'S FARM with S cross-wing, the hall originally with a single aisle, recorded early in the C14. Behind, C17 maltings, enlarged in the C18, renovated in the C19, now a house. Seven-bay timber-framed and weatherboarded range with square brick kiln.

BELSTEAD'S FARM, 1 m. SE. Late C15 with two gabled cross-wings, largely rebuilt in 1678 – the date is on the central chimneystack. Of the same date probably the staircase with moulded balusters.

CROXTON'S MILL, nearly ¾ m. S. C18 timber-framed and weatherboarded water mill. Three storeys and loft, with hoist in N gable of steep-pitched roof. Now offices.

LITTLE WARLEY
Brentwood

A long, thin parish, like its neighbours Great Warley and Childerditch, with church and hall on low ground to the S.

ST PETER. A small church, restored and repaired piecemeal in the C19. Brick W tower dated 1718 with chequer pattern, diagonal buttresses and parapet. C15 ragstone nave, some windows with Perp tracery. Early C16 brick chancel, heavily buttressed (later) on the N side. E wall C19, stock brick with triple lancets. Timber S porch, c. 1500. Nave roof with tie-beams and crownposts. – SEATING. At the back of nave, some early C16 benches. Otherwise late C16 or early C17 box pews, including choir stalls. – STAINED GLASS. In tower window, fragments of C15 glass, re-set. – MONUMENTS. Brass with finely drawn demi-figure of Anne Terrell (i.e. Tyrell, of Little Warley Hall) †1592, 10 in. (25 cm.). – Anne Strutt †1641 and her husband Sir Denner Strutt †1661, of Little Warley Hall. Standing wall monument. Recumbent effigies on shelves, the wife above and behind the husband, who was probably added later. Big baldacchino and coarsely carved putti lifting up the curtains. Attributed by K.A. and E. Esdaile to *William Wright*. – Mary Strutt †1658, Sir Denner's third wife. Standing wall monument. Reclining figure in a shroud; cheek propped on elbow. Attributed to *Thomas Burman* (AW). – Father Time, early C17 alabaster figure, reclining, from a lost monument.

LITTLE WARLEY HALL, immediately S. Quite small, but originally longer at the W end; what remains is the hall (one-storey with moulded beams and simple fireplace), and service end. Lovely early C16 brick in English bond, with vitrified headers in diaper pattern. Stepped gable over the porch, next to it the three-light hall window and then the massive hall chimneystack, broad below and ending in two twisted shafts. Staircase of c. 1600 with flat balusters.

On wooded land at the top of the hill, the site of WARLEY BARRACKS. Opened 1805, owned by the East India Company between 1843 and 1861, closed in 1960 and mostly demolished.

REGIMENTAL CHAPEL, Clive Road (Essex and Royal Anglian Regiments). 1855–7, started by *A.J. Green*, continued after his death in 1855 by *Sir Matthew Digby Wyatt*, his successor as the East India Company's surveyor. In the Early Christian Italianate style which Wyatt's brother Thomas Henry had made famous at Wilton, and praised by the authorities as a model military chapel. Yellow and a little red brick with coupled round-arched windows. Nave, aisles, and short chancel with apsidal sanctuary. Plainer SW campanile by *Sir Charles Nicholson*, 1956. Dark, dignified interior, mainly red brick, and stone columns with imitation Early Christian capitals. – FURNISHINGS by *F. E. Howard* with advice by *Nicholson*, following dedication as the Essex Regiment Chapel in 1925, including screens, seating, pulpit, lectern, and W gallery. – STAINED GLASS. Apse windows by *Christopher Webb*, 1928, and heraldic rose window by *Geoffrey Webb*, 1930. Aisle windows by *A.K. Nicholson*.

Apart from the chapel, the principal surviving building is the former depot officers' mess, BLENHEIM HOUSE, on its N side. 1878, stock brick with rusticated quoins and round-headed ground-floor windows. On the site of the main barracks, FORD MOTOR COMPANY offices by *T.P. Bennett & Son*, 1962–4. Six storeys and penthouse, T-plan, the long main front to Eagle Way of glazing separated by a protruding stone framework with stone cladding on the other elevations. Opposite, THE MARILLAC (nursing home, former officers' mess), 1939. Neo-Georgian stock brick with Ionic porch. Also N of Eagle Way, in BECKET CLOSE and ESSEX WAY, housing by *Clifford Culpin & Partners*, c. 1964. Mostly grey brick.

LITTLE WIGBOROUGH
Great and Little Wigborough

ST NICHOLAS. Late C15 nave, chancel, and narrower W tower, the top rebuilt 1885–6 by *J. Clarke* following the 1884 earthquake. Clarke used much septaria; the older fabric mainly Kentish rag. The S side lies open towards the Blackwater estuary. – IRONWORK. Communion rail, lectern, and above all the bracket used for raising the cover of the font, all scrolly and artistic and presumably due to *Clarke*. Contrast is provided by part of the frame of a Zeppelin which came down nearby in 1916, hanging over the tower arch.

LITTLE YELDHAM

ST JOHN THE BAPTIST. Late C14 nave, proved by the discovery in 1999 of true medieval bricks datable to *c.* 1380–1400. The chancel, exceptionally out of line with the nave, is C15. Also C15 the belfry, resting inside the nave on four posts with cross-beams on arched braces. W wall rebuilt and nave re-seated in 1874; further restoration by *J.P. Seddon*, 1891. He added the S porch and N vestry, the latter separated from the chancel by an open arcade. His also the stone CHANCEL SCREEN and attached PULPIT, altogether too overpowering for such a modest church. – FONT. Octagonal, Perp, with quatrefoils etc and shields. – STAINED GLASS. E window by *G.E.R. Smith*, 1955.

OLD RECTORY, SE, by *Seddon*, 1890. Rambling gabled brick and half-timbering, but the SE cross-wing survives from the original timber-framed building.

RED HOUSE, ¼ m. NNW. Early C17, the timber frame exposed on the SW and SE fronts. The SE front is jettied, on brackets. Rear stair hall with 'Ipswich' window, dated 1679.

STONE AND FAGOT INN (now The Crazy Boar), North End, ¾ m. SE. 1915, the first pub designed by *Basil Oliver*, who made his name in this field. Considerably altered and extended by the *Architecture & Design Partnership Ltd*, 2000–1.

LOUGHTON*

Churches 568
Public Buildings 570
Perambulations:
1. The centre and north-east: High Road, The Uplands 571
2. North-west: York Hill and Baldwins Hill 572
3. South-west: Ollard's Grove, Nursery Road 573
4. South-east: Station Road, Aldeton Hill,
Tycehurst Hill 574
5. North-east: Loughton Hall and Debden 575

Loughton lies in a corridor between Epping Forest on the NW and the River Roding on the SE. Particularly where it merges into the Forest it is unexpectedly picturesque and hilly, and this, combined with the ready access to London that the railway has provided since 1856, resulted in a large number of good late C19

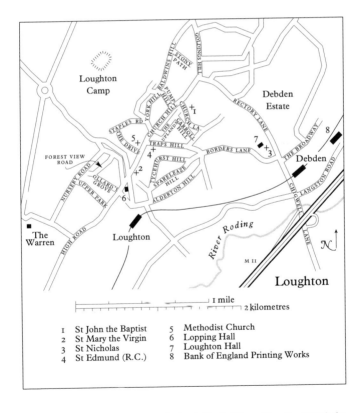

1 St John the Baptist
2 St Mary the Virgin
3 St Nicholas
4 St Edmund (R.C.)
5 Methodist Church
6 Lopping Hall
7 Loughton Hall
8 Bank of England Printing Works

*I am indebted to Chris Pond, and his book *The Buildings of Loughton* (2003), for the identification and dating of many of the buildings described, especially those in the perambulations.

and early C20 houses for discerning commuters. The shift of population towards the High Road resulted in the replacement of St Nicholas as the parish church by St John the Baptist in 1846; a further shift later in the C19, towards the railway, resulted in the building of St Mary the Virgin. In the eastern part of the town is the Debden Estate, developed by the LCC after 1945.

CHURCHES

St John the Baptist, Church Lane. 1845–6 by *Sydney Smirke*. It is a surprise here to find him using the fashionable Neo-Norman. The material is gault brick, which does not help the Norman spirit; *The Ecclesiologist* considered it 'a most unsatisfactory production'. The plan is without aisles, but with transepts and crossing tower. The vaults used throughout are no doubt plaster. Chancel extended in the same style by *W. E. Nesfield*, 1876–7. Reordered with nave altar 1983, but leaving the chancel intact. – PULPIT, low CHANCEL SCREEN, REREDOS, SEDILIA, PISCINA, chancel walls and floor all lavishly fitted out between 1877 and 1915 in marble, alabaster, mosaic and *opus sectile* by *James Powell & Sons*. Nesfield himself designed the paving in front of the altar, marble scenes from the Old Testament; other designers include *J. W. Brown* and *Charles Hardgrave*. Also First World War memorial, 1922, with kneeling figure of St George in *opus sectile* – SCULPTURE. Ferracotta Madonna and iron pricket stand by *Nancy Coulson*, 1992. – STAINED GLASS. Chancel windows by *Powell*, one on N side (Virgin and Child) designed by *Ada Currey*, 1901, three E windows 1907. W window by *Jennifer Conway*, 1995–6. Round window in S transept by *Hugh Winn*, 2002.

CHURCH HOUSE, SW of the church, built 1846 as Sunday School and verger's accommodation. Neo-Gothic with windows and stone facings said to come from old St Nicholas.

St Mary the Virgin, High Road. 1871–2 by *T.H. Watson*. Random Bargate stone with bonding courses of red tile. Nave with E bellcote and apse, S aisle and porch; N aisle added by Watson 1883, principally to shore up the N wall which had settled badly. The clerestory has foiled windows outside, but the rere-arches are of two low lights with a separate circle above. The general effect is rather grim and austere, so it is surprising to find some very good carving: on the exterior of the S porch, scenes from the life of the Virgin, 1872, and on the circular piers of the arcades, capitals of the most riotous naturalism, C13 in inspiration, a quite exceptionally large variety of local flora and fauna, completed in 1887. The pier and capital nearest the S door replaced *c.* 1949. Lady Chapel (S aisle) by *Martin Travers*, designed 1942, installed 1946, and for him very restrained. – SCULPTURE. Stone panel above pulpit by *Lindsey Clark*, 1951. – WAR MEMORIAL. Vellum, with illuminated inscription by *Graily Hewitt*, 1923.

St Nicholas, Rectory Lane. 1876–7 by *W. E. Nesfield*. After the opening of St John the Baptist, only the chancel of the medieval parish church was retained (as a mortuary chapel), but this too was demolished when Nesfield's church was built a few yards to the w. Its w wall forms part of the boundary with Loughton Hall (*see* p. 575); a hooded 'Queen Anne' doorway leads through the garden wall to the s. Short nave, short raised chancel, N vestry and s porch. w bellcote added 1890. – REREDOS. Heavy carved oak, by *Nesfield*, 1879. – AUMBRY. Late C16, with elaborately carved doors between columns. – TILES. Nave dado, reproduction C16 Spanish tiles by *Frederick Garrard*. – STAINED GLASS. Two kneeling figures of *c.* 1500 in tracery of N and s windows. – MONUMENTS. From old St Nicholas. Part of brass of William Nodes †1594, 23½-in. (60-cm.) figure with smaller figures of children. – Brass of George Stonnard †1558 with his wife Mary, 20½ in. (52-cm.) figures. – John Stonnard †1540 and two wives, figures *c.* 24 in. (60 cm.), and Abel Guilliams †1637, under carpet and not visible, the latter attributed to *Francis Grigs* (AW). – Signed marble tablets to Mary Ismay †1808 by *Druitt*, Nicholas Pearse †1825 by *M.W. Johnson*, Mary Cooke †1840 by *H. Hopper*. – Sarah Pearse †1845 by *Cox & Sons*, iron with red enamel lettering. – E of the church a very Gothic churchyard monument to Mary French †1860, in the shape of a shrine with steep-pitched roof.

ST EDMUND OF CANTERBURY (R.C.), Traps Hill. 1957–8 by *Tooley & Foster*. Concrete frame, exposed internally, and brick walls, of which the N (liturgical w) wall, with a large central window occupying most of the gable over the w door, is as much as one normally sees. The side walls zigzag with full-height w-facing windows in the manner of Coventry Cathedral; otherwise the plan is traditional, including s chapel, w narthex and enclosed baptistery, and w gallery. – SCULPTURE. Stations of the Cross by *John Skelton*. Incised panels of Ancaster stone. – Panel on exterior of w wall (Annunciation) by *P. Lindsey Clark*. Doulting stone. – Christ in Glory by *Michael Lindsey Clark*. Figure in artificial stone on reinforced concrete cross, originally standing in shallow pool next to the w door. – STAINED GLASS. Jewel window over altar and engraved glass door panels by *John Hutton*.

ST THOMAS MORE (R.C.), Willingale Road. By *E. Bower Norris*, 1953. Pale brown brick. Plain, with no E window but a cross set in an arched recess, and small NE bell-turret.

METHODIST CHURCH, High Road. 1986–7 by the *Goodrow Consultancy* (architect, *Bernard Gooding*, engineer, *Ronald Rowson*), replacing that by *Gordon & Gunton*, 1903. Welcoming front opening to the road. Five glazed bays separated by cruciform panels, and at the E end a polygonal projection containing an office and meeting room topped by a short spire with a cross made of optical fibres. The worship area lies behind a large foyer/café, separated by a screen incorporating stained glass by *Ian Carthy*. Interior dominated by the timber roof, supported on massive glue-laminated beams curving up to roof-lights. Hall, vestry and other facilities behind.

UNION CHURCH (Baptist and United Reformed Church), High Road. Of the group of buildings designed by *James Cubitt* – manse, 1879, Salcombe College, 1886, and schoolroom, 1898 – only a small LODGE survives. The church, 1861, was replaced in 1972–3 by the present forbidding mass of yellow brick by *Michael Pollard*.

CEMETERY, Church Lane. Opened 1887. Timber-framed mortuary chapel at the entrance.

PUBLIC BUILDINGS

PUBLIC LIBRARY, Traps Hill. 1976 by *Elidir Davies*. Brick, with glazed panels, opaque between the floors. Some of these panels wrap round the corners where the building steps back in a zigzag, others nestle in the re-entrant angles.

PUBLIC LIBRARY, Rectory Lane, Debden. By *H. Conolly*, County Architect (architect in charge, *K.W. Benoy*), c. 1961. A good corner design and typical of this period's branch libraries. Brick with a clerestory, on two sides of a courtyard, the other two sides delimited by a perimeter beam raised on columns.

LEISURE CENTRE, Traps Hill. 2000–3 by *GLR Architects*. The aluminium roofs dominate, monopitch and, over the pool hall, butterfly, supported on glue-laminated trusses that project beyond the eaves, with continuous clerestory glazing. Relatively low walls of concrete blocks, pinkish and grey, incorporating a high proportion of granite aggregate.

LOPPING HALL, High Road and Station Road. *See* Perambulation 4.

EAST 15 ACTING SCHOOL (University of Essex), Rectory Lane. Based in Hatfields, a two-storey five-bay stock brick house with central pedimented doorway and rainwater head dated 1795; C19 red brick extensions behind. In the grounds the CORBETT THEATRE, a C15 timber-framed aisled barn with brick and flint walls. The frame came from Ditchling (East Sussex), re-erected here and extended, with new walls, in 1966.

DEBDEN PARK HIGH SCHOOL, Willingale Road. 1999–2001 by the *Architects Co-Partnership* and *Jarvis Construction*. Brick plinth with cedar cladding above, and aluminium windows. A series of three-storey department blocks, linked by a central 'street'.

EPPING FOREST COLLEGE, Borders Lane. Built as Lucton Secondary Modern School, 1950, and St Nicholas Primary School, 1948, by *H. Conolly*, County Architect, both good examples of his early post-war work. Lucton has a distinctive tower with patterned brickwork. Main block of two storeys separated by panels of fluted concrete, with patterned concrete baffles between the ground-floor windows to control glare. Brought together in 1991 with central library, offices, etc. by *RMJM*.

RODING VALLEY HIGH SCHOOL, Alderton Hill. The core is of 1908 by *Herbert Tooley*, combining Shaw's Queen Anne with Philip Webb. Three storeys with large windows, those on the third floor of Sparrowe's House pattern set in large pebble-dashed gables with roofs that sweep down into the first floor. Chimney-like bell tower. Numerous C20 extensions.

INFANT AND JUNIOR SCHOOLS, Staples Road. Boys' school, 1887, with infants' department added 1891, by *James Cubitt*. Stock brick with red brick dressings, and a very successful composition along a narrow sloping site. Separate girls' school (now infants), 1911–13, by *Herbert Tooley*.

RAILWAY STATION, Station Approach. By *J. Murray Easton* of *Stanley Hall & Easton & Robertson*, 1939–40, for the London & North Eastern Railway, in preparation for its transfer to London Underground's Central Line. Double-height ticket hall, flat-roofed and box-like, but tunnel-vaulted inside with large arches filled with glass bricks at either end. Steel-frame construction faced with narrow pale buff bricks with deeply recessed pointing. Entrance flanked by shops and screen wall. Platforms at a higher level, with boldly cantilevered concrete roofs. Original fixed seating with signage. Signal box and electricity substation in same style as ticket hall.*

PERAMBULATIONS

Exploring Loughton is best done in a number of separate perambulations, and even so some of the buildings are quite far apart. Moreover, anyone who persists in thinking that Essex is flat will be disabused. Much can be done by car, but not Perambulation 2.

1. The centre and north-east: High Road, The Uplands

The centre is the crossroads by St Mary's Church. It is best not to linger in the HIGH ROAD. Between St Mary's and the Methodist Church to the NE, only one building of interest, THE LAST POST pub, built as the Post Office, 1932, by *A. Scott* of the *Office of Works* and a good example of the type, brick with Portland stone dressings and unusually fine carving round and over the door. Shortly before the Methodist Church, on the NW side, THE DRIVE, laid out by the prolific local architect *Edmond Egan* with houses designed mainly by his pupil *Horace White*, c. 1900–10: Arts and Crafts cottage-style, with tile-hanging, half-timbering, and brick-nogging.

Continuing N up the High Road, shortly after the Methodist Church the road broadens out into KINGS GREEN at the start of Church Hill. On the Green itself, WAR MEMORIAL by *T.J. Weatherall*, 1920. On the W side, a row of characteristic brick cottages by *Horace White*, 1909, in the 'Garden City' style with flat-roofed dormers. On the N side of Kings Green, ZIZZI (formerly the King's Head pub), 1908, and in York Hill the WHEATSHEAF, 1904, vernacular style, also by *White*, and

---

*The bus garage in Church Hill by *Yorke Rosenberg & Mardall*, 1954, was demolished in 1992.

between them a former temperance refreshment house and cottages, 1898, nominally by *Egan* but at the end of his life and very likely also by White.

Opposite Zizzi, THE UPLANDS leads first SE and then turns NE, an early C20 development, with the largest house at its highest point in CARROLL HILL: No. 19, PITREAVIE, by *Frank Baggallay*, c. 1904. Rendered, with a steeply pitched roof of green slates. Each end gable has a pair of chimneys either side of a window. Opposite, a cut through to CHURCH LANE, and immediately on the N side is ELM LODGE, a well-preserved late 1920s house with rounded corners and metal windows that follow them. Green pantiles. To the SE, on the other side, No. 49, LIMBER, a large Wrenaissance brick house, c. 1936–7. Two storeys and seven bays. The central bay breaks forward with an open pedimented gable and doorcase with deep, open segmental pediment. Outer bays break further forward and have hipped roofs. Dentilled cornice.

Church Lane leads into TRAPS HILL. Opposite the junction TRAPS HILL HOUSE and PRIORS, two timber-framed and plastered houses semi-detached but at right angles. Priors, which faces away from Traps Hill (now in Rowans Way) has a C16 core, with a C17 block added to its SW corner and then further additions in the C19, including the present three-storey front with two bay windows under a veranda. Traps Hill House was added to the NW end of Priors in the C18, also extended and refronted in the C19 with one canted bay and one bow, both two-storey. Heading W downhill, on the N side is ROSE FARM, C17 timber-framed and weatherboarded, and then on the S side Nos. 29 and 31, two similar houses, probably by *Sir Frank Baines*, c. 1928, one for his brother: painted brick, tile-hanging, still in the Arts and Crafts tradition. At the bottom of Traps Hill we are back in the High Road, opposite the Methodist Church.

2. North-west: York Hill and Baldwins Hill

The character of the streets here is quite unlike the rest of Loughton: hilly, narrow and winding, punctuated by little greens and, at the top, open on one side to Epping Forest.

YORK HILL leads out of the NW corner of Kings Green. A short way along, STAPLES ROAD leads off to the l. with the schools described above and at the far end an unspoilt row of good late C19 houses, notably FOREST VILLA (No. 7), 1882 with rooftop belvedere, and at the far end SHAFTESBURY RETREAT (No. 3), a two-storey *cottage orné* built in 1879 to provide non-alcoholic refreshments for visitors to Epping Forest. Back in York Hill, No. 98, SOUTHBANK, by *James Cubitt* for Loughton's historian W.C. Waller, 1888, an Arts and Crafts detached house with double weatherboarded gable. On reaching YORK HILL GREEN one is rewarded with views right across London to the Kentish hills. On the E side of the green THE GARDENERS' ARMS, late C17, and PUMP HILL,

C17–C18, all prettily weatherboarded. On the N side Nos. 111–15 York Hill, a terrace of mid-C19 cottages, timber-framed and brick faced.

WOODBURY HILL, W of York Hill Green, has another house by *Cubitt* for Waller, 1888–9, now divided (Nos. 7–9). Tucked away right on the edge of the Forest, WOODBURY HOLLOW, 1906 by *M.H. Baillie Scott* for the Zimmermann siblings. Arts and Crafts cottage, pebbledash and half-timbering with high gables, and with original doors and other high-quality interior woodwork. A little further on LOUGHTON LODGE, late C18 with early C20 additions, then WOODPECKERS (No. 37) by *Kenneth Lindy*, 1959, for himself. Wooden, cabin-like, with balconies and large windows to take advantage of the view over the Forest.

After York Hill Green, York Hill is blocked to cars but leads to Baldwins Hill. Where they meet, ASH GREEN HOUSE, formerly the home of W.C. Waller: large early C19 house, stucco, with Gothick windows and trellised porch with tented canopy, additions by *Cubitt* dated 1885 and a pebbledashed block along the road of 1903. In BALDWINS HILL, which looks down over the Forest to the W, No. 9, an unspoilt Modern Movement house with flat roof, metal windows in curved corner, etc., and on the other side No. 40, a wooden chalet imported from Switzerland in 1849.* Sir Jacob Epstein lived at No. 49, then No. 50, between *c.* 1921 and 1950, and the social reformer Muriel Lester at Nos. 47 and 49 (Albion Place, dated 1878). Off the SE side of Baldwins Hill, in Whitakers Way, MONKWOOD COTTAGE, by *W. R. Lethaby* for the social investigator Hubert Llewellyn Smith, with deep eaves, and a large lead rainwater hopper dated 1896. Pitched roof with copings and roughcast walls, giving the house a somewhat Scottish appearance.

It is now necessary to retrace one's steps a short distance to the Forester's Arms and STONY PATH, which leads down the hill to the SE past WHITAKER'S ALMSHOUSES, Arewater Green, 1845: terrace of six in a half-H plan, stock brick with depressed curved hoodmoulds. Stony Path leads down to Goldings Hill, near Rectory Lane (*see* Perambulation 5), with Church Hill leading back to Kings Green to the SW.

3. South-west: Ollard's Grove, Nursery Road

OLLARD'S GROVE, S of St Mary, runs steeply up the hill W of the High Road. Some way uphill, No. 40 is by *H.H. Francis*, 1892, for himself. An irregular composition: part brick with some Gothic windows: part false half-timbering. Several houses in similar vein, here and in parallel streets. At the top of Ollard's Grove, No. 49 FORESTVIEW ROAD (Sherwood), by *T. Philips Figgis*, *c.* 1905, probably for S.H. Warren, a local

---

* Ashfield Lodge, noted by Pevsner as 'a piece of ingenious and imaginative design' by *Turner Powell*, 1914, was demolished *c.* 1968.

antiquary and palaeontologist. Brick, render, and tile-hanging, angled to take advantage of the view, and taller on the garden side where the ground drops sharply away. A path to the l. leads through to NURSERY ROAD, and 100yds uphill to the SE is DRAGONS, 1882–3 by *Edmond Egan*. Here the local domestic style is elaborated to an outlandish degree, with decorative bargeboards, double-height bay windows with the upper parts jettied and separated by friezes of terracotta plaques, and dragons on the gables. Much of the decorative carving and modelling was done by the client, H.M. Fletcher, a ship-builder. Ornate wrought-iron gate, with dragons, by *Ludwig Spanlang* of Munich. A little further on, Upper Park leads back down to the High Road. At the bottom, former lodges of what was originally a private estate: that on the E side of the High Road, on the corner of Lower Park Road (PLYMOUTH LODGE), the more elaborate, with a large half-timbered gable.

4. South-east: Station Road, Alderton Hill, Tycehurst Hill

STATION ROAD runs S from the crossroads by St Mary. On the corner is HOLMDALE (No. 199 High Road), with Gothic spirelets and gables with decorative bargeboards, built by *Edmond Egan*, *c*. 1878, as his own residence. Now a car show-room. In Station Road itself, LOPPING HALL, 1883 by *Egan*, paid for by the Corporation of London to compensate for the withdrawal of the right of Loughton's inhabitants to take wood (by lopping) from Epping Forest. Stock brick with red dress-ings and Gothic windows. Tower on Station Road with steep pyramidal slate roof and main entrance in base; an excellent terracotta bas-relief over the door depicts the loppers at work. Extended 1904, 1937, and 1962. Built by *Egan* at the same time were by Nos. 195–197 High Road, brick and half-timbered shops, originally with dwellings over.

Opposite Lopping Hall, the LOUGHTON CLUB, 1901. Brick, partly rendered, with a segmental pediment over the entrance and octagonal lead cupola hinting at Queen Anne Revival. Probably by *Horace White*, who designed WHITE LOPPING (No. 10) next door for himself, *c*. 1910. Painted brickwork in the Arts and Crafts tradition. Also in Station Road, No. 16, by *R.C. Foster*, 1912. Rendered walls with asymmetrical gables and timbered porch, the sort of detached suburban house that became commonplace after 1918 but must have looked very striking when new. On the other side of the road, several houses of the 1880s, probably by *H.H. Francis*: half-timbered with prominent gables and verandas. At the far end No. 58, Hetton House, by *Dovetail*, 2004–5, a three-storey block of flats with corner turret and balconies that evokes the spirit of the 1870s villa it replaced.

At the bottom of Station Road is the Station (*see* Public Buildings) to the l., SAINSBURY'S supermarket to the r. The latter by *Pick Everard*, 2002–3, boldly combining Modern Movement formality with sinuous curves. Projecting towards the street a two-storey rendered drum, flat-roofed with 1930s-style glazing, the upper floor on pilotis and the lower floor set well back; the rest dominated by sweeping curved roofs of patinated copper, cutting down into buff brick walls.

But turn l. from Station Road into ALDERTON HILL, and once past the Roding Valley High School (*see* Public Buildings) we are in a broad street of large detached houses, of all styles and none, and quite spread out up the hill. Early C20 BROOK HOUSE (No. 8), on the corner of Brook Road, is by *Alfred Moulton*, for himself. Mainly half-timbered, but the corner is chamfered to reveal a recessed porch, balcony, and gable end in variously patterned brickwork. Further up on the same side, MEADOWSIDE (No. 22), also early C20, again designed by the owner, *Arthur Erith*, a builders' merchant. Austere stock brick. Internal alterations for his widow by his nephew, *Raymond Erith*, 1930–1, including a fireplace moved to Westgate House, Dedham (q.v.) in 1938.* On the s side, MANSARD (No. 57), by *Edward Maufe* for the printer Harold Curwen, 1926. A forbidding street elevation, with a lot of mansard roof and only a low painted wall, but opening out on the garden side with loggia and balcony. Near the top of the hill, on the same side, ALDERTON HALL. Late Medieval timber-framed and, unusually for a house of its size, weatherboarded. Two-bay hall with cross-wings, but with many later additions combining to create a randomly picturesque effect.

From the top of the hill, Spareleaze Hill leads down into TYCEHURST HILL. Plenty more large comfortable houses but a couple of surprises among them, both flat-roofed Modern Movement. First PEMBERLEY (No. 82) by *P. D. Hepworth*, 1935–6. Rendered brick, and quite large, but spoilt by alterations to the windows etc. Smaller, but in original condition externally, MERROW BROW or DOWN (No. 38), by *P. Wynne Williams*, 1935, with Crittall windows including bays with rounded corners. At the bottom of Tycehurst Hill, Brook Road leads back via a footpath to St Mary on the r.

5. North-east: Loughton Hall and Debden

The Loughton Hall estate was bought by the London County Council in 1944 and developed as the Debden Estate. It was one of the 'out-county' estates built to ease the housing shortage in London and has the character of the pre-war cottage estates. 4,321 dwellings were built between 1945 and 1953. LOUGHTON HALL itself stands on the w side of Rectory Lane behind St Nicholas (*see* Churches) and, like the church, is by *Nesfield*. An excellent building, every bit as good as Norman Shaw's at the same time (cf. Chigwell) and very similar in style to Shaw (they had been partners in the 1860s), except that Nesfield was on his way down and Shaw was still on his way

---

* *Erith* designed his uncle's tombstone in Loughton Cemetery †1926, and also a house in the garden of 22 Alderton Hill, 1934 (dem.).

up. Completed in 1878, the client was Rev. J.W. Maitland, whose sister was married to Nesfield's cousin. Brick and plastering. Symmetrical s (garden) front with three bay windows, the outer straight-sided, the middle canted, two entrances with remarkably classical details and three gables. The symmetry is, however, broken by an off-centre cupola and chimneystack. Similar effect on the N (entrance) front, which has only two bays that rise to three storeys through the hipped roof: one bay rests on the Ionic porch of the entrance, the other starts at first-floor level. Remodelled internally by *Tooley & Foster* with *H. Conolly*, 1951, as a community centre for the Debden Estate; now part of Epping Forest College (*see* Public Buildings).

SE of Loughton Hall and St Nicholas, THE BROADWAY, the shopping centre for the estate, by the *LCC Architect's Dept*, 1953–8. Very impressive frontage of two storeys of flats above shops in a long, unbroken, gentle curve either side of a wide street. Brick, with a continuous shallow canopy and a low walk-through halfway along where the windows have aprons carved with reliefs of fauna. It is all very un-English; if the subject of the reliefs was industrial rather than natural, one would say Eastern European.

SE of the railway, off Chigwell Lane, Debden Estate's industrial area, the most important building being the BANK OF ENGLAND PRINTING WORKS, Langston Road. By *Easton & Robertson*, 1953–6, with *Ove Arup & Partners* as consulting engineers, but designed before the War. The outstanding element is the printing hall, an unbroken space over 850 ft (260 metres) long and 130 ft (40 metres) wide, vaulted by an asymmetrical, very effective curve which rises very slowly from the N but falls steeply to the s, to obtain as much N light as possible. The whole vault is of reinforced concrete and glass and conveys a sense of the grandest spaciousness. On the s side, as well as a smaller hall of the same shape, the administrative block, three storeys with a central five-bay, six-storey tower forming the office entrance. Partly of brick laid in double stretcher bond with Portland stone dressings, partly with the structural members of reinforced concrete exposed and with brick panels in a variety of unstructural bonds. Only the canteen block has been demolished.

On the corner of Chigwell Lane and Langston Road, a five-storey headquarters building for Higgins Group by *David Wood Architects*, 2004–5. Glass-walled but with an external framework of metal louvres.

THE WARREN, ⅞ m. SW of St Mary's within Epping Forest. Originally built as a hunt standing for Henry VIII (cf. Queen Elizabeth's Hunting Lodge, Chingford); some of the timbers visible inside. By 1747 it had become the Reindeer Tavern, converted to a private house by *Repton c.* 1812–15. Mostly weatherboarded but the main front stuccoed, of two storeys and eight bays with a central two-bay pediment and off-centre porch with tented lead roof. N of the house an OBELISK on ball feet, said to come from Wanstead House. ¼ m. s of The

Warren, WARREN HALL (formerly Warren Hill House, now flats), a large brick house of *c.* 1874 that incorporates an C18 staircase and panelling from a house in Kensington. Stables with Gothic turret 1883, probably by *Edmond Egan.*

LOUGHTON CAMP, 1 m. NW of St Mary's within Epping Forest. Early Iron Age encampment, well sited on a spur. Roughly oval in shape, covering an area of 6½ acres. There is a single rampart and a 45-ft (14-metre) wide ditch. The location of the original entrance is doubtful.

MAGDALEN LAVER   5000

ST MARY MAGDALEN. Nave with blocked Norman window in the N wall and blocked circular windows in the W wall. Walls of flint rubble, the lower parts laid herringbone-wise, with Roman brick and dressings of tufa, limestone, and clunch. W doorway with Roman brick dressings. Chancel with remains of C14-looking windows, but most of them belong to *Chancellor*'s restoration of 1873–5. Timber W tower, weatherboarded. It was built in 1535 and replaced a small late C14 one for which the tie-beams with queenposts survive in the W part of the nave. The tower has a centre with four posts carrying beams with queenposts. The posts are cross-strutted. There are narrower N, S, and W aisles outside the square formed by the four posts. The tower aisles have pent-roofs, and above the bell-chamber is a pyramid roof. – SCREEN. Much restored, but what remains is interesting because of its relatively early date, probably not later than *c.* 1350. Four openings on each side, separated by slender circular shafts with shaft-rings, and carrying an ogee arch. Circles with quatrefoils in the spandrels. Straight top. – COMMANDMENTS BOARD (chancel N wall). Large, early C18, very nicely painted. – STAINED GLASS. Chancel N †1895 by *W. Ramsey.* Nave N to D.B. Smith †1872, drowned at Shanghae [*sic*]. – MONUMENTS. Rev. George Kindleton †1667.* Marble tablet with segmental pediment and skull and crossbones. Oval inscription within a wreath supported by piles of books. – William Cole †1729/30. Fine white marble tomb-chest built (before his death) against the S wall W of the porch. On steps, with gadrooned slab and winged cherubs on the front. Achievement of arms on wall above. Black marble ledger slab inside, no doubt originally in chancel. – His nephew and heir William Cole †1729/30. Inscription on *trompe l'œil* drapery.

BUSHES, ¾ m. ESE. House of *c.* 1500, extended in the early C17, and restored 1933, when the timbers were exposed. The W front has a continuous jetty.

WYNTERS ARMOURIE, nearly 1 m. WSW. A complicated house, whose present appearance dates from *c.* 1935 – when it was restored and the timbers exposed – but its present form from

---

* Instituted as rector in 1631, dispossessed in 1644, restored in 1662.

the C16 and C17. It began as a C14 aisled hall; evidence survives of the base cruck that formed the centre truss, an unusual method of construction. Two-bay gabled parlour / solar cross-wing (w), the E service end rebuilt as a cross-wing in the late C16 or early C17. About the same time a floor was inserted into the w bay of the hall, which was given a façade gable.

MALDON

8000

The best way to approach Maldon is by water, but failing that the view from the sea-wall on the N side of the River Blackwater gives a good overall impression of the town, with the Hythe in the foreground and an interesting skyline that rises gradually to the site of a Saxon *burh* on the w edge of the town centre. Maldon enjoyed great prosperity as a port in the Middle Ages, stagnated between 1500 and 1700, revived in the C18 and continued to prosper in the C19 following the opening of the Chelmer and Blackwater Navigation in 1797 (*see* Introduction, p. 52) and of the railway in 1847. It is now a small and relatively unspoilt market town.

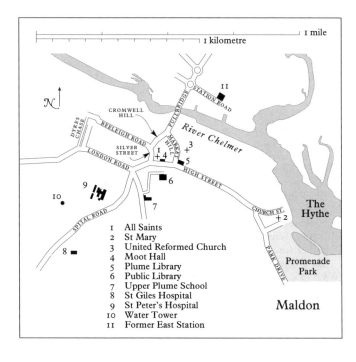

1 All Saints
2 St Mary
3 United Reformed Church
4 Moot Hall
5 Plume Library
6 Public Library
7 Upper Plume School
8 St Giles Hospital
9 St Peter's Hospital
10 Water Tower
11 Former East Station

CHURCHES

ALL SAINTS. Long s side to the High Street without a break
between s aisle and Darcy (s) Chapel, with small STATUES in
the buttresses of local historical figures (St Cedd, Byrhtnoth,
etc.) by *Nathaniel Hitch*, 1907. The C13 W tower lies back a
little. It is unique in England in that it is triangular, probably
to fit a constricted site. It has lancets (also towards the nave),
a hexagonal shingled spire, and three spirelets. The rest is
externally somewhat confusing. Brick nave of 1728, gothicized
in the C19, perhaps in 1876–7 when the N vestry was added
and extensive repairs made. N chapel late C15, and the chancel
and Darcy Chapel earlier C15. The architectural interest lies in
the s aisle, exceptionally lavishly executed inside. The exterior
does not betray this. Of its windows all but one are C19. The
easternmost is C14, but clearly earlier than the interior. It is of
three lights, with ogee reticulation above, i.e. a Dec motif, but
a band of Perp panelling below this.

Inside, the C14 window cuts into the arcading that distinguishes the aisle. The arcading is in two tiers. On the s wall
there is first a tier of blank ogee arches with renewed capitals
and renewed headstops, and above this a rich framing of the
windows by arches alternating with blank arches to fill the wall
between the windows. The jambs and voussoirs of all these
arches are decorated with trails of roses. At the aisle's W end
the lower tier of arches is higher, but the style is the same.
Other unusual features of this unusual aisle are the SEDILIA
below the easternmost window, and the crypt, reached by a
spiral stair in the outer wall. It is vaulted and has depressed-
pointed transverse arches – also C14. Nothing is known that
would explain the splendour of this aisle, reminiscent, as
Pevsner noted, of the Ely Lady Chapel, though with a good
many reductions. The date of this is *c.* 1340, and that seems a
convincing date for the s aisle of All Saints too. Additional
proof is the arcade towards the nave with its filleted quatrefoil
piers of Purbeck marble and its finely moulded arches. The
nave is wide and bare and has little atmosphere. A N arcade
must have been ripped out in 1728, and the two C18 arches
into the chancel and the N chapel now stand incongruously
side by side. The Darcy Chapel has a three-bay arcade to the
chancel with piers of the not unusual four-shafts-four-hollows
section and moulded arches. The N chapel's arcade, also of
three bays, has simply octagonal piers and double-hollow-
chamfered arches; rebuilt 1800, according to a stone panel in
one of the spandrels.

FONT and REREDOS. 1866–7, the main survivals of an extensive refitting of the church by *William Adams*. Caen stone, with
painted panels on the reredos by *Robert Nightingale*. Of the
same date the wooden LECTERN, carved by *Polley* of Coggeshall. – ALTAR, CHOIR STALLS and other chancel woodwork
by *P. M. Beaumont*, 1905–10, made by *S. Marshall*. – SCREEN
to Darcy Chapel (originally chancel screen). By *F. W. Chancellor*, 1925. – PULPIT, 1951, and BENCHES, 1930 onwards, by

Bryan Saunders. – ROYAL ARMS. Stuart, carved and painted wood. – STAINED GLASS. E window, 1902, and tower window, 1908, by *T. F. Curtis, Ward & Hughes*. In Darcy Chapel, pieces of the E window by *Clutterbuck*, 1848, in the E and a S window, rearranged 1950 following bomb damage. Three-light S window by *A.K. Nicholson*, 1928. In S aisle, from E to W: *William Morris* of Westminster †1916; *Lawrence Lee* with *Beth Glasser*, 1977; *G.E.R. Smith*, 1948; *F.W. Cole*, 1950 (over S door). – MONUMENTS. A number of good C17 wall monuments, the best to Thomas Cammocke †1602, two wives, and children. Kneeling figures, the man frontal, the wives in profile, separated by Corinthian columns supporting an entablature and an arch over the middle bay; children below. – Sarah, wife of John Jeffrey and widow of William Vernon, †1638. Urn in a niche flanked by Doric pilasters, supporting an entablature with achievement of arms in a broken pediment. Attributed to *Edward Marshall* (GF). – Mary Vernon †1647. Similar to the previous, but with Corinthian columns and cherubs on the urn, a conceit unusual before the C18. Also attributed to *Marshall* (AW). – John Jeffrey †1657, again attributed to *Marshall* (GF). Inscription on plain tablet, with broken pediment, arms, and swags etc. on the surround.

ST MARY THE VIRGIN. At the E end of the town, above the Hythe: a landmark for sailors and an essential component of picturesque views of the town. Big, heavy W tower with uncommonly massive buttresses; early C14. Upper part rebuilt in brick with stepped battlements, 1636. Shingled spire on octagonal weatherboarded base. The nave N wall revealed as Early Norman by a small window close to the porch. The interior shows that the Norman nave was as wide as the present one, quite a remarkable fact, proved by the responds of the Norman chancel arch, which are wider than the present chancel arch, restored with C14 bits. Chancel rebuilt in the early C19. S aisle all of 1885–7 by *Chancellor*; he restored the nave, and at the same time *Ewan Christian* restored the chancel. S extension (The Octagon) by *Purcell Miller Tritton & Partners*, 1992–3. – FONT. Perp stem with bowl of *c.* 1700. – COMMUNION RAIL. With twisted balusters, *c.* 1700. – REREDOS. By *P. M. Beaumont*, 1914, made by *S. Marshall*. Three painted panels. Now on W wall. – In Lady Chapel, 'English' ALTAR with riddel posts etc. by *F.W. Chancellor*, 1938–9. – PULPIT. From Mashbury. C17, octagonal, with panelled sides. – ROOD FIGURES. From St Andrew, Plaistow, by *James Brooks*, 1867–70. Coloured in the 1930s by *Randall Wells*. – STAINED GLASS. E window by *Heaton, Butler & Bayne*, 1912. – Nave N by *Wm. Pearce & E. Cutler*, 1920 (First World War memorial, the central light a copy of *James Clark*'s 'The Great Sacrifice'). – S aisle (Battle of Maldon Millennium Window) by *Mark Angus*, 1991.

ST PETER. *See* PLUME LIBRARY, below.

ASSUMPTION OF OUR LADY (R.C.), Victoria Road. 1924–5, by *Geoffrey Raymond* (*Scoles & Raymond*). Dec. Brick with stone dressings.

BAPTIST CHURCH, Butt Lane. By *P. M. Beaumont*, 1896. E.E.,
stock brick with red brick bands and arches. Schoolroom by
William Hayne, 1914.

UNITED REFORMED CHURCH (Congregational), Market Hill.
Rebuilt 1800–1, and although large the domestic character
is evident on the pargetted side walls. Classical front by *C.
Pertwee*, 1875–7: ground-floor entrance loggia with four Ionic
columns, arched windows above and a pediment. At the same
time were provided vestries and an enlarged gallery, which
extends round the whole of the interior. Between church and
road, the former BRITISH SCHOOL, 1843, 'altered and new
builded' 1890: red brick, with stock brick and stone dressings,
and windows with lozenge-pattern cast-iron glazing bars.

FRIENDS' MEETING HOUSE, Butt Lane. 1820–1. Nice, quiet
brick house of three bays by five, with arched windows and
hipped roof. The old trees of the graveyard give it a peaceful,
secluded feeling.

CEMETERY, London Road. Opened 1855. Brick chapel with gault
brick dressings. Cottage by *P. M. Beaumont*, 1902, with half-
timbered and jettied first floor.

PUBLIC BUILDINGS

MOOT HALL, High Street. Built as a house by Sir Robert Darcy,
possibly as early as the 1420s: a narrow, plain brick tower,
probably at first of two storeys with first-floor hall. The solar
is now part of the neighbouring building (No. 39 High Street).
The ground-floor room, which might originally have been
floored, was used for storage. The house was raised to three
storeys later in the C15, with a small annexe at the NW angle
and a higher octagonal stair-turret at the NE. The brickwork is
in English bond, and in the W wall can be seen original window
loops. In the stair-turret is a virtuoso display of rising tunnel
vaulting on the spiral stair that is the equal of the similar stair
at Faulkbourne Hall (q.v.). The house was purchased by the
Corporation in 1576 and converted for use as a moot hall,
when a balcony was first built over the pavement; the present
balcony, with four Doric columns, is of 1810. Also of that date
is the first-floor courtroom (disused, but fittings intact). The
ground-floor room was converted into a gaol, with exercise
yard at the rear; it served as the police station from 1839 until
1914. The second-floor room, used as the Council Chamber
since 1687, has panelling and a chimneypiece of 1810. Fenestration mainly C19. On the roof, a timber bell-cage of 1881.

POLICE STATION, West Square. 1913, probably by *F. Whitmore*,
County Architect. Brick with stone dressings. Deep modillion
cornice and gable with scrolled feet.

PLUME LIBRARY, Market Hill. Built *c.* 1698–9 and bequeathed
to the town by Dr Thomas Plume (†1704). The site is that of
the medieval church of St Peter, which became redundant at
the Reformation and is said to have collapsed *c.* 1665. That an

archdeacon of Rochester should have felt a library to be of more use to his native town than the rebuilding of a parish church is a noteworthy sign of the period about 1700. What remains of the old church is the C15 W tower, with Perp W window, angle buttresses, and battlements. Plume made this a vestibule, with a floor inserted in the lower stage that cuts across the tower arch, providing access to each level of his new building on the site of the nave. This takes the form of a five-bay, two-storey brick house with wooden cross-windows, stone quoins and keystones. Extended by two bays to accommodate the National School, 1817. On the ground floor was a school-room (now the Maeldune Centre), on the first floor the library, its collection of about 5,000 volumes still kept in their original peninsular bookcases. Other fittings include reused C17 pan-elling and a C17 overmantel. Tower restored by *Ewan Christian*, 1875–6, *F. W. Chancellor*, 1929, and *Purcell Miller Tritton & Partners*, 1980–1, when its NE stair-turret, originally higher, was reduced. The C17 building restored by *David E. Nye*, 1931–2.

PUBLIC LIBRARY (and Social Services offices), White Horse Lane. 1992–3 by *Stephen Greenberg & Dean Hawkes* (project architect, *Deborah Bentley*), using materials and forms (colon-nade, yellow and red brick, pitched slate roof) that relate to The Friary (*see* Perambulation) and other neighbouring buildings.

ALL SAINTS' PRIMARY SCHOOL, London Road. 1840, enlarged 1897 and 1901 by *P. M. Beaumont*. Brick, with stock brick dress-ings, and steep roof with dormers. The central, earliest part has scalloped roof tiles and windows with cast-iron lattice case-ments similar to the former British School, Market Hill (*see* above, United Reformed Church).

UPPER PLUME SCHOOL (former Grammar School), Fambridge Road. 1906–7 by *P. M. Beaumont*. Brick, two storeys, front of twelve bays plus three wider gabled bays and central clock turret. Additions include the hall, 1931–2, no doubt by *J. Stuart*, County Architect.

LOWER PLUME SCHOOL (former Elementary School), Mill Road. By *A. S. G. Ley*, c. 1910–11, and various additions. Brick. Long, low front with straight gables, taller hall with louvred cupola behind.

ST GILES HOSPITAL, Spital Road. A leper hospital founded, it is said, by Henry II in 1164. All that survives is part of the transepts and of the chancel of a chapel on quite an ambitious scale. The scanty details point to the end of the C12: shafts attached to the angles of the crossing piers and a W window in the N transept. Both transepts seem originally to have had E chapels. The three lancets of the S transept S wall are an E.E. alteration. In about 1922, within the space of the crossing, an apse was found, and immediately S of it the beginning of some-thing which looked like a second apse of the same size. These foundations are in all probability pre-Norman. The standing walls are of septaria and flint rubble, with much Roman brick and later brick repairs, and limestone dressings.

St Peter's Hospital, Spital Road. Former workhouse by *F. Peck*, 1873. Brick, with stock brick bands and arches. Long and unattractive symmetrical front of three storeys, punctuated by short projecting gabled wings, with a central clock tower. Freestanding chapel (now hall) in front with lancets and octagonal chancel. Stock brick with red brick bands and arches.

Promenade Park. On the s bank of the Blackwater, laid out in 1894, with entrance lodge (now Maldon District Museum) and gates. Sea-water swimming lake opened 1905. Statue of Byrhtnoth, heroic loser of the Battle of Maldon in 991, by *John Doubleday*, 2006.

Water Tower, Cherry Garden Road. 1934 by *K. Holst & Co.* Concrete. Circular tank with balustrade on twelve square columns with round arches between them. Small domed turret with flagpole.

PERAMBULATION

The perambulation consists mainly of the High Street, between the two parish churches, with digressions to either side. The best buildings are concentrated towards the upper (w) part of the town, but the waterfront is the logical place to start. Between the Hythe and Fullbridge little of architectural value, but a generally very attractive scene of boatyards and workshops, some replaced by imaginative housing near Fullbridge completed in 2003. Where Church Street joins the Hythe, The Jolly Sailor pub, a picturesque amalgam of early C16 and early C19. St Mary's looms above it.

Church Street leads into the bottom of the High Street, where the first point of interest is Nos. 160–164, a pair of early C15 Wealden houses. The l. house is still jettied, its neighbour underbuilt with shopfront. Nos. 140–144, further w on the same side, also timber-framed, with cross-wings of the first half of the C16, but the hall rebuilt in the C17. Then as a complete contrast, King George's Place, a long three-storey Modern brick block by *David E. Nye*, 1934–5, which originally included the Embassy cinema at its E end. Also by Nye the row of cottages round the corner in Wantz Road. w of the junction with Wantz Road, on the N side, No. 105, early C19 timber-framed with a stuccoed brick front and two full-height segmental bows, and on the s side Nos. 92–94, apparently a purpose-built C15 warehouse. On the same side No. 86, a C17 gabled cross-wing joined on to the C15 cross-wing of a house that forms part of No. 88. Back on the N side, the Swan Hotel is a merchant's house of *c.* 1400, extended to the rear and given a brick front early in the C19. The front was 'restored' in the early C20 with half-timbered gables, balcony etc. The original layout was probably of an open hall in the middle, floored *c.* 1600, with shops at the front of the cross-wings. Next, across an alley, Nos. 69–71 has three gables, the central one a C16 cross-wing, with C17 additions including the decorated carriage arch to the r. Church House, C18 timber-framed and rendered at right angles to the street, faces St Peter's churchyard. On the w side of the churchyard Market Hill (*see* below) leads down to Fullbridge.

w of Market Hill, the character of the High Street is more densely c18 and c19, at least as far as the frontage is concerned, for example Nos. 54–56 (s side), with two storeys of mid-c18 chequered brick above the shop fronts, nine bays wide with scalloped soffits to the windows and heavily modillioned eaves. Next Nos. 52 and 52A, with a smart mid-c18 five-bay brick refronting, with brick pilasters at the ends, those on the second floor fluted and tapering. Nos. 50 and 50A are later and taller, early c19 gault brick with giant pilasters and two first-floor bow windows. WOOLWORTHS, by *W. B. Brown*, *c.* 1970, is acceptable infill for its date, but to the w much more commercial imagination is shown where the front of BUDGENS supermarket is set back behind a Doric colonnade that echoes the portico of the Moot Hall opposite (*see* Public Buildings, above). This is part of a remodelling in 1981–2 by *Downs Morgan Partnership* of the c18 brick frontage, its two upper storeys of five bays, the central bay with a Diocletian window over a Venetian window. On the High Street's N side, various commercial premises of mixed styles. No. 51, built as the Post Office, has a half-timbered jettied first floor and gabled dormers; by *P. M. Beaumont*, early c20. No. 47, its tall narrow frontage topped with a shaped gable, is dated 1893. Nos. 43 and 45 was originally the Literary and Mechanics' Institute with Corn Exchange to the rear. 1859–60 by *T. Roger Smith*: stock brick with stone dressings, seven bays with central three-bay pediment and round-arched windows.

Back on the s side is the KING'S HEAD CENTRE, a remodelling of a hotel by *John Fairhead*, 1994–5. The c18 painted brick front of four bays, with porch on slender Doric columns, has a cross-wing to the l. also brick-fronted. This conceals part of the timber framing of one or perhaps two late c15 Wealden houses, and at the rear a c17 maltings. Imaginative timber-framed and weatherboarded buildings added in the 1990s create a courtyard behind. Bas-relief bronze of Edward Bright, the 'fat man of Maldon' †1750, by *Catharni Stern*, 2000. This courtyard is a good way to reach WHITE HORSE LANE, with the Library on the far side and beyond it THE FRIARY, 1805–7, on the site of a house of *c.* 1570, itself replacing the Carmelite house founded in 1292–3. Two separate houses, red brick with gault brick fronts and Greek Doric porticoes, with differences in detail of fenestration etc. Contemporary stable block, and c20 extensions for the East Essex Adult Community College, including a single-storey block by *Stephen Greenberg & Dean Hawkes*, 1992–3, in similar style to their Library (*see* Public Buildings). On part of the friary site, to the N, the (early c19?) walls of the WALLED GARDEN include reused materials from the c16 house. Archaeological excavations in 1990–1 revealed portions of the friary buildings, including part of the late c13 or early c14 cloister.

Now back to the High Street, at the point where it broadens out into what was the medieval marketplace in front of All Saints, with *F. W. Chancellor*'s WAR MEMORIAL of 1921. The street then curves gently away from the centre with a variety of attractive houses on both sides. Just before the top, on the N side, Nos. 1–3 has a plastered front with parapet concealing what is probably the oldest timber-framed building in Maldon, thought to be mid C14. Hall and two cross-wings. OAKWOOD HOUSE, opposite, with two two-storey canted bays and rusticated doorcase, is timber-framed, early C19 but with fragments of an earlier building.

Oakwood House looks over WEST SQUARE, with the Police Station (*see* Public Buildings) on the E side, and on the N a fine Georgian brick house (No. 2 London Road), now offices. Three-bay S front, with two shallow projections either side of a doorcase with open pediment, five bays to London Road with similar doorcase. Dog-leg staircase with column-on-vase balusters. On the square's W side, Nos. 3–7, C15 with an early C19 front: former hall with two jettied and gabled cross-wings. LONDON ROAD is mainly of interest for the large, mid-C19, stock brick, semi-detached houses along the W side. Among them the OLD COURTHOUSE (former County Court), 1858 and probably by *Charles Reeves*, converted to a house by *G. Vale*, 1996–7. Single-storey, stock brick with stone dressings, with a row of five round-headed windows and free-standing royal arms above the parapet. Former chambers at the front, double-height courthouse to the rear, with inserted gallery.

At the end of London Road, just before the by-pass, DYKES CHASE, and at its N end PHOENIX HOUSE by *Plater Inkpen*, c. 1986. Two storeys, mainly brick, with steep roofs leading up to a central lantern, a feature derived from local examples of lanterns or belvederes on buildings along BEELEIGH ROAD (reached by a footpath), e.g. the Franciscan Convent (MOUNT VIEW), a large gault brick house dated 1880 (for John Sadd) with red brick and terracotta dressings, and on the opposite corner of West Chase a timber-framed and weatherboarded house (No. 37) of 1908 with corrugated zinc roof built round a central double-height living hall.

Beeleigh Road leads back to SILVER STREET, with THE WHITE HOUSE on the corner of Cromwell Hill, C16 with C19 painted brick front, then CHANDLERS, late C16 and C17 with two gables and C19 canted bays, and finally on the N side THE BELL, timber-framed with an early C19 gault brick front and late C16 range to the rear. A lane between it and the N side of All Saints leads to ALL SAINTS' VICARAGE, its timbers exposed on the S front as part of restoration in 1902, when oriel and bay windows and porch were added. Two jettied cross-wings with hall between, the W cross-wing the earliest part and probably built for the chantry priest funded by a bequest of Sir Robert Darcy, 1448. Fragments of wall paintings in the same part, principally on the ground floor. The S side of Silver Street, opposite the W end of All Saints, is dominated by the

BLUE BOAR HOTEL, with an impressive early C19 five-bay, three-storey front of Suffolk white bricks. Tuscan porch and carriage arch. Through this can be seen the original timber-framed structure, notably the late C14 jettied range at right angles to the street. The main building includes remains of a mid-C16 hall.

The final stage of the perambulation is MARKET HILL, for which it is necessary to retrace one's steps E along the High Street. Market Hill is steep and gently curving, a rare combination in Essex, and contains a number of fine merchants' or ship-owners' houses. Most prominent, well sited on the W side, HILL HOUSE, early C19 timber-framed and plastered, three bays and three storeys with belvedere. Downhill, on the same side, HILLSIDE, a tall group with a gabled wing at the N end. Purpose-built as the workhouse, 1719, extended (and raised by a storey) in 1834, but converted to separate houses in 1874 when superseded (see St Peter's Hospital, above). Facing, a very attractive row steps down the hill, including THE OLD CUSTOM HOUSE. Late C16 with an early C18 five-bay front of blue brick with red dressings. No. 12, higher up, has in a first-floor room C18 wall paintings of two figures, and on the ground floor an overdoor painting of a landscape and birds.

FULLBRIDGE, at the foot of Market Hill across the Chelmer, developed as Maldon's riverside industrial area, helped, from 1847, by the railway (closed 1966). It starts with a few worth-while houses on the l., and on the r. FULLBRIDGE HOUSE stands at right angles to the street to present its gault brick front to the bridge, a good effect. Largely rebuilt in 1827, with a C17 or earlier timber-framed core and a bakehouse of similar age to the NE. Between Fullbridge House and the river FULL-BRIDGE MILL, now offices, c. 1879. Stock brick, a three-storey block with pedimented gable end and a lower three-storey block projecting towards the road with a pedimented gable whose sides are interrupted by a single step. Pilasters between bays on both blocks.

A little further N stand the remains of MALDON IRON-WORKS, founded here in 1853 by *Joseph Warren*. Two three-storey yellow brick ranges of 1875 in parallel with gabled ends to the street, with oculi and windows set in round arches. Inside, cast-iron columns support deep transverse beams. On the other side of the roundabout, a large former GOODS SHED for the branch line from Witham and further E the former EAST STATION, now offices. 1847–8, perhaps by *H.A. Hunt*. Red brick with stock brick dressings, in a pretty Jacobean style, with shaped gables and nine-bay arcade. This industrial heritage has been drawn on to good effect in more recent buildings: for example on the ironworks site, TRAFALGAR HOUSE by *Baldwin Design Ltd*, 2003, three storeys, red and stock brick, and on a much bigger scale TESCO by *Biscoe & Stanton*, c. 1991–2, extended 2001–2. Brick, with arches and gables picked out in reconstituted stone. Further W, three BRIDGES of Maldon by-pass, which opened 1990 and follows the line of the old railway, continue the theme (*County Council Architect & Planning Depts*, project architects *George Corderoy & Co.*).

MALDON HALL, ¾ m. SW of All Saints. Early C16, cased in C18 brick, part painted, on a moated site. Three-bay E front and early C19 cast-iron veranda on S front. To the NW, a five-bay, mid-C17 weatherboarded barn, converted to house (Headland Barn) by *Plater Inkpen Vale & Downie*, *c.* 1985, with sympathetic extensions including midstrey.

MANNINGTREE

1030

The historic parish is very small, only 22 acres, so that by the middle of the C19 it was already spilling over into Lawford and Mistley. The old parts of the town are chiefly the cross formed by the High Street and South Street, which together constitute a largely unspoilt C18 and C19 townscape, with the Stour Estuary and quay forming a picturesque backdrop to the N.

ST MICHAEL AND ALL ANGELS. Demolished 1967, a loss to the town that would have been inconceivable twenty years later. 1616, with various C19 and C20 alterations and additions. A fragment of the W wall remains embedded in the wall of No. 42 High Street.*

METHODIST CHURCH, South Street. Bold and elaborate composition of 1807. White brick with stone dressings. Five-bay façade, with a projecting three-bay loggia and side bays added *c.* 1900 to form a portico *in antis* with two Greek Doric columns. Above that three round-headed windows separated by pilasters, then a three-bay pediment, and finally a timber cupola, also *c.* 1900. Beside it the much humbler building of 1795 which it superseded, with pedimented gable and three arched windows.

THE HIGH STREET has an almost entirely Georgian appearance. The biggest of the houses, many with Greek Doric doorways or porches, is No. 50, seven bays, one of an impressive row to the E of the site of St Michael that tails off very attractively with No. 56, FORGE COTTAGE and FORGE STUDIOS, leading through a central carriageway to a courtyard, and ENGLISH TERRACE forming a continuation of High Street which here turns sharply N. On the opposite corner Nos. 59–65, a terrace of three-storey, early C19 brick cottages, very tall, and curved. W of the site of St Michael the street broadens slightly with an island block, Nos. 25–27, more C18 brick. Nos. 38–42 on the S side, however, demonstrate vividly that older work often lies behind the façades: a massive C16 brick chimneystack with six octagonal shafts is visible from the street, but the C16 origins of the house, with a C15 outbuilding, are best seen from Stour Street behind. On the W wall of

---

*The altarpiece painting of 'The Risen Christ' by *John Constable*, 1821–2, is now in St Mary, Dedham. Various monuments transferred to St Mary, Mistley.

No. 25, at the corner with South Street, an open metalwork SCULPTURE, 'The Manningtree Ox', by *Colin Wilkin*, 2000.

W of South Street, High Street's S side is dominated by the classical PUBLIC LIBRARY, built as the Corn Exchange in 1865, converted to an R.C. church by *Raymond Erith*, 1966–7, and the library since 1980; then the POST OFFICE of 1939, the *Office of Works'* usual well-mannered Neo-Georgian. On the N side, the C18 brick façades of the WHITE HART and WISTERIA HOUSE conceal an early C16 timber-framed hall house with rear cross-wings, the hotel carriageway cutting through part of the hall.

The crossing with SOUTH STREET forms the town's centre. To the N, only one building of interest, an early C15 house and shop, now a restaurant, mostly rebuilt in the C16, restored 1974 by the *County Architect's Dept* (job architect, *James Boutwood*). To the S, an unbroken stretch of good houses run uphill, the most prominent HILL HOUSE (No. 52) and PROSPECT HOUSE (No. 48), overlooking the triangular green halfway up, and at the top, closing the view nicely, GROVE HOUSE (No. 59). All have gault brick façades, *c.* 1800, with Grove House the largest, five bays and three storeys. Earlier houses at the junction with Stour Street; on the E side No. 17 is of C15 origin and includes a hall at the rear with octagonal crown-post. Between Nos. 29 and 31, set back from the street, the former MECHANICS' INSTITUTION by *Teulon*, 1849. Neo-Elizabethan brick, reading room with lecture room behind. Hidden at the W end of the green the former CONGREGATIONAL CHAPEL of 1823, plain brick, square but with rounded corners that incorporate curved sashes.

South Street leads in to BROOK STREET, with a few attractive C18 and C19 cottages on the hill running back down to the junction with the High Street and Station Road; on the SW corner a cast-iron MILEPOST, cast by *O. Bendall* of the Lawford Ironworks, 1834. A short way along STATION ROAD to the W LEANDER COTTAGES (Nos. 57–61), 1925: a group of three made to look like two, brick with stone dressings and three dormers in the deep tiled roof.

Opposite the bottom of Brook Street, NORTH STREET, with early C19 MALTINGS and prominent brick kiln with slate pyramidal roof; now flats. North Street becomes QUAY STREET; on the S side, W of Stour Street, a former warehouse, early C19 gault brick with heavy rustication. This in turn leads to THE WALLS, with further extensive MALTINGS built by Edward Norman of Mistley, 1806–28. Brick, slate roofs, with a pair of large kilns and third smaller one, also now converted.

WATERWORKS, Mill Hill. Two tall stock brick pump houses, late C19, with full-height round-headed windows. Single-storey office building, red brick and domestic in character, with carved brickwork in the gables including the date, 1908.

MANUDEN

ST MARY. Flint, with battlemented W tower and recessed spire. N transept *c.* 1400. Nave rebuilt and S aisle and porch added 1863–4 by *Thomas S. Lansdown*, chancel rebuilt and N vestry added 1866–7 by *Woodyer*. The latter work is of noticeably better quality. Nave roof largely original C15. – SCREEN. Sumptuous for Essex, with large one-light divisions. Dado panel with quatrefoil frieze at the foot, blank tracery, and two top friezes. Cusped and crocketed ogee arches are the main motif above, surmounted by panel tracery. Broad straight cornice. – STAINED GLASS. E window by *Jones & Willis* to members of the Thomas family of Manuden House †1869, 1892 and 1915.

MANUDEN HALL, 200yds ENE. Impressive four-bay W front. Four stepped gables of unequal size with pinnacles on the apexes, the second bay with the entrance projecting slightly. But seen from the E it is a modest, plain C19 building, much smaller than the entrance would indicate. The original mid-C16 brick house, of five bays, was severely damaged by fire in 1889, and rebuilt on a smaller scale behind the façade; only the N wall and the two gables r. of the entrance are original, as are probably the windows below them – on the upper floor mullioned, on the ground floor mullioned and transomed. All the individual lights are arched. The S front would seem to be a rebuilding of the fifth bay of the W front. In the garden, a single-storey brick FOLLY by *James Boutwood*, 2000, whose form mimics the gables.

Manuden has an especially pretty village street with timber-framed cottages with jettied upper floors N and S of the church. Further W, a small assortment of Georgian houses, including CLEEVE HALL, built as the vicarage and refronted in 1725, and dominating the N end of the village, MANUDEN HOUSE, early C19, five bays with later C19 and C20 additions. In front a straight stretch of road with good iron railings on both sides, laid out by John Thomas. Cottages which he demolished were replaced by six pairs dated 1857 at the village's S end.

MARDEN ASH
Ongar

Originally a hamlet of High Ongar, but now joined to Chipping Ongar. The boundary is Cripsey Brook.

ST JAMES. 1957–8 by *Laurence King*, replacing a church of 1882–3 destroyed by a bomb in 1945. Nave and shallow polygonal chancel with slender SW bell-tower. Stock brick and pantiles, with round-headed windows and W door.

MARDEN ASH HOUSE, Stanford Rivers Road. Late C17, refronted in the mid C18. Large, of nine by six bays, two storeys with parapet. Ionic pedimented doorcase. Inside, a handsome staircase with twisted balusters, and in one room an Adamesque ceiling. C18 stable block with clock turret and cupola (now houses). N of the house a picturesque single-storey COTTAGE, tall thatched roof with deep eaves that rise to accommodate the pointed windows and door. Opposite, DYERS, a smaller house of C16 or C17 origins with a C18 plastered brick front and doorcase with fluted Ionic pilasters.

In Stondon Road, N side, NEW HOUSE FARM of *c.* 1600, reduced in size in the C19. Rough rendered, with two gables and a central gabled two-storey porch. Original rear stair-turret and a central chimneystack of six octagonal shafts. Inside, three panelled rooms on the ground floor. On the S side, KNOWLE-TON HALL, the remaining portion of The Gables, a large house by *J. P. Pritchett*, 1888: brick ground floor, jettied first floor originally with exposed timbers, now tile-hung.

MARGARET RODING

ST MARGARET OF ANTIOCH. C12 nave, C14 chancel, with bell-cote and N vestry of 1855. In the nave W wall an odd two-light window which may be C17, and above it a small Norman window. Restored Norman S doorway with two orders of columns. The capitals are scalloped, one column is zigzag-carved. Curved lintel, the tympanum with diaper pattern. Zigzag arches and a billet hoodmould. Norman windows on the N and S sides of the nave. Chancel windows late C14. Inside the chancel a low ogee-arched recess and damaged SEDILIA and PISCINA, also a corbel S of the (C19) E window with a caryatid demi-figure. – FONT. Octagonal, Perp, with traceried stem and quatrefoils with shields on the panels. – DOORS in chancel and nave with some mid-C12 ironwork. – CHEST. Dug-out, iron-bound, two compartments with five locks and a further fastening for a padlock. Ornamental ironwork on the lids, C12 and C13. – WALL PAINTINGS. In chancel, *c.* 1860–70, figures of saints, Christ in Majesty, Annunciation and angels, possibly by an amateur but within a professionally painted architectural framework. – Chamber ORGAN by *William Pilcher*, 1842. – STAINED GLASS. E window by *Lavers & Barraud*, *c.* 1861. Chancel S by *Mayer & Co.*, 1902. Nave S (First World War memorial) by *James Clark*, based on his painting 'The Great Sacrifice'. Three small nave windows by *Clayton & Bell*, one dated 1876.

GARNISH HALL, E of the church. Of C18 appearance but possibly earlier. Central pediment and porch, sash windows, but a homely pargetted front.

BRICK HOUSE, ½ m. SE. Timber-framed two-storey house of *c.* 1680–1700 with a five-bay brick façade, of which there are countless examples in Essex, except that here the façade is contemporary. It would not have looked out of place in London at the time. In Flemish bond with blue flared headers and flat arches of gauged brickwork over the windows. Narrow recesses at each end, on each floor, and wooden modillions beneath the cornice. Mid-C19 porch and rear extensions.

MARGARETTING

6000

St Margaret should be visited by all for its splendid C15 timber w tower, on ten posts (like Blackmore). The free-standing posts are connected from N and S by three pairs of arched braces. From E to W between posts two and three and posts three and four on both sides there are also arched braces, but lower and smaller. Cross-strutting above these. Outside, the tower has a vertically weatherboarded ground floor. The roof is hipped on N, S, and W, but straight on the E and higher than the nave roof. The bell-stage is straight again and on it sits a splay-foot spire, all shingled. The two-light W window with a little tracery is original, the N and S windows renewed. The N porch also is of timber and contemporary. Four-centred doorway with tracering spandrels, cusped bargeboarding and one-light side openings. The rest of the church is essentially C15 and early C16, but the flint rubble of the N wall, with some Roman brick, has survived from the C12. The S arcade has first one bay, then a piece of wall, and then another three. The piers are quatrefoil, and the arches four-centred with double-hollow-chamfered moulding. Restoration by *Chancellor*, 1868–70, who rebuilt the E wall and S porch, and renewed the windows.

FONT. Octagonal, Perp, with quatrefoils carrying flowers, a crown, a mitre, a head with tongue put out. Nice ogee-domed COVER. – REREDOS. 1877, by *Earp*. With three deeply carved stone panels, depicting the Feeding of the Five Thousand. Wooden dado below by members of the village carving class, 1893–6. – SCREEN. C15 dado with elaborate blank tracery, restored 1870. Upper part by *F. W. Chancellor*, 1919–20, as war memorial. – PLASTERWORK. On chancel E wall, patterns and symbols in low relief with scenes of the Annunciation and Nativity. By *Philip Robson*, 1918. – STAINED GLASS. In the three-light E window the Tree of Jesse, dated by John H. Hall to 1451–9 and most likely by a local craftsman rather than, as previously suggested, John Prudde. Moved from a nave N window in 1869–70 by *Lavers, Barraud & Westlake* and restored: of the twenty-two figures, two were completely new and four partially restored, the new glass marked with a cross. Nonetheless impressive as a complete C15 composition: four medallions with two figures each in the sidelights, Jesse, three medallions, and the seated Virgin in the centre light. – S aisle W also by *Lavers, Barraud & Westlake*, and perhaps the tower window. – Chancel N 1903 by *W. Aikman*. – Two nave N windows by *Clayton & Bell*, 1877. – MONUMENTS. Brass of James Gedge of Shenfields (i.e. Killigrews) †1556 and wife Mary. His head missing, her figure 22½ in. (57 cm.). Palimpsest of various brasses, the oldest piece with hands of a priest, *c.* 1390. – John Tanfield †1625. Alabaster, with painted kneeling figures of man and wife with children behind. – Richard Benyon †1774 and his son Richard †1796. Both by *Richard Westmacott Sen.*, both with sarcophagus, the later monument larger and more elaborate.

Right in front of the church, which is cut off from Margaretting Hall and village by the railway, the OLD VICARAGE, an attractive gault brick house of 1822. Porch with tented canopy on trellis supports, and three little round-headed dormers. Earlier house kept as the rear wing.

KILLIGREWS, 2 m. NE. Late C15 house, of which the moat survives with its original brick revetment. At the angles of the wall two ornamented turrets of the same date: octagonal with battlements and crocketed brick pyramid roofs or spires. The house, known as Shenfields until the mid C18, was remodelled after 1714, with a five-bay brick w front and pedimented doorcase with Roman Doric columns. Additions by *Chancellor & Son*, 1912–13, mainly to the NE corner, and a five-bay E range added in the 1920s. Early C17 panelling in a ground-floor room. Formal, sunken walled garden with pavilion SW of the house, outside the moat, probably also 1920s.

NEW COPTFOLD HALL, 1¾ m. NNE. By *Stuart Martin*, 2002–5, for Simon Upton. Neo-Georgian, the six-bay entrance front of brick, with Serlian front door, the other sides stuccoed with quoins simply incised. On the site of the service wing of Coptfold Hall, rebuilt in 1862, of which the stables and chapel remain, and which replaced the house of 1751 by *Sir Robert Taylor*.

PEACOCKS, ¾ m. NE. Charming Georgian brick house, like a Cheltenham villa, standing in a small park. Extended early in the C19, and given a tetrastyle Greek Doric portico, the front possibly stuccoed at the same time. Seven bays, two storeys and attics, with panels above the first-floor windows. Three-bay pedimented centre, an outer bay each side set slightly back, then a further bay, lower and narrower, set further back, with a blind window on the first floor and round-headed recess on the ground floor. Painted brick LODGE with tetrastyle pilastered front.

8020

MARKSHALL

Coggeshall

ST MARGARET. Demolished 1933, the foundations still visible. The medieval church had been rebuilt in the mid C18 and remodelled by *James Brooks*, 1872–5.★

MARKS HALL. The mansion N of the church, rebuilt by Robert Honywood *c.* 1605–9 and enlarged in the second half of the C18, was demolished in 1950. The estate has been developed as a visitor attraction and arboretum since 1971, centred on large ponds N of the house: three shown on a survey of 1764, the two smaller ones combined by 1838, formed by damming Robin's Brook, with a series of cascades (mostly rebuilt). To

★ Monuments in St Peter-ad-Vincula, Coggeshall, and Hollytrees, Colchester.

the S a brick bridge, *c.* 1800, with good cast-iron railings. On the W bank of the larger pond a C18 walled garden, laid out by *Brita von Schoenaich*, 1998–2003. The VISITOR CENTRE is a C15 weatherboarded barn, ¼ m. S of the house, moved from Bouchier's Grange, 1 m. SE, in 1991.

MARKS TEY

9020

ST ANDREW. W tower with a mix of brick, rubble and pudding-stone at the base, then brick, with diagonal buttresses and stair-turret. The top damaged in the Civil War and replaced (even the battlements) with vertical weatherboarding. Recessed shingled spire. Much puddingstone in the nave and chancel also. In the nave (S side) one small Norman window, and plain Norman N and S doorways. These and the windows have surrounds of Roman brick, found also in the quoins. Chancel C14. S porch C15, of timber, plain. 'Thoroughly' restored by *E. J. Dampier*, *c.* 1884–5. Utilitarian brick N extension by *Duncan Clark & Beckett*, 1967–8. – FONT. C15. Octagonal. The remarkable thing is that it is of oak. Stem with tracery panels with roses in the centres, bowl with tracery panels formerly with seated figures. – STAINED GLASS. E window by *F. C. Eden*, 1925. Nave SE to Arthur F. Erridge, master glass-painter, 1968, made by *J. Wippell & Co.* and signed with both their marks. Nave SW by *Auravisions*, 2001. – MONUMENTS. Rev. Peter Wright †1839. By *Henry Lufkin*. Marble tablet, with restrained classical decoration. – First World War memorial. Brass, with figures of St Michael and a soldier, each about 23 in. (58 cm.).

MASHBURY

6010

CHURCH. Flint and stone rubble nave and chancel, and C16 brick S porch. On the N side a Norman window and a plain Norman doorway, on the S side also a Norman window and a doorway with one-scallop capitals, decorated abaci, and zigzag arches. The belfry rests on four C15 posts with two arched braces. Restoration, including new nave roof, by *F. Whitmore*, 1873, and again *c.* 1890–4 (probably by *A. Y. Nutt*), when the tiny W bellcote was added. Now redundant and privately owned.* – DOOR. C12 ironwork on the N door. – STAINED GLASS, C14 fragments, N window, including the figure of a Saint.

BAILEYS, 1 m. NNW. Early C16 farmhouse with two gabled and jettied cross-wings. Porch added 1614 and probably at the same time the tall central gable, supported on a moulded bressumer and carved brackets, all purely for display. Small square GRANARY with pyramidal roof to W.

---

*Pulpit now in St Mary, Maldon.

MATCHING

ST MARY THE VIRGIN. Flint rubble. C15 battlemented W tower, late C14 S aisle wall, and C13 N and S arcades (W parts only, with circular piers and double-chamfered arches). The rest 1875 by *A. W. Blomfield*, who extended the nave by one bay to the E, rebuilt the chancel, N aisle, and S porch, and added a N organ chamber and vestry and S transept. The S doorway and one S aisle window (square-headed) survived. Stone carving (e.g. REREDOS) by *Earp*, woodcarving by *Rattee & Kett*, the chancel ceiling stencilled by *Heaton, Butler & Bayne*. – FONT. Octagonal, Perp, with quatrefoils with shields and flowers. – Good Jacobean PULPIT with strapwork decoration, given in 1624. – BENCHES. Four, C16, plain. – STAINED GLASS. E window, 1899, S aisle 1887 and 1902, all by *Powell & Sons*, designed by *Penwarden*, *Henry Holiday*, and *J. W. Brown* respectively. N aisle by *Heaton, Butler & Bayne*, 1907. – MONUMENTS. Brass of John Ballett †1638 and wife Rose, with children. Main figure 28½ in. (72.5 cm.). – Nicholas Ashton †1716. With putti, skulls, and leaf sprays, excellently carved. – In churchyard, S of tower, Thomas Bishop †1788. Tomb-chest with flaming urn and railings.

The church and its surroundings make an extremely pleasing picture. To the W, the MARRIAGE FEAST ROOM, late C15 with continuous jetty along the W front. It was built, according to Morant, 'for the entertainment of poor people on their wedding day'. The upper floor is one large room, with crown-post roof. To the N, the former VICARAGE, C17 timber-framed and plastered, remodelled *c.* 1770, with an incongruous brick wing by *G. E. Pritchett*, 1884. To the S, MATCHING HALL, the NW cross-wing C15, the SE cross-wing and main range (with façade gable) *c.* 1600. N of the house, two square service buildings, C17, perhaps larders. Square brick dovecote with pyramidal roof, *c.* 1700, SSW of the hall, and seven-bay aisled weatherboarded barn to SW, *c.* 1600. NE of the church, a small lake with a mid-C19 brick fishing lodge (LILY POND COTTAGE).

In addition, two quite separate settlements: Matching Green and Matching Tye, ¾ m. SE and SW respectively. MATCHING GREEN is large and triangular, with houses along each side. The best are along the E: THE LIMES, early C18 brick, two storeys and five bays with Tuscan porch and segment-headed windows, and a two-storey canted bay on the garden front; MAY TREES, late C17 timber-framed with two-storey, three-bay C18 brick front; and MOAT HOUSE, set back a little, a hall house of *c.* 1500 with gabled and jettied cross-wing to the r. and a large C20 cross-wing to the l. On the W side of the Green, LASCELLES, a large C14 house with two gabled and jettied cross-wings. At the SE corner, the PRIMARY SCHOOL, 1866 by *G. E. Pritchett*, for the parishes of High and Little Laver. Brick, with combined chimney and bellcote. Adjacent hall, of white brick with stone dressings, built 1874 as a chapel of ease (ST EDMUND) for High Laver.

MATCHING TYE is a much more compact group of buildings, individually unremarkable but sitting well together. Most
striking is GAINSBOROUGH COTTAGE, two cottages of the
C18 or C19 converted to a single house in the C20 with much
picturesque but misleading detail added, e.g. part of a shell-
hood of *c.* 1700, with carved wooden brackets in the shape of
putti, and a date of 1692. SW, MATTHEWS CHAPEL (former
Congregational Chapel), now a house. 1875 by *George Perry*.
Stock brick, with red brick decoration, and a rose window
above the W porch.

MOOR HALL, 2 m. W. Formerly in the parish of Harlow (Old
Harlow, *see* p. 466) and, in the second half of the C19, the seat
of one of that town's great benefactors, J.W. Perry Watlington.
The house, rebuilt between 1805 and 1810 and enlarged later
in the C19, was demolished *c.* 1960. Part of the stable block
and a thatched lodge with entrance gates survive, as well as
evidence of early C19 landscaping. The line of the road follows
Repton's suggestion, 1808, taking it further from the house.

STOCK HALL, Matching Green, 1 m. ESE. Mid-C16 timber-
framed and plastered, within a double moat: the inner one
surrounds the house, the outer one the outbuildings. The E
cross-wing, demolished before the Royal Commission visited,
was rebuilt in 2001, when a late C16 or early C17 wall painting
was discovered, depicting a colourful floral stem motif. Early
C17 rear additions, resulting in four gables, with a lower C18
service wing.

MAYLAND 9000

ST BARNABAS. Rebuilt 1866–7 by *P. C. Hardwick*, about 300 yds
s of the old church. Nave and chancel, with tall S porch and N
vestry, all of Kentish rag. E.E. with cusped lancets, but now
lacking the bellcote on the nave's E gable. – STAINED GLASS.
The best feature of the church, unexpected in such an out-of-
the-way place. Apart from the war memorial window by *Jones
& Willis*, 1920, all by *Powell & Sons*, and the variety demonstrates just how much freedom their individual designers had.
Most of it by *Henry Holiday*, notably the E window; W by *Henry
Casolani*, 1866; 'Faith' (nave N) by *J. W. Brown*, 1876.

Former BOARD SCHOOL, ½ m. S. By *Chancellor*, 1875–6, with
later additions. Stock brick with red brick and stone dressings.

MAYLANDSEA COUNTY PRIMARY SCHOOL, The Drive. By the
County Architect's Dept, 1990. Two square blocks with sweeping pyramidal roofs rising to ventilators, rather like a distillery.

The church stands on a hill S of the village, and most of the
houses are at Maylandsea, on roads leading down to the Blackwater estuary. These have names like Imperial Avenue,
Wembley Avenue, and The Esplanade, suggesting they were
laid out in the 1930s in a spirit of optimism that proved unjus-
tified. Among the suburban housing, some labourers' cottages
designed by *Charles Holden*, 1906, relics of a 'farm labour

colony' established by Joseph Fels, an American soap manufacturer and philanthropist, to provide smallholdings as an alternative to emigration. Holden designed three types of stock brick semi-detached cottages and two single cottages. Largely unaltered examples survive at Nos. 24–26 and 60–62 Nipsells Chase.

MESSING
Messing-cum-Inworth

ALL SAINTS. The nave is C14, the chancel C13, as can be seen from a blocked window on its N side. Nave roof datable by its heraldry to c. 1360, and includes a single hammerbeam frame against the chancel arch. W tower rebuilt in brick by *J.B. Watson*, not at all Essex in style, 1839–40. He also added N and S transepts, the N damaged in the 1884 earthquake and taken down by *Chancellor*, who also carried out a general restoration, 1885–6. What makes the church worth a visit are the chancel fittings: the PANELLING and STALLS of 1634: not choir stalls, but communion stalls, where communicants would sit to receive the sacrament, with the altar placed lengthwise in the chancel. The ornament is entirely Jacobean, but with hardly any strapwork; the stall fronts with rusticated oval frames, the backs with rusticated blank arches separated by Corinthian pilasters. – Unusually fine ROYAL ARMS of Charles I, dated 1634, originally hung no doubt in the chancel arch. Carved in high relief with inscription below; on the reverse, arms of the Prince of Wales above those of the patron and donor, Hanameel Chibborne.* – STAINED GLASS. E window contemporary with the panelling etc. and attributed to *Abraham van Linge*. The Works of Mercy and figures of Faith, Hope, and Charity. – N and S chancel windows by *Wilkinson Bros*, 1882. In S transept, figure of St Cecilia, c. 1939, transferred from the chapel of Prested Hall, Feering, 1996. – Iron-bound dug-out CHEST, C14. – BRASS to a Lady, c. 1540; 20-in. (51-cm.) figure. Some nice houses in the village, which forms a T with the churchyard along the S side of the stem. At the W end of The Street, the OLD SCHOOL HOUSE, C18 brick but with three windows and two blocked hoodmoulded doorways that probably date from the building becoming a school in 1836. Before that it was almshouses, then workhouse; since 1911 the village hall. Halfway down on the N side, YEW TREE COTTAGE, with C15 gabled and jettied cross-wing, part of the original hall with later inserted chimney, the W part rebuilt in the C18. At the E end, THE OLD CROWN, C17 timber-framed and plastered with C19 brick front and three canted bays beneath a lean-to roof. Next to it FORGE HOUSE, early C16 with exposed timbers.

---

* Chibborne also donated a set of communion plate in 1634.

BOURCHIER'S HALL, S of the church. C15–16. Large jettied and gabled cross-wing with lower hall range to the W and later E additions.

MESSING PARK, ½ m. SSW. Elevated from farmhouse to country house by Golding Griggs after 1775. Gault brick on three sides. Five-bay NE front, the centre breaking slightly forward with Doric porch and tripartite window above. On the NW front two two-storey shallow bows, on the SE pilasters and windows set in segmental arches. The older house visible at the rear, early C18 but with internal evidence of the C16.

MIDDLETON

8030

ALL SAINTS. Nave and chancel of flint rubble, rendered, the chancel 2 ft (60 cm.) longer than the nave. The church is of some importance, especially for its Norman features. The S doorway has colonettes with scalloped capitals and two orders of zigzag. The inner order is of a remarkable design. Polygonal shafts decorated down each side by a chain of triangles. Another such column (reused?) is in a C13 recess at the E end of the S aisle. The capitals are scalloped or with volutes and slight leaf decoration. The chancel arch, also with columns, has decorated abaci. The arches are provided with a zigzag moulding and another with zigzags and a kind of stylized tongues lapping into them. In the nave N and S walls two identical C14 recesses on short triple shafts. Porch Early Tudor. Restored by *Anthony Salvin Jun.*, 1852–3, who added the N vestry (later organ chamber), and presumably also the open timber spirelet seen in old photographs, since replaced by a weatherboarded belfry. – DOOR. In S doorway, C15 with traceried panels. – PAINTING. Annunciation. Italian, early C17; perhaps by a follower of *Veronese*. Presented by Rev. Oliver Raymond, from his own large collection, as an altarpiece; replaced by the carved oak REREDOS erected to his memory in 1889. – ROYAL ARMS. C16, carved in wood, after the Act of Supremacy (1534). – STAINED GLASS. E window in the style of *Warrington*, one of a good collection of various dates, *c.* 1840–87. – MONUMENT. Incised slab to James Samson, a priest †1349, 7 ft (2.1 metres) long. The style is Flemish rather than English, with an elaborate architectural surround, but the slab is of Purbeck marble, and we know too little of such pieces to decide against English authorship. The head of the figure unfortunately is renewed.

QUEEN'S BEECHES (former rectory), S of the church. Large early C19 house of grey gault brick. By the drive, E of the church, a pond with classical fragments artfully arranged (one with carved inscription 'CAVE STAGNUM'), and to the N a small Gothic FOLLY erected by Rev. Oliver Raymond, 1841. Gault brick, flint, and fragments from Lavenham church, Suffolk (see the de Vere mullets).

9020

MILE END (or MYLAND)

A suburb of Colchester, with no character as a village.

St Michael and All Angels. By *E.C. Hakewill*, 1854–5. The medieval church stood ½ m. s; its foundations can be seen in Rectory Close. Hakewill's is E.E., Kentish rag with Caen stone dressings, and shingled NW spire. N organ chamber and vestries by *Duncan Clark & Beckett*, 1933–4. – Stained glass. Chancel and two nave s windows by *T. Wilmshurst*, 1855–c. 1874. Nave s western window by *E. J. Prest*, 1902. – Parish Hall (former school). By *Hakewill*, 1870–1, partly with materials from the old church. Enlarged 1884.

Primary School, Mill Road. 1905–6 by *C.E. Butcher*. Brick, nicely detailed, with distinctive wooden bellcote.

Hospitals. *See* under Colchester, p. 279–80.

Mile End (or Myland) Hall (St Helena's Hospice), Barncroft Close. Medieval manor house with C14 two-bay hall; contemporary s cross-wing, N cross-wing rebuilt. C18 range added to e front, with further C19 additions. Single-storey brick additions by *Alan Bragg*, 1983–7.

Opposite the church, an interesting Arts and Crafts house by *E. E. May*, 1907: roughcast, three gables to the front, with a canted oriel over the front door and large staircase window. In the s of the parish, N of the railway, commercial buildings include a large office building (Crowe House) next to the station by *Arthur Willter Associates* for Philips, 1975. The use of local brick fails to disguise its bulk. Off the bottom of Turner Road, *Aukett Associates'* Asda Supermarket, 1997 is considerably more stylish, with a dramatic internal space.

In Severalls Lane, 1½ m. ene, Phoenix Square, the former Trebor Factory by *Arup Associates*, 1978–80, now mixed use. An inspiring building, dark brown brick with exposed steelwork painted bright red. In the foreground, three single-storey blocks, the flat roofs formed of pre-cast concrete, each bay topped by a truncated pyramid with skylight; behind rises the former power plant, almost entirely glazed and still a deliberate feature although shorn of its chimneys.

1030

MISTLEY

Mistley's unusual character is the result of two strong but very different influences: an extremely wealthy landowning family in the C18, and maltings in the late C19. Its position on the s shore of the Stour estuary led to Mistley becoming a major centre of the malting industry, and some of the most technologically advanced malthouses in the country were built here.

St Mary and St Michael (formerly St Mary). Of the medieval church (at Mistley Heath, 1 m. ese) only the outline can be seen. It became redundant when a new church was built in 1735 as part of the Rigby family's scheme for developing the village (*see* below). The present building is by *Wadmore &*

Baker, 1868–70. Early Dec, Kentish rag with Bath stone dressings, SW steeple with spire and E apse. Largely unaltered interior, with some good carving, notably to the PULPIT and the corbels of the chancel arch, although of the chancel decorations of 1885 (by *Simpson & Sons*) only the ceiling survives. – FONT. Small stone basin on baluster from the 1735 church, as well as the massive one of 1870, alabaster on dwarf columns of serpentine. – REREDOS. Painted triptych by *Heaton, Butler & Bayne.* – ORGAN CASE. Made for Worcester Cathedral, 1667, with elaborate gilded carving. – ROYAL ARMS of 1816–37, cast iron, made by *Coleman & Wallis* of Colchester for St Michael and All Angels, Manningtree. – STAINED GLASS. By *Clayton & Bell*, 1870–1920, the w window (1886) a particularly spirited depiction of the Last Judgement. – MONUMENTS. Mostly from the two earlier churches, and also from Manningtree; including a lengthy panegyric to Richard Rigby †1788: 'no man ever went beyond him in doing good to all his acquaintance'. – Fanny Cox †1826 by *J. Browne*, 1830. Draped urn.

Edward Rigby was a successful linen draper who bought an interest in the estates of the Earl of Oxford in 1680, and established a right to the lands of Mistley on the earl's death in 1703. His son Richard made a fortune as a factor to the South Sea Company and built Mistley Hall and laid out a new village by the river, known as Mistley Thorn, with a wharf and brick and lime kilns. His son, also Richard, later M.P., inherited in 1730 at the age of eight, and returned from the Grand Tour with ambitious plans. In these he was to be helped by his appointment as Paymaster General of the Forces in 1768, one of the most lucrative jobs in England. He began by altering MISTLEY HALL, making the grounds picturesque in the fashionable landscape style, building Gothic and Chinese temples, bridges, etc.; *Horace Walpole* was a visitor and lent a hand, reporting great improvements by 1750. About 1774 Rigby called in *Robert Adam*. His unexecuted design for a magnificent saltwater bath by the river is in the Soane Museum. It is not certain whether his designs for the dining and drawing rooms of the Hall were carried out, but his suite of entrance lodges and gates of 1782 were. Only one LODGE survives (at the crossing of the Colchester–Mistley and Manningtree–Clacton Roads), a small, square single-storey building of white brick with stone dressings. HOPPING BRIDGE on the Manningtree–Mistley road is also by Adam, but only the S side remains unmutilated, a single span of red and yellow brick with stone dressings. Rigby died in 1788, leaving 'near half a million of public money'. In 1844 the property was sold and the Hall demolished. The STABLE BLOCK survives, red brick with gault brick on the N front facing the house, and, to the S, DAIRY HOUSE, farmhouse and associated buildings of *c.* 1777. Much of the park retains its character, despite the railway driven through the upper part in 1854.

MISTLEY HALL, Clacton Road (Acorn Village residential home). Built 1846 next to Richard Rigby's kitchen garden, some of whose walls still stand. Brick, all but the s front stuccoed and ashlar-lined. Three-bay entrance (E) front, the central bay breaking forward with pediment and porch enclosing steps up to front door. Outbuilding on w side flint-faced with brick quoins and decorative arches in white brick and clinker. SE, an ornamental TUNNEL, its walls lined with flint, clinker and coloured glass waste.

VILLAGE. Most of the buildings were erected by Richard Rigby II. The centrepiece is FOUNTAIN SQUARE, with FOUNTAIN HOUSE, THE GRAPE VINE and GRAPE VINE COTTAGE on the N side, originally four cottages: nine bays wide with a partly projecting circular porch on Tuscan columns, a blind Diocletian window above it, and three-bay pediment. By *Adam*, 1779, as is the round POND in the middle of the square on which appears to float a swan, water flowing from its beak. The row of cottages on the High Street's N side w of Fountain Square, and all but the westernmost house on the s side including the THORN HOTEL, are of about the same time, the grandest being Acacia House on the corner of The Green, with Greek Doric porch. On the N side of THE GREEN, a row of twelve cottages, possibly built by Rigby as almshouses, c. 1778: brick with gault brick dentilled eaves, central band and pilasters. EAST LODGE on the s side is mainly C18, probably also for Rigby, and has a grotto room lined with shells, flints, slag and glass.

At the far w end of the High Street stood the new CHURCH, a plain brick rectangle consecrated in 1735. To this *Adam* added in 1776 square towers at each end, and porticoes with two pairs of Tuscan columns each on the two long sides. The result was extremely original and far from religious-looking. The towers were adorned with free-standing Tuscan columns, each with a piece of projecting entablature on top, as if they were angle buttresses gone classical. Above the entablature was a square storey with four pediments, and then a slim circular drum with attached Ionic columns and a crowning dome. The duplication of the towers so far distant from each other was not aesthetically wholly successful. The intervening nave prevented them from being seen as one, and today that is even more difficult, since the two towers alone survive (known as MISTLEY TOWERS). The nave was pulled down in 1870 following the construction of St Mary (*see* above), and the portico columns were reused to continue the motif of the buttressing by columns on the sides where formerly the nave stood. This buttressing motif, even if derived from Roman precedent, is handled very daringly, and no doubt impressed Sir John Soane a great deal. Restored by *Raymond Erith*, 1955–6.

Opposite Mistley Towers, on the road to the C19 church, the NORMAN MEMORIAL HALL by *W. D. Caröe*, 1911. Brick and roughcast, the side windows set in deep arched recesses as if between buttresses. In NEW ROAD, s of the church, a row of villas of c. 1840, notably DORSET HOUSE, with gault brick front, three bays divided by Ionic pilasters and porch.

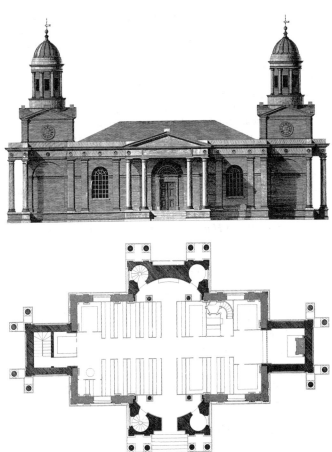

Mistley Towers.
The church as remodelled by Robert Adam, 1776

Back in the High Street, E of Fountain Square, the C19 takes over, principally in the shape of a group of MALTINGS built 1896–1904 for Free, Rodwell & Co., and incorporating many of the technological innovations of *Robert Free*. Only No. 2, on the S side of the High Street, remains in use. No. 1, on the quayside, is partly converted to residential and commercial units. Up to eight storeys, brick with stock brick pilasters, arches, etc., and ironwork by *J.R.M. Fitch* of Lawford Ironworks. Nos. 3 and 4 to the SE in School Lane (now flats) also of red and white brick, with terracotta panels of sunflowers. No. 7, demolished following a fire in 1995, was said to be the tallest maltings in the country.

Amongst the maltings, the attractive RAILWAY STATION, *c.* 1854, probably by *F. Barnes*. Brick with stock brick dressings, two pedimented gables facing the street. In School Lane, the former NORMAN SCHOOLS by Barnes, 1856, extended by *Baker & May*, 1899, an expensive job of grey brick with round-headed windows. Of the C19 housing that makes up most of New Mistley E of the railway, a conspicuous example is ALMA HOUSE, three bays, three storeys, stock brick with rusticated quoins, Tuscan porch, and the name proudly emblazoned.

FURZE HILL BUNKER, Shrubland Road, ½ m. SE. Anti-aircraft operations room, 1951, from 1963 the county's Emergency Headquarters. Decommissioned in 1993. Two-storey semi-sunken structure of reinforced concrete.

ST JOHN, Horsley Cross Street, 2 m. S, by *Charles Buckeridge*, 1862–3, a simple chapel and school of red and black brick with circular apse admired by *The Ecclesiologist*; converted to a house by *Basil & David Hatcher*, *c.* 1972, and much altered.

MORETON

ST MARY THE VIRGIN. Early C13 nave and chancel with lancets, of flint rubble with limestone and clunch dressings. Brick W tower, rebuilt 1787, with diagonal buttresses and battlements and short recessed spire. Interior restored 1864–9, in part at least by *Chancellor*, which was perhaps when the N vestry was added; many of the windows renewed later in the century. Chancel roof tree-ring dated 1510–38, but restoration of the nave ceiling in 2002 showed the timbers behind it to be original C13. Fragments of WALL PAINTING of that date, mainly red and of a foliate or leaf-scroll pattern, at eaves level. – FONT. Square, of Purbeck marble, *c.* 1200. On one side the familiar row of shallow blank round arches, four in number, on two sides fleurs-de-lys, and on the fourth sun, moon, and a whorl. – PULPIT. 1868–9, incorporating moulded top rail and carved panels of *c.* 1600. Hexagonal. – PAINTING. C18 copy of La Madonna del Divino Amore by *Giovanni Francesco Penni*. – STAINED GLASS. Chancel S, Good Shepherd, *c.* 1891. Nave S by *G. Maile & Son*, 1945.

Former RECTORY, SW of the church. Painted seven-bay Georgian front with pedimented doorcase, but mainly C17 with a massive brick chimneystack at the S end.

The centre of the village, 300 yds W of the church, is very attractive in an unassuming way: the road from the S crosses Cripsey Brook by a narrow C18 brick bridge and curves gently up to a T-junction. One building in particular stands out: BLACK HALL, with exposed timbers and a gabled cross-wing at the N end jettied on two sides. The S cross-wing no longer survives but the hall (horizontally subdivided in the C16) still has two openings into the former screens passage and a roof truss with tie-beams on arched braces and moulded crown-post. Said to have been the meeting place of the Guild of All Saints, founded 1473.

LITTLE ROOTHING, ½ m. NE. By *Edward Maufe*, 1923. Large but cottage-like house, two storeys with half-hipped roof with gablets that comes down to ground-floor level either side of a two-storey porch on the N side, and terrace on the S. Roughcast walls, metal windows, and two groups of tall brick chimneystacks with diagonal shafts.

MOUNT BURES

9030

On a hill overlooking Bures and the River Stour. The Normans built a CASTLE here, of which the mound survives, 200 ft (62 metres) across and *c.* 35 ft (11 metres) high. This lies N of the church, the bailey to the W.

ST JOHN THE BAPTIST. With crossing tower, no doubt explained by the connection with the castle. But the present tower, with its shingled splay-foot spire, is a rebuilding of 1875 by *Thomas Harris*, who added the short transepts and N vestry. Further restorations in 1908 and 1936. Otherwise all is Norman, mainly of flint rubble. The Roman quoins of the old part can easily be distinguished from the new bricks. Norman windows (with Roman brick dressings) high up in the W wall (reticulated C14 window below), in the S wall, blocked, and in the N wall, where there is also a plain Norman doorway. S porch Perp, brick and flint, with three-light windows and a stone doorway with decorated spandrels. – PISCINA. Two octofoiled drains, C13 or C14, in C19 recess. – SCULPTURE. St John the Baptist by *David Dobson*, 1959.

IRON AGE BURIAL. In 1849 the tomb of a British nobleman was found SE of the mound, near the railway. It consisted of a triangular vault, each side 7 ft (2.1 metres) long. The finds, dated to just before or just after the Roman conquest, included iron firedogs, amphorae, a glass bottle, and Gallo-Belgic platters. Excavation of an Iron Age ditch in the same area in 1984 failed to reveal the burial's precise location.

MOUNTNESSING

6090

ST GILES makes a handsome picture alongside MOUNTNESSING HALL, late C16 with an C18 brick façade of seven windows (and another false one). The main interest of the church is its C15 belfry standing as an independent timber structure in the nave's W bay. It has six posts, cross-beams supported by impressively tall arched braces, and trellis-strutting higher up. The E pair of braces rest on polygonal responds with concave sides. Big buttressing struts in the aisles of the church. The church itself is basically C13, of mixed rubble, but only the N aisle is in anything like its original state. The N and S arcades have circular piers and double-chamfered arches. Moulded capitals, except for one capital and one respond on the N side which are enriched by stiff-leaf and a grotesque head; lancets in N wall. Brick W front with a date-plate of 1653 set in a frame with open pediment, six buttresses, and heavy S-cramps for securing the belfry timbers. Brick chancel of 1805. S aisle rebuilt as part of a thorough restoration by *Bodley & Garner*, 1889–90, extended E to form organ chamber and vestry 1890–1. S porch rebuilt 1912–13, small N extension by *Gerald W. Barrett*, 2002. – COMMUNION RAIL. Early C18, with fine twisted balusters. – PULPIT. By *Bodley & Garner*, with sounding board. – FONT. Octagonal, with carvings of fishes, flowers and other devices; late C15, from All Saints, Hutton. Pedestal and COVER by *Bodley & Garner*. – ORGAN CASE. Also by *Bodley & Garner*, 1891. – PICTURE. On E wall, Moses and Aaron. Formerly part of a reredos, 1726, from St Martin, Little Waltham, installed here 1888. – CHEST. Of dug-out type; perhaps C13. – STAINED GLASS. E window by *James Powell & Sons*, 1869, designed by *Holiday*. N aisle by *Kempe*, 1891. – MONUMENTS. Edmund Pert †1676. White marble, with achievement of arms and drapery, erected by 'the disconsolate widdow'.

ST JOHN, Church Road. Mission church, now church hall. Corrugated iron, 1873, by *Samuel C. Hemming & Co.*; transepts added 1887, and W porch 1895, by *John Cross*, builder, of Hutton.

THOBY PRIORY, 2 m. NW. Founded for Augustinian Canons in the first half of the C12 and dissolved 1525. Only fragments remain of the early C14 building, part of the S wall of the presbytery and S nave arcade.

BACONS FARM, 1 m. N. Moated farmhouse, early C19 brick, incorporating an early C17 timber-framed building. Pair of mid-C19 estate cottages to the E, brick with stock brick dressings and elaborate metal casements.

TILEHURST, 1 m. N. For Sebastian Petre, *c.* 1884, with minor alterations in 1904. Unmistakably the work of *George Sherrin*, his grandest house in the neighbourhood, and the closest he came to designing a full-blown country house, although the language is still suburban. Sprawling composition, facing W across the valley; two storeys with attics and at one side of the main block a square tower with belvedere. Brick with limestone dressings; a variety of gables with false timber-framing each in a different regional style, oriels with brick-nogging, and a timber gallery on the garden side. Original features, including staircase, on the ground floor, but otherwise considerably altered inside. Stables and cottage adjoining to the S, with separate lodge and elaborate wrought-iron gates to the N. Walled kitchen garden.

WINDMILL, 1½ m. NW. Post mill, 1807, on sixteen-sided brick roundhouse. Restored by *Vincent Pargeter*, County Millwright, 1979–83, and in full working order.

MOYNS PARK*

Moyns is one of several manors within the parish of Steeple
Bumpstead, established by 1086. Part of the moat remains,
probably C13 or C14, but the present house dates from the C16.
It is U-plan, and behind the late C16 main façade, which faces
NW, lie two lower and older wings. The delightful SW WING is
the earlier and dates from 1537–40, half-timbered with brick
infillings, jettied upper storey, and three gables of which the S
one (part of the cross-wing added to the S end of this range
c. 1552) is higher and broader than the others. The SW wing
was probably an extension to a small earlier house on the site
of the present NW range, but of this nothing survives, because
about 1575–80 Sir Thomas Gent, a Baron of the Exchequer
and Steward of the lands of the Earl of Oxford, began an ambitious rebuilding. First he extended and reconstructed the SW
range towards the NW, to provide some coherence to what had
previously been an accretion of lodgings, with a small gallery
overlooking the garden to the SW. On the other side of the
courtyard he built the NE RANGE with long gallery at first-floor
level; this was completed by his son Henry, c. 1605–25, by the
construction of the outer block of rooms facing NE.

Thomas's main achievement, however, was the construction
of the principal NW RANGE, which towers over the two wings.
Tree-ring dating shows that the roof timbers for this were felled
in 1591 and 1592, and work was halted by Thomas's death in
1593, leaving the W end unfinished (this is structurally separate and is tree-ring dated to c. 1606) and the interiors as bare
shells. The seven-bay façade is of brick with stone dressings
and represents an unusual type, with big gables near each end,
two smaller ones in between, and three bay windows between
the gables instead of below them. The outer two bay windows
are polygonal, the centre one starts rectangular to hold the
porch but is also continued polygonal above. The ground floor
has two-transomed windows; the bay windows continue these
on the upper floor as well. At the back of the façade and dominating its appearance from a distance are tall chimneystacks
with polygonal shafts, that on the l. replaced, probably in the
1820s. The ground floor was intended to provide a great hall
entered through the main door in the centre of the NW range,
with the hall to the r. of the screens passage and service rooms
and kitchen to the l.; on the first floor the best apartment, with
great chamber over the hall; and on the top floor, a long gallery,
once subdivided but now opened up again.

Some remodelling of the INTERIOR took place in the early
C18. Two rooms at the end of the NW range were panelled, with
a drawing room at the W end beyond the original hall, and the
main stair (the original position of which is uncertain) was
built or rebuilt; little of this survives as it was again rebuilt
c. 1910. More radical alterations were made for George William

*I am grateful to Paul Drury for much new information included in this account.

Gent in the 1820s: he created a dining room and library at the E end of the main block in place of the kitchen and other service rooms, which were moved to the NE range, and at the other end added to the drawing room a bay window with Neo-Tudor details in Roman Cement; on this side of the house he made a walled garden next to the forecourt.* The house remained in the Gent family until 1879. After use as a military hospital during the Second World War significant internal alterations were made by *Michael Tapper* for Ivor Bryce, 1956–8, principally the subdivision of the first floor to provide bedrooms and bathrooms; also extensive outbuildings in a curiously Hollywood-Hispanic style for Bryce's stud farm.

C19 LODGES to the E of the house, at Birdbrook, and SE; the latter, Pheasant Lodge, is the prettier. It has a two-storey central porch and pargetted decoration above the windows and incorporates older carved timbers.

MUCKING
Thurrock U.A.

(ST JOHN THE BAPTIST.† W tower, nave, chancel, S aisle, and S chapel of Kentish rag. Almost entirely rebuilt by *J. H. Banson*, 1849–52, except for the chancel, which was restored by *J. A. Hunt*. Perp three-light E window, and blocked C13 arcade to a former N chapel, whose lancets, when it was pulled down, were reused. The arch to the S chapel is C15 and the S aisle has a C13 two-bay arcade with treble-chamfered arches. The pier is circular and has a big stiff-leaf capital, with two faces between the leaves. One is a so-called Green Man, that is a face with leaves sprouting from his mouth. The S doorway to the tower, which serves as a porch, has recognizable C15 parts. Plain SEDILIA in the chancel. – STAINED GLASS. E window and two others by *Percy Bacon*. – MONUMENT. Graceful little alabaster monument of Elizabeth Downes †1607, with kneeling figure between ornamented pilasters.)

In the churchyard's SE corner is the former SCHOOL, 1855. Stone, Perp, and small.

ST CLERE'S HALL, ¾ m. NW (golf clubhouse). C17, remodelled and enlarged for James Adams in 1735, when it was known as New Jenkins. Adams (whose monument is in the churchyard at Stanford-le-Hope) was Clerk of the Stables to King George II, 1727–60, and the character of the house suggests that he employed designers and craftsmen from Court circles. On the E side a timber-framed and plastered wing, a remnant of the original house. The main house of chequered brick, five bays, two storeys with attics, and crenellated parapet. Doorway

---

* *Thomas Willement* was working at the house in 1823 and there is stained glass in St Mary, Steeple Bumpstead (q.v.) which was made for the dining room at Moyns.
† In the process of being converted to a house in 2002–5; no access possible.

altered, with large keystone and single urn, formerly three. The
back of the house much more fanciful, with a projecting canted
bay flanked by stair towers and single-storey wings, all crenellated. The wings have blind round windows above the sashes.
The Entrance Hall is separated from the room with the bay by
a wooden screen that can be raised like a portcullis to make
one large room. The Hall and another smaller ground-floor
room, as well as the main first-floor room, have painted panels
above the doors depicting pastoral idylls, landscapes and
seascapes, one after Watteau's 'The Island of Cythera'. The
overmantel in the upper room depicts the goddess Diana
bathing.

NORTH RING, about ½ m. w. Site of a circular Bronze Age
enclosure (*c.* 900 B.C.), 125 ft (38 metres) in diameter, excavated in 1978 (since destroyed). Evidence of a central round
building and other round and rectangular buildings.

MUNDON

8000

ST MARY. Nave, chancel, and low timber w tower. The latter
early C16 and remarkable in design, with a square centre and
N, S, and W aisles, the W aisle connected by triangular pieces
to N and S aisles (cf. Navestock). The aisle roofs are tiled and
start about 8 ft (2.5 metres) from the ground. The square upper
part is boarded. The nave, of plastered rubble, has an early C14
N window with Y-tracery. On the S side a brick window and a
blocked archway into a (demolished) chapel must be early C16.
The brick chancel, with original E and N windows, is early C18.
Timber N porch, *c.* 1600, with pendants hanging from the
lower eaves ends of the gable and carving in the spandrels, considered by Cecil Hewett the finest of its kind in Essex. Redundant since 1970 and leased to the Friends of Friendless
Churches in 1975, for whom it was repaired by *Laurence King*,
and *Julian Limentani* of *Marshall Sisson*. The humble, decayed
interior has great charm, with C18 BOX PEWS and PULPIT, C19
CHOIR STALLS and simple ROOD SCREEN, and remains of C18
WALL PAINTING, notably in the chancel (Creed, Commandments and Lord's Prayer in *trompe l'œil* panels and, above the
E window, billowing curtains).

WHITE GATE FARM, Vicarage Lane, ½ m. WNW. By *Chancellor*,
1866, as the vicarage. Brick, and rather gaunt, especially now
that it is painted.

WHITE HOUSE, ¾ m. NNW. Mid C17, prettily restored by *Mr
Jennings*, 1935–9. Exposed timbers on S front, the main five-
bay portion with jettied upper storey and a massive chimneystack to the r., and beyond it a slightly lower three-bay
in-line kitchen. 1930s porch with crowstepped gable, using old
bricks. Moulded and deeply carved beams inside.

Running NE from White House to the Blackwater Estuary the
remains of a private CANAL, with sea lock at the far end, built
1832 for J. Marriage.

NAVESTOCK

St Thomas the Apostle. Nave N wall with plain Norman doorway; s aisle, s chapel, and s arcade E.E. Circular piers and double-chamfered arches of wood plastered and whitewashed in imitation of stone. This can be seen at the E end, where the plaster has been removed, also from the four arches that spring from the last pier to N, S, E, and W. How many other 'stone' arcades in Essex churches are in fact timber? One blocked lancet in the s chapel, one long lancet in the s aisle. Early C14 chancel with Dec windows – the E of three lights with reticulated tracery. In the nave N wall at its E end a wide recess, E.E., with a shaft on the l. carrying a stiff-leaf capital. Probably in the C15 a s porch was added, rebuilt 1955. Restored by *Chancellor* with a light hand, 1895–1904, including renewal of windows, new choir stalls and chancel paving, and restoration of the church's most remarkable feature, its timber tower. This stands to the W not of the nave but of the aisle. It is oblong and has N and S aisles and in addition a W aisle connected with the others by triangular pieces (cf. Mundon). The tower is carried on four heavy posts that rise directly from the ground, which requires unusually long timbers; each with an octagonal shaft attached diagonally towards the centre. These shafts carry rib-like arched braces meeting in the middle in a foliage boss. Tree-ring dated 1365–91. Walls of tower and church rendered, with weatherboarded belfry and shingled splay-foot spire. – Pulpit. 1966. Made by *John Enkel*, designed and with carving by *Gwynneth Holt*. – Good ironwork on three Doors: N, four straps, *c.* 1100, s and chancel s, ornamental strap hinges, C13. – Organ. Mid C19, from Lord Southwood's house at Highgate, London.

Monuments. Mainly to the Waldegrave family, whose vault lies outside the N wall of the chancel, and singularly modest. 1st and 2nd Earls †1741 and 1763, very large, but all inscription and minimal decoration, by *John Dixon*. – William Lord Radstock †1797 by *William Behnes* with profile head. – Edward Waldegrave †1809, shipwrecked returning from the Battle of Corunna, by *John Bacon Jun*. Prostrate weeping female and a triumphant cherub on the back of a lion higher up. – 6th Earl †1835 by *E. Gaffin*. Sarcophagus. – 7th Earl †1846, with bust by *Behnes*. – Viscount Chewton †1854, wounded in the Battle of Alma and died at Scutari. Bas-relief bust by *M. Noble*. – Also Ann Snelling †1625. Tiny reclining marble figure with tinier baby in her arms. – John Greene of Bois Hall †1653. Frontal demi-figure, painted, in judge's robes, flanked by Corinthian pilasters supporting an entablature and broken pediment with ten painted shields. Attributed to *Joshua Marshall* (AW). – Rev. James Ford †1850 by *Samuel Manning Jun*. Elaborate C15-style surround, like a miniature Gothic Revival chimneypiece.

Navestock Hall. The manor was sold to Sir Edward Waldegrave in 1553 and it remained in the family until 1898.

The 1st Earl built a large house about ¼ m. NE of the church, dem. 1811. Grounds remodelled by *Capability Brown* from 1763, including Lady's Pond, which survives NE of the church. C19 ICE HOUSE on N side of churchyard. The present HALL, SE of the church, is early C16 with exposed timber framing and a rainwater head dated 1767 on the S front, but extensively rebuilt following bomb damage in 1940. NW of the house a medieval BARN, and beyond it a square GRANARY, C15 or C16 but rebuilt 1788, according to a carved inscription.

BOIS HALL, 1 m. E. Five- by five-bay block, formerly with rain-water heads dated 1687, and extensively altered in 1953 and 1974–9. Two-storeyed with parapet. Tuscan porch.

DUDBROOK, 1¼ m. E. Probably mid C18 but considerably altered in the C19, including work by *George Devey* for Lady Waldegrave and Lord Carlingford, 1875–8. Painted, of irregular plan with a vaguely Italianate character including a small tower at the centre. Now a residential home.

The village consists of a number of scattered settlements, principally Navestock Heath, Navestock Side (the main centre of population), and Horseman Side. On the N side of NAVESTOCK HEATH, ¾ m. SSE, MARLEY'S (former rectory), 1867: large, three-storey red brick house with yellow and black brick decoration and stone porch. Diagonally across the Heath, LOFT HALL, late C18 brick.

At HORSEMAN SIDE, 1½ m. SSW, an attractive row of houses and cottages including HOUGHTONS, Late Medieval with exposed timbers, and an unusually large PUDDING-STONE, over 6 ft. (2 metres) high, found locally, erected to commemorate the Millennium, 2000.

More nice houses at NAVESTOCK SIDE, 1½ m. SE, and at the corner of Princes Road THE BLACK MILL, now a house, built as a steam mill *c.* 1860–70. Very striking, with black weather-boarding, slate roof, projecting gabled hoist loft, spikes and ornamental bargeboards, and an elaborate wrought-iron weathervane. Two and three storeys and attics, but seeming much taller. On the opposite corner, THE FORGE, early C16 house with cross-wing at E end, rebuilt in the C17 with forge added in the C19.

NAZEING

4000

ALL SAINTS. Norman nave with rere-arch of one window. Flint rubble, partly rendered. C15 N aisle with arcade piers of the familiar four-shaft-four-hollow type where capitals are introduced only for the shafts. Wave-moulded arches. Timber S porch also C15. Its floor is made of tiles set closely on end. Brick W tower with blue diapers, diagonal buttresses, battlements, and higher stair-turret; early C16 or possible C15 (cf. Nether Hall, Roydon). Restored and re-seated by *John Bentley* of Waltham Abbey, 1873–4; further restoration, including new chancel arch, N vestry and organ chamber, by *W.F. Lyon*,

1890–1. N extension (Pilgrim Room) by *L. Jones*, 1999. – FONT. Perp, octagonal, with quatrefoils carrying shields. The stem is earlier, perhaps Norman. – CHEST. Oblong, with flat lid, heavily iron-bound; ascribed to the C14. – SEATING. C15 bench with poppyheads. Also two early C16 bench ends, with poppyheads carved with faces, incorporated in a screen. – STAINED GLASS. E window †1858 by *Clayton & Bell*, nave S lancet by *T. Willement*, 1854. – Nave S by *G. Maile & Son*, 1952. – N aisle by *Goddard & Gibbs*, designed by *Peter Cormack*, 2006. – MONUMENT. James Bury †1825 by *T. Harling*. The usual female figure by an urn. His very large tomb, with railings, is beside the S porch.

NAZEING PARK, ⅔ m. S. *James Lewis* published his design for additions in 1797, although this was modified in execution. Stock brick, mainly stuccoed. Four-bay centre of three storeys with two-storey Ionic colonnade, flanked by two-storey canted bays. Contemporary stable block to the N, stock brick with two-bay pediment and domed cupola.

GREENLEAVES, 1 m. WSW. Early C15 hall house with two jettied and gabled cross-wings, part weatherboarded and part plastered. Contemporary weatherboarded barn behind the house, four bays with hipped two-bay midstrey and queenpost roof.

NEWPORT

ST MARY THE VIRGIN. Big church, formerly collegiate, mainly of flint and pebble rubble. It lies back, away from the main road. Its chief accent is the W tower, with embattled polygonal turrets, rebuilt by *G.E. Pritchett*, 1856–8. Restoration of the nave followed in 1858–60, apparently under the supervision of the clerk of works, *Mr Whitehead*, the chancel in 1911. The church has a crossing and transepts, dating from the C13, as is shown by the forms of the arches separating them (responds with nailhead ornament) and the two N and one (blocked) S lancets. The chancel is wide and not too high and in its masonry also C13. S arcade early C14 with octagonal piers and double-chamfered two-centred arches. To the same time belongs the S aisle W window. N arcade Early Perp with sturdy quatrefoil piers with hollows in the diagonals, slightly decorated capitals, and double-wave-moulded arches. Two-storey S porch and nave clerestory, C15, the latter rebuilt 1859–60. Chancel clerestory brick, later C16.

FONT. Octagonal, with heavy gabled trefoil arches, an unusual design, probably early C13. Restored and given new base in 1860. – FONT COVER. Oak, C15. Central post with four crocketed supports. – ALTAR. C19, with three C16 German or Flemish reliefs. – Fragments of a C15 SCREEN, with six-light divisions with broad panel tracery, restored 1860. – LECTERN. Oak, also C15, with octagonal base and stem, tracery panels, and tracery in the triangle between the top book-rests. – PULPIT. Stone and marble, large and elaborate, by *Teulon*,

1860. – ALTAR CHEST. A portable altar, an extremely interesting later C13 piece. The lid of the chest, when raised, forms the reredos, with paintings inside of the Crucifixion, the Virgin, St John, St Peter, and St Paul, each within a cusped arch – very early examples of oil painting on wood. The front has three friezes of ornament, circles, shields, and lozenges, the latter filled with C19 copies of ornament cast in pewter. – STALLS. 1860, reusing some C16 poppyheads. Not *in situ*. – STAINED GLASS. In N transept, two lancets with C13 and C14 glass, with several whole figures (St Katherine, St Michael). Rearranged and fixed by *Heaton, Butler & Bayne*, 1894. By the same firm, chancel N †1909, and probably also two windows at the S aisle's W end, and one in N aisle, *c.* 1887–91. – Chancel S, three windows by *Lavers, Barraud & Westlake*, 1870s. – S transept E †1887 by *Clayton & Bell*. – MONUMENTS. Brasses of Thomas Brond †1515 in civilian dress, and wife Margery, with children, the larger figures about 19 in. (48 cm.). – Katherine Nightingale †1608 and her husband Geoffrey, in civilian dress, the larger figure 27 in. (68 cm.). – Dame Grace Brograve †1704, wife of Giles Dent, builder of Shortgrove Hall, †1712, erected after his death. White marble. Inscription on *trompe l'œil* drapery, shields above, skulls below, resting on a winged cherub's head. – Joseph Smith of Shortgrove Hall †1822. By *Henry Westmacott*. Draped urn and lengthy inscription.

GRAMMAR SCHOOL. Founded by Joyce Frankland, 1588. The original school building was rebuilt in 1836–9 (*see* Church House, below). In 1875–8 the school moved to a new site on the northern edge of the village, the architect being *W.E. Nesfield*, who had recently been working in Saffron Walden. Highly picturesque, like a small-scale Oxbridge college in the style of a C17 manor house. Brick. Built round a courtyard with covered inner walkway, like a cloister, the entrance on the E side in the middle of what was originally a screen wall. Opposite the entrance the dining hall (now classroom), with dormitory above lit by two large dormers with shaped gables. Coved eaves. On the N side the original schoolroom, now part of the library. On the S side, the Headmaster's House (now offices), differentiated on the sides away from the courtyard by having panel pargetting on the first floor and, on the S front, a three-storey porch with double overhang. Modest and sympathetic additions by *G.E. Pritchett*, 1896, *James S. Cooper*, 1911–12, and *H.II. Dunn*, 1913. More radical alterations by *W.J. Kieffer*, 1919–21, included extending the schoolroom to form a Memorial Hall. In 1926–7 the *County Architect's Dept* remodelled the entrance to the courtyard by adding a single-storey block on the W side, in line with the Memorial Hall.

Post-war additions include free-standing boxy brick Assembly Hall E of the old school, 1957–8, by *Clifford E. Culpin* with *H. Conolly*, County Architect, extended 1990; music suite to its S, single-storey with pitched roof, by *A.P.G. Borley*, 1988, extended by *The Kenneth Mark Practice*, 2004; classrooms by *Culpin* along Bury Water Lane, 1958–9, predominantly large windows with some brick cladding, joined to 'B' block, 1997, by *Lyster Grillet & Harding*, which echoes aspects of Nesfield's building. Buildings N of Bury Water Lane include 'E' block, 1977, by the *County Architect's Dept* (project architects, *D. Webber* and *C.P. French*), a good example of the concrete panel system which was then the standard for Essex school buildings; and Sixth Form Centre, 1998, and sports hall, 2002, by *Lyster Grillet & Harding*.

SHORTGROVE HALL, ¾ m. NE The old house, rebuilt by Giles Dent in 1684, was gutted by fire in 1966. Its replacement, by *Cowper Griffith Associates*, 2000–1, is much smaller, but its form is derived from the original and it incorporates parts of the C17 cellars and N wall with niche. Brick, two storeys and attics, and hipped roof, with corner pavilions and a portico *in antis* with square columns. Heavy cornice. Five wide windows, widely spaced. Two-storey garage with pyramid roof. The house holds its own in its setting, for behind it looms the C18 brick STABLE BLOCK, converted to housing by *Biscoe & Stanton*, 1975. Two storeys, with clock tower and open cupola topped with a dome over the central archway, now blocked. Eleven bays, the outer bays and the central, pedimented bay stepping slightly forward. *Matthew Brettingham*, father and son, were working at the house between 1758 and 1769, and this may be part of their improvements. It stands on the E side of a large yard, with formal gardens behind it laid out in the mid C19 by *William Chater* in the C18 walled kitchen garden. N of the yard, a square brick DOVECOTE, also C18. The grounds round the main house (with ha-ha) and the park were laid out by *Capability Brown*, commissioned by Percy Wyndham, later Earl of Thomond, in 1753. A series of boundary plantations survive, including Temple Plantation on the W, which led to a temple by Brettingham (dem.). Just inside the W entrance to the park, a three-arched stone BRIDGE by *Brettingham* over the River Cam, *c.* 1758–62. Gateway with brick piers and stone caps with urns and elaborate wrought-iron gates with overthrow perhaps also by Brettingham.

VILLAGE

Newport was once a market town on the main road to Cambridge, and this gives it a dignity not usually found in a place of such relatively small size. The best buildings lie along the main road, but the area round the church has great charm. On the churchyard's S side, CHURCH HOUSE, 1836–9 by *William Ward*, a rebuilding of the original Grammar School (*see* above), now parish rooms. Brick, with ornamental bargeboards, two oriel windows and hoodmoulds. Beyond it PARSONAGE HOUSE (former vicarage). Mid-C19 brick with tall ornamental chimneys. In WICKEN ROAD, opposite the approach to the church, GOODRICKS and GOODRICKS COTTAGE with long-wall jetty, C16 or C17, next to BRIGHTON COTTAGE, early C19 with Gothick glazing. On the E side of the churchyard, in CHURCH

STREET, a picturesque row of timber-framed cottages. Beside them the street runs N into ELEPHANT GREEN, a triangular space with nice buildings on all sides, including ROOKES HOUSE, Georgian brick, three bays, two storeys with attics, parapet and mansard roof. At the N end of the Green BELMONT FARMHOUSE, late C17 with a Georgian brick front, the main five-bay block with parapet and stucco dentilled cornice.

This brings us to BELMONT HILL, the continuation northwards of the High Street. On the E side a row of timber-framed houses, notably No. 7, with exposed timbers and jettied upper storey. Then THE LINKS, built as the House of Correction, now flats. 1774–5, the design approved but probably not by *William Hillyer*, County Surveyor. Five-bay stock brick front with rusticated quoins and round-headed windows. Central three bays breaking slightly forward, with stone panel in the pediment carved with fetters. Red brick behind, with rear wings forming a half-H. Opposite, the TOLL HOUSE, early C19 timber-framed and plastered, with painted notice of tolls payable for the bridge.

N of this the main road splits from the old road, which (as BRIDGE END) runs to the r., bisected by the railway viaduct. Just before the viaduct, on the W side, THE OLD PRIORY, C15, the upper storey mainly jettied. After the viaduct, a most attractive row leads to CROWN HOUSE, one of Newport's two outstanding houses. Late C16 or early C17, pargetted with gar-lands, swags, and large leafy branches in 1692, when also the inviting big shell-hood was added. Beyond it to the N TUDOR HOUSE, C15, with exposed timbers on the jettied upper storey and on both storeys of the jettied solar cross-wing at the N end. C16 chimneystack of four shafts with moulded bricks and spurred caps.

The GREAT or LEPER STONE, ¼ m. further N, is a large glacial erratic. It stands near the site of the medieval Hospital of St Mary and St Leonard, stones from which (including C13 half-octofoil responds) are built into the wall behind.

Now it is necessary to retrace one's steps up Belmont Hill to the straight and wide HIGH STREET. On the W side, S of Wicken Road, THE OLD FORGE, C16 or C17 with timbers exposed on the jettied upper storey, and cart entrance at the N end of the ground floor. On the same side, further S, NEWPORT HOUSE, Georgian brick of five bays and two storeys and attics, with a good pedimented Tuscan doorcase. This is opposite Newport's other outstanding house, MONK'S BARN. Exposed timbers and brick-nogging. The earliest part on the l., late C15 or early C16, on the jettied upper floor of which is an oriel (renewed), its coving carved (badly) with a demi-figure of the Virgin and Child and two ministering angels. Then a two-bay hall, early C16, set slightly back but with a new single roof over both portions. The wing to the r. is later C16, with jettied upper storey to balance the original, but a lower roof, giving the front the form of a Wealden house, but without the continuous roof-line.

On the same side of the High Street, s of Debden Road, the OLD VICARAGE, early C16 with cross-wings, both jettied and gabled and with exposed timbers, and then THE GEORGIANS, C18 brick. Three-bay, two-storey front, with brick pilasters at either end, and two two-storey canted bays. Square oriel over central doorway. Back on the w side, THE WHITE HOUSE, C18 timber-framed and plastered, two-and-a-half storeys with a three-storey cross-wing on the r. To its l. THE OLD MANSE, C18 brick with dormers in the mansard roof. Further s, on the same side, a pair of mid-C19 cottages (PENDEAN and POND CROSS COTTAGE) presumably inspired by Monk's Barn: timber-framed, with brick nogging, jettied upper floor, ground-floor oriels, and latticed iron casements.

In STATION ROAD, off the E side of the High Street, brick industrial buildings prompted by the railway, which opened in 1845: THE NEW GRANARY, now offices, with dressings of black engineering brick, and former MALTINGS, 1853–4, with two conical kilns at one end. STATION in the standard plain Tudoresque style, with additional buildings by *W. N. Ashbee*, c. 1885.

NORTH BENFLEET

7080

ALL SAINTS. Away from the village but close to the moated site of North Benfleet Hall (dem.). Small and of little interest outside, except for one early C16 brick window (renewed) of two lights with panel tracery. The brick tower of 1903 does not betray the timber construction of the C15 belfry inside, with braces between the posts from E to W as well as from N to S. Trellis struts higher up. And this heavy timbering in turn does not betray a window of *c.* 1200 hidden in the nave's Norman w wall. Nave refaced in Kentish rag in the mid C16, the chancel rebuilt in the same material by *G.E. Street*, 1870, when the s vestry was added.*

NORTH END
Great Waltham

6010

BLACK CHAPEL. The rare survival of an entirely timber-framed ecclesiastical building, and the rare case of a medieval chapel with attached priest's house. There is no satisfactory explanation of the origin of the chapel, nor of its name. Nave and chancel in one, the house set to the w at right angles and projecting N. The house has two original windows, now blocked, and remains of the roof, but the earliest part of the structure is the C14 tie-beam in the chancel. The chapel inside looks

74

---

*Closed 1994, no access to the interior in 2004.

lovely – not in the original, but in an early C19 way. At this time the tie-beams and posts in the nave were removed (tie-beams reinstated 1975–6) and BOX PEWS constructed along the s side, with a central two-decker PULPIT flanked by Gothick casements that rise into s dormers. Tiny W GALLERY with a necessarily tiny BARREL ORGAN. N aisle and vestry added 1838, and schoolroom at the NW corner of the house, all in keeping. – SCREEN. Humble C15 work. – Four long BENCHES. Also C15, of simple design, rearranged at the beginning of the C19 to face the pulpit. – WALL PAINTING. Fragment of early C17 arcading at the foot of the stairs to the W gallery. – ROYAL ARMS. Of Queen Anne, dated 1714, over the chancel arch; Creed, Lord's Prayer and Commandments in chancel probably of the same date.

ABSOL PARK, 1 m. N. C17 timber-framed and plastered farm-house, altered in the C18, standing near the centre of a medieval deerpark acquired by Richard Rich in 1538. Project-ing two-storey gabled W porch with pedimented doorway. NE of the house is a complete moat, and to the N a C17 timber-framed eleven-bay barn.

BROOK HOUSE, ½ m. NNE. C15, with jettied front. N and s cross-wings, the s wing projecting slightly. Alterations by *David E. Nye*, 1932, when the s wing was extended westwards and a C16 barn added as an extension to the house beyond the N wing. On the chimney-breast of a ground-floor room in the s wing a wall painting of heavy scrolls and a central motif.

NORTH FAMBRIDGE 8090

HOLY TRINITY. Small, brick, with arched windows in the E and s walls, described as 'new-built' by Morant, so probably not long before the ROYAL ARMS, dated 1764. No chancel. Half-timbered narthex and vestry at W end by *Chancellor & Son*, 1912. – STAINED GLASS. E window by *D. Marion Grant*, 1964, amid the mud-flats.

s of the church, by the River Crouch, a good estuarine scene: FERRY BOAT INN and cottages, C18, timber-framed and weatherboarded.

NORTH WEALD BASSETT 4000

ST ANDREW. Mainly Dec, see the s arcade of octagonal piers with double-chamfered arches and the flowing tracery of the s chapel windows. The E window has the unmistakable hallmark of ogee reticulation, refixed when the chancel was rebuilt in 1869 by *J. T. Smith*; nave restored 1865, with vestry and organ chamber added 1888–9. Flint rubble, with Early Tudor brick W tower. Diagonal buttresses and battlements and W window of brick with Perp panel tracery. Interior reordered by *Laurence*

King & Partners, 1964–5, following a fire, with a simple, dignified chancel.* – STATIONS OF THE CROSS. By *Rev. John Pelling*, 2005. Oil on canvas. – STAINED GLASS. E window by *Francis Stephens*, 1967. – S chapel E, 1910, and tower window, 1927, by *Kempe & Co.* – C14 tabernacles in the S chapel S windows. – S aisle (by font) by *Powell & Sons*, 1957. – MONUMENTS. Brass to W. Larder †1606 and wife Marie (18½-in. (47.5-cm.) figures) with incised figures of children. – In churchyard, by NE corner of chancel, three very finely carved and well-preserved headstones: Joseph Whittingham †1793, his son Thomas †1737, and Ann Thorowgood †1749. – Small Second World War cemetery with *Blomfield*'s Cross of Sacrifice, 1953.

ALL SAINTS, Foster Street. Mission church, *c.* 1873. Cruciform, with battlemented crossing tower. Dec tracery. Disused since 1961, now a house.

The main centre of the parish has little of architectural interest apart from the KING'S HEAD pub, C15 hall house with gabled cross-wings, the hall block rebuilt in the C17. Restored 1927, when the timbers were exposed and many new ones added.

LATTON PRIORY, 2 m. WNW of St Andrew. Founded *c.* 1200 for Augustinian Canons. All that survives is the crossing of the church, now part of a barn. C14, with piers (of clunch, with capitals of a harder stone) to the main sides consisting of big semicircular shafts and very thin shafts between. Moulded arches. Short stretches of the flint-rubble walls of the transepts and nave, with blocked doorways and a blocked sexfoiled window. SE buttress of the S transept largely of brick, of the Coggeshall type, i.e. early C13. There is no certainty of the extent and plan of the monastic buildings. E of the crossing, on the site of the presbytery, a late C17 timber-framed barn, and S of the crossing a similar barn, C19. Early C18 brick farmhouse to the SW. Five bays, two storeys and attics with gambrel roof, and single-storey C19 additions.

WHITE FRIARS, E of St Andrew. 1827–9 by *C.R. Cockerell*, for his brother Henry, as the vicarage. Brick ground floor, plastered first floor, now painted. 'Elizabethan', meaning straight gables and one Tudor arch inside. Cost £1,600, which the architect thought 'very astonishing for the quantity of rooms and convenience'.

NORTH WEALD MOBILISATION CENTRE, I m. SE. The northernmost redoubt of a defensive line that ran from here to Guildford (Surrey), conceived in 1888 to counter a possible German invasion (*see* Introduction, p. 76). Semicircular earthworks surround concrete underground ammunition stores beneath artillery positions, with caretakers' quarters, 1890–3, and other storage buildings, 1903–4, above ground. Acquired by the Marconi Wireless Telegraph Co. as a radio station, 1919, now abandoned; concrete mast bases litter the surrounding fields.

---

*Chancel screen removed at this time now in St Mary, Crimplesham, Norfolk.

NORTON MANDEVILLE   5000
High Ongar

ALL SAINTS. A modest country church in coursed flint with stone dressings. Some reused C12 fragments and a small fragment of a spiral-carved Norman column with projecting moulding (part of a PILLAR PISCINA) tell of an earlier church on the site. The present nave and chancel seem C14, as does the timber belfry, which rests on a tie-beam. Restored by *Chancellor & Son*, 1902–3, who rebuilt the nave roof reusing the C14 octagonal crown-posts, and added the s porch. – FONT. Square bowl of Barnack stone, four attached shafts with moulded capitals and bases; late C12. – PULPIT. Includes some C18 mouldings. Wrought-iron HOURGLASS STAND on the wall adjacent. – SCREEN. 1903, but incorporating C15 tracery. – Six early C16 open BENCHES in the nave, very robustly carved. – STAINED GLASS. Nave N, 1895, by *Lavers, Barraud & Westlake*, as is perhaps the E window, which commemorates the Chancellors' restoration.

NORTON HALL, NW of the church. Rebuilt 1864, when the farm was sold by Merton College, Oxford, who had owned it since 1490. Norton Hall, its range of MODEL FARM BUILDINGS, and two pairs of semi-detached cottages, brick with black brick decorations and all of a piece, form an impressive ensemble; was *Chancellor* responsible?

NORTON MANOR, 1½ m. E. Three-bay house; two storeys and attics. Plastered front with three straight gables, and canted bays on the two outer bays. Behind is brick, including three massive chimneystacks, each with three octagonal shafts, the s stack dated 1613. C18 and later additions either side of the rear staircase tower.

ORSETT   6080

ST GILES AND ALL SAINTS. Norman nave – see the s doorway with primitive volute capitals, arch with zigzag, hoodmould with billet, curved lintel, and tympanum with diapers divided into triangles. In the s wall near the porch, a small round-headed window, possibly Norman. Evidence of a C13 N aisle is provided by the circular piers and one-stepped, single-chamfered arches of the arcade's first two bays. In the C14 the chancel was built and the N aisle widened. The chancel E window is of four lights with cusping and a quatrefoil in a circle on top. The s window and those of the s organ chamber are of two lights in the same style. The SEDILIA have detached shafts and moulded capitals. Of the C14 also the E part of the N arcade with piers with four demi-shafts and four hollows in the diagonals and moulded arches. Next in time comes the tower, placed at the aisle's w end in the C15 and occupying its first C13 bay. It is partly of stone and partly of C17 brick (repairs 1610 and 1678, the latter date on the parapet) and has big diagonal buttresses, a thick NW stair-turret, brick battlements, and spire

dated 1694. The Whitmore (N) Chapel dates from *c.* 1500.
Church repaired by *Robert Wallace*, 1837, after a fire, re-seated
1849, and in 1865 the transeptal S chapel, organ chamber, and
small N vestry were added by Rev. James Blomfield.* Extensively restored by *Sir Charles Nicholson* and *Edward Fincham*,
1926–7, following another fire, which destroyed the roofs.

FONT. Perp, octagonal, with buttressed stem and panels
with rosettes and shields. – PULPIT. Panelled sides in two
tiers, dated 1630 in the enriched frieze. – SCREENS. Chancel
screen by *Comper*, 1911. Screens on N and S sides of chancel
by *Nicholson*, 1927, that on the S side surmounted by a trellis
with gilded vines. – SCULPTURE. Below W window, five C18
Italian panels: Annunciation, Holy Family, Mourning of the
Dead Christ, Ascension, Pentecost. – HATCHMENTS. In the
Whitmore Chapel, a collection of thirteen, 1751–1927. –
STAINED GLASS. E window, E window of organ chamber and
S chapel W by *Wailes*, *c.* 1848–58. Chancel S by *Heaton, Butler
& Bayne* to Rev. James Blomfield †1877. Whitmore Chapel E
and western N window by *Ward & Hughes*, 1893–4, to Louisa
Margaret Emily Whitmore of Orsett Hall †1892, including
morbid portraits of her on her deathbed (with husband and
children) and as the Virgin Mary in an Annunciation scene. W
window by *Kempe & Co.*, 1922. – MONUMENTS. From
damaged brasses: 7½-in. (19-cm.) figures of children from
brass to Thomas Latham †1485; 5½-in. (14-cm.) figures of six
daughters, *c.* 1520; 9 in. (23 cm.) kneeling figure of a civilian,
c. 1535. – In Whitmore Chapel, an impressive collection of
monuments, starting with Sir John Hart †1658. Broad standing wall monument with black columns, entablature with narrower segmental pediment, and reclining figure with cheek
propped up on elbow. Attributed to *Thomas Stanton* (GF). –
Elizabeth and John Baker †1796 and 1801, monument with
small female figure with urn, above inscription plate; by *Charles
Regnart*. – Three by *Richard Westmacott*: Dame Jane Trafford
Southwell †1809, mourning female, urn, and standing angel;
Charlotte Baker †1818, figure of Hope; Richard Baker of Orsett
Hall †1827, standing wall monument with two angels, one har-
vesting corn with a sickle, the other just taking off. – In church-
yard, Captain Samuel Bonham of Orsett House †1745.
Pyramid on bulgy sarcophagus.

PRIMARY SCHOOL, School Lane. By *T. Bird* of Gravesend,
1848–50, with later additions. Tudor Gothic.

ORSETT HALL, ½ m. ENE (now a hotel). Georgian stock brick;
drawings at the house dated 1776 signed by Richard Baker (the
owner) and *Philip Kemp*. Seven bays, two storeys and attics,
with slate mansard roof. The end bays have Venetian windows
set in arched recesses on the ground floor and round-headed
windows above, with two similar bays on the l. return and
another on the r. Tuscan porch with open pedimented hood.

---

* Grandfather of Sir Reginald Blomfield.

C19 and C20 additions. Inside, C18 staircase with twisted balusters. The room in the SE corner has mid-C17 work presumably reused from the earlier house: fireplace with strapwork pilasters with terminal figures, carved figures of Hope and Charity in the overmantel, and a contemporary plaster ceiling with ribs and stylized leaf and flower motifs between.

ORSETT HOUSE, ⅓ m. w. 1740, for Captain Samuel Bonham. Brick. Five bays, two-and-a-half storeys with parapet. Pedimented doorcase with Tuscan pilasters. Now flats.

The church stands on the N side of the HIGH ROAD, just before it forms a T-junction to the E with Rectory Road, and here the village has retained its character. Opposite the church, a row of C15 and C16 timber-framed, gabled houses, part weatherboarded. Adjoining them to the E CHURCH HOUSE by *Gerald Shenstone & Partners*, *c.* 1974, a contemporary but sympathetic addition with brick ground floor and black weatherboarded first floor. In RECTORY ROAD, BIRCH COTTAGE, C15 or C16, thatched, with exposed timbers on the gabled and jettied crosswing. N along Rectory Road, on the corner of Malting Lane, CHURCH ROW, late C19 brick cottages, each bay of the long side separated by buttresses, the gable end to Rectory Road jettied with exposed timbers and a ground-floor oriel.

W of the church, on the N side of the High Road, the village pound and LOCK-UP, the latter moved to its present site in 1938. Probably early C18, with black weatherboarding. N along Pound Lane, OLD HALL FARM. Mid-C15 two-storey crosswing with exposed timbers and jettied gable. Original four-light windows. Early C17 timber-framed extension encased in C19 stock brick, as well as C19 stock brick additions. Behind, BISHOP BONNER'S PALACE, or rather the earthwork where the palace is said to have stood. Bonner was bishop of London in the reigns of Henry VIII and Mary, but the age of the earthwork is not known. It consists of a circular enclosure of 200 ft (62 metres) internal diameter with a rectangular bailey to the N. Some parts are surrounded by ditches. Large rectangular fishpond 200 yds W.

WINDMILL, Baker Street, ¾ m. WSW. Late C18 smock mill, fully restored. Adjoining early C19 stock brick steam mill converted to a house.

OSEA ISLAND

9000

Great Totham

A privately owned island in the Blackwater estuary, bought by the teetotal philanthropist F.N. Charrington (of the brewing family) in 1903. Here he built a home for inebriates, now the MANOR HOUSE, *c.* 1906, and *c.* 1910 a convalescent and holiday home for his Tower Hamlets Mission of Mile End, London. Now CHARRINGTON HOUSE (flats). Poured concrete, with Voyseyesque tapering chimneys and pebbledashed walls. Both by *P. M. Beaumont*. Most of the other buildings, including a former CHAPEL, date from the island's occupation by the Navy during the First World War; also a weatherboarded FARMHOUSE, C17 with C18 additions.

7040

OVINGTON

ST MARY THE VIRGIN. Nave and chancel in one, S porch, and W belfry resting on four rough posts inside the nave. Cross-beam on the two E posts. The windows indicate the C14 as the date for nave and chancel, the latter restored (with new E window) *c.* 1865. Walls of flint rubble, apart from stonework fragments inserted in the early C20 by the rector's wife, *Margaret Anna Brett* (cf. Tilbury-juxta-Clare).* – FONT. C12. Very large circular bowl. The base no doubt due to Mrs Brett. – MONUMENT. NE of the church, chest-tomb of Thomas Chickall of Ovington Hall †1840. Tuscan columns at the corners, but side panels with four-centred arches and foliated decoration in the spandrels. By *Charles Harding* of Ballingdon.

9090

PAGLESHAM

ST PETER. Mainly ragstone. On the N side three original Norman windows, much restored, and most of the church was rebuilt in the C15. Also in the C15 the W tower was added, with diagonal buttresses, a three-light W window with Perp panel tracery, and battlements. *Teulon* may have worked on the church *c.* 1865, but the main restoration came in 1883, when the N nave vestry and organ chamber, and S porch, were added. – PILLAR PISCINA. On E wall. Square bowl in the form of a scalloped capital, mid C12, the shaft renewed. – DOORS. In tower arch, and quite out of proportion, the inner great W doors of Westminster Abbey, removed in 1967. Late C19 or early C20. – STAINED GLASS. E and W windows *c.* 1883, not very good. – Chancel S by *William Glasby*, 1929. – MONUMENTS. On the chancel floor, a number of C17 and C18 head-stones, formerly in the churchyard. The usual displays of skulls, hourglasses etc., but better preserved than usual.

Although close to Southend, Paglesham feels remote. On the E side of the church CHURCH HALL, C17 faced in Georgian brick. Three-bay front with tripartite windows, later porch with doorway on attached Tuscan columns. Nice C18 cottages W of the church, and THE PUNCH BOWL pub, weatherboarded, its three storeys introducing a somewhat more townish scale. Between them a row rebuilt in the early 1970s, trying out some of the principles that would be enshrined in the Essex Design Guide: brick and weatherboarded ground floor, tiled roof with dormers. More weatherboarding at FINCHES AND MAULES

---

* As at Tilbury, she also painted the interior, but this has been covered over.

further on round the corner, very attractively done in an C18
way although the house dates back to the C16. By contrast
INGULFS, ½ m. WSW, built as the rectory by *Teulon*, 1861–2,
Neo-Gothic brick. Like a small country house with outbuildings, stables, cottage, etc., and picturesquely irregular, including service stair-tower with hipped roof and bellcote.

At Paglesham Eastend, 1¼ m. ESE, more weatherboarded cottages, and the C17 PLOUGH AND SAIL pub. Also CUPOLA
HOUSE (formerly Lunts), with brick façade added in 1803 to
a C17 house. Semicircular Tuscan portico, but no cupola.

PANFIELD   7020

ST MARY AND ST CHRISTOPHER. C15, mainly of flint and
pebble rubble, restored by *R.J. Withers*, 1858. He virtually
rebuilt the chancel, with five-light Perp E window, adding the
N chancel aisle (now organ chamber) and vestry. Nave
restored, and the timber W belfry given its band of quatrefoils
and slender splay-foot shingled spire. The belfry rests on posts
inside. C15 S porch with pretty side openings. Tomb recess in
the nave N wall with depressed pointed arch. – REREDOS. 1858.
Stone, carved by *Earp*. Five panels, inlaid with coloured
marbles. – SCREEN. By *E. Geldart*, 1898. Three two-light openings with rood figures, probably made in Bruges. – PULPIT.
With reused early C16 tracery panels. – STAINED GLASS. C15
glass in a nave N window, including two whole figures of saints.
– Withers introduced glass by *Lavers & Barraud* in the E and
W windows, with quarries by *Powell* in the chancel S windows.
E window blown out in the Second World War, replaced by
M.C. Farrar Bell, 1956. – MONUMENTS. Susan Kynaston
†1733. Marble, with achievement of arms in broken pediment.
– Thomas Stevens †1809. By *J. Challis* of Braintree. Large and
plain, with just an urn.

PANFIELD HALL. Small but exceedingly interesting. There is
some evidence that it was once much larger, perhaps quadrangular, reduced in the 1740s. All brick, dating from the late
C15 or early C16. This earliest part now lies in the middle, and
has some diapering on the N (entrance) front. Parts of the S
front were refronted in the C18 in chequered brick, with
exposed timbers and brick-nogging on the first floor of a
gabled wing that projects to the S as well as on the W front.
Much of the hall roof can be seen inside, including some fine
pierced tracery in the spandrels, and serpentine wind-bracing.
Also inside, on the top floor, a gable window that now looks E
into the roof-space of a second hall range that was added
c. 1570, perhaps the alteration or completion of earlier work.
Chimneystack on S side with three tall (rebuilt) shafts. More
original windows of plastered brick, mullioned and transomed,
with ovolo moulding. At the E end a four-stage porch-tower,
added perhaps in the C17. Pedimented round-arched doorway,
then two floors with straight windows with one transom, and

at the top a small round-arched window. Ogee dome. C18 NW
wing with half-hipped roof, exposed timbers and brick-
nogging. W of that a C20 wing, also with half-hipped roof. Mid-
C20 extension at the W end of the S front.

GREAT PRIORY FARM, 600 yds NNW, near the site of Panfield
Priory. Late Medieval farmhouse, but with sashed front and
pedimented doorcase, and C17 N extension. Facing the house
a fine range of farm buildings. First an early C17 weatherboarded granary, square, on staddle-stones. Then two aisled
barns, both plastered and weatherboarded, dating from the late
C13. The first was rebuilt, with a higher roof, in the C17, but
the other, which is thatched, has its structure substantially
intact. Aisle walls and roof rebuilt, and midstrey added, in
the C15.

PATTISWICK
Bradwell

ST MARY MAGDALEN. Redundant, 1983; sympathetically converted into a house by *Patrick Lorimer* of *ARP Architects*,
1990–1. The nave is C13 (one re-set lancet in the N vestry), the
chancel C14 (two S windows each of two lights under one
pointed head). Between nave and chancel, a tie-beam and
above it a timber-framed 'tympanum', like a gable. The nave
roof has a tie-beam with octagonal crown-post, and the C15
belfry rests on two straight tie-beams. C16 S porch rebuilt, and
N vestry and organ chamber added, as part of restoration by
E.J. Dampier, 1881–2. – PULPIT by Dampier, executed by *L.J.
Watts*. – STAINED GLASS E window, probably 1881–2, and
SCREEN, 1908, remain *in situ*.

PEBMARSH

ST JOHN THE BAPTIST. C14, mainly of flint rubble. The W tower
comes first (see its lower windows) but it was added to an existing nave, lower and narrower than the present one, as can be
seen from the stonework on the inner W wall. Nave and chancel
rebuilt soon afterwards, and N and S aisles added, all with
Dec windows, the most fanciful being the N aisle E. The
arcades have piers with semicircular shafts to the arches and
semi-polygonal ones to the nave and aisles (cf. e.g. St Peter,
Colchester, and St Gregory, Sudbury, across the Suffolk
border). The arches are double-chamfered. The SEDILIA are
most ornate, of two seats only, the third lost when the chancel
was shortened in the C16; with crockets, finials, and headstops.
W tower completed in the early C16 in red brick, with blue
diapers, battlements, and stunted pinnacles. C18 cupola. Of the
C16 and also in brick the embattling of the church and the
unusually elaborate S porch, with a blank stepped gable over
the entrance and another stepped gable above. Figure of St

St John the Baptist, Pebmarsh.
Brass to Sir William Fitzralph, *c.* 1331–8

John by *Alec Miller*, 1928. Restorations in 1861 by *H.W. Hayward*, 1876, including the addition of an organ chamber, and 1906 by *S. Gambier Parry*. – PULPIT. Reused tracery panels, perhaps from bench ends. – STAINED GLASS. C14 bits in chancel and N aisle windows. E window by *Clayton & Bell*, 1879. S aisle E, 1911, and S (First World War memorial) by *Heaton, Butler & Bayne*. N aisle E by *Hugh Easton*, 1934.* –

p. 623 BRASS. Sir William Fitzralph, engraved *c.* 1331–8. The earliest and one of the most important brasses in Essex. Large figure (66 in. (168 cm.)), cross-legged, with a hood of mail.

In Mill Lane, opposite the church, WEAVER'S COTTAGE, single-storey with a very large thatched roof, *c.* 1500, and at the bottom MILL HOUSE. This once belonged to the flour mill (dem. *c.* 1900) that was converted to silk-throwing by George Courtauld in 1799, the beginning of the Courtaulds' silk business.

MARVELS GREEN FARMHOUSE, ½ m. SSW. A well-preserved, typical mid-C15 Essex hall house (tree-ring dated 1458–9). Two-bay hall, floored in the late C16, with crown-post roof. Two-bay extension of *c.* 1560. Some timbers exposed on the earlier building, and close studding on the extension.

RAFE HALL, 400 yds E. Former rectory, for Hon. and Rev. E.H. Grimston, 1842, in the style of a smart Italianate villa with deep portico and four-storey tower.

STANLEY HALL, 1¼ m. WSW. Late C16, originally L-plan. E wing demolished 1871 and the remainder purchased and restored by *Percy Middleditch* in 1929. He exposed the timbers on the main front, which has brick-nogging on the ground floor. Middleditch introduced panelling and other fittings as well as new woodwork carved by *E. Beckwith*, and a collection of C16 and C17 Dutch, Flemish and German STAINED GLASS, mainly heraldic, from Hartrow Manor, Stogumber, Somerset. Three gables to the main front, two jettied, the third with jettied first floor. New E wing and other rear additions by *A.S.G. Butler*, 1951–4. On a moated site, the gardens laid out by Middleditch with rather theatrical, Tudoresque buildings, walls, gate piers etc.

WORLD'S END FARMHOUSE, 1¼ m. SW. Late C16, with exposed timbers and long-wall jetty to the front. Well stair with solid treads in rear tower.

9010

PELDON

ST MARY THE VIRGIN. Big W tower with angle buttresses, battlements, and higher embattled stair-turret. Kentish rag with some flint decoration, notably four crosses on the S side.

---

*Pevsner wrote in 1954: 'So much is said (and done) nowadays against Victorian glass that one should consider seriously whether Clayton & Bell's is not more legitimately stained glass than Mr Easton's, which is always reminiscent of line drawings daintily water coloured.'

Stone nave with early C16 brick buttresses and clerestory. The clerestory windows of two lights. The nave roof is of hammer-beam type, with moulded principals, purlins, collars and braces. Curious short chancel, white brick and stone in the lancet style and looking early C19, by *Marshall Sisson*, 1953. It replaced the longer one rebuilt 1858–9 by *J.M. Roberts* of Dedham as part of a general restoration; the chancel arch and general style are Roberts's. – FONT. Purbeck marble. Plain, octagonal, on eight small shafts. Late C12 or C13, much restored. – STAINED GLASS. In nave S window, panel by *G.J. Baguley*, c. 1870, from St Peter-in-the-East, Oxford. W window by *A.A. Orr*, c. 1926, from Rockley Chapel, Wilts. Installed 1990. Nave N by *Gay Hutchings*, 2002.

OLD RECTORY, SW of the church. By *W.G. & E. Habershon*, c. 1852, sadly deprived of much of its original character.

Several good timber-framed houses round the village, all hall houses apart from PRIEST'S HOUSE, S of the church. C15 with some of the frame exposed on the N side, the jettied front underbuilt. PELDON HALL, NE, is early C14, with two gables to S front. E wing late C16, C18 alterations and additions. Mid-C14 five-bay aisled barn. In Lower Road, GAMES FARM, early C15, originally a two-bay open hall with floored end bay of which much of the original frame survives, including screens doorways and crown-post. C16 inserted floor and C17 extension. ½ m. SW, SAMPTON WICK, early C14, the hall floored in the C17, the two-storey cross-wing retaining an original ogee-headed doorway and crown-post roof, and HARVEY'S FARM, C15 with gabled cross-wings, that on the N C15, the S early C17. ¾ m. SE, KEMP'S FARM, C17, and HOME FARM, C14 or C15.

BRICK HOUSE FARM, Lower Road. C18 farmhouse remodelled by *Chancellor*, 1884, retaining original staircase and other internal features. Three bays square, two storeys with attics in steep pyramidal roof.

PENTLOW   *8040*

ST GREGORY AND ST GEORGE. Nave and chancel are Norman. The apse is completely preserved, with its three windows. As for the nave, the W doorway survives. It leads into the tower, one of the round towers of Essex, probably C14, the date of the windows. That the tower is later than the nave is apparent from the doorway, which on the outside is enriched by columns (one order with decorated scalloped capitals) and the little animal's head above the arch. The N chapel was added to the chancel c. 1600. It has stepped brick gables (now rendered) to the W and E and Late Perp windows. The E window seems C15 and may be reused. The chapel has a charming panelled tunnel vault. It houses the MONUMENT to Judge George Kempe †1606, his son John †1609 and his wife Elinore, three recumbent effigies on a tomb-chest with kneeling children against the front of the chest. On the wall a tablet with a verse inscription. Church restored and re-seated 1886 by *W.M. Fawcett*, who removed the w gallery, rebuilt the s porch, and erected a weatherboarded TOOLSHED in the churchyard. – FONT. Against the N wall. Square, with angle colonettes, Norman. The sides decorated with a cross and interlace and leaves, a star, branches etc. – all very stylized. Square COVER with canted front; C15. Niches with nodding ogee arches. The canopy with buttresses, canopies, etc., crocketed and ending in a finial. – STAINED GLASS. Chancel s by *A.K. Nicholson*, 1927. Nave s by *Percy Bacon*, 1931. – MONUMENTS. Edmund Felton †1542 and wife Frances. Tomb-chest with shields on cusped panels; no figures. – Rev. Edward Bull †1871, his wife Elizabeth †1844 and daughter Winifred †1845. Gothic wall tablet by *Lufkin & Keogh* of Sudbury. – On outside wall of N chapel, tablet placed by Rev. E.W. Mathew to Sarah Stone †1809, servant to the Brise and Mathew families, to encourage 'those in like situations to observe whatever is honest, commendable, and of good report'.

PENTLOW HALL. An uncommonly fine manor house of *c.* 1500. E wing remodelled in the C18 and plastered, with a projecting pedimented bay, but otherwise the timberwork is exposed. Open mortices on the W side show that the house originally extended further in that direction. The central part of the S front, facing the church, is jettied and the first floor, with a broad twelve-light oriel window, appears original. The Hall has linenfold panelling, a fireplace decorated with heads and heraldry, and at the back carved brackets which were originally outside and part of the rear jetty.

PENTLOW TOWER HOUSE, ¾ m. SSE. Built as the rectory for Rev. Felix Bull, *c.* 1880; stables by *Chancellor*, 1899–1900. Brick, much of it moulded. The TOWER was erected by Rev. Edward Bull as a monument to his parents, 1859. Hexagonal, 90 ft (28 metres) high, battlemented. Brick with gault brick dressings and burnt brick decorations. Designed and executed by *L. Webb* of Sudbury under the supervision of *John Johnson* of Bury St Edmunds. Said at the time to afford a view of forty-one churches, sixty windmills, and two castles.

PENTLOW MILL, 400 yds NW. Long two-storey range, C18, timber-framed and brick-faced, with weatherboarded lucam.

PLESHEY

HOLY TRINITY. Cruciform, which it owes to the fact that it was built to serve a college of nine chaplains, two clerks and two choristers. Pleshey College, founded in 1393, was suppressed in 1546; its buildings, which stood to the S, and the church's chancel, were demolished. The nave was purchased by the parishioners, fell into disrepair, and was rebuilt in brick in 1708. The chancel was rebuilt *c.* 1750 by Samuel Tufnell. Most of this was swept away in the restoration of 1868 by *Chancellor*, and the only remains of the medieval church are the crossing arches to the N, S, and W of *c.* 1400. Chancellor gave his church a picturesque and restless S show front, the walls faced in pebble rubble with Bath stone dressings and flint voussoirs to the windows and doors. The distinguishing feature is the stair-turret at the E end of the crossing tower. Heavy timber S porch with double rows of stumpy columns. – STAINED GLASS. E, W, and S transept S windows by *O'Connor*, 1868. – MONU-MENTS. Sir William Jolliff [*sic*] †1749. With big urn, rocaille monument, and three cherubs' heads at the foot. Safely attrib-uted to *Henry Cheere* by M. I. Webb. – Samuel Tufnell of Lan-gleys, Great Waltham †1758, nephew and co-heir of Jolliffe, probably also by *Cheere* (cf. the Comyns monument at Writtle). Standing wall monument with excellent bust on top of a straight-sided sarcophagus and in front of a grey obelisk.

PLESHEY CASTLE. A good example of the motte-and-bailey type. In existence by the mid C12, Back Lane marking the posi-tion of the earlier bailey N of the mound. William de Mande-ville inherited the estate in 1167 and was given permission to fortify the castle by Henry II. This probably resulted in the construction of the present kidney-shaped upper bailey S of the mound, and the outer bailey or town enclosure. The mount is 55 ft (17 metres) high and 295 ft (91 metres) across at the foot. Early C20 excavations revealed foundations of the keep, a late C12 rectangular building 67 ft (21 metres) by 56 ft (17 metres). The moat is crossed by a single-span brick BRIDGE, probably built by Thomas of Woodstock, Duke of Gloucester, who held the castle from 1380 to 1397 – a remarkably early date for a structure entirely of brick. At the upper bailey's W end was a CHAPEL, excavated in the 1960s: built of stone in the early C14 on the site of a mid-C13 wooden structure, refurnished and redecorated by Thomas of Woodstock. The castle had been abandoned by the mid C16.

Pleshey was an attempt by the Mandevilles of Great Waltham to found a new town, something they had done successfully at Saffron Walden. It did not thrive, perhaps because it was too far from the Chelmsford to Walden road, but the fortunate result is that the village has never grown beyond its C12 enclo-sure. Several attractive cottages, some thatched, less remark-able in themselves than for the way in which they are laid out round the castle and its moat. Exceptions are MOUNT HOUSE at the E entrance to the village (early C19, red brick behind a gault brick façade with segmental flat-topped porch on Tuscan columns and half-columns) and PEACHFIELD at the N entrance (former vicarage, red brick, *c.* 1800).

DIOCESAN HOUSE OF RETREAT, E of the church. Built 1908–9 as an Anglican convent. Simple CHAPEL by *Newberry & Fowler*, 1932–3. Rendered walls with white brick dressings, pan-tiles, and W bellcote. Small CLOISTER in similar style, 1959.

PURFLEET

Thurrock U.A.

Purfleet, which lies in the western portion of the historic parish of West Thurrock, was sufficiently remote in the C18 to be chosen by the Government as the site for the testing and storage of gunpowder, at a safer distance from London in the event of accident than the older magazines at Greenwich. Later in the century Samuel Whitbread opened a chalk quarry, and the first cement factory opened in 1871, but in the C19 Purfleet was also a popular destination for day-trippers from London.

PRIMARY SCHOOL, Tankhill Road. 1889, with teacher's house 1892. Brick, with bands of stone and flint. Separate block of banded yellow and red brick by the *County Architect's Dept* (project architect, *James Boutwood*), *c.* 1986–7, with rendered gables giving the effect of pediments.

ROYAL HOTEL (originally Bricklayers Arms), High Street. Early C19. Brick, rendered and painted. Three-storey, five-bay river front with seven-bay ground-floor colonnade of square piers, partly glazed, and first-floor glazed veranda with tented lead roof on cast-iron supports. Many later extensions. ROSE COTTAGE, opposite, is brick with polygonal chimneys, dated 1896 with Samuel Whitbread's initials. The Whitbreads (of the brewing family) developed the chalk quarry, building a terrace of twelve single-storey stock brick workers' COTTAGES (later converted to six) in Church Hollow (The Dipping), 1790. At the same time a CHAPEL, schoolhouse and master's house were built (derelict and inaccessible in 2004). On the s side of LONDON ROAD, near the railway, BOTANY COTTAGES, workers' housing for the Steam Ship Coal Owners' Association, 1905, and 1 m. further E JARRAH COTTAGES, similar housing for the Purfleet Wharf and Saw Mills Co., 1904–6, pebbledashed with the companies' ownership prominently displayed in gables. Opposite Jarrah Cottages, HIGH HOUSE, C17 with early C18 farm buildings and an impressive late C17 octagonal brick DOVECOTE, with coved eaves cornice. Over 500 nesting boxes, with outer wooden door and inner iron door for security.

POWDER MAGAZINE, Centurion Way. The establishment closed in 1962. Of five stock brick magazines by *James Gabriel Montresor*, Royal Engineers, 1763–5, only one remains; the other four, and the Storekeeper's (later Ordnance) House, 1767, were demolished in 1973. Each magazine was 150 ft (46 metres) long, 52 ft (16 metres) wide, with walls up to 5 ft 3 in. (1.6 metres) thick, comprising two brick-vaulted chambers with single-span slate roof. Internal wooden fittings, including a crane that slides on a beam the length of the building. Also surviving the chapel-like PROOF HOUSE, *c.* 1765, for testing gunpowder, with open-pedimented gables and round-headed windows, and square CLOCK TOWER, 1767–8. Lower stage with round-headed arches in each face, pedimented upper stage (with clock), then a square wooden bell-turret with square dome and weathervane.

RSPB Environment and Education Centre, Tankhill Road, by *van Heyningen & Haward*, 2003–6. A model for sustainable design. Overhanging upper storey clad in timber, borards of white, grey, orange, etc. irregurlarly arranged like camouflage or plumage, with two roof cones for natural lighting and ventilation. The bird sanctuary was, until 2000, a rifle range.

Van den Berghs and Jurghens (now Unilever), just w of the Queen Elizabeth II Bridge. Food factory, 1924, with office building at the front in a style appropriate for a Dutch company. Stone and red brick, the central bay (of seven) with an open segmental pediment.

Dartford Tunnel. Under the Thames, from Purfleet to Dartford. Pilot tunnel 1936–8, main tunnel 1957–60, opened 1963; engineers *Mott Hay & Anderson* and *Coode & Partners*, consultant architects *Trehearne & Norman, Preston & Partners*. 4,685 ft (1,442 metres) long, up to 100 ft (31 metres) deep, lined with cast-iron segments 28 ft 2 in. (8.7 metres) in diameter. Second tunnel built alongside 1972–80.

Queen Elizabeth II Bridge. 1988–91, to supplement the 122 Dartford Tunnel following completion of the M25 to N and S of the Thames in 1984–6. Cable-stayed bridge, then the longest in Europe and third-equal longest in the world. Main span of 1,463 ft (450 metres) flanked by back spans of 588 ft (181 metres) each, the roadway 9,237 ft (2,872 metres) in all and rising to 211 ft (65 metres) above the river. Composite steel and concrete deck suspended from 112 cables anchored to steel pylons, two at each end, 273 ft (84 metres) high. Superstructure by *Cleveland Structural Engineering* with *Dr-Ing. H. Homberg & Partner*, foundations and substructure by *Trafalgar House Technology*; consulting engineers, *Sir William Halcrow & Partners*.

Channel Tunnel rail link. Twin tunnels, 2003, under the Thames from Swanscombe (Kent), 4 m. long and up to 130 ft (40 metres) below the surface of the river, emerging E of the Queen Elizabeth II Bridge and continued by a ¾-m. viaduct under the bridge and over the Dartford Tunnel approach roads. By *Rail Link Engineering*, a consortium of *Arup Group*, *Bechtel, Sir William Halcrow & Partners*, and *Systra*.

PURLEIGH   8000

All Saints. Ambitious embattled w tower, restored 1914 with American money in memory of Lawrence Washington, rector 1633–43, great-great-grandfather of George. Angle buttresses with three set-offs, bands of flint and stone and cream-coloured brick, and also some flint and stone chequerwork. The windows indicate a C14 date. Brick S porch with a four-centred doorhead and two-light W and E windows. Early C14 chancel, see the intersected and cusped three-light E window and the similar two-light N and S windows, also the SEDILIA and PISCINA, where, however, ogee arches occur at the tops of the cusping. Nave arcades with thick short octagonal piers and double-chamfered arches. Those of the S arcade die against the vertical continuation of the piers; the arcade itself largely rebuilt as part of *Chancellor*'s restoration, 1891–3. N extension by *Inkpen Downie*, 2002–3. – PULPIT. Elegant piece of *c.* 1700; staircase with twisted balusters, nicely framed panels, and garlands hanging down the angles. – COMMUNION RAIL. Early C18? The balusters not twisted, but no longer of C17 forms. – ALTAR. 'English' altar, 1938, with carved and painted REREDOS by *R. Hedley* of Newcastle, replacing that of 1756 (now at W end, dismantled) with large paintings of Moses and Aaron by *I. Fairchild*. – CHANDELIER. Brass; given in 1758. – STAINED GLASS. Early C14 tabernacles in the heads of chancel N and S windows. Later C14 tabernacles in a S aisle window. E window and S aisle E, 1932, and S aisle W, 1950, by *A.K. Nicholson*. – MONUMENT. In churchyard, on S side of chancel, John Strange †1658. Chest-tomb with three achievements of arms by *Thomas Cartwright the Elder*, 1659.

The church is well sited on the top of what is, in these parts, a considerable hill. Below it, immediately W, the OLD RECTORY, 1883 by *Chancellor*: large, picturesquely irregular, brick and tile-hanging with exposed timbers in the gables. On the churchyard's E side, THE BELL pub, formerly two houses, dating back to the C15, with C18 brick stables.

Former SCHOOL and master's house, Church Hill. 1807, enlarged 1872. Two-storey brick and weatherboarded house and two single-storey brick schoolrooms, that of 1872 with Gothic windows.

At NEW HALL, ½ m. NNE, farm buildings by *Chancellor*, 1868: brick with stock-brick dressings, including an aisled barn with large central arched entrance.

MOATED MOUND, 350 yds S. Diameter 250 ft (77 metres).

QUENDON
Quendon and Rickling

ST SIMON AND ST JUDE. Curious-looking but attractive, thanks to three distinctive features: the nave roof, which covers the aisles in a single sweep; the conspicuously small chancel, rebuilt in the C16; and the timber bellcote by *Stephen Dykes Bower*, 1963, replacing a C19 bell-turret. The three-bay aisle arcades, circular piers and arches with two slight chamfers, are early C13, but restored like the rest of the building by *George Perry* of Bishop's Stortford, 1861. He rebuilt the S aisle, which had been demolished some years earlier, and added the small N vestry. The aisle windows were replaced by Dykes Bower, who in 1965–8 restored the S porch and rebuilt the roof. The interior is almost entirely due to him, notably the painted and gilded chancel roof, executed by *Campbell, Smith & Co.* The chancel walls were panelled, new oak pews installed, the SCREEN (erected 1921 in memory of the architect A. Winter Rose †1918) heightened and extended to incorporate a LECTERN on the S side and two return stalls in the chancel;

the oak of the 1885 PULPIT was toned to match. – ORGAN CASE. C18, said to come from the chapel of Jesus College, Cambridge; restored 1938. Dykes Bower was organist here for fifty-seven years. – STAINED GLASS. E window by *W.B. Simpson & Sons*, 1882. – MONUMENTS. Thomas Turner of Numan [*sic*] Hall (now Quendon Hall) †1681. Marble tablet with Ionic columns, scrolled pediment and three coats of arms, gilded and painted by *Dykes Bower*.

QUENDON HALL. On the N side of the only medieval park in Essex to have survived still with its deer. Part of the manor of Quendon, purchased by Thomas Newman in 1553, who built a half-H house which he called Newman Hall. From this a staircase at the E end survives substantially. Thomas Turner remodelled the house *c*. 1680; there are grounds for attributing this to *Henry Winstanley* of Littlebury, who was clerk of the works at Audley End and had family links with Quendon.* The house was refaced in red and blue brick, and the space between the two arms of the H filled in, with an entrance hall and gallery above. So it then had a flat front with two gabled one-bay side-parts, and a centre of nine much more narrowly spaced bays. The centre is divided – irregularly, one is surprised to see – by giant Tuscan pilasters. The rhythm is 1:2:1:2:2:1. The fourth bay is wider and has the doorway with a fine straight top on richly carved brackets. The roof had dormer windows until a fire, following which the attic was removed by *Poulton & Freeman*, 1957. Additions to N front, 1866, remodelled in 1908–9 as part of extensive alterations and additions by *Forsyth & Maule*. These included the addition of a SW wing at an oblique angle. Very little of the old interior survives, having been reconstructed by the 3rd Earl of Inchcape, with decorations by *Campbell, Smith & Co.*, 1970. – Fine octagonal DOVECOTE to the W, C17, red and blue brick with tiled roof and lantern for bird access. – PARKGATE COTTAGE, ½ m. S of the house. Mid C19, picturesquely detailed with a very large ornamental chimney.

The village consists of the houses along the E side of Cambridge Road.† S of the turning to the church the OLD RECTORY, largely the rebuilding in 1725 of a C17 house. Jettied upper storey at the N end of the W front and a canted bay in the centre. Present RECTORY by *Dykes Bower*, *c*. 1960, gault brick with Regency-style veranda. Further S, Dykes Bower's own house, QUENDON COURT, a nice five-bay, two-storey brick house of *c*. 1750. Impressive doorcase with pilasters, ornamental frieze and pediment. C19 wing with curved gable projects at the S end of the W front. Dykes Bower lived here from 1934 until his death in 1994; he added a single-storey drawing office with clock turret and cupola.

---

* Information from Alison Barnes.
† For the W side, *see* Rickling.

RADWINTER

St Mary the Virgin. Of the medieval church, very little remains: the western three bays of the nave, with s arcade of *c.* 1280, and mid-c14 n arcade. Everything else was rebuilt during the long incumbency (1865–1916) of Fred Bullock, the fourth of five members of his family to hold the living between 1758 and 1925. He made the unusual choice, in 1867, of *W. E. Nesfield* as his architect, and the otherwise domestic nature of Nesfield's work is evident in much of the detailing, e.g. the castellated rainwater heads with their fashionable Japanese pie-dish motifs, and painted tiles in the s vestry. Walls of flint, with bands of tiles of irregular length and spacing. Nesfield extended the nave by one bay eastwards, which necessitated rebuilding the chancel and the s vestry; he also rebuilt the aisles. The chancel was made higher. He kept the nave's essential character, retaining and continuing the arcade piers which on the s side are quatrefoil with thin round shafts in the diagonals – all shafts carrying fillets – and on the n octagonal, both with moulded arches. Nave roof mainly c14; tie-beams, curved braces with traceried spandrels, octagonal crown-posts with capitals and four-way struts. The church was rededicated in 1870. Nothing more of significance was done until 1886, by which time Nesfield had retired from practice, and Bullock employed the young *Temple Moore*, who is responsible for some of the church's most striking and characteristically High-Church features. He restored the c14 porch, unique in Essex for being dragon-beamed, adding the jettied upper storey (but following a design by Nesfield), and then rebuilt the w tower, 1887–8, and added the two-storey n vestry. Inside, he was responsible for the decoration of the wrought-iron chancel SCREEN with its pretty scrollwork, designed by Nesfield but not made until the 1880s, the painted chancel ceiling, the painted decoration of the ORGAN CASE, and the positioning of the reredos, as well as the FONT and PULPIT, 1892. Other notable decorated features are the rood beam with crucifix, aumbry (with painted inner door), churchwardens' staves, and two cupboards in the tower for hymn books and music. Moore continued Nesfield's domestic style in the n vestry, with its fire-places and Delft tiles.

REREDOS. A remarkable piece. The central portion, bought by Bullock in 1888, was made in Brussels *c.* 1510 and restored *c.* 1880 by *François Malfait*. It has six panels with scenes from the life of the Virgin, small free-standing figures against shallow carved backgrounds, probably originally decorated with gesso and paint. Wings added by *Temple Moore*, with six painted panels. Removed for conservation in 2003 and replaced in a lower position, and the altar moved forward of the e wall. – PAINTINGS. Triptych (chancel, formerly in n aisle). c15, Italian, perhaps Sienese or South German. Demi-figure of Virgin and Child in the centre, two saints on the wings. – Christ with the children by *Isaac Alexander Gibbs*, beside font.

– STAINED GLASS. Fragments of medieval glass in chancel and N vestry windows. E window 1870, N aisle E 1892. – In S vestry, three windows depicting SS Gabriel, Michael and Raphael. Signed by *Nesfield*, 1870, the only stained glass he is known to have designed. – Remaining windows by *Gibbs* (*Gibbs & Howard*), 1882–8, following a coherent programme: in the S aisle parables and miracles, in the N aisle angels as described in the Old and New Testaments; at the W end of each aisle, scenes illustrating baptism and Holy Communion.

On the SW edge of the churchyard, the OLD VICARAGE. A two-cell, two-storey house built, according to documentary evidence, shortly before 1520. Jettied at the E end, garderobe tower at the W. Facing the church to the S, CHURCH VIEW (cottages), C16 or C17 with gabled cross-wing to the l.

The VILLAGE was devastated by a fire in 1874 and Bullock, as *de facto* squire, was active in rebuilding it. *Nesfield* built the row of shops and cottages in CHURCH HILL, opposite the E end of the church, 1874–5, and *Moore* designed the ALMSHOUSES N of the church (originally six, now converted to three), 1887, and the 'READING ROOM' (parish hall with cottage) next to it, 1889. Both architects use pargetting, Moore in an exuberant, Baroque way. Opposite the parish hall the PRIMARY SCHOOL, 1853, enlarged 1877, flint and brick with fish-scale slate roof and cast-iron casements with delicate glazing bars.

RADWINTER MANOR (former rectory), nearly ¾ m. NW. Probably by *H. W. Inwood*, whose design was exhibited at the R.A. in 1812 and described as 'now building'.* Painted brick. Two-storey, five-bay front, the wider central bay stepping slightly forward with a gable (perhaps originally pedimented) and Doric portico. Now subdivided.

NEWHOUSE FARM, ¾ m. W. Late C18 or early C19 brick front; only the massive square chimneystack betrays a C17 core. The three l. bays are particularly fine, with tuck pointing and gauged brickwork; the outer two bays project slightly, each forming a two-storey arched recess in which the windows are set. Cornice and parapet with three balustraded panels. In the l. return (largely covered by a C19 conservatory) the cornice is broken by a blind arched recess in a small straight gable. A fourth bay added to the r. in the same style but of lower quality.

THE GRANGE, ¾ m. SSW. Later C16, timber-framed with panel pargetting. At the rear a three-storey gabled staircase wing with two jetties, and a fine brick chimneystack. The shafts have been rebuilt but the diapered base is original.

RAMSDEN BELLHOUSE

7090

ST MARY. The important part is the timber W belfry, tree-ring dated 1413. Free-standing, on four posts with heavy braces

---

* Other designs survive by *Robert Lugar*, 1807, and *M. G. Thompson*, as well as an unsigned design, similar to that executed, dated 1808.

from N to S. Weatherboarded aisles on N, S, and W. Splay-foot shingled spire. Original W door and doorway. S porch of about the same date, with coarse timbers, much restored. Chancel rebuilt in brick, 1812, the nave N wall in stone rubble by *Chancellor*, 1880–1, when the S wall was repaired; the roofs, with Tudor details, were retained. – CHEST. Heavily iron-bound, 7 ft (2.1 metres) long. C17 or earlier. – CHAIRS. Two in chancel, thickly carved, early C18. – STAINED GLASS. E window by *Heaton, Butler & Bayne*, 1892. Chancel S (Millennium window) by *Susan McCarthy (Auravisions)*. – MONUMENTS. In churchyard, by S door, a good group of early C18 headstones, with the usual emblems of mortality.

RAMSDEN CRAYS

ST MARY. C15 belfry, weatherboarded with shingled splay-foot spire. It stands on four posts with heavy braces from N to S. The remainder thoroughly restored by *Chancellor*, 1869–70, who rebuilt the chancel and W wall, added a N vestry, and refaced the nave, all in Kentish rag. Some C15 windows reused, also one lancet, probably C13. Redundant 1993, now a house.

RAMSEY AND PARKESTON

ST MICHAEL. Nave and chancel rendered, but the C15 W tower of septaria, flint, and pebbles, the upper part repaired in brick. In the nave N wall a variety of styles entertaining to follow: one C12 window, a C12 doorway with decorated abaci, a C13 lancet, a simple C14 two-light window. Other early C14 types of two lights in the S wall, where the arrangement of the windows is completely haphazard. The S doorway is a handsome C15 piece, decorated in one order with fleurons, in the other with figures of a king and a queen and small suspended shields. The chancel is just as varied. It has a C14 recess in the N wall with a curiously wilful arch on short shafts and a late C14 chancel arch with small demi-figures of angels in the capitals, but E, N, and S windows and roof are of 1597. The windows very domestic, with straight tops and transoms. The roof has collar-beams on scrolly braces more like brackets, and is ceiled. S porch rebuilt 1816. Restoration by *W.D. Caroë*, 1913–14; N hall *c.* 2000. – PULPIT. Early C17 with panelling moulded below, blank-arched above in the way familiar in Elizabethan furniture, and yet another tier of small foliage panels above these (cf. Great Horkesley). – S DOOR. C15, with attached shafts that originally supported figures. – WALL PAINTING. One C15 head high up above the second S window from the E in the nave, and another fragment by the N doorway. – ROYAL ARMS. 1727. The remarkable thing is that they were placed over Commonwealth arms of 1651, painted on boards, which have thus survived. – MONUMENTS. Daniel Burr †1782 and wife Elizabeth †1783. 'This unadorned memorial is erected by their children';

nonetheless an elegant piece using coloured marbles. – In churchyard, s of porch, E.F. Burbidge †1852. Large, with draped urn and weeping foliage, enclosed by a fence of iron anchors.

Across the road, a cast-iron HORSE TROUGH and drinking fountain erected *c.* 1920 but probably C19. Six supports in the form of horses' hoofs and fetlocks.

MICHAELSTOW HALL, NE of the church. 1902–3, in the comfortable Neo-Georgian style of the day, similar to houses by Ernest Newton. Brick with alternating brick and stone quoins and hipped slate roofs. Two storeys and attics, with a single-storey billiard room to the l. of the main front. This has two two-bay wings flanking an Ionic porch. Venetian window on the garden front lighting the main stair. Stable block and coach house to the E, the latter's entrance set back behind a pair of Tuscan columns. In institutional use since 1939, with many ugly additions.

ROYDON HALL, 1¾ m. w. Timber-framed and plastered house of *c.* 1570, jettied along the s front and also along the w wall of a cross-wing that projects at the E end. The interesting feature is the contemporary brick w gable. Straight, not stepped, flanked by polygonal turrets with pinnacles, one pinnacle also corbelled out on the apex of the gable, and below it two pedimented windows (blocked) above each other. The E wall has remains of something similar but only as far as eaves level, with pedimented windows inserted *c.* 1968. Along the N side three external chimneystacks, the tops rebuilt in gault brick.

SUNCOURT, Wrabness Road, 1¼ m. NW. 1937 by *F. G. Vincent-Brown* of Dovercourt. Large Modern Movement house with flat roof and Crittall windows.

WINDMILL, ½ m. w. Post mill of the Suffolk type, with three-storey round-house and small weatherboarded body. Moved to this site from Woodbridge in 1842, restored in the 1970s. Sails and much of the machinery survive.

PARKESTON QUAY (Harwich International Port). Built by the Great Eastern Railway to provide an easy connection between train and ship, and named after their chairman, Charles Parkes. Opened 1883; extended twice in the C20. Main STATION building (formerly hotel) two storeys, brick with stone dressings, oriels overlooking the platform, and central clock tower. Large additions of 1972. A rather depressing little railway village sprang up nearby, including a former SCHOOL, 1888. Two blocks along Coller Road and Hamilton Road, with teacher's house on the corner. Brick, with stock brick arches over the Neo-Gothic windows. A permanent church (ST PAUL) was not built until 1914, by *E.D. Hoyland*: of terracotta blocks, inside and out, with a sweeping pantiled roof that has three dormers in the w face leading up to a bellcote. Half-hexagonal baptistery at the w end with porches to either side and larger half-hexagon for the sanctuary. Elaborate timber roof supported on posts that form narrow aisles.

PARKESTON CEMETERY. 1909–10 by *F.G. Vincent-Brown*, including chapel with W narthex and short tapering NW tower with spike.

7090

RAWRETH

ST NICHOLAS. C15 W tower, W wall and S arcade. The rest rebuilt by *Hopper*, 1823, but replaced in 1881–2 by *E. Geldart*, mainly on the old foundations, but with a new N aisle and porch and a longer chancel (which is also higher than the nave). Of ragstone, with flushwork, notably on the porch, which also incorporates red tilework to create quite a jazzy effect. Damaged in the 1884 earthquake and again during the Second World War, following which the S aisle was taken down and the arcade walled up. – Geldart designed all the FITTINGS for the church, made by *Cox, Sons, Buckley & Co.* and shown at the Ecclesiastical Art Exhibition, 1882. The painted panels of the REREDOS depict the institution of the Holy Eucharist and its Old Testament types, the sacrificial offerings of Noah and Melchizedech. This theme was to be continued in the STAINED GLASS of the E window, but most of the windows were blown out in 1944. The altar itself has decorated panels and at least one frontal survives, embroidered by *Harriett Anne Kemp*, the rector's wife. – BRASS to Edmund Tyrell †1576 and wife. Kneeling figures (14 and 13 in. (36 and 33 cm.)) on stone tablet with side-columns and a round arch. In the decoration the motifs are still Gothic.

BATTLESBRIDGE. *See* p. 125.

8090

RAYLEIGH

A little town with three visual and historical accents: the church, the castle, and the windmill.

HOLY TRINITY. Mainly of ragstone rubble, with flint and other materials. The stone of the big, tall W tower, documented as being under construction in 1396, probably came from the castle. Diagonal buttresses and higher stair-turret, W doorway and three-light W window. Most of the church was rebuilt in the late C14 and early C15, although fragments of C12 work survive in the chancel. The show front is the S side with the embattled S aisle, the embattled S chapel built by William Alleyn in 1517, and the delightful early C16 brick porch, with two-light brick side windows and stepped battlements on a trefoil-arched corbel-frieze. The S doorway is clearly C13 and reused. The aisle windows are all large, of three lights, Late Perp. The N chapel has a four-light E window with Perp panel tracery. Light and spacious interior, thanks to the aisle windows. Four-bay arcades on thin piers of the four-shaft-four-hollow type, two-centred arches. Tall tower arch, broad chancel arch. The S chapel opens into the chancel with one broad Perp arch on responds with concave sides. Rood stairs on the N side complete with cusped upper exit. Original roofs, much repaired. Under the tower the beam of a C17 gallery. Principal restoration by *Sedding & Wheatly*, 1912–14, when the N vestry was enlarged, ceilings removed, and plaster stripped from the porch. Extensive N additions by *MEB Partnership*, c. 1989–94, including Parish Centre with cloister, linking to an earlier hall.

SCREENS. Between N aisle and N chapel, with cusped single-light partitions and castellated top beam. C15. From Runwell, erected here in 1921, the date of the screen between the S aisle and the S chapel. This has more elaborate tracery, cusped and crocketed, and, in place of a rood, a carved tableau of a First World War soldier below a crucifix. – Chancel screen by *Sir Charles Nicholson*, 1933, reused as inner S porch by *David Ferguson*, 2003. – REREDOS, PANELLING, and PULPIT also by *Nicholson*, 1933. – FONT. 1871, by *C.C. Rolfe*. Of Caen stone, unusually massive, and deeply carved, with a more delicate, traceried cover. Nice brass plaque by *Hart, Son, Peard & Co.* COVER by *Clarke & Son*, 1927. – CHOIR STALLS by *Rolfe*, 1873.[*] – CHEST. Dug-out type, under the tower. – STAINED GLASS. E window, 1921. W window by *Powell & Sons*, 1927. – BRASS to a civilian and wife, c. 1450. Male figure originally 20½ in. (52 cm.), head missing. In doorway between N aisle and Parish Centre. – The S chapel houses the most important piece in the church, the Alleyn MONUMENT of c. 1517. Recess with flat niches in the back wall, cambered and panelled ceiling, and tomb-chest with three large, richly cusped quatrefoil panels.

OUR LADY of RANSOM (R.C.), London Hill. By *T. H. B. Scott*, 1934, although not completed until 1965, when the S aisle and sanctuary were built. Brick, Italianate, with round-arched windows. Tall gabled nave and lower, narrow, flat-roofed aisles. Interior also brick but buff-coloured. Four-bay nave arcades with semicircular arches.

BAPTIST CHURCH, High Street. 1798–9. Rendered and painted brick. Former entrance front with open-pedimented gable and three round-arched windows above triple entrances. Single-storey extension to the l. forming new entrance, also with three round-arched openings, by *K. Cheeseman*, 1979–82, when the interior of the original chapel was reordered. Galleries partly retained. Separate schoolroom, 1864: stock brick with red dressings.

CHRIST CHURCH (United Reformed, originally Rayleigh Tabernacle), Crown Hill. 1898 by *F. Woodhams*. Dec Gothic. Brick with terracotta dressings, including Art Nouveau lettering. Caley Memorial Hall 1914.

SALVATION ARMY CITADEL (originally Wesleyan Methodist), High Street. 1885. Stock brick with red dressings. Gabled front

---

[*] Rev. E. Geldart wrote in 1881 that the choir stalls 'would stand a mild siege' and the font was one 'of which the Pharaohs might make use to replace a worn-out Pyramid'.

with triple lancets set in an arched recess. Schoolroom in similar style, 1902.

RAYLEIGH MOUNT. Motte-and-bailey castle, mentioned in the Domesday Book, and probably built by Swein, son of Robert fitz Wimarc, c. 1070. The motte or mound is 50 ft (15 metres) above the ditch and stands at the E end. The Inner Bailey follows to the E, and the Outer Bailey, added in the late C12, lay further E, coming up to the line of Bellingham Lane. The earthworks were originally fortified by stockades. The castle had fallen into disuse by the mid C13 and permission to quarry stone was granted by Richard II in 1394.

Within the area of the Outer Bailey stands the WINDMILL, a brick tower mill of 1809 and the tallest in Essex. Cap and non-working sails reinstated by millwrights *Lennard & Lawn*, 1974.

The HIGH STREET retains its ancient shape, widening at the point where the market was held before running uphill to the church at the N end, but all too few of its older buildings. The view of the church is partly blocked by the former NATIONAL SCHOOL, 1864, brick with large Gothick windows and shaped bargeboards. Opposite, BARRINGTONS (council offices), 1844, five bays, stock brick with portico of two pairs of Ionic columns, extended 1965–6. To its NE a row of C18 timber-framed and weatherboarded cottages (now a shop), and facing the church's E end No. 18 HOCKLEY ROAD, C18 timber-framed, the three-bay front of stock brick with pedimented doorcase but the other walls weatherboarded. Round the corner from Barringtons, on the E side of the High Street, KINGSLEIGH HOUSE, late C18 brick, three storeys and five bays and a doorcase with open pediment. Nothing more until the street widens, with a large town house (now LLOYDS BANK) on the W side, Early Victorian plastered brick, three storeys, with Tuscan pilasters and a one-bay pediment. Adjoining it to the S, on the corner of Crown Hill, YE OLDE CROWN, C17 and part-weatherboarded but with a C19 plastered front with pilasters. On the E side a further sense of the marketplace is given by the late C19 cast-iron PUMP and HORSE TROUGH, flanking the MARTYRS' MEMORIAL (marble obelisk), 1908. Near them No. 91, dating back to 1400, with a single gabled cross-wing, and then the SPREAD EAGLE, late C16 but much altered. Just beyond Crown Hill, on the W side, No. 102, built c. 1933 as the Westminster Bank by *W.B. Sinclair*. Neo-Georgian brick. Single-storey with hipped roof. Three bays, two tall sash windows and an even taller doorcase with half-pilasters and entablature that comes right up to the eaves cornice.

In CROWN HILL, NW of the High Street, the DUTCH COTTAGE, dated 1621, although looking tidier and more C18 than the two similar cottages on Canvey Island (q.v.). Timber-framed and plastered, octagonal, with circular thatched roof, circular central chimneystack, and two rather rustic pedimented doorcases.

RAYLEIGH LODGE, The Chase, ½ m. ESE. Timber-framed, C16 or earlier. Three-bay Georgian brick front with a pedimented Tuscan portico, and later additions. Now a pub.

RAYNE   7020

ALL SAINTS. The glory of the church is its unusually fine Tudor w tower, built in brick by Sir William Capel *c.* 1510. Blue brick diapering, quatrefoil frieze at the foot, blank stepped gable above the w window with a finial on the apex, castellated frieze below the bell-openings, and embattled top with pinnacles and a curious stepped pinnacle as a roof to the stair-turret. Dull brick nave, chancel, N vestry and s porch by *Vulliamy*, 1839–41; chancel 'restored' 1867, sanctuary and s vestry added by *E.J. Tench*, 1913–14. – FONT. C14, octagonal with carved emblems of the Evangelists etc. Installed 1884; heavily restored. – WOODWORK. In chancel, several pieces of C15–C17 work, probably Flemish, including the aumbry, sedilia, priest's stall, and reredos panels. Installed 1913–14. – CHANCEL SCREEN. 1901, oak, carved by *J.L.W. Rudken*. – STAINED GLASS. Sanctuary windows by *Norwich Glass Co.*, 1914.

RAYNE HALL. NW of the church, and separated from it by a fine C16 brick WALL with moulded brick doorway. The manor was acquired by Sir William Capel in 1486, and his son Sir Giles †1556 seems to have been responsible for extensive remodelling of the house, which probably dates from the C14. Half-H plan with wings extending SW; two storeys, timber-framed and rough-rendered. Central range with long-wall jetty now underbuilt and central entrance with single-storey porch leading into the single-storey hall. s cross-wing also with long-wall jetty but with moulded bressumer exposed. C16 doorways in hall with the Capel badge (an anchor) carved in the spandrels, good C16 linenfold panelling and heavy moulded ceiling beams. Broad formal stairs, an early example, with more heraldic carving in the spandrels of the opening, leading to the great chamber on the first floor (now subdivided). Timber-framed building behind, connected by a passage, probably the kitchen. C16 BARNS SW of the house, of five and seven bays.

W of the church and hall THE GREEN, with TUDOR COTTAGE on the s side, C16 with jettied and gabled cross-wings, altered in the C17, and on the w side MARY'S COTTAGE (No. 13 Shalford Road), small C18 timber-framed cottage with Gothic windows in the gable end. Behind it the village LOCK-UP, brick, *c.* 1819.

Several good houses along Stane Street, of which the most conspicuous is RAYNE HOUSE: C18 brick, three storeys, the entrance to the side, and running the length of the five-bay front a delicate cast-iron veranda with curved glass roof. Next to it TURNERS, C16, timber-framed with C18 and C19 windows, plastered on the front but with exposed timbers at the side, and then NETHER HOUSE, C17 with an C18 pedimented doorcase. E of Rayne House, THE SWAN, attractive C16 pub, with gables and bay windows.

RETTENDON

ALL SAINTS. One of the most prominently sited churches in Essex, on high ground and with a tall W tower. Mainly ragstone rubble. Plain, Late Norman S doorway and C13 chancel (see the shafted splays of the E window, inside a small lancet, and the trefoiled PISCINA and SEDILIA). The rest mostly Perp, restored 1895–8 by *Chancellor & Son*, who rebuilt the S porch, the S wall of the nave and chancel, and the roofs. The tower has diagonal buttresses, SE stair-turret, large W window (with tracery that may be C17), battlements, and a low pyramid roof. N aisle arcade with short octagonal piers with concave sides and double-hollow-chamfered arches, single-bay N chapel with the same characteristics, and two-storey N vestry. – Chancel STALLS with pretty poppyheads, decorated e.g. with a dog, a lion, a bear, a monkey, incorporated in work by *W. B. Polley*, 1898. Also some traceried panels that perhaps originally formed part of a rood screen. – STAINED GLASS. Fine E window by *Henry Holiday*, 1919. – BRASSES. Civilian and two wives, *c.* 1535, the main figure 17½ in. (44.5 cm.), with children below. On a stone slab of *c.* 1200, its edges deeply carved with foliage, birds, etc. – Richard Cannon †1605 and his half-brother Richard Humfrie †1607. Similar figures, about 23½ in. (60 cm.) – The surprise of the church is the MONUMENT to Edmund Humphrey †1727, signed by *Samuel Chandler*, and reckoned by Gunnis to be one of the most important early C18 monuments in England. Large marble affair, filling the N chapel's E wall. Humphrey is shown reclining, with two putti behind him. Above him, his parents and grandparents, four standing figures arranged triptych-wise with two single figures in niches in the wings and a couple higher up together in one niche. Open segmental pediment above them, supported by Corinthian columns, broken by achievement of arms, and flaming urns to either side. Intricate marble pavement in front.

BISHOP OF ELY'S STABLES, NE of the church.* C16 brick barn with three straight gables on the S side. Now a house.

RETTENDON PLACE, SE of the church. Large stock-brick house dated 1884, extended by *Chancellor & Son*, 1900. On the earlier part some good decorative brickwork, especially in the gables.

OLD RETTENDON HALL, ½ m. N. C18 timber-framed and weatherboarded, with a three-bay brick front dated 1743.

GIFFORD'S FARM HOUSE, 1⅓ m. WNW. C16 T-plan house, weatherboarded, with gabled and jettied cross-wing.

HYDE HALL, 2¼ m. NNE. Late C16 farmhouse, with an early C17 weatherboarded barn. Gardens covering 24 acres, laid out

---

*The bishops of Ely owned the parish in the Middle Ages.

from 1955 by *Dick & Helen Robinson*, and given to the Royal
Horticultural Society, 1993, for whom *Colvin & Moggridge* pro-
duced a master plan in 1996.
BATTLESBRIDGE. *See* p. 125.

RICKLING

4030

Quendon and Rickling

ALL SAINTS. The nave is E.E., as witnessed by one small lancet
at the nave's W end. This now opens into the W tower, added
in the early C14. At the same time the S aisle was added and
the chancel rebuilt, the latter noticeably off-centre. The tower
has low diagonal buttresses. The top stage is early C16, originally with brick quoins and battlements but rebuilt 1973 in
stone and flint to match the rest of the church. The chancel
windows are typical of their date. So is the two-bay arcade,
with a quatrefoil pier and arches of one quadrant and one
hollow-chamfered moulding. Nave restored 1865, chancel
1889. – N recess in chancel with very low tomb-chest, like a
seat, and a big ogee arch. S recess with a tomb-chest with six
quatrefoils with shields. – REREDOS. Elaborately carved oak,
1879, with central panel depicting the Adoration of the Lamb;
Flemish. – SCREEN. Typical of the C14. The divisions are broad,
of four lights separated by shafts with shaft-rings, and the
tracery is of squashed circles with ogee ending at top and
bottom. Finer tracery within these. – PULPIT. C15 with panels
with blank tracery and at the foot alternating pairs of quatrefoils and wheels of three mouchettes. – STAINED GLASS. Two
nave N windows by *Powell & Sons*, 1855 and 1862; also S aisle
S, 1889. – E window, 1896, a striking depiction of Christ
calming the storm on Galilee. Possibly by *E.R. Frampton* for
Clayton & Bell.
PRIMARY SCHOOL, Rickling Green. 1873 by *G.E. Pritchett*.
Brick, minimally decorated. Former National School opposite:
1830, extended by *W. M. Brookes*, 1845.
RICKLING HALL, ¾ m. S. The remains of an extremely interesting house, built *c.* 1490–1500 in the bailey of a Norman
castle; the mound survives to the S. It was one of the earliest
medium-sized residences in Essex to be built in brick, but
although moated was relatively modest and unostentatious. It
was quadrangular, and the courtyard and buildings on all four
sides survive. Only the Great Hall (S range E side) has gone.
In the C17 the offices and kitchen to its W were stripped out
and the building used as a barn, with the residential accommodation concentrated in the E range, to which a staircase
tower was added in 1620. The W range was rebuilt as a granary
and byre apparently at the same time. The best-preserved part
is the gateway into the courtyard from the N, i.e. opposite the
Hall, the entrance marked by a slight raising of the roof-line
over the four-centred arch. Also in existence a few cusped
and pointed windows, apparently not *in situ*. Extensively

remodelled 1968–70: E range refronted and drawing room added S of the staircase tower, Neo-Georgian and indeed just the sort of alterations that might have been made in the C18. At the same time the E wall of the barn on the S side of the courtyard was rebuilt, and arched openings inserted in the S wall. Brick COTTAGE immediately N of the house also c. 1500.

Next to the church the former RECTORY, gault brick, 1847 but still with a Regency air, and CHURCH END FARM, late C18 red brick, which has in the yard behind it an unusual square DOVECOTE of flint with brick quoins, probably C18.

The actual village is at Rickling Green 1¼ m. SE, and along the W side of Cambridge Road.* Several nice timber-framed cottages, some thatched, down each side of RICKLING GREEN: e.g. on the W side, YEW TREE COTTAGE, C17, originally a row of three, and on the E side TUDOR COTTAGE, C17–C18 with exposed timbers. Also on the E side THE CRICKETERS pub, C18 or early C19 to which a wing was added later in the C19, when the old block was refronted to match the new in red brick with stock brick quoins and dressings. In RICKLING GREEN ROAD, RICKLING HOUSE COTTAGES, C17 timber-framed and plastered with a higher, weatherboarded C19 addition.

There is a slight broadening of CAMBRIDGE ROAD to mark the presence of the village, with a granite drinking trough and fountain, 1887, the latter within an octagonal timber shelter (restored 1954). S of this, RICKLING CORNER COTTAGES, C17 with C19 Gothic windows, and to the N THE LILACS, a pretty early C18 cottage. Set back from the road, RICKLING HOUSE, C18, large, painted brick, with early C19 and later additions. Further N, STREET FARMHOUSE, c. 1800, brick with heavily rusticated quoins and window surrounds, and GRAPE COTTAGE, flint-fronted, with a lozenge-shaped panel (decorated with bottle ends) dated 1835. Towards the N end of the village the former COACH AND HORSES INN, timber-framed of late C16 origin but refaced in brick, probably in the early C19, divided by pilasters into five bays.

7040   RIDGEWELL

ST LAURENCE. All Perp, of flint and pebble rubble, except for an unexplained, probably reused, piece of C13 blank arcading in the N wall of the vestry. W tower with angle buttresses, some flint decoration at the foot, battlements, and a higher stair-turret. Embattled S porch. Windows with Perp tracery. N arcade with piers with semi-polygonal shafts, small to the two-centred arches, and large, without capitals, to the nave. The N aisle widens at the E end, presumably to accommodate an altar. Clerestory with embattled sill. N chapel with octagonal pier and semi-octagonal responds carrying embattled capitals. Delicately detailed nave roof with collar-beams on arched braces,

* For the E side, see Quendon.

every second resting on defaced figures which stand on corbels. All beams and rafters moulded. – SCREEN. Four divisions of the dado remain, with elaborate tracery including mouchette-wheels. Two of the panels have red and gold decoration. – PULPIT. C17, plain. – LECTERN. Octagonal, its heavy foot decorated with fleurons. C15 (book-rest replaced). – FONT. Octagonal. C14 stem with fleurons in panels. Bowl 2003, carved by *John Green*. – BIER. Oak, C15, with octagonal legs and telescopic handles.

The church is set back down a lane with the VICARAGE facing it to the W. 1841–2. Three-bay gault-brick front with Roman Doric portico and corner pilasters. Sides and rear of red brick but with gault brick pilasters. Then ST LAWRENCE LODGE, converted from the National School: 1865, enlarged 1872. Gothic brick porches with stone dressings and black diapering. The lane leads off the E side of THE GREEN, with a C19 cast-iron pump by *Ransomes* of Ipswich. Tapering sides and ball finial. Pretty cottages on the N side of The Green, some thatched, although not THE NOOK and OAK COTTAGE, which can just still be seen to be a long-jetty house, early C16, beneath later additions. On the SE side, RICHMOND HOUSE, C18 timber-framed and plastered with a three-bay, two-storey front and pedimented doorcase with paired columns. To the N, on the NE side of CHAPEL ROAD, the KING'S HEAD pub, long-jetty house of *c.* 1500 with an C18 or early C19 brick front, and next to it WADES FARM (now divided), with a prominent gabled and jettied cross-wing to the l. This, with its large external chimneystack, forms a late C16 addition to an early C15 two-bay hall and integral service end to the r. A little further W, on the S side, APPLETREES, late C14: two-bay hall, with late C16 inserted floor, and storeyed bays at each end. Restored by *Donald Purkiss*, 1978, with a large rear extension.

MILL HOUSE, Stambourne Road, 700 yds WSW. Late C15, thatched. Two-bay hall with service bay to the l. and parlour and solar bay to the r. Timber-framed chimney inserted in the C16.

PANNELLS (formerly Hill Farm), 500 yds ENE. Main range gabled at both ends and jettied at the S. Additions on the W side include a N-facing range with three projecting gables. Original carved bargeboards with pendants, and bressumer with foliate carving and date 1589.

RIVENHALL

8010

ST MARY AND ALL SAINTS. The medieval church was 'a rude and unseemly structure' in the eyes of Lord Western, who commissioned *J. A. Repton* to remodel it in 1838–9. Archaeological investigations in the 1970s and 1990s showed that more of the original fabric survived beneath the render than had been thought, as can be seen from the chancel N wall, where the render has been removed. Nave and W part of the chancel date to the C10 or C11 (see small round-headed chancel windows), with an apsidal E end added late in the C11, extended and straightened c. 1300. W tower added in the C15, of which the foundations are visible; this collapsed and was rebuilt in brick, inside the foundations, 1714–17. Repton's work was largely cosmetic: the walls (mainly flint, rubble, with some Roman brick and stone) were rendered, polygonal buttresses rising to turrets added to the tower, similar buttresses at the angles of the nave and chancel, and battlements to the tower and nave. Windows replaced with simple Y and intersecting tracery. Plain white interior with coved ceiling with thin narrow transverse ribs. Further work by *S.C. Parmenter* of Braintree, 1877–8, included taking out the W gallery, lowering the floor, opening up two square-headed side windows at the E end of the nave, and adding the S porch. Octagonal N vestry by *Laurence King & Partners*, 1974, in a depressing dark brick. – FONT. Outside, near S porch, octagonal font of c. 1300. – COMMUNION RAILS. With twisted balusters, c. 1700. – WALL PAINTING. Detached fragment (Late Medieval) on N wall of nave. – CLOCK. Drop dial clock by *Christian Lange*, 1871, with Gothic case. Presented by Sir William Tite to the workmen's hall (now dem.) founded by Henry Dixon of Durwards Hall. – ROYAL ARMS. Of James II, painted.

STAINED GLASS. The best in Essex; purchased by the rector, Bradford Denne Hawkins, from the church of St Martin at Chenu, NW of Tours, in 1839, and assembled in the E window in 1840. He paid 400 francs for the glass and 89 francs for its removal; the cost of transporting it to London was £5 10s. 3d. Two large frontal figures of archbishops, and four roundels (Christ in Majesty, the Entombment, the Annunciation, and Virgin and Child) of c. 1170–80; of exceedingly good quality. – Knight in armour, inscribed 'Robert Lemaire', mid C13. – Demi-figure of a bishop saint, St Anthony, and the Adoration of the Magi, C16. – More fragments of C16 and earlier glass in nave windows, some it moved from the E window in 1948 as part of rearrangement by *Joan Howson* (further rearrangement of the E window by *Chapel Studio*, 1991). – Small nave N by *Comper*, 1919.

MONUMENTS. Raphe and Elizabeth Wyseman †1608 and 1594. Standing wall monument of alabaster and marble, with tomb-chest, recumbent effigies on a rolled-up mat, kneeling children below; topped with funerary HELM. Erected by Wyseman c. 1598 and attributed to *Garat Johnson the Elder* (AW). – Samuel Western †1699. Good monument with segmental pediment, scrolls, flowers, and cherubs' heads. Attributed to *William Woodman the Elder* (GF). – Thomas Western †1706. Cast-iron floor slab, with arms. – William Western †1729. Big black sarcophagus in front of a black obelisk; no effigy. – Olive Western †1823. Black and white marble with urn and coloured arms. By *P. Shout*. – Hannah Harriott †1831. By *William Carr* of Maldon. A competent piece, with urn, erected by the ladies of Rivenhall Place to their former governess. –

Sarah Hawkins †1832. Simple marble tablet in the classical taste by *Peter Rouw*. – Charles Callis Western, Baron Western †1844. By *Clarke* of Wigmore Street. Suitably large and Gothic, with standing female figures in niches either side of the inscription, crocketed ogee arch and pinnacles, and battlemented top. – Five sons of James and Susannah Davey †1837–54. Of no artistic pretensions, but a rare monument to working men. Originally on an outside wall.

PRIMARY SCHOOL, on S side of churchyard. School and master's house, 1855, enlarged by *Harcourt Runnacles*, 1873: Gothic, flint with stone dressings. Stock brick additions by *Stanley Bragg Partnership*, 2001.

RIVENHALL HALL, N of the church. Late C16, with jettied cross-wings.

RIVENHALL PLACE, nearly 1 m. NNW. C.C. Western attained his majority in 1788 and in 1789 consulted *Humphry Repton* about redesigning his park and house. Repton's more ambitious proposals for Raphe Wyseman's Tudor house were not executed, but it was refronted and then considerably reduced in size for Western's uncle, Rev. Thomas Walsingham Western, *c.* 1796–1800, following Western's move to Felix Hall, Kelvedon (q.v.).

Rendered brick E front of seven bays and two-and-a-half storeys, with cement quoins and segment-headed windows. C19 semicircular Tuscan porch. The two r. hand bays step slightly forward, betraying the N cross-wing of the Tudor house; on the N front is a Tudor chimneystack of three (rebuilt) octagonal shafts, and the gable end of the cross-wing is Tudor brick with an original three-light window. Another Tudor chimneystack in the middle of the W side, serving the Tudor hall, and also the tall round-headed window of the late C17 staircase tower. The S side is a long brick façade (partly, formerly entirely rendered), eight bays, although some of the third-floor windows are false, set in a high parapet concealing a hipped roof. Single-storey additions on the W side by *Plater Claiborne*, 2001–3. Inside, much C16–C18 panelling. Principal staircase, late C17, of three-and-a-half flights round a square open well, with twisted balusters, goes only to the first floor. The attics are reached via a winder stair, probably late C16.

At least part of *Repton*'s scheme for the medieval deerpark was executed. It was enlarged to the S, so that the house and newly formed lake became more central, and in 1796 the public road from Rivenhall to Braintree was moved to the E and N of the park. Stable block rebuilt NW of the house (now PARK HOUSE) from designs provided by *William Wilkins*, 1789–90. He also redesigned the brick bridge across the lake, which forms the main approach to the house, preserving a datestone of 1693; rebuilt 1963.

KELVEDON PARK (formerly Durwards Hall), 1¼ m. SE. 1850, for Dr Henry Dixon of Witham. Neo-Tudor, stock brick with paler brick dressings. Three storeys and attics. Two gabled cross-wings with single-storey canted bays and central gabled porch. Service wing to the l., of same height and style, and single-storey conservatory to the r., by *Chancellor*, 1885. Interior remodelled as offices by *Kilngrove Architectural Ltd*, 1998–9, with a large two-storey rear extension by *John Finch Partnership*. Side walls and link of dark glazing, with broad piers of brick to match the old building, a juxtaposition that works surprisingly well.

OLD RECTORY, ¾ m. SSW. Early Georgian brick. Two storeys and attics, with parapet. SE front of three bays with single-storey wing to the SW. To the NW a C16 or C17 wing with exposed timbers. Good C18 staircase with turned balusters.

ROMAN VILLA. Excavated 1971–3. Outside the churchyard to the E, N wing of a high-status villa from A.D. 70–80, facing a courtyard with presumed E and W wings projecting from it. Second building partly under the present chancel.

ROCHFORD

The town is quite separate from the church and Hall, and the separation became especially obvious when the railway arrived in 1889 and cut off the town completely.

ST ANDREW. The *pièce de résistance* is the big tall W tower of brick, with diapers of vitrified headers, angle buttresses, a higher SE stair-turret, a big three-light Perp brick window, and battlements. Above the W door the arms of Thomas Butler, Earl of Ormond †1515. Also of brick the C16 N vestry, perhaps originally a chapel, with two surprising and charming half-timbered gables, entirely domestic in character. The body of the church is of ragstone rubble with some flint and septaria; C14 N aisle, otherwise mostly late C15 to early C16. The S side was the show side. It has on the aisle and the porch battlements faced with stone and flint chequerwork. The E view is dominated by the five-light chancel and three-light aisle and vestry windows. The interior has three-bay arcades on octagonal piers with double-chamfered arches. Uncommonly tall tower arch. Judiciously restored by *William Slater*, 1862–3, including a new nave roof reinstating the clerestory. Organ chamber slipped in between the N aisle and N vestry later in the C19. – ALTAR RAILS. With twisted balusters; *c.* 1700. – STAINED GLASS. Chancel S windows by *O'Connor* and *Joseph Bell* of Bristol, 1863, both very strongly coloured. – E window, 1886, and S aisle two-light †1891 by *Powell & Sons*, designed by *Charles Hardgrave* and *J. W. Brown* respectively. Also by *Powell* the two S porch windows †1914, and N aisle W, 1930. – S aisle W by *Jones & Willis*, 1919. – BRASS. Maria Dilcock †1514. 11½ in. (29-cm.) figure.

CONGREGATIONAL CHURCH (Presbyterian), North Street. 1740, brick, enlarged 1838 when the front was altered and rendered.

ROCHFORD HALL. Sadly mutilated remains of a building which was once of great size and some architectural importance, more than half destroyed by fire in 1760 and further damaged by bombs in the Second World War. The manor of Rochford was bought by Richard, Lord Rich, in 1550 and he died there in 1567. There is little doubt it was he who rebuilt the house. The age of the earlier building is not known for certain, but it was extensively refurbished in 1430–3 by Joan Beauchamp, Lady Abergavenny. Later owners included Thomas Butler, Earl of Ormond, and Sir Thomas Boleyn, Viscount Rochford, father of Anne. Built mainly of stone, much of it reused from the earlier building and probably also from Prittlewell Priory, which Rich owned. Brick dressings, the whole building originally plastered. It must have been nearly 200 ft (62 metres) square, about twice its present size, with at least five courtyards. The present building represents the surviving NE corner, and the N front, with four gabled bays, gives some idea of the original appearance. Although the windows have been altered the outlines of the original openings are still clearly visible. These were large and oblong and must have had a transom and four lights – similar perhaps to Sutton Place, Surrey. The gables are straight, and from the centre of each rises an octagonal chimney on a shaft. At the NE corner is an octagonal crenellated angle tower, with a polygonal staircase tower on the internal corner that has its original newel stair. Some original windows with arched heads and hoodmoulds on the inner walls. The E front, rendered and sashed after the 1760 fire, also has four straight gables, but with pinnacles (now just stumps) rather than chimneys. Little survives in the interior (now a golf club) until one reaches the attics, which are in remarkably unaltered condition. The carpentry of the roof and floors is sophisticated for its date, suggesting the presence or influence of London craftsmen. W of the surviving four bays of the N front stood a big broad projecting central bay, now gone. Beyond it the remainder of the N front, part of the W front, and part of the internal range behind the central bay stood up to first-floor level; converted to barns after the fire of 1760. This NW part of the complex, including the base of the NW angle tower and staircase tower, was rebuilt as four houses by *Malcolm Ginns*, 1986–9, an attractive and imaginative pastiche.

HOSPITAL, Union Lane. Begun as the workhouse by *William Thorold*, 1837 (dem.). Later buildings included the INFIRMARY by *Henry Stock*, 1857–8 (dem.), CHAPEL of *c.* 1865, and free-standing BOARDROOM by *Norman Evans*, 1923–4. Developed in the 1930s as Southend Municipal Hospital by *Frank W. Smith* in a very progressive style. Main hospital and administration block, started 1938, two storeys with four projecting bays, each with full-height glazing of clear and opaque glass, for sun lounges. The ISOLATION BLOCK for TB patients, designed 1933–4 and opened by 1939, has a staggered, V-shaped plan, with two-storey flat-roofed curved bay at the point and

V-shaped rooms projecting from the sides, all fully glazed. This and the tall brick BOILER HOUSE with soaring chimney converted to housing by *George Traer-Clark*, 1999–2000; further housing covers much of the grounds.*

POLICE STATION, South Street. 1914, probably by *F. Whitmore*, County Architect. Brick and terracotta, almost Baroque in its detailing. Seven-bay façade with central open segmental pediment, and single-bay wings breaking forward at either end.

RAILWAY STATION. 1889 by *W.N. Ashbee*, including brick stationmaster's house with large half-timbered gable, original canopies, and lattice footbridge. Brick goods shed probably of the same date, converted to a community centre (The Freight House) by *Kenneth Cheeseman*, 1983.

PERAMBULATION. The little town's centre is the crossing of East, West, North, and South Streets, an ingeniously managed crossing – from the visual if not the traffic point of view – in which no two roads run straight on. South Street comes to a dead end, with North Street continuing much narrower, and East Street starting in a NE direction and then bending round. Moreover, the MARKET SQUARE lies along West Street and separated from North Street by a thin partition of shops, i.e. almost as enclosed as an Italian piazza. It is a surprising space to find in a South Essex town and its character is still largely genuine. The best building is on the w side, No. 34 West Street, seven-bay Georgian brick with a fine doorway on attached Tuscan columns. On the s side the KINGS HEAD INN, painted brick with three canted bays, C18 and C19, overshadowed to its r. by BARCLAYS BANK, a three-storey stock brick palazzo by *Chancellor*, *c.* 1865. Next to it the former CORN EXCHANGE, now Women's Institute Hall, also by Chancellor, also stock brick, 1866: three round arches in the gabled front with a raised and gabled apex. At the far end of West Street LORD RICH'S COTTAGES, a row of six almshouses founded 1567 and probably built by Rich's grandson Robert, Earl of Warwick early in the C17; brick, single-storey with two projecting gabled bays.

In NORTH STREET and off to the e in WEIR POND ROAD, a number of attractive weatherboarded cottages. In EAST STREET, No. 24, C18 three-bay timber-framed house, weatherboarded on the returns but with a sashed and plastered front and pedimented doorcase. Set back on the N side, KING'S HILL, dating back to *c.* 1300 but with a wing and internal features of the C17. The stateliest houses are to be found in SOUTH STREET, the greater number Georgian, of which the largest is No. 19: five bays, three storeys, red brick with yellow brick front and a stableyard with coach house behind. This and most of the buildings on the E side to its l. are now offices of Rochford District Council, including Rochford's oldest house, No. 17, restored 1982–3 by *Philip Blower* of the Council Architects Section. Central hall late C13, l. cross-wing added shortly after, r. cross-wing late C14. Both cross-wings jettied. Fine

*Construction of new hospital buildings by *Devereux Architects* started in 2006.

brick chimneystack inserted in hall *c.* 1500 with three brick niches over the opening, one with corbelled trefoiled heads. Hall floored *c.* 1600 but opened up again in the restoration of 1982–3; crown-post roof. Opposite, No. 24, built as the court house, 1859: five-bay gault brick façade with rustication, keystones, aprons to the windows and heavy eaves cornice decorated with black brick crosses.

At Stroud Green, ¾ m. w, THE GLEBE, Hall Road, painted brick and stucco, by *Dent Hepper*, 1808, as the rectory. ½ m. further on THE LAWN, a handsome white-painted house enlarged by *John Johnson* for Major George Davis Carr after 1796. Johnson's work is probably the two-storey, five-bay E front with balustraded parapet and Ionic porch. Extended twice in the C19. Seven-bay Ionic loggia on S front and pediments on E and S fronts added in the 1930s. W of The Lawn, ARK HOUSE, 1962 for David Keddie by *David Allford* of *Yorke, Rosenberg & Mardall*. Tightly planned two-storey house, 2-in. (5 cm.) white brick with large windows, timber panels, and deep timber fascia beneath a flat roof. S-facing, with a high-ceilinged living room raised above the sunken garage, and other rooms arranged round a large central staircase hall. Sympathetically extended *c.* 1975.

DOGGETTS FARM, 1¼ m. NNE. C16 farmhouse with early C19 gault brick front and stable block with clock dated 1856. SW of the house a mid-C19 purpose-built barn, gault brick and weatherboarding, housing a wooden and cast-iron horse engine and associated milling machinery.

ROXWELL

ST MICHAEL AND ALL ANGELS. C14 nave and chancel, restored out of recognition. Flint-rubble walls, tall timber W spire dated 1891 but resting on C15 or C16 timbers. N aisle and vestry by *C. R. Ainslie*, 1854. – REREDOS. In chancel, by *Chancellor*, 1872. Painted panels added 1881, with new altar and altar rail by *E. C. Lee*. In N chapel, made up of parts of Durham Cathedral organ case, built in 1684, and erected as chancel screen, 1886, by *Polley* of Coggeshall. Moved to its present position 1981. The pieces exhibit that characteristic mixture of Baroque and Gothic which had been made fashionable at Durham by Bishop Cosin in the second third of the C17. The cornice has Baroque leaves, but the posts are decorated with bits of Gothic tracery. – PULPIT. Stone, by *Chancellor*, for Great Waltham, 1862–3, moved here in 1894. – POOR BOX. Free-standing, heavy oak, late C19, intertwined branches in a massive version of Art Nouveau. – STAINED GLASS. Two panels of 1600, with biblical stories and German text. Each panel only the size of a page in a book of hours.* E window by *Clayton & Bell*, 1872, incorporating fragments of older glass. N aisle W by *Henry*

*Not on view.

Holiday, 1919–20, N aisle N by *Lawrence Lee* with *Janet Christopherson*, 1976. – Several MONUMENTS to the Bramstons of Skreens, including Sir John Bramston †1654, white marble draped tablet with various martial emblems. – Mrs Mary Byng †1774. Stone obelisk and in front of it a cherub leaning on an oval portrait medallion. Across the SW corner of the chancel. – Maria Herlock †1821. By *Charles Regnart*. White marble on black ground with classical motifs freely arranged.

PRIMARY SCHOOL. Built by T. W. Bramston, 1834. Workhouse-like small brick house with two-storey centre and symmetrical single-storey wings.

In the village centre, several pretty cottages, notably a weather-boarded group dating back to the C17 immediately opposite the church with early C19 bays supported on cast-iron pillars. E of the church, BROADGATES, two-storey C18 brick house set back from the street, four bays with central Tuscan portico and timber-framed outbuildings. W of the church, on the S side of the road, LITTLE DUKES, the remaining gabled and jettied cross-wing of a C15 house with main block rebuilt in the C17. Behind it, across Roxwell Brook, DUKES, tall, timber-framed, two gables with exposed timbers to the E and six of various sizes to the W. The taller gables represent the original C16 house, the lower ones an addition of 1666. Three fine chimneystacks.

BOARDS FARM, 1m. S. Timber-framed and weatherboarded, probably late C16, with cross-wings to l. and r. and a large brick chimneystack with two octagonal shafts to the l.*

HOE STREET FARM, ¾ m. SE. *c.* 1600, with exposed timbers. In a first-floor room a painted imitation of panelling and, on the chimney-breast, the Stuart arms and the date 1606.

NEWLAND HALL, 1m. NW. Late C15 or early C16 two-bay open hall forms the plastered W front. S cross-wing demolished, and on the N side a three-bay, two-storey lodging range added in the first half of the C16. This retains at least some of its original brick-nogging, an early example: six different decorative patterns on the S side and another two on the N.

SKREENS, 1¼ m. ESE. The house built for Thomas Bramston, 1728, and altered by *John Johnson c.* 1769–71, was demolished *c.* 1920. A thatched LODGE survives at the W entrance, with rustic veranda and Gothick windows, said to be of 1812.

At Cooksmill Green, 1½ m. S, HOME FARM, late C15 or early C16 timber-framed and plastered house, two storeys and attics with three gables on the E and W fronts.

ROYDON

ST PETER. A cemented church hall by *Harold Mileson*, 1971, connects to the S door and obscures most of the church's S side – astonishingly insensitive. After that one is not so surprised by

---

* Benedict Otes, opposite, is in Writtle, q.v.

the reordering of 1969, which placed the ALTAR (by *Angela Godfrey*, 1972) in the middle of the N aisle's N wall, with the chancel redesignated the Colte Chapel. *J. Clarke*'s restoration of 1854–6, which made no additions, was by contrast a model of restraint. C13 nave with one renewed S lancet. Next to it one Dec and one Perp window. N aisle dates from *c.* 1330, see the windows (E and W of three lights with ogee-reticulated tracery) and the arcade (short octagonal piers and double-chamfered arches). Later C14 W tower with angle buttresses and battlements. Chancel rebuilt early in the C15. – FONT. An interesting piece of *c.* 1300. Octagonal with, in the four diagonals, four heads, men who are neither saints nor clerics, but look like workmen. They wear hats with rolled-up brims. – SCREEN. The side parts of five lights each with plain broad ogee arches and no tracery above them – C14, no doubt. – STAINED GLASS. Chancel N by *Heaton, Butler & Bayne*, 1926, incorporating late C15 quarries. – N aisle, over altar, by *John Hayward*, 1970. – MONUMENTS. In chancel, brasses of Thomas Colt †1467 and wife, his figure 3 ft (91.5 cm.) long; John Colt †1521 and two wives and children, the largest figure 25½ in. (65 cm.); and John Swifte †1570, 3 ft (90 cm.) long. – Elizabeth Stanley †1589. Mural brass with inscription and realistic scene including five children. – Margaret Colt †1602. Tablet framed by enriched pilasters with achievement of arms. – Francis Butler †1721. Marble tablet with cherub's head below and urn with swags above. – In the churchyard a fine headstone for R. Crowe †1779, with Rococo decoration.

The church stands to one side of a large green at the High Street's N end. To its S TEMPLE FARM, late C16 or early C17, timber-framed but mostly cased in brick, with C18 and C19 brick additions; and facing the green CHURCH HOUSE, a small C15 weatherboarded hall house with C16 jettied cross-wing. S of Church House the timber LOCK-UP or cage, 1828; the stocks a replacement of 1947. Across the green, THE DOWER HOUSE, C17 timber-framed clad in chequered brick *c.* 1700, with a late C16 weatherboarded and thatched barn alongside. Further up the High Street, on the W side, a terrace of six three-storey stock brick workers' COTTAGES, apparently built speculatively *c.* 1840 when the railway was being constructed. Windows with segmental heads and cast-iron pivot frames.

The railway runs alongside the STORT NAVIGATION, completed 1769, with a new cut in the NW corner of the parish including BRICK LOCK, with a little brick lock-keeper's cottage with Gothick windows dated 1830. The cut by-passes ROYDON MILL, late C19, two storeys of stock brick and weatherboarded third storey. Timber-framed former RAILWAY STATION, *c.* 1841, mostly weatherboarded, with a curved portico on the road front with coupled columns.

NETHER HALL, 1½ m. SW. Gatehouse and part of the curtain wall of a manor house that was almost certainly built by Thomas Colt †1467, a date supported by tree-ring dating. Brick with blue brick diaper and stone dressings. Of the two towers flanking the single gateway one stands upright, semi-octagonal, three storeys high and decorated with trefoiled corbel friezes. The other has collapsed, and one now looks into the porter's lodge that was behind it. To its r., the intact garde-robe and staircase towers, the latter with vaulted brick spiral stair. Partial restoration in 1993–4 showed that the brick construction was supported by a framework of lacing timbers joined together by iron fixings, and vertical iron rods, a highly unusual method that suggests the involvement of foreign craftsmen. To the s, i.e. outside the moated enclosure, is a farmyard with a late C14 or early C15 house on the w side. Gabled and jettied cross-wings. Crown-post hall roof with sooted timbers. To the l. a further gabled and jettied cross-wing, C16 or C17. E of the house a weatherboarded aisled barn, c. 1400, to the SE a C17 weatherboarded granary.

₇₀₉₀

RUNWELL

ST MARY. The best things are the two C15 timber porches. The side openings are arched and cusped. Over the gateway is a crown-post. The main difference between N and S is that the one has quatrefoils, the other trefoils in the spandrels of the arches. w tower with diagonal buttresses, battlements, and a recessed spire. Higher stair-turret. Nave and chancel in one. Double hagioscope. Four-bay s arcade with short circular piers and double-chamfered arches – the only reminder of the C13 in a church otherwise entirely Perp. Restored by *Chancellor* in 1867, and again in 1907–9 by *W. F. Unsworth*, when the chancel was restored to its length before shortening *c.* 1400. Unsworth also rebuilt the s aisle w wall, underpinned the aisle arcade and the rebuilt the wall above it, opened out the roof, restored the s porch, and added the s vestry. – SCREEN, with rood. By *Unsworth*, the corpus added 1941. – POOR BOX. Oak, hollowed-out, iron-bound. – STAINED GLASS. Fragments of C13 or C14 glass in s aisle E window, and of C15 glass in vestry. E window, 1907, and chancel N †1924 by *Heaton, Butler & Bayne*. Chancel N †1903 by *Ernest Geldart*, made by *Taylor & Clifton*, 1909. w window by *J. N. Lawson*, 1958. – MONUMENTS. Brasses of Eustace and Margaret Sulyard of Fleming's †1547. 12-in. (30-cm.) kneeling figures between pilasters carrying a pediment. – Edward Sulyard †1692, 'the last of his house and family', signed by *Thomas Cartwright the Elder*. Inscription on *trompe l'œil* marble drapery. Both monuments and a number of other features in the church were painted in the 1940s, an unfortunate attempt at brightening the interior.

RUNWELL HOSPITAL.* 1934–7 by *Elcock & Sutcliffe*, for the boroughs of East Ham and Southend-on-Sea, to accommodate 1,032 psychiatric patients on a 500-acre site. Basically sym-

---

* Much of the site is due to be redeveloped for housing.

metrical layout, centred on the administration building (two storeys, eleven bays stepping forward in two stages, with copper-covered clock tower) with boiler house in line behind it and separate, widely spaced wards and treatment blocks to either side. The latter mainly one- and two-storey, with wide verandas and solaria. To the N, a group of farm buildings, to the SE the chapel and nurses' home (THE LODGE, three storeys and attics, twenty bays punctuated by two canted stair towers), and staff housing by the S entrance. Creamy-white brick used throughout, with artificial stone dressings on more important buildings, and Neo-Georgian detailing. Staff houses more Modern in style with flat roofs, Crittall windows, and contrasting bands of dark brick. Highly unusual chapel (ST LUKE'S CHURCH). Pale brick walls and pantiles, creating a sort of Hispano-Moorish effect. Narthex, nave, chancel, transeptal S Lady Chapel and N vestry, apsidal sanctuary, and a massive squat tower over the chancel with a prominent curved NE stair-turret. Mansard roofs to nave and transepts. The nave windows (Crittall, square-headed) break through the eaves into the lower slope of the roof, with little semicircular dormers in the upper slope. Inside, the walls and ceiling of the nave form one continuous curve, with a wall separating nave from chancel with one large and two small round-arched openings. Complete Art Deco FITTINGS including ALTAR with riddel posts, and aluminium LIGHT FITTINGS in the form of Biblical oil lamps.

Runwell now runs into Wickford and the two cannot be differentiated, but the N of the parish is rural and contains other buildings of interest.

FLEMING'S, 1½ m. NNW. Fragment of a larger house of *c.* 1600. Brick, with cement dressings. The showpiece is a two-storey bay window on the N side with five-light windows, on the ground floor with one transom, on the upper floor with two. The room formed a corner of the house, as on the upper floor there is another large window towards the E. The N bay has a gable with obelisks. The chimneystack with diagonal shafts on the E front is renewed, but correctly. Two-bay block to the W dated 1810. On the E side of the entrance a single-storey outbuilding with a two-centred stone doorway and bread oven at the N end.

In Chalk Street, 2 m. N of the church, a mission church (St Andrew) with cottage by *Chancellor*, 1895. The very plain church has, since *c.* 1990, been transformed into CHERRY CHAPEL, a glorious pastiche of the Gothic Revival, complete with stained glass (including a window by *Mayer* of Munich) and matching garage.

SAFFRON WALDEN*

See also AUDLEY END, LITTLE WALDEN,
ST AYLOTTS, SEWARDS END

Churches 654
Castle 658
Public Buildings 658
Perambulations:
  1. High Street and streets to the west 661
  2. Market Place and streets to the east 664
  3. Suburbs: South of Audley Road 668
The Vineyard 669
Battle Ditches 669

Saffron Walden is a town of exceptional interest, and has managed to preserve much of its medieval character. After the Norman Conquest a settlement grew up around the castle founded by Geoffrey de Mandeville, with two parallel streets, Church Street and Castle Street, E of the present High Street. As the town grew the market moved away from the castle, to the S, where the streets still follow the line of the medieval market rows. The town's main peiod of prosperity was between about 1400 and 1700, based like many East Anglian towns on the wool trade, but also, unlike them, on the growing and selling of saffron, an expensive commodity used for dyeing and as a medicine. The town became known as Saffron Walden (rather than Chipping, i.e. Market, Walden) in the C16. The most obvious sign of this prosperity is the church, but it is also evident from the large number of high-quality timber-framed buildings. By the C19, the town's most important industry was malting: at the end of the C18 there were forty-one maltings. The Quaker Gibson family were leading maltsters and brewers, who moved into banking and spent much of their fortune on buildings and institutions (many by *William Beck* and *Edward Burgess*, themselves Quakers) which still dominate the town. The town's principal benefactors had until then been the Braybrooke family of Audley End (*see* p. 95), built on the site of Walden Abbey W of the town.

CHURCHES

ST MARY THE VIRGIN. One of Essex's largest parish churches, with a total length of nearly 200 ft (62 metres), and lying in such a commanding position, on a hill, higher than the surrounding streets, that it can be seen as prominently from the N as the S. It is also one of the most lavishly designed – in a style entirely from across the border, East Anglian of the Suffolk and even more the Cambridgeshire brand of Perp. There are indeed certain features which make connections

---

* Of many books on the town, *The Buildings of Saffron Walden* by Martyn Everett and Donald Stewart (2003) provides the best architectural information.

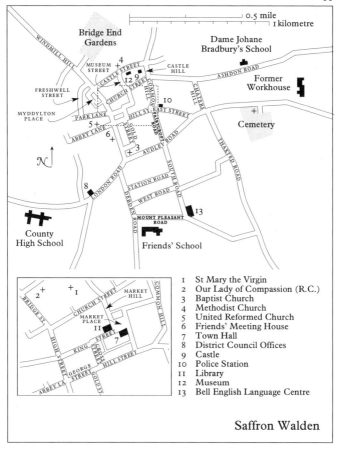

1   St Mary the Virgin
2   Our Lady of Compassion (R.C.)
3   Baptist Church
4   Methodist Church
5   United Reformed Church
6   Friends' Meeting House
7   Town Hall
8   District Council Offices
9   Castle
10 Police Station
11 Library
12 Museum
13 Bell English Language Centre

Saffron Walden

with King's College Chapel and Great St Mary more than likely. The C13 church was rebuilt between *c.* 1450 and *c.* 1525, beginning with the chancel and ending with the chancel arch, the nave clerestory, alterations to the chancel chapels, and the completion of the W tower. A contract of 1485 exists with *Simon Clerk* and *John Wastell.* Clerk was master mason at Eton *c.* 1460 and at King's College Chapel *c.* 1480; Wastell succeeded Clerk at King's and was one of the most distinguished masons of his generation. The church has been the subject of several restorations, but externally the only major post-medieval change is the tall octagonal spire added in 1831 by *Rickman & Hutchinson.* The first restoration, 1790–3 by *R. W. F. Brettingham,* particularly affected the interior; much of this was undone by *R. C. Hussey,* 1859–60. *Butterfield,* 1873–8, mainly did repairs. The surviving parts of the earlier church comprise a crypt partly below the S aisle and partly below the S porch, and the arcades from the chancel into the N and S chapels, and from these chapels into the aisles. These indicate a church with a crossing and transept, narrower aisles, and a s porch.

EXTERIOR. The material is largely clunch. The W tower has setback buttresses, decorated battlements, and at the corners big panelled polygonal pinnacles like turrets. The tall octagonal stone spire of 1831 has crockets and two tiers of dormers, the lower one of two lights with a transom. The total height is 193 ft (59 metres). The aisles, clerestories, and chancel chapels are all embattled and have pinnacles. There are large, wide four-light windows in both aisles with elaborate but not very interesting panel tracery, equally large windows of different, somewhat closer panel tracery in the chancel chapels, a C19 five-light E window, and three-plus-three-light clerestory windows of the early C16. At the E end of the nave clerestory are two polygonal turrets with crocketed stone roofs clearly dependent on King's College Chapel as completed in 1515. The two-storey s porch (whose upper storey contained a meeting room for the guild of the Holy Trinity, and later the Town Council) is also embattled. It has a four-light upper window. On the E wall is a fragment of a C11 cross-shaft built into the base. The N porch has only one storey, and is pinnacled. The porches are all that differentiate the two sides of the church.

Now for the INTERIOR, starting with the porches, which again show their differences. The s porch vault is more elaborate than that of the N: a two-bay fan vault with two bosses (cf. Cambridge customs of the early C16) as against a simple one-bay tierceron vault of star shape. In the nave, the seven-bay arcades are very tall with lozenge-shaped piers enriched by four attached shafts and with hollows and finer connecting mouldings in the diagonals. Only the shafts towards the arches have capitals. The shafts to the nave run upwards unbroken (except for a thickening at the main horizontal course) to the springers of the roof and only there have capitals. The diagonal members have no capitals at all. The spandrels of the arches are closely decorated with tracery as at Great St Mary's Cambridge and of course also at Lavenham and other Suffolk churches. The horizontal course has fleurons, the clerestory mullions are carried down in panels to the string course. The ROOFS are original everywhere, low-pitched and adorned variously with bosses, tracery, badges, etc. The deep wall-pieces of the chancel roof are carved with standing figures. As for other enrichments, the N aisle's three eastern bays have blank wall arcades with different intricately carved heads. The easternmost bay especially is worth studying. The figures in the spandrels represent King David, St John, Doubting Thomas, the Virgin, the Scourging of Christ, the Agony in the Garden. They are clearly earlier than the aisle and must for some reason be reused material. The chancel arcades have quatrefoil piers and moulded capitals and arches. The C13 CRYPT is divided into four bays and has single-chamfered arches and ribs springing from semi-octagonal responds.

REREDOS. 1867, of Caen stone, by *William Smith*. Carving by *J. Forsyth*, painting by *Ward & Hughes*, part of a scheme which included the decoration of the E wall, now painted over. – FONT. Octagonal, C15 to early C16, with quatrefoils and fleurons. – ROOD SCREEN. 1923–4 by *Sir Charles Nicholson*, carved by *E. Beckwith*. Figures added 1951. – ORGAN CASE. One side still in the pretty Gothick state of 1824, the other by *J.F. Bentley*, 1885. – PAINTING. Copy of Correggio's 'Il Giorno' by *Rev. M.W. Peters*, presented in 1793. – SCULPTURE. Fragment of an alabaster panel, *c.* 1410, in the S porch, N wall. Part of a former reredos; another fragment in Saffron Walden Museum. – STAINED GLASS. Early C15 head in S aisle W window. – Heraldic glass over door to N porch (originally in N chapel E window) and in S chapel E window by *James Pearson*, 1792. – E window by *Ward & Hughes*, 1866, also sanctuary N and S. – N chapel E by *Burlison & Grylls*, 1904. – N aisle, three by *James Powell & Sons*, 1888 (designed by *C. Hardgrave*), 1908 or -9, and 1912 (by *J.H. Hogan* and *John Brown*). – S aisle, from E to W: Four Evangelists by *Lavers & Barraud*, 1859; *Ward & Hughes*, 1870; Annunciation by *Powell*, 1916; *Lavers & Barraud*, 1858. – Tower window by *Henry Holiday* and *Powell*, 1888.

MONUMENTS. In S aisle, incomplete brass of Richard Wild †1484, vicar; 37-in. (94-cm.) figure, head now missing. Other brasses with figures, *c.* 1430–1530, collected in N aisle. – Thomas Lord Audley, Lord Chancellor, †1544 by *Cornelius Harman*. Black touchstone tomb-chest decorated with wreaths round medallions and ornamented pilasters in the taste of the tomb of Henry VII in Westminster Abbey; back-plate with splendidly carved coat of arms between pilasters (S chapel, moved from chancel in 1793). – Tomb-chest for John Leche †1521, with lid and inscription but no figures (N chapel, moved from chancel in 1793). – One side of a tomb-chest, N wall, N aisle, with three circular panels. – Thomas Baron †1656/7. Marble tablet with segmental pediment, on which recline weeping cherubs. Attributed to *Thomas Cartwright the Elder* (AW). – Two sons of Lord and Lady Braybrooke †1854 in the Crimea, by *T. Milnes*. With flags and other militaria.

OUR LADY OF COMPASSION (R.C.), Castle Street. Converted in 1906 from a C16 barn. Short brick tower with pyramidal spire, porch and cloister by *Hibbs & Walsh Associates*, 2004–5, with reordered sanctuary by *Anthony Delarue Associates*.

Former BAPTIST CHAPELS, London Road and Hill Street. *See* Perambulations 1 and 2.

BAPTIST CHURCH, High Street. By *Searle, Son & Hayes*, 1879. Brick with stone dressings. Tall gabled front with round-headed and circular windows. Galleried interior. Behind, in Audley Road, the earlier chapel of 1774–5, with C20 inserted floor. Brick, with burnt headers. Two tiers of windows, the lower with segmental, the upper with round heads.

GOLD STREET CHAPEL. *See* Perambulation 2.

METHODIST CHURCH, Castle Street. 1865. E.E. Stock brick with red dressings.

UNITED REFORMED CHURCH (formerly Congregational), Abbey Lane. 1811. Brick, with stuccoed front. Big open pediment and Ionic tetrastyle porch. Galleried interior, remodelled 1888. Behind, a rather ugly school, white brick with bands of red, by *H.N. Goulty* of Brighton, 1861.

FRIENDS' MEETING HOUSE, High Street. Brick with stone dressings, with Tudor-style windows and two straight gables. 1791, rebuilt 1879.* New entrance and interior remodelled 1969.

CEMETERY, Radwinter Road. 1855–7, by *Middleton & Pritchett*, with landscaping by *William Chater*. Asymmetrical layout, with ragstone Gothic lodge and Dec chapel.† NW tower incorporating porch with bellcote and short spire. Stock brick and flint mortuary. Small Second World War cemetery, with *Blomfield*'s Cross of Sacrifice.

CASTLE

Large fragments of the flint-rubble walling of the C12 keep. Built by 1139, but dismantled by Henry II in 1158. The keep had a forebuilding to the W which was ascended from the S along the W wall of the keep by a staircase. In 1796 *Placido Columbani* and *Richard Ward* built the turret for Lord Howard de Walden in brick faced with flint, as a signalling station.

PUBLIC BUILDINGS

TOWN HALL, Market Place. A properly townish brick house of 1761–2, of which part of the front and one side can still be seen, but bursting from its face is a large half-timbered, gabled addition by *E. Burgess*, 1878–9, which projects over the pavement on a three-bay stone Gothic arcade. This continues in the same vein as a large rear block at the rear. One wonders why they bothered to keep any of the C18 building; perhaps the intention was to create an impression of a medieval moot hall insensitively extended in the C18. Burgess's additions (paid for by G.S. Gibson) provided a council chamber and committee room on the ground floor, and grand staircase leading up to a large hall at the back and courtroom at the front.

COUNCIL OFFICES, London Road. Former General Hospital by *W. Beck*, 1864–6, restored and extended for Uttlesford District Council by *Darbourne & Partners*, 1988–90. Beck's first building for the town, won in competition; the cost was met by a legacy of £5,000 from W.G. Gibson. Exuberant Ruskinian Gothic in brick, with white brick and stone dressings. Plate tracery. Shallow H-plan, with a chimney gable in the centre and two gabled wings. Open porch on granite columns. In front and to the l., Darbourne & Partners' block projects at

---

* Apparently not, as one might expect, by *E. Burgess*.
† Second (Nonconformist) chapel dem.

right angles, using similar materials in a late C20 idiom, and with a central gable complementing Beck's work. In the angle between the two, a secondary entrance and glazed link, leading to the civic suite of council chamber etc.

POLICE STATION, East Street. 1884–6 by *Henry Stock*, County Surveyor. Neo-Tudor, still quite domestic but on a large scale. Paired gables at the front and a tall porch with shaped gable. The W side has plastered gables with bargeboards, the E side a chimneystack in a crowstepped gable.

PUBLIC LIBRARY, Market Square. 1847–8 by *Richard Tress*, as the Corn Exchange. In an exuberant Italianate style. Symmetrical tripartite façade with a central arch flanked by coupled giant columns and supporting a mighty clock and cupola on big scrolls etc. The lower flanking sides have open pedimented doors. Like so many exchanges it also included a savings bank, post office, and news room. The main space was originally open, but it was roofed over after being acquired by the Council in 1882. The roof level was raised in 1975 for the conversion to library and arts centre by *Ralph Crowe*, County Architect, when a gallery was inserted. Tress's building is linked to the earlier TOWN LIBRARY, a stuccoed palazzo on King Street. The ground floor takes the form of a five-bay Tuscan arcade, with round-headed windows above to light the Reading Room, which must be the most civilized public room in Essex. It houses the collection of the Saffron Walden Literary and Scientific Institute, founded 1832, moved here in 1853. The Town Library was enlarged and remodelled in 1888–9 at the instigation of Mrs Gibson, and fitted with fine bookcases from the Gibsons' Hill House, High Street. To this date must belong the pretty hanging sign, decorated with saffron crocuses.

MUSEUM, Museum Street. 1834, an early example of a purpose-built museum, erected by the town's Natural History Society. Symmetrical Neo-Tudor, two storeys, with a hall on the E side. Might *Harrison* or *Rickman*, then working at Audley End, have supplied the design?

BELL ENGLISH LANGUAGE CENTRE, South Road. By *E. Burgess*, 1882–4, as a teacher training college for the British and Foreign School Society (given by G.S. Gibson). Queen Anne style, three storeys with wings. Centre block with three asymmetrical gables and two two-storey bays, one rectangular and one splayed. Attached school to the N, 1901, presumably also by *Burgess*. Later additions include some by *R. Robertson*, 1938.

COUNTY HIGH SCHOOL, Audley End Road. By *Richard Sheppard*, 1952–3. Excellently planned and uncommonly extensive. Most recent additions include a multi-purpose hall and five classrooms by *Bland, Brown & Cole*, 2005.

FRIENDS' SCHOOL, Mount Pleasant Road. 1877–9 by *E. Burgess*. Founded in 1702, at Clerkenwell, and in 1825 moved to Croydon. Following outbreaks of typhoid in 1875, Saffron Walden was chosen for its healthy location, accessibility by railway from London, and the town's strong Quaker tradition;

the Gibsons gave the land. The main block, facing N, is of two and three storeys, brick with terracotta dressings sparingly used and a few Gothic and Tudor details, e.g. little buttresses with cusped gablets. Boys and girls were housed at opposite ends of this range, with a large Dining Hall and Lecture Room (now Library) in the middle. The Dining Hall, with open timber roof, projects from the main façade, and in the angle is a five-storey entrance tower with stepped battlements. To the r. is the kitchen court with gateway and half-timbered upper storey, and l. a lower extension of 1903, and l. of that the former Gymnasium (now drama studio) and indoor swimming pool, 1902, all by Burgess.

All the school's later buildings are in brick, unless otherwise stated, and generally quite plain. To the r. of the main block, the free-standing ASSEMBLY HALL by *Johns & Slater*, 1936, with metal windows. Extended by *Jolly & Millard*, 1984, as Music School. W of the Assembly Hall, at the corner of Mount Pleasant Road and Debden Road, the JUNIOR SCHOOL (Croydon House), a house of 1840 faced in flint with stock brick dressings, altered and extended by *Johns & Slater*, 1930. S of that, a single-storey classroom block of 1950, the first building for the school by *Kenneth Bayes* of the *Design Research Unit*, who prepared an ambitious but unexecuted scheme for expansion in 1946. Flint-faced concrete blocks, clerestory window, and flat concrete roof. To the S, the OCTOPUS GALLERY, converted by *Philip M. Cowell* in 1975 from the old reservoir of the town's waterworks, constructed 1862. Stock brick vaults on short square columns, the exterior walls rendered. Beside it the WATER TOWER, 1913 by *A.H. Forbes*, Borough Surveyor. 92 ft (28 metres) high, with four stages of round-headed recesses.

At the main building's E end is a two-storey classroom block (Essex Wing) by *Bayes*, 1961, forming a small courtyard. Also by Bayes, The Laurels, 1950, a small house S of Essex Wing, with a peculiar mansard roof that continues awkwardly over a porch-like projection. On the main building, a small extension by *Burgess* of 1901 between Essex Wing and the original part, and at the W end a three-storey classroom and art room block by *Fred Rowntree & Ralph W. Thorpe*, 1922, 'Queen Anne' with coved eaves and half dormers.

S of the main group, various detached buildings, including classroom blocks by *Johns & Slater*, 1936, and an early C18 wrought-iron gate from the old school at Croydon, thought to be designed by *Thomas Robinson*. Small timber Cricket Pavilion by *Paul V. Mauger*, 1925. At the far S of the site, the former SANATORIUM (now Gibson House) by *Burgess*, 1913, but quite unlike his other work. Originally single storey, with pantiles and rendered walls, it has the air of a colonial bungalow.

DAME JOHANE BRADBURY'S SCHOOL, Ashdon Road. 1881 by *E. Burgess* as the Grammar School. Endowed by Dame Johane Bradbury in 1525, the style appropriate to that date. Gymnasium added 1896, further extensions in 1931.

Former WORKHOUSE ('The Spike'), Radwinter Road. By *James Clephan*, 1835–6, based on a model plan by *Sampson Kempthorne* for 300 inmates. Stock brick. Three storeys, cruciform, with an octagonal central block and square pavilions at the end of each wing. The round-headed windows grouped in threes are one of Clephan's hallmarks. Converted to flats by *Stefan Zins Associates*, 1999, with new entrance block.

BRIDGE END GARDENS. Begun by Atkinson Francis Gibson (†1829) and laid out in earnest by his son *Francis Gibson* from 1838 onwards, in collaboration with a local nurseryman, *William Chater*. Compartmented plan of small gardens divided by walls or hedges. In the Dutch Garden, a square brick pavilion, and on the Summerhouse Lawn an octagonal gault brick pavilion, the interior decorated by *L. G. Fry* in 1927 as a memorial to Francis Gibson. In the wall separating the Dutch Garden from Summerhouse Lawn, an archway with *Coade* stone keystone with a female head, 1794; another *Coade* keystone in the gardens' NE corner. Maze of 1840 replanted 1986, with central SCULPTURE by *Hamish Horsley*, 'The Mermaid', 2005. Restoration by *Liz Lake Associates* and *Elizabeth Banks Associates* began in 2003.

Former GASWORKS, Thaxted Road. 1836. Two brick and stucco entrance buildings, with pedimented gable ends and pilasters. Very early survivals.

Former WATERWORKS, Debden Road. *See* Friends' School.

PERAMBULATIONS

1. The High Street, its continuations, and streets to the west

The town really starts, on the SW approach (London Road), with the former Hospital, now Council Offices (*see* Public Buildings), and just beyond it a former Baptist Chapel (now a house) of 1822. Opposite, gault brick and stucco villas of about the same date, and a house of red brick with burnt headers and thin stone pilasters, early C19 with mid-C19 and early C20 additions. After this, DEBDEN ROAD comes in from the r. (Nos. 11–13 mid C19 with red and white bricks in bands, chequers, and even key pattern; *see also* Perambulation 3), and London Road curves round to the l. and the HIGH STREET begins.

On the l., No. 79, a picturesque brick cottage of *c.* 1870 with pretty iron casements, then Nos. 77 and 77A, Late Medieval, remodelled in the C19 with brick sides and rear. Two gables with decorative bargeboards continued across the front eaves. HILL HOUSE (No. 75), stuccoed brick, was built in 1818–21; later owned by G. S. Gibson, and remodelled and extended for him in the 1860s;* converted to flats by *Kenneth Mark*, 1982. At the back an Italianate loggia with carved capitals. The High Street now runs downhill, essentially Late Georgian in

* Possibly, on stylistic grounds, by *R. Tress*.

character, e.g. No. 73 with typical ornamental motifs. On the other side No. 74, five-bay, two-storey house with Tuscan door-case, and the earlier No. 72, with brick quoins and a doorway with rusticated brick pilasters. No. 67 opposite has an especially elegant early C18 doorway, but is timber-framed and of C16 origin, as is No. 65. Nos. 61–63 provide a complete contrast: High Victorian Gothic brick with stone dressings by *W. Beck*, 1864. Further on, THE TEMERAIRE (No. 55) must be *c.* 1830, with its heavy Tuscan doorcase. No. 53 has a Greek Doric porch and two bow windows of the same date.

We are now at the bottom of the hill, at a crossroads with Abbey Lane to the l. and George Street to the r., and as the street narrows we enter a different period. This is heralded by Nos. 44–46 on the SE corner (formerly the Greyhound Inn), early to mid-C16 with gabled cross-wing and jettied front with embattled bressumer. First, though, a diversion down ABBEY LANE, for examples of mid-C19 philanthropy, starting with a row of cottages for employees of the Gibson family, 1840–50. Single-storey centre range with two-storey cross-wings at each end, gault brick with stone dressings, and Neo-Tudor windows. Bargeboarded gables to the wings. Then, after the United Reformed Church (*see* above), the KING EDWARD VI ALMSHOUSES, founded 1400, refounded 1549, rebuilt in 1782 and again in 1829–33; design supplied by *Henry Harrison*, who had been working at Audley End for Lord Braybrooke, with construction supervised by *William Nash* of Royston, who made minor changes. Brick, with composition dressings, in a thin Tudor Gothic style. Long two-storey range of twenty-two bays, with a gabled cross-wing at each end and in the middle a chapel with Perp window. In front and to the sides separate blocks in similar style but white brick, 1840 (E) and 1881 (W) paid for by the Gibsons – the wealthy, Nonconformist middle class taking on part of the aristocracy's role. At the back of the site (on Park Lane), two gault brick houses of 1847 form part of the group. Beyond the Almshouses, Walden Lodge and the entrance to Audley End park (q.v.).

Now we return to the High Street, whose next section is dominated, on the W side, by the POST OFFICE, a fine seven-bay C18 brick front with a three-bay pediment and doorway with carved brackets. Interior reconstructed *c.* 1973 by the *Property Services Agency*. On the E side, CROSS KEYS HOTEL, on the corner of King Street, with exposed timbers, jettied along both street fronts with a dragon post on the corner. It dates from the C15, and the corner block was originally a shop, entered from King Street. On the High Street front, a first-floor frieze window with traceried lights, largely restored. N block C16. Then a complete change at the corner of Church Street, a very attractive early C19 gault brick house with rounded corner. Shopfront with attached Corinthian columns, corner doorway and above it a window, also with columns, and cast-iron balcony. The house opposite needs to the seen from the side: early C19 gault brick front with cement pilasters, the front half of the roof hipped slate, the back half tiled over the earlier, timber-framed part of the building.

N of Church Street, the long rendered range of the SAFFRON HOTEL, the central part of which (l. of the carriage opening) is *c.* 1500, with an early C19 front. At the far end of the row, No. 4 has two gabled and jettied cross-wings; N side also jettied. The exposed timbers in the gables are not original, but the interior construction suggests that the S wing is late C14 or early C15, the N wing mid to late C15. On the W side, No. 7 is early C19 brick with an elegant stuccoed front, including two shallow canted bays. No. 3 has on its side wall a row of three arched recesses and the date, 1848. Back on the E side, on the corner of Castle Street, THE CLOSE, late C15 and early C16, with exposed timbers, the hall range jettied. It formed the N part of a larger house; the S part was encased with brick (for Francis Gibson) in 1854, then dismantled and re-erected (without the brick) at West Grinstead (West Sussex) in 1934, when the retained N part was restored.*

BRIDGE STREET continues the High Street at this point. Here, right at the beginning, at the corner of Myddylton Place, stands the best medieval house of Saffron Walden (Youth Hostel), long and low, with exposed timbers and a courtyard. It is jettied along MYDDYLTON PLACE, with two charming upper oriel windows, and at the corner a diagonally-set carved bracket on a carved post. Inside, the most interesting feature is the original screen with a wide arch in the middle and smaller and lower doorways l. and r. The spandrels of the centre arch have leaf carving. The house seems to date from *c.* 1500. In the C18 it was used as a malthouse, when the hoist loft was added at the front (hoist wheel still *in situ*) and a small brick extension at the rear. Further down Myddylton Place, MYDDYLTON HOUSE is C16 with C18 additions and a C19 gault brick front. Beyond it, WALDEN PLACE (now flats), standing in its own grounds, almost a country house. Mid-C18 brick, five bays, two-and-a-half storeys, with a pedimented doorcase with Roman Doric pilasters.

The Youth Hostel continues along Bridge Street with a lower, jettied building of *c.* 1600, then down again to what was a late C16 barn, with a wagon way though the middle bay and then a weatherboarded section. On the E side, a small gault brick house dated 1838, built by the Gibsons. Back on the W side, Nos. 5–7 are late C15, jettied, with screens passage, then on the corner No. 1 FRESHWELL STREET, C15, jettied along both fronts, and very cosily plastered. Shallow first-floor oriel to Bridge Street. Inside, remains of medieval shop openings with arched heads. Along Freshwell Street, FRESHWELL HOUSE, C16 and C17 timber-framed and plastered with an C18 brick front including pedimented doorcase with Gibbs surround. Also a row of two-storey brick 'Almshouse Tenements' built by G.S. Gibson, 1881.

---

*Some C16 panelling, not original to the house, reused at Elsenham Place (q.v.).

Back in Bridge Street, No. 15 appears to be a large early C18 house: plastered front of three storeys and seven bays, with quoins and modillion cornice. But the N wall has a C17 brick chimneystack with four octagonal shafts and a blocked, three-light, pedimented window. The core of the house is late C15. Opposite, the EIGHT BELLS, C15 and late C16, has a jettied front. Bressumer carved with leaves and four original upper windows with plaster coving underneath. Carved dolphins below the centre window downstairs. Bridge Street ends with rows of C15 and C16 jettied cottages on both sides; Nos. 24–26 and 27–31 are Wealden-type. SWAN LODGE (*see* under Audley End, p. 105) marks the end of the town.

2. Market Place and streets east of the High Street

CASTLE STREET lies to the N of the church and castle, long and quiet and nicely varied. It begins on the N side with two timber-framed houses of *c.* 1600, refronted in gault brick, with decorated bargeboards dated 1843. The S side takes longer to get going, being taken up with the outbuildings of The Close (*see* High Street, Perambulation 1); No. 2, TRINITY HOUSE, has a gault brick pilastered front of *c.* 1840, but is timber-framed, *c.* 1700. It stands opposite the alleyway to Bridge End Gardens (*see* Public Buildings), down which is the FRY ART GALLERY, which presents to the outside world little more than a door in a gault brick wall. Built in 1856 to house the collection of Francis Gibson, which passed by descent to the Fry family, and now home of the North West Essex Collection of work by Edward Bawden, Eric Ravilious, and others (cf. Great Bardfield). Top-lit entrance hall and corridor with walls marbled by *Mark Fry*, 1987, leading to two top-lit galleries.

Still on the N side, WALSINGHAM HOUSE (No. 35), was the Grammar School, the front block rebuilt in 1825; brick, two storeys and three bays. Extended to the rear in 1852 to join up to a timber-framed schoolroom which is inscribed over the doorway '1655 Aut Disce Aut Doce Aut Discede' (either learn, or teach, or go away). Opposite, a narrow pathway gives a fleeting view of the church. E of the path No. 8, early C19 gault brick, formerly The Wheatsheaf pub. Back on the N side, BELLINGHAM BUILDINGS, almshouses of *c.* 1879. Brick with jettied, half-timbered upper floors, either side of the entrance to a small courtyard. Then an interesting row (Nos. 41–51) whose jettied fronts and recessed bays show them to have been three late C15–early C16 Wealden-type houses. No. 55, at the end of the row, is a C15 hall house with the unusual feature of an undershot cross-passage, i.e. the passage is part of the cross-wing rather than being at the end of the hall range.

Shortly after this the street widens out where it is joined by Museum Street from the S. On the SW corner the former VIC-ARAGE, now doctors' surgery, 1793 by *William Ivory*. Brick, two storeys and three bays, C19 trellised porch. Stone plaques with Latin inscriptions record the original construction, and conversion in 1987. s of the vicarage, Nos. 2–6 MUSEUM STREET, a terrace of three early C19 gault brick houses. Three storeys, one bay each, with horizontal sliding slashes. On the E side of Museum Street the corner curves to follow the line of the inner bailey of the Castle, with Nos. 11–15, a late C15 timber-framed and plastered house with jettied front that was originally of Wealden type, then No. 17, three-storey red brick with gault brick dressings dated 1863. Projecting gabled entrance bay with round-arched windows.

Castle Street continues, mostly quietly (Nos. 77–81 the noisy exception, High Victorian brick with yellow and black dressings and three gables with scalloped bargeboards), until CASTLE HILL is reached. From here one can walk s, round the grounds of the Castle, to reach CHURCH STREET, which runs parallel to Castle Street. On the s side, a short row of early C19 houses, notably No. 33 (THE GRANGE), gault brick with stuccoed front. Tuscan doorcase and projecting pedimented bay of three storeys with shallow two-bay bow. The main interest of Church Street lies further down with a group of four houses at the corner of Market Hill. These are among the most precious of Saffron Walden, dating from the C14 and C15, and with jettied gables of many sizes, curved brackets, moulded bressumers, and the most lively C17 enrichments in plaster, geometrical patterns, foliage, birds, and also figures. On one of the houses (formerly the SUN INN) appears the date 1676 and two figures in C17 dress, variously interpreted as Thomas Hickathrift and the Wisbech Giant, or Gog and Magog. A stork and initials record a restoration in 1871 by the then owner, G.S. Gibson. Further w, on the N side, CHURCH PATH with its row of pretty late C16 cottages (once one building, with continuous jetty and exposed timbers) leads up to the church, and then two timber-framed houses with C18 brick fronts, No. 8 Church Street of four bays and No. 6 of six, dating back to the C15 and C17.

It is best now to return to Market Hill and so arrive at the MARKET PLACE. In spite of the sad loss in 1969 of the Rose and Crown (*c.* 1600, with a front of *c.* 1700, restored by *W.E. Nesfield* in 1872–4; dreary replacement by *W. Saunders & Partners*), this remains a great ensemble, C19 in its chief accents and much of it due to the Gibson family. W.S. Gibson, as we have seen, paid for the new Town Hall on the s side, and on the E side is his bank (Gibson, Tuke & Gibson, now BARCLAYS), 1873–5 by *Nesfield*, adjoining the Rose and Crown (and replacing premises at No. 13 Market Hill, 1864). An original, self-certain Neo-Tudor design that looks a good deal later than it is. Brick, with stone dressings. Two bold, very long four-light transomed windows close together on the ground floor. Next to them a tall and deep two-centred arch up which the stairs lead from street level to the banking hall, and to the r. of that a smaller entrance to the offices, with Franco-Flemish early C16 style detail. The spandrels of the main arch are carved with storks, Gibson's emblem. This, and carving of interior woodwork, was by *J. Forsyth*. The lead parapet is decorated with irregularly spaced ornamental discs, much used by Nesfield and his erstwhile partner Norman Shaw, who called them 'pies'. The building is higher than those surrounding it, with tall chimneys that make it almost as prominent a landmark as the church.

The third Gibson feature is the extravagant Gothic DRINKING FOUNTAIN in the middle of the square by *J. F. Bentley*, executed by *T. Earp*, exhibited at the International Exhibition of 1862, and presented to the town by Mrs Gibson the following year. Its four sides are carved with Biblical scenes set in cusped tabernacles.

As for the square's other two sides, the W is dominated by the former Corn Exchange, now Library (*see* Public Buildings), while the N is occupied by a nine-bay building, originally C18 but much altered in the C19 and C20, the three l. bays of which have a nice early C19 iron balcony with tented canopy.

KING STREET leads out of the SW corner of the Market Place. On the N side, the splendid sequence of mid-C19 library buildings is followed by the rather less elegant commercial display of the former Post Office and row of shops by *Benison & Bargman*, 1889. High gabled brick fronts. Between the two and set back from the street, LIME TREE COURT, a three-storey house of *c.* 1800. Gault brick, the first two storeys and the centre three (of five) bays ochre-washed. The pedimented centre bay has a Venetian window with stucco Adam-style ornament, the bays either side with round-headed windows in rusticated surrounds and little balustrades to the windows above. Adam-style decoration inside. The whole gives the impression of striving to be fashionable and genteel in too mean a space. Then King Sreet narrows; between Nos. 22 and 26 a tall early C16 carriageway with pilasters and decorated spandrels. The timber-framed buildings to either side of the alley frame a view of the church spire.

The important buildings of King Street are, however, on the S, either side of Cross Street. On the SW corner, Nos. 17–21, is a Late Medieval hall house whose hall range has a plastered front of *c.* 1800. The r. cross-wing is gabled with original bargeboards and a pretty, early C19 oriel. The l. cross-wing is most interesting, for its C15 timber frame is exposed, and jettied to N and E with moulded angle posts. Along its E side are two pairs of medieval shop openings, with four-centred arched heads. The same feature (as well as a doorhead) can be seen on the W wall of a building on the other side of Cross Street (former Hoops Inn), but the front has been very much altered. No. 13, late C15, has a nice early C19 double shopfront.

Cross Street leads through the market rows, narrow streets following the medieval pattern, to George Street, continued to the E in HILL STREET. No. 5 is early C18, see the carved brackets of the doorway with the characteristic upcurved frieze, and the red and blue-black brick chequerwork. Dog-leg staircase with turned balusters and Corinthian newel posts. Much extended in the mid C19, as can be seen from JUBILEE GARDENS – which also allows a view of the back of Nos. 1–3, unexpectedly picturesque Mid Victorian, if one ignores the C20 additions. In the gardens, a Victorian-style octagonal BAND-STAND by *The Kenneth Mark Practice*, *c.* 1991–2. Opposite the bottom of Market Street, the reused stone gateway to the Cattle Market, 1831.

At the end of Hill Street, Nos. 25–25A, timber-framed and plastered with C20 pargetting, was a Baptist Chapel of 1744, superseded in 1792 by a building with double-hipped roof behind it (now in commercial use, reached via Elm Grove). Hill Street leads into EAST STREET, with the Police Station (*see* Public Buildings) and then the former BOYS BRITISH SCHOOL (now offices), dated 1838, a nice, neat, gault brick building, nine bays wide and low, with a three-bay centre of attached Tuscan columns. Nos. 17–37, on the same side, are a row of early C19 weavers' cottages, flint with brick dressings, two storeys to the street but three storeys behind.

Instead of going directly into East Street, one can turn from the end of Hill Street up COMMON HILL. On its w side THE PRIORY, with an Elizabethan s half and C17 N half. Fine chimneystack with diagonally placed shafts. Two-storey porch with an upper window made Venetian in the C18. Attached to the N end a little gazebo, early C19 flint and brick. On the Common's E side, in CHATERS HILL, large C19 houses take advantage of the view, including EASTACRE (formerly The Grove, now divided), 1804 by *William Robinson*, a local architect and builder, for himself. Main block of three bays and two storeys with bays and Ionic porch. Large C19 conservatory with sweeping serpentine roof. Nearby, on the Common, a TURF MAZE of medieval origin. First recorded in 1699; it was re-cut then and on several occasions in the C19 and C20. It consists of a series of concentric circles cut into the turf, the largest about 95 ft (29 metres) in diameter, surrounded by a low bank, with a low mound in the middle, and four bastion-like low mounds round the circumference.

We now have to return to the centre, but shall do so by way of AUDLEY ROAD, which forks off from East Street near the bottom of Chaters Hill. Just after the fork, on the s side, FAR-MADINE, a two-storey, three-bay brick house of *c.* 1800 with Doric porch, now flats. On the N side, behind Nos. 21–29, facing terraces inscribed 'Artisans Buildings 1882' in the stucco string course. Two large mid-C19 houses on the corners of South Road and Fairycroft Road, then on the s side REED LODGE, a wonderful early C19 *cottage orné*, gault brick with tall chimneys and steep thatched roof. On the N side, entrance gates to Elm Grove, *c.* 1835, one of the Gibson family homes; the house has been demolished, but a brick and flint garden folly ruin can be seen in Elm Grove, off Fairycroft Road. It is surrounded by brick bungalows and flats with monopitch roofs by *Byrd & Tyler Associates*, *c.* 1972.

Audley Road comes out at the top of the High Street, by the Baptist Church. A short way downhill is GOLD STREET, in many ways the most delightful street in Saffron Walden. It begins rather surprisingly, with a C19 brick and weather-boarded workshop that has achieved a picturesqueness its original occupiers could never have anticipated. Next to it the GOLD STREET CHAPEL, its narrow brick front with simple shaped gable and pedimented doorway belonging to a much more urban back street than this. But then comes a row of modest C17 houses, timber-framed and plastered, that turn the corner; and the street slopes gently down to the N. On the far side of the valley, seeming to float above the buildings of King Street, is the whole S side of St Mary the Virgin, with a clear view through the clerestory windows. Down the E side of Gold Street, a terrace of two-storey brick 'blind-back' houses, i.e. originally built with windows only at the front. Dated 1810, four pairs stepping down the hill, with cast-iron casements. Near the bottom a large late C18 house (Nos. 23–27), brick, with three canted bays and a large two-storey carriageway. This led through to maltings, redeveloped as housing; at the far end a doctors' surgery by *Ian Steen*, 1988. Plastered exterior with sweeping pantiled roof, exposed brick inside with high glazed waiting area. Down the W side, a variety of timber-framed houses, Nos. 34–38 early C16 with exposed timbers, an original arched doorhead and pair of arched shop windows (one now part of a doorway), and DOLPHIN HOUSE (No. 6), refronted *c.* 1700 with a charming plaster frieze and a dolphin. At the bottom of Gold Street we are back in George Street.

3. Suburbs: South of Audley Road

The final perambulation is very much shorter than the others, but worth taking for the quite different aspect of the town that it reveals. It begins with SOUTH ROAD, the continuation of Fairycroft Road S of Audley Road. On the W side, ALPHA PLACE, two facing terraces of three-storey gault brick cottages, dated 1850. They must have seemed very stark when new. Then comes STATION ROAD, with the former railway station (now two houses), 1865 by the Saffron Walden Railway Co.'s engineer, *John Sampson Pierce*. White brick, H-plan, the wings with rusticated quoins and open-pedimented gables. THE RAILWAY pub, almost opposite, very similar in style and no doubt the same date. Good distant view of St Mary the Virgin down Station Street. S of the old railway line, picturesque flint and brick semi-detached houses of *c.* 1850 with bargeboarded gables, then two terraces (Nos. 26–40) of later C19 houses, brick with black diapers and white bands and very muscular.

At the top of South Road the former Training College (*see* Public Buildings, Bell English Language Centre), and then MOUNT PLEASANT ROAD, which has, on its S side, the Friends' School (*see* Public Buildings), and on the N a variety of largeish houses that were built in its wake. The most extraordinary of these are Nos. 9–10, semi-detached but asymmetrical, 1890 by *William Bell & Sons*, the town's leading builders, for the Bell family's own use. Fronted with reused stone rubble (including fragments of gravestones), partly hung with green slate; the roof also of green slate. Irregular fenestration, including two pretty first-floor oriels, and a polygonal corner turret with copper roof. No. 12 is less extreme but shares some features, as well as boasting a large half-timbered gable.

Mount Pleasant Road leads into DEBDEN ROAD, with on its w side No. 64, another example of the High Victorian style that is dotted about the town. A particularly virtuoso display of polychromatic brickwork, with white and black lozenges and relieving arches etc., and panels of flint on the side elevations. Gables with pierced bargeboards and prominent chimneystack. Off Debden Road, in WEST ROAD, more examples of large late C19 houses, mostly semi-detached, some with half-timbering, one apparently built of stone, heavily rusticated. Debden Road comes out into London Road (*see* Perambulation 1), just before the beginning of the High Street.

THE VINEYARD, Windmill Hill, ½ m. NW of St Mary. 1864 by *W. Beck* for W. M. Tuke, G.S. Gibson's brother-in-law and fellow banker. Large High Victorian Gothic house, brick with stone dressings. Two storeys and attics, with gables and half-dormers, and small bell-tower with weathervane. Porch added after 1908. Planned round a large staircase hall, the drawing room and dining room projecting from it in short wings to the w and s. Lower service wing to the N. *J.F. Bentley* prepared designs for the drawing room chimneypiece, 1866, and ten years later for panelling and painted ceiling, but it is uncertain whether these were carried out. NE of the house, THE COACH HOUSE, from 1966 the home of the photographer *Edwin Smith* and his wife Olive Cook. Smith, who had trained as an architect, added a Regency-style hall and porch decorated with trellis-work. Garden ornaments include two massive ball finials from Knightsbridge Barracks, London, by *T. H. Wyatt*, 1880 (dem. 1966).

BATTLE DITCHES. At the w end of the town, immediately s of the line of Abbey Lane, a bank and ditch runs s for 484 ft (149 metres) and then turns sharply to the E for a further 495 ft (152 metres). Sections cut across the bank and ditch in 1959 indicated that the earthwork was constructed in the C13 as part of the town extension at that period. In the SW corner, excavated in the C19, were found over 200 Romano-British and Anglo-Saxon (probably Christian) burials.

ST AYLOTTS *5040*
2 m. NE of Saffron Walden

An important moated house that belonged to the abbots of Walden Abbey. The earliest mention of the site is in 1248, and it is possible that the moat dates from this time; a chapel is recorded in 1444. The present house, however, is a rebuilding of 1500–1 by John Sabysforth, abbot from 1484 until his death in 1509. Following the dissolution of Walden Abbey in 1537 St Aylotts was granted to Sir Thomas Audley, but apart from internal partitioning of the ground-floor rooms (most of which were reinstated in 1994–6) the building has remained substantially unchanged.

It is of eight bays and two storeys. The standard of construction is high throughout, although there is relatively little carved decoration other than the bressumer of the jettied upper floor which is in part decorated with scrolls. This storey is plastered and pargetted up to the steep, high tiled roof, which is broken along the SW side by two soaring chimneystacks. These are of brick, the material used for the ground floor, which is diapered on the NE side near the entrance. Some stone windows, notably one of three lights and a semi-octagonal bay of six in a room at the S end. This was the abbot's parlour (now kitchen), with a large fireplace in the SW wall; the opposite end of the room, with the bay, may have been used as an oratory. A polygonal stair-turret opens off the parlour leading up to the abbot's solar and bedchamber, rooms which originally formed a self-contained suite separate from the rest of the first floor. The original doorways survive and the fireplace in the solar has an embattled lintel of oak enriched with a flowing band of foliage and a thin foliage scroll. Garderobe beside the fireplace. The abbot's parlour opens into the hall, the spandrels of the doorway decorated with scallop shells denoting St James the Apostle, one of the Abbey's patrons. In the hall's SW wall a fireplace, with stone surround, and on its far side a screen with two openings (originally three – the middle one opened into a passage – and also with decorated spandrels) beyond the main entrance to the house, which is on the NE side. Behind the screen were two service rooms, one of which has been removed, leading into the kitchen (now drawing room) with its fireplace in the N wall. In the SW wall is a secondary entrance and a doorway through to another staircase which (together with a garderobe) is in a shallow projection. Above are two heated lodgings at the N end, over the kitchen, and over the hall a large heated withdrawing chamber or gallery (now subdivided) and an inner chamber, presumably accommodation for visitors. The spacious attics may have had more windows originally than the present single opening in the S gable; the roof has tie-beams on arched braces with collar-beams and two rows of wind-braces.

The apparent conventionality of the layout on the ground floor is complicated by the fact that it had an E wing on the entrance side whose extent and purpose remain unknown. It may perhaps have contained a chapel. On its site, N of the polygonal stair-turret, stands a late C16 or early C17 two-storey outbuilding, timber-framed with lath and plaster infill. It probably came from elsewhere and may originally have been a dovecote. A C17 barn that stood NE of the house, outside the moat, has been demolished.

ST LAWRENCE

ST LAWRENCE. Rebuilt 1877–8 by *Robert Wheeler*. Perp. Nave, lower chancel, and belfry. Kentish rag with dressings of Bath stone and stock brick. Fragments of stone from the old church incorporated in the vestry wall, and in the nave N wall a reused C14 PISCINA.

SALT HOUSE, 1½ m. NW, by *Alison Brooks Architects*, 2003–4. On the waterfront of the Blackwater estuary, at one end of a row of weatherboarded cottages. Clad in tropical hardwood, with a hipped slate roof twisted in a way that reflects the irregular plan. On floating piles capable of being raised in the event of a rise in sea level.

ST OSYTH

Legend relates that Osyth (or Osgyth) was married to Sigehere, C7 king of the East Saxons, who, once he accepted that their marriage was not going to be consummated, gave her the village of Chich (modern St Osyth) where she founded a nunnery. From there she was kidnapped by Danish pirates and beheaded for refusing to worship idols.

ST OSYTH PRIORY (later abbey) was established for Augustin- *p. 672* ian canons by Richard de Belmeis, bishop of London, shortly after 1120. A few fragments of the original building remain, and more from the C13. Late in the C15 the Priory's most important feature, the Gatehouse, was built, and in 1527 Abbot John Vintoner added the Bishop's Lodging. After dissolution in 1539 the abbey passed to Thomas Cromwell, to Princess Mary, and in 1553 to Thomas, 1st Lord Darcy, who made further additions. It remained with Darcy's descendants until 1714, after which it was owned by the earls of Rochford and then by an illegitimate branch of the family, the Nassaus. From 1863 to 1909 it was owned by Sir John Johnson, a London corn merchant, who made extensive alterations. For much of the second half of the C20 it was a convalescent home.

The state of the buildings in the C13 will first be examined. The priory church lay NE of the present Gatehouse, its site now laid out as gardens. The cloister was to the N of the church, surrounded as usual by domestic ranges on the W, N, and E sides, of which only fragments survive. On the ground floor of the W range were the cellars, or rather storerooms. Two of these with single-chamfered ribs across, dating from the C13, exist in the range SE of the Bishop's Lodging. Opposite, in the E range, in direct communication with the N transept of the church, to make access easy at night, was the Dormitory. Of this several chambers of the undercroft can still be seen. They are of the earliest period, roughly cross-vaulted. In the N range was the Refectory. All that exists of this is a piece of blank arcading at its E end, fine C13 work. Of equally high quality is the passage the other side of that E wall, converted into a chapel in 1866.

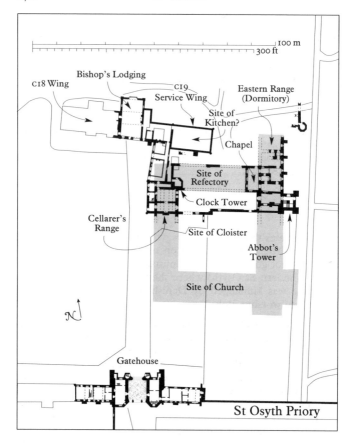

100 m
300 ft

C18 Wing
Bishop's Lodging
C19
Service Wing
Eastern Range
(Dormitory)
Site of
Kitchen?
Chapel
Site of
Refectory
Clock Tower
Cellarer's
Range
Site of Cloister
Abbot's
Tower
Site of Church
N
Gatehouse
St Osyth Priory

This is the best piece of the earlier Middle Ages at St Osyth,
with two slender Purbeck shafts dividing it into six bays and
with tripartite, elegantly filleted ribs. In addition, N of the site
of the Refectory is a corner of a C13 building, perhaps the
kitchen, with two semicircular responds. The capitals can no
longer be recognized in their details.

We have no means of ascertaining C14 and early C15 alterations or additions of any size. But in the late C15 the GATE-
HOUSE was built, the most splendid survival of the abbey. It
vies with the gatehouse of St John's Abbey at Colchester for
first place among monastic buildings in Essex. As at St John's,
the façade to the outer world is much more magnificent than
that to the monastery. It has a wall covered with flushwork
panelling, from the quatrefoil frieze at the base to the chequer-
pattern of the battlements. The tall carriageway has a two-
centred arch with lively carvings of St Michael and the Dragon
in the spandrels. Pedestrian entrances to either side. There are
tall slender niches above all three entrances, the higher middle

one with a canopy reaching right up to the two-light upper windows. To the l. and r. of this centre are very broad polygonal towers of three storeys. Inside the Gatehouse is an elaborate two-bay lierne vault with carved bosses. It springs from slim wall-shafts, the middle one on each side carrying thirteen ribs. The outer side towards the monastery has no flushwork panel tracery, only chequer and diaper patterns. It has only one wide gateway but four turrets, the outer two square, the inner two half-hexagons. The spandrels of the gateway are decorated with angels in quatrefoils holding shields.

The Gatehouse has two-storey embattled ranges to either side. The r. (E) one must be much older; for, invisible from the outside, its E bay contained originally a C13 gateway of two orders, of which a blocked arch can be seen on the inside. The rest of the range C15, like the Gatehouse; one of the rooms contains WALL PAINTINGS, in poor condition and very indistinct. However, at right angles to the l. range, projecting to the S, are the remains of another range. There is no more left of it than its E wall, with a round-headed gateway apparently of the C14. So here was yet another building connecting the priory with the outer world.

The next enrichment was the BISHOP'S LODGING by Abbot John Vintoner. He (like e.g. the abbots of Forde (Dorset) and Muchelney (Somerset) at the same time) built a mansion for himself which, though attached to the abbey, could compete with that of any nobleman. It is of diapered brick, which by then had become the fashionable building material, and extends N of the C13 cellarer's range (i.e. W of the site of the Refectory) and then turns W to face the great Gatehouse. Here Abbot Vintoner built a triple gateway not quite in line with the older Gatehouse and above it his own hall with a magnificent tall oriel window of six lights. The window itself was renewed in 1866, when the range behind was remodelled, but the corbelling, base, and head are original, as well as the stone panelling of the jambs and the arch of the oriel inside. It is all of the richest, though the motifs are not fanciful nor indeed imaginative – mostly cusped panelling, quatrefoils, and shields. Only at the head does the new Italian style make an appearance – one of the earliest in Essex. There are small naked figures and Renaissance leaves, and the date: 1527.

The Lodging's return range to the S is much lower and plainer, with straight gables and straight-headed windows of several lights, each light with an arched head. No attempt is made to match the oriel front nor to show symmetry in any other way. Inside this building on the ground floor there is much good panelling, not *in situ*, exhibiting vine ornament (for Vintoner), initials, dolphins, etc.

Lord Darcy was granted the priory in 1553, and set about creating a vast and splendid mansion from the monastic buildings, but it is difficult to evoke what it was like when he and his son John, 2nd Lord Darcy, lived there. The church and much around the cloister had been pulled down. The Refectory perhaps became the Great Hall. At the SE end of the E (dormitory) range of the former cloister Darcy built the ABBOT'S TOWER, proudly proclaiming the new lord's ownership. It has a square stair with solid newel leading up to a new upper dormitory storey containing several rooms of some size. The exterior has polygonal turrets, square on the ground floor, windows still similar to those of Abbot Vintoner, and is faced with chequer-work of limestone and septaria. Lord Darcy also remodelled the range S of the Bishop's Lodging, incorporating the C13 cellars. Brick and septaria chequer-work and forms still entirely Perp, with polygonal angle turrets or buttresses. Behind this another tower was built, octagonal on a square base, which now carries a pretty C18 timber lantern and clock. Moreover a completely new detached range was put up N of the old Dormitory. Of this only one angle with a polygonal turret stands upright. Into what kind of pattern can all this have formed itself? The answer probably is: none. No symmetry was attempted, just as no Renaissance decoration was used.

A brick range connecting the clock tower and the old dormitory range was built *c.* 1600, but of this only the S wall remains. Then decay set in. Nothing was kept up, and when the 3rd Earl of Rochford, who acquired the property in 1714, wanted convenient accommodation, he added what is in effect a red brick villa with a bow window to the W side of the Bishop's Lodging. The final major phase of work came in 1866–9, when the owner, John Johnson, rebuilt the Bishop's Lodging behind Abbot Vintoner's gateway and oriel. The main interest here lies inside, notably in the room lit by the oriel which contains elaborate Neo-Gothic doorcases, chimney-pieces, panelling, and furniture of a character more Continental than English. To the E of this Johnson added a service wing, and created a CHAPEL from the C13 passageway at the E end of the Refectory. This was given a floor of encaustic TILES and several STAINED GLASS windows, including depictions of Osyth, Sigehere, Richard of Belmeis, and Abbot Vintoner.*

A word needs to be said about the outbuildings that enclose the courtyard SW of the house. The range W of the Gatehouse is continued by a large C16 BARN. Stone on the N side, timber-framed and weatherboarded on the others. Tie-beams with arched braces inside. At right angles to this a range of mid-C19 brick STABLES, and then after a gap a detached C16 building of unknown purpose, built of medieval stone rubble and brick. The cottage at its N end has a C13 roof with smoke-blackened timbers, so was an original outbuilding (possibly a bakehouse or brewhouse) to the abbey. More outbuildings behind these of various dates, and beyond them the precinct WALL which runs round the W, S, and E sides of the priory.

---

*The windows may date from *c.* 1882: cf. the chancel of St Peter and St Paul, restored by Johnson in that year.

N of the house the outline of the medieval LITTLE PARK can still be traced. On its W side the remains of a SHELL HOUSE, marked on a map of 1762 (with another building now vanished) as a hermitage. The grounds were landscaped by the 4th Earl of Rochford, who succeeded in 1738 and converted the immediate surroundings of the priory into a picturesque garden with ruins.

ST PETER AND ST PAUL. The parish church lies just outside the abbey precinct, SE of the site of the priory church. It is in one way most remarkable, in that its large nave has brick piers and brick arches. The impression on entering is of a North German more than an English church. This nave with its aisles dates 29 from the early C16. The work was initiated by Abbot Vintoner and was probably going on at the same time as his additions to the abbey, i.e. *c.* 1527. The nave has a hammerbeam roof, and the aisles have flat roofs with moulded (S) and richly foliated (N) beams. A new chancel was also contemplated, as the responds of a wide and tall chancel arch prove; these contain squints which line up with the anticipated location of the new high altar. But the new chancel was not built, and much lower and narrower arches, perhaps originally meant to be temporary, connect the ambitious Tudor nave with the older church. The older church, at first hardly noticed, was, however, also quite ambitious. It dates mainly from the C13 and had a chancel and long transepts with E chapels or rather an E aisle. These were shortened in the C16. However, the chancel is still that of the C13 (one blocked S window), and the transepts still have thin E piers carrying triple-chamfered arches. The piers are circular, the N with four, the S with eight attached shafts. There is indeed, though almost unnoticeable, some evidence of a yet earlier age. The W wall contains the S respond of a Norman arcade, plain with the simplest capital.

Now the exterior. Two C13 chancel windows survive, their mullions and tracery lost. The E window is Perp of an unusual tracery pattern. In the S transept aisle's E wall are two early C14 windows. The S transept S window goes with the chancel E end. N and S aisle windows are latest Perp, of four lights with depressed heads and the simplest panel tracery. But the S aisle and its porch are diapered brick, whereas the N aisle is faced with flint and septaria, much patched with C18 and C19 brick, and the window orders are of flint and red brick. This aisle looks as if it might well be of post-Reformation date, but if so it reuses the N doorway, which has symbols of the Virgin and St Katherine carved in the spandrels. The W tower was in existence when the nave and aisle were built. It was probably attached in the C14 to the Norman nave. It has big angle buttresses with three set-offs, and battlements. A curious connection, including a squinch, was made in the C16 between the S aisle and the stair-turret. Chancel restored 1882, the nave 1899, when the N porch was added; all the work of *A. W. Blomfield*.

FONT. Octagonal, with panels containing a head of St John, an angel holding a shield, heart and flowers, etc. –

COMMUNION RAIL. Unusual 'sheepfold' pattern, a replacement in stone, 1882, of a wooden rail of the same shape. Within the rails a MOSAIC floor. – SCREENS. To N transept and tower, C19, formerly in the chapel of Whitelands College, Chelsea, installed 1930. STAINED GLASS. In chancel, three windows commemorating the restoration of 1882, one depicting the martyrdom of St Osyth. The E window looks like *Clayton & Bell*. – S transept aisle E by *Heaton, Butler & Bayne*, 1911. S aisle W by *G.E.R. Smith* of *A.K. Nicholson Stained Glass Studios*: designed 1940, installed 1951. – MONUMENTS. In chancel, two large standing wall monuments facing each other, almost identical in design. They commemorate the first and second Lord Darcy, Thomas †1558 and John †1581, and their wives. Erected by the third (and last) Lord Darcy, Thomas †1639. They date from *c.* 1620 and are attributable to *William Wright* (GF). Alabaster and marble tomb-chest with recumbent effigies, the husband behind and a little higher than the wife. Restrained background; no columns, no strapwork. – Lucy Countess of Rochford †1773. Standing wall monument with a straight-sided sarcophagus, and on it two urns, erected by her husband the 4th Earl. No effigy. Signed by *William Tyler*. – In S transept aisle, Briant Darcie (Darcy) †1587. Marble tablet with columns and arms. – John Darcy †1638. Recess containing tomb-chest with recumbent alabaster effigy. Against the back wall, brass plate with inscription and signature of *Francis Grigs*, 1640. – LYCHGATE. 1909 by *F.A. Rogers*.

The church is tucked away in CHURCH SQUARE, which has some nice C16 and C17 timber-framed cottages and on the N side the ST OSYTH SOCIAL CLUB, 1911 by *H.P.G. Maule* (*Forsyth & Maule*) as the Johnson Institute. Brick, with a stepped gable over the entrance. The village centre is the crossroads NE of the church, each of the roads different in character. Leading N, COLCHESTER ROAD, with the impressive precinct wall of the abbey on the W side. Houses on the E side include Nos. 36–38, C15 with long-wall jetty and gabled crosswing, timbers exposed. Nothing special in Clacton Road to the E, but SPRING ROAD, to the S, includes THE OLD HOUSE and LITTLE PRIORY, originally a single house. Two jettied crosswings with gables and a third smaller gable between them. The l. cross-wing and central range late C15, but the r. cross-wing has a crown-post roof with moulded base and capital datable to *c.* 1300. The cellar of this wing is lined with brick contemporary with the timbers above, an extremely early example of the use of medieval brick. W of the crossroads is THE BURY, a triangular green in front of the Priory, leading to MILL STREET. The tide mill at the head of St Osyth Creek has gone but the OLD MILL HOUSE is on the N side, C18 or early C19, red brick with a gault brick façade and very smart Roman Doric porch.

ST CLERE'S HALL, ½ m. SSE. The extremely rare case of a surviving aisled hall. It is in the centre of a C14 house with cross-wings, i.e. of H-plan. There is one pair of sturdy octagonal piers, and they carry, just like the posts in barns, braces along as well as across. These timbers have been carbon-dated to *c.* 1350. The roof runs straight down over the aisles, again as in barns. The N front has two gables, one jettied with a pretty C18 bow window below the overhang, the other underbuilt. In the latter, which has brick-nogging in the gable, can be seen the space where a projecting window frame once sat. Much C16 alteration in the cross-wings, including the extension of the E wing in brick. The staircase in its present form seems to be Jacobean. Timbers exposed on three sides, weatherboarded on the S, with an C18 turret looking out towards the sea.

PARK FARM, 1 m. NE. On part of the abbey's Great Park. The house is late C14, timber-framed and rendered, the ground floor faced in brick. Inside were two painted panels (now in Colchester Castle Museum), contemporary with the house but not necessarily made for it. One depicts the Virgin, the other a female figure, perhaps St Osyth. W of the house a pair of stone URNS, similar to those on the Rochford monument in the parish church.

MARTELLO TOWERS. 1809–12 (*see* Introduction, p. 76). One at Point Clear, 2½ m. W, another at Seawick, 2 m. ESE. A third, on Beacon Hill above Point Clear, was demolished in 1967. The one at Point Clear, now a museum, appears never to have been rendered, and retains a Second World War observation post.

SALCOTT

9010

ST MARY. C14 nave, late C15 S porch and W tower, flint and septaria with limestone dressings, all much renewed by *Chancellor:* tower restored 1876–7, nave restored (N wall rebuilt) and chancel added 1892–3. – PULPIT. C18, hexagonal, with elegant inlaid stars in the centre of the oak panels. – STAINED GLASS. E window by *William Lawson (Faith Craft Works)*, 1930. Chancel S by *Kempe*, 1897.

Several timber-framed houses along the street, of which the best is HORN FARM, the C15 cross-wing of a former hall house with jettied upper floor. Three-bay aisled barn to its W (now a house) tree-ring dated 1339, one of the oldest in Essex.

OLD VICARAGE. *See* Virley.

SANDON

7000

ST ANDREW. Nave and chancel Norman, see the remains of Roman brick quoins, also W of the chancel E end which is a Perp addition. N aisle C14, as shown by the three-bay arcade. This has semi-polygonal shafts to the nave and semicircular ones to the arches – all with capitals. The arches have two quadrant mouldings. Early in the C16, in the favourite Essex fashion, the battlemented W tower and S porch were erected in brick, with blue diaperwork. The tower has a much higher polygonal stair-turret, and a little brick dome. The brick W window is of three lights. The porch is distinguished by a rib vault and stepped battlements on a trefoiled corbel-frieze. Moderate restoration by *Chancellor & Son*, 1903–4, included removing plaster from the exterior walls, which are of flint rubble and puddingstone. Meeting room linked to N aisle by *K.C. White & Partners*, 1993; diapered brickwork to complement the C16 additions. Nave roof replaced in 1878, preserving a single C15 hammerbeam frame. – PILLAR PISCINA. C12, the shaft ornamented with spiral fluting and beading. – CHOIR STALLS. On N side, 1856, by *Henry Ringham*, with carved ends incorporating C17 work. – PULPIT. A fine, not at all showy, C15 piece. Its foot and stem are preserved, which is rare. The stem is a polygonal pier and the connection to the pulpit proper is trumpet-shaped. Simple traceried panels. Restored by *Ringham*. – DOOR. Originally the N door, uncovered in 1993, now displayed on the organ loft wall. Mid C14. – The church possesses a PAX,* that is a small wooden board for the Kiss of Peace to be given at services, of which very few survive; *c.* 1500. On one side is a painted Crucifixion. – PICTURE. St Andrew. By *Lynton Lamb*, who lived in the village. Presented in 1972. – STAINED GLASS. E window by *Heaton, Butler & Bayne*, 1920. Chancel N by *Horace Wilkinson*, 1929. Tower window, 1912, by *A.J. Davies* of the Bromsgrove Guild: Virgin and Child surrounded by angels, most of the colour provided by the angels' red wings. – BRASS to Patrick Fearne †1588 and wife, with kneeling figures (about 9 in. (24 cm.)).

The church stands in an immaculate churchyard with a green on the E side, and would present a perfect village scene were it not for the A12 on one side and power lines on the other. On the green's N side, SANDON PLACE, C16 with jettied crosswings, much altered. S of the church, the OLD RECTORY, 1756 (rainwater head). Painted brick. Five bays, with three-bay broken pediment and a doorway with attached Tuscan columns connected with a window which has volutes at the bottom.

BRIDGE FARM, ½ m. E. Early C17 timber-framed and plastered farmhouse, prettily dressed up in the mid C19 with hood-moulded Gothic windows, bargeboards to the two gables, and a veranda between the cross-wings, as well as cast-iron Gothic railings along the road. Brick BRIDGE over Sandon Brook by *Hopper*, 1817. Single span, with circular abutment piers.

WOODHILL, 1½ m. E. Five-bay, three-storey C18 house of red and blue brick. Doorway with pedimented Tuscan porch on r. bay. Single-bay two-storey addition to l., with Venetian window set in an arched recess, then a Diocletian window, then a Dutch gable with date (1798) and initials (of Samuel Charles Carne) in a circular panel. Addition in same style to the r.,

* Not on view.

dated 1868, with initials of Frederic Carne Rasch. Then a C19 extension protrudes before a third gabled addition, 1893, for Katherine Anne Rasch. The composition echoed on the garden front, but spoilt by later additions.*

SEWARDS END
Saffron Walden

5030

ST JAMES. Brick 'school chapel', 1847, to which was added, on the S side, a small church, 1870–1. Lancet style, with polygonal apse, S porch, and belfry with flèche.

VILLAGE HALL. 1994–5 by *The Kenneth Mark Practice*. Brick, square, with pyramidal slate roof and porticoes on the E and W sides.

A number of interesting houses along WALDEN ROAD, beginning at the W end with POUNCE HALL, early C17 timber-framed and plastered with a taller, gabled later C17 cross-wing. On the S side, CAMPIONS, L-plan, *c.* 1580, with some exposed timbers. Its extensive scheme of wall paintings of *c.* 1600 was largely destroyed early in the C20, but in an upstairs room survives a rich representation of tapestry that appears to hang behind elaborate arcading, its columns apparently resting on a tiled floor. Where the road bends N, ELMS FARM, timber-framed with a nice pargetted front and a decorated lozenge panel with the date, 1676, although the house may be older. SE of this corner, THE TOWERS, an intriguing mid-C19 brick house. Square, two storeys and three bays, and at each corner a three-storey tower with ogival roof, like a smaller version of Hallingbury Place, Great Hallingbury (dem.). Castellated porch, and castellated parapets between the towers.

SHALFORD

7020

ST ANDREW. Prettily situated with a stream running through the churchyard. Mainly flint rubble, restored 1871–2 by *C.C. Rolfe*, who added the N vestry and organ chamber. Otherwise C14. W tower with clasping buttresses. In the chancel and the N aisle some early C14 windows, but the most unusual motif is the straight-headed two- and three-light windows with a kind of reticulated tracery straightened out, and these are early Perp, i.e. later C14. The N and S aisle arcades rest on piers with four major and four keeled minor shafts. The arches are two-centred and have headstops. Early C14 SEDILIA with cusped arches on polygonal shafts and no ogee forms. Most remarkable are the three large and almost identical tomb-recesses, one in the N aisle, one in the chancel S wall, and one in the S aisle. No effigies, but that in the S aisle is probably the oldest, for Humphrey

---

*Two statues by *Samuel Carpenter* from the façade of Moulsham Hall, Chelmsford, formerly stood in front of Woodhill.

de Northwood, *c.* 1330, that in the chancel for his son John
†1362, and that in the N aisle possibly for Sir Roger de Scales
†1386, successive lords of the manor. Two hold tomb-chests
with indents for brass figures. All three have canopies with thin
buttresses and large cusped arches and ogee gables with crockets and finials. In the gables of two is a quatrefoil in a circle.
The third has the quatrefoil cusped. The one in the chancel
moreover has to the l. and r. of the gable large shields. – FONT.
C15, Hexagonal. Traceried stem, bowl with two small quatrefoils with shields in alternate panels, trefoils and quatrefoils on
the rest. – SCREEN with simply traceried lights, late C14. –
STALLS (W end of nave). Two, with poppyheads. Early C16. –
COMMUNION RAIL. *c.* 1700, with twisted balusters. – STAINED
GLASS. Many C14 fragments, including arms of the Northwood
family and its alliances. Mainly in the E window, also in a
window of the N aisle and the S aisle E. Main lights of the latter
by *Clayton & Bell* to Richard Marriott †1870. – MONUMENTS.
William Bigge of Redfants †1616. Mural brass with shields,
skull, and texts. – Richard Marriott of Abbot's Hall †1813.
White marble urn, inscription, shield etc. on grey marble background, a very smart effect. – STRAW DECORATION. Reredos
(now at W end), text over chancel arch, and two banners,
worked in plaited straw. Shown at the International Exhibition,
London, 1872.

SHALFORD HALL. The C17 house was all but destroyed during
the Second World War, and a new one built in the ruins by
Edward Samuel & Partners, 1967. Consent was given provided
the old walls were not disturbed, and the house was not visible
from the public road. So it is long and low, with low-pitched
roof of concrete pantiles. Walls include reclaimed bricks, but
most of the S front is of laminated pine rails, bolted to pine
mullions. On the N side, old walls enclose an entrance court.

The best houses are in the outlying parts of the parish:

ABBOT'S HALL, I m. ESE. Two-storey, five-bay gault brick house
of 1823, with three-bay service wing to the r. of 1879, three
storeys but the same height. Two-storey, two-bay ballroom
extension to the l., 1920.

ANCELLS IN THE HOLE, I m. SW. C16, of interest for the wall
painting in a ground-floor room. Female figure in late C16
dress.

REDFANTS MANOR, ¾ m. WNW. Very attractive combination of
a timber-framed hall house to which a brick wing was added
in the C16. On the l. a C14 cross-wing with underbuilt jetty,
extended to the rear later in the C14. Then a two-bay hall with
two-storey jettied porch on the r., still timber-framed: late C16
or early C17, replacing an earlier, lower hall. At the back a C16
staircase tower. To the r. of the porch the C16 wing, with cross-
wing to the r., considerably higher than the earlier part. Diapered brick with brick windows. One large room on the ground
floor and two above. In a first-floor room of the l. cross-wing,
wall paintings dating to the last quarter of the C16, or very early
C17, showing men hunting.

SHEERING

ST MARY THE VIRGIN. Flint rubble, with a NW quoin of Roman brick providing evidence of Norman origins.* Unbuttressed C13 W tower, completed or restored and embattled in the C16 in brick, restored 1906 by *T.G. Jackson*. Fine staircase of solid oak treads behind a partition, probably C16. Nave and chancel C14, including the Early Perp E window, two-storey N vestry (no longer floored), and S porch. Various C19 and C20 restorations and additions, including the addition of the N aisle and organ chamber by *G.E. Pritchett*, 1902–3. Triple chancel arch *c.* 1875. Unusual nave roof, C14, of gambrel form with both queen- and kingposts. – FONT. 1903, a copy of the C12 original that is now in the tower. Square bowl with shallow blank arcading and detached corner shafts. – Single STALL, probably C14 and part of the original choir stalls. Carved heads on the arms. – WALL PAINTING. C14 consecration cross on nave S wall. – STAINED GLASS. In the head of the E window, a complete late C14 Coronation of the Virgin with two censing angels and eight orders of angels. The rest of the window by *Powell & Sons*, 1889, who also did the chancel S (designed by *Charles Hardgrave*), 1888. Tower window by *John Hayward*, 1974. – MONUMENT. Alice Margaret Douglas †1947. By *Gilbert Bayes*, with charming bas-relief head.

OLD RECTORY, S of the church. Refronted and extended 1835–7 in Tudor Gothic style. Earlier parts C17 timber-framed, remodelled *c.* 1770 and faced in gault brick.

SHEERING HALL, 1 m. SW. Formed from a late C15 Wealden house and an early C16 hall house abutting it at right angles. The Wealden house has one storeyed end that is jettied on both sides, an unusual feature in Essex. The hall house has one integral storeyed end and a storeyed cross-wing. Two large aisled barns to the N, C17 and *c.* 1600.

AYLMERS, 1¼ m. WSW. Good early C17 house with three gables on the E front, the middle one on the three-storey porch. Studding exposed, and much restored; the best original work the ground-floor oriel on the N elevation, with guilloche carving. Nice outbuildings to the N, including a contemporary weatherboarded barn.

DURRINGTON HALL, opposite Aylmers. A C17 timber-framed house largely rebuilt by Samuel Feake †1757, further embellished by his son. More or less a hollow square, mainly plastered brick. Showpiece entrance (W) front, albeit on a small scale. Three-bay pedimented centre with Corinthian porch flanked by niches and first-floor window with segmental pediment. Single-storey canted bays to l. and r. and first-floor Venetian windows. The S range is the original house, its front remodelled by the elder Feake, with five windows not quite evenly spaced, pedimented on the first floor. To the r. of them two further bays, the return of the four-bay E range of

---

* Also some fragments of diapering formerly recorded in the church.

c. 1860. The plainer N range mid C18. To the N a C17 timber-framed house altered in the C19 and C20 to form servants' quarters, and beyond a coach house and stables mainly of gault brick, *c.* 1800, with clock tower and cupola. Walled garden NE of the house.

At LOWER SHEERING, 1½ m. NW, an extensive range of disused C19 MALTINGS alongside the railway and Stort Navigation, now converted to flats and commercial use, parts dated 1865–7. The complex includes a rare purpose-built pneumatic malting, with conical kiln.

5000

SHELLEY

Ongar

St PETER. By *Habershon & Fawckner*, 1888, the third church on the site: the medieval one was rebuilt in 1810 in what Habershon & Fawckner called 'the worst style of bastard gothic'. Their chosen style was 'C12 transitional E.E.' Chancel, nave and N aisle, with a small S porch and a NW tower with splay-foot spire forming the main entrance. Knapped flint and stone dressings on the outside, brick with stone dressings and black brick decoration on the inside. All its original fittings, including STAINED GLASS E window. – MONUMENTS. From the medieval church, in the base of the tower, including Agnes Greene †1626, painted stone. Kneeling figures with husband and children.

The church is surrounded by fields with farm buildings on its N side, including a picturesque C18 cart lodge and dovecote, and on its W SHELLEY HALL. C14 hall house (date of 1869 on the porch refers to cladding in gault brick) with cross-wing at the N end and perhaps originally another at the S. Smoke-blackened crown-post in the roof. Hall floored in the late C16 and a second wing built to the N; door lintel dated 1587, about the same date as a large carved oak chimneypiece in the entrance hall (not *in situ*). In the attic, crudely painted late C16 or early C17 WALL PAINTINGS incorporating a variety of contemporary motifs, including huge nightmarish flowers and a large fantastical bird. Former early C19 LODGES, one on Moreton Road (Gothic Cottage), another (thatched) on Fyfield Road.

PRIMARY SCHOOL, Milton Crescent. By the *County Architect's Dept*, 1993. Brick, with white bricks to lighten the space beneath the deep eaves. Sweeping, slightly splayed slate roof with hipped ends running the length of the building; its apex glazed, lighting a central corridor around which the teaching areas are arranged.

6000

SHELLOW BOWELLS

St PETER AND St PAUL. Rebuilt in brick, 1754: nave and short chancel separated by a heavy, rather low chancel arch. Large arched windows, two on each side of the nave, large domestic-looking W door, and small timber W belfry with squared domical roof. C19 Gothic W and E windows. Converted to a house by *Patrick Lorimer* of *ARP Architects*, 1973–4, with minimal intervention. Further alterations by *James Boutwood*, 1999–2000.

SHENFIELD

Brentwood

6090

Shenfield means to many a railway station, opened 1886, where the Southend line branches off, and the built-up area merges seamlessly into Brentwood and Hutton. The old centre of the village, round the church, lies ½ m. W.

ST MARY THE VIRGIN. The most interesting part is the timber N arcade, late C15 or early C16. Originally five bays, with piers of four attached shafts and four hollows in the diagonals. Sixth (easternmost) bay added 1867–8, when the arcade's four-centred arches, removed in the 1830s, were reinstated by *W. G. Bartleet*. He also extended the chancel (already extended by him in 1863, when he rebuilt the nave and chancel walls), adding a small N organ chamber (enlarged 1886). Cement rendering obscures this almost total rebuilding of the original, probably C15, fabric.* Timber S porch and W tower, both C15, the latter with an especially tall and thin shingled spire. Substructure of eight posts grouped in pairs from W to E, big braces to hold the cross-beams, trellis-strutting along the N and S walls above. In the nave N wall, an early C16 brick doorway with shallow crenellated projection. NW vestry rebuilt 1899–1900, extended by *Richard Burbidge*, 1984, when the NE vestry was also added. – FONT. Octagonal, with various carved devices, including a 'Green Man', in quatrefoils. Late C14. Originally from Shenfield, from 1895 to 1949 it was in All Saints, Marsworth, Bucks, whose vicar, *F. W. Ragg*, restored the bowl and made (or designed) the base. – REREDOS. By *Frans Vermeylen*, 1873. Oak triptych, with deeply carved panels, coloured in 1920. – WALL PAINTING. 'Suffer the Little Children' by *Heaton, Butler & Bayne*, 1900. – STAINED GLASS. By *Kempe*: E window 1893, chancel S 1896, N aisle 1900. – Nave S by *Powell & Sons*, 1936. – MONUMENTS. Elizabeth Robinson †1652 aged sixteen. Reclining and shrouded, with infant in swaddling clothes in her left arm, the other hand resting on a skull. No superstructure. Attributed to *Thomas Burman* (AW). – Good C18 headstones in churchyard: to George Gross †1737/8 on N side, to Richard Moss †1760 at W end.

SHENFIELD HALL, N, with many gables facing the church, including a two-storey jettied porch. This is late C16, part of alterations to the medieval hall. S, by the old main road, OLD

---

* A restoration by *Teulon*, announced in *The Ecclesiologist* in 1858, was not carried out.

SHENFIELD PLACE, 1689 by *Robert Hooke*. Partly stuccoed brick. Five-bay, two-storey S front with two dormers in the hipped roof and two large chimneystacks on each return. Early C18 staircase with twisted balusters, but otherwise much altered and extended.

FRIENDS' MEETING HOUSE, Hutton Road. By *Hubert Lidbetter*, 1957. Brown brick, hardly more than a bungalow.

PUBLIC LIBRARY, Hutton Road. 1961 by *H. Conolly*, County Architect. Brick, with a large full-height window.

PRIMARY SCHOOL, Hall Lane. By *Bartleet*, 1865, extended 1869.* The main feature is the clock tower, added 1893. Single-storey block with pyramidal roof, 1990, and large two-storey additions to main block by *W.S. Atkins*, 1997–8.

BRICK HOUSE FARM, 1 m. NW. S front with three bargeboarded gables and gabled two-storey porch. This has a round-arched doorway and a date of 1623.

7030   SIBLE HEDINGHAM

There are two main centres of interest, the immediate neighbourhood of the church and the road S of the junction of Swan Street and Alderford Street, ½ m. SE.

ST PETER. Except for the W tower, a church dating from about 1330–40. The window tracery is typical. The W window of the tower also belongs to that period, although the tower itself, with its angle buttresses carried up in four set-offs and its stepped battlements, is of the early C16. Buttresses are also carried down into the inside of the church. The quatrefoil clerestory windows are not original, but the back-splays may indicate that the form is correct (cf. Little Sampford). The arcades between nave and aisles and the chancel arch have octagonal or semi-octagonal supports and double-chamfered arches. Organ chamber between N aisle and N vestry by *F.W. Chancellor*, 1921–3. Hammerbeam roofs in chancel and nave by *F. Chancellor*, 1889–90 and 1897 respectively, as part of general restorations, but at the W end of the S aisle two bays of a very richly carved early C16 roof, including emblems of the de Veres and Bourchiers. – REREDOS. Twelve apostles, painted on zinc, early 1870s, the central panel of the Crucifixion missing. – STALLS. By *F.W. Chancellor*, 1929. – ROYAL ARMS of William III, carved and painted wood, nicely done. – STAINED GLASS. E window †1892 and tower window by *Heaton, Butler & Bayne*. – MONUMENT. In S aisle, cenotaph for Sir John Hawkwood †1394. Low tomb-chest, decorated with six cusped panels holding shields. Big ogee arch flanked by buttresses. The spandrels have Perp panelling. Hawkwood, the son of a tanner at Sible Hedingham, rose to be a *condottiere* of the Florentine army and son-in-law of the Duke of Milan. He is buried in

---

*In 1954 Pevsner thought it 'specially revolting . . . but very typical of minor High Victorian work'.

Florence Cathedral, where a fresco by Paolo Uccello commemorates him.

STRICT BAPTIST CHURCH, Swan Street. Opened 1864,
although the threshold has 1868 marked out in pebbles. A very
simple brick building, set back from the street, but as if to compensate for this a dazzling front with stock brick dressings and
stock and black brick diapers and other patterns. Wide bargeboarded gable.

PRIMARY SCHOOL and former teacher's house, School Road.
1843 by *Webb & Morgan*. Plain brick. Enlarged 1960.

PUBLIC LIBRARY, Swan Street. A good example of the type
being built by the County Architect, *H. Conolly*, in the early
1960s. Brick walls behind and clear of the steel uprights that
support the roof, which extends as a canopy at the front.
Glazed front and continuous clerestory.

PERAMBULATION. The church is set on quite a hill and dominates the old part of the village below it to the S. To its N,
PRAYORS FARM, C17 timber-framed and plastered with lattice
glazing bars. To its E, facing into the churchyard and separated
from it by wrought-iron railings and gate, GREYS HALL.
Painted brick, *c.* 1714. Two storeys with cellars and attics. Three
windows on the first floor, two wide windows on the ground
floor, but panels in the balustrade and scars in the brickwork
suggest it was originally five bays. Pedimented doorcase. A
quite different appearance at the back, facing Rectory Road,
with three full storeys owing to the sloping ground and a roof
of four small hipped gables. Central staircase tower with two
tall windows.

Below the church the OLD RECTORY, built by Rev. Moses
Cooke, *c.* 1714. Large even by the standards of the day. Brick,
with a seven-bay front of two storeys and attics, parapet, and
Ionic porch of stone. Parapet higher on the garden front, which
has a large two-storey canted bay. Three-bay carriage house
with semicircular windows over the doors. Cast-iron railings
with anthemion panels. Looking down Rectory Road, THE
WHITE HORSE, C15 with a large jettied cross-wing to the r.
and smaller cross-wing to l. In CHURCH STREET to the S, up
the hill on the other side of the valley, CRESWELLS, C16
timber-framed and plastered with panel pargetting on the
front. Chimneystack with eight octagonal shafts. Painted on
the chimney-breast of a first-floor room, scenes probably based
on plates in Andrea Alciati's *Emblematum libellus*.

Now SWAN STREET, the main (Roman) road running N–S
through the village. At the junction with Rectory Road, ¼ m.
ENE of the church, THE SUGAR LOAVES, C15 with exposed
timbers. Two-bay hall to the l., unusually high, to the r. of
which can be seen the outline of a carriage archway. C19 extension r. of that. Little then until No. 49, ½ m. S, opposite the
junction with Alderford Street: early C16 with long-wall jetty
with moulded bressumer and brackets and close studding.

ALDERFORD STREET itself leads down to Alderford Mill (*see*
below). A very attractive group of houses on the N side, one

c16 with exposed timbers, another c18 with two full-height bows and Tuscan doorcase with open pediment. On the s side, a large former maltings barn, now houses. c18, timber-framed, part faced in brick, part weatherboarded. On the corner of Swan Street, ALDERFORD GRANGE, c16 timber-framed and plastered with an c18 painted brick façade, the main part of six bays.

Back in Swan Street, on the w side THE SWAN, c15 on half-H plan, the space between the wings filled in in the c17, and with a c19 brick façade. On the e side, up the hill, Nos. 32–38, four (originally six) ALMSHOUSES, 1884. Picturesque c17 style with irregular roof-line, dormers, ground-floor oriels, and tall chimneys. Further s, Swan Street becomes POTTER STREET, with HAWKWOOD MANOR on the w side. Early c16, with two cross-wings lower than the main range. The front remodelled c. 1700, including a fine doorcase with fluted, roughly Corinthian pilasters, segmental pediment, and frieze rising in the middle. Finally in QUEEN STREET, the continuation s of Potter Street, THE BRIDGE HOUSE, late c15 or early c16 with exposed timbers and jettied cross-wings to l. and r., HALF MOON HOUSE, c16 with two projecting cross-wings, one jettied, and BRICKWALL HOUSE, c16 with exposed timbers and, facing the road, a tiled veranda or penthouse.

BAYKERS, 1 m. s. Large c16 house with exposed timbers. Two gabled cross-wings at the front, four gables to the rear. Chimneystacks with three and five octagonal shafts. Single-storey brick studio added for the painter Edward Killingworth Johnson, 1867.

ROOKWOODS, Yeldham Road, 700 yds N. Regency gault brick. Two storeys, hipped slate roof with deep eaves. Three-bay front, the central bay recessed with balcony over porch. Ancillary buildings erected by Mark Gentry, owner of Hedingham Brick Works, 1887–8, making good use of the firm's wares, especially ornamental bricks. Large stable block NW of the house, the end wall a Dutch gable punctuated by four pilasters with ball finials, and a smaller stable block with attached kennel. Two-storey cottage E of the house with much decorative brickwork, including panels and friezes with sunflowers, and by the main road a similarly ornate single-storey lodge.

ALDERFORD MILL, ¾ m. SE. c18 water mill, weatherboarded above brick ground floor. Tiled gambrel roof with dormers and hoist loft at one gable end. Machinery complete. Owned, and being restored, by Essex County Council.

HULL'S MILL. *See* Great Maplestead.

SILVER END

Silver End was a hamlet in the northern part of Rivenhall until Francis Henry Crittall chose it as the site for a model village in which to continue the provision of housing for his workers that he had begun at Clockhouse Way, Braintree (q.v.). The foundation stone of the first house was laid on 17 April 1926 and between then and 1932 over 470 houses were built, as well as shops, village hall, hotel, two churches, a school, and a subsidiary factory employing disabled ex-servicemen.*

ST FRANCIS. Thatched and weatherboarded barn, converted 1929–30 by *W. F. Crittall* and *C. G. Holme*,[†] who inserted green-painted Crittall doors and windows. Interior decorated in strong colours, blue ceiling with gold bands at each end, although toned down in a redecoration of 1982, when a N extension was added. – FONT. By *Crittall*, carved from a solid trunk of oak by *Rev. A.A. Hunt*. – ALTAR RAILS, READING DESK and PULPIT by *Crittall*, made by Crittall workers. – STAINED GLASS. E window by *Leonard Walker, c.* 1930.

ST MARY (R.C.), Sheepcotes Lane. 1966 by *Martin Evans*. In plan like a snail's shell, white brick walls and timber roof growing round and up from a reinforced concrete column, the intention being to allow for enlargement into a circular building.

CONGREGATIONAL CHURCH, Silver Street. By the *Crittall Development Co.*, 1930. Conventional, with rendered walls and pitched roof.

PRIMARY SCHOOL, School Road. 1929 by *J. Stuart*, County Architect. Traditional brick and pitched roof, single storey, with very large Crittall windows.

VILLAGE. The planning consultant was *Captain Richard Reiss*, a director of Welwyn Garden City and Hampstead Garden Suburb. To lend variety, a number of different architects were employed, starting with *C. Murray Hennell*, *C.H.B. Quennell*, and *Sir John Burnet & Partners*, the latter's chief designer being *Thomas Tait*, assisted by *Frederick MacManus*. *George E. Clare* and *James Miller* made later contributions, as did the *Crittall Development Co.*'s in-house architects. Hennell had worked on various garden cities, including Letchworth and Welwyn, and was responsible for the village plan, as well as for setting a traditional Garden City tone for much of the housing: brick, pitched roofs, with almost Neoclassical touches. By contrast, Tait and MacManus introduced the International Modern Style for which Silver End has become famous: brick rendered and painted to resemble concrete, with flat roofs. Both styles, needless to say, used Crittall windows. The company sold the village to the local authority in 1968, but although many of the houses are now in private ownership, most are unaltered and in good condition.

Opposite St Francis in Western Road, the former CRITTALL WORKS by *Brown & Burgess*, 1926, brick, much altered. To the r., along BOARS TYE ROAD, on the N side a row of traditional

---

*Also a piggery, designed by *Hennell*, 1926, 'so luxurious it was often mistaken for a church', according to Graham Thurgood; dem. Attribution of individual buildings relies heavily on Thurgood's article 'Silver End Village 1926–32', *Thirties Society Journal*, 3 (1982), 36–42.
[†] Holme was editor of *The Studio* and lived at the Old Rectory, Rivenhall (q.v.).

houses by *Hennell*, 1926–7, and then on the S side three large detached houses, LE CHATEAU by *Tait*, for Daniel F. Crittall, and WOLVERTON and CRAIG ANGUS by *MacManus* for managers: all 1927, Modern, and the most stylish houses in the village, with 'V' windows that finish in three finials, and Art Deco metal gates and balcony railings. They lie opposite SILVER STREET, which has the best stretch of Modern workers' houses, in a variety of designs, mostly semi-detached with some terraces of four; the lower half, Nos. 1–32, by *Mac-Manus*, 1927–8, Nos. 33–60 by the *Crittall Development Co.*, 1928, and Nos. 69–75 by *Miller*, 1929–30. *Miller* was also responsible for houses in the continuation of Silver Street, where it becomes FRANCIS WAY, and in BROADWAY, which runs across it; here the Silver Street designs are modified, and the houses built without cavity walls, to make economies that were necessary in the harsher climate after 1929.

Broadway leads into the village centre, a small circus with the CENTRAL BUILDING (village hall) on its S side: by *Hennell*, 1927–8, two storeys, stock brick. Inside, carved WAR MEMORIAL board by *W.F. Crittall*, executed by *E. Beckwith*, 1948. Next to it a parade of shops, single-storey brick, originally the CO-OPERATIVE DEPARTMENT STORES by *Messrs Joseph*, 1928, rebuilt following a fire in 1951. Opposite, the former HOTEL, also by Messrs Joseph, 1928, now a residential home: two storeys, brick, pitched roof with dormers. On the N side of the circus the former TEA ROOM, single storey, originally thatched, by the *Crittall Development Co.*, 1927, and the MEMORIAL GARDENS, laid out by *W.F. Crittall*, 1948–51, including a Japanese garden; gates made from Crittall window sections in memory of F.H. Crittall, 1952, and W.F. Crittall, 1956. On the far side of the gardens, in Francis Way, MANORS, F.H. Crittall's own house, by *Quennell*, 1927: seven bays with a central single-bay open pediment and porch, and flanking bungalows for staff, a very stripped-down sort of Neo-Georgian.

The remaining houses of interest, W of the village centre, are all traditional, and mostly by *Hennell*: Nos. 19–25 FRANCIS WAY, Nos. 1–24 TEMPLE LANE, and the whole of VALENTINE WAY (No. 15 Temple Way, on the corner of Valentine Way, has the ceremonial foundation stone for the whole village), 1926–7. Valentine Way in particular shows the influence of Welwyn Garden City, the houses arranged as pairs and blocks of eight according to Louis de Soissons's pattern there, and with three 'courts' of houses set back from the street on one side. Following on from *Hennell*, Nos. 26–60 Temple Lane by *Quennell*, 1927, traditional to the extent of blind pedimented brick doorcases in the middle of semi-detached houses, and Nos. 1A–12A Temple Lane by *Clare*, 1928, with rendered walls and pantile roofs, no better than good interwar council housing.

SHEEPCOTES FARM, ¾ m. NE. Timber-framed and plastered, *c.* 1700, with a brick front dated 1785. In a ground-floor room a painted representation of arcading with elaborate pendants, early C17 (cf. No. 3 Knights Templar Terrace, Kelvedon).

SOUTH BENFLEET

ST MARY. A biggish church, as medieval churches in this part of the county go. Ashlar, rubble and flint. Big W tower with angle buttresses at the foot, and a recessed spirelet of 1706 replacing a larger spire. The original windows indicate an early C14 date. Nave with Perp clerestory, embattled S and N aisles, both Perp, but the S aisle earlier and remodelled when the N aisle was added. The chancel also Perp. The most rewarding part of the church outside is the timber S porch, late C15, unusually ornate, with panel tracery in the spandrels of the doorway, an embattled beam, tracery panels in the gable, cusped bargeboarding, and a fine two-bay hammerbeam roof inside. On entering the church one becomes aware of the much earlier origin of the nave. The W wall has a plain Norman doorway (into the later tower, now concealed by a screen) and above two unusually large blocked Norman windows. Was there once a higher middle window or a circular window between them? The nave is impressive by its height. The carved stone corbels between the clerestory windows tell of an earlier, lower roof. The height of the present roof, C17, allows for two small windows above the chancel arch. The S arcade has octagonal piers, the later N arcade piers with four attached shafts and four hollows in the diagonals. The arches on both sides are double-chamfered. The chancel roof has tie-beams with crown-posts and four-way struts. Restoration by *William White*, 1861, included lowering the level of the nave floor to reveal the bases of the piers, repairs to the porch, re-seating the nave, and new E window. He also removed the gallery of 1824 by *Jonathan Savill*.

More significant is the church's long association with *Sir Charles Nicholson*. His parents lived at Hadleigh House, on the parish's NE boundary, and he worked on the church between *c.* 1890 and his death in 1949. He is buried on the S side of the tower beneath a stone he designed for his first wife Evelyn Louise †1927. As well as caring for the actual building (especially the restoration of the S aisle, 1924–5), he designed most of its FURNISHINGS AND FITTINGS.* – REREDOS. 1890–1, gilded border 1925, with paintings by his mother *Sarah Nicholson* (repainted by *E. A. Hunt*, 1958). Riddel posts now removed but one pair set back as panels with paintings by his daughter *Barbara Nicholson*. – COMMUNION RAIL, 1922. – FONT. C13 circular stem with C19 corner pillars added to support a square bowl, probably by *White*, 1871. – FONT COVER and PULPIT, 1925. – ROOD SCREEN. 1931, rood loft and figures 1933. Six

* Also the village's WAR MEMORIAL, 1919–20, and (with *H.C. Corlette*) school buildings (dem.).

bays plus wider central opening, with ogee heads and web-like tracery. Painted panels with figures of saints by *Barbara Nicholson* are part of Nicholson's CLERGY AND CHOIR STALLS, 1928–30. – PEWS. S aisle, 1924–5. In nave, mostly by *White*, very simple. – ORGAN LOFT. 1927. Paintings of angels by *Sarah Nicholson*, 1897, done for the organ when it was in the chancel; enlarged and rebuilt on w gallery by *Harrison & Harrison* to a specification by *Sir Sydney Nicholson*, Sir Charles's brother. – PAVING. In chancel, Italian black and white marble, *c.* 1730. – STAINED GLASS. A complete scheme by *A.K. Nicholson*, starting with the S aisle, 1925–6, continued after his death in 1937 by *G.E.R. Smith* and the *A.K. Nicholson Studios*. Figures of saints and prominent churchmen and women set in clear glass. E window, 1948, replacing glass of 1861 by *Clutterbuck* damaged during the War.

ANCHOR INN, corner of High Road and Essex Way. Refronted in the late C19, with brick cladding on ground floor, but with C14 timber frame and crown-post roof. There was originally a carriageway through the middle. Its unusual plan form, and absence of sooting on the roof timbers, is thought to indicate that it was a public building, such as a guildhall or court hall, or perhaps the College of Canons referred to by Morant. Upstairs, remnants of late C16 wall paintings, part of alterations at that time.

OLD VICARAGE, Vicarage Hill. By *George Devey*, 1846, and probably his first independent commission, before he got to know the Kentish Wealden style that he made his own. Ragstone, with ashlar and brick dressings. Front elevation with two gables, that on the r. cut into by an outsize, irregular chimney-breast.

SHIPWRIGHTS, Benfleet Road. *See* Hadleigh.

8080

SOUTHEND-ON-SEA*

p. 692 Southend-on-Sea had a population of 160,000 in 2001, little changed in forty years, whereas between 1871 and 1901 it leapt from 2,800 to nearly 29,000. As a town Southend dates from 1892, when it was incorporated; '-on-Sea' was officially added the following year. Southend-on-Sea comprises six medieval parishes, with Prittlewell at its centre; Southend grew out of Prittlewell, but by 1892 had overtaken its mother parish in importance. Southchurch, to the E, was absorbed in 1897, Leigh-on-Sea to the W in 1913, and finally in 1933 Eastwood to the NW and North and South Shoebury (including Shoeburyness) to the E of Southchurch. These parishes have grown together to the extent that it is almost impossible, on the ground, to tell where one ends and the next begins, but they are treated separately below to make the account of the town more manageable. In addition, Westcliff-on-Sea, between Southend and Leigh-on-Sea, and Thorpe Bay, between Southchurch and South Shoebury, are

---

*Since 1998 a unitary authority.

sufficiently distinct to warrant individual attention. Southend proper, including Clifftown, will here be described first, the adjoining places after.

Southend	691
Eastwood	699
Leigh-on-Sea	700
North Shoebury	704
Prittlewell	705
Southchurch	708
South Shoebury	709
Thorpe Bay	712
Westcliff-on-Sea	712

SOUTHEND

The name 'Sowthende' first appears in a will of 1481 to denote an area in the southern part of the manor of Prittlewell. Until the C18 there were no buildings along this part of the shore. Then after about 1700 oyster cultivation was begun. Within twenty years the whole of the foreshore from Southchurch to Leigh was leased as oyster feeding grounds, and huts for the oystermen were built in region of the present s end of Southchurch Avenue. In 1767 a very humble terrace of two-storey brick cottages was built near the fishermen's huts. This was Pleasant Row (now demolished). Visitors in small numbers were coming to Southend to bathe in the sea, but it was not until 1791 that a syndicate was formed to develop a resort at 'New Southend'. It was then that The Terrace was built, renamed Royal Terrace in 1804 after Princess Caroline of Brunswick, wife of the Prince Regent, stayed in Nos. 7, 8, and 9, and thereby boosted the resort's popularity; the first pier was built in 1829–30. Further stimulus to growth was provided by the railway: first the London, Tilbury & Southend, 1856, which led to the development of Clifftown, followed by the Great Eastern in 1889. Southend declined sharply in the latter part of the C20, the result partly of changing holiday habits, partly of competition from Basildon and then Lakeside (West Thurrock) as shopping centres, but major developments such as the University of Essex's Southend campus and improvements to the pier and Esplanade are doing much to reverse this.

CHURCHES[*]

ALL SAINTS, Southchurch Road. Built to provide for the area of Prittlewell known as Porters Town, the first portion (chancel, s chapel, two bays of nave and aisles) 1886–8 by *James Brooks*, extended by two bays 1896–7. w end with rose window completed with a further two bays, including organ gallery, by *Sir Charles Nicholson*, 1932–4. Nicholson had added a N chapel and

---

[*] *Walter Tapper*'s magnificent St Erkenwald, Southchurch Avenue, begun in 1905 but never completed, was demolished in 1995.

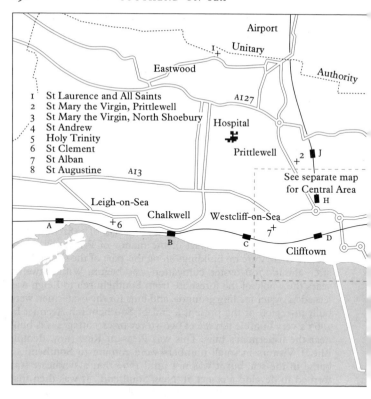

1 St Laurence and All Saints
2 St Mary the Virgin, Prittlewell
3 St Mary the Virgin, North Shoebury
4 St Andrew
5 Holy Trinity
6 St Clement
7 St Alban
8 St Augustine

vestries, 1924–5, connecting to the VICARAGE, although the hall he envisaged, that would have completed the Anglo-Catholic complex, was not built. The church is a long, tower-less building of even red bricks, although the breaks between the stages are still clearly visible. Inside, square chamfered piers without capitals, decorated by broad alternating bands of brick and stone. The roof very high up, of a semicircular wagon type. The chancel arch has a large triple arch above, as the chancel is not lower than the nave. The E end is straight and has two tiers of lancets, the upper tier stepped. – STAINED GLASS. E window by *Clayton & Bell*, 1993. – S chapel E by *L. Grossé-De Herde* of Bruges, 1896.

ST JOHN THE BAPTIST, Church Road. By *T. Hopper*, 1840–2, the new town's first Anglican church. A modest Neo-Norman building, entirely obscured by gradual additions. Aisles 1869, chancel 1872–3 by *Slater & Carpenter*; their successor *B. Ingelow* extended the nave to the W, 1906, then the chancel to the E, 1912, and added the N chapel, S vestries, transepts, and narthex, when the church was deemed complete and many of the fittings installed (including a fine alabaster REREDOS). Coursed ragstone, with lancets and plate tracery. The interior is better than one might expect from the muddled exterior, although the

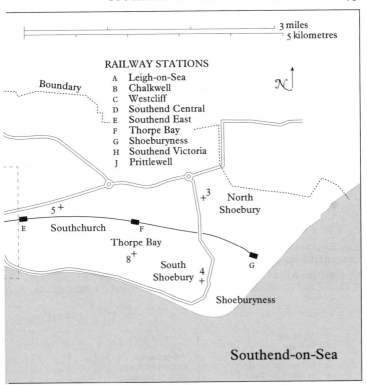

3 miles
5 kilometres

RAILWAY STATIONS

Boundary

A Leigh-on-Sea
B Chalkwell
C Westcliff
D Southend Central
E Southend East
F Thorpe Bay
G Shoeburyness
H Southend Victoria
J Prittlewell

N

+3 North Shoebury

5+

E Southchurch F

Thorpe Bay
8+ South Shoebury 4+

G

Shoeburyness

Southend-on-Sea

functioning of the building has been improved at the expense of its spatial qualities by enclosing the aisles. – SCREENS. By *Sir Charles Nicholson*, carving by *Harry Hems*. Dwarf chancel screen with high curved beam and cross, 1925. War Memorial screen to N chapel, 1919, with carving of 'Sacrifice' in place of rood. Corresponding screen in S transept, 1926, with figure of Christ symbolizing Peace. – Nicholson and Hems also modified the 1873 stone PULPIT, 1928. – STAINED GLASS. E window 1908, W 1927, N chapel E 1928, N chapel N *c.* 1901 (from St Edmund, Forest Gate), all by *Kempe*. – In N aisle, an undated window by *Burlison & Grylls*, another by *Willett Windows*, U.S.A., 1965. – In N transept, single-light window †1944 by *David Maile*. – In S aisle, 1907 by *Jones & Willis*, and tall triple lancets in S transept by *Powell & Sons*, 1950.

ST MARK, Hamlet Road. By *Edward Wright*, 1885, as a Baptist tabernacle. E.E. Stock brick with courses of black brick, and stone dressings. Schoolroom and caretaker's house on N side, 1892. The orientation was reversed in 1901 for the C. of E., the porch becoming the sanctuary, and gallery moved to W end. S porch rebuilt by *Cabuche & Hayward*, 1908. – PISCINA and other fittings from Little Stambridge (dem. 1891). – ROOD SCREEN, PULPIT, and LECTERN, 1913, the screen large for the

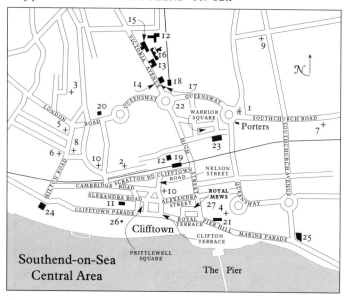

Southend-on-Sea
Central Area

The Pier

1 mile

2 kilometres

1	All Saints	14	Central Library
2	St Mark	15	Civic Centre
3	St Barbara	16	Police Station
4	St John the Baptist	17	Central Museum
5	St Alban the Martyr	18	Victoria Station
6	Our Lady (R.C.)	19	Central Station
7	Sacred Heart (R.C.)	20	Nazareth House
8	Avenue Baptist Church	21	Palace Hotel
9	Bournemouth Park United	22	Victoria Plaza
	Reformed Church	23	Swimming Pool
10	Methodist Church	24	Cliffs Pavilion
11	Former Synagogue	25	Kursaal
12	South East Essex College	26	War Memorial
13	Court House	27	The Royals Shopping Centre

space but very open. – STAINED GLASS. Chancel windows by
Jones & Willis, one dated 1935. Sanctuary windows 1959–62.
SACRED HEART (R.C.), Southchurch Road. By *B.R. Parkes*,
1909–12. Brick with stone dressings. Romanesque. Four-bay
nave and aisles, and apsidal sanctuary with N and S chapels.
SW porch, intended as the base of a tower. – Tudor-Gothic
presbytery to E and parish hall to S by *Burles & Harris*, 1911.
UNITED REFORMED CHURCH (Congregational), Chelmsford
Avenue. 1900, by *Burles & Harris*. Brick with stone dressings.
W front with large Perp window whose tracery continues up to
a little gable and spirelet.
UNITED REFORMED CHURCH (Clifftown Congregational
Church), Nelson Street. 1865 by *W. Allen Dixon*, enlarged by
E.J. Hamilton, 1889, with Memorial Hall by *Douglas Smith &
Barley*, 1925. Kentish rag with Bath stone dressings, 'in the

Geometric style' of the C14 (*Builder*). SW tower with octagonal bell-chamber and spire.

SYNAGOGUE, Alexandra Road. *See* Perambulation.

PUBLIC BUILDINGS

CIVIC CENTRE, Victoria Avenue. By *P.F. Burridge*, Borough Architect, 1960–7. Proposed before the Second World War, revived 1956. Sixteen-storey office block with four-storey Council Suite at right angles to it on the N side of a public square; on the S side, two-storey Court House (magistrates' and county courts, opened 1966), and set back a little on the E side, three-storey Police Station (opened 1962). In the NE corner of the site, buildings of South East Essex College (former College of Technology, begun 1958), up to six storeys. A good feeling of spaciousness and unity about the whole complex, with much use of Portland stone cladding, combined with blue panels on the Police Station. On the ground floor of the Council Suite, a cloister-like arcade with shallow pointed arches and ceremonial bronze entrance doors by *Don Foster*. Inside, elliptical staircase faced with Cippolino marble, with polished aluminium balustrade and mahogany handrail. Coat of arms in Council Chamber by *William Mitchell*; fibreglass, resin, and mosaic. The pointed arches continue round the office block and Police Station. Court House plainer, the entrance set back in a little courtyard.

CENTRAL LIBRARY, Victoria Avenue. 1971–4, by the Borough Architect, *R. Horswell*, in succession to *N.P. Astins*. Three principal storeys and basement, ground and first floor glazed, second floor concrete and slightly overhanging, on concrete columns. Inside, galleries round a large open well, with the walls of the central service core clad in ceramic tiles, an abstract design by *Fritz Steller*.

CENTRAL MUSEUM, Victoria Avenue. 1905–6 by *H.T. Hare*, as the Carnegie Library.* Edwardian Baroque. Brick, with generous stone dressings. Five-bay front, wider gabled bays at either end and the three central bays separated by giant Ionic pilasters. Large tripartite windows in the gabled bays, the openings separated by pilasters, on the first floor in a variant of Venetian form topped with open segmental pediments. Smaller windows have openings separated by balusters, with swags below. Enlarged 1927.

PRITTLEWELL PRIORY MUSEUM. *See* PRITTLEWELL PRIORY, p. 705.

SWIMMING POOL, Warrior Square. 1967–9 by *P.F. Burridge*. Exposed steel frame with black brick cladding and dark grey concrete panels, the pool hall mainly glazed.

LEISURE AND TENNIS CENTRE, Garon Park. By *Taylor Woodrow* and *Percy Thomas Partnership* (design and build), 1994–6. Two

---

*Hare's Technical College, Victoria Circus, 1901–2, was demolished in 1971.

large sports halls with curving monopitch metallic roofs that rise gently towards a central wedge containing offices, changing rooms etc. Rotunda entrance at the wide end of the wedge.

SOUTH EAST ESSEX COLLEGE, High Street. 2001–4 by *KSS Architects*. Seven storeys, stepping down to four at the rear, the front mainly glazed but with some metallic cladding and a red 'Skylon' marking the entrance. Behind the front and along the S side a vast atrium with curved walls, also stepping down, of EFTE panels (plastic cushions, increasingly opaque towards the top) on a steel frame. Inside the atrium, one wall of balconies providing access to teaching rooms, offices, etc., and in the open space a large red 'pod', like a giant egg, housing a 250-seat auditorium, and a group of six linked mushroom-like raised dining and meeting areas on two levels.

HOSPITAL, Prittlewell Chase. By *Adams, Holden & Pearson*; design selected 1927, built 1929–32. Stock brick, with dressings of red brick, Portland stone, and artificial stone. Three storeys. Central administration block with two internal courts, and two long ward blocks projecting to the S. The ends of these were originally open solaria. Much extended, including tower block, 1966–71, with external mosaic of serpent and rod.

SOUTHEND VICTORIA STATION. By *W. N. Ashbee*, 1889, for the Great Eastern Railway, in his usual rather domestic style. Brick, with stone dressings, and straight gables. In response, the London, Tilbury & Southend Railway rebuilt SOUTHEND CENTRAL STATION the same year (enlarged 1899), nondescript brick but with a nice porte cochère on iron columns on the N side.

PORTERS, Southchurch Road. Manor house, once standing quite on its own, bought by Sir Charles Nicholson in 1912 to save it from demolition. He lived there until 1932, when he sold it to Southend Corporation, who opened it in 1935 as the town's Civic House and Mayor's Parlour (with a small extension on the W side). Brick, *c.* 1600, but with evidence of an earlier, possibly early C16 half-H building remodelled later in the century, the space between the gabled cross-wings on the N front being filled in and the S front being rebuilt further out. The symmetry of the N front is broken by the off-centre porch. The windows are mullioned and transomed, of four and five lights, and of three in the gables. Stumps of small polygonal shafts on the gable-tops. Inside, the Hall has early C16 linenfold panelling (reused), moulded ceiling beams, an early C17 screen, an Elizabethan fireplace, and in the panelling five panels of demi-figures, very Mannerist, *c.* 1535. They are probably French and may represent five of the Nine Worthies. The room over the Hall has an open roof with curved braces. Elizabethan fireplaces in this and several other rooms. The Parlour in the E wing and Mayoress's Room above it have early C18 panelling. Two staircases, both originally of the newel type, one rebuilt straight in the C19.

PERAMBULATION

The PIER in its present form dates from 1888–91, when it was
rebuilt by engineers *Brunlees & McKerrow*; extended 1897–8
by the same firm with *C. H. Driver*, succeeded by *Sir John Wolfe
Barry*, and further extended in 1927–9 to its present length of
1⅓ m. – reputedly the longest pleasure pier in the world, with
trippers carried its length on a narrow-gauge railway reconstructed in 1984–6. Fires in 1959, 1976, and 1995 destroyed
most of the older superstructure. Entrance pavilion by *Peter
Emptage Associates*, 2002–3, with sinuous roof and fully-glazed
semicircular stair-tower, and bridge across the Esplanade. At
the pier head, LIFEBOAT STATION by *Bondesign Associates*,
2000–2. Timber-clad, with zinc-clad wave-form roof, and
glazed circular stair-tower. These two additions are resolutely
contemporary, where the temptation might have been to
indulge in Victorian pastiche – a welcome boldness that is
followed across the Esplanade, where a tower with lift and
viewing platform by *Stanley Bragg Architects*, 2004–5, is
connected by a bridge to the top of Pier Hill, with associated
landscaping.

Southend at its most jolly (or vulgar) can be seen along MARINE
PARADE, E of the Pier. That it was not always thus is evident
from the Regency bow fronts of the upper storeys (one with
canopy) of the first few buildings and, further along, the Hope
Hotel, *c.* 1780, an eight-bay stuccoed front with continuous
cast-iron balcony on one half. The KURSAAL at the far end of
Marine Parade (music hall, ballroom, etc.), 1898–1901 by
George Sherrin and *John Clarke* with engineer *R. J. Gifford Read*,
perhaps hastened the decline. Brick with stone dressings, low
except for two large gables with segmental pediments, and
behind this a large square lantern with Corinthian columns
topped by a Wrenian dome. The lantern lights an inner glass
dome over an ornate balconied two-storey entrance hall, but
the rest of the L-plan building was rebuilt internally as a leisure
complex by *John Breley Design Associates*, 1996–8. It is all that
remains of a larger amusement park, on a 26-acre site, that
included an Eiffel Tower, circus, parade of sixty shops, and
Marine Park.

PIER HILL, at the W end of Marine Parade, presents another
form of vulgarity: the PALACE HOTEL by *James Thompson &
Greenhalgh*, 1896–1904. Six storeys, more where the ground
falls away down Pier Hill, with a round tower and tourelles
(now decapitated), tiers of balconies with awnings and a con-
servatory-like projection along the whole of the long S side.
Magnificently exuberant in its heyday, now very subdued.*
Next to it, in line with the Pier and along the E side of the High
Street, THE ROYALS shopping centre by *Building Design Partnership*, 1985–8. Pale brown brick with bands of red, and two

---

*Planning permission granted in 2005 for renovation by *John Lyall Architects* as
hotel and conference centre.

malls with barrel-vaulted glass roofs at right angles to each other meeting at a glass-domed octagon.

The ROYAL HOTEL, on the opposite corner, marks the transition to gentility. It and ROYAL TERRACE were built in 1791–3. The hotel, enlarged 1824, has a semicircular Tuscan porch to the High Street and above it a Venetian window that belonged to the Assembly Room. Stock brick, with stuccoed ground floor, and along the S side a covered balcony with ornamental cast-iron supports. Similar balconies, all different and C19 additions, on all the fifteen houses that make up Royal Terrace, which are stock brick, some stuccoed. The centre is distinguished by five pilasters. The hotel, together with Nos. 1–2 Royal Terrace and No. 1 High Street (PRINCESS CAROLINE HOUSE), restored and remodelled internally by the *Rolfe Judd Group Practice*, 1980. w of the entrance to Royal Mews, three tall gabled brick houses of 1887, perhaps by *G. Sherrin*, who built the smaller house behind them in 1888.

CLIFFTOWN begins a little further w. The moving spirits were Sir Morton Peto, E.L. Betts, and Thomas Brassey, contractors responsible for the London, Tilbury & Southend Railway, together with the Lucas Bros builders. Peto acquired a lease on the land in 1859 and a prospectus for sale of houses was issued in 1871. The houses, all of stock brick but some stuccoed, were designed by *Banks & Barry*, and in four classes, ranging from the grand (Clifton Terrace, facing the sea, five storeys with canted bays and balustrade) to the humble (Scratton Road, facing the railway, two storeys, plain). Second- and third-class houses all had views of the sea, even if only an oblique glimpse: open spaces (Prittlewell Square) and the careful angling of the streets ensured this, even two streets back in Cambridge Road. Clifftown Congregational Church (*see* Churches) was an important part of the composition. Nelson Street, N of the church, was the shopping street for the estate; on the w side a terrace of gabled three-storey blocks connected by two-storey blocks with shop windows on the ground floor, now offices.

More variety w of Prittlewell Square, e.g. Nos. 28–30, two pairs of semi-detached houses with curved verandas, and then some late C19 three-storey blocks of flats with tiers of verandas and balconies. In the gardens opposite Clifftown Parade, *Lutyens*'s WAR MEMORIAL, 1920, a Portland stone obelisk, its base and pedestal remarkably subtly proportioned; and a STATUE of Queen Victoria by *J. H. Swynnerton*, 1897, seated on a Perp pedestal by *Edward Goldie*.★ In Alexandra Road, one street back from the front, a former SYNAGOGUE (now day nursery) by *Bertram R. Parkes*, 1911–12. Brick with stone dressings, the style Byzantine-cum-Romanesque.

★ Originally at the top of Pier Hill, prompting Pevsner to write in 1954 that Queen Victoria was 'pointing without any enjoyment towards the pier'. He thought the statue 'extremely funny'.

The HIGH STREET can now be tackled, and one might as well approach it via Nelson Street and Clifftown Road, because there is little to enjoy s of the railway bridge, indeed little enough to the N. Here, on the w side, a building for the University of Essex by *Peter Emptage Associates*,★ due to open in 2007. On the E side, on the corner of Warrior Square, a fine corner building by *Bromley & Watkins* for (but no longer) Boots the Chemists, 1915, faced in stone with two main storeys above the shopfront, a domed corner turret, and large Flemish gable. On the opposite corner, and continuing back to WARRIOR SQUARE, the former KEDDIE'S Department Store. The original 1890s store, eleven bays with Giant Ionic columns, fronts the High Street. Behind it, in 1960–4, *Yorke, Rosenberg & Mardall* built an extension fronting Warrior Square, with eight storeys of offices on a five-storey podium, including basement, of which the second and third floors were for car parking (cf. their Cole Bros, Sheffield). Faced in white tiles, the practice's favoured material at that time, and very clinical as a result. Podium (now a hotel) extended to the whole width of Warrior Square in 1971, and later in the 1970s the block on the corner opposite Boots was filled in. This is now the only part to retain its tiles.

Back in the High Street, N of Keddie's, a row of shops (Nos. 148–164; No. 166 rebuilt) by *James Thompson & Greenhalgh*, 1896, each with a first-floor veranda behind a three-bay arcade and above that an oriel window with half-timbered gable. After that, VICTORIA PLAZA shopping centre by *Bernard Engle & Partners*, 1968–73, with three levels of shops attached to a large multi-storey car park and ten-storey office block. Built at the same time as part of a major reorganization of the N end of the High Street that included the demolition of old Technical College and the construction of Queensway. N of Queensway, VICTORIA AVENUE has on its w side a row of tall blocks of government and other offices built in the 1960s and 70s in the wake of the Civic Centre opposite, including VICTORIA HOUSE by *H.G. Huckle & Partners*, 1962, CARBY HOUSE by *D. Francis Lumley*, 1963, PORTCULLIS HOUSE by *E. H. Banks*, 1965, and ALEXANDER HOUSE, 1972.

EASTWOOD

ST DAVID, Rayleigh Road. By *H.T. Rushton* of *Sir Charles Nicholson & Rushton*, 1965–6. Cruciform, with a very slender central timber flèche with aluminium finial, the roof supported on laminated timber beams. Cedar-clad gable ends showing above pale brick gabled projections on all four sides. Entrance on s side, altar on N side of the main worship area, with Lady Chapel behind it flanked by vestries. – MURAL over arch behind altar by *Mary Harris Tiler*. – Contemporary vicarage to the N.

★ On the site of the Astoria Cinema by *E.A. Stone* with *T.R. Somerford*, 1935.

ST LAURENCE AND ALL SAINTS, Eastwoodbury Lane. The
Norman church is recognizable only inside. The N wall above
the arcade shows three Norman outer windows. The wall
below was pierced in the C14 by two broad arches with much
wall left standing between. The chancel is C13, as its lancets
indicate. The w tower, added to the s of the nave, can be
ascribed to the same century on the strength of its w lancet.
Its upper part is weatherboarded, and ends in a hipped and
then needle-thin shingled spire. Three-bay s arcade with octagonal piers and double-chamfered arches may be c. 1300. The
tower arch is of the same design. The exterior of the s aisle is
remarkable for its pretty brick porch (early C16) and the two
plastered gables on the s aisle wall (C16 or C17?). Below the
gables the upper part of the rubble walls have been rebuilt in
brick. C15 timber priest's chamber in the N aisle. Re-seating
and repairs by *William White*, 1873, brick N choir vestry 1966.
– FONT. Norman, circular, tapering, and very large, with intersected arches. – DOORS. Its two doors with ironwork of
c. 1170–80 are what the church will be visited for. The N door
(re-hung 1966 with ironwork facing inwards) has ironwork in
two-and-a-half tiers of large curves and small tendrils between.
The s door also has large C-curves, with oak scrolls, straps and
other ironwork added in the first half of the C14. – STAINED
GLASS. E window by *Cox, Sons, Buckley & Co.*, 1887. s aisle
(St Laurence), 1964, and three-light w, 1978, by *F.W. Skeat*. –
BRASS to Thomas Burrough †1600. 25-in. (63-cm.) figure in
civil dress.

JESUS CHRIST OF LATTER DAY SAINTS, Grovewood Avenue.
By the Church Architectural Department of Salt Lake City,
U.S.A., modified to British requirements by *Graham &
Baldwin*, 1963. Low pale-brick walls, mostly glazed, the end
wall of concrete blocks with a central stone panel, and a small
brick corner tower (cf. Lexden).

COCKETHURST, Whitehouse Road, ½ m. WSW of St Laurence,
where it is depicted in the w window. Late C16 or early C17
brick house, five bays and two storeys and attics, with shaped
gables at each end, and a gabled porch. Rear wing also with
shaped gable.

LEIGH-ON-SEA

Leigh, alone of the older constituent parts of Southend,
retains some of its individual character. The maritime heritage is
apparent in the parish church and its memorials, while the High
Street below it, separated from the rest of Leigh by the railway,
still feels like a fishing village.

CHURCHES AND PUBLIC BUILDINGS

ST CLEMENT. High above the riverfront, and mainly of ragstone.
C15 w tower with diagonal buttresses, w door with shields in
the spandrels, three-light w window, battlements and higher

stair-turret. C15 N aisle with four-light W window (Perp panel tracery) and three-light N windows. Early C16 S porch of diapered brick, with thick brick doorway and two-light E and W windows. Squashed clumsily against its E side the S aisle of 1897 by *Geldart*, the E end completed by *Nicholson*, 1913 (Lady Chapel), who added N vestries at the same time. Chancel extended by *C.F. Hayward*, 1872. – REREDOS. By *Geldart*, 1893. Mahogany, the figures very finely carved (in Belgium). – FONT. C15, from St Swithin, Norwich. Octagonal. Against the stem four lions sejant facing outwards, against the bowl four lions guardant and four demi-figures of angels holding shields. COVER by *H. & K. Mabbitt*, c. 1983. – SCREENS. To Lady Chapel, by *Geldart*, originally the chancel screen of St Margaret of Antioch, Stanford-le-Hope. Wrought-iron gates by *Bodley* from St Matthew, Great Peter Street, Westminster. – At E end of N aisle by *Nicholson*, 1919, with tracery in the form of fishing nets.

STAINED GLASS. Very pictorial painted E window of the Crucifixion, with sinister grey clouds, perhaps C18 but said by Kendrick to be from Munich. – Chancel S of two lights with replicas of two of *Reynolds*'s figures for New College Oxford (Faith and Hope), with incongruous Gothick canopies added. Also painted; by *Eginton*? – Chancel N by *F. Preedy*, 1872, its companion now in the E window of the vestry. – Lady Chapel E 1913 and two S windows, 1922 and 1929, by *Horace Wilkinson*. – S aisle by *Powell*, 1868, with medallions by *E.J. Poynter*, and a second window †1869 with decorative quarries. – In tower, W window by *Geldart*, made by *Percy Bacon & Bros*, 1893; N by *Francis Stephens*, 1971, who also designed the eastern window of the N aisle †1968. – N aisle W 1958 and western window 1952 by *W. Wilson*. To the E, Good Shepherd by *Mayer & Co.*, c. 1875, side lights added 1887, then St Andrew by *William White*, 1887. – MONUMENTS. Brass to Richard Haddok †1453 and wife Christine with seven sons and three daughters, also their son John, his wife Alice, and their eight sons and three daughters. The largest figure 19 in. (48 cm.). – Richard Chester †1632, Elder Brother of Trinity House, and wife Elizabeth, with four sons and one daughter. 18-in. (46-cm.) figures. – Civilian (18-in. (46-cm.) figure) and wife, c. 1640. – Robert Salmon †1641, Master of Trinity House, with frontal demi-figure between pilasters. Attributed to *Thomas Stanton* (GF). – In churchyard, a number of good chest-tombs near the E end, including Capt. William Goodlad †1639, Chief Commander of the Greenland Fleet and Master of Trinity House, with scroll borders to the inscription and rusticated arched end panels, and Sarah Goodlad †1685 with large acanthus leaves.

ST JAMES THE GREAT, Elmsleigh Drive. By *Laurence King*, 1969. Brick. Asymmetrical pyramidal roof with glazed gablet on the W side. – STAINED GLASS. By *John Hayward*, 1974 (Lady Chapel).

ST MARGARET, Lime Avenue. *Graham Lloyd* was appointed architect in 1927, but for the construction, 1930–1, he and

Nicholson were joint architects; N aisle by *Sir Charles Nicholson & Rushton*, 1938. What distinguishes the church from others by Nicholson is its Early Christian inspiration and basilican form, and for this Lloyd can take the credit; but when it came to the development of that basic idea, it seems probable that Nicholson was dominant. Concrete, roughcast, with brick bands and dressings, and pantile roof. Nave with round-arched W door, round window above that, lunette clerestory windows, round-arched aisle windows, and apsidal E end with three small round-arched windows. S vestries connected by a covered walk to a large hall by *Laurence Selby*, 1966. Remarkably restful interior, with an arcade of Tuscan columns; open timber roof, lightly painted. Reordered by *Kenneth Cheeseman*, 1986, with a nave altar on a circular stone plinth. – HIGH ALTAR by *Nicholson*; also PULPIT, no longer *in situ*. – SCULPTURE. St Margaret by *Gilbert Bayes* (niche over W door). – Our Lady of Walsingham by *Anton Wagner* (S aisle). – STAINED GLASS. Lady Chapel E by *Terence D. Randall* and *Francis Stephens*, 1950.

OUR LADY OF LOURDES AND ST JOSEPH (R.C.), Leigh Road. By the parish priest, *Fr. F.W. Gilbert*, 1924–5, a near-replica of *Nicholson*'s St Alban Westcliff-on-Sea (*see* below). Nave and aisles with N and S porches, a pair of gables on the S side, SE tower with Lady Chapel at the base, and blind arcading on the E wall. The main differences are that Gilbert's church has a short spire (envisaged by Nicholson), and there is a presbytery on the N side. Walls faced in mainly random stone, quarried near Glasgow, with sacred emblems on the tower and E end. W extension by *A. J. Newton* (*Burles, Newton & Partners*), 1965–6, with W gallery and conversion of N porch to baptistery. – Most of the FITTINGS also by *Gilbert*, including ROOD BEAM, COMMUNION RAILS, and PULPIT, the latter with figures of the Evangelists and supported by cherubs. REREDOS as at St Alban, covering the E wall. – STAINED GLASS. S aisle (St Thomas More), 1933, and porch window, 1940, by *Paul Woodroffe*. Others by *Whitefriars Stained Glass Studios* (including five-light W, shortened 1965–6), and *Goddard & Gibbs*, 1962–75.

CONGREGATIONAL CHURCH, Pall Mall. By *Smee & Houchin*, 1909. Dec, with corner tower and recessed spirelet. Brick with stone dressings. HALL by *Norman G. Harland*, 1934, in a contemporary style with Gothic references.

HIGHLANDS METHODIST CHURCH, Sutherland Boulevard. 1955–6 by *A. G. Gentry*. Brick, in a very stripped-down Gothic style that echoes the Neo-Perp chapel of 1927 alongside, now used as a hall.

WESLEY METHODIST CHURCH, Elm Road. 1903–4 by *F. E. Smee*. Stock brick, with an elaborate ragstone front that includes flushwork, pinnacles, and Art Nouveau tracery. Unaltered galleried interior. – STAINED GLASS. E window by *Goddard & Gibbs*, 1947, perhaps also the porch window (Second World War memorial, 1946), and other later windows. Also some original windows with Art Nouveau ornament. – Halls etc. at the rear by *Kenneth Cheeseman*, 1962–3, new

National Schools, Leigh-on-Sea.
Drawing by J. Clarke, 1852

entrance 2003. To the E, in North Street, school buildings (including earlier chapel) by *Smee*, 1897–8, enlarged 1931–2.

POLICE STATION, Elm Road. By *J. W. Liversedge*, Council Surveyor, 1911–12, the surviving portion of a larger block of council offices. Free Edwardian Baroque. Deep porch with rusticated round-arched entrance, pedimented gable with a first-floor Venetian window with an exaggerated keystone that sticks up into an open pediment, bands of stone and alternate brick and stone quoins. Stone plinth with vermiculated rustication. Was Liversedge also responsible for the LEIGH COMMUNITY CENTRE, 1914, a short distance to the N?

PUBLIC LIBRARY, Broadway. Built as the rectory, 1838, for Rev. Robert Eden. Tudor Gothic, of chequered brick. Two storeys and attics. Four-bay N front with gabled dormers and porch, and on the other three fronts gables with decorative bargeboards, hoodmoulded windows, various bays and oriels, and clusters of tall chimneys. At the SW corner an octagonal turret. Opened as the library in 1928, with a new rectory (now WATSON HOUSE, offices) to the E by *Nicholson*, 1925, an irregular brick composition.

ST MICHAEL'S SCHOOL, Hadleigh Road. Opened (in existing buildings) 1922, with chapel by *Sir Charles Nicholson*, 1933. Very simple, with roughcast walls, pantile roof, narrower chancel with blank arcade of three round arches in the E wall.

PERAMBULATION

HIGH STREET. The general effect is picturesque but not the least precious, with a few weatherboarded huts but no individual house of special interest apart from THE CROOKED BILLET at the w end, late C16 timber-framed with a cross-wing to the r., faced in C19 brick. THE BOATYARD RESTAURANT by *Frank Smith*, 2000, is a stylish conversion of a boat shed; attached to it and fronting the street a C16 timber-framed house demolished in 1952 but rebuilt in 2004–5.

Between the High Street and the church, a few nice houses in LEIGH HILL, particularly PROSPECT VILLAS, weatherboarded with long veranda facing s, and at the top, opposite the E end of the church, CARLTON TERRACE, 1886, with first-floor veranda. Both verandas have trellis supports. On the s side of the churchyard, the former NATIONAL SCHOOLS, now a house, by *J. Clarke*, 1847. Kentish rag. Separate schoolrooms for boys, infants, and girls on three sides of a quadrangle, with houses for a curate and teacher at the angles.

p. 703

N of the church, C19 and C20 brashness dominates, culminating in the GRAND HOTEL at the E end of Broadway, 1899: brick with stone dressings, seven bays facing s, segmental pediments over the first-floor windows, triangular ones on the second floor, a two-storey oriel over the entrance, and shaped gables. But the residential streets are worth exploring for quieter late C19 and early C20 domestic architecture: e.g. in VERNON ROAD off Marine Parade to the w, No. 10 (Gable Cottage, Arts and Crafts with pargetting) and No. 17 (Ingeholm, roughcast with gabled fronts and bays) that would not look out of place in Frinton. To the E, off Grand Parade, in LEIGHCLIFF ROAD, Nos. 62 and 64 in similar style, and at No. 43 an extension by *Cottrell & Vermeulen Architecture*, 1996, weatherboarded on the first floor but contemporary in style and contrasting nicely with its turn-of-the-century host. No. 53, brick with bays angled to catch views of the sea, is by *Parker & Unwin*, 1902–3.

NORTH SHOEBURY

ST MARY THE VIRGIN, North Shoebury Road. Wide and rather low chancel, early C13 with lancets. Also C13, but later, the s aisle, later demolished. The arcade piers and arches are still recognizable, octagonal piers with moulded capitals. In the nave N wall one window of *c.* 1300: Y-tracery, cusped. The w tower is in its lower parts also C13, see the w windows. Later, big diagonal buttresses were added and the top parts with a weatherboarded pyramid roof in two steps, the upper with broaches. C18 s porch. Restored and reseated by *W. Benton*, 1883–5, who probably inserted the large window in the s arcade's E bay. – FONT. C12 Purbeck marble. Square bowl on square stem with four attached shafts. The sides undecorated, but on the top in the four corners fleurs-de-lys. – STAINED GLASS. E window by *Powell & Sons*, 1866, with medallion of the Ascension by *E.J. Poynter*. – MONUMENTS. Fragment of a coffin lid with an exceptionally richly adorned foliated cross and some letters; early C13. – John Milnes †1768, Elizabeth

Ibbetson †1796, and John Ibbetson †1804, three similar designs by *R. Cooke* with grey steles above white marble tablets. One has a weeping female leaning on an urn, copied by *Noakes & Pearce* for Elizabeth Jones †1846.

NORTH SHOEBURY HOUSE, Poynters Lane, ½ m. NE. Georgian brick front of five widely spaced windows with central Tuscan porch. Timber-framed range behind.

ANGEL INN, Parsons Corner, ¼ m. NNW. C17, timber-framed and weatherboarded, part thatched, attractively restored and extended by *M. Ginns*, *c*. 1990–5.

PRITTLEWELL

Prittlewell is the 'mother parish' of Southend, and its early origins, evident from a C7 doorway in the parish church, were further demonstrated by the discovery in 2003 of a C7 BURIAL CHAMBER beside Priory Crescent, ⅓ m. NNE of the church. The objects found in it were of high value and from a variety of countries, including copper-alloy vessels, glass jars, a gold belt buckle, Byzantine silver spoon, and two gold crosses. These indicate the high rank of whoever was buried there, and the crosses have led to the suggestion that it might be the grave of Sæberht, first Christian king of the East Saxons, who died in 616 or 617.

PRITTLEWELL PRIORY (Museum), Priory Park. The priory was founded from Lewes, the chief Cluniac Benedictine house in England, *c*. 1110. Of the buildings little survives. What is most prominent now is the refectory on the S side of the former cloister, and the W range of the cloister, containing the Prior's quarters, with a C15 roof, restored 1918–21 by *Philip M. Johnston* with *W. A. Forsyth*. The church adjoined the cloister on the N, and only part of the core of the S wall remains, but the foundations were excavated in 1954. The excavations revealed three building periods: the original small Oratory of *c*. 1100, choir and apse of 1170, and nave aisle and N transept of 1280. The REFECTORY, contemporary with the nave and apse, has its original, though much restored, doorway with two orders of columns and crocket capitals and a pointed arch with zigzag and dogtooth decoration. The two eastern bays were added in 1922, restoring the building to what was then thought to be its original length, although later excavations showed it to have been longer. Inside the refectory, no more of original work left than one lancet with keeled shafts and dogtooth decoration, and the splay at the foot going up so steeply that the exterior form is a pointed trefoil. Against the same wall a fragment of an arch with nailhead ornament, re-set. C15 roof with tie-beams, crown-posts, and four-way struts. On display are WALL PAINTINGS by *Alan Sorrell*, four panels painted for Southend Library, 1933–7. The WEST RANGE is two storeyed, the upper storey with exposed timber-framing, the lower storey faced in brick. The Prior's Chamber on the first floor has a roof similar to the refectory's, and a fireplace moved to its present position in 1920. The gabled southern end of the w range and the four-bay w front are Georgian, cemented, with a C19 porch.

To the w of the Priory is the CROWSTONE, re-erected in 1950, which stood on the foreshore at Chalkwell and marked the seaward end of the jurisdiction of the City of London over the Thames. It is an obelisk and was put up in 1755. Its successor of 1837 is still *in situ* (*see* Westcliff-on-Sea).

ST MARY THE VIRGIN, East Street. A large church, built mainly of Kentish rag, standing, with quite a lot of space all round, in a position which has lost much of its character. Large w tower of the Tudor period, with diagonal buttresses in three set-offs and above them corner turrets with crocketed spirelets. w door with shields in the spandrels, a three-light w window with niches to the l. and r., three-light bell-openings, and battlements with flint and stone chequer decoration. The same decoration over the w door, on the battlements of the nave N wall, chancel, and s aisle walls, and the two-storey porch. The nave N wall and the N and E walls of the chancel are Norman, although to the E of the pulpit in the chancel N wall is a C7 Saxon doorway arch with Roman brick voussoirs. It is also visible inside. The s aisle windows are big, of three lights; Late Perp. On the N side the nave clerestory is visible. Other Norman evidence is the two small blocked windows which now appear above the arcade in the s aisle. They were once the nave s windows. On entering the building the surprising thing is that so prosperous a church should have no N aisle. This lopsidedness remains a little disturbing. The eight-bay s arcade consists of a w portion of three bays, with heavy octagonal piers without proper capitals – the Norman wall just pierced – then three bays of the late C15 with slimmer octagonal piers with concave sides and arches with one wavy and one hollow-chamfered moulding, and then the two bays of the s chapel (Jesus Chapel), of similar design and date. Restored by *Ewan Christian*, 1870–2, who stripped the plaster off the internal walls and replaced the roofs, adding angels to the hammer-beams in the chancel (painted and gilded decoration by *Stephen Dykes Bower*, 1965–6). Porch, tower, s aisle and chancel restored by *P. M. Johnston* and *W.A. Forsyth*, 1921–31. N vestry by *Comper*, 1909, extended by *O.H. Cockrill*, 1957.

FONT. Perp, octagonal, with concave sides with roses, crossed spears, etc. – DOOR. Early C16, with panels with blank crocketed ogee arches. – COFFER. Two carved panels from the C14 front of a coffer, one with winged beasts, one with ornate tracery. – COFFIN LID. C13, with raised cross. – BANNER. St Cedd. Designed by *Nicholson* for the Church Congress, held at Southend, 1920, made by the *Municipal School of Art*. – STAINED GLASS. E window of Jesus Chapel, twelve panels of early C16 glass depicting Biblical stories. German, some derived from drawings by *Dürer*. Installed 1889, re-set by the *A.K. Nicholson Studios*, 1946. – Chancel s (re-set) and s aisle w by *Alexander Gibbs*, 1872. – s aisle (Crucifixion), two s porch windows, 1922, and E window, 1928, by *Percy Bacon*. – Jesus Chapel S by *Caroline Townshend & Joan Howson*, to J.E. Watts-Ditchfield, first bishop of Chelmsford, †1923. – The remaining C20 windows by *G.E.R. Smith*, made by the *A.K. Nicholson Studios*, *c.* 1938–56, many including depictions of local buildings. The finest is the Tabor window, 1941, in the N wall, unusually detailed and rich for its date. – MONUMENT. Mary Davies †1623. Black marble tablet in carved alabaster surround with painted achievement of arms. – WAR MEMORIAL and LYCHGATE opposite W door by *P. M. Johnston*.

ST LUKE, St Luke's Road. 1959–60 by *H.T. Rushton*. Mainly brick, with some Kentish rag and panels of green slate and low-pitched copper roof. The laminated timber roof frame divides to form an arched passage down each side of the nave. – PAINTING on sanctuary ceiling and STAINED GLASS (two windows of proposed scheme of six) by *Mary Harris Tiler*, 1960.

ST PETER, Eastbourne Grove. By *Humphrys & Hurst*, 1963. Square plan, wide nave and low aisles, with Lady Chapel and choir on the N side. Yellow brick, broken up by projecting blocks of ashlar on the W wall and panels of cobblestones on the S. Large windows in transeptal gables. The roof supported by pre-cast concrete A-frames, the two eastern pairs angled so that they meet to indicate the sanctuary. Good range of contemporary fittings, including paired PULPITS (or pulpit and lectern) with stalls, almost a re-invention of the two-decker.

BOURNEMOUTH PARK UNITED REFORMED CHURCH (Congregational), Central Avenue. Of corrugated iron, an unusually large specimen. 1904, moved to its present site in 1924, with brick and stucco hall ('school-chapel') by *Burles, Harris & Collings*, 1924–5.

EAST STREET CENTRE (former primary school), East Street. Kentish rag. By *Wenham & Blake*, 1868, extended by *A.J. Martin*, 1895.

BOURNEMOUTH PARK PRIMARY SCHOOL, Bournemouth Park Road. 1905–7, by *Greenhalgh & Brockbank*. Brick with stone dressings. Varieties of Dutch gables and cupolas.

ST MARY'S C. OF E. PRIMARY SCHOOL, Boston Avenue. By *Henry T. Hare*, 1912–3, as the Secondary School for Girls. Very tame Baroque, brick with stone dressings. Long façade with barely projecting wings and entrance, and a little cupola. Enlarged 1920, part now converted to flats.

PHOENIX HOSPITAL, Prittlewell Chase. 2003–5 by *Peter Emptage Associates*. Stock brick, render, and glass. Two storeys, with prominent corner stair-tower.

In EAST STREET, No. 30, C18 five-bay house of two storeys with attics, of blue and red brick. Pedimented Doric doorcase. Opposite the W end of the church, No. 255 VICTORIA AVENUE, restored by *Malcolm Ginns* following a fire in 1998, has been tree-ring dated to 1407. Jettied front with one large and one small gable, the larger further jettied above an oriel window. On the first floor an open hall with crown-post roof.

Nos. 269–75 is a C15 hall house with two jettied cross-wings, but with a cartway later driven through the N end of the hall block. Between them, the SPREAD EAGLE by *W. H. Pertwee & Howard*, 1925–7, and on the corner of West Street the BLUE BOAR by *Edward Wright*, 1888, good examples of pub architecture of their different dates.

N of Prittlewell Park, along PRIORY CRESCENT, the former EKCO wireless factory, 1930 onwards, including offices by *E. Edward Briggs*, 1932–3, and research laboratory by *Wells Coates*, 1935–6. The former has a long brick front with three-storey stone-faced entrance; the latter of two storeys, plastered brick, with rounded corners and strip windows.*

PRITTLEWELL CAMP, 1 m. NE of the church. Early Iron Age encampment, roughly elliptical, measuring 800 ft (243 metres) from N to S and 650 ft (198 metres) from E to W. Part of the southern rampart survives.

SOUTHCHURCH

HOLY TRINITY, Southchurch Boulevard. A modest Norman church, as can still be seen from the S, restored by *W. Slater* in 1855–7. On the N side of this *Comper* built a new church in 1906, reducing the old church to an aisle. Comper's was the same length as the old one, with nave and chancel, N chancel aisle, and low battlemented NW vestry. To this *F. C. Eden* added a long chancel, 1931–2. The new church remains unfinished on the N side. Light and spacious, large windows with simple flowing tracery. Kentish rag walls artfully dotted with large knapped flints. The old nave is Norman. Its S doorway is in position, with one order of colonettes with one- and two-scallop capitals, and zigzag and roll moulding in the arch. The N doorway was re-erected as the W doorway of the new church. It also has one order of colonettes, one-scallop capitals, and zigzag in the arch, but in addition a billet-decorated hood-mould. In the old S side is one C13 lancet and one C14 window with segmental head. In the chancel are on the S as well as the N side C13 lancets. In the new church, reused, one lancet and one small Norman window. At the W end of the old church a C15 belfry resting on eight posts. W wall rebuilt by Slater. – Of most interest are the two RECESSES in the old chancel, that in the S wall early C14, ogee-headed on short shafts, that in the N wall a combined funeral monument and Easter sepulchre. It consists of a low segmental arch under which stands a low tomb-chest with cusped arch-head decoration, and above, the more spacious four-centred, cusped arch of the Easter Sepulchre itself. – PISCINA. In the old chancel, C13 with attached shafts. – In the old nave, remains of C12 double piscina in the form of scalloped capitals. – STAINED GLASS. In the old church, various windows typical of the 1850s. – In the

---

*Wells Coates also designed wireless sets for Ekco; and cf. Shipwrights, Hadleigh.

new church, w window and adjacent n window by *Comper*, 1918–21. e window by *G.E.R. Smith*, 1956, richly detailed with pictures of local buildings etc. but too much plain glass. – MONUMENT. Elizabeth Asser Drew †1761. Elegant wall monument of coloured marbles, with covered urn against a grey obelisk.

E of the church the former NATIONAL SCHOOL and teacher's house by *Slater*, 1851, enlarged 1894. Coursed ragstone, tall gabled windows with plate tracery. w of the church the former RECTORY, now flats. Two-storey stock brick, the upper floor now painted on the n front. Two bays, *c.* 1830–5, extended by four bays with canted bay on the s front in the 1850s, and a further wing to w.

CHRIST CHURCH, Colbert Avenue. By *Nicholson*, 1921, but the nave, with s arcade, is only what was intended to be the n aisle of a very much larger church. Late Perp, brick with stone dressings. – STAINED GLASS. By *James Powell & Sons*: e 1939, nave n and w 1949, the last unusually rich. – Church Centre on s side, *c.* 1997, forming new entrance.

HAMSTEL JUNIOR AND INFANT SCHOOLS, Hamstel Road. By *Laurence T. Weaser*, 1912. Three low brick blocks with shaped gables.

SOUTHEND ADULT COMMUNITY COLLEGE, Ambleside Drive. 1902–3 by *Burles & Harris*, as Southchurch Hall School. Brick with stone dressings. Very large, with prominent shaped gables and two little towers each with a copper-covered cupola. Striking entrance with curved walls and roof by *Peter Robins Associates*, 2002–3.

SOUTHCHURCH HALL (Museum), Southchurch Hall Close. Mid-C14 manor house (tree-ring dated 1321–63), surrounded by a moat that was dug in the late C12. In-line service block and hall. One cross-wing, to the r., rebuilt in the mid C16 and extended to the s, with jettied upper storey on the n side. Restored for the Borough by *P.M. Johnston*, 1929–31, when the porch was rebuilt, and most of the s side was tile-hung; elsewhere the timbers are exposed. Exhibition room of the same date on the s side, to balance the w wing, by *R.H. Dyer*, Borough Surveyor. The interior has the rare survival of a hall still open to the roof. Original central truss, with tie-beam, octagonal crown-post with capital, and four-way struts. Some fragments of C14 timberwork: a doorway and some tracery. By the bridge over the moat, on the n side, excavated foundations of a stone gatehouse and garderobes, late C13.

SOUTH SHOEBURY

South Shoebury includes Shoeburyness, the point of land which marks the end of the n bank of the Thames. This was selected by the Army for artillery experiments in the 1840s. The buildings of Shoebury Garrison (*see* below) were soon followed by other development, and by the end of the C19 Shoeburyness had become the dominant part of the parish.

St Andrew, Church Road. Norman nave and chancel, ragstone and flint rubble, with original simple N doorway, slightly more elaborate S doorway (one order of colonettes, roll moulding in the arch, and billet decoration of the hoodmould) and an original chancel N window. In addition some C13 lancets, a Perp nave S and a Perp chancel E window. Early C14 W tower with diagonal buttresses. C18 brick battlements. C15 timber porch. Inside, the chancel arch is Norman, with one order of columns (scallop capitals), and in the arch a roll moulding and a double zigzag. To the N and S of the arch curious recesses, more clearly recognizable on the S side. They consist of a blank arch next to the chancel arch and, at right angles, a second blank arch in the N and S walls of the nave respectively. The S recess has shafts at the outer sides of the two arches and one corbel for the two inner sides. Was all this for side altars? Nave roof with tie-beams on curved braces (tracery in the spandrels) and polygonal crown-posts with capitals. Opened up by *Nicholson*, who restored the church *c.* 1894–1902 and added the all-too-plain S vestry. Earlier restoration, including re-seating, by *W. Slater, c.* 1857. – STAINED GLASS. E window by *Margaret G. Thompson* (*Lowndes & Drury*), 1949. Chancel S ('The Bread of Life') by *W.F. Dixon*, late C19. Nave S, small window (St Andrew and St Peter) probably by *O'Connor, c.* 1852, large window by *H. Stacy Marks* for *James Powell & Sons*, 1858. Nave N (Pilgrim's Progress) by *Cox, Sons, Buckley & Co.*, 1881. – MONUMENTS. R.W.Yorke, son of Philip Yorke of Erdigg, †1854 at South End. Sarcophagus, urn, and weeping tree. By *T. Gaffin.* – In churchyard, First World War MEMORIAL, *Sir Reginald Blomfield*'s 'Cross of Sacrifice' with bronze sword.

GARRISON CHURCH OF ST PETER AND ST PAUL, Chapel Road. *See* Shoebury Garrison, below.

St George and the English Martyrs (R.C.), Ness Road. 1938–9 by *T. H. B. Scott*. Brown brick, making a strong impression on the street. Tall tower with Romanesque doorway, three statues in niches above it, and a round window above that. The roof-line steps down in three stages to the presbytery, 1927, also by Scott. Plain vaulted interior with W balcony.

POLICE STATION (former council offices) and FIRE STATION, High Street. By *Burles & Harris, c.* 1909. Stock brick with rusticated red brick pilasters, stone windows, and stone doorcase with rusticated pilasters and open pediment.

SHOEBURYNESS COUNTY HIGH SCHOOL, Caulfield Road. Classroom block, dining hall and 'covered street' by *Steven Kearney* of *Southend-on-Sea Borough Council Property Division*, 2002–3. Rendered blockwork and red cedar cladding.

SHOEBURYNESS HOTEL, High Street. By *William Stewart*, 1899. Large gable with decorative plaster frieze on brick Ionic pilasters.

SOUTH SHOEBURY HALL, SE of church. Timber-framed, probably C16, with two-storey, three-bay Georgian brick front.

MANOR HOUSE, Suttons Road, 1¼ m. NE and in a Ministry of Defence prohibited area. Brick, dated 1681. Symmetrical front with shell-hood over the doorway. Hipped roof with dormers with triangular and segmental pediments and central cupola – a well-known type of the second third of the C17.

RED HOUSE, Wakering Road, 1 m. NE. Brick, dated 1673. Still with a gable, but the brick panel with initials and date has an architrave and a small pediment.

SHOEBURY GARRISON. The British School of Gunnery was established in 1859 (the date on a lodge-like house with latticed glazing that marks the entrance to the site from Ness Road), but buildings for the garrison were started c. 1847. The firing ranges closed in 1998 and redevelopment of the site for housing by *Gladedale Homes* (master plan by *Allen Tod Architecture*) began in 2000, retaining most of the garrison buildings but including four timber-clad blocks of apartments by *Hawkins Brown* facing the sea. The centrepiece of the garrison is a group of buildings for gunnery cadets known, because of its unique layout, as HORSESHOE BARRACKS, by *Capt. T. Inglis R.E.*, 1859. Stock brick, as are nearly all the garrison buildings. The shape is more accurately that of the Greek capital letter omega, with eight two-storey, ten-bay blocks round a circular parade ground, and on the S side, closing the neck of the omega, a single-storey guardhouse and offices with central gateway. High central arch and two lower arches, square clock tower and square cupola, with voussoirs and other dressings in paler brick. Separate washhouses and cookhouses to the rear.

Opposite the gateway, Warrior Square Road, with married officers' quarters of 1860 on the E side, leads to THE TERRACE, 1861–2, three gabled blocks with more spacious accommodation for married officers and the surgeon. Behind this, the GARRISON CHURCH OF ST PETER AND ST PAUL. By *J. Egan Roper*, 1866, and intended for dual use as a school. E.E., ragstone. Nave with bellcote, lower shallow chancel, transepts, and NE vestry. Re-fitted and decorated by *Rev. Alfred Malim*, chaplain 1884–93, in part to his own designs, including the PULPIT, 1887, and REREDOS, 1889.* He also initiated a scheme, not completed, of colourful and original STAINED GLASS by *Campbell, Smith & Co.*, 1891 onwards, including the E window, chancel N and S and transept windows. NW window, 1902, and two nave N windows, 1926, by *Kempe*. – MONUMENT. Col. W.A. Fox Strangways, Commandant, and others †1885 in an accidental explosion. Mural brass by *Gaffin*.

E of Horseshoe Barracks, in HOSPITAL ROAD, the former hospital and staff quarters by *Capt. R.S. Beatson R.E.*, dated 1856. Five bays, the centre bay stepping slightly forward with open pediment, Venetian window, and enclosed porch. Deep bracketed eaves. To either side, single-storey terraces of N.C.O.s' housing by *Capt. Sykes R.E.* and *Inglis*, 1861. E of Hospital Road, the GUNNERY DRILL SHED, 1859, with lecture room added 1908. Stock brick with coupled red brick pilasters and cornice. Nine-bay free-span north-light roof. Then a twenty-one-bay range of OFFICERS' QUARTERS, 1871, two storeys and basement.

---

*Also the altar, *c.* 1885, now in the Garrison Church, Colchester (q.v.).

In MESS ROAD to the S, facing the sea, the OFFICERS' MESS. Originally a coastguard station, *c.* 1825, extended 1852, 1861–2, and 1898, the latter being the date of the ballroom on the N side and seventeen-bay accommodation block on the S. S of the Mess, BEACH HOUSE, stuccoed, 1856–7, and beyond it the heavy quick-firing BATTERY, 1898, of mass concrete. Other garrison buildings include, on the W side of Mess Road, the COMMANDANT'S HOUSE, 1851, extended 1860 and later, and in Beach Road, off Mess Road to the W, two POWDER MAGAZINES, 1852–3.

Outside the main garrison enclosure to the N, off Rosewood Lane, two long two-storey blocks of married soldiers' quarters. Brick, mid C19. Flats on the upper floor are reached by an external walkway on iron columns.

ENCAMPMENT. Very fragmentary remains, now mostly obliterated by the barracks; Rampart Street marks the NE corner. The camp is ascribed to the Danish chieftain Hasten and has been dated *c.* 894.

THORPE BAY

More regularly laid out than much of Southend, with straight roads running back from the esplanade, and in the middle an island in which sits:

ST AUGUSTINE, St Augustine's Avenue. 1934–5 by *W. H. Allardyce*, with Nicholson as consulting architect. Its tall W tower, with vestigial pilaster-like buttresses, seems even taller because of the surrounding bungalows. Simplified Perp. Brick, with Clipsham stone dressings on only some of the doors and windows. Undivided nave and chancel with shallow-pitched roof and narrow aisles (Bath stone arcades); wider aisles, and a S chapel, were planned as a future extension. – STAINED GLASS. E window, 1937, and others by *James Powell & Sons*. W window by *Francis W. Skeat*, 1958.

CHRIST CHURCH, Colbert Avenue. *See* Southchurch.

THORPE HALL, Thorpe Hall Avenue. Golf clubhouse since 1907, and the ground floor completely rebuilt and extended in the last quarter of the C20. The gables can still be seen, two on each of the N and S fronts, but the doorway with brick pediment and three balls noted by Pevsner has disappeared, and the date of 1668 cannot be verified.

WESTCLIFF-ON-SEA

A late C19 creation, following the opening of the railway station in 1895; the ecclesiastical parish was formed three years later.

CHURCHES

ST ALBAN THE MARTYR, St John's Road. 1898–90, completed 1903–4, an early and extremely interesting work of *Sir Charles Nicholson*, or rather at that time *Nicholson & Corlette*. Flint and rubble with brick dressings. Nave and aisles, N and S porches, N transept and vestries and larger S transept, visible on the outside by two gables with large Dec windows, leading into the Lady Chapel at the base of the SE tower. This is hardly taller than the nave roof, and has battlements. The nave has a spacious six-light W window and arcades with chamfered square piers. No E window, but a blind arcade on the exterior and inside a full-height REREDOS with carved figures in niches and Nativity scene, 1920 (First World War memorial, together with sanctuary panelling). The chancel roof is prettily painted. – ROOD SCREEN. By *Nicholson*, 1904, carved by *H.K. Kuchemann*. – FONT. From St Mary-le-Bow in London, inscribed 'Gift of Francis Dashwood Esq 1673', and given to the church in 1899. Octagonal stem with large leaves going up its lower part. Bowl with thick fluting. Contemporary octagonal domed wooden COVER, also carved with leaves etc. – STAINED GLASS. In addition to a large number of windows by *A.K. Nicholson* (notably the W window, 1927), a nave N window signed by *W. Sharp* of Southend, 1904. N transept by *John Hayward*, 1971. – N of the church, the original corrugated-iron mission church, 1892, now used as a hall, and the former VICARAGE, also by *Nicholson*.

ST ANDREW, Westborough Road. 1934–5 by *Newberry & Fowler*. All brick, including gable crosses, with pantile roof, and lancet windows, five stepped at the W end and aisle windows also stepped in groups of five. W narthex, nave, narrow aisles, a S transept that does no more than mark an entrance, chancel with S aisle and N chapel and N vestries.

ST MICHAEL AND ALL ANGELS, Leigh Road. By *Nicholson*, begun 1926, the first phase completed 1929, N and S aisles 1954–6, W end 1965–6 (by *H.T. Rushton*). The original design included a W tower with spire. Brick, with battlements all round, and flowing stone tracery. High chancel, the E end a half-hexagon; pointed Lady Chapel on S side, two-storey vestries etc. on N side with blind arcades of round-headed arches. Very simple lofty interior. – FONT. By *T.B. Huxley-Jones*, 1963. – STAINED GLASS. Three three-light chancel windows, 1930, and two-light Lady Chapel window, 1933, by *A.K. Nicholson*. Also in Lady Chapel, two-light window by *Luxford Studios*, 1962, and three-light S windows by *A.K. Nicholson Stained Glass Studios* and *G.E.R. Smith*, 1959, and *Chapel Studio*, 1990. Epiphany window by *F.W. Skeat*, 1969.

ST SAVIOUR, King's Road. By *Hoare & Wheeler*, who first built a temporary church (now hall), 1906–7, before embarking upon the present one: nave 1910–11, transepts 1923, chancel, S chapel, vestries, etc. (by *Ward, Hoare & Wheeler*), 1933–5. SW porch, the base of a tower that was never built. Dec, of Kentish rag, the interior plastered brick. Very wide nave, with narrow aisles and clerestory. – STAINED GLASS. E window by *W. Aikman*. – In S aisle, windows by *F.C. Eden* with *George Daniels*, c. 1927, and *A.K. Nicholson*, c. 1955.

OUR LADY HELP OF CHRISTIANS AND ST HELEN (R.C.), Milton Road. 1868–9 by *Thomas Goodman*, with carving by

Earp. E.E. Stock brick with stone dressings and some red brick, the latter used more obviously to decorative effect on the interior. *A.J.C. Scoles* added the s aisle, 1899–1900, and N aisle, 1902–3, more or less following Goodman's original scheme. Also by *Scoles* the school on the N side, 1898–9. – STAINED GLASS. A number of windows by *Hardman*, 1952–63, replacing ones damaged in the Second World War. – PRES-BYTERY. By *Leonard Stokes*, 1887, looking very domestic with plastered walls and prominent brick chimney. But the unusual placing of the front door at the base of the chimneystack is a later alteration. – Also by *Stokes* a wing of the convent to the s (now St Bernard's High School). It has a gable decorated by a Baroque niche and mullioned and transomed windows – a typical Stokes mixture. Other parts of the convent are by *W. J. Wood*, 1888, *B.R. Parkes*, 1909, and *Fr. Benedict Williamson & J.H.B. Foss*, 1912–13.

NAZARETH HOUSE (R.C. Poor Sisters of Nazareth), London Road. On the site of an earlier house, Milton Hall, to which *F. W. Tasker* added a CHAPEL, 1875–6. Plain and cusped lancets, with w rose window, now rendered. Additions by *Pugin & Pugin*, 1913.★

ST BARBARA, ST PHANOURIOS AND ST PAUL (Greek Orthodox), Salisbury Avenue. Built as a Nonconformist chapel, *c.* 1899–1904. Brick with stone dressings. Curious-looking, with a large but not tall sw tower that makes the aisled nave seem even smaller than it would otherwise. – STAINED GLASS. s aisle window by *Jones & Willis*, 1933.

AVENUE BAPTIST CHURCH, Milton Road. 1900–1 by *F. E. Smee* of *Smee, Morice & Houchin*. An expensive-looking building, although the projected tower over the entrance porch was never built. Brick with Bath stone dressings. Reticulated tracery and other flowing Dec forms. Attractive extension with hall etc. on N side by *K. Cheeseman*, 1993–4, which borrows flint chequerwork from the old building.

METHODIST CHURCH, Park Road. By *Elijah Hoole*, 1871–2. Called by a local writer of the later C19 'one of the greatest ornaments of Southend'. Ragstone, laid like crazy paving. w window with bare plate tracery. No tower, only frontal angle turrets. Hall in similar style, 1902. Closed 1997.

TRINITY METHODIST CHURCH, Argyll Road. 1901 by *G. & R.P. Baines*. Late Perp, freely treated. Brick, with tracery and dressings of white Cosseyware, a form of moulded brick. Broad w front with porch, octagonal turret to the l. and small, square, tapering tower to the r. Large addition of 1923.

ST GEORGE'S UNITED REFORMED CHURCH (formerly Crowstone Congregational Chapel), King's Road. A relatively modest chapel by *Burles & Harris*, 1910, with a small tower and spire behind battlements, became an appendage to a vast new church by *George Baines*, 1924. Kentish ragstone, with Dec

★ Other buildings, including a three-storey block by *Pugin & Pugin*, 1899–1900, are due to be redeveloped.

tracery. Apsidal E end and transepts with two gables each. Reordered 2001 by *Lewis Patten*, when a new W entrance was added, the worship area of the 1924 church made smaller and given galleries to create additional rooms elsewhere, and the 1910 church converted to flats. – STAINED GLASS. E window of 1924 church by *Powell & Sons* (First World War memorial).

WESTCLIFF UNITED REFORMED CHURCH (Congregational), King's Road. 1914. Ragstone, with Perp tracery, and the base only of a NW tower. To the r., halls etc., the entrance set in a little tower with short square spire, noticeably similar to the nearby 1910 chapel by *Burles & Harris* (*see* above).

SYNAGOGUE (Southend and Westcliff Hebrew Congregation), Finchley Road. 1967–8 by *Norman Green*. Reinforced concrete frame with panels of brown brick. From the exterior might equally be, for example, a leisure centre.

PUBLIC BUILDINGS

PUBLIC LIBRARY, London Road. By *P. F. Burridge*, 1958–60, a very light, elegant, and welcoming design. Single storey, steel-framed with yellow brick walls but the front and rear walls almost entirely glazed. Flat roof with a central clerestory that has a ridge-and-furrow roof.

CHALKWELL HALL SCHOOLS, London Road. 1907–8 by *Clare & Ross*. 'Queen Anne' brick, with sash windows, quoins and modillion cornices. Main school two storeys, very tall, with projecting wings and gables with open pediments. Separate single-storey infants' school.

WESTBOROUGH PRIMARY SCHOOL, Macdonald Avenue. 1911. Single storey, brick. What makes it interesting are additions by *Cottrell & Vermeulen Architecture*, from 1993. These include a single-storey timber-framed classroom block, 1996, the walls partly glazed, partly rendered, and in one area clad with polycarbonate sheets so that the structure can be seen; and an after-school club, 2001, that is clad in cardboard, decorated with drawings of origami by *Simon Patterson*. The structure is part timber and part cardboard, with the roof supported on eleven cardboard tubes. By the same architects, at MILTON HALL PRIMARY SCHOOL, Salisbury Avenue, a C-plan range of eight steel-framed, brightly painted classrooms and separate nursery *c.* 1996.

CLIFFS PAVILION. By *P. F. Burridge*. The building was started in 1939, then abandoned, and not resumed until 1955; opened 1964. The finished building is definitely post-war in appearance, with mosaic cladding and zigzag roof. What looks 1930s – a two-storey glazed bar, with semicircular end wall, on the sea side – belongs to a major refurbishment by *Tim Foster Architects*, 1991–2, which also increased the capacity of the auditorium by inserting a cantilevered balcony.

PALACE THEATRE, London Road. 1912 by *Cabuche & Hayward*. Four-storey brick façade with stucco decoration, a mainly symmetrical but otherwise improper assemblage of pilasters, scrolls, panels, cartouches, balustrade, etc. Extended with studio theatre 1982.

Westcliff has no clearly defined boundaries or characteristics, but abounds in late C19 and, especially, early C20 houses of the kind one associates with the seaside, with balconies and turrets for (sometimes impossible) sea views. Good examples along the front, e.g. WESTCLIFF PARADE towards Southend, including one (No. 28, with polygonal turret) lived in by the theatre architect Frank Matcham, and a Neo-Jacobean semi-detached pair with two-storey bows and shaped gables dated 1899, now part of the Westcliff Hotel of 1891. w of Cliffs Pavilion, PALMEIRA AVENUE was developed c. 1901–4 by *James Edmondson*, including Palmeira Mansions with balconies and bays angled for sea views. Further w, ARGYLL HOUSE, a large block of flats with streamlined balconies and curved corner windows by *Howis & Belcham*, 1937, and in PEMBURY ROAD the bracingly-named OZONE COTTAGE (No. 20) by *Parker & Unwin*, 1902–4. Roughcast, narrow front with central canted bay rising through the eaves like a large dormer.

Other interesting houses in the streets N of the Railway Station, beginning with Westcliff Towers, 1903, at the S end of DITTON COURT ROAD. Further up, No. 34, a modest house of c. 1902 by *H. Leon Cabuche*, c. 1902, single-storey with a large dormer and veranda. In PRESTON ROAD, No. 35, by *H. Fuller Clark*, c. 1902, part brick and part rendered, combines elements of Arts and Crafts, Voysey, and Mackintosh; on the opposite side a characteristic house with balconies and half-timbering dated 1903. In CANEWDON ROAD, w of Hamlet Court Road, SUNRAY HOUSE, a small block of flats with metal windows and multi-coloured sun-burst above the entrance; by *O.H. Cockrill*, 1934. On the corner of Canewdon Road and HAMLET COURT ROAD, the former Capital and Counties Bank by *Greenhalgh & Brockbank*, 1901–2. Flamboyant commercial architecture with gables and, on the corner, prominent entrance rising though a turret to a cupola. Further N, No. 51 ANERLEY ROAD by *Walter Tapper*, 1901–2. 'Queen Anne' brick with hipped roof, modillion cornice and quoins. Two-storey, seven-bay front; central doorcase with shell-hood on carved brackets. Built for Dr W.H. Morgan, including surgery and waiting room with separate entrance.

Further early C20 development of the CHALKWELL HALL estate, e.g. a pair of large semi-detached houses on the corner of Chalkwell Avenue and Galton Road by *Clare & Ross*, c. 1904; other interesting houses in Imperial Avenue and Seymour Road. The Hall itself a dull, stuccoed house of c. 1830, three bays and three storeys, standing in Chalkwell Park, opened 1903. About ½ m. N, in CLATTERFIELD GARDENS, a Modern Movement house (No. 62) by *Neil Martin-Kaye*, 1932–3. Two storeys with flat roof. Rendered brick with metal windows, including corner windows and 'V' window to the stairs. Behind it the WHITE HALL, 1931, a tennis clubhouse by *Martin-Kaye* for the same client, N.T. Thurston, who planned a large Modernist development. Another flat-roofed house, with some exposed brickwork, at No. 52.

On Chalkwell Beach, the CROWSTONE, an obelisk erected in 1837 to mark the seaward limit at that time of the City of London's jurisdiction over the Thames.

SOUTH FAMBRIDGE
Ashingdon

8090

ALL SAINTS. Rebuilt 1846, just a chapel. Nave and chancel in one, with W porch and bellcote. Stock brick with stone dressings, and lancets.

OLD FERRY HOUSE, ¾ m. NW. Late C18 brick. Asymmetrical front with three windows on two storeys and pedimented doorcase. Gutters supported on wooden brackets, a nice touch.

SOUTH HANNINGFIELD

7090

ST PETER. Nave, chancel and belfry with splay-foot spire. The nave is of *c.* 1200. It has a small and another lengthened original window in the N wall, and one in the S wall. In the S wall in addition a two-light C15 window, with PAINTING of very pretty foliage scrolls in the jambs. The belfry, probably C14, rests on four posts with big curved braces and is self-supporting. Chancel rebuilt 1850 – see the S and E walls of brick, the others being of rubble with limestone dressings. Nave, tower and S porch restored by *Chancellor*, 1883–4. – DOOR with iron hinges, *c.* 1400. – STAINED GLASS. E window by *G.E.R. Smith* (*A.K. Nicholson Stained Glass Studios*), 1952. Small nave N window by *Valerie Green*, 1995.

SOUTHMINSTER

9090

ST LEONARD. A largish, odd, and aesthetically unsatisfactory church. The exterior has an unfinished look, which demonstrates the extent to which church restorers in the C19 imposed unity upon buildings assembled piecemeal; here there was only a restoration of the interior, which did for the inside what was never done for the outside. But it means that the history of the building can be easily read, from the S side, where the different strata are obvious. At the bottom, stone, and the S doorway shows this to be Norman; Norman also the internal W window above the triple-chamfered C14 tower arch. Then comes a layer of flint, including the clerestory, showing how the nave was heightened in the C15 (sundial 1814); finally a layer of brick, which belongs to 1819. The W tower is mainly C15 on a C12 base. It has one big diagonal buttress and there are the remains of flint-and-stone-ornamented battlements. The best feature of the church is that rare thing in Essex, a stone-vaulted N porch with a star-shaped tierceron vault and bosses. It dates from the C15 and has two-light side windows; above the entrance three richly canopied and crocketed niches. Iron gates and overthrow by *Michael Hoyle*, 1997, contemporary in style but wholly satisfactory. It is at the E end that things go awry.

A licence was granted in 1702 to rebuild the chancel, much smaller than the existing one; this was in turn rebuilt in 1818–19 by *Hopper*, who provided a five-sided chancel and transepts, cemented on the exterior, in 'the plainest Gothick'. This is recorded in an unusually elaborate painted notice on the N wall. Hopper also raised the nave roof, giving it and the chancel plaster rib vaults of entirely unconvincing weight. Then in 1891 *Rev. W. H. Lowder* was appointed to the living. He had trained under Butterfield and was therefore competent to act as his own architect. He took down Hopper's W gallery, screened off the transepts to provide a vestry and organ chamber on the N side and separate chapel on the S; the chancel was raised, screen and choir stalls added, as well as an elaborate stone reredos and arcading round the E end like the seating in a chapter house. Some of the carving was executed by Lowder himself (including the PULPIT, the oak REREDOS in the side chapel, and two of the Caen stone figures on the main reredos); most of the fittings were executed by *Luscombe* of Exeter. – FONT. Perp, octagonal, with decorated foot, stem, and bowl. The ornament is chiefly the usual quatrefoils, but the overall effect is graceful. – BENCH ENDS. Two, of the C15, with poppyheads, in the chancel. – BRASSES. Civilian and wife, *c.* 1560; 21- and 20-in. (53- and 51-cm.) figures. – John King †1634; 15-in. (38-cm.) figure. – STAINED GLASS. Three windows (nave S and tower) by *Heaton, Butler & Bayne*, 1910 and 1932.

BAPTIST CHAPEL, Burnham Road. 1861. Brick, with gault brick detailing and windows that taper in the Egyptian manner. Now a house.

MEMORIAL HALL. By *A. H. Mackmurdo*, 1933. Plain brick front with Regency-style decoration over the door and windows. One of the village halls erected under the auspices of the Rural Community Council for Essex (*see* also Great Totham).

POLICE STATION, Queenborough Road. By *F. Whitmore*, 1901; an outpost of authority, including magistrates' court and houses for a superintendent and a married constable. Brick with stone dressings and broad shaped gables.

In Hall Road, a WATER PUMP by *Richmond & Son*, engineers, Chelmsford, 1832; erected by the Governors of the Charterhouse, the principal landowners.

SOUTH OCKENDON

Thurrock U.A.

ST NICHOLAS. Striking exterior, mainly knapped flint with Reigate stone dressings, restored 1865–6 by *Richard Armstrong*.* Best of the old work is the Late Norman N doorway, moved when the C15 N aisle was added, restored 1865. Three orders of supports, the middle colonettes spiral-fluted and enriched by shaft-rings. The three orders of voussoirs of three-dimensional varieties with zigzag motif. The date *c.* 1180. Of the C13 the fine circular W tower, although the top stage with Norman openings and battlements is Armstrong's. Perp N chapel, two-and-a-half-bay N arcade (octagonal piers and double-chamfered arches), and rood stair-turret on the S side. S aisle and vestry (now organ chamber), 1865–6. – HOUR-GLASS STAND. Wrought iron, C17. – STAINED GLASS. Tower window by *Benjamin Finn*, 1998. Seated figure of Christ against an intensely glowing orange background. – MONUMENTS. Brass to Sir Ingram Bruyn †1400. 53-in. (134-cm.) figure in armour (head missing), with fragments of canopy. – Brass to Margaret Barker †1602. 30-in. (76-cm.) figure. – Sir Richard Saltonstall †1601, Lord Mayor of London. Standing wall monument of alabaster. The usual kneeling figures, painted, with six sons and nine daughters in the 'predella'. – George Drywood †1611. Marble tablet with Ionic pilasters. – Philip Saltonstall †1668 as a result of falling from his horse in Belhus Park. Restrained Baroque, with broken segmental pediment, swags, and putti heads.

HOLY CROSS (R.C.), Easington Way. 1960–1 by *H.B. Towner*. Brick, with stone dressings. Low aisles and squat W tower with pyramidal pantiled roof. Foundation stone and figure of Christ over W door by *Joseph Cribb*.

South Ockendon ceased to be a village with the building of LCC housing estates W of the railway after the Second World War. Nonetheless the Green on the N side of the church survived, dominated by the ROYAL OAK, with Late Medieval N cross-wing and hall range, the remainder C17. Attached to its N end a single-storey building with Gothick windows, which with a similar detached building across the lane frames the entrance to SOUTH OCKENDON HALL. Rebuilt 1862 (by *Richard Armstrong*?), stock brick, with the big moat of the previous Hall adjoining. Crossing the moat a brick bridge and the ruins of a stone gatehouse, partly rebuilt in C17 or C18 brick. 400 yds S of the Green, in South Road, QUINCE TREE FARM, early C16 with exposed timbers, and gabled and jettied N cross-wing.[†]

---

* Armstrong also restored St Mary Magdalene, North Ockendon, 1858, and rebuilt nearby All Saints, Cranham, 1873 (London Borough of Havering; *see London 5: East*).

[†] The early C19 smock mill by the Hall noted in previous editions has gone. The rectory, just N of Quince Tree Farm, was dem. *c.* 1970. Ockendon Courts Secondary School by *Denis Clarke Hall*, praised by Pevsner, closed in 1971.

GROVES, North Road, ¾ m. NNE. Length of garden wall and tall gateway with round-headed arch and Doric pilasters, all in brick, *c.* 1600, the remains of a manor house demolished at the end of the C18.

LITTLE BELHUS, ¾ m. SW. Largish weatherboarded late C16 house with much panelling inside. The most handsome feature is the gateway into the walled garden with a steep curly gable. Restored and converted to three dwellings by the *GLC Dept of Architecture and Civic Design*, 1966, and hemmed in by housing of the same era.

THE MOUNT, 270yds NE of South Ockendon Hall. Barrow, 150ft (45.7 metres) in diameter and 17ft (5.1 metres) high. Roman and Iron Age pottery has been found.

SOUTH WEALD

5090

Brentwood

One of the largest parishes in the county, which until the late C19 included much of what is now Brentwood.

ST PETER, Weald Road. A large church in a fine position and with a surprisingly big W tower of *c.* 1500, ashlar-faced, with angle buttresses, battlements, and higher stair-turret; repaired in 1692, according to a date on the N side. The medieval church consisted of C12 nave and chancel, from which the Norman S doorway survives. It has one order of columns with zigzag-carved shafts, a carved lintel, an arch with zigzag decoration, and a tympanum with diaper ornament, little squares divided into two triangles. Chancel rebuilt and lengthened in the mid C13, when the N aisle was added. This was rebuilt in the C15, slightly wider than the nave. *James Savage* repaired and re-seated the church, 1837–8, adding a S gallery and extending the existing N gallery, but all this was swept away in 1867–9 when *Teulon* effectively rebuilt the church, all but the W tower, and even here the top stage was renewed. The client for both campaigns was the redoubtable and wealthy C.A. Belli, vicar 1823–76. The N aisle became the nave, with new chancel and N vestry; the old nave became the S aisle, with a chapel in place of the old chancel. The walls appear to have been rebuilt from the ground up, although Teulon's plans indicate that more of the N and W walls of the old N aisle were preserved than the S and E walls of the old nave. The arcade is reconstructed but reusing the original piers (four circular, one octagonal), and the double-hollow-chamfered arches follow a C13 model. Walls predominantly flint, with various other fragments, in which Teulon incorporated putlog holes for decorative effect. CARVING of St Peter's keys on S aisle wall presumably by *Earp*, who was responsible for the interior stone carving; wood-carving by *Polley* of Coggeshall. Depressing N extension by *Laurence King*, 1980.

Elaborate carved marble and alabaster REREDOS and low chancel wall with bronze gates by *E.C. Lee*, 1885. – SCREEN.

Painted and gilt iron screen between chancel and s chapel by
Sir Gilbert Scott, 1877, made by *Francis Skidmore*. – FONT. 1662,
polygonal, with thick leaves sprouting up the stem. – STAINED
GLASS. In tower window, two late C15 panels, probably
Flemish. – E window to Belli, 1886, chancel s 1907, s chapel E
and s, 1888 and 1929, all by *Kempe*. s aisle by *Clayton & Bell*,
c. 1878. – HELM. In s chapel. Burgonet, of plain design, C17.

    MONUMENTS. Brass (s chapel) of Sir Antony Browne †1567,
the bottom half only of a kneeling figure, 11½ in. (30 cm.), until
1867 on top of a chest-tomb between chancel and N aisle.
Other brasses removed at this time now at w end of nave,
c. 1450–1500, all small; also Arthur Crafford †1606, 24½-in.
(62-cm.) figure, and two kneeling boys, Robert Picakis and
Allen Talbott †1634, 7½ in. (19 cm.). – Hugh and Dorothy
Smith †1745 and 1755. Standing wall monument with sarcophagus and grey obelisk, erected 1757. Against the obelisk a
large roundel with two profiles facing each other. Unsigned. –
Sir Richard Neave of Dagnams★ †1814. Wall monument in the
form of a sarcophagus, by *E. Gaffin*. – The Ven. F.J.H.
Wollaston †1823 with profile: 'He went to bed in perfect health
October 11th 1823, and was found a corpse on Sunday
morning, reader reflect!!!' Said to be by *Francis Chantrey*. –
Rev. Charles Tower †1825, draped tomb, by *C. H. Smith*. – John
Tower, Rear Admiral of the Blue †1837, white and grey marble
with flag and anchor, by *T. Denman*. – C.J. Fox †1856 by *T.
Gaffin*, inscription on open book. – Mary Tower †1865 by *T.
Hall*, inscription within a wreath of flowers. – C.T. Tower
†1867, large chest-tomb of granite and coloured marbles. – In
sw corner of churchyard, O.E. Coope of Rochetts †1886 by his
nephew *E.C. Lee*, 1887, carved by *Earp, Son & Hobbs*. Sicilian
marble. Large horizontal cross resting on five short shafts, the
slab carved with orchids. – LYCHGATE. By *Teulon*.
ST PAUL, Mores Lane, Bentley. By *E.C. Lee*, 1877–80, as a chapel
of ease to St Peter. E.E., flint with Westwood stone dressings,
and with many of the characteristics seen at his slightly later
St Thomas, Brentwood. Nave, chancel, s aisle, NW porch, NE
tower and tall splay-foot shingled spire with lucarnes. Well
detailed, with excellent carving by *Thomas Earp*. – REREDOS.
1883, by *Earp*; alabaster. – LORD'S PRAYER, COMMAND-
MENTS and CREED. Painted on chancel N wall. – STAINED
GLASS. E and w windows by *Clayton & Bell*, *c.* 1880. Nave N,
E to W: *C. E. Kempe & Co.*, 1927 and 1931, *G.E.R. Smith*,
c. 1948, and *Goddard & Gibbs*, 1992. s aisle, four signed by *G.
Maile*, one dated 1989, and another by *G.E.R. Smith*, *c.* 1953.
– Free-standing CHURCH HALL at SE corner, 1989. – Curate's
house, now the OLD VICARAGE, s of the church, also by *Lee*,
1878–80. Brick with tile-hanging.
St Peter's lies more or less in the centre of the parish, with a
    pretty group of houses and other buildings around it, especially

★ *See London 5: East*, p. 164.

the TOWER ARMS, dated 1704, red brick with chequered burnt headers, five-bay, two-storey, with hipped roof and dormers. At the top of Wigley Bush Lane THE COTTAGE, early C19 with veranda, opposite HIGH HOUSE (originally The Grange) by *E.C. Lee*, *c.* 1875, for O.E. Coope of Rochetts. S along Wigley Hall Lane, on the E side LUPTONS, timber-framed and brick, rendered, dating back to the C17, and then the BROWNE AND WINGRAVE ALMSHOUSES by *Teulon*, 1854. A picturesque, long, low group of ten houses and chapel, stepping down the hill. Brick with stone dressings, asymmetrically composed. Octagonal shelter for water pump.* A little further S the former VICARAGE (now Weald Hall), for Rev. C.A. Belli, 1824–5. By *Hardwick*, probably *Philip*, in which case one of his earliest works; *C. R. Cockerell*, a relation of Belli's, amended the plan, which he found 'v contrived'. Large, white brick, with seven bays to the road and tetrastyle Corinthian portico on the S side overlooking the valley.

WEALD COUNTRY PARK. Weald Hall, demolished 1950, stood NW of St Peter.† It was built in the mid C16, and received a new S front in the early C18. The only surviving building is known as QUEEN MARY CHAPEL, Weald Road, originally a garden house or lodge. C16, brick, in the same style as the main house with octagonal corner turrets. Extended *c.* 1830 and *c.* 1970. Next to it a brick granary, *c.* 1800, on square staddlestones. The landscape survives, however, as a public park, bought by Essex County Council in 1953. A plan of 1738 shows a formal layout with avenues radiating from a lake NE of the house, of which the lake and some lines of trees remain. Immediately E of the house can be seen steps which led up to a stone BELVEDERE TOWER, heightened by Thomas Tower after 1752. Demolished 1954, but the mound and steps survived. In the SE of the park SOUTH WEALD CAMP, a Late Iron Age univallate hill-fort, in very poor condition. Rampart and steep scarp slope, with traces of an external ditch, roughly circular in shape, enclosing about 7 acres. Ditch re-cut C10 to C12 when the fort was incorporated into South Weald deerpark, and remodelled in the C18 as a landscape feature.

At Brook Street, ¾ m. SSE, MARYGREEN MANOR HOTEL. Early C16 cross-wings, the hall rebuilt in the late C17. Exposed timbers and C19 canted bays beneath the jetties. Rear additions include a brick chapel with stone dressings, 1948. Almost opposite, the GOLDEN FLEECE (now Harvester), plastered, with two jettied cross-wings. The smaller (W) cross-wing, with crown-post roof, *c.* 1400, hall and E cross-wing early C16.

The parish contains an unusually large number of substantial houses, a reflection of its rural location within easy reach of London.

---

*The primary school opposite, also by *Teulon*, 1856, at the expense of Rev. Charles Belli, dem. 1968.

†Panelling, stonework, and a painting of the house attributed to *William van der Hagen* were removed to Brentwood School (q.v.).

COXTIE HOUSE, Coxtie Green Road, 1¼ m. NNW. By *J. R. Moore Simpson*, 1937–8. Neo-Georgian brick. Three-bay entrance front with Tuscan doorcase, seven-bay garden front.

DYTCHLEYS, Coxtie Green Road, 1¾ m. NW. Said to be dated 1729. Seven-bay brick house of two-and-a-half storeys with a three-bay pediment and Tuscan porch. C18 Gothick stables on E side of house with a Chinoiserie tower at one end. All derelict in 2005.

GILSTEAD HALL, Coxtie Green Road, S of Dytchleys. Dated 1726. Fine nine-bay brick house with parapet, doorway with broad segmental pediment, and a large entrance hall, the staircase having Corinthian newel posts and alternating fluted and twisted balusters. Converted to flats 1988.

GREAT ROPERS (Ursuline Preparatory School), Great Ropers Lane, 1¾ m. SSE. 1772 (rainwater head). Yellow brick. Three-storey, three-bay entrance front with central pediment, and Tuscan porch with open pediment. Bowed ends. Large C19 additions.

HOU HATCH, Weald Road, 1¼ m. NW. Probably dating back to the C17. Six-bay brick entrance (NE) front of 1903, with projecting porch. Elsewhere early C19 yellow brick, including six-bay garden (SE) front. The park had been laid out by 1777, with further landscaping by *J. B. Papworth*, *c.* 1824.

LEVERTON HOUSE (formerly Boyles Court), Dark Lane, 1½ m. SSE. 1776 by *Thomas Leverton*. Brick. N elevation of five bays of which the central three break forward, with low ground floor, *piano nobile*, upper floor, and attics behind a parapet and three-bay pediment. Tuscan portico with six square columns. Lower pavilions, set back, each with one big Venetian window, two-and-a-half storeys, connected to the main block by two-storey single-bay links. S elevation probably the original entrance front, with central blind Venetian window, the present ground-floor entrance hall the result of C19 alterations by the Lescher family, when the fine staircase, with delicate balusters of thin alternating shapes and carved tread ends, was rebuilt. Further alterations, mainly to the top storey, following a fire in 1973. Now a children's home; adjoining the S side, LEVERTON HALL secure unit by *W. S. Atkins* (*Rick Broadley*), 1996–7. Like a converted stable, albeit an unusually long one: brick, single storey, with sash windows separated by reconstituted stone pilasters, two pedimented bays to break up the elevation and a larger projecting pedimented bay at the S end. Long unbroken slate roof with three louvres.

LINCOLNS, Lincolns Lane, 1¼ m. NNW. E cross-wing *c.* 1500, hall and W cross-wing rebuilt in late C16. C17 weatherboarded barn to the S and another timber-framed and weatherboarded building, also *c.* 1500, possibly a detached kitchen. Further S, LINCOLNS COTTAGE, early C16 with ground-floor timbers exposed. Unusual plan of six bays in line, with evidence of a three-bay hall at the N end with an upper room at the gable end supported on a richly moulded beam, and an unusually early (for Essex) queenpost roof.

MASCALLS, Mascalls Lane, 1¼ m. SSE. Early C19 rendered brick, with later C19 additions. Mainly two storeys. Three-bay entrance front with projecting pedimented central bay, and linked pavilions to either side. Garden front with two canted bays and, to the l., a round stair with conical roof and lantern. Early C19 stables to N.

MILLFIELD (Millfield Business Centre), Ashwells Road, 400 yds NE of St Paul. Large brick house with Dutch gables by *E.C. Lee*, 1882–6; remodelled 1911 by *A. Winter Rose*, including new main entrance, SW wing with billiard room and garden entrance, and garden layout.

PILGRIMS HALL, Ongar Road, Pilgrims Hatch, ½ m. SE of St Paul. Early C19 two-storey brick farmhouse, given two stuc-coed bow-fronted wings with a decorative cast-iron balcony between, *c.* 1814. Further extended *c.* 1860 and then in 1913 by *Horace Farquharson*, who added a wing with a third bow to the r. and on the l. laid out a terrace with pergola and beyond it a sunken garden.

ROCHETTS, Weald Road, ½ m. NW of St Peter. C18 house, largely destroyed by fire 1975. From 1784 to 1823 the seat of Sir John Jervis, later Admiral the Earl of St Vincent, who built the major part, which was timber-framed and faced with mathematical tiles. What survives is mainly a C19 brick wing, with parapet. Early C19 circular thatched LODGE, with C20 additions, as well as entrance gates that date from later occupancy by O.E. Coope (*see also* Berechurch Hall), for whom *George Devey* carried out alterations and additions, 1866–73. Park laid out by St Vincent, including an ornamental lake N of the house that links visually to that of Weald Hall. At St Vincent's Hamlet, NW, ROCHETTS FARM, with a pair of very quirky cottages by *E.C. Lee* for Coope, *c.* 1875 (cf. High House, above): brick with projecting upper storeys, part-exposed timber framing, and gabled roofs.

WARLEY HOSPITAL. *See* Brentwood.

8090

SOUTH WOODHAM FERRERS

A proposal for developing the southern part of Woodham Ferrers (q.v.) was published by Essex County Council in 1971. Quite separate from the older part of the parish on the hill to the N, it already had a population of some 4,500, centred on the railway station. Changes in government policy enabled the County Council to purchase more land and put forward more ambitious proposals for a small town of 18,000 residents on a 1,300-acre site, much of it replacing irregular plotland devel-opment. Construction of the infrastructure by the Council began in 1975, the first houses were built in 1976, and the town centre's first buildings opened in 1978. The target of 4,700 dwellings was largely achieved by the early 1990s, although some building is still in progress. As well as residential areas (with three primary schools), mostly in the southern part of the town, there are two small industrial areas near the railway, a central area with shops, secondary school, church, and other public buildings, and open space to the s, w, and e, including a country park along the River Crouch.

Development of the town was closely regulated by the County Council, and the individual private developers had to follow tight design briefs based on the *Design Guide for Residential Areas* published by the Council in 1973. As a result, South Woodham Ferrers became the embodiment of the *Design Guide* and the model for hundreds of smaller-scale developments that have followed since. The pilot scheme was a group of eighteen houses in FENNFIELDS ROAD in the NW of the town by *Stanley Keen & Partners*, 1976, including the first 'mews court' layout, and in the mix of materials that was to become so familiar: brick, plaster, and weatherboarding. If it now looks a little commonplace, that is only because it has been so widely imitated; and it is instructive to compare the new housing with what was already there, e.g. in THE CHASE, just to the e of Fennfields Road, or along the main pre-existing thoroughfares of HULLBRIDGE ROAD and CLEMENTS GREEN LANE. Other early phases of development were along HAMBERTS ROAD in the NE of the town and COLLINGWOOD ROAD in the SE, including COLLINGWOOD SCHOOL, brick with pantiled roof and little clock tower. In the SW quarter, GANDALF'S RIDE also provides good examples of the variety of styles of housing that could be achieved within the constraints of the *Design Guide*, including a not entirely successful attempt to create a little village centre round CHETWOOD SCHOOL and pub opposite.

The CENTRAL AREA was developed by Associated Dairies Ltd (Asda) and their architects *Holder & Mathias Partnership*, 1977–8. Although the *Design Guide* was concerned only with residential areas, it was decided to apply it to the Central Area also, and this is what in particular caused derision in the architectural press because of its make-believe re-creation of an old town centre that never existed in reality. The main commercial building is the ASDA SUPERSTORE, disguised as a large brick barn with tiled roof, the entrance marked by a pair of weatherboarded 'midstreys' – the first of many such barn-style superstores. On the N side is a weatherboarded clock tower – the weatherboarding in fact plastic cladding – heightened in 1985 when the superstore was enlarged. The tower stands on the edge of QUEEN ELIZABETH II SQUARE, opened 1981, with [121] later BANDSTAND. Here the attempt at illusion becomes a little trying. On the N side of the square is what appears to be a brick chapel, the ground floor a shop, and next to it a former corn exchange perhaps, but in fact a bank – also brick, two storeys with round-headed windows separated by giant pilasters, and an attic storey beneath deep eaves of a slate roof. Most of the buildings, however, are small-town Essex vernacular, brick and plaster and weatherboarding with some 'jettied' upper storeys, irregularly arranged in a picturesque manner.

More successful, because less contrived, is TRINITY
SQUARE to the N, reached by a narrow pedestrian street
(HERALDS WAY) along one side of which are shops with classrooms of the town's secondary school on the upper floors. This
rare integration of school and community continues on the NE
side of the square with the WILLIAM DE FERRERS CENTRE,
1982–3, comprising the main school buildings but incorporating the Public Library and other community facilities. On the
NW side, HOLY TRINITY CHURCH, 1982 (shared by C. of E.,
R.C., and Methodist). Irregular hexagonal worship area, two
sides of which are common with adjoining C. of E. and R.C.
primary schools. Church and Centre by the *County Architect's
Dept* (project architects *W.G. Apps*, *J. Breavington*, and *C.P.
French*). Brick and pantiles, but with tent-like slate roof on the
church. Also of note the HEALTH CLINIC in Merchant Street,
c. 1987, by the *County Architect's Dept* (project architect, *Laurie
Wood*), white rendered walls with stained hardwood joinery and
pantile roof.

CHAMPIONS HALL, Kingsway. C18 timber-framed and plastered. Two storeys and attics, with three bays and dormers on
the E front. To its E, on the corner of Burnham Road and Hullbridge Road, C17 and C18 cottages with exposed timbers. All
much restored and extended in the C20.

SPAINS HALL

6030

1 m. NW of Finchingfield

Named after the family of Hervey de Ispania or d'Espagne, who
held the property at Domesday (cf. Willingale Spain and
Spaynes Hall, Great Yeldham). In the C14 the estate passed to
the Kempe family, and the present house is the result of a
rebuilding by John Kempe, *c.* 1585, although fragments of the
previous building survive, dating to the first half of the C15.
Alterations were carried out by (Sir) Robert Kempe, *c.* 1637.
In 1760 the house and estate were purchased by Samuel
Ruggles, clothier, of Bocking; the family assumed the additional surname Brise in 1827. Samuel's son John made various
alterations during his ownership, 1764–76, and further work
was carried out at the end of the C18 and early C19. Some of
this was undone at the end of the C19, but no significant
changes have been made since.

59   Most of the house is of brick. The main (SW) front is of two
storeys with attics, and has eight shaped gables, not all identical
in detail. They are of different sizes and arranged apparently
in no system. Apart from that on the l. hand bay, an addition
of the 1890s, the gables probably belong to a remodelling of
the front dated 1637 on five very fine decorated rainwater
heads. The windows are mullioned or mullioned and transomed and again quite casually placed, although only those on
the upper storey are original rather than C19 replacements of
C18 sashes. The exception is the nine-light window of the hall,

r. of the entrance, but even here the top row of lights, and the second transom, are C19. The porch with two upper storeys is near the centre, more or less balanced by a projection to its l. A broader projection to the r. of the hall contains the main staircase. The SE front has a single-storey canted bay, castellated and with pinnacles and cement mouldings, based on more extensive but unexecuted proposals made by *J.A. Repton* in 1824. Sashes on the first floor. The return has a large, two-storey canted bay that probably dates from the 1760s, its castellated parapet perhaps added later. Set back from the SE front is the rear wing of the house, the façade rebuilt or refenestrated at the end of the C18 but with a distinctive cupola and weathervane dated 1768. The dome rests on a rusticated drum pierced by six arches, surrounded by a ring of Tuscan columns, alternately paired and single. The N part of the NE front and the whole of the NW front have no regularity to them and constitute the service side of the house. Two bargeboarded gables on the NW front, timber-framed and plastered, with C17 oriels on the first floor. Between the gables is one bay of a king-post roof, very rare in Essex, and belonging to the previous house of the first half of the C15. Its mouldings show that it was intended to be seen, but the absence of smoke-blackening means that it cannot have been for an open hall; a cross-wing seems more likely.

Inside, the main room is the Hall, entered directly from the porch. Dado of reused C16 or C17 panelling, moulded wallplates and moulded and carved beams. Stone chimneypiece by *William Ward*, *c.* 1837, who may also have designed a screen (removed in the 1890s). At the SE end is the Drawing Room, whose fireplace goes with the alterations of 1637. At the opposite end of the room, framing the canted bay of the 1760s, a timber arch with Doric frieze on fluted pilasters, Greek-key decoration on the soffit, and rustication that links it to the 1768 cupola. Main staircase also at this end, *c.* 1600. Narrow, dog-leg, with turned balusters. Off the NE side of the Hall, the rear wing with Dining Room, vestibule and small drawing room, belonging to the remodelling of the wing at the end of the C18. At the NW end of the Hall is the Library, with late C18 fittings, and a broad, straight C18 stair with a Venetian window on the landing. In a room on the first floor at this end an elaborate carved fireplace.

Humphry Repton reported on the grounds in 1807 and he may have influenced the present form of the Lake SE of the house, made from two of a string of eight fishponds shown on a survey of 1618. The furthermost of these also survives. The pond nearest the house was an extension of the moat, filled and incorporated in the garden in the early C19. On the NE side an extremely large, spreading cedar tree, planted *c.* 1670. From the NE corner of the rear wing of the house runs a brick wall, at the end of which is a square two-storey building known as the PRAYER HOUSE. Mainly brick but partly faced in rubble, with battlements and angle turrets. Shown on the 1618 survey, but rebuilt in the first half of the C19, and now lying in the kitchen garden enclosed by a wall dated 1828.

NE of the house SPAINS HALL FARMHOUSE, probably an C18 conversion of a C17 farm building, and opposite the NW front – where there is the only obvious surviving portion of the moat, now dry – a square C18 brick dovecote and mid-C19 coach-house and stables, timber-framed and plastered on brick plinth.

ROMAN BUILDING. The site lies in the field known as Further Brixted, ¾ m. W. Excavations in 1931–2 revealed a rectangular building measuring 67 by 47 ft (20.4 by 14.3 metres) with stone footings supporting a timber-and-daub superstructure. The central room had a hypocaust and produced fragments of painted wall plaster and window glass. Pottery and coins suggest an occupation beginning in the mid C2.

SPRINGFIELD

Springfield is topographically confusing. The medieval parish extended as far W as the River Chelmer, but White's 1848 Directory already treated it as a suburb of Chelmsford and in 1907 it was absorbed into the municipal borough. Most of 'old' Springfield – the parish church, houses round Springfield Green, Springfield Hall – is therefore actually in Chelmsford, but is included here for convenience. 'New' Springfield – the present civil parish – consists mainly of large housing developments built since the 1970s: North Springfield, Chelmer Village, and Beaulieu Park.

ALL SAINTS. Norman nave, as proved by one N window with Roman brick surround and one S, now blocked; mainly flint rubble. Early C14 chancel and N vestry. The renewed windows are shafted inside and have hoodmoulds with headstops. Headstops also above the PISCINA. The C14 W tower with set-back buttresses was repaired and partly rebuilt in brick in 1586, as an inscription on the S face records. NW stair-turret by *Chancellor* as part of a restoration of the tower, 1883–4; he also extended the vestry, 1887. Main restoration by *J. Clarke*, 1867, which included removing cement and plaster from the exterior, re-seating, and adding the S porch. Large brick N extension by *Bryan Thomas & Partners*, 1979, enlarged 1988. – PANELLING. Frieze of arabesque ornament, early C17, in back of sedile. The rest of the chancel panelling is C16, removed from Dynes Hall, Great Maplestead (q.v.) in 1947. – SCREEN. Tall, with one-light divisions with cusped arches. Dado with various blank tracery motifs. Much restored, the cornice added 1840, as part of a restoration of the chancel by *J.A. Repton*. – PULPIT. 1902, carved by *W.B. Polley*. – FONT. Early C13, and the best of the date in Essex, especially the E side with big, lush stiff-leaf scrolls. Two large rosettes each on the other sides. Base renewed 1867. – PAINTINGS. Moses and Aaron, 1643. Now on w wall. – In blocked nave N window, Millennium 'window' by *Ken Rolf*, 2001. – ROYAL ARMS. 1791. On wood, nicely painted on both sides with carved surround, hanging from a beam. – STAINED GLASS. In a chancel S window, roundels with fragments of Flemish or similar glass, C16 and C17. Two-light chancel S by *Clutterbuck*, 1851. E window by *Joan Howson*, 1952. Nave N and S by *D. Marion Grant*, 1960–1. – MONUMENTS. Brass to Thomas Coggeshall †1421. 32-in. (82-cm.) figure, in armour. – Thomas Brograve †1810. By *Peter Rouw the Younger*. Tablet with Greek Revival decoration. In base of tower, with a number of other monuments moved in 1867. – Richard Coates †1822, engineer of the Chelmer and Blackwater Navigation. Brass by *E. Matthews*, 1867, with nautical scene. In S porch, which was built in his memory.

HOLY SAVIOUR, Chelmer Village. By *David Ruffle Associates* (project architect, *Joe Hobbs*), 1984–5, including vicarage and hall annexe. Brick, with pitched slate roof that splays towards the base to accommodate a clerestory window. Of church-like form, with lower chancel, but more like a village hall in character and detailing.

HOLY TRINITY. *See* Chelmsford.

COUNTY POLICE HEADQUARTERS. *See* Chelmsford.

PRISON. *See* Chelmsford.

THE BISHOPS' PRIMARY SCHOOL, North Springfield. 1986 by *Thomas, Mowle & Chisnall*, extended 1992. Banded brick, arranged round a central glazed courtyard. Glazed entrance block set back behind two wings with pyramidal slate roofs. Chiefly of interest for the small circular LIBRARY by *Colin St John Wilson & Partners*, built at the same time and of the same materials as the main school, with a lantern interrupting the conical roof. The form was partly inspired by circular mausolea, as the library is a memorial to Wilson's father, Bishop of Chelmsford 1929–50. Within the drum is an aedicule, its metal canopy pierced with holes to represent the constellations of the Zodiac.

All Saints stands at the NW corner of SPRINGFIELD GREEN, surrounded by the old trees of Springfield Place and other houses. SPRINGFIELD PLACE, early C18 brick, with S front of nine bays and two-bay projecting wings, two storeys and attics. Segment-headed windows, Diocletian windows in the attic floor of the wings. Ionic doorcase, pedimented window above, and eaves cornice all of stone. Coachhouse to r. has a central pedimented bay with two blocked carriage entrances. Converted to houses by *Melville Dunbar Associates*, 1982, who also adapted the main house. – In the NE corner of the Green, a pair of ALMSHOUSES by *J. Clarke*, 1878. Single-storey, the entrance squeezed between two large half-timbered gables. – To the S of the church SPRINGFIELD DUKES (now The Priory Hospital), a seven-bay, two-storey Early Georgian brick house with a one-bay segmental pediment and a projecting frame round the central window. Sides and rear remodelled by *Arthur Needham Wilson*, *c.* 1906, in Arts and Crafts style with tile-hung

bays and casement windows. Extensive late C20 hospital buildings. – The OLD RECTORY, sw of the church, also Georgian
brick (rainwater head dated 1752). Five-bay, two storey E front,
central one-bay projecting pediment with brick quoins.

SPRINGFIELD HALL, ¾ m. NW. Late C16, timber-framed and
plastered, the three-bay s front encased in gault brick, late C18
or early C19.

SPRINGFIELD LYONS, ½ m. SE. Early C17 timber-framed and
plastered, with larger late C17 addition to the E, and to the w
a brick addition of *c.* 1800 with later C19 yellow brick and stone
canted bays. Heavily restored by *Barber Casanovas Ruffles* following fire damage, 2000–1, and converted to offices, with the
addition of a large contemporary N block.

Of the housing developments that make up 'new' Springfield,
BEAULIEU PARK, 1 m. NE of All Saints, is the most prominent.
The main developers were *Countryside Properties*; work on the
infrastructure started in 1998 and the first houses were ready
for occupation in 1999. Countryside Properties completed
their sectors in 2002, other developers in 2004. The layout is
relatively generous, the main approach a broad avenue leading
to a circus of ten four-storey detached houses. The houses are
the usual, slightly improbable assortment – plastered Essex
vernacular, Georgian brick (some with Dutch gables), Late
Georgian Gothick, Early Victorian stock brick and stucco, etc.
– imaginatively detailed on the whole but repeated just too
often to be convincing. The real problem with Beaulieu Park
is that it is, as yet, rather lifeless – the traffic may be calmed
but the car still rules – and it encroaches inexcusably upon the
surroundings of New Hall, Henry VIII's Beaulieu, from which
it derives its pretentious name.

BARNES MILL LOCK, 1 m. SSE, SANDFORD LOCK and BRIDGE,
1½ m. SE, and CUTON LOCK, 1½ m. ESE. On the Chelmer and
Blackwater Navigation, opened 1797 (*see* Introduction, p. 52).
BARNES MILL, converted to residential use in 1975, is timber-
framed and weatherboarded, *c.* 1800. W of the mill, the FOX
AND RAVEN pub, formerly Barnes Farm, late C16 timber-
framed with an early C18 stuccoed front. Three wide bays with
central pediment.

SPRINGFIELD LOCK and MILL. *See* Chelmsford.

EARTHWORK, E of Springfield Lyons. Late Bronze Age enclosure, excavated 1981–3. Oval ditch, about 70 yds (65 metres)
in diameter, enclosing a bank. There was an internal timber
rampart and, in the centre of the enclosure, a round timber
house. Later used as a Saxon cemetery (*see* Introduction,
p. 11).

STAMBOURNE

ST PETER AND ST THOMAS. Impressive and powerful C11 W
tower, unusually broad. Unbuttressed, with two large windows
fairly high up on the w, N, and s sides, an arch to the nave with

decoration on the N abacus, and later battlements. C14 S doorway, but part of the nave S wall at least is C11 or C12. The rest C15 to C16, largely due to the generosity of the Mackwilliam family, who acquired the three manors of Stambourne by *c.* 1420. They added the C16 N aisle and chapel, also the brick S porch, and generally overhauled the building; one bell dated 1583 indicates major work to the tower, including an obvious rebuilding of the NW corner in dressed stone as opposed to the prevailing flint and pebble rubble. All windows Late Perp, several of three lights with depressed heads and intersecting tracery. One nave S window has four lights, and the E jamb inside is decorated by two niches with elaborate canopies, one above the other. The three-bay N arcade has slim octagonal piers with partly wave-moulded arches. The N chapel is only one bay long, but the E respond has a quite exceptional enrichment: a niche for a figure and above it a shield with the Mackwilliam arms, a beautifully carved helmet and as a back-   44 ground a spray of leaf-work. Early C16. The N aisle, chancel and N chapel roofs are attributed by John Harvey to *Thomas Loveday,* the N aisle's especially good, with the Mackwilliam motto carved on two of the spandrels, as well as on the chancel roof. Re-seated and repaired by *Gordon Macdonald Hills,* 1873–4. – FONT. Octagonal, with traceried stem and the usual quatrefoils and shields on the bowl. – SCREEN. Also given by Henry Mackwilliam. One-light divisions with ogee tops and simple panel tracery above. The dado on the N side painted with figures of saints – an East Anglian rather than Essex tradition. The quality of the paintings is low. – STAINED GLASS. Fragments in the E window, given by Henry Mackwilliam, and datable by the heraldry to shortly before 1532. In the tracery, the armorial pedigree of the family; at the bottom, kneeling figures of Henry's mother Christian, and a male figure in armour assumed to be her husband Edward. Other fragments in side windows.

STAMBOURNE HALL, NE of the church. L-plan, dating back to the C15. It consists of a hall house, facing SW, and at right angles to it a later, separate five-bay house facing SE, the two combined in the C17. The inner faces of the L remodelled in the C19, with large sash windows, gables, and a small single-storey extension, but the outer faces largely untouched.

MOONE HALL (formerly the Red Lion), opposite the church. Long-wall jetty house, tree-ring dated 1488–1515. Two storeys, with a gabled cross-wing to the l., that to the r. replaced by a single-storey brick extension.

STAMBRIDGE   9090

ST MARY THE VIRGIN AND ALL SAINTS, Great Stambridge. Evidence, although very slight, of a Saxon church. In the N wall of the nave and chancel indications of blocked small round-headed windows, and the wall itself is too thin for Norman work; also a small piece of wall on the S side of the tower. The S aisle was added *c.* 1300: see the S arcade of three bays with octagonal piers and double-hollow-chamfered arches. Tower and N porch C15; the former has an embattled brick parapet of *c.* 1800. Restored 1881 by the rector, *G. W. Keightley*, who acted as his own architect. His is the C14-style hammerbeam roof that runs the length of the building; also the five-sided N vestry, and the organ chamber, an extension eastwards of the S aisle. Floors tiled throughout by *Campbell & Co.*, apart from tessera work by *Oppenheimer & Co.* of Manchester in front of the altar. – FONT. Octagonal, Perp, with concave sides and quatrefoiled panels with shields etc. – WOODWORK. Benches, pulpit, reading desk, altar and communion rails made in Bruges for *Buckley & Co.* as part of Keightley's restoration. – STAINED GLASS. E window †1862 by *Lavers & Barraud.* This and other indifferent glass of the period is eclipsed by *Henry Holiday*'s nave N window, 1898, when he was doing his best work. Figures of Faith and Love against a background of dense foliage. – Another nave N by *Alfred R. Fisher* of *Whitefriars Stained Glass Studios*, 1971, commemorating John Winthrop (1588–1659), first Governor of the Massachusetts Bay Colony and founder of Boston. – In S aisle, memorial window to Emily Alice Keightley †1905, the rector's daughter and co-founder of the Ratcliff Settlement in East London, including her portrait. – S aisle W to Phoebe Allen †1865 from Little Stambridge.

Keightley also built the RECTORY (now Old Rectory Nursing Home), 1880, ¾ m. N, presumably to his own design. Of grey ragstone, like the church, with extensive brick additions.

LITTLE STAMBRIDGE HALL, 1 m. NW. C16 timber-framed, faced with Georgian brick, and later additions. Five-bay main range with cross-wing to the r., on the outer wall of which is an original chimneystack. E of the Hall is the site of Little Stambridge church, dem. 1891.*

OLD HOUSE, Ballards Gore (former Shepherd and Dog Inn), 1½ m. NNE. Mainly C15, with exposed timbers and one jettied cross-wing. The picturesque effect is enhanced by Gothic heads to the casements.

6080

STANFORD-LE-HOPE
Thurrock U.A.

ST MARGARET OF ANTIOCH. Dominated by its big tower at the E end of the N aisle, which was rebuilt in 1883–4 (see the Latin chronogram on the N wall, with figure of St Margaret in a niche, translated on the E wall) by *E. Geldart*, inspired by the tower of Prittlewell. He also added the W porch and vestries, 1890–1, and LYCHGATE, 1892. Restoration had started in 1877–8 under *M. H. Linklater*, a grand scheme that remained

---

*Piscina and other fittings in St Mark, Hamlet Road, Southend.

incomplete when he became a priest. Otherwise the building, of ragstone rubble with some flushwork, can be traced back to the C12 – see the two windows visible inside in the N and S walls of the nave close to the chancel. The nave W wall is also C12. The N arcade is clearly E.E. with alternating octagonal and circular supports and one-stepped arches with two slight hollow chamfers. The S arcade – the usual change – has octagonal piers only and double-chamfered arches, i.e. C14. C14 also the chancel, see the SEDILIA and the low ogee-headed recess in the N wall (restored by *Harry Hems*, 1877–8). In the recess a tomb-chest of *c.* 1500. – FONT. Octofoil plan, C13, on nine supports. Moved to N side of chancel arch as part of reordering from 1994. – SCREEN (E end of N aisle, not *in situ*). Incorporates seven bays of tracery from a screen of *c.* 1400, simple and graceful.* – STAINED GLASS. E window by *Lavers, Barraud & Westlake*, 1878. Chancel S by *T.F. Curtis, Ward & Hughes, c.* 1905. Easternmost window in S aisle †1868 by *N.H.J. West-lake*. Nave and N aisle W windows by *Geldart*, 1891, made by *Ward & Hughes*. Among his best, golden and richly glowing. N aisle E by *Kempe*, 1901.

MONUMENTS. In N aisle, Richard Champion of Hassenbrook Hall †1599, with pilasters and shield of arms, and to another Champion, early C17, but with incomplete inscription. Corinthian columns and cherubs reclining on the broken pediment, and the upper part of a skeleton in the base. – In S chapel and S aisle, a number of large wall monuments to the Fetherstones of Hassenbrook Hall, including Anna Maria †1690, with Ionic columns and swags of fruit and flowers. – Sir Heneage †1711 with two weeping cherubs and between them a relief of ill-assorted bones, attributed to *William Woodman the Elder* (GF). – Sir Henry †1746 with the heads of three winged cherubs set in a broken segmental pediment on square Corinthian columns. Signed by *Thomas Bellamy*. – In the churchyard another display of bones: monument to James Adams †1765 of New Jenkins (St Clere's Hall, Mucking, q.v.). By *William Winchester*. Big tomb-chest with rounded lid and on this crudely carved cherubs, Bible, skeleton, Father Time etc. At the back a baldacchino with curtains raised, which, in less rustic monuments, is a C17, not an C18, motif.

INFANTS AND JUNIOR SCHOOL, Corringham Road. Plain, stock brick, begun 1840, including additions by *James Brooks*, 1875. Late 1970s Infant School with large and colourful ceramic MURAL by *Lisa Hawker* in collaboration with staff and children, 2001. New Junior School by the *County Architect's Dept* (project architects, *Peter Heather* and *Richard Horley*), *c.* 1985–6. Axial plan, with twelve classrooms sharing two glazed courts and central hall. Rendered blockwork walls and a series of shallow-pitched steel roofs painted red and blue.

HASSENBROOK SCHOOL, Hassenbrook Road. 1951–3 by *Gerald Lacoste & Partners* and in good shape still. Secondary school

---

* Chancel screen by *Geldart* now in St Clement, Leigh-on-Sea.

for 600 children. A spreading plan, mostly single-storey, but with a vertical accent provided by a Swedish-looking clock tower away from the main entrance, hall, and gymnasium. Pale brown brick enlivened by odd patterns, e.g. basket-weave, with panels of bricks set vertically and sunken.

Not much remains of the village, least of all the optimistically named Green opposite the E end of the church. A rare survival is HASSENBROOK HALL, ½ m. N. Early C17 timber-framed with two brick gables facing SE, and a third added probably later in the C17, overlooking a large walled garden. In the walls, a series of niches or bee boles, and opposite the house a four-centred gateway surmounted by a triangular pediment with a circular opening in the tympanum. Entirely hemmed in by 1970s housing.

ST CLERE'S HALL. *See* Mucking.

WATER TOWER, Wharf Road. By *Brian Colquhoun & Partners*, *c.* 1958. Concrete. Round tank on four slender tapering legs.

5000   STANFORD RIVERS

ST MARGARET. Mostly of flint rubble, unattractively rendered. C12 nave with original W window high up, two N and two S windows. The round arch of the original S door can be discerned in the plaster inside. The chancel is Dec, see the windows, raised in the C16 (in brick) when clerestory windows were inserted. No chancel arch. C19 E window. Good timber N porch; late C15, now blocked. Weatherboarded belfry on four posts as usual with leaded splay-foot spire. Unusual open timber W porch, 1817, when the W gallery was erected and probably also the S porch converted to a vestry, supervised by *Robert Footit*. Nave roof with tie-beams on braces and crown-posts. – FONT. Of the usual Purbeck type of *c.* 1200, but of Barnack stone. Octagonal with two shallow pointed arches to each side. – SCREEN. Bits of tracery reused in the W gallery. – BENCHES. Twelve oak benches; plain ends with two buttresses each. C15. – COMMUNION RAIL. With turned balusters. Probably those ordered following an archdeacon's visitation in 1683. – SANCTUARY LAMP. By *J. McCarthy*, 1934. Hanging from an elaborate early C18 wrought-iron pendant from Suttons, Stapleford Tawney. – PAINTING. Below the W gallery, Nativity scene in contemporary local setting by *Fyffe Christie*, *c.* 1961. – STAINED GLASS. E window by *F.W. Skeat*, 1951–2. – BRASSES. Thomas Greville †1492. 7-in. (19-cm.) figure of chrisom child. – Robert Borrow †1503, 18 in. (47-cm.) figure in plate armour, and wife Alys. Both under the altar. – On S wall of nave, Anne Napper †1584. Kneeling figure, 11 in. (29 cm.), with six children. Set in stone tablet with pilasters and round arch.

Former WORKHOUSE, ¾ m. SE. 1830–1, for nine parishes. Gault brick, three storeys, with a central three-bay straight gable and hoodmoulds. Two later wings, also with straight gables, and school house and infirmary by *C. Pertwee, c.* 1870. Closed 1930 and converted to industrial use.

LAWNS, 1½ m. SW. Late C16 or early C17 with two jettied cross-wings and two very fine, uncommonly tall chimneystacks, one with six octagonal shafts, the other with three.

LITTLEBURY HALL, 1 m. E. Late C16 or early C17 and, unusually for Essex, with a brick ground floor and timber-framed upper storey. Only part of the original house survives, the two-bay hall and N cross-wing. Remodelled in the early C19 when the S cross-wing was demolished and the N front given bay windows on the ground floor and sash windows above. S of the Hall a disused WATER MILL, *c.* 1840. Timber-framed and weatherboarded on a brick base.

ONGAR PARK, 2¼ m. NW. The 1,200-acre park, a rectangle with rounded corners bisected by a Roman road, apparently grew out of a 'deerhay' mentioned in a will of 1045, and according to Oliver Rackham may be the prototype of English deerparks; certainly the oldest in Essex, and unusually large. Survived intact until about 1950, its outline still discernible. Near its centre, ONGAR PARK LODGE, a small timber-framed and plastered house, C16 or earlier. NE of this, ONGAR PARK HALL, of similar date, partly faced in brick in the C19. Brick farm buildings by *Beadel, Son & Chancellor* for Capel Cure of Blake Hall (Bobbingworth), 1854, remodelled 1884 by the influential Scottish agriculturalist Primrose McConnell.

STANSTED AIRPORT
Stansted Mountfitchet and Takeley

5020

Stansted Airport began as a United States Air Force base, the first runway being built in 1942–3. After the War it entered civilian service, although its first purpose-built terminal was not constructed until 1969. In 1985, planning permission was granted to expand the airport to take 15 million passengers a year, making it (with Heathrow and Gatwick) London's third airport. This expansion was phased, the first part carried out in 1986–91,* the second in 2000–2. Planning permission for expansion to 25 million passengers a year was granted in 2002, using the existing runway and without extending the airport's boundaries. Further expansion, for a second runway E of the present one and nearly doubling the area of the airport, is under discussion in 2006.

The main architectural feature is the TERMINAL BUILDING by *Foster Associates* with *BAA Consultancy* (structural engineers, *Ove Arup & Partners* and *BAA Consultancy*), 1986–91. It is remarkable for its elegance and apparent simplicity: long and low, and although of three storeys, only one storey is visible on the landside. Five bays wide, with a two-bay extension,

117

---

*Five listed buildings were demolished, one of which was re-erected at Battlesbridge and two at Wat Tyler Park, Pitsea (Basildon).

indistinguishable to the casual eye, by *Pascall & Watson*, 2000–2. This main storey has front and back walls of glass, allowing the arriving passenger to see right across the building to the runway, indicating the principle behind the plan of 'straight line progress' from landside to airside and vice versa. The vast roof, made up (originally) of 121 canopies with shallow squared domes and triangular skylights, is supported on 36 steel 'trees' which barely disrupt this clear view. The sub-sequent cluttering of the interior with shops and restaurants has unfortunately detracted from this effect. Baggage handling and offices are located below the main concourse, and below that is another vast space, as impressive in its more rugged way as the first, of the RAILWAY STATION that provides a mainline link to London. To board aircraft, passengers are taken by dri-verless trains to satellites: one in 1991, two more added in 1998 and 2002.

Landscaping by *Adrian Lisney & Partners* did much to min-imize the impact of the airport, so that the terminal barely rises above the surrounding countryside. The main visual element is the CONTROL TOWER, 1995–6, little more than a concrete cylinder 197ft. (61 metres) high. The other building of inter-est is the DIAMOND HANGAR 1m. SW of the Control Tower by *Faulks Perry Cully & Rech* (consulting engineers, *Sir Frederick Snow & Partners*), 1987–9, for aircraft maintenance. Two equilateral triangles, large enough to hold two Jumbo jets in an uninterrupted space, the broadest span over 550ft (170 metres). Wrapped round two sides of the hangar are three floors of offices.

STANSTED MOUNTFITCHET

5020

ST MARY. Former parish church, outside the village next to Stansted Hall; redundant 1990 (now in the care of the Churches Conservation Trust). Nave and chancel faced with flint and given a thoroughly Victorian appearance by *F.T. Dollman*, 1887–8. W tower rebuilt (in brick, embattled, with 'Hertfordshire spike') in 1692, paid for by Sir Stephen Langham; windows added by Dollman. All this serves to conceal the church's Norman origins, apparent from the N and S doorways of *c.* 1120, and from the chancel arch inside. The S doorway has three orders of columns carrying scalloped cap-itals, arch with zigzag and saltire-cross decoration, and a tym-panum on a curved lintel, with diaper-work. The N doorway (reused) has three orders of columns, with scalloped capitals, and the rest also very similar to the S. The chancel arch has capitals with incised zigzag decoration, the arch itself with zigzag and an outer Norman 'bell-flower' motif. The C13 chancel has inside tall blank shafted arcades embracing the windows. The E end (renewed by Dollman) was similar, as is shown by the angle shafts (with shaft-rings). On the N side an E.E. arch into the Lancaster Chapel and a plain C14 arch; the

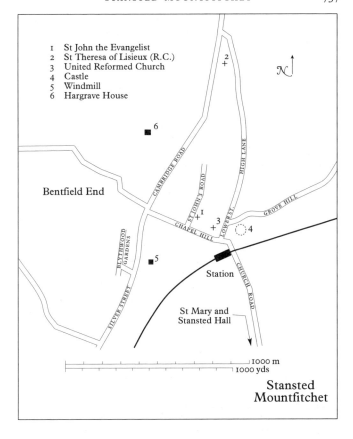

1 St John the Evangelist
2 St Theresa of Lisieux (R.C.)
3 United Reformed Church
4 Castle
5 Windmill
6 Hargrave House

Bentfield End

Station

St Mary and
Stansted Hall

1000 m
1000 yds

Stansted
Mountfitchet

latter marks the extension of the chapel eastwards, when it was given Dec windows. The E.E. arch has responds with capitals decorated with volutes at the angles and between them stiff-leaf in the E, upright three-lobed leaves in the W respond. N aisle added as part of a restoration by *J. Poolman* of Cambridge, 1829, but rebuilt by Dollman, who also removed galleries, re-seated the nave, re-fitted the chancel, repositioned the N doorway, and added the S porch. All windows renewed apart from three at the E end of the Lancaster Chapel. Also by Dollman the striking nave roof, coved on the S side and brought forward from the wall on a series of marble shafts and corbels to align it with the tower. Lancaster Chapel refitted by *Stephen Dykes Bower*, 1950–2.

FONT. A big heavy circular piece with coarse angle volutes, *c*. 1300. Early C17 COVER; plain, ogee in outline, with foliage finial. – COMMUNION RAIL. Graceful; C18. In Lancaster Chapel, by *William Bainbridge Reynolds*, early C20. – REREDOS. Pink alabaster, depicting the Risen Christ, phoenix, and Tree of Life, 1903. – CHOIR STALLS. By *Duncan Clark & Beckett*, made by *Bryan Saunders*, 1928. – STAINED GLASS. E window by *Hardman*, c. 1890. Nave S, eastern window, c. 1886, and N aisle, c. 1876, by *Clayton & Bell*. Nave S, two middle windows by *Wallace Howard*, c. 1901 and 1903, the former with inscription added by *A.K. Nicholson*, 1934; Lancaster Chapel E by *William Warrington*, 1859. – MONUMENTS. In a recess in the N wall of the Lancaster Chapel, cross-legged Knight of c. 1300, possibly either Sir Richard de Lancaster †1291 or his son Sir John †1334. – At E end of N aisle, raised tomb, not in its original state, of Hester Salusbury †1614. Coloured recumbent effigy wearing the fashionable high hat. To it belongs the CARTOUCHE on the N wall, a text surrounded by thirty pieces of silver, a shield with the Instruments of the Passion and the crown of thorns as a crest, etc., indicating *Epiphanius Evesham* as the author of both (according to K.A. Esdaile); the overtly Roman Catholic symbolism is unusual. – Her father, Sir Thomas Myddelton, late Lord Mayor of London †1631. Uncommonly sumptuous standing wall monument with bulky sarcophagus-like base decorated with skulls, recumbent effigy, between coupled black marbled columns carrying a shallow coffered arch. Straight top with achievement. Outside the columns two standing angels and inside also two, of specially good quality, holding the inscription plate. – W.H. Torriano †1828, with mourning female figure, by *E. Gaffin*. – T.M. Welsh †1832 by *Charles Smith*, austerely classical. – Harriott Croasdaile †1847, an elegant scroll with the serpent of eternity, by *T. Gaffin*. – H. C. Gardner, Baron Burghclere, †1921, by *John Coleridge*, restrained and heraldic. – A.W. Blyth †1928, billowing cartouche by *Martin Travers*.

ST JOHN THE EVANGELIST. By *W.D. Caröe*, 1887–9, one of his earliest churches. Conventional layout: nave and S aisle with short transepts, the E end of the S aisle fitted up as a Lady Chapel in 1905. But there are quirky details, such as the canted W balcony and a squint between the Lady Chapel and the high altar that incorporates a piscina, and decorative touches such as an elaborate aumbry. The material, inside and out, is a light-red brick from Birchanger, with Bath and Ketton stone dressings on the exterior and a range of stones for the interior of the chancel – Ketterton, Casterton, Weldon, Corsham and Stoke Ground – to give a varied effect, now lost, because the stonework has been painted over. Late Perp (with touches of Art Nouveau in the tracery), treated very freely in the SW tower, 1894–5, which stands clear of the nave and bristles with gargoyles, pinnacles, stepped battlements, and a lantern-shaped ending of the stair-turret. – FITTINGS. By *Caröe*, including the oak choir stalls (where Perp starts to fuse into Renaissance), bronze LECTERN (made by *Singer & Son*), organ cases by *Alfred Robinson*, and an unusual PULPIT with sides sloping in towards the top. Carving by *Nathaniel Hitch*; sanctuary pavement (*opus alexandrinum* and *sectile* mosaic) by *R. Davis*. Overpowering REREDOS, 1929. – Caröe's LIGHT

FITTINGS have been reused as flower stands. – STAINED
GLASS. E window by *Burlison & Grylls*, 1902. Lady Chapel E
by *Horace Wilkinson*, 1929.

ST THERESA OF LISIEUX (R.C.), High Lane. 2002 by *James
Boutwood*. A large church by early C21, indeed any, standards.
Its shape is based on the Barley Barn at Cressing Temple (q.v.),
i.e. a large hipped roof with gablets and a 'midstrey' in the
middle of the long wall. But the material is brick, and the midstrey is half-hipped, with most of the gable glazed. Other
windows little more than slits. The midstrey is the main
entrance, with the sanctuary opposite. This also is in the form
of a midstrey, but with a solid wall behind the altar that carries,
on the outside, a simple cross. Striking interior, the open roof
partly lined with timber; carved and painted wooden bas-relief
SCULPTURES by *Stephen Foster*. To the r. of the church a HALL,
smaller but not very much, and also barn-like, but plainer. To
the l. of the church the PRESBYTERY, rather commonplace by
comparison.

UNITED REFORMED CHURCH, Chapel Hill. By *Jasper Cowell* of
Henham, 1864. 'Italian, freely treated': front stuccoed in imitation of stone, with a large plain pediment, between corner
towers of stock brick. Next to it the former BRITISH SCHOOL,
red brick with stone dressings, also by Cowell, 1862.

FRIENDS' MEETING HOUSE, Chapel Hill. By *Paul V. Mauger*,
1967. Originally a factory-made timber building, encased in
brick and tile in 1994.

CASTLE. Less than ¼ m. E of St John. Small circular inner bailey
having once probably possessed a stone keep, and a small
bailey to its E. Destroyed 1215 and not rebuilt; a small piece of
flint-rubble walling remains on the S side of the ring.

The village consists chiefly of two parallel streets, Lower Street
to the E and Silver Street/Cambridge Road (the line of the
Roman road) to the W, joined by Chapel Hill, with St John the
Evangelist halfway up. W of St John's, on the N side of CHAPEL
HILL, the HERMITAGE, a C19 summerhouse, and opposite,
THE OLD COURTHOUSE, built 1854 as the Central Hall for
the Stansted Literary Institute. Tetrastyle Ionic portico. At the
junction with Cambridge Road an elaborate cast-iron fountain
by *Macfarlane & Co.*, 1871, beneath a canopy. Across the road,
an unusually tall C19 mile iron. To the S, on the W side of
SILVER STREET, stood BLYTHWOOD, a large house by *Caröe*
for Sir James Blyth, 1885–6; the house itself destroyed by fire
in 1926, but the stable block remains (in Blythwood Gardens)
as well as the model DAIRY, 1892, now much altered. *p. 740*

CAMBRIDGE ROAD runs N from the junction with Chapel Hill,
on its E side No. 2, WESTERN HOUSE, C17 with a five-bay,
two-storey brick front with pedimented doorway of
c. 1726. Next to it, a good piece of flamboyant Victorian commercial architecture, red brick with stock brick and black brick
detailing and other embellishments, dated 1878. A little further
N the equally exuberant Co-operative Stores, 1901, with stone
carvings of the Horn of Plenty, Hive of Industry, and Dove of

Blythwood, Stansted Mountfitchet.
Model dairy

Peace. Opposite and further N, a number of C17 and C18 cottages, including Nos. 23–25 and No. 41, both dated 1759 in the plaster. Also on the W side, but set back, HARGRAVE HOUSE (care home) by *G.E. Pritchett*, 1875, extended *c*. 1880 and 1898. Neo-Jacobean brick with stone dressings and Flemish gables. Three storeys, with large conservatory at one end of the garden front. At the corner of Croasdaile Road, MONUMENT to Henry and Mary Croasdaile †1797, urn on a pedestal.

LOWER STREET, at the bottom of Chapel Hill, is the real centre of the village and has the best houses, the most conspicuous SAVAGES on the W side, a well-preserved C15 hall house with exposed timbers, jettied front and two gabled cross-wings. Next to it TUDOR HOUSE, late C16, plastered with jettied upper storey and coved plaster eaves cornice. Decorative carving around the doorway. No. 47 has nice C19 Gothick detailing. At the N end BREWERY HOUSE, C18 brick with a doorway with fluted pilasters, ornamented frieze and fanlight, and C19 additions. On the E side, the DOG AND DUCK pub, a good bit of weatherboarding, dating back to *c*. 1700. The S end of the street is dominated by the MOUNTFITCHET SOCIAL CLUB, 1888, by *Arthur Sanders*, a local shopkeeper: brick with some half-timbering and a steep slated tower that gives it a Hanseatic look. The mid-late C19 KINGS ARMS HOTEL turns the opposite corner nicely with two prominent gables, a little octagonal castellated turret and much eccentric detail.

S of here, Church Road leads towards St Mary and Stansted Hall (*see* below). Immediately over the railway line, BRIDGE HOUSE, early C16 with exposed timber framing on the upper storey, and a gabled projecting bay on the W front resting on two posts to form an open porch. Further S, on the W side,

FULLERS HOUSE, former almshouses, 1883. Two storeys, brick with jettied, half-timbered upper storey to the front and two deep wings behind enclosing a courtyard.

Running E from Lower Street, GROVE HILL, at the top of which are two large houses by *John S. Lee*, HAWTHORNS and GORSEFIELD, the latter a butterfly-plan house of 1906–7 with two angled wings either side of the entrance. Gorsefield is of brick, roughcast, with casement windows on the entrance front and sash windows on the garden front; Hawthorns brick with elm weatherboarding on the first floor, and large sash windows throughout in the style of Philip Webb.

BENTFIELD END, W of Cambridge Road, forms a separate hamlet, with a number of attractive houses. Nos. 16–18 Bentfield Green is a Wealden-type house, C15–C16, with jettied upper storeys at the E and W ends and a jettied upper window to No. 18. HOLE FARM, early C16, the ground floor encased in brick in the C18 and the upper storey plastered and incised in imitation of ashlar, has a good collection of farm buildings ranging from the late C16 to the mid C19.

STANSTED HALL (Arthur Findlay College). Large Neo-Jacobean house by *Richard Armstrong*, 1871–6, for William Fuller-Maitland, replacing an earlier house that stood closer to the church. Brick with stone dressings, with shaped gables and a forest of tall chimneys. Full-height porch with oriel bow. Symmetrical main block of two storeys and attics, with former orangery on the SE side linked to the house by a colonnade. Some good interiors, especially the gallery out of which the staircase rises, with Neo-Jacobean chimneypieces, panelling and ceiling. NW of the house, an arched carriageway and lodge at the entrance to the park from Stansted Mountfitchet; to the SE, stables (more shaped gables), walled kitchen garden, and two cottages with iron latticed casements.

Further E, at Burton End, BURTON BOWER, a planned farm with large brick barn and single-storey ranges (converted to residential use in 1999) that was part of the estate. *Repton* made a Red Book for the old house and park in 1791, but all that seems to have been carried out (and not until 1867) was the re-routing of the public road to the S side of the church away from the house.

NORMAN HOUSE, Alsa Street, 1 m. NNE of St John. Large, irregular, mainly stuccoed. Early C18, with extensive C19 alterations, and further alterations and additions including remodelling of the entrance front by *W.J. Kieffer & H.S. Fleming*, 1925. Wide doorcase with Corinthian pilasters, swept-up frieze, and flat hood on carved brackets. Opposite, NORMAN HOUSE COTTAGE, C17 with exposed timbers on the jettied E front.

THREMHALL PRIORY, 1¾ m. SE of St Mary. Augustinian priory, founded in the C12, of which nothing remains but the rectangular enclosure with part of moat and fishpond. C18 brick house, seven bays and two storeys, with C19 additions, in ruinous state; walled garden on E side with two-storey garden house in one corner.* Farm buildings including an C18 brick granary and square dovecote, plastered and weatherboarded with pyramidal roof, to W of house, restored and extended for commercial use by *Cowper Griffith Associates*, 2001–2.

WINDMILL, ¼ m. SW of St John. Tower mill, 1787, last worked in 1910 and in good condition.

STANSTED AIRPORT. *See* p. 735.

9020

STANWAY

Lying between the W approaches (from London and Maldon) to Colchester, to which it is now joined.

ALL SAINTS, Great Stanway. In the grounds of Stanway Hall (now part of Colchester Zoo), and in ruins since the early C18. Tower, nave and N porch, originally late C13 but much rebuilt following the fall of the tower in the late C14. The tower is of bands of flint and stone rubble with some brick, an important early example of its use. Early in the C17 Sir John Swinterton adapted the church as his private chapel, removing the N aisle, which was replaced by brick windows, adding the porch, blocking the chancel arch and inserting a three-light brick window.

ST ALBRIGHT, Little Stanway. The nave is C12, see the S doorway and one S window, two N windows, and the restored W window (all with much Roman brick). Chancel added 1825–6 by *William Lay*, then rebuilt, with the addition of S aisle, S chapel, and N porch, by *Sir Gilbert Scott*, completed by *John Oldrid Scott*, 1878–80; W gallery removed. The two-bay arcade between the chancel and chapel is original work of *c.* 1500, from St Runwald, Colchester. Scissor-braced nave roof, eight of the western couples probably as old as the nave itself. Belfry restored and raised by J.O. Scott, 1889. – FONT. Octagonal, Perp, with panels and shields and with the chalice and host surrounded by rays. Defaced during the Civil War. Oak cover by *H. & K. Mabbitt*, 1955. – CHOIR STALLS. By *J.O. Scott*, made by *Polley* of Coggeshall, 1889. – STAINED GLASS. E window, S aisle W and another S aisle window by *Kempe*, 1892 and 1910, with his characteristic faces. – S aisle (St Stephen and St Alban) by *Powell & Sons*, 1905. Nave S (angel) by *Clayton & Bell*, 1889. Nave N by *Heaton, Butler & Bayne*, *c.* 1910.

Former WORKHOUSE (Lexden & Winstree Union), London Road. 1836 by *Foden & Henman*. Brick, still Georgian in the details. Four three-storey ranges, within a large open octagon, connecting to a taller central octagon that was the master's house. Domestic-looking two-storey entrance and administration block on N side.

Stanway has no real centre, and most of the interesting buildings are to be found along London Road. Immediately W of St

---

*Façade of house retained as part of office development under construction in 2005–6.

Albright, COMRIE HOUSE (St Mary's School), built as the rectory, 1875–6: large, Neo-Gothic brick. To the E (N side), CATCHBELLS, timber-framed with two cross-wings dating back to the early C15 and C18 brick front. 1 m. NNE, BEACON END FARM (now offices), another hall house, the W wing early C14, the E wing and central hall late C14, the hall floored in the late C16, also with C18 brick front.

OLIVERS, 1 m. ESE of All Saints. U-plan, two storeys and attics, with seven-bay entrance (W) front and five-bay S front, both brick, the former early C18 (rainwater heads dated 1716, although possibly not *in situ*), the latter late C18 or early C19; on W front, three centre bays have windows in arched recesses, over a semicircular Doric porch. Timber-framed, the earliest part the N wing, C15. Much of the interior remodelled by *Miles Park, c.* 1968. In the garden, galvanized steel sculpture by *Ben Coode-Adams, c.* 2000. Late C17 octagonal DOVECOTE, SW, weatherboarding on brick plinth, with original lath-and-plaster nesting boxes. N of Olivers, LITTLE OLIVERS, C16 and C17 with pretty weatherboarded front.

STREAMLINES, Dyers Road, ¾ m. N of All Saints. Well named and well preserved Modern Movement house by *Charles R. Brown* of Colchester, 1935–6. Two storeys, with flat roof and Crittall windows, including corner windows. Rendered brick walls with continuous bands of blue bricks (now painted) between the first-floor windows.

GOSBECKS PARK, 1 m. NE of All Saints. Part of the site of Camulodunum, the farmstead of Cunobelinus (†*c.* A.D. 40) within the fortified settlement, and later an important Romano-British settlement. The outlines of a Romano-British temple (*c.* A.D. 60–80) within a portico and of a semicircular theatre (the largest known in Britain) are marked out. An exceptionally large and fine statuette of Mercury found here is in Colchester Castle Museum. 1 m. W, near the Bellhouse pit, was a high-status burial site, dating from the mid CI B.C. to *c.* A.D. 60, excavated between 1987 and 1997.

STAPLEFORD ABBOTTS

5090

ST MARY. Rather plain W tower, 1815, stock brick with stone dressings, and nice, small N chapel of red brick, dated 1638. The chapel windows, a remarkable fact, are round-arched and no longer Perp. All the rest, including N vestry and S porch, by *Thomas Jeckyll,* 1861–2. The effect of random stone laid like crazy paving is not successful,[*] but otherwise the detailing is good, including carving on the porch and round the doorways, and the doors themselves. The windows have geometrical tracery. Crown-post roof with nailhead moulding on the tie-beams. – PULPIT. Good late C16 or early C17 piece with blank

---

[*] Pevsner thought the church 'hideous'. This now seems unduly harsh, even given his known antipathy towards the 1860s.

arches in the panels. – TILES. By *Minton,* on the chancel floor, but, most unusually, with more elaborate ones (designed by *Pugin*) on the E wall as a dado, and because of their position in very good condition. – STAINED GLASS. Very fine, small early C14 figure of Edward the Confessor (N vestry). – E window by *Lavers, Barraud & Westlake,* 1869. – Chancel s †1891 by *A.L. Moore* (Annunciation), and 1921 by *W. Aikman.* – MONUMENTS. Francis Stonard †1604. Slate tablet with panels of carved and painted alabaster. In tower, with other monuments formerly in the chancel. – Sir John Abdy of Albyns †1758. Standing wall monument with large putto standing by an oval medallion with frontal, rather vacant, portrait. Open pediment on brackets at the top. – First World War memorial. By *W. Aikman.* Alabaster, with mosaic medallion of St George and the Dragon.

OLD RECTORY FARM, SW of the church. Late C18, timber-framed and rendered, with early C19 brick additions. Wide three-bay front with pedimented portico, two storeys with attics, and dormers in the slate mansard roof.

ALBYNS, ½ m. NE. The house, of *c.* 1620 but incorporating a smaller C16 house, was demolished 1954 following war damage. Its best interiors had already been shipped to the United States before the war. There remains, to the r. of the site of the house, a section of C17 garden wall, terminating in a low, square pavilion with ogival roof. To the l., the former service range (now ALBYNS MANOR), that was separated from the house by a yard. Early C17 brick, with straight gables and mullioned windows. Original N cross-wing and C20 S cross-wing. It contains part of the staircase from Albyns, with flat openwork strap decoration and square newels with moulded finials. E of this an C18 brick coachhouse, H-plan, with clock tower and hexagonal cupola. C19 octagonal brick lodge 500 yds NW of the house.

OLD SCHOOL HOUSE, Bournebridge Lane, 1 m. S. Two-storey, five-bay front of red and blue brick, with a stone plaque over the door identifying it as Knolls Hill Free School, built by Sir John Fortescue-Aland in 1734.

STAPLEFORD TAWNEY

ST MARY THE VIRGIN. Nave and chancel assigned to the C13, on the strength of renewed lancets and the blocked N doorway. S chapel, which lies across the division between nave and chancel, of about the same date. All flint rubble with limestone dressings. C15 or C16 belfry on four posts; low E–W braces, higher N–S braces. Above the beams carried by the braces is cross-strutting in all four directions. S porch and N vestry added as part of restoration by *John Turner,* 1862, which included renewing the windows, re-seating, and taking down the late C18 W gallery. Further work in 1884 when the open roof was boarded in. Parish room on N side of nave by *Tony*

Mitchell of *Herbert & Partners*, 1998–9, sympathetic in form and materials. – REREDOS. Mosaic of the Last Supper, by *Salviati & Co.*, 1883. – COMMUNION RAILS. C17, with square tapering openwork balusters. – MONUMENTS. William and Margery Scott †1491 and 1505. Slab, originally the top of a raised tomb. No figures, but remains of marginal inscription and fine achievement of arms, and indent of cross. – Grace Addison †1727. Marble. Lengthy inscription between Corinthian pilasters, a very lavish monument to a servant who gave twenty-two years' service. – Augusta Smith †1845. Gothic. By *Clarke* of Wigmore Street. – In churchyard, two C12 stone coffins, one complete with lid. – Monument marking the vault of the Smith family of Suttons, erected for Susannah Smith †1796. Fluted oval sarcophagus on base and four steps, with coat of arms. By *J. Bonomi*, 1797.

OLD RECTORY, ⅓ m. N. Good Georgian brick front, but the irregular spacing of the windows and the chimney betray the older house behind: *c.* 1700, but incorporating an Early Medieval core. Staircase hall and room with bay window added as part of renovations *c.* 1820. Nice setting with walled garden and range of C18 weatherboarded outbuildings.

SUTTONS, ⅔ m. SE. Manor house, remodelled with brick and stucco *c.* 1815. The main block two storeys, five bays, with lower wing to the r., formerly balanced by another to the l. Orangery to SW by *Bonomi*, 1796.

STEBBING

6020

ST MARY THE VIRGIN. An unusually well-preserved C14 church, the principal alterations being the Perp clerestory and E window. Even the N vestry is contemporary, and was probably originally a chapel. Flint rubble, formerly rendered. The date suggested by the Royal Commission is *c.* 1360, but it may be rather earlier. The tracery of most of the windows has Dec forms, and the SEDILIA and DOUBLE PISCINA look no later. The W tower (with angle buttresses, battlements, and recessed shingled spire) has a W window with (renewed) reticulated tracery. The S porch is given one original feature: the side openings are small and of quatrefoil shapes (cf. Great Bardfield), one on the l., two on the r.; walls raised (in brick) in the C16. The N and S arcades of the large nave inside have piers of an uncommon section, four slim polygonal shafts and in the diagonals four round ones. Complex arch mouldings in the two-centred arches. Headstops.

The one distinguishing, and at the same time most effective, feature of the church is the stone ROOD SCREEN, filling the whole of the tall chancel arch (cf. Great Bardfield). It consists basically of three stepped lancets with clustered shafts and mouchettes in the spandrels. Buckler in 1856 shows little more than this framework, but in 1884 *Woodyer* restored all the mid-C14 details of ogee arches, quatrefoils, and ballflower decoration. This must be conjectural, Woodyer filling the side arches with tracery where there may only have been cusping, and in the middle inserting an embattled transom through the arch at the point of its springing. This was to hold, on three plinths, the rood figures, but Woodyer supplied only a central cross. Some original fragments are reused as a CREDENCE. – The chancel roof is of shallow pitch, six cants with arched braces carrying tracery in the spandrels, and collar-beams. Wall-plates with foliage trails and battlements; embattled purlins. The nave roof is flat-pitched. The principals rest on brackets, the sub-principals start with figures of angels. Two bosses on each sub-principal. – REREDOS (N aisle). Very defaced. Traces of a rib pattern in the soffit. Early C16. – COMMUNION RAIL. C18, with alternating slim balusters. – Two MODELS of the church by *Henry Fitch*, 1850, one shown at the Great Exhibition. – STAINED GLASS. S aisle E by *A.K. Nicholson*, *c*. 1924. – BRASS to a widow, *c*. 1390 (nave). 47½-in. (120-cm.) figure.

The village consists mainly of a nice group of houses near the church and, quite separate, the High Street. On the E side of the churchyard is THE CHANTRY, late C14 or early C15 with exposed timbers and jettied upper storey. S of the church, RUFFELS PLACE, seven houses by *Melville Dunbar & Associates*, 1998, a good mix of Essex Design Guide vernacular with one Georgian-style brick-fronted house, the scale more generous than usual. To the W, CHURCH FARM, C15 or C16 timber-framed and plastered, with square DOVECOTE behind, then PRIORS HALL (formerly Parsonage Farm), with a two-and-a-half-storey front of exposed timbers. Hall and cross-wing *c*. 1400, the roof of the cross-wing raised *c*. 1490. Hall rebuilt *c*. 1600, with one-and-half storeys over a long-wall jetty. Rear range, incorporated in the main building in the C20, originally a separate late C15 structure, perhaps a kitchen.

Church Farm faces down the HIGH STREET, and the view back towards it is of an almost ideal, but utterly unpretentious, village street: the road gently curving, lined with a mixture of houses, mostly timber-framed, some with exposed timbers. The oldest is probably TWEED COTTAGE, next to the White Hart on the W side. Late C13, with a cross-wing to the r. and a blocked mullion window showing through the plaster. Also on the W side, the former FRIENDS' MEETING HOUSE, now a village meeting room. Brick, mostly red and blue chequer, but also diapered, dated 1674 on a panel of carved bricks over the door. Hipped roof, the hipped end facing the road, giving a pyramidal effect. Entrance originally on the N side, flanked by segment-headed windows; the two large windows on the E front, and small porch on Tuscan columns, early C19. At the N end of the High Street the PRIMARY SCHOOL and teacher's house, *c*. 1876. Brick, gabled, the central gable with decorative verges continued upwards to a bellcote.

Off the W side of the High Street, in MILL LANE, the former CONGREGATIONAL CHURCH, now in commercial use.

Rebuilt 1793, with various C19 additions. Opposite, built 1877 as its Sunday School, the VILLAGE HALL, with two cottages. The builder, perhaps also the designer, was *James Brown* of Braintree. Brick, with yellow brick bands and moulded brick decoration, and a central gable with pilastered doorway. Behind it, the former British School, 1842. Further down Mill Lane, TAN FARM, with exposed timbers. C17 range along the road, behind it and at right angles a mid-C15 jettied range. At the bottom, TOWN MILL, late C17 or early C18 weather-boarded water mill with adjoining painted brick mill house.

N of this the MOUNT of a former castle, 44 ft (13.4 metres) high, next to STEBBING PARK, mid-C16 timber-framed and plastered. Rear wing partly jettied with C17 bay window on ground floor, and C18 sashed entrance (N) front. ½ m. further N, BRAN END MILL. C19 brick, two main floors, the bays separated by pilasters. Now flats. C18 timber-framed and plastered mill house across the stream.

PORTERS HALL, 1 m. ESE. Large C16 moated house. Hall and cross-wings, that on the l. with a two-storey bay window. At the back of the house an outbuilding, older than the Hall, with exposed timbers and long-wall jetty on one side and original mullioned windows. Large C17 barn by the road. ¼ m. s of Porters Hall, CANONFYLDE (formerly Canfield Farm). Mid C16, one cross-wing jettied. Restored and extended *c.* 1920 by *Fred Rowntree.*

STEEPLE

ST LAWRENCE AND ALL SAINTS. Rebuilt by *Chancellor*, 1881–3, reusing material from the medieval church that stood 600 yds to the w, including the C14 s doorway and one late C14 window in the nave N wall. As at Creeksea, he indulged in an orgy of mixing into his brown stone walls bricks and fragments of dressed stone entirely at random and in all directions. Conventional plan – nave and chancel, belfry – except that the w end of the nave is divided off by a circular pier into two bays. Late E.E. style, with cusped lancets. – PILLAR PISCINA with spiral fluted shaft. C12. – STAINED GLASS. Single-light window w of s door by *Cox, Sons, Buckley & Co.*, 1885.

STANSGATE PRIORY, 1¾ m. N. The priory was Cluniac, founded probably early in the C12. Of all that the Royal Commission could still describe in 1923, only one wall now remains visible, N of Stansgate Abbey Farm, and that has been rebuilt.

CONGREGATIONAL CHAPEL, 1857, and PECULIAR PEOPLE'S CHAPEL, 1877, both brick with stock brick dressings and pointed windows, the latter now a house.

VILLAGE HALL. 2003–4 by *Inkpen Downie*. Brick and weatherboarding. Hipped pantiled roof with gablet at one end, the entrance marked by a curved wall and gable.

STEEPLE BUMPSTEAD

ST MARY. There was here a remarkably large C11 church. The w tower belonged to it (see its lower windows, open and blocked), as did the chancel (see its quoins). The diagonal buttresses of the tower, and also the buttresses that project into the nave, were added later, and the E half of the upper stages was rebuilt in brick in the early C16. Also of brick are the tops of the aisles and of the late C14 s porch, and the whole clerestory, indicating extensive work at that time; otherwise mainly flint rubble. Most of the exterior features belong to the restoration of 1877–80, the chancel by *Ewan Christian* and the nave by *Frank Whitmore*; this included adding an organ chamber to the N side of the chancel and rebuilding the vestry, re-roofing the chancel at a higher level, and renewing most of the tracery, including the E window. But in the N aisle are still two fairly reliable windows. They look late C14 or early C15. The N arcade and the identical s arcade may well belong to the same date. They have piers with semi-polygonal shafts, those to the arches with capitals and those to the nave without. The early C16 s aisle roof, attributed by John Harvey to *Thomas Loveday*, is particularly fine. It has carved tie-beams and ridge, and a carved rose pendant hangs from the middle of each principal tie-beam.

FONT. Octagonal, Perp, with quatrefoils carrying shields. – BENCHES. Two in the nave incorporating panelling dated 1568. Also some poppyheads and some more panelling. – POOR BOX. Iron-bound, on panelled stem, *c.* 1500. – BOSS. On vestry door, replica of an C8 boss, probably Irish (original now in the British Museum). – HELM. Late C16, N aisle, E end. – STAINED GLASS. In s aisle, the eastern window arranged with glass (probably by *Willement*) from Moyns Park, as part of the monument to George Gent, 1834. Other windows re-set by *David Sear* (*Lincolnshire Stained Glass Studio*), 1998, incorporating C19 glass from the Stained Glass Repository and (E window) formerly in tower window. N aisle 'Te Deum' window by David Sear, 2000. – MONUMENTS. Richard Bendish †1486, Richard Bendish †1523 and John Bendish †1585. C17 stone tablet, partly painted, in three bays separated by Composite half-columns supporting an entablature and cresting. – Sir Henry Bendyshe †1717. Standing wall monument by *Thomas Stayner*. Sir Henry is shown elegantly reclining with his elbow on a cushion, like a French prelate. By his side a tiny baby. Spiral columns and a rich pediment with seated putti. A first-rate work. – Sir John and Martha Bendyshe †1707 and 1705. By *J. Pickford & W. Atkinson*, erected *c.* 1740 (cf. their monument to John Pyke †1738 at Birdbrook). Large, with the usual obelisk and in front of it a big putto and an oval medallion with two profile portraits. – George Gent of Moyns Park †1818, erected 1834. Marble, massive, like a chest-tomb, beneath a window that forms part of the ensemble. By *Downes* of Bocking. – Eliza Mary Gent †1848 and her husband George William Gent †1855. Elaborate Gothic tablet by *Samuel Cundy*.

CONGREGATIONAL CHURCH. By *Charles Bell*, 1883. Gothic, brick with stone dressings, two turrets on the front facing the street, that on the l. much taller than the other. Lecture hall behind. Interior fittings largely unaltered.

MOOT HALL. Late C16. Two storeys, the upper floor jettied, with exposed timbers. The ground floor, with small four-centred arches, was originally open (cf. Thaxted Guildhall), enclosed in the C18 for use as a school. Restored 1890 and 1923.

VILLAGE HALL. By *Argent Building Co.*, 1994. Double-height main hall flanked by lower wings and single sweeping pantile roof. Pale brown brick.

The village has much to offer in the small area of the triangle formed by Church Street, Chapel Street and North Street. Facing the S side of the church PARSONAGE FARM, mainly timber-framed but with a late C16 brick cross-wing. On CHURCH STREET, the former NATIONAL SCHOOL, 1848, and attached house, 1854, both enlarged 1875; brick. A number of pretty houses along Church Street, notably (on the N side) the OLD MANOR HOUSE, with two-storey canted bays either side of the front door as part of the C18 refronting of a late C16 house – see the brick chimney towering above. Brick LOCK-UP, late C18 or early C19, on the S side, against the churchyard wall. Near the W end of the street, BRIDGE CRESCENT, dated 1849, a short terrace of two-storey brick cottages with a satisfying curve that becomes convex where it turns into the street.

A path leads past the Crescent through to NORTH STREET, emerging opposite its most prominent building, FREEZE'S FARM: late C17 timber-framed with an elegant six-bay sashed front of *c.* 1800. Beside this, FREEZE'S BARNS, a development (*c.* 2002) built to look like barn conversions. At the N end of the street, opposite Claywall Bridge, the former BRITISH SCHOOL, now a house, dressed flint with stock brick dressings, 1847. The continuation of North Street leads to The Endway, with BRICK HOUSE on the l. With brick-nogging, chimneystack dated 1571. Returning to Claywall Bridge, at the bottom of CHAPEL STREET No. 39 has an C18 sashed front of four bays with a two-bay addition to the NW and Tuscan porch. Massive C16 chimneystack with four octagonal shafts. On the E side of Chapel Street, ANCIENT HOUSE, C15, with jettied cross-wing at the N end and integral service bay at the other, and on the W ROSE COTTAGE, timber-framed, set at an angle to the road and incongruously attached to a late C19 brick villa.

Chapel Street becomes Finchingfield Road, on the S side of which stood BOWER HALL, built for Sir Henry Bendyshe in 1717, the year he died and the baronetcy became extinct. Demolished 1926; a pretty stock brick and flint LODGE is incorporated into a late C20 house.

LATCHLEYS, 1 m. SW. Timber-framed and plastered manor house of which the SE wing is Early Tudor. In it one room with foliage-decorated beams and bosses carved with roses, pomegranates, etc. Early C17 staircase with a square well and heavy turned balusters. S of the house a C16 brick bridge of two arches across the unusually wide moat. SSE of the house a five-bay, early C16 aisled barn, weatherboarded.

MOYNS PARK. *See* p. 605.

STIFFORD

Thurrock U.A.

ST MARY. Square, short C13 W tower with splay-foot spire. Steep primitive wooden stair inside. Nave with two-bay S arcade also C13 (circular pier, double-chamfered broad, depressed, pointed arches). The responds more remarkable than the pier, especially the E respond with a head corbel, and original colouring; fine mouldings. Late C13 the S chapel: lancets with cusped rere-arches. Sign of an earlier Norman past is the plain N doorway. Restored by *Henry Stock (Snooke & Stock)*, 1861–3. His are the chancel arch and roof, and N porch. He also rebuilt and enlarged the S aisle, using a lot of puddingstone; elsewhere flint and ragstone rubble predominate. – PULPIT. 1611, of the type then usual. Fixed to it a wrought-iron HOURGLASS STAND, C17. – FONT. Plain square bowl, C13, with central pedestal of three grouped shafts, and four corner columns. – DOOR, on the N side, with reused C12 ironwork, including two large C hinges. – STAINED GLASS. E and S chapel windows by *Powell & Sons*, 1863; also S aisle, 1868, with panels by *Holiday* (part re-set randomly following bomb damage). – S aisle W by *Leonard Walker*, 1929. St George against a largely abstract background of slab glass. – Nave N by *Clayton & Bell*, 1883, and *F.C. Eden* with *George Daniels*, 1930. – MONUMENTS. Many brasses, the best in the chancel: Ralph Perchehay, rector of Stifford †1378. Large demi-figure in mass vestments, 15 in. (38 cm.). – In nave, shroud brass of a priest holding inscribed heart, 20 in. (50 cm.), *c.* 1480. – On S chapel wall, John Ardalle †1504 and wife Anne, and William Lathum and wife Susan, both †1622, 18½-in. (47-cm.) figures; Ann Lathum †1627, 12½-in. (31-cm.) figure, and Elizabeth Lathum †1630, 13½-in. (34-cm.) figure. – Wall monuments in W tower: Anne Silverlock †1642. Inscription in alabaster frame beneath broken segmental pediment. – Sir Nathaniel Grantham †1708. White marble cartouche with skull and weeping cherubs.

FORD PLACE, ½ m. WNW. The 'excellent house dated 1655' described by Pevsner in 1954 was gutted by fire in 1987, destroying the 'extremely rich late C17 plaster ceiling' that was the house's most important feature. The date appeared on shaped gables which, the fire revealed, were part of the remodelling of a late C16 brick house. Main front of nine bays added *c.* 1747. Attached C17 wall enclosing an unusually large garden and including a gardener's cottage, also derelict.

Some attractive C17 and C18 thatched cottages along the High Road near the church, and on the N side COPPID HALL, seven-bay mid-C18 brick. Doorcase with attached Tuscan columns and pediment. Further E, Stifford Lodge, now LAKE-

SIDE MOAT HOUSE. Rebuilt in the mid C18, extended early in the C19, partly remodelled by *C.M. Shiner*, *c.* 1903, and greatly enlarged after becoming a hotel in 1966. The original stuccoed block is of five bays and three storeys with lean-to veranda.

Off Clockhouse Lane, ½ m. WSW of the church, a housing development, 2002–4, on the site of the Ardale School, built as a children's cottage home village for the Stepney Union by *Frank Baggallay*, 1901. The WATER TOWER has been preserved, the top stage with deep machicolations and shallow pyramidal roof. Shorter stair-towers with similar roofs clasp two corners. Also PRINCIPAL HOUSE, semi-detached with canted bays.

The area round the church, separated from the rest of the parish by the A13, is generally known as North Stifford. S of the A13 is Chafford Hundred (*see* West Thurrock). To the W, in Stifford Clays, where development began in 1952, WILLIAM EDWARDS COMPREHENSIVE SCHOOL, by *Richard Sheppard, Robson & Partners*, 1962–3, enlarged 1976. Mainly single storey, stock brick.

STISTED

ALL SAINTS. A church of odd external shape, due mainly to the tower which stands at the E end of the S aisle; this was rebuilt on old foundations in 1844 for Onley Savill-Onley, the chancel re-roofed and restored at the same time by the rector, Charles Forster. The nave W wall and N and S porches are also C19. Chronologically the history of the church begins with the N arcade of five bays, or rather three with odd narrower arches at either end. The arcade is of *c.* 1180–90 and has short circular piers with very good square foliage capitals. The E capital is a little later: round with heads at the corners. The S arcade has in the corresponding place a capital of the same type. The others are without carving. The N and S arches have only one slight chamfer. The chancel belongs to the same time as the E capitals. It has a fine group of five (renewed) stepped lancets; lancets also on the N and S sides. Finally there are the N and S aisle walls with C14 Dec windows of no special interest. S aisle screened off to form a meeting room by *Gerald W. Barrett*, 1991. – REREDOS. Crucifixion by *Holiday*, made by *Powell & Sons*, 1877–83; mosaic and *opus sectile*. Also decorative tiles on E wall. – PULPIT with panelled sides, one with a coat of arms, early C18. – CHANCEL SCREEN. By *John A. Cheston*, 1926. – PAINTING. Adoration of the Magi, by *Gaspar de Crayer*. – STAINED GLASS. Collection of fragments in chancel windows, presented by Onley Savill-Onley, 1844. E window Flemish and French, mainly C16 and C17, from the cloister of the former Monastery of Steinfeld, Germany. First window on the S side includes C14 and C15 English tabernacle work, and the second a fine kneeling female figure, C15. Chancel N to Rev. Charles Forster †1871 by *Heaton, Butler & Bayne*. W windows to Onley Savill-Onley

†1890 by *A.O. Hemming*, 1892. S aisle by *R.W. Coomber* (*J. Wippell & Co.*), 1966. – MONUMENTS. On chancel N wall, brass to Elizabeth Wiseman †1584; 10-in. (25-cm.) figure of woman and daughter praying. – Arthur Savill-Onley †1843 of 'hooping cough', aged 8; mourning cherub, by *E. Gaffin*. – Charles Savill-Onley †1843 with profile portrait, by *Gaffin & Co.* – Caroline Savill-Onley †1845, rising heavenwards. By *E.H. Baily*. – Louise Harvey Carter †1849 by *T. Gaffin*.

STISTED HALL (Prince Edward Duke of Kent Court residential home). 1823–5 by *Henry Hakewill*, the construction supervised by *John Penrice*, for Charles Savill-Onley. Yellow brick with stone dressings. Five-bay entrance front with slightly project-ing corner bays and a big purely Greek Ionic tetrastyle portico (porte cochère) with pediment. Plain S front of seven bays and elegant deep-eaved service wing to the N. NORTH LODGE and gates in King's Lane. Most of the park now a golf course.

The village consists principally of THE STREET which runs N from the church. Many of the houses and cottages were rebuilt between 1853 and 1878 (some dated) for Onley Savill-Onley by *Thomas Watts* and his son *John Lent Watts*, builders. Highly picturesque, brick, half-timbered and roughcast with deco-rated bargeboards and elaborate Neo-Tudor chimneys. At the S end a row of six flint cottages, *c.* 1830, and at the N end an elaborate flint double cottage, now a single dwelling, with a single central chimneystack similar to that on the nearby North Lodge, suggesting it might be contemporary with the Hall and also by *Hakewill*.

GLEBE HOUSE, ¼ m. further N, was built 1839 as the rectory for Rev. Charles Forster; plastered brick and slate, two storeys, the main block of three windows with two full-height canted bays on the garden front.

STISTED MILL, King's Lane ½ m. ESE. Pretty weatherboarded watermill on the River Blackwater, C18 (operating in 1775), extended in the C19, converted to a house 1977.

STOCK

ALL SAINTS. The C15 belfry is the most interesting part. Square ground floor with four posts set inside so as to form a Greek cross with four small corner spaces. The W arm has a doorway with three tracery panels over, the N and S arms each have one three-light traceried wooden window. The tracery differs slightly. The centre is braced from N to S as well as E to W. The arms have N–S braces. Trellis-strutting above from E to W and N to S. The upper part of the belfry has a gabled projection on the E side. Tall bell-stage and tall thin splay-foot spire. Weather-boarding dark and vertical below, white and horizontal above. Timber also the C15 S porch, with six ogee-arched openings on the W and E sides, restored 1937. The late C14 doorway has blank panel tracery above. The church itself is of mixed rubble. Three-bay N arcade with octagonal piers and double-hollow-chamfered arches, that is C15. Three-bay crown-post roof in N aisle. Nave restored and chancel rebuilt 1847–8, N chapel 1904 (as organ chamber). Restoration and refurnishing of nave by *Laurence King & Partners*, 1981 (including decoration by *Campbell, Smith & Co.*), who also designed the exemplary N sacristy and vestry, 1986, executed by *Gerald Shenstone & Partners*, 1988–9. – FONT. Octagonal bowl, plain stem and base, C15. Oak COVER by *Francis Stephens*, 1970. – SCULPTURE. Limewood rood figures by *Gwynneth Holt*, 1955 (N aisle). – STAINED GLASS. E window, chancel S, and W of S door by *Reginald Bell*, 1948–50; two nave S windows and N chapel E by *M.C. Farrar Bell*, 1951–9. Chancel S lancet by *David Wasley*, 1986. – BRASS to Richard Twedye †1574; 18-in. (45.5-cm.) figure in armour.

OUR LADY AND ST JOSEPH (R.C.), Mill Road. By *P.P. Pugin*, 1890–1, as St Joseph's School; used as a church since 1937, when a shallow sanctuary was added. Brick, with the large windows associated with schools rather than churches. Reordering and other alterations by *Burles, Newton & Partners*, 1970–1. – LECTERN and CELEBRANT'S CHAIR by *Mabbitt*, 1970. – PAINTING. Flight into Egypt. Probably School of *Chiari*. – STAINED GLASS. In chancel, arms of Petre and Gillow families by *Moira Forsyth*, 1978.

CHRIST CHURCH (Free Church, formerly Congregational), High Street. 1887–9 by *C. Pertwee*. Brick with stock brick dressings and decorative panels, and cast-iron glazing bars.

LILYSTONE HALL, 500 yds SW. 1847, gault brick, the main block three bays, two storeys, with giant pilasters and Greek Doric porch. Set-back wings to l. and r., and also on the r. a private R.C. chapel jutting forward. By *C.A. Buckler* for the Gillow family, 1879. Simple Neo-Norman, with apse. House and chapel now flats.

The church lies on one side of the village, separated from it by a large expanse of glebe. On the NE side of this the old RECTORY, brick with stock brick dressings, by *H.E. Kendall Jun.*, c. 1841, altered by *Chancellor*, 1900–8. SW of the church BELLMANS FARM, C18 door and sashes added to a timber-framed house with two gabled cross-wings, and then BISHOP'S HOUSE, i.e. the residence (since 1980) of the R.C. Bishop of Brentwood. By *Sherrin*, 1896, as the presbytery. Brick with tile-hanging, extended in similar style c. 1980. Across the road a range of four late C17 brick ALMSHOUSES, single storey, founded by Richard Twedye †1574, and the former NATIONAL SCHOOL and master's house, 1839, enlarged 1896.

The centre of the village is NE of Mill Road, where the HIGH STREET broadens out with a long Green down one side, and a number of good houses, the smartest COPT HALL, C18 brick, five bays, two storeys with attics in the tiled mansard roof. At the N end, GREENWOODS, an early C19 stuccoed house with, at right angles, a smart late C19 Neo-Tudor wing, with the entrance in the inner angle. Brick ground floor with stone dressings, continued on the NW front through a two-storey canted bay. Large half-timbered gables. Expensive interior with panelling etc. Large N additions by *Citiscape Developments* for conversion to hotel and spa, opened 2002. E of the High Street, Nos. 14–16 BIRCH LANE by *Clive Plumb*, 1972–3. Pebbledash and weatherboarding and a complicated roofscape. Later additions in the same style.

WINDMILL, ½ m. E of the church. A well-preserved brick tower mill of *c.* 1816. Large boat-shaped cap, overhanging at the rear, the only remaining example of a type once common in s Essex.

BARROW, 600 yds SW. Diameter 55 ft (17 metres).

STONDON MASSEY

5000

ST PETER AND ST PAUL. Nave and chancel Early Norman. Two original windows remain on the N side and two on the s; also both doorways, though that on the N is blocked. They are completely plain and unmoulded. Walls of flint rubble with Roman tiles laid in both herringbone and chevron patterns. The only later medieval addition of importance is the belfry, tree-ring dated 1408, which is placed a little E of the W end. It rests on four posts carrying tie-beams and connected with them by arched braces. There are also beams in the E–W direction forming a square with the others. Belfry and shingled splay-foot spire rebuilt 1888. General restoration, 1849–51, including new s porch, E window and N vestry, and taking down a N gallery of 1825. In 1873–4 the vestry was rebuilt, an organ chamber added N of the chancel and on the N side of the nave a mortuary chapel, the latter with a fine brick vaulted roof; W gallery and ceiling also taken down, opening up the belfry. By *E. Swansborough*, showing his usual lack of sensitivity: the new work good in itself, but making no attempt to harmonize with the old. – FONT. Perp, octagonal. Bowl with quatrefoils carrying fleurons. – SCREEN. Plain one-light divisions with ogee arches and a minimum of panel tracery above them. Late C15. – PULPIT and READER'S DESK. Dated 1630. Good work with strap decoration and bands of diamonds. Originally a three-decker, rearranged 1849–51. – MONUMENTS. Brasses of John Carre †1570, 'citizen of London, an ironmonger free and also a marchaunt venturar', and two wives (17½-in. (44-cm.) figures), and Rainold Hollingworth †1573 and wife (18-in.; 46-cm figures). The latter is a palimpsest. – In churchyard, by w window. Mrs Mary Vaughan †1775. Large chest-tomb with three cherubs' heads at one end and a flaming urn entwined with serpents.

p. 26

STONDON HALL, NE of the church. C16 straight timber-framed range with later cross-wings, that on the s side early C17, brick with two-storey canted bay.

STONDON MASSEY HOUSE, ¼ m. s. 1800 by *John Oldham*, rector 1791–1841, as the rectory. Brick, two storeys, three bays square, each face having a three-bay pedimented gable with deep eaves and exposed purlins. Oldham is said to have been his own architect, but he later acknowledged the assistance of *Repton*, perhaps in the laying out of the grounds.

STONDON PLACE, ¾ m. SSE. The home, for the last thirty years of his life, of the composer William Byrd (†1623), but rebuilt 1706–7 and again following a fire in 1877, although only the chimneys are obviously of that date. Brick, two storeys. Elegant garden front of nine bays of which the outer three are semicircular.

GILES COTTAGES, Ongar Road, 1¼ m. SE. Brick terrace of four, originally almshouses founded 1574, rebuilt 1860. Some of the C16 timber frame survives. Porches with shaped bargeboards and leaded windows with Gothic tracery.

STOW MARIES

ST MARY AND ST MARGARET. Very odd-looking, of rubble, flint, and brick. C14 chancel, taller than the nave; this is C15 (see the N window of three lights with panel tracery) but was heightened in brick early in the C16, to which the trefoil-arched corbel-frieze and the stepped E gable belong. Squat wooden W steeple. Restored 1870, probably by *G.R. Clarke*, who designed the brick former SCHOOL on the churchyard's N side, 1870–2. N vestry 1912, rebuilt 1950–1. – ALTAR. Late C19, good of its kind, with three painted panels depicting Gabriel appearing to Zacharias, Mary, and Daniel. – BRASS. Mary Browne †1602. 18½-in. (47-cm.) figure, with three sons and four daughters, remounted on nave wall.

OLD RECTORY, S of the church. Painted brick, *c.* 1799. Three bays, two storeys, the ground-floor windows and front door set in arched recesses. C19 additions on S side.★

At Flambirds Farm, 1 m. NW, remains of a First World War AIR-FIELD, one of a number of Flight Stations set up to defend London. Operational 1916, closed 1919. Single-storey brick buildings, some rendered, no more than functional, but a rare survival.

STRETHALL

ST MARY THE VIRGIN. The chancel arch has been described as 'one of the finest examples of Anglo-Saxon workmanship in smaller parish churches'.† It is plain towards the chancel, but towards the nave has triple pilaster-strips continued over the archway as a hoodmould. Similar strips on the imposts, which have a lower chamfered face enriched with lozenges. The flint-rubble nave is also Saxon; see the long-and-short work at the

---

★ Mrs Beryl Board has noticed the very close similarity between the rectory and Brentry Hill, Glos., by *H. & J.A. Repton*, 1802.
† R.M. and J. Taylor, *Anglo-Saxon Architecture* (1965).

w quoins, and a small window high up in the nave w wall. This now opens into the plain, square w tower, the lower stage of which is Norman, the upper stages C14. Chancel C15, much restored in the 1860s and 70s, when the s porch and N vestry were added. – FONT. Late C12, a crude tapering bowl on four shafts with C19 central shaft. – STAINED GLASS. Three windows by *Clayton & Bell* (E 1872, nave N 1880s and 1901), illustrating nicely the development of the firm's style. – MON-UMENTS. Brass of a priest, *c.* 1480, the figure 27½ in. (69 cm.). Reused as monument to Thomas Abbott †1539, the inscription a palimpsest first used for Margaret Siday, *c.* 1460. – John Gardyner †1508. Tomb-chest with quatrefoil decoration in a recess in the chancel N wall, four-centred arch and cresting.

The church stands next to a farmyard with OLD HALL to the NW, C17 timber-framed, mostly plastered but part faced in brick, with gabled jettied cross-wing to the s. N end rebuilt in brick in the C19. The village lies across the fields ¼ m. s. At its w end, MANOR COTTAGE, thatched, C15 or C16 with exposed timbers, single storey and attics with a two-storey block at the w end. 150 yds E, the OLD RECTORY, early C15, jettied at both ends. Hall floored in the C16, when a chimneystack and garderobe were also added.

6040

STURMER

ST MARY. Away from the village, amid trees, with Sturmer Hall (C16, but so restored as to be entirely C20 in appearance) to the w. CII nave, the only evidence the un-rebated N doorway with a lintel decorated with a chequer pattern. C12 s doorway with one order of columns carrying scalloped capitals, zigzag in the arch, two heads like projecting knobs at the top of the door jambs, and a tympanum decorated with two ornamental crosses and two rosettes. The latter may mean sun and moon, but why two crosses? And why this completely unplanned arrangement? The chancel is Norman too, as shown by two small N windows. The E angles have quarter-round shafts with spiral fluting and cushion capitals. The chancel was altered in the E.E. style, when three smallish separate lancets were inserted at the E end. C14 w tower with diagonal buttresses and pyramid roof. Early C16 brick s porch with stepped gable. Nave restored and re-seated 1877, chancel restored 1883. The nave roof (attributed by John Harvey to *Thomas Loveday*) has double hammerbeams, but they are small and the spandrels decorated with rather thin tracery. w organ gallery by *F.W. Chancellor*, 1929–30.

LINNETTS, 1 m. ESE. Small thatched hall house. Late C15 or early C16, with two-bay hall, integral service end to the l. and integral storeyed parlour and solar to the r. Wall painting of a deer in solar. Inserted floors and chimneystack, C17, but otherwise largely unaltered.

BARROW, ¼ m. NNW. Bronze Age bowl barrow.

SUTTON

ALL SAINTS. A small church, rather heavily restored by *Slater & Carpenter* in 1868–9. Nave and chancel of ragstone rubble, with shingled belfry and pyramid roof. It rests on eight posts, or rather on four, each of which has as a reinforcement an additional post along the N and S wall of the nave. Thus a kind of nave with aisles is created. But the curved braces start from the wall-posts and meet in the middle, while the trellis-strutting connects the nave posts from E to W. It is probably C14. The rest basically Norman, notably the good chancel arch with one order of columns with scalloped capitals and a corresponding roll moulding in the nave. Ornamental painting, renewed. Norman windows in the nave, and remains in the chancel. Also in the chancel a C13 lancet, as well as other lancets and the three-light nave windows of 1869. Also C13 the nave S doorway with three orders of columns and manifold moulding of the arches. The S porch has a round-headed doorway dated 1633; rectangular side openings with half-balusters, now blocked, and early C17 PANELLING, probably reused. – FONT. C13, of the Purbeck type, with five pointed shallow arcades on each side. Base probably 1869. – COMMUNION RAIL. Later C17, with turned balusters. – S DOOR. C12 outer face and remains of ironwork now inside, with new outer face dated 1869. – STAINED GLASS. Three E lancets no doubt by *Clayton & Bell*, c. 1869. – Chancel N to Philip Benton of Beauchamps and Little Wakering Hall †1898, looks like *Heaton, Butler & Bayne*. From St Mary Magdalene, Shopland (dem. 1957). – MONUMENTS. Brass of Thomas Stapel †1371, from Shopland. In armour, but nothing remaining below the knees; originally 43 in. (109 cm.) long. – Charles Tyrell †1695. Marble, like a headstone. From Shopland. – Chester Moor Hall †1771. Bas-relief of a mourning female in a cemetery, in classical surround with Composite pilasters etc. and obelisk. Signed by *G. Wilson*, architect, and *W. Vere*. Hall, of Sutton Hall, was the inventor of the achromatic telescope.

SUTTON HALL, E of the church. Smoke-blackened timbers indicate a hall house dating back to the late C14, much altered in the C16, including a staircase tower on the E side with jettied gable. Faced in brick and extended to the rear in the second quarter of the C18, with later additions.

CROWSTONE PREPARATORY SCHOOL, 300 yds N. Former National School, 1873, by *E. Saunders*. Stock brick on red brick plinth, with three large gabled windows.

BEAUCHAMPS, 1¼ m. ESE. Timber-framed, the main front of four widely spaced bays plus an off-centre two-storey porch. This front formerly had elaborate pargetting, dated 1688, and the present date is not original. One good plaster ceiling with two oval wreaths.

TAKELEY

HOLY TRINITY. Quite a large church, and quite on its own. Norman quoins in the nave, with some Roman bricks, but mainly flint rubble. One nave N window of C16 brick, above a blocked N doorway with Roman brick jambs. Generally restored 1859–61, and the chancel in 1874, when *Ewan Christian* built the chancel arch and added the N organ chamber. Chancel E.E. with much-renewed lancet windows. The windows are shafted inside. C14 S aisle with characteristic (restored) window and arcade of octagonal piers and double-chamfered arches. The easternmost respond and arch, however, are a little earlier, say *c.* 1300, evidence of a S transept preceding the S aisle; the western window in the S wall of the aisle appears to have been reused from the transept. C15 S porch and W tower. The latter has diagonal buttresses, doorway with shields in the spandrels, three-light W window and a niche above it. Reordering of W end, to provide vestry in tower etc., by *John Glanfield & Partners*, 2003–5. – FONT COVER. Very tall, with a lavish display of crocketed nodding ogee arches and buttresses and flying buttresses with crocketed pinnacles, tier above tier. C15 but much restored, including in 1847 by *William Ollett Jun.*, who also restored the C15 hexagonal PULPIT, with pinnacled ogee arches set in cinquefoiled panels. – SCREEN. 1910, a fine piece. Eight lights, with elaborate tracery, fan vaulting supporting the richly carved beam, and rood figures. – CUPBOARD. Late C16, with linenfold panelling. Originally a font-case. – STAINED GLASS. Chancel S signed by *O'Connor*, 1861, who might well have done the E window, 1859, and others. – BRASS with inscription recording the benefaction of Mrs Hannah Knollys, 1689.

A large part of the parish is covered by Stansted Airport (q.v.),★ and more of it will be lost if the proposed second runway is built. Most of what is left of the village lies along the old Bishop's Stortford–Dunmow Road (Roman Stane Street). The more interesting buildings are at TAKELEY STREET, ½ m. SW, beginning with STREET FARM, early C17 with a pretty little C19 porch and windows, then the GREEN MAN, late C16 with a gabled cross-wing. Further W, JOSEPHS, one bay of a C15 hall house with the frame exposed at the point where the remaining bays were chopped off, and jettied cross-wing. Then RAYLEIGH COTTAGE, a hall house of *c.* 1400 with floored end bays and thatched roof, and CLOCK HOUSE, *c.* 1600, with long-wall jetty and exposed timbers.

AKLOWA, 500 yds SE of the church. Built as the vicarage, 1874–5, by *Chancellor*, replacing a building of 1837 by *James Edmeston*. Brick, with bands and panels of ornamental bricks, and stone dressings. Irregular composition, with gables, short projecting wings, and porch with open timber sides.

★ Three timber-framed houses at Coopers End, about 1 m. NNW of the church, were dismantled to make way for the airport and re-erected at Battlesbridge and Pitsea, Basildon (q.v.).

BASSINGBOURNE HALL. The house by *Joseph Sanderson*, *c.* 1746, on an older moated site, stood about ¾ m. NW of the church, i.e. under Stansted Airport. A pair of stuccoed lodges survive on the N side of Takeley Street, possibly those described as 'new-built' by *George Byfield* in 1784.

SHEERING HALL, 1½ m. NE. C19 front of painted brick, two large and one small central gable with decorative bargeboards. C20 bays. Behind the two l. gables a C15 house with crown-post roofs and high ceilings.

WARISH HALL, 1 m. ENE. Late C13 aisled hall, on the site of the former Priory of St Valery. Much of the frame survives, with sooted rafters and one original doorway. Plastered exterior, with C18 and C19 sashes, canted bay, two small oriels, and projecting wing to r. C17 wing to l. that includes an original window with sliding shutter. Complete moat, with C17 brick bridge.

TENDRING

1020

ST EDMUND KING AND MARTYR. The curious feature of the church is the roof truss close to the W end. It stands just above the N and S doorways, so the ingenious carpenters framed these by posts, then connected them by a gable, and from these gables started the braces of what is now a hammerbeam but probably started as a tie-beam, its centre removed at some time. The tracery detail of the gables is clearly C14, and not too late in the century either. The circles with wheel figures of mouchettes might be mistaken for the Late Flamboyant sometimes found in England in the early C16 under Flemish or French influence, but the pointed trefoils etc. cannot be so late. The S doorway now leads into the S aisle which, together with the W tower, was added by *Henry Stone* in 1876. He also rebuilt the chancel E wall, all in Kentish rag, although the tower, with recessed polygonal spire, has some flushwork. Older walls of flint rubble, rendered. C14 timber porch, C13 nave and chancel, see two N windows. – FONT. Octagonal, with elaborate foliage and shields in the panels. – STAINED GLASS. W window (reused) by *Thomas Baillie & Co.*, 1863. Nave N by *Horace Wilkinson*, 1928. Chancel N (Annunciation) by *Rosemary Rutherford*, 1967. – MONUMENT. Edmund Saunder †1615, small, alabaster, with kneeling figure.

N of the church the former National School, now VILLAGE HALL: small, Neo-Jacobean brick with black diapers and straight gables, dated 1842. NW of the church, TENDRING HALL, C17, with two gabled cross-wings and a large gabled dormer in the middle of the main range.

Former METHODIST CHAPEL, Tendring Green, 1 m. NNW. By *F. Barnes*, 1869. Kentish rag. Now a house.

PRIMARY SCHOOL, ⅓ m. NNE. 1896 by *J. W. Start*, with C20 additions. Brick, with separate teacher's house.

Former WORKHOUSE, Tendring Heath, 1½ m. NW. by *Scott & Moffatt*, 1836–8. Austere single-storey brick entrance block with central pedimented gatehouse, even more prison-like than most workhouses and with none of the prettiness that Scott achieved elsewhere. Three-storey block behind it with taller central section. Remodelled 1899, probably by *F. Whitmore*, whose designs for an infirmary were approved in 1895. Now offices and residential home.

TERLING

ALL SAINTS. The best part is the brick W tower of 1732 by *Anthony Goud*, with stone quoins and arched openings with rusticated surrounds. The rest, of flint rubble apart from the brick vault on the N side of the chancel, is not impressive from outside. N aisle and porch, 1849, completely renewed S aisle and SW vestry, 1856–7. The chancel seems to be C13. It has one small lancet window on the N side, and otherwise windows of *c.* 1300. Nice C15 timber S porch. Inside, four-bay C15 S arcade with octagonal piers with concave sides and wave-moulded arches, copied on the C19 N arcade. The S aisle and probably the S porch were paid for by John Rochester, who died in 1444. The low many-moulded tower arch is proof of the existence of a previous C13 tower. Spire rebuilt and windows renewed by *J. G. P. Meaden*, 1945, following war damage. – REREDOS. 1905. Alabaster, with a copy of *Thorvaldsen*'s statue of Christ. – FONT. C13, octagonal, of Purbeck marble, with two shallow blank pointed arches on each side; C19 stem and shafts. – COMMUNION RAIL. Early C18, with slim twisted balusters. – BRASSES. In S aisle, male and female figures, the former in early Tudor armour, 37 and 35 in. (94 and 89 cm.), thought to be Robert Rochester †1508 and wife Elizabeth. – Two mural groups of kneeling figures, in Purbeck frames: William and Elizabeth Rochester †1558 and 1556, six sons and four daughters, engraved *c.* 1581; John Rochester †1584, two wives, four sons and eight daughters.

UNITED REFORMED CHURCH. Modest brick Independent Chapel of 1752–3 but looking late C17: three bays, hipped roof, with cross-windows, the effect spoilt by a porch added as part of alterations in 1895–6, which included re-seating and the removal of a gallery. Vestry added *c.* 1840 and further additions at rear 1998–9. Inside, a brass CHANDELIER with dove finial and hexagonal panelled PULPIT, both C17.

The village is especially attractive, with a large number of picturesque timber-framed houses. Church and chapel face each other across the green; next to the chapel a pair of ALMSHOUSES, now a single dwelling, built to celebrate the coming-of-age of J.W. Strutt of Terling Place in 1863. E of this VINE COTTAGE and CHURCH VIEW, originally a single house with that rare thing, a two-bay aisled hall with both aisles still present. Probably early C14. Two-bay cross-wing to the r.

(C15?), three-bay cross-wing to the l. (with late C14 crown-post roof), both with jettied upper floors; single-storey hall, floored in the C16, with a brick chimney dated 1613. Tucked in behind, a late C20 development of courtyard houses, just right in terms of scale and design. On the E side of the green, the delightful TUDOR HOUSE with exposed timbers, jettied cross-wings, and a large C16 W chimneystack decorated with a blank stepped gable. The house dates from the first half of the C15 and still has the original crown-post truss of the central hall. Late C16 panelling in another room. C15 granary to the NW. More good houses along The Street and Owl's Hill, including the OLD VICARAGE, C14 or C15, a high-quality small house, and OWL'S HILL HOUSE, two-bay hall house dating back to the late C14 with two-bay jettied cross-wing. SW of the green, across the River Ter, a mill dam and wheel chamber of a former water mill, the dam built by John Strutt in 1767 as part of a water-supply system for the village, with some surviving machinery of c. 1870.

TERLING PLACE. 1770–7 by *John Johnson*, substantially remodelled by *Thomas Hopper* 1818–21. There were two earlier houses [78] closer to the church, the first a palace of the bishops of Norwich, exchanged by Henry VIII at the Reformation for St Osyth's Priory and then acquired by his Lord Chancellor Thomas Audley.

In 1761 the estate was purchased by John Strutt, M.P. for Maldon, whose family had been accumulating a fortune as millers at Moulsham, outside Chelmsford, since the C17. He commissioned Johnson to rebuild the house a few hundred feet further S, away from the church. The new position appears to have been suggested by *Nathaniel Richmond*, who also laid out the park to the S. Work on brickmaking began in 1770, although plans did not arrive until the following year. The estimated cost was £5,722 8s. The Strutts were able to move into part of the house in 1773 and the final bill was paid in 1777.

Johnson's house is of white brick and quite plain. The entrance was on the S side, the house being of seven bays, five bays deep; behind the three-storey main block was a two-storey kitchen wing, separated from the stables by a yard. John Strutt's successor, John Holden Strutt, married a daughter of the Duke of Leinster, and seems to have felt obliged to emulate the splendour of his father-in-law's seat at Carton, Co. Kildare, for in 1818–21 he had the house remodelled by *Hopper*. Low two-storey service wings were added to E and W, swept back at an oblique angle, ending in little temple fronts *in antis* with pediments; these made the old kitchen wing redundant, and the entrance was moved to the house's N side. The garden front, as the S side now became, was given four attached Ionic columns on the first floor, Johnson's pediment was raised to the level of the parapet with a cornice inserted above the capitals, and his round arches on the ground floor were faced with stone and given moulded keystones. On the N side a porch with Tuscan columns was built, flanked by short projecting blocks.

One of these houses the new staircase, reusing Johnson's wrought-iron balusters. The area of the old staircase was transformed into a proud double-height Saloon. It is a perfect Neo-Greek room of its date. Its chief decoration is a frieze by *Richard Westmacott*, 1823, based on that of the Parthenon, then a very recent British acquisition – it was first displayed at the British Museum in 1817. A gallery runs round the room above the frieze with a beautiful cast-iron railing and Ionic columns of iron painted to resemble yellow marble – the middle ones on each side are in fact chimneys. The ceiling is made into a shallow saucer-dome.

Beyond the Saloon, along the garden front, Johnson's house had a Dining Room to the l. and Drawing Room to the r., separated by an entrance corridor. Hopper turned the Dining Room into the Library, taking in the entrance corridor. A new Dining Room was formed on the l. of the Saloon, nearer to the kitchens in the new E wing. The Drawing Room is the only room by Johnson that survives substantially intact; its plasterwork ceiling is decorated with four ovals incorporating female figures, suspended from ribbon ties. Much redecoration was done, however, in 1850, including a regrettable colouring and embellishment of the Drawing Room ceiling, and in 1854 a conservatory was built in the angle between the W wing and the main house. The W wing was largely converted in 1884 to house the laboratories of John William Strutt, 3rd Baron Rayleigh, who was awarded the Nobel Prize for Physics in 1904. An observatory dome was added as part of restoration work following a fire in 1930. In 1996–7 the E wing, containing Hopper's domestic offices, was rebuilt by *Quinlan Terry* for the 6th Baron Rayleigh, retaining only the S wall, to provide family rooms and farm office. Also by Terry the elegant Palladian SUMMERHOUSE in the walled garden E of the house, 1999: Ionic temple front in white brick and Portland stone.

KENDALLS, Norman Hill, ½ m. WNW of the church. Largely unaltered small house of the mid C17. Three-bay main range with two-bay cross-wing, both parts with crown-post roofs almost complete.

THE MALTINGS (formerly Eyart's Farm), Flack's Green, ¾ m. W. Early C17 house, extended in the C18. Carved bracket below the jettied upper storey in the form of a grotesque crouching figure.

RINGERS FARMHOUSE, 1¼ m. SW. Small, two-storey farmhouse, with central hall and two cross-wings. Built in the early C16, but of timbers that formed part of a larger structure about two centuries older – very probably the bishop's palace by the church that was demolished in the Early Tudor period. Removal of the C16 floor in 1984 (when the C16 central chimneystack was rebuilt) revealed the original roof timbers, far too massive and well carved for a house of this size. Timbers in the E (service) cross-wing also reused, but the parlour/solar cross-wing newly built in the C16. Unusually wide doorway to the screens passage, with tracery decoration in the spandrels, no doubt also reused.

WINDMILL, ½ m. NW. Early C19 smock mill, possibly moved here in 1818. The last commercially working mill in Essex, now converted to a house. No sails or machinery.

THAXTED

Thaxted in the C14 and C15 was one of the most prosperous towns of Essex. Its present population of about 2,500 makes one forget that it vied in business importance with Saffron Walden and indeed many towns now ten and twenty times as populous. Yet only by remembering that can the size of the church be understood. Now, being essentially unspoiled and well supplied with attractive houses, it is prosperous in a different way.

CHURCHES

St John the Baptist. The church, as we see it now, appears at first all of one piece, proud, spacious, clear and a little frigid inside, and outside dominated by its splendid tall steeple. The spire reaches 181 ft (55.1 metres) up; the church is 183 ft (55.7 metres) long. The material is pebble rubble. Apart from clunch for the chancel clerestory, ashlar is not used; but otherwise, in innumerable details, it is obvious that much money was spent on the building. It is embattled all round, pinnacles are used in addition to battlements, decorative friezes of ornament or figures appear here and there, and so on. The church, in its earliest parts of c. 1340 but rebuilt in the C15–C16, has often been restored, notably by *R. Creed*, 1896–1901, with further work (mainly to the tower, but including also the removal of cement facing from the whole church) by *Randall Wells*, 1910–12, and *Sir Charles Nicholson*, 1925, but not much has been changed. Storms in 1757 and 1763–4 blew out the windows of the chancel clerestory and the transepts respectively, and they were rebuilt in simplified form.* Further storms in 1814 brought down the spire, but the reconstruction by *John Cheshire*, 1822, was accurate.

The tower has set-back buttresses, but the angles are not of 90 degrees. They form two sides of a polygon. At the top of the tower battlements and panelled pinnacles connected by flying buttresses to the spire. This is of the Northamptonshire type, with crockets and three tiers of dormer windows. Niches to l. and r. of the W door and W window. The aisle windows have depressed heads and panel tracery, mostly of four lights – more uniform on the N side than the S – and five at the W end. The chancel chapels have long, straight-headed four-light windows, identical on the N and S sides and again with panel tracery. The E window is huge, of five lights, and has an odd mixture of Perp detail and intersections. Both porches are two-storeyed, but that on the S side (the earlier, built c. 1380) is

---

* Restoration work in 2004–5 revealed stonework from the earlier clerestory windows, showing them to have been as wide as the chancel chapel windows.

slightly less sumptuous. Even so it has a main s doorway and subsidiary doorways to the E and W, a three-light side opening, and a star-shaped tierceron vault. The N porch vault has liernes as well and many bosses. This porch is taller than the other, in fact almost as high as the transept, which is most effective when one looks at the church from the NW. The doorway has roses in the spandrels and two large panels with shields over it, two upper windows side by side, with fleuron surrounds, a turret at the NW angle which is higher than the porch, and a figure-frieze below the battlements. There are even headstops to the gables of the first set-offs of the buttresses. A similar figure-frieze below the battlements can also be noticed in the N transept, and there are many more minor enrichments, gargoyles, etc.

28 The INTERIOR in its present form is white and bared of all major furnishings, though there are plenty of smaller objects of devotion about, mostly brought in during the incumbency of Conrad Noel, 1910–42. The surprising lightness is partly due to the fact that most of the windows have clear glass. The arcades are the earliest elements of the church. They date from *c.* 1340. The piers are quatrefoil with very thin shafts in the diagonals. The two-centred arches have mouldings with two quadrants. The hoodmoulds rest on comparatively big headstops. The crossing arch belongs to the same C14 church.

The C15 rebuilding proceeded as follows: s transept late C14, N transept *c.* 1400, N aisle widened and N porch added *c.* 1445; steeple probably late C15, chancel and chancel chapels, crossing arches to the N, S, and E, and clerestory *c.* 1510. The date of the s transept can be deduced from the fine blank arcading below the s window, with alternating pointed and coupled ogee arches, all crocketed richly. The date of the N transept appears in the corresponding arcading on the N side and the fine REREDOS on the E wall with ogee-headed niches and a frieze above, in which Christ appears between censing angels. Fragments of another reredos can be seen on the E wall of the s transept. The tall tower arch and the vault inside the tower must be C15. The chancel arcades of *c.* 1510 have an interesting, very complex pier section: semicircular shafts to the arches, but to the chancel a combination of thin shafts and thin hollows not having a capital but turning round to the l. and r. above the arches to form frames. In the arch spandrels is broad simple openwork tracery. The roofs are low-pitched, although their history is not entirely straightforward. The nave roof dates from *c.* 1530–60, but has a lot of reused timbers; the chancel roof seems to have been rebuilt (in part at least) in 1562, but again incorporates older timbers, tree-ring dated 1413–36. Tie-beams are used only in the chancel. The figures of the brackets and the bosses will repay some attention. The E bay of the s chapel roof is ceiled, with a carved boss depicting a Chalice and Host.

COMMUNION RAIL. With twisted balusters; *c.* 1700. – LECTERN. 1896, with painted decoration by the *Marquis d'Oisy*, 1930s. He gave the same treatment to two cupboards, the statue of St Thomas à Becket (N chapel), and two *coronae lucis* in the S chapel and nave. – PULPIT. A fine late C17 piece with garlands hanging down the angles between the panels. Hexagonal, with sounding-board. The staircase with twisted balusters does not belong. – FONT CASE AND COVER. Late C15. Case with two tiers of traceried panels hiding the font completely. Top with buttresses, canopies, finial, etc., a little broader and heavier than at Littlebury. – SCREENS. At the E end of the N and S aisles, parts of the lower half of C15 screens, with elaborate tracery. – To N and S chapels, late C17, low, with a frieze of thick openwork foliage scrolls. – DOOR. In the N doorway, with traceried panels, C15. – BENCHES. A number of tall bench ends of the mid C17, probably Flemish, carved with *memento mori* and a variety of other motifs. From the chapel of Easton Lodge, Little Easton (q.v.). – SCULPTURE. In S transept, early C14 Madonna, French or German. – Praying hands (N aisle). Bronze, by *Eric Kennington, c.* 1937. – Rev. Conrad Noel †1942. Bronze head by *Gertrude Hermes*. – STELLA. By *Randall Wells*, 1910 (made for St Mary's, Primrose Hill, London, but never installed there). Very large, of iron, counterbalanced. – WALL PAINTING. In one of the spandrels of the S arcade, fragment of the martyrdom of Thomas à Becket. – ROYAL ARMS. Over S door, of Queen Anne, before the Union. Painted on wood, cut out rather than framed, and very large. – BANNERS. Six, hanging in the chancel, copies by *Jane Stagg*, 1996, of the 1920s originals. – Processional banners by *Alec & Margaret Hunter*, the earliest 1917. – TAPESTRY. Rebecca at the well. Flemish, mid C16. – STAINED GLASS. Many figures and other fragments have been distributed over N and S windows. The most notable are the C15 and early C16 figures of saints in the N windows (reset by the *Kempe* studio, 1907, who added the head of a saint in the r. hand of four lights to a N aisle window), the late C14 figure in the S transept S window, and the stories from Genesis, with small figures of Adam and Eve, of *c.* 1450, in a S aisle window. – E window, S chapel S, and N chapel E by *Kempe*, 1900, 1906 and 1907 respectively. S chapel E by *Gamon & Humphry*, 1910. – MONUMENTS. Brass to a priest (chancel), *c.* 1450, just over 3 ft (93 cm.) long. – Thomas Swallow †1712. Ledger stone by *Edward Stanton*, lettering by *John Le Neve*. The dearth of monuments more than anything tends to give Thaxted that curious atmosphere of remoteness which one cannot help feeling directly one enters.

BAPTIST CHURCH, Park Street. 1832–3, enlarged to the front later in the C19. Brick, with rendered front and three-bay pediment.

UNITED REFORMED CHURCH, Bolford Street. Late C18, enlarged in 1828, 1857, and 1876. The different stages can be clearly seen in the brickwork. Of 1876 the stock brick dressings and the towering front (by *C. Pertwee?* – cf. Great Dunmow, Maldon), which has transept-like returns with

pedimented gables: triple-arched loggia entrance, three tall
round-arched windows above that, and three-bay pediment.
Galleried interior, of two tiers at the w end.

PUBLIC BUILDINGS

54 GUILDHALL. The Guildhall is the hub of Thaxted, vying with
the church as the focal point of the view up the main street,
and arguably more famous because more unusual. Long
thought to have been built in the last quarter of the C14 as a
hall for a guild of cutlers, it now seems certain that it was a
market hall and council chamber, and tree-ring dating shows
that it was built in the third quarter of the C15, to which it
belongs stylistically. Alterations were made in 1715, and in
1910–11 the building was restored by *Ernest Beckwith*, following on from his work at Paycocke's, Coggeshall (q.v.). Major
repairs, mostly structural, were carried out in 1974–5 by *James
Boutwood* of the *County Architect's Dept.*
The building is three-storeyed, free-standing on three sides,
and on each of those three sides are not one but two jetties. It
has a double-hipped crown-post roof that until the C18 ended
in twin gables. Also in the C18 the walls were pargetted; this
covering was removed by Beckwith, who in the fashion of the
time blackened the timbers; they were more correctly limewashed in 1974–5 – an interesting example of changing attitudes to treatment of timber-framed buildings. The ground
floor is open, with simple arches between the posts; Beckwith
took out the original carved ogee arches, believing them to be
later insertions. One contemporary doorhead can be seen on
the N side, brought from another house in the course of repairs
by *Marshall Sisson*, 1948–51. Next to this, in the building's NW
corner, is an C18 lock-up, and the staircase also is C18. In the
centre of the ground floor, a massive timber post supports the
entire structure. The arches on the first floor are also Beckwith's, allegedly based upon a single example that he found,
while the second-floor oriels are entirely conjectural. The
first floor originally had continuous window openings on all
three sides, and the second-floor windows facing Town Street
were originally twice as wide as they now are. Inside, the first
and second floors are divided into rooms, although whether this
was originally the case, particularly on the first floor, is a matter
of debate. There is also a basement, with brick and flint walls.
PRIMARY SCHOOL, Bardfield Road. 1880, by *George Perry &
John Slater*, with separate master's residence. Gabled, brick,
with thin bands of black brick. School hall in front of the old
building, 1996–8, and additional classrooms etc. behind,
2001–2, by *Robert Hutson Architects* (partner-in-charge, *Peter
Heather*).

PERAMBULATION

The town as a whole is very perfect, chiefly because there is truly
not one house in it that would appear violently out of place.

All is in scale, nothing too high or too ostentatious, mostly white, cream, pink plastering or exposed timber-framing. The walk starts at the W end of the church, which lies high up at one end of the town, visible as a climax from everywhere. To the S, a row of early C18 ALMSHOUSES with C19 detailing – hoodmoulds, bargeboards – on the end wall, restored by *Peter Cleverly*, 1975. Alongside is THE CHANTRY, C17 timber-framed, plastered and thatched, converted from almshouses in 1933 by *Thomas Rayson*, who added a semicircular extension at the S end. These two frame a view towards the WINDMILL, which forms the other climax in the landscape. Brick tower mill of 1804, built for John Webb, landowner and innkeeper, the bricks made at his own works. Fully restored in stages since 1972, with new fantail and sails. Opposite the church's N porch lies the SWAN HOTEL, C17 timber-framed behind a long, Late Georgian front of painted brick with three pedimented doorcases. This leads to the corner of NEWBIGGEN STREET, the entry to the town from Saffron Walden, which has a pleasing variety of mostly undemonstrative houses on both sides. The exceptions have exposed timbers – e.g. No. 25, C17, originally jettied, with an original four-centred doorhead – and medieval hall houses can also be discerned, e.g. Nos. 16–20 and 40–42, with gabled cross-wings. At the far end on the E side, the former VICARAGE, C17 timber-framed and plastered with a staircase tower at the back, refronted in the C18, and just before it No. 48, early C15 with crown-post roof, thought to have been built as a guildhall. WATLING LANE, tucked away behind the W side of Newbiggen Street, contains some nice C17 thatched cottages.

Back to the Swan Hotel, where WATLING STREET runs downhill alongside the church. Two Late Medieval houses, one with exposed timbers, and then CLARANCE HOUSE, the only ambitious C18 house in Thaxted. Rainwater heads give the date, 1715, and the initials of William Heckford, an apothecary and surgeon, and his wife Elizabeth. It has a seven-bay, two-storey front with segment-headed windows, cement keystones, and a doorway with a segmental pediment carried on Corinthian pilasters. The frieze below the pediment rises characteristically in the middle. Simpler doorway with segmental pediment on the garden front and a single C19 bay, others of which, until 1951, also marred the street front. Contemporary panelling, staircase with alternate turned and twisted balusters, and garden walls. After that more modest houses climbing down the hill, of C18 appearance but No. 16, for example, with an intact C15 timber frame and crown-post roof over a first-floor hall.

So the Guildhall is reached in the best position of the town (described above), at the top end of Town Street, where it forks. Between the two main prongs, immediately r. of the Guildhall, STONEY LANE leads up to the churchyard. In it, just behind the Guildhall, an early C14 house, remodelled in the C18 with C20 panel pargetting, and then a very picturesque group of three three-storey houses jettied at each floor, with exposed studs. They date from the first quarter of the C15 and have many original window openings as well as original cellars. The furthest has in addition original traceried heads, original staircase with solid treads, and on the first floor a room with an extensive scheme of late C16 or early C17 wall paintings depicting flowing flowery stems interspersed with a variety of motifs, exotic birds, and animals.

TOWN STREET is a much quieter sight. It is broad, to accommodate what was once a thriving market, and it needs to be understood that it continued further SE than it now does, the houses between Mill End and Orange Street forming an island that now occupies the upper part of the market place. The best houses are close to the Guildhall, on the S side, where the land belonged to the medieval manor, whose gardens were bounded by Town Street and Park Street. No. 25 has a front with C18 detailing, three canted bay windows, and a doorcase with Tuscan columns and pediment tucked in under a long-wall jetty, enriched here and below the parapet with modillions. The front is a remodelling of shops (over cellars) that projected from an early C14 hall, of which part of the frame and fine roof with octagonal crown-post can be seen to the rear. Then No. 23, which has a rear range that might be of similar age but a three-storey, five-bay Georgian brick front spoilt by C19 bays. No. 19, the home of Gustav Holst between 1917 and 1925, is late C18. But that is overshadowed by the three-storey RECORDER'S HOUSE, whose C15 overhangs are supported on the ground floor as well as the first by two canted oriel windows each, a remarkable sight. The lower ones are C19 shop windows but the upper ones are C15 and rest on original sills carved with a griffin and the arms of Edward IV. No. 9 is C17 and still has two gables of the kind which elsewhere, e.g. on the Guildhall, were later replaced.

The N side of Town Street has two main points of interest, one at each end. Opposite the Guildhall, THE PRIORY has a Neo-Georgian front of 1938 with two bow windows on the ground floor and an iron balcony above, but inside the remains of a late C14 hall with crown-post roof. Evidence of much wall painting inside the house, including an early C17 scheme that was destroyed in the process of uncovering a C16 monochrome pattern beneath. Near the lower end a shop, No. 18, formerly the Duke's Head Inn and originally a hall house whose cross-wing has been concealed by the raised roof and parapet. The front was originally jettied and the l. part of the shop preserves the C14 ceiling of what was the inn's carriageway and may originally have been the upper end of the hall. Outside it a C19 cast-iron PUMP, octagonal with traceried panels and ogee cap.

At the foot of Town Street, roads branch off in various directions. MILL END is the main thoroughfare, with the STAR INN on the s side, its C18 sashed front and hipped roof concealing a late C14 hall house with two cross-wings. At the top of the hill, opposite Bardfield Road, an interesting group of buildings, now part of a factory. The first is brick, built in 1813 as

a Baptist Chapel. Three-bay front facing down Mill End with
the entrance set in a wide arched recess. Two similar recesses
along the side wall. Next a timber-framed and plastered building, with underbuilt long-wall jetty. Finally an early C16 building, with diapered brickwork and on the rear elevation a corbel
table with trefoiled arches. A short distance along Bardfield
Road, CLAYPITS FARM, C15 or earlier hall house with two
cross-wings.

Down Park Street, which leads s from the foot of Town Street,
lies PARK FARM, early C16 with a probably original chimneystack and some original ceilings. Long-wall jetty with
exposed studs on the upper floor, original windows and a
doorway that once led to the upper floor of a porch. Beyond
it No. 36, also C16 with exposed timberwork on the jettied
upper floor, and between them a C16 flint wall with some C16
and C18 brick and a number of C14 carved stones.

Among C20 housing N of Town Street, WEATHERHEAD
CLOSE by *Gerald Lacoste, c.* 1949. Mainly small blocks of two-
storey houses, roughcast and painted, many with one or two
gabled cross-wings, laid out round a large green.

BOROUGH FARM, Bolford Street, ¼ m. SW. Late C14. Hall to the
r., then a higher cross-wing, jettied with exposed timbers. This
was originally gabled, but the roof-line was presumably
changed when the extension to the l. was built in the early C16.
This also has exposed timbers and continues the jetty.

PRIOR'S HALL, ¾ m. SSE. Late C15, with gabled cross-wings,
much restored in 1898 in the house style of the Maynard
(Easton Lodge) estate.

At Cutlers Green, nearly 1 m. WSW, MAYNARDS CROFT, formerly a Maynard estate farmhouse. C19, quaintly thatched,
including porch and bays, but much bigger in every dimension
than its quaintness would indicate.

HORHAM HALL. *See* p. 496.

THEYDON BOIS

ST MARY. By *Sydney Smirke*, 1850–1. The medieval church stood
next to the Hall. A new church was built on the present site
by *J. O. Abbott & W. G. Habershon* of St Neots, 1843–4, but it
was 'unsoundly constructed'. A smug inscription in the porch
warns:

> Gain, Reader, gain from the catastrophe
> Lesson of service for Eternity.
> In the foundation mainly was the flaw
> That did the fabrick unto ruin draw.
> Examine well on what foundation stands
> The hope of Heaven which in thine heart expands.

Smirke's church is small, brick, and rather ugly, with an unconventional SW tower-cum-porch with copper-covered splay-foot

spire. Dormer windows on N side. Large N extension by *T. Venn*, 2003–4, replacing *Caroë*'s vestry and organ chamber of 1926. – PULPIT. Nice piece in the C18 style with back panels and small canopy. By *Paul Waterhouse*, 1900. – ROYAL ARMS. James I, painted. – STAINED GLASS. Nave N by *Clayton & Bell*, 1897, and *Jones & Willis* †1932. Nave S †1928 by *A.K. Nicholson*. – MONUMENTS. J.M.G. Dare †1810. Tablet with draped urn. By *H. Rouw*. – S. Wild †1817. Memorial with details of bequest of his wife Elizabeth †1844. By *T. Marsh*. – Diana Hamilton †1853. By *W.T. Hale*. Inscription in a round border, like a lifebelt. – LYCHGATE. 1914. Brick and stone. Pitched roof that on the road side extends over little aisles containing seats, an original and attractive design.

Former SCHOOL, on S side of churchyard. Plain gault brick, 1840, by *G. Bridges*. Extended 1894 and 1903. Now offices.

THEYDON HALL, 1¼ m. SE. Late Georgian yellow brick. An earlier timber-framed range to the rear now demolished.

PARSONAGE FARM, ¾ m. ESE. Late C15 or early C16, of Wealden type. Jettied front with exposed timbers, interrupted by bays and oriels that probably date from restoration in 1920.

COAL DUTY OBELISK, 1 m. SSE. Slender stone obelisk, beside the railway line, *c.* 1861.

THEYDON GARNON

ALL SAINTS. The historical interest of the church lies in the fact that the brick W tower is dated 1520 by an inscription (S side, now all but illegible) and the brick N aisle 1644 (E gable). In the tower blue bricks are used as well but apparently without system. W doorway and W window in all probability C18. The original bell-openings have two lights, and there are battlements. Of 1644 also is the five-bay aisle arcade inside. It is entirely of timber (cf. Shenfield), with octagonal piers and round arches. Of the other parts of the church, which are of flint rubble, the chancel seems to be C13, see one S lancet restored and reopened in 1934. The E window is quite ambitious C15 work. As for the nave, the prettiest feature, the two dormers, probably dates from 1644. Various restorations by Rev. Sir Cavendish Foster Bt, rector 1843–87: one of 1863–4 by *Jekell*, presumably *Thomas Jeckyll*, which included new N aisle windows, otherwise mainly internal, including removal of the W gallery of 1774; another of 1885. Small N vestry and organ chamber by *E.P. Warren*, 1891–2. Against the inside W wall an oak door frame from the C15 PRIEST'S HOUSE that stood a few yards W of the church. – PULPIT, with large detailed tester, staircase with elegant twisted balusters, and attached reader's desk, *c.* 1710. – COMMUNION RAIL. With twisted balusters, 1683–4. – CHEST. Oak, with iron straps, with ornamental pattern of nailheads, and brass plate recording gift by Sir John Archer, 1668. – STAINED GLASS. Chancel E and S by *Arthur J. Dix*, the former designed by *Warren*, 1896–7, with later commemorative panels, the latter 1918. Chancel N, rather better, by *Holiday*, made by *Powell & Sons*, 1890–1.

The special character of the interior is chiefly derived from the large number of MONUMENTS and other mural adornments, including a good collection of HATCHMENTS, BEQUEST BOARDS, and unusually large ROYAL ARMS of George III painted by *Russell* of Chigwell, 1762. – Brass to William Kirkeby, rector, †1458, the figure *c.* 3 ft (96 cm.) long, with engraved orphreys; re-set on N wall of chancel in C19 with new inscription. – Recess in chancel N wall, containing a tomb-chest with two cusped lozenges on the front. The arch is depressed, a straight horizontal on quadrant curves, and has a quatrefoil frieze above. Kneeling figures against the back wall of a man in armour and a woman, each 12½ in. (30 cm.), with smaller figures of two sons and three daughters, *c.* 1520. – Similar recess in s wall with indents of kneeling figures. – Ellen Branch †1567, small grey stone tablet with ogee arch. Inside the arch a brass plate with kneeling figure. – Denton Nicholas M.D. †1714, white marble with cherubs and a very elaborate canopy with *trompe l'œil* drapery. Attributed to *Thomas Stayner* (GF). – Several monuments to members of the Archer family of Coopersale House. The oldest is that of Sir John †1681, white marble with Corinthian columns and scrolled pediment, by *William Stanton*, 1683. The most spectacular is to William Eyre Archer †1739, a standing wall monument with a grey sarcophagus, and a paler grey obelisk. Two seated cherubs l. and r. of the sarcophagus. Against the obelisk hovers another cherub just above a dual portrait medallion of the deceased and his wife Susannah †1761. By *Peter Scheemakers*. – Lady Mary Archer †1776, erected *c.* 1800. Very elegant and restrained classical design in white and grey marble by *John Bacon Jun.*

THEYDON PRIORY, Coopersale Lane, SW of the church. Built as the rectory, the core early C17 rebuilt in the C18. Main (S) front of five bays, the centre bay breaking forward with a fine pedimented doorcase. Considerable C19 and C20 additions broadly in keeping. Between it and the church its replacement as rectory by *Bailey & McConnal* of Walsall, 1895–8. Brick, some of it decorative, almost amounting to Queen Anne Revival.

FITZWILLIAM COTTAGES, ⅓ m. SE. Terrace of four early C17 almshouses, now two cottages. Single-storey, timber-framed, brick-fronted. The charity was founded in 1602.

GAYNES PARK, 1¾ m. NNE.* The manor dates back to the C13, and a well-built brick house is documented in the C17, but it was rebuilt in the mid C18. Further alterations, including partial refronting in stock brick with round-headed windows on the ground floor, probably followed its acquisition by William Coxhead Marsh in 1811. Most of the N side, and all

---

*I am grateful to Paul Drury for sharing his unpublished report on the house.

of the E and S sides, were rebuilt in 1868–70 by Thomas Coxhead Chisenhale Marsh in an extravagant style that is mainly Tudor but with more than a touch of Scottish Baronial, and faced in Kentish rag. Good collection of decorative terracotta chimney pots by *Doulton* of Lambeth and *H. Lundy* of Stamford, one dated 1867. This rebuilding remained incomplete at Marsh's death in 1875; presumably he had intended to create a new house round a small central courtyard. Further work was carried out by his son William in 1901. A number of the principal rooms still have their late C19 or early C20 panelling, including the library with narrow gallery, but they are not on the same rugged dramatic scale as the exterior. Brick STABLES NE of the house probably also *c.* 1811. Now empty, after a period of institutional use. – SOUTH LODGE, ½ m. WSW. C16 or C17 timber-framed and plastered with weatherboarded ground floor. Rustic porch.

THEYDON MOUNT

ST MICHAEL. Rebuilt in brick by Sir William Smith of Hill Hall, 1611–14, following a fire. The W window has intersected tracery, so has the E. The other windows are of two lights under straight hoodmoulds, and the brick surrounds are rendered in imitation of stone. The details do not seem to differ between W parts and chancel. Yet the bricks and the building are too different to allow for the same date. Did the chancel in fact not need rebuilding in 1611, but does it date from 1577, when Sir Thomas Smith was interred in the new vault below it? The W tower is not high. It has diagonal buttresses and battlements and a (later?) recessed shingled spire. The stair-turret adjoins the W tower on the S and ends in a segmental gable. The windows are double slits of very odd shape. The S porch has a more elaborately shaped gable and a four-centred doorway and above it an uneasily balanced aedicule of Tuscan pilasters with pediment. The nave roof has collar-beams on arched braces which form semicircles.

REREDOS. Coupled Corinthian pilasters l. and r. of the E window, the dado panelling continued below the window. Late C17. – FONT. Unusually small, of black and coloured marble, attached to the wall. Rectangular bowl, on a pillar, and above it a niche with shell-head and mask, as if about to spout water. Contemporary with the church and said to come from Italy, where it was probably intended as a stoup. – BENCHES. Plain, early C17. – HELM. One, C17, in the chancel, with surcoat or tabard. – HATCHMENTS. Nine, including a good display (combined with ROYAL ARMS) at the W end. – MAIDEN'S GARLAND. Dome-shaped ash frame decorated with sprigs of box and paper ribbons etc., *c.* 1700. – WALL PAINTINGS. Creed and Lord's Prayer, early C17 black-letter inscriptions. Curiously incorporated in MONUMENTS to the First World War and Sir

Robert Hudson †1927. – STAINED GLASS. E window by *W.G. de Glehn*, made by *E. & C. O'Neill*, 1920. Strikingly modern figures and strong colours.

MONUMENTS. An impressive series to the Smith family of Hill Hall, crowding the small chancel and spilling out into the nave. Sir Thomas †1577 (on his career *see* below). Standing wall monument. Alabaster figure stiffly reclining, head propped up on elbow. Shallow coffered arch behind the figure, flanked by two Ionic columns with an entablature carrying two black obelisks and a large achievement. Fine inscription plate with bold strapwork and fruit surround under the arch. Attributed to *Giles de Witte* (AW), in which case it must date from after de Witte's arrival in England in 1585. – Sir William †1626 and wife. Standing wall monument with two effigies both stiffly reclining with head on elbow; he a little higher and behind her. The background more or less as before but the effect is richer, with Composite columns and figures in the spandrels. Kneeling figures of children against the front of the tomb-chest. Attributed to *Maximilian Colt* (GF). – Sir William †1631 and two wives. Standing wall monument with recumbent effigy. Big kneeling figures of wives and son behind and above. Attributed to *John & Matthias Christmas* (GF). – Sir Thomas †1668. Standing wall monument, of black and white marble, with no superstructure. The effigy again reclining, head propped up on elbow. Thick angle volutes ending in cherubs' heads. Attributed to *Jasper Latham* (GF). – Sir Edward †1713, simple white marble tablet, with a cherub's head at the foot. By *Edward Stanton*. – Sir William Smyth †1823 by *Stephen Radburn*. Marble tablet with draped urn and oil lamps, perhaps deliberately intended to balance the similar monument to Rev. Sir William Smyth †1777. – Rev. Sir Edward Bowyer Smijth †1850. Large Perp Gothic tablet with ogee canopy and crocketed pinnacles, supported on angels. By *W. Osmond* of Salisbury.

HILL HALL*

Hill Hall, in spite of its moderate size and its outwardly early C18 appearance, is one of the most important earlier Elizabethan houses in the country, for two reasons: it has some of the earliest classical decoration on any surviving building in Britain, and it contains a series of wall paintings that have no equal as examples of the interior decoration of the period. Their preservation is miraculous, for the house was not only remodelled on several occasions, but was gutted by fire in 1969 after being used for some years as a prison. In 1980 the shell was taken into the care of the Department of the Environment, transferred to English Heritage in 1984. They conserved the exterior, returning it substantially to its appearance in 1939.

*The account of the house relies extensively on research by Paul Drury, that of the wall paintings on research by Muriel Carrick.

The Elizabethan house is due to Sir Thomas Smith, who died in 1577 and is buried in the church. He was unquestionably a remarkable man. Born in 1513, he graduated and lectured at Cambridge, went to Paris, Orleans and Padua in 1540–2, took a D.C.L. at Padua, got interested in the minutiae of Greek pronunciation, became Vice-Chancellor of Cambridge University, and in 1547 went into politics to serve Protector Somerset. Somerset, as is witnessed by all that is recorded of Old Somerset House of *c*. 1546–9, was the leader of an architectural group believing in the Renaissance as a style rather than as a fashion of decoration. Their work – Sharington of Lacock Abbey and Thynne of Longleat were the other chief members – has more affinities with France than with Italy. Smith was M.P. for Marlborough and Provost of Eton; as a staunch Protestant he was out of favour during Queen Mary's reign, but in 1562 was sent to France as Ambassador. While there he must have taken an interest in architecture; for Lord Burghley in a letter of 1568 refers to a French book on architecture which he had seen at Smith's house, and the inventory of his library (at Queens' College, Cambridge) includes, besides three editions of Vitruvius and John Shute's *First and Chief Grounds of Architecture*, Hans Blum's *Quinque columnarum descriptio . . . conscripta per Ioannem Blum* (1550), Jacques Androuet du Cerceau's *Livre d'architecture* (1559), and Philibert de l'Orme's *Nouvelles inventions pour bien bastir* (1561). In France Smith travelled with the Court, for instance to Toulouse. In 1566 he was back in England, and spent three years in retirement in Essex; it was during this time that he carried out much of the rebuilding of Hill Hall.

The basic structure is simple: the house is built round a courtyard, with the entrance on the N side and Great Hall opposite; and further ranges to the NW. The history of the various phases of construction is more complex and has only come to light as a result of archaeological investigation since 1969. The Theydon Mount estate came to Smith in 1554 on his marriage to Philippa, widow of Sir John Hampden. There was a house on the site dating back to *c*. 1200, rebuilt at the end of the C15, of which little is known. It was in use until the late C17 and traces of its basement have been excavated. Smith rebuilt this house in 1557, but the work was shoddy (the bricks were set in loam, not mortar), and he started again ten years later, building first the N and W sides of the courtyard, 1567–8, and the other two sides in 1572–3. For the first phase, it seems likely that Smith was his own architect, using local craftsmen; the details of the capitals are taken from Blum, but the general effect, with a lack of symmetry and some curious proportions, is clumsy. The S and E sides, on the other hand, are more sophisticated, and incorporate terracotta mouldings that may have been supplied by foreign makers: the vogue for architectural terracotta, seen for example at Layer Marney (q.v.), was generally confined to the 1520s. The French influence is at its most apparent on the courtyard elevations, with cross-windows separated by two orders of short attached columns, Doric below, with an incorrectly spaced metope frieze, and Ionic above; then elaborate dormers, with attached Corinthian columns, rising above the upper entablature on the s side. Comparison has been made to the French châteaux of Assier and Azay-le-Rideau, both built some forty years previously. The name of Smith's architect for the later work is known from his will. He left £20 to *Richard Kirby*, 'cheefe Architecte overseer and M[aste]r of my workes for the p[er]fecting of my howse according to the plott', to be paid out on completion of the house, and work was in progress when Smith died: probably the rebuilding of the NW range, *c.* 1576–81.

The most surprising features are on the external elevations of the s and e ranges: on each elevation, four giant Doric engaged columns, two and two, on tall bases not carrying more than fragments of entablature. This is a unique occurrence in England and indeed in Europe, although at Kirby Hall (Northants), of 1570–5, the pilasters of the courtyard elevations are also of the giant order. These columns were retained in the major rebuilding of the e front, which in 1714 was given an entirely Baroque appearance: stone quoins, big stone dressings for the windows surmounted by segmental arches, and a three-bay, slightly projecting centre with a big pediment decorated with garlands and the arms of Sir Edward Smith, 3rd baronet, who inherited in 1713, and his wife Ann Hedges, who died in 1719. The next major phase came in 1789, with the erection of the Neoclassical portico on the N front. In 1791 *Repton* produced a Red Book for the house and park and his recommendations for some internal reorganization were carried out; also at this time the classical details of the courtyard and s and e fronts were remodelled in Roman cement and *Coade* stone (happily removed after 1984), work completed by 1815. The w front was rebuilt in 1844 and between 1872 and 1895 a small extension was built at the SW corner.

Extensive alteration were made by *Sir Reginald Blomfield* for Mr and Mrs Charles Hunter, 1909–12. This included remodelling the NW range to provide servants' quarters, building a new kitchen block on the w side of the forecourt, reconstructing the southern end of the w side of the courtyard, and a drastic replanning of the interior. Much was lost as a result of this, including the Elizabethan hall screen, but the 1969 fire made the loss academic.

The INTERIOR has been almost entirely reconstructed as apartments by the *P. J. Livesey Group*, 2000–1, but on the first floor of the NW corner, the only part of the interior to survive the fire (apart from the chimneypiece in the Great Hall, remodelled during the first substantial alterations to Sir Thomas's house between 1668 and 1698) are the WALL PAINTINGS of c. 1570. They presumably once extended throughout the N and W ranges. Figurative wall paintings of this date and of this quality are very rare. They came to light in 1934. In the w corner room of the N range (perhaps Sir Thomas's *Studioli*) are four scenes from the life of King Hezekiah from 2 Chron.: 28–32, forming a deep decorative frieze on the upper part of the wall. The paintings display a Low Countries influence and *Lucas d'Heere* has been suggested as the artist. There are fragments of a fifth scene, probably from the same cycle, but so far it has not been identified. The Cupid and Psyche cycle of wall paintings is taken from the story in the *Golden Ass* by Apuleius, possibly copies of engravings by *Jacques Androuet Du Cerceau* which in turn had been copied from engravings by The Master of the Die and Agostino Veneziano after designs by Michiel Coxcie. A copy of Apuleius was in Smith's library, but it has not survived and it is not known which edition it was. Unlike the Hezekiah paintings, these cover the full height of the walls, with life-size figures, and are painted to appear as tapestries with wide borders of fruit and flowers. Only a small part of the cycle remains *in situ*. Two sections, removed in 1938, are now at the Victoria and Albert Museum. Fragments from the same palette can be found elsewhere in the house.

The surrounding LANDSCAPE has suffered as much as the building itself, not least because the southern end of the park was lost to the M25. Sir Thomas Smith made a garden to the S of the house, with ponds originally on three sides, two of which survive. *Repton*'s suggestions for alterations to the grounds, which included moving the kitchen garden and making a new approach to the house from the S, were at least partly carried out. *Blomfield* built terraces to the W of the house and also the hexagonal brick hut by the S pool, and remodelled the W pool for bathing. To the latter *Philip Tilden* added a classical temple, 1927–8, and laid out a sunken garden (in a position corresponding to the missing E pool; now filled in) and a rose garden further SE of the house, for Sir Robert and Lady Hudson.

THORNDON HALL
Brentwood

Thorndon Hall and park date back to *c.* 1412, when Lewis John enclosed 300 acres of land and built a lodge just to the N of the parish church of St Nicholas, West Horndon. The house was rebuilt by John, later 1st Lord Petre, who purchased the estate in 1573, and laid out gardens around it. But it remained subsidiary to the main seat, Ingatestone Hall, until Robert, 8th Lord Petre, moved to it after his marriage in 1732. It was partially remodelled by *Giacomo Leoni*, 1733–42, and an elaborate scheme of formal gardens and landscaping was drawn up by *Sieur Bourginion*, probably based on Lord Petre's own design. Both house and grounds were incomplete when Robert died in 1742. His son, also Robert, abandoned the old house, which was damaged by fire in 1757, and built a new one on a site 1¼ m. to the N. It was designed by *James Paine*, 1763–70, with interiors completed by *Samuel Wyatt*, 1777–1801. The landscape was remodelled by *Capability Brown*, 1766–72, with

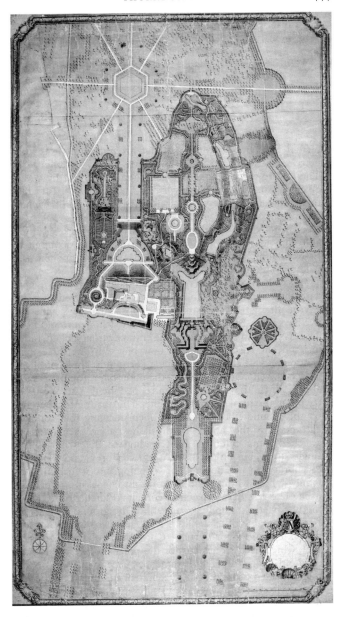

Thorndon Hall.
Design for formal gardens and landscaping by Sieur Bourginion

Thorndon Hall.
Elevation by James Paine

further work by *Richard Woods* after his appointment as Lord
Petre's surveyor in 1783. The house was gutted by fire in 1878.
The E wing was restored as a self-contained house by *George
Sherrin*, 1894, with further work by *Detmar Blow c.* 1913, but
the main part and the W wing remained a shell until the whole
building was bought in 1976 by *Thomas Bates & Son*, who
reconstructed the interior as flats. Part of the park became a
golf club in 1921, much of the remainder was acquired by
Essex County Council in 1939 and 1951 and opened as a
country park in 1971.

Paine's house is a big rectangular block, eleven bays wide
with three main floors and a mezzanine, connected by nine-
bay quadrants to three-storey pavilions, three bays wide and
five bays deep. Stock brick on a rusticated stone ground floor.
This has right in the middle of the entrance front a plain, rather
insignificant Tuscan doorcase, now blocked. The three main
windows above this have aedicule surrounds; the central one
is arched. Venetian windows in the outer bays. Top balustrade,
above which the three-bay centre pediment just rises. The
pavilions also have centre pediments. The quadrants are arched
on the ground floor (originally open, forming the 'common
entrance' to the house) with niches above separated by
attached Ionic columns. That leading to the W pavilion is
single-storey, but on the E side is of two storeys and contained
the library on the upper floor, opening into a 'tribune', i.e.
family gallery within the double-height chapel in the pavilion
itself. The rest of this pavilion contained kitchens etc., while
the W pavilion (entirely rebuilt above the ground floor in the
1970s) contained the stables.* The showpiece of the house is
the six-column giant portico (Corinthian columns) on the S
side, which used stones cut for the portico of *Leoni*'s remodelled old Thorndon Hall. It stands, as usual with Paine, above
the rusticated ground floor. Decorative carving in the tympanum was never completed, and Paine's published design shows
that he intended greenhouses to either side of the S front that
would have balanced the pavilions and hidden the backs of the
quadrants. Behind the portico is now an open courtyard with
stairs and balconies providing access to the flats.

---

* At the time of the 1878 fire the largest of the stables had just been converted into
a skating rink.

The principal evidence of *Brown*'s landscaping is New Hall Pond, 750 yds SSE of Thorndon Hall, remodelled (probably by *Woods*) later in the C18. Mounds E and W of the house survive from the 8th Lord Petre's earlier landscaping, remains of which are also to be found in the southern part of the present country park: Old Hall Pond, with a ziggurat or pyramid on its northern bank, and Octagon Plantation to the E. W of Old Hall Pond is the site of old Thorndon Hall, excavated 1957–9, and beyond it Pigeon Mount, the mound of a dovecote or similar structure that formed part of the old Hall's formal gardens.

LION LODGE and GATEWAY, ¾ m. WSW. Probably by *Paine, c.* 1766. Pair of cubical stuccoed lodges, with arched recesses in the outer faces and in them roundels with male and female heads. Rusticated stone piers with *Coade* stone swags, rams' heads, and lions. OCTAGON LODGE, 900 yds NW. Late C18, possibly by *Woods*. Plastered brick.

CHANTRY CHAPEL, 400 yds SW. By *W. W. Wardell*, 1854, for William, 12th Lord Petre. Nave, sanctuary, sacristy and bell-turret, with coffin lift to vault below. Ragstone, Dec, and small – only 18 by 30 ft (5.5 by 9 metres) internally – but finely detailed, with elaborate carving outside and especially inside. Hammerbeam roof bristling with angels, painted and gilded, and encaustic floor tiles, so that even in its present sorry state (much vandalized; the windows, which had glass by *Hardman & Co.*, have been cemented over) its original character still shines through. Walled KITCHEN GARDEN to the N, contemporary with new Thorndon Hall.

HATCH FARM, ¾ m. S. By *Samuel Wyatt*, 1777. Built as an animal feeding place for the park; partly converted to housing in the C19 and C20. Brick, with slate and pantiled roofs. Central two-storey fodder store, with high lunette windows, with a yard on three sides around which are single-storey feeding ranges, with stalls behind a colonnade of brick columns with stone Tuscan capitals and bases. On the W side of the central building a weatherboarded GRANARY, the frame of *c.* 1600 and probably reused.

THORPE-LE-SOKEN

1020

ST MICHAEL. Mostly rebuilt by *William White*, 1875–6. The early C16 brick W tower was allowed to remain. Blue brick diapers, diagonal buttresses. Bell-openings of two lights with a circle as tracery – all in brick. A pretty weathervane of 1902 on a kind of needle spirelet. Nave, chancel, N and S aisles, N porch and N and S chapels of stone rubble, with limestone and red sandstone dressings, all by White apart from the C15 N aisle and N porch of *c.* 1500, which were heavily restored, refaced and given new windows. Geometric tracery, arcades of round columns with simple carving, all correct and somewhat lifeless. Timber W gallery by *Jeffrey Couzens*, 1991. – FONT. Octagonal, Perp; the sides have star-shaped panels with shields. – SCREEN. S chapel, originally chancel screen. C15. The tracery of each division is of two intersected ogee arches, cusped and crocketed, with carved inscription: 'This loft is the bachelers made by ales, Ihesu be ther med'. – STAINED GLASS. Good collection of windows, 1876–*c*. 1893, by *Clayton & Bell*. – MONUMENT. Stone effigy of a knight in chain-mail, his legs crossed; *c*. 1300. It lies under a later C14 canopy with thin diapered angle buttresses and a cusped and sub-cusped ogee arch. Thick band of crocketing with large bossy leaves.

BAPTIST CHURCH. Modestly set back from the High Street, and entirely domestic in character. Timber-framed, *c*. 1802, with roughcast front and weatherboarded sides, two tiers of sash windows and a large pedimented canopy over the central door. Gallery on iron stanchions, 1820.

THORPE HALL. The C17 house rebuilt or remodelled by *M.G. Thompson* for J.M. Leake, 1822–5, with C20 additions for Viscount Byng, was demolished in 2002. The gardens remain, laid out from 1913 by *Lady Byng* with *Robert Wallace*, including sunken rose garden, cascade, and rock garden.

Nice village street, with at its centre the BELL INN, on the N side of the churchyard, restored 2001 by *Last & Tricker Partnership* after a serious fire. Long five-bay range facing the church, built as the church house or hall for the Guild of St Margaret, *c*. 1500, with a taller wing facing the street added in the mid C16. End wall to road jettied with overhanging gable and carved bressumers. The other highlights are at the extremities. At the NW end, COMARQUES, largish Georgian, brick. Seven bays, two storeys with attics behind a parapet. Above the central doorcase, with pediment and attached Ionic columns, a Venetian window, and above that a Diocletian window in the three-bay pediment. Attributed to *Sir Robert Taylor* on the strength of the characteristic glazing bars on the main front, with a central octagonal pane (cf. Braxted Park); a brick inscribed *W. Whatey*, 1755, probably refers to the master builder. Alterations and additions by *E.A. Rickards* for his friend the novelist Arnold Bennett, who lived here 1913–21.

Opposite, the OLD VICARAGE, 1823–4 with later C19 additions: gault brick three-bay front, Greek Doric portico, the ground-floor windows in arched recesses. Apparently by *Joseph Parkins*.

At the other end of the High Street, just beyond the church, THE ABBEY, which, rendered and painted as it mostly is, now looks rather Neo-Tudor of 1840, but is original, with one crow-stepped end gable and a two-storeyed embattled porch. Over the porch an odd crocketed pinnacle. The material is brick, the date can hardly be later than 1550; its present name dates from the late C18. To the N, in Landermere Road, former POLICE STATION and magistrates' court, 1853 by *Hopper* on the model of Halstead (q.v.). Tudor Gothic.

1 m. s, off Station Road, MALTINGS by *Robert Free*, *c*. 1874–8: long, three-storey block with a pair of kilns near the centre and a third behind. Stock brick with red brick dressings. Next to

them the former KING EDWARD VII pub, 1901, with two large shaped gables and balconies with decorative ironwork.

THORRINGTON

ST MARY MAGDALENE. Fine East Anglian W tower, especially interesting because it can be dated. A BRASS inscription commemorates John and Margery Deth †1477 and 1483, 'specialis benefactor istius ecclie et campanilis ejusdem' (benefactor of this church and bell-tower). The tower is of brick faced with knapped flint, with diagonal buttresses, a three-light W window, two-light openings, and battlements with flushwork panels – all in the style of neighbouring Brightlingsea but more modest. The church itself is of pebbles with stone dressings – the N aisle looks as though it were a cobble pavement put up vertically – with the conspicuous exception of the C14 S porch, which has brick quoins and dressings on the pattern of the Norman use of Roman bricks. Restored (except the tower) by *Ewan Christian*, 1866–7: upper part of the walls rebuilt with new roof, gallery of 1813 removed, and new floors, pews, and other furnishings. His is the ornate and lifeless N arcade. – FONT. Octagonal, Perp. Stem with buttresses and tracery panels, partly defaced, bowl with leaves and shields. – Late C17 wrought-iron HOURGLASS STAND by pulpit. – COMMANDMENTS painted on metal, very colourful and decorative, by *G.A. Read* of Colchester, 1873. – STAINED GLASS. E window and others, decorative, part of Christian's restoration. – BRASS. John Clare †1564 and family. Only one of his two wives (18-in. (46-cm.) figure) and some children remain.

METHODIST CHURCH. 1905, by *Eade & Johns*. Chapel with schoolroom and vestry. Brick with stone and stock brick dressings.

GATEHOUSE FARM, 1 m. SW. In front of a nondescript farmhouse dated 1883 is the eponymous gateway: early C16 brick with stone jambs, finished with a moulded and crowstepped gable.

At the head of Alresford Creek, 1 m. WSW of the church, a TIDE MILL dated 1831, maintained in working order by Essex County Council. White-painted weatherboarding on brick plinth with cast-iron water wheel at the W end. Three storeys with loft and lucam. The MILL HOUSE stands above the mill to the E, C19 brick front with reused C18 porch. 84

THUNDERSLEY

ST PETER. The small medieval church, whose eaves are no more than 9 ft (2.7 metres) from the ground, was transformed in 1965–6 by the building of a new nave in place of the chancel of 1885, by *Alan J. Frost* of *Donald W. Insall & Associates*. The new portion also has low eaves, but is higher and longer than the old, and repeats the steep roof of the old part on a much bigger scale. Side walls mainly window, narrow strips like vertical weatherboarding, but the E wall of stone-like brick with shallow projecting chancel, very tall because of the sloping ground. This makes the shingled W belfry, C15 with splay-foot spire, look even smaller than it would otherwise. Wide, airy interior, the laminated timber framing of the roof exposed with boards between the frames. The old nave, used as a W-facing Lady Chapel, is separated from the new by a very large window. Arcades of N and S aisles of the first half of the C13. Circular piers with stiff-leaf capitals of upright leaves and slightly double-hollow-chamfered arches. Large three-light Perp W window, framed internally by the timber substructure of the belfry. – FONT. Small, octagonal, Perp with quatrefoil panels. – HELM. C16, probably funerary.* – STAINED GLASS. In the old part, N aisle by *T.F. Curtis, Ward & Hughes*, 1898, S aisle by *Chapel Studio*, 1984, incorporating fragments of C15 glass, and W window, 1901, to Rev. W.W. Talfourd, including a small photograph of him. – In the new part, full-height N and S sanctuary windows by *Ray Bradley*, 1966, representing Peter the man and Peter the saint.

The church is on a hill with wide, if not particularly inspiring, views to the W. Thundersley is now part of the dormitory miles along the A13, and has no character as a village, but THUNDERSLEY LODGE still stands, ⅔ m. ESE. C16 timber-framed, faced with red and black brick, with many alterations and additions, notably an extension of 1901 with shaped gable.

SOUTH EAST ESSEX SIXTH FORM COLLEGE (SEEVIC), Kiln Road/Runnymede Chase. 1970–2 by the *County Architect's Dept* (principal architect in charge, *Jack Sorrell*, project architect, *Derek Heath*). Built on the SEAC system, part faced in brick, part with asbestos cement panels, and part with softwood cladding. One- and two-storey, round two large and three small courts, with octagonal drama and music workshop at the SW corner and sports hall to the N.

TILBURY
Thurrock U.A.

ST JOHN THE BAPTIST. By *Sir Arthur Blomfield & Sons*, 1902–3, replacing a temporary church of 1883. Brick with stone dressings. Two bays of an intended four-bay nave, with polygonal W baptistery, N and S aisles, and S porch. There was originally a clerestory, taken down in 1919, and there was a temporary roof and E end until the church was completed by *Harold Mileson*, c. 1965, still very much short of Blomfield's intentions. – STAINED GLASS. Three charming small baptistery windows by *Reginald Hallward*, 1904.

---

*Accompanying SWORD stolen in 1965.

OUR LADY STAR OF THE SEA (R.C.), Dock Road. By *R.L. Curtis*, 1906–7. E.E. Bright yellow brick with red brick dressings. PRESBYTERY and CONVENT OF MERCY in the same materials.

ST ANDREW'S COMMUNITY CHURCH (Methodist), Calcutta Road. 1966, by *K. Cheeseman*. Octagonal, with short spire.

TILBURY DOCKS. Authorized by Parliament in 1881, constructed by the East and West India Dock Company, and opened in 1886; engineers, *August Manning* and *Donald Baynes*, with *F. C. Ahlfeldt*. Unlike the existing London docks upstream, with their large warehouses, Tilbury was a transit dock for both cargo and passengers, so that the railway, which had come to Tilbury (with a loop down to the river for the Gravesend ferry) in 1854, was an essential element of the scheme. The original docks consisted of a MAIN DOCK, 1,800 ft (549 metres) long and 600 ft (183 metres) wide, with three branches off it, each 1600 ft (488 metres) long and 300 ft (91 metres) wide, linked to a tidal basin by three locks to the S. By 1900, the port was handling a million tons of cargo each year. In 1909 the Port of London Authority took over and set about expansion. The main dock was extended westwards in 1912–17, and again in 1929, when a new lock was opened that is now the only entrance, from the W. The size of the docks was approximately doubled, 1963–70, to accommodate container ships, which signalled the end for the docks upstream. Along the river, a concrete cargo jetty (now disused) was opened in 1921 and passenger terminal in 1930. For the latter the PLA's architect, *Sir Edwin Cooper*, designed RIVERSIDE STATION (now closed) and BAGGAGE HALL (now London International Cruise Terminal), 1925–30.[*] Formal Neo-Georgian brick and Portland stone, with symmetrically placed cupolas, big stone surrounds of arches à la Somerset House, etc. Baggage Hall of thirteen bays, Riverside Station eleven, the latter joined to a five-bay block, partly a (former) pub. A future extension to the Baggage Hall, never built, would have balanced the Station. The vast basilica-like hall (now subdivided), 273 ft (83 metres) long and 75 ft (23 metres) wide, with aisles and barrel-vaulted central portion. Inside, at the W end, First and Second World War memorials, including STAINED GLASS by *Christopher Webb*, 1952. The hall is built on a ferro-concrete platform and connected by booms and walkways to the floating LANDING STAGE, on which is a two-storey timber building of waiting rooms and offices, by engineers *F. Palmer* and *F.W. Davis*.

A small town rapidly grew up NE of the docks, all now replaced by housing of varying quality. Some of the best was built 1920–7 by the Urban District Council (District Surveyor, *S.A. Hill-Willis*), particularly in the N either side of St Chad's Road

---

[*] Fire station and housing NW of the Baggage Hall built for the Authority earlier in the 1920s by *Cooper* have been demolished, as has the Tilbury Hotel by *E.A. Gruning*, 1886 (bombed in 1944).

and Feenan Highway, and including housing by *Pepler & Allen*,
e.g. in NORTH VIEW AVENUE, SOUTH VIEW AVENUE, and
the circle where they meet. The centrepiece of the new Tilbury
was CIVIC SQUARE, an ambitious scheme by *Adshead &
Ramsey* with council offices, concert hall etc. in the middle of
a large square flanked by piazza-like rows of shops and flats.
Only partially executed, 1922–4, with single-storey Neo-
Georgian offices (the central feature, like a Georgian town hall
raised on columns over an open space, was not built), and a
row of shops along the N side, the shopfronts separated by
attached Tuscan columns and with two floors of flats above. In
the W of the town, some dismal housing of the 1960s on the
Broadway Estate, but between DARWIN ROAD and ADE-
LAIDE ROAD a small block by *Sergison Bates* (job architect, *Tim
Rettler*) for the New Islington and Hackney Housing Association, 2002–3. Ten flats on two floors, the upper floor reached
by outside stairs and balcony. Semi-prefabricated open-panel
timber frame, faced on the front with timber and elsewhere
with cement panels. Assisted self-build, with unskilled young
people working alongside the contractors.

TILBURY FORT

Built in 1670–83 against the Dutch and French, to command the
Thames in conjunction with New Tavern Fort at Gravesend
on the S side of the river. Designed by a Dutchman, *Sir Bernard
de Gomme*, a military engineer under Charles II. In plan it is a
pentagon, though one of the five bastions, nearest the river,
was never built. Another enclosed a blockhouse of 1539 (cf.
East Tilbury) which survived, altered, until a major remodelling begun in 1868 under *Colonel Charles Gordon*. These alterations were in turn masked by emplacements of *c.* 1913. The
profile of the fort is low and the main construction is of brick-
revetted earthworks, with such buildings as there are of brick
also. It is protected by inner and outer moats on the W, N, and
E sides; surviving outworks include a covered way on the land
between the two moats, and the ravelin in the inner moat. Two
wooden bridges over the moats rebuilt in 1982.

64   The main entrance is the WATER GATE on the S side, the
fort's principal architectural feature, and unlike the Landport
Gate on the N side designed consciously for display as well as
for defence. It is slightly later and less ornate than that of the
Plymouth Citadel, earlier and more ornate than those at
Portsmouth. All the display is on the stone S façade. It has a
ground floor of the triumphal arch type, with four Ionic demi-
columns, an archway with depressed head and trophies in the
spandrels, and an upper storey only as wide as the central part
below. Two Corinthian columns either side of a round-headed
niche carry a segmental pediment with the Stuart arms. To the
l. and r. of the upper part are thickly carved trophies including cannons. The type of gateway derives from C17 France; the
style is more robust and a little fussier than that of Sir Christopher Wren.

Inside the Water Gate the GUARDROOM, late C17 (rainwater heads dated 1715 probably a later addition), and CHAPEL on the upper storey with tall round-headed windows. Most of the interior of the fort is taken up with a large (2½-acre) parade ground. On the E the site of the soldiers' barracks, on the W side a terrace of OFFICERS' HOUSES, 1772. Stock brick. Two storeys, twenty-three bays, central round-headed doorway under a ground-floor open pediment with a circular window above, and six other doors, although the original arrangement may have been for twenty-two separate quarters. Behind the terrace, earth-covered powder magazines of the 1860s. In the middle of the N side are the earlier POWDER MAGAZINES, 1716,* with massive buttresses lacking their original finials, blast walls added 1749, and reconstructed internally in the 1860s and given flat-domed roofs. Between them the LAND-PORT GATE with gatehouse over, the gateway itself of Portland stone, but with minimal decoration.

TILBURY-JUXTA-CLARE

7040

ST MARGARET. In the fields under a few large trees. C15 nave and chancel (Perp windows). Brick tower added by Elizabeth de Vere, Countess of Oxford, in 1519, according to a renewed inscription. Blue brick diapering, diagonal buttresses, battle-ments, and a higher stair-turret. Walls embellished with frag-ments of carved stonework collected by *Margaret Anna Brett*, wife of Rev. C.W. Brett, rector 1898–1943. – PULPIT with two tiers of arches with plaited ornament in each panel; Elizabethan. – WALL PAINTINGS. Late C15 fragments, with late C16 overpainting, on nave walls. Chiefly ornamental, but also a scene with a man on a white horse in front of a house which exhibits clearly its brick-nogging between the timber studs. In the chancel, in imitation of the ornamental parts of the old work, very rustic decoration by *M. A. Brett*. – STAINED GLASS. Fragments of C15 glass in E window, re-set by *John Hayward*, 1980.

TILBURY HALL, 250 yds SW. T-plan house, at the centre of which is the former cross-wing of a C14 aisled hall, the latter rebuilt in the late C15 or early C16. Later C16 additions.

TILBURY COURT, ¼ m. SE. Built 1882 by Lewis John Way of Spencer Grange, Great Yeldham. Brick with burnt headers, three irregular gables, now shorn of its service wing.

TILLINGHAM

9000

ST NICHOLAS. Between 604 and 616, but probably in 608, the parish of Tillingham was granted to Mellitus, Bishop of

---

*When *Nicholas Hawksmoor* was designing for the Royal Ordnance at Tilbury and elsewhere, but there seems to be no direct evidence to link him with these buildings.

London, by King Ethelbert of Kent, to help finance his Monastery of St Paul. The Dean and Chapter of St Paul's Cathedral are still the patrons of the living. Parts of the present church are C12 or earlier: the W half of the chancel and the N nave wall, notably the N door. Walls of septaria and flint rubble, originally rendered; this covering reinstated on the chancel's S and E walls, 2001. The chancel was extended in the C13 and has three stepped E lancets and a quatrefoil above and single lancets on the N and S sides – all renewed outside, probably as part of the restoration of the chancel by *C. R. Ainslie*, 1855. The plain SEDILIA and PISCINA also belong to the C13. C14 S arcade of four bays with octagonal piers and double-chamfered arches, covered up when the S aisle was taken down in 1708 and renewed when the aisle was rebuilt (and S porch added) by *Chancellor* as part of his restoration of the nave, 1864–6. The chancel arch of the same style. The W tower also C14, with angle buttresses and W window of two cusped lights with pointed quatrefoil in the spandrel. Later battlements, the tower restored in 1887–8, including new staircase turret, again by *Chancellor*. Then in 1890–1 he replaced the nave and chancel roofs, added the N organ chamber and vestry, introduced steps up to the sacrarium and provided the sanctuary walls with their marble cladding. – FONT. Late Norman, with plain square bowl with attached angle shafts. Carved foliage. – STAINED GLASS. E window by *Frederick Drake* of Exeter, 1897, who also did the six side windows, since replaced by *A.K. Nicholson Studios*. – BRASS to Edward Wiot †1584, nicely detailed kneeling figure, 11½ in. (30 cm.) (chancel S wall, behind a door in the panelling).

Attractive village street widening just S of the church into a green (The Square). The buildings are predominantly weatherboarded, but there are also three pairs of brick and tile-hung cottages by *Chancellor*, more Sussex than Essex, erected by the Dean and Chapter of St Paul's in 1881. No fewer than four PUMPS, of which the most elaborate is opposite the W end of the church. Brick PRIMARY SCHOOL on the W side of The Square by *Wild Stammers* of Southminster, 1861, enlarged 1881 by *Chancellor*, who also did the schoolmaster's house, 1874.

5020   TILTY

Foundation of a Cistercian ABBEY in 1153 (dissolved 1536). It was laid out as usual with the church S of the cloister, the refectory N, the chapter house and dormitory E, and cellarer's quarters W of it. To the E of the main group was the infirmary, with double-aisled hall. The buildings are recorded in a map by *Ralph Agas* of 1594, but all that survives above ground is a few fragments of the E wall of the cellarer's range with springers of a vault, and the W wall of the refectory. Brick was used in the construction, as well as flint rubble and clunch. But 150 yds to the S is the parish church of Tilty, ST MARY THE VIRGIN, once the *capella extra portas* of the monastery (cf. Coggeshall). The nave is E.E. with lancets, and very similar to the Coggeshall chapel. The three w lancets are particularly handsome. The two plain doorways on the N and S sides are also original. The chapel was, as at Coggeshall, originally nave and chancel in one – see the E window on the S side, with a higher sill than the others to leave space for the double piscina and aumbry. Below the piscinae, a small area of C13 masonry pattern, with zigzag border, in red and grey-blue, all that remains of extensive internal coloured decoration. S porch probably C17. The w belfry and cupola seem to be C18 or early C19. The overall effect (apart from the small C19 N vestry) is unusual and charming, the walls plastered and painted a shade of ochre. But *c.* 1330 was added the chancel, taller, wider, and much more ambitious, the gift of a rich man, or the beginning of a larger rebuilding scheme. It is in the sumptuous style of the moment. Here the flint and stone is left exposed, with chequerwork at the base of the E wall, and a five-light E window the tracery of which is of a very personal style. Niches outside to the l. and r. of the window, placed at an angle and cutting halfway into the buttresses, a large three-light N window of more usual character, and a two-light S window with a higher sill to allow for the sedilia and double piscina below. These have cusped arches, the cusping also being of quite a personal pattern. The windows are shafted inside and have hoodmoulds with headstops. Headstops also to the l. and r. of the sedilia–piscina group. Most of the glass is clear, and the lightness of the chancel interior is most striking, enhanced by the removal of the C18 plaster ceiling by *H. T. Rushton* in 1975.

S. Dykes Bower made various changes to the interior, mainly 1959–62, including reconstructing the 'gallery', no more than a small enclosure, at the w end. His are the C17-style PULPIT, and the FONT, both incorporating fragments of stonework from the abbey; the sounding board of the pulpit and the wooden FONT COVER have pretty decorative painting attributed to the *Marquis d'Oisy* (cf. Thaxted). – STAINED GLASS. Heraldic panels in w window by *Pilgrim Wetton*, 1952, who also designed the CRUCIFIX on the tympanum above the tie-beam that separates the chancel from the nave. – BRASSES to Gerard Danet, Councillor to Henry VIII, †1520, wife Mary, with five sons and six daughters, the main figures about 3 ft (93 cm.). – George Medeley †1562 and wife Mary, 2-ft (61 cm.) figures, with three sons and two daughters. – Margaret Tuke †1590, with kneeling figures, including three sons, three daughters, and three infants, the main figure 12 in. (30 cm.).

TILTY GRANGE, ¼ m. w. Early C16 with one gabled cross-wing. C17 porch and other additions. To the w an impressive seven-bay weatherboarded BARN, early C17, now a house.

MILL, NW of the abbey ruins. Brick water mill with weatherboarded lucarne. Early C18, heightened in the C19, with C19 machinery largely intact.

8010 TIPTREE

ST LUKE. 1855–6 by *Ewan Christian*. Brick and Caen stone, with shallow polygonal apse and w bellcote. 'Partakes somewhat of the Norman style', said the *Builder* (although the tracery is Dec), and 'has a rather peculiar appearance'. S extension by *Bryan Thomas & Partners*, 1975. – PULPIT. By *E. Geldart*, 1907. – STAINED GLASS. Apse windows by *Clutterbuck*. w window by *A.K. Nicholson Stained Glass Studios*, 1951.

UNITED REFORMED CHURCH. By *F. Barnes*, 1864, on the site of a chapel of 1750. White brick with red brick detailing and lancets. Large hall on w side, complementary in style and materials, by *Lewis Patten*, 2003–4, as well as minister's house.

THURSTABLE SCHOOL. By *H. & H.M. Lidbetter* in association with the County Architect, *H. Conolly*, 1957. Brick, with pitched roofs. Considerably enlarged in the 1970s.

TIPTREE HALL, nearly 1 m. SSW. John Mechi bought 130 acres of poor-quality land in 1841 and established an experimental farm, although even his successful methods did not protect him from the agricultural depression of the 1870s and he died bankrupt in 1880. He built the present house, of stuccoed brick, four bays and two storeys with Tuscan porch. Part of Mechi's model farmstead survives.

TIPTREE PRIORY, 2 m. SW. Fragment of an Elizabethan brick mansion. What remains looks now excessively tall and rather gaunt. It was the l. half of the frontage of a house which in addition had one or perhaps two lower wings coming forward. The chief features are a doorway with a four-centred head and a big steep pediment above and a number of transomed four- and five-light windows, some of them (especially those in the E wall) reused.

The parish of Tiptree Heath was created in 1859 out of portions of six parishes; before that the village did not exist as a sepa- rate entity, and the Heath (which stretched from Messing to Heybridge) was shared by no fewer than fourteen parishes. The steady growth of the village is largely due to A.C. Wilkin, who in 1885 progressed from fruit-farming to jam-making, and the coming of the railway in 1904. The latter closed in 1951, but development continues apace. In an otherwise undistinguished main street TESCO stands out. By the *Saunders Partnership*, 2002: boldly contemporary, powder-coated steel cladding with large areas of glass set back behind deep canopies, and corner pavilions like brick-legged tables. Large tile panel by *Ned Heywood* and *Julia Land* depicts aspects of Tiptree's heritage.

WATERWORKS, Grange Road. Pumping station, *c.* 1935, for the South Essex Waterworks Co., in their Modern Movement style. Concrete, with tall windows of glass blocks. Employees' housing to the w. Water was pumped from Langham on to the reservoir at Abberton (qq.v.).

WINDMILL. Brick tower mill, with a datestone of 1775 (no sails). Now a house.

TOLLESBURY

St Mary. Nave and w tower CII, see the nave N and S windows
high up and the rere-arch of the S doorway. The imposing brick
tower, its lower stages of rubble and flint, was heightened
in brick about 1600 and has stepped battlements. Chancel
rebuilt and S porch added as part of a general restoration by
Habershon & Brock, 1871–2. N vestry 1955. – REREDOS. Painted
by *Christopher Webb*, 1938. – FONT. Small, octagonal, 1718, with
an inscription: 'Good people all I pray take Care. That in ye
Church you doe not sware. As this man Did'. – STAINED
GLASS. E window by *Kempe*, 1902, also the two small nave
windows (St George and St Cedd), 1921. 'Seafarers' window'
in N wall by *Derek Wilson*, 1963. – MONUMENTS. Brasses to
Thomas Freshwater †1517 (in civilian dress) and wife, figures
19 in. (48 cm.), with a group of nine daughters and indent for
two sons. – Damaged brass of a woman, possibly Margaret
Ransom, *c.* 1510, 14-in. (36-cm.) figure. – Jane Gardiner of
Bourchier's Hall †1654. Handsome tablet with oval inscription
plate surrounded by fanciful scrolls and crowned by a scrolled
pediment.

Congregational Church. By *C. Pertwee*, 1874, with minister's house to N and schoolroom to E. Yellow and red striped
brick. Interior reordered by *Plater Inkpen Vale & Downie*, 1991,
including STAINED GLASS by *James Dodds* and *R. Costley*.

Tollesbury Hall, S of the church. The surviving portion of
a C13 aisled hall with integral service bay and two-bay parlour-
solar crossing at the E end, the latter rebuilt in the C16. Aisles
removed when the floor was inserted in the C16.

The centre of the village is a large square (in fact a triangle) by
the church; in the SE corner, the LOCK-UP, a small weatherboarded shed with pyramidal roof of *c.* 1700, much renewed.
The rest of the village has a curiously urban air, perhaps owing
to the railway that arrived in 1904 (and closed in 1951). In
ELYSIAN GARDENS, SW of the church, a brick MONUMENT,
square and topped by a dome, erected 1852 by Captain Jeremiah Easter, to commemorate Nelson and Wellington and the
planting in 1839 of the now vanished gardens. Off East Street,
THE MOUNT, including a house by *John Fairhead*, 1969–70.
Traditional materials (brick and black weatherboarding) but
otherwise pure Modern Movement: flat roof, projecting semicircular upstairs living room balanced by semicircular staircase. Sympathetically extended with a second semicircular
projection, *c.* 2002. Further E, at the end of WOODROLFE
ROAD, a row of four picturesque timber sail lofts, 1905–11,
refurbished 1984–5 by *Plater Inkpen Vale & Downie*, one their
own office.

Bourchier's Hall, 1 m. NW. The remnant of an aisled hall.
C14 roof with tie-beams, curved braces forming a two-centred
arch, octagonal crown-post with capital and four-way struts.
C16 staircase wing on part of the site of the former E aisle, with
C17 additions to the E. Behind it, BOURCHIER'S LODGE,
c. 1600, with C20 brick-nogging.

TOLLESHUNT D'ARCY

9010

ST NICHOLAS. All Perp with embattled w tower with diagonal buttresses, and embattled s aisle. Of stone rubble, the chancel rendered. In the Darcy Chapel, on the N side of the nave, one brick window. Restored by *Pye & Hayward*, 1879–80 (including new benches and choir stalls, pulpit, and floor of *Minton* tiles), and more extensively in 1897–8 by *E. Geldart*. This included removing the w gallery and opening out the w window, and rebuilding the C16 N vestry with the E wall further w, opening up the chancel N window. Hagioscope from the Darcy Chapel to the chancel discovered and restored. Extensive stencilled decoration, of which only the chancel ceiling survives. – REREDOS. 1898, probably by *Geldart*; now on chancel s wall. Triptych, the middle panel a copy of a painting of the Holy Family by *William John Müller*, the side panels copies of angels by *Fra Angelico*. – ORGAN. Console in chancel made *c.* 1845 and formerly in the chapel at Bowood, Wilts. Elaborately carved with panels of St Cecilia and women at prayer inside the doors, and topped with a scallop said to come from an organ designed by *William Kent* for a house in Charles Street, London. Rebuilt by *R.H. Walker & Son*, 1957–8, with the pipes in an over-large w gallery by *Carden & Godfrey*. – SCULPTURE. Painted plaster bas-relief of a kneeling angel by *Robert Anning Bell*. – STAINED GLASS. In the Darcy Chapel, N window with fragments of C14–C16 glass, and an early C17 tulip, an unusually early representation of that flower. – E window by *Alexander Gibbs*, 1880. Chancel s by *A.L. Wilkinson*, 1954. Nave N (Millennium Window) designed by *Michael Smee*, made by *Andrew Fawcett*, 2000. – In porch, w by *Wilkinson*, 1964, E by *Joseph Nuttgens*, 1967.

MONUMENTS. In chancel, monument of Sussex marble thought to be to Thomas Darcy †1558. In s wall, recess with depressed segmental top and a quatrefoil frieze above. Indents of brasses in the back wall. Converted into SEDILIA. In N wall, what appears to be the front of the tomb, with three diamond-shaped panels and indents for three heraldic brasses. – Thomas Darcy †1593, erected by his wife Camilla Guicciardine of Florence. The usual design of marble wall monument, two kneeling figures and smaller figures of three sons and six daughters. Attributed to *Garat Johnson the Elder* (AW). – In Darcy Chapel, a collection of BRASSES, the oldest being part of Robert le Wale †1362 and his wife Matilda. Flemish, with ornamental background of a vine, the Creed on a ribbon running through it. In the central panel, the Virgin and Child. The two outer panels are engraved on both sides, with the symbols of SS Mark and Luke and figures of SS Bartholomew, Philip, James the Less and Thomas. The Wale inscription was reversed and used for Anthony Darcy †1540 (now mounted separately). 47-in. (119-cm.) figure, and very curious, because he is shown wearing armour that is a mixture of the C15 and C16. – 26-in. (66-cm.) figure of a man in armour, the top of his helmet and other details missing. Probably John de Boys †1419. Now mounted with him, a woman, 27-in. (68.5-cm.) figure, thought to be his wife Margaret. – 18-in. (45-cm.) figure of a Lady, possibly Katherine Darcy †1535; on the reverse, part of the brass of an abbot or bishop in vestments, c. 1400. – Philippa Darcy †1559. 20-in. (50-cm.) figure.

D'ARCY HALL, s of the church. Built (or rebuilt) by Anthony Darcy, c. 1500–10. Two ranges, formerly three; that on the E demolished 1789–90, when the w range was rebuilt. The N range, although uniformly rendered and with C18 and C19 windows, retains many original internal features. On the ground floor, original entrance doorway leading to the screens passage with two wooden doorways and one original door to the buttery and pantry on the r. On the l., single-storey hall, with large fireplace. Above, the original tie-beams, crown-posts and four-way struts of the roof of the upstairs chamber survive, with no blackening, the room now subdivided and with a ceiling introduced. In the entrance hall of the w wing, very fine reused panelling of c. 1525–30, partly with linenfold, partly with Early Renaissance foliage, vases, medallions with heads, etc., including the initials A.D. and the Darcy arms. To the NE a late C16 rectangular brick DOVECOTE; hipped roof with gablets that were the original entry for the birds, and an C18 timber louvre. Fine MOAT, with a single BRIDGE of four round arches dated 1585 built of bands of brick and stone.

The village street N of the church is dominated by D'ARCY HOUSE. Fine seven-bay Georgian brick front with four attic dormers behind a high parapet. To its r. D'ARCY COTTAGE, it smaller size more than compensated for by an impressive pedimented doorcase with attached Ionic columns (said to have come from D'Arcy House). Road junction with a very tall maypole and on the N side MAYPOLE HOUSE, with charming C19 trellis porch.

TOLLESHUNT KNIGHTS

ALL SAINTS. Ceased to be a parish church in 1957, and no village anywhere near. C12 nave, the chancel rebuilt and extended in the C14; C15 N door and one C15 window on each side of the nave. Various C19 restorations, including one of 1877–8 by *Richard Armstrong*, when the w bellcote was added, and another in 1896 by *E. J. Dampier*, when the timber porch was rebuilt on the brick base of c. 1600. Interior reordered for the Eastern Orthodox Community with the E end screened off to form a vestry and an open ironwork iconostasis. – MONUMENT. Knight of c. 1380, holding his heart in his hands. Much defaced.

The Eastern Orthodox Community was established in the OLD RECTORY in 1959, the first community house of the Greek Orthodox Church in England. Additional buildings include a refectory, 1975–8, chapel (ST SILOUAN THE ATHONITE) by

Alan Bragg, 1982–5, the latter a plain box of rendered brick with western narthex, triple apse and bell-tower and only a narrow strip of windows high up, both with extensively painted interiors by members of the community, and a residential building by *Geof Clark*, 1984–8, decorated externally with mosaics.

In Darcy Road, WOODACRE by *Penoyre & Prasad*, c. 1991. Housing for people with learning disabilities, mostly set round a courtyard. Brick and stained timber cladding, with mono-pitch aluminium roofs.

TOLLESHUNT MAJOR

ST NICHOLAS. A humble church of nave and chancel, the S porch added by *E. Geldart*, 1888, as part of restoration. His also the N vestry, where there had once been a N chapel. Pudding-stone predominates. At the W end, in about 1545, Stephen Beckingham of Beckingham Hall decided to place a splendid brick tower, much too big for the older building. It is patterned with diapers of blue brick and has diagonal buttresses with four set-offs and very low battlements. The W windows are of three and two lights, the bell-openings of three with a depressed pointed head. C14–C15 roofs, with the remains of supports for a belfry at the W end of the nave. – FONT. Against the S wall. Half an octagon, Perp, with rosettes and shields. – WALL PAINTING. On S wall, remains of a C15 figure.

BECKINGHAM HALL, NE of the church. The manor was granted to Stephen Beckingham by Henry VIII in 1543. This house was greatly reduced in size in the C18 and is now unremarkable, part timber-framed and part brick, with a plain early C19 front. But to the SW is an extraordinary enclosure of Early Tudor brickwork, over a hundred feet (30 metres) square, indicating that something much more impressive once stood here. A gate-house forms the centre of a long wall, which is partly diapered. To the NW of this a corner turret, as thin as a pinnacle, and to the SE another turret which serves as the gatepost of a gateway of which the other post is also a turret, and which were prob-ably once joined by an archway. The gatehouse has two circu-lar turrets to the outside, one of which continues as a chimney, and two to the inside. The doorways have four-centred heads, and above them are two-light windows. The house that Beck-ingham built to go with this grand entrance can be deduced from two estate maps, as well as from the NE wall of the present house, the brickwork of which matches that of the gatehouse. A map by John Walker of 1616 shows a three-storey house with three gables, but by 1637 (the year after the house passed out of the family) it had been transformed into an E-plan house of two storeys with six gables, aligned with the gatehouse. Until 1912 it contained a piece of ornamental panelling, now in the Victoria and Albert Museum, dated 1546. The panels have fine Early Renaissance decoration, rather in the style of the stalls and screen of the chapel of King's College, Cambridge. The central bearded demi-figure in a medallion is especially comparable. They are probably the work of a Fleming or Italian woodcarver, or of an English one who had received a good training.

TOPPESFIELD

7030

St Margaret of Antioch. Brick w tower, 1699. On the w side together with other names that of the bricklayer, *Daniel Hill*, is recorded. The tower has arched windows and turrets at each corner with obelisk pinnacles. The distinguishing feature is the parapet, with two troughs on each side which meet at little plinths that originally carried more pinnacles. Nave and chancel c14, the walls of flint rubble, plastered. s aisle with an arcade on octagonal piers, carrying double-chamfered arches. The chancel on its s side has a group of cusped arches, first a low broad recess containing a tomb-chest with quatrefoil decoration, then two single SEDILIA and then the PISCINA. Windows all Perp. Porches c15, w gallery probably the same date as the tower but with a late c18 or early c19 front of reused panelling. – STAINED GLASS. In the tracery of the s aisle E window, fragments of c15 glass: Coronation of the Virgin and censing angels. – E window by *E.R. Frampton*, perhaps 1895, when the church was restored. – Chancel s †1908 by *Mayer & Co.* – MONUMENTS. Knight of *c.* 1260, cross-legged with flat-topped pot-helmet, Purbeck marble. Beneath the organ, as are brasses of John Cracherood †1534 and wife, and William and Elizabeth Cracherood †1585 and 1587. – Dorcas Smyth †1633, signed by *John Colt the Younger*. A display of emblems, without effigy: for Spes a heart, for Charitas a hand pointing upward, and for Fides a dove, now missing. A lamb and beehive presumably denote two of Dorcas' other qualities, humility and industry. Scrolled pediment supported on piles of books with devotional titles.

The centre of the village is a triangular space at the top of the main street, with a pump under a large timber shelter in the middle, painted brick CONGREGATIONAL CHAPEL of 1881 on the w side, and the church up a lane to the E. Opposite the church, CHURCH FARM HOUSE, *c.* 1500, the front jettied and partly underbuilt. The first floor was originally an undivided space, probably a guildhall. On the w side of the main street, set back from the road, BERWICK HALL, early c17 but much altered, and to its s the early c16 OLD RECTORY. On the E side, cottages, some thatched, including No. 59, *c.* 1600 with cross-wing to the r., *c.* 1700, and a simple arcade scheme of painting on the first floor. At the s end, blocks of two and three cottages (Nos. 63–65 and 67–71) by *George Truefitt*, *c.* 1859–62. Brick, with bands of black brick and striped relieving arches, although one of the block of three (which cost £284 to build) has been rendered. N of the chapel, at the beginning of

STAMBOURNE ROAD, a terrace of six cottages, with jettied half-timbered upper storey, perhaps also by Truefitt.

TOPPESFIELD HALL, ½ m. SE. Late C16, its external appearance largely early C20, but with some original panelling and an early C17 fireplace from OLIVER'S FARM, ¼ m. S. The latter also late C16 but with earlier origins. Of two storeys, both unusually high. Chamfered beams with lamb's-tongue stops and the posts of the ground-floor hall with carved jowled heads. Two-storey porch, and rear staircase tower, by *James Blackie*, 2003–4.

BRADFIELDS, 1 m. SW. Mainly C16. Cross-wing to the r. jettied, with exposed timber framing, along the return. The rest plastered, including the l. cross-wing added in the C17 or C18, with C18 sashes and doorcase. Inside, some C16 wall paintings with flower and leaf designs.

CUST HALL, ⅔ m. SSW. Plastered E front with jettied upper storey, partly underbuilt; carved bressumer; smaller, plainer range facing N. Both parts of *c.* 1500, but the E range has been moved here from elsewhere and both its floors were originally undivided, suggesting that it was a guildhall or other public building.

HOSES, nearly 1 m. SSW. C15 or C16. Two gabled and jettied cross-wings, the upper parts of which are plastered. The rest of the E front has exposed framing with brick-nogging.

At GAINSFORD END, 1½ m. SW, a few good thatched cottages; GAINSFORD HALL, C16 with a range of weatherboarded farm buildings; and a brick TOWER MILL dated 1869, now derelict but with some machinery intact.

TWINSTEAD

99　ST JOHN THE EVANGELIST. 1859–60 by *Woodyer*. The fourth church on the site: the medieval church was rebuilt in 1791,* but replaced shortly afterwards by a building deemed in 1858 to be 'very inferior with no ecclesiastical character attaching to it'. Woodyer's church is every bit as ecclesiastical as one could hope for, although the plan is modest: nave, chancel, bellcote, S porch and small N vestry. Brick, with patterns of black-and-white bricks used on the outside to make a narrow blank arcade, and on the inside to create more dazzling effects of arcades, arches and trellis. Stone chancel SCREEN, the arches of equal height and embellished with ornamental brasswork and gilt cross, Caen stone REREDOS with painted and gilt panels, SEDILIA beneath a low pointed window (like the head of a full-size window), *Minton* and *Poole* encaustic TILES, especially colourful in the chancel. Metalwork by *Filmer & Mason*, stonework by *Keogh* of Sudbury. – FONT. Octagonal, stone

---

* Foundation stone built into the garden wall of Twinstead Hall, with the names of *John Bradford*, carpenter, and *Isaac Slythe*, bricklayer and mason.

inlaid with marble, on a central stem and eight small marble shafts. Painted wooden COVER with elaborate wrought-iron lifting frame, the counterweight in the shape of a dove. – STAINED GLASS. Chancel windows by *Hardman*. Remarkably good. – MONUMENTS. Brass to Marie Wyncoll †1610, her husband Isaac †1638, and five daughters, the main figures 25 in. (63 cm.). – In churchyard, Marianne Pocklington †1860 and Frances Shortland †1877. In the form of a churchyard cross, the base decorated with encaustic tiles.

SPARROW HALL, ¾ m. WSW. Late C16, with a very tall, original chimneystack. Restored by *Basil Oliver*, 1928–9.

UGLEY

ST PETER. Early C16 brick W tower with low diagonal buttresses and battlements. Flint-rubble nave, the S wall W of the door and the N wall probably C13. The rest 1862–5 by *William Brown* of King's Lynn: chancel restored (all new windows), S chapel rebuilt, N chapel, vestry and organ chamber added. – STAINED GLASS. E window by *Morris & Co.*, 1882. Panels by *Burne-Jones* (painted by *Bowman* and *J.H. Dearle*), and by *Pozzi*, in background of patterned quarries by *Singleton*, with scrolls and other tracery by *George Campfield*. Repairs by *Titcomb*, 1905. – Chancel S, *c.* 1866, and others of *c.* 1893. – MONUMENTS. Samuel Leightonhouse of Orford House †1823. By *J. Bacon Jun.* and *S. Manning Sen.* Draped urn.

UGLEY HALL. Two-storey, five-bay range of painted brick. Middle three bays *c.* 1840, extended later in the C19 and C20. Gardens on S side laid out by *Brenda Colvin*, 1937, including raised herbaceous borders.

The main centre of population is at UGLEY GREEN, 1 m. SSE. A few thatched cottages, including THE OLD PLACE, C17 but much extended, and two large late C19 or early C20 houses: TUDOR PARK, mock-Tudor with exposed timbers, gabled and jettied cross-wings, tall chimneys, etc., and GREEN PLACE, Arts and Crafts vernacular with tile-hanging, irregularly distributed gables, bays etc. On the E side of the Green, the former SCHOOL by *G. E. Pritchett*, 1851. Brick with stone dressings.

ORFORD HOUSE, 1 m. SSW. Built *c.* 1700 by Admiral Edward Russell, created Earl of Orford in 1697. It stands beside the Cambridge road, almost exactly half-way between London and Orford's principal seat at Chippenham Park, near Newmarket. Brick, two storeys and attics, the W (road) front originally of six bays with segment-headed windows. Extended by two bays to the l. and two-storey canted bay added by Isaac Whittington (†1773). Asymmetrically placed pedimented doorway on attached Doric columns. Garden front also probably six bays originally, extended by three bays in the late C18 and with a large two-storey bow added. Pedimented Doric porch. Inside, the room with the canted bay has a fine carved chimneypiece, overmantel with fruit basket in broken pediment, and door

surrounds, and Rococo plasterwork ceiling. Stable block with
tall clock tower immediately behind the house, and to the NE
a timber-framed and plastered dovecote on chequered brick
base. Square, with square louvre breaking the pyramidal roof.

THE SQUARE, 300 yds N of Orford House, a picturesque group
of seven mid-C19 cottages in three blocks. Exposed timber
framing, brick nogging, jetties, brick chimneys and other C17-
style elements.

ULTING

ALL SAINTS. Delightfully situated by the Chelmer and Blackwater Navigation. Essentially C13: see the lancet windows in
chancel and nave and the S doorway. The other windows, as
well as the timber belfry, N porch and S vestry, date from the
restoration by *Chancellor*, 1871–3; characteristic reuse of old
materials, for example round the W windows. – FONT. Of
Purbeck marble, early C13, on a C19 base; not square but octagonal, with only one of the usual blank arches per side. The
angles of the octagon are chamfered.

In Crouchmans Farm Road, the former VICARAGE, c. 1845. Neo-
Tudor yellow brick, its iron casement windows with elaborately
latticed glazing bars; additions by *Chancellor*, 1873. The painter
and photographer Humphrey Spender bought the house in
1948 and then in 1968–9 built for himself and his wife THE
STUDIO in the garden behind, one of the earliest works of
Richard Rogers, then in partnership with his wife *Su* (engineer,
Anthony Hunt). One of two executed experiments by Rogers
for a steel-framed structure (the other being a house for his
parents in Wimbledon), built as far as possible with factory-
made components: the width of the buildings, for example, is
determined by the width of the available sheeting for the roof.
In theory, the house was a prototype for a system that was
capable of mass production. Composed of two separate single-
storey pavilions, aligned N–S to minimize the effect of the sun.
The main building contains the living accommodation, its long
sides (42 ft (12.8 metres)) entirely glazed; the secondary building was Spender's studio, top-lit by a single sawtooth roof-
light, with carport at one end. The structural system is
immediately apparent, the stanchion and girder trusses being
not only visible, but painted bright yellow, in contrast to the
unpainted walls of plastic-covered corrugated steel sheeting.
The blank end walls have diagonal steel bracing cables which
are not, however, structural.

Between the church and the vicarage, the former NATIONAL
SCHOOL, 1865. Brick with stone dressings and moderate polychromatic brick decoration. The gable end fits a lot into a small
space: open porch, carved stone band, a pair of pointed
windows, and fancy bargeboards.

ULTING HALL, ¾ m. NNE. Timber-framed and plastered, C16
or earlier, very nicely improved c. 1800. As well as the usual

sashed front and pedimented doorcase, this included a prominent single-storey bow and, inside, a circular staircase with gallery supported on Tuscan columns.

STAMMER'S (formerly Tanhouse) FARM, 1 m. E. With fine late C16 projecting chimneystack. The lower part has a blank stepped gable; the two shafts are set diagonally. Late C20 extension on E side.

THE ELMS, Maldon Road, 1½ m. NE. Late C18 brick, three bays, three storeys. Ground-floor windows in recessed segmental arches (cf. Crix, Hatfield Peverel) either side of a Tuscan doorway. To the w, BAYTREE COTTAGES by *Chancellor*, brick and false half-timbering, *c.* 1873, built for John Piggot of The Elms.

HOE MILL LOCK, ½ m. SE. Lock and lock gates of the Chelmer and Blackwater Navigation, opened 1797 (*see* Introduction, p. 52). Brick with granite coping stones and quoins; also lock-keeper's cottage, with gault brick front. *Robert Mylne* was consulted in 1796 over this particular stretch of the navigation, where a new cut was required.

UNIVERSITY OF ESSEX *0020*

The University lies between Wivenhoe and Colchester. The site is that of Wivenhoe Park and its grounds (*see* below), a total of about 204 acres, and was chosen in 1961. The house was acquired a year later, and a further 63 acres were bought in the 1970s. Professor Albert Sloman was appointed first Vice-Chancellor in 1962. The master plan was presented later that year, and the first students were admitted in 1964. Teaching took place in the existing mansion (now known as Wivenhoe House) and temporary huts while construction of the new buildings got under way; these were first occupied in 1965.

From the start, Essex was to be radically different from the other new universities of post-war England. The architect was *Kenneth Capon* of the *Architects Co-Partnership*, whose scheme 116 planned for a university of 20,000 students, a huge number for its date. In planning terms too Capon's design was entirely *p. 798* novel in attempting to create a compact urban environment within the parkland setting. The academic, social and administrative functions were to be grouped into an unbroken chain of buildings laid out along the line of the valley that runs down from the two lakes N of the mansion towards the River Colne to the w; a third lake was created w of the existing two. The form of the buildings was to be that of a rectangular snake folded round five squares (numbered one to five from w to E), with five small hexagonal buildings in the open courts this created; the squares were raised on stilts and a service road ran beneath, entered from the w. At the E end was to be the Library and, in the new lake itself, an administration block. Traditional halls of residence were dispensed with, and instead student accommodation was to be in up to thirty-one tower blocks,

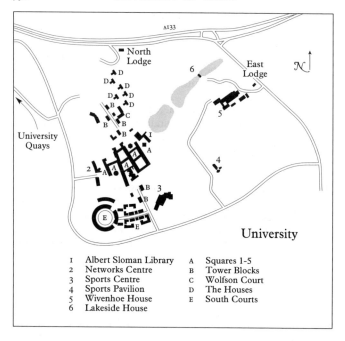

1	Albert Sloman Library	A	Squares 1-5
2	Networks Centre	B	Tower Blocks
3	Sports Centre	C	Wolfson Court
4	Sports Pavilion	D	The Houses
5	Wivenhoe House	E	South Courts
6	Lakeside House		

eighteen on the N side of the valley and thirteen on the S. Sloman's vision was of an academic community in an urban setting, with the buildings kept separate from the diluting effect of traffic and residential buildings; the continuous form of the buildings was meant to enable flexibility and to break down barriers between academic disciplines. Capon's vision was of an Italian hill-town with tower blocks clustered after the manner of San Gimignano.

In fact Essex became a by-word for student unrest in the 1960s, and at least some of the blame for that was placed upon the shortcomings of the buildings, and especially of the TOWER BLOCKS, partly because accommodation was cramped, and partly because there were not enough of them: only six were built, four to the N and two to the S (built later, and made slightly more spacious in response to criticism), before the policy of tower blocks was finally abandoned in 1979. As structures, they are more successful, remarkable for being of load-bearing engineering brick, although the colour – dark blue or grey – makes them sombre under a normal English sky. Of the ACADEMIC BUILDINGS, only about two-thirds were completed: the podia for all five squares were laid, but only three were fully enclosed, and only one hexagon was built, N of Square 4. They have pre-cast column-and-beam construction in high-quality concrete with the pattern of shuttering boldly exposed. The free-standing LIBRARY (named after Sloman) was built between Square 5 and the new lake, its four floors of open-access book stacks fully glazed; extension by *Stanley Bragg*, 1998. Between the Library and the lake, completely underground, is the THEATRE; on the surface, 'Réquiem', stone and slate sculpture by *Ana Maria Pacheco*, 1986–95. On the dam dividing the two old lakes stands the Vice-Chancellor's residence, LAKESIDE HOUSE, which appears to float on the water. Other buildings erected during this first stage of development, 1964–70, were the lecture theatres S of Square 3 by *H. T. Cadbury-Brown*, an irregular massing of halls opening off a central stair hall that creates an ever-changing pattern of levels and vistas, and the sports pavilion to the SW of Wivenhoe House by *Gasson & Meunier*.

The overall impression of the campus is that of buildings which harmonize well with the landscape. The eastern portion of the site, which corresponds roughly to the C18 park, is still mostly parkland and playing fields, with Wivenhoe House at its centre and Lakeside House nestling unobtrusively by the water. Capon's central complex follows the contours of the valley in which it sits; approached from the E, the scale is human, with a gentle progression through the squares to the W. It is only when seen from outside, and particularly from the W (and below), that the sheer size of many of the blocks is appreciated. The massing of the tower blocks changes as one moves round the campus; the 'San Gimignano effect' may never have materialized, and the view from the far side of the Colne is not quite what Capon must have hoped for, but seen from the NW, where the blocks are not quite in line, something of the effect can be gauged.

Development since 1970 has been sporadic. In 1977 *Faulkner-Brown Hendy Watkinson Stonor* built the indoor SPORTS CENTRE to the E of the southern towers, of bright orange and cream brick and shaped to complement the lecture block and sports pavilion. It was designed to be capable of easy extension and this duly happened in 1997 and 2001, by the *University of Essex Estates Section*. N of the Sports Centre, an iron sculpture (untitled) by *Amilcar de Castro*, 1980. *H. T. Cadbury-Brown* added an octagonal GALLERY building N of Square 5 in 1985. Residential accommodation was extended, first with WOLFSON COURT N of Square 4, a one-off by Cadbury-Brown, 1982. L-plan, brick, low-lying, and visually unrelated to anything else – a deliberate riposte, it would seem, to the towers. Beyond that, a group of six two- and three-storey T-plan residential blocks (THE HOUSES) by *Roff Marsh Partnership*, 1991–2. Day nursery W of the N towers by the *University of Essex Estates Section* with Roff Marsh, 1993; nearby a sculpture by *Nigel Hall*, 'Views of the Interior', 1992.

Nicholas Hare Architects produced a twenty-year development plan for the university in 1991, which has given more coherence to the most recent wave of building and also confirmed the departure from Capon's original scheme, with buildings scattered more widely over the campus away from

the central core. The first result was a large residential development in the SW corner of the site, SOUTH COURTS. The first
phase of this, by Hare, was completed in 1993; phases two and
three were completed in 1996 and 2000 by the *Charter Partnership* to Hare's overall design. The result is rather like an
interwar Dutch housing estate, tree-lined streets and courts in
pale yellow brick. N of the Courts, an iron sculpture by *Franz
Weissmann*, 'Fita decrescente no espaço', 1992. Also by Hare
the drum-shaped R.A. BUTLER BUILDING, 1991, on the S side
of Square 2, and the SQUARE 1 BUILDING, with gull-wing
roof, 1993. This lies at the western edge of the academic buildings, on the S side of Valley Road; on the N side, the NET-
WORKS CENTRE by *John Miller & Partners*, 2002–4, its smooth
whiteness contrasting with the rugged grey of much else
around it. Another building with gull-wing roof, by *Stanley
Bragg*, for the DEPARTMENTS OF HISTORY, ACCOUNTING,
FINANCE, AND MANAGEMENT, leads off the N end of Square
4; completed 2002. At the S end of Square 3, an extension to
the BIOLOGICAL SCIENCES FACULTY by *Cullum & Nightingale*, 2001–3, with specialist greenhouses on a flint-clad base.
Curved LECTURE HALL by *Patel Taylor*, SE of Square 5, 2005–6,
with rumpled stainless-steel cladding.

Between the railway (with elegant metal footbridge) and
River Colne, UNIVERSITY QUAYS, a development of 773
study-bedrooms by *Dawe & Geddes Architects*, 2002–3. Blocks
in various combinations of brick, render, and timber-cladding,
some facing the river, some into a street, and some in a curvilinear court. In the latter, a painted steel sculpture, 'Tú y Yo',
by *Armando Varela*, 2004.

WIVENHOE HOUSE was built by Isaac Martin Rebow, whose
father Isaac Lemyng Rebow had purchased the estate in 1734.
Rebow engaged *Thomas Reynolds* of London in 1759, although
work had started the year before; the contract (in the sum of
£3,654) and specification survive. The final payment to
Reynolds was made in 1761. Payments to *Matthew Brettingham
Sen.* in 1762 and 1766 for visits and drawings may relate to
plasterwork and other internal decoration. The park was laid
out by *Richard Woods*, designed 1765, executed 1777–81, with
two lakes separated by a dam below the house to the N. Its
appearance is known from a painting by Constable, 1816;*
close to his viewpoint is a sculpture, 'Standing Stone', by *John
Maine*, 1987. Much of Woods' scheme survives, as well as part
of a boathouse at the eastern end of the upper lake.

Isaac Rebow's house was of two storeys with raised cellars
and attic, the main façade of five bays with the centre slightly
stepped forward and bows on the side elevations; Woods' plan
of the park shows service wings to either side. In 1846–53 it
was remodelled by *Thomas Hopper* for John Gurdon Rebow.
The basic form seems to have been retained but it was given
a thoroughly Tudor appearance: brick with stone dressings, all

---

* Now in the National Gallery of Art, Washington DC.

very elaborate with curved gables, showy strapwork, termini etc. The w wing disappeared, the E was rebuilt as stables. Estate cottages along Clacton Road and Colchester Road are in the same style and no doubt Hopper's work also.

At the same time the park was overhauled by *William Andrews Nesfield*, who probably also laid out gardens near the house, now gone. The two picturesque LODGES date from this time: single-storey, octagonal, with Gothick windows and the roof projecting beyond the walls to form a veranda. The N lodge marks the former main entrance to the park, and is more elaborate with carving round the windows and doors; the E lodge is simpler, as it serves the stables.

The estate was sold in 1902 to Charles Gooch, whose son sold it to the University and moved to Wivenhoe New Park (*see* Greenstead). In 1977 Wivenhoe House was refurbished as a hotel and conference centre, and in 1986–8 was given a banal extension to the SE by *Bryan Thomas Macnamara*. At the same time the John Tabor Building was built as an extension to the stables, by *Roff Marsh Partnership*. Galvanized steel sculpture, 'Spinney', N of the stables, by *Robert Simon*, 1989.

UPSHIRE

4000

Waltham Abbey

ST THOMAS. By *Freeman & Ogilvy*, 1901–2, paid for by Sir Thomas Fowell Buxton Bt of Warlies, a simple building of great quality in the best Arts and Crafts tradition. Perp; nave, chancel and N aisle, roughcast exterior with dressings of Chilmark stone, all consciously based on Essex precedent, including a self-supporting timber W belfry and short shingled spire. Nave roof with crown-posts, and timber N arcade (cf. nearby Theydon Garnon, although the detailing is closer to Shenfield's). – METALWORK, including door furniture, light fittings and weathervane, by *W. Bainbridge Reynolds*. – PLASTERWORK. Decorative chancel ceiling by *L.A. Turner*, also responsible for stone- and woodcarving.

Upshire was a hamlet of Waltham Abbey, with no church before 1902, although *c.* 1855 Sir Edward Buxton (who purchased Warlies in 1851) built a combined chapel and school, designed by *Teulon* (dem.). On Upshirebury Green, at the top of Horseshoe Hill, BURY FARMHOUSE and attached cottages, mainly C18, an attractive weatherboarded group. THE BURY, to the W, two-storey five-bay Georgian brick, remodelled and extended by *K.M.B. Cross c.* 1929 with canted bays.

UPSHIRE HALL, ¾ m. SW. Five-bay Georgian brick front, two storeys and attics, with a central first-floor canted bay, pebbledashed, supported on Doric columns and forming a porch. Two-bay C19 stock brick extension to the l.

WARLIES PARK, ¼ m. N (now offices). The house dates back to the C17 but what can now be seen comes in two strongly contrasting parts. Georgian S front, with a two-storey bow-fronted

Ionic portico in the middle of a seven-bay façade. To the N Sir
T.F. Buxton added a service wing, 1879, designed by *Teulon* in
his unmistakable style: heavily picturesque, e.g. with elephantine brackets carrying a gabled overhanging upper storey, in
grey brick with red and black brick dressings. More successful
STABLE BLOCK to the NW, brick with black diapering, patterned slate roofs, and clock tower, dated 1862; probably also
by Teulon. Grounds landscaped in the first half of the C18,
probably by *William Shenstone*. E of the house, a handsome
ROTUNDA with six Tuscan columns, erected 1737. To the NE a
brick OBELISK, originally stuccoed, said to mark the spot
where Boudicca took poison after being defeated by the
Romans; another, ⅔ m. NW, supposedly where she died.

WOODREDON FARM, nearly 1 m. SSE. Early C18 five-bay, three-
storey brick front with pedimented wooden porch. On the N
side of the house a group of model dairy FARM BUILDINGS by
Maurice Chesterton, *c.* 1931, now stables. Painted brick. The
main building (milking parlour) has a high pantiled roof with
wooden louvre. To the N, WOODREDON HOUSE (Upshire Residential Home), built by T.F.V. Buxton in 1889, extended 1926.
Brick, large, and irregular, with half-timbered gables, square
and canted bays, and tall chimneys. To 1926 belongs the
entrance: doorway with pilasters and broken segmental pediment, above it a large round-headed window set in an aedicule
with open triangular pediment. Probably at this time the fine
C18 staircase with twisted balusters was installed, said to come
from Warlies Park.

VIRLEY

ST MARY. Described by Rev. Sabine Baring-Gould in his novel
Mehalah (1880) as 'a small hunchbacked edifice in the last
stages of dilapidation'. The earthquake of 1884 dealt the *coup
de grâce*, but the ruin still stands. The only feature of strictly
architectural interest is the chancel arch. Transitional style, i.e.
round arch of Reigate stone (the middle fallen) with two slight
chamfers, resting on semi-octagonal responds. Remains of the
nave and chancel walls a mix of Roman brick, septaria, flint
and Kentish rag, including some rare C13 peg-tiles capping
putlog holes etc.

The ruin stands in the grounds of the OLD VICARAGE of
Salcott-cum-Virley. 1880 by *Chancellor*. Brick, with a single
gable to one side of the main front.

WAKES COLNE

ALL SAINTS. Nave, lower chancel, and belfry. Norman windows
in the N and S walls, plain Norman S doorway, and N doorway
with one order of one-scallop capitals and a roll moulding. The
thickness of the chancel walls shows that there was once a

crossing tower, taken down in the C14 when the chancel – perhaps originally longer – was rebuilt. Brick E wall probably 1862, when the church was repaired and re-seated and the S vestry added. In the N and S nave walls one Dec window each, and in the S wall in addition one early C16 three-light brick window. The C15 belfry rests on four posts in a row from N to S with cross-beams and arched braces and a tie-beam a little further E, also with arched braces. War memorial SCREEN, 1920, between the four posts, an unusual and successful design. Chancel reordered by *Duncan Clark & Beckett*, 1936–7, including CHOIR STALLS and other woodwork by *H. & K. Mabbitt.* – FONT. Octagonal, late C12, with three shallow blank arches on each side of the bowl. From Messing, 1848; Purbeck marble base by *Watts* of Colchester, 1930. – WALL PAINTINGS. On E wall of nave, diaper of black roses on white ground, C16. Saints and angels on E wall of chancel, and a separate figure of Christ on N wall, 1911, by *Hemming & Co.*, one panel signed *R.H. Corbould.* – STAINED GLASS. Chancel S signed by *H. Hughes*, 1876, and the N window †1873 no doubt his also. W window by *Jones & Willis*, 1925. – MONUMENTS. William Tyffin †1617. Alabaster frame with shield of arms. – Herbert Brett †1875. Tablet surmounted by an anchor and coiled rope. By *J. Bedford.*

CHAPPEL AND WAKES COLNE STATION. Opened 1849, rebuilt 1890–1, when the original station became the stationmaster's house. Brick. Booking hall and platforms up a double flight of steps. Still in use, but most of the buildings occupied by the East Anglian Railway Museum. In addition to the original signal box, 1891, others from Mistley and Fotherby, Lincs; also a cast-iron urinal from Cockfield, Suffolk.

The village is scattered, with the church lying in the S of the parish near the River Colne. On the N side of the churchyard the former SCHOOL, now offices. 1871–2, brick, extended 1892–3 with tile-hanging and large leaded windows. Former RECTORY, now Wakes Colne House, across the road to the N. Timber-framed, rebuilt by 1747, encased in grey brick and greatly enlarged in the 1840s, including a three-storey service wing to one side.

WAKES HALL, ¼ m. WNW. Gault brick villa, built between 1825 and 1838. Three bays, with Greek Doric porch, and a bow on the W side. On the other side a later C19 three-storey tower, similar to (but smaller than) that at the rectory. Used as a residential home since 1964, with various extensions. Single-storey LODGE in front of the house, and behind it farm buildings including a six-bay brick CART LODGE with Diocletian windows on the upper floor.

CREPPING HALL, 1¼ m. E. Attractive plastered front. Crosswing dating from the C16, remodelled in the C18, and again *c.* 1905, with a large two-storey canted bay. To the r. of this a lower range that contains the remains of a hall, originally aisled, and one which moreover includes in its construction something very rare in Essex, a base cruck, supporting a crown-post roof. It has been tree-ring dated 1301–37.

NORMANDY HALL (formerly Normans Farm), 1 m. NNW. Aisled hall house, of which the S aisle remains, tree-ring dated 1368. The central truss of the hall is without supporting arcade posts, but rests on the arcade plates. Contemporary jettied cross-wing at the E end. S of the house an outbuilding, probably a detached kitchen, tree-ring dated 1527.

OLD HOUSE FARM, ⅔ m. NE. Jettied cross-wings and exposed timber framing. One cross-wing may be C14, to which the hall and other cross-wing were added in the C15. Upper floor of the hall added in the C17, nicely pargetted.

WAKES COLNE PLACE, ¼ m. ESE. Timber-framed, L-plan, C17 or earlier, refronted in gault brick shortly before 1813. Four-bay fronts to NE and SE, with Tuscan porch on the NE and on the SE two large single-storey bows. Further alterations to the rear later in the C19.

WATCH HOUSE, ⅓ m. E. C16, with cross-wing to l., lower cross-wing to r., and a third gable to the hall between them.

WATER MILL, ¼ m. SE of the church. Brick, with hipped and gambrelled slate roof, and adjoining two-storey house and offices; c. 1840, altered and extended by *Beadel, Son & Chancellor*, 1857. Now houses.

4000

WALTHAM ABBEY*
See also HIGH BEACH, UPSHIRE

Holy Cross and St Lawrence	804
Other Churches and Public Buildings	811
Perambulation	812
Royal Gunpowder Mills	814

Waltham Abbey is still a little town, not a suburb of London. The low-lying ground to the W, along the River Lea, seems to have saved it from joining up with the continuous built-up area along the eastern border of Hertfordshire that extends from North London, while the M25 provides a more recent barrier along the S side. The parish church and abbey site dominate the old part of the town, the bulk of which lies to its E.

HOLY CROSS AND ST LAWRENCE

The church is no more than a fragment of what it was: Norman nave, C14 chapel, C14 W wall, C16 W tower, and C19 E wall. It is frustrating that so little survives, for successive churches on the site were significant buildings both before the Conquest and later. Excavations have produced fragmentary evidence for a C7 timber church, rebuilt in stone possibly in the late C8. According to a late C12 account, it acquired the name Holy Cross c. 1030 after Tovi, an associate of King Cnut, presented

---

* The old name for the town, Waltham Holy Cross, has now officially disappeared, perhaps to avoid confusion with Waltham Cross just to the W in Hertfordshire.

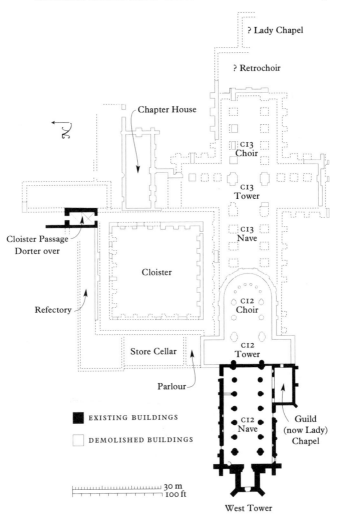

Waltham Abbey, Holy Cross and St Lawrence.
Plan, including demolished portions of the abbey

a miraculous 'bleeding' crucifix of black stone, discovered on his estate at Montacute, Somerset. The added prestige which this gave to Waltham may explain the choice of the site by King Harold for a foundation of secular canons, and the building of a third church dedicated in 1060. Some masonry in the s transept at the E end of the present building may date from this time.*

---

* P.J. Huggins interprets this, together with other archaeological evidence, as the remains of a continuous transept of continental (Carolingian/Ottonian) type (*Archaeol. J.*, vol. 149, 1992).

After the Battle of Hastings Harold's body was, it is claimed, brought here for burial. The grand rebuilding on Norman lines is undocumented, but appears to have taken place in the early C12, possibly incorporating a wall of the earlier transept, and adding a crossing with a tower as well as twin western towers. Excavations have established that the E end of this building had an ambulatory, with chapels added later; the surviving seven-bay aisled nave was probably completed in the second quarter of the C12. The next precise date is 1177, when Waltham was re-established by Henry II as a priory of Augustinian canons, one of three religious foundations undertaken by the king in expiation of the murder of Thomas à Becket. In 1184 it was given the dignity of a 'mitred abbey' and it soon became one of the most prosperous and important abbeys in the kingdom. The earlier E arm was demolished (it is now marked out in the grass) and E of the crossing arose a building whose magnificent scale is known only from excavations:* it had its own seven-bay nave, crossing, aisled transepts and straight-ended choir of perhaps six bays, with a possible retrochoir and Lady Chapel beyond. It must have dwarfed the Norman parts completely. The whole complex, with its double transepts, may have looked something like Canterbury Cathedral in the C13. A cloister was built on the N side of the new nave with a chapter house to its E at the end of the N transept. The old nave, retained for parochial use, was divided off by a screen, c. 1300, a S chapel W of the old S transept was added (for the Guild of the Holy Sepulchre; now Lady Chapel) in the C14, and a C14 building campaign also provided a new W front, following the demolition of the W towers.

The E parts of the abbey were pulled down after the Dissolution, when the site passed to Sir Anthony Denny. The old crossing tower fell in 1553, bringing the transepts down with it, and the W tower was built in 1556–8. On the site of the S transept the Dennys erected a family burial chapel (dem. 1817), and a private entrance was made into the church through the E wall blocking the N aisle. *Edward Lapidge* made internal alterations in 1818–19 (removed 1859–60). A tentative start on restoration was made by *Ambrose Poynter* in 1853, but the major work was by *William Burges*: new E end 1859–60, restoration of the S chapel as a Lady Chapel 1874–5, and other works finally completed in 1877. It was a pioneering restoration in that he deliberately chose not to re-create the building as it might once have been but to preserve its character as a fragment of a once-larger structure, and with him worked a team of artists and craftsmen of the first rank. He was succeeded by *J. A. Reeve*, who restored the tower in 1904. Major repairs were carried out in the C20 by *Laurence King*, 1960–4, and *Alan J. Frost* of *Donald W. Insall & Associates*, 1984–9. N vestries were built in 1874 and 1950.

---

* Fragments of reused stonework can be seen in various locations.

A tour of the EXTERIOR should start at the E end, that is at the former crossing of the Norman church. *Burges*'s E wall is built upon the screen separating the parish and monastic churches; it has an unfinished look with which other architects of his time would never have been content. The E shafts and capitals of the NW crossing pier survive (restored), and the start of an inner and outer gallery arch with chevron, and a billet hood-mould. Older blocking and a doorway to the church remain in the N transept. The S transept wall, now forming the E wall of the projecting Lady Chapel, retains a blocked Norman clerestory window. Below is a round-headed window with side-shafts, resting on a string course; underneath is exposed coarse rubble masonry, laid herringbone-wise, a technique used in the C11 and early C12. Its date has been much debated; it has been claimed as a remnant of the transept of Harold's mid-C11 church. Raised above an undercroft is the Lady Chapel, restored as such by *Burges* in 1874–5 with *Reeve* as clerk of works. On the S side it is of flint and stone bands, with buttresses enriched with recesses. The windows had been blocked up by the C19; Burges restored the S windows with entirely conjectural tracery, but the unusual W window is based on surviving evidence: three times two lights with a straight head and Dec tracery. The exterior of the nave is simple: aisle windows with nook-shafts with some zigzag decoration, circular gallery windows and clerestory windows much rebuilt in brick (likewise on the N side). The Norman S doorway of two orders, with an upcurving lintel and zigzag in the arches, is in its surface, it seems, wholly C19. The westernmost bay of the S aisle was part of the early C14 rebuilding campaign. W buttresses with pretty niches. In one niche a figure of Harold by *Elizabeth Muntz*, 1964.

The W TOWER was added in 1556–8, the upper part rebuilt in 1778 and repaired in 1798 (*M. Layton*, mason) and again in 1810–11 by *S.S. Saxon*. The upper part as it now appears belongs to the restoration of 1904 by *Reeve*. It has irregular flint and stone chequerwork below and ashlar facing to the upper parts. The stones were taken, it is said, from the old crossing tower. The buttresses are placed diagonally and end in battlemented tops, also in a diagonal position. Each side has two-light bell-openings. The outer W portal of the tower is reused C14 work, with three orders of columns with foliated capitals and fleurons in the arches, all very defaced.

Within the tower are visible the remains of the C14 W FRONT. The portal is single. It is deep enough to allow for a very shallow vault, which is carried on four shafts. The outer ones are a normal order of portal columns, the inner are placed on diagonally set seats which form the sides of little vaulted portal niches. The jambs and arch of the doorway are decorated with fleurons. Above the doorway is a gable and in the spandrel a circle with head in a quatrefoil. To l. and r. of the doorway are beginnings of blank shafted niches as were so usual in English church fronts. This portal and the W end of the S aisle were the extent of Poynter's restoration of 1853, with carving by *Samuel Hanchet*.

12 The INTERIOR is much more impressive. The Norman nave has something of the sturdy force of Durham Cathedral, though neither its size nor its proportions. The obvious visual similarity is the use of bold grooved patterning on the eastern piers. The nave is of seven bays; the western two, including the wider final bay for the W towers, were altered in the C14. The elevation of the rest, as in most major Anglo-Norman churches, is of arcade, gallery and clerestory, here more evenly divided than at Durham, where the arcade is proportionately taller. The arcades have supports alternating between composite piers and subordinate round ones. The composite piers, of oval form, broader E–W, have a buttress-like broad flat projection to the nave with demi-shaft attached running up to the ceiling without any break apart from the clerestory sill. The capitals are big and heavy, single- or double-scalloped. Both major and minor piers, with the exception of the easternmost circular pair, have shafts on their aisle sides, to support transverse arches between aisle vaults. The large gallery is comparable to churches in eastern England such as Ely and Norwich; here it is disconcertingly deprived of its floor so that the aisles are now much higher than they were meant to appear. The gallery is now unsubdivided, but inner shafts suggest subordinate arches were intended. The clerestory has the usual English arrangement of a wall passage and, towards the nave, an arcade of three arches for each bay, with the middle arch wider and taller.

The numerous discrepancies of detail in the Norman work have led to much debate over the date and order of construction of the nave. The grooved minor columns appear only in the eastern bays, the first pair with spirals, the second with chevrons. These bays also have arches with more deeply cut chevron decoration, a feature also of the former W crossing arch above the present E wall. This richer ornament, as Eric Fernie has suggested, is likely to have had a liturgical significance, as a setting for a nave altar W of the crossing. A similar hierarchy is found in other churches with decorated nave columns; both Durham, begun 1093, and Dunfermline, begun 1128, and of remarkably similar dimensions to Waltham Abbey, have a progression of decorated columns with the spiral ones at the E end (the association of spiral columns with sacred places can be traced back to St Peter's tomb at Rome). There were indeed close links with Durham from the late C11, as the Durham bishops owned land at Waltham.

The first bays would have had to be constructed as part of the initial campaign, in order to support the crossing, which formed part of the clergy's portion of the church. Other variations – for example the different base and capital of the easternmost column, and the corbel head above – point to a building break after the first bays, and minor changes of design during the building of the rest of the nave. There are differences also between the N and S sides in the treatment of the gallery responds (simpler on the s side) and treatment of the corbels to the wall shafts (plain on the s side).

The E wall above the medieval screen, as we have seen, is by *Burges*, 1859–60. He was inserting a wall where there had never been one before the C16, so there was no question of restoration, and he therefore chose not to replicate the style of the nave. He decided 'to fill it with a composition of the most beautiful architecture known to us', then generally accepted to be that of the early C13. So, consciously or not, he made up for the absence of all the C13 structure that had been demolished in the C16. The wall provides a powerful contrast to the silent severity of the nave, with plenty of carved figure-work that includes scenes from Aesop's fables. Above the reredos three lancets with short marble columns, the inner pair coupled, with thick shaft-rings and thick crocket capitals, and above it a giant rose window in a round-headed arch with an inner order of the same short columns. But the eye has been prepared for the E wall by the PAINTED CEILING which Burges inserted, based on the one at Peterborough. It is compartmented, twenty-nine of the lozenge-shaped panels being filled with canvases by the young *E.J. Poynter*, representing 'The Economy of the World': the Four Elements, the Past and Future, the Signs of the Zodiac, and the Labours of the Months. Burges also lowered the floor of the nave, removed old pews and galleries, restored the N aisle and s clerestory (two C14 windows in the N aisle were reconstructed), and added the w organ gallery, cantilevered out above tall coving.*

Off the s aisle, one of the Norman aisle windows now opens into the C14 Guild Chapel, restored by *Burges* as the Lady Chapel in 1874–5 (*see* above). This is an unvaulted space, with blind E wall covered with painting (*see* below) and a delightful feature to its w window, a detached three-light arcade with pierced spandrels. The undercroft is of two bays with chamfered ribs and small windows decorated by headstops.

REREDOS. 1876, by *Burges*, modelled by *T. Nicholls*, coloured and gilded by *Charles Campbell*. Deeply carved panels depicting the Annunciation, Shepherds, Adoration of the Magi, and Flight into Egypt. – ALTAR and SEDILIA also by *Burges*, richly carved in black American walnut. – SCREENS. At the E end of the N aisle, heavy construction and simple tracery indicating a C14 date. – Between the s aisle and Lady Chapel, 1886 by *J.A. Reeve*. Glazed 1998 with engraved panels by *David Peace*. – PULPIT. Good, mid C17. At the angles tapering pilasters, in the panels elaborate frames crowned by broken segmental pediments. With sounding board.[†] – SCULPTURE. At E end of s aisle, exceedingly fine small early C14 figures below arcading from a former reredos. – Seated stone figure of the Madonna, head and child missing. Dated to *c.* 1380 on the evidence of

---

* Replacing *Lapidge*'s gallery of 1818–19, the organ for which was donated by Thomas Leverton.
[†] Marble pulpit by *Burges*, 1876, now in Epping Forest District Museum.

her costume. Found in a garden in Sun Street; now in Lady Chapel undercroft. – Late C13 or early C14 COFFIN LID with floriated cross. – WALL PAINTING. Large C14 Doom on Lady Chapel E wall, discovered during Burges' restoration. – ROYAL ARMS. On W gallery, of Elizabeth I, carved and painted. Under the tower, 1662, painted; also large CHARITY BOARDS, including the Leverton bequest of 1830.

STAINED GLASS. The E window is an early work by *Burne-Jones*, 1861, made by *Powell & Sons*. A Tree of Jesse spread over three lights, and Creation scenes in the lobes of the round window above. In its vigorously stylized composition and figure design and its glow of colour it is amongst the best glass done in the C19, much bolder than most of Morris & Co.'s glass and much richer in the scale of colours used. Almost as remarkable and as daring the E window of the S aisle by *Henry Holiday*, 1867, also made by Powell. Many more windows installed under Burges' direction were destroyed in the Second World War. A false window by *Holiday*, painted in oil on silver foil for the opening in the S wall above the entrance to Lady Chapel undercroft in 1861, is now placed nearby. – Lady Chapel S windows, *c.* 1929–37, and one N aisle window, 1947, by *A. K. Nicholson*, later *G. E. R. Smith* and the *A.K. Nicholson Studios*. Inevitably very anaemic by comparison with the C19 work; rather bolder the N aisle E window by *Francis Stephens*, painted by *Gordon Beningfield*, 1966, to commemorate the 900th anniversary of the consecration in 1060, and the restoration of 1964. The architect Laurence King is depicted kneeling in one corner.

MONUMENTS. Several matrixes of lost brasses, including a fine early C14 one to an abbot. – Edward Stacy †1555 and wife Katherine †1565. Rectangular mural brass with kneeling figures and verse. – Thomas and Magdalen Colte †1559 and 1591, erected by her in 1576. Mural brass with kneeling figures in round-arched Purbeck frame. – Sir Edward Denny †1600 and wife. Standing wall monument by *Bartholomew Atye & Isaac James*. Two reclining painted effigies, the man behind and a little above the woman, with children along the tomb-chest. Shallow coffered arch (and, originally, flanking columns). In the spandrels figures of Fame and Time. Strapwork cartouche against the back wall. – Lady Elizabeth Greville †1619. Only the stiff alabaster figure is preserved, a recumbent figure now turned sideways. – Francis Wollaston †1684. Marble bust. N aisle; associated wall monument now in tower. – Capt. Robert Smith †1697. Tomb-chest carved with navigational instruments and an allegorical relief of the ship Industria negotiating the rock of Socordia (sloth). To the l. and r. arms and cherub's head used instead of volutes. By someone not far from *Grinling Gibbons*. – James ('A Lover of Literature & the Polite Arts') and Hester Spilman †1763 and 1761. Fine monument with the usual cherub standing by a sarcophagus against a grey obelisk. Two portrait heads in profile at the foot. Attributed to *Henry Cheere* (GF). – James Austin †1803. By *J. Kendrick*, 1805.

Covered urn against a grey obelisk. – Caroline Chinnery
†1812. Plain, elegantly shaped urn on a pillar. On the urn in
good lettering the one word 'Caroline'. – Thomas Leverton
(the architect) †1824. By *J. J. P. Kendrick*, designed by Leverton's great-nephew *T. L. Donaldson*. Angel weeping over an
urn.* – BOER WAR MEMORIAL, *c.* 1902. Red and white
alabaster. Mourning female figures (Fame and Grief) leaning
against a list of 'Rough Riders' killed in South Africa.
Very little remains of the MONASTIC BUILDINGS. The abbey
GATEHOUSE survives, N of the W front of the church. This is
of the later C14 and has a wide entrance for carriages and a
small one for pedestrians. The larger entrance has on the
outside angels (defaced) as label stops. Of the angle turrets
only one is preserved. In the S wall are original 'great bricks'.
NE of the church is a PASSAGE which led N from the NE angle
of the cloister. It is of two bays, rib-vaulted on shafts with
waterleaf capitals, and must belong to the late C12. On its E
side stood Abbey House, built *c.* 1600 no doubt with material
from the abbey ruins, enlarged early in the C18 and demolished
c. 1770.† Evidence of it can be found in the wall running E: a
chimney, blocked windows, and gatepiers marking the S
entrance to the forecourt. Further E a moated area, probably
a C15 cemetery and later part of the Abbey House gardens, and
on the E side of that, along Crooked Mile, part of the precinct
wall. NE of the cloister passage are the excavated foundations
of the medieval abbey forge and further N, beyond Abbey View
ring road, the remains of fishponds. Between the forge and the
ponds, STONEY BRIDGE, late C14, single span, stone, with the
remains of vaulting ribs. Abbey farm buildings have been
excavated nearby.

OTHER CHURCHES AND PUBLIC BUILDINGS

ST THOMAS MORE AND ST EDWARD (R.C.), Monkswood
Avenue. 1903 by *John Wills & Sons* of Derby, for the
Methodists. Brick with stone dressings. Free Perp, with octagonal turrets either side of the W window, and a battlemented
section with straight hoodmoulded windows – all quite
respectable until the squat corner porch tower is reached. This
has diagonal buttresses, rising to square crocketed pinnacles
also diagonal (cf. the abbey), gables between the pinnacles
behind which rises a slate pyramid on which is perched an
octagonal bell-turret beneath a short spire.
BAPTIST CHURCH, Paradise Street. 1836. Tudor Gothic, stock
brick, with two porches. Schoolroom added 1879.
JEWISH CEMETERY, 2 m. ESE. By *Lewis Solomon, Kaye & Partners*, 1959–60. One large hall for burial services, two smaller

---

* The monument in the churchyard to Thomas Leverton's brother Lancelot †1784,
and other members of the family, E of the church, was erected and presumably
designed by Leverton.
† Early C16 carved oak panelling now in Epping Forest District Museum.

halls for memorial services (one now used as an office), linked by a covered walkway, also a hand-washing unit beneath a circular concrete canopy. The halls have curved, copper-covered timber roofs, curved end walls and tapering side walls of random squared York stone with tracery of reconstituted stone in the form of the Star of David.

TOWN HALL, Highbridge Street. By the council's engineer and surveyor, *W.T. Streather*, 1904. Brick with stone dressings. Three-storey porch tower with a French-looking roof, two bays to the r. of it, one to the l., and then a cross-wing with shaped gable and large round-arched window on the first floor. Large hall behind with half-hipped roof and more shaped gables, seen also on a smaller scale on the public conveniences.

POLICE STATION, Sun Street. 1874–5 by *F. H. Caiger*, architect to the Metropolitan Police, within whose jurisdiction the town then fell. A little stock brick palazzo. Two storeys and five bays, with a heavy stuccoed doorcase with pilasters. Stucco bands, red brick arches to the windows with stucco keystones, and red brick between the painted or stuccoed brackets that support the deep eaves.

LIBRARY and MUSEUM, Sun Street. The Museum occupies No. 41, an appealing early C16 timber-framed house. Street front remodelled in the late C19 with applied half-timbering, a gable and a gabled dormer, a window with a segmental pediment, and an ogee-arched doorway (blocked). Plastered and pebbledashed E front remodelled in the C18, with sash windows. Now entered through the lobby of the adjacent Library, via a doorway in a wall that is a life-size version, cast in fibreglass, of a section of the Bayeux Tapestry, sculpted by *Philip & Jean Jackson*. Library building by *M.G. Booth* of *ATP Group Partnership*, 1984–6. Brick, two storeys, nine bays, with round-arched openings on the ground floor: small window, taller wider doorway, two small windows, taller wider window, two small windows, taller wider doorway, small window.

PERAMBULATION

The interesting parts of the town cover a small area. It is worth walking W from the church to see how it closes the view at the end of HIGHBRIDGE STREET. This has one good building on its S side, THE OLD COURTHOUSE, dated 1704 on the pedimented Doric porch. Brick with rusticated stucco quoins, two storeys and seven bays, and a passageway at one end under a round rusticated arch. Next to it a mid-C19 Tudor Gothic building and then No. 23, earlier C19 stock brick, the first-floor windows set in arched panels. On the N side, behind the street front, ROMELAND, site of the former cattle market, from which the DRINKING FOUNTAIN, 1878, and THE CROWN, C17 timber-framed and plastered, remain. Housing for Epping Forest District Council by *Ronald Bradshaw*, c. 1979, appropriately urban in character using materials (stock brick, weatherboarding) that echo those in Highbridge Street.

By the W end of the abbey, the VICARAGE, late C16 or early C17 timber-framed and plastered with gabled cross-wing to the r., quite a contrast both to the church and to the former COCK INN, rebuilt 1894 in red and stock brick, three storeys with three gables, an oriel, and a little cupola, challenging the Town Hall (*see* above) opposite. The buildings opposite the S side of the church are disappointing, unless one is amused by No. 5 CHURCH STREET, a Victorian stock brick villa converted to offices *c.* 1965 in the most insensitive manner. But things improve towards the E end of Church Street, with a nice row of houses leading one into MARKET SQUARE, where the historic scale of the buildings has been maintained. On the N side, THE WELSH HARP, C15 or C16 with exposed timbers, and a gateway through to the churchyard. On the W side, on the corner of Leverton Way, No. 20, also C16, with jettied upper storey and dragon post. A little to the S, in SEWARDSTONE STREET, No. 22, a three-storey, five-bay brick front with rainwater heads dated 1722, but rebuilt behind as part of a large development of flats.

Back to the Market Square, and on the E side No. 1 SUN STREET, but facing the square: C17 with jettied upper storey and carved dragon beam, carefully restored by *Prior Manton Tuke Partnership*, *c.* 1991–4, with new buildings in KING HAROLD COURT off Sun Street and Nos. 7–8 Market Place. The rest of Sun Street is of modest mainly C19 urban character, and peters out somewhat at its E end, but with some older buildings, e.g. THE SUN, recorded in 1633, with two pedimented doorcases and two large first-floor sashes, as well as the Police Station, Library and Museum (*see* Churches and Public Buildings). In SOUTH PLACE, off Sun Street, Nos. 2–3 was probably once a yeoman's house, C16 or C17. Painted brick ground floor with sashes, plastered first floor with sliding casements, and weatherboarded side walls.

GILWELL PARK (Scout Association headquarters), 2½ m. SSE. C16 or early C17 timber-framed house, remodelled in the last quarter of the C18 for Leonard Tresilian.* Wings added, the ground floor built further forward at the front with a canted bay over the front door, and the whole building clad in slate panels and painted. Tudor Gothic window surrounds and some Gothick glazing bars. Jagged black chimney pots, like slate, but made by *Coade*, dated 1797. Acquired by the Scout Association in 1919. N wing by *Fred Rowe*, 1962–3, entirely in keeping. To the S a stable-like block of brown brick with red brick dressings, 1926, and behind this two blocks of 1993–4 by *Broadway Malyan* that combine the appearance – brick and white render – of the older buildings. These contrasts are continued in the large contemporary office building by *T.P. Bennett Architects*, 2001, that joins on to the S. W of the house, MONUMENT to W.G. Chinnery †1802 (urn on pedestal) and a COLUMN

---

* Son-in-law of Henry Holland, but there is no evidence that Holland designed the alterations.

erected in 1812 to celebrate Caroline Chinnery's recovery from illness, but the gesture was premature and both children are buried in Waltham Abbey. Further s GILWELL FARM, timber-framed and weatherboarded, c. 1700. At the N end of the park GILWELLBURY, brick house with tile-hanging by *Arthur Needham Wilson*, 1907. Development of camping facilities planned for completion in 2007; the first accommodation lodge (stone and weatherboarding, with grass roof) and ablution unit completed in 2003 by *T.P. Bennett Architects*.

WARLIES PARK and WOODREDON. *See* Upshire.

AMBRESBURY BANKS. *See* Epping Upland.

ROYAL GUNPOWDER MILLS
Beaulieu Drive

The manufacture of gunpowder and other explosives was the principal industry of Waltham Abbey for over two hundred years. In the C17 a fulling mill on a branch of the River Lea was adapted for the purpose. In addition to the water power for the mills, an advantage of the site was that the gunpowder could be conveniently transported by barge along the Lea Navigation to the magazines at Purfleet (q.v.) and Woolwich. As the site developed, a system of canals (on three levels) was built to produce a head of water to drive the water wheels. They also provided a means of transporting material, later supplemented by a light railway. In 1787 the mills were purchased by the Board of Ordnance and expanded rapidly during the Napoleonic Wars. By the mid C19 experiments were being made with new forms of explosive to replace gunpowder; in 1863 a plant was set up for the production of guncotton, and in 1885 a new site was acquired to the s of the town (Quinton Hill) for increased production of guncotton and nitroglycerine. These two substances combine to make cordite, manufacture of which started in 1891, and which was the main product of the factory until production ceased on this site in 1943. After the Second World War the buildings were adapted for use as an experimental station for the research and testing of explosives. The establishment closed in 1991; the Quinton Hill site has been redeveloped but the main site, covering 175 acres, is now a museum and nature reserve.

The oldest standing buildings are in the SW corner of the site: the GUNPOWDER MIXING HOUSE and SALTPETRE MELTING HOUSE, 1787–1800, and WALTON'S HOUSE (superintendent's office), 1789 with C19 additions. Brick. The older part of Walton's House of two storeys and three bays, the other buildings single-storey with pyramid roofs. Nearby a brick 1960s lecture theatre and library, with curved glazed entrance by *Thomas Ford & Partners* (partner-in-charge, *Clive England*), who restored or repaired a number of buildings on the site, 1998–2001.

To the NE of this group, a BOILER HOUSE and ENGINE HOUSE AND MECHANICS' SHOP, 1856–7, built to house engines to drive the first of the steam-powered incorporating mills (now demolished). Both stock brick with some red brick dressings, and nicely detailed with dentil cornices, pilasters, etc. s of them a large POWER HOUSE, *c.* 1910, extended 1916, for the central production of electricity. In the SE corner of the site, in POWDERMILL LANE, THE LODGE, for senior officers. Early C19 stock brick, two storeys and three bays, with deep eaves. Later C19 central porch and rectangular oriels.

N of the engine house and mechanics' shop a row of four GUNPOWDER INCORPORATING MILLS, with a fifth behind them to the E, 1861–89, converted for cordite incorporation *c.* 1898–9. Adapted after 1945 for use as laboratories, but the earliest has been at least partially restored (by *Thomas Ford & Partners*). Single storey, T-plan, the stem to the E housing the boiler, with a taller engine house at the intersection. To either side of this three bays separated by brick walls, but the outer walls of each bay originally of felt panels within a steel framework, designed to blow out in the event of an explosion (partially reconstructed on the 1861 building). Along the w side a raised veranda for access to the light railway. Adjacent to the mills a number of small stock brick EXPENSE MAGAZINES for the temporary storage of gunpowder, 1861 and later. Across Queen's Mead to the w an incongruously picturesque LABORATORY, 1897, extended 1902: exposed timbers with brick infill on the ground floor and pebbledash on the first floor, which overhangs slightly. Further N, a battered, oval brick structure survives from an earlier production method, an early C19 horse-powered CORNING HOUSE. Adapted for use as a gunpowder press *c.* 1850 when a hydraulic pump and cast-iron water wheel were installed alongside in a brick building with curved roof covered in corrugated iron, the original sheets of which have survived. But the northern part of the site has mainly buildings associated with later developments: NITRATING HOUSE, 1896, part of the nitroglycerine factory, a massive brick ring banked up with earth that formerly housed an internal wooden structure; guncotton DRYING STOVE, 1897, also a brick ring, with metal drying racks; and the QUINAN DRYING STOVE, 1935, an innovative and unique steel-framed, concrete building with arched roof, named after its designer *Kenneth B. Quinan*. At the very N of the site is the brick GRAND MAGAZINE, rebuilt 1867–8, where gunpowder was stored before being loaded on to barges for transport to Purfleet.

On the E side of the site, a second NITROGLYCERINE FACTORY at New Hill, 1941, essentially the same design as the 1895–6 plant but of concrete, with associated washing houses, water-settling houses, and mixing houses. Other structures include massive concrete TRAVERSES for containing explosions, one E-plan, 1882–4, for two free-standing gunpowder moulding houses; a brick hydraulic gunpowder PRESS HOUSE, 1879; cast-iron AQUEDUCTS, 1878–9 and *c.* 1914; and a number of semicircular cast-iron BRIDGES.

WALTON-ON-THE-NAZE

'No monuments known' to the Royal Commission – that means,
no building prior to 1700. The medieval parish church of
Walton-le-Soken, recorded as a ruin by Morant, was lost to the
sea in 1796. The modern history of Walton starts with the Marine
Hotel, 1829, and pier, 1830, both by *John Penrice* of Colchester
(pier constructed by *Joseph Salmon* of Beaumont; both dem.).
Penrice also laid out some terraces, but it was Peter Bruff, from
1855, who had the greater impact upon the development of the
resort. By 1859 it was sufficiently fashionable for Ford Madox
Brown to bring his family here on holiday; the view over the town
that he painted is in Birmingham City Art Gallery. Bruff brought
the railway to Walton in 1867, and built a new pier between the
STATION (by *F. Barnes*, now flats) and Penrice's, which rapidly
fell into disuse and finally collapsed in 1880. Walton is now overshadowed by Clacton as a popular resort, although Bruff's pier
remains a prominent feature.

ALL SAINTS. By *Henry Stone*, 1873–82, W tower 1895–6, replacing a building of 1804. Nave, chancel and S aisle, Kentish rag
with Bath stone dressings, in a dull E.E. – STAINED GLASS.
E window to Peter Bruff †1900. S aisle S by *Jeremy Russell*,
made by *Shades of Light*, *c.* 1982.

EMMANUEL CHURCH (Methodist/United Reformed), Station
Street. 1878 by *Charles Pertwee*, added to the N of an earlier
building. Kentish rag with Bath stone and brick dressings.
Unusual W end, polygonal with gabled window over W door.

PRIMARY SCHOOL, Standley Road. By *Tomkins, Homer & Ley*,
1909. Brick, with tall windows set in a row of four shaped
gables.

PERAMBULATION. The PIER is the best place to start; Bruff's
pier, that is, of 1869–71. Extended 1897–8 to 2,610 ft (803
metres), the engineers *Kinniple & Jaffrey*. The superstructure
is post-war and no more than utilitarian. Immediately opposite, CLIFTON BATHS or music hall (later a hotel, now a bar)
opened by Bruff in 1862. Stock brick with red brick dressings
and a small Italianate tower; Art Deco PUBLIC TOILETS to one
side, *c.* 1930. Above and behind this THE PARADE, parts of
which were built by Bruff as South Crescent and South Terrace
in 1859. S of the pier, ranks of BEACH HUTS climb the shallow
cliff, impressive in their mass. N of the pier, just beyond the site
of the old pier and Marine Hotel, only a straggling and
unkempt fragment remains of *Penrice*'s original scheme, Nos.
40–44 MARINE PARADE, three-storey stuccoed houses with
pilasters and little first-floor balconies. Another more modest
terrace, two storeys, behind the front in OLD PIER STREET,
and at its far end, on the corner of the High Street, the
former PORTOBELLO HOTEL, another part of the early C19
development.

In the HIGH STREET, little of interest. On the N side, opposite
Old Pier Street, the former TOWN HALL by *Alphonzo Migotti*,
1900, brick with Bath stone dressings. On the S side, the

PUBLIC LIBRARY occupies the former National School, Gothic brick of 1853 with additions by *Horace Darken*, 1871–2, and later in the C19. Opposite, a terrace of four houses of the 1830s. Off the High Street to the NW, SAVILLE STREET gives further flavour of the early resort: GOTHIC HOUSE, brick with hoodmoulded windows, some more terracing, including a pair with full-height shallow-bowed fronts and cast-iron balconies, and on the corner of NORTH STREET, set back, a charming weatherboarded house with Gothick detailing.

The N end of the High Street meets up with the seafront, and after ¼ m. N comes another attempt to establish Walton as a smart resort, this time by John Warner of Hoddesdon, the bell-founder. In 1836 he built EAST TERRACE, three storeys, stuccoed. The southernmost house of the terrace was his own, five bays projecting slightly, and distinguished by a Greek Doric porch. The terrace has now been extended by six bays to the S, replacing the single-storey lodge that was intended as the preamble to the new-town-to-be. Behind the terrace, in HALL LANE, Warner built for his mother East Cliff Cottage, now GOTHIC COTTAGE, in the then popular style with barge-boarded gables. A terrace of cottages in GREEN LANE, similarly Gothic, must belong to the same project. N of East Terrace, the former lifeboat house, now WALTON MARITIME MUSEUM: 1884, extended 1899. Brick with tile hanging and a delightful little oriel window over the entrance. Presumably by the R.N.L.I.'s architect, *C.H. Cooke* (cf. Clacton-on-Sea). To its l. more utilitarian coastguard cottages, 1891. Back in Hall Lane, No. 46, a picturesque thatched and weatherboarded house, originally a row of cottages, perhaps C18.

N of here the character changes yet again. At the top of Hall Lane, Robert Warner, son of John, established a FOUNDRY, *c.* 1875, a subsidiary of the firm's London premises, and engaged *T. A. Cressy* of Clacton to lay out workers' housing. Some of the brick foundry buildings survive, as well as terraced housing. Larger houses further out along NAZE PARK ROAD and OLD HALL LANE, almost up to the standard of Frinton, and early C20 convalescent homes, including POPLARS, 1909, with two projecting, pavilion-like wings and a large central gable.* Finally THE NAZE is reached, a headland of rapidly eroding cliffs that looks N towards Harwich and encloses the Walton backwaters (setting of Arthur Ransome's *Secret Water*) to the w. NAZE TOWER by *William Ogbourne*, for the Corporation of Trinity House, was built 1720 as a seamark (bricklayer, *Daniel Fisher*). Brick, tall and slim, octagonal, three slightly tapering stages, opened to the public in 2004 when its battlements were reinstated. NE, WALTON HALL, a farmhouse to which was added in 1802 a three-storey stuccoed block, two bays square. Restored from a state of advanced dereliction in 2003–5.

---

*Built as the Poplar Hospital for Accidents' Convalescent Home.

MARTELLO TOWER, unhappily located in a caravan park off Kirby Road. 1810–12 (*see* Introduction, p. 76). Brick with stone dressings and remains of rendering. Broad and not high. Another tower nearer the sea was sold in 1835 and demolished.

WEELEY

ST ANDREW. Early C16 brick W tower, with diagonal buttresses and battlements. Brick W doorway. The rest by *E.C. Robins*, 1880–1: nave, chancel, N aisle, vestry and N porch. Also brick, but lifeless by comparison, in a Neo-Late Perp. Fortunately the proposed heightening of the tower was not carried out. – STAINED GLASS. E window by *F. H. Spear*, 1947.

METHODIST CHURCH, The Street. 1870 by *John Leaning*. Small, with minimal black brick decoration and stone dressings. Narrow round-headed windows.

PRIMARY SCHOOL. 1866–7 by *H. Darken*. Brick, much extended.

HILLSIDE HOUSE. By *C.F. Hayward*, 1858. Brick, roguish Gothic, with gables and a bell-turret, but derelict in 2005.

WENDEN LOFTS*

ST DUNSTAN. Rebuilt 1845–6, in knapped flint. W tower, nave, N aisle with six-bay arcade, and short chancel. Perp. Of the earlier church, it seems that only the Norman S doorway was reused. Semicircular arch of two orders, with zigzag ornament. Now in private ownership; interior dismantled in 1958, some fittings transferred to Elmdon (q.v.) and the Hamlet Church (*see* below).

LOFTS HALL, NW of the church. The late C16 house burnt down in 1935. Designs for its replacement were prepared by *Ian B.M. Hamilton* that same year, but the new house was not built until 1963–5 (*Ian Hamilton & Alan Chalmers*). Neo-Georgian, seven bays and two storeys. Hamilton also converted and extended a C19 lodge, published in 1938. Large brick DOVECOTE, E of the church. Late C16 or early C17. Octagonal, with octagonal louvre on the roof, about 1,500 nests, and 'potence', i.e. revolving ladder for reaching the nests.

THE HAMLET CHURCH, Upper Pond Street, ¾ m. S. C16 or early C17 barn, converted to a church by Rev. Robert Wilkes of Lofts Hall, 1859. Weatherboarded and thatched, with Gothic windows, S porch, and tiny bellcote, a very picturesque sight, next to CHURCH HOUSE, also thatched. Simple interior, with plain pine BENCHES. – FONT. Classical. Marble bowl on stone stem. From St Dunstan (*see* above), as is the COMMUNION RAIL, with twisted balusters.

---

*Access to St Dunstan and Lofts Hall was refused in 2004.

WENDENS AMBO   5030

The name means 'both the Wendens', i.e. Great Wenden and Little Wenden, united in 1662. Nothing remains of Little Wenden.

St Mary the Virgin. The church is best approached from the w, with the thatched cottages of Church Walk on the l. contributing to a view that is a favourite with publishers of scenic calendars. Norman w tower, with Hertfordshire spike. It has a w doorway with Roman bricks, remains of small windows higher up, and bell-openings with colonettes. The tower arch towards the nave is also Norman, unmoulded on simple imposts. Tower battlements evidently later. E.E. s arcade of circular piers with one-stepped pointed arches. The s doorway (with colonettes) and the w lancet window of the same period. The N arcade is later. It has octagonal piers and double-chamfered arches. N aisle rebuilt by *James Barr*, 1847,* and extended to the w to balance the C15 vestry at the w end of the s aisle; chancel arch renewed. Nave clerestory, *c.* 1500, with three windows each side, of which the easternmost are of brick, added only a few years later. The date of the chancel, *c.* 1300, is indicated by two cusped lancet windows. s organ chamber added by *E. Geldart*, 1895–6, who also carried out a general restoration that included rebuilding the s porch and replacing the crown-post roof of the nave. – PULPIT. Good late C15 piece. Nine-sided, slightly tapering, with exaggeratedly high crocketed pinnacles in the panels. – FONT. Octagonal, *c.* 1400. C16 domed COVER with a ball finial. – SCREEN. With one-light divisions with crocketed ogee arches and panel tracery, broad and not very refined. Late C15, restored 1847. – BENCHES. A number of late C15 bench ends, including one with a carving of a boar with its foot on a mirror. – WALL PAINTINGS. On s wall of chancel, remains (probably only the uppermost of three tiers) of an interesting cycle of *c.* 1330 depicting episodes from the life of St Margaret. On N wall, fragment of a late C16 black-letter inscription. – STAINED GLASS. Fragments of medieval and C16 fragments re-set in a chancel N window, 1986. – s aisle †1888 by *Clayton & Bell*. – N aisle by *Peter Caller*, 2002 (Annunciation, including a bird's-eye view of the village). – MONUMENTS. Brass of William Loveney, *c.* 1410. 44-in. (112-cm.) figure, in armour. – Ambrose Andrews †1718. Tablet with flamboyant display of drapery, cherubs' heads, etc.

Wenden Hall, s of the church. C15 two-bay raised aisle hall, one storey and attics, with an C18 wing to the w, two storeys and attics. Mostly timber-framed and plastered with some plastered brick. The form of the hall was revealed during restoration by *Edwin Smith* in the 1960s.

Wenden Place, w of the church. Three-bay C18 timber-framed and plastered range, with an early C19 brick cross-wing at the E end. This has a pedimented gable within which is an arched recess. Arched recesses along the three-bay return also.

* Rev. John Barr, curate of Wendens Ambo 1846–57, may have been his brother.

AUDLEY END RAILWAY STATION. 1845, by *Sancton Wood* and
Francis Thompson. Gault brick. Arched windows with stucco
surrounds, and a large stuccoed porte cochère with arched
entrance on piers with banded rustication. Opposite the
approach road, RAILWAY COTTAGES (row of nine). Mid C19,
flint with brick dressings, windows with iron lattice casements,
the front divided by pilasters.

WEST BERGHOLT

ST MARY (OLD; vested in the Churches Conservation Trust,
1976). Very prettily sited beside the Hall, right outside the
village. Of the C11 building, much of the N wall survives, with
blocked Saxon doorway. The usual mix of materials, including
Roman tiles, septaria and puddingstone. Chancel enlarged and
squared off in the late C13, S aisle and porch added early C14.
Dec windows to S aisle, low S arcade of octagonal piers and
double-chamfered arches. Timber belfry C14–C15, with low
four-sided spire. Early C19 W gallery on Tuscan columns with
triglyph frieze. – ROYAL ARMS. Of James I, painted on the
tympanum over the chancel arch. – Of 1816–37, on front of W
gallery. Cast iron, by *Coleman & Wallis* of Colchester. –
STAINED GLASS. E window by *F. C. Eden*, 1928, when the
stonework was also replaced. – MONUMENTS. Robert Brad-
brook †1877. Heavily carved Gothic tablet by *Watts*. – J.T.
Argent †1894. Brass cross by *Quilter* of Colchester.
ST MARY (NEW), in the centre of the village. 1903–4 by *Sir Arthur
Blomfield & Sons*. E.E., pebbledashed with brick dressings.
Only three bays of the nave and S aisle were built.
WEST BERGHOLT HALL. A Georgian town house, not at all in
harmony with its rural surroundings, but very splendid
nonetheless. Seven bays, three storeys, brick, doorway with
open pediment, Venetian window above, tripartite semicircular
window above that, and three-bay pediment on top. Delightful little coachhouse between it and the church, part brick part
weatherboarded.
A number of good houses between the old church and the River
Colne to the S. COOKS HALL and HORSEPITS FARM, the
former partly and the latter entirely with exposed timbers.
Inside Horsepits, wall painting of the Sacrifice of Isaac, and a
cartouche dated 1628. Between Horsepits and Cooks Hall, the
OLD RECTORY, *c.* 1700, faced in gault brick in the late C18
and given an impressive pedimented doorcase. Below Cooks
Hall, COOKS MILL, of which only the house remains, early
C19 brick.
Off Colchester Road, ½ m. SE of the new church, MALTINGS
PARK ROAD, houses and flats, *c.* 1989–90, based round mid-
C19 brewery buildings, the main block three storeys of brick
with a further weatherboarded storey.

WEST HANNINGFIELD

ST MARY AND ST EDWARD. The timber W tower is built on a Greek cross plan, the square upper part provided with an odd W oriel in the C17 to accommodate a larger peal of bells. On the ground floor to the S two Gothick windows, on the upper floor to the N timber tracery with trefoils visible behind the louvres. The construction inside is especially interesting, with arched braces in all four directions, buttressing struts in the arms of the cross, and on the upper floor of the centre arched braces diagonally across like ribs and meeting in a centre key block with a grotesque face. Probably C15, originally clad in wattle and daub; now weatherboarded with splay-foot spire, partially rebuilt and slated by *Carl Rother* of Frankfurt, 1886.

The church itself, to which the tower is connected only by the E arm of the cross, is of flint, pebble rubble and pudding-stone, rendered on the S side; Norman nave, as witnessed by the rere-arch of a N window, the remains of a C13 chancel (see the traces of E windows), C14 S arcade and S aisle, timber S porch with crown-post roof of *c.* 1500, and an early C16 brick chancel, its E wall largely rebuilt in 1831. Most of the windows are probably *c.* 1810 (Gothick), when a S vestry, now demolished, was added. The five-bay S arcade stands on octagonal piers and has double-chamfered arches. The chancel has two- and three-light brick N windows, probably C17. Restoration in 1888 including taking down the W gallery, re-seating and re-paving, and raising the level of the chancel floor. – FONT. Perp, octagonal, small. – COMMUNION RAIL. Late C17 with alternately twisted and turned balusters, moved in 1888 to form a low chancel screen. – CHEST. Of the dug-out type, uncommonly long (over 8 ft (2.4 metres)), heavily iron-bound; late C13. – PANELLING round organ. Early C17, from the W gallery. – MONUMENTS. Brass to Isabel Cloville, 12-in. (30-cm.) demi-figure, with indent of her son John †1361. – John Erdeswicke †1622. Floor slab, now worn smooth, but recorded as bearing the effigy of a child and as having been signed by *Epiphanius Evesham*.

CLOVILE HALL, 1¼ m. WNW. Formerly known as Fullers or the Meeting House. C16, L-plan; extended to the N, and S front refaced, late C19 and C20. Tall W wing, in the attic floor of which are two rooms with remarkably good and well-preserved paintings of arabesques, with centaurs, putti, fishes etc. Symmetrical compositions. In one room red and white, in the other grey and white. In the latter the date 1615.

ELMS FARM, 1 m. WNW. C16, remodelled in the early C17, with two symmetrical jettied gables, two-storey canted bays beneath them, and carved figures supporting the eaves and gables. A third gabled bay to the W, demolished by the time of the Royal Commission's survey, was rebuilt as part of a general restoration, 1984–8.

HANNINGFIELD RESERVOIR. 1952–6, covering 900 acres. By the N end, in Middlemead, some well-detailed staff housing by *R. A. Boxall Associates*, 1955–6. Brick, with little porches.

WEST HORNDON

ST FRANCIS. By *Peter Grist* and *Mark Hale* of *LAP Architects & Interior Designers Ltd*, 2000–1. Traditional plan and materials, but with an airiness and modernity not always associated with churches. Nave and chancel in one, and a spirelet at the E end. Walls of square pine logs laid horizontally in a boat-like frame of laminated pine crucks, prefabricated in Finland. Tall slate roof and three gabled windows along each side; no E window, but two corner windows either side of the end wall. Small gabled N and W porches, with the main entrance on the s side where the church connects to an existing building.

The medieval parish church, St Nicholas, stood about 1 m. N, on the s side of old Thorndon Hall (q.v.). It was demolished c. 1735 to open up the view from the house and a new church built at Ingrave (q.v.), to which brasses were transferred.

WEST MERSEA

ST PETER AND ST PAUL. A Benedictine priory was established here in 1046 and it seems likely that the lower part of the w tower dates from then – Late Saxon rather than Early Norman. Of that time one N and one s window, also the severely plain tower arch inside. The tower has no buttresses, but Roman brick quoins. The upper part, with handsome two-light transomed bell-openings and battlements, is probably C14. That is the date of the rest of the church, with N porch added in the C15. Upper part of chancel rebuilt in brick in the C16, also brick E window of the s aisle. Nave heightened in brick in 1833, when the s arcade was rebuilt. C18 s vestry, hall added 1971, extended by *Purcell Miller Tritton & Partners*, 1992. – FONT. Of the Purbeck type, C13, octagonal, with two of the usual shallow blank pointed arches to each side. – PAINTING. Pretty cartouches with biblical inscriptions above the s arcade. The date must be 1833. – SCULPTURE. Fragment of Saxon carving, built into s aisle wall by s door. C10–C11 grave cover? – Lunette in the style of Della Robbia, Christ and three angels. Clearly no earlier than the mid C16. Similar panel of the Annunciation. – ROYAL ARMS of George IV, 1823. Carved. – STAINED GLASS. E window by *Mary Lowndes*, 1905. s aisle by *Lisa McFarlane*, 2005.

MERSEA ISLAND SCHOOL, Barfield Road. School and house by *Horace Darken*, 1871–2. Domestic Gothic, brick with stone dressings. Additional classrooms by *J. W. Start*, c. 1897, with two broad gabled wings and bell-turret on little columns.

THE HALL stands on the SE side of the church, four bays wide, C16 timber-framed and plastered, but with a big hipped roof, and a canted bay with little sweeping roof echoing that on the pretty C19 porch. Otherwise most of the interest lies along the COAST ROAD to the w, beginning with YEW TREE HOUSE, early C18, of blue bricks with red dressings. Two storeys, five bays, with segment-headed windows and parapet, and Tuscan doorway. Wrought-iron gate and brick piers. Then a little square with weatherboarded and brick cottages set back from the road. At the far end, about ½ m. ENE of the church, a nice group of houses round the bottom of THE LANE: Carriers Close (Late Medieval, black weatherboarding), The Old Victory (mid C19, roughcast, with veranda), and Nos. 1–3 The Lane, dated 1624. In FIRS CHASE, S of The Lane, THE FIRS, dated 1756 but with later windows and porch. Brick, five bays, two storeys and attics.

NE of the church, No. 20 YORICK ROAD ('Casa Pantis') by *Baillie Scott & Beresford*, 1923. Late Arts and Crafts, painted brick, with hipped roof coming down to first-floor level at each end and the porch set in a little tower-like projection. In HIGH STREET NORTH, Brick House, dated 1766, with jagged *Coade* chimney pots, and in EAST ROAD Myrtle, chequered brick, two storeys and attics, dated 1741, then Brierley Hall, roughcast, *c.* 1800. Two-storey, three-bay front, with round-headed window above Greek Doric portico.

MERSEA MOUNT, 1½ m. NE. Romano-British burial mound, 110 ft (38.5 metres) in diameter and 22 ft 6 in. (6.8 metres) high. Its contents were remarkable. The excavators found in 1912 a small chamber, 18 in. (46 cm.) square and 21 in. (53 cm.) high, constructed of Roman tiles. Inside the chamber was a small square lead casket containing a glass bowl 1½ in. (4 cm.) high. In the bowl were the cremated remains of an adult. Sherds in the body of the mound suggested a date of A.D. 100–20.

ROMAN VILLA. Remains, no longer visible, were uncovered in the C18 of at least one house on the site of the church, churchyard, and Hall. These included a mosaic pavement. Other remains have been found in front of Yew Tree House.

WHEEL TOMB, 200 yds E of the church. Excavated 1896; no visible remains. A small hexagonal room from which radiate six walls to an encircling wall 65 ft (20 metres) in diameter, the whole resembling a spoked wheel in plan. Similar tombs are found elsewhere in the Roman Empire.

WEST THURROCK
Thurrock U.A.

5070

ST CLEMENT (old). As famous for its setting as for any qualities of its own: until 1939 it was stuck rather forlornly in the marshes, but now it can only be seen against the backdrop – dramatic in its own way – of the Procter & Gamble detergent factory. The marshland has given way to industrial wasteland. Handsome C15 W tower with diagonal buttresses and stripes of flint and stonework. Battlement brick top. Outside the W door are the foundations of the original (C12) circular nave. Such a thing is normally associated with the Knights Templar or Hospitaller (cf. Little Maplestead); land that formed the manor of Purfleet was granted to the Knights Templar in the late C12.

To the chancel of this church were added N and S aisles, the two-bay arcades with circular piers and double-chamfered arches. One tiny window at the W end of the N aisle and plain N doorway, early C13. Then follows the chancel, mid C13, extended later in the century when the N and S chapels were added. Their windows are cusped lancets (chancel N and S), and two cusped lancet lights and a quatrefoil above (N chapel E, with two blank lancets to the l. and r. Was this originally a stepped-lancet group?). The N chapel N windows are C14. So are the octagonal piers to the N and S chapels. S chapel rebuilt early in the C19 (brick with panels of knapped flint), with major repairs to the whole church by *C.M. Shiner*, 1906–7. Restored 1987–90 by Procter & Gamble following redundancy in 1977, but most of the furnishings and fittings dispersed or damaged in the interim.

FONT. Octagonal, with tall oak cover. From All Saints, Grays, together with a carved and painted figure of St Hugh of Lincoln by *Sir Charles Nicholson, c.* 1932. – STAINED GLASS. Various small bits in E window and N chapel. Late C13 or early C14. – TILES. In N chapel, re-set, early C14 fleurs-de-lys, foliage, eagle, etc. – MONUMENTS. Coffin lid of Purbeck marble with foliated cross, C13. – Nicholas Ferobaud †1315. Indent of foliated cross and half-effigy of a priest (21½ in. (55 cm.)), with marginal inscription in Lombardic capitals. – Brass to Humphrey Heies †1584 and son †1585. Replica made from rubbing of lost originals, 1990. Figures in civilian dress, 18¾ and 16¼ in. (47.5 and 41.5 cm.) – Katherine Redinge, daughter of Humphrey Heies, †1591. Replica figure, 18¾ in. (47.5 cm.), with original inscription. – Sir Christopher Holford †1608 and Lady Holford. Two stiff reclining alabaster figures, not in their original context. Attributed by Esdaile to *Bartholomew Atye* and *Isaac James*.

CHAFFORD HUNDRED. Planned development of 5,000 houses on 600 acres, partly in former chalk quarries, begun 1988, the master plan and first houses by the *Barton Willmore Partnership*. Architectural distinction is provided by *Laurie Wood*'s crescent-shaped, timber-framed and rendered CHAFFORD GORGES VISITOR CENTRE, 2006, and *Nicholas Hare Architects*' CHAFFORD HUNDRED CAMPUS, 2000–1, a 'lifelong learning' complex comprising nursery, primary and secondary schools, adult education, and public library. Classroom blocks to either side of the central spine, an atrium up to three storeys high. Flat-roofed, with projecting eaves and brises-soleil supported on slender columns. Walls clad in pre-cast concrete panels with large expanses of glazing giving a crisp, clean look lacking in the 'traditional' housing that surrounds it.

LAKESIDE SHOPPING CENTRE. 1987–90 by *Chapman Taylor Partners* (partner in charge, *Henry Herzberg*), with 230 shops on a 120-acre site, enlarged 1998 to 320 shops on a 200-acre site. Three-storey mall, clad in yellow and red brick, the main feature a glazed dome over the central atrium with short lattice-work spire. By the lake a jolly building clad in blue profiled metal sheeting giving the effect of vertical weather-boarding. Large multi-storey brick-clad car parks with corner towers along the lake by *Tooley & Foster Partnership*, 1993, and another with pedestrian suspension bridge connecting to Chafford Hundred railway station, 1996–9.

PURFLEET, including river crossings. *See* p. 628.

See p. 628.

WEST TILBURY 6070
Thurrock U.A.

ST JAMES. Well placed on the edge of the escarpment looking S towards the Thames. Flint and ragstone rubble, restored by *W. Benton*, 1879–80, which included renewing all the windows (C14 in the chancel) and the chancel arch. The tower followed in 1883, with N porch and vestry. Fragments of Early Norman windows and on the S side near the W end one deeply splayed lancet, re-set. Converted to a house after 1984, without subdividing the interior. – STAINED GLASS. Chancel S †1933 by *C.E. Moore*. Nave S, 1919, by *T. F. Curtis, Ward & Hughes*, who probably also did the two single-light chancel windows. W window by *James Powell & Sons*, 1925. – MONUMENTS. Lady Gordon †1811 and Louisa Pritchard †1818. Two plain tablets by *R. Watson* of Gravesend.

A pleasant grouping of houses round The Green 300 yds N of the church, including on the E side MANOR FARM. Timber-framed and weatherboarded, C17 with later additions, including a large semicircular bay at the S end. To the N, in Blue Anchor Lane, MARSHALL'S COTTAGE. Early C15, part weatherboarded. Single-storey hall and two-storey jettied cross-wings.

WETHERSFIELD 7030

ST MARY MAGDALENE. Low, massive early C13 W tower without buttresses, of flint and pebble rubble. Small lancet windows, two-light bell-openings separated by a polygonal shaft. Their position proves that the tower was not meant to be taller. Short shingled spire in two stages that gives it a rare, German rather than English shape. Early C14 chancel, see the E window with reticulated tracery, also the S chancel window and another re-set in the vestry's E wall. Inside the chancel, blank arcading, low N recess, and double PISCINA. N and S aisle windows late C14 (renewed) – straight-headed with the Early Perp version of reticulation (cf. Shalford). The interior confirms the date of the tower: low, unmoulded, but pointed arch towards the nave. It also introduces a new period. The S arcade is clearly C13, but probably later than the tower. Circular piers and double-chamfered arches, and the E respond with stiff-leaf on a defaced head corbel. The N arcade is yet later: octagonal piers, and double-chamfered arches, but a short vertical piece first, rising from the capitals and dying into the arch. That goes with the date of the aisles. C15 S porch, brick clerestory, and nave roof. N porch rebuilt 1750. Restoration by *Ewan Christian*, 1874–7, who added the S organ chamber and vestry.

FONT. In S porch. Hexagonal bowl, buttressed and panelled stem. C15. – SCREEN. Quite tall, of one-light divisions, each with an ogee arch, and panel tracery above. Mainly C15. – STAINED GLASS. Many fragments, in various windows, C14 to C16. – E window and chancel N. 1879 and 1881 by *C. Champigneulle* of Bar-le-Duc, France, and quite unlike what English artists were producing at this time. Pictorial, using vivid colours, yet gloomy in effect. N window to a soldier killed in 1880, whose uniformed body is shown being mourned by angels. – Another chancel N by *Ward & Hughes*, 1890. Chancel S by *Kempe & Co.*, 1909. N aisle N by *Eric Dilworth*, 1959. – MONUMENTS. Tomb-chest with alabaster effigies, not of high quality. Thought to be Sir Roger Wentworth †1539 and wife. The FUNERAL HELM on the wall above probably belongs to it. – Joseph Youngman alias Clerk †1682. Slate tablet in stone surround with *trompe l'œil* drapery below and achievement of arms above. – Mott family, after 1752, one of the many, often very fine, and hardly ever signed Rococo tablets of various marbles which occur in Home County churches. Urn above, as usual, and cherub's head below. It is similar to, but simpler than, the monument to Sir William Jolliffe †1749 at Pleshey, attributed to *Cheere*. – Joseph Clerke †1790, by *E. Thompson*, also of various marbles and in similar style.

UNITED REFORMED CHURCH (former Congregational Chapel). 1707, rebuilt 1822, as a roundel in the pedimented gable proudly proclaims, but the gable itself was rebuilt in stock brick, probably in 1861 when the chapel was enlarged. Gault brick front below a line of dentils. A brick under the eaves is carved with the name of *J. Fitch*, perhaps the architect or builder. Four round-headed windows over two straight-headed windows and two pedimented doorcases. Behind the front, red brick, two distinct builds. Galleried interior. – MONUMENT. E of the church, Mariann Legerton †1829 and family. Brick mausoleum with niches either side of a blocked doorway, and pitched slate roof – rather like a large dog kennel.

The village is visually very satisfying, with three roads converging on a green that lies W of and lower than the parish church. But it is the chapel (*see* above) on its N side which dominates the green, in spite of being set back. Partially obscuring the view of it an incongruous former schoolroom, 1876. Gothic Revival, brick with stock brick and stone dressings. To the r. of the approach to the chapel THE MANSE, late C16 with two feature gables and tall chimneystack. Good early C19 cast-iron railings and piers. To the l., CHAPEL COTTAGE, early C17, joined on to CASTLE HOUSE, early C16, the latter with continuous jetty.

The HIGH STREET runs E uphill from the green. On the N side, ST GEORGE'S HOUSE, early C16 with a sashed front of *c.* 1800. THE HOODS, further E, has an early C16 range to the rear, timbers exposed, and in front a parallel range of the late C17. On the S side, early C19 brick terraces dominate, including two three-storey houses. At the eastern edge of the centre, GOWER HOUSE, four almshouses by *E. F. Bisshopp*, 1895. Single storey, brick, with large square bay windows, optimistically described by the architect as Elizabethan.

BRAINTREE ROAD runs S from the green. On the W side the BREWERY TAVERN, 1879, brick with stock brick dressings and moulded bricks in two gables facing the street. Behind it, buildings of the former Hope Brewery, 1840s, including boilerhouse and square chimney. Converted to a house in 1952. To the S, on the same side, SIMM'S FARM, C16, part weatherboarded and part plastered. Cross-wing fronting the road with jettied gables, the N bressumer carved with spiral leaf design, pendants etc., and on the E wall a pargetted panel, late C17, with foliage and scrollwork. Further S, RUSSELL'S FARM, also C16, opposite BROOK FARM, a hall house of *c.* 1400 that now forms the service wing behind a late C17 range of two storeys and attics that was remodelled in the C18 and given a four-bay sashed front. Crown-post of the medieval hall visible inside. Behind the house a small C17 building, part brick and part timber-framed; originally maltings, later converted to a brewhouse. Continuing S, on the W side, WETHERSFIELD PLACE, Georgian brick of five bays and two storeys with mansard roof, and various C19 additions.

GREAT CODHAM HALL, 2½ m. SE. Seven-bay, two-storey entrance (N) front with C20 sashes and pargetting. But the façade is not quite symmetrical, and although the middle three bays step forward, as one might expect, the two r. hand bays step further forward, as one might not. The oldest part of the house lies behind the middle three bays, tree-ring dated to 1327–70, probably built by Sir John de Coggeshall †1361, and thought to be the cross-wing of a now vanished hall. Moulded and carved ceiling beams visible inside, and one crown-post in the roof. Wings added to the r. and l. in the C16 and early C17 respectively, the five-bay C17 wing of interest for its row of rooms entered from a corridor, as in a college or inn. C18 improvements, including the staircase and panelled dining room. Alterations in the 1930s, mainly to the W front overlooking the Pant valley, with two double-height bows; between them a Venetian window. Opposite the W front, an C18 brick DOVECOTE. Square, two storeys, with pyramidal roof and octagonal wooden cupola. Doorway with pointed arch and above it two blind windows, also pointed. To the N, a cottage that was originally a manorial CHAPEL. Small, single-cell, of flint rubble now rendered but with some stone dressings revealed; *c.* 1300.

CODHAM MILL, 2½ m. SE. C18 watermill and house in a continuous range, the mill weatherboarded, the house plastered, with plaster quoins.

WETHERSFIELD MILL, 1¼ m. SE. Three-storey weatherboarded watermill with a brick extension of the same height, converted to a house by *Melville Dunbar*, 1974. Separate mill house, 1856.

Brick with white brick dressings. Two projecting gabled bays either side of the entrance with decorative bargeboards and finials.

AT ROTTEN END, 1½ m. SE, THE PRIEST HOUSE. Early C16 with long-wall jetty, with two-storey, two-bay hall flanked by parlour and solar bay to l. and service bay to r. The central chimneystack has a panel of diapered brickwork with three trefoiled heads. To its N, GOLDEN RILL and ROTTEN END FARMHOUSE, originally one house. Late C16 with a large cross-wing at the N end. Then SPICES, early C15 hall and cross-wing and to the r. a higher mid-C16 extension at a slight angle. Further rear extensions. NE, early C16 former granary, part weatherboarded.

BLACKMORE END. *See* p. 142.

8030

WHITE COLNE

ST ANDREW. Very thoroughly restored by *C.J. Moxon*, 1869–72, who rebuilt most of the walls (flint rubble, with stone dressings), added the S vestry (rebuilt 1890) and N porch, and heightened the W tower, giving it battlements and a recessed shingled spire. Roman brick quoins are evidence of the C12 origins of the nave; chancel and tower C14. Inside behind the pulpit three odd niches, the taller central one pointed, the outer two round. – PULPIT. Usual C17 piece unusually enriched. Hexagonal, with, at the angles, term pilasters with Jacobean-style ornament. But on three of the panels, in relief, well-carved figures of the Virgin, St James the Great, and St Augustine of Hippo. The style is not English. Can it be Flemish? – PAINTINGS. On the W wall, but probably intended to flank the altar, large figures of St Andrew and St Peter by *A.I. Whalley*, 1881. – STAINED GLASS. Tower window, 1869, and E window, 1884, by *Ward & Hughes*. Chancel S by *T.F. Curtis, Ward & Hughes*, 1898, and presumably also the chancel N, 1896. – LYCHGATE. 1923, by *E. Beckwith*.

Former VICARAGE, E of the church, 1868–9 by *Moxon*. Brick, with black diapers and string courses. Part rebuilt following a fire in 1952. W of the church the former NATIONAL SCHOOL, now a house, by *H.W. Hayward*, 1863, extended 1884. Gothic. Brick with stone dressings.

The main centre of population is at COLNEFORD HILL, nearly 1 m. SW, with houses round a triangular green. On the SE side, COLNEFORD HOUSE has a two-storey, seven-bay front, richly pargetted, mostly big foliage scrolls, dated 1685 and with the initials of George and Elizabeth Toller, the best of its kind in the county. Two C16 brick chimneys and reused C15 timbers. Below it, running down to the River Colne, a nice row of mainly Late Medieval houses, some plastered, some weatherboarded, punctuated by gabled and jettied cross-wings of former hall houses.

CHALKNEY MILL. *See* Earls Colne.

WHITE NOTLEY

St Etheldreda. c11, arguably pre-Conquest. The chancel arch
is the only immediately visible early feature. It is dressed with
Roman bricks. To its l. and r. two round-headed niches. In the
chancel s wall outside can be detected traces of an c11
doorway, window, and se quoin. The chancel was remodelled
in the c13, its lancets renewed during restoration in 1874–5.
The s aisle and s arcade are c. 1250. Circular piers and double-
chamfered arches. The n aisle and n arcade a little later, with
the same arches but octagonal piers. c14 s porch with plainly
cusped bargeboarding. c15 belfry on four posts, with cusped
arched braces on polygonal shafts high up. n vestry and organ
chamber by J. Oldrid Scott, 1885–8. The frame of the e window
of the vestry is a reused Saxon grave marker. c14 chancel roof,
with four shields dated 1638–9 recording refurbishment of the
chancel. – REREDOS. Mosaic. 1879, by James Powell & Sons,
designed by Holiday. – FONT. Octagonal, Perp, traceried stem,
bowl with quatrefoils with leaves or grotesque heads. – DOOR.
c14, traceried. – SCREENS. n and s aisles, e end, early c16 and
early c15 respectively. – CHEST. Big dug-out, with bevelled lid,
c13? – WALL PAINTING. Extensive remains at the e end of the
nave, mostly indistinct. On the s wall, two (of three) tiers of
what appears to be a Passion cycle. Similar in style to Fairstead
and Belchamp Walter, i.e. c. 1325–30. – STAINED GLASS. In
vestry e window, upper half of the figure of a king (?), c13. e
window †1903 by Heaton, Butler & Bayne.

White Notley Hall. c16, quite large, with the central hall
well preserved. s front with a gable at either end, two storeys
and attics, plastered, with false quoins. Single-storey c19
additions to the r. The back of the house shows the central
portion and the e wing to be timber-framed, c. 1530, but the
w wing to be about fifty years later, and of brick, not plastered
as it is on the front elevation. Six gables at the back, including
one for the staircase tower, with its original newel stair. At right
angles to the house at its nw corner a c16 CART LODGE.
Diapered brickwork on the ground floor, open on the side
away from the house, the upper floor timber-framed with
brick-nogging.

Pennett's Farm, ¾ m. nw. Main two-storey range of c. 1600.
At the n end the single-storey, two-bay hall of c. 1400 survives,
still open to the roof. This has one original truss, with tie-beam
on arched braces, crown-post, and four-way struts.

WHITE RODING

St Martin. Norman nave with Roman brick quoins, two plain
doorways, some original windows, and a plain one-stepped
chancel arch. Chancel E.E. with a recess in the w wall s of the
chancel arch. Large w tower c. 1500 with diagonal buttresses
and battlements; spire taken down in 1959. Early c17 timber s

porch. N vestry added by *Somers Clarke* as part of a general restoration, 1878–9; the W window and two nave S windows date from this time. Plain, spacious interior, with good crown-post roofs: nave 1250–1300, chancel mid C14. – S DOOR. Norman, of unusual construction, with C13 decorated iron-work. – FONT. Norman, square, of Purbeck marble with zigzag decoration and incised concentric circles in the spandrels on the top. – MONUMENTS. In nave, to Rev. John Maryon †1760 and Sir Thomas Maryon Wilson, erected 1822, both large and impressive. On either side of chancel arch, memorials to Queen Victoria and King Edward VII by *Rev. J.E. Long*, rector 1893–1925, who left his mark upon the church in many small ways. A memorial to his daughter and wife Emily †1872 incor-porates a portrait medallion of Long sculpted by himself and cast in bronze at the rectory in 1911. His also the REREDOS, 1903, and weathervane.

One or two interesting houses along CHURCH LANE, including CHURCH COTTAGE, early C19 timber-framed and plastered with thatched roof, Gothick detailing, and a central cross-wing whose upper storey projects to form a porch supported on wooden posts. White-brick TOWER MILL at the far end: 1877, the last corn mill to be built in the county. No sails.

CAMMAS HALL, 1¼ m. N. Large late C16 house with cross-wings and staircase wing, and original chimneystack with four diag-onal shafts.

COLVILLE HALL, ½ m. W. Good early C16 house with later addi-tions. It forms the E side of a yard with outbuildings on the other three sides, a remarkable ensemble, ranging in date from the C12 to C17. The most striking is on the W side, a timber-framed building with brick nogging, an exquisite piece of its type; second quarter of the C16. Two storeys, jettied on the E side, with stables on the ground floor and a large room, perhaps a manorial courtroom, above. S of the house an Early Tudor brick gateway; pediment with remains of three octago-nal pinnacles over four-centred arch.

LUCAS FARM, 1 m. ENE. High-quality L-plan house with exposed timbers. Early C16 N wing with long-wall jetty, wing with two-storey porch added to its S end later in the same century.

WICKEN BONHUNT

ST MARGARET. *John Hanson Sperling* was rector here, 1856–62, long enough to restore the church and build the rectory, acting as his own architect. He was the author of *Church Walks in Mid-dlesex* (1849), and a contributor to *The Ecclesiologist*, so thought he knew what he was doing. St Margaret's dates from the C12, and had a round tower, but the oldest surviving part is now the C13 chancel. This Sperling restored in 1857, and in 1858–9 rebuilt the nave and tower; drawings by *G.E. Pritchett* survive for the chancel stalls, but there is no other evidence that he contributed to the restoration, and Sperling was not shy about claiming the credit. All was done in accordance with the best ecclesiological principles, and the *Ecclesiologist* approved: *Minton* TILES in the chancel, CHANCEL SCREEN (carved by *Rattee & Kett*) with a triangular canopy surmounted by a floriated gilt cross derived from the Ecclesiological Society's *Instrumenta ecclesiastica*, and a stone PULPIT designed by *G. E. Street*. The w face of the wall above the chancel arch is decorated with motifs in stamped plaster using the technique invented by *Benjamin Ferrey*. But the result is rather lifeless, and there are surprising lapses: the chancel is lower than the nave, there is no vestry, and there was a stove in the chancel next to the priest's stall. The only significant change to the church since has been the replacement of the E window by *A. W. Blomfield*, 1868, and the rebuilding of the spire on a much smaller scale by *F. W. Chancellor*, 1935.

FONT. Norman; plain, massive, square. – ALTAR. English altar with riddel posts, 1935, by *Chancellor*; also ALTAR RAILS. – MONUMENTS. J. J. Bradbury †1731, signed by *H. Scheemakers*. Relief scene flanked by volutes showing the ten-year-old Bradbury rising above the clouds escorted by putti. – STAINED GLASS. Sperling installed glass by *Lavers & Barraud*: the five side windows in the chancel, and sexfoils in the two nave N windows on the N side of the nave. E window by *Clayton & Bell*, 1868, who also did the remaining nave windows, 1877–9. – MOSAIC CROSS (chancel S) by *Powell's*, 1887. – BANNER of St Margaret, designed by *Bodley*, and worked by the Ladies' Ecclesiastical Embroidery Society, *c.* 1860.

Sperling's RECTORY (now Wicken House Residential Centre) came first, 1856; it cost £5,000 and had its own chapel, complete with stalls and stained glass. Miraculously, given its size and uncompromisingly Victorian appearance,* it survives, E of the church. In between, a small SCHOOL (now a private house), of the same materials, red and yellow brick, and about the same date; could this be by Sperling also, or is it too pretty?

CHAPEL OF ST HELEN, Bonhunt Farm, ¾ m. E. A complete Norman chapel of nave and chancel with a number of plain original windows and some re-set fragments of circular shafts. Used as a barn for many years, reconsecrated in 1975; no fittings. There was a substantial Saxon settlement in the adjoining fields, dating from *c.* 700–850.

BRICK HOUSE, less than ¼ m. SW. Small compact brick building with one shaped and one altered gable, *c.* 1600, with a rear wing added *c.* 1660. Transomed four-light windows. Later doorcase with segmental pediment and cartouche with arms of the Bradbury family, who built the house. Above it a circular niche with the bust of a Roman emperor. On the parapet, at one corner, a stone figure in Roman dress.

* Described by Pevsner in a footnote as 'gruesome'.

WICKFORD

St Catherine. Rebuilt 1875–6 by *Henry Stone*. E.E., stone rubble. Nave, chancel, N vestry and organ chamber, and S porch; a N aisle was planned but not built, as can be seen from the blind arcade. Timber w bellcote with attractive openwork frame and shingled splay-foot spire. Some materials from the old church reused, including a c15 window in the N wall of the vestry, and the chancel roof of *c.* 1500. Brick choir vestry by *John Leech*, 1934, extended by *Wykeham Chancellor & Bragg*, 1957. – REREDOS. By *William Butterfield*, from All Saints, Margaret Street, London. Stone with inlaid coloured marbles. – STAINED GLASS. E window by *A.L. Moore & Co.*, nave N †1919 by *A. L. Moore & Son.* – Another nave N by *Jones & Willis*, 1936. – Nave S (with masonic emblems) by *Arthur S. Walker* of *G. Maile & Son*, 1947. – LYCHGATE by *Stanley Bragg*, 1949.

St Andrew, London Road. 1963–4 by *Tooley & Foster*. Pale brown brick and, on the outside, not particularly church-like, apart from a weatherboarded w tower with pyramidal spire. Inside, the laminated-wood portal frames stand clear of the walls, creating narrow aisles, with a deeper recess for the choir at the SE corner.

WICKHAM BISHOPS

The older part of the village, including the medieval parish church (St Peter), lies along the River Blackwater. The main centre of the village, including the present parish church (St Bartholomew) lies at the top of the hill 1 m. NE.

St Bartholomew. By *Ewan Christian*, 1849–50, an ambitious design, relatively early in his prolific career. Given by Sarah Leigh in memory of her father, Rev. Thomas Leigh †1848 (cf. Goldhanger). E.E., Kentish rag with Caen stone dressings; nave, chancel, N and S aisles, and S transept. w tower and a very tall (nearly 111 ft (34 metres) altogether) splay-foot spire with lucarnes, shingled but looking as if it would rather be in stone. Fittings include octagonal FONT with tall wooden cover, large Caen stone PULPIT, and oak ALMS BOX on a pedestal, all well carved. Good extension to S by *Plater Inkpen Vale & Downie* (project architect, *G. Vale*), 1994–5: pale brick, square plan, with a two-way gabled roof that creates an interesting variety of planes. – ORGAN CASE. By *E. Geldart*, 1899, made by *Percy Bacon & Bros.* – ALTAR. Carved oak front framing a painted panel of the Lamb of God with censing angels. Six matching panels with figures of saints etc. on E wall. Probably all 1911. – STAINED GLASS. E window by *Gamon & Humphry*, 1911. – MONUMENTS. Sarah Leigh. 'Founder's tomb' in recess on N side of chancel. – In churchyard, three headstones to members of the Wood family by *William Butterfield*, 1891.

ST PETER. Nave and chancel, late CII, with late CI6 S porch and the remains of a W belfry. Mostly of flint rubble but with some Roman bricks, especially the quoins of the chancel and NE quoin of the nave. Superseded by St Bartholomew (q.v.) and allowed to become semi-ruinous; leased to the Friends of Friendless Churches, 1975, and in 1996 repaired by *Julian Limentani* of *Marshall Sisson* for use as a studio by the stained-glass artist Benjamin Finn. – ALTAR. Stone, very simple, by *Rory Young*, 2002. – FONT. Octagonal, mid CI5. – SCULPTURE. Stone figure of St Peter by *Nicholas Hague*, 2003.

VILLAGE HALL. By *John Finch Partnership*, 2005. Stock brick, with courses of black and red brick, and timber cladding higher up. Basilica-like, with single-storey side aisles and narthex, double-height hall with clerestory, and a slight apse at the two-storey E end.

FAIRPLAY HOUSE (Outdoor Education Centre), ½ m. NE of St Peter. By *C.H.B. Quennell*, c. 1926–8, for Valentine Crittall (originally 'Crockies'), with later additions. Long house, two storeys and attics, with half-hipped pantile roof and Crittall windows. Painted brick, also partly inside, giving an austere, almost industrial feeling. Glazed quadrant at one end leading to former squash court.

HIGH HALL, ½ m. ENE of St Bartholomew. Mid-CI9 Neo-Jacobean. Brick with stone dressings. Symmetrical front with two straight gables, two-storey porch with octagonal clasping buttresses ending in twisted pinnacles and small gable. Former coach house (now house) on W side, in similar vein.

WICKHAM HALL, 1,000 yds SE of St Peter. Mainly CI8 red brick with black headers. Double range, two storeys and attics, with five-bay front. Lower, earlier timber-framed N wing. Moat almost complete.

WICKHAM PLACE, 500 yds N of St Peter. Lovely, wide Queen Anne front of blue brick with red dressings. Two storeys and deep panelled cornice. Central pediment with oval window. Adjoining it to the r. a more conventional CI8 façade of chequered brick. To the r. of this was until 1975 a large mill, of which the sluices etc. remain. Good brick road BRIDGE to SW over the River Blackwater, 1774–6. Three main arches, with two culverts added by *John Johnson*, 1799.

In BEACON HILL, 1 m. ENE of St Bartholomew, LITTLE RUFFINS, by *A.H. Mackmurdo* for his brother-in-law H.W. Carte, 1901–2, but lacking the eccentricity of neighbouring Great Ruffins (Great Totham, q.v.), and considerably altered. Also by Mackmurdo the 'MOTOR HOUSES' in Kelvedon Road, SW of Little Ruffins, c. 1910: cottages on three sides of a square, the ground floor of black weatherboarding and the upper floor a slate mansard roof. Planned as staff accommodation and garaging for Great Ruffins. SNOW'S CORNER, ½ m. NE of St Bartholomew, was designed by Mackmurdo as the post office, with telephone exchange and house, 1905; rough-cast, it looks like an unexceptional building of the 1920s or 30s and has lost the impact it must have had when first built, with its projecting turret-like corners.

VIADUCT, 500 yds N of St Peter. 1847–8, carrying the branch line from Witham to Maldon (closed 1966) over the River Blackwater. Engineer *Joseph Locke*, contractor *Thomas Jackson*. Low, and made of timber. Restored by Essex County Council 1995–6.

WICKHAM ST PAUL

8030

ALL SAINTS. In 1505 £20 was bequeathed for the building of the tower. It is a fine specimen, though not high. Brick with blue brick diapers, diagonal buttresses, high stair-turret, battlements, and brick pinnacles. Brick W doorway (blocked) and W window of three lights with depressed pointed head and intersecting tracery. C14 nave, chancel, and S porch of plastered flint rubble, with N transept and vestry added by *A.W. Blomfield*, 1866. To him also is due the Victorian character of the chancel, including the encaustic TILES on the floor, E wall, and REREDOS. – CHEST. Heavily iron-bound; C13. – SCREEN. With one-light divisions, ogee heads and some panel tracery above. – STAINED GLASS. Dreadful E window, probably 1866, but a very good one on the S side of the sanctuary by *Clayton & Bell*, 1879, and two delightful nave windows by *John Hayward*, 1979 and 1995, the latter incorporating C15 fragments.

WICKHAM HALL, NW of the church. Mid-C19 painted brick. Five-bay N front, with just two large windows on the ground floor flanking the porch, which has two pairs of columns.

The village lies round a large green ½ m. SE, with a few thatched cottages by a pond on its N side, although the general scene is not as picturesque as this might suggest.

CATLEY CROSS HOUSE, 1½ m. SE. Late C16, timber-framed with brick infill, plastered. One-and-a-half storey hall and service end with two-storey cross-wing to l. Inside, an unusually large number of original features survive, including door openings, inglenook fireplace, and stairs with solid treads.

WIDDINGTON

5030

ST MARY THE VIRGIN. Flint and stone rubble, restored by *Ewan Christian*, 1872–4, including a new W tower to replace the C15 one that had fallen in 1771. Of the same time the large imitation Perp windows on the N and S sides of the nave. The E window, however, and the chancel S window are original early C14 work. Inside one notices an earlier history of the chancel. There is one Norman N window and there is the surround of the Dec S window, *c.* 1260, with shafts, much dogtooth decoration, and good stiff-leaf capitals. – SCREEN. By *Guy Dawber*, 1911, made by the rector, *J.W. Court*, and seven local craftsmen. Also by Dawber the FIRST WORLD WAR MEMORIAL, a simple oval tablet with good lettering. – STAINED GLASS. Chancel N, C14 shields of France and England, and panel with a sundial, hourglass and crown dated 1664, restored 1999. – Nave N †1903 by *Heaton, Butler & Bayne*. – The restoration of the church was largely funded by Francis Smith, and his name (or that of his son Griffiths Smith) is to be found on six windows, dated 1874, as well as on the tiled decoration of the E wall of the sanctuary, probably all the work of *Powells*. Smith also gave the LYCHGATE, presumably designed by Christian. – BRASS to a Civilian, *c.* 1460; 18½-in. (47-cm.) figure in loose belted cloak, feet missing.

WIDDINGTON HALL, E of the church. Gabled S front; at the E end are the remains of the C15 hall and buttery wing with an original pointed-arched doorway between them. Extended to the W in the C16 and also to the N. The latter is the main point of interest, a long (five-bay), relatively narrow two-storey block built as a manorial court. The upper floor is undivided save by the roof timbers. N and W fronts of this wing of brick with black diapering and a massive chimney at the N end, but the E side, away from public view, timber-framed.

OLD RECTORY, W of the church. Timber-framed, C16 or C17, refaced in brick in the C18. Fine S side with two slightly projecting wings, and good stables behind.

PRIORS HALL, 250 yds W.* One of two manors in Widdington, given by William the Conqueror to the Abbey of St Valéry-sur-Somme in Picardy, confiscated by Edward III in 1377 and given to William of Wykeham. He used it to form part of the endowment of New College, Oxford, who owned it until 1922. The eastern portion of the house is a Late Saxon chapel, with long-and-short quoins of Barnack stone now exposed on the N side; the original walls are of flint rubble. In the E wall is a blocked doorway, with a small blocked round-headed window above, originally leading to the chancel, now demolished and replaced by a late C20 extension; another blocked doorway, plastered over, in the S wall near what would have been the W end of the chapel. In 1395–1400 the building was re-roofed and converted to a dwelling; thermographic imaging has revealed what appears to be a blocked double-height window in the middle of the S wall, which might have been inserted to light the W end of the hall. A timber-framed extension was added at this time, probably what is now the W end of the house. The open hall was floored in the C16 and a timber-framed rear extension added to the W end *c.* 1700, extended in the C19. Immediately S of the house a timber-framed OUTBUILDING, probably a malthouse, the central five-bay section (with crown-post roof) built with timber felled in 1490–1, with a 1½-bay extension to the E dated to 1563–4 and a two-bay extension to

* I am grateful to Mrs Pam Walker for sharing the results of her research, undertaken with Dr Ian Tyers and the Archivist of New College, Oxford.

the w, 1580s. NW of the house a magnificent eight-bay aisled BARN, weatherboarded with crown-post roof, dated on documentary and tree-ring evidence to 1440–2. At the E end a raised floor inserted in the C18 to provide an area for drying corn. Two gabled entrance bays on the S side with original bargeboards. On the N side, remains of the moat.

The village has several attractive cottages, particularly around THE GREEN below the church, but it owes its distinctive character to the same Francis Smith who was responsible for restoring the church. In 1843 he built BISHOPS at the S end of the High Street on the site of a C16 house, stuccoed, with rusticated quoins and decorative motifs on the chimneystacks. In 1867 he rebuilt MARTINS FARMHOUSE on the corner of Cornells Lane in gault brick with red brick decoration, retaining much of the original timber-framed structure behind. Then on the W side of the High Street he erected a number of cottages, notably six semi-detached pairs, one dated 1868. The form of each is similar but with differences in detailing, using various combinations of red, black, and yellow brick, flint, and bottle ends.

Towards Debden a fine group of farmhouses. First SWAYNES HALL, ½ m. E of the church, with pargetting on the E front including panels with flowers, fleurs-de-lys and lions, and the date 1689. Short wings on the W side extended in the 1950s with entrance hall between. Contemporary five-bay aisled barn. Close by, to the E, MOLE HALL, late C16, L-plan, with on the NW front a two-storey former porch, jettied and gabled, and two more gables. Entirely moated. ½ m. E of Mole Hall, THISTLEY HALL, c. 1670, almost identical to New Amberden Hall, Debden (q.v.), ½ m. SE. Brick, the five-bay front chequered. Two storeys and attics with dormer windows and central doorcase with open pediment. Roof at the rear comes down to the ground floor. Original dog-leg staircase with turned balusters. ¼ m. S of Thistley Hall, AMBERDEN HALL. Late C18 front range, brick, two storeys and three bays with Roman Doric portico flanked by canted bays. Behind this what is probably the surviving NW range of a very substantial house of c. 1560, mainly brick. Central chimneystack with six octagonal shafts, and in the E wall a blocked four-light window with brick mullions and one transom. Above it a frieze with sexfoil flowers. Original fireplaces, including one in the attic with a frieze of Tudor roses. The brick wall of the garden on the W side is partly the remains of the larger house but seems mostly to have been built in the C17 reusing the old bricks. To the E of the house a small brick building contemporary with the main building, with some original brick windows; perhaps originally a chapel, now a house. Nine-bay weatherboarded barn to NW, c. 1570. Three sides of a moat to the S of the house, and remains of another to the N.

WIDFORD

6000

Borough of Chelmsford

ST MARY. Rebuilt by *J.P. St Aubyn*, 1862, paid for by Arthur Pryor of Hylands (cf. Galleywood). Kentish rag with Bath stone dressings. Dec. w tower with very tall broach spire and four pinnacles that appear unfinished. Nave, N aisle, chancel, S porch, and N vestry with organ chamber over it. This adds to the interest externally, and internally results in an elaborate opening into the chancel at high level. Four-bay N arcade with alternate round and octagonal piers. A small amount of stone carving by *T. Earp*. Good open timber roofs, and much other quality work, including CHOIR STALLS. – STAINED GLASS. E window by *Powell & Sons*, 1862, dark rich colours. – MONUMENTS. William Hucks †1804, by *Richard Westmacott*. Marble tablet with classical decoration. – In churchyard, Sarah, Viscountess Falkland †1776. Stone pyramid on a square base, very substantial. Designed by *George Gibson*, made by *Edward Pierce*, 1778.

There is little to show that Widford was once a village. SW of the church the OLD RECTORY, *c.* 1818, gault brick, doorway in stone and stucco surround flanked by canted bays. About 200 yds NW of the church, but separated from it by the A414 and on an industrial estate, WIDFORD HALL (now offices), late C17 with a nice, plain brick front of two storeys and three bays. More of the village in Widford Road, E of London Road, including No. 44, an early C19 single-storey gault brick cottage with hoodmoulded Gothick sashes, and a later C19 corrugated-iron chapel, now the VILLAGE HALL.

HYLANDS. *See* p. 500.

WILLINGALE

5000

Willingale Doe and Willingale Spain were two adjoining parishes, with the curious distinction of sharing the same churchyard: St Christopher Willingale Doe lies on its N side, St Andrew Willingale Spain on its S. St Christopher is the larger church. It has a W tower (with diagonal buttresses and battlements), whereas St Andrew has only a belfry. The benefices were united in 1929, and in 1992 St Andrew was vested in the Churches Conservation Trust, for whom it was extensively repaired by *Simon Marks*, 1993–5.

ST ANDREW is the older church. The nave has in the N wall two Norman windows and a plain Norman doorway, in the S wall one window and a doorway. These and the quoins make much use of Roman bricks; otherwise of flint rubble with courses of puddingstone. The chancel is C15, as is the belfry resting on a tie-beam carried by two posts with arched braces. Restoration by *Ernest Geldart*, 1891–2, included the rebuilding of the S porch, addition of the N vestry, ALTAR and REREDOS, painted decoration of the chancel (of which only traces now remain),

and some very jazzy encaustic tile paving. – FONT. Octagonal,
C14, with traceried stem and quatrefoils carrying roses and
heads. Oak COVER by *Geldart*. – DOOR in N doorway, with
uncommonly extensive C12 ironwork, divers long stems with
leaves besides the usual scrolled strap-hinges. – STAINED
GLASS. E window by *Cox & Sons*, *c*. 1870.

ST CHRISTOPHER. Restored by *J. Clarke*, 1852–3, and even at
the time it was thought that he went too far; the flint exterior
has no untouched features.* He added the N aisle, rebuilt the
C15 tower and fitted up its base as a vestry. C14 chancel and
nave (see the S doorway), C15 porch. – FONT. Octagonal, Perp,
with traceried stem and quatrefoils carrying shields. – STAINED
GLASS. E window by *Saunders & Co.*, *c*. 1878. W windows
(tower and N aisle) also by Saunders, designed by *Geldart*,
1879–80. – Good window to Major Arthur T. Saulez †1917
(nave S). – MONUMENTS. Brass to Thomas Torrell †1442,
knight in armour, the figure 37 in. (93 cm.) long. – Brasses to
Ann Torrell †1582 (palimpsest) and Dorothy Brewster †1613,
figures 24 and 22½ in. (61 and 58 cm.). – Robert Wiseman
†1641 and Richard and Mary Wiseman †1618 and 1635. Large
monument, marble and alabaster with painted lettering, attributed to *William Wright*. Reclining figure of Robert flanked by
two columns and behind a third. Above the entablature carried
by these are two smaller figures, Richard and Mary, kneeling
under two arches. – Lady Winifred Wyseman †1684, oval tablet
in white marble with laurel-wreath frame and shield of arms.
Probably by *William Stanton* (GF). – John Salter †1744, Lord
Mayor of London, tablet with obelisk and urn in different
coloured marbles.

OLD RECTORY, Willingale Doe. For Rev. John Bramston, rector
from 1797, and (unusually for a parsonage) moated. Similar in
style to the front block of Torrell's Hall (*see* below), and possibly also by *John Johnson*: three storeys, gault brick with a plain
stone band at first-floor height, and Doric porch.

OLD SCHOOL and SCHOOL HOUSE, N of the churches. 1863 by
Chancellor, with black brick decorations. Sympathetically
extended after 1985 to form a private house.

DUKES, 700 yds NNW. Farmhouse with exposed timbers on the
upper storey. Low hall between two jettied cross-wings built in
the second quarter of the C16, soon replaced by a two-storey
hall with crown-post roof, with brick chimneystack and stair-
tower added at the rear.

TORRELL'S HALL, ¾ m. NNW. Late C16 with numerous alterations and extensions, the most significant the two-storey, three-
bay front (S) block added by *John Johnson* for John Crabb, who
acquired the house in 1800. Gault brick, tripartite windows
with segmental heads, and central fluted Doric porch leading
into a coved entrance passage. The rest of the house of red

---

* George Buckler wrote in 1856 that 'it has undergone such considerable alterations,
as almost to deprive it of its antiquarian interest'.

brick, with a group of mid-C19 MODEL FARM BUILDINGS on the N side.

WARDEN'S HALL, ¼ m. SW. For John Salter, *c.* 1720–40. Brick, five bays and two storeys, the middle three bays breaking slightly forward; central doorcase with Gibbs surround in painted wood and segment-headed windows.

WIMBISH

5030

ALL SAINTS. Norman nave: see one S window and the S doorway, with two orders of columns, one of them spiral-carved and with volute capitals, the other smooth and with one-scallop capitals; both have plaited rings below the capitals. C13 alterations to this Norman nave are not easy to understand. The only evidence is a blank pointed arcade outside, just above the Norman window. What was its purpose? Inside, the N arcade is also C13. It has quatrefoil piers and double-hollow-chamfered arches. S porch, with upper room, C15. Chancel also C15, but largely rebuilt as part of the restoration of 1872 by *W.O. Milne*, who also removed a gallery and N vestry. N aisle restored by *F. Woodhouse*, 1879, its roof dated 1534 in one of the graceful tracery spandrels of the braces, and attributed by John Harvey to *Thomas Loveday*. W tower destroyed by lightning in 1740, its replacement (within the W end of the nave) completed by 1755; a scheme of 1883 by *Nelson Jones* to rebuild it beyond the W wall got no further than taking down the C18 one. – SCREEN to Thunderley (N) Chapel. One-light divisions with ogee heads and mouchettes above; late C14. – COMMANDMENT BOARD. Dated 1580. – STAINED GLASS. In Thunderley Chapel, fragments of C14 glass. – In chancel, N and S windows by *Gibbs & Howard*, 1888, and a two-light window by *A.J. Dix*, about the same date. – MONUMENTS. Sir John de Wautone †1347 and wife. An unusual and delightful piece. Two small brasses (his effigy, part missing, originally 19 in. (48 cm.) long), both in the elegant, swaying attitudes of that age. The style is very similar to that of the most accomplished of English brasses, that of Sir Hugh Hastings at Elsing in Norfolk (†1347). Fragments of a cross-head in the form of an ogee quatrefoil around the figures, and at the foot the indent of an elephant and castle. – Mary Wiseman †1654. Painted board with inscription, including an approximate anagram of her name ('Mi jesu rais me anu') and a long verse ending 'She to her sexe a patterne stood / Of all thats imitably good'.

No village near the church, just the weatherboarded HALL on the S side, with a large C17 weatherboarded barn, and the gabled OLD VICARAGE on the E, C17 or C18 brick remodelled in the C19.

BROADOAKS MANOR, 2 m. S. Partly moated brick house, the surviving wing of a house whose taller main range extended to the S. Tree-ring dating of the timbers in the outer parts of the structure – the N and W fronts – has shown that it was built in the

late 1570s or early 1580s, probably for Thomas Wiseman
(†1585). The principal original feature is the gable at the w end
of the N front. The ground floor has a six-light window with
one transom, the first floor a six-light window with two transoms, and the (straight) gable a low four-light window. Clunch
dressings. On the w front four four-light windows, two on the
ground floor with one transom and two on the first floor with
two transoms. The E front has two gables, that on the l. early
C18, when the re-entrant corner was filled in. Most of the S
front is C19 brick and tile-hanging, where the rest of the house
joined on. Splendid chimneystacks, all with octagonal shafts,
the tops renewed. Little in the way of original interior fittings,
but a fine, quite classical fireplace on the first floor. Of clunch,
with Doric pilasters and dentilled cornice, a panelled frieze
with strapwork and another panel with a row of trefoiled pendants. Excellent, gently curving newel stair, oak with turned
balusters, by *Kay Pilsbury*, 2001–4, part of a restoration that
included reinstatement of the windows on the w front, and a
single-storey extension to the SW. In the attic, a room formerly
used as a chapel. Its fireplace conceals the priest-hole in which
Father John Gerard successfully hid in 1594.

TIPTOFTS, 1¼ m. WNW. One of the most valuable survivals of
medieval domestic architecture in Essex, although from
outside that is hardly discernible. It is not known who built it,
but timbers in separate parts of the house have been tree-ring
dated to 1282–1327 (hall) and 1287–1329 (s cross-wing). From
1562 until the late 1980s it was owned by Brasenose College,
Oxford, who encased the E (entrance) and N fronts in brick in
the third quarter of the C19. The visitor is thus quite unpre-
pared for what lies within. A low passage to the l. of the C19
front door leads into the original HALL, which is largely complete and, moreover, an aisled hall, and, what is more, a hall
not horizontally subdivided. So, standing in it, one sees one
slim detached quatrefoil pier with fillets to the shafts and a
moulded capital just as in a church, and the pier opposite now
partly in a later wall, so that the existence of the second (E)
aisle can only be deduced from the existence of the mortice of
a former horizontal strut. The piers carry traceried curved
braces with the very simple motif of a large pointed trefoil. On
the tie-beam stands an octagonal crown-post with capital
which in its turn carries four-way struts, again exactly as in
Essex churches. There were originally three roof trusses in the
hall, the middle pair resting not on shafts but on hammer-
beams to gain more space in the centre of the hall. The third
pair is not visible. Clearly visible, however, at the s end of the
hall are one two-centred arch, part of a second and indications
of a third, and doorways leading to the buttery, kitchen, and
pantry in the s cross-wing in the way familiar from larger
houses and university colleges. In the w wall can be seen part
of the trefoiled head of a window. The middle of the hall is now
filled with a C16 brick chimneystack, and the floor to the N was

inserted at about the same time. In the C17 the E aisle was obscured by the addition of a two-storey extension, balanced by the extension of the C15 N cross-wing in the C19 followed by refronting in brick. Complete moat, with C18 and C19 farm buildings to the N and square brick dovecote to the E.

WITHAM

8010

Churches   842
Public Buildings   844
Perambulations   845

Witham is best considered as three separate parts: Chipping Hill, p. 842 the area round the parish church; Newland Street, the former main road from London to Colchester; and the housing that has encircled the old town since the 1960s. Chipping Hill is the original centre of the town, which grew up around the market that was held here. In 1212 the Knights Templar, who had held the manor of Witham since 1147, were granted a charter to hold a weekly market along the Roman road ½ m. SE of the church. This was the origin of Newland Street, and although the market at Chipping Hill continued to be held weekly until the C15, thereafter the area declined and the focus of the town's commercial activity shifted.

Daniel Defoe described Witham as 'a pleasant, well-situated market town' in 1722, and in 1736 Dr James Taverner established a spa at Powers Hall End, ½ m. W of the church, the water coming from a chalybeate spring discovered in the C17. Buildings were erected (including an assembly room moved from New Hall, Boreham), but the spa did not long survive Taverner's death in 1746. However, it brought a period of prosperity to the town which is reflected in the architecture of Newland Street. Witham was also the half-way point on the two-day coach journey from London to Harwich, and a further boost was given to the town when Princess Charlotte stayed the night in 1761 on her way to marry King George III. All this changed with the arrival of the railway in 1843, which further separated Chipping Hill from Newland Street.

The growth of the town was unremarkable until 1964, when the council entered into a Town Development Agreement with London County Council to expand the population from 10,000, as it then was, to 25,000 by 1981. Five new residential areas were designated, to take 3,000 homes. To accompany this growth, an industrial area was developed on the E side of the town, mostly between the town and the by-pass, which had opened in 1965; office development was concentrated on the site of The Grove, on the SE side of Newland Street. Educational and leisure facilities were also provided.

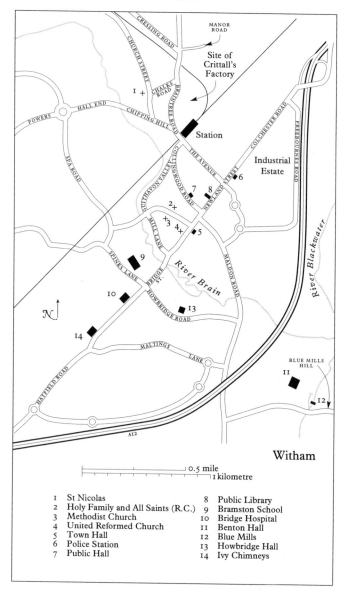

Witham

1 St Nicolas
2 Holy Family and All Saints (R.C.)
3 Methodist Church
4 United Reformed Church
5 Town Hall
6 Police Station
7 Public Hall
8 Public Library
9 Bramston School
10 Bridge Hospital
11 Benton Hall
12 Blue Mills
13 Howbridge Hall
14 Ivy Chimneys

CHURCHES

St Nicolas. A large church, mainly of flint and pebble rubble with some Roman brick, well positioned on rising ground to the N of Chipping Hill Green. Almost entirely C14: W tower with diagonal buttresses and a W window with Dec tracery, nave and both aisles, embattled porch, and chancel. Embattled

ragstone rubble N vestry added later in the same century; originally floored, with a stair-turret in one corner. Only the N and
s chancel chapels are C15, the former slipped in between the N
aisle and the vestry with a single Perp window taking up most
of the wall. The s doorway (re-set) is the one surviving piece
of evidence of an earlier church: *c.* 1200 with three orders of
columns and voussoirs partly with three-dimensional zigzag
and partly with keeled roll mouldings. N and s aisle windows
of the same pattern of tracery as the w window of the tower,
the porch windows different but of the same character. One s
aisle window is different, but also Dec. The chancel E window
(renewed 1844) has ogee reticulation. The arcades of four bays
have the curious piers consisting of a square with big attached
demi-shafts that are found also at Halstead and Feering, and
arches with a double wave moulding. Tall steep tower arch on
semicircular responds. The C15 s chapel opens in two bays into
the chancel. The pier has an odd section as if reused or
re-tooled. It consists of four shafts connected by deeply undercut hollows. Two C19 restorations, both by *J. Clarke*, and
restrained. In 1849–50 he removed a w gallery, exposing the
tower arch and w window, re-seated the nave, and carried out
general repairs, and in 1877 removed side galleries and rebuilt
the upper part of the tower, adding a stair-turret on the N side.
– SCREEN. Of tall lights arched and cusped at the top and with
cusped ogee arches a little lower down. Original late C15 up to
the ogee arches; above that, i.e. the loft, by *E. Geldart*, made
by *W.B. Polley*, 1891. – ROYAL ARMS of William III, finely
carved in the round (s chapel, originally intended to hang from
chancel arch). – SCULPTURE. Small wooden relief of the
Nativity (s chapel). Mannerist and not English. – FUNERAL
HELMS (s chapel). One late C16, two C17. – STAINED GLASS.
Tower window by *Wailes*, 1850, given by Sir Gilbert Scott in
memory of his clerk of works, Henry Green Mortimer †1849,
a native of Witham, killed while engaged on the building of
Scott's Nikolaikirche, Hamburg. Other windows 1846–1911,
typical of their date.

MONUMENTS. John Southcote †1585 and his wife Elizabeth.
Plain tomb-chest with recumbent effigies, he in judge's robes.
Good quality; painted alabaster. At w end of N aisle (originally
in chancel); accompanying tablet with side columns and
achievement of arms in N chapel. – Mary Nevell †1592 erected
by her husband Francis Harve 1593, with kneeling couple
facing each other across a prayer desk; painted alabaster and
marble. Attributed to *Garat Johnson the Elder* (AW). – George
Lisle †1687, black and white marble tablet with shield of arms,
supported by a winged cherub's head. – Robert Barwell †1697,
white marble with cherubs' heads and achievement of arms,
an elegant and sophisticated affair with inscription in Latin and
Greek. Attributed to *John Nost* (GF). – William East †1726.
Large monument filling a blocked window on N side of
chancel, by *Stanton & Horsnaile*; excellent bust above a big
inscription tablet. Columns l. and r. supporting a broken and

open segmental pediment. Cherubs standing l. and r. and reclining on the pediment. – Hannah, wife of William Henry Pattisson †1828, and their son William Henry Pattisson and daughter-in-law Sarah Frances †1832, drowned in the Lac de Gauve, High Pyrenees, France. Bas-relief above the lengthy inscription shows the unfortunate couple being reunited with Hannah in the clouds above the scene of their demise. By *C.A. Rivers*, 1834. – In the base of the tower, a good collection of C18 and C19 painted BEQUEST BOARDS, as well as the Creed and Lord's Prayer. – In churchyard, s of s door, HEADSTONE of Matthew Nichols †1700, with skull and crossbones.*

HOLY FAMILY AND ALL SAINTS (R.C.), Guithavon Street. 1840–2 by *John Brown* of Norwich, as a chapel of ease to St Nicolas.† Flint and white brick. Large, in the lancet style. w end with very big bellcote. Nave without aisles and, oddly enough, a tripartite chancel, that is a chancel with aisles of two bays – all this vaulted. Closed 1969, reopened as a Roman Catholic church following alterations by *Plater Inkpen*, 1987–9, including new furnishings and fittings and inserted floor at w end to create a hall, but incorporating stained glass, Stations of the Cross, font and other fittings from the old church in Avenue Road, by *D.C. Nicholls*, 1851 (now a house). – Presbytery also by Plater Inkpen. – Churchyard extended 1867, with cast-iron railings by *Davey, Paxman & Davey*.

METHODIST CHURCH, Guithavon Street. 1961. Original brick chapel by *C. Pertwee*, 1863–4, now used as hall.

UNITED REFORMED CHURCH, Newland Street. Rebuilt 1840, by *James Fenton*. White brick, of five bays with five-bay pediment. Reordering by *Plater Inkpen*, 1984–6, including removal of pews and reconstruction of gallery. Meeting rooms at rear and on N side by *Plater Inkpen Downie*, 1997.

PUBLIC BUILDINGS

TOWN HALL. *See* Perambulation 2.

POLICE STATION, Newland Street. 1937 by *J. Stuart*, County Architect. Dignified Neo-Georgian, set back from the street, with projecting wings, and magistrates' courts behind. Court reception area, 1992.

PUBLIC HALL, Collingwood Road. By *E. J. Dampier*, 1893–4. A graceless composition of brick with stone dressings; veranda and balcony in front.

CHURCH HOUSE, Collingwood Road. By *Chancellor & Son*, 1909–10. Two-storey church hall in rather heavily detailed brick and pebbledash, the arcaded lower storey having the appearance of an open loggia.

PUBLIC LIBRARY, Newland Street. Originally a private house (White Hall), then a school, later a cinema. C18 façade, five

---

* The 2nd edition of *Essex* states that the PULPIT is by *Bodley*, but the attribution cannot be verified.
† Brown also designed a school to the s (dem.).

bays, rusticated ground floor and pilasters rising through two upper storeys, restored by the *County Architect's Dept* (project architects, *James Boutwood* and *John Came*), 1981, and replacement portico added. Offices at the front, galleried library occupying the former auditorium behind.

BRAMSTON SCHOOL, Spinks Lane. By *J. Stuart*, 1937, a traditional stripped classical design in brick; considerably extended *c.* 1971.

BRIDGE HOSPITAL, Hatfield Road. Former workhouse, 1837–9, by *Scott & Moffatt*, additions by *Whitmore*, 1897. Brick, with polygonal central block and high arched gateway. Closed 2003.

MEMORIAL GARDEN, Newland Street. War Memorial by *Sir Charles Nicholson*, 1920: stone cross and screen wall incorporating a bronze bas-relief by *Gilbert Ledward* of a soldier kneeling in front of St George.

SAUL'S BRIDGE, Maldon Road. Single-span cast-iron bridge over the River Brain, by the County Surveyor, *Robert Lugar*, 1814, made by *Ransome & Son* of Ipswich.

PERAMBULATIONS

1. Chipping Hill

Starting at the centre of CHIPPING HILL, the triangular Green on the S side of the church is lined by a very satisfying group of timber-framed houses. The oldest building is THE FORGE, on the corner of Church Street, restored by the *County Architect's Dept* (supervising architect, *James Boutwood*), 1979. The core is a hall house dating to *c.* 1375, with cross-wings added *c.* 1425 and 1500; the smithy, still working, is an extension of *c.* 1650. On the opposite corner, the WHITE HORSE INN, late C16. E of Church Street, BRAMSTONS, C16 altered and enlarged in the mid C19, then THE RECESS, and TEMPLE VILLAS, large mid-C19 houses that reflect the revived prosperity of the area following the arrival of the railway. Facing down Chipping Hill THE GRANGE, *c.* 1720, restored 1971 when the porch was added.

Turning back now towards the church, on the S side of Chipping Hill, No. 29, BROOKCOTE HOUSE, by *George Sherrin*, 1896, described as a 'small cottage residence' but to our eyes a large house, the front to the street a playful irregular composition of three gables each bigger than the last. This and Earlsmead (1899, dem.), were designed by Sherrin for Joseph Smith & Sons, builders, a development prompted no doubt by the proximity of the railway station. BARNARDISTON HOUSE is C16 with a seven-bay Georgian front, then W of Moat Farm Chase No. 43, with continuous jettied front, mid C17, attached to No. 45, C15 or early C16, the jettied gable forming the end of a house that formerly extended further W. The end wall of No. 43 has a nice oriel window and pretty pargetting under the gable. Finally in this section, Nos. 51–53, a hall house with cross-wings of *c.* 1400, one gable jettied, the other underbuilt, with painted decoration inside including the date 1606. The brick chimney that was inserted *c.* 1600 projects at its base through the front wall, with a little arched alcove, now filled in, on the street. No. 55 is an extension to the house of *c.* 1710.

Down the hill is CHIPPING HILL BRIDGE over the Brain, 1770 by *Samuel Humphreys* and *Charles Malyon*, Witham bricklayers. On the far side the stock brick MILL HOUSE, 1856. Weatherboarded mill destroyed by fire in 1882, but rebuilt in similar style as an extension to the house by *Geary & Black*, 2001–4. Just beyond it SPRING LODGE, gault brick, early C19. Along the N side of POWERS HALL END, the substantial C16 brick wall of WITHAM PLACE, the house itself demolished *c.* 1850. ¾ m. further on SPA HOUSE, the only visible evidence of Dr Taverner's spa, incorporating a C17 timber-framed house; much altered in the C19.

Returning towards the church, the old VICARAGE can be seen on the l., the surviving part of a large timber-framed house of *c.* 1700 encased in brick for the Rev. George Sayer, vicar 1722–61. He also landscaped the grounds to the N and W of the house, with the help of *Philip Southcote*, whose father's seat was Witham Place.*

The path through the churchyard leads to CHURCH STREET, the E side dominated by the former parish WORK-HOUSE (Nos. 28–40) dated 1714; the dormer-lit attic was built as a single long workroom that extends the whole length of the building. The building was divided in 1839 after the construction of the new workhouse (*see* Bridge Hospital) in Hatfield Road. Nos. 24–26, C15 with a gable at one end and projecting upper storey, probably housed the master. N of the brick Board School, 1902, a nice row of early C18 cottages, Nos. 44–48B. On the street's W side, No. 11 is the most elegant house in the Chipping Hill area: *c.* 1720, five bays, two storeys and attics, and a careful display of brickwork: red brick in Flemish bond with burnt headers below the ground-floor windows, then burnt headers laid in header bond with red brick dressings, and segmental arches of gauged brick over the windows.

A most startling contrast to the village-like atmosphere of Chipping Hill is made in BRAINTREE ROAD to the E, although its rural origins can still be detected: Nos. 55–59, just S of Chalks Road, is a terrace of three cottages, 1855, well-detailed stock brick designed to look like a single house. S of here, in WHITE HORSE LANE (now separated from Chipping Hill by Bellfield Road), former seed warehouses erected by Thomas Cullen in what was then the bottom of the garden of his house, No. 16 Chipping Hill: one timber-framed and weatherboarded, late C19, and the second of brick, 1920s. But what one chiefly notices is the supermarket and car park occupying the site of the Crittall Manufacturing Co.'s factory, 1919, demolished

---

*Horace Walpole called the result 'one of the most charming villas in England'; the grounds included a cascade and a bath house.

1992; workers' housing by *C.H.B. Quennell*, 1924–6, survives to the N in Rickstones Road (Nos. 6–8) and Manor Road. E of Crittalls' site the railway and, on the far side, Baird's maltings.[*]

2. Newland Street and neighbourhood

NEWLAND STREET is entirely separate from Chipping Hill; there was no direct public road between the two until Collingwood Road was opened in 1872. The best place to start is the Memorial Garden (*see* above) on the corner of The Avenue.[†] Witham's C18 prosperity led almost always to refronting, rather than complete rebuilding; Newland Street needs to be seen from behind as well as in front. On the NW side the remarkably unified C18 character of the street starts with some flourish at AVENUE HOUSE, seven windows wide. C16, cased in early C18 chequered brick but refronted in red brick in 1757 (rainwater head). The shell-hooded doorcase and heavy wooden cornice look earlier; No. 2 is a three-bay addition. Nos. 6–12 form a terrace built for servants of The Grove in 1828: gault brick, with a pediment over the central double doorcase echoed at roof level. Then ROSLYN HOUSE, also gault brick, refronted in 1720. Nine bays and two storeys with a pedimented Tuscan doorway; a delicate C19 glasshouse projects towards the street, and to the rear a C17 wing. From here, the original timber framing of the late C16 house can be seen. Opposite, FREEBOURNES COURT, a development of commercial buildings but of domestic character, managing not to overwhelm the timber-framed C16 farmhouse that forms its centre. STATUE of Dorothy L. Sayers by *John Doubleday*, 1984. She looks across to the Library (*see* above), behind which lies WHITEHALL COURT, sheltered housing by *Roy Belsham*, 1986. Gault brick is the preferred material on the NW side of the street, whatever the style of building, and it is used again for TIPTREE VILLA, dated 1876, modestly Tudor Gothic and nicely preserved with front garden and iron railings, and again for Nos. 22–26, a five-bay house flanked by two of three bays each, making what appears to be a nice Georgian terrace, but in fact the remodelling of a building dating back to the C15, restored by the *County Architect's Dept* in 1975. This is apparent not just from the rear and sides, but also from the way in which the joists of the upper floor cut across the fanlights over the front doors. Cast-iron railings, *c.* 1866, by *Davey, Paxman & Co*. Back on the SE side, a standard Neo-Georgian POST

---

[*] The commercial buildings N of the maltings replaced *Chamberlin Powell & Bon*'s Cooper Taber seed factory, 1954–6, demolished in spite of its reputation as one of the best industrial buildings of its time.

[†] The Avenue was originally a private road leading to The Grove, planted with a double row of limes in the C18; at the NW end of this, a surviving gatepier and Wrenaissance LODGE by *George Sherrin*, 1898. The house was demolished in 1932; the garden wall runs along the SE side of Newland Street and part of the gardens are now occupied by offices, GROVE HOUSE, 1972.

OFFICE, 1939, a good neighbour to No. 5, HIGH HOUSE, two storeys but originally three, apparently based on a design in *Abraham Swan*'s *Collection of Designs in Architecture* (1757), with a prominent white stucco frontispiece contrasting with the brick to either side. Then THE RED LION, the first of the coaching inns, which as a group seem to have chosen not to have moved with the times and to have kept their antique appearance: this one has a late C14 cross-wing with a crown-post roof, with the NE wing rebuilt in the C17 using old timbers. Nos. 11–15 have C19 Picturesque woodwork applied to them, while Nos. 29–33, delicately pargetted, are closer to their original state. Almost opposite, THE GEORGE, C17 with remodelled front, partly demolished to make way for Collingwood Road.

The staggered junction of Newland Street with Collingwood Road and Maldon Road is an important point and it is therefore all the more regrettable that this was chosen for the one serious interruption to an otherwise harmonious scene: NEWLANDS SHOPPING CENTRE, *c.* 1967–8 by *Wimpey*, an unlovely development of brown brick and concrete wholly at odds (apart from its height) with its neighbours. The buildings opposite have been managed better; the GROVE CENTRE, by *Leslie Jones & Partners* for Charville Estates, 1985–8, makes little impact on the street, but behind is a substantial development including a supermarket and sixteen shop units, pleasant enough in the inoffensive manner inspired by the Essex Design Guide, although the one old building on the site (Superdrug) was mercilessly over-restored. The buildings are staggered, two storeys with pitched tiled roofs, and there is a church-like clock tower as focal point.

On the SE corner of Maldon Road is THE WHITE HART, dating from the C15, with a smart C18 brick building to the rear that presumably overlooked gardens. On the SW side of MALDON ROAD the former BAPTIST CHAPEL, rebuilt 1846, a simple white pedimented brick front, now offices, and then FREELANDS, a yellow and red brick villa by *Chancellor*, 1862. On the other side an early C19 villa (No. 31), the gault brick front of three bays between pilasters, and the former FRIENDS' MEETING HOUSE (now Masonic Hall), *c.* 1809, plain brick with hipped roof.

Returning to Newland Street, on the SE side THE SPREAD EAGLE, the most flamboyant of the inns, C16 behind a façade of Early Victorian picturesqueness, with its carriageway still open. Then the road broadens out, gradually contracting as it goes away from the centre, and the serious business begins with Nos. 55 and 57, both C18 brick, three storeys, and both now banks. No. 57, with C19 porch, was WITHAM HOUSE, home of the Pattisson family, the site purchased by Jacob Pattisson in 1740. W.H.E. Pattisson laid out parkland SW of the house in the 1840s, and in 1901 this was donated to the town as a public PARK; wall-mounted DRINKING FOUNTAIN by *S. Gambier Parry*, 1913, with mixed Gothic and classical decoration. GUITHAVON STREET, opposite, was formed in 1841 by Pattisson to open up a route to All Saints' Church and school that were then being built on ground he donated. On the S side Nos. 3–17, a brick terrace of 1843 with parapet and stuccoed cornice, four of the doors paired under elliptical arches. No. 19, large, detached Neo-Tudor brick with stone dressings, is an early example of a purpose-built savings bank, 1850, now offices. On the N side, PENHALIGON COURT, mixed development of flats and shops by *Wimpey Homes*, 1989, brick with slate and tile roofs and appropriate in scale. Beyond the church, Old Parsonage Court, a late 1980s housing development based round the parsonage of *c.* 1849 that lies W of what appears to be a replacement parsonage in the domestic Gothic style of the 1860s.

Back to Newland Street. BARCLAYS BANK (No. 59), 1939, sits well between its neighbours; to its r. the TOWN HALL, occupying a three-storey, three-bay brick town house, with recessed cast-stone Tuscan porch. Refronted in the mid C19 to conceal a late C15 timber-framed building with a C16 wing at the rear. Then a very pleasant row of shops (including some good C18 shop windows) and houses (now offices), notably No. 87, brick, three bays with round-headed window on first floor, steps up to front door with fanlight and ornamental railings. No. 63 is in fact an early C15 hall house, which retains a crown-post roof, altered in the C16 and refronted in the C18. Opposite, the United Reformed Church (*see* Churches), set back from the street. The shop at No. 92 occupies two C16 houses on timber frames behind a brick front, with an elegant curved Regency staircase. THE BATTESFORD COURT pub is also C16, with a Tudor brick chimney at the E end, and a brick front of seven bays that makes the building seem bigger than it is: the top row of windows is false. Perhaps it was meant to rival Nos. 117–119 opposite, a double house of five plus five bays and two-and-a-half storeys over a cellar. Early C18, burnt brick with red brick dressings, the red carried vertically through the storeys; each house with its central pedimented doorway. Behind No. 121, the chance survival of single-storey cottage with brick-vaulted cellar beneath. Nos. 125–127 and 129 now form the doctors' surgery, but were formerly two C17 houses. Nos. 125–127 has a fine C19 porch on spiral columns; the side elevation of No. 129 is pargetted, but it has a brick front, with canted bays either side of the doorway, and the best fanlight in the street, late C18 cast iron.

Across the road again HIGHWAY COTTAGE, a small late C14 hall house with one cross-wing (the second now forms part of No. 120), has kept its medieval appearance, and is perhaps the oldest surviving house in the town. Hall roof raised and first floor inserted in the mid C17. No. 120 (formerly a school) has an ornamental C19 façade and, inside, a large fireplace lined with blue-and-white Delft tiles. No. 126 appears to be another early C18 house. Five bays, two windows with little curly brick decoration of the lintels; the centre window arched. The arched window is a motif with which we are now familiar – it occurs also at Nos. 85 and 87, and on the other side at No. 74 – as we are with the use of burnt headers, although little of it appears here squeezed in between the ample red brick dressings. But, yet again, this is the refronting of a much older building, in this case revealed by renovations carried out in 1995: a medieval cross-wing and remnants of an adjacent cross-wing flanking the space previously occupied by the open hall, datable to the C15.

Newland Street ends at the bridge over the River Brain. Its continuation is BRIDGE STREET; on the SE side, Nos. 23 and 27, early C16 with exposed timbers, finely carved jetty brackets and beams, with No. 25 fitted between them later in the century. Nos. 59–67 have their name (Paragon Terrace) and date (1869) spelt out in brickwork, with railings by *Davey, Paxman & Davey*. Before the bridge, MILL LANE runs N along the river valley; where this becomes known as GUITHAVON VALLEY is the OLD MILL HOUSE, brick, *c.* 1730 with a façade about fifty years later, but earlier features, including C17 brickwork in the cellar. At the far end of this road, a pair of cottages (Nos. 57–59 Collingwood Road) dated 1827. Stock brick with nice ogee heads to the windows.

3. Outer Witham

Beyond the two historic centres lies the result of the expansion of the town in the 1960s and 1970s. The first housing was built on the N side of Cressing Road, occupied in 1966, based on the Radburn principle, i.e. laid out around courtyards and designed to separate pedestrians and cars, which have their own access roads. The Templars County Infants School was opened in the same year. Then came the Spa Estate in the W, off Spa Road, and finally housing at Powers Hall End, with new schools at Howbridge, 1966, and Powers Hall End, 1969. The council also developed private housing for sale off Highfields Road. Other private housing includes Barwell Way on the site of The Grove, *c.* 1976, an early application of the principles of the Essex Design Guide.

On the industrial estate on the W side of the town next to the A12, the former MARCONI-ELLIOTT MICROELECTRONICS FACTORY, Freebournes Road, by *Anthony B. Davies & Associates* (architect in charge, *R. S. Chesher*), 1966–7. Low and sleek, clad in panels of compressed asbestos cement with stove-enamelled finish. Extended 2000–1. In Stepfield, SOCIAL SERVICE SUPPLIES LTD, warehouse and printing works by *Edward Cullinan*, 1966–7. White modular concrete blocks with long ranges of sloping aluminium-framed windows in the roof.

BENTON HALL, Blue Mills Hill, 1½ m. SE. C17. Chimneystacks with octagonal shafts.

BLUE MILLS, Blue Mills Hill, 1½ m. SE. A very charming group. Early C19 weatherboarded mill, and adjoining C18 brick mill house. Late C18 BRIDGE over the River Blackwater. Three arches, brick, with contemporary cast-iron tie-plates; culverts by *John Johnson*, 1799.

BLUNT'S HALL, Blunts Hall Road, ¾ m. SW. C17, timber-framed and plastered, with S front of grey gault brick, extended in the C19 and C20.

HOWBRIDGE HALL, Howbridge Road, 1 m. S. Timber-framed house of *c.* 1580 with sashed front. Restored *c.* 1924 for himself by *Basil Ionides*, who introduced much in the way of panelling, cupboards, fireplaces etc.

DENHOLM COURT, Maltings Lane, 1½ m. S. Residential conversion of C16 or C17 maltings, part weatherboarded and part brick-faced, with conical oast house at E end. To the W, on the S side of the road, a good group of mid-C19 brick cottages.

POWERS HALL, 1 m. W. Late C16, refaced in the C18 in buff-coloured gault brick. Fine seven-bay barn to the SE, C15, and another of five bays with aisles, C17.

EARTHWORK. Iron Age fort, two concentric banks and ditches constructed *c.* 350–50 B.C. This was bisected by the railway in 1843 and the road bridge marks the approximate centre of the mound; the earthwork is most clearly seen from the SE, where it slopes down to the River Brain.

IVY CHIMNEYS, Hatfield Road. Excavations in 1970–80 revealed evidence of a Romano-British temple complex, *c.* A.D. 80, built in the middle of a large banked and ditched enclosure dating from 400 B.C. A large square timber temple was erected in the late C3, replaced by a rectangular one in the mid C4 that may have been used for Christian worship.

WIVENHOE

ST MARY THE VIRGIN. The W tower is of *c.* 1500, mixed rubble and flint, with diagonal buttresses and a moulded plinth of flint chequerwork; surmounted by an elegant early C18 wooden cupola. The rest of the church almost entirely rebuilt by *E. C. Hakewill*, 1859–60; the structure had been weakened by the insertion of a gallery by *Joseph Parkins*, 1832–3, which had involved taking down part of the N arcade. The two western bays of the arcades are mid C14, as is most of the wall of the N aisle and the W walls of both N and S aisles; chancel and N chancel aisle rebuilt, and new S chancel aisle added. All in a rich mix of rubble with stone dressings, the old work incorporating Roman bricks, and new Dec tracery throughout. The chancel aisles make the interior surprisingly spacious. Solid, well-carved oak SEATING, and stone PULPIT and LECTERN placed side by side, the latter rising out of a low wall at the chancel step. – FONT. Octagonal, Perp, with quatrefoils and shields; bowl only, the stem and base 1923. – STAINED GLASS. E window and N chancel aisle E by *William Warrington*, S aisle W and tower window by *Castell*, all 1860. S aisle E to John Gurdon Rebow of Wivenhoe Park †1870 by *Lavers, Barraud & Westlake*. N aisle W by *Hardman*, 1900. – Fine BRASSES to

William, Viscount Beaumont †1507, figure of 56 in. (142 cm.) but with a triple canopy with crocketed gables etc. making the whole plate over 9 ft (279 cm.) long; in armour, his feet resting on an elephant and castle, the emblem of the Beaumonts. Next to him his second wife (subsequently wife of the 13th Earl of Oxford), Elizabeth Scroope †1537, 58 in. (147 cm.), also in an architectural surround, dressed in a heraldic cloak originally filled with coloured enamels. They lie just below the sanctuary step, and are palimpsests, dating from *c.* 1410. – In the sanctuary itself, a modest and pleasingly crude brass to Elizabeth's chaplain, Thomas Westeley †1535, 14 in. (35 cm.), in mass vestments.

CONGREGATIONAL CHURCH, High Street. 1962 by *L. & D. Kemble*, superseding the chapel of 1846 by *James Fenton* in Quay Street, a large classical building, now flats.

RAILWAY STATION. 1886 by *W. N. Ashbee*, in the Domestic Revival style favoured by the Great Eastern Railway. Brick, with tile-hanging in the gable.

WATER TOWER, Tower Road. 1901–2 by *Sands & Walker*, engineers, of Nottingham. Brick with stone dressings and pyramidal roof. 77 ft (24 metres) high and appropriately massive, but nicely detailed.

5 The QUAY is pretty as such quays are, if the houses are well looked after, and there is a good balance of old and new, domestic and commercial buildings. A sprinkling of nice bow and bay windows; Maple Cottage, Trinity House, and Quayside Cottage form a particularly attractive C17 row, with early C19 cast-iron railings by *Richard Coleman* of Colchester. Only to the W, on the site of the town's main shipbuilding yard, do things start getting out of hand, with a development by *Edward Irish Partnership* for Persimmon Homes, 2000, with houses of every size and style – Tudor, Georgian, vernacular – jumbled together. Picturesque streets just behind the waterfront, e.g. Black Buoy Hill, lead on to streets of 1860s terraced cottages either side of the railway, the earliest and most attractive ALMA STREET, with Alma House (built as the Swedenborgian Chapel, 1864), three storeys with decorative bargeboards, closing the vista.

The best house is in EAST STREET just s of the church: GARRISON HOUSE. It has a gorgeous display of mid-C17 pargetting on the N side, as good as any in the county: large scrolls arranged round basic cross-shapes. Jettied upper storey and an original doorway on the S side, among the carving the date 1676. Inside, remains of C17 and C18 painted schemes, including a little river scene. Owned by the S.P.A.B., 1928–86, restored by *Marshall Sisson* in 1948, and by *Essex County Council* in 1987–8. A number of other good houses at the lower end of the HIGH STREET; more pargetting on Nos. 11–13, a vine-trellis motif under the eaves, also elaborate painted arcading in a first-floor room.

THE FALCON and FALCON YARD on the N side of the churchyard is a particularly blatant example of an C18 brick façade slapped on to an earlier structure, the timber framing of which is exposed down the side. N of the railway line, on the E side of the High Street, Nos. 84 and 86, early C19 gault brick façade with a tall central gable hiding an earlier timber-framed building. On the w side, the site of WIVENHOE HALL (dem. 1927), which dated back to *c.* 1530; part of the boundary wall survives, also an C18 garden building or cottage, a tetrastyle portico with a nondescript brick structure behind, now a house. In REBOW ROAD, off the E side, a row of six brick almshouses, 1873. ½ m. further N, at Wivenhoe Cross, ROPERY HOUSE (No. 16 The Avenue), described as 'newly bricked' in 1789. Two storeys, and attics behind parapet; five bays, with pedimented doorcase, and a later sixth bay on the l.

WIVENHOE NEW PARK. *See* GREENSTEAD.

WIVENHOE HOUSE. *See* UNIVERSITY OF ESSEX.

WIX

1020

Wix Priory was founded *c.* 1123 by Walther, Alexander and Edith Mascherell, and dissolved in 1525. Only the foundations have been found, and are not exposed.

ST MARY THE VIRGIN. Built in 1744 out of the ruins of the priory church, on the site of the original nave; the N wall incorporates the C13 N aisle arcade, and in the E wall of the nave is a blocked C14 doorway. The old parts are of rubble with limestone dressings; otherwise brick, although part of the W wall is faced in reused ashlar. *Wadmore & Baker* tried (not very successfully) to make the church more ecclesiastical in 1887–8 by replacing wooden windows with stone, inserting an open timber roof, and adding a raised, semi-octagonal chancel. W porch by *F.G. Vincent-Brown*, 1937. – STAINED GLASS. Three chancel windows by *Clayton & Bell*. – N of the church, a timber BELL-CAGE (cf. Wrabness); a rebuilding in 1975 by *George Paskell & Son* of the C17 original.

WIX ABBEY. Brick house, *c.* 1570, its chief feature the projecting porch crowned by a stepped gable. Entrance with round arch and steep pediment, above this a three-light one-transom window of which only the pediment (lower and broader) is original, and on the second floor another such window, completely preserved, with a smaller pediment. There were originally wings projecting forward on this front, but of these only the stump of the N wing remains.

POND HALL, ¾ m. NW. C17 timber-framed and plastered, with an early C19 five-bay stuccoed front. Windows with hoodmoulds, two of them round-headed, and Tuscan porch. Two fine sets of C19 wrought-iron gates by *Barnard, Bishop & Barnard* of Norwich, *ex situ*.

WOODHAM FERRERS
Woodham Ferrers and Bicknacre

ST MARY THE VIRGIN. Nave and aisle, chancel, belfry. With the exception of the latter, essentially *c.* 1250–1330. The N and S arcades come first, three bays with alternating circular and octagonal piers, alternating also in a N–S direction across the nave. Moulded capitals and double-chamfered arches. Niches in the E responds of N and S arcades and on first pier of S arcade. Clerestory C19, but with C13 splays. Chancel arch of the same style, but the chancel is in one way noticeably later: the windows have bar tracery with quatrefoils in circles. That can hardly be earlier than *c.* 1275. The aisle windows have usual two-light Dec tracery. There was originally a late C15 W tower, but its brick replacement of 1715 has also been demolished and the tower arch bricked up; small belfry and spire, painted white, added 1793.* Patches of flint and stone flushwork remain to indicate the character of the tower. C15 timber S porch, with six cusped arched openings on each side and a par-getted gable. The belfry rests on a big tie-beam, not on posts, as usual. 'Thorough' restoration by *Charles Pertwee*, 1884, included re-seating and opening up the nave roof. Chancel restored and N vestry added 1894. – FONT COVER. Ogee-shaped, of thin ribs. – CHANCEL STALLS. Four benches, C15, with poppyheads. – WALL PAINTING. C15 Doom above chancel arch, with Christ seated in the centre on a rainbow, his arms upraised displaying the stigmata. The rest very indis-tinct. – ROYAL ARMS of George III, *c.* 1788, carved in wood. – STAINED GLASS. In chancel, C14 shields of France and England. – MONUMENTS. Cecilie Sandys, wife of the Arch-bishop of York, †1610/11, erected 1619. Attributed to *William Wright* (GF). The usual alabaster design with a kneeling figure in profile, but in addition Father Time on the l., a missing figure on the r., and Victories on the semicircular pediment. What will be remembered as exceptional and enchanting is the background behind the figure and the whole area of the ped-iment, all carved into an arbour of roses. Floor slab now built into the W wall outside.

EDWIN'S HALL, 1 m. E. Fragment of a larger house, built by Edwin Sandys at about the time of his appointment as Arch-bishop of York in 1576, on the site of an earlier C16 house and probably incorporating parts of it. Brick with black diapers. What now stands has a front to the S of irregular shape. The two-storey l. part has the original porch and a C19 two-storey bay beneath a straight gable. The r. part is set back and rises to three storeys, and has an original two-storey bay. This part ends in a later parapet, and may originally have possessed gables. The return has a late C19 single-storey bay where the house originally continued to the E, but how far and in what direction it continued is a matter of conjecture. There may have

---

* Described by James Hadfield in 1848 as 'most tasteless'.

been a wing on the E side to match that on the W; there is hardly enough space between the house and the moat for the house to have continued round to form a courtyard. The windows are of stone with mullions and transoms. At the back a brick window and big original chimneystacks. One good panelled room inside and another with panelling from Fremnells, Downham.* Remains of an outer moat, as well as the complete inner moat.

WOODHAM MORTIMER

8000

St Margaret. Rebuilt 1891–2 by *S. Gambier Parry*, retaining only the S wall and E end, but largely following the existing form of the building, including the N transept added by *Hopper* in 1840–4. Parry revealed the Norman and Dec windows in the S wall, and the rere-arch of the S doorway is also Norman. Parry's church has all the characteristics of the area – built largely of septaria, with S porch and western belfry and splay-footed timber spire – but the N aisle, with tall dormer windows, is wholly his and characteristic of the date, while the N transept (as organ chamber) leading to a N vestry (enlarged 1907) is an unusual composition which creates interesting internal spaces. The structure of the belfry, resting on a tie-beam rather than posts, appears to be modelled on that of Woodham Ferrers. – FONT. C13 round bowl on a C15 octagonal brick base. – PULPIT, ALTAR and ORGAN CASE incorporate early C17 carving, probably from the old church. – STAINED GLASS. Good group of windows by *Heaton, Butler & Bayne*, 1892, three in the chancel and one in the tower; small window W of S door added to commemorate Queen Victoria's Diamond Jubilee. – MONUMENTS. Brass to Dorothie Alleine †1584 aged three; 9-in. (22-cm.) figure (including head, now missing) and inscription beginning 'A litle impe, here buried is'. – Nicholas Griffinhoofe †1789 by *Randalll*, New Road, London. – In churchyard, tomb-chest of Dr Peter Chamberlen †1683, Court Physician and pioneer obstetrician: ornate tomb decorated with skulls, gravediggers' tools etc, giving details of his life and verses of his own composition.

Woodham Mortimer Hall. C17 brick front with four shaped gables masking a C16 timber-framed wing. The rectangular projection was probably the original porch. Mullioned and transomed windows replaced by sash windows. On the W side one two-light brick window. Original chimneystacks. OBELISK, opposite, erected 1825 by the Coopers' Company, to commemorate William Alexander's bequest of his estate at Woodham Mortimer.

Woodham Mortimer Lodge, ⅔ m. SE. Georgian brick. Two storeys and attics, five bays with central three-bay pediment.

* Mid C16, submerged by Hanningfield Reservoir.

Brick STABLES to r., also pedimented, dated 1824. Farm buildings behind house, part of the original complex, include a brick
BARLEY BARN, rebuilt 1827.

WOODHAM MORTIMER PLACE, ½ m. WSW. C18 gault brick
front range. Six bays with Doric portico, stucco quoins and
balustrade with pierced panels. Behind and parallel, a timber-
framed range, C17 or earlier. C18 stable block to the S, part
brick, part timber-framed and plastered, and to the W more
stables, C16 or C17 brick, with gabled dormers.

SALTER'S FOLLY (formerly Nursery Farm), 1 m. SW. A modest
two-storey, three-bay house, the rear range early C17, the front
range added c. 1680–90. Refronted in brick in the early C18
(the brickmaker said to be *Obediah Barker*), burnt headers laid
in header bond with red dressings, but much altered. Inside,
remarkable paintings on the staircase wall and landings of a
Bacchanalian procession, late C17 or early C18. On wooden
panels, and whether painted *in situ* or brought in is unknown.
A further panel above the fireplace in an upper room depicts
a city (probably London) in flames.

WOODHAM WALTER

St MICHAEL. Brick, small, but historically interesting, in that it
was built in 1562–3, consecrated 1564: the only church in Essex
built during the reign of Elizabeth I. Yet it is still essentially
Gothic. It has, it is true, stepped gables at the W and the E end,
where that of the N vestry together with that of the chancel
form a pretty E view, but otherwise the windows are Perp,
straight-headed, with each light arched and cusped, the walls
have buttresses, the arcade to the N aisle has piers superficially
similar to the familiar four-shaft-four-hollow type (but the
hollows are straightened out) and double-hollow-chamfered
arches. The roofs also are of the usual Perp types. This is partly
explained by the fact that materials from the old church were
reused, including the bell-frame and roof structures of the nave
and chancel, C14, and the C15 arcade and roof of the N aisle.
Re-seated by *Chancellor*, 1866–7, and generally restored
1878–9, when the plaster ceiling was removed and most of the
windows renewed. – FONT. Large, octagonal, Perp, the stem
decorated with tracery, the bowl with quatrefoils. From the old
church. – REREDOS, PANELLING etc. Heavily carved wood, by
Chilton Mewburn, 1901–4. – ROYAL ARMS. Painted, on wood,
dated 1660. – STAINED GLASS. Fragments of C15 glass in N
aisle and nave S windows. E window by *Ward & Hughes*, 1879,
W window by *T.F. Curtis, Ward & Hughes*, 1898. – MONU-
MENTS. H.A. Chaplin †1905. By *H. Maryon*. Bronze bas-relief
of the scientist looking through a microscope. – J.W. Gregory
†1932. Bronze bas-relief by *W. Marsden*, 1934.

The medieval church was probably ½ m. SE, next to the site of
WOODHAM WALTER HALL, of which only fragments of brickwork and surrounding earthworks can now be discerned. The

C17 brick house now known as Woodham Walter Hall, formerly Oak Farm, was built as a warren or lodge. In the centre of the village, N of the church, the BELL INN, early C16 with C17 and later additions; exposed timbers, jettied gabled wing on the l. with carved bressumer. A picturesque group with a row of cottages to the r. and on the green in front a cast-iron SIGNPOST by the *Maldon Ironworks*.

THE WARREN, ½ m. WSW. Late C17 timber-framed house, altered and extended *c.* 1905 by *Read & Macdonald*.* They also built stables E of the house and a pair of Voyseyesque entrance LODGES, roughcast with battered walls, nearly ½ m. SE, and *c.* 1926 WAYSIDE COTTAGE E of the house and two pairs of cottages on Herbage Park Road and Common Lane. Weatherboarded barns S of the house, one dated 1744 but reusing medieval timbers, converted to golf clubhouse in the 1930s.

WEST BOWERS HALL, ¾ m. NW. Late C16 or early C17 with some exposed timbers on the main (E) front, which is jettied. Gabled staircase tower in the middle, possibly original but more probably added later in the C17. Cross-wing to the r. by *K. M. B. Cross*, 1930–2, painted brick, with two-storey canted bay. Detached garage and galleried store by *Geoffrey Vale*, 1986. Brick and weatherboarding in the local vernacular style, with a continuous run of windows under the eaves of the half-hipped roof.

RUSHES LOCK, 1½ m. Lock, gates and weir of the Chelmer and Blackwater Navigation, opened 1797 (*see* Introduction, p. 52). Brick, with granite coping stones and quoins.

WORMINGFORD 9030

ST ANDREW. Norman W tower of coursed rubble with Roman brick quoins. Original windows and bell openings. C17 brick parapet with battlements and crocketed pinnacles. Norman nave with one blocked S window and evidence of another. The N aisle and N windows early C14, chancel later C14. Four-bay arcade with smallish octagonal piers and arches with two quadrant mouldings. Restored 1869–70 by *Chancellor*, who rebuilt the C15 S porch (reusing the original archway) and N vestry. His is the fine nave roof, with panels of pierced tracery. – REREDOS. 1894. A showy affair of marble and alabaster. – LECTERN. Oak, carved by *S. J. Tufnell*, 1949. – SCREEN. Part of former chancel screen, now in tower arch. Three bays with elaborate tracery. C15, much restored. – STAINED GLASS. C14 bits in chancel windows. E and two other chancel windows by *O'Connor*, 1869. N aisle E by *G.E.R. Smith*, 1950. – BRASSES. Civilian, *c.* 1460, 22 in. (56 cm.); civilian and two wives, *c.* 1590, the largest 16 in. (41 cm.). – In churchyard, a number of early C19 CHEST-TOMBS of John Constable's uncle and family; also headstone of John Nash R.A. †1977.

*A grander scheme published in *Academy Architecture*, 1910, was not carried out.

Opposite the church CHURCH HOUSE, C16 with a later C16 S wing of brick. This has five-light transomed windows in the front and a (rebuilt) shaped gable of unusual form. To its N CHURCH COTTAGES, pleasingly simple, dated 1750. CHURCH HALL lies N of the church, early C16 with gabled cross-wings.

JENKINS FARM, 1 m. S. Especially attractive, with exposed timbers. The date 1583 is on one of the carved brackets supporting the first floor of the porch. This is jettied, with a further jettied gable.

ROCHFORDS, 1¼ m. S. Early C18 plastered front doing little to conceal the house's medieval origins. C15 cross-wing to the N of the main C16 range, which was floored from the outset.

WORMINGFORD HALL, ¾ m. WSW. C16, considerably altered and extended in the mid C20 by the owner, *S. J. Tufnell*, who did much of the carving on bressumers etc., as well as importing panelling and other features.

WRABNESS

1030

ALL SAINTS. Small, plain church. C12 nave and lower chancel, the latter rebuilt in the C14 and reroofed after partial collapse in 1697. Norman N doorway. Pretty C15 S doorway, with fleurons and hung-up shields in the voussoirs. The nave has a hammerbeam roof, not a frequent feature in Essex, its angels (if that is what they were) removed. Chancel restored 1893 by *J. C. Bourne*, who replaced the E window, although the reduction in the opening probably dates from 1697. Bourne also restored the nave, 1907–8, extending it (in flint; the rest of the church rendered) two bays westwards, and adding the S porch and N vestry. The steeple disappeared in the C18 and was replaced by a timber BELL-CAGE, a little shed like a village lock-up quite independent of the church. – FONT. Octagonal, Perp, with deliberately defaced figures of the Evangelists and their symbols. – COFFIN LID. Purbeck marble, with foliated cross on stepped calvary, C13; removed from the chancel in 1697, built into the wall of the porch in 1908.

Former METHODIST CHAPEL, Harwich Road. By *Eade & Johns*, 1907–8. Perp. Brick, with stock brick dressings, including 'Tudor' chimney.

WRITTLE

6000

One of the largest parishes in the county and historically of great importance. The manor belonged to Earl Harold at the time of Edward the Confessor, and was owned by the Crown until it was granted to Sir William Petre by Queen Mary in 1554. It formerly included the parishes of Roxwell, Highwood, and part of Chignall.

ALL SAINTS. Big and not very high w tower, rebuilt in 1802, the work paid for and supervised by a parishioner, *Henry Lambirth*. Stone rubble with brick angle buttresses and battlements, its three tiers of round-headed windows replaced in 1924 to give a more Gothic appearance. Nave and aisles of stone, embattled. The nave arcades and the clerestory 1878–9, part of a restoration by *Chancellor*, with the exception of two original piers, both circular. These belong to the c13, as does the E wall of the chancel. The exterior walls of the aisles have some Dec windows, indicating their age. The chancel chapels are later c14, as is the two-storey N vestry. Brick chantry chapel on S side of S aisle, built after the death of William Carpenter, vicar to 1526. Off the N aisle a much smaller chantry chapel, hardly more than a recess, c15. Nave roof of low pitch resting on wooden demi-figures of angels. Easternmost beam records restoration in 1740 (*Reginald Branwood*, carpenter, of Writtle), the westernmost in 1802. Numerous c19 restorations, besides Chancellor's: *Snooke & Stock*'s of 1864 has probably been undone, but *A. W. Blomfield*'s restoration of the chancel, 1885–6,* can be seen in the stonework of the E window and the mosaic REREDOS, and *J. S. Corder* opened up the tower arch in 1893. E end restored by *Purcell Miller Tritton* following fires in 1974 and 1991.

FONT. Square, with slightly tapering sides and attached shafts at the corners. Caen stone, *c.* 1170. – CHANCEL STALLS with early c16 poppyheads and fronts with openwork foliage scrolls of the early c18. – Also c15 BENCHES with poppyheads, one with a bird, another with a seated dog, etc. – SCREENS. To N and S chapels, by *F. W. Chancellor*, 1929. Between chancel and S chapel, originally chancel screen, 1909, also by Chancellor (carving by *Edward Usborne*), cresting added 1929. Tower screen by *G. J. Wragg*, 1955, made by *H. & K. Mabbitt*. – Very fragmentary WALL PAINTINGS, e.g. St George above the N door. c15? – STAINED GLASS. In N vestry, arms of William of Wykeham, dated 1619. Chancel E, 1914, by *H. W. Bryans*, S by *A. K. Nicholson*, 1950. – S chancel chapel E by *Jane Gray*, 1992; S by *Percy Bacon*, designed by *G. H. F. Prynne*, 1901. – S aisle chapel by *Clayton & Bell*, 1870. – S aisle by *Ion Pace*, 1899, and *C. C. Powell* (Queen Victoria memorial), 1902. – N aisle by *H. W. Bryans*, 1906 and 1919, and *Horace Wilkinson*, 1937.

MONUMENTS. A large number of brasses, all now in the N chapel and aisle. Man in armour (Bedell family) with wife, six sons and two daughters, *c.* 1500; male figure 31 in (79 cm.). – Civilian and four wives, *c.* 1510, with three groups of children; male figure 17½ in. (44 cm.). – Thomasin Thomas †1513 with father, grandfather and grandmother; largest figure 30½ in. (77 cm.). – Constans Berners †1524; 15 in. (38 cm.). – Edward Bell †1576, with wife, three sons and daughter; male figure 20 in.

*The firm's invoices are signed by *Reginald Blomfield*, then still working in his uncle's office.

(51 cm.). – William Pinchon †1592 and wife, his figure missing, hers 21 in. (53 cm.). – Edward Hunt †1606. Mural brass with kneeling figures of Hunt and wife with skull. – Edward Bowland †1609 and wife †1616; male figure 23 in. (58 cm.). – Altar tomb of Richard Weston of Skreens, Roxwell, †1572. Three cusped lozenges with brass shields of arms. No effigy. – Edward Eliott of Newland Hall, Roxwell †1595 with wife and children, small, with kneeling figures. – Sir Edward Pinchon and wife Dorothy (Weston), made in 1629 by *Nicholas Stone* for £66 13s. 4d. Allegorical monument on the theme of man as a crop, sown, tended, reaped, and renewed by God. Angel of the Resurrection (originally with sickle) standing on the rock of Christ, in front of which are garnered sheaves. The figure reaches up above a broken segmental pediment, which is on pilasters elaborately decorated with agricultural tools, and points towards the Sun of Righteousness. Two seated angels wearing large reapers' hats to l. and r. Below, a winnowing fan, bearing the inscription, and corn shovel with coat of arms. It is a slightly modified version of Stone's monument to Joyce Austin (Lady Clarke) †1626 in Southwark Cathedral, commissioned and almost certainly designed (at least as far as the iconography is concerned) by her son *William Austin*. – Elizabeth Knightbridge †1658. Alabaster cartouche with scroll-work, arms, etc. – Sir John Comyns of Hylands, Lord Chief Baron of the Court of Exchequer, †1740. Bulgy sarcophagus with life-size bust above. Urns to l. and r. Rococo ornament. Signed *H. Cheere*. Erected 1759.

UNITED REFORMED CHURCH (Congregational), The Green. 1885, by *C. Pertwee*. 'Queen Anne': brick, with round-arched windows and a pretty little white-painted turret.

PUBLIC LIBRARY, The Green. Former Board School, 1870s. Brick, with gabled front and high round-arched window beneath a segmental pediment.

LONGMEADS COMMUNITY CENTRE, Redwood Drive. Large brick house by *Chancellor*, 1873, for Robert Woodhouse. Entrance front with three straight gables, long garden front with three polygonal bays, each different. Window jambs, mullions, hoodmoulds, etc. in moulded brick, with bands of decorative brick made to Chancellor's design.

WRITTLE COLLEGE, Lordship Road. By *J. Stuart*, County Architect, 1938–40. His usual mild Neo-Georgian, brick with a little Clipsham stone, with two symmetrically projecting wings and a centre lantern of the Swedish variety. Behind it, two halls of residence. These form the E side of a garden; on the W side the Strutt Hall of Residence, 1957–8 by *H. Conolly*, and on the S side the Harvey Halls of Residence, three four-storey blocks, 1966–9 by *A.R. Dannatt & Son*. Beyond the Strutt Hall, two- and three-storey halls of residence by *Ash Design*, 1993–8. S of the main building, Recreation Centre by *Conolly*, 1964, and Chapel, 1966.

Further S, the site of KING JOHN'S HUNTING LODGE, excavated 1955–6. Built in 1211, comprising a hall, kitchen, and gatehouse surrounded by a rectangular moat, about 320 by 200 ft (97.5 by 60 metres), with fishponds (now reservoir) to the E. The moat survives, and on the W side of the enclosure are some foundation walls belonging to a later phase of building. The original buildings were probably destroyed by fire at the end of the C13, rebuilt in the early C14, with new buildings (timber-framed, on brick footings) in the C15. These were surveyed by royal commissioners in 1521. In 1554 the estate was granted to Sir William Petre, and by 1566 the only building remaining was LORDSHIP BARN, S of the fishponds. Weatherboarded, aisled, of six bays, with two gabled porches on the N side. Tree-ring dated 1441–75.

On the E side of Lordship Road, the Rural Business Centre by *Sustainable Ecological Architecture Ltd*, 2003. S wall mainly glass, the others timber-clad or plastered, with pitched roof incorporating solar panels, designed for energy efficiency. At STURGEON'S FARM, ¾ m. W of the main buildings, a two-storey, five-bay house of white brick with Ionic porch, and a range of contemporary brick farm buildings, one dated 1821.

WRITTLE BRIDGE, over the Wid. 1891 by the County engineer, *Percy J. Sheldon*, with *Westwood Baillie & Co.* Steel and concrete, with ornamental cast-iron parapets.

PERAMBULATION. Writtle possesses one of the most attractive village greens of Essex. It is roughly triangular, with the best houses along the SE side in front of the church. Framing the approach to the church, Aubyns and Mundays, both timber-framed. AUBYNS, *c.* 1500, has exposed timbers. Restored by *H.P. Cart de Lafontaine, c.* 1927, the hall range rebuilt following a fire in 1936. Jettied cross-wings, the W one on two sides, with on the ground floor towards Church Lane three blocked openings with four-centred heads, indicating a shop; also a blocked original doorway. MUNDAYS, C17, is plastered with a shell-hooded entrance. NE of Aubyns, MOTTS HOUSE, late C16 timber-frame with a Georgian brick front of seven bays, later extended. Of the buildings on the W side, Nos. 27 and 29 are most prominent, a late medieval house with slightly projecting gabled wings at each end. Off the W side, in CHANCERY PLACE, two brick houses by *David Brewster*, 1969, for himself and his parents. Single-storey, but with little galleries in the apex of the roof. In the SW corner of the Green a C18 malt kiln, timber-framed on brick base, now part of a house conversion; octagonal lantern added by *F.W. Chancellor*, 1924–5. On the N side, Nos. 32–36 were refronted in 1888 with surplus stone left over after the rebuilding of the church tower. To the SE, No. 22 (Greenbury), C18 timber-framed and plastered with a five-bay, three-storey brick front with a heavy plaster cornice between the first and second floors. The SE end of the Green leads into ST JOHN'S GREEN, much smaller but with a number of nice houses, e.g. Nos. 4 and 5 on the W side, C18, one timber-framed and plastered, the other brick.

On the S side of the churchyard, the OLD VICARAGE, brick, rebuilt 1760, enlarged 1772–3, with a five-bay E front. The very

substantial brick walls of its former garden can be seen along
Lodge Road and Romans Place, of various builds but including a date of 1656. Along the N side of ROMANS PLACE an
attractive row of houses with Georgian brick fronts.

At Newney Green, 1¾ m. W:

BENEDICT OTES. Timber-framed and plastered. Central stack
of six octagonal chimneys dated 1644, although the house may
be older.*

MOOR HALL.† The cross-wing, with underbuilt jetty, is probably mid C14. It was the service end; the other cross-wing was
in existence in 1673, but has since disappeared. Hall range
rebuilt in the late C16, two storeys and attics, with two tall
gabled bay windows and gabled porch. The gables have decorated bargeboards and pendants and ornamented bressumers.
Inside the house the hall screen survives partly, with one two-
centred arch and another with a broad ogee head and quatrefoil tracery above.

NEWNEY HALL. Late C16, timber-framed and plastered with
tile-hanging on the first floor. Jettied cross-wings.

HYLANDS. *See* p. 500.

WRITTLE PARK. *See* Highwood.

---

*Boards Farm, opposite, is in Roxwell (q.v.).
†Dating and other information kindly provided by Mrs Anne Padfield.

GLOSSARY

Numbers and letters refer to the illustrations (by John Sambrook) on pp. 874–881 .

ABACUS: flat slab forming the top of a capital (3a).

ACANTHUS: classical formalized leaf ornament (4b).

ACCUMULATOR TOWER: *see* Hydraulic power.

ACHIEVEMENT: a complete display of armorial bearings.

ACROTERION: plinth for a statue or ornament on the apex or ends of a pediment; more usually, both the plinth and what stands on it (4a).

AEDICULE (*lit.* little building): architectural surround, consisting usually of two columns or pilasters supporting a pediment.

AGGREGATE: *see* Concrete.

AISLE: subsidiary space alongside the body of a building, separated from it by columns, piers, or posts.

ALMONRY: a building from which alms are dispensed to the poor.

AMBULATORY (*lit.* walkway): aisle around the sanctuary (q.v.).

ANGLE ROLL: roll moulding in the angle between two planes (1a).

ANSE DE PANIER: *see* Arch.

ANTAE: simplified pilasters (4a), usually applied to the ends of the enclosing walls of a portico *in antis* (q.v.).

ANTEFIXAE: ornaments projecting at regular intervals above a Greek cornice, originally to conceal the ends of roof tiles (4a).

ANTHEMION: classical ornament like a honeysuckle flower (4b).

APRON: raised panel below a window or wall monument or tablet.

APSE: semicircular or polygonal end of an apartment, especially of a chancel or chapel. In classical architecture sometimes called an *exedra*.

ARABESQUE: non-figurative surface decoration consisting of flowing lines, foliage scrolls etc., based on geometrical patterns. Cf. Grotesque.

ARCADE: series of arches supported by piers or columns. *Blind arcade* or *arcading*: the same applied to the wall surface. *Wall arcade*: in medieval churches, a blind arcade forming a dado below windows. Also a covered shopping street.

ARCH: Shapes *See* 5c. *Basket arch* or *anse de panier* (basket handle): three-centred and depressed, or with a flat centre. *Nodding*: ogee arch curving forward from the wall face. *Parabolic*: shaped like a chain suspended from two level points, but inverted. Special purposes. *Chancel*: dividing chancel from nave or crossing. *Crossing*: spanning piers at a crossing (q.v.). *Relieving or discharging*: incorporated in a wall to relieve superimposed weight (5c). *Skew*: spanning responds not diametrically opposed. *Strainer*: inserted in an opening to resist inward pressure. *Transverse*: spanning a main axis (e.g. of a vaulted space). *See also* Jack arch, Triumphal arch.

ARCHITRAVE: formalized lintel, the lowest member of the classical entablature (3a). Also the moulded frame of a door or window (often borrowing the profile of a classical architrave). For *lugged* and *shouldered* architraves *see* 4b.

ARCUATED: dependent structurally on the arch principle. Cf. Trabeated.

ARK: chest or cupboard housing the

tables of Jewish law in a synagogue.

ARRIS: sharp edge where two surfaces meet at an angle (3a).

ASHLAR: masonry of large blocks wrought to even faces and square edges (6d).

ASTRAGAL: classical moulding of semicircular section (3f).

ASTYLAR: with no columns or similar vertical features.

ATLANTES: *see* Caryatids.

ATRIUM (plural: atria): inner court of a Roman or C20 house; in a multi-storey building, a toplit covered court rising through all storeys. Also an open court in front of a church.

ATTACHED COLUMN: *see* Engaged column.

ATTIC: small top storey within a roof. Also the storey above the main entablature of a classical façade.

AUMBRY: recess or cupboard to hold sacred vessels for the Mass.

BAILEY: *see* Motte-and-bailey.

BALANCE BEAM: *see* Canals.

BALDACCHINO: free-standing canopy, originally fabric, over an altar. Cf. Ciborium.

BALLFLOWER: globular flower of three petals enclosing a ball (1a). Typical of the Decorated style.

BALUSTER: pillar or pedestal of bellied form. *Balusters*: vertical supports of this or any other form, for a handrail or coping, the whole being called a *balustrade* (6c). *Blind balustrade*: the same applied to the wall surface.

BARBICAN: outwork defending the entrance to a castle.

BARGEBOARDS (corruption of 'vergeboards'): boards, often carved or fretted, fixed beneath the eaves of a gable to cover and protect the rafters.

BAROQUE: style originating in Rome *c.*1600 and current in England *c.*1680–1720, characterized by dramatic massing and silhouette and the use of the giant order.

BARROW: burial mound.

BARTIZAN: corbelled turret, square or round, frequently at an angle.

BASCULE: hinged part of a lifting (or bascule) bridge.

BASE: moulded foot of a column or pilaster. For *Attic* base *see* 3b.

BASEMENT: lowest, subordinate storey; hence the lowest part of a classical elevation, below the *piano nobile* (q.v.).

BASILICA: a Roman public hall; hence an aisled building with a clerestory.

BASTION: one of a series of defensive semicircular or polygonal projections from the main wall of a fortress or city.

BATTER: intentional inward inclination of a wall face.

BATTLEMENT: defensive parapet, composed of *merlons* (solid) and *crenels* (embrasures) through which archers could shoot; sometimes called *crenellation*. Also used decoratively.

BAY: division of an elevation or interior space as defined by regular vertical features such as arches, columns, windows etc.

BAY LEAF: classical ornament of overlapping bay leaves (3f).

BAY WINDOW: window of one or more storeys projecting from the face of a building. *Canted*: with a straight front and angled sides. *Bow window*: curved. *Oriel*: rests on corbels or brackets and starts above ground level; also the bay window at the dais end of a medieval great hall.

BEAD-AND-REEL: *see* Enrichments.

BEAKHEAD: Norman ornament with a row of beaked bird or beast heads usually biting into a roll moulding (1a).

BELFRY: chamber or stage in a tower where bells are hung.

BELL CAPITAL: *see* 1b.

BELLCOTE: small gabled or roofed housing for the bell(s).

BERM: level area separating a ditch from a bank on a hill-fort or barrow.

BILLET: Norman ornament of small half-cylindrical or rectangular blocks (1a).

BLIND: *see* Arcade, Baluster, Portico.

BLOCK CAPITAL: *see* 1a.

BLOCKED: columns, etc. interrupted by regular projecting

blocks (*blocking*), as on a Gibbs surround (4b).

BLOCKING COURSE: course of stones, or equivalent, on top of a cornice and crowning the wall.

BOLECTION MOULDING: covering the joint between two different planes (6b).

BOND: the pattern of long sides (*stretchers*) and short ends (*headers*) produced on the face of a wall by laying bricks in a particular way (6e).

BOSS: knob or projection, e.g. at the intersection of ribs in a vault (2c).

BOWTELL: a term in use by the C15 for a form of roll moulding, usually three-quarters of a circle in section (also called *edge roll*).

BOW WINDOW: *see* Bay window.

BOX FRAME: timber-framed construction in which vertical and horizontal wall members support the roof (7). Also concrete construction where the loads are taken on cross walls; also called *cross-wall construction*.

BRACE: subsidiary member of a structural frame, curved or straight. *Bracing* is often arranged decoratively e.g. quatrefoil, herringbone (7). *See also* Roofs.

BRATTISHING: ornamental crest, usually formed of leaves, Tudor flowers or miniature battlements.

BRESSUMER (*lit.* breast-beam): big horizontal beam supporting the wall above, especially in a jettied building (7).

BRICK: *see* Bond, Cogging, Engineering, Gauged, Tumbling.

BRIDGE: *Bowstring*: with arches rising above the roadway which is suspended from them. *Clapper*: one long stone forms the roadway. *Roving*: *see* Canal. *Suspension*: roadway suspended from cables or chains slung between towers or pylons. *Stay-suspension* or *stay-cantilever*: supported by diagonal stays from towers or pylons. *See also* Bascule.

BRISES-SOLEIL: projecting fins or canopies which deflect direct sunlight from windows.

BROACH: *see* Spire and 1C.

BUCRANIUM: ox skull used decoratively in classical friezes.

BULL-NOSED SILL: sill displaying a pronounced convex upper moulding.

BULLSEYE WINDOW: small oval window, set horizontally (cf. Oculus). Also called *œil de bœuf*.

BUTTRESS: vertical member projecting from a wall to stabilize it or to resist the lateral thrust of an arch, roof, or vault (1c, 2c). A *flying buttress* transmits the thrust to a heavy abutment by means of an arch or half-arch (1c).

CABLE OR ROPE MOULDING: originally Norman, like twisted strands of a rope.

CAMES: *see* Quarries.

CAMPANILE: free-standing bell-tower.

CANALS: *Flash lock*: removable weir or similar device through which boats pass on a flush of water. Predecessor of the *pound lock*: chamber with gates at each end allowing boats to float from one level to another. *Tidal gates*: single pair of lock gates allowing vessels to pass when the tide makes a level. *Balance beam*: beam projecting horizontally for opening and closing lock gates. *Roving bridge*: carrying a towing path from one bank to the other.

CANTILEVER: horizontal projection (e.g. step, canopy) supported by a downward force behind the fulcrum.

CAPITAL: head or crowning feature of a column or pilaster; for classical types *see* 3; for medieval types *see* 1b.

CARREL: compartment designed for individual work or study.

CARTOUCHE: classical tablet with ornate frame (4b).

CARYATIDS: female figures supporting an entablature; their male counterparts are *Atlantes* (*lit.* Atlas figures).

CASEMATE: vaulted chamber, with embrasures for defence, within a castle wall or projecting from it.

CASEMENT: side-hinged window.

CASTELLATED: with battlements (q.v.).

CAST IRON: hard and brittle, cast in a mould to the required shape.

Wrought iron is ductile, strong in tension, forged into decorative patterns or forged and rolled into e.g. bars, joists, boiler plates; *mild steel* is its modern equivalent, similar but stronger.

CATSLIDE: *See* 8a.

CAVETTO: concave classical moulding of quarter-round section (3f).

CELURE OR CEILURE: enriched area of roof above rood or altar.

CEMENT: *see* Concrete.

CENOTAPH (*lit.* empty tomb): funerary monument which is not a burying place.

CENTRING: wooden support for the building of an arch or vault, removed after completion.

CHAMFER (*lit.* corner-break): surface formed by cutting off a square edge or corner. For types of chamfers and *chamfer stops see* 6a. *See also* Double chamfer.

CHANCEL: part of the E end of a church set apart for the use of the officiating clergy.

CHANTRY CHAPEL: often attached to or within a church, endowed for the celebration of Masses principally for the soul of the founder.

CHEVET (*lit.* head): French term for chancel with ambulatory and radiating chapels.

CHEVRON: V-shape used in series or double series (later) on a Norman moulding (1a). Also (especially when on a single plane) called *zigzag*.

CHOIR: the part of a cathedral, monastic or collegiate church where services are sung.

CIBORIUM: a fixed canopy over an altar, usually vaulted and supported on four columns; cf. Baldacchino. Also a canopied shrine for the reserved sacrament.

CINQUEFOIL: *see* Foil.

CIST: stone-lined or slab-built grave.

CLADDING: external covering or skin applied to a structure, especially a framed one.

CLERESTORY: uppermost storey of the nave of a church, pierced by windows. Also high-level windows in secular buildings.

CLOSER: a brick cut to complete a bond (6e).

CLUSTER BLOCK: *see* Multi-storey.

COADE STONE: ceramic artificial stone made in Lambeth 1769–c.1840 by Eleanor Coade (†1821) and her associates.

COB: walling material of clay mixed with straw. Also called *pisé*.

COFFERING: arrangement of sunken panels (coffers), square or polygonal, decorating a ceiling, vault, or arch.

COGGING: a decorative course of bricks laid diagonally (6e). Cf. Dentilation.

COLLAR: *see* Roofs and 7.

COLLEGIATE CHURCH: endowed for the support of a college of priests.

COLONNADE: range of columns supporting an entablature. Cf. Arcade.

COLONNETTE: small medieval column or shaft.

COLOSSAL ORDER: *see* Giant order.

COLUMBARIUM: shelved, niched structure to house multiple burials.

COLUMN: a classical, upright structural member of round section with a shaft, a capital, and usually a base (3a, 4a).

COLUMN FIGURE: carved figure attached to a medieval column or shaft, usually flanking a doorway.

COMMUNION TABLE: unconsecrated table used in Protestant churches for the celebration of Holy Communion.

COMPOSITE: *see* Orders.

COMPOUND PIER: grouped shafts (q.v.), or a solid core surrounded by shafts.

CONCRETE: composition of *cement* (calcined lime and clay), *aggregate* (small stones or rock chippings), sand and water. It can be poured into *formwork* or *shuttering* (temporary frame of timber or metal) on site (*in-situ* concrete), or *pre-cast* as components before construction. *Reinforced*: incorporating steel rods to take the tensile force. *Pre-stressed*: with tensioned steel rods. Finishes include the impression of boards left by formwork (*board-marked* or *shuttered*), and texturing with steel brushes (*brushed*) or hammers (*hammer-dressed*). *See also* Shell.

CONSOLE: bracket of curved outline (4b).

COPING: protective course of masonry or brickwork capping a wall (6d).

CORBEL: projecting block supporting something above. *Corbel course*: continuous course of projecting stones or bricks fulfilling the same function. *Corbel table*: series of corbels to carry a parapet or a wall-plate or wall-post (7). *Corbelling*: brick or masonry courses built out beyond one another to support a chimney-stack, window, etc.

CORINTHIAN: *see* Orders and 3d.

CORNICE: flat-topped ledge with moulded underside, projecting along the top of a building or feature, especially as the highest member of the classical entablature (3a). Also the decorative moulding in the angle between wall and ceiling.

CORPS-DE-LOGIS: the main building(s) as distinct from the wings or pavilions.

COTTAGE ORNÉ: an artfully rustic small house associated with the Picturesque movement.

COUNTERCHANGING: of joists on a ceiling divided by beams into compartments, when placed in opposite directions in alternate squares.

COUR D'HONNEUR: formal entrance court before a house in the French manner, usually with flanking wings and a screen wall or gates.

COURSE: continuous layer of stones, etc. in a wall (6e).

COVE: a broad concave moulding, e.g. to mask the eaves of a roof. *Coved ceiling*: with a pronounced cove joining the walls to a flat central panel smaller than the whole area of the ceiling.

CRADLE ROOF: *see* Wagon roof.

CREDENCE: a shelf within or beside a piscina (q.v.), or a table for the sacramental elements and vessels.

CRENELLATION: parapet with crenels (*see* Battlement).

CRINKLE-CRANKLE WALL: garden wall undulating in a series of serpentine curves.

CROCKETS: leafy hooks. *Crocketing* decorates the edges of Gothic features, such as pinnacles, canopies, etc. *Crocket capital*: *see* 1b.

CROSSING: central space at the junction of the nave, chancel, and transepts. *Crossing tower*: above a crossing.

CROSS-WINDOW: with one mullion and one transom (qq.v.).

CROWN-POST: *see* Roofs and 7.

CROWSTEPS: squared stones set like steps, e.g. on a gable (8a).

CRUCKS (*lit.* crooked): pairs of inclined timbers (*blades*), usually curved, set at bay-lengths; they support the roof timbers and, in timber buildings, also support the walls (8b). *Base*: blades rise from ground level to a tie- or collar-beam which supports the roof timbers. *Full*: blades rise from ground level to the apex of the roof, serving as the main members of a roof truss. *Jointed*: blades formed from more than one timber; the lower member may act as a wall-post; it is usually elbowed at wall-plate level and jointed just above. *Middle*: blades rise from half-way up the walls to a tie- or collar-beam. *Raised*: blades rise from half-way up the walls to the apex. *Upper*: blades supported on a tie-beam and rising to the apex.

CRYPT: underground or half-underground area, usually below the E end of a church. *Ring crypt*: corridor crypt surrounding the apse of an early medieval church, often associated with chambers for relics. Cf. Undercroft.

CUPOLA (*lit.* dome): especially a small dome on a circular or polygonal base crowning a larger dome, roof, or turret.

CURSUS: a long avenue defined by two parallel earthen banks with ditches outside.

CURTAIN WALL: a connecting wall between the towers of a castle. Also a non-load-bearing external wall applied to a C20 framed structure.

CUSP: *see* Tracery and 2b.

CYCLOPEAN MASONRY: large irregular polygonal stones, smooth and finely jointed.

CYMA RECTA and CYMA REVERSA: classical mouldings with double curves (3f). Cf. Ogee.

DADO: the finishing (often with panelling) of the lower part of a wall in a classical interior; in origin a formalized continuous pedestal. *Dado rail*: the moulding along the top of the dado.

DAGGER: *see* Tracery and 2b.

DALLE-DE-VERRE (*lit.* glass-slab): a late C20 stained-glass technique, setting large, thick pieces of cast glass into a frame of reinforced concrete or epoxy resin.

DEC (DECORATED): English Gothic architecture *c.* 1290 to *c.* 1350. The name is derived from the type of window tracery (q.v.) used during the period.

DEMI- or HALF-COLUMNS: engaged columns (q.v.) half of whose circumference projects from the wall.

DENTIL: small square block used in series in classical cornices (3c). *Dentilation* is produced by the projection of alternating headers along cornices or stringcourses.

DIAPER: repetitive surface decoration of lozenges or squares flat or in relief. Achieved in brickwork with bricks of two colours.

DIOCLETIAN OR THERMAL WINDOW: semicircular with two mullions, as used in the Baths of Diocletian, Rome (4b).

DISTYLE: having two columns (4a).

DOGTOOTH: E.E. ornament, consisting of a series of small pyramids formed by four stylized canine teeth meeting at a point (1a).

DORIC: *see* Orders and 3a, 3b.

DORMER: window projecting from the slope of a roof (8a).

DOUBLE CHAMFER: a chamfer applied to each of two recessed arches (1a).

DOUBLE PILE: *see* Pile.

DRAGON BEAM: *see* Jetty.

DRESSINGS: the stone or brickwork worked to a finished face about an angle, opening, or other feature.

DRIPSTONE: moulded stone projecting from a wall to protect the lower parts from water. Cf. Hoodmould, Weathering.

DRUM: circular or polygonal stage supporting a dome or cupola. Also one of the stones forming the shaft of a column (3a).

DUTCH or FLEMISH GABLE: *see* 8a.

EASTER SEPULCHRE: tomb-chest used for Easter ceremonial, within or against the N wall of a chancel.

EAVES: overhanging edge of a roof; hence *eaves cornice* in this position.

ECHINUS: ovolo moulding (q.v.) below the abacus of a Greek Doric capital (3a).

EDGE RAIL: *see* Railways.

E.E. (EARLY ENGLISH): English Gothic architecture *c.* 1190–1250.

EGG-AND-DART: *see* Enrichments and 3f.

ELEVATION: any face of a building or side of a room. In a drawing, the same or any part of it, represented in two dimensions.

EMBATTLED: with battlements.

EMBRASURE: small splayed opening in a wall or battlement (q.v.).

ENCAUSTIC TILES: earthenware tiles fired with a pattern and glaze.

EN DELIT: stone cut against the bed.

ENFILADE: reception rooms in a formal series, usually with all doorways on axis.

ENGAGED or ATTACHED COLUMN: one that partly merges into a wall or pier.

ENGINEERING BRICKS: dense bricks, originally used mostly for railway viaducts etc.

ENRICHMENTS: the carved decoration of certain classical mouldings, e.g. the ovolo (qq.v.) with *egg-and-dart*, the cyma reversa with *waterleaf*, the astragal with *bead-and-reel* (3f).

ENTABLATURE: in classical architecture, collective name for the three horizontal members (architrave, frieze, and cornice) carried by a wall or a column (3a).

ENTASIS: very slight convex deviation from a straight line, used to prevent an optical illusion of concavity.

EPITAPH: inscription on a tomb.

EXEDRA: *see* Apse.

EXTRADOS: outer curved face of an arch or vault.

EYECATCHER: decorative building terminating a vista.

FASCIA: plain horizontal band, e.g. in an architrave (3c, 3d) or on a shopfront.

FENESTRATION: the arrangement of windows in a façade.

FERETORY: site of the chief shrine of a church, behind the high altar.

FESTOON: ornamental garland, suspended from both ends. Cf. Swag.

FIBREGLASS, or glass-reinforced polyester (GRP): synthetic resin reinforced with glass fibre. GRC: glass-reinforced concrete.

FIELD: see Panelling and 6b.

FILLET: a narrow flat band running down a medieval shaft or along a roll moulding (1a). It separates larger curved mouldings in classical cornices, fluting or bases (3c).

FLAMBOYANT: the latest phase of French Gothic architecture, with flowing tracery.

FLASH LOCK: see Canals.

FLÈCHE or SPIRELET (*lit.* arrow): slender spire on the centre of a roof.

FLEURON: medieval carved flower or leaf, often rectilinear (1a).

FLUSHWORK: knapped flint used with dressed stone to form patterns.

FLUTING: series of concave grooves (flutes), their common edges sharp (arris) or blunt (fillet) (3).

FOIL (*lit.* leaf): lobe formed by the cusping of a circular or other shape in tracery (2b). *Trefoil* (three), *quatrefoil* (four), *cinquefoil* (five), and *multifoil* express the number of lobes in a shape.

FOLIATE: decorated with leaves.

FORMWORK: see Concrete.

FRAMED BUILDING: where the structure is carried by a framework – e.g. of steel, reinforced concrete, timber – instead of by load-bearing walls.

FREESTONE: stone that is cut, or can be cut, in all directions.

FRESCO: *al fresco*: painting on wet plaster. *Fresco secco*: painting on dry plaster.

FRIEZE: the middle member of the classical entablature, sometimes ornamented (3a). *Pulvinated frieze* (*lit.* cushioned): of bold convex profile (3c). Also a horizontal band of ornament.

FRONTISPIECE: in C16 and C17 buildings the central feature of doorway and windows above linked in one composition.

GABLE: For types see 8a. *Gablet*: small gable. *Pedimental gable*: treated like a pediment.

GADROONING: classical ribbed ornament like inverted fluting that flows into a lobed edge.

GALILEE: chapel or vestibule usually at the w end of a church enclosing the main portal(s).

GALLERY: a long room or passage; an upper storey above the aisle of a church, looking through arches to the nave; a balcony or mezzanine overlooking the main interior space of a building; or an external walkway.

GALLETING: small stones set in a mortar course.

GAMBREL ROOF: see 8a.

GARDEROBE: medieval privy.

GARGOYLE: projecting water spout often carved into human or animal shape.

GAUGED or RUBBED BRICKWORK: soft brick sawn roughly, then rubbed to a precise (gauged) surface. Mostly used for door or window openings (5c).

GAZEBO (jocular Latin, 'I shall gaze'): ornamental lookout tower or raised summer house.

GEOMETRIC: English Gothic architecture *c.* 1250–1310. *See also* Tracery. For another meaning, *see* Stairs.

GIANT or COLOSSAL ORDER: classical order (q.v.) whose height is that of two or more storeys of the building to which it is applied.

GIBBS SURROUND: C18 treatment of an opening (4b), seen particularly in the work of James Gibbs (1682–1754).

GIRDER: a large beam. *Box*: of hollow-box section. *Bowed*: with its top rising in a curve. *Plate*: of I-section, made from iron or steel plates. *Lattice*: with braced frame-work.

GLAZING BARS: wooden or some-times metal bars separating and supporting window panes.

GRAFFITI: *see* Sgraffito.

GRANGE: farm owned and run by a religious order.

GRC: *see* Fibreglass.

GRISAILLE: monochrome painting on walls or glass.

GROIN: sharp edge at the meeting of two cells of a cross-vault; *see* Vault and 2c.

GROTESQUE (*lit.* grotto-esque): wall decoration adopted from Roman examples in the Renaissance. Its foliage scrolls incorporate figurative elements. Cf. Arabesque.

GROTTO: artificial cavern.

GRP: *see* Fibreglass.

GUILLOCHE: classical ornament of interlaced bands (4b).

GUNLOOP: opening for a firearm.

GUTTAE: stylized drops (3b).

HALF-TIMBERING: archaic term for timber-framing (q.v.). Sometimes used for non-structural decorative timberwork.

HALL CHURCH: medieval church with nave and aisles of approxim-ately equal height.

HAMMERBEAM: *see* Roofs and 7.

HAMPER: in C20 architecture, a visu-ally distinct topmost storey or storeys.

HEADER: *see* Bond and 6e.

HEADSTOP: stop (q.v.) carved with a head (5b).

HELM ROOF: *see* 1c.

HENGE: ritual earthwork.

HERM (*lit.* the god Hermes): male head or bust on a pedestal.

HERRINGBONE WORK: *see* 7ii. Cf. Pitched masonry.

HEXASTYLE: *see* Portico.

HILL-FORT: Iron Age earthwork en-closed by a ditch and bank system.

HIPPED ROOF: *see* 8a.

HOODMOULD: projecting moulding above an arch or lintel to throw off water (2b, 5b). When horizontal often called a *label*. For label stop *see* Stop.

HUSK GARLAND: festoon of stylized nutshells (4b).

HYDRAULIC POWER: use of water under high pressure to work machinery. *Accumulator tower*: houses a hydraulic accumulator which accommodates fluctuations in the flow through hydraulic mains.

HYPOCAUST (*lit.* underburning): Ro-man underfloor heating system.

IMPOST: horizontal moulding at the springing of an arch (5c).

IMPOST BLOCK: block between abacus and capital (1b).

IN ANTIS: *see* Antae, Portico and 4a.

INDENT: shape chiselled out of a stone to receive a brass.

INDUSTRIALIZED or SYSTEM BUILDING: system of manufac-tured units assembled on site.

INGLENOOK (*lit.* fire-corner): recess for a hearth with provision for seating.

INTERCOLUMNATION: interval be-tween columns.

INTERLACE: decoration in relief simulating woven or entwined stems or bands.

INTRADOS: *see* Soffit.

IONIC: *see* Orders and 3c.

JACK ARCH: shallow segmental vault springing from beams, used for fireproof floors, bridge decks, etc.

JAMB (*lit.* leg): one of the vertical sides of an opening.

JETTY: in a timber-framed building, the projection of an upper storey beyond the storey below, made by the beams and joists of the lower storey oversailing the wall; on their outer ends is placed the sill of the walling for the storey above (7). Buildings can be jettied on several sides, in which case a *dragon beam* is set diagonally at the corner to carry the joists to either side.

JOGGLE: the joining of two stones to prevent them slipping by a notch in one and a projection in the other.

KEEL MOULDING: moulding used from the late C12, in section like the keel of a ship (1a).

KEEP: principal tower of a castle.

KENTISH CUSP: *see* Tracery and 2b.

KEY PATTERN: *see* 4b.

KEYSTONE: central stone in an arch or vault (4b, 5c).

KINGPOST: *see* Roofs and 7.

KNEELER: horizontal projecting stone at the base of each side of a gable to support the inclined coping stones (8a).

LABEL: *see* Hoodmould and 5b.

LABEL STOP: *see* Stop and 5b.

LACED BRICKWORK: vertical strips of brickwork, often in a contrasting colour, linking openings on different floors.

LACING COURSE: horizontal reinforcement in timber or brick to walls of flint, cobble, etc.

LADY CHAPEL: dedicated to the Virgin Mary (Our Lady).

LANCET: slender single-light, pointed-arched window (2a).

LANTERN: circular or polygonal windowed turret crowning a roof or a dome. Also the windowed stage of a crossing tower lighting the church interior.

LANTERN CROSS: churchyard cross with lantern-shaped top.

LAVATORIUM: in a religious house, a washing place adjacent to the refectory.

LEAN-TO: *see* Roofs.

LESENE (*lit.* a mean thing): pilaster without base or capital. Also called *pilaster strip*.

LIERNE: *see* Vault and 2c.

LIGHT: compartment of a window defined by the mullions.

LINENFOLD: Tudor panelling carved with simulations of folded linen. *See also* Parchemin.

LINTEL: horizontal beam or stone bridging an opening.

LOGGIA: gallery, usually arcaded or colonnaded; sometimes free-standing.

LONG-AND-SHORT WORK: quoins consisting of stones placed with the long side alternately upright and horizontal, especially in Saxon building.

LONGHOUSE: house and byre in the same range with internal access between them.

LOUVRE: roof opening, often protected by a raised timber structure, to allow the smoke from a central hearth to escape.

LOWSIDE WINDOW: set lower than the others in a chancel side wall, usually towards its W end.

LUCAM: projecting housing for hoist pulley on upper storey of warehouses, mills, etc., for raising goods to loading doors.

LUCARNE (*lit.* dormer): small gabled opening in a roof or spire.

LUGGED ARCHITRAVE: *see* 4b.

LUNETTE: semicircular window or blind panel.

LYCHGATE (*lit.* corpse-gate): roofed gateway entrance to a churchyard for the reception of a coffin.

LYNCHET: long terraced strip of soil on the downward side of prehistoric and medieval fields, accumulated because of continual ploughing along the contours.

MACHICOLATIONS (*lit.* mashing devices): series of openings between the corbels that support a projecting parapet through which missiles can be dropped. Used decoratively in post-medieval buildings.

MANOMETER or STANDPIPE TOWER: containing a column of water to regulate pressure in water mains.

MANSARD: *see* 8a.

MATHEMATICAL TILES: facing tiles with the appearance of brick, most often applied to timber-framed walls.

MAUSOLEUM: monumental building or chamber usually intended for the burial of members of one family.

MEGALITHIC TOMB: massive stone-built Neolithic burial chamber covered by an earth or stone mound.

MERLON: *see* Battlement.

METOPES: spaces between the triglyphs in a Doric frieze (3b).

MEZZANINE: low storey between two higher ones.

MILD STEEL: *see* Cast iron.

MISERICORD (*lit.* mercy): shelf on a carved bracket placed on the underside of a hinged choir stall seat to support an occupant when standing.

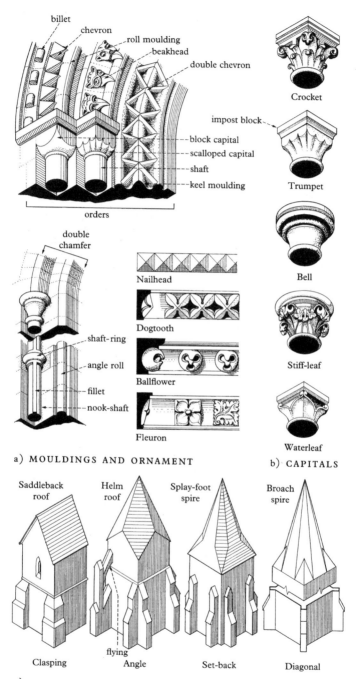

a) MOULDINGS AND ORNAMENT

b) CAPITALS

c) BUTTRESSES, ROOFS AND SPIRES

FIGURE 1: MEDIEVAL

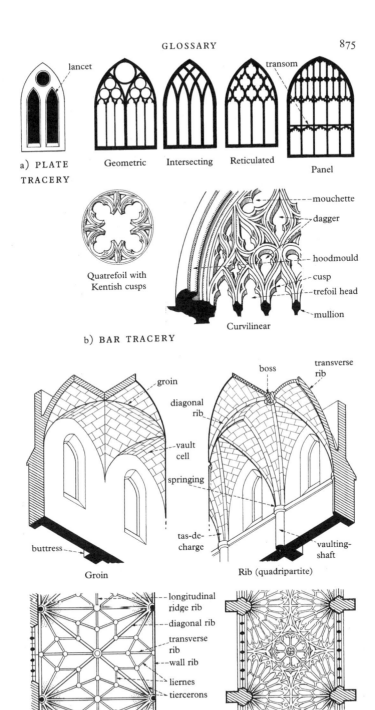

a) PLATE TRACERY

lancet

Geometric   Intersecting   Reticulated   Panel

transom

b) BAR TRACERY

Quatrefoil with
Kentish cusps

Curvilinear

mouchette
dagger
hoodmould
cusp
trefoil head
mullion

c) VAULTS

groin
diagonal rib
vault cell
springing
buttress

Groin

boss
transverse rib
tas-de-charge
vaulting-shaft

Rib (quadripartite)

longitudinal ridge rib
diagonal rib
transverse rib
wall rib
liernes
tiercerons

Lierne   Fan

FIGURE 2: MEDIEVAL

ORDERS

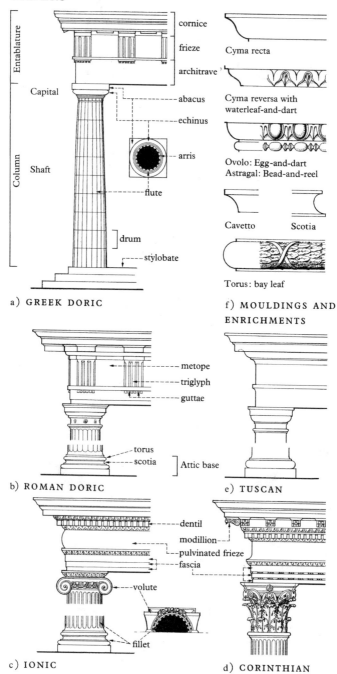

a) GREEK DORIC

- cornice
- frieze
- architrave

Cyma recta

Cyma reversa with
waterleaf-and-dart

Ovolo: Egg-and-dart
Astragal: Bead-and-reel

Cavetto   Scotia

Torus: bay leaf

f) MOULDINGS AND
   ENRICHMENTS

- Capital
- Column
  - Shaft
- Entablature

- abacus
- echinus
- arris
- flute
- drum
- stylobate

b) ROMAN DORIC

- metope
- triglyph
- guttae
- torus
- scotia } Attic base

e) TUSCAN

c) IONIC

- volute
- fillet

- dentil
- modillion
- pulvinated frieze
- fascia

d) CORINTHIAN

FIGURE 3: CLASSICAL

a) PORTICO

Anthemion & Palmette Guilloche Key pattern

Rinceau Husk garland Vitruvian scroll

Console Diocletian window Acanthus

Broken pediment Lugged architrave

Segmental pediment Shouldered architrave

Venetian window

Open pediment Swan-neck pediment Gibbs surround

b) ORNAMENTS AND FEATURES

FIGURE 4: CLASSICAL

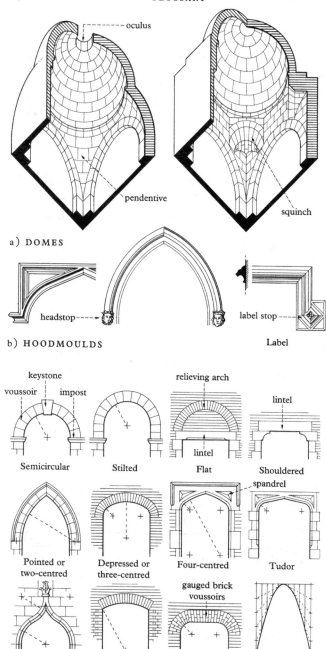

a) DOMES

b) HOODMOULDS

Label

c) ARCHES

FIGURE 5: CONSTRUCTION

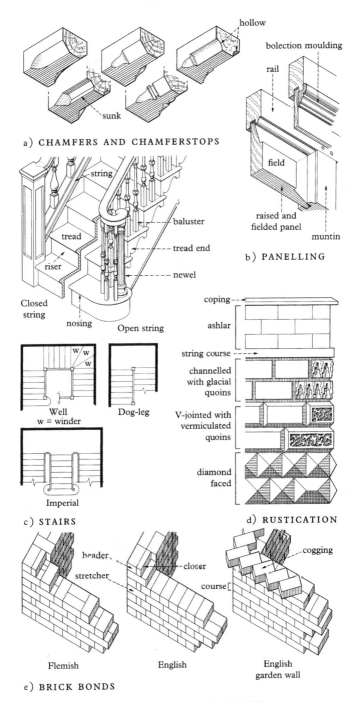

a) CHAMFERS AND CHAMFERSTOPS

hollow

bolection moulding

rail

field

raised and
fielded panel

muntin

b) PANELLING

string

baluster

tread

tread end

riser

newel

Closed
string

nosing

Open string

w w
w

Well
w = winder

Dog-leg

Imperial

c) STAIRS

coping

ashlar

string course

channelled
with glacial
quoins

V-jointed with
vermiculated
quoins

diamond
faced

d) RUSTICATION

header

closer

stretcher

course

cogging

Flemish

English

English
garden wall

e) BRICK BONDS

FIGURE 6: CONSTRUCTION

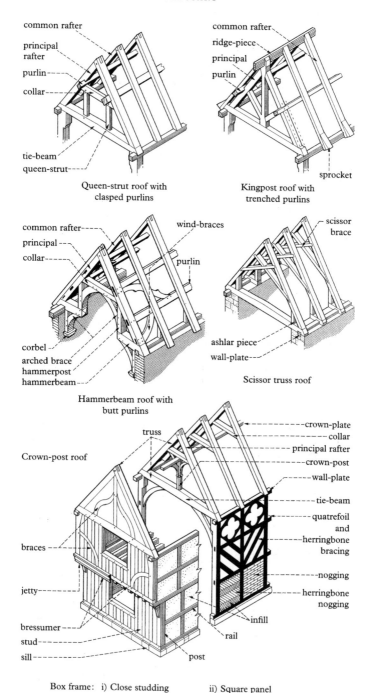

Queen-strut roof with
clasped purlins

- common rafter
- principal rafter
- purlin
- collar
- tie-beam
- queen-strut

Kingpost roof with
trenched purlins

- common rafter
- ridge-piece
- principal
- purlin
- sprocket

Hammerbeam roof with
butt purlins

- common rafter
- principal
- collar
- wind-braces
- purlin
- corbel
- arched brace
- hammerpost
- hammerbeam

Scissor truss roof

- scissor brace
- ashlar piece
- wall-plate

Crown-post roof

- truss
- crown-plate
- collar
- principal rafter
- crown-post
- wall-plate
- tie-beam
- quatrefoil and herringbone bracing
- nogging
- herringbone nogging
- infill
- rail
- post
- braces
- jetty
- bressumer
- stud
- sill

Box frame: i) Close studding   ii) Square panel

FIGURE 7: ROOFS AND TIMBER-FRAMING

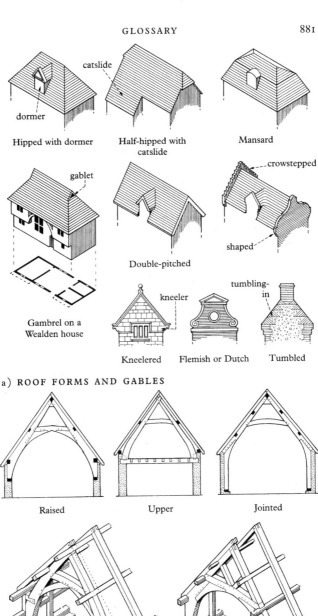

dormer

catslide

gablet

crowstepped

shaped

kneeler

tumbling-in

Hipped with dormer

Half-hipped with catslide

Mansard

Gambrel on a Wealden house

Double-pitched

Kneelered

Flemish or Dutch

Tumbled

a) ROOF FORMS AND GABLES

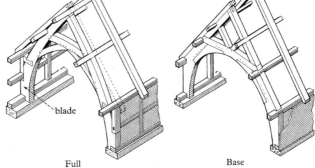

Raised

Upper

Jointed

blade

Full

Base

b) CRUCK FRAMES

FIGURE 8: ROOFS AND TIMBER-FRAMING

MIXER-COURTS: forecourts to groups of houses shared by vehicles and pedestrians.

MODILLIONS: small consoles (q.v.) along the underside of a Corinthian or Composite cornice (3d). Often used along an eaves cornice.

MODULE: a predetermined standard size for co-ordinating the dimensions of components of a building.

MOTTE-AND-BAILEY: post-Roman and Norman defence consisting of an earthen mound (motte) topped by a wooden tower within a bailey, an enclosure defended by a ditch and palisade, and also, sometimes, by an internal bank.

MOUCHETTE: see Tracery and 2b.

MOULDING: shaped ornamental strip of continuous section; see e.g. Cavetto, Cyma, Ovolo, Roll.

MULLION: vertical member between window lights (2b).

MULTI-STOREY: five or more storeys. Multi-storey flats may form a *cluster block*, with individual blocks of flats grouped round a service core; a *point block*, with flats fanning out from a service core; or a *slab block*, with flats approached by corridors or galleries from service cores at intervals or towers at the ends (plan also used for offices, hotels etc.). *Tower block* is a generic term for any very high multi-storey building.

MUNTIN: see Panelling and 6b.

NAILHEAD: E.E. ornament consisting of small pyramids regularly repeated (1a).

NARTHEX: enclosed vestibule or covered porch at the main entrance to a church.

NAVE: the body of a church w of the crossing or chancel often flanked by aisles (q.v.).

NEWEL: central or corner post of a staircase (6c). Newel stair: see Stairs.

NIGHT STAIR: stair by which religious entered the transept of their church from their dormitory to celebrate night services.

NOGGING: see Timber-framing (7).

NOOK-SHAFT: shaft set in the angle of a wall or opening (1a).

NORMAN: see Romanesque.

NOSING: projection of the tread of a step (6c).

NUTMEG: medieval ornament with a chain of tiny triangles placed obliquely.

OCULUS: circular opening.

ŒIL DE BŒUF: see Bullseye window.

OGEE: double curve, bending first one way and then the other, as in an *ogee* or *ogival arch* (5c). Cf. Cyma recta and Cyma reversa.

OPUS SECTILE: decorative mosaic-like facing.

OPUS SIGNINUM: composition flooring of Roman origin.

ORATORY: a private chapel in a church or a house. Also a church of the Oratorian Order.

ORDER: one of a series of recessed arches and jambs forming a splayed medieval opening, e.g. a doorway or arcade arch (1a).

ORDERS: the formalized versions of the post-and-lintel system in classical architecture. The main orders are *Doric*, *Ionic*, and *Corinthian*. They are Greek in origin but occur in Roman versions. Tuscan is a simple version of Roman Doric. Though each order has its own conventions (3), there are many minor variations. The *Composite* capital combines Ionic volutes with Corinthian foliage. *Superimposed orders*: orders on successive levels, usually in the upward sequence of Tuscan, Doric, Ionic, Corinthian, Composite.

ORIEL: see Bay window.

OVERDOOR: painting or relief above an internal door. Also called a *sopraporta*.

OVERTHROW: decorative fixed arch between two gatepiers or above a wrought-iron gate.

OVOLO: wide convex moulding (3f).

PALIMPSEST: of a brass: where a metal plate has been reused by turning over the engraving on the back; of a wall painting: where one overlaps and partly obscures an earlier one.

PALLADIAN: following the examples and principles of Andrea Palladio (1508–80).

PALMETTE: classical ornament like a palm shoot (4b).

PANELLING: wooden lining to interior walls, made up of vertical members (*muntins*) and horizontals (*rails*) framing panels: also called *wainscot*. *Raised and fielded*: with the central area of the panel (*field*) raised up (6b).

PANTILE: roof tile of S section.

PARAPET: wall for protection at any sudden drop, e.g. at the wall-head of a castle where it protects the *parapet walk* or wall-walk. Also used to conceal a roof.

PARCLOSE: *see* Screen.

PARGETTING (*lit.* plastering): exterior plaster decoration, either in relief or incised.

PARLOUR: in a religious house, a room where the religious could talk to visitors; in a medieval house, the semi-private living room below the solar (q.v.).

PARTERRE: level space in a garden laid out with low, formal beds.

PATERA (*lit.* plate): round or oval ornament in shallow relief.

PAVILION: ornamental building for occasional use; or projecting subdivision of a larger building, often at an angle or terminating a wing.

PEBBLEDASHING: *see* Rendering.

PEDESTAL: a tall block carrying a classical order, statue, vase, etc.

PEDIMENT: a formalized gable derived from that of a classical temple; also used over doors, windows, etc. For variations *see* 4b.

PENDENTIVE: spandrel between adjacent arches, supporting a drum, dome or vault and consequently formed as part of a hemisphere (5a).

PENTHOUSE: subsidiary structure with a lean-to roof. Also a separately roofed structure on top of a C20 multi-storey block.

PERIPTERAL: *see* Peristyle.

PERISTYLE: a colonnade all round the exterior of a classical building, as in a temple which is then said to be *peripteral*.

PERP (PERPENDICULAR): English Gothic architecture *c.* 1335–50 to *c.* 1530. The name is derived from the upright tracery panels then used (*see* Tracery and 2a).

PERRON: external stair to a doorway, usually of double-curved plan.

PEW: loosely, seating for the laity outside the chancel; strictly, an enclosed seat. *Box pew*: with equal high sides and a door.

PIANO NOBILE: principal floor of a classical building above a ground floor or basement and with a lesser storey overhead.

PIAZZA: formal urban open space surrounded by buildings.

PIER: large masonry or brick support, often for an arch. *See also* Compound pier.

PILASTER: flat representation of a classical column in shallow relief. *Pilaster strip*: *see* Lesene.

PILE: row of rooms. *Double pile*: two rows thick.

PILLAR: free-standing upright member of any section, not conforming to one of the orders (q.v.).

PILLAR PISCINA: *see* Piscina.

PILOTIS: C20 French term for pillars or stilts that support a building above an open ground floor.

PISCINA: basin for washing Mass vessels, provided with a drain; set in or against the wall to the S of an altar or free-standing (*pillar piscina*).

PISÉ: *see* Cob.

PITCHED MASONRY: laid on the diagonal, often alternately with opposing courses (*pitched and counterpitched* or *herringbone*).

PLATBAND: flat horizontal moulding between storeys. Cf. stringcourse.

PLATE RAIL: *see* Railways.

PLATEWAY: *see* Railways.

PLINTH: projecting courses at the

foot of a wall or column, generally chamfered or moulded at the top.

PODIUM: a continuous raised platform supporting a building; or a large block of two or three storeys beneath a multi-storey block of smaller area.

POINT BLOCK: see Multi-storey.

POINTING: exposed mortar jointing of masonry or brickwork. Types include *flush*, *recessed* and *tuck* (with a narrow channel filled with finer, whiter mortar).

POPPYHEAD: carved ornament of leaves and flowers as a finial for a bench end or stall.

PORTAL FRAME: C20 frame comprising two uprights rigidly connected to a beam or pair of rafters.

PORTCULLIS: gate constructed to rise and fall in vertical grooves at the entry to a castle.

PORTICO: a porch with the roof and frequently a pediment supported by a row of columns (4a). A portico *in antis* has columns on the same plane as the front of the building. A *prostyle* porch has columns standing free. Porticoes are described by the number of front columns, e.g. tetrastyle (four), hexastyle (six). The space within the temple is the *naos*, that within the portico the *pronaos*. *Blind portico*: the front features of a portico applied to a wall.

PORTICUS (plural: porticūs): subsidiary cell opening from the main body of a pre-Conquest church.

POST: upright support in a structure (7).

POSTERN: small gateway at the back of a building or to the side of a larger entrance door or gate.

POUND LOCK: see Canals.

PRESBYTERY: the part of a church lying E of the choir where the main altar is placed; or a priest's residence.

PRINCIPAL: see Roofs and 7.

PRONAOS: see Portico and 4a.

PROSTYLE: see Portico and 4a.

PULPIT: raised and enclosed platform for the preaching of sermons. *Three-decker*: with reading desk below and clerk's desk below that. *Two-decker*: as above, minus the clerk's desk.

PULPITUM: stone screen in a major church dividing choir from nave.

PULVINATED: see Frieze and 3c.

PURLIN: see Roofs and 7.

PUTHOLES or PUTLOG HOLES: in the wall to receive putlogs, the horizontal timbers which support scaffolding boards; sometimes not filled after construction is complete.

PUTTO (plural: putti): small naked boy.

QUARRIES: square (or diamond) panes of glass supported by lead strips (*cames*); square floor slabs or tiles.

QUATREFOIL: see Foil and 2b.

QUEEN-STRUT: see Roofs and 7.

QUIRK: sharp groove to one side of a convex medieval moulding.

QUOINS: dressed stones at the angles of a building (6d).

RADBURN SYSTEM: vehicle and pedestrian segregation in residential developments, based on that used at Radburn, New Jersey, USA, by Wright and Stein, 1928–30.

RADIATING CHAPELS: projecting radially from an ambulatory or an apse (*see* Chevet).

RAFTER: see Roofs and 7.

RAGGLE: groove cut in masonry, especially to receive the edge of a roof-covering.

RAGULY: ragged (in heraldry). Also applied to funerary sculpture, e.g. *cross raguly*: with a notched outline.

RAIL: see Panelling and 6b; also 7.

RAILWAYS: *Edge rail*: on which flanged wheels can run. *Plate rail*: L-section rail for plain unflanged wheels. *Plateway*: early railway using plate rails.

RAISED AND FIELDED: see Panelling and 6b.

RAKE: slope or pitch.

RAMPART: defensive outer wall of stone or earth. *Rampart walk*: path along the inner face.

REBATE: rectangular section cut out of a masonry edge to receive a shutter, door, window, etc.

REBUS: a heraldic pun, e.g. a fiery cock for Cockburn.

REEDING: series of convex mouldings, the reverse of fluting (q.v.). Cf. Gadrooning.

RENDERING: the covering of outside walls with a uniform surface or skin for protection from the weather. *Limewashing*: thin layer of lime plaster. *Pebble-dashing*: where aggregate is thrown at the wet plastered wall for a textured effect. *Roughcast*: plaster mixed with a coarse aggregate such as gravel. *Stucco*: fine lime plaster worked to a smooth surface. *Cement rendering*: a cheaper substitute for stucco, usually with a grainy texture.

REPOUSSÉ: relief designs in metalwork, formed by beating it from the back.

REREDORTER (*lit.* behind the dormitory): latrines in a medieval religious house.

REREDOS: painted and/or sculptured screen behind and above an altar. Cf. Retable.

RESPOND: half-pier or half-column bonded into a wall and carrying one end of an arch. It usually terminates an arcade.

RETABLE: painted or carved panel standing on or at the back of an altar, usually attached to it.

RETROCHOIR: in a major church, the area between the high altar and E chapel.

REVEAL: the plane of a jamb, between the wall and the frame of a door or window.

RIB-VAULT: *see* Vault and 2c.

RINCEAU: classical ornament of leafy scrolls (4b).

RISER: vertical face of a step (6c).

ROACH: a rough-textured form of Portland stone, with small cavities and fossil shells.

ROCK-FACED: masonry cleft to produce a rugged appearance.

ROCOCO: style current *c.* 1720 and *c.* 1760, characterized by a serpentine line and playful, scrolled decoration.

ROLL MOULDING: medieval moulding of part-circular section (1a).

ROMANESQUE: style current in the CII and CI2. In England often called Norman. *See also* Saxo-Norman.

ROOD: crucifix flanked by the Virgin and St John, usually over the entry into the chancel, on a beam (*rood beam*) or painted on the wall. The *rood screen* below often had a walkway (*rood loft*) along the top, reached by a *rood stair* in the side wall.

ROOFS: Shape. For the main external shapes (hipped, mansard, etc.) *see* 8a. *Helm* and *Saddleback*: *see* 1c. *Lean-to*: single sloping roof built against a vertical wall; lean-to is also applied to the part of the building beneath. Construction. *See* 7. *Single-framed* roof: with no main trusses. The rafters may be fixed to the wall-plate or ridge, or longitudinal timber may be absent altogether. *Double-framed* roof: with longitudinal members, such as purlins, and usually divided into bays by principals and principal rafters. Other types are named after their main structural components, e.g. *hammerbeam*, *crown-post* (*see* Elements below and 7). Elements. *See* 7. *Ashlar piece*: a short vertical timber connecting inner wall-plate or timber pad to a rafter. *Braces*: subsidiary timbers set diagonally to strengthen the frame. *Arched braces*: curved pair forming an arch, connecting wall or post below with tie- or collar-beam above. *Passing braces*: long straight braces passing across other members of the truss. *Scissor braces*: pair crossing diagonally between pairs of rafters or principals. *Wind-braces*: short, usually curved braces connecting side purlins with principals, sometimes decorated with cusping. *Collar* or *collar-beam*: horizontal transverse timber connecting a pair of rafter or cruck blades (q.v.), set between apex and the wall-plate. *Crown-post*: a vertical timber set centrally on a tie-beam and supporting a collar purlin braced to it longitudinally. In an open truss lateral braces may rise to the collar-beam; in a closed truss they may descend to the tie-beam.

Hammerbeams: horizontal brackets projecting at wall-plate level like an interrupted tie-beam; the inner ends carry *hammerposts*, vertical timbers which support a purlin and are braced to a collar-beam above.

Kingpost: vertical timber set centrally on a tie- or collar-beam, rising to the apex of the roof to support a ridge-piece (cf. Strut).

Plate: longitudinal timber set square to the ground. *Wall-plate*: plate along the top of a wall which receives the ends of the rafters; cf. Purlin.

Principals: pair of inclined lateral timbers of a truss. Usually they support side purlins and mark the main bay divisions.

Purlin: horizontal longitudinal timber. *Collar purlin* or *crown plate*: central timber which carries collar-beams and is supported by crown-posts. *Side purlins*: pairs of timbers placed some way up the slope of the roof, which carry common rafters. *Butt* or *tenoned purlins* are tenoned into either side of the principals. *Through purlins* pass through or past the principal; they include *clasped purlins*, which rest on queenposts or are carried in the angle between principals and collar, and *trenched purlins* trenched into the backs of principals.

Queen-strut: paired vertical, or near-vertical, timbers placed symmetrically on a tie-beam to support side purlins.

Rafters: inclined lateral timbers supporting the roof covering. *Common rafters*: regularly spaced uniform rafters placed along the length of a roof or between principals. *Principal rafters*: rafters which also act as principals.

Ridge, ridge-piece: horizontal longitudinal timber at the apex of the roof supporting the ends of the rafters.

Sprocket: short timber placed on the back and at the foot of a rafter to form projecting eaves.

Strut: vertical or oblique timber between two members of a truss, not directly supporting longitudinal timbers.

Tie-beam: main horizontal transverse timber which carries the feet of the principals at wall level.

Truss: rigid framework of timbers at bay intervals, carrying the longitudinal roof timbers which support the common rafters. *Closed truss*: with the spaces between the timbers filled, to form an internal partition.

See also Cruck, Wagon roof.

ROPE MOULDING: *see* Cable moulding.

ROSE WINDOW: circular window with tracery radiating from the centre. Cf. Wheel window.

ROTUNDA: building or room circular in plan.

ROUGHCAST: *see* Rendering.

ROVING BRIDGE: *see* Canals.

RUBBED BRICKWORK: *see* Gauged brickwork.

RUBBLE: masonry whose stones are wholly or partly in a rough state. *Coursed*: coursed stones with rough faces. *Random*: uncoursed stones in a random pattern. *Snecked*: with courses broken by smaller stones (snecks).

RUSTICATION: *see* 6d. Exaggerated treatment of masonry to give an effect of strength. The joints are usually recessed by V-section chamfering or square-section channelling (*channelled rustication*). *Banded rustication* has only the horizontal joints emphasized. The faces may be flat, but can be *diamond-faced*, like shallow pyramids, *vermiculated*, with a stylized texture like worm-casts, and *glacial* (frost-work), like icicles or stalactites.

SACRISTY: room in a church for sacred vessels and vestments.

SADDLEBACK ROOF: *see* 1c.

SALTIRE CROSS: with diagonal limbs.

SANCTUARY: area around the main altar of a church. Cf. Presbytery.

SANGHA: residence of Buddhist monks or nuns.

SARCOPHAGUS: coffin of stone or other durable material.

SAXO-NORMAN: transitional Romanesque style combining Anglo-Saxon and Norman features, current *c.* 1060–1100.

SCAGLIOLA: composition imitating marble.

SCALLOPED CAPITAL: *see* 1a.

SCOTIA: a hollow classical moulding, especially between tori (q.v.) on a column base (3b, 3f).

SCREEN: in a medieval church, usually at the entry to the chancel; *see* Rood (screen) and Pulpitum. A *parclose screen* separates a chapel from the rest of the church.

SCREENS or SCREENS PASSAGE: screened-off entrance passage between great hall and service rooms.

SECTION: two-dimensional representation of a building, moulding, etc., revealed by cutting across it.

SEDILIA (singular: sedile): seats for the priests (usually three) on the S side of the chancel.

SET-OFF: *see* Weathering.

SETTS: squared stones, usually of granite, used for paving or flooring.

SGRAFFITO: decoration scratched, often in plaster, to reveal a pattern in another colour beneath. *Graffiti*: scratched drawing or writing.

SHAFT: vertical member of round or polygonal section (1a, 3a). *Shaft-ring*: at the junction of shafts set *en delit* (q.v.) or attached to a pier or wall (1a).

SHEILA-NA-GIG: female fertility figure, usually with legs apart.

SHELL: thin, self-supporting roofing membrane of timber or concrete.

SHOULDERED ARCHITRAVE: *see* 4b.

SHUTTERING: *see* Concrete.

SILL: horizontal member at the bottom of a window or door frame; or at the base of a timber-framed wall into which posts and studs are tenoned (7).

SLAB BLOCK: *see* Multi-storey.

SLATE-HANGING: covering of overlapping slates on a wall. *Tile-hanging* is similar.

SLYPE: covered way or passage leading E from the cloisters between transept and chapter house.

SNECKED: *see* Rubble.

SOFFIT (*lit.* ceiling): underside of an arch (also called *intrados*), lintel, etc. *Soffit roll*: medieval roll moulding on a soffit.

SOLAR: private upper chamber in a medieval house, accessible from the high end of the great hall.

SOPRAPORTA: *see* Overdoor.

SOUNDING-BOARD: *see* Tester.

SPANDRELS: roughly triangular spaces between an arch and its containing rectangle, or between adjacent arches (5c). Also non-structural panels under the windows in a curtain-walled building.

SPERE: a fixed structure screening the lower end of the great hall from the screens passage. *Spere-truss*: roof truss incorporated in the spere.

SPIRE: tall pyramidal or conical feature crowning a tower or turret. *Broach*: starting from a square base, then carried into an octagonal section by means of triangular faces; and *splayed-foot*: variation of the broach form, found principally in the south-east, in which the four cardinal faces are splayed out near their base, to cover the corners, while oblique (or intermediate) faces taper away to a point (1c). *Needle spire*: thin spire rising from the centre of a tower roof, well inside the parapet: when of timber and lead often called a *spike*.

SPIRELET: *see* Flèche.

SPLAY: of an opening when it is wider on one face of a wall than the other.

SPRING or SPRINGING: level at which an arch or vault rises from its supports. *Springers*: the first stones of an arch or vaulting rib above the spring (2c).

SQUINCH: arch or series of arches thrown across an interior angle of a square or rectangular structure to support a circular or polygonal superstructure, especially a dome or spire (5a).

SQUINT: an aperture in a wall or through a pier usually to allow a view of an altar.

STAIRS: *see* 6c. *Dog-leg stair*: parallel flights rising alternately in opposite directions, without an open well. *Flying stair*: cantilevered from the walls of a stairwell, without newels; sometimes called a *Geometric* stair when the inner edge describes a curve. *Newel stair*: ascending round a central supporting newel (q.v.); called a *spiral stair* or *vice* when in a circular shaft, a *winder* when in a rectangular compartment. (Winder also applies to the steps on the turn.) *Well stair*: with flights round a square open well framed by newel posts. *See also* Perron.

STALL: fixed seat in the choir or chancel for the clergy or choir (cf. Pew). Usually with arm rests, and often framed together.

STANCHION: upright structural member, of iron, steel or reinforced concrete.

STANDPIPE TOWER: *see* Manometer.

STEAM ENGINES: *Atmospheric*: worked by the vacuum created when low-pressure steam is condensed in the cylinder, as developed by Thomas Newcomen. *Beam engine*: with a large pivoted beam moved in an oscillating fashion by the piston. It may drive a flywheel or be *non-rotative*. *Watt* and *Cornish*: single-cylinder; *compound*: two cylinders; *triple expansion*: three cylinders.

STEEPLE: tower together with a spire, lantern, or belfry.

STIFF-LEAF: type of E.E. foliage decoration. *Stiff-leaf capital see* 1b.

STOP: plain or decorated terminal to mouldings or chamfers, or at the end of hoodmoulds and labels (*label stop*), or stringcourses (5b, 6a); *see also* Headstop.

STOUP: vessel for holy water, usually near a door.

STRAINER: *see* Arch.

STRAPWORK: late C16 and C17 decoration, like interlaced leather straps.

STRETCHER: *see* Bond and 6e.

STRING: *see* 6c. Sloping member holding the ends of the treads and risers of a staircase. *Closed string*: a broad string covering the ends of the treads and risers. *Open string*: cut into the shape of the treads and risers.

STRINGCOURSE: horizontal course or moulding projecting from the surface of a wall (6d).

STUCCO: *see* Rendering.

STUDS: subsidiary vertical timbers of a timber-framed wall or partition (7).

STUPA: Buddhist shrine, circular in plan.

STYLOBATE: top of the solid platform on which a colonnade stands (3a).

SUSPENSION BRIDGE: *see* Bridge.

SWAG: like a festoon (q.v.), but representing cloth.

SYSTEM BUILDING: *see* Industrialized building.

TABERNACLE: canopied structure to contain the reserved sacrament or a relic; or architectural frame for an image or statue.

TABLE TOMB: memorial slab raised on free-standing legs.

TAS-DE-CHARGE: the lower courses of a vault or arch which are laid horizontally (2c).

TERM: pedestal or pilaster tapering downward, usually with the upper part of a human figure growing out of it.

TERRACOTTA: moulded and fired clay ornament or cladding.

TESSELLATED PAVEMENT: mosaic flooring, particularly Roman, made of *tesserae*, i.e. cubes of glass, stone, or brick.

TESTER: flat canopy over a tomb or pulpit, where it is also called a *sounding-board*.

TESTER TOMB: tomb-chest with effigies beneath a tester, either free-standing (tester with four or more columns), or attached to a wall (*half-tester*) with columns on one side only.

TETRASTYLE: *see* Portico.

THERMAL WINDOW: *see* Diocletian window.

THREE-DECKER PULPIT: *see* Pulpit.

TIDAL GATES: *see* Canals.

TIE-BEAM: *see* Roofs and 7.

TIERCERON: *see* Vault and 2c.

TILE-HANGING: *see* Slate-hanging.

TIMBER-FRAMING: *see* 7. Method of construction where the structural frame is built of interlocking timbers. The spaces are filled with non-structural material, e.g. *infill* of wattle and daub, lath and plaster, brickwork (known as *nogging*), etc. and may be covered by plaster, weatherboarding (q.v.), or tiles.

TOMB-CHEST: chest-shaped tomb, usually of stone. Cf. Table tomb, Tester tomb.

TORUS (plural: tori): large convex moulding usually used on a column base (3b, 3f).

TOUCH: soft black marble quarried near Tournai.

TOURELLE: turret corbelled out from the wall.

TOWER BLOCK: *see* Multi-storey.

TRABEATED: depends structurally on the use of the post and lintel. Cf. Arcuated.

TRACERY: openwork pattern of masonry or timber in the upper part of an opening. *Blind tracery* is tracery applied to a solid wall. *Plate tracery*, introduced *c.* 1200, is the earliest form, in which shapes are cut through solid masonry (2a). *Bar tracery* was introduced into England *c.* 1250. The pattern is formed by intersecting moulded ribwork continued from the mullions. It was especially elaborate during the Decorated period (q.v.). Tracery shapes can include circles, *daggers* (elongated ogee-ended lozenges), *mouchettes* (like daggers but with curved sides) and upright rectangular *panels*. They often have *cusps*, projecting points defining lobes or *foils* (q.v.) within the main shape: *Kentish* or *split-cusps* are forked (2b). Types of bar tracery (*see* 2b) include *geometric(al)*: *c.* 1250–1310, chiefly circles, often foiled; *Y-tracery*: *c.* 1300, with mullions branching into a Y-shape; *intersecting*: *c.* 1300, formed by interlocking mullions; *reticulated*: early C14, net-like pattern of ogee-ended lozenges; *curvilinear*: C14, with uninterrupted flowing curves; *panel*: Perp, with straight-sided panels, often cusped at the top and bottom.

TRANSEPT: transverse portion of a church.

TRANSITIONAL: generally used for the phase between Romanesque and Early English (*c.* 1175–*c.* 1200).

TRANSOM: horizontal member separating window lights (2b).

TREAD: horizontal part of a step. The *tread end* may be carved on a staircase (6c).

TREFOIL: *see* Foil.

TRIFORIUM: middle storey of a church treated as an arcaded wall passage or blind arcade, its height corresponding to that of the aisle roof.

TRIGLYPHS (*lit.* three-grooved tablets): stylized beam-ends in the Doric frieze, with metopes between (3b).

TRIUMPHAL ARCH: influential type of Imperial Roman monument.

TROPHY: sculptured or painted group of arms or armour.

TRUMEAU: central stone mullion supporting the tympanum of a wide doorway. *Trumeau figure*: carved figure attached to it (cf. Column figure).

TRUMPET CAPITAL: *see* 1b.

TRUSS: braced framework, spanning between supports. *See also* Roofs and 7.

TUMBLING or TUMBLING-IN: courses of brickwork laid at right-angles to a slope, e.g. of a gable, forming triangles by tapering into horizontal courses (8a).

TUSCAN: *see* Orders and 3e.

TWO-DECKER PULPIT: *see* Pulpit.

TYMPANUM: the surface between a lintel and the arch above it or within a pediment (4a).

UNDERCROFT: usually describes the vaulted room(s) beneath the main room(s) of a medieval house. Cf. Crypt.

VAULT: arched stone roof (sometimes imitated in timber or plaster). For types see 2c. *Tunnel* or *barrel vault*: continuous semicircular or pointed arch, often of rubble masonry.

Groin-vault: tunnel vaults intersecting at right angles. *Groins* are the curved lines of the intersections.

Rib-vault: masonry framework of intersecting arches (ribs) supporting *vault cells*, used in Gothic architecture. *Wall rib* or *wall arch*: between wall and vault cell. *Transverse rib*: spans between two walls to divide a vault into bays. *Quadripartite* rib-vault: each bay has two pairs of diagonal ribs dividing the vault into four triangular cells. *Sexpartite* rib-vault: most often used over paired bays, has an extra pair of ribs springing from between the bays. More elaborate vaults may include *ridge ribs* along the crown of a vault or bisecting the bays; *tiercerons*: extra decorative ribs springing from the corners of a bay; and *liernes*: short decorative ribs in the crown of a vault, not linked to any springing point. A *stellar* or *star* vault has liernes in star formation.

Fan-vault: form of barrel vault used in the Perp period, made up of halved concave masonry cones decorated with blind tracery.

VAULTING SHAFT: shaft leading up to the spring or springing (q.v.) of a vault (2c).

VENETIAN or SERLIAN WINDOW: derived from Serlio (4b). The motif is used for other openings.

VERMICULATION: *see* Rustication and 6d.

VESICA: oval with pointed ends.

VICE: *see* Stair.

VILLA: originally a Roman country house or farm. The term was revived in England in the C18 under the influence of Palladio and used especially for smaller, compact country houses. In the later C19 it was debased to describe any suburban house.

VITRIFIED: bricks or tiles fired to a darkened glassy surface.

VITRUVIAN SCROLL: classical running ornament of curly waves (4b).

VOLUTES: spiral scrolls. They occur on Ionic capitals (3c). *Angle volute*: pair of volutes, turned outwards to meet at the corner of a capital.

VOUSSOIRS: wedge-shaped stones forming an arch (5c).

WAGON ROOF: with the appearance of the inside of a wagon tilt; often ceiled. Also called *cradle roof*.

WAINSCOT: *see* Panelling.

WALL MONUMENT: attached to the wall and often standing on the floor. *Wall tablets* are smaller with the inscription as the major element.

WALL-PLATE: *see* Roofs and 7.

WALL-WALK: *see* Parapet.

WARMING ROOM: room in a religious house where a fire burned for comfort.

WATERHOLDING BASE: early Gothic base with upper and lower mouldings separated by a deep hollow.

WATERLEAF: *see* Enrichments and 3f.

WATERLEAF CAPITAL: Late Romanesque and Transitional type of capital (1b).

WATER WHEELS: described by the way water is fed on to the wheel. *Breastshot*: mid-height, falling and passing beneath. *Overshot*: over the top. *Pitchback*: on the top but falling backwards. *Undershot*: turned by the momentum of the water passing beneath. In a *water turbine*, water is fed under pressure through a vaned wheel within a casing.

WEALDEN HOUSE: type of medieval timber-framed house with a central open hall flanked by bays of two storeys, roofed in line; the end bays are jettied to the front, but the eaves are continuous (8a).

WEATHERBOARDING: wall cladding of overlapping horizontal boards.

WEATHERING or SET-OFF: inclined, projecting surface to keep water away from the wall below.

WEEPERS: figures in niches along the sides of some medieval tombs. Also called mourners.

WHEEL WINDOW: circular, with radiating shafts like spokes. Cf. Rose window.

WROUGHT IRON: *see* Cast iron.

INDEX OF ARCHITECTS, ARTISTS, PATRONS AND RESIDENTS

Names of architects and artists working in Essex are given in *italic*. Entries for partnerships and group practices are listed after entries for a single name.

Also indexed here are the names/titles of families and individuals (not of bodies or commercial firms) recorded in this volume as having commissioned architectural work or owned or lived in properties in the area. The index includes monuments to members of such families and other individuals where they are of particular interest.

Abbott & Co. 240
Abbott (J. O.) & W. G. Habershon 769
Abdy family 510, 512, 744
Abdy, Sir Anthony-Thomas 512
Aberdeen, David du R. 461
Aberdeen (David du R.) & Partners 116n.
Abergavenny, Joan Beauchamp, Lady 647
Abraham, Esmond 501
Abraham, Robert 62, 468
Acharya, Larrisa 228
Ackroyd, Jane 456
Ackworth, Sir Jacob 142
AD Architects 464
Adair, John & William Robert 103
Adam, Robert 50, 52, 96, 98, 100, 101, 102, 104, 166n., 476, 599, 600
Adams family 445
Adams, James 606, 733
Adams, William 93, 579
Adams, Holden & Pearson 70, 696
Addedomaros (British king) 302
Adsetts, Ernest 455, 456
Adshead & Ramsey 784
Adye, Charles S. 466
Adye, Thomas 54, 549
Aedas AHR 211
Agas, Ralph 786
AHA Architects 456
Ahlfeldt, F. C. 783
Ahrends, Burton & Koralek 71, 117, 119
Aikman, W. 109, 554, 591, 713, 744
Ainslie, C. R. 649, 786
Albemarle, George Monck, 1st Duke of 157
Alciati, Andrea 685
Aldridge, John 388, 391
Alexander, D. A. 474
Alexander, John W. 92
Alexander, Rosemary 391

Alexander, William 855
Alken, Sefferin 101
Allardyce, W. H. 712
Allen, Bill 463
Allen, E. P. 212
Allen, Dr Matthew 64
Allen, Mike 467
Allen, Snooke & Stock 361
Alleyn, William 636–7
Allford, David 649
Allford Hall Monaghan Morris 72, 416
Allom, Thomas 476
Alston family 396
Altham family 455, 456
Amec Design & Management 465
Amor, John 235
Amos, G. S. 135
Anderson, J. Macvicar 472
Anderson, S. 165
Anderson, W. E. Ellery 561
Andrews, Mr and Mrs Robert 186
Angelico, Fra 790
Angello-del-Cauchferta, François 414
Anglian Architects 456
Angold, Paulinus 455
Angus, Mark 580
Annys-Dhont, C. 160
Appleton, Sir Henry 192
Apps, W. G. 211, 726
Arabin, Richard 489
Archer family 771
Archer, E. A. H. 441
Archer, E. P. 315, 317
Archer, James 266
Archer, Sir John (C17) 770
Archer, John (C18) 304
Archer, Robart 195
Archer-Houblon, Miss 304
Architects Co-Partnership 73, 74, 241, 461, 570, 797, Pl. 116
Architecture & Design Partnership Ltd 566

Arderne, Sir Peter 454, 456
Argent Building Co. 749
Arkwright family 456
Arkwright, Elizabeth 459
Arkwright, Joseph 458
Arkwright, L. W. 459
Armstrong, Douglas G. 148
Armstrong, June 464
Armstrong, Richard 65, 184, 719, 741, 791
Arnold (Cedric) & Hyatt 208
ARP Architects 522, 622, 683
Arrowsmith (A. W.) & Co. 277
Arts Team @ RHWL 229
Arup Associates 177, 598
Arup Engineering 317
Arup Group 629
Arup, Ove 69, 193, Pl. 113
Arup (Ove) & Partners 576, 735
Ash Design 860
Ashbee, C. R. 59, 497–8
Ashbee, W. N. 56, 185, 278, 368, 503, 525, 614, 648, 696, 852
Ashurst, Robert 195
Ashurst, Sir William 195
Associated Architects & Consultants 463
Astins, N. P. 695
Atkins, W. S. 74, 149, 211, 281n., 419, 684, 723
Atkins (W. S.) Property Services 169
Atkinson, T. W. & C. 160
Atkinson, William 501
ATP Group Partnership 812
Attfield & Jones 357
Atye (Bartholomew) & Isaac James 46, 810, 824
Audley family 133
Audley, Sir Henry 133
Audley, Sir Thomas Audley, Lord 45, 47, 95, 98, 277, 657, 670, 761, Pl. 42
Aukett 215
Aukett Associates 598
Auravisions 339, 593, 634
    see also *McCarthy, Susan*
Austin, George 147
Austin, William 860
Austin-Smith, Salmon, Lord Partnership, The 116n., 464
Aylett, Thomas 510

BAA Consultancy 735
Backhouse & Co. 276
Bacon, John Jun. 55, 147, 395, 492, 608, 771
Bacon, John Sen. 55, 102, 209, 433, 501
Bacon, Percy 191, 554, 606, 626, 707, 859
Bacon (Percy) & Bros 90, 176, 196, 393, 440, 498, 518, 554, 701, 832
Bacon & Manning 478, 520, 795

Badeley, Dr John 216
Baggallay, Frank 63, 572, 751
Bagshaw, John 328–9
Bagshaw, R. J. 328, 329
Baguley, G. J. 625
Bailey, H. Roberson 432
Bailey Lewis 190
Bailey & McConnal 771
Bailey & Walker 432, 534
Baillie (Thomas) & Co. 125, 759
Baillie Scott see Scott, M. H. Baillie; Scott (Baillie) & Beresford
Baily, E. H. 55, 214, 752
Baines, Sir Frank 572
Baines, G. & R. P. 714
Baines, George 67, 714
Baker, Frederick M. 384
Baker, J. L. 524
Baker, Richard 618
Baker, T. H. 240, 241, 242, 243n., 289
Baker, W. Lewis 65, 524
Baker & May 270, 283, 372, 534, 602
Baldwin Design Ltd 586
Ball, Peter Eugene 205
Ball, Raymond 183
Banks, E. H. 699
Banks, T. Lewis 61, 480, Pl. 100
Banks (Elizabeth) Associates 661
Banks & Barry 66, 698
Banson, J. H. 606
Barber Casanovas Ruffles 547, 730
Barefoot (Peter) & Partners 341
Baring, Hon. Cecil 230
Baring, T. C. 489
Barker, Obadiah 856
Barker, R. T. 525
Barker, Robert 505
Barker (R. T.) & A. H. Kirk 64, 176, 178, 525
Barleyman, John 352
Barnadiston, Nathaniel (fl. 1809) 554
Barnadiston, Col. Nathaniel (fl. 1884) 555
Barnard, Peter and Marget 377
Barnard, Bishop & Barnard 276, 853
Barnes, Frederick 56, 61, 269n., 271, 329, 441, 535, 602, 759, 788, 816
Barnsley Hewett & Mallinson 159, 229
Barr, Edward 543–4
Barr, James 341, 546, 819
Barr, Rev. John 819n.
Barrett family 107
Barrett, Gerald W. 123, 386, 400, 604, 751
Barrett, John 107
Barrett-Lennard family 107
Barrington family 478
Barrington, J. S. 479
Barritt, C. M. H. 265
Barron, Edward 443

Barry, Sir John Wolfe 697
Bartleet, W. G. 65, 117, 175–6, 232, 254, 683, 684
Bartlett, Percy J. 283
Barton Willmore Partnership 824
Basevi, George 49, 145
Basildon Council 119, 122
Basildon Development Corporation 111, 115, 117, 118, 119, 120, 122, 125
Baskett, Charles Edward 277
Baskett, Charles Henry 277, 297
Bateman, Viscountess 434
Bates (Thomas) & Son 778
Bawden, Edward 388, 390, 664
Bawden, Richard 129, 389
Baxter, R. D. C. 124
Baxter (Alan) & Associates 111
Bayes, Gilbert 661, 702
Bayes, Kenneth 660
Bayliss & Co. 520
Baynard, Geoffrey 548
Bayne, Robert 268
  see also Heaton, Butler & Bayne
Baynes, Donald 783
Baynes, T. M. 234, 235
Bayning family 541
Beadel, James 420
Beadel (James) & Son 57
Beadel, Son & Chancellor 217, 220, 225, 735, 804
Beatson, Capt. R. S., R.E. 711
Beauchamp, Joan *see* Abergavenny, Lady
Beaumont family 852
Beaumont, G. F. 250
Beaumont, Sir George (b. 1753) 403
Beaumont, Sir George (d. 1762) 402
Beaumont, P. M. 90, 250, 252, 326, 332, 333, 511, 579, 580, 581, 582, 584, 619
Bebb, Maurice 166
Beck, William 64, 345, 654, 658–9, 662, 669
Beckingham, Stephen 792
Beckman, Martin 481
Beckwith, Edward 509
Beckwith, Ernest 110, 147, 148, 204n., 252, 253, 331, 354, 377, 389, 408, 410, 421, 425, 510, 533, 624, 657, 688, 766, 828
Bedford, F. O. 489
Bedford, J. 803
Behnes, William 55, 608
Beighton, Graham 168, 277, 301, 314, 316
Belcher, John 61, 276, Pl. 97
Beleschenko, Alex 210
Belham & Co. 232
Bell family 669
Bell, Anning see Bell, Robert Anning
Bell, Charles 61, 91, 240, 243n., 345, 468, 749
Bell, Daniel 306, Pl. 17

Bell, James 402
Bell, Joseph 646
Bell, Ken 287, 341
Bell, M. C. Farrar 91, 397, 621, 753
Bell, Reginald 303, 753
Bell, Robert Anning 232, 790
Bell & Beckham 90
Bell (William) & Sons 669
Bellamy, Thomas 54, 733
Belli, Rev. Charles A. 173, 720, 721, 722n.
Belmeis, Richard de, Bishop of London 400, 671
Belsham, Roy 847
Belshaw, Walter A. 374
Belsky, Franta 278
Belsom, David 340
Bendall, O. 588
Bendlowes, Edward 388
Bendlowes, William 389, 391
Bendyshe, Sir Henry 748, 749
Benham, W. Gurney 277, 289
Beningfield, Gordon 184, 233, 810
Benison & Bargman 666
Bennett, Arnold 780
Bennett, Austin 551
Bennett (T. P.) Architects 813–14
Bennett & Hunt 101
Bennett (T. P.) & Son 125, 177, 566
Benoy 452
Benoy, K. W. 192, 570
Benson, Philip 190
Bentall, E. H. 488
Bentall, William 488
Bentley, Deborah 582
Bentley, John 609
Bentley, John Francis 60, 148, 657, 666, 669
Benton, W. 704, 825
Benyan, Richard 247
Beriffe family 179–80, 181
Berk, Meir 215
Betts, E. L. 698
Bevan, C. H. 149
Bevington & Son 110
Bewsey, J. C. N. 441
Bickerdike, John 463
Bicknell, John 465
Bicknell, Stephen 205
Bilham, Edward C. 518
Binney, Sir George 496
Binns & Charles 95
Binyon, Brightwen 278, 295
Birch, John 66, 149, 381, 444, 480
Birch Wolfe family 91
Birchall Scott 233
Bird, Hugo R. 174, 179
Bird, T. 618
Biscoe & Stanton 300, 586, 612
Bishop, Bertram 464
Bishop, J. R. 212
Bisshopp, E. F. 555, 827
Blackburn, Bewicke 56

Blackie, James 248, 794
Blacking, W. H. R. 161, 232
Blair-Warren, Rev. J. C. 556
Bland, Brown & Cole 659
Blatch, John 204
Bleecker, Tessa 280
Blomfield, A. C. 214, 370
Blomfield, Sir Arthur William 58, 123,
    129, 143, 161, 204, 226, 266, 268,
    271, 350, 410, 435, 440, 488, 509,
    515, 594, 675, 831, 834, 859
Blomfield, C. J. 510
Blomfield, Rev. James 618
Blomfield, Sir Reginald 316, 356, 556,
    616, 618n., 658, 710, 775–6, 859
Blomfield (C. J.) & Morgan 410
Blomfield (Sir Arthur) & Sons 139,
    265, 356, 399, 782, 820
Bloomfield, Alan 310
Blore, E. 87
Blount, G. R. 172
Blow, Detmar 778
Blower, Philip 648
Bly, C. L. 269
Blyth, Sir James 739
Boal, A. 114
Boatswain, Jason 416
Bodley, G. F. 226, 336, 345, 389, 539,
    701, 831, 844n.
Bodley & Garner 59, 248, 345, 499,
    604
Bodley & Hare 345, 395
Boehm, Sir (Joseph) Edgar 373, 551
Boggis, Thomas 285
Boleyn family 647
Boleyn, Thomas see Rochford,
    Viscount
Bolton, William 155
Bondesign Associates 697
Bonham, Captain Samuel 618, 619
Bonner, Bishop 619
Bonomi, J. 745
Booth, M. G. 812
Booth & Ledeboer 456, 461
Booth & Poulson 461
Borges (P. Andrew) & Associates 299,
    363, 562
Borley, A. P. G. 611
Borromini, Francesco 324
Botolph, St 19, 438
Boudicca 14, 257, 277, 802
Boulton & Paul 325
Bourchier family 30, 440–1, 549–50,
    684
    see also Essex, Earl of
Bourchier, Bartholomew, Lord 444
Bourchier, Sir Henry 487
Bourginion, Sieur 776
Bourne, J. C. 858
Boutwood, James 67, 75, 245, 248,
    253, 588, 589, 628, 683, 739, 766,
    845
Bouygues Consortium, The 183

Bowden (Mark) & Co. 395
Bowe, Daniel J. 242
Bowen, Doug 536
Bowen, J. P. 476
Bower, Stephen E. Dykes 66, 67, 205,
    248–9, 334, 356, 425, 630–1, 706,
    737, 787
Bowles, F. W. S. 432
Bowman 522, 795
Bowyer-Smith, Sir Edward 496
Boxall, R. A. 328, 457
Boxall (R. A.) Associates 821
Boyes, H. C. 423
Boys, William and Susan 286
Bradbury, Dame Johane 660
Bradford, John 794n.
Bradley, Ray 782
Bradshaw, Ronald 812
Bragg, Alan 331, 381, 415, 436, 598, 792
Bragg, Stanley 116n., 118, 485, 799,
    800, 832
Bragg (Stanley) Architects 403, 697
Bragg (Stanley) & Associates 192,
    291, 292, 326, 387
Bragg (Stanley) & Partners 170
Bragg (Stanley) Partnership 113, 124,
    278, 279, 283, 645
Braithwaite, John 55, 175, 213, 535
Bramston family 650
Bramston, Rev. John 838
Bramston, T. W. 650
Bramston, Thomas 650
Brand Hollis (Brand), Thomas 504
Brand, J. E. C. 189
Brand (M. P.) Ltd 150
Brand, Thomas see Brand Hollis,
    Thomas
Brandon, J. R. 61, 283, 294
Brandon & Blore 276n.
Brandon-Jones (John), Ashton &
    Broadbent 73, 174
Brandon-Jones & Andrew Thorne 174
Branwood, Reginald 859
Brassey, Thomas 698
Braybrooke family 545, 654, 657
Braybrooke, 1st Baron 96
Braybrooke, 3rd Baron 63, 97, 98,
    101, 102, 662
Braybrooke, 5th Baron 544
Brazdys, Antanas 454, 462, 472
Breavington, J. 726
Breeze, Gary 249
Breley (John) Design Associates 697
Bremer (Colchester) 87
Bremer, William 269
Brennand-Wood, Michael 74, 149
Brett, Rev. C. W. 785
Brett, Margaret Anna 620, 785
Brett (Lionel) & Kenneth Boyd 116n.
Brettingham, Matthew Jun. 612
Brettingham, Matthew Sen. 612, 800
Brettingham, R. W. F. 104, 655
Brewster, David 118, 119, 125, 861

Bridgeman, Charles 427, 480
Bridges, G. 770
Bridges, George 525
Bridges, Mark 534
Briggs, E. Edward 708
Brightman, Hilary 165
Brimilcombe, Geoffrey 464
British Railways Eastern Region
    Architect's Department 114, 465
Britten & Gilson 205
Britton, J. P. 199
Broadbent, Hastings, Reid & New 441
Broadley, Rick 169, 723
Broadway Malyan 813
Bromley & Watkins 699
Brookes, W. M. 641
Brooks, James 59, 347, 421, 580, 592,
    691, 733
Brooks, William 410
Brooks (Alison) Architects 71, 671
Browell, W. R. 126
Brown (Colchester) 393
Brown, Capability 49, 96, 103–4, 107,
    304, 309, 409, 479, 609, 612, 776,
    779
Brown, Charles R. 743
Brown, Cuthbert 212
Brown, Ford Madox 816
Brown, H. K. 385
Brown, Harold 377
Brown, J. W. 185, 568, 594, 595, 646
Brown, James 747
Brown, John (fl. 1840) 844
Brown, John (fl. 1912) 657
Brown, Ralph 453, 458
Brown, W. B. 584
Brown, William 795
Brown & Burgess 295, 328, 687
Browne, A. E. 509
Browne, Sir Anthony 175
Browne, J. 134, 478
Browne, John 37
Browne, Robert H. 235
Browning, Edward 479, 518
Brownlow, George Washington 130, 131
Bruff, Peter 55–6, 199, 237, 369, 816,
    Pl. 96
Brunlees & McKerrow 697
Brunton (John) Partnership 291
Bryans, H. W. 859
Bryant (Peregrine) Architects 288
Bryant Harvey Partnership 416
Bryce family 140
Bryce, Ivor 606
Buckeridge, Charles 142, 602
Buckingham, George Villiers, 1st
    Duke of 155, 158
Buckingham, Michael 500
Buckler, C. A. 753
Buckler, J. C. 105
Buckley (Michael) & Co. 120, 732
    see also Cox & Buckley; Cox, Sons,
    Buckley & Co.

Budworth, P. J. 437
Building Design Partnership 697
Bull family 626
Bull, Rev. Edward 626
Bull, Rev. Felix 626
Bullock family 350, 351, 632
Bullock, Sir Edward 351
Bullock, Rev. Fred 632–3
Bullock, Hannah 54, 350
Bullock, Jonathan 351–2
Burbidge, Richard 106, 683
Burcombe, A. A. 124
Burges, William 58, 806–10
Burgess, Edward 61, 62–3, 563, 654,
    658, 659–60
Burgh, Hubert de 438
Burles & Harris 694, 709, 710, 714,
    715
Burles, Harris & Collings 707
Burles & Newton 116n., 192
Burles, Newton & Co. 121
Burles, Newton & Partners 116, 172,
    174, 458, 702, 753
Burlison & Grylls 60, 144, 166, 228,
    248, 345, 389, 441, 510, 657, 693,
    739
Burman, Thomas 46, 474, 517, 565,
    683
Burne-Jones, Sir Edward 60, 110, 369,
    431, 503, 554, 795, 810, Pl. 104
Burnet (Sir John) & Partners 69, 687
Burnet (Sir John), Tait & Lorne 148
Burnet (Sir John), Tait & Partners
    462
Burnett, Florence 549
Buro Happold 114
Burrell, Rev. H. J. 59, 544
Burrell, John 294
Burridge, P. F. 695, 715
Burroughs, Humphrey 160
Burrow, H. 376
Burton, Decimus 144
Burton, John 267
Buss, A. E. 228, 554, 561
Butcher, C. E. 269, 290, 301, 515, 598
Butcher & Abrams 521
Butler, A. S. G. 304, 624
Butler, R. A. 436
Butterfield, William 89, 97, 98, 265,
    410, 433, 439, 655, 718, 832
Butterworth, James 329
Buxton, Sir Edward, Bt 801
Buxton, Edward North 347, 480
Buxton, Noel 252
Buxton, T. F. V. 802
Buxton, Sir Thomas Fowell, Bt 801,
    802
Byfield, George 759
Byng, Lady 780
Byrd, William 755
Byrd & Tyler Associates 667
Byrhtnoth 579, 583
Byron, John 111, 119

Byron, Mary Jane 518

Cabuche, H. Leon 716
Cabuche & Hayward 693, 715
Cachemaille-Day, N. F. 384
Cadbury-Brown, H. T. 71, 457, 458, 799
    see also Crabtree (William) and H. T. Cadbury-Brown
Cadbury-Brown (H. T.) & Partners 465
Caiger, F. H. 812
CALA 466
Cales, W. 161
Calfhill, James 150
Caller, Peter 819
Came, James 845
Campbell, Charles 809
Campbell & Co. 732
Campbell, Smith & Co. 226, 422, 425, 630, 631, 711, 753
Campbell Jones, Sons & Smithers 370
Campfield, George 795
Canadian Central Mortgage & Housing Group 463
Cane, Percy 520
Cant, B. R. 271
Canute, King 94, 438
Capel family 85, 639
Capel, Sir Giles 639
Capel, Sir William 639
Capel-Cure family 86
    see also Cure
Capel-Cure, Isabel 85
Capel-Cure, Laurence 86
Capon, Kenneth 73, 797–9, Pl. 116
Capronnier, J. B. 265
Carden, Andrew 315
Carden & Godfrey 315, 422, 502, 790
Care Design Group 294
Cargill, Campbell F. 405
Carle, B. De 318
Carle, Robert De 321
Carlingford, 1st Baron 609
Carlyle, Lady (Isabel) 418
Carne, Samuel Charles 678
Caröe, W. D. 59, 129, 199, 320–1, 322, 497–8, 600, 634, 738, 739, 770
    see also Christian & Caröe
Caroline of Brunswick, Princess 691
Carpenter, R. C. 58, 477–8, 558
    see also Slater & Carpenter
Carpenter, Samuel 679n.
Carr, Major George Davis 649
Carr, William 487, 644
Cart de Lafontaine, H. P. 861
Carte, H. W. 833
Carter, George 266
Carter, John 53, 318, Pl. 70
Carter, William 376
Carter & Co. 114n., 475
Carthy, Ian 348, 374, 569
Cartwright, Thomas the Elder 46, 630, 652, 657

Carwardine, H. H. 331–2, 333, 334
Casolani, Henry 595
Casson, Sir Hugh 436
Castell, George 851
Castelnau-Bucher, Lestocq de 173
Castro, Amilcar de 799
Catchpool, Thomas 296
Catherine Ruth, Sister 499
Cautley, H. Munro 440
Cawthra, Hermon 168, 340
Cazalet, Mark 205
CD Partnership 464
Cedd, St 18–19, 165, 205, 208, 579, 706, 789
Cerceau, Jacques Androuet Du 776
Chadwick, Lynn 453
Challis, John 55, 129, 168, 350, 621
Chamberlain & Partners 279
Chamberlin Powell & Bon 847n.
Chambers, Walter 297
Chambers, Sir William 504
Champigneulle, C. 826
Champion, Richard 733
Champion de Crespigny, Sir Claude 422, 423
Chance & Co. 184
Chancellor, F. G. M. 385
Chancellor, Frederic 57, 58n., 61, 62, 64, 89, 119, 138, 139, 142, 144, 147, 153, 158, 161, 165, 167, 182, 186, 194, 197, 201, 204–5, 207, 208, 213, 214, 216, 217, 219, 220, 221, 222, 223, 225, 243n., 311, 312, 316, 335, 355–6, 373, 377, 379, 387, 388, 397, 405, 412, 424–5, 426–7, 428, 433, 436, 458, 459, 460, 479, 488, 490, 491, 492, 502, 518, 542, 548, 549, 563, 577, 580, 591, 595, 596, 602, 607, 617, 625, 626–7, 630, 634, 646, 648, 649, 652, 653, 677, 684, 717, 728, 747, 753, 758, 786, 796, 797, 802, 838, 856, 857, 859, 860, Pls. 13, 92
    see also Beadel, Son & Chancellor; Chancellor & Son
Chancellor, Frederic Wykeham 57, 94, 110, 128, 147, 198, 204n., 220, 307, 311, 317, 337, 349, 354, 356, 406, 413, 480, 533, 579, 580, 582, 585, 591, 684, 756, 831, 859, 861
Chancellor (Wykeham) & Bragg 124, 832
Chancellor & Son 62, 147, 148, 158, 176, 201, 212, 218, 309, 311–12, 332, 341, 417, 501, 510, 527–9, 531, 532–3, 592, 615, 617, 640, 678, 844
Chandler, Samuel 54, 640, Pl. 71
Channon, Henry ('Chips') 513
Chantrey, Sir Francis 55, 162, 721
Chapel Studio 644, 713, 782
Chapman, J. W. 241, 243
Chapman Taylor Partners 824
Chapple, David 115

Charles II, King 96
Charlotte, Princess 841
Charrington family 527
Charrington, F. N. 619
Charter Partnership 800
Chater, William 612, 658, 661
Chatto, Beth 343
Cheere, Sir Henry 54, 159, 206, 386, 546, 627, 810, 826, 860
Cheers, H. A. 62, 212, 332
Cheers & Smith 279
Cheeseman, Kenneth 67, 270, 437, 637, 648, 702, 714, 783
Cheffins, William 479
Chelmsford Borough Council 220
Chelmsford Borough Engineer's Department 220
Chesher, R. S. 850
Cheshire, John 763
Chesterton, Maurice 802
Cheston, John A. 751
Chetwood, H. J. 356
Chetwood & Grant 356–7
Chewton, Viscount 608
Chiari (School of) 753
Chibborne, Hanameel 596
Chinnery family 811, 813–14
Chipchase & Lambert 102
Chiswell family 318, 319
Chiswell, Peter (formerly Muilman) 318
Chiswell, Richard 318
Chiswell, Richard Muilman Trench 318
Christian, Ewan 58–9, 106, 248, 378, 419, 471, 487, 521, 522, 541, 580, 582, 706, 748, 758, 781, 788, 826, 832, 834–5
Christian & Caröe 497
Christiani & Nielsen 193
Christie, Fyffe 734
Christie-Miller, W. 183n.
Christmas, Gerard 134
Christmas, John & Matthias 537, 773
Christopherson, Janet 430–1, 650
Christy, Miller 225
Church, Jabez 443
Churchill, John 514
Cipriani, G. B. 102
Citiscape Developments 754
Clare, George E. 687–8
Clare, John 64, 489
Clare & Ross 211, 214, 312, 413, 715, 716
Clark, Duncan W. 108, 265, 280, 283, 285, 441, 555
Clark, Geof 792
Clark, H. Fuller 716
Clark, J. W. 169, 332
Clark, James 580, 590
Clark, Jenny 135
Clark, John K. 184
Clark, Jonathan 417

Clark, Lindsey 568
Clark, Michael Lindsey 207, 569
Clark, Mona 550
Clark, Philip Lindsey 441, 569
Clark (John) Associates 215
Clark (Duncan) & Beckett 88, 199, 268, 280, 285, 295, 299, 331, 395, 593, 598, 738, 803
Clark & Fenn 394
Clarke (Wigmore Street) 55, 645, 745
Clarke, G. R. 755
Clarke, H. F. 392
Clarke, John (C18) 145
Clarke, John (C19) 697
Clarke, Joseph 62, 64, 95, 132, 173n., 184, 207, 225, 235, 244, 252, 253, 262, 304, 326, 349, 367, 368, 422, 432, 440, 459, 460, 464, 478–9, 480, 508, 513, 550, 566, 651, 703, 728, 729, 838, 843
Clarke, Somers 830
  see also Micklethwaite (J. T.) & Somers Clarke
Clarke & Son 637
Clarke (E.) & Son 232
Claughton, Bishop T. L. 315
Clayton & Bell 7, 60, 92, 142, 147, 161, 168, 189, 205, 207, 208, 232, 249, 265, 277, 303, 306, 321, 331, 341, 376, 380, 389, 395, 397, 402, 406, 408, 412–13, 417, 418, 454, 481, 499, 510, 525, 539, 543, 544, 550, 590, 591, 599, 610, 611, 624, 641, 649, 676, 680, 692, 721, 738, 742, 750, 756, 757, 780, 819, 831, 834, 853, 859
Cleaver, Rev. Euseby Digby 120
Cleeve, Alexander 437
Clegg, Charles 280, Pl. 48
Clephan, James 63, 661
Clerk, Simon 655
Cleveland Structural Engineering 629
Cleverly, Peter 767
Clopton, Dr Poley 536
Clutterbuck, Charles 60, 367, 440, 441, 546, 580, 690, 729, 788
Cnut see Canute
Coade 53, 100, 102, 104, 166, 204n., 205, 208, 215, 307, 309, 318, 402, 472, 473, 483, 501, 661, 775, 779, 813, 823
Coade & Seely 53
Coakes 480
Coates, Richard 52, 729
Coates, Wells 69, 198, 372, 438, 708
Cobham, Charles 384
Cockerell, C. R. 426, 616, 722
Cockerell, F. P. 64, 480, Pl. 88
Cockerell, Henry 616
Cockrill, O. H. 706, 716
Coesvelt, William Gordon 373, 374
Coggeshall, Sir John de 827
Colchester Borough Architect 294

Coldwell, E. W. 442, 443, 445
Coldwell, Coldwell & Courtauld 68, 442, 445
Coldwell & Nicholls 68, 169
Cole, Frederick W. 86, 228
Cole, John 294
Cole, John J. 129–30
Coleman, Richard 289, 534, 852
Coleman & Morton 428
Coleman & Wallis 55, 140, 327, 421, 515, 542, 599
Coleridge, John 738
Collins, Harold 278, 295
Collins, Henry & Joyce 291, 292, 301, 454
Collis, John 217
Collister (E. R.) & Associates 124, 221
Colquhoun (Brian) & Partners 734
Colt family 651
Colt, John the Younger 46, 793
Colt, Maximilian 502, 773, Pl. 45
Colt, Thomas 651
Columbani, Placido 104, 658
Colvin, Brenda 795
Colvin & Moggridge 641
Comerford, Hebe 452
Comper, Sir Ninian 67, 147, 386, 618, 706, 708–9
Comyns, Sir John 216, 500, 860
Condron, Michael 211, 279–80
Connolly, Kitty 416
Conolly, Harold 73, 77, 118, 210, 212, 229, 278, 279, 328, 453, 454, 457, 561, 570, 576, 611, 684, 685, 788, 860
Conran Roche 464
Constable, John 48, 88, 319, 321, 438, 520, 587n., 800, 857
Conway, Jennifer 228, 563, 568
Conyers family 309
Conyers, Rev. Edward 348
Conyers, Sir John 307, 309
Conyers, John II 307, 309
Coode & Partners 629
Coode-Adams, Ben 353, 364, 743
Cook, Olive 669
Cooke, C. 424
Cooke, C. H. 243, 545, 817
Cooke, Rev. Moses 685
Cooke, R. 705
Cooke, Thomas 478
Coomber, R. W. 752
Coombs, Roger 120
Coope, Octavius E. 65, 134, 173, 721, 722, 724
Cooper, Sir Edwin 70, 783
Cooper, Eric P. W. 189
Cooper, James S. 611
Cooper, Muriel 186
Cooper, Sir Richard P. 368
Cooper, Samuel 140
Cooper-Abbs, G. B. 473
Cope (F. C.) & C. Eales 383

Copeland, W. J. 349
Copland, Edward 222, 223
Copland, John Jun. 223
Copland, John Sen. 222
Coppinger, Siobhan 416
Corbould, R. H. 803
Corder, D. M. 123, 561
Corder, J. S. 859
Corderoy (George) & Co. 587
Cordingley & McIntyre 210
Corlette, H. C. 689n.
Cormack, Peter 610
Cornelisen, Elizabeth 285
Costley, R. 789
Cottingham, L. N. 62, 399, Pl. 91
Cottingham, N. J. 399
Cottingham, R. M. J. 399n.
Cotton, Henry 459
Cotton, K. S. 115, 119
Cotton, T. M. 114
Cottrell & Vermeulen 241, 457
Cottrell & Vermeulen Architecture 704, 715
Coulman 482
Coulson, Nancy 183, 207, 208, 431, 568
Cound Page 372
Countryside Properties 72, 217, 219, 415, 564, 730
County Architect's Department 74, 136, 149, 168, 182, 189, 192, 193, 199, 210, 211, 212, 241, 248, 250, 253, 277, 278, 279, 301, 314, 316, 343, 373, 376, 385, 428, 443, 465, 588, 611–12, 628, 682, 726, 733, 766, 782, 845, 847
County Council Architect & Planning Depts 587
Court, J. W. 834
Courtauld family 52, 66, 68, 149, 152–3, 167, 169, 221, 442–3, 624
Courtauld, Mrs C. C. 152
Courtauld, Dr Elizabeth 442
Courtauld, George I (1761–1823) 169, 624
Courtauld, George III (1830–1920) 148, 381, 442
Courtauld, Mrs George 149
Courtauld, John Sewell 68, 168, 446
    see also *Coldwell, Coldwell & Courtauld*
Courtauld, Dr Richard 441
Courtauld, Samuel 52, 66, 146, 152, 381, 382, 436, 442, 444
Courtauld, Samuel Augustine 143, 147, 148, 152, 356, 442, 443
Courtauld, Sydney 149, 152
Courtauld, William Julien 68, 148, 151, 152, 168, 169, 170, 210, 381, 446
Couzens, Jeffrey 779
Coverdale, Joseph 504
Cowdray, Viscount 285

Cowell, Jasper 487, 739
Cowell, Philip M. 660
Cowper Griffith Associates 356, 612, 742
Cox, Mrs 524
Cox, A. 386
Cox, Alan 307
Cox & Buckley 393
Cox & Son/Sons 110, 187, 189, 263, 306, 569, 838
Cox, Sons, Buckley & Co. 180, 360, 422, 437, 498, 541, 636, 700, 710, 747
Crabb, John 838
Crabtree, William 116n.
Crabtree (William) and H. T. Cadbury-Brown 116n.
Crabtree (William) & Wladyslaw Jarosz 116n., 459
Craig, Teddy 551
Crampton, Sean 174
Crayer, Gaspar de 751
Creed, Richard 401, 405, 406, 539, 540n., 763
Cressall, W. T. 270, 280, 287, 298, 442
  see also *Goodey & Cressall*
Cressy, T. A. 242, 243n., 817
Cribb, Joseph 405, 563, 719
Crittall family 68
Crittall, Daniel F. 688
Crittall, Francis Berrington 68, 149
Crittall, Francis Henry 69, 170, 223, 686, 688
Crittall, Valentine 833
Crittall, W. F. 69, 148, 171, 222, 407–8, 687–8
Crittall (firm) 148, 190, 340
Crittall Development Co. 687–8
Croasdaile family 738, 740
Crompton, R. E. B. 222
Cromwell, Thomas 671
Crondon, Michael 123
Croppenburgh, Joas 192
Cross, John 604
Cross, K. M. B. 538, 801, 857
Crosse family 46n.
Crowe, Ralph 73–4, 77, 659
Crowe, Sylvia 71, 111, 450, 452, 457
Crowe & Careless 173
Crowest, T. B. 120, 424
Cruickshank & Seward 289
Cubitt, James 570, 571, 572–3
Cubitt, Lewis 64, 280n.
Cubitt & Co. 349
Cubitt Nichols 208
Cubitt (James) & Partners 463
Cullen, Thomas 846
Cullinan, Edward 850
Cullum & Nightingale 800
Culpin, Clifford E. 462, 611
Culpin (Clifford) & Partners 116n., 427, 463, 566
Cundy, Samuel 748

Cunobelinus 13, 255, 302, 743
Cure family 145
  see also Capel-Cure family
Cure, Capel 85, 145, 735
Cure, Cornelius 502, Pl. 38
Cure, William Jun. 502
Cure, William Sen. 502
Currey, Ada 185, 460, 568
Curtis, R. L. 783
Curtis, Samuel 164
Curtis, T. F. 338
Curtis, W. J. 321
Curtis (W.) & Sons 91
Curtis (T. F.), Ward & Hughes 364, 464, 580, 733, 782, 825, 828, 856
Curwen, Harold 575
Cutler, T. W. 64, 489
Cutte, Sir John 47, 496
Cutte, John and Elisabeth 497
Cutts, J. E. K. 137, 327n.
Cutts, J. E. K. & J. P. 327, 343, 559

Dabrowski, J. H. 534
Dacre, Thomas, Lord 107
Dampier, E. J. 249, 264, 268, 362, 434, 563, 593, 622, 791, 844
Dampier, Rev. W. J. 249
Daniel, Terry 129, 143
Daniell, F. Stanley 299
Daniell, Dr Richard 287
Daniels, George 424, 432, 713, 750
Dannatt (A. R.) & Son 860
Dannatt (Trevor) & Partners 120
Dapré, Anton 494
Darbourne & Partners 658
Darcy family 671, 676, 790–1
Darcy, Anthony 790–1
Darcy, Sir Robert 581, 585
Darcy, Thomas, 1st Lord 43, 671, 673–4, 676
Darcy, John, 2nd Lord 673, 676
Darken, Horace 181, 328, 392, 476, 817, 818, 822
Dashwood, Francis 713
Davey, Charles 297
Davey, Paxman & Co. 847
Davey, Paxman & Davey 844, 850
Davidson, William 169, 442
Davies, A. J. 678
Davies, Anthony B. 111
Davies, Elidir 570
Davies, Philomena 455
Davies (Anthony B.) & Associates 121, 850
Davis, F. W. 783
Davis, James 215
Davis, Louis 60, 430–1, 510
Davis, R. 738
Dawber, Guy 432, 834–5
Dawber (Sir Guy), Fox & Robinson 287
Dawe & Geddes Architects 300, 800
Dawes, Rev. Sir William 150

Dawson, N. J. 86
Day, Lewis F. 402
Dean, Basil and Mercy 551
Dean, Beryl 205
Dean, Christopher 458, 472
Deane family 46, 413–14
Deane, Anne, Lady 46, 414
Deane, Sir Anthony 472
Deane, James 271, 273–6, 285–6, 287, Pl. 83
Deane, William 415
Deare, John 374
Dearle, J. H. 503, 522, 795
De Carle see Carle
Deedes, Rev. Cecil 277
Defoe, Daniel 6n., 261, 841
Delarue, Anthony 206
Delarue (Anthony) Associates 657
Delvaux, Laurent 482
Denman, T. 721
Denny family 806
Denny, Sir Anthony 806
Denny, Sir Edward 46, 810
Dent, Giles 611, 612
Denton, Stephen 320
Design Buro, The 280
Design Planning Associates 504
Design Research Unit 454n., 512, 660
Devall, John 98
Development Corporation see Basildon Development Corporation
De Vere see Vere
Devereux, Alan H. 243
Devereux Architects 648n.
Devereux Partnership, The 280
Devey, George 609, 690, 724
De Zoete see Zoete
DGI International 465
d'Heere, Lucas 776
Dickens, Charles 200, 226, 230
Dilworth, Eric 826
Disney family 373
Dix, Arthur J. 770, 839
Dixon, Dr Henry 644, 645
Dixon, John 608
Dixon, Joseph 104
Dixon, W. Allen 694
Dixon, W. F. 710
DLA Architecture 201n.
Dobson, David 603
Dobson (George) & Son 298, 299
Dodds, James 789
d'Oisy see Oisy
Dolby, William 514
Dollimore, Colin 120
Dollman, F. T. 226, 229, 736–7
Donaldson, T. L. 811
Doreward family 147, 149, 150
Dorman, Joseph 55, 145, 413, 493
Doubleday, John 137, 147, 173, 180, 224, 583, 847
Doubleday, William 250
Doulton 152, 772

Dovetail 574
Downes 389, 748
Downes, H. 355
Downie (Norman) Associates 278
Downs Morgan Partnership 584
Drake, Charles 480
Drake, Frederick 786
Draper, John 303
Drew, R. W. 479
Drinkwater, George 149
Driver, C. H. 697
Druitt (Mile End Road) 384, 402, 569
DTZ 111
Dubois, Nicholas 96, 100
Du Cane family 393, 422
Du Cane, Hon. Lady 422
Du Cane, Ella 422
Du Cane, Peter (1718–1803) 393–4
Du Cane, Peter II (1741–1822) 393
Du Cane, Peter III (1778–1841) 394
Dudley, Rev. Henry Bate 166
Duffield, Richard 368
Dunbar, Melville 72, 827
Dunbar (Melville) Associates 121, 251, 253, 729
Dunbar (Melville) & Associates 151, 746
Duncanson, E. Ford 136
Dunn, H. H. 611
Dunn & Watson 217
Dunthorne Parker 284
Dürer, Albrecht 706
Dyck, Anthony Van 102
Dyer, Charles 428
Dyer, D. 462
Dyer, R. H. 709
Dyke, D. N. 169, 290
Dykes Bower see Bower

Eade & Johns 781, 858
Earle, Edward 492
Earley (Dublin) 228
Earp, Thomas 226n., 268, 269, 418, 431, 522, 529n., 591, 594, 621, 666, 714, 721, 837
Earp & Son 173
Earp, Son & Hobbs 90, 721
East Anglian Renovations 333
Easter, Captain Jeremiah 789
Eastern Region Architect's Department 114, 465
Easton, Hugh 521, 624
Easton, J. Murray 69, 571
   see also Hall (Stanley), Easton & Robertson
Easton & Robertson 69, 576
Easton & Robertson, Cusdin, Preston & Smith 459
Eaton, Geoff 212
Eaton, John 531
Ebbetts & Cobb 306
ECD Architects 466

ECD Partnership 218
Eden, F. C. 67, 424, 432, 593, 708, 713, 750, 820
Eden, Rev. Robert 703
Edis, R. W. 86
Edmeston, James 758
Edmondes, John 313
Edmondson, James 716
Edward the Elder, King 18, 277
Edward III, King 31, 438
Edward VII, King 94, 387, 464, 830
Edwards, C. H. 328
Edwards, Carl 185, 315, 406
Edwards, Jennifer 216
Edwards, Joseph 55, 134, 265
Edwards & Powell 315
Egan, Edmond 65, 185, 571–2, 574, 577
Eginton, Francis 701
Ehrlich, Georg 205
Elcock & Sutcliffe 70, 652
Elliot, John 538
Elliot, T. 523
Ellis, Clifford & Rosemary 372
Ellisdon, Richard 269
Elliston, John 377
Elmes, Patrick 352
Elmslie & Franey 561
Elsam, Richard 381, 446
Elsworth Sykes & Partners 459
Emberton, Joseph 69, 189, Pl. 112
Emett, Rowland 114
Emptage (Peter) Associates 212, 697, 699, 707
England, Clive 814
Engle, Bernard 177
Engle (Bernard) & Partners 699
English Heritage Property Co. 349–50
Enkel, John 608
Epstein, Sir Jacob 573
Erith, Arthur 575
Erith, Raymond 70, 75, 161, 319, 320–1, 322, 323, 324, 325, 366, 406, 411, 434, 515, 516, 524, 556, 575, 588, 600, Pl. 118
Erith, Robert 516
Erith & Terry 524, 556
Erkenwald, St 19
Erridge, Arthur F. 303, 593
Escreet, Rev. John 59, 485
Essex County Council 852
Essex, Viscount Bourchier, Earl of 127n., 550
Essex, James 96, 101, 318
Essex Property Services Dept 453
Etchells, Frederick 69, 373
Eudo Dapifer 272, 277
Evans, Alan 205
Evans, Martin 67, 687
Evans, Norman 647
Evans, Roger 466
Evans (Roger) Associates 466
Evans (Charles) & Co. 339

Everard family 425
Everard, Sir Richard 425
Evesham, Epiphanius 45, 46, 355, 738, 821, Pl. 43
Evetts, Leonard 249
Ewart, C. B., R.E. 281

Fabbrucci, Aristide Luigi 277
Fagan, Peter 280
Fairchild, I. 630
Fairhead, John 113, 114, 292, 584, 789
Fairhursts Design Group, The 207
Fairview Homes 223
Faith Craft Works 91, 173, 384, 677
Falconer (Peter) & Partners 454n.
Falconer Partnership 266
Farley, J. S. 421
Farmer, William 349
Farmer & Brindley 277
Farquharson, Horace 724
Farrell (Terry) & Co. 454
Faulkner-Brown Hendy Watkinson Stonor 799
Faulks Perry Cully & Rech 736
Fausett, Shelley 461
Fawcett, Andrew 392, 488, 790
Fawcett, W. M. 626
Feake, Samuel 486, 681
Fearnhead, Jonathan 440
Fehr, H. C. 285
Feilden & Mawson 229
Fels, Joseph 66, 596
Fenner, Rachel 280
Fenton, James 53, 60, 136, 168, 197, 208, 215, 220, 222, 223, 224, 357, 435, 503, 844, 852
Ferguson, David 168, 187, 221, 484, 503, 562, 637
Ferguson, John 503
Ferguson (Richard) Associates 208, 221
Ferrey, Benjamin 831
Fetherstone family 733
Field, R. 122
Figgis, T. Philips 573
Filmer & Mason 794
Finch, W. A. 63, 235, 243
Finch (John) & Associates 207
Finch (John) Partnership 358, 646, 833
Fincham, Edward 618
Finn, Benjamin 264, 487, 719, 833
Firmin, W. R. 131
Fisher, Alfred R. 732
Fisher, Daniel 817
Fitch, Henry 746
Fitch, J. 826
Fitch, J. R. M. 601
Fitz Geoffrey, Maurice 134
Fitzralph, Sir William 30, 624
Fitzroy Robinson 125, 204, 475
Fitzroy Robinson Partnership 547
Fitzwalter, Walter and Elizabeth 549, Pl. 39

Flaxman, John 55, 478, 482, 517
Fleetwood-Walker, Bernard 210
Fletcher, H. M. 574
Fletcher, Rosamund M. B. 148
Fletcher Priest 114
Flight & Robson 472
Flint, Ernest 152, 153
Flitcroft, Henry 157
Flower, Gerald 69, 184
Flower, Henry 172
Foden & Henman 63, 742
Foord-Kelsey, Mrs 455
Footit, Robert 734
Forbes, A. H. 660
Forbes, Ian 93
Ford, Capt. W. H. 76
Ford (Thomas) & Partners 814–15
Fordham, John 354
Forrest, G. Topham 77
Forster, Rev. Charles 751–2
Forsyth & Maule 631, 676
Forsyth, J. (C18) 460
Forsyth, J. (C19) 189, 657, 666
Forsyth, Moira 753
Forsyth, W. A. 705, 706
Fortescue-Aland, Sir John 744
Foster, Rev. Sir Cavendish, Bt 770
Foster, Don 695
Foster, Rev. John 367
Foster, John 279
Foster, Joseph 388
Foster, Michael 356
Foster, Peter 114
Foster, R. C. 185, 574
    see also Tooley & Foster
Foster, Stephen 739
Foster (Tim) Architects 715
Foster Associates 74, 735, Pl. 117
Fowke, William 418
Fowler, C. Hodgson 363, 493
Fox-Edwards, Patricia see Gibberd,
    Lady
Foyster, R. C. 192
Frampton, E. R. 110, 402, 412, 508,
    641, 793
Frampton, J. 335
Francis, Messrs 515
Francis, H. H. 573, 574
Franey, F. 560
Frankham Consultancy Group 212
Frankland, Joyce 611
Franks, Ronald H. 495n.
Fraser, Ian 149, 465
Free, Robert 601, 780
Freeland, Henry 527–9
Freeman & Ogilvy 801
French, C. P. 199, 612, 726
French, G. R. 263
Freshwater, Sally 149
Frew, Hilary 455
Fricker, Henrietta 367
Frink, Elisabeth 452, 454, 461n.
Frith, Norman 461

Fromings, Hedy 280
Frost, Alan J. 781, 806
Fry family 664
Fry, L. G. 661
Fry, Mark 664
Fry, Drew & Partners 71, 457
Fuller, Kate Baden 280
Fuller, Hall & Foulsham 465
Fuller-Maitland, William 741

Gaffin, Edwin 55, 608, 721, 738, 752
Gaffin, Thomas 55, 154, 349, 424,
    721, 738, 752
Gaffin & Co. 711, 752
Gahura, František 69, 340
Gainge, George 204
Gainsborough, Thomas 48, 166, 186
Galli, Pietro 501
Galloway, Douglas 111, 114
Galton, Capt. Douglas, R.E. 282
Gamon & Humphry 345, 348, 433,
    765, 832
Gandon, James 431
Gansel, David 335
Gardener, W. M. 474
Gardner (Starkie) & Co. 277
Garrard, Frederick 569
Garrard, George 55, 114, 122, 147, 455
Gasson & Meunier 799
Gate, Sir Geoffrey 490
Gatley, A. 517
Geary, Ronald 291, 324, 432, 515, 516
Geary (Ronald) Associates 153
Geary & Black 421, 435, 846
Gee, Mrs Mary 333
Geldart, Rev. Ernest 59, 90, 168, 180,
    196, 268, 348, 349, 360, 379, 392–3,
    417, 422, 432, 433, 437, 482, 518,
    541, 542, 562, 621, 636, 637n., 652,
    701, 732, 733, 788, 790, 792, 819,
    832, 837–8, 843, Pl. 102
Gent family 606, 748
Gent, George (1724–1818) 748
Gent, George William (1782–1855)
    310, 605–6, 748
Gent, Henry 605
Gent, Sir Thomas 605
Gentry, A. G. 702
Gentry, G. D. 125
Gentry, Mark 686
George Trew Dunn Beckles Willson
    Bowes 183
George Trew Dunn Partnership 183
Gepp, Edward (C18) 216
Gepp, Rev. Edward (C19) 491
Gernand, Bruce 279
Giambologna 278
Gibbens, Rev. William 59, 225
Gibberd, Sir Frederick 71, 372,
    447–50, 452, 453, 454, 455n., 456,
    459, 462, 464, 468, 471–2, Pl. 114
Gibberd, Patricia Fox-Edwards,
    Lady 450

Gibberd (Frederick) & Partners 291, 385, 452, 454, 469, 470
Gibberd (Frederick) Partnership 280
Gibbon, Thomas 402
Gibbons, Grinling 478, 551, 810
Gibbs, Alexander 90, 515, 706, 790
Gibbs, Isaac Alexander 632
Gibbs, James 480
Gibbs, Samuel 411
Gibbs & Howard 60, 318, 633, 839
Gibson family 63, 654, 659–60, 662, 663, 665
Gibson, Mrs 659, 666
Gibson, Alexander 454n.
Gibson, Atkinson Francis 661
Gibson, Francis 661, 663, 664
Gibson, G. S. 658, 659, 661, 663, 665, 669
Gibson, George 837
Gibson, W. G. 64, 658
Gilberd, William 264, 277
Gilbert, Alfred 551
Gilbert, Fr. F.W. 702
Gilbert, I. C. 234
Gilbert (I. C.) & Fothergill Watson 234
Gilbey, Sir Walter 344
Giles, Francis 56
Giles, Tam 115
Gill, Colin 210
Gill, Eric 170, 405, 425, 431, 455, 552
Gill, J. H. 244
Gillow family 753
Gilpin, William Sawrey 104
Ginns, Malcolm 647, 705, 707
Gladedale Homes 711
Gladman, Jerome 455
Gladman, Paul 71, 317
Glanfield (John) & Partners 758
Glasby, William 620
Glascock, Edward 77
Glascock, Richard 514
Glasser, Beth 580
GLC Dept of Architecture and Civic Design 720
Glehn, W. G. de (formerly von Glehn) 321, 773
Gloucester, Thomas of Woodstock, Duke of 627
GLR Architects 570
Gn'design 317
Goalen, Gerard T. 67, 454, 455, 462, 463
Goddard, R. W. K. 240n.
Goddard & Gibbs 95, 174, 206, 228, 237, 240, 348, 380, 389, 431, 441, 473, 554, 561, 610, 702, 721
Godfrey, Angela 461, 651
Godwin, Keith 453
Godwin, T. S. 132
Goldfinger, Ernö 69, 184
Goldie, Edward 135, 698
Goldie, Child & Goldie 135
Gomme, Sir Bernard de 76, 784

Gooch, Mr and Mrs Charles Jun. 434, 801
Gooch, Charles Sen. 801
Goodey, J. F. 66, 270, 287, 293, 295, 297, 298
Goodey & Cressall 62, 270, 279, 280, 287, 291, 293, 297, 298, 442, 535
Gooding, Bernard 466, 569
Goodman, Thomas 60, 713–14
Goodrow Consultancy 67, 569
Goodyear, Herbert 283, 289
Gordon, Colonel Charles 339, 784
Gordon, William 114n., 207
Gordon & Gunton 569
Gordon (Alex) Partnership 219, 280
Gordon & Tait 103
Gosling family 349
Gosling, E. C. 181
Gosling, Robert 349
Goud, Anthony 155, 760
Gough, T. 165
Gough, William P. 373
Gould, Roy 67, 181, 240, 495, Pl. 108
Gould, F. Carruthers 277
Gould, G. H. B. 242, 243, 244, 495, 515
Gould Grimwade Shirborn Partnership 368
Goulty, H. N. 658
Gowan, James 336
Graham, John 469, 499
Graham & Baldwin 499, 534, 537, 700
Grant, Charles 505
Grant, D. Marion 615, 729
Grant, T. F.W. 356
   see also Chetwood & Grant
Grassin, Didier 205
Gray, Charles 273–6, 285
Gray, George Kruger 168, 210
Gray, Jane 180, 330, 859
Gray, Milner 512
Greaves, Len 174
Green family 523
Green, A. J. 77, 565
Green, Edward 523
Green, J. L. 411
Green, Rev. John 558
Green, John 643
Green, Jonathan 419
Green, Norman 715
Green, Valerie 330, 717
Greenberg, Bill 550
Greenberg (Stephen) & Dean Hawkes 582, 584
Greenhalgh & Brockbank 494, 707, 716
Greenhill, Rev. William 349, 350
Greening, Alan 123
Greenwood, Thomas 222
Greiffenhagen, Maurice 168
Grey of Wilton 396
Griggs, Golding 597
Grigs, Francis 46, 168, 206, 569, 676

Grimes, Joseph 199, 335, 365, 392
Grimston, Hon. and Rev. E. H. 624
Grimwade, Roy 296
Grist, Peter 822
Grossé-De Herde, L. 692
Grout, Henry 552
Gruning, E. A. 783n.
Gryce, Nicholas le 87, 88
Grylls, Harry 166
Guelfi 380
Guicciardine, Camilla 790
Guild of Handicraft 498
Gurdon, John 319–20
Guy, Henry 207, 212
Guyon, Sir Mark 415
Gwynne, Patrick 438

Habershon, W. G. & E. 625
  see also Abbott (J. O.) & W. G.
  Habershon
Habershon & Brock 789
Habershon & Fawckner 682
Hagen, William van der 176, 722n.
Hague, Nicholas 833
Hakewill, E. C. 86, 126, 400, 598, 851
Hakewill, Henry 49, 752
Hakewill, J. H. 331
Halcrow (Sir William) & Partners
  629, Pl. 122
Hale, Mark 822
Hale, W. T. 770
Hall, Chester Moor 757
Hall, Denis Clarke 719n.
Hall, John 221
Hall, Nigel 799
Hall, T. 721
Hall (Stanley), Easton & Robertson
  69, 373, 571
Hall (John) & Son 326
Hallward, Reginald 176, 229, 430–1,
  503, 508, 782
Halpern & Partners 453
Hambley, J. C. & William 366
Hamilton, E. J. 694
Hamilton, Ian B. M. 818
Hamilton, Paul 465
Hamilton (Ian) & Alan Chalmers 818
Hammond, Frederic 521
Hamnett, Victor 450
Hampden, Lady (Philippa) 774
Hanbury, Charles 446
Hanbury, Osgood 254
Hanchet, Samuel 808
Handisyde, Cecil 459
Handyside & Henderson 278
Hardgrave, Charles 196, 413, 440,
  568, 646, 657, 681
Harding, Charles 55, 129, 620
Hardman, Beryl 414
Hardman (John) & Co. 159, 162,
  168, 196, 263, 349, 367, 380, 409,
  432, 433, 437, 466, 478, 503, 536,
  714, 738, 779, 795, 851

Hardman (John) Studios 126
Hardwick, Philip 722
Hardwick, P. C. 64–5, 349, 595, Pl. 87
Hardy, R. B. 410
Hare, Cecil G. 395, 540n.
Hare, Henry T. 61, 695, 707
Hare, Nicholas 72
Hare (Nicholas) Architects 73, 357,
  799–800, 824
Harland, Norman G. 702
Harland & Fisher 466
Harley, Edward *see* Oxford and
  Mortimer, 2nd Earl of
Harling, T. 610
Harlow Development Corporation
  Design Group (HDC Design Group)
  450, 453, 457, 458, 459, 461, 463,
  464, 465, 470
Harlow District Council 458
Harman, Cornelius 45, 197, 657, Pl.
  42
Harold, Earl *see* Harold, King
Harold, King 805–6, 858
Harrington & Ley 371
Harris, Charles 418
Harris, D. W. 468
Harris, E. Vincent 68, 152, 168, 169,
  170, 210
Harris, Mark 234
Harris, Renatus 539
Harris, Thomas 603
Harris (J. Seymour) & Partners 113,
  453
Harrison, Henry 63, 97, 105, 186,
  394n., 659, 662
Harrison, John Haynes 307
Harrison & Harrison 690
Harsnett, Samuel, Archbishop of
  York 45, 228–9, 277
Hart, Michael 210
Hart, T. G. 348, 463
Hart, T. H. 392
Hart & Son 249
Hart, Son, Peard & Co. 380, 637
Hartley, Matthew 294
Hartshorne, Albert 268
Hartwell, Charles 242
Harvey family 231, 485
Harvey, Sir Eliab 485
Harvey, Philip 112
Harvey, William 46, 485, Pl. 46
Harvey & Ashby 395
Hasten (Danish chieftain) 712
Hatcher, Basil & David 495, 602
Hawken, Anthony 459
Hawker, Lisa 212, 733
Hawkins, Rev. Bradford Denne 644
Hawkins Brown 711
Hawks, H. N. 214
Hawksley, Thomas 346
Hawksley, T. & C. 518
Hawksmoor, Nicholas 785n.
Hawkwood, Sir John 30, 684

Haylock, William 93
Hayne, Rev. L. G. 162
Hayne, William 67, 207, 240, 370, 372, 410, 500, 581, Pl. 106
Hayward, C. F. 269, 368, 421, 443, 444, 446, 522, 529, 701, 818
Hayward, H. H. 197, 296, 368, 402
Hayward, H. W. 62, 263, 265, 267, 279, 285, 288, 297, 331, 396, 440, 519–20, 624, 828
Hayward, John 127, 143, 174, 206, 651, 681, 701, 713, 785, 834
Hayward, Richard 534
Hayward, William 164
Hayward (H. H.) & Son 264n.
HDC Design Group see Harlow Development Corporation Design Group
Heal, A. V. 540, 551, 553
Hearn, J. 289
Heath, Derek 782
Heather, Peter 733, 766
Heaton, Butler & Bayne 60, 90, 91, 107, 143, 166, 180, 212, 233, 249, 266, 267, 268, 270, 331, 344, 377, 378, 384, 397, 399, 410, 481, 490, 493, 534, 562, 580, 594, 599, 611, 618, 634, 651, 652, 676, 678, 683, 684, 718, 742, 751, 757, 829, 835, 855
Heckford, William and Elizabeth 767
Hedley, R. 630
Hemming, A. O. 205, 335, 752
Hemming (A. O.) & Co. 88, 174, 303, 326, 563, 803
Hemming (Samuel C.) & Co. 604
Hems, Harry 233, 348, 693, 733
Hening & Chitty 471
Henman, C. & W. 174
Hennell, C. Murray 69, 687–8
Henniker family 402
Henniker, Sir Brydges 406
Henrion, Daphne Hardy 455
Henry II, King 582, 806
Henry VIII, King 2, 43, 47, 76, 142, 155, 158, 576, 761
Henshaw, Nicola 280
Hepper, Dent 649
Hepworth, Barbara 457
Hepworth, P. D. 575
Herbert & Partners 745
Hering family 487
Hermes, Gertrude 765
Hervey, Rev. Lord Charles Amelius 399
Hervey d'Ispania (or d'Espagne) family 726
Herzberg, Henry 824
Heseltine, Arnold 429
Heseltine, Evelyn 176, 178, 429, 431
Heskett, Philippa 384
Hewett, Cecil 31–2, 74
Hewitt, Graily 568

Heywood, Ned 788
Hibbs & Walsh Associates 225, 657
Hicklin, Stephen 211
Hicks, David 129, 140, 514
Hicks, Joseph 103
Higgins & Thomerson 226, 228
Hill, A. E. 179
Hill, Daniel 793
Hill, Judy 512
Hill, Oliver 69, 372–3, Pl. 110
Hill, W. J. M. 556
Hill-Willis, S. A. 783
Hillier Group, The 465
Hills, Gordon Macdonald 731
Hills, M. R. 303–4
Hills, Philip 303–4
Hillyer, William 51, 77, 208, 411, 613
Hinchcliff, John 55, 410
Hinchliffe, T. 452, 457, 462
Hinde, Jacob 520
Hiner (J. P.) & Associates 182
Hinsley & Co. 241
Hiscott, Robin 231
Hitch, Nathaniel 393, 579, 738
Hoare, Benjamin 47, 155, 157
Hoare, Richard 155
Hoare & Wheeler 308, 309, 713
Hobbs, Joe 121, 729
Hobcroft, John 101, 102n., 104, 105
Hockley, Daniel 91
Hodge, John 170
Hodges, Rev. Henry 88
Hogan, J. H. 228, 431, 509, 657
Holden, Charles 66, 595–6
    see also Adams, Holden & Pearson
Holder & Mathias Partnership 73, 725, Pl. 121
Holich, G. M. 531
Holiday, Henry 60, 138, 205, 310, 454, 473, 478, 536, 594, 595, 604, 640, 649–50, 657, 732, 750, 751, 771, 810, 829
Holland, Henry 318, 813n.
Holland, Richard 318, 319, Pl. 70
Hollins 176
Holman & Goodrham 63, 500
Holme, C. G. 69, 687
Holroyd, Charles 106–7
Holst, Gustav 768
Holst (K.) & Co. 583
Holt, Adam 49, 195, 304
Holt, Gwynneth 182, 207, 608, 753
Homberg (Dr-Ing. H.) & Partner 629
Homer & Sharp 65, 371
Honywood, Mary 249
Honywood, Robert 592
Honywood, W. P. 422
Hooke, Robert 684
Hooker, Thomas 538
Hoole, Elijah 714
Hooper, H. R. 476
Hooper, Raymond 456
Hope Foundry Co. 551

Hopper, Humphrey 180, 485, 536, 569
Hopper, Thomas 49, 51, 61, 64, 77,
   138, 150, 155, 162, 177, 197, 211,
   280, 316, 345, 402, 442, 481, 483,
   509, 512, 522, 552, 558, 636, 678,
   692, 718, 761, 780, 800–1, 855,
   Pl. 78
Horkesley family 555
Horley, Richard 733
Hornor, Edward 442
Horseman, W. G. 486
Horsley, Hamish 661
Horsnaile, C. 331
   see also *Stanton & Horsnaile*
Horsnell, Alick 297
Horswell, R. 695
Houblon family 408–9
Houblon, J. A. 408
Houblon, Jacob 409, 479
Houghton-Brown, Geoffrey 512
Howard family 284, 559
   see also Norfolk; Northampton;
      Suffolk
Howard, F. E. 185, 249, 565
Howard, John Howard, Lord 284
Howard, Wallace 738
Howard & Pank 363
Howard de Walden, Lord 658
Howe, James 427
Howe, L. G. 428
Howell & Bellion 161
Howell Killick Partridge & Amis 115
Howes, Allan 341
Howis & Belcham 716
Howson, Joan 644, 729
   see also *Townshend (Caroline) &
      Joan Howson*
Hoyland, E. D. 635
Hoyle, Michael 718
Hubert, S. M. 345, 488
Huckle (H. G.) & Partners 699
Huddart, R. M. F. 516
Hudson (Pentonville) 207
Hudson, Sir Robert and Lady
   772–3, 776
Hughes, H. 386, 803
Hughes, James O'Hanlon 168
Hughes, M. E. Hughes 532
Humphrey, Edmund 640, Pl. 71
Humphreys, Samuel 846
Humphrys, Derrick 451
Humphrys & Hurst 67, 124, 437, 451,
   707
Hunt, Rev. A. A. 687
Hunt, Anthony 796
Hunt, Arthur 333
Hunt, E. A. 689
Hunt, G. J. 379
Hunt, H. A. 503, 586
Hunt, J. A. 606
Hunt, Reuben 333, 421
Hunter, Alec & Margaret 765
Hunter, Mr and Mrs Charles 775

Hunter, Hugh 184
Hurlock, Rev. J. T. 520
Hurst, R. W. 437
   see also *Humphrys & Hurst*
Hussey, R. C. 315, 419, 655
Hutchings, Gay 270, 625
Hutchinson (Colchester) 303
Hutson, Robert 135
Hutson (Robert) Architects 766
Hutton, John 205, 569
Huxley-Jones, Thomas Bayliss 114,
   140, 182n., 204, 205, 516, 713
Hyklott, William 89
Hyll, Johannes 89

I'Anson, E. 89
Ibberson, H. G. 478
Inchcape, Baron (later 1st Earl of
   Inchcape) 547
Inchcape, 3rd Earl of 631
Ingelow, B. 692
Inglis, Capt. T., R.E. 711
Inkpen Downie 154, 163, 488, 630,
   747
   see also *Plater Inkpen Downie*;
      Plater Inkpen Vale & Downie
Inman & Jackson 108
Insall, Donald 131
Insall (Donald W.) & Associates 75,
   781, 806
Inwood, H. W. 633
Ionides, Basil 127, 851
Irish (Edward) Partnership 852
Ison, Walter 496–7
I. T. 467
Ivory, William 96, 664

Jackson, A. B. 87, 108, 376–7, 377,
   424
Jackson, C. d'O. Pilkington 206
Jackson, F. A. 268
Jackson, Sir T. G. 266, 320, 542, 681
Jackson, Thomas 834
Jackson & Edmonds 210
Jackson, Philip & Jean 812
Jacob, Nicholas 164, 520, 563
Jacquet (Vauxhall Bridge Road)
   545
Jago, W. 545
James, Michael 459
James, Thomas 393
Janssen, Bernard 95
Jarvis Construction 570
Jebb, Joshua 51, 211
Jebb, Philip 105
Jeckyll, Thomas 743, 770
Jekell 770
Jellicoe (G. A.) & Partners 116n.
Jennings, Mr 607
Jerram Falkus Construction Ltd 216
Jervois, Colonel W. F. D. 339
Jewell, H. H. 151, 152, 161
John, Lewis 776

Johns, W. E. F. 168
Johns & Slater 660
Johns, Slater & Haward 189, 328
Johnson, Abraham 483
Johnson, Edward Killingworth 686
Johnson, Garat the Elder 129, 132, 162, 269, 644, 790, 843
Johnson, Hugh 418
Johnson, John (1732–1814) 49, 51, 53, 77, 155, 166, 204–5, 206, 208–9, 215, 273, 355, 356, 393–4, 483, 519, 649, 650, 761–2, 833, 838, 851, Pls. 77–9
Johnson, John (1811–91) 169, 626
Johnson, Sir John (St Osyth Priory) 671, 674
Johnson, M. W. 126, 344, 478, 569
Johnson, Malcolm 279
Johnston, Philip M. 197, 705, 706, 707, 709
Johnstone, Fred 232
Jolley, W. J. 327
Jolliffe, Sir William 627, 826
Jolly & Millard 660
Jones, Graham 427, 465
Jones, Inigo 48, 158
Jones, Ivor Roberts 90
Jones, Joyce 470
Jones, L. 610
Jones, Nelson 839
Jones, W. Campbell 283
Jones (Leslie) Architects 454
Jones (Leslie) & Partners 848
Jones & Willis 148, 189, 235, 240, 267, 321, 373, 422, 429, 471, 484, 589, 595, 646, 693, 694, 714, 770, 803, 832
Joseph, Messrs 69, 407, 688
Junols, John 487

Kadishman, Menashe 463
Kafik, Vladimir 69, 340
Katz & Vaughan 340
Kauffmann, Angelica 166, 307
Kay, Rev. William 413
Kaye, Captain C. W. C. 339
Kaye (Sidney), Firmin & Partners 114
Kearney, Steven 710
Keddie, David 70, 649
Keeling, Joseph 362
Keen (Stanley) & Partners 725
Keightley, Emily Alice 732
Keightley, G. W. 59, 732
Kellner, W. W. 514
Kemble, L. & D. 852
Kemp, Derek 376
Kemp, Harriett Anne 636
Kemp, Philip 618
Kemp & Tasker 169
Kempe family (Finchingfield and Spains Hall) 360, 726
Kempe family (Pentlow) 625

Kempe, C. E. /Kempe (C. E.) & Co. 147, 187, 207, 228, 263, 307–8, 309, 321, 345, 396, 481, 518, 536, 604, 616, 618, 677, 683, 693, 711, 721, 733, 742, 765, 789, 826
Kempe, John 726
Kempe, Sir Robert 361, 726
Kempe (C. E.) & Co. see Kempe, C. E.
Kempthorne, Sampson 63, 661
Kendall, H. E. Jun. 175, 232, 310, 505, 753
Kendall, H. E. Sen. 56
Kendall & Pope 64, 175, 491
Kendrick, J. 55, 810
Kendrick, J. J. P. 55, 811
Kennedy, R. T. 463
Kennington, Eric 765
Kent, Messrs C. 544
Kent, Aileen 320
Kent, William 790
Kent Blaxill & Co. 240
Keogh, Edward 55, 129, 140, 794
  see also Lufkin & Keogh
Key, William D. 422
Kieffer, W. J. 611
Kieffer (W. J.) & H. S. Fleming 741
Kilngrove Architectural Ltd 646
Kindersley, D. 418
King, Dennis G. 102, 106, 180
King, Laurence 66, 67, 162, 173, 174, 176, 184, 206, 336, 378, 389, 454, 589, 607, 701, 720, 806, 810
King, Thomas 55, 140, 318
King & Lister 269
King (Laurence) & Partners 174, 615–16, 644, 753
King (Thomas) & Sons 411
Kinniple & Jaffrey 242, 816
Kinsman, Edmund 308
Kinward, Thomas 231n.
Kirby, Richard 775
Kirby Adair Newson Partnership 169
Kirk & Kirk 283
Kirk, Ben 283
Kirk, Robert 525
Knapp, Stefan 472
Knevynton, Ralph de 30, 107
Knight, John and Anna 54, 380, 382–3
Knight, Samuel 485
Knightley, T. E. 177n., 431
Kortwright, Cornelius 501
KSS Architects 73, 696
Kuchemann, H. K. 713

Labouchere, P. C. 501
Lack (Charles) & Sons 246
Lacoste, Gerald 458, 769
Lacoste (Gerald) & Partners 733
Laing, David 61, 282, 325, 534
Laing, G. E. 264
Laing, Gerald 362
Laing Homes 137

Lake (Liz) Associates 661
Lamb, E. B. 406
Lamb, Lynton 678
Lambert, Maurice 112
Lambert Scott & Innes 278
Lambie, John 210
Lambirth, Henry 859
Land, Julia 788
Landscape Partnership, The 164, 242
Lange, Christian 644
Langham, Sir Stephen 736
Langley, Batty 49, 159, 286
Langsford, W. C. 240
Langston, H. H. 89
Lansdown, Thomas S. 589
LAP Architects & Interior Designer Ltd 822
Lapidge, Edward 806, 809n.
Large, Richard 496
Larke, Thomas 506
Last & Tricker Partnership 780
Latham, Jasper 773
Latham Architects 279
Lavers, N. W. 147
Lavers & Barraud 374, 467, 590, 621, 657, 732, 831
Lavers, Barraud & Westlake 147, 154, 160, 186, 249, 269, 373, 377, 436, 481, 492, 536, 591, 611, 617, 733, 744, 851
Lavers & Westlake 270, 510
Law, Henry 415
Law & Edwards 271
Lawrence, A. K. 210
Lawrence, E. E. 192
Lawrence, F. W. 315
Lawson, J. N. 95, 206, 228, 431, 441, 652
Lawson, William 91, 677
Lay, William 280, 742
Layton, M. 807
LCC Architect's Dept 576
Leach (W. Perry) & Sons 549
Leake, J. M. 780
Leaning, John 818
Ledward, Gilbert 845
Lee, E. C. 59, 65, 134, 173, 649, 720, 721, 722, 724
Lee, F. G. 192
Lee, George 297
Lee, John S. 741
Lee, Lawrence 430, 563, 580, 650
Leech, John 832
Legerton, Owen 385
Legg, John 425
Leigh family 378, 832
Leigh, Rev. C. B. 378
Leigh, Sarah 832
Leigh, Rev. Thomas 832
Lemaire, Robert 644
Le Neve, John 765
Lennard & Lawn 638
Leoni, Giacomo 221, 482, 508, 776–8

Lescher family 723
Lester, Alfred 363
Lester, J. H. 534
Lester, Muriel 573
Lethaby, W. R. 65, 573
Leverton family 811
Leverton, Thomas 723, 809n., 811
Levitt Bernstein Associates 452
Lewis, E. Wamsley 69, 373
Lewis, J. C. 482
Lewis, James 246, 610
Lewis, John 523
Lewis, Neville 210
Lexden Restorations 253
Ley, A. S. G. 582
    see also Harrington & Ley;
    Tomkins, Homer & Ley
Ley Colbeck & Partners 148
Lidbetter, Hubert 684
Lidbetter, H. & H.M. 788
Lightoler, T. 105, 500
Lilleshall Co. Ltd 518
Lilley, Thomas 243
Limbrick (Stephen) Associates 290
Limentani, Julian 607, 833
Lincolnshire Stained Glass Studio 748
Lindsey, W. H. 328
Lindsey-Smith, C. H. 464
Lindy, Kenneth 573
Linford, W. J. 461
Ling, Mary Stella 352
Linge, Abraham van 46, 596
Linklater, M. H. 732
Lisney (Adrian) & Partners 736
Liversedge, J. W. 703
Livesey (P. J.) Group 775
Livi, Igor 539
Llewelyn Davies Yeang 183
Lloyd, Graham 66, 701–2
Lloyd-Winder, Matthew 396
Locke, John 491
Locke, Joseph 834
Lockwood family 517
Lockyer, J. M. 207
Lockyer, James 494–9
Logan, Eric 427
Long, Rev. J. E. 59, 830
Lorimer, Patrick 68, 225, 522, 622, 683
Loveday, Thomas 25, 196, 376–7, 731, 748, 756, 839, Pl. 33
Lovejoy, Derek 115
Lovell, James 54, 206
Low, W. Ralph 218
Lowder, Rev. W. H. 59, 718
Lowe, Deborah 280
Lowndes, G. A. 479
Lowndes, Mary 60, 138, 516, 822
Lowndes & Drury 205, 402, 441, 710
Lucas, Thomas 299
Lufkin, George 55, 134, 140, 268, 269, 321, 335, 542
    see also Slythe & Lufkin

Lufkin, Henry 55, 162, 266, 509, 523, 542, 593
Lufkin & Keogh 626
Lugar, Robert 51, 77, 296, 554–5, 633n., 845
Lukin, Lionel 404
Lumley, D. Francis 699
Lund, Giuseppe 205
Lundy, H. 772
Lupton, George 402
Luscombe (Exeter) 718
Luther, John 514
Lutyens, Sir Edwin 230, 431, 516, 558, 698
Luxford, F. L. 402, 560
Luxford Stained Glass Studios 431, 713
Lyall (John) Architects 697n.
Lyon, R. 210
Lyon, W. F. 609
Lyons (Eric) & Partners 463
Lyster Grillet & Harding 212, 612

Mabane, Bert 210
Mabbitt, Kenneth 441
Mabbitt, H. & K. 140, 266, 306, 334, 338, 342, 395, 433, 548, 701, 742, 753, 803, 859
Macarthy, John H. 123
McCarthy, J. 734
McCarthy, Susan 140, 143, 310, 431, 634
MacCarthy, W. E. 493
McConnell, Primrose 735
McCowan, Alex 450
Maccreanor Lavington 111
McCrossan 277
McFarlane, Lisa 822
Macfarlane & Co. 149, 739
MacGregor, J. E. M. 234
McKenzie & Moncur 105
Mackintosh, Charles Rennie 716
Mackmurdo, A. H. 65, 166, 220n., 422–3, 718, 833, Pl. 90
Mackwilliam family 29, 731, Pl. 44
McMahon, Thomas, Bishop of Chelmsford 172
MacManus, Frederick 69, 687–8, Pl. 111
McMullen, A. L. 378
McMurdie, S. C. 379
McMurdie & Wagstaffe 379
McWilliam, F. E. 454, 467
Madden, Tita 534
Magens, Nicolas 54, 180, Pl. 72
Maguire & Murray 216, 461
Maile, David 693
Maile, G. 721
Maile (G.) & Son 331, 364, 384, 485, 602, 610, 832
Maine, John 800
Maitland, Rev. J. W. 576
Maklouf, Raphael 172

Malcott, John 393
Maldon Ironworks 586, 857
Malfait, François 632
Malim, Rev. Alfred 281, 711
Malyon, Charles 846
Manasseh, Leonard 122
Manasseh (Leonard) & Partners 463
Mander (N. P.) Ltd 205
Mandeville family 627
Mandeville, Geoffrey de 654
Mandeville, William de 627
Manley, Robert 508
Mann, H. W. 212
Manning, August 783
Manning, Charles 139
Manning, Samuel Jun. 608
Manning, Samuel Sen. 55, 138, 348, 395, 433, 520, 795
    see also *Bacon & Manning*
Mansfield, Isaac 427
Mantell, Robert 128
Manwood family 182
Marcanik, A. 340
Margetts, Paul 333
Mark, Kenneth 661
Mark (The Kenneth) Practice 245, 563, 611, 667, 679
Markham, F. A. 478
Markrow, Paul 136
Marks, Henry Stacy 147, 710
Marks, Simon 837
Marney family 526, 530, 555
Marney, Sir Henry Marney, 1st Baron 43, 47, 526–30
Marney, John, 2nd Baron 526–30, 555
Marnock, Robert 349
Marriage, Edward 295
Marriage, J. 607
Marriott family 680
Marriott, Rosemary Smith 563
Marsden, W. 856
Marsh, John 135
Marsh, Roff 158, 279, 289
Marsh (Roff) Partnership 279, 799, 801
Marsh, T. 770
Marsh, Thomas Coxhead Chisenhale 772
Marsh, William 772
Marsh, William Coxhead 771
Marshall, Edward 46, 86, 228, 245, 485, 580, Pl. 46
Marshall, Joshua 245, 608
Marshall, Samuel 393, 441, 579, 580
Martin, A. J. 707
Martin, Christopher 137
Martin, J. W. 242
Martin, Mary 461n.
Martin, Stuart 592
Martin, Thomas (Alresford Hall) 88
Martin, Thomas (Victoria Street) 499

Martin, William 458, 460
Martin-Kaye, Neil 716–17
Martindales 319
Mary, Princess (C16) 671
Maryon, H. 856
Maryon Wilson family 398
Mascherell, Walther, Alexander and Edith 853
Masey, Cecil 294
Masham family 491
Mason, Edmund 204
Mason, George 53
Mason, Paul 456
Mason, William 58, 181, 264, 334
Massen, C. 189
Matcham, Frank 716
Matcham (Frank) & Co. 385
Mathew, Rev. E. W. 626
Mathews, H. E. 243n.
Mathews Serjeant Architects 135, 183
Matthews, E. 729
Mattick, Stephen 407
Maufe, Edward 575, 603
Mauger, Paul V. 67, 153, 208, 660, 739
Mauger (Gavin) & Associates 462
Mauger (Paul) & Partners 137, 455
Maule, H. P. G. 676
May, E. E. 279, 534, 598
    see also Baker & May
May, Edward 443
Mayer & Co. 172, 174, 229, 489, 520, 544, 590, 653, 701, 793
Maynard family 546, 551, 769
Maynard, Arne 398
Maynard, Sir Henry 54, 549, 550–1, 552
Maysent family 147, 151
Meaden, J. G. P. 760
Meadows, Rev. W. S. H. 231
MEB Partnership 135, 637
Mechi, John 788
Medland, James 233–4
Mellitus, Bishop of London 18, 785–6
Mellor (Ray) Associates 300
Messenger, Peter 412
Mewburn, Chilton 856
Meyrick, Col. Augustus 186
Michener, Thomas 425
Micklethwaite (J. T.) & Somers Clarke 147
Middleditch, Percy 624
Middlesex, Lionel Cranfield, Earl of 309
Middleton & Pritchett 658
Midgley, Kenneth 310
Migotti, Alphonzo 816
Mildmay family 46, 206, 221, 537
Mildmay, Thomas 222
Mildmay, Sir Walter 315–16
Mildmay, William 222
Mileham, C. H. M. 375
Miles, E. J. 210

Mileson, Harold 650, 782
Miller, A. T. 360
Miller, Alec 624
Miller, James 687–8
Miller, Sanderson 382, 500
Miller (John) & Partners 800
Milligan, Rev. H. M. 59, 89
Millington, Sir Thomas 382
Mills, Frederick 117
Mills, John 465
Mills, Jon 386
Mills (Edward D.) & Partners 158, 159, 392
Milne, W. O. 839
Milne & Hall 185
Milnes, T. 657
Milsom Architects 477
Minoprio, Anthony 201
Minter family 186
Minton 91, 744, 790, 794, 831
Mitchell, Arnold 387n.
Mitchell, K. A. 158, 159
Mitchell, Tony 744–5
Mitchell, William 452, 695
Mitchell & Houghton 555
Mollo, Eugene 386
Mollo & Egan 169
Monchaux, Paul de 279
Monck, George see Albemarle, 1st Duke of
Monro & Partners 215
Monson, E. C. P. 457
Montagu, Duke and Duchess of 157
Montagu, Major-General 272
Montgomery, Sir John 351
Montgomery, Sir Thomas 351
Montmorency, R. M. De 561
Montresor, James Gabriel 628
Moore, Mr (London) 331
Moore, A. L. 142, 232, 744
Moore, Charles E. 370, 548, 825
Moore, Henry 452
Moore, J. 393
Moore, J. F. 55, 103, 478
Moore, Leslie 237–40
Moore, Rupert 140, 304, 515
Moore, Temple 59, 64, 237–40, 632–3, Pls. 105, 107
Moore (A. L.) & Co. 139, 832
Moore (A. L.) & Son 120, 832
Morant, Rev. Philip 87
Morant (George) & Son 316
Morgan, Ivor H. 534
Morgan, J. D. 309
Morgan, Lisa Z. 374
Morgan, Dr W. H. 716
Morgan, William de 530
Morice, William 234
Moring 491
Morley family 408
Morley, John 445–6
Morley, Henry Parker, Lord 408
Morris, Charles 485

Morris, F. E. 270
Morris, William 60, 107, 327, 369
Morris & Co. 110, 162, 350, 431, 473, 503, 522, 554, 795, 810
Morris (William) & Co. (Westminster) 86, 228, 268, 548
Morrison, Shirley 395
Mose, John 104
Moss, Thomas Jun. 208
Moss, Thomas Sen. 208
Mott Hay & Anderson 514, 629
Moulton, Alfred 575
Mountjoy, Alan 306
Mowbray (A. R.) & Co. 185, 542
    see also Wippell Mowbray
Moxon, C. J. 828
Moy, W. A. 267
Muilman family 318
Muilman, Peter (later Peter Chiswell) 318
Müller, William John 790
Mumford, A. G. 264
Munby, A. E. 356
Municipal School of Art 706
Munnings, Sir Alfred 325
Muntz, Elizabeth 807
Murdoch, Andrew 204
Murduck, Malcolm 94
Murphy (Richard) Architects 466
Murphy Philipps 346
Murray, H. G. 232
Mussi, Cleo 280
Myddelton, Sir Thomas 45, 738, Pl. 47
Mylne, Robert 52, 797

Naish & Mitchell 495
Nash, W. T. 63, 149
Nash, William 63, 662
Nassau family 671
National Building Agency 464
Naunton, Maurice 114, 119, 122
Neave, Airey 374
Neave, Penelope 374
Nesfield, William Andrews 801
Nesfield, William Eden 60, 62, 65, 568–9, 575–6, 611, 632–3, 665–6
Nevill family 313
Nevill, Ralph 431
Nevinson & Newton 162
Newberry & Fowler 67, 627, 713
Newbery, Robert J. 240
Newdigate, Sir Roger 307–8
Newman, J. T. 63, 375, 513
Newman, Thomas 631
Newman (Dudley), Elliott & Archer 317
Newman, Jacques & Round 279
Newton, A. J. 116, 172, 192, 702
    see also Burles & Newton; Burles, Newton & Co.; Burles, Newton & Partners
Newton, Ernest 635
Neylan, Michael 462

Neylan & Ungless 462
Nicholls, Cliff 353
Nicholls, D. C. 60, 232, 233, 507n., 844
Nicholls, T. 466, 809
Nicholls Associates 353
Nichols, F. M. 524
Nichols, Francis 524
Nichols, Sir Philip 524
Nicholson family 689–90
Nicholson, A. K. 66, 95, 176, 205, 240, 310, 431, 441, 517, 535, 565, 580, 626, 630, 690, 713, 738, 746, 770, 810, 859
Nicholson, Barbara 689–90
Nicholson, Sir Charles 59, 66–7, 95, 122, 160, 201, 204, 369, 384, 437, 485, 565, 618, 637, 657, 689–90, 691, 693, 696, 701, 702, 703, 706, 709, 710, 712–13, 763, 824, 845
Nicholson, Sarah 689–90
Nicholson, Sir Sydney 690
Nicholson & Corlette 712
Nicholson (Sir Charles) & Rushton 418, 699, 702
Nicholson (A. K.) Stained Glass Studios 182, 198, 205, 370, 395, 424, 523, 557, 676, 690, 706, 707, 713, 717, 786, 788, 810
Nickson, R. S. 342
Nightingale, Robert 579
Nightingale Associates 328
Nixey, E. Robbins 126, 241
Noakes & Pearce 705
Noble, M. 608
Noel, Rev. Conrad 764, 765
Nollekens, Joseph 55, 233, 336n.
Norfolk, Thomas Howard, 4th Duke of 95
Norman, Edward 588
Norman & Dawbarn 116n., 458
Norris, Dom Charles 67, 455
Norris, E. Bower 569
Northampton, Henry Howard, 1st Earl of 95
Northwood, Humphrey and John de 679–80
Norwich Glass Co. 639
Nost, John 843
Nugent, Robert, Earl 382
Nutt, A. Y. 153, 154, 225, 364, 424–5, 428, 557, 593
Nuttgens, Joseph 790
Nuttgens, Patrick 114
Nutting, Jos. 441
Nye, David E. 582, 583, 615

Oakley, Sir John 514
Oates, Captain L. E. G. 377
O'Connor, Michael 110, 425, 627, 646, 710, 758, 857
Office of Works 137, 165, 169, 178, 214, 287, 290, 405, 571, 588

Ogbourne, William 817
Oisy, Marquis d' 551, 764–5, 787
Oldham, John 754–5
Oldofredi, G. 278
Olins, Rob 74, 241
Oliver, Basil 405, 443, 495, 555, 566, 795
Oliver, Rev. William 145
Ollett, W. 402
Ollett, William Jun. 545–6, 758
Olmius family 313
    see also Waltham
Olmius, Herman 313, 558
Olmius, John see Waltham, 1st Lord
O'Neill, E. & C. 773
O'Neill & Fordham 207, 441
Oppenheimer & Co. 732
Orchard, J. S. 288
Orford, Admiral Edward Russell, Earl of 795
Ormiston, H. 114
Ormond, Thomas Butler, Earl of 155, 646, 647
Orr, A. A. 488, 625
Osmond, W. 773
Osyth, St 671
Oxford, Elizabeth, Countess of 785, 852
Oxford, Earls of 21, 30–1, 45, 193, 599
    see also Vere (de) family
Oxford, Aubrey de Vere, 1st Earl of 193
Oxford, Robert de Vere, 3rd Earl of 478
Oxford, 6th Earl of 478
Oxford, 13th Earl of 195, 852
Oxford, John, 15th Earl of 45, 197
Oxford and Mortimer, Edward Harley, 2nd Earl of 480

Pace, Ion 425, 557, 859
Pacheco, Ana Maria 799
Page, Barrie 241, 250, 373
Page, G. H. 181, 284, 295
Page, Peter 279, 537
Page, R. J. 291, 321, 370–3
Paine, James 48, 776–9
Pakington & Enthoven 69, 433
Palmer, Ada 229, 231
Palmer, Benjamin 362
Palmer, F. 783
Palmer, William 460
Palmer & Holden 214
Palmer (E. William) & Partners 467
Pank, Philip 70, 363
Papworth, E. G. 509
Papworth, J. B. 374, 501, 723
Pargeter, Vincent 108, 505, 604
Paris, Matthew 29, 397
Paris, William 473
Park, Miles 161, 307, 743
    see also Tweddell (Noel) & Park

Parke, E. Hamilton 386
Parker, C. W. 352
Parker & Unwin 704, 716
Parkes, Bertram R. 694, 698, 714
Parkes, Charles 635
Parkins, Joseph 265, 515, 780, 851
Parlby, George 466
Parmenter, S. C. 535, 644
Parris, Robert 85
Parry, S. Gambier 268, 330, 350, 422, 624, 848, 855
Parsons, Ben 550
Parsons, Sir Humphrey 476
Pascall & Watson 736
Pasco, Joseph 406
Paskell (George) & Son 853
Patel, Trupti 385
Patel Taylor 800
Patrick, George 339
Patten, Lewis 715, 788
Patterson, Simon 715
Pattisson family 848
Pattisson, Jacob 848
Pattisson, W. H. E. 848
Paxman, James 276, 278, 298, 300
    see also Davey, Paxman & Co.;
        Davey, Paxman & Davey
Paycocke family 247, 249
Paycocke, Thomas 249, 252
PCKO 71, 466
Peace, David 809
Peache family 527
Peacock, Joseph 118, 122, 160
Pearce, Edward 54, 91
Pearce, H. W. 88, 199
Pearce, Walter J. 402
Pearce (Wm.) & E. Cutler 580
Pearson, J. L. 94, 167–8, 432
Pearson, James 318, 657
Peck, F. 583
Peck, John 517
Peckitt, William 102
Peers, C. R. 165
Peeters, Hendrik 306
Peeters, Pierre 306
Pelling, Rev. John 616
Penni, Giovanni Francesco 602
Pennystone, Thomas 77
Penoyre & Prasad 72, 416, 792, Pl. 123
Penrice, John 270, 752, 816
Penrose, F. C. 235
Pentreath, Ben 483
Penwarden 480, 594
Pepler & Allen 244, 784
Pepys, Samuel 472
Perkins, Mark 253
Perkins (Mark) Partnership 298
Perry, George 62, 471, 487, 595, 630
Perry, Heather 443
Perry (George) & John Slater 766
Pertwee, Rev. Arthur 180

Pertwee, Charles 57, 61, 64, 133, 148, 180, 208, 211, 213, 219, 222, 249, 358, 402, 419, 422, 424, 488, 503, 510, 537, 581, 735, 753, 765, 789, 816, 844, 854, 860

Pertwee, William Hart 57, 212, 213, 358

Pertwee, Charles & W. H. 69, 222, 386

Pertwee (W. H.) & Howard 214, 708

Peters, Mr 306

Peters, Rev. M. W. 657

Peto, Harold 552–3

Peto, Sir Morton 698

Petre family 60, 494, 753, 776

Petre, John, 1st Lord 494, 776

Petre, Robert, 8th Lord 49, 508, 776, 779

Petre, Robert, 9th Lord 506, 507, 776

Petre, William, 11th Lord 503

Petre, William, 12th Lord 60, 779

Petre, Lionel, 16th Lord, and Lady Rasch 506, 507

Petre, Joseph, 17th Lord 506

Petre, Sebastian 604

Petre, Sir William 47, 502, 504, 506, 858, 860, Pl. 38

Peyman, H. P. 162

Phillips, Douglas 550

Phillips, George R. 268

Phillips, J. R. Spencer 154, 317

Phillips, John 96

Phillips, William 294

Phillips Stained Glass Studio 550

Phipson, R. M. 442

Physick, R. 180

Pick Everard 574

Pick Everard Keay & Gimson 281

Pickford (J.) & W. Atkinson 54–5, 140, 748

Pierce, Edward 837

Pierce, John Sampson 668

Pietzch, Siegfried 494

Piggott, John 797

Pilcher, William 590

Pilsbury, Kay 106, 477, 840

Pilsbury (Kay) Architects 404

Pinder, William 197

Piper, John 67, 451, 453n.

Piper, Thomas 147

Pitcher, Mrs Scott 455

Pite, Arthur Beresford 368–9, 371

Pither, John 100

Pitman & Cuthbertson 129, 139

Plant, W. G. 121, 280

Plater Claiborne 161, 422, 645

Plater Inkpen 585, 844

Plater Inkpen Downie 163, 844

Plater Inkpen Vale & Downie 488, 587, 789, 832

Playne, B. 185

Pleydell-Bouverie, David 69, 199

Plumb, Clive 71, 118, 119, 120, 125, 330, 413, 754

Plume, Dr Thomas 581–2

Pole, Sir John de la 237

Pollard, Michael 570

Pollard Thomas & Edwards 70, 244

Polley, W. B. 143, 249, 250, 354, 397, 579, 640, 649, 720, 728, 742, 843

Poole (tiles) 794

Poole family 145

Poole, A. J. 113

Poole, Robert 197

Poolman, J. 737

Pope, Alexander 360, 380

Poplack, Dudley 105

Portakabin 457

Porter, Richard 77

Portsmouth, Elizabeth, Countess of 96, 98, 104

Potter, Robert 204–5

Potter, Thomas 394

Potter (Robert) & Richard Hare 206

Poulton, W. F. 270

Poulton & Freeman 116n., 631

Powell, C. C. 431, 859

Powell, C. E. 198

Powell, Hugh 555
    see also Edwards & Powell

Powell, Hugh L. 184

Powell, Nathanael 185

Powell, Turner 573n.

Powell & Moya 459

Powell (James) & Sons 60, 85, 95, 138, 140, 162, 182, 185, 196, 228, 233, 263–4, 265, 277, 304, 321, 349, 368, 376, 408, 409, 413, 422, 431, 435, 440, 464, 466, 478, 480, 489, 509, 510, 530, 536, 541, 554, 568, 594, 595, 604, 616, 621, 637, 641, 646, 657, 681, 683, 693, 701, 704, 709, 710, 713, 715, 742, 750, 751, 771, 810, 825, 829, 831, 835, 837

Power, Cyril E. 384

Pownall, F. H. 384

Poynter, Ambrose 806

Poynter, E. J. 58, 701, 704, 809

Pozzi 795

Preedy, F. 701

Prest, E. J. 598

Price, John 268

Prior, Matthew 441, 480

Prior Manton Tuke Partnership 813

Pritchett family 554

Pritchett, G. E. 62, 90, 108, 139, 302, 346, 350, 408, 409, 468, 479, 480, 491, 493, 521, 553–4, 590, 594, 610, 611, 641, 681, 740, 795, 830

Proctor Matthews Architects 71, 466

Property Services Agency 115, 210, 652

Prowse, Thomas 307

Prudde, John 591

Pryer, G. H. 550

Prynne, G. H. F. 859
Pryor, Arthur 375, 837
Pugh, Dr Benjamin 214
Pugh, Dennis E. 511
Pugh (Dennis E.) Associates 353
Pugin, A. W. N. 270, 281, 482
Pugin, E. W. 328
Pugin, P. P. 753
Pugin & Pugin 714
Pulham (James) & Son 104
Purcell Miller Tritton 93, 128, 242, 267, 269, 285, 440, 547, 554, 563, 859
Purcell Miller Tritton & Partners 273, 276, 318, 460, 461, 481, 580, 582, 822
Purkiss, Donald 643
Pye, George Gard 240, 293, 297, 475
Pye & Hayward 790
Pyghtle Works 210
Pyke family 140, 141, 748
Pym, John 349
Pyrton, Sir William 541

Quail, Paul 229, 370
Quennell, C. H. B. 68–9, 171, 222, 223, 687–8, 833, 847
Quilter, George 820
Quinan, Kenneth B. 815

Rackham (David) Partnership 240
Radburn, Stephen 773
Radley, Len 429
Raffles, W. Hargreaves 191
Ragg, F. W. 683
Rail Link Engineering 629
Ramsey, W. 577
Randall, Charles 139, 855
Randall, Terence D. 384, 702
Rank, J. Arthur 455
Ransom, F. 543
Ransome & Son 845
Ransomes 643
Raphael 414
Rasch, Frederic Carne 679
Rasch, Katherine Anne 679
Ratcliffe & Burridge 357
Rattee & Kett 389, 408, 594, 831
Ravilious, Eric 198, 388, 390, 664
Rayleigh, John William Strutt, 3rd Baron 760, 762
Rayleigh, 6th Baron 762
Raymond family 129–31
Raymond, Geoffrey 580
Raymond, George 60
Raymond, Rev. J. M. St Clere 129–31
Raymond, Rev. Oliver 597
Rayner, Abraham 331
Rayner, P. J. 404
Rayson, Thomas 767
Rea, Betty 469
Read 480
Read, Charles 189
Read, G. A. 781

Read, Nicholas 54, 180, Pl. 72
Read, R. J. Gifford 697
Read & Macdonald 857
Rebecca, Biagio 100, 102, 103
Rebow, Sir Isaac 268, 273, 290
Rebow, Isaac Lemyng 800
Rebow, Colonel Isaac Martin 88, 800
Rebow, John 54, 268
Rebow, John Gurdon 800, 851
Redgrave, John 304, 409
Reeve, Francis 469
Reeve, J. A. 806–7, 809
Reeves (of Bath, sculptor) 55, 402
Reeves, Charles 152, 177, 585
Regnart, Charles 55, 384, 618, 650
Reid (Richard) Architects 345
Reinagle, Philip 235
Reiss, Captain Richard 687
Rennie, John 52, 474
Renton Howard Wood Levin 114
Repton, Humphry 49–50, 145, 186, 317, 380, 418, 427, 501, 512, 538, 576, 595, 645, 727, 741, 755, 775–6
Repton, J. A. 50, 58, 206–7, 317, 643–4, 727, 728
Repton, H. & J. A. 317, 755n.
Rettler, Tim 784
Reveler, John 218
Reynolds, Sir Joshua 701
Reynolds, Thomas 800
Reynolds, William Bainbridge 737, 801
Reynolds-Stephens, William 59, 429–30, 431, Pl. 103
Reyntiens, Patrick 174
Rice, Rev. H. 410
Rich, 3rd Lord see Warwick, 1st Earl of
Rich, Sir Hugh 380
Rich, Sir Richard Rich, 1st Lord 42–3, 45, 47, 354–5, 357, 429, 438, 531–3, 615, 647, Pl. 43
Rich, Robert, 2nd Lord 354, Pl. 43
Richardson, A. E. 92
Richman, Martin 218
Richmond, Nathaniel 761
Richmond & Son 718
Richold, P. 536
Rickards, E. A. 780
Ricketts, Rachel 541
Rickman, Thomas 105, 417, 659
Rickman & Hutchinson 655
Ridley, T. D. 358
Rigby family 598–9
Rigby, Edward 599
Rigby, Richard (I, d. 1730) 599
Rigby, Richard (d. 1788) 599–600
Ringham, Henry 267, 367, 395, 678
Rivers, C. A. 844
Rivers, Thomas 105
RMJM 570
Roberts, D. 385
Roberts, David 271

Roberts, Gilbert C. 368
Roberts, J. M. 320, 625
Robertson, R. 659
Robins, E. C. 818
Robins (Peter) Associates 709
Robinson, A. Douglas 370, 371
Robinson, Alfred 738
Robinson, Thomas 660
Robinson, William 667
Robinson, Dick & Helen 641
Robson, Philip 591
Rochester family 760
Rochester, John 760
Rochford, Earls of 671
Rochford, 3rd Earl of 674
Rochford, 4th Earl of 675, 676
Rochford, Sir Thomas Boleyn,
    Viscount 155, 647
Rodin, Auguste 452
Rogers, Mrs 205
Rogers, F. A. 676
Rogers (Richard) Partnership 217
Rogers, Richard & Su 70, 121, 796, Pl.
    115
Rolf, Ken 729
Rolfe, C. C. 233, 637, 679
Rolfe Judd 411
Rolfe Judd Group Practice 698
Rome, William 312
Rookwood, Sir Henry Selwin-
    Ibbetson, Lord 480
Roper, Grace Faithfull 90, 296, 323,
    325, 326
Roper, J. Egan 711
Roscoe, Frank 169, 381
Rose, A. Winter 552, 630, 724
Rose, Abbot 460
Rose, Carol 270
Rose, Joseph 100, 101, 102, 104
Rose, Russell W. 287
Ross, A. D. C. 418
Ross, Peter 317
Rossi, Charles 209
Rossi, J. C. F. 55, 402
Rothenstein, Michael 388
Rother, Carl 821
Rothermel, Rolf 538
Roubiliac, L. F. 55, 331, 485
Round family 273, 276
Round, C. G. 138, 297
Round, James 273
Round, John 315–16
Round, Susan Constantia 316
Rouw, Henry 55, 145, 770
Rouw, Peter the Younger 55, 145, 147,
    360, 424, 645, 729
Rowe, Fred 813
Rowe, R. R. 439
Rowntree, Fred 225, 242, 558, 747
Rowntree, Kenneth 388
Rowntree, Douglas W. & Colin 558
Rowntree (Fred) & Ralph W. Thorpe
    660

Rowson, Ronald 569
Rubens, P. P. 235
Rubinstein, Gerda 462, 472
Rudken, J. L. W. 639
Ruffle, David 72
Ruffle (David) Architects 405
Ruffle (David) Associates 121, 179,
    219, 503, 729
Ruggles (and Ruggles-Brise) family
    360, 726
Ruggles, John 726
Ruggles, Samuel 726
Runnacles, Harcourt 645
Runtz (Ernest) & Co. 499
Rush family 344
Rushbury, Henry 168, 210
Rushton, H. T. 699, 707, 713, 787
Rushton, T. J. see Nicholson (Sir
    Charles) & Rushton
Russell (Chigwell) 55, 771
Russell, Jeremy 816
Ruszkowski, Zdzislaw 451
Rutherford, John 182
Rutherford, Rosemary 67, 162, 182,
    240, 441, 759, Pl. 109
Rysbrack, John Michael 54, 380

Sabysforth, John 670
Sacré, Lester H. 387
Sadd, John 585
Sæberht, king of the East Saxons 18,
    19, 705
Sainsbury (J.) Architects & Engineers
    Dept 169
St Aubyn, J. P. 326, 375, 522, 837
St Aubyn & Wadling 286
St Clere family 315
St Pancras Ironwork Co. 528
St Vincent, Sir John Jervis, Admiral
    the Earl of 724
Sale (H. B.) Ltd 523
Salisbury, Frank O. 356
Salisbury, H. J. 108, 237, 379
Salmon, Joseph 161, 816
Salter, John 839
Salviati & Co. 331, 745
Salvin, Anthony Jun. 597
Samuel (Edward) & Partners 70, 680
Sandby, Thomas 519
Sanders (Euston Road) 392
Sanders, Arthur 740
Sanders, J. 561
Sanders, T. W. 442
Sanderson, John 307–9, 479
Sanderson, Joseph 479, 759
Sanderson, Philip 205
Sandles, Tony 374
Sands & Walker 852
Sandys, Cecilie 45, 854
Sandys, Edwin, Archbishop of York
    854
Sargeant, Jamie 526
Saunders, Bryan 331, 580, 738

Saunders, E. 757
Saunders, Paul 103
Saunders Architects 450
Saunders & Co. 838
Saunders (W.) & Partners 665
Saunders Partnership 465, 788
Savage, James 173n., 720
Savill, Alfred 229
Savill, Jonathan 185, 689
Savill-Onley family 752
Savill-Onley, Charles 752
Savill-Onley, Onley 164, 751–2
Saville, Rev. John 294
Saville, Joseph 150
Saxon, S. S. 807
Sayer, Rev. George 846
Scales, Sir Roger de 680
Scamell, George 387
Scargill, Walter 267
Scarlett, James 444
Scheemakers, Henry 55, 831
Scheemakers, Peter 54, 55, 350, 771
Scheuermann, J. A. 244
Schoenaich, Brita von 593
Schreiber, David 193
Scoles, A. J. C. 60, 714
Scoles, J. J. 58, 60, 158, 207, 269
Scoles (A. J. C.) & C. Raymond 241,
    270, 580
Scott, A. 571
Scott, Sir George Gilbert 58, 62, 160,
    264, 268, 310, 315, 352, 353, 435,
    721, 742, 843
Scott, George Gilbert Jun. 403
Scott, John Oldrid 185, 742, 829
Scott, M. H. Baillie 65, 573
Scott, T. H. B. 534, 637, 710
Scott, Thomas Jun. 377
Scott, W. G. 474
Scott, William Langston 403n.
Scott (Baillie) & Beresford 823
Scott & Moffatt 63, 136, 405, 435,
    441, 760, 845, Pl. 98
Scully, Stephen 207
Sear, David 748
Searle & Hayes 189
Searle & Searle 515
Searle, Son & Hayes 657
Sedding & Wheatly 637
Seddon, J. P. 232, 566
Seely & Paget 433, 436
Seeman, Enoch 100
Sefre Architects 228
Selby, Laurence J. 334, 702
Selwin-Ibbetson see Rookwood, Lord
Sergeant, G. 421, 434, 525
Sergison Bates 70, 784
Seymour Harris see Harris
Shades of Light 816
Shaen, Samuel 483
Shakespear, George 96
Sharp, W. 713
Sharpe, Sir John 247

Sharpe & Paley 522
Shaw, Henry 97, 98, 101
Shaw, Norman 65, 229, 570, 575, 666,
    Pl. 89
Sheldon, Percy J. 861
Shelton, J. T. 372–3
Shelton, Roderick 118
Shennan, William 104
Shenstone, William 802
Shenstone (Gerald) & Partners 521,
    619, 753
Shepherd, Miss 185
Shepherd, Edward 49, 155
Sheppard, Richard 659
Sheppard (Richard) & Partners 71,
    73, 229, 456, 457
Sheppard Robson 210, 291
Sheppard (Richard), Robson &
    Partners 751
Sherman, Edmund 323
Sherrin, Frank 503, 504
Sherrin, George 57, 64, 65, 66, 149,
    152, 224, 240, 330, 333, 374, 442,
    444, 483, 504, 505, 510, 511, 604,
    697, 698, 753, 778, 845, 847n., Pl.
    4
Shiner, C. M. 187, 385, 751, 824
Shout, P. 644
Shrigley & Hunt 148, 237, 478, 539
Shuffleton, John 529
Siborne, Captain H. T. 339
Sievier, R. W. 474
Simkin, W. R. 277
Simon, Henry 213, 218
Simon, Robert 801
Simpson, Donald 181
Simpson, J. R. Moore 723
Simpson (W. B.) & Sons 207, 440,
    599, 631
Sinclair, G. 145
Sinclair, Robert 56
Sinclair, W. B. 638
Singer & Son 738
Singh, Rajindar 216
Singleton 795
Sipson Gray Associates 218
Sisson, Marshall 69, 70, 106, 291,
    323, 373, 524, 555, 607, 625, 766,
    833, 852
Skeat, Francis W. 370, 437, 512, 700,
    713, 734
Skelton, John 205, 451, 569
Skidmore, Francis 721
Slater, John 223
Slater, William 58, 62, 109, 558, 646,
    708–9, 710
Slater & Carpenter 692, 757
Slowman, Gerald W. 229
Slythe, Isaac 794n.
Slythe & Lufkin 441
Smart, Mr 402
Smart, Gordon 189
Smee, F. E. 702–3, 714

Smee, Michael 790
Smee & Houchin 385, 702
Smee, Morice & Houchin 714
Smirke, Robert Sen. 166
Smirke, Sydney 58, 568, 769
Smith family (Cressing Temple) see Smyth
Smith family (Hill Hall) 45, 773
Smith, Anne E. 537
Smith, C. H. 467, 721
Smith, C. Raymond 482
Smith, Charles 738
Smith, Rev. Charles Lesingham 59, 545–6
Smith, D. Jennings 72
Smith, Donald 205, 541
Smith, Sir Edward 773, 775
Smith, Edwin 669, 819
Smith, F.W. 228
Smith, Francis 835, 836
Smith, Frank 704
Smith, Frank W. 70, 647
Smith, G. E. R. 182, 198, 205, 310, 424, 557, 566, 580, 676, 690, 707, 709, 713, 717, 721, 810, 857
Smith, Geoffrey 421
Smith, Griffiths 835
Smith, Hubert Llewellyn 573
Smith, J. O. 401
Smith, J. T. 615
Smith, Jeremy 333
Smith, Percy F. 366
Smith, R. Moffat 61, 467
Smith, Ray 385
Smith, Rev. Ron 343
Smith, T. Roger 584
Smith, Thomas 467, 471
Smith, Sir Thomas 772, 773, 774–6
Smith, William 657
Smith, Sir William 496, 772–3
Smith (Douglas) & Barley 694
Smith (Roger) & Gale 271
Smith, Son & Gale 243
Smith (G.) & G. B. Williams 185
Smyth family (Berechurch Hall) 134
Smyth or Smith family (Cressing Temple) 312, 313
Smyth, Dorcas 46, 793
Smyth, Sir John 313
Smythies, Francis 296
Sneezum, Thomas 123
Snooke & Stock 750, 859
Snow (Sir Frederick) & Partners 736
Soane, Sir John 304, 321, 324, 411, 600
Solis, Virgil 97
Solomon (Lewis), Kaye & Partners 811
Somerford, T. R. 699n.
Sorrell, Alan 705
Sorrell, Jack 136, 212, 782
Soukop, Willi 458
Southcote, Philip 846

Southend-on-Sea Borough Council Property Division 710
Southgate, F. G. 137
Southwick, Alfred 240
Soward (John) & Son 380
Spalding, Fred Jun. 207
Spanlang, Ludwig 574
Sparrow, Basil 380, 381
Sparrow, James Goodeve 380, 381
Sparrow, John (C17) 377
Sparrow, John (C18) 77
Spear, Francis H. 279, 818
Spear Studios 182
Spence, Sir Basil 111
Spence (Basil) & Partners 116n.
Spencer, Lady Anne see Bateman, Viscountess
Spender, Humphrey 796
Sperling, Charles 415
Sperling, Henry 414
Sperling, Rev. John Hansom 58, 830–1
Spiers, K. J. 279
Spooner, Charles 59, 441
Squire, William J. 374
Stabler, Harold 59, 480
Stagg, Jane 765
Stammers, Wild 786
Stanhope, D. A. 182, 453
Stanley, Charles 54, 551
Stanton, Edward 233, 510, 765, 773
Stanton, Thomas 133, 398, 455, 487, 618, 701
Stanton, William 55, 206, 510, 771, 838
Stanton & Horsnaile 402, 843
Stanton Williams 212n.
Start, J. W. 88, 283, 294, 328, 392, 759, 822
Stayner, Thomas 54, 560, 748, 771
Stedman, F. C. 244
Steen, Ian 668
Steen (Ian) Associates 357
Steller, Fritz 695
Stephen, King 246
Stephens, Francis 143, 165, 184, 233, 489, 616, 701, 702, 753, 810
Stephenson, Edward 391
Stephenson, Robert 56, 545
Stern, Catharni 216, 518, 584
Steven Bros & Co. 326
Stevens, Richard 46, 154
Steward-Watling, H. 328
Stewart, Mrs A. C. 303
Stewart, Donald 439
Stewart, Patricia 93, 537
Stewart, William 710
Stewart & Hendry 119
Steyning 419
Stock, Henry 62, 77, 125, 148, 360, 383, 403, 545, 647, 659, 750
    see also Allen, Snooke & Stock; Snooke & Stock
Stokes, Leonard 228, 714

Stone, E. A. 699n.

Stone, Henry 335, 368–9, 515, 759, 816, 832

Stone, Nicholas 46, 309, 860

Stoneham, J. C. 383–4

Stones, Alan 509

Stopes family 295

Stopes, H. 295

Streatfeild, T. E. C. 185, 187

Streather, W. T. 812

Stredder, F. C. 367

Street, G. E. 58, 62, 204n., 330, 401, 437–8, 481, 499, 614, 831

Strutt family 47, 565, 761

Strutt, John 761

Strutt, John Holden 761

Strutt, John William *see* Rayleigh, 3rd Baron

Stuart, John 68, 69, 70, 77, 137, 148, 174, 181, 182, 209, 212, 217, 241, 280, 346, 385, 561, 582, 687, 844, 845, 860

Suffling, E. R. 160, 245, 327

Suffolk, Thomas Howard, 1st Earl of 95–8, 100

Suffolk, 6th Earl of 96

Sulman, John 107

Sulman & Rhodes 245, 322

Sulyard family 652

Sumner, Heywood 431

Sussex, Earls of 45, 154

Sussex, Thomas Radcliffe, 3rd Earl of 154, 155, 157, 159

Sustainable Ecological Architecture Ltd 861

Suter, R. George 479

Sutton, Baptista 46, 550

Swaine, Bourne & Son 486

Swansborough, Edward 300, 303, 492, 754

Swash, Caroline 180

Swein (son of Robert fitz Wimarc) 638

Swinnerton, Sir John 742

Swynnerton, J. H. 698

Sydes, John 428

Sykes, Capt., R.E. 711

Sykes, Arthur 242, 243

Sykes, Steven 170

Symons, A. J. A. 360

Systra 629

T., I. 467

Tait, Thomas 69, 687–8

see also Burnet (Sir John), Tait & Lorne; Burnet (Sir John), Tait & Partners

Talbot, Roger 120

Tallakarne family 94, 484

Tangram Architects & Designers 459

Tanner, Joseph 185

Tappen, George S. W. 178

Tapper, Michael 606

Tapper, Walter 67, 691n., 716

Tapper (Michael) & J. Anthony Lewis 129, 140

Tarring, J. 348

Tasker, Countess 60, 176, 431

Tasker, F. W. 60, 173, 176, 240, 431, 714

Tasker, John 514

Tate, William 307, 309

Taunton, Donald B. 126

Taverner, Dr James 841, 846

Tawke, A. S. 494

Tayler & Green 121

Taylor, Isaac 234n.

Taylor, J. H. 346

Taylor, Peter 146

Taylor, Sir Robert 170, 461n., 482, 592, 780

Taylor, Robert 393

Taylor, Robert Sen. 130, 393

Taylor, W. G. 147

Taylor, Wendy 115

Taylor & Clifton 652

Taylor & Collister 388

Taylor & Hunt 211

Taylor Woodrow 695

Tench, E. J. 639

Terry, Dame Ellen 551

Terry, Quinlan 67, 70, 166, 172–3, 321, 322, 323, 365, 366, 398, 406, 516, 762, Pls. 119, 120

see also Erith & Terry

Tessier, Stephen 325

Teulon, S. S. 58, 64, 138, 226n., 265, 294, 429, 588, 610, 620, 621, 683n., 720–1, 722, 801, 802

TFP Architects 356, 387

Thatcher, J. E. 266

Theakston 418

Theed, W. 467

Thomas family 589

Thomas, Sir A. Brumwell 70, 241

Thomas, Brian D. L. 397

Thomas, Bryan 270–1, 341, 343, 475

Thomas, John 589

Thomas, Russell 436

Thomas (Bryan) Macnamara 801

Thomas, Mowle & Chisnall 729

Thomas (Bryan) & Partners 88, 265, 728, 788

Thomas (Percy) Partnership 279, 459, 695

Thomas of Leighton 269

Thomond, Percy Wyndham, Earl of 612

Thompson, A. 210

Thompson, E. 826

Thompson, Francis 56, 400, 820

Thompson, M. G. 51, 53, 64, 280, 324, 472, 533, 633n., 780

Thompson, Margaret G. 710

Thompson, Robert 281

Thompson (James) & Greenhalgh 697, 699
Thompson, W. & C. 482
Thorman, Patricia 464
Thorn, C. T. 510
Thorne 321
Thornhill, Sir James 383
Thorold, William 213, 647
Thorpe, John 48, 95, 309n.
Thorvaldsen, B. 199, 501, 760
Threlfall, Philippa 503
Thrussell, Gary 416
Thurrock U.D.C. Architect's Dept 385
Thurston, N. T. 717
Tibbalds Monro 112–13
Tilden, Philip 552–3, 776
Tiler, Mary Harris 699, 707
Titcomb 554, 795
Tite, Sir William 644
To, Frederick E. 228
Tod (Allen) Architects 711
Toller, George and Elizabeth 828
Tomkins, Mrs 371
Tomkins, Homer & Ley 370, 371, 372, 816
Tooley, Herbert 186, 229, 346, 570, 571
Tooley & Foster 86, 176, 213, 229, 356–7, 374, 461, 569, 576, 832
Tooley & Foster Partnership 133, 178, 825
Torrigiano, Pietro 482
Tovi (C11) 804
Tower, Thomas 722
Tower, Walter E. 307, 309
Town, W. H. 64, 280
Towner, H. B. 207, 719
Townsend, Charles Harrison 59, 176, 429, Pl. 103
Townshend (Caroline) & Joan Howson 515, 707
Tradescant, John the Elder 159
Traer-Clark, George 648
Trafalgar House Technology 629
Travers, Martin 310, 490, 568, 738
Traylen, J. C. 533
Trehearne & Norman, Preston & Partners 629
Trench family 318
Tresham, Henry 104
Tresilian, Leonard 813
Tress, Richard 61, 659, 661n.
Tristram, Professor 550
Troughton, Captain John 502, Pl. 45
Truefitt, George 793–4
Trundle Foulkes & Co. 135
Tubbs, Ralph 116n., 461
Tubbs (Percy), Son & Duncan 69, 373
Tuffin, Ferraby & Taylor 293
Tufnell family 47, 364
Tufnell, Captain Edward 426
Tufnell, John Jolliffe II 426
Tufnell, S. J. 857, 858
Tufnell, Samuel 425–7, 626–7

Tufnell, W. M. 483
Tufnell, Col. W. N. 154, 364
Tufnell, William 427
Tuke, W. M. 669
Tullio Lombardo 145
Turner, Edward 77
Turner, J. Goldicutt 557
Turner, John 744
Turner, L. A. 801
Turner, S. C. 371
Turner, Thomas 631
Tweddell, Noel 111, 450, 470n.
Tweddell (Noel) & Park 217
Twedye, Richard 753
Twiss, Brig.-Gen. William 76
Tyler, Richard 184
Tyler, William 55, 360, 676
Tyley, T. 373
Tyrell family 154, 336–7, 565, 757
    see also Tyrrel
Tyrell, Edmund 636
Tyrell, John (C17) 337
Tyrell, Col. Sir John 155, 483
Tyrell, Sir Thomas 336
Tyrrel family 92
    see also Tyrell
Tyson, Richard, M.D. 425

Umfreville, Rev. Charles 163
University of Essex Estates Section 799
Unsworth, W. F. 652
Upton, Simon 592
Usborne, Edward 859

Vale, Geoffrey 162n., 254, 561, 585, 832, 857
    see also Plater Inkpen Vale & Downie
van Heyningen & Haward 628–9
Vanbrugh, Sir John 48, 96, 100
Vane, D. C. W. 385
Varela, Armando 800
Venn, Tim 90, 165, 182, 192, 265, 422, 429, 434, 482, 523, 770
Vere (de) family 197, 331, 332, 333, 559, 597, 684
    see also Oxford, Earls of
Vere, Aubrey de (fl. 1100) 332
Vere, Aubrey de (II, fl. 1135) 477
Vere, William 55, 486, 757
Vermeylen, Frans 683
Veronese (follower of) 597
Vestey, Edmund 93
Victoria, Queen 277, 278, 327, 329, 347, 464, 489, 698, 830, 859
Vincent-Brown, F. G. 495, 635, 636, 853
Vining, J. R. 392
Viñoly, Rafael 286n.
Vintoner, Abbot John 43, 671, 673–4, 675
Voysey, C. F. A. 65, 297, 371, 429, 619, 716, 857, Pl. 94
Vulliamy, Lewis 346, 489, 639

Wadhwa, D. C. 298
Wadmore & Baker 598–9, 853
Wagner, Anton 702
Wailes, William 94, 130, 207, 321, 411, 539, 618, 843
Waite, William 55, 498
Wakeford (Kenneth), Jerram & Harris 217, 453
Wakering, Bishop 562
Walde, E. H. S. 229
Waldegrave family 160, 608
Waldegrave, Earls 608
Waldegrave, 1st Earl 608–9
Waldegrave, Sir Edward 608
Waldegrave, Edward 523
Waldegrave, Lady (Frances) 609
Wale, John 331
Walford, Thomas 139
Walker, Arthur S. 384, 832
Walker, J. W. 484
Walker, James 330
Walker, John 206, 507
Walker, Leonard 147, 233, 687, 750
Walker, Russell 443
Walker, William 516
Walker (R. H.) & Son 790
Wall, Samuel 287
Wallace, Robert 618
Wallace, Robert W. 285, 409, 780
Waller, W. C. 572, 573
Wallis, Joseph 181, 283, 365, 820
    see also *Coleman & Wallis*
Wallis, Richard 406
Walpole, Horace 195, 383, 599, 846n.
Walter, James 341
Walters 522
Waltham, John Olmius, 1st Lord 157–9, 206
Waltham, 2nd Lord 157–9
Warboys, Rowland & Surinder 422
Ward 87
Ward, A. L. 542
Ward, Francis Burdett 215
Ward, Richard 104, 658
Ward, Simon 549
Ward, William 612, 727
Ward & Hughes 154, 263, 338, 386, 410, 541, 618, 657, 733, 826, 828, 856
    see also *Curtis (T. F.), Ward & Hughes*
Ward, Hoare & Wheeler 713
Ward (Ronald) & Partners 372
Ward, William & Richard 331
Wardell, W. W. 60, 779
Ware, Isaac 393
Ware, Samuel 350
Warham Guild 249
Warmington, Miss 326
Warmington, E. J. 326
Warner, John 817
Warner, Robert 817

Warners (Cripplegate) 549
Warren, E. P. 770
Warren, Joseph 586
Warren, S. H. 573
Warrington, William 264, 266, 321, 393, 597, 738, 851
Warwick, Frances Maynard, Countess of 405, 550, 552–3
Warwick, Robert, 3rd Lord Rich, 1st Earl of 354–5, 648
Warwick, Francis, 5th Earl of 551
Washington, Lawrence 629
Wasley, David 753
Wastell, John 655
Waterfield, Humphrey 69, 184
Waterhouse, Alfred 183n.
Waterhouse, Paul 770
Watkins, David 149
Watkins, Jesse 455
Watlington, J. W. Perry 466, 468, 469, 470, 595
Watson 554
Watson, Fothergill 234
    see also *Gilbert (I. C.) & Fothergill Watson*
Watson, J. B. 525, 596
Watson, Mary Spencer 456
Watson, R. 825
Watson, T. H. 568
Watts, John Lent 752
Watts, L. J. 253, 264, 267, 268, 277, 321, 622, 803
Watts, Thomas 752
Watts-Ditchfield, J. E. 206, 707
Way family 433
Way, Lewis John 785
Weaser, Laurence T. 709
Weatherall, T. J. 571
Webb, A. W. R. 462
Webb, Christopher 161, 331, 370, 565, 783, 789
Webb, Geoffrey 168, 534, 565
Webb, John 767
Webb, L. 626
Webb, Maurice 525
Webb, Philip 570, 741
Webb, Stephen 207, 375, 493
Webb & Morgan 309, 685
Webbe family 30, 319, 321
Webbe, Thomas 321, Pl. 41
Webber, D. 612
Weber, Rudi 489
Webster, William 125
Wegg, George 286
Weir, William 486, 562
Weissmann, Franz 800
Wellesley & Wills 513, 514
Wells, Frederick 211
Wells, H. G. 551, 552
Wells, Randall 580, 763, 765
Wells, W. C. 222
Wenham & Blake 707
Wentworth, Sir John 379, 380, 381

Wentworth (James) & Son 128
Wescomb, Nicholas 519
Wesley, Anne 416
Western family 644
Western, Charles Callis, Baron 512, 643, 645
Western, Rev. Thomas Walsingham 645
Westlake, N. H. J. 348, 733
    see also Lavers, Barraud &
        Westlake; Lavers & Westlake
Westlake, T. M. 189
Westmacott, Henry 611
Westmacott, Sir Richard 55, 360, 560, 618, 762, 837
Westmacott, Richard Sen. 591
Westminster Marble Co. 373
Weston, Sir Thomas de 342
Westwood Baillie & Co. 861
Wetton, Pilgrim 402, 787
Whall, Christopher 498
Whalley, A. I. 828
Whatey, W. 780
Wheeler, Robert 671
Wheeley, John 273
Whewell, William 478
Whistler, Laurence 362
Whitaker, Charles W. 242
Whitbread family 628
Whitbread, Samuel 628
White, Horace 65, 571–2, 574
White, William 58, 62, 120, 140, 149, 304, 310, 413, 414, 435, 441, 466, 484, 504, 537, 538, 689–90, 700, 701, 779
White (Gordon) & Hood 292
White & Mileson 173
White (K. C.) & Partners 270, 678
White (J. P.) & Son 210
Whitefriars Stained Glass Studios 304, 370, 515, 534, 702, 732
Whitehead, Mr 610
Whitehead (John) & Associates 434
Whitelaw, William 321
Whitmore family 618
Whitmore, Frank 64, 77, 209, 213, 216, 280, 364, 428, 474, 511, 581, 593, 648, 718, 748, 760, 845
Whitmore & Binyon 358
Whittingham, A. Bensly 224
Whittington, Isaac 795
Whymark, David 249, 393
Wild, J. W. 207
Wilhelm II, Kaiser 327
Wilkes, Rev. Robert 818
Wilkin, A. C. 788
Wilkin, Colin 588
Wilkins, William 645
Wilkinson, A. L. 180, 228, 370, 392, 480, 515, 790
Wilkinson, Horace 233, 266, 471, 678, 701, 739, 759, 859
Wilkinson, Sara 90

Wilkinson Bros 596
Wilkinson Eyre 73, 218–19, 453
Willement, Thomas 139, 207, 374, 606n., 610, 748
Willett, William 289
Willett Windows 693
William the Conqueror 30, 272
William of Wykeham 835, 859
Williams, Lesley 431
Williams, Sir Owen 69, 407
Williams, P. Wynne 575
Williams, Ron 466
Williams & Winkley 207
Williams-Ellis, Clough 471
Williamson, F. J. 161
Williamson (Fr. Benedict) & J. H. B. Foss 714
Willis, Alan 73, 74, 77, 169, 210, 253, 319, 503
Willis, S. W. Ward 551
Willmott, Ellen 431
Willmott, Frederick 431
Wills (John) & Sons 811
Willter (Arthur) Associates 598
Wilmshurst, Thomas 352, 598
Wilson, Arthur Needham 186, 350, 729, 814
Wilson, Corinne 529
Wilson, Derek 789
Wilson, G. 757
Wilson, John 278
Wilson, R. V. 118, 125, 330
Wilson, W. 701
Wilson, Mason & Partners 465
Wilson (Colin St John) & Partners 729
Wilson (R. V.) & Clive Plumb 330
Wilson-Webb, S. 335
Wilton, Joseph 55, 517
Wilton, William 101
Wimpey 333, 848
Wimpey Construction 458
Wimpey Homes 849
Winchester, William 55, 733
Winmill, C. C. 484, 486, 562
Winn, Hugo 568
Winsley, Arthur 266, 299
Winstanley, Henry 48, 545n., 631
Winter, Faith 169
Winter, John 184
Wippell (J.) & Co. 197, 433, 473, 593, 752
Wippell Mowbray 431
Wise, W. 480
Wiseman, A. E. 215, 220, 404
Wiseman, Robert 46, 838
Wiseman, Thomas 840
Withers, R. J. 58, 417–18, 621
Witte, Giles de 773
Wonnacott, Thomas 64, 386
Wood, E. J. 118
Wood, George 160
Wood, J. Mackworth 281

Wood, Laurie 726, 824
Wood, Sancton 56, 400, 545, 820
Wood, W. H. 88
Wood, W. J. 396, 424, 562, 714
Wood, W. T. 506
Wood, W. W. 218, 388
Wood (David) Architects 576
Wood (Laurie) Architects 296
Wood (John S.) Chartered Surveyors
  183
Woodhams, F. 637
Woodhouse, F. 839
Woodhouse, Robert 860
Woodhouse & Mitchell 218
Woodley (Torquay) 55, 492
Woodman, William the Elder 644, 733
Woodroffe, Paul 702
Woods, Michael 270
Woods, Mike 453
Woods, Richard 49, 88, 104, 107, 155,
  159, 307, 337, 483, 514, 778, 779,
  800, Pl. 82
Woodthorpe, Edmund 359
Woodward, John 477
Woodyer, Henry 58, 195–6, 305, 320,
  354, 367, 415, 429, 466–7, 468,
  536, 589, 745–6, 794, Pls. 35, 99
Woolley, Sarah 210
Woore, Edward 205
Worley, Robert 123
Wormleighton, Francis 480
Wragg, G. J. 859
Wray 482
Wray, George 213
Wray & Fuller 182
Wren, Sir Christopher 54, 191, 445,
  542, 784
Wright family (Kelvedon Hall) 60,
  513–14
Wright, Edward 693, 708
Wright, John 481, 482–3

Wright, William 46, 249, 377, 414,
  498, 565, 676, 838, 854
Wrightson, W. H. 410
Wrinch, Raymond C. 524
Wyatt, B. D. 553
Wyatt, J. D. 191
Wyatt, James 307, 309
Wyatt, James 546
Wyatt, Sir Matthew Digby 77, 565
Wyatt, Samuel 776, 779
Wyatt, Thomas Henry 280, 436, 553,
  565, 669
Wyborne, John 438
Wylson, Johannes 89
Wyseman family 54, 397–8, 644, 645
Wythes, E. J. 307, 309
Wythes, George 199, 307

Yeldham, John 418
Yorke family 411
Yorke, F. R. S. 71, 457
Yorke, Rev. Philip 411
Yorke, R. W. 710
Yorke, Rosenberg & Mardall 70, 73,
  116n., 117, 461, 571n., 649, 699
Young, John (1830–1910) 123, 124,
  176, 415, 429
Young, John (C20) 279
Young, Joseph 354
Young, Keith 213
Young, Rory 833
Young, William 552
Young & Hall 64, 213, 243
Young & Marten 429
Younger, Alan 303
Youngs, Roy E. 467

Zimmermann, Elizabeth and William
  573
Zins (Stefan) Associates 661
Zoete, Walter De 527–9

INDEX OF PLACES

Principal references are in **bold** type; demolished buildings are shown in *italic*.

Abberton **85**
  Reservoir 69, **85**, 788
Abbess Roding **85–6**
  St Edmund 27, 46, **85–6**, 373, 557
Abridge **86**
Albyns *see* Stapleford Abbotts
Alderford Mill *see* Sible Hedingham
Aldham 29, **86–7**
Alphamstone **87–8**, 415n.
Alresford **88–9**
  Alresford Hall and the Quarters
    49, **88–9**, Pl. 82
Alresford Creek *see* Thorrington
Althorne 59, **89**
Ambresbury Banks *see* Epping
  Upland
Ardleigh *10, 11–12, 17*, **89–90**
  St Mary the Virgin 24, 58, **89–90**,
    395
Arkesden **90–1**
  St Mary the Virgin 21, 46, 54,
    90–1
Ashdon **92–3**
  Guildhall 39, **92**
  Rose and Crown Inn 44, **92**
Asheldham **93**
  Asheldham Camp 12, **93**
Ashen **94**, 484
Ashingdon **94–5**, 438
Auberies *see* Bulmer
Audley End 44, 47, 48, 53, **95–106**,
    440, Pls. 61, 63
  Audley End Village and College
    of St Mark (almshouses) 44,
    51, **105–6**
  park, stables etc. 44, 49, 96,
    103–5, 545
  Railway Station *see* Wendens
    Ambo
  railway tunnel *see* Littlebury
Aveley *1*, **106–7**
  Belhus 47, 49, **107**, *500*
  St Michael 30, **106–7**
Aythorpe Roding **107–8**
  windmill 51, **108**, Pls. 85, 86

Bardfield Saling (or Little Saling) 53,
    108–9
  St Peter and St Paul 21, 23, 28,
    46, **108**
Barling **109**

Barnston 22, **109–10**
Barrington Hall **479**
Barstable *see* Basildon (neighbourhoods)
Basildon xviii, *1, 2, 4*, 71, 73, **110–25**,
    691
  housing 71, 110–11, 112, 115–16,
    117
  industrial areas **124–5**
  neighbourhoods 71, 73, 111,
    115–24
    Barstable **116–17**
    Chalvedon 116n., **117**
    Dunton 111, **117–18**
    Felmore **118**
    Fryerns 116, **118–19**
    Ghyllgrove 116
    Kingswood 116
    Laindon 110, 115, 116, **119**
    Langdon Hills 3, 4, 110, 115,
      120–1; All Saints 27, 47, **120**
    Lee Chapel North 116, **121**
    Lee Chapel South 116, **121**
    Nevendon **121–2**
    Noak Bridge 72–3, 116, **122**
    Pitsea 110–11, 115, **122–3**,
      735n., 758n.; *St Michael 68*,
      123
    Vange 110, 115–16, **123–4**; All
      Saints 29, **123–4**
  public buildings 111, **114–15**, 116,
    124
    Gloucester Park 111, **115**
    railway station 111, **114**
  town centre **110–15**, 123
Bata Estate *see* East Tilbury
Battlesbridge xviii, **125**, 735n., 758n.
  tide mill 52, **125**
Baythorne Hall see Birdbrook
Beauchamp Roding **125–6**
Beaulieu see Boreham (New Hall)
Beaumont-cum-Moze **126**
  Beaumont Hall 48, **126**, 418
  Beaumont House 6, **126**
Beckingham Hall *see* Tolleshunt
  Major
Beeleigh Abbey 19, 42, **127–8**
Belchamp Hall see Belchamp Walter
Belchamp Otten 21, **128**
Belchamp St Paul **128–9**, 140
  St Andrew 28, **128–9**

Belchamp Walter **129–31**
　Belchamp Hall 47, **130–1**, Pl. 76
　St Mary 27, 29, 30, **129–30**, 349,
　　829
Belhus see Aveley
Berden **132–3**
　Berden Hall 43–4, **132–3**
　Berden Priory *19*, **133**
　St Nicholas 22, **132**, Pl. 21
Berechurch **133–4**, 298
　Berechurch Dyke **302**
　Berechurch Hall 65, 134, 724
　St Michael 27, **133–4**
Berners Roding **134**
Bicknacre **134–5**
　Bicknacre Priory *19*, **134–5**
Bigods **405–6**
Billericay 2, **135–6**
　churches 60, **135–6**, 138
　Norsey Wood earthworks 10,
　　138
　public buildings **136–7**
　　Mayflower High School 73,
　　　136
　　workhouse (former) 63, **136–7**
　streets and houses 71, **136–8**
Birch **138–9**
　Birch Hall *47*, 64, **138**
　Post Office Cottages 57, **138**, Pl.
　　92
　St Peter 58, 60, **138**, 525
Birchanger 21, **139**
Birdbrook **139–41**
　Baythorne Hall 35, **140–1**
　Community House 129, **140**
　St Augustine of Canterbury 53,
　　55, **139–40**, 748
Black Chapel *see* North End
Blackmore 2, **141–2**
　Jericho Priory *47*, **142**
　St Laurence and *Augustinian pri-
　　ory 19*, 21, 23, 24, 26, **141–2**,
　　591
Blackmore End xviii, 68, **142–3**
Black Notley **143–4**
　St Peter and St Paul 29, **143**
　Stanton's Farm 34, **144**
Blake Hall *see* Bobbingworth
Bobbingworth **144–5**
　Blake Hall 49, **145**
Bocking **146–53**, 167n.
　churches etc. **146–8**, 153
　　Franciscan Convent 60, **148**
　　St Mary 24, 25, 29, **146–7**
　Mill Hill earthwork **153**
　mills 51, *52*, **150**, **151**
　public buildings **148–9**, 152
　　Church Hall 66, **149**
　　Cottage Hospital 64, **149**
　　Tabor Science College 74, **149**
　　Village Hall 68, **148–9**
　　workhouses (former) 63, **149**,
　　　150

　streets and houses 66, **149–53**,
　　170, 444
　　Bocking Hall 34, **149**
　　Bocking Place 66, **152**
　　Bradford Street 39, 40, **150–2**
　　Wentworth House 50, **151**
　　Woolpack Inn 40, **151**
Boreham *16*, **153–9**
　Boreham House 47, 49, 51, **155**,
　　157, Pl. 80
　New Hall 2, 43, 47, 48, 60, 75,
　　155–9, 730, 841, Pl. 60
　St Andrew 20, 21, 45, 46, **153–4**
Borley 46, **159–60**
Bowers Gifford 30, **160**
Boxted **160–2**
　Songers 34, **162**
Boyles Court (Leverton House)
　723
Bradfield **162–3**
Bradwell **163–4**
　Holy Trinity 5, 29, 30, **163–4**, 233
Bradwell Lodge *see* Bradwell-on-Sea
Bradwell-on-Sea **164–7**, 423
　Bradwell Lodge 49, **166**, 519, Pl.
　　79
　Roman fort (Othona) 17, 19, **165**
　St Peter-on-the-Wall 17, *18*, 19,
　　20, **165**, 389, Pl. 7
　St Thomas 53, **165–6**
Braintree 2, *15*, 56, 68, **167–71**
　churches **167–8**
　　St Michael the Archangel 22,
　　　46, **167–8**
　Courtauld works 52, 169, **171**
　Crittall works 68–9, **170**, 171n.
　public buildings 61, 68, **168–9**
　　Town Hall 68, **168**
　　William Julien Courtauld
　　　Hospital 68, **169**
　streets, houses and commercial
　　buildings 4, **169–71**
　　Braintree Freeport Designer
　　　Village 73, **171**
　　Clockhouse Way 69, **171**, 686
　　Swan Inn 39, **170**
Braxted Park **393–4**
Brays Grove *see* Harlow (neighbour-
　hoods)
Brentwood 50, **171–9**
　churches etc. **172–4**, 177
　　Cathedral (R.C.) 60, 67,
　　　172–3, 174, Pl. 119
　　St George the Martyr 67, **173**
　　St Thomas of Canterbury 59,
　　　173–4, 721
　public buildings **174–5**, 177n., **178**
　　Brentwood School 51, 60, 62,
　　　175–6, 332, 431, 722n.
　　Shen Place Almshouses 64,
　　　178
　　Town Hall (council offices)
　　　73, **174**

Warley Hospital (former
Essex County Lunatic
Asylum) 64, **175**
streets, houses and commercial
buildings 50, 72, 73, **176–9**, 284
Brightlingsea 3, 42, **179–81**
All Saints 23, 24, 54, 89, **179–80**,
Pl. 72
United Church (Wesleyan) **181**,
392
Brizes *see* Kelvedon Hatch
Broadoaks **839–40**
Broads Green *11*
Broomfield **182–3**
Broomfield Hospital 69, **182–3**
Library 73, **182**
Priors **183**, 225
St Mary 21, **182**
Broxted **184**
Hill Pasture 69, **184**
St Mary 24, **184**
Buckhurst Hill xviii, **185–6**
Bulmer **186–7**
Auberies 48, **186**
Bulphan 1, 68, **187**
Bures Hamlet xviii, **188**
Burnham-on-Crouch **188–90**
Library 73, **189**
Minefield Control Tower 77, **190**
Royal Corinthian Yacht Club 4,
69, **189–90**, Pl. 112
St Mary the Virgin 23, **188–9**, 559
Buttsbury **190–1**

Camulodunum *see* Colchester;
Stanway
Canewdon 54, **191–2**, 388
Cann Hall *see* Great Clacton
Canonium *see* Kelvedon
Canvey Island 76, **192–3**, 638
Labworth Café 69, **193**, Pl. 113
Library 73, **192**
Castle Hedingham 61, **193–8**
churches etc. **195–7**
nunnery 19, 197, 198
St Nicholas 21–2, 25, 27, 28,
29, 45, **195–7**, 354, 395,
441n., Pl. 15
Hedingham Castle 5, 30–1, 49,
193–5, Pl. 50
Chadwell St Mary **198–9**
Sunspan 69, **198–9**
Chafford Hundred *see* West
Thurrock
Chalvedon *see* Basildon (neighbour-
hoods)
Chappel **199**
viaduct 55, 56, **199**, Pl. 96
Chelmer and Blackwater Navigation
52, 213, 488, 519, 539, 578, 797,
857
Chelmsford 1–2, 4, 50, 52, 57, 76,
200–24

churches etc. *19*, **201–8**, *222*
Cathedral (former parish
church of St Mary) 2, 24, 27,
46, 53, 54, 60, 67, 68, 200,
201–6, **216**, Pl. 26
cemeteries **208**, 220
Dominican friary 200
Friends' Meeting Houses 53,
67, **208**, **217**
Holy Trinity 58, **206–7**
Our Lady Immaculate (R.C.)
60, **207**
industrial buildings 201, **213**,
217–18, *222*
Crompton 201, **222**, **223**
Marconi buildings 201,
217–18, 221, 388
Moulsham Mill 52, **213**
railway station and viaducts
56, **213**
Springfield Lock and Basin
52, **213**
Springfield Mill (now
Riverside Inn) 52, **213**
Moulsham 15, **213**, **215**, **221–2**,
679n.
public buildings **208–20**
Anglia Ruskin University 73,
218–19; Central Campus and
Frederic Chancellor Building
(former public library etc.)
61, 201, **217**, 218; Rivermead
Campus 73, 201, **218–19**
Chelmsford and Essex Centre
(former Essex and
Chelmsford Infirmary and
Dispensary) 64, **212–13**
Corn Exchange 61, 201, 217n.
County Hall (and extension)
68, 70, 74, **209–10**
King Edward VI Grammar
School 62, **212**
Moulsham Bridge 51, **215**
National Schools (former) 57,
216, **222**
Police Stations **210–11**, **216**
Prison 51, **211**, 489
Public Library *see* Anglia
Ruskin University *above*
St John's Hospital (former
workhouse) 63, **213**
Shire Hall 49, 51, 200, **208–9**,
212, 213, Pl. 77
Roman (Caesaromagus) 15, 17,
200
streets, houses and commercial
buildings 50, 66, 201, **214–24**
Boarded Barns Estate 201,
220
Church Street **216**
Duke Street 201, **216–17**, **219**
High Chelmer Shopping
Precinct 201, **214**, 217n.

High Street 200–1, **214–15**
Melbourne Park 201, **220**
Moulsham Hall 221, 679n.
Moulsham Street 200, **215**,
221–2
New London Road 66, 201,
215, **222–4**
New Street **217–19**
Southborough Lodge (origi-
nally New House) 68, **223**
Springfield Road **220–1**
Tindal Square **214**
town centre **214–17**
The White House 68–9, **222**
Chickney 10, **224**
Chignall *16*, *17*, **225**
Chobbings Farm 41, **225**
St James 68, **225**
St Nicholas (Chignall Smealey)
27, 28, **225**
Chigwell *15*, **226–32**
churches etc. **226–8**
St Mary 21, 45, **226–8**
public buildings **228–30**
Chigwell Hall 65, **229–30**, 575,
Pl. 89
Chigwell School 51, 62,
228–9, **230**
West Hatch High School 73,
229
Rolls Park 47, *231*
Chigwell Row **232**
Childerditch xviii, **232–3**, 505n.
Chipping Ongar 2, **233–5**
castle 31, 234
St Helen (R.C.) 60, **233**
St Martin of Tours 20, 45, 55,
233–4
Chrishall 30, **235–7**
Church Langley *see* Harlow (neigh-
bourhoods)
Clacton-on-Sea 1, 7, 8, 55, **237–44**,
368, 816
churches etc. **237–41**
Our Lady of Light and St
Osyth (R.C.) 60, **240**
St James 59, **237–40**, Pl. 107
St Paul 67, **240**, Pls. 108, 109
public buildings **241–3**
Bishops Park College 74, **241**
Martello Towers 76, **242**
Middlesex Hospital
Convalescent Home (for-
mer) 64, **243**
Ravenscroft Primary School
74, **241**
Town Hall 70, **241**
streets, houses and commercial
buildings 237, **242–4**
Jaywick 8, 70, 71, **244**
Clavering **244–6**
The Bury 33–4, **246**
Old Guildhall 39, 75, **245**

St Mary and St Clement 29, 30,
46, **244–5**
Clifftown *see* Southend-on-Sea
Clovile Hall *see* West Hanningfield
Coggeshall 2, *15*, **246–54**
churches etc. **246–50**
Abbey and Grange Barn 3, 6,
19, 33, 74–5, 163, **246–8**, 251,
305, 352
St Peter-ad-Vincula 25, 67,
248–9, 352, 592n.
public buildings **249–53**
Primary School 74, **250**
Sir Robert Hitcham's Free
School 62, **252**
streets and houses 246, 248,
250–4, 332n.
Holfield Grange 65, **254**
Paycocke's 246, **252**, 766, Pl.
53
Colchester 1–2, 3, 18, 50, 57, 58, 75,
254–302
Camulodunum and Roman
Colchester (Colonia
Victricensis) 13–15, 17, 30,
255–60, **301–2**
Balkerne Gate 14, 256, **259**,
293, Pl. 48
dykes 12, **301–2**, 412
Temple of Claudius and the-
atre 257, **259–60**, **265**, 273–4
walls 255, 256, **257–9**, 276,
289, 291
Castle 5, 30, 200, 259–60, 261,
262, **272–6**, 305, Pl. 49
churches etc. *19*, 68, 261, 262,
263–72
All Saints, High Street (now
Natural History Museum)
263, 285
All Saints, Shrub End 262,
263–4
Castle Methodist Church 67,
270
Cemetery, Mersea Road 61,
271
Congregational Church, Old
Heath 61, **270**, Pl. 101
Crutched Friars 261
Culver Street chapel 270
Friends' Meeting House (for-
merly St Mary's House;
1802–3) **270–1**
Garrison Church of St Alban
the Martyr **281**, 711n.
Grey Friars *261*, **286**
Holy Trinity 20, 133, **264**, Pl.
8
*Methodist Chapel, Maidenburgh
Street 270*
Methodist Church, Wimpole
Road **270**, 298
St Botolph 58, **264–5**, 332

St Botolph's Priory 19, 20, 261, **271–2**, 292, Pl. 10
St Giles 29, 264, **265**, 301
St Helen's Chapel 260, **265**
St James the Less (R.C.) 58, 60, **269–70**
St James and St Paul (former St James the Great) 24, **265–6**, 294, 299
St John the Evangelist, Ipswich Road 58, 262, **266**
St John's Abbey 19, 24, 261, 265, **272**, 281, 672, Pl. 36
St Leonard-at-the-Hythe 23, **267**
St Martin 60, 261, **267–8**, **334**
St Mary-at-the-Walls 54, 172, **268**
St Mary Magdalen 261n., *269*
St Nicholas, High Street 58, 261n., *262,* 263, 264, **284–5**
St Paul, Belle Vue Road 262
St Peter 24, 29, **268–9**
St Runwald 261n., *263,* 286, 297, 742
United Reformed Church, Lion Walk *60–1,* **271**
dykes *see* Camulodunum and Roman Colchester *above*
industrial buildings 262, 263, **280–1**, **294–5**, **299–300**
 Bourne Mill 44, **299**, Pl. 66
 Marriage's mills 262, **295**
 Paxman works 262, **300**
public buildings 262, **276–87**, **301**
 arts building 286n
 almshouses 51, **290**, **293**, **298**, **299**
 Bluecoat School, Culver Street **277**
 Board Schools 62, **279**
 bus station 286
 Colchester Garrison and cavalry barracks 77, 262, **281–2**
 Corn Exchanges (former) 61, **282–3**, **294**
 District General Hospital 263, **279–80**
 Eastern Counties Asylum 64, 280n.
 Essex County Hospital 51, 64, **280**
 moot hall 261, 276n.
 Police Station 169, **277–8**
 Public Libraries 70, **278**, **291**
 railway stations 56, **278**
 Royal Grammar School 62, **279**
 Severalls Hospital (former) 64, **280**
 Sixth Form College 260, **279**
 Telephone Exchange 263, **287**

Town Hall 61, 200, 261, 262, **276–7**, Pl. 97
town walls and gates 5, 14, 17, 261, **291**, 292
Water Tower ('Jumbo') 255, 262, **280–1**, Pl. 48
St Botolph's Priory *see* churches etc. *above*
St John's Abbey *see* churches etc. *above*
streets, houses and commercial buildings 14, 39, 50, 262, 280n., **282–301**
 Balkerne Hill and Lane 263, 283n., **293–4**
 Bourne Mill *see* industrial buildings *above*
 Church Street **293**
 Crouch Street **293–4**
 Culver Centre 263, 290, **291**
 Culver Street 260, 261, **291–2**
 The Cups 262
 Dutch Quarter 75, 261, 262, **286–8**
 East Hill 261, 262, **294–5**
 East Hill House 261, **286**
 East Stockwell Street 14, **288**
 East Street **296**
 Flagstaff Road 272, 281
 Foundry Yard *261*
 Head Street 14, **290**
 High Street 14, 261, 262, 271, 276, **282–6**
 High Woods estate 262
 Hollytrees 50, 261, 273, 276, **285**, 592n.
 Hythe Quay and Hythe Hill 261, 262, 267, **299–300**
 Lexden Road 66, 262, **296–8**
 Lion Walk 14, 260, 261, **291**
 Lion Walk Centre 263, 271, **273**
 Maidenburgh Street 14, 260, 265, *270,* **288**
 Maldon Road 262, 286n., **297**
 The Marquis of Granby 39, **289**
 Mersea Road 272, 281, 300n.
 Middleborough 263, **289**
 Military Road 281, **298–9**
 The Minories 49, **285–6**, Pl. 83
 Napier Road 272, **281**
 New Town Road **298–9**
 North Hill 14, 39, 260, 261, **288–90**
 Old Heath Road **299**
 Queen Street **292–3**
 St John's Green **300**
 Southway 263, **301**
 West Stockwell Street 261, **286–8**, Pl. 6

suburbs and outer areas 262–3, **294–302**
 The Hythe 261, 262, 267, **299–300**
 New Town 66, 262, **298–9**
 Old Heath 261, 262, 270, **299**
 Sheepen 13, 255, **302**
 Shrub End 262, 263
 West Donyland 298
 see also Berechurch; Greenstead; Lexden; Mile End; Stanway
Cold Norton **302–3**
Colne Engaine **303–4**
 St Andrew 27, **303**
 Village Hall 68, **303**
Colneford Hill *see* White Colne
Colne Priory *see* Earls Colne
Colville Hall *see* White Roding
Comarques **780**
Coopersale 62, **304–5**
 Coopersale House 49, **304**
Coopers End *see* Takeley
Copford **305–7**
 Copford Hall 49, **306–7**
 St Michael and All Angels 20–1, 25, 29, 274, **305–6**, 350, 354, 400, 486, 560, Pl. 17
Copped Hall 47, 157n., **307–9**
Cornish Hall End **309–10**
Corringham xvii, 2, 56, **310–11**
 Coryton xvii, 123, **311**
 St Mary 21, 28, 30, **310**
Cranes *see* Basildon (industrial areas)
Creeksea **311–12**
 All Saints 57, **311**
 Creeksea Place 57, **311–12**
Cressing 36–7, **312–14**
 Cressing Temple 3, 31–2, 33, 37–8, 40, **312–14**, Pls. 51, 52
 Rook Hall 42, **312**
Crix *see* Hatfield Peverel

Danbury 3, 4, 52, 71, **314–17**
 Danbury Park (Danbury Place or Palace) 51, 57, 64, **315–16**
 Riffhams 50, 154, **317**, 537–8
 St John the Baptist 23, 28, 30, 75, **314–15**, 419
D'Arcy Hall *see* Tolleshunt d'Arcy
Debden **317–19**
 airfield (RAF Debden) 76, 246
 New Amberden Hall **319**, 836
 St Mary the Virgin and All Saints 53, **317–18**, Pl. 70
Dedham 48, 70, 75, **319–26**
 churches **319–21**, 322
  St Mary the Virgin 23, 24, 27, 28, 30, 46, **319–21**, Pl. 41
 public buildings **321–4**
  Assembly Rooms 319, **321**
  Grammar School 50, **322**
 streets and houses 70, **322–6**, 575

Great House 70, **324**, Pl. 118
Shermans 50, 70, **323–4**, Pl. 75
Dengie 6, **326**
Doddinghurst **326–7**
Doreward's Hall **150**
Dovercourt 66, **327–30**, 472
 Alexandra Hotel 65, **330**
 public buildings **328–30**, 474
  Beacon Hill Fort 76, **330**
  spa 50, 328
Down Hall *see* Hatfield Heath
Downham **330**, *855*
Dunmow *see* Great Dunmow
Dunton *see* Basildon (neighbourhoods)
Durolitum 15
Durrington Hall **681–2**
Durwards Hall *see* Rivenhall
Dynes Hall *see* Great Maplestead
Dytchleys *see* South Weald

Earls Colne 66, **330–4**
 churches etc. **330–2**
  Colne Priory *19*, *20*, 49, 197, **331–2**, 352
  Friends' Meeting House 53, **331**
  St Andrew 55, **330–1**
 Grammar School 62, **332**
East Donyland **334–5**
 St Lawrence 46, 53, 267, **334–5**
Eastern Counties Railway 55–6, 213
East Hanningfield **335–6**
 medieval church 29, *335*
East Horndon **336–7**
 All Saints 27, 42, 135, **336–7**, 424
 Heron Hall *42*, **337**
Easthorpe 20, **337–8**
East Mersea **338**
 blockhouse 76, *338*
Easton Lodge *see* Little Easton
East Tilbury **338–40**
 Bata Estate xvii, 4, 69, **340**
 Coalhouse Fort 76, 77, **339–40**, 784, Pl. 95
 St Catherine 22, 47, **338–9**
Eastwood 690, **699–700**
 see also Southend-on-Sea
ECR *see* Eastern Counties Railway
Edwin's Hall **854–5**
Eight Ash Green xviii, **341**
Elmbridge Hall *see* Fyfield
Elmdon **341–2**, 818
Elmstead 2, **342–3**
 Market Field School 74, **343**
 St Ann and St Laurence 23, 29, 30, 54, **342–3**
Elsenham **343–5**
 Elsenham Place 43, **344**, 663n.
 St Mary the Virgin 21, **343–4**
Epping **345–7**
 Epping Forest 2–3, **347**

St John the Baptist 59, **345**
see also Coopersale
Epping Upland **347–8**
    All Saints 345, **347–8**
    Ambresbury Banks 12, **348**

Fairstead 29, **348–9**, 829
Farnham **349–50**
    Hassobury 64–5, **349–50**, Pl. 87
    St Mary the Virgin 62, **349**
Faulkbourne **350–2**
    Faulkbourne Hall 6, 42, **351–2**,
      581, Pl. 57
    St Germanus 5, 21, 29, 54, **350**
Feering **352–4**, 596
    All Saints 23, 27, **352**
    Feering House 44, **353**
    Prested Hall **353**, 596
Felix Hall *see* Kelvedon
Felmore *see* Basildon (neighbour-
    hoods)
Felsted 2, **354–9**
    almshouses 57, 64, **357**
    churches **354–5**, 357
      Congregational Chapel 53,
        357
      Holy Cross 5, 21, 22, 42, 45,
        354–5, Pl. 43
    Felsted School 51, 57, 62, 353,
      355–7
      Old School House (former
        guildhall) 39, **355**
Finchingfield 2, **359–62**, Pl. 3
    St John the Baptist 21, 23, 24, 28,
      29, 55, **359–60**
    windmill 51, 359, **362**
Fingringhoe **362–3**
    Grange Farm 70, **363**
    St Andrew 24, 28, 29–30, 46, **362**
    tide mill 52, **363**
Fobbing 1, 6, **363–4**
Ford End 57, **364–5**
Fordham **365–6**
Foulness 77, **366–7**
Foxearth 62, **367–8**
    St Peter and St Paul 28, 130n.,
      367
Frating **368**
Frinton-on-Sea 3, 55, **368–73**
    churches **368–70**
      Free Church 67, **370**, Pl. 106
      St Mary Magdalene 66,
        369–70
      St Mary the Virgin 60, **368–9**
    streets and houses xvii, 65, 66,
      69, **370–3**
      Brookmead 65, **371**
      Easton Way 69, **373**
      The Homestead 65, **371**, Pl.
        94
      The Round House **372**, Pl.
        110
Fryerning 65, **373–4**

St Mary 27, **373–4**, 505, 557, Pl.
    30
Fryerns *see* Basildon (neighbour-
    hoods)
Further Brixted *see* Spains Hall
Fyfield **374–5**
    Elmbridge Hall 63, **375**
    Fyfield Hall 31, 33, 166, **375**
    St Nicholas 21, **374–5**

Galleywood **375–6**, 837
Garrison House *see* Wivenhoe
Gaynes Park *see* Theydon Garnon
Gestingthorpe *17*, **376–7**
    Gestingthorpe Hall 49, **377**, Pl.
      81
    St Mary 22, 25, 27, **376–7**, 395,
      Pl. 33
Gibberd Garden *see* Harlow
Gilstead Hall *see* South Weald
Gilwell Park *see* Waltham Abbey
Glazenwood **164**
Goldhanger 59, **378**, 488
Good Easter 22, **378–9**
Gosbecks *see* Stanway
Gosfield 15, 66, **379–83**
    Gosfield Hall 43, **381–3**
    Gosfield Place *381, 446*
    St Catherine 46, 54, **379–80**
Grays *see* Grays Thurrock
Grays Thurrock (or Grays) 1, 4,
    383–6
    All Saints **384**, 824
    Carnegie Library *187*, 385n.
    The Dell 64, **386**
    St Peter and St Paul 22,
      383–4
Great Baddow 7, **386–8**
    Pontlands Park 57, **388**
    St Mary the Virgin 27, 46, 54, 68,
      386
Great Bardfield 2, **388–91**
    St Mary the Virgin 23, 24, 28, 29,
      60, **388–9**, 745
Great Bentley 181, **392**
Great Braxted 20, **392–4**
Great Bromley **394–6**
    St George 23, 24, 25, **394–6**
Great Burstead 135, **396–7**
Great Canfield **397–8**
    Badgers 70, **398**
    castle 31, **398**
    St Mary the Virgin 20, 21, 29, 54,
      397–8, Pl. 18
Great Chesterford 76, **399–400**
    All Saints 22, **399**
    Old Vicarage 39, **399**
    Primary School 62, **399**, Pl. 91
    railway station 56, **400**
    Roman fort and town 15, 17, 18,
      400
Great Clacton **400–1**
    Cann Hall 39, **401**

St John the Baptist 20, 21, 26, 305, **400**
Great Codham Hall **827**
Great Dunmow (or Dunmow) 2, *15*, **401–6**
  churches **401–2**
    St Mary the Virgin 22, 24, **401–2**
    United Reformed Church 61, **402**, 765
  public buildings **402–3**
    Boyes Croft and maltings (now museum) 37, **404**
    Police Station 61, **402**
    workhouse (former) 63, 137, **405**
  streets and houses **403–6**
    Clock House 44, **403**
    Merks Hall 70, **406**, Pl. 120
Great Eastern Railway 56, 691
Great Easton **406–8**
  motte and bailey 31, **407**
  New Farm 69, **407–8**
  St John and St Giles 21, **406**
Great Graces *see* Little Baddow
Great Hallingbury **408–9**, *679*
  Hallingbury Place 409, 679
Great Henny **409–10**
Great Holland **410**
Great Horkesley **410–12**
  All Saints 28, **410–11**, 634
  Chapel Cottage 42, **411**
  Horkesley Hall (Littlegarth School) **411**
  Pitchbury Ramparts **412**
Great Leighs **412–13**
  St Mary 21, **412–13**, Pls. 13, 25
Great Maplestead **413–15**
  Dynes Hall 48, **415**, 728
  House of Mercy 88, **414–15**
  St Giles 46, 58, **413–14**
  school and house 62, **414**
Great Myles's *see* Kelvedon Hatch
Great Notley xviii, 72, **415–17**
  Discovery Centre 72, **416–17**, Pl. 123
  Notley Green Primary School 72, **416**
Great Oakley **417**
Great Parndon *see* Harlow (neighbourhoods)
Great Ruffins *see* Great Totham
Great Saling **417–18**
  St James the Great 58, **417–18**
  Saling Grove 50, **418**
  Saling Hall 48, **418**
Great Sampford **418–20**
  St Michael 22, 23, 315n., **418–19**
Great Stambridge *see* Stambridge
Great Tey **420–1**
  St Barnabas 16, 20, 21, 199, **420–1**
Great Totham 2, 3, 4, 65, **422–3**, 718

Great Ruffins 65, **422–3**, 833, Pl. 90
Lofts Farm 10, **423**
Great Wakering 336n., **423–4**
Great Waltham **424–9**
  Broads Green *11*
  Fitzjohn's Farm 35, **428**
  Langleys 44, 47, 49, **425–7**, Pl. 62
  Littley Park **429**, 533
  St Mary and St Lawrence 21, 24, 46, **424–5**, 649
  see also Ford End; North End
Great Warley **429–32**
  Christ Church 58, **429**
  St Mary the Virgin 59, 176, **429–31**, Pl. 103
Great Wigborough 58, **432**
Great Yeldham **433–4**, 726
  Land Settlement Association houses 69, **434**
  St Andrew 28, 55, **433**
Greenstead 262, **434–5**
  Wivenhoe New Park 70, **434–5**
Greenstead Green xviii, 58, 62, **435–6**
Greensted **436–7**
  St Andrew 20, 32, **436**

Hadleigh **437–8**
  Hadleigh Castle 31, 48, **438**
  National School (former) 62, **437–8**
  St James the Less 20, 58, **437**, Pl. 11
  Shipwrights 69, **438**, 708n.
Hadstock 94, **438–40**
  St Botolph 19, 20, 28, **438–9**, Pl. 9
Hallingbury Place *see* Great Hallingbury
Halstead **440–6**
  churches 53, 61, **440–2**
    Adams' Brewery Chapel 54, **445**
    Holy Trinity 58, 59, **441**, Pl. 98
    St Andrew 23, 30, 435, **440–1**
  public buildings **442–5**
    Hospital 64, **442**
    Police Station 62, **442**, 780
    Public Library (former Corn Exchange) 61, **442**
  streets and houses 66, 68, **442–6**, Pl. 4
  Townsford Mill 52, **444**, Pl. 4
Hare Street *see* Harlow (neighbourhoods)
Harlow xviii, 1, 2, 4, 71, 73, **446–72**
  churches 451, **454–5**, 458–62, **464**, 466–8, **471**
    Baptist Church, Fore Street 61, **467–8**
    Baptist Church, Potter Street 53, **471**

Methodist Church, High
  Street 61, **468**
Our Lady of Fatima (R.C.)
  67, **455**
St Andrew, Netteswellbury
  460–1
St John the Baptist (former),
  Old Harlow **467**, 472
St Mary, Great Parndon **464**
St Mary-at-Latton 67, **454–5**
St Mary, Little Parndon **460**
St Mary Magdalene, Potter
  Street **471**
St Mary and St Hugh, Old
  Harlow 29, **466–7**
St Paul, Playhouse Square 67,
  451
St Thomas More (R.C.)
  458–9
Gibberd Garden **471–2**
industrial areas and buildings
  447, **464–5**
  Gilbey's 447, 454n.
  New Frontiers Science Park
    465
  Pinnacles 447, **464–5**
  Pitney Bowes 447, **465**
  Temple Fields 447, **464–5**
neighbourhoods 71, 73, **454–71**
  Brays Grove **460–2**
  Church Langley 71, 451,
    465–6
  Great Parndon *19*, 446, **462–4**
  Hare Street **458–60**
  Katherines **465**
  Kingsmoor **462–4**
  Latton Bush 456, 460, **460–2**
  Little Parndon 144, 446,
    458–60
  Mark Hall North 447, **454–8**
  Mark Hall South 447, **454–8**
  Netteswell 446, **454–8**, 460;
    Monks Barn, Netteswellbury
    33, 38, **461**
  Newhall 71, **465–6**
  Old Harlow 446, **466–71**
  Passmores **462–4**
  Potter Street **471**
  Staple Tye 447, **462**
  Stewards **462–4**
  Summers **465**
  Tye Green **460–2**
public buildings 447, **452–4**
  Churchgate School **468**
  Civic Centre 450, **452**
  Fawbert and Barnard's
    Primary School 62, **468**
  Harlow Town Station **465**
  Leisure Centre 450, 452
  Princess Alexandra Hospital
    459
  Sportcentre 450, **454**
  Town Centre **452–4**

Romano-British remains 12, 16,
  452, **471**
streets, houses and commercial
  buildings 73, 447–51, **452–4**,
  456–8, **459–60**, **461–4**
  Bush Fair 447, 452, **461**
  Harlowbury 33, **470**
  Katherines **464**
  The Lawn **456**, Pl. 114
  Mardyke Road 447, **457**
  Mark Hall 456, 470
  Millhurst **468**
  Momples Road 447, **458**
  Pearson (former Longman
    Green) offices 447, **464–5**
  Pinnacles **465**
  Queen's Head **468**
  The Stow 447, **456**
  Town Centre 447, **451–4**
Harlowbury *see* Harlow
Harwich 1, 2, 3, 5, 56, 327, **472–7**
  churches etc. *328*, **472–4**, 475
  St Nicholas 53, **472–4**
  Guildhall 51, **474**
  The Redoubt 76, **474**
Hassenbrook Hall **734**
Hassobury *see* Farnham
Hatfield Broad Oak **477–80**
  Hatfield Forest 2–3, 409,
    479–80
  St Mary the Virgin and *priory 19*,
    54, 55, 58, **477–8**, Pl. 40
Hatfield Forest *see* Hatfield Broad
  Oak
Hatfield Heath xviii, **480–1**
  churches **480**
    Holy Trinity 59, **480**
    United Reformed Church 61,
      480, Pl. 100
  Down Hall 64, **480–1**, Pl. 88
Hatfield Peverel **481–3**
  Crix 48, **483**, 797
  Hatfield Place 48, **483**
  Hatfield Priory 48, 49, **482–3**
  St Andrew and *priory 19*, 21, 68,
    481–2
Hatfield Place *see* Hatfield Peverel
Hatfield Priory *see* Hatfield Peverel
Hawkwell 68, **484**
Hazeleigh xviii, **484**
Hedingham Castle *see* Castle
  Hedingham
Helions Bumpstead 94, **484–5**
Hempstead **485–6**
  St Andrew 23, 46, 55, 59, **485**, Pl.
    46
Henham **486–7**
  St Mary the Virgin 23, 28, 29, 55,
    486
Heybridge *18*, **487–8**
  Heybridge Basin 52, **488**
  The Towers 64, **488**
High Beach **488–9**

Lippitts Hill Camp 76–7, **489**
Lippittshill Lodge (former asylum) 64, **489**
Suntrap Forest Education Centre (former convalescent home) 64, **489**
High Easter **490–1**
St Mary the Virgin 21, **490**, Pl. 1
High Garrett **152–3**
High Laver **491–2**, 594
Mashams 35, 41, **491–2**
High Ongar **492–3**
St Mary 21, **492**, Pl. 14
High Roding 2, **493**
All Saints 28, 29, **493**
Highwood xviii, 2, **493–4**
Hill Hall *see* Theydon Mount
Hockley 50, **494–5**
Holfield Grange *see* Coggeshall
Holland-on-Sea xviii, 244, **495–6**
Horham Hall 42, 47, **496–7**, Pl. 58
Horkesley Hall (C17/C18; Littlegarth School) **411**
Horkesley Hall (C19) 49, **555–6**
Horndon-on-the-Hill **497–9**
Old Market Hall 40, **499**
St Peter and St Paul 22, 55, 59, 119, **497–8**
Hutton **499–500**
churches **499–500**
All Saints **499–500**, 604
Hutton and Shenfield Union Church 67, **500**
Hutton Hall 49, **500**
Poplar Union Training School (former) 63, **500**
Hyde, The 373, *504*
Hylands 48–9, 50, **500–1**

Ingatestone **502–7**
churches **502–3**, 507n.
St Edmund and St Mary 27, **502**, 529, Pls. 38, 45
St John the Evangelist and St Erconwald (R.C.) 60, **503**
public buildings **503–4**
almshouses 64, **503–4**
Railway Station 56, **503**
streets and houses 50, 65, 374, **503–7**
Chapel Croft 72, **503**
Hyde, The 373, *504*
Ingatestone Hall 43, 47, 60, 503, **506–7**
Mill Green 502, **505–6**
Ingrave 49, **508**
St Nicholas 52, **508**, 822, Pl. 68
Inworth 29, **508–9**
Ivy Chimneys *see* Witham

Jaywick *see* Clacton-on-Sea
Jericho Priory *see* Blackmore

Katherines *see* Harlow (neighbourhoods)
Kelvedon **509–13**
churches etc. **509–10**, 512
St Mary the Virgin 60, 68, **509–10**
mills (Easterford and Grey's) **613**
Roman (Canonium) *16*, *509*
streets and houses **510–13**
Felix Hall 47, 49, **512–13**
Knights Templar Terrace **510**, 689
Kelvedon Hall *see* Great Braxted; Kelvedon Hatch
Kelvedon Hatch **513–14**
Brizes (Peniel Academy) 49, **514**
churches **513**
Old St Nicholas 53, **513**
Great Myles's 49, **514**
Kelvedon Hall 48, 60, **513–14**
nuclear bunker (former) 77, **514**
Killigrews *see* Margaretting
Kingsmoor *see* Harlow (neighbourhoods)
Kirby-le-Soken 55, **514–15**
Kynochtown 311

Laindon *see* Basildon (neighbourhoods)
Lakeside Shopping Centre *see* West Thurrock
Lamarsh 21, 60, **515–16**
Lambourne **516–18**
St Mary and All Saints 53, 55, **516–17**, Pl. 69
Langdon Hills *see* Basildon (neighbourhoods)
Langenhoe *xviii*, *58*
Langford **518–19**
Langford Grove 47, *51*, 166, *519*
St Giles 20, **518**
Langham **519–21**
waterworks 69, 85, **521**, 788
Langley 4, **521**
Langleys *see* Great Waltham
Latchingdon 68, **522**
Latton *see* Harlow (neighbourhoods)
Latton Priory *see* North Weald Bassett
Lawford 69, 70, **522–5**
Lawford Hall 65, **523–4**
St Mary 6, 22, 29, **522–3**, Pls. 23, 24
school (former) 65, **524**
Lawn, The **649**
Layer Breton **525**
Layer de la Haye **525–6**
waterworks 69, 85, **526**
Layer Marney **526–31**
Layer Marney Tower 30, 43, 47, 57, **526–9**, 774, Pl. 56
St Mary the Virgin 27, 30, 45, **529–30**

Leaden Roding 28, 119, **531**
Lea Navigation 52, 814
Lee Chapel North *see* Basildon
  (neighbourhoods)
Lee Chapel South *see* Basildon
  (neighbourhoods)
Leez Priory 19, 22, 42, 47, 57, 354,
  429, 528, **531–3**, 558
Leigh-on-Sea 62, 690, 691, **700–4**
  St Clement 46, **700–1**, 733n.
  St Margaret 66, **701–2**
  see also Southend-on-Sea
Leverton House **723**
Lexden 262, 263, **533–5**
  Lexden Dyke and Tumulus **301–2**
  viaduct 56, **535**
Lindsell 23, 29, **535**
Lippitts Hill Camp *see* High Beach
Lippitts Lodge *see* High Beach
Liston **536**
  Liston Hall 47, **536**
Little Baddow **536–9**
  churches **536–7**
    St Mary the Virgin 30, 58,
      536–7
    United Reformed Church 53,
      537
  Great Graces 44, **538**
  Old Riffhams 48, **538–9**
  Water Hall 35, **539**
Little Bardfield 20, **539–40**
Little Bentley 62, **540–1**
Little Birch *see* Birch
Little Braxted **541–2**
  Little Braxted Hall 37, **542**
  St Nicholas 20, 59, **541**, 560, Pl. 102
Little Bromley **542**
Little Burstead **542–3**
Littlebury 48, **543–5**
  Holy Trinity 24, 28, 59, **543–4**,
    765
  Littlebury and Audley End rail-
    way tunnels 56, **545**
  Ring Hill **104**, **545**
  Winstanley's house 48, 545n.
Littlebury Hall *see* Stanford Rivers
Little Canfield 28, 59, **545–6**
Little Chesterford **546–7**
  Little Chesterford Manor 31,
    546–7
  St Mary the Virgin 54, **546**
Little Clacton **547–8**
Little Dunmow **548–9**
  Grange Farm 37, **549**
  St Mary and *priory 19*, 22, 23, 30,
    54, 332, 531, **548–9**, Pls. 16, 39
Little Easton **549–53**
  Church Row 65, **551**, Pl. 93
  Easton Lodge 46, 47, 54, 64, 76,
    403, 405, 407, 550, **552–3**, 765,
    769
  St Mary 29, 46, 47, 54, 127n.,
    550–1

Little Hallingbury **553–4**
  St Mary the Virgin 60, **553–4**
  Wallbury (hill-fort) 12, 412, **554**
Little Henny xviii, **554–5**
Little Holland *see* Holland-on-Sea
Little Horkesley **555–6**
  Horkesley Hall 49, **555–6**
  Priory 19, **556**
  St Peter and St Paul 75, **555**
Little Laver 27, 373, **557**
Little Leighs **557–8**
  St John the Evangelist 29, 30,
    557–8
  see also Leez Priory
Little Maplestead **558–9**
  St John the Baptist 23, 27, 58,
    558–9, 823
Little Oakley 17, **559**
Little Parndon *see* Harlow (neigh-
  bourhoods)
Little Ruffins *see* Wickham Bishops
Little Saling *see* Bardfield Saling
Little Sampford **559–60**
  St Mary the Virgin 23, 24, 46, 54,
    559–60, 684
Little Stambridge *see* Stambridge
Little Tey 29, **560**
Little Thurrock **560–1**
Little Totham 28, **561–2**
Little Wakering 109, **562–3**
Little Walden 76, **563**
Little Waltham *11*, 15, **563–4**
  St Martin 53, **563**, 604
  The Street 37, **564**
Little Warley **564–6**
  St Peter 46, **565**
  Warley Barracks 77, **565**
Little Wigborough 5, 58, **566**
Little Yeldham 434, **566**
Littley Park *see* Great Waltham
Lofts Farm *see* Great Totham
Lofts Hall **818**
London, Tilbury & Southend
  Railway 56, 691, 698
Loughton 2, 3, 56, **567–77**
  churches etc. **568–70**
    Methodist 67, **569**
    St John the Baptist 58, 60,
      568
  Loughton Camp 12, **577**
  public buildings **570–1**
    Public Library 73, **570**
    Railway Station 69, **571**
  streets, houses and commercial
    buildings 65, **571–7**
    Bank of England Printing
      Works 69, **576**
    Debden Estate 71, **575–6**
    Lopping Hall 347, **574**
    Loughton Hall 65, 569, **575–6**
  The Warren **576–7**
Lower Sheering *see* Sheering
Lyons Hall 153

Magdalen Laver **577–8**
 St Mary Magdalen 26, 28, **577**
 Wynters Armourie 34, **577–8**
Maldon 2, 3, 18, 52, 56, **578–87**
 churches etc. **579–87**, 765
  All Saints 18, 22, 23, **579–80**
  Friary 19, 584
  St Mary the Virgin 21, **580**,
   593n.
  St Peter 581–2
 public buildings *18*, **581–7**
  Moot Hall 6, 42, 351, **581**n
  St Giles Hospital 19, **582**
  St Peter's Hospital (former
   workhouse) 63, **583**
 streets, houses and commercial
  buildings 18, **583–7**
  All Saints Vicarage 39, **585**
  Fullbridge 583, **586**
  High Street 39, **583–5**
  King's Head (former) 39, **584**
  Maldon Hall **587**
Manningtree 50, **587–8**
 Public Library (former Corn
  Exchange) 61, **588**
 St Michael and All Angels 321,
  343, *587*, 599
Manuden 28, **589**
Marden Ash xviii, **589–90**
Margaret Roding **590**
 Brick House 50, **590**
 St Margaret of Antioch 21, 29,
  590
Margaretting **591–2**
 Killigrews 42, 591, **592**
 St Margaret 25, 29, **591**, Pl. 31
Mark Hall 456, 470
Mark Hall North *see* Harlow (neigh-
  bourhoods)
Mark Hall South *see* Harlow (neigh-
  bourhoods)
Marks Hall *see* Markshall
Markshall **592–3**
 Marks Hall *47*, 517, **592–3**
 St Margaret 249, 285, *592*
Marks Tey 28, **593**
Mashams *see* High Laver
Mashbury 580, **593**
Matching **594–5**
Mayland 66, **595–6**
 Primary School 74, **595**
Merks Hall *see* Great Dunmow
Messing **596–7**
 All Saints 46, 47, 353n., **596**, 803
Middleton 21, 30, 47, **597**
Mile End (or Myland) **598**
Mill Green *see* Ingatestone
Mistley **598–602**, 803
 churches **598–9**, *600*, 602
  Mistley Towers 52, 600
  St Mary and St Michael (and
   medieval church) 60, 587n.,
   598–9

Furze Hill Bunker 77, 489, **602**
 village 50, **600–2**
Moone Hall *see* Stambourne
Moreton **602–3**
Moulsham *see* Chelmsford
Mount Bures 21, 27, **603**
Mountnessing **603–4**
 Thoby Priory 19, **604**
 Tilehurst 65, **604**
 windmill 51, **604**
Moyns Park 43, 140, **605–6**, 748
Moze *see* Beaumont-cum-Moze
Mucking 17, **606–7**
 North Ring 10, 11, 16, 18, **607**
 St Clere's Hall **206–7**, 733
Mundon 26, **607**, 608
Myland *see* Mile End

Navestock **608–9**
 St Thomas the Apostle 22, 26,
  29, 75, 358–9, **608**
Nazeing **609–10**
Nether Hall *see* Roydon
Netteswell *see* Harlow (neighbour-
  hoods)
Nevendon *see* Basildon (neighbour-
  hoods)
New Amberden Hall *see* Debden
New Hall *see* Boreham
Newland Hall *see* Roxwell
Newport 18, **610–14**
 public buildings **612–14**
  Grammar School 62, **611–12**
  *Hospital of St Mary and St
   Leonard 19*, 613
  House of Correction (former;
   The Links) 51, **613**
 St Mary the Virgin 22, 27, 28, 29,
  610–11
 streets and houses **612–14**
  Crown House 40, 50, **613**, Pl.
   55
  Monk's Barn 41, **613**
  Shortgrove Hall *47*, 48n., 49,
   612
Noak Bridge *see* Basildon (neigh-
  bourhoods)
Norsey Wood *see* Billericay
North Benfleet **614**
North End **614–15**
 Black Chapel 54, **614–15**, Pl. 74
North Fambridge **615**
North Shoebury *18*, 690, **704–5**
 see also Southend-on-Sea
North Stifford *see* Stifford
North Weald Bassett 76, **615–16**
 Latton Priory 19, **616**
 St Andrew 28n., **615–16**
Norton Mandeville 27, **617**

Old Harlow *see* Harlow (neighbourhoods)
Old Riffhams *see* Little Baddow

Orford House *see* Ugley
Orsett *12*, **617–19**
    Orsett Hall 44, **618–19**
    St Giles and All Saints 21, 23, 25,
      55, **617–18**
Osea Island xviii, 8, *76*, **619–20**
Othona (Roman fort) *see* Bradwell-
  on-Sea
Ovington **620**

Paglesham **620–1**
Panfield *19*, 58, **621**, 621–2
Parkeston *see* Ramsey and Parkeston
Parndon Hall **459**
Passmores *see* Harlow (neighbour-
  hoods)
Pattiswick 68, **622**
Peacocks **592**
Pebmarsh *17*, *52*, **622–4**
    St John the Baptist 27, 30, **622–4**,
      Pl. 32
Peldon **624–5**
Pentlow 20, 21, 24, 28, **625–6**
Pinnacles *see* Harlow (industrial
  areas)
Pipps Hill *see* Basildon (industrial
  areas)
Pitchbury Ramparts *see* Great
  Horkesley
Pitsea *see* Basildon (neighbourhoods)
Pleshey *13*, *16*, **626–7**
    Holy Trinity 54, **626–7**, 826
    Pleshey Castle 6, 31, **627**
Pontlands Park *see* Great Baddow
Potter Street *see* Harlow (neighbour-
  hoods)
Prested Hall *see* Feering
Priors *see* Broomfield
Prior's Hall *see* Widdington
Prittlewell *18*, 518, 690, 691, **705–8**
    churches etc. 691, **705–7**
      Prittlewell Priory *19*, 647,
        705–6
      St Mary the Virgin *19*, 24,
        706–7, 732
      St Peter 67, **707**
    Crowstone **706**
    Prittlewell Camp *12*, **708**
    see also Southend-on-Sea
Purfleet 1, 4, 48, **628–9**
    Powder Magazine 77, **628–9**
    Queen Elizabeth II Bridge **629**,
      Pl. 122
Purleigh 57, **629–30**
    All Saints 6, 46, **629–30**

Quarters, The *see* Alresford
Quendon **630–1**
    Quendon Hall 48, **631**
    St Simon and St Jude 67, **630–1**
Quinton Hill *see* Waltham Abbey
  (Royal Gunpowder Mills)

Radwinter 15, **632–3**
    Old Vicarage 39, **633**
    St Mary the Virgin 22, 25, 60, 65,
      632–3, Pl. 105
    village 64, 65, **633**
Ramsden Bellhouse **633–4**
Ramsden Crays **634**
Ramsey and Parkeston 1, 472, **634–6**
    Parkeston Quay (Harwich
      International Port) 56, **635**
    Roydon Hall 44, **635**
    St Michael 45, 47, **634–5**
Rawreth 59, **636**
Rayleigh 2, 7, **636–9**
    Holy Trinity 27, **636–7**
    Rayleigh Mount 31, **638**
    streets and houses 123, 193,
      638–9
    windmill 51, **638**
Rayne **639–40**
Rettendon **640–1**
    All Saints 54, 60, **640**, Pl. 71
Rickling 23, 28, **641–2**
Ridgewell 28, **642–3**
Riffhams *see* Danbury
Ring Hill *see* Littlebury
Rivenhall *13*, *17*, *18*, **643–6**, 687
    Kelvedon Park (formerly
      Durwards Hall) 57, **645–6**
    Rivenhall Place 50, **645**
    Roman Villa 16, 17, **646**
    St Mary and All Saints 29,
      643–5, Pls. 19, 20
Rivers Hall **162**
Rochetts **724**
Rochford 2, **646–9**
    Ark House 70, **649**
    Corn Exchange (former) 61, **648**
    Hospital (former Workhouse) 70,
      647–8
    railway station 56, **648**
    Rochford Hall 43, 47, **647**
    St Andrew 27, 58, 529, **646**
Rolls Park *see* Chigwell
Rowhedge *see* East Donyland
Roxwell **649–50**
    Newland Hall 37, 41, **650**
    St Michael and All Angels 53–4,
      649–50
Roydon **650–2**
    Nether Hall 42, 609, **651–2**
    St Peter 27, 68, **650–1**
Roydon Hall *see* Ramsey and
  Parkeston
Runwell **652–3**
    Runwell Hospital 70, **652–3**
    St Mary 46, 637, **652**
Ryes, The **554–5**

Saffron Walden 2, 4, 75, **654–69**
    Battle Ditches **669**
    castle 31, 654, **658**
    churches **654–8**, 667

Benedictine monastery *19*
cemetery 61, **658**
St Mary the Virgin 5, 20, 22,
  23, 24, 25, 45, 197, 320n.,
  654–7, Pls. 27, 42
United Reformed Church
  (formerly Congregational)
  53, **658**
public buildings **658–61, 668**
  Bell English Language Centre
    (former British and Foreign
    School Society teacher train-
    ing college) 63, **659**
  Council Offices (former
    General Hospital) 64, **658–9**
  Museum 61, **659**
  Police Station 62, **659**
  Public Library (former Corn
    Exchange) 61, **659**
  schools 62–3, **659–60**
  Town Hall 51, 61, **658**
  workhouse (former) 63, **661**
streets, houses and commercial
  buildings 39, 654, **661–9**
  Barclays Bank (formerly
    Gibson, Tuke & Gibson) 65,
    665
  The Close 344, **663**
  Hill House 659, **661**
  King Edward VI Almshouses
    63, **662**
  Myddylton Place 39, **663**
  Sun Inn (former) 41, **665**
St Aylotts 41, 352, **669–70**
St Clere's Hall *see* Mucking; St
  Osyth
St Lawrence **671**
  Salt House 71, **671**
St Osyth *11*, **671–7**
  Martello Towers 76, **677**
  St Clere's Hall **676–7**
  St Osyth Priory (Abbey) 19, 24,
    42, 43, 401, **671–5**, Pl. 37
  St Peter and St Paul 5, 22, 24, 43,
    46, 55, 529, **675–6**, 677, Pl. 29
Salcott **677**
Saling Grove *see* Great Saling
Saling Hall *see* Great Saling
Sandon 27, 28, **677–9**
Sewards End **679**
Shalford **679–80**
  St Andrew 23, 24, 30, **679–80**,
    825
  Shalford Hall 70, **680**
Sheepen *see* Colchester (suburbs and
  outer areas)
Sheering **681–2**
  maltings 52, **682**
  St Mary the Virgin 29, **681**
Shelley **682**
Shellow Bowells 53, 68, **682–3**
Shenfield 24, 46, **683–4**, 770, 801
Shipwrights *see* Hadleigh

Shoebury Garrison *see* South
  Shoebury
Shoeburyness *see* South Shoebury
Shopland *xviii*, **757**
  St Mary Magdalene 165, 191, **757**
Shortgrove Hall *see* Newport
Shrub End *see* Colchester
Sible Hedingham **684–6**
  Alderford Mill 52, **686**
  Public Library 73, **685**
  St Peter 23, 30, **684–5**
Silver End xvii, 4, 69, 152, 171, 340,
  686–9, Pl. 111
  St Francis 69, **687**
  St Mary (R.C.) 67, **687**
  Sheepcotes Farm 44, **689**
Skreens **650**
Songers *see* Boxted
South Benfleet 67, **689–90**
Southchurch 690, **708–9**
  Holy Trinity 58, 67, **708–9**
  public buildings 62, **709**
  Southchurch Hall 35, 37, **709**
  see also Southend-on-Sea
Southend-on-Sea 1, 3, 55, 66, 690,
  690–717
  churches etc. 67, **691–5**, 698, 732n.
    All Saints 59, **691–2**
    St Erkenwald 67–8, 691n.
  Cliftown 66, 691, **698–9**
  public buildings **695–7**
    Central Museum (former
      Library) 61, **695**
    Hospital, Prittlewell Chase 70,
      696
    Pier 3, 691, **697–9**
    South East Essex College 73,
      695, 696
    Southend Central and
      Victoria Stations 56, **696**
  streets, houses and commercial
    buildings 65, 73, 691, **697–9**
    Keddie's 73, **699**
    Porters 43, **696**
    Royal Terrace 50, 691, **698**
  see also Eastwood; Leigh-on-Sea;
    North Shoebury; Prittlewell;
    Southchurch; South Shoebury;
    Thorpe Bay; Westcliff-on-Sea
South Fambridge **717**
Southfields *see* Basildon (industrial
  areas)
South Hanningfield **717**
Southminster **717–18**
  Memorial Hall 423, **718**
  St Leonard 21, 59, **717–18**
South Ockendon 107, **719–20**
  St Nicholas 21, **719**
South Shoebury 690, **709–12**
  churches **710, 711**
    Garrison Church of St Peter
      and St Paul 281, **711**
    St Andrew 20, 508, **710**

Manor House 50, **710–11**
Shoebury Garrison 77, 709,
  711–12
see also Southend-on-Sea
South Weald **720–4**
  St Paul 59, **721**
  St Peter 21, 58, **720–1**
  streets, houses and commercial
    buildings **721–4**
    Dytchleys 49, **723**
    Gilstead Hall 49, **723**
    Leverton House (Boyles
      Court) **723**
    Weald Country Park and
      Weald Hall 47, 176, **722**
    Wingrave Almshouses 58, 64,
      722
South Woodham Ferrers xviii, 71–3,
  724–6
  Queen Elizabeth II Square
    725–6, Pl. 121
Spains Hall **726–8**, Pl. 59
  Roman building (Further
    Brixted) **728**
Spaynes Hall **434**
Spencers **434**
Springfield 8, 50, **728–30**
  churches **728–9**
    All Saints 16, 27, 415n., **728–9**
    see also Chelmsford
  locks 52, **213**, **730**
  Springfield Lyons earthwork 8–9,
    11, 18, **730**
  streets and houses 201, 221,
    729–30
    almshouses 64, **729**
    Beaulieu Park 72, 201, **730**
Springfield Lyons *see* Springfield
Stambourne **730–1**
  Moone Hall 39, **731**
  St Peter and St Thomas 21, 25n.,
    28, 29, **730–1**, Pl. 44
Stambridge **731–2**
  Little Stambridge Church 693, *732*
  St Mary the Virgin and All Saints
    59, 60, **731–2**
Stane Street 15, 250, 307, 401, 639, 758
Stanford-le-Hope **732–4**
  St Margaret of Antioch 54, 55,
    606, 701, **732–3**
Stanford Rivers **734–5**
  Littlebury Hall 41, **735**
  St Margaret 28, **734**
  workhouse (former) 63, **734–5**
Stanley Hall **624**
Stansgate Priory *see* Steeple
Stanstead Hall **436**
Stansted Airport 1, 4, 74, 75, 123,
  735–6, 759, Pl. 117
  Middle Bronze Age settlement
    9–10, 12, 13
Stansted Mountfitchet **736–42**
  Castle 31, **739**

churches etc. **736–9**
  St John the Evangelist 59, **738–9**
  St Mary (former parish
    church) 21, 23, 30, 45, **736–8**,
    Pl. 47
  St Theresa of Lisieux (R.C.)
    67, **739**
Stansted Hall 50, 65, **741**
Thremhall Priory 19, **741–2**
windmill 51, **742**
Stanton's Farm *see* Black Notley
Stanway 263, **742–3**
  Gosbecks (part of
    Camulodunum) 12, 13, 15, 17,
    255, 302, **743**
  Lexden and Winstree workhouse
    (former) 63, **742**
  St Albright 286n., **742**
Stapleford Abbotts **743–4**
  Albyns 44, 47, **744**
  St Mary 27, 29, 45, **743–4**
Stapleford Tawney 734, **744–5**
Stebbing **745–7**
  Friends' Meeting House 53, **746**,
    Pl. 73
  St Mary the Virgin 23, 28, 388–9,
    745–6, Pl. 35
Steeple **747**
  St Lawrence and All Saints 57,
    311, **747**
  Stansgate Priory 19, 747
Steeple Bumpstead **748–50**
  Congregational Church 61, **749**
  Moot Hall 40, **749**
  St Mary 25n., 54, 55, 606n., **748**
Stewards *see* Harlow (neighbour-
  hoods)
Stifford 6, **750–1**
  Ardale School (Stepney Union)
    63, *751*
  St Mary 30, **750**
Stisted **751–2**
  All Saints 22, **751–2**
  Stisted Hall 49, 276, **752**
  The Street 65, 164, **752**
Stock 60, **752–4**
  All Saints 68, **752–3**
  windmill 51, **754**
Stondon Massey 6, 46, **754–5**
Stort Navigation 52
Stow Maries 755
  Flambirds Farm airfield 76, **755**
Strethall 20, 438, **755–6**
Sturmer 25n., **756**
Sumners *see* Harlow (neighbour-
  hoods)
Sutton 55, **757**

Takeley 19, 75, **758–9**
  Aklowa (former vicarage) 57, **758**
  Coopers End 123, 125, 758n.
  Holy Trinity 28, **758**, Pl. 34
  Priory 19, 759

Temple Fields *see* Harlow (industrial areas)
Tendring 63, **759–60**
Tendring Hundred Railway 56
Terling **760–3**
  All Saints 24, 52, **760**
  Terling Place 47, 49, 51, **761–2**, Pl. 78
  United Reformed Church 53, **760**
Thames Gateway 75, 111
Thaxted 2, 57, 75, **763–9**
  churches **763–6**
    St John the Baptist 23, 24, 28, 29, 53, **763–5**, 787, Pl. 28
  Guildhall 40, 75, **766**, Pl. 54
  streets, houses and commercial buildings 39, **766–9**
    Clarance House 50, **767**
  windmill 51, **767**
Theydon Bois **769–70**
Theydon Garnon **770–2**
  All Saints 24, 27, 55, **770–1**, 801
  Gaynes Park 65, 305, **771–2**
  Theydon Priory **771**
Theydon Mount **772–6**
  Hill Hall 43, 44, 50, **773–6**, Pl. 67
  St Michael 45, **772–3**
Thistley Hall *see* Widdington
Thoby Priory *see* Mountnessing
Thorndon Hall 48, 49, 60, 506, 508, **776–9**
  Old Thorndon Hall 42, 776, 778, 779, 822
Thorpe Bay 690, **712**
  Thorpe Hall 48, **712**
  see also Southend-on-Sea
Thorpe-le-Soken **779–81**
  Baptist Church 53, **780**
  Police Station (former) 62, **780**
  St Michael 30, **779–80**
Thorrington **781**
  St Mary Magdalene 27, **781**
  tide mill (Alresford Creek) 52, **781**, Pl. 84
Thremhall Priory *see* Stansted Mountfitchet
Thundersley 7, **781–2**
Thurrock *see* Grays Thurrock
Tilbury 1, 2, 6n., **782–5**
  churches etc. *18–19*, **782–3**
  streets and houses 70–1, **783–4**
  Tilbury Docks 56, 70, **783**
  Tilbury Fort 76, **784–5**, Pl. 64
Tilbury-juxta-Clare 434, **785**
  church 27, 620, **785**
Tillingham **785–6**
Tilty **786–7**
  St Mary the Virgin and *Tilty Abbey* 19, 22, 108, 248, **786–7**, Pl. 22
Tiptofts *see* Wimbish
Tiptree **788**

Tiptree Priory 19, **788**
  waterworks 69, **788**
Tiptree Heath *see* Tiptree
Tollesbury 20, **789**, Pl. 2
Tolleshunt d'Arcy **790–1**
  D'Arcy Hall 43, **791**
Tolleshunt Knights **791–2**
Tolleshunt Major **792–3**
  Beckingham Hall 43, 344, **792–3**
Toppesfield 30, 46, 52, **793–4**
Townsford Mill *see* Halstead
Twinstead **794–5**
  St John the Evangelist 58, **794–5**, Pl. 99
Tye Green *see* Harlow (neighbourhoods)

Ugley **795–6**
  Orford House 48, **795–6**
  St Peter 60, **795**
Ulting **796–7**
  The Studio 70, **796**, Pl. 115
University of Essex 73, 255, 263, 434, 691, **797–801**, Pl. 116
  Wivenhoe Park (Wivenhoe House) 51, 64, 73, 797, **800–1**
Upshire **801–2**

Vange *see* Basildon (neighbourhoods)
Virley **802**

Wakes Colne **802–4**
  All Saints 21, **802–3**
  Crepping Hall 34, **803**
  Normandy Hall 35, **804**
Walden Abbey *see* Audley End
Wallbury *see* Little Hallingbury
Waltham Abbey 57, **804–15**
  Holy Cross and St Lawrence (*Abbey*) 6, 19, 20, 22, 29–30, 43n., 45, 46, 47, 58, 60, 531, **804–15**, Pls. 12, 104
  Royal Gunpowder Mills 52, 77, **814–16**
  streets and houses **812–14**
    Abbey House 811
    Gilwell Park **813–14**
Waltham Forest 2–3
Walton-le-Soken 816
Walton-on-the-Naze 1, 8, 55, 56, **816–18**
  Martello Tower 76, **818**
  Poplars (Poplar Hospital convalescent home) 64, **817**
Warley Barracks *see* Little Warley
Warlies Park **801–2**
Warren, The *see* Loughton
Water Hall *see* Little Baddow
Weald Hall *see* South Weald
Weeley **818**
Wenden Lofts xviii, 341, **818**

Wendens Ambo **819–20**
  Audley End Railway Station 56, **820**
  St Mary the Virgin 28, **819**
West Bergholt **820**
  St Mary (old) 47, **820**
  West Bergholt Hall 50, **820**
Westcliff-on-Sea 690, **712–17**
  churches etc. **712–15**
    Nazareth House (R.C.) 60, **714**
    Our Lady Help of Christians and St Helen (R.C.) 60, **713–14**
    St Alban the Martyr 54, 59, 66, 702, **712–13**
    St Andrew 67, **713**
    St George's U.R. Church (former Crowstone Chapel) 67, **714–15**
    St Michael and All Angels 66, **713**
  Crowstone 706, **717**
  see also Southend-on-Sea
West Donyland *see* Berechurch; Colchester (suburbs and outer areas)
West Hanningfield **821**
  Clovile Hall 44, **821**, Pl. 65
  Hanningfield Reservoir **821**, 855n.
  St Mary and St Edward 46, **821**
West Horndon xviii, 508, 776, **822**
West Mersea **822–3**
  St Peter and St Paul and *priory* 19, 20, 60, **822**
  wheel tomb 17, **823**
West Thurrock xvii, **823–5**
  Chafford Hundred and Campus 72, **824**
  Lakeside Shopping Centre 73, 691, **824–5**
  St Clement (old) 21, 384n., **823–4**
West Tilbury **825**
  St James 339, **825**
Wethersfield 2, 24, **825–8**
White Colne **828**
White Notley 16, 20, 29, 349, **829**
White Roding **829–30**
  Colville Hall 37, 41, **830**
  St Martin 59, **829–30**
Wicken Bonhunt *18*, **830–1**
  St Margaret 21, 55, 58, **830–1**
Wickford **832**
Wickham Bishops 65, **832–4**
  St Bartholomew 378n., **832**

viaduct 56, **834**
Wickham St Paul **834**
Widdington **834–6**
  Prior's Hall 20, 31, 38, **835–6**
  Thistley Hall 319, **836**
Widford 376, **837**
Willingale 726, **837–9**
  St Andrew (Willingale Spain) 29, **837–8**
  St Christopher (Willingale Doe) 46, **838**
Willingale Doe *see* Willingale
Willingale Spain *see* Willingale
Wimbish **839–41**
  All Saints 22, 25n., 30, **839**
  Tiptofts 33, 34, 35, 140, **840–1**
Witham 2, 18, 50, 56, **841–51**
  churches **842–4**
    Holy Family and All Saints (R.C.) 60, **844**
    St Nicolas 23, 352, **842–4**
  public buildings **844–5**, **850**
    Bridge Hospital (former workhouse) 63, **845**
    Saul's Bridge 51, **845**
    spa *50*, 157n., *841*, **846**
    Roman (Ivy Chimneys) **851**
  streets and houses 50, 841, **845–51**
Wivenhoe **851–3**, Pl. 5
  St Mary the Virgin 30, **851–2**
  streets and houses **852–3**
    Garrison House 40, 75, **852**
    Wivenhoe Hall 853
    Wivenhoe New Park *see* Greenstead
    Wivenhoe Park/House *see* University of Essex
  water tower 335, **852**
Wix **853**
  St Mary the Virgin and *priory 19*, **853**
  Wix Abbey 44, **853**
Woodham Ferrers 45, 724, **854–5**
Woodham Mortimer 44, **855–6**
Woodham Walter 45, **856–7**
Wormingford **857–8**
Wrabness 853, **858**
Writtle **858–62**
  All Saints 28, 46, 54, 627, **859–60**
  Lordship Barn 48, **861**
Wynters Armourie *see* Magdalen Laver